The Franco-Prussian

THE Franco-Prussian War

CHAPTER XV.

Popular Feeling in Paris—Excitement on hearing of the Fighting around Metz and Hostile Feeling against the Government—Appointment of General Trochu as Governor of Paris, and brief Biographical Notice of him—Complete Exemplification of his Views with regard to the French Army—His First Proclamation to the Inhabitants of Paris—Favourable Reception of it by all Parties—Cheering Assurances of M. Thiers as to the Capacity of Paris to withstand a Siege—His Proposal to make a Waste of the Country surrounding the Capital, and to bring the Inhabitants and their Produce within the City—False Statements made by the Government as to the Battles around Metz and the reputed slaughter in the Quarries of Jaumont—The Feeling of the Extreme Opponents of the Government—The First Arrivals of the Wounded in Paris—Execution of Spies—Fearful Atrocity at Hautelaye—Important Decree published by the Empress appointing a Committee of Defence—Proclamation of General Trochu to the National Guard—Sketch of the Sieges of Paris, and Historical and General Description of the Fortifications—Activity displayed in placing the latter in a thorough State of Defence—Armament of the Forts—Gunboats launched on the Seine to assist in the Defence of the City—Minute Information possessed by the Germans as to the Fortifications of Paris—Improved Tone in the Feeling of the Parisians, and Activity manifested in the Organization of the Troops—Expulsion of the Germans and of all the "Dangerous" Classes, and Voluntary Exodus of the Well-to-do Classes and Foreigners—Closing of the Theatres—Arrival of the Outside Population within the City, with Huge Droves of Sheep and Cattle—The Country aroused at the Danger of the Capital—A Loan of £30,000,000 rapidly subscribed for—Proceedings in the Corps Législatif—Impressive Remarks by M. Thiers—The Party of the Left gradually gaining the Upper Hand—Important Communication from the Government and Reply from the Inhabitants—Statement to the Corps Législatif by Count Palikao relating to the Sortie from Metz and Battles around Sedan—The Surrender of the Emperor and his Army still kept from the People—Great Agitation in the Chamber, and demand of M. Jules Favre that the de facto Government should cease—Levy en Masse—Instances of the Changeability of the French Character—The Sad Feeling in Germany caused by the Fearful Losses in the Battles around Metz, and increased determination to put down France effectually—Behaviour of the French Wounded—Remonstrances of the well-known Authoress, Fanny Lewald, against the Attention shown to the French Prisoners—Increasing Feeling of Hostility against the French Government and People—Germany's wishes with regard to Alsace and Lorraine—Protests against Foreign Interference in the Struggle—The Jubilation in Berlin and other German Cities on the Reception of the News of the Surrender of the Emperor and the French Army at Sedan.

HAVING brought the narrative of the events connected with the war to the surrender of the emperor and his army at Sedan, we suspend the further description of active operations in the field, to glance at the situation of affairs in the French capital, where most important political and other matters had naturally occupied the attention of the authorities and people generally. We shall also, at the same time, briefly notice the feeling manifested in Germany.

In Chapter IX. we described the progress of events and the state of the public mind in the French and Prussian capitals down to the emperor's fete day (August 15)—a day which had been fixed on by many enthusiastic Frenchmen for the triumphant march of their troops into Berlin! As already stated, the usual festival was not celebrated; and the Parisians suffered keenly from suspense and mortification occasioned by the early disasters of the campaign. The festival of the church, however, was duly honoured. On the day following the festival (August 16) the city was again plunged into a state of the most intense excitement, when it became known that severe fighting had been going on upon the banks of the Moselle, the details of which were, in vain, eagerly sought for; while the excitable disposition of the Parisians was embittered by the minister of the Interior posting a despatch to the effect that "some travelers" had reported a great battle, in which 40,000 Prussians were placed *hors de combat*. Taught a lesson by the false news spread after the battle of Woerth, this proceeding of M. Chevreau only served to increase the hostile feeling of the people, whose menaces began to be formidable.

The 17th of August deserves especial notice as the day on which General Trochu, who afterwards played so important a part in the defence of the capital, was appointed governor of Paris. Nothing could have shown more clearly the precarious condition of the empire than this appointment. General Trochu had displayed the qualities of an able soldier and a high-minded gentleman; but his sympathies were professedly Orleanist, and little in accord with the regency of the empress. He had likewise requested of the emperor a command in the army of the Rhine, which was refused. He had, however, been sent to the camp at Toulouse to organize the troops, and was subsequently appointed to the command of the twelfth army corps stationed at the camp at Châlons, whence he was recalled for the defence of the capital.

This general, Louis Jules Trochu, was born in 1815, and educated at the military school of St. Cyr. He was appointed lieutenant in 1840, captain in 1843, and subsequently served in Algeria, where he became the favourite aide-de-camp of Marshal Bugeaud, who had remarked his great bravery at the battle of Isly. He became major in 1846, and colonel in 1853. During the Russian war he served in the Crimea as aide-de-camp to Marshal St. Arnaud, gaining by his gallant conduct at the siege of Sebastopol the commander's cross of the Legion of Honour. After the Marshal's death he was promoted to the rank of general, and commanded a brigade of infantry until the end of the war. During the Italian campaign of 1859, which ended with the victory of Solferino, he served with distinction in command of a division. In 1861 he was promoted to the rank of grand officer of the Legion of Honour, having then been in the army twenty-five years, and served in eighteen campaigns, in one of which he was wounded. General Trochu was also elected a member of the consulting committee of the Etat Major, and chosen in the place of his father a member of the Conseil Général of Morbihan, in the canton of Belle Isle. In 1866 he helped greatly in the reorganization of the army, and in the following year published anonymously a book entitled "The French Army in 1867," which passed through ten editions in six months. In it he severely criticized the organization of the army, and especially the changes introduced into it under the empire, which tended to render the soldiery a caste, severed in interest and feeling from their civilian countrymen. He maintained that its manoeuvres were antiquated, its organization very imperfect, and "that the main secret of success in every war was to be more completely prepared for action than the enemy;" a theory strikingly exemplified in the Prusso-Austrian war of 1866, and still further verified by the French reverses during the late conflict.

General Trochu's appointment as governor of Paris was mainly owing to the acknowledged merits of this treatise; and so highly were his qualifications valued by the community, that it was only by promptly installing him in the office the government prevented a proposition in the Corps Législatif to place him in it. Count de Palikao, however, in announcing the appointment, was careful to state that it had no political signification. On the morning following his appointment the general issued the subjoined proclamation:—

"Inhabitants of Paris,—In the present peril of the country I am appointed governor of Paris and commander-in-chief of the forces charged with defending the capital in a state of siege. Paris assumes the role which belongs to her, and desires to be the centre of great efforts, of great sacrifices, of great examples. I associate myself with it with all my heart. It will be the pride of my life and the brilliant crowning of a career till now unknown to the most of you. I have the most implicit faith in the success of our glorious enterprise, but it is on one condition, the nature of which is absolute, imperative, and without which our united efforts will be powerless. I mean good order; and I understand by that not only calmness in the street, but in-doors, calmness of mind, deference for the orders of the responsible authority, resignation under those experiences which are inseparable from the situation, and, finally, that grave and collected serenity of a great military nation which takes in hand, with a firm resolution, under solemn circumstances, the conduct of its destinies. I will not refer, in order to secure to the situation that equilibrium which is so desirable, to the state of siege and of the law. I will demand it from your patriotism, I shall obtain it from your confidence, while I myself repose unbounded confidence in you. I appeal to men of all parties, belonging myself, as is known in the army, to no other party than that of the country. I appeal to their devotion; I entreat them to restrain by moral authority those ardent spirits who cannot restrain themselves, and to do justice by their own hands on those men who are of no party, and who perceive in our public misfortunes only the opportunity of satisfying detestable desires (*appétits*). And in order to accomplish my work—after which, I assure you, I shall retire into the obscurity from which I emerge—I adopt one of the old mottoes of my native province of Brittany, 'With God's help, for the country' ('Avec l'aide de Dieu, pour la patrie').

"GENERAL TROCHU."

This proclamation was greatly approved by the inhabitants of Paris, and favourably commented on by journals of nearly every shade, especially for its patriotic spirit, firmness, and modesty. In relation to that part of it which speaks of summary justice being done by the people, the general subsequently explained as follows:—"A time may come when Paris, threatened at all points, and subjected to all the hardships of a siege, will be, so to speak, given over to that particular class of rascals (*gredins*) who in public misfortunes only see an opportunity for satisfying their detestable appetites. These are the men, as you know, who run through the affrighted town, crying out, 'We are betrayed!' who break into houses and plunder them. These are the men whom I told all honest folk to lay hold of in the absence of the public force, which will be required on the ramparts. That was what I meant." It is noticeable that General Trochu simply announced his appointment, without indicating the authority whence it emanated.

These proceedings, coupled with declarations by M. Thiers as to the capacity of the fortifications of the capital to withstand a siege, somewhat cheered the spirits of the Parisians. At the sitting of the Corps Législatif he (M. Thiers) also expressed a hope that, in case of necessity, Paris would be able to offer an invincible resistance to the Germans. With a view to this, and in order to secure abundance in the capital, he suggested that a waste should be made around it, and that the inhabitants of the surrounding country, with all their produce, should take refuge in it.

As regards the communication of news from the front, the government fell into the error of their predecessors. The truth respecting the battles around Metz on the 14th, 16th, and 18th of August, which led to the investment of Marshal Bazaine and his entire army within the lines of the "maiden" fortress, was uniformly withheld from the people. The minister of War spoke of the affair of the 14th as a brilliant combat, in which the enemy had sustained severe losses; but refused to give any details of the engagement. A despatch subsequently published intimated that the French had been able to carry their wounded into Metz; that the Prussians were compelled to retire to their former lines; that they had been repeatedly repulsed in an unsuccessful attempt to carry the French position; and that Bazaine had rejoined MacMahon, with the prospect of a decisive victory.

In published despatches it was also announced that in the battle of the 16th Marshal Bazaine had repulsed the German army, had everywhere maintained his ground, and that his troops had passed the night in the position they had conquered. The place, however, whence the latter announcement had been issued was not mentioned; and although the despatch had been sent on the night of the 16th, it was not published in Paris till the 18th. The actual state of affairs was subsequently learned from German despatches published in the English newspapers. No information was communicated respecting the hard-fought battle of Gravelotte on the 18th, but the Parisians were firmly persuaded that a great victory had been obtained; and on Friday (19th) the Boulevards were crowded with enthusiastic multitudes singing the Marseillaise and shouting "Vive la France!" "Vive Bazaine!" "Vive l'Armée!"

In the Chamber, on Saturday, August 20, although no despatch was produced from Bazaine, Count Palikao made the following communication:—"The Prussians have circulated the report that they gained advantages over our troops on the 18th. I wish formally to state the contrary. I have shown to several deputies a despatch, from which it appears that three Prussian corps united made an attack upon Marshal Bazaine, but that they were repulsed and overthrown into the quarries of Jaumont (*culbutés dans les carrières de Jaumont*)." The minister likewise intimated that Bismarck's cuirassiers had been cut to pieces, and the Prussian troops had sustained great loss, while Bazaine's position secured to him entire freedom of action. These statements were at the time loudly cheered; but subsequently, pressed by the Left, Count Palikao failed to substantiate them. Assailed by M. Gambetta, he said that a premature communication of good news from the seat of war would imperil the success of the commander's plans; but the Opposition contended that if there was only bad news it could not come too soon, since, until the country was made aware of the worst, it would not nerve itself for the sacrifices to which it would have to submit.

It was, however, well understood in Paris that the success of Bazaine was absolutely necessary to meet the circumstances. When on the 15th Count Palikao announced in the Chamber that on the 13th the marshal had shaken off the Germans, and rejoined MacMahon, there appeared in the Paris journals on the same day long articles showing the critical character of the dangers which had been surmounted, and congratulating Bazaine on his safety. Little did the writers know that the information they had received was utterly opposed to the facts; and it was but indifferent consolation they subsequently professed to find in believing that their favourite general had failed to shake off the hold of the German strategists, only because he had resolved to engage the enemy with the best troops of France, while the raw levies were being drilled into efficiency in the camp at Châlons!

The reticence of the government, combined with the flagrant distortion of the actual facts, had the usual damaging effects. The inhabitants of the capital, in their feverish discontent, encouraged the fabrication of false news. Thus, according to the *Liberté*, on the 18th the Prussians were totally defeated, leaving 40,000 wounded on the battle-field, and had to demand leave to send them to Germany through Belgium and Luxemburg. Imaginative writers also described "the terrific drama of the Quarries of Jaumont, near Metz, where 20,000 Prussians were represented to have been precipitated into an abyss with vertical sides and a depth of 100 feet, and afterwards buried *en masse* with sand by Belgian peasants employed at ten francs a day, while groans yet issued from the mass on the fourth day after the catastrophe, a catastrophe which caused many French soldiers who witnessed it to burst into tears." On the other hand, the most alarming rumours were current that the French army had been utterly beaten and destroyed. The following extract from the *Centre Gauche* (subsequently suppressed) shows the feeling of the extreme opponents of the government at this time:—"How absurd are the organs which boast of a 'victory.' Is it victory because the emperor just escaped being made prisoner? Is it victory because our army was not cut in two on the Moselle? Is it victory because, after four days' fighting, we at length shook off an enemy which all that time had harassed our retreat? If it is victory, where are the prisoners, the guns, and the flags to show for it? If the Prussians should take the emperor prisoner, let them keep him. Not a particle of our national genius or honour will go with him. Let his wife and son share with him the carefully prepared luxuries of an opulent exile. At all events, may the hand which traced the proclamation abandoning Metz to its fate draw up no more bulletins of the grande armée on the banks of the Meuse. May such sad comedies be spared us in future. He is already called by his former flatterers in the Corps Législatif, His Majesty Invasion III., and it is notorious that only to avoid difficulties while the enemy is at our gates his deposition is postponed for a short time by a tacit compromise."

Added to the restlessness engendered by uncertainty, the heart of Paris was further saddened by the arrival of the battered remnants of cavalry regiments, reduced to mere handfuls by the vicissitudes of the campaign. Weary, footsore, and wounded, the chargers passed along the thoroughfares; while the troopers, thin and haggard, looked like men who had fought hard and fared badly. Not even the march of troops still in course of being forwarded to the front could now awaken the enthusiasm of the Parisians, and regiment after regiment passed through the streets in silence. Meantime, many of the rioters at La Villette were condemned; "spies" were executed; reports were in circulation implicating even the ladies of the palace, and the mind of the capital was agitated by news of outrages in the provinces. An outrage of a specially frightful character was perpetrated on the deputy mayor of Beaussac. Misinterpreting a remark made by the unfortunate gentleman as favourable to the Prussians, a mob of some 200 ruffians attacked him with barbarous ferocity, and having wounded and battered his person, kindled a fire in the market-place of Hautelaye, and literally burnt him alive.

The serious turn which the course of events had taken was evidenced by the following decree, published in the *Journal Officiel* of the 21st August, signed by the empress and countersigned by the Count de Palikao:—

"Napoleon, by the grace of God and the national will, emperor of the French. To all present and to come, salutation. We have decreed and do decree as follows:—1. The Defence Committee of the fortifications of Paris is composed of general of division Trochu, president; Marshal Vaillant, Admiral Rigault de Genouilly, Baron Jerome David, minister of Public Works, general of division Baron de Chabaud la Tour, Generals Guiod, d'Autemarre, d'Erville, and Soumain. 2. The Defence Committee is invested under the authority of the minister of War with the powers necessary for carrying out the decisions at which it may arrive. 3. For the execution of such decisions our minister of War will attach to the Defence Committee such generals, military intendants, and other officers as may be required. 4. The Defence Committee will meet every day at the War Office. It will receive a daily report of the progress of the works and armaments, the stores of ammunition and provisions. 5. The Committee will report its proceedings every day to the minister of War, who in turn will report to the Council of Ministers. 6. Our minister of War is charged with the execution of this decree. Done at the Palace of the Tuileries, 19th of August, 1870, for the emperor, by virtue of the powers intrusted to her.

"EUGENIE."

To the names given in this proclamation, the Chambers, contrary to the wishes of the executive, subsequently persisted in adding others; and three deputies, MM. Thiers, De Talhouet, Dupuy de Lôme, and two senators, General Mellinet and M. Béhic, were placed on the Committee of Defence.

General Trochu also issued the following proclamation, which was published in the same number of the *Official Journal*:—

"To the national guard, the national garde mobile, to the land and sea troops in Paris, and to all the defenders of the capital in a state of siege. In the midst of events of the utmost gravity, I have been appointed the governor of Paris and commander-in-chief of the forces assembled for its defence. The honour is great, but for me equally so is the danger. Upon you, however, I rely to restore by energetic efforts of patriotism the fortunes of our army, should Paris be exposed to the trials of a siege. Never was a more magnificent opportunity presented to you, to prove to the world that a long course of prosperity and good fortune has in no degree enervated public feeling nor the manhood of the country. You have before you the glorious example of the army of the Rhine. They have fought one against three in heroic struggles, which have earned the admiration of the country, and have inspired it with gratitude. It wears now mourning for those who have died.

"Soldiers of the Army of Paris. My whole life has been spent among you in a close intimacy, from which I now derive hope and strength. I make no appeal to your courage and your constancy, which are well known to me. But show by your obedience, by a firm discipline, by the dignity of your conduct and behaviour, that you have a profound sense of the responsibilities which devolve upon you. Be at once an example and an encouragement to all. The governor of Paris,

"TROCHU."

From these proceedings on the part of the governing authorities, the people saw clearly the dangers of the position. Notwithstanding the "glorious example" and "heroic struggles" of the army of the Rhine, the facts came out that Bazaine was shut up in Metz; that the camp at Châlons had been broken up and evacuated; and that the Crown Prince of Prussia, with a powerful army, was pursuing the southern route in order to attack Paris. The attention of the capital was thus centred upon the fortifications which thirty years before had been constructed by the ministry of M. Thiers—now a member of that Committee of Defence whose duty it was to place those structures on a war footing.

Before proceeding further with our narrative, we think it cannot fail to be interesting if we here give a very brief sketch of the sieges of Paris prior to that of 1870—71, and a short historical and general description of the fortifications which proved so effective during its investment on the present occasion, and of which a plan is annexed.

It is worthy of note that the first mention we have of Paris in history is connected with the record of an investment. Fifty years before Christ it was a stronghold of the Gauls, when Labienus, the most able of Caesar's generals, marched an army against it, and after crossing the Seine forced the insurgents to evacuate it, after Vercingetorix, the chief of the Gauls, had burned what there was of a city. Paris was originally confined to an island, formed by a river and surrounded by inaccessible swamps. After the Germans conquered France, Chlodwig, the leader of the invading tribe, reconstructed ancient Lutetia, and made it the centre of the new empire. When the authority of his descendants began to decline, the defence of Paris against a foreign enemy gave a prestige to one of their generals that enabled him to usurp the throne of the decaying dynasty. Nearly 900 years after Christ, Charles le Gros, a degenerate scion of Charlemagne, was attacked by the Normans. A helpless imbecile, he had no choice but to make his peace with the predatory bands. On the occasion of a second raid, however, Paris gallantly held out for a whole year under the command of Count Otto, one of the king's nobles. By this feat of arms Otto acquired such renown, that on Charles' death, in 888, the Frankish nobility elected him king. A nephew of his, Hugh Capet, was the ancestor of the Bourbons.

Meantime, the German conquerors of France, absorbed by the subject of nationality, had quarrelled with the old country whence they had proceeded. In 978, when the German emperor Otto II. was celebrating the festival of St. John at Aix-la-Chapelle, he was surprised by King Lothaire of France at the head of an army of 30,000 men. Otto, however, crossed the frontier on the 1st of October, and marched straight upon Paris, overcoming all resistance in his way. Before winter set in he stood at the foot of Montmartre, and invested the city. But to ward off the hosts attempting its rescue he had to detail a portion of his army, which was eventually decimated by the cold of winter and disease. He was ultimately obliged to withdraw without effecting his object, and returned the way by which he came.

The strength of the place having thus been proved by experience, King Philip Augustus, at the beginning of the thirteenth century, extended its fortifications, adding several hundred towers to the walls. In the latter part of the fourteenth century King Charles V. surrounded the new suburbs with a fresh enceinte, built a citadel called the Bastille, and constructed a fort on the Isle of St. Louis. Notwithstanding these new defences, the English, after the battle of Agincourt, 1420, took Paris. The Maid of Orleans, attempting to recapture it in 1429, was repulsed; but seven years later, through the gallantry of Dunois, the Bâtard Royal, the English were obliged to evacuate it.

King Henry IV. was the next to assail the devoted capital. As he was a Protestant, it would not recognize his authority. Having defeated the Catholic League at Ivry, 17th March, 1590, he approached the city by forced marches; and occupying Corbeil, Lagny, and Creil, cut off the supply of provisions, then chiefly received by the river. He next planted his guns on Montmartre, and from this commanding position left the Parisians to choose between starvation and bombardment: 15,000 of the inhabitants died of hunger before negotiations were opened with the king. At that very moment, however, the Spaniards, who assisted the Catholic League, sent General Prince Farnese with a large army from Belgium to the rescue. Henry was thus compelled to raise the siege, and only entered Paris four years later, when, having embraced Catholicism, he was welcomed with the greatest enthusiasm.

The power of France rapidly increasing, Paris remained more than 200 years unvisited by an invading army. In the reign of Louis XIV. the mere idea of the foreigner venturing into the heart of the country had come to appear so preposterous, as to lead to the razing of the fortifications. Louis XV., in 1726, again encircled the city with a wall, which, however, was not intended for military purposes; and as an open town Paris passed through the storms of the Revolution.

In 1814 the allied armies appeared in front of Paris to avenge the deeds of Napoleon I. At that time Joseph Bonaparte acted as regent, and a few redoubts, hastily thrown up, were all the impediments in the way of the enemy; 25,000 regulars under Marmont and Mortier, and 15,000 national guards, with 150 guns, formed the city garrison. The allied sovereigns arrived on the evening of the 29th of March at the château of Bondy, and resolved to attack Paris by the right bank of the Seine. They planned three simultaneous attacks. That on the east, under Barclay de Tolly, with 50,000 men, was to carry, by Passy and Pantin, the plateau of Romainville; that on the south, under the Prince Royal of Würtemburg, with about 30,000 troops, was to pour through the wood of Vincennes on the barriers of Charonne and the Trône; the third by the north, in the plain of St. Denis, was to be headed by Blucher himself, and to march on the right of Montmartre, Clichy, and Etoile. On the French side, Marmont had to scale the escarpments of Charonne and Montreuil, and establish himself on the plateau of Romainville; while Mortier, traversing the exterior boulevard from Charonne to Belleville, and descending by Pantin, La Villette, and La Chapelle, to the plain of St. Denis, established his right wing on the canal of the Ourcq, his left at Clignancourt, at the foot of Montmartre. Marmont, finding the Russians in possession of Romainville, with 1200 men threw himself on their rear-guard and drove them back on Pantin and Noisy. Barclay de Tolly, vexed at his repulse, resolved to retake Romainville, and called up his reserve. General Mezenzoff, who had been repulsed in the morning, pushed forward his stubborn grenadiers and won the height. The Russian cuirassiers, driving along the plateau of Montreuil, tried to charge the retiring French infantry, but were repelled. The French batteries, served by mere Polytechnique lads with skill and devoted courage, kept up a most determined plunging fire with great effect. Ledru des Essart's young guard had also reconquered, tree by tree, the wood of Romainville, and thus outflanked the Russian troops. Marshal Mortier had already taken up his position on the plain of St. Denis. On the north, Blucher was advancing over the plain of St. Denis. The bulk of the Prussian infantry advanced to the foot of Montmartre; General York's corps, on the left of the allies, moved on La Chatelle; and the corps of Kleist and Woronzoff, still more to the left, bore down on La Villette. The Prince Royal of Würtemburg also advancing, and carrying the bridge of St. Maur, made a circuit round the forest and attacked Charenton by the right bank. The brave national guards had tried to defend the bridge at Charenton with l'Ecole d' Alport; but finding their rear in danger, they abandoned the position, and pushed across the country to the left of the Seine. The allied forces were now in line, and the firing commenced in one broad belt. To the north Prince Eugene fell on Pantin and Près St. Gervais, and grappled with the Boyer de Rebeval and picked divisions of the young guard. The French, driven out, rallied, however, at the foot of the height, and supported by well-posted artillery, returned to renew the struggle for the unhappy villages. On the plateau of Romainville there was equally hard fighting, but the French had not the same success. Pressed on both flanks, Marmont struck a bold blow for life rather than for victory. He threw himself in front of four battalions, formed in column, and pushed like a battering-ram straight at the Russian centre. Twelve cannons loaded with grape gave a rude welcome to the intruders, Marmont being at the same moment attacked in front and in flank. The four French columns fell back after a furious hand-to-hand fight. Marmont was already weighed down by his assailants, when a daring officer, named Ghesseler, broke from a wood with 200 men, and rushed at the Russian columns, to give time to Marmont to retreat towards Belleville. Bravely as they had resisted, the French were everywhere outnumbered; and along the line from St. Denis to the Barrière du Trône, the allies, according to Thiers, had lost already 10,000 men, the French 6000. The allies, however, dreaded the return of

Napoleon, and the blow of despair he might strike. About three in the afternoon Brigadier Paixhan placed heavy guns on the declivity of Mènilmontant by Belleville, and Chaumont. His gunners waited with stern calmness for the masses of Russians and Germans, whose front ranks were mowed down by the relentless fire. The allies, however, pushed on and attacked Marmont in the rear; who, to prevent being cut off, collected his forces, and rushed on the Russian grenadiers, whom he broke and drove back beyond the barrier, and then resumed the defence at the octroi wall. Mortier, in the plain of St. Denis, was also in an all but hopeless condition, though he still kept a brave front to the enemy. The divisions at La Villette were now in the centre of a mass of Russians and Germans, when Mortier rushed with part of the old guard down on La Villette, and drove out the Prussian guard with great carnage. But fresh masses poured in, and drove him over the plain into the barriers of Paris. The heights of Montmartre were then wrested from a handful of sappers, and subsequently the Clichy barrier, which the national guards, under Marshal Moncey, were bravely defending. As M. Thiers says eloquently, when he reaches this point in his history: "Such was the termination of two and twenty years of victory. The triumphs at Milan, Venice, Rome, Naples, Cairo, Madrid, Lisbon, Vienna, Dresden, Berlin, Warsaw, and Moscow, now closed disastrously before the walls of Paris." Marmont, desirous of saving the city from ruin and bloodshed, sent three officers to Prince Schwartzenberg to propose terms. At that moment General Dejean arrived in breathless haste, to announce that Napoleon would appear within two days with 600,000 men, and that, therefore, the enemy must be resisted at any cost, or cajoled by a sham parley. But it was too late; the imperial star was waning, fortune had hidden her face. The allies refused to resume negotiations till Paris surrendered, and hostilities were suspended. The marshals consented to save Paris by evacuating it that night, and retiring to Fontainebleau. Meanwhile, Napoleon was flying to save the city, but at Fromenteau he met General Belliard, and heard the fatal news that struck him like a thunderbolt. He sat down by the two fountains on the Juoisy road, hid his face in his hands, and, in those moments of agony, struck out a great plan to still save France, which, however, it was not permitted him to accomplish. On March 31 Frederick William III. of Prussia, and Alexander I. of Russia, made their entry into the city.

The following year witnessed a repetition of the feat. On the 2nd of July, 1815, the Prussians, under Blucher, took Montrouge and Issy by storm, while Wellington forced his way into the northern and eastern suburbs, and on the 7th the English and Prussian guards once more trod the Boulevards.

Projects for fortifying Paris had been entertained from the Revolution in 1789. Since the works opposed to the Allies in the operations above referred to had utterly failed, Napoleon I. had other plans in view in the latter years of his reign, and while at St. Helena ordered a memorial of his intentions to be drawn up. After the revolution of 1830 the project was again revived, and in 1831 the works were commenced by Louis Philippe; but on the return of peace, after the siege of Antwerp, they were abandoned for a second time.

It was reserved for M. Thiers, in 1840, to carry out the projects to their fullest extent. Louis Philippe had made up his mind to fortify the capital, and with his council and generals held that the best system of defence was the erection of several fortresses, built in front and around it. The Opposition in the Chamber, on the other hand, contended that the only way to fortify the city efficiently was to build a rampart all round it. At this juncture the duke of Orleans, the intelligent but unfortunate heir-apparent to the throne, proposed a new project, combining the two plans, viz., to have Paris fortified with circular ramparts as well as with detached fortresses.

The opponents of the scheme, however, declared that the notion of a siege or of an assault of the capital of the civilized world, with its public monuments, its riches, and its population of near two millions, was insensate. How could whole legions of men be got to occupy all the points of that vast *enceinte*? Even if they could be got together it would, with the city blockaded, and the enemy's flying columns devastating the country, be impossible to feed them, not to speak of the multitude of refugees from the surrounding villages and towns who would be forced to take shelter within its walls. Nor would it be possible to keep in order such a mass of human beings on the brink of famine, liable to frequent panics and seditions, and but too ready to impute their disasters to treason. If Paris was to be defended it should be at the frontier. In a political point of view, a series of bastilles, enveloping in a circle of fire the city which represents the whole of France, would be full of peril to liberty and the free institutions of the country. The idea of fortifying Paris was not merely an illusion, it was a menace and a danger; and the treasure which it was proposed to lavish on it, the amount of which could not be fixed beforehand, but which, in any case, must be enormous, would be more usefully spent in making roads, canals, railways, steamships, &c.

The defenders of the project, which was submitted to a committee consisting of M. Billault, General Bugeaud, Matthieu de la Redorte, Allard, Liadéres, General Boguereau, Bertin, Odillon Barrot, and Thiers, contended that, far from exposing Paris to a siege, the fortifications would for everprevent it. The capital was not more than six days' march from the frontier, and the centralization in it of all the impulsive forces of the nation rendered France utterly incapable of resistance were Paris taken. When it was entered in 1814 and 1815 all France surrendered. Paris, as an open city, seemed to invite the enemy, who would be anxious only to hurry on and strike the decisive blow. Paris fortified, that sort of war would be impossible, and the enemy would be obliged to employ regular tactics, to take fortified places, and to secure his communications before venturing to approach the interior of France. That which without fortifications was little more than a *coup de main*, would become with fortifications an undertaking of magnitude and hazard. And should Paris be besieged, it would certainly know how to defend itself. Valenciennes, Lille, Mayence, Dantzic, Hamburg, and Strassburg had proved that the genius of Frenchmen was not less fitted for sieges than for battles. It was likewise asked how Paris could be fed. The question should be—How an army that besieged Paris could be fed? In ordinary times the capital always had provisions for five weeks at least, and in case of invasion little effort would suffice to supply it for two months; and where was the army of 200,000 or 300,000 men that could live a single month concentrated in such a space? Moreover, how could Paris, with fortifications eighteen leagues in circumference, be blockaded? The besieging army should extend on a front of twenty-two leagues, cut up stream and down stream by the great course of the Seine! The attempt would be madness. A good deal had been said about terrorism, panic, want of confidence, &c. To this it was replied that before the first line of outer works was carried Paris would certainly be delivered—either the army, which there would have been time to reform, or the want of supplies, would force the enemy to retire. Regarding the danger to liberty, where, it might be asked, could be found a tyrant so barbarous, and withal so stupid, as to fire on his capital, and confound in his wrath friends and foes? With respect to expense, even exaggerating all the calculations, it would scarcely amount to 160,000,000 francs; and what was that compared to the 2,000,000,000 francs which two invasions cost France?

At the sitting of the Chamber of Deputies on the 1st of February, 1840, the bill for carrying out the fortifications, which had been amended in some matters of detail and completed by some guarantees, was again presented, and passed by 237 votes against 162. Its adoption was chiefly owing to the Opposition, who were the majority in the committee, and had named the reporter who supported it during the debate with remarkable talent. M. Odillon Barrot, then the leader of the Left, defended the bill in the tribune. The Radical or Republican Opposition had the patriotism to abstain from all opposition on a question which so deeply concerned the defence of the country. They not only did not oppose, but combated in the columns of the *National*, then their principal organ under the management of Armand Marrast, the objections brought forward against the fortifications; and a speaker of the extreme Left, M. Arago, in a speech which attracted much attention, defended the system of the *enceinte continuée*. Having passed the Chamber of Deputies, it was carried up to the Peers on the 11th of February, when, after a discussion which lasted six weeks, it passed by a majority of 147 against 85.

M. Thiers and his cabinet entered heartily into the work, and the duke of Orleans, with the concourse of officers of the *génie*, submitted plans of the fortifications to a full council of the ministers, which were ordered to be executed under the direction of Marshal Dode de la Brunnerie. The district in which the city is situated is crossed by four longitudinal roads— 1. From Paris to Strassburg by Meaux, Château Thierry, Epernay, and Châlons, now skirted by a railway. This was the route taken by Blucher's army in its march to Paris. 2. From Paris to Châlons by Meaux, Fertèsous-Jouarre, Montmirail, and Champaubert. This route Blucher took in his first march in 1814, when his army was destroyed by Napoleon in the battles of Champaubert, Montmirail, Château Thierry, and Vauchamps. 3. From Paris to Vitry by Langwy, Coulommiers, Fertè Gaucher, Sezanne, and Fère Champenoise. The allies took this route in 1815, in their last march on Paris, when they defeated at Fère Champenoise and Fertè Gaucher the corps of Marmont and Mortier. 4. From Paris to Nogent-sur-Seine by Brie Comte Robert, Mormans, Nangis, and Provins. This was the route taken by Schwartzenberg's army in its first march on Paris, when it was beaten by Napoleon at Mormans, Nangis, and Montereau. These four roads are intersected by four cross-roads:—1 . From Châlons to Troyes by Arcis. 2. From Epernay to Troyes by Vertus, Fère Champenoise, and Plancy. 3. From Epernay to Nogent by Montmirail and Sezanne.

The city, placed between the confluence of the Marne, the Oise, and the Seine, in the midst of a wide plain, is divided into two unequal parts by the river, from 200 feet to 300 feet in breadth, which runs from east to west, forming an arc of a circle. On the right bank of the Seine, the height of which is about 80 feet above the level of the sea, rise the hills of Montmartre, 426 feet high; of Belleville, 311 feet; of Mènilmontant, and of Charonne. On the left bank are the heights of Mont Valérien, 495 feet; of St. Cloud, 306 feet; of Sévres, Meudon, and Issy. The district lying to the north of the Seine is the larger and lower of the two; that to the south of the river is considerably higher. Twenty-one bridges keep up the communications. The form of the city may be compared to an ellipse, somewhat flattened on the right side, the longer axis of which is about nine miles. According to the census of 1866, Paris had 1,825,274 inhabitants, and 90,000 houses. The systematic reconstruction of the interior of the city, which Napoleon III. caused to be executed by the eminent prefect of the Seine, M. Haussmann, completed the works of fortification. These form probably the most complete and extensive military engineering works ever constructed. As will be seen from the accompanying plan, the fortress consists of a continuous inclosure (*enceinte continuée*) of a roughly pentagonal form, embracing the two banks of the Seine, bastioned and terraced with ten mètres (about 33 English feet) of escarpment faced with masonry. The general plan of the enceinte presents 94 angular faces (fronts), each of the medium length of 355 mètres (about 1450 feet), connected by curtains, with a continued fosse or line of wide wet ditches in front, the bottom laid with masonry, of the medium depth of six mètres; thence to the top of the parapets of earth raised over the wall is a height of 14 mètres in all, or about 46 feet. This is for artillery, &c., and forms entrenchments for the defenders. The continuous outline of the work is broken by V-shaped projections, the two sides of each of which are commanded by a flank fire, and thus every part of the front may be swept by the guns of the garrison. At different points are drawbridges, magazines, &c., and several military roads of communication. The distance of this regular zone or belt from the irregular cutting formed by the octroi wall of the capital varies from two-fifths of a mile to nearly two miles. Taking as a point of departure the western extremity of Bercy, on the right bank of the river, it crosses the road to Charenton, traverses the avenues of St. Maudè and Vincennes, goes to the south end of Charonne, behind Père la Chaise to Belleville, then to Romainville, and, crossing the Poute de Flandre, reaches the Pont de Flandre at La Villette. Thence passing westward, it proceeds to La Chapelle St. Denis, crosses the great northern road, leaves Montmartre to the left, and traversing various routes, &c., passes by Clignancourt to Batignolles, &c., till it reaches the eastern point of the park at Neuilly, when crossing the road it cuts into the upper part of the wood of Boulogne and ends at Auteuil. Resuming the line on the opposite bank, it incloses the suburbs of Grenelle, Vaugirard, cuts the line of the Versailles Railway, leaves Montrouge outside, passes Gentilly, traverses the plain of Ivry, and crosses the line of the Orleans Railway before arriving at its limit opposite Bercy, on the left bank. The entire circle of inclosure comprises a length of 35,914 yards (upwards of 20 miles).

In their outer extent the ditches are of considerable width, and the escarpment is lined with a wall which is covered by the glacis. The military road inside is paved. Near to this, and frequently parallel to it, embracing the entire series of fortifications, is the line which joins all the railways running into Paris and their eight termini. Sixty-six gates are pierced in the fortifications. On the north side of the city the hill of Montmartre, which, as before stated, is 426 feet high and 318 feet broad, forms a commanding eminence close on the boundary, inaccessible on all sides except that towards the town. It is a position of surpassing strength, and, if well defended with artillery, almost impregnable. Montmartre is separated from Belleville by the plain of St. Denis. These three positions—the plateau of Belleville, 460 feet high, and extending from 984 feet to 4920 feet in breadth, the hill of Montmartre, and the plain of St. Denis—form the natural defences of Paris; and as it was evident in the late campaign that the Prussians had determined on marching on the city, these positions, especially the heights of Montmartre, were strengthened, and a fine battery of naval guns established, worked by a detachment of the sailors from the fleet.

The exterior fortifications (*forts detaches*) present sixty-one fronts, and are so many small but complete fortresses, with lodgings for at least 500 men each, and dwellings for the officers. Adopting the line traced in the preceding description of the *enceinte*, the first in order is the Fort de Charenton; 2, the Fort de Nogent; 3, the Fort de Rosny; 4, the Fort de Noisy; 5, the Fort de Romainville; 6, the Fort de l'Est; 7 and 8, Couronne du Nord and Fort de la Briche, one on either side of St. Denis; 9, Fort du Mont Valérien; 10, Fort de Vanves; 11, Fort d'Issy; 12,. Fort de Montrouge; 13, Fort de Bicêtre; and 14, Fort d'Ivry.

The detached forts may be considered in three groups. One group formed the north-east line from St. Denis to the north of Montmartre. On the left of St. Denis, close to the railway leading to Enghien and Montmorency, and behind the confluence of the canal of St. Denis, with the Seine, is the fort of La Briche, covering the branch of the railway to Pontoise to the north; on the other side of the stream of Rouillon, the fort of La Double Couronne du Nord, containing in it the crossing of the principal north, north-eastern, and north-western roads; and on the south-east the fort de l'Est, a regular bastioned square. These three points are united by ramparts and ditches which can be readily filled, and which are covered by the redoubt of Stains. At 4400 paces to the south-east of Fort de l'Est is that of Aubervilliers, an irregular bastioned pentagon. Between the two passes the railway to Soissons, and behind this line the canal of St. Denis. The earth which was dug out of the canal formed before it a sort of parapet fortified by three redoubts. At a distance of 4200 paces from the other side of the Canal de l'Ourcq and of the Strassburg Railway, on the continuation of the height of Belleville by Pantin, stands the fort of Romainville, a bastioned square, 1800 paces from the principal wall of defence. A series of intrenchments extends from the fort towards the Canal de l'Ourcq, while on the other side two redoubts defend the passage. Further off to the east and to the south, still on the outer side of the same line of hills, and almost in a line parallel to the railway to Mulhouse, the works of the fortifications, which are united by a paved road, are continued at about equal distances—the forts of Noisy (3500 paces), Rosny (3200 paces), and Nogent (3800). There ends the line of hills which begins near Belleville, and descends by a steep incline towards the Marne. Between the above-named forts are placed at short intervals the redoubts of Noisy, Montreuil, Boissière, and Fontenay. The Marne, which is here 100 paces in breadth, forms a natural defence, fortified also by an intrenchment of 2800 feet in length, consisting of a parapet and ditches covering the isthmus of Saint Maur, where a bridge crosses the Marne. The two extremities of the intrenchment are flanked by the redoubts of Faisanderie and Gravelle, which the railway of

Vincennes and La-Varenne passes. All these works inclose in a semicircle the castle of Vincennes, in which is the principal arsenal of Paris, on the edge of the great field for manoeuvring artillery close to the Marne. On the other bank of this river, in the triangle formed by the union of the Seine and the Marne near Alfort, on the right side of the Lyons Railway, is the fort of Charenton, a bastioned pentagon which closes the first line of defence. What adds to its strength is that the *enceinte* inclosed by the fortifications serves admirably for an intrenched camp, in which 200,000 men may be placed.

The next group of detached forts form the southern line of exterior defences. Opposite Fort Charenton, at a distance of 4000 paces, on the left bank of the Seine, begins the southern line, with the fort of Ivry, another bastioned pentagon, which commands the neighbourhood. In a straight line, nearly from east to west, the forts of Bicêtre, covering the road to Fontainebleau, Montrouge (a bastioned square), Vanves (an irregular bastioned quadrilateral), and Issy (a bastioned pentagon), follow at equal distances of about 3000 paces. The last-named rises to a height of about fifty feet above the Seine, which here leaves the city. Between them are the railways of Limours and Versailles.

The third group of detached forts are those on the western side of Paris. This line of outside defence is naturally very easy, for the Seine, flowing in the direction of the north and north-east, turns towards St. Denis by St. Cloud, Boulogne, Surennes, Puteaux, Courbevoie, Neuilly, Asnières, Clichy, and St. Ouen, places on the banks of the river. Between it and the town is the celebrated Bois de Boulogne. On the line indicated five bridges cross the Seine; and near the station at Asnières, on the left bank, the railways from Dieppe, Normandy, St. Germain, and Versailles unite, and cross the river by a common bridge. A single fort, but the largest and strongest of all—that of Mont Val6ien, a large bastioned pentagon, situate 415 feet above the Seine, and from which there is a magnificent view of Paris—commands this space. A paved road joins Mont Valérien with the Bois de Boulogne, by the bridge of Surennes.

The distance from Fort Mont Valérien to the nearest of those about St. Denis is nearly seven miles, and from the fort of Issy about four miles. Consequently at this point there was a great gap in the system of defence; a defect met by the construction of extensive works, on the plan organized for the defence of Sebastopol by General Todleben, between Mont Valérien and the sides of Meudon, at Montretout, which commanded the valleys of Sévres and Ville d'Avray. The extreme diameter is that between Mont Valérien and the Fort de Nogent. It follows exactly the parallel, and at a distance of 27,000 paces, or nearly eleven miles; while in the southern direction the greatest distance between St. Denis and the fort of Bicêtre is 20,000 paces, or eight miles. A line of circumference joining the exterior forts would be twenty-six miles, or twelve and a half hours' march. All the exterior forts possess bastions, and the forts of Noisy, Rosny, and Nogent have hornworks. The scarps and counterscarps are as high as those of the fortifications of Paris; covered ways, with trenches of masonry and bomb-proof powder magazines, are everywhere. All the forts communicate by telegraph with Paris, and with each other.

To place the fortifications in a condition for active defence, at the period at which we interrupted our narrative, in order to give the preceding description of them, 12,000 "navvies" worked day and night to cut through the roads and carry the fosse completely round the walls. The smaller gates were blocked up by the banks of earth and strengthened on the inside by palisades. Dams were constructed across the Seine by which the waters could be forced into the trenches. Three gates only, those of Bercy, Italy, and Orleans, were left open, which were approached by drawbridges and defended by massive outworks. The trees which grew upon the glacis were cut down to within a foot or two of the ground, and the sharpened stumps left standing to impede the advance of a storming party. On every bastion from eight to ten twelve-pounders were mounted to the number of about 1200, and the outlying forts were armed with heavy naval breech-loaders, throwing projectiles of great weight, and served by marine artillerymen. From St. Denis to Vincennes, and thence to Issy, the forts are so close that their cross-fire sweeps the intervening space; and between Issy and Mont Valérien to St. Denis, as before stated, intermediate works were constructed.

These detached forts, thus placed with reference to the range of their guns, and supporting one another, were capable of filling the spaces between them as with a hail of iron or a wall of fire. Within their protection an army could manoeuvre with freedom, or retreat in safety. The actual armaments of the detached forts—which were subsequently materially strengthened by supplementary defences—were approximately as follows:—The southern forts, Issy, Vanves, Montrouge, Bicêtre, and Ivry, mounted from forty to seventy guns each; the eastern forts, Charenton, Nogent, Noisy, Rosny, Romainville, and Aubervilliers, from fifty to seventy; the northern forts of St. Denis, Forts de l'Est, du Nord, and de l'Ouest, from forty to sixty guns; and Mont Valérien, the only fort on the western side of the city, was armed with about eighty cannon. There was also a strong field of artillery drawn up in the Champs Elysées, the Palais de l'Industrie, and other localities.

Besides upwards of 2000 heavy guns mounted on the forts and ramparts of the city, and manned by 18,000 sailors, the flower of the French navy, several light gun-boats were launched upon the Seine, to assist in the defence of the city, placed under the command of Captain Thomaset. These small vessels were very broad in the beam in proportion to length, being iron-plated, and the decks were covered with iron. Each vessel contained two guns, pointing forward in a fine with the keel, with a slight training limit to each side. Two large helms with double screw were fixed, and in six small projections on each side the forecastle, covered loop-holes for musketry.

While, however, the French authorities were putting Paris into a state of defence, the Germans had the most minute information of every addition to the fortifications. The officers were furnished with maps of France more complete than any which the French possessed; and in particular the defences of the capital were perhaps not better known to M. Thiers and General Trochu than to Count von Bismarck and General von Moltke.

During the last days of August, as the situation grew more serious, an improved tone was manifested by the inhabitants of the capital. General Trochu likewise showed great activity in the organization of the troops, and took energetic measures for the expulsion of German residents from Paris. To effect this the following decree was issued:—"Article 1. Every person not a naturalized Frenchman, and belonging to one of the countries actually at war with France, is called upon to quit Paris and the department of the Seine within the space of three days, and to leave France or to withdraw into one of the departments situated beyond the Loire. Article 2. Every foreigner coming within the scope of the preceding injunction who shall not have conformed to it, and shall not have obtained a special permission to remain, emanating from the governor of Paris, shall be arrested and handed over to the military tribunals to be judged according to law.

"The Governor of Paris, TROCHU."

A further order was issued to rid Paris of that loose class of society which finds its opportunity in times of national trouble. Accordingly a great number of arrests were made from the disreputable dens and suspicious *cafés* of the city; while a raid was made upon the ranks of the courtesans, whose language and gestures after arrest were a public scandal. Several thousands of these worse than "useless mouths" were conveyed to villages outside the fortifications. Most of the theatres were also closed, the musicians and other attendants joining the ranks of the army. There was moreover a voluntary exodus of the well-to-do classes, of ladies and children, and of foreigners of all nationalities, who hurried to the railway stations in order to escape from the city. Side by side with the movement outward, thousands of farmers and peasants living in the environs flocked in with vehicles crammed with furniture, and waggons laden with corn and flour and all kinds of agricultural produce. This immigration was hastened by the action of the government, who had invited farmers to deposit their stores in the municipal warehouses free of all charge, and threatened that all grain remaining outside the walls would be burnt, to prevent it falling into the hands of the enemy. Huge droves of sheep and cattle arrived from the provinces, and were placed in the beautiful grounds of the Bois de Boulogne and other open spaces; the pens covered many acres, and a market was rapidly constructed. The preparations to receive the invaders were made with a ruthless hand. The handsome entrance gates from the Avenue de l'Impératrice to the Bois de Boulogne gave way to a massive bulwark in stone; the line of gilded railings at La Muette was replaced by a high wall, loopholed for musketry; and the woods upon the glacis were cut down.

The danger to the capital effectually roused the nation. Recruits poured into the various dépôts with great rapidity. Regiment after regiment passed through Paris for the protection of its outer defences; masses of gardes mobiles were drilled at the camp of St. Maur, and thousands volunteered for the corps of francs-tireurs and other irregular troops. Many aged men, among whom were Auber the composer, and Carnot, grandson of the celebrated military organizer mentioned in Chapter V., also joined the ranks. Fortunately, too, although composed of most discordant elements, the various bodies of defenders showed great confidence in the character and sagacity of the governor.

The ministry of Count Palikao, while displaying great activity in raising troops to meet the contingency, by calling out all old soldiers between twenty-five and thirty-five years of age, all officers formerly in the army up to sixty, and all able-bodied generals up to seventy, also put forth strenuous efforts to obtain the necessary military equipments. Large demands were made upon foreign markets, and much satisfaction was felt at the discovery of 300,000 Chassepots which were not known to be in store. The patriotism of the people at this juncture was strikingly manifested in the readiness with which they replenished the coffers of the government. On the 21st of August a decree was issued announcing a new loan for the sum of 750,000,000 francs (about £30,000,000). The subscription opened on the 23rd, and on the 25th the *Official Journal* stated that more than the amount had been received.

The proceedings in the Corps Législatif during this period of intense interest to the Parisians, were of a most unsatisfactory nature, and similar scenes to those recorded in Chapter IX. were repeated in the Chamber. Great difficulty continually arose from the incapacity of the Legislature. There was, however, one honourable exception. M. Thiers, who so boldly opposed the declaration of hostilities, and was reviled by the Chamber for doing so, forgot past slights, and applied himself with all the vigour and ardour of youth to the work of the national defence. His appointment by the government to the Committee of Defence was approved by acclamation of the Chamber; and a few words of his address are worthy a place in the records of the crisis. Although his voice was feeble, there was something peculiarly impressive in the tone and manner in which he said:—"Believe me, gentlemen, that I do not desire at this moment to create difficulties for the government or for you, for they would also be difficulties for the country itself; but I have all my life endeavoured to keep my conduct perfectly clear, not in the eyes of blind partisans, for whom nothing is clear, but with just and prudent men. And I cannot consent that the slightest cloud of doubt should rest upon the act to day imposed upon me. What I yesterday was I to-day am; I do but bring an unofficial and devoted co-operation to the common work—unfortunately a very inadequate co-operation; I say it, believe me, without false modesty! . . . The efforts of everybody are inadequate in the emergency in which we find ourselves. I ask your pardon for these details and beg you to excuse them, but I desire that my conduct and my life shall be for my country, and for all parties whatsoever, as clear as daylight."

Subsequently, the veteran statesman of seventy-three years was out for hours before breakfast, superintending the arming of the fortifications, and giving the benefit of his suggestions to the officials in charge.

But during this period the more resolute party in the Chamber was gradually gaining the upper hand, although the fierce onslaughts of the Left, generally headed by M. Gambetta, whose impetuosity was most remarkable, were pretended to be treated either with threats or contempt; while General Trochu, whose popularity was his great crime, was opposed by the empress, and regarded with ill-concealed suspicion by the cabinet, as explained more fully in the note at the end of the chapter. Count Palikao stated publicly in the Chamber that he would suffer no distribution of arms to be made to the national guard by "one of his subordinates;" and a disposition was even shown by some members of the Right to place the general at the bar of the Chamber, to ask explanations relative to his proclamation to the people and the army of Paris; but an officer so valuable as Trochu could not be sacrificed thus lightly. Ernest Picard, in the *Electeur Libre*, said, "We cannot believe the position of General Trochu to be seriously menaced; the government will not brave public opinion; if it has any doubt as to what that opinion is, let it go to the next review of the national guard."

It was soon felt, however, that it was no time for internal discord, and on the 26th of August M. Chevreau made the following communication to the Corps Législatif:—

"Messieurs,—The army of the Crown Prince appeared yesterday and the day before to be retreating, but it is now marching onwards. It is the duty of government to inform the Chamber, France, and the Parisian population of this fact. I need not add that the Committee of Defence is taking every measure for the eventuality of a siege. The utmost reliance may be placed on the energy of the minister of War and of the governor of Paris, and we on our part believe we may rely on the valour of the Parisian population."

This statement drew forth a spirited reply signed by the eighteen mayors of the capital:—"Monsieur le Ministre,—You announced to the Corps Législatif that the enemy was marching on Paris. The citizens of our arrondissements are ready for every sacrifice, every act of devotion and courage. They will receive the enemy with calm and resolution. The inhabitants of Paris will prove to the whole world that France is still the grand nation. Let the enemy come. We await him with arms in our hands. The mayors of Paris will be in the front rank of the defenders of the country."

Notwithstanding the gravity of the situation, the Bourse held firm, and the greatest activity prevailed in the city. The Chamber, too, did not fail to applaud the gallant conduct of Strassburg, which was declared to have "merited well of the country." A firm protest was also entered by M. Andre against malevolent aspersions as to alleged dealings of the Protestant population of the provinces with the enemy; certain honourable pastors having been pursued with the cry of "A bas les Prussiens." The deputy was loudly cheered, and the good sense of the Chamber possibly saved the country from the dangers of a religious war.

The opening days of September brought news to Paris unfavourable to the French cause. The contending armies were closing in. Success was already attending the enemy's operations; and after being puffed up with falsehoods regarding the exploits of their army, the Parisians were rudely awakened to the truth that their two greatest generals, with the flower of their troops, had been signally defeated. In the Corps Législatif, on Saturday, September 3, Count Palikao, very much depressed, made the following statement:—

"Messieurs les Députés—I have promised to tell you the whole truth, and I am now here to keep my promise, painful as it is to do so. The news I have to give is even yet not official; but it comes from a certain source. Marshal Bazaine, after a great engagement and some advantages, has been obliged to fall back upon Metz; but he may perhaps yet make sorties. There is the first bad news. The next is that of a battle fought near Mézières by Marshal MacMahon. There was a long series of combats attended by reverses and successes. A part of the Prussian army was driven into the Meuse; but after a terrible fight our army was obliged to retreat either to Mézières or Sedan, and a few took refuge in Belgium. There is other serious news in circulation about another battle fought by Marshal MacMahon, but as the government has no official news it cannot give details for fear of being accused of alarming the country. We therefore come here to-day to make a fresh appeal to the whole valid force of the nation. The mobile national guard is organized throughout France. A part of it will come to assist in the defence of Paris, and the rest will be sent to reinforce the regular army. I trust that France, responding to our appeal, will enable us to drive the enemy out of the country."

Thus at last the truth was told, with one all-important reservation, that of the surrender of the emperor and his army. The statement of the minister, however, caused great agitation, and M. Jules Favre intimated that the time had come for the *de facto* government to cease. The country must henceforth rely on itself. Before the Chamber separated a resolution was passed that a levy *en masse* of the nation should be made forthwith.

The development of the crisis illustrated the truth of Carlyle's estimate of the French nature, "so full of vehemence, so free from depth." One day towards the close of August, a large black cloud hovering over Paris took a shape which was thought to betoken victory, and the crowds on the boulevards eagerly accepted the auspicious omen; on the 3rd of September, when the news of defeat began to spread among the citizens, their depressed and despairing attitude was saddening to witness; next day, when the news was received of the crowning disaster of Sedan and the capture of the emperor, Parisians, frantic with joy, were rushing into each others arms, and shouting and singing with the glee of school-boys set free for a holiday. In the cry of "Vive la République!" they forgot the awful peril of their position; that the enemy was steadily advancing; that the flower of their army had been cut down on the red battle-field; and that the effective force with which they could oppose the victorious Prussians was comparatively small and inefficient. Enough that Paris had effected a revolution, and was delivered from imperialism!

But the events of this day, September 4, must form the first subject of the succeeding chapter of our narrative.

The progress of events which led to the collapse of the imperial *régime* in France naturally caused great satisfaction throughout Germany. The opening victories of the campaign inspired her people with confidence, and prepared them for the news of further successes. Great irritation, however, was felt at the manner in which their opponents professed to regard their victories. Even the defeat of MacMahon at Woerth and Frossard at Forbach were made light of, and the Vosges mountains, according to French journalists, were to be the grave of the Prussian troops. "Two more such victories as they had won, and the German army would cease to exist." Such statements, so little in accordance with the facts, incited the Germans to caricature the failure of the French programme, and to display cartoons the reverse of flattering, especially after receipt of the news that Nancy, the chief city of Lorraine, had capitulated without a battle in its defence, thus placing in the hands of the Germans the direct line of railway between Metz and Paris.

The issue of the hard-fought battles around Metz produced in Germany a subdued feeling of exultation. The people saw the importance of the advantage obtained by their commanders in isolating Marshal Bazaine and cutting in two the army of the Rhine; but they had hardly the heart to exult over the news of victory so dearly purchased. As the king had written to his queen from the battle-field that he could scarcely bring himself to ask after his acquaintances, so many of them were dead or maimed, the joy of the inhabitants generally was sensibly damped by the same cause. The terrible slaughter of the 16th and 18th August more particularly cast a gloom over the nation. At Berlin the people received the news with melancholy thankfulness, and no demonstrations were made in the streets. But in the absence of outward displays, their interest in the sanguinary events of the war was the more intense, and the wish to prevent a recurrence of them was general. Although the German army was not composed of mercenary soldiers, but citizens in uniform, the pith and flower of the country, who were being slaughtered in those murderous contests, the universal cry was to "put down France," and render it impossible for her again to indulge in "military promenades" at the expense of her neighbours. In fact, though shocked at the frightful bloodshed and the untold miseries it entailed upon their families, the Germans were yet firmly determined to crush the enemy before mentioning terms.

Germany indeed had sad experience that close upon the heels of victory follows the ghastly shadow of suffering. Into the larger cities of the Fatherland, after the sanguinary battles of the middle of August, poured continuous streams of wounded men, many with the impress of death upon their faces. Train after train brought regiment upon regiment of sufferers, stretched on beds extemporized to receive them; all the surgeons available, besides many strangers and foreign volunteers, troops of sisters of charity, and bands of girl and woman nurses, assiduously sought to relieve the sufferings of the wounded, and friends and enemies were treated with equal kindness. Especially in the earlier stages of the war, the Germans displayed great general philanthropy, and their kindness to the individual Frenchman was beyond all praise. That, however, which raised their indignation was the employment of the Turcos, who even when wounded bit at the very fingers which tended them, and actually attempted to outrage the sisters of charity. For that crime ten of their number were shot off-hand at Berlin in one day. "Conceive," said the Germans, "these men masters of our towns, with our wives and daughters at their mercy;" and they became the more embittered against the French.

A sterner feeling was also enkindled among many by the lavish attentions bestowed upon the French wounded and other prisoners by German ladies. In the *Cologne Gazette*, a well-known authoress (Fanny Lewald) reminded them that such benevolent proceedings had their limits, and, addressing the women of Germany, concluded with the following:—"You would not be worthy of the German men who are standing in the field for us and our country if you could forget but for a moment who are the authors of the fearful misfortune brought upon hundreds of thousands of Germans, if you could forget what you owe to the memory of our fallen heroes, to the anguish of the mourners, to your country, to your fellow-women, and to your own dignity. We should not forget the man in the prisoner, the wounded, the Frenchman; but we should not, and will not, forget that he is at this moment our enemy and the enemy of our country. Let him testify on his return that we are merciful and know what is becoming, and what we owe to ourselves. Do not let us substantiate the caricatures with which, at the expense of German women, French vanity and immorality filled the soldiers knapsacks when they started." Indeed the hostile feeling towards both the French government and people was manifestly deepening, and such articles as the following from the *Staats Anzeiger* found a hearty response in public opinion:—

"Three battles have been fought in the short space of time between the 14th and the 18th. In each of them the main army of the French, headed by the guards and commanded by its most able generals, has been defeated. Let us place laurel wreaths on the coffins of our departed brothers, to whose self-sacrifice we are indebted for these victories; but let us acknowledge that we are witnessing a judgment of God Almighty. God is punishing a people which obstinately persists in insolence and blindness even in the hour of trial, and of whose moral depravity we see such appalling proofs before us. High and low in France behave at this moment with equal frivolity. Lies are incessantly propagated at our expense, to stir the passions of the populace against us. A hollow grandiloquence appeals in vain to the patriotism of the inhabitants. Fanatic party divisions interfere with all real devotion to the country, and as they cannot vanquish our armies they presume to hate us as a race, and to injure, oppress, and expel the few Germans living among them. The infamies perpetrated against German residents in France will be a lasting stain upon that country. In the meantime, our sons and brothers are fighting the good fight of Germany. Many have already sealed with their blood the vow they took; none have given way before the enemy, and all have manifested that spirit of moral elevation and discipline, the symbol of which the Prussian colours have ever been. We celebrate their exploits, and we mourn the dead. In seeing the noblest of our race taken from us by an untimely death we have one consolation. If our fathers warded off the unjust attacks of France without deriving any permanent benefit from their efforts it will not be so this time. We shall settle accounts with this race, so eaten up with arrogance and the lust of conquest, which has threatened and endeavoured to humiliate us for centuries, and which has robbed Germany of some of her finest provinces. The Lord, who has helped us to overcome the lying mendacity and frivolity of France, will not permit our victims to be offered up in vain. He will bless our aged king, and accord him the noble privilege of establishing a safe and durable peace, guarded by our united, our free, upright, and pious Fatherland."

A still more notable production appeared in the official *Provincial Correspondenz*, broadly intimating that the social and political disorganization displayed by France could not have supervened so soon unless her people had been morally corrupt long before. After noticing her arrogant claims to take the lead in European affairs, the writer continued:—"By the reviving power of Germany this overweening superiority of one state is at last to be reduced to its proper limits. . . . In a state of perfect intoxication the French government and people entered upon the war. Events which have recently occurred could not but arouse them from their dreams. Yet the same giddiness, the same deficiency in moral sense, which have conjured up the evil, are noticeable in their conduct. . . . What has surprised us most is the precipitation with which extreme measures are adopted by the ministry and sanctioned by the Chambers. Steps which in great and well-ordered states are, as a rule, only resorted to in the lust extremity, we find resolved upon after a few preliminary disasters. This betrays a state of corruption and internal rottenness more intense and more comprehensive than one could have imagined to exist. Not by her misfortunes in war, but by her pitiable self-despair, France has forfeited the prestige she so long regarded as her due."

Sentiments similar to these were widely disseminated by the German press, and contemporaneously an article appeared in the *Provincial Correspondenz*, headed "Germany's wishes with regard to Alsace and Lorraine," which contained the following:—

"These provinces which were torn away from the German empire have become France's chief points of support for menacing attacks upon Germany. How should it be possible, after the glorious victories of the German army, after the re-conquest of two old German provinces, and after the heavy and costly sacrifices by which our triumph has been gained; how should it be possible to avoid the irresistible conviction that the honour and the safety of Germany imperatively demand the removal of the lasting shame—a German country serving as a starting point for German enslavement? The European powers, true to the attitude of neutrality which they have assumed, will not arbitrarily endeavour to arrest the consequences of the war, so long as no substantial European interest is injured by the conditions of the treaty of peace. The German people, however, is conscious that in its demand it does not aim at any preponderance over other nations which might endanger the so-called European equilibrium, but that it seeks only a firmly established peace, which it intends to wring for itself and for other nations from the old enemy of the peace of Europe."

Large public meetings, also, were held in Germany, protesting against foreign interference, and contending that the mere substitution of one form of government for another in France would not afford the necessary guarantees against another war of aggression. Since 1552, it was said, France, under every possible form of government, and under the control of the most opposite parties, had never ceased to extend her territory at the expense of her neighbours, and Germany had been the principal sufferer. The time had at length come when the Fatherland must cease to be molested by her, and secure for itself a long period of peace. Alsace and Lorraine must again form an integral portion of the German empire.

This resolve on the part of the Germans was greatly favoured by the subsequent course of events; and while they watched with intense interest the movements of the combatants on the field, many of the well-informed anticipated to some extent the gradual closing in of their warlike hosts upon the bewildered and disorganized French. But no anticipations could have come up to the reality; and when, early on Saturday, September 3, a telegram proclaimed the astounding news of the crowning victory at Sedan and the surrender of the French army, Berlin immediately gave way to unwonted jubilation. Unter den Linden was crowded, and everywhere the city became alive with processions. Flags and banners were exhibited in endless profusion, and wreaths and streamers covered the great monument of Frederick the Great, and every other public situation. The veteran Marshal TVrangel was early on his way to the palace to offer his congratulations; and on returning to his residence in the Pariser Platz was attended by an enthusiastic crowd, who cheered him as he passed the sentries at his gate, waved flags under his windows, and sang "Borussia." These jubilant demonstrations continued throughout the day, and were followed in the evening by brilliant illuminations from almost every dwelling, public and private; the unusual glare increased by torchlight processions and displays of fireworks. Similar scenes occurred in every corner of Germany. In all the larger cities the moment the capture of Napoleon and his army became known, the population rushed into the streets, and assembled in the churches, town-halls, and other places of public resort. Schools and workshops, and, in some cases, even the courts of justice, were closed. Everywhere the bells were rung and royal salutes fired in honour of the day. In many towns meetings were improvised on the market-place; in others, a regular service was celebrated in the churches; and rarely, indeed, had the places of worship been so filled as they were on that Saturday and the ensuing Sunday. All the various capitals had their processions, and forwarded congratulatory telegrams to the king of Prussia and the Crown Prince of Saxony. Important and cordial addresses were presented to King William of Prussia, thanking him and the army for their achievements in the field, insisting upon the annexation of Alsace and Lorraine as the only means of securing Germany from future attack, and recommending the immediate reunion of Northern and Southern Germany. Thus the victors, rejoicing over their marvellous successes in the field, eagerly sought, at the same time, to possess themselves of the fruit of their conquests.

The intelligence of the emperor's surrender created a profound sensation in England and throughout all the nations of the Continent, while the Atlantic cables flashed the news across the seas to the Western hemisphere. East and west alike, men looked on in surprise and bewilderment, exclaiming, in the words of the Jewish patriot, "How are the mighty fallen!"

NOTE.

The exact circumstances attending General Trochu's appointment as governor of Paris were neither known nor understood correctly until he himself laid them before the National Assembly sitting at Versailles in June, 1871, and in the course of his statement on that occasion considerable light was thrown upon some of the incidents of this part of our narrative. After describing the causes of the military decadence of France, General Trochu, on the occasion referred to, said that as early as the commencement of August, he, being the only general in Paris, perceived the importance of the capital being prepared to withstand a siege. He wrote a letter to the emperor to that effect, warning him that all other events were secondary, and that an army of succour collected before Paris was the only resource left. The general also asked for the recall of the army of Marshal Bazaine, subsequently to be joined by that of Marshal MacMahon, which was unanimously approved by a conference of generals, but political considerations prevented this measure from being carried out. This support failing, the safety of Paris was thenceforth seriously compromised. General Trochu was present at a conference held on the 17th August at Châlons, at which the emperor, Marshal MacMahon, Prince Napoleon, and several other officers were present. The question discussed was whether the emperor should give up the command of the army or abdicate altogether, the emperor himself being desirous of resuming the reins of government. General Trochu accepted, with the title of Governor of Paris, the task of preparing for the return of the emperor, on the express condition that the army of Marshal MacMahon should be ordered to fall back on the capital to act as an army of succour. The appointment was couched in the following terms:—"General Trochu, appointed governor of Paris and commander-in-chief, will immediately start for Paris; he will precede the emperor by a few hours. Marshal MacMahon will march on Paris with his army." The general also received the following order:—"Camp of Châlons, August 17, 1870. Mon cher Général,—I appoint you governor of Paris and commander-in-chief of all the forces intrusted with the defence of the capital. Immediately on my arrival at Paris you will receive communication of the decree officially conferring these functions upon you; but in the meanwhile take all the measures that may be necessary to fulfil your mission. Receive, mon cher général, the assurance of my friendly feelings—Napoleon." The empress, however, distrustful of what was being done, formally opposed the return of the emperor. Count Palikao, too, received General Trochu coldly; refused to allow the army of Marshal Bazaine to come to Paris; and decided to send all disposable reinforcements to Verdun and Metz. The peculiar fact, too, that no authority was given by General Trochu for his appointment was also fully explained in his speech before the National Assembly, to which we are referring. On presenting himself to the empress on the night of the 17th of August, General Trochu said, "I have brought with me the proclamation in which I desire to make known to the population that I have been appointed governor and commander-in-chief during the siege. That proclamation begins thus:—' In the presence of the peril that threatens the country, the emperor has appointed me governor of the capital is in a state of siege.' The empress here interrupted me. 'General, the emperor's name must not appear in a proclamation at a time like this.' 'But, madam, I represent the emperor. I said that I would come here to defend him. I cannot address the population of Paris without referring to the emperor, and saying that it is by his orders that I have undertaken the defence of the capital.' 'No, general, believe me. In the present state of the public mind there would be serious objections to allow this reference to the emperor.' Thereupon it was struck out." Farther on in this remarkable speech, General Trochu fully confirmed the inharmonious nature of his relations with Count Palikao and the empress. In their views of the situation of affairs the governor and the minister strongly disagreed, and General Trochu was regarded with a distrust which was shared in by all the imperial authorities. "The council of the empress," continued the general, "consisted of the ministers of the privy council, of the president of" the Corps Législatif, and of the president of the Senate. I experienced at its hands great and growing distrust; my loyalty, my sincerity were insufficient to disarm those who showed me so plainly their feelings." In fact, for some days the general was virtually relieved from his command, and until the time of the revolution on the 4th of September was at constant variance with the minister of War.

To this defence of General Trochu before the National Assembly, Count Palikao subsequently replied in a letter to the president. That document, however, essentially confirmed the statement of General Trochu, especially as to the unfortunate relations existing between him and the count. The latter admits that the general conceived that the whole war should be reduced to the defence of Paris, with MacMahon's army hovering at a distance round the capital till it gathered strength to come to the rescue. His plan was laid before the emperor's council at Châlons: it was approved and intrusted to Trochu himself for execution. Trochu, however, found himself, on arriving at Paris, in a subordinate position. His scheme clashed with the views of the War minister, which were also those of the empress-regent and of her cabinet, who held at that moment the supreme power. Count Palikao's own plan was to reinforce MacMahon at Châlons, so as to enable him to defend the line of the Marne, and even to recover lost ground on the Mease and the Moselle, eventually advancing to the release of Bazaine at Metz. In pursuance of this strategy, both

Trochu himself and the emperor's council, in whose name he spoke, were utterly ignored. By Palikao's own admission, Trochu was "taught his place," "it being the habit of the minister never to discuss with his subordinates when he had orders to give them." The most serious charge made by Count ' Palikao against General Trochu in his letter was, that when he returned to Paris from Châlons, "in pursuance with the order which he communicated to the Chamber, he brought back with him eighteen battalions of the Paris mobiles who were quartered there." "We all know," I continued Count Palikao, "the innate gallantry of the Parisians under fire, and all the world is equally aware of the dangers their presence in Paris must bring about. So that, instead of leaving at Châlons these eighteen battalions, who, at a given moment, might have performed prodigies of valour and decided the issue of a battle, the general brought back in his train a phalanx of revolutionists, whose presence here must further complicate our trying situation. Several of these battalions belonged to the most dangerous quarters of the town. By this step we were deprived of so many men against the enemy, who were arrayed against the cause of order, as experience proved soon after, under the very eyes of General Trochu." Count Palikao also intimated that matters were rendered still worse by a proclamation, in which General Trochu asserted that "the mobiles had a right to be in Paris, and to stay there." He further admitted that he ceased to communicate with the general, and added, "As to his presence at the Council of Ministers, he was summoned to attend whenever a question which came within his province was to be discussed, and he was admitted whenever he wished to be present. But I must frankly confess that in the midst of the urgent business to be transacted during those critical times, the length of the speeches which the general's great facility of elocution led him to indulge in were greatly dreaded."

It is thus easy to perceive that some, at least, of the misfortunes of France at this time arose as much from a conflict of opinion as from a collision of authority. The division was not, however, only between the two generals; it was also, as we have proved in a previous chapter, between the government in Paris, presided over by the empress, and the government in the field, with the emperor at the head of its councils. The views of the former prevailed, and resulted in the catastrophe of Sedan, involving alike the ruin of the regency, of the empress, and of the dynasty of Napoleon.

CHAPTER XVI.

Overthrow of the Second Empire—General Trochu called upon to assume the Government of the Country—Midnight Sitting of the Corps Législatif—M. Jules Favre moves that the Emperor and his Dynasty have forfeited all Rights conferred by the Constitution—Government Proclamation on Sunday, September 4, admitting the Surrender of the Emperor and his Army—Its effect on the Parisians—The National Guard fraternize with the People, and the Gendarmerie allow them to proceed to the Corps Législatif—The Scene inside the Chamber—The National Guard replace the Soldiers on guard outside—The crowd calls for the immediate Dethronement of the Emperor and the Proclamation of a Republic—The National Guards and the Citizens at last invade the Chamber—The President is driven from the Chair, the décheance voted by an immense majority, and the New Republic established—The Extraordinary Scenes in the City on the News becoming known—Public Proclamation of the Republic by M. Gambetta—The Palace of the Tuileries entered by the Crowd, and everything connected with the Imperial regime destroyed—Protest of a Meeting of the Deputies against the Proceedings in the Chamber—A Provisional Government formed of all the Members for Paris except M. Thiers—The Last Sitting of the Senate—The Opinion of the American Ambassador on the Events—Biographical Notice of M. Jules Favre, the new Minister of Foreign Affairs—Flight of the Empress from Paris, and safe arrival in England—Proclamation of the new Government decreeing the Formation of the Republic and granting an Amnesty for all Political Offences—Important Circular by M. Jules Favre, blaming the Emperor for the War and throwing the onus of continuing it upon the King of Prussia, but asserting that the French will cede neither "An Inch of their Territory nor a Stone of their Fortresses"—The feeling produced by the Circular in France and abroad—The Prospects of Peace increasingly doubtful—The Military Spirit throughout the Country aroused—Disturbances in Lyons—Extraordinary Proceedings—Excitement in Marseilles and other towns—Re-appearance of the Extreme Section of the Press—Magniloquent Addresses of Victor Hugo—Arrival of the Orlean Princes in Paris, but their offer to serve the Government declined—Address of the Comte de Chambord—Characteristic Letter from Garibaldi—A Constituent Assembly to be called—Another Important Circular by M. Favre—Unremitting Exertions to Provision and Defend the City—Review of the whole Armed Force in Paris by General Trochu, and subsequent General Order—Destruction of the Bridges leading to Paris, and of the Woods near the City—Removal of the Government to Tours—Fruitless Mission of M. Thiers to the different European Courts—The Financial Position of Affairs—Recognition of the Republic by the United States of America—Manifestation of Feeling on the part of the Germans in America—Acknowledgment of the Republic by Italy, Switzerland, Belgium, Spain, and Portugal—Action of the British Government on the Subject—Meetings of the Working Classes and Deputation to the Prime Minister, Mr. Gladstone—Interesting Letter of M. Guizot—Feeling in Germany on hearing of the Proclamation of the Republic, and of its prompt recognition by the United States—The action of England treated with indifference—Impulse given to the cause of German Unity by the Events of the War.

THE news of the French disaster at Sedan sealed the fate of the second empire. Scarcely seven weeks had elapsed since the declaration of hostilities was made with a "light heart" by the Ollivier ministry. During that time the capital of France had been deluded with false reports of successes. Even when the fact of the crushing reverses she had sustained became generally known, the people still clung to their belief in the invincibility of their army, and cast the blame of defeat, first upon the cabinet, which crumbled under the heel of popular displeasure, and subsequently upon the emperor and his generals. These circumstances paved the way for the events which form the subject of the present chapter.

We have already shown that in the Corps Législatif on Saturday afternoon (September 3) Count de Palikao prepared the public mind for the reception of the disastrous intelligence. A similar statement was made in the Senate by Baron Jerome David. The ministerial statements roused public indignation, though very few were yet aware that the emperor was a prisoner. But later in the evening, on the publication of confused reports in the special editions of the papers, an assemblage of about 6000 persons sent a deputation to General Trochu, calling upon him to assume the government of the country. He replied that he was not in a position to respond to such a proposal, but would do his duty in defending Paris. This answer was received with shouts of "Abdication!" "Abdication!" Another assemblage of about 10,000 persons sent a deputation to him with the same object, and got a similar reply, which was followed by cries of "Abdication!" "France for ever!" "Trochu for ever!" The Boulevards were densely crowded, and though the people were silent, the approaches to the Chamber were guarded by a strong force of cavalry and infantry.

While the Legislative Body were still in session at midnight on Saturday, Count de Palikao communicated the news of the surrender of the emperor and the capitulation of the army, and asked the Chamber to postpone discussion as to what should next be done till the following day; but M. Jules Favre rose and moved that the emperor and his dynasty should be declared to have forfeited all rights conferred by the constitution. He also demanded the appointment of a Parliamentary committee to be invested with powers to govern the country and take measures for expelling the enemy from French territory, and that, in the meantime, General Trochu should be maintained in his post as governor of Paris. This proposal was received with profound silence, broken only by a protest from M. Pinard. The Chamber thereupon resolved to hold a sitting at noon on the following day, Sunday, September 4.

Early on the morning of this day the cabinet posted the following proclamation, which was also published in the *Journal Officiel*, signed by the full council of ministers:— "Frenchmen! a great misfortune has befallen the country. After the three days of heroic struggles kept up by the army of Marshal MacMahon against 300,000 enemies, 40,000 men have been made prisoners. General Wimpffen, who had taken the command of the army, replacing Marshal MacMahon, who was grievously wounded, has signed a capitulation. This cruel reverse does not daunt our courage. Paris is now in a state of defence. The military forces of the country are being organized. Within a few days a new army will be under the walls of Paris, and another is in formation on the banks of the Loire. Your patriotism, your concord, your energy will save France. The emperor has been made prisoner in this contest. The government co-operates with the public authorities, and is taking all measures required by the gravity of these events."

By this intelligence the Parisians seemed for a time to be well-nigh paralyzed. The streets were deserted; the shops were either not opened, or were closed again long before the usual hour. The faces of the few stragglers who might be seen reading the ominous placards, were expressive of doubt and anxiety as to what might be their effect. Even on the principal boulevards, between ten and eleven o'clock, comparatively few persons were abroad. Everything wore that look of silent and suppressed emotion which in Paris has so often proved the premonitory signal of a coming explosion. About eleven o'clock, however, vast bodies of men approached from the Boulevard Montmartre, all armed, and displaying a perfect forest of bayonets. In a moment the whole scene on the boulevards changed. The *trottoirs* suddenly became densely crowded, and every window and balcony filled with the heads of eager spectators. The column proved to be national guards, and though in every sort of attire, they marched in excellent order, with each officer in his place. Loud cries of "La déchéance! La déchéance!" "Vive la France!" and "Vive la Republique!" were raised, equally by the national guards and the people, with a vehemence and unanimity which left no doubt as to the nature of the movement which was taking place. The cry of "La déchéance" especially was repeated by the national guards; and the shout of "Vive la Republique!" was universal. An order had been issued by General Trochu for the national guards to muster in force around the Chamber, and they were now evidently marching from all points of the city towards the Place de la Concorde, which rapidly filled with a prodigious multitude, and glittered with thousands of bayonets. The number of armed men, almost all of whom had a musket, was appalling. But complete unanimity prevailed, and in the satisfaction of putting down the imperial government and crying "La déchéance," the news of the morning—the German invaders, the defeat, indeed every other fact and feeling—seemed to be forgotten. There was an entire absence of hostile demonstration. The crowd in the Place de la Concorde continued to increase. The gates of the Tuileries gardens were closed, and one or two soldiers only were visible inside; but the imperial flag still floated above the palace. As each successive battalion of the national guard debouched into the Place, it was hailed with deafening shouts, which were answered with like enthusiasm. Often the entire battalion raised the butt-ends of their muskets in the air, and flourished them in token of complete sympathy with the crowd, in the midst of which numbers of ladies were walking about without apprehension. Every now and then the multitude caught up the refrain of the *Chant du Depart* or other revolutionary air, and sang it in chorus with inspiring effect. The whole scene resembled some immense jubilation or Sunday *fête*. Civilians gathered twigs from the neighbouring trees and stuck them in their hats, while every garde national inserted one into the end of his musket, so that the entire Place soon presented a display of green branches instead of bayonets. The men marched steadily across the Place and up to the Pont de la Concorde in front of the Corps Législatif, where a slender body of gendarmerie à, cheval had been drawn up across the entrance to the bridge, who had received orders from Count de Palikao to "do their duty," and prevent the invasion of the Chamber. When the head of the column came up, the officer in command of the gendarmerie refused to let it pass, and the national guard were brought to a stand-still. There was much angry vociferating by the crowd, and gesticulation and remonstrance, followed by menace, on the part of the captains of the citizen troops. The gendarmerie, expecting to be attacked, drew their swords, and so frightened the spectators as to send them to the rear. It was an anxious moment: some of the horses, pressed by the crowd, got restive, and the officers, mounted and foot, found it difficult to negotiate. Suddenly there was a cheer from the spectators; the gendarmerie opened its ranks, and the national guards, with drums beating and colours flying, passed on to the bridge. When half across, however, another obstacle presented itself in the shape of a squadron of helmeted troops belonging to the municipal guard. The civic troops, uncertain how to act, halted for a few minutes, until orders were sent them from the Chamber to wheel about, and on the steps of the Corps Législatif some fifty deputies were immediately observed, who uncovered and cheered. There was a responsive cheer from the populace; again the drums of the national guard were sounded, and the men effected the passage of the bridge without bloodshed. The various battalions then took possession of every available space outside the Chamber, the general crowd following them unimpeded across the bridge.

Meanwhile, a noonday sitting was being held inside the Chamber, and before the other proceedings commenced, M. de Keratry complained of the presence of a great body of regular troops massed about the Corps Législatif, contrary to the orders of General Trochu. Count de Palikao then brought in a *projet de loi* signed by the empress, for instituting a council of government and national defence, to consist of five members elected by the Legislative Body, himself occupying the post of lieutenant-general of the council. M. Jules Favre claimed priority for his motion already proposed, to the effect that the emperor and his dynasty had forfeited all rights conferred on them by the constitution. M. Thiers also brought forward a proposition, signed by forty-five members of the left and right centres, to appoint a commission of government and national defence. The Chamber declared urgency for all the three propositions *en bloc*, and they were collectively referred to the bureaux with a view to the appointment of the commission. The sitting was then suspended for a short time, during which the crowd penetrated into the Salles des Quatre Colonnes and de la Paix. In the latter, M. Jules Ferry, mounting on a bench, amid cries of "Vive la Rcpublique!" "Vive Ferry!" informed the multitude that he had given Count de Palikao his word that the people would not enter the hall where the deputies of the Corps Législatif deliberated. M. Ferry having called upon the national guard to defend the entry, the soldiers on guard retired, and the crowd continued calling for the dethronement, which, they urged, ought to be immediately proclaimed. M. Ernest Picard then addressed them, saying that the Chamber was about to pronounce on this very question, and begged them to wait patiently the decision of the deputies, which could not but be favourable to the unanimous demand of the people. M. Emmanuel Arago next came forward, observing "that they knew for what the democratic party in the Chamber had combated, but that it was for the people to decide who should govern them." He was followed by the president, M. Schneider, who had been requested by several deputies and officers of the national guard to speak. He had always, he said, been devoted to the empire and his country; and he begged the crowd to allow the Chamber to deliberate calmly, and not to let it appear that their representatives acted under popular pressure. "Before all," said he, "we must save France," which produced shouts of "Yes, yes! Vive la Republique?" Meanwhile, M. Glais Bizoin, in the Salle des Quatre Colonnes, called on the people in the name of liberty not to compromise what they were about to proclaim; and M. Ferry, conducted into the Salle de la Paix by several national guards, was invited to address the assemblage there. "Citizens," he said, "I do not call on you to evacuate the Corps Législatif, but be calm and allow us to deliberate." M. Steenackers followed in a similar strain; but the crowd insisted on getting into the "Salle des Séances," clamoured about the members to be designated to form a provisional government, and a paper, on which was written the names of seven deputies of the Left, was hung on the statue of Minerva. The pillars and walls were also covered with demands for the dethronement of the emperor and the proclamation of the republic, which were re-echoed by the incessant clamours of the crowd.

Inside the Chamber there was an attempt to get through business, amid cries of "down with Bonaparte." M. Gambetta ascended the tribune, and thrice addressed the galleries; while groups of citizens and national guards invaded and persistently kept the floor of the Chamber. President Schneider occupied the chair for the last time, and addressed a few words to the Corps Législatif, represented by the Left and a few members of the Right who had timidly taken their seats. Count de Palikao shortly appeared, but M. Brame was the only minister who faced the storm. In spite of a spirited protest by M. Schneider against all attempts at intimidation, there arose fierce cries for the republic, the Chamber was again invaded by a fresh rush of the mob, the benches were taken by storm, and the president was driven from his chair. In the midst of this scene of utter confusion the new republic was born. Numerous slips of paper were passed eagerly from hand to hand, containing the names of persons who should be appointed to form a new government, and many deputies were summoned, all of them belonging to the Left, excepting M. Thiers. M. Jules Favre then gained possession of the tribune, and proclaimed the downfall of the Bonapartist dynasty, backed by M. Gambetta, who acted as "reporter." The *déchéance*, indeed, had been previously voted in committee by the immense majority of 195 deputies to 18.

Outside the Chamber it was immediately known that the *déchéance* had been pronounced and the republic proclaimed. The shout which arose left no doubt as to the opinion of those present upon what had been done. The cry of "à l'Hôtel de Ville!" was soon after raised, and the whole body of national guards began to move in that direction. On their way they removed the eagles from the flagstaffs, and the frightened householders followed the example, throwing them amongst the crowd. Arrived at the Place de la Concorde, the populace forced the sergents-deville to give up their swords, which were immediately broken, and the fragments thrown at the feet of the statue representing Strassburg, which had been crowned with flowers on the preceding day.

As the army had made common cause with the national guards there was, of course, no fear of armed collisions. The scene at the barracks of the Quai d'Orsay was thus graphically depicted by an eye-witness, and was a specimen of what took place in other parts of the capital:—"From the windows of those great barracks, formerly peopled with troops every man of whom was supposed to be ready to die for his emperor, I saw soldiers smiling, waving handkerchiefs, and responding to the cries of 'Long live the Republic!' raised by gendarmes, cavalry, soldiers of the line, national guards, and people, below. Well-dressed ladies in open carriages shook hands with private soldiers and men in blouses, all crying 'Long live the Republic!' Nay, strangers fell on each others' necks, and kissed each other with 'effusion.' In the neighbourhood of the Pont Neuf, I saw people on tops of ladders busily pulling down the emperor's busts. I saw the busts carried in mock procession to the parapet of the Pont Neuf and thrown into the Seine; clapping of hands and hearty laughter greeting the splash which the graven image of the mighty monarch made in the water."

The scene which took place at the Hôtel de Ville, to which the more prominent members of the Left had retired, was almost equally extraordinary. The mob soon became masters of the building, and vented their rage on everything connected with the emperor or his family. Portraits of him and the empress were cut to pieces and thrown out of the window to be trodden upon by the people, the number of whom was now enormous. A discussion arose as to the choice of the flag to be used by the new government, but the tricolour was ultimately decided on—the proposal of some workmen to adopt a red one having been objected to by MM. Gambetta and Schoelcher. As soon as the provisional government had actually been formed, a deputation from them went to the prison of St. Pelagie, and demanded the release of M. Henri Rochefort, a most violent republican, and one of the members for Paris, who was confined there for a political offence. The officials at once acceded to the demand—thus acknowledging the authority of the new rulers as readily as every one else—and he was triumphantly drawn through the streets to the Hôtel de Ville; where on appearing at the window he was vehemently cheered by the vast crowd below. At forty-five minutes past four, M. Gambetta appeared at one of the windows, MM. Jules Favre and E. Arago standing a little behind him, and then and there he publicly proclaimed the republic, and the installation of a provisional government. This proclamation was received with every possible demonstration of enthusiasm, and a few minutes afterwards the Phrygian cap of liberty was planted on the top of the flagstaff in place of the eagle.

Meanwhile the crowd, in company with national and mobile guards, moved towards the Tuileries, tore down the eagles that surmounted the railings, and bursting open the gates made their way to the reserved garden, where a considerable number of voltigeurs of the guard were massed. A deputation sent in advance to hold a parley with the general in command, informed him that the republic had been proclaimed, and that the people demanded entrance to the palace. At this moment the imperial flag was lowered, the signal that the empress had fled from the Tuileries. The general then mounted upon a chair, and expressed his willingness to march out the troops, providing the post was confided to the charge of the national guards. This agreed to, the crowd was allowed to roam at will over the apartments of the palace, which were deserted by all except the servants in the kitchen.

The people, however, were soon cleared out by a detachment of national guards, who throughout the day behaved with great propriety. As in all Parisian tumults, the wits were busy, and covered several prominent places with "Appartements a louer," "liberté, egalité, fraternité," and other stock phrases of the previous revolution. The crowd, however, unlike that of 1848, not only did not destroy the furniture, but showed some disposition to respect property. Then, however, as on the following day, they busied themselves in erasing and destroying every vestige of the imperial regime. Thus many of the public buildings were defaced, and the shopkeepers, either from predisposition or force, speedily removed all tokens of imperial patronage, even to the vignettes on Exhibition prize medals. All portraits and photographs of the imperial family immediately disappeared, and the Avenue de l'Impératrice and other thoroughfares associated with the cast-off dynasty were renamed after republican or patriotic celebrities.

The deputies who left the Chamber when it was invaded met in the afternoon at the president's residence; vice-president Alfred le Roux presided. It was agreed to advise the nomination of a committee of government elected by the Corps Législatif; the Chamber, at the same time, protesting that it recognized in no single body of citizens the right of controlling the destiny of the country. A deputation was then appointed to wait upon the deputies of the Left at the Hôtel de Ville, for the purpose of inculcating the necessity of reliance upon the representatives of the nation, the only legal and organized force, in the forming of a government and combining of efforts against the enemy. The bearers of the proposal were informed that it could not now be entertained, as the republic had already been proclaimed and accepted by the people. It was promised, however, that some of the members of the provisional government should attend an evening meeting of the deputies. At this sitting, which took place under the presidency of M. Thiers, and comprised nearly 200 members of the Corps Législatif, amongst them MM. Jules Favre and Jules Simon, it was explained that the new government were anxious to have the support of the deputies, though these, it was considered, might be able to render better service to the country in the departments. "If," added M. Favre, "you will kindly give the new government your ratification, we shall be grateful to you for it; if, on the contrary, you refuse it, we shall respect the decisions of your conscience, but we shall preserve the entire liberty of our own." He also stated that M. Rochefort was a member of the provisional government, which comprised all the deputies for Paris except M. Thiers, who had refused to form part of it. The veteran statesman, however, counselled a passive concurrence in accomplished facts. "Our duty," said he to M. Favre, "is ardently to desire your success in the defence of Paris. We desire this because your success would be that of our country." Nothing, however, came of this interview, beyond the issue of a protest on the part of the deputies present against the events of the afternoon. The exclusion of other members than those of Paris from the government, was justified by M. Favre on the ground that the defence of the capital was their primary duty.

The Senate on that eventful Sunday had also held its last sitting. M. Rouher took the chair at noon, and warmly protested against the proposition of M. Jules Favre for dethroning the dynasty. The protest evoked some applause, and one or two senators cried, "Vive l'Empereur!" M. Baroche said a few words in defence of the empire, as did also Prince Poniatowski; but with these feeble and expiring forms the body became defunct.

Referring to these events, the American minister wrote to his government:—"In a few brief hours of a Sabbath day I have seen a dynasty fall and a republic proclaimed, and all without the shedding of one drop of blood."

At six o'clock in the evening a decree naming the members of the provisional government was issued, stating that the *déchéance* had been pronounced by the Corps Législatif, the republic proclaimed at the Hôtel de Ville, and a committee of national defence had been appointed.

The provisional government originally consisted of the following members:—General Trochu, president; Emmanuel Arago; Cremieux, minister of Justice; Jules Favre, minister for Foreign Affairs; Jules Ferry; Gambetta, minister of the Interior; Gamier Pages, Glais Bizoin, Pelletan; Ernest Picard, minister of Finance; Rochefort; and Jules Simon, minister of Public Instruction. Subsequently General Leflô, minister for War; Admiral Fourichon, minister of Marine; M. Dorian, minister of Public Works; M. Magnin, minister of Agriculture and Commerce; Count de Keratry, prefect of police; and M. Etienne Arago, were added—forming eighteen members in all.

Jules Claude Gabriel Favre, the minister for Foreign Affairs, and vice-president of the Committee of Defence, was one of the most distinguished members of the new cabinet. He was born at Lyons in 1809, and took a prominent part in the revolution of 1830, being at the time a law student at Paris. Practising as a barrister at Lyons, he warmly espoused the cause of the working classes, and gained great distinction by his ultra-radical opinions. In 1835, at the Paris bar, he especially distinguished himself in a speech before the Cour des Pairs, when, commencing with *Je suis Republicain*, he pleaded for four hours, though he was then dangerously ill. In the revolution of February, 1848, he was appointed secretary-general of the ministry of the Interior, took a prominent part in the prosecution of Louis Blanc and Caussidiére for the attempted insurrection of the 15th May, and refused to join in the vote of thanks to General Cavaignac. After the election of Louis Napoleon as president, Jules Favre became one of his bitterest opponents; and though he acquiesced in the vote for the Italian expedition, he objected to the direction it was taking, and demanded that the president and ministry should be proceeded against. On the *coup d'état* of the 2nd December, M. Favre retired from political life for six years, refusing to swear fidelity to the new *régime*. He reappeared in the Corps Législatif as a Paris deputy in 1858, and defended those involved in the Orsini conspiracy with such power that, in reference to his speech, the procureur-général said, "En presence de l'echafaud qui se dresse on avait élevé une statue pour celui qui doit y monter." In the general elections of 1869 he was rejected by his native town, but was elected for the seventh circonscription of Paris. He was known as the author of a number of political pamphlets, and in 1868, in company with MM. Henon and E. Picard, founded *L'Electeur*, a weekly political journal.

It had become evident about mid-day that the Tuileries was no longer a safe residence for the empress, and she determined on immediate flight. As she passed into the streets a *petit gamin* recognized her, and shouted "Voilá l'Imperatrice!" which called forth from the crowd the rejoinder, "A la guillotine!" No violence, however, was offered her Majesty, who hastened to the house of a friend. As it was considered hazardous to travel by railway, she left Paris without luggage of any kind, and drove to the little northern port of Deauville. An English cutter yacht, the *Gazelle*, lay in the harbour, ready to sail on the following day for England with Sir John and Lady Burgoyne. A few hours before the time appointed for the Gazelle to weigh her anchor the empress presented herself, announced her rank and difficult position, and claimed the protection of Sir John as an English gentleman. Lady Burgoyne was at once introduced to the empress, who became her guest for the voyage across the Channel. At seven o'clock on the morning of the 7th September the Gazelle left for England, and reached Ryde on the afternoon of the 8th. The empress then crossed by steamer to Portsmouth and proceeded to Hastings, where she was joined by the Prince Imperial, who had already arrived in England. After her flight a despatch was found on her table from M. Pietri, the prefect of the police, announcing that the situation was grave; that the national guards were hostile; and that the troops would not inarch.

The officials of the imperial *régime* had shown themselves quite as fully alive to the dangers of the situation as the empress. Count de Palikao and his colleagues in the ministry fled immediately after the proclamation of the republic, and the "official majority" instantly disappeared. In fact, as soon as it became really known that the emperor had succumbed, his wife, his son, his throne, his system, and his supporters, shared in the general collapse. An exodus of the able-bodied youth of the capital followed, and as the Germans approached, England, Belgium, and other countries received an influx of of visitors from Paris evading the *levée en masse*. Thus France rewarded him who had given her the first place in Europe for eighteen years, and during the same time had preserved her internal quiet, and held in order the turbulent masses of Paris.

On Monday morning (September 5) the *Journal Officiel* was superseded by the *Journal of the French Republic*, which contained the following proclamation:—"Frenchmen! The people have disavowed a Chamber which hesitated to save the country when in danger. It has demanded a republic. The friends of its representatives are not in power, but in peril. The republic vanquished the invasion of '92. The republic is proclaimed. The revolution is accomplished in the name of right and public safety. Citizens! watch over the city confided to you. To-morrow you will be with the army avengers of the country." A decree of the ministry dissolved the Corps Législatif, and abolished the Senate and the presidency of the Council of State. The manufacture and sale of arms was declared absolutely free, and a complete amnesty proclaimed for all political crimes and offences. Four prisoners, sentenced to death for their participation in the La Villette riots on the 14th August, were also released.

A proclamation was also issued to the army, in the following terms:—"When a general has compromised his command, it is taken away from him. When a government has imperilled by its faults the safety of the country, it is deposed. This is what France has just done. In abolishing the dynasty which was responsible for our misfortunes, France accomplished an act of justice, and at the same time performed an act of necessity for her own preservation. The nation has only to depend upon herself, and only to reckon upon two things—the revolution, which is invincible; and your heroism, which has no equal, and which, amid undeserved reverses, excites the astonishment of the world. We are not the government of a party, but a government of national defence; and have but one object and one will—the safety of the country by means of the army and the nation grouped around the glorious ensign which made Europe draw back eighty years ago. To-day, as then, the name of the republic signifies the hearty union of army and people in the defence of the country."

All public functionaries of every class were released from their oaths; the ambassadors to England, Austria, and Russia were dismissed; and all Germans not in possession of special permissions were ordered to leave the departments of the Seine and Seine-et-Oise within twenty-four hours. Count de Nieuwerkerke was dismissed from his post of superintendent of the fine arts and museums. New prefects were appointed all over France; new mayors in all the Paris arrondissements; and M. Gambetta, the minister of the Interior, addressed the following letter to all the provisional administrators and prefects of departments:—"In accepting power at a time of such danger to the country we have accepted great perils and great duties. The people of Paris who on the 4th of September found themselves again in existence, after so long an interval, have so understood the emergency, and their acclamations plainly mean that they expect from us the preservation of the country. Our new republic is not a government which permits of political dissensions and empty quarrels. It is, as we have said, a government of national defence, a republic of war to the knife against the invader. Support us, then, citizens, animated, like ourselves, by the paramount desire of saving the country, and prepared to shrink from no sacrifice. Into the midst of these improvised workers bring the coolness and vigour which should belong to the representatives of a power resolved on everything in order to vanquish the enemy. Sustain every one, by your unlimited activity in all the questions which concern the armament and equipment of the citizens and their military instruction. All prohibitory laws, all the restrictions so unfortunately placed on the manufacture and sale of arms, have disappeared. Let every Frenchman receive or seize a gun, and place himself at the disposal of the authorities. The country is in danger! Day by day information will be given you respecting the details of your duties. But do much spontaneously, and especially endeavour to gain the co-operation of all minds, so that by a gigantic and unanimous effort France may owe its deliverance to the patriotism of all its children."

The fact that the revolution had been achieved without bloodshed gave rise to the hope in some quarters that peace might be established. But the illusion was speedily dispelled. On the 6th September M. Favre, vice-president of the government of national defence and minister of Foreign Affairs, addressed to the French diplomatic agents abroad the following very important and historical circular:—

"Sir,—The events which have just taken place in Paris explain themselves so well by the inexorable logic of facts, that it is useless to insist at length on their meaning and bearing. In ceding to an irresistible impulse, which had been but too long restrained, the population of Paris has obeyed a necessity superior to that of its own safety; it did not wish to perish with the criminal government which was leading France to her ruin; it has therefore pronounced the deposition of Napoleon III. and of his dynasty: it has registered it in the name of right, justice, and public safety; and the sentence was so well ratified beforehand by the conscience of all, that no one even among the most noisy defenders of the power that was falling raised his voice to uphold it. It collapsed of itself under the weight of its faults, and amid the acclamations of an immense people, without a single drop of blood being shed, without any one individual being deprived of his personal liberty; and we have been able to see—a thing unheard of in history—the citizens, upon whom the popular voice conferred the perilous mandate to fight and to conquer, not thinking for a moment of their political adversaries, who but the day before threatened them with execution. It is by refusing to their adversaries the honour of being subject to any sort of repression, that they have shown them their blindness and their impotence. Order has not been disturbed for a single moment. Our confidence in the wisdom and patriotism of the national guard and of the whole population permits us to affirm that it will not be disturbed. Rescued from the shame and the danger of a government which has proved itself a traitor to all its duties, each one now comprehends that the first act of the national sovereignty, at last reconquered, must be one of self-control—the seeking for strength in respect for right. Moreover, time must not be lost: the enemies are at our gates; we have but one thought, namely their expulsion from our territory. But this obligation, which we resolutely accept, we did not impose upon France. She would not be in her present position if our voice had been listened to. We have energetically defended, even at the cost of our popularity, the policy of peace; we still maintain the same opinion with increasing conviction. Our heart breaks at the sight of these human massacres wherein is sacrificed the flower of two nations, that a little good sense and a great deal of liberty would have preserved from such frightful catastrophes. We cannot find any expression capable of rendering our admiration for our heroic army sacrificed by the incapacity of the supreme commander, but showing itself greater in its defeats than in the most brilliant victory: for in spite of the knowledge of faults which compromised its safety, the army has immolated itself with sublime heroism in the face of certain death—redeeming thus the honour of France from' the stain cast upon her by her government. All honour to the army! The nation looks towards it with open arms! The imperial power wished to divide them: misfortune and duty join them in a solemn embrace sealed by patriotism and liberty. This alliance renders us invincible. Beady for every emergency, we look with calmness on the position of affairs made what it is, not by us, but by others. This position I will explain in a few words, and I submit it to the judgment of my country and of Europe. We loudly condemn the war, and while protesting our respect for the rights of peoples, we asked that Germany should be left mistress of her own destinies. We wished that liberty should be at the same time our common tie and our common shield. We were convinced that these moral forces would for ever insure peace, but as a sanction we claimed an arm for every citizen, a civil organization, and the election of leaders. Then we should have remained invincible on our own soil. The government of the emperor, which had long since separated its interests from those of the country, opposed that policy. We take it up with the hope that, taught by experience, France will have the wisdom to put it into practice. On his side the king of Prussia declared that he made war, not against France, but against the imperial dynasty. The dynasty has fallen to the ground. France raises herself free. Does the king of Prussia wish to continue an impious struggle, which will be at least as fatal to him as to us? Does he wish to give to the world of the nineteenth century the cruel spectacle of two nations destroying one another, and in forgetfulness of humanity, reason, and science, heaping corpse upon corpse, and ruin upon ruin. He is free to assume this responsibility in the face of the world and of history. If it is a challenge, we accept it. We will not cede either an inch of our territory or a stone of our fortresses. A shameful peace would mean a war of extermination at an early date. We will only treat for a durable peace. In this our interest is that of the whole of Europe, and we have reason to hope that, freed from all dynastic considerations, the question will thus present itself before the cabinets of Europe. But should we be alone, we shall not yield. We have a resolute army, well-provisioned forts, a well-established enceinte, and above all, the breasts of 300,000 combatants determined to hold out to the last. When they piously lay crowns at the feet of the statue of Strassburg, they do not obey merely an enthusiastic sentiment of admiration, they adopt their heroic *mot d'ordre*—they swear to be worthy of their brethren of Alsace, and to die as they have done. After the forts we have the ramparts, after the ramparts we have the barricades. Paris can hold out for three months and conquer. If she succumbs, France will start up at her appeal and avenge her. France would continue the struggle, and the aggressor would perish. Such is, sir, what Europe must know. We have not accepted power with any other object; we will not keep it a moment if we should not find the population of Paris, and the whole of France, decided to share our resolutions. I sum up these resolves briefly, in presence of God who hears me, in the face of posterity which shall judge us. We wish only for peace; but if this disastrous war, which we have condemned, is continued against us, we shall do our duty to the last, and I have the firm confidence that our cause, which is that of right and of justice, will triumph in the end. It is in this manner that I invite you to explain the situation to the minister of the court to which you are accredited, and in whose hands you will place a copy of this document. Accept, sir, the expression of my high consideration.

"JULES FAVRE.
"Minister of Foreign Affairs,
"*September* 6, 1870."

This document attracted much notice. By the journals of Paris and the people generally it was received with great satisfaction, and it had a favourable effect on the Bourse. But in all these proceedings neutral nations saw little hope for a peaceful solution of the quarrel. It was seen that the republic could not avoid the responsibility of the previous reign; that it was held to answer for the acts of the imperial government, the war among the rest; because, whatever the sentiments of French republicans, the rule of the deposed emperor had been accepted and maintained by the majority of the French people. In the language of the *Siécle*, he was the man "whom the misguided country had accepted as chief." Even the democratic *ouvriers* of France, addressing their brethren across the Rhine, did not scruple to repeat the declaration made to the coalition of Europe in 1793, that "the French people concludes no peace whatever with an enemy occupying its territory." But the reference implied a misapprehension of facts. The coalition marched against France unchallenged and unprovoked, to re-establish the ancient monarchy in all its privileges. The German armies appeared on French soil because they were attacked by the armies of France, and with every demonstration of popular enthusiasm. There were other difficulties in the way of peace. The government undoubtedly wished for peace, but it could not say so. In the first place, an extreme republican party was prepared instantly to denounce any concession to the enemy as treason, and would have been borne to power in their stead had it promised an ever-credulous public to bring victory back to the standards of France. The government felt that the national honour would scarcely be safe if hard conditions were accepted while

Paris was unattacked and Metz and Strassburg untaken; and thus the prospect of peace became increasingly doubtful.

The revolution in Paris was at once followed by an impulse to the military spirit throughout the country. In most of the provincial towns a numerous response was made to the levy en masse of the provisional government, and squads of recruits, of all ages and all ranks, assembled in the public squares for the purpose of being drilled, but very few had at this stage either arms or uniform. The drill sergeants were generally old soldiers, who, having retired from the army, were following various civil avocations.

The new *régime*, however, was not established without more or less difficulty in some of the larger cities, notably in Lyons. By stifling open discussion the imperial system had driven the people to seek political information in secret reunions; and many of the working men of Lyons were deeply imbued with the spirit of Socialism and Communism. The *canaille* of the city, moreover, had been reinforced by many of the dangerous classes who had been expelled from Paris by General Trochu. The news of the emperor's surrender was fully known early on the morning of the 4th of September, and at eight o'clock a large crowd assembled in front of the Hôtel de Ville, speedily invaded the edifice, arrested the prefect, M. Sencier, constituted themselves a Comité du Salut Public, and proclaimed the republic, thus forestalling the capital by several hours. Happily the day ended without accidents, and the *bourgeoisie*, having formed themselves into a garde nationale, ransacked the forts until sufficient arms had been secured. When, however, the prefect appointed by the provisional government, M. Lacour, arrived, he found the Lyons committee comfortably installed in the Hôtel de Ville, and little disposed to resign their functions. He was informed that these gentlemen considered their appointments to be quite as valid as his own; and they retained a body guard of chosen men at their disposal day and night. In the course of a few days they abolished the octroi, thus depriving the town of ten millions of francs per annum. They also issued a decree that priests should serve in the army like other people, and no person was allowed to leave the town without permission. Many gentlemen who had filled public offices were arrested, although in most cases they were not detained more than a few hours. The patriotic citizens of the committee, on the principle that services rendered to the state should be paid for, generously voted themselves a certain sum per day out of the public purse. The prefect avoided a collision, and in the meantime hastened forward the election of the municipal council. The committee were induced to quit the Hôtel de Ville and take up their position in the central bureau de police in the Rue Luizerne; but the red flag, the emblem of the advanced party, was still allowed to float over the town-hall. After the municipal elections a certain number of the more intelligent and respectable members of the original committee were chosen, and the council entered upon its duties under the presidency of the mayor, M. Hénon, formerly deputy for the Rhône; but the amateurs of the Rue Luizerne were not disposed to part with the sweets of office. M. Baudy, a former colleague, was deputed to explain that their services could now be dispensed with, as there was a regularly elected council to do the work, and that in any case their salary would be stopped. M. Baudy, however, was reproached as a renegade, a traitor, and a pickpocket, and put under confinement. But the councillor's constituents having sent a threatening message to the Rue Luizerne, he was released. A few days later the Comité du Salut Public ceased to exist; but its members, powerless in public, were indefatigable in secret. They also received a powerful ally in the person of "General" Cluseret, an ex-officer of the French army, who had been holding meetings, accusing the existing administration of a want of vigour, and calling upon the people to rise and turn them out. At a meeting in the Rotonde, it was resolved that all existing authority should be done away with; that everything should be left to be settled by the justice of the people; that taxes should be abolished; that all moneys required for the good of the country should be furnished by the rich; that the payment of private debts should not be enforced by laws; and that all the officers of the army should be ejected! The inflammatory speeches in which these resolutions were urged had the desired effect. A demonstration was immediately got up; the Hôtel de Ville was taken; the prefect arrested; and the municipal council abolished. The ringleaders then harangued the crowd from the balcony. The Citoyen Saigne, a plasterer, proceeded to appoint the Citoyen Cluseret commander-in-chief of all the military forces of the south of France; an appointment which M. Cluseret, with becoming modesty, accepted—promising to save the country. His first step was to call up the Quartier de la Croix Rousse, and then to seize the general in command at Lyons. The inhabitants were in apprehension of disturbance. The assembly was sounded all over the town, and the gardes nationales flew to arms. The first battalion to arrive was composed of Cluseret's friends of the Croix Rousse; but they proceeded to the town-hall and set the prefect at liberty. Other bodies came up with loaded rifles, when the "general" and his colleagues retired, vowing to return with sufficient strength to carry all before them, but in this valorous intention they failed. The prefect subsequently informed the garde nationale that he had received unlimited powers from the government over the regular troops, so as to be able to deal effectively with any attempt at disturbance. He was everywhere well received, and the soldiers swore to support him to the utmost.

At Marseilles, also, great excitement followed the news of the surrender of the emperor. The people rushed *en masse* to the Bourse, decapitated the statue of Napoleon, and derisively rolled the trunk through the streets and flung the eagles into the port. They pitched inkstands at the picture of the imperial family, breaking furniture, tearing curtains to shreds, and finally regaling themselves from the cellars. The news was received at Bordeaux with similar popular manifestations. An equestrian statue of the emperor, erected in the Allées de Tourny, was torn from its base, and in falling broke into fragments. Thousands of people then paraded the streets, and shouted "Vive la Republique!" before the Hôtel de Ville. Similar proceedings took place at Toulouse, where an informal committee was constituted in much the same manner as at Lyons.

With the earliest days of the revolution reappeared the extreme section of the press, which had been suppressed during the Palikao ministry. The *Marseillaise* attacked the provisional government. The *Reveil* and the *Rappel* were moderate in their tone, but enthusiastic in their praise of the republic. In the latter journal, Victor Hugo, who had returned to "save Paris," issued to the German people a magniloquent address, which commenced as follows:—"Germans, he who speaks to you is a friend. Three years ago, at the epoch of the Exposition of 1867, from exile, I welcomed you to our city. What city? Paris. For Paris does not belong to us alone. Paris is yours as well as ours. Berlin, Vienna, Dresden, Munich, Stuttgart, are your capitals; Paris is your centre. It is at Paris that one feels the heart of Europe beating. Paris is the city of cities; Paris is the city of men. There was Athens, there was Rome, there is Paris. Paris is nothing but an immense hospitality. To-day you return there. How? As brothers, like you did three years ago? No, as enemies. Why? What is this sinister misunderstanding? Two nations have made Europe. Those two nations are France and Germany. . . . This war, does it proceed from us? It was the Empire which willed it. The Empire is dead. It is well. We have nothing in common with that corpse. It is the past, we are the future. It is hatred, we are sympathy. It is treason, we are loyalty."

M. Victor Hugo also addressed a long and inflated epistle to the Parisians, for the purpose of encouraging them under the anticipated hardships of the siege:—"Two adversaries," said the writer, "are in presence at this moment. On one side is Prussia, with 900,000 soldiers; on the other Paris, with 400,000 citizens. On one side, force; on the other, will. On one side, an army; on the other, a nation. On one side, night; on the other light. It is the old contest between the Archangel and the Dragon which is recommencing. It will have now the same termination as before; Prussia will be cast down. This war, frightful as it is, has hitherto been but trifling; it is about to become great. I am sorry for you, Prussians, but it is necessary that you should change your method of dealing."

Among the arrivals in Paris at this period were the Orleans princes, the Duc d'Aumale, the Duc de Chartres, and the Prince de Joinville, who under the Palikao ministry had previously offered their services, which were not accepted. On the 7th September they reached the capital from Brussels, and communicated with the government of national defence; presuming that, as exceptional laws had been practically repealed by the revolution, the decree which exiled them was also set aside, and expressing their desire to be allowed to serve their country *in propria persona*. The government, however, apprehensive that their presence might be misconstrued, declined their offer; and in very courteous and sympathetic terms appealed to them, in the name of patriotism, to depart, upon which they immediately left the capital. Meanwhile, the Legitimist candidate for the French throne, the Comte de Chambord, issued an address in which he said:—"Amid all these poignant emotions, it is a great consolation to see that public spirit, the spirit of patriotism, does not allow itself to be cast down, but rises with our misfortunes. Above everything it is necessary to repulse the invasion, to save at any price the honour of France, the integrity of its territory. Every dissension must be forgotten at this moment, every after-thought put aside. We owe our whole energy, our fortune, our blood, to the deliverance of our country. A true mother will rather abandon her infant than see it perish. I experience the same feeling, and say incessantly, May God save France, though I should die without seeing it again!"

General Garibaldi also, writing from Caprera, September 7, addressed the following to his friends:—"Yesterday I said to you, War to the death to Bonaparte; I say to you to-day, We must help the French republic by all possible means. I am an invalid, but I have offered my self to the provisional government of Paris, and I hope it will not be impossible for me to perform some work. Yes, my fellow-citizens, we should regard assistance to our brothers of France as a sacred duty. Our mission will not certainly consist in combating our German brethren, who, being as the arm of Providence, have overthrown in the dust the germ of the tyranny which weighed upon the world; but we should sustain the only system which can assure peace and prosperity among nations."

To strengthen the authority of the provisional government, the ministry, on the 8th of September, issued in the *Journal Officiel* the following proclamation for the appointment of a Constituent Assembly:—"Frenchmen,—In proclaiming four days ago the government of the National Defence, we ourselves defined our mission. Power was lying in the dust. What had commenced by a crime finished by a desertion. We simply grasped the helm which had escaped from powerless hands. But Europe has need to be enlightened. It is necessary that she should know by irrefragable testimonies that the entire country is with us. It is necessary that the invader should meet on his route not only the obstacle of an immense city resolved to perish rather than yield, but an entire people erect, organized, represented—an assembly, in short, which can carry into all places, and in spite of all disasters, the living soul of the country. Consequently, the government of the National Defence decrees:—Art. 1. The electoral colleges are convoked for Sunday, the 16th of October, for the purpose of electing a National Constituent Assembly. Art. 2. The elections will be held by collective voting, conformably to the law of the 15th of March, 1849. Art 3. The number of members of the Constituent Assembly will be 750. Art. 4. The minister of the Interior is charged with the execution of this decree. Given at the Hôtel de Ville of Paris, September 8, 1870."

This proceeding was regarded as of the first importance, and subsequently the provisional government fixed on the 2d of October for the elections. M. Jules Favre issued a second diplomatic circular, dated the 17th September, the language of which was more moderate in its tone than that of the document already quoted. The minister of Foreign Affairs thus concluded—"I will sum up our entire policy. In accepting the perilous task which was imposed upon us by the fall of the imperial government we had but one idea; namely, to defend our territory, to save our honour, and to give back to the nation the power emanating from itself, and which it alone could exercise. We should have wished that this great act might have been completed without transition, but the first necessity was to face the enemy. We have not the pretension to ask disinterestedness of Prussia. We take account of the feelings to which the greatness of her losses and the natural exaltation of victory have given rise to her. These feelings explain the violence of the press, which we are far from confounding with the inspirations of statesmen. These latter will hesitate to continue an impious war, in which more than 200,000 men have already fallen. To force conditions upon France which she could not accept, would only be to compel a continuance of the war. It is objected that the government is without regular power to be represented. It is for this reason that we immediately summon a freely-elected Assembly. We do not attribute to ourselves any other privilege than that of giving our soul and our blood to our country, and we abide by its sovereign judgment. It is therefore not authority reposed in us for a day. It is immortal France uprising before Prussia—France divested of the shroud of the empire, free, generous, and ready to immolate herself for right and liberty, disavowing all political conquest, and all violent propaganda, having no other ambition than to remain mistress of herself, and to develop her moral and material forces, and to work fraternally with her neighbours for the progress of civilization. It is this France which, left to her free action, immediately asks the cessation of the war, but prefers its disasters a thousand times to dishonour. Vainly those who set loose a terrible scourge try now to escape the crushing responsibility, by falsely alleging that they yielded to the wish of the country. This calumny may delude people abroad, but there is no one among us who does not refute it as a work of revolting bad faith. The motto of the elections in 1869 was peace and liberty, and the *plébiscite* itself adopted it as its programme. It is true that the majority of the Legislative Body cheered the warlike declarations of the duke of Gramont; but a few weeks previously it had also cheered the peaceful declarations of M. Ollivier. A majority emanating from personal power believed itself obliged to follow docilely and voted trustingly; but there is not a sincere person in Europe who could affirm that France freely consulted made war against Prussia. I do not draw the conclusion from this that we are not responsible. We have been wrong, and are cruelly expiating our having tolerated a government which led us to ruin. Now we admit the obligation to repair by a measure of justice the ill it has done; but if the power with which it has so seriously compromised us takes advantage of our misfortunes to overwhelm us, we shall oppose a desperate resistance; and it will remain well understood that it is the nation, properly represented in a freely-elected Assembly, that this power wishes to destroy. This being the question raised, each one will do his duty. Fortune has been hard upon us, but she is capable of unlooked-for revolutions, which our determination will call forth. Europe begins to be moved; and sympathy for us is being reawakened. The sympathies of foreign cabinets console us and do us honour. They will be deeply struck by the noble attitude of Paris in the midst of so many terrible causes for excitement. Serious, confident, ready for the utmost sacrifices, the nation in arms descends into the arena without looking back, and having before its eyes this simple but great duty, the defence of its homes and independence. I request you, sir, to enlarge upon these truths to the representative of the government to which you are accredited. He will see their importance, and will thus obtain a just idea of our disposition." In the previous chapter we recounted the energetic measures of the authorities for the defence and provisioning of the capital. On the morning of the day (September 4) when the republic was proclaimed, the Crown Prince of Prussia and the Crown Prince of Saxony, accompanied by the king of Prussia and Count von Bismarck, started on their march to Paris. As the German armies drew nearer day by day, unremitting exertions, which had been commenced by the Count do Palikao, were continued to man and provision the city, and to put the *enceinte* and the detached forts in a condition to sustain a lengthened siege, while the surrounding belt of country was cleared of its inhabitants. The completeness of these preparations was amply attested by subsequent events, and the prolongation of the siege.

 On the 14th September a grand review of the whole armed force in Paris was held by General Trochu. Apparently the spectacle was one of the most stirring on record, and for the first time in twenty years Paris appeared openly and fully armed. The troops consisted of soldiers of the regular army, national guards, and the garde mobile, to the number of 300,000, who were drawn up in line, extending from the Place de la Bastille to the Arc de Triomphe. The number of regular troops was considerably increased by the return of General Vinoy and his army, who had failed to join MacMahon before the battle of Sedan, and also by the scattered remnants of defeated soldiers who had managed to make good their escape. As General Trochu, accompanied by a brilliant staff, rode along the ranks, he was received with great enthusiasm, amid cries of "Vive Trochu!" and "Vive la Republique! "The feeling of the troops was admirable; but, beyond the regulars, few were armed with the Chassepot, and the uniform of many consisted only of the *kepi*. While the troops marched back to their quarters after the inspection the air resounded with patriotic songs, and the muzzles of many of their muskets were ornamented with bouquets and tricoloured flags, which gave a lively and brilliant appearance to the scene. The governor subsequently issued the following general order:—

"To the National Guards of Paris and the Gardes Mobiles of Paris and the Departments,—Never before has any general witnessed so grand a spectacle as that which you have presented; three hundred battalions of citizens organized and armed, enveloped by the entire population of the city, unanimously proclaiming the determined defence of Paris and of liberty. If those foreign nations which doubt you, if the armies which are marching upon you, could only have heard that, they would have understood that misfortune has done more in a few weeks to rouse the soul of the nation than long years of prosperity have done to abase it. The spirit of devotion and of sacrifice has infused itself into you, and to it you owe that hearty union which will prove your safety. With our formidable effective force the daily guard of Paris will be 70,000 men. If the enemy by a fierce attack, or by a surprise, or by effecting a breach, should pierce our protecting fortifications, he would encounter barricades which are being prepared, and his columns would be driven back by the successive attacks of ten reserves stationed at different points. Remain, therefore, perfectly assured, and know that the *enceinte* of Paris, defended as it is by the persevering efforts of public spirit, and by 300,000 muskets, is impregnable. National guards of the Seine and gardes mobiles, in the name of the government for the National Defence, of which I am towards you but the representative, I thank you for your patriotic solicitude for the cherished interests which you have in charge. Now let us proceed to work in the nine sections of the defence. Let there be everywhere order, calmness, and devotion; and remember that you are charged, as I have previously informed you, with the police of Paris during this critical period. Prepare to bear your task with constancy, and then you will not fail to conquer."

The provisional government meanwhile completed its preparations against the impending investment of the capital. Communications with the departments were abandoned, bridges were destroyed, sometimes too hastily, telegraphs severed, obstacles placed in the path of the advancing enemy, and the woods near Paris filled with combustibles. In the beautiful woods of the Seine and Marne, the forests of Lagny, De Ferrières, Clamart, Bellevue, Bondy, and the woods around St. Cloud, openings were effected by the axe of the garde mobile and francs-tireurs, large numbers of whom were told off for the service. The *Journal*

Officiel published decrees authorizing the minister of justice, M. Cremieux, to transfer the criminal chamber to Tours; and placing 40,000 francs at the disposal of the Scientific Committee of Defence. All legal appeals were suspended, together with the octroi duties upon the importation of goods. The government further decided to sit at a town in the interior of France during the siege; and besides M. Cremieux, the minister of Marine and M. Glais-Bizoin established themselves at Tours, where they were joined by Lord Lyons and several other foreign ambassadors. The envoys of the United States, Belgium, and Switzerland resolved, however, to remain in Paris.

While the government were thus taking their measures of defence, M. Thiers was sent to England, and thence to Vienna and St. Petersburg, charged with a diplomatic mission. But the difficulties in the way of the veteran statesman were insurmountable. Count von Bismarck had determined to decline all intervention, and the courts of Europe, to whom M. Thiers was delegated, thus found no favourable opportunity to enter upon negotiations.

It is worthy of notice, too, that before the government had been in existence a fortnight they had the courage to abolish the entire system of police surveillance. A short time before the Prussians finally invested the capital, M. de Keratry, the prefect of police, addressed to the provisional government a report recommending the suppression of an institution which had proved a ready and efficient instrument in the hands of successive governments for seventy years. The system had been most abused under Napoleon I., by whom it was founded in 1800, and who had extended its powers during his reign. So great was the importance attached to it, that at the change of each *régime* the first care of the victors was to secure its influence.

A brief review of the financial condition of the country, prior to the final investment of Paris, will be found suggestive. The trade bills under discount at the bank of France amounted at the close of June to £26,000,000. On the 8th of September they had increased to £57,000,000, or nearly 120 per cent.; and while the aggregate of cash and bullion in the bank continually diminished, the paper circulation increased. The weekly drain of the precious metals is represented by the following table:—

	Cash and Bulletin in Bank of France.		French Bank Notes in Circulation	
	Amount.	Weekly Decrease.	Amount.	Weekly Increase.
July. . . . 7 .	£50,723,000	—	£57,557,000	—
" . . . 14. .	49,809,000	£914,000	58,209,000	£652,000
" . . . 21. .	48,590,000	1,219,000	58,808,000	599,000

" . . . 28 . .	45,775,000	2,815,000	61,092,000	2,284,000
August . . . 4 . .	43,875,000	1,900,000	61,044,000	48,000
" . . . 11 . .	41,142,000	2,733,000	61,344,000	300,000
" . . . 18 . .	36,244,000	4,898,000	66,705,000	5,361,000
" . . . 25 . .	34,742,000	1,502,000	68,340,000	1,635,000
September . . 1 . .	33,764,000	978,000	69,206,000	866,000
" . . . 8 . .	32,320,000	1,444,000	69,800,000	594,000

On the 12th August the bank suspended payments in specie, and the following week nearly £5,000,000 was withdrawn. At the same time the note circulation was increased by upwards of £5,250,000.

With regard to the foreign relations of the provisional government, it may be stated that the republic was early recognized by the United States of America. On the 5th of September M. Favre officially notified its institution to the American ambassador, Mr. Washburne, who, on the day following, replied:—"I have the satisfaction of announcing to you that I have received from my government a telegram empowering me to recognize the government of the National Defence as the government of France. I am consequently ready to enter into relations with the government, and, if you wish it, to treat with it on all the matters arising out of the functions with which I am invested. In making this communication to your excellency, I beg to tender to yourself and to the members of the government of the National Defence the congratulations of the government and people of the United States. They will have learnt with enthusiasm the proclamation of the republic which has been instituted in France without the shedding of one drop of blood, and they will respond heartily and sympathetically to the great movement which they hope and believe will be fertile in happy results for the French people and for humanity at large. Enjoying for nearly a century immeasurable benefits from a republican government, the people of the United States cannot but witness with the deepest interest the efforts of the French people, attached to them by the bonds of a traditional amity, who seek to found institutions by which will be assured to the present generation, as well as to posterity, the invaluable right of living, by working for the welfare of all." M. Jules Favre, in acknowledging this letter, hailed as a happy augury for the French republic that the American government should have been the first to recognize and countenance it. Subsequently a large gathering of citizens visited the American legation, and gave enthusiastic cheers for the United States. The crowd then waited on M. Jules Favre, who replied, "I am happy to hear of your demonstration. I am, as you know, the personal enemy of war, which divides and tears in pieces mankind. I retain the hope of an honourable peace; but if it is necessary, we will sacrifice everything to the very last for the defence of the country."

In the United States the successes of the German arms, and the surrender of Napoleon, caused exuberant rejoicings among the German population and those of Teutonic origin, as well as among a large part of the nation itself, whose sympathies were against the French empire. In Philadelphia long processions, bearing torches and transparencies, and led by the German musical societies, went singing through the streets, while the offices of the newspapers favourable to the German cause were serenaded, as well as the residence of the German consul. With this feeling throughout the country, there was a general hope of a speedy peace. On the intelligence of Napoleon's downfall, the premium on gold fell from above 117 to 113%.

The news of the establishment of the republic in Paris, however, caused a sensible diminution of the sympathy with the Germans, and, combined with the overwhelming defeats inflicted on the French, excited a general desire for peace on moderate terms. France was more frequently spoken of as "our ancient ally," and, as already stated, the government promptly recognized the republic. Nevertheless, with France as a military nation, or with her military standards of morality, there was little sympathy. The democrats, however, gained courage in their denunciations of Germany from the French defeats, and the Irish grew more noisy than ever in their demonstrations of fellow-feeling, especially with the disasters of MacMahon, who was generally believed amongst them to be the lineal descendant of an Irish king. There was undoubtedly a strong dislike of the Germans in the country.

The new government in Paris was also acknowledged by Italy, Switzerland, Belgium, Spain, and Portugal. Switzerland expressed a hope that the republic "would be able shortly to procure for France the blessings of an honourable peace, and to consolidate for ever liberty and democratic institutions." Chevalier Nigra informed M. Jules Favre that he had received instructions from Florence to keep up relations with the provisional government in every way conformable to the sympathies existing between the two countries. A similar statement was made by Senor Olozaga, the Spanish ambassador, to whom M. Jules Favre replied, "It is precisely at this cruel moment for France that we see clearly manifested the wisdom which would join in one single tie three nations that really form but one family, and awaiting only the signal of liberty to recover their family titles."

The action of the British government at this juncture caused considerable discussion both in England and France. The fall of the empire and the proclamation of a republic gave a new character both to the French resistance and the German invasion, which greatly influenced opinion in England, particularly amongst the political leaders of the working classes, in relation to the war. While up to Sedan the public sympathies generally were with the German cause, a change of phase in the politics of the war wrought a change of feeling in English working men. Mass meetings were held in favour of the French, and an address was issued by the International Working Men's Association with the same object. On the evening of the 10th September a large gathering of the working classes took place under the presidency of Mr. Edmond Beales. While France was blamed for the initiation of a war of conquest, Germany was called upon by the meeting to exercise moderation and magnanimity in her hour of triumph, especially as the republican government then in power was composed of the very men who had protested against and denounced the imperial policy. The English cabinet was also urged to use every effort to procure the cessation of hostilities, and to prevent the territorial spoliation of France. Again, on the 13th September, a deputation, organized by the Labour Representation League, waited upon the Right Honourable W. E. Gladstone. The deputation, which consisted of about 100 representatives of the leading London and provincial trade societies and industrial organizations, expressed to him that great dissatisfaction existed throughout the country, and especially amongst the working classes, at the non-recognition of the French republic by her Majesty's government, and urged that the spoliation of France by any annexation of her territory by Germany would sow the seeds of a future war, and lead to complications dangerous to the peace of the whole of Europe. They therefore prayed her Majesty's government to use their influence with the German government not to insist upon any annexation of territory as the terms of peace. By this course, the deputation believed that the terrible war might be brought to a speedy and honourable termination, without further humiliation to the French nation. In the course of an elaborate reply, Mr. Gladstone said that her Majesty's government had acted on the principle of international arbitration when the war was on the point of breaking out, and had done their utmost to prevent it. But although he shared the desire of the deputation that bloodshed should cease, they must expect great nations to claim for themselves to be in the first instance, and in the last resort, the proper judges of their own affairs. Any opportunity for mediation, however, would be eagerly seized by her Majesty's government. With regard to the recognition of the provisional government the premier continued:—"Even if the men who constitute that government were questionable in point of character, I do not think it would be for us to criticize them; but, on the contrary, I believe them to be men of honour, character, and intellect. Therefore do not suppose anything like a cessation of intercourse is signified by the fact that official recognition has not taken place. I am far from saying that the great question of recognition is unimportant; because undoubtedly the question of recognition is an acknowledgment that a combination of men has acquired a certain position, and that recognition undoubtedly strengthens them. I think we have no business to inquire whether France prefers one government or another. If it could be shown we are proceeding on principles less favourable to the government of France than any other government, we should be adjudged wrong in the face of the whole world. Our business is to proceed upon principles of perfect equality, and look impartially upon any government that may be established in France, independently of its being democratic, parliamentary, monarchical, or whatever it may be. Then what is the principle on which we are to proceed? That we acknowledge it as the government of France which France chooses to accept for herself. But, as it is not our business to lag behind in that respect, so it is not our business to go before France. Before the government exercising power in France has been recognized, are we to be expected to pronounce an opinion which France has not expressed? What is the position of the French government exercising power in Paris and Tours? How did they describe themselves? They are not themselves carrying out the government. They have been appointed for the calling together of some body—referring their case to that body, and deriving their title from the approval of that body. Now, surely it is plain that we cannot travel faster than France in this matter; and we cannot travel faster than the present government of France. The recognition of the late empire of France did not take place until after the vote of the people. The vote of the people took place on the 1st of the month, and the recognition took place on the 4th. We were in hopes the vote of France was going to take place on Saturday next; and if it did take place, we would not have been less prompt than any former government has been to recognize that which has been established. But if you step in before the judgment of the people, you are really recognizing that which the great, high-minded, and civilized people of France have not recognized themselves."

The general feeling amongst moderate and intelligent Frenchmen at this time was admirably expressed in a letter from the veteran statesman, M. Guizot, to an English friend, in the course of which he said—"If we were only beginning this unhappy war, I would tell you frankly what I think of its evil origin and its lamentable errors; and I am sure that a large majority of the French nation think as I do about it. But we are not beginning the war. The opinion of the French nation on the main points of the question is unchanged; but no one thinks about them now, and, indeed, we cannot and ought not to think about them. For the present we ought to occupy ourselves—and, in fact, we do occupy ourselves—with war, and war only. We are engrossed by it, not only because of the unexpected reverses which we have experienced, but also, and above all, because of the designs which the Prussians manifest, and the character which they have stamped upon this war. On their part it is manifestly a war of ambition and for the sake of conquest. They proclaim loudly that they intend to take back Alsace and Lorraine, provinces which have been ours for two centuries, and which we have held through all the political vicissitudes and chances of war. The Prussians do more even than this. Although they occupy these provinces very partially and only temporarily, they already presume to exercise the rights of sovereignty over them. They have issued a decree in Lorraine abolishing our laws of conscription and recruiting for the army. Ask the first honest German whom you meet if this is not one of those acts of victorious ambition which pledge a nation to a struggle indefinitely prolonged, a struggle which can only be terminated by one of those disasters that a nation never accepts—one that if it experiences it never forgives. Be sure that France will never accept the character and consequences which Prussia desires to give to the war. Because of our first reverses we have our national honour to preserve, and because of the claims of Prussia we have to defend and keep our national territory. We will maintain these two causes at any price and to the very end. And let me tell you, and that without presumption, that, being as resolute as we are, we are not seriously uneasy as to the result of this struggle. At the very beginning the Prussians made an immense effort; there is another effort yet to be made; it is on our part, and it has, as yet, scarcely begun. We were greatly to blame that we were not better prepared at first; but with all our shortcomings we have seen what our troops are worth, and this will be seen and felt more and more as time goes on. We are superior to the Prussians in men, money, and territory, and we will equal them in perseverance, even should they persevere, as they will need to do if their projects are to have any chance of success. The age is with us, and we will not fail the age. This, I tell you in all frankness and sincerity, is the actual condition of facts and of men's minds in France. I am very anxious that it should be known in England, and that there should be no mistake there as to our national sentiments and the possibilities of the future. I devoted my whole political life to creating and maintaining bonds of friendship and unfettered alliance between France and England. I thought, and I still think, that this alliance is a pledge of the moral honour of the two nations, of their material prosperity, and of the progress of civilization throughout the world. I can recall the sorrow and apprehension which I felt in 1857, when I thought that the power of England was endangered by the great Indian mutiny. I remember also that the sentiments of France at that time were in complete harmony with my own. It is therefore with sorrow, not unmixed with surprise, that I now see many Englishmen so openly hostile to France."

We have already described the jubilation of the German people after the news of Napoleon's surrender. But their satisfaction was somewhat modified by the proclamation of the republic, and especially by the tone of Jules Favre's first circular, which presented terms of peace that could not be conceded. The German press insisted that the altered circumstances could not affect these terms, and "trusted that the German giant, who so long had had nothing but his head free to think and dream with, while his hands and feet were fettered, would now, when for the first time free and conscious of his strength, make a right use of it by retaining Alsace and Lorraine, no matter how 'unstatesman-like' that might appear to his neutral friends, patrons, and advisers."

Considerable dissatisfaction was felt at the promptitude with which the French republic was recognized by the United States, and still more by the heartiness of the letter of the American minister to Jules Favre. "Mr. Washburne," said the *National Zeitung*, "doubtless is a sound republican, but he is deemed a weak politician; and the fate of the Germans in Paris should have been placed in abler hands by the German governments. He simply received from Washington by telegraph authority to recognize the new republic, which was a matter of course in regard to the views and principles prevailing there. The rest are his own personal sentiments. Of these he would have done well to address a share to the Germans, whose protection he has taken upon himself, and who are persecuted and put under ban by Monsieur Gambetta more cruelly than they were before."

The action of England was treated with something like indifference in Germany. It was generally thought Great Britain might, by a timely and energetic interference, have prevented the breaking out of the war; but since nothing had been done to avert the storm, the Germans were not disposed to admit any interference in ulterior negotiations, or regarding their dictation of the conditions of a peace so dearly purchased. Confident of victory, exasperated by the cruel sacrifices to which the country had been subjected, and naturally indignant at the unwarrantable and unprovoked attack made upon it, they regarded the exactions proposed by their rulers as a minimum which could not be reduced by an iota. They were also somewhat indignant at the treatment accorded to the captive emperor at Wilhelmshöhe, where he could not, they alleged, have received more attention had he been a guest instead of a prisoner. In the endeavour to tone down this feeling, the semi-official journals indicated that Count von Bismarck had not wholly given up the Bonapartist dynasty.

An immense impulse was given to the cause of German unity by the events of the war. With the accounts brought to Berlin of general rejoicings for victories, came announcements of meeting after meeting, and resolution after resolution, all tending to show the united spirit of the nation, north and south. At a cabinet council, held on the 9th September, the Bavarian government decided on taking the initiative in opening negotiations with Prussia, with a view to accession to the North German Bund. After a warm expression of thanks to the army and its leaders, and of confidence in those at the head of affairs, it was declared that Germany, now united as she had never been before, had fought her battles and beaten the enemy without allies, and would therefore conclude a peace without the interference of neutrals. The French must be brought to feel themselves defeated before lasting peace could be hoped for; and a false generosity would only encourage fresh aggressions. The recovery of Alsace and Lorraine held out the only guarantee against that hankering after German territory which had been displayed under every new government in France. As the Germans went united to the war, so should peace also find them united, by the fusion of the southern and northern states, and the acquisition of long-lost territories. One people, one army, one Diet, one constitution, were the guarantees of lasting peace for Germany and for Europe. These sentiments found ready assent amongst the various other states, and thus were the shadows broadly cast of important coming events.

NOTE.

In his celebrated "Defence Speech," before the National Assembly, at Versailles, in June, 1871, to which we alluded at the end of the previous chapter, General Trochu gave the following account of the transactions of this memorable 4th of September, so far as he was personally concerned:—"In the morning I went to the Tuileries. I saw the empress regent surrounded by many anxious persons. She herself was perfectly calm. I addressed to her these few words:—'Madam, the hour of great dangers has arrived. Strange things are taking place here, but this is not a time for recrimination. I remain at my post, but be assured that the crisis is a serious one.' I received neither from the War Office nor the Tuileries any orders, news, or notice of any kind. About one o'clock in the afternoon I saw General Lebreton, the questeur of the Corps Législatif. He said to me: 'General, the peril is at its height; there is a tremendous crowd on the quay about to break into the House—the troops have allowed the mob to break through their lines. You alone, by a personal effort, may perhaps stave the danger off.' I replied, 'General, I am the victim of an unprecedented situation. In fact, I have no command; I did not order the troops you mention to be posted where they were.' Here, gentlemen, I beg to say that I am thoroughly convinced that if I had been in command the case would have been precisely the same. I further said to General Lebreton, 'Look here, general, you want me single-handed to stop the advance of half a million of men who are surging up towards the Assembly; and yet you must know as well as I that it cannot be done; but as you make this demand in the name of the Corps Législatif, I will attempt the effort, though I am well assured of its failure.' Ten minutes later I was on horseback, on my way to the Corps Législatif. At the same moment I despatched General Schmitz to the Tuileries to inform the empress of what I was going to do. I was accompanied by two aides-de-camp, and had no difficulty in getting through the Carrousel, though the place was crowded, because nobody seemed to want to penetrate into the Tuileries; but when I got to the quay I had great difficulty in moving through the huge mass, which stretched from a long way beyond the Pont Nenf, far up in the Champs Elysées. I witnessed, not without fear or emotion, such a sight as I had never beheld, although I had seen both 1830 and 1848. An immense multitude of men, women, and children, wholly unarmed, and in which kindliness, fear, anger, and good nature were oddly mingled, surged up all around me and wholly prevented my advance; men with sinister faces threw themselves on my horse's reins, and shouted, 'Cry "Vive la Sociale!"' Yes, gentlemen, 'Vive la Sociale.' I said to them, 'I will not cry anything at all; you want to bind my free will—you shall not do it.' Other men, understanding my position, remonstrated, and shouted, 'He's right.' It took me nearly an hour to get to the corner of the Pont de Solferino. There I was compelled to come to a stand-still. I had long since lost my two aides-de-camp, and could neither go forward nor back. I kept parleying with the crowd, trying to get them to open a way for me, when a tall man elbowed himself up. I did not know him; he was under the influence of great emotion. He said, 'General, where are you going?' 'I am going to try and save the Corps Législatif.' 'The Corps Législatif has been invaded. I was there—I saw it. I give you my word it is so. I am M. Jules Favre.' M. Jules Favre added, 'That is the culminating disaster; here is a revolution being consummated in the midst of the disasters of our armies. You may be sure that the demagogues who are going to try and turn it to account will give France her death-blow if we don't prevent it. I am going to the Hôtel de Ville: that is the rendezvous of the men who wish to save the country.' I replied, 'Monsieur, I cannot take such a resolution at present;' and we parted. It took me about an hour longer to get back to the Louvre. Whilst these events were taking place, the empress had left the Tuileries. General Schmitz had found her gone, and had been received by Admiral Jurien de la Gravière, who had remained at the palace. The official historiographers, whose narratives I have read, generally add—'The principal functionaries of state crowded round the empress to take leave of her; alone General Trochu did not appear.' No, I did not appear, because at that time, instead of paying compliments of condolence to the empress, I was making an attempt personally to protect the Corps Législatif, at the request of General Lebreton. A little after my return to the Louvre a group of persons, utterly unknown to me, presented themselves. The person who led them said, 'I am M. Steenackers, a deputy. I am sent to you with these gentlemen to tell you that a real drama is being enacted at the Hôtel de Ville; it is surrounded by the mob; deputies have met there to form a Provisional Government; but there are no troops; there are no soldiers; there are no means of enforcing any decision that may be arrived at; they imagine that your name will be a kind of sanction, and that the troops dispersed all over Paris would rally round you.' I asked for five minutes to see my family, and went to the Hôtel de Ville. What I saw there was striking enough. There were the same enormous crowds as during the morning, but very much more mixed. Shouts, clamours, and threats arose on every side. The Hôtel de Ville itself was filled with so dense a crowd that it was only by devious ways that I was able to reach a closet, about four times the size of this tribune, in which the Provisional Government had stationed itself by the light of a solitary lamp. I didn't know whether the men I saw there for the first time—with the exception of M. Jules Favre, whom I had seen during the day—were really usurpers, vultures soaring down on power as a prey; but they did not look like it. I felt that they and I were exposed to a great peril. One of them said, 'General, in this formidable crisis we are especially anxious that the government should not fall into the hands of the people in the next room. Just now, taken aback by the suddenness of events, they are assembled, but they are not yet armed; but they will be tomorrow. If you consent to be the minister of War of the Provisional Government to-morrow, the officers and soldiers in Paris will gather round your name, and there will be some means of enforcing the measures that must be taken for the preservation of order in Paris.' I replied, 'Before making up my mind it is my duty to go to the War office and acquaint the minister, who is my chief, of what is going on here.' I went and found General Palikao in his office a prey to intense grief; he thought that his son, a clever young officer, had been killed at Sedan. On this occasion he received me with the greatest cordiality. 'General,' he said, 'the revolution is a fait accompli; if you don't take the direction of affairs it is all up with us; if you do, probably the result will be just the same; but the soldiers will rally round you.' I returned to the Hôtel de Ville, where I found the Provisional Government had received during my absence an addition to its numbers in the person of M. Rochefort. I told them, 'If you want me to be of any use at this fearful crisis I must be at the head of affairs. M. Jules Favre is president; I must be president in his place.' Such, gentlemen, in a very condensed form, is the history of September 4."

In his letter to the President of the National Assembly, referred to at the end of the previous chapter, Count Palikao, referring to this part of General Trochu's defence, said:— "On the morning of the 4th the council met as usual, and only broke up at half-past eleven, as the ministers had to go to the Chamber; none of the persons whose duties called them elsewhere were therefore with the empress—we all knew the dangers of the situation as well as the governor of Paris. I was the last to leave the Corps Législatif. I had strenuously contended with the insurgents in the *Salle des pas Perdus* until the very last moment, exposed to the brutality of an infuriated mob, excited against me by a member of the Extreme Left; and was only rescued from the hands of these misguided men by my aide-de-camp, Lieutenant-colonel Barry, and Captain de Brimont, my orderly officer. I had one last duty to fulfil—to wait upon the empress. It was three o'clock when I got to the Tuileries; at that hour the guard were leaving their posts and the mob had invaded the palace. The empress had gone, no one knew whither. It was therefore impossible for me to take her orders. I returned to the ministry at four o'clock; the Revolution had conquered through an insurrection doubly criminal, from the fact of its taking place before a victorious enemy. At five o'clock General Trochu called upon me, to inform me that he had replaced me at the War Office; he wished to know my opinion as to what he had to do. He did not mention his meeting M. Jules Favre, nor what he had done during the day. I replied, that as disturbances might entail the greatest calamity, the presence of men of order such as he could not but be useful. He could not ask me—nor could I give him—advice as to what his conscience might dictate. I have not seen him since."

CHAPTER XVII.

The Situation and Possibilities on both sides after the Battle of Sedan—The great mistake of the French in not constructing Intrenched Camps and making the Sea the Base of their Operations for the relief of Paris—Commencement of the March of the Germans on Paris the day after the Battle of Sedan—Their Forethought and Organization—The Routes taken and System adopted by the Armies in their March to the Capital—Escape of a French Corps which had been sent to assist MacMahon—No resistance offered to the Germans—Their Arrival at Rheims, and Surrender of the City—Catastrophe at Laon, which caused the Explosion of the Powder Magazine in the Citadel—The Commandant declared innocent by the Germans—Letter from him to his Wife on the General State of Affairs—Description of Laon and its History—Skirmishes as the Germans approached nearer to Paris—Their Investment of the City—General Trochu's Plans—Engagement between the French under General Ducrot and the Germans under the Crown Prince of Prussia, on September 17—The French are completely defeated—A more severe Engagement on the 19th, in which the Germans are again Victorious—Disgraceful Conduct of part of the French Troops—Manifesto of General Trochu on the Subject—Entry of the Germans into Versailles—Sketch of the Palace, in which their Headquarters were established, and Town—Negotiations for an Armistice—Count von Bismarck's opinion on the general Situation—His difficulty in dealing with "the Gentlemen of the Pavement"—The German intention of starving the City out, and the only Terms on which Germany could consent to Peace—Meeting between Jules Favre and Count von Bismarck at Ferrières—Epitome of the Reports issued by each on their Interview—The French Government reiterate their Determination not to cede "an Inch of their Territory, or a Stone of their Fortresses"—The Action taken by the English Government between both Belligerents—The Operations of the Besiegers up to the end of September—The Feeling in Germany—Speech and Imprisonment of Dr. Jacoby—Events in Italy—The French Troops withdrawn from Rome on the outbreak of the War, and the Italians at once determine to take possession of the City—Enthusiasm in the Army—Triumphant Entry of the Troops on the 20th of September, after three hours' fighting—The Fall of the Temporal Power proclaimed—A Plebiscitum declares unmistakably in favour of the New Order of Things.

BEFORE proceeding further, it may be of service that we pass in brief review the situation and possibilities on both sides, at the time to which our narrative now reaches, as they were estimated by an able writer in the *Quarterly Review* for January, 1871.

First, as to France. Starting with the assumption that Paris could resist for three months, we find the French bent on continuing the struggle—a determination which appears to have been intensified by every fresh disaster; but the only elements of success were supplied by the superior numbers and wealth of the defenders. Of able-bodied men there was no lack; but they were at first without arms and without officers to organize them. Especially were they deficient in field artillery, a deficiency for which no amount of courage or numbers could make up. The action of the civilian prefects in many cases disgusted the officers of the regular army; and the hoisting of the red flag at Lyons and Marseilles, referred to in the previous chapter, threatened at one time to divide the French people into two hostile camps.

While such was the state of affairs without the city, the temper of the Parisian populace could not be counted on. Dissensions were known to exist, and the Belleville clique, headed by Flourens, were noisy and violent. As already stated, the armed force at the disposal of Trochu was of a mixed character, consisting of regular troops, mobiles, and national guards; the regulars greatly disheartened by the events of the war. This force too, wanted organization, and was very imperfectly armed. The garrison was almost destitute of field artillery. Guns had to be cast, and the horses and gunners trained, while the enemy was thundering at the gates. Until this was effected, sorties in force, though the soul of the defence, could not be successfully undertaken.

Thus the composition and equipment of the garrison were in every respect so inferior to those of the approaching besiegers, that the salvation of the city depended absolutely on the formation of such an army without the walls as, in co-operation with the army within, might be able to drive the Germans from their prey. Now, the organization, arming, and provisioning of such a force required both time and a place where, secure from molestation, it might be drilled, and disciplined, and supplied with all the *matériel* and provisions necessary to enable it to take the field with any prospect of success. Such a place the sea alone could furnish. During the whole war the sea was at the command of France, and should have constituted the base of operations for the relief of Paris. Three harbours, Bordeaux and Havre being two of them, might have been fixed on as the rallying points for the whole of the French levies; by united and ceaseless effort on the part of all who were able to labour, entrenched camps might have been constructed round those ports, the flanks resting on the sea; and the works armed with heavy guns from the fleet, which should have been recalled to the defence of France and divided between the three ports, to which the whole available merchant-marine should have been constantly employed in bringing field-guns and breech-loading rifles for the equipment of the armies, as well as the stores of food and forage required for their maintenance in an advance on Paris. The three camps, each garrisoned by 150,000 fighting men, and armed with guns very superior to any the Germans could bring against them, would easily have defied attack, and divided the operations of the enemy. To assail them, indeed, it would have been necessary to employ three powerful armies, so widely separated from each other in a hostile country as must have rendered intercommunication tedious and difficult; and those armies could not even have been brought into the field, and provided with the requisite heavy guns, except by abandoning the siege of Paris.

The defence of the three camps, on the other hand, might be considered as one; since they could have maintained constant and rapid communication by steam, and reinforced each other according to need. As soon as they were ready to take the field, the French marine could have easily transported the armies of the two southern camps to Havre, from which an united army of 450,000 men might have marched to raise the siege of the capital. To the last a screen of troops should have been maintained as far as possible in advance of the two camps; but all serious engagements in the open country, where success might be doubtful, and especially all attempts to defend open towns, should have been avoided.

After Sedan the only organized army remaining to France was shut in at Metz, under Bazaine, and consisted of 150,000 men, exclusive of the regular garrison of the fortress. This force was now hemmed in by strong lines of circumvallation, and invested by the first and second German armies under General Manteuffel and Prince Frederick Charles, consisting of seven corps and three divisions of cavalry, reinforced later by one infantry division. Thus, a German force, never probably exceeding 210,000 men, spread over a circumference of twenty-seven miles, which was divided into two parts by the Moselle, was found sufficient to hold fast 150,000 French occupying the centre of the circle, and with every strategical advantage in their favour.

At Strassburg a French garrison of 19,000 was besieged by 70,000 Germans. By one Prussian division, under the grand duke of Mecklenburg, a garrison of 2000 mobiles was besieged at Toul, whose cannon, commanding the railroad from Nancy by Châlons and Epernay to Paris, compelled the Germans to unload their trains some distance east of the town, to transport their supplies on wheels by a long detour, and to reload them on trains to the west of the fortress. Thus the persistent defence of the garrison, which only surrendered in the last days of September, contributed largely in delaying the operations of the besiegers of Paris. Thionville, Longwy, Montmèdy, and Mézières, all held French garrisons, and prevented the Germans from using the railroad passing by these places to Rheims and Paris. Thionville and Montmèdy were blockaded, and the blockades of Bitsche and Phalsburg were continued; they were defended chiefly by mobiles, and occupied about 18,000 German troops.

To compensate somewhat for their inferiority in the field, the French, as fighting in defence of their own soil, had this advantage, that instead of being limited to one general line of retreat, they could, in the event of defeat, retire in any direction save the one barred by the enemy. With such an extent of seaboard and a powerful fleet they would have been secure of finding safety and support on reaching any point on the coast where local conditions were favourable; and this circumstance would evidently give them a real tactical advantage in battle.

Turning, now, to the Germans. The capture of Paris was the one great object they proposed to themselves in continuing the war, as its attainment, they considered, would lead to the immediate submission of France. The siege of the capital, therefore, was the one great central operation to which all the other military movements were accessory. Had the Germans foreseen the resistance they would have to encounter, it is not improbable that, after Sedan, they would have offered terms of peace which the French might have accepted; but they were under the impression that Paris would yield on the mere appearance of their forces before it, and thus they were committed to a tedious and difficult enterprise, the duration of which gave France all the chances arising from the mutability of human affairs in general, and the changes which time might work in the opinions and conduct of the other European powers.

Destitute as France was at this period of any organized military force in the field, the most obvious way of reducing her to subjection was to prevent the assembling and training of such a force, by sending strong movable columns of the three arms into every district. But from the large extent of France it was impossible, even with the overwhelming numbers at the disposal of the Prussian monarch, to coerce in that manner more than a small portion of her area. The German columns could command only the ground on which they encamped, with a certain zone around it; and the fire of hatred and resistance, smouldering over the whole surface of the country, would thus be stamped out in one quarter only to burst forth with increased violence in another. To this it was owing that the French government was left so long unmolested at Tours, as it would have been hazardous, in view of the strength of the garrison, to detach to so great a distance from Paris a large force from the investing armies, and a small one would have run the risk of being overpowered.

The base of operations for all the German forces was formed by the fine of frontier extending from Saarbrück on the north to Basle on the south, and all their movements were necessarily regulated by that consideration.

The lines of communication for the army engaged in the primary operation of the siege of Paris took their departure from the northern half of this base; and on these lines were situated all the strong places excepting Strassburg, such as Thionville, &c., which the Germans were besieging at the period of the fall of Sedan. The southern half formed the base of operations for the troops engaged in the siege of Strassburg, and for those subsequently employed in reducing Schlestadt, Neu Brisach, Belfort, &c.; as well as for the armies operating by Dijon towards Lyons, and to the south of Belfort towards Besançon.

The position of the investing army at Paris formed a secondary base, from which radiated the different columns acting towards Orleans, Chartres, Dreux, Evreux, Amiens, St. Quentin, &c.; the capital being, as it were, the centre of the wheel, of which these columns represented the spokes. The object for which they were employed, was the collecting of supplies, and preventing the siege from interruption by the different bodies of French troops which were organizing all over the country.

With these explanations clearly apprehended, the movements of the German forces, which otherwise would appear confused, will assume in the mind of the reader a methodical and symmetrical arrangement.

On the evening of the 2nd September, the day on which the surrender of Sedan was consummated, the German armies received their marching orders, and on the morning of the 3rd broke up in different directions, *en route* for Paris. The readiness and rapidity with which they resumed their march were noteworthy. An army of 120,000 prisoners, with their personal arms, artillery, camp baggage, ammunition, military train, and military stores, had to be received and transported on a sudden emergency. The transport, store, and commissariat services were thus put to a severe strain; and the victors were hampered in proportion to the magnitude of their victory. The men and horses which came into their hands required to be fed, and the sick to be provided for. The ease, however, with which all this was accomplished was equally astonishing with the victory itself, and showed extraordinary forethought and organization. The demolition of the French army and capture of the emperor seemed only a little episode, by which the stern purpose of the invaders remained unshaken and unaltered. Their goal was Paris; and orders were issued that by the 14th of September the battalions were to be each in position at a distance of ten leagues from the city.

The eleventh corps and first Bavarians, both belonging to the third Prussian army, were detailed to escort the prisoners to Pont-à-Mousson, whence, having handed over their charge to the tenth corps, employed before Metz, they were to make all speed to join the Crown Prince of Prussia in his march to Paris.

The third and fourth armies marched on the capital by two different routes. The third, under the Crown Prince of Prussia, passed by Rethel, Rheims, and Epernay, to the south bank of the Marne; and continued its march by Montmirail to Coulommiers, whence the different corps diverged to take up their respective investing positions from Lagny, on the Marne, towards Versailles. The Crown Prince of Saxony, with the fourth army, moved his columns to the south-west, but without encroaching on the roads to the west of the line formed by Remilly, La Besace, and Le Chêne. They passed by Vouziers, Rheims, and generally by the north bank of the Marne to Claye, whence the several corps diverged to their respective positions for continuing the investing line from Lagny on their left, round by Gonesse to St. Denis and Argenteuil, north of the city. The tracks of the two crown princes intersected each other at Rheims. That one army of 80,000 men, with all its trains and impediments, should, without serious inconvenience, have been able to cut across the march of another numbering 120,000, added another proof to the excellence of the working staff amongst the Germans.

Each army marched in parallel columns, the lateral communication between which, as well as between the two armies, was kept up by the cavalry; and in particular, the outward flanks of both were protected by strong bodies of mounted troops. Their front was, at the same time, covered by a chain of advanced guards, at a distance of from twenty to thirty miles, in communication with each other by means of cavalry patrols, thus forming a continuous circle, either for protection or conveying information, enveloping the head of the line of march of both armies.

A new French corps d'armée, which had been formed in Paris, under the command of General Vinoy, was despatched by rail to Soissons, Laon, Marie, Vervins, &c., to join MacMahon on his way from Rheims to Stenay, to attempt the relief of Bazaine at Metz. This thirteenth corps consisted of the four last regiments of infantry and two of light cavalry that had arrived from Algeria, and the *débris* of one of MacMahon's cuirassier brigades; to which were added *regiments de marche* composed of fourth battalions and depôts. The corps, however, did not get beyond Mézières; but retreating as quickly as possible, escaped by rail, via Laon, Soissons, and Villers-Cotterets, to Paris, before the first-named town surrendered to the cavalry division of Duke William of Mecklenburg.

The march of the Germans met with little opposition. After the defeat at Sedan, although France still had considerable elements of military power, they were for a time so disorganized that they could offer but a feeble resistance to the advance of the enemy. As yet, however, hardly a single fortress of the invaded country had fallen; and Bazaine was still in occupation of Metz with an immense force. The Germans had not, indeed, mastered even one of the main roads or railways necessary to maintain their communications with the interior and with the frontier of Germany, but they still pressed forward, not doubting that Paris would soon be within their reach. Their march was well described by a correspondent of the *Daily News*:—"All through the fertile province of Champagne, down the straight roads, with their lines of poplar trees, and among the pleasant villages on the vine-covered slopes, the Prussians advanced towards Paris. There was a great bend to the northward when the Crown Prince swung round upon MacMahon, and pinned him in against the Belgian frontier at Sedan. There was a momentary pause after the success of September—a pause merely to rest the exhausted troops; then a second movement, as decided and almost as rapid as that of the shutting in of MacMahon. The German forces returned to the main road to their promised goal. They came slanting back to the line of the Marne, and occupied village after village and town after town, with astonishing quickness. The French had no time to prepare a systematic defence. Before the national guard could even be armed, far less exercised, those fluttering pennants of black and white which told of the Prussian lancers, or those spiked helmets of the Prussian dragoons, were seen approaching. Everything had to be abandoned. The armed force, such as it was, dispersed or retreated, and the people submitted themselves to the inevitable in the way of war contributions." On and on marched the invaders. Heralded by their trusty cavalry, the immense armies moved in open order, although never beyond the reach of their prescient strategist, who required but a few hours' notice to mass them for any possible contingency. Dr. Russell also wrote as follows to the Times on the subject:—"One thing which causes astonishment to me is the perfect impunity with which the Prussian communications have been preserved. Their military administration is most vigorous, and its apparent severity prevents bloodshed and secures their long lines against attack. It is 'Death' to have any arms concealed or retained in any house. It is 'Death' to cut a telegraph wire, or to destroy anything used for the service of the army. What can a disarmed population, however hostile and venturesome, attempt even against small bodies of armed men who always move with caution, and against troops who do not make night marches unless in large bodies? The Prussian cavalry are everywhere. There is no neglect, no *insouciance*. Nothing is taken on trust. The people in the towns and villages are quite aghast."

On the 5th of September the Germans entered the ancient cathedral city of Rheims. In the morning a few cavalry soldiers entered the town, one of whom was attacked by an old Frenchman; the hussar fired his pistol, wounded his assailant, and then, with his companions, galloped out of the city. In the afternoon a large body of troops appeared, followed by the main army, whereupon the mayor formally surrendered the town, and the king of Prussia's headquarters were established in the episcopal palace.

A notable incident occurred when the Germans, under the Duke William of Mecklenburg, arrived at the fortress of Laon, which General Vinoy's corps left early on the morning of the 6th September. On the evening of that day three uhlans presented themselves at the gate, and demanded admission; but the gardes mobiles fired on them, and they were dismounted and made prisoners. On the following day three more uhlans arrived with a flag of truce. One was admitted, after having had his eyes bandaged; but General Theremin d'Hame, the commandant of the citadel, would not treat with him on account of his inferior rank. On the 8th of September more Prussians appeared; a lieutenant-colonel presented himself as *parlementaire*, and was received by General d'Hame, who refused to surrender the citadel, but the maire came to terms for the town. On the 9th, however, the general received a telegram from the War minister to surrender, as the place was not in a state to defend itself. Two officers of the mobile were sent to the Prussian camp to make the announcement; and accordingly, towards noon a corps of Prussian infantry, a thousand strong, preceded and followed by cavalry, escorting a group of superior officers, entered the town with their band playing. A portion of this force immediately marched to the citadel, just before occupied by the mobiles, who laid down their arms and were declared prisoners of war on parole. At the moment the mobiles were defiling the powder magazine exploded, causing fearful consternation in the ranks both of friends and foes. Fifty Germans and 300 gardes mobiles perished in the catastrophe, and several hundred soldiers and civilians were more or less severely wounded. Roofs were blown off the houses and windows broken, both in Laon and the neighbouring village of Vaux. This sanguinary incident naturally caused great irritation among the Germans, who immediately placed the commandant under arrest. The king of Prussia ordered a judicial investigation to be made into the cause of the explosion, which resulted in establishing the complete innocence of General Theremin d'Hame, who died shortly after of his own injuries. The perpetrator was declared to be a certain inspector of artillery, missing after the catastrophe, and believed to have had no accomplices. By a portion of the French press the perpetrators of the barbarous deed were eulogized as devoted patriots, who preferred death to dishonour. The following abbreviation of a touching letter, written by the unfortunate General to Madame d'Hame shortly after the explosion, shows that he held a contrary opinion, and gives a glimpse of the condition of affairs at the period of which we are writing:—"You will be in great anxiety on my account, beloved. To-day I am able to write and comfort you, which the injuries to my head would not let me do before. A hard trial has fallen on me. You know that sixteen days since the command of this department was assigned to me, without staff, or a single man or officer of the regulars. I was left alone with a battalion of mobiles, who had been called out on the 8th of August. The men, terrified at the rumours flying about, deserted wholesale, and were reduced one half. We had no means of resistance, and a telegram from the minister told me, if necessary, to fall back on Soissons. Unhappily this came too late. The Prussian summons to surrender arrived soon after it, and there was no means of withdrawal. After two days of parleying, I was obliged to surrender, the citadel being in face of a whole army corps. When the duke of Mecklenburg entered he was astonished to see who had defended the place—mere peasants in blouses, many of them without a cartridge-box. The duke had asked me whether I was related to F. Theremin, formerly of our foreign office, and I had scarcely answered this, and one or two other friendly questions, when a terrific explosion covered the ground with dead and dying. The event was so surprising that one could only attribute it to treason, and to-day it is manifest to all that the garde d'artillerie is alone responsible for it. Yet all my life long I shall be grieved that so rascally a deed was perpetrated where I had the command. Happily the duke and his brigadier, Count Alvensleben, are only slightly wounded. I was to have had my freedom, and my sword had been given back to me. All is changed now. I am a prisoner and in hospital, and know not when I may be well and free again. But as soon as permitted I will, by a pass, hasten to you and my daughter, who must, for the present, use her Christian faith to bear the trial that has come upon us." A month after the above was written General d'Hame died of his wounds.

The town of Laon is situated seventy-five miles north-east of Paris, and is the capital of the department of the Aisne. Its traditionary history extends back to the reign of Clovis, and during the Carlovingian dynasty it formed a part of the possessions of the crown. The city was surrounded by an ancient wall, and possessed a handsome cathedral dating from the twelfth century. The fortress had sustained frequent sieges, and in 1594 was taken from the League by Henry IV. During the campaign of 1814 it was the scene of a sanguinary engagement between Napoleon I. and Marshal Blücher, in which, after a conflict of great obstinacy and varying success, the French were finally beaten, with a loss of forty-eight guns and between 5000 and 6000 prisoners.

After the affair at Laon the German armies continued to advance uninterruptedly (with the exception of a few futile attempts at obstruction by the felling of trees and the blowing up of bridges) towards Paris, which, as previously arranged, they approached by three main roads, the one from Soissons, through Villers-Cotterets and Dommartin; the second from Meaux, through which they had come from Epernay and Château-Thierry; and the third from Provins, through Brie, which leads to the junctions of the rivers Seine and Marne, close to Paris on its south-east side. When they reached so near the capital their progress was not allowed altogether undisputed. At Château Thierry a Prussian reconnoitring party was driven back by a body of French cavalry. At Montereau and Melun engagements took place between uhlans and francs-tireurs, and heavy fighting occurred near Colmar between these irregulars and the Germans, in which the French sustained defeat and lost several prisoners.

It was in the suburban village of Créteil, on the Marne, two miles in front of the Fort de Charenton that the Prussian scouts made their first appearance on the 16th September. Two days before, the main body of the German armies had reached the streams which fence Paris on its eastern front. The Crown Prince of Saxony was posted at Meaux, on the Marne, and the Crown Prince of Prussia at Melun, on the Seine, with the design of converging from those points on their destined prize. The fortifications of the city, however, saved it from a sudden attack, although, as yet, they were comparatively ill armed, and had not the support of an army outside. Their unprotected state enabled the invaders from the first to seize positions which gave them the power of effectually investing the capital, and which never could have been occupied had the French possessed an army of such strength as that with which MacMahon undertook his fatal march to Sedan.

General Trochu, who well knew the importance of preventing the enemy from closing in on the city, had endeavoured, as far as was in his power, to retard the investment, and to strengthen the external line of the defences where they were weakest. With this object he had stationed troops outside the eastern and southern forts, with orders to attack the Germans in flank as they advanced, and, if possible, to drive them back; and he had constructed, and partly armed, works on the heights which, from Clamart to Châtillon, command the forts of Issy, Vanves, and Montrouge, along the southern verge of Paris.

With any considerable number of good troops and an adequate field artillery, General Trochu would at this time have made it impossible for the Germans to take up their investing line on such an enormous circumference without defeating again a French army. The French, holding the centre, might have struck vigorously at different portions of the force closing round the city, and might have cut it into fragments before it found time to construct entrenchments and batteries, to tighten its hold upon its victim.

On the 18 th September, a feeble fragment of the French regular army, under General Vinoy, attacked the leading columns of the Crown Prince of Saxony as they debouched into the valley of the Marne; but it was soon forced to fall back before them. The next day another attack was made by the French between St. Denis and Gonesse with a similar result; in the evening, on the southern side, they put forth an effort more vigorous and protracted, but still fruitless. On the 17th, the third army, under the Crown Prince of Prussia, was headed by the fifth corps, which, at Villeneuve St. George threw pontoon bridges over the Seine, by which the fifth, sixth, and second Bavarian corps passed, to take up their positions in the investing line from the Seine westward by Sévres to Bougival, north-west of the city. To cover this operation, the seventeenth infantry brigade of the fifth corps, supported by two squadrons and two batteries, occupied a strong position on the heights of Limeil, extending across the high road to Melun and the Lyons railway, to Boissy St. Leger. Five companies occupied the woods of the Château Brevannes, at the foot of the hill on the Paris side of the position. At two p.m. eight battalions of French regulars, and two batteries, under the command of General Ducrot, debouched from Charenton on the tongue of land lying between the Seine and Marne. The ground was admirably chosen, as both flanks of the attacking force were covered by rivers; but notwithstanding the advantage of their position, the French were defeated and driven back in wild confusion by the five German companies posted in the woods of Brevannes, aided by the two batteries on the heights of Limeil. On the 18th, the fifth German corps, covered by a squadron of cavalry on the side towards Paris, advanced with its leading division (ninth) to Bièvre, and the tenth division to Palaiseau. The head of this column had a slight skirmish with some French troops posted to the north of Bièvre, near Petit Bicêtre, in the afternoon. On the same day the second Bavarian corps had crossed the Seine and occupied Longjumeau (on the left bank), while the head of the sixth corps arrived at the bridge, and prepared to pass it early the next morning, in the meantime constructing another bridge.

On the morning of the 19th the following corps commenced their march: the fifth on Versailles, in two columns, by Bièvre and Jouy; the Bavarians on Chatenay, by Palaiseau; the sixth on Chenilly, by Villeneuve le Roi and Orly. The head of the ninth division (fifth corps), after debouching from Bièvre, was again attacked by a French force in the fortified position at Petit Bicêtre, but the attack was soon repulsed. The division was about to resume its march on Versailles when it was once more attacked, and this time so vigorously and by so large a force (the whole of the French fourteenth corps), that it was very hard pressed. But one Bavarian brigade, which had reached Chatenay, came to its assistance at Villa Coublay (on the summit of the plateau); and another, advancing on Sceaux, threatened the enemy's flank, whilst a third marched on Bourg-la-Reine, to cut off his retreat; the remaining brigade of the Bavarian corps meanwhile occupying Croix de Bernis. The tenth division, fifth corps, arriving on its march from Palaiseau, at Jouy, at this time, was, with the reserve artillery, also directed on Villa Coublay, and the fire of the latter, from the plateau, caused the French to evacuate their position at Petit Bicêtre, and retreat rapidly on Châtillon, so that the fifth German corps was enabled to resume its march on Versailles soon after eleven o'clock a.m. By their retrograde movement the French were brought into closer contact with the advance of the Bavarians at Bourg. To gain time to carry off the guns which had been placed in the earthworks near Châtillon, they occupied a strong position along the edge of the plateau and towards Meudon, bringing twenty-six field guns into battery, and even threatening Fontenay and Plessis with attacks which seemed sufficiently serious to cause the Bavarian general, Von Hartmann, to suspend the advance of the two brigades in front until he could bring the other two up to their support. A pause thus ensued in the fire on both sides. About an hour after, it was again opened with renewed vigour by the Bavarians, who, perceiving that the enemy was withdrawing his "position" guns and preparing to retreat, made a general attack and carried the redoubt at three p.m., capturing eight pieces of artillery, and driving the French under the guns of forts Vanves and Montrouge. During these proceedings the sixth corps crossed the river, and advancing on Villejuif and Vitry, by Choisy, Orly, and Thiais, came up on the right of the Bavarians; but its further progress was arrested by the fire of a large French redoubt on the heights above Villejuif. On the evening of the 19th the third army occupied the line of Bougival, Sévres, Meudon, Clamart, Bour-gla-Reine, L'Hay, Chevilly, Choisy-le-Roi, and, in conjunction with the Würtemburg division, the space between Choisy-sur-Seine, and Monneuil-sur-Marne. On the morning of the 20th the city was thus invested on all sides.

The behaviour of a part of the French troops engaged in the combats around the city rendered of no effect the superior advantages of their position. They had belonged to regiments of MacMahon's own corps; but demoralized through repeated defeats, they fled panic-stricken from the field at the first appearance of danger, and refused to renew the contest. The losses of the French were few in killed and wounded, but the number of prisoners was variously estimated at from 2000 to 3000, besides the eight guns captured in the redoubt, as already mentioned. On the German side the Crown Prince of Prussia reported that the investing of the city had been effected with little loss—the chief casualties occurring in the seventh regiment. In Paris the establishment of a court-martial for the trial of "cowards and deserters" was proclaimed by the minister of War; and General Trochu issued to the garrison of the capital a manifesto containing the subjoined passage, which strikingly illustrates some of the difficulties with which the French military leaders had to contend:—"In the fight of yesterday, which lasted during nearly the whole day, and in which our artillery, whose firmness cannot be too highly praised, inflicted upon the enemy enormous losses, some incidents occurred which you ought to be made acquainted with, in the interest of the great cause which we are all defending. An unjustifiable panic, which all the efforts of an excellent commander and his officers could not arrest, seized upon the provisional regiment of zouaves which held our right. From the commencement of the action the greater number of those soldiers fell back in disorder upon the city, and there spread the wildest alarm. To excuse their conduct the fugitives have declared that they were being led to certain destruction, while, in fact, their strength was undiminished, and they had no wounded; that cartridges were deficient, while they had not made use, as I ascertained for myself, of those with which they were provided; that they had been betrayed by their leaders, &c. The truth is, that these unworthy soldiers compromised from the very beginning an affair from which, notwithstanding their conduct, very important results were obtained. Some other soldiers of various regiments of infantry were similarly culpable. Already the misfortunes which we have experienced at the commencement of this war had thrown back into Paris undisciplined and demoralized soldiers, who caused there uneasiness and trouble, and who from the force of circumstances have escaped from the authority of their officers and from all punishment. I am firmly resolved to put an end to such serious disorders. I order all the defenders of Paris to seize every man, all soldiers and gardes mobiles, who shall be found in the city in a state of drunkenness, or spreading abroad scandalous stories and dishonouring the uniform which they wear." The misfortunes caused by these panic-stricken troops were increased by the French engineering department having constructed the redoubt captured by the Germans between the villages of Châtillon and Clamart, apart from the permanent defences of the city. When the Germans crossed the Seine the work was unfinished, and should have been dismantled and destroyed; but was left, armed, to fall into the hands of the enemy, who immediately transformed it into a redoubt facing towards forts Vanves and Montrouge. Captain Bingham, in his "Siege of Paris," says, that had the Prussians followed up their advantage the city would have been at their mercy—the regular troops being demoralized and the mobiles and national guards being quite untrained. The people felt highly indignant that after so many lessons their soldiers should again have allowed themselves to be so ignominiously routed; and there was a loud outcry against the Zouaves especially, who, as representatives of the late *régime*, were denounced as dastardly praetorians, fit to act against unarmed citizens, but useless when opposed to armed troops.

The entry of the Germans into Versailles may be noticed in a few sentences. On the 18th of September three death's head hussars presented themselves at one of the town gates and demanded a parley with the authorities, but the make refused to treat with any soldier under the rank of a general, or who was not furnished with full powers. The next morning the demand was renewed by an aide-de-camp, followed by a single cavalry soldier, and a long discussion ensued. Since six o'clock the cannon had been booming on the road from Versailles to Sceaux, about three miles from the town. The aide-de-camp required accommodation for the wounded, and the keys of all forage stores. These demands having led to a warm debate, the officer departed to consult his general. In less than an hour an aide-de-camp to the general commanding the fifth corps arrived, and the discussion was renewed. At a quarter past eleven a.m. M. Rameau, the newly-appointed maire, taking his station at the Paris gate, read the conditions of capitulation at last agreed to, which were:— "1. That property and person should be respected, as also public monuments and works of art. 2. The confederate German forces should occupy the barracks with their soldiers, but the inhabitants were to lodge the officers, and soldiers also, if the barracks should afford insufficient accommodation. 3. The national guard should retain its arms, and, for the common interest, should be intrusted with the internal police of the town, except that the confederates should occupy at their discretion the gates at the barriers. 4. There should be no requisition for money, but the town should supply at money rates all that might be needed for the passing or stationary forces. 5. On the same day the Grille des Chantiers would be opened to allow the fifth corps to enter." Shortly before ten o'clock the German columns began to defile through the Rue des Chantiers. The procession lasted until past five o'clock in the afternoon, the total number of troops being variously estimated at from 25,000 to 40,000 men. Versailles was immediately fixed on as the headquarters of the Crown Prince and king of Prussia, and so remained till the end of the siege. The palace of Versailles, in which the German headquarters were established, was founded in 1661 by Louis XIV., being erected on the site of an old hunting lodge of Henry IV., situated in the midst of a large forest. The timber, however, was soon cleared, and a splendid park formed twenty miles in circumference, the grounds laid out in a style of great magnificence, and a supply of water obtained for the ornamental fountains at an enormous outlay. It is reported that the palace, grounds, and waterworks cost upwards of £40,000,000 sterling, and an outlay of 10,000 francs has to be incurred every time the whole of the fountains are played. The palace itself is in the Ionic style, and more remarkable for its vastness than its architectural beauty; but the rooms and galleries are most elaborately decorated, and stored with the choicest works of art. Versailles had always been a favourite residence of royalty; and although the palace and gardens suffered considerably during the first revolution, they were fully restored and improved by Louis Philippe, whose object was to make Versailles a grand historical museum. The town of Versailles itself has an interesting history, and contains several handsome monuments and an old cathedral dedicated to Our Lady. In 1815 it was occupied by the Prussians under Blucher, and pillaged by the troops.

Previous to the investment of the capital negotiations had been entered into for an armistice. Even before the German headquarters had arrived at Rheims, on its march to Paris, Earl Granville, the English Foreign minister, had conveyed intimations to Count von Bismarck that the provisional government were anxious to discuss terms of peace. The proclamation of the republic, however, and the institution of the provisional government, were viewed with little favour by the German chancellor, and he intimated that he could not recognize M. Favre as minister of Foreign Affairs for France, or as capable of binding the nation. In the course of a conversation, reported about this time by a correspondent of the *Standard*, Count von Bismarck observed:—"When I saw the emperor, after his surrendering himself a prisoner, I asked him if he was disposed to put forward any request for peace. The emperor replied that he was not in a position to do so, for he had left a regular government in Paris, with the empress at its head. It is plain therefore that, if France possesses any government at all, it is still the government of the empress as regent, or of the emperor." When asked if the flight of the empress and of the prince imperial might not be regarded as an abdication, he said very positively he could not so construe it. The empress had been forced to go by the "gentlemen of the pavement," as the Corps Législatif had been obliged to suspend its sittings, but the actions of these "gentlemen" were not legal.

They could not make a government. "The question was," continued the count, "Whom does the fleet still obey? Whom does the army shut up in Metz still obey? Perhaps Bazaine still recognizes the emperor. If so, and we choose to let him go to Paris, he and his army would be worth considerably more than the gentlemen of the pavement and the so-called government. We do not wish to dictate to France her form of government: we have nothing to say to it; that is her affair." Count von Bismarck also significantly added: "The present is the twenty-fifth time in the space of a hundred years that France has made war on Germany on some pretext or other. Now, at least, our terrible disease of divided unity being cured, we have contrived, by the help of the hand of God, to beat her down. It is idle to hope to propitiate her."

A large section of the German people thought it highly improbable that Paris could withstand the rigours of a siege; and Colonel von Holstein took a bet of 20,000 francs with M. de Girardin that the Prussian army would defile before his house in the Avenue du Roi de Rome by the 15th of September. This, however, was not the opinion of Count von Bismarck, who publicly declared that the German policy was not immediately to attack the capital. "We shall," said he, "enter the city without attacking it; we shall starve it out." He is also credited with having used the expression, that the Parisians would be made "to stew in their own juice." In the conversation to which we have just alluded the conditions of peace were freely canvassed. "For the improvement of the frontier," said the German chancellor, "we must have Strassburg, and we must have Metz; and we will fight ten years sooner than not obtain this necessary security." Count von Bismarck admitted that the French would regard with a rancorous hatred the possession of these two fortresses; but he suggested that, as it was already, France would never forgive the Germans for the complete overthrow of their grand army. They must therefore secure material guarantees against future attack. The above conversations were generally confirmed by official circulars issued by Count von Bismarck from Rheims on the 13th and Meaux on the 16th of September, in which he threw the entire responsibility of the war upon France, and assumed that Prussia was a highly pacific and ill-used nation. But these sentiments appear to have been used, in every case, simply as a preface to the fact that Germany was now determined to "strengthen her frontier," which she could not adequately do till Metz and Strassburg were in her possession.

Previous to the final investment of the capital, and while the German armies were on the march, negotiations of an official character were, however, entered into. The report of M. Jules Favre, issued on the 21st September, stated that the day after it was established the provisional government received the representatives of all the powers in Paris. North America, Switzerland, Italy, Spain, and Portugal officially recognized the French Republic, and the other powers authorized their representatives to enter into semi-official relations with the new government. On the 10th of September M. Favre asked Count von Bismarck if he was willing to enter into negotiations as to the conditions of an arrangement. He replied that he could not entertain any proposal in consequence of the irregular character of the provisional government, but asked at the same time what guarantees that government could offer for the execution of any treaty that might be concluded. Earl Granville, who had acted as intermediary, considered it desirable that M. Favre should proceed to the Prussian headquarters; and on the 16th September Count von Bismarck decided to receive him, first at Meaux, and subsequently at Ferrières. In the course of these interviews, M. Favre declared the fixed determination of France to accept of no condition which would render the proposed peace merely a short or precarious truce. Count von Bismarck said that, if he believed a permanent peace possible, he would conclude it without delay; but he thought the provisional government was not to be depended on, and that its overthrow by the populace, should Paris not be captured in a few days, was a very probable event. "France," he added, "will as little forget the capitulation of Sedan as Waterloo or Sadowa, which latter did not concern you." On being pressed by M. Favre to state exactly his conditions of peace, he replied that the possession of the departments of the Upper and Lower Rhine, of the Moselle, with Metz, Château-Salins, and Sonines, was indispensable, as a guarantee for the security of his country, and that he could not relinquish them. He acknowledged the force of the objection, that the consent of the people of those districts to be thus disposed of was more than doubtful, and that the public law of Europe would not permit him to act without that consent; but he added, "As we shall shortly have another war with you, we intend to enter upon it in possession of all our advantages." M. Favre urged that the European powers might regard the claims of Prussia as exorbitant, and that France "will never accept them. We can perish as a nation, but we cannot dishonour ourselves. The country alone is competent to decide upon a cession of territory. We have no doubts as to its sentiments, but we will consult it." The charge that Prussia, carried away by the intoxication of victory, desired the destruction of France, Count von Bismarck utterly denied; but to a demand for time to allow of the meeting of the Constituent Assembly, he, according to M. Favre, replied that for the purpose an armistice was necessary, which he could on no account grant. At the second interview, however, on the evening of the 19th of September, at Ferrières, he appeared to consent to an armistice of fifteen days; and next day, at eleven a.m., he sent M. Favre the following conditions, namely, the occupation of Strassburg, Toul, and Phalsburg; and as the French minister had stated that the Assembly would meet in Paris, one of the forts commanding the capital—Mont Valérien, for instance—must be placed in the hands of the Germans. M. Favre said that it would be a more simple arrangement to give up Paris at once. Count von Bismarck replied, "Let us seek some other combination." M. Favre then proposed that the Constituent Assembly should meet at Tours, in which case no guarantee relative to Paris would be required. Against a further demand that the garrison of Strassburg should surrender as prisoners of war, M. Favre expressed himself in terms of strong indignation. Upon this Count von Bismarck went to consult the king, who accepted the second combination, but insisted on the surrender of the garrison of Strassburg as proposed." "My powers were now exhausted," continued M. Favre; "I rose and took my leave, expressing to him my conviction that we should fight as long as we could find in Paris an element of resistance." On his return to the capital he forwarded to Count von Bismarck the following despatch:—

"M. le Comte,—I have faithfully expressed to my colleagues in the government of National Defence the declaration that your excellency has been good enough to make to me. I regret to have to make known to your excellency that that government has not been able to accept your propositions. They will accept an armistice having for its object the election and meeting of a National Assembly; but they cannot subscribe to the contingent conditions. As to myself, I can say with a clear conscience that I have done my utmost to stop the effusion of blood, and to restore peace to two nations which would be so much benefited by that blessing. I have only been stopped by an imperious duty, which required me not to yield the honour of my country, which has determined energetically to resist such a sacrifice. I and my colleagues associate ourselves without reserve in that determination. God, our judge, will decide on our destinies. I have faith in his justice.—I have, &c.

"(Signed), JULES FAVRE.

"*Sept.* 21, 1870."

The French minister concluded his report to his colleagues, with regard to the whole negotiations, as follows:—"I have done, my dear colleagues; and you will think with me that, if I have failed in my mission, it has still not been altogether useless. It has proved that we have not deviated. From the first we have conducted a war which we condemned beforehand, but which we accepted in preference to dishonour. We have done more; for we have laid bare the equivocation on which Prussia relied, and let Europe now assist us in dissipating it altogether. In invading our soil, she gave her word to the world that she was attacking Napoleon and his soldiers, but would respect the nation. We know now what to think of that statement. Prussia requires three of our departments: two fortified cities—one of 100,000, the other of 75,000 inhabitants; and eight or ten smaller ones, also fortified. She knows that the populations she wishes to tear from us repulse her; but she seizes them nevertheless, replying with the edge of the sword to their protestations against such an outrage on their civic liberty and their moral dignity. To the nation that demands the opportunity of self-consultation she proposes the guarantee of her cannon planted at Mont Valérien, and protecting the scene of their deliberations. That is what we know, and what I am authorized to make public. Let the nation that hears this either rise at once or at once disavow us when we counsel resistance to the bitter end."

This memorandum of M. Jules Favre drew forth a reply from Count von Bismarck, addressed to the North German embassies and legations. The language of this document approached the extreme of curtness, not unmixed with a tone of scorn. On the whole, however, the German chancellor admitted that M. Favre had endeavoured to convey an accurate account of the transaction, although the drift of his entire argument was not the conclusion of peace, but of an armistice which was to precede it. Count von Bismarck continued:—"As to our terms of peace, I expressly declared to M. Favre that I should state the frontier we should claim only after the principle of cession of territory had been publicly conceded by France. In connection with this the formation of a new Moselle district, with the arrondissements of Saarbrück, Château Salins, Saargemund, Metz, and Thionville, was alluded to by me as an arrangement included in our intentions; but I have not renounced the right of making such further demands as may be calculated to indemnify us for the sacrifices which a continuance of the war will entail. M. Favre called Strassburg the key of the house, leaving it doubtful which house he meant. I replied that Strassburg was the key of our house, and we therefore objected to leave it in foreign hands. Our first conversation in Château Haute Maison, near Montoy, was confined to an abstract inquiry into the general characteristics of the past and present ages. M. Favre's only pertinent remark on this occasion was that they would pay any sum, 'tout l'argent que nous avons,' but declined any cession of territory. Upon my declaring such cession to be indispensable, he said, in that case, it would be useless to open negotiations for peace; and he argued on the supposition that to cede territory would humiliate—nay, dishonour—France. I failed to convince him that terms such as France had obtained from Italy, and demanded from Germany, without even the excuse of previous war—terms which France would have undoubtedly imposed upon us had we been defeated, and in which nearly every war had resulted down to the latest times—could have nothing dishonourable in themselves to a nation vanquished after a gallant struggle; and that the honour of France was of no other quality or nature than the honour of all other countries." Count von Bismarck further said that the conversations at Ferrières took a more practical turn, referring exclusively to the question of an armistice; and this, he contended, disproved the assertion that he had refused such a question under any conditions. "In this conversation," he continued, "we both were of opinion that an armistice might be concluded, to give the French nation an opportunity of electing a Representative Assembly, which alone would be in a position so far to strengthen the tide to power possessed by the existing government as to render it possible for us to conclude with them a peace valid in accordance with the rules of international law. I remarked that to an army in the midst of a victorious career an armistice is always injurious; that in the present instance, more particularly, it would give France time to reorganize her troops and to make defensive preparations; and that, therefore, I could not accord an armistice without some military equivalent being conceded to us. I mentioned as such the surrender of the fortresses obstructing our communications with Germany; because, if by an armistice we were to be detained in France longer than was absolutely necessary, we must insist upon increased means of bringing up provisions. I referred to Strassburg, Toul, and some less important places. Concerning Strassburg I urged that, the crowning of the *glacis* having been accomplished, the conquest of that place might be shortly anticipated; and that we therefore thought ourselves entitled to demand that that garrison should surrender as prisoners of war. The garrisons of the other places would be allowed free retreat. Paris was another difficulty. Having completely inclosed this city, we could permit it renewed intercourse with the rest of France only if the importation of fresh provisions thereby rendered possible did not weaken our own military position and retard the date at which we might hope to starve out the place. Having consulted the military authorities and taken his Majesty's commands, I therefore ultimately submitted the following alternative: 'Either the fortified place of Paris is to be given into our hands by the surrender of a commanding portion of the works, in which case we are ready to allow Paris renewed intercourse with the country, and to permit the provisioning of the town; or, the fortified place of Paris not being given into our hands, we shall keep it invested during the armistice, which latter would otherwise result in Paris being able to oppose us at its expiry, reinforced by fresh supplies, and strengthened by new defences.' M. Favre peremptorily declined handing over any portion of the works of Paris, and also refused the surrender of the Strassburg garrison as prisoners of war. He, however, promised to take the opinion of his colleagues at Paris respecting the other alternative under which the military *status quo* before Paris was to be maintained. Accordingly, the programme which M. Favre brought to Paris as the result of our conversations, and which was rejected there, contained nothing as to the future conditions of peace. It only included an armistice of from a fortnight to three weeks, to be granted on the following conditions, in order to enable the election of a National Assembly to be held: Firstly, in and before Paris the maintenance of the military *status quo*; secondly, in and before Metz the continuance of hostilities within a circle hereafter to be more accurately defined; thirdly, the surrender of Strassburg with its garrison, and the evacuation of Toul and Bitsche, their garrisons being accorded free retreat. I believe our conviction that this was a very acceptable offer will be shared by all neutral cabinets. If the French government has not availed itself of this opportunity for having a National Assembly elected in all parts of France, those occupied by us not excepted, this indicates a resolve to prolong the difficulties which prevent the conclusion of a valid peace, and to ignore the voice of the French people. From all we see here, the conviction is forced upon us, as it no doubt is likewise upon the rulers at Paris, that free and unbiassed general elections will yield a majority in favour of peace."

It will thus be seen that the negotiations failed to procure peace. The ministers in Paris issued a proclamation reiterating their determination not to cede "an inch of territory, or a stone of a fortress." As a sequel to this proclamation a manifesto of the delegation at Tours appeared as follows: "To France! Before the investment of Paris, M. Jules Favre, minister for Foreign Affairs, wished to see M. de Bismarck to learn the intentions of the enemy. Here is the declaration of the enemy: Prussia wishes to continue the war, and to reduce France to the rank of a second-rate power; Prussia claims Alsace and Lorraine, as far as Metz, by right of conquest; Prussia, to consent to an armistice, has dared ask for the surrender of Strassburg, of Toul, and of Mont Valérien. Paris, enraged, would sooner bury itself beneath its ruins. To such insolent pretensions, in fact, we answer only by a struggle *à outrance*. France accepts this struggle, and relies on her children."

The correspondence subsequently published by the British government, relating to this period, showed more clearly the significance of the above negotiations. The English foreign minister, Earl Granville, had all through the proceedings acted with dignified consistency, abiding by the propositions that England would make no attempt at mediation unless with the concurrence of both belligerents; that where military questions came in, the government would rigidly abstain from offering any opinion; and that England would not formally recognize the government of National Defence until it had received an express recognition from the French nation. But any project of successful mediation was rendered difficult on account of the ground taken by the combatants. On the one hand, the Germans had stated that they must and would have territory; while, on the other, the republican government held to their famous declaration that they would yield neither an inch of territory nor a stone of any fortress. And then, again, the French cabinet never felt exactly secure of its own position, and repeatedly acknowledged that in order to bind the nation it ought to have the sanction of a National Assembly; while at the same time the calling together of that Assembly was indefinitely postponed, and even the councils general suspended. To add to the difficulties of the situation, the Germans soon perceived that they had miscalculated the resistance which Paris would make, and therefore in negotiating would not yield a single point which they considered of military importance. There were also indications that some divergence of opinion existed among the German leaders. Count von Bismarck foresaw political difficulties which Germany might be creating for herself, and wished the war to end; while General von Moltke thought of nothing but how to carry on the war so as to lose no advantage that could be obtained. The principal objection to an armistice was that the German position round Paris was so fraught with danger, that the possibility of diplomatic successes could not be set against the peril of giving Paris three weeks more breathing-time, while the armies behind the Loire were being organized.

The active operations of the besiegers from the period of the final investment of the city up to the end of September were carried on with vigour and with caution. No immediate attack was made upon the outworks, but the capital was effectually blockaded in a circumference of about forty miles. On the 23rd the French attacked the besieging force at Drancy, Pierrefitte, and Villejuif. The fight was sustained by the sixth Prussian corps; and in the two last-mentioned localities the advantage was in favour of the French; but as the sorties in either case were hardly pushed beyond the range of the heavy guns of the forts, they were evidently intended by General Trochu only as military training for the troops, and were in themselves of little or no importance. Meanwhile the Germans, amounting to from 200,000 to 230,000 men, occupied the heights surrounding the city, fortified their various positions, and established batteries, supported by infantry connected with each other by squadrons of cavalry, which were kept in unceasing movement. All this time the heavy siege guns of the Germans were arriving, and the camp was kept in constant watchfulness by reports from inside Paris that "its defenders, especially the garde mobile, demanded an immediate sortie in force." To this treacherous impatience General Trochu eventually yielded; and on the 30th of September General Vinoy directed a large force of all arms again to the south-east, where the sixth Prussian corps was strongly intrenched. In this action the French were repulsed after two hours' fighting, and retired under cover of their forts. Their loss amounted to upwards of a thousand men, including several hundred prisoners. The German official account admitted a loss of only 200—the troops having fought chiefly under cover. The Crown Prince of Prussia commanded in person, and the French General Giulham was killed.

Many of the German journals at this period regarded the annexation of the provinces of Alsace and Lorraine almost as good as accomplished. The large majority of the people, likewise, were resolved that these provinces should be united to Germany. "If we make no military conquest," said they, "we have no lasting peace, but only a short truce; we must always remain in full military equipment; there can be no thought of reducing our armaments in time of peace, and any one can foresee the effect of this on our internal development." Expressive of the same feeling, the New *Prussian Zeitung* said:—"Germany can conclude with France such a peace only as, by giving her a strong position against

France, will make her wholly indifferent as to what passes in France. In the possession of Alsace and German Lorraine, in the possession of Strassburg and Metz—the two opening doors for French plundering expeditions—Germany will have the guarantees of peace in her own hands, and, secured by this possession, she can quietly look on at whatever explosion volcanic France in the distance gives herself up to." Still, a section of the German people regarded the annexation of these provinces with disfavour. A writer in the *Cologne Gazette* represented the inhabitants of Lorraine as thoroughly French in all their physical and intellectual characteristics, and condemned the proposed acquisition of that territory. Other writers expressed the same views, which were held by a considerable number of German democrats and conservatives. But a public meeting at Königsberg for the consideration of the subject of annexation was specially distasteful to the Prussian authorities. At that meeting Dr. Johann Jacoby, a politician of republican tendencies, made the following remarkable speech:—"The chief question, the decision of which alone has any importance for us, is this: Has Prussia or Germany the right to appropriate Alsace and Lorraine? They tell us Alsace and Lorraine belonged formerly to the German empire. France possessed herself of these lands by craft and by force. Now that we have beaten the French, it is no more than what is right and proper that we should recover from them the spoil, and demand back the property stolen from us. Gentlemen! do not let yourselves be led away by well-sounding words, and though they offer you the empire of the world, be not tempted to worship the idols of power. Test this well-sounding phrase, and you will find that it is nothing but a disguise of the old and barbarous right of force. Alsace and Lorraine, they say, were formerly German property, and must again become German. How so, we inquire? Have, then, Alsace and Lorraine no inhabitants? Or are, perchance, the inhabitants of these provinces to be regarded as having no volition, as a thing that one may at once take possession of and dispose of just as one likes? Have they lost all their rights through the war, have they become slaves, whose fate is at the arbitrary disposal of the conqueror? Even the most ardent and incarnate partisans of annexation allows that the inhabitants of Alsace and Lorraine are in heart and soul French, and wish to remain French. And however much they might have offended us, it would be contrary to all human justice should we try to Germanize them compulsorily, and incorporate them against their will either with Prussia or any other German state. Gentlemen! There is an old German proverb, which has been raised to a universal moral law on account of its being so true—'Do not unto others what you would not they should do unto you.' What should we and our 'national Liberals' feel if at some future time a victorious Pole should demand back and seek to annex the provinces of Posen and West Russia? And yet the same grounds might be urged for this that are now brought forward to support an annexation of Alsace and Lorraine. No, Gentlemen! It is our duty to oppose such tendencies of national egotism. Let us hold fast to the principles of justice as much in public life as in private life! Let us openly declare it to be our deep and inmost conviction that every incorporation of foreign territory against the wishes of the inhabitants is a violation of the right of self-constitution common to all people, and therefore as objectionable as it is pernicious. Let us, without being led astray by the intoxication of victory, raise a protest against every violence offered to the inhabitants of

Alsace and Lorraine. Only he who respects the liberty of others is himself worthy of liberty."

General Vogel von Falckenstein, who during the war exercised all but supreme power over the district under his control, immediately arrested Dr. Jacoby, as well as the chairman of the meeting, Herr Herbig, both of whom were conveyed to the fortress of Lötzen. Dr. Jacoby, however, protested by letter to Count von Bismarck; and the authorities, either not prepared to sanction the extreme measure of General Falckenstein, or unwilling to arouse a feeling of irritation among the democrats of Germany and Europe at large, subsequently ordered the release of Dr. Jacoby and his colleague. But undoubtedly the great national party firmly adhered to the policy of annexation, and their leaders were already foreshadowing a federal constitution, in which an imperial crown should be awarded to the house of Hohenzollern.

To describe, briefly, one of the "incidents" arising out of the war, it is necessary to look for a little at the state of matters in Italy. For many years it had been the aspiration of Italian statesmen to accomplish the unity of that country, by making Rome the capital. But although this desire was almost universally shared by the people, it could not be carried into effect in consequence of the occupation of the city by French troops, to support the temporal power of the pope. On the outbreak of the war, however, the French government immediately determined to evacuate Rome, and an announcement of their purpose was made by M. Ollivier on the 30th of July. These proceedings greatly alarmed the pope and the clerical party; but the Italians saw their opportunity was come, and resolved to embrace it, notwithstanding that intimations were rife that Prussia would interfere on behalf of Pius IX. The popular excitement was intense, and even the loyalty of portions of the papal troops appeared doubtful. Some of the French regiments, on their march for embarkation to Marseilles, shouted "Vive l'Italie!" the papal legions of Antibes refused to garrison Civita Vecchia, were engaged in constant strife with the German carabineers quartered with them, and many of them deserted, while the attitude of the inhabitants became sullen and threatening. Before leaving Rome, General Dumont told Cardinal Antonelli that the emperor had exacted from the Italian government guarantees for the protection of the pope; to which the cardinal replied, "There are three persons who do not believe in these guarantees: the emperor, yourself, and I." Eight Italian ironclads were ordered to cruise before Civita Vecchia as soon as the French had embarked. To meet the emergency, great activity prevailed in the pontifical war department; the troops were armed with the most approved weapons, recruits sought from the bandit population of the Abruzzi, and the urban guard mobilized.

All uncertainty, however, was speedily dispelled by the action of the Italian ministry. On the 29th of August the people of Florence were startled by the following announcement in the *Gazetta d'Italia*:—"All those whose terms of lease for apartments, separate lodgings, shops, and public-houses have expired, or are about to expire, are informed, that in one of the latest councils of ministers held here, it was decided that the immediate and decided transfer of the government from this provisional capital to Rome shall take place before the end of September next."

By the disasters to the French arms, the catastrophe of Sedan, and the revolution of the 4th September, Italian statesmen considered themselves as freed from their engagement, and that a bold and rapid attack upon the temporal power of the papacy was the only security against the revolutionary contagion. To meet contingencies, the army was raised to 300,000 men. The spirit of the troops was excellent, and on the official declaration reaching the camp, all the tents were illuminated. On the 8th of September a manifesto was sent to the pope by Victor Emmanuel, through Count Ponza di San Martino, embodying the following propositions:—The pope to retain the sovereignty over the Leonine portion of Rome, and all the ecclesiastical institutions of the city. The income of the pope, the cardinals, and all the papal officers and officials to remain unchanged. The papal debt to be guaranteed. Envoys to the pope and cardinals to retain their present immunities, even though not residing in the Leonine city. All nations to be freely admitted to the Leonine city. The Catholic clergy in all Italy to be freed from government supervision. The Italian military, municipal, and entail laws to be modified as regards Home. These propositions Pius IX. refused to entertain.

On the morning of Sunday, September 11, the king ordered the Italian troops to enter the papal territory. They consisted of 50,000 soldiers, in five divisions, led by Generals Mazé de la Roche, Cozenz, Ferrero, Angioletti, and Bixio, under the supreme command of General Cadorna. At the approach of General Bixio, on Sunday night, the garrison at Montefiascone withdrew without striking a blow. At Aprona, on Monday, a brigade of Italian troops, on crossing the papal frontier, were enthusiastically received. At Bagnorea, twenty zouaves and officers surrendered. At Civita Castellana the zouaves fired upon General Cadorna's vanguard; but on receiving a few shots in return, at once surrendered. Viterbo was occupied without opposition, and no serious resistance was offered to the royal army on its march to the capital. General Cadorna issued a proclamation to the Romans, assuring them that he did not bring war, but peace and order, and that "the independence of the Holy See will not be violated."

The division of General Bixio approached Rome from Civita Vecchia by the left, or west, bank of the Tiber; the division of Angioletti came from the south, out of the Neapolitan territory; and the other divisions, which had entered the Papal States from Tuscany, approached the city on its eastern side. It was therefore ordered that Bixio should attack the western gate, called Porte San Pancrazio, by which the French took the city in 1849; that Angioletti should attack that of St. John Lateran; while the rest of the army should direct their efforts against Porta San Lorenzo, Porta Pia, and a part of the city wall, between Porta Pia and Porta Salara, where the papal zouaves had taken up their position. The garrison, exclusive of some of the pope's Italian troops who refused to fight, numbered above 9000 men—the zouaves, the carabineers, the Antibes legion, the dragoons, the squadriglieri, and the gendarmes. The gates of the city were barricaded and fortified by ramparts of earth. The defence was commanded by General Baron Kanzler. The garrison had sixty pieces of artillery; and the walls, built of solid brick, and forming a circuit of thirteen miles about the city, were of great height and thickness, having been erected to a great extent in the times of the ancient Roman empire, in the reign of Aurelian.

At five o'clock on the morning of the 20th September the Italian artillery opened on the city, accompanied by a sharp interchange of musketry between the papal zouaves and the royal bersaglieri, with the loss of life on both sides. After about three hours' fighting, each division of the Italian forces had succeeded in opening a breach; and when they poured into the city, prepared to charge with the bayonet, the papal soldiers beat a hasty retreat. On this the pope ordered General Kanzler to capitulate; a white flag was waved all along the line, and a messenger informed General Bixio that a treaty had been opened with General Cadorna. The number of killed on the Italian side was 21, including 3 officers; and of wounded, 117, of whom 5 were officers. Of the papal troops, 6 zouaves were killed, and 20 or 30 wounded. The prisoners amounted to 10,400 of all arms.

During these proceedings the pope had taken refuge in the Vatican, and sent to the various diplomatic agents a protest against the action of the Italians. The citizens, however, crowded to the capitol to proclaim the fall of the temporal power, but were fired upon by the squadriglieri, who still retained their arms. A vast multitude subsequently assembled at the Coliseum, where, in accordance with an intimation from the Italian authorities, they elected a provisional giunta, composed of forty-two members, the leading liberals of the city. In the evening, the political prisoners in Castello and St. Michele were liberated by the soldiers and the populace. In St. Michele prison, Cardinal Petroni, condemned for life, had already been a captive for nineteen years; the Doctor Luigi Castellozzo, Count Pagliani, Giulio Ajani, and (Jesare Sterbini, were also lying under the same sentence. Victor Emmanuel had given instructions that the papal territory should not be formally annexed to Italy until a plebiscitum had been taken. In the meantime the elected giunta, in the midst of considerable indications of the tumultuous disposition of the inhabitants, prepared the way for the popular vote. The principal dissatisfaction was occasioned by the fact that the rule of the Leonine city had been secured to the pope, an arrangement which 6000 inhabitants of the Borgia deeply resented, and showed their resentment by popular demonstrations.

The formula of the plebiscitum was, "The Romans, in the belief that the Italian government will guarantee the free exercise of his spiritual authority to the Holy Father, answer *Yes*." The vote was taken on the 2nd of October, amidst great popular enthusiasm, resulting in 136,681 voting Yes, and 1507 No.

The total collapse of the pontifical *régime*, and the occupation of Rome by the Italian government, form a remarkable epoch in the history of Europe; yet so completely were the minds of men engrossed by the startling occurrences of the war, that these events received at the time a comparatively small amount of attention, and a brief notice in the columns of the European press. In a few days, with a mere show of resistance and a minimum of internal commotion, were accomplished the dream of generations, and the fulfilment of the long-cherished but almost hopeless aspirations after unity by the Italian people.

CHAPTER XVIII.

Extensive Siege Operations of the Germans in September—Description of Strassburg and its Fortifications, and Sketch of its History—Brief Biography of General Uhrich, the Governor—State of the City after the Battles of Wissembourg and Woerth—Number and Description of the Garrison at the Commencement of the Siege—Council of War Determines on a Vigorous Resistance—Proclamation of General Uhrich—Number and Description of the Besieging Force under General von Werder—The Positions occupied by them—Commencement of Hostilities on 12th August—The Superiority of the German Artillery over that of the French—Reconnaissances by the French—Commencement of the Bombardment, in earnest, on 21st August, causing great Destruction of Property and Loss of Life—The Germans consent to spare the Cathedral as much as possible—General Uhrich again refuses to Surrender—The Bombardment is discontinued, and a Regular Siege commenced—Strange Apathy of the French during the Proceedings of the Besiegers—Extraordinary Completeness of the German Works—Great Sortie on 2nd September—The hopes of the Besieged raised by a piece of extraordinary False News—General Uhrich refuses to believe in the Disaster at Sedan—M. Valentin, the Prefect of the Lower Rhine, appointed by the Republican Government, reaches the City after a very Narrow Escape—Hospitality of the Swiss towards the Aged and Destitute Inhabitants, whom the Germans permitted to leave—Fearful State of the City during the Latter Part of the Siege, and Gallant Conduct of the Inhabitants—Capture of Three Lunettes by the Germans—Two Breaches made in the Walls preparatory to the intended Storming—Final Demand for Surrender, with the Alternative of an Immediate Assault—Song written during the Siege to be Sung by the Troops as they marched into Strassburg—Determination of the Governor t3 capitulate—Proclamation announcing the Fact to the Inhabitants and Garrison—German Preparations to receive the French Delegates—Disgraceful Conduct of some of the French Soldiers whilst Surrendering—Triumphant Entry of Part of the German Army into the City—Affecting Scenes as the Inhabitants emerged from the Cellars in which they had lived so long—German Rejoicings on 30th September, the day on which the City had been taken from them 189 years before—Impressive Religious Services—Speech of General Werder—The Fearful Effects of the Bombardment on the City—The Irreparable Loss of the Library—State of the Cathedral—Total amount of Damage done to the City estimated at £8,000,000—The Aspect of the Botanic Garden, which had been used as a Burying-Ground—Destruction of Kehl, opposite Strassburg, by the French—Quantity of Shot, &c., fired during the Siege of Strassburg—Number and Value of the Guns captured by the Germans—The Siege of Toul—Description of the Town—Gallantry of the Inhabitants and Garrison—Determination of the Germans to Storm the Town averted by its Capitulation—Reasons for adopting such a course on the part of the French—Scenes in the Town on the Entry of the Germans.

FALL OF STRASSBURG AND TOUL.

IN Chapter X., describing the march of the third German army into France, after the defeat of MacMahon at Woerth, we stated that the Badish troops in it were despatched to lay siege to the fortress of Strassburg. We now proceed to relate the chief events of that siege, from the time the city was first invested to its fall on September 28, and also the leading incidents connected with the siege of Toul, which was likewise invested by a portion of the Crown Prince's army a few days after Strassburg.

About the third week in September the Germans were, in fact, prosecuting four important sieges; any one of which would, in ordinary times, have been regarded as a great operation.

Strassburg, the centre of the defence of the French frontier of the Rhine, and one of the strongest fortified cities in Europe, was besieged by a corps of about 60,000 men, composed of one division of Badish, one of Prussian, and one of Prussian guard landwehr troops, with pioneers and garrison artillery from the South German states. Toul, on the direct Line of railway to Paris, was surrounded by a Prussian division, under the Grand-duke of Mecklenburg Schwerin, and still blocked all communication to the capital from South Germany. Metz, the centre of the defence of France between the Meuse and the Rhine, the strongest fortress in all France, surrounded by forts forming an entrenched camp, and held not only by its own garrison, but by the army under Marshal Bazaine, was invested by seven Prussian army corps and three divisions of cavalry—altogether, about 200,000 men. And above all, Paris, defended by more than half a million of armed and disciplined men, was shut in by the third German army, under the Crown Prince of Prussia, and the fourth, under the Crown Prince of Saxony, numbering more than 250,000 men. It will be remembered that in his interview with M. Jules Favre, described in the preceding chapter, the only conditions on which Count von Bismarck would consent to an armistice, were that the fortresses of Strassburg, Toul, and Phalsburg should be placed in the hands of the Germans. As the French were not disposed to accede to these conditions, the conference ended. Two of the fortresses named were, however, destined to fall immediately. While M. Jules Favre and Count von Bismarck were conferring at Ferrières, General Uhrich and a council of war were deliberating as to the surrender of Strassburg, which capitulated on the 28th of September.

At the time to which our history refers, Strassburg was a French fortified town of the first rank, situated in the valley of the Rhine and of the Ill. Its extensive series of fortifications formed roughly an isosceles triangle, having for its base the southern front, which, at its eastern extremity, close to the Rhine, was defended by a pentagonal bastionned fort. The Germans made their principal attack on the north-west. The two fronts covered by the river Ill could be easily inundated, and the ditches were generally full of water. The north front, like the two others, was composed of a strong system of bastions, with lunettes and fortified works, communicating with the interior by a double line of casemates. Both extremities were defended, the northern by Fort des Pierres, and the southern by Fort Blanche. A military road ran at the foot of the ramparts.

The founder of the fortress, Daniel Speckel, Speckle, or Specklin, was born at Strassburg in 1536, and was at first a mould cutter and silk embroiderer, but subsequently took to the study of architecture. After travelling extensively in the north of Europe he settled at Vienna in 1561, and entered the service of the imperial architect, Solizar. In 1576 he formed an engagement with Duke Albert of Bavaria, and erected several buildings at Ingolstadt; but in 1577 he was called to his native town, and commissioned to construct the fortifications, a wooden model of which, previously made by him, was placed in the town library. In 1589 he completed the task, and died in the same year. Vauban built the citadel, and subsequently outworks were added.

Strassburg was never taken by force until the late war in 1870. When in 1681 it surrendered to the French, it had disarmed itself by the dismissal of the regular Swiss militia; and on the 30th September in that year it was surprised by a French force, drawn together under the pretext of manoeuvring in the neighbourhood. On the 28th of September, 1870, it fell, after a long and laborious siege, into the hands of a combined Prussian and Baden corps. Louis XIV. took it just as he had Nancy a few years before, in the midst of peace, and without even giving himself the trouble of declaring war, or assigning a reason for his rapacity. He knew that the German empire, torn to pieces by a religious feud, was not in a position to avenge the injury which the Grand Monarque therefore thought himself justified in committing. In vain the captured city sent envoys and special messengers to the emperor and Imperial Parliament, soliciting assistance in ridding it of those whom it then considered foreigners and enemies. Domestic quarrels were then rife in Germany, and combined action hopeless.

As often as France has aimed at dominion on the Rhine (1688-97, 1703, 1733, 1796, &c.), the outlet for attack on Germany was strengthened by the fortification of Kehl, immediately opposite Strassburg. Kehl, indeed, sustained a two months' siege by the Austrians in the winter of 1796-97. The Rhine fortress, scarcely accessible in consequence of its being surrounded by water, was first invested by the Russians and Badeners on the 7th of January, 1814. It was cannonaded, but without success, on the 14th of February. On the 13th of April the entry of the allies into Paris and the deposition of Napoleon was first known in Strassburg; on the 14th the white flag of the Bourbons was hoisted, on the 16th there was an armistice, on the 2nd of May Kehl was razed, and on the 5th the blockade of Strassburg was raised, the besieging army settling itself in the neighbourhood. On Napoleon's return from Elba, in 1815, the garrison and citizens of Strassburg were among his first supporters. In the end of June, and of course subsequently to the second deposition of the emperor (June 22), the French army, under General Rapp, after several engagements, was shut up in Strassburg by the Crown Prince of Würtemburg. On the 4th of July the Würtemburgers were replaced by Austrians and Badeners. A sortie by General Rapp on the 9th of July, against Hausbergen, caused the loss of many men on both sides. This was the last deed of arms. On the 22nd of July an armistice was concluded, and on the 30th the Bourbon dynasty was recognized by the garrison, which was disarmed and dismissed on the 6th of September, and on the 15th the blockade was raised.

The resolute resistance of Strassburg in the siege of 1870, the heroism of its governor, General Uhrich, the intrepidity of its garrison, the patriotic devotedness of its inhabitants amidst a bombardment of unprecedented severity, during a contest which began on the 17th of August and ended on the 28th of September, have secured for the unfortunate city an undying record in military annals. General Uhrich, the gallant veteran whose name is associated with the heroic defence, had been long known in the French army as a brave and skilful officer. A true son of Alsace, born at Phalsburg in 1802, at eighteen years of age he left the military school of St. Cyr to join the third light infantry as sous-lieutenant. Captain in 1834, and colonel of his old regiment in 1848, Jean Jacques Alexis Uhrich was made general of brigade in 1852, and in the second year of the Crimean war became general of division. In the Italian campaign he was attached to the fifth army corps, and in 1862 received the grand cross of the legion of honour, having been made commander in 1857. For some time after he was in charge of one of the territorial sub-divisions of the army of Nancy. In 1867 he retired from active service, but on the outbreak of the war with Germany he asked and obtained the command of Strassburg. His firmness in the panic which followed the rout at Woerth, and during the terrible bombardment of the city, won praise even from his enemies.

Strassburg had been chosen as headquarters of the first corps d'armée of Marshal Mac Mali on; but on the 2nd of August he quitted the place with his divisions, leaving a garrison composed of the eighty-seventh regiment of the line, of the depôts of the eighteenth and ninety-sixth regiments, and of the tenth and sixteenth battalion of chasseurs.

On August 5 the town was plunged into deep consternation, the news of the battle and defeat at Wissembourg having arrived in the middle of the night. By the next day, however, the bustle and excitement had nearly died away; and notwithstanding the appalling tidings, crowds of officers sat outside the cafés as usual, lounging, smoking, and chaffing, all wearing a pacific and unexpectant air, truly disheartening to anxious citizens, who considered that but twenty-four hours before their brethren in arms had suffered a bloody check not easily forgotten. A sound of distant cannonading was heard throughout the day; and while rumours that another battle of greater importance still was then raging, waggons full of wounded drove at a slow pace through the streets.

At nightfall on Sunday, the 7th, the first fugitive from the fatal field of Woerth entered the city. All the inhabitants had turned into the streets, and the tumult was beyond description. Bells began to toll from every steeple, and from one end of the town to the other rang the fearful cry, "MacMahon is defeated; our army is put to flight!" Soon there set in a stream of soldiers with bare heads, covered with blood and dirt, wearied with a protracted struggle, famished with hunger, dying of thirst, beaten, and humbled. At seven o'clock a panic seized upon all citizens, for the news spread like wildfire that the enemy was fast approaching the town. There was a rush to the arsenal for arms. The drawbridges were pulled up, and for the first time the inhabitants passed the night expecting to hear the thunder of cannons, for it was generally supposed that the siege of Strassburg would be the immediate consequence of the disaster of Woerth.

In this grave crisis, General Uhrich immediately assembled a council of war to consider the resources of the city, and the best course to be adopted. Admiral Excelmans had arrived with a detachment of sailors and marines to serve a flotilla of gun-boats, which were never forthcoming, and he now undertook to remain and assist in the defence. The director of the custom-house formed with his men a battalion of 500 douaniers, and two regiments, one of cavalry and one of infantry, were formed out of the unpromising material which, flying from Wissembourg and Woerth, had taken refuge behind the Strassburg outposts. The garrison was thus found to consist of 7000 infantry, including sailors and douaniers, 600 cavalry, 1600 artillery, a battalion of mobiles, and 3000 national guards, forming altogether an effective force of 15,000 men. The barracks, fitted up with beds, could accommodate 10,000 men. The supplies consisted of bread for 180 days, and provisions for 60 days; but the quantity of live stock was limited. The council of war unanimously decided on resisting, and that the garrison should be divided into three bodies, one-third for the service of the ramparts, another third for marching, and the last for reserve. It was also decided to put the supplies in cellars for security against the bombardment, to turn out of the town all persons of loose character, and to urge the aged, the women, and the children, to leave at once. The following day the council, under the presidency of General Uhrich, held several meetings, at which measures were taken for the defence of the city and resolutions formed to resist to the utmost extremity.

On the 9th of August an envoy, bearing a flag of truce, approached the fortifications, and on behalf of the general commanding the enemy made the usual summons to surrender. From the Saverne gate, by which the envoy entered, to headquarters, he was accompanied by the townspeople, who cried in German, so that he might understand, "We will not surrender." When he had delivered his message to General Uhrich, the latter, by way of reply, opened the window and showed him the people, who cried out, "Down with Prussia! Long live France! No surrender!" Next morning the following proclamation was issued to the inhabitants of Strassburg:—

"Unfounded rumours and panics have been spread within the last days in our brave city; some individuals have dared to assert that the place would surrender without defending itself. We energetically protest, in the name of the courageous population, against that cowardly and criminal weakness. The ramparts are armed with 400 cannons, the garrison composed of 11,000 men and of the national guard. If Strassburg is attacked, Strassburg will be defended so long as a soldier, a biscuit, or a cartridge is left. The brave can be tranquillized, the others may leave.

"GENERAL UHRICH."

"10th August, 1870."

Marshal MacMahon's corps d'armée had retreated on Saverne, Luneville, and Châlons. The investment of Strassburg was likely to follow the defeat of the first corps. For the purpose, therefore, of watching the movements of the enemy, the march of its columns and of its convoys, General Uhrich's first care was to establish an observatory, which was formed by the erection of a platform on the highest tower, not the spire, of the cathedral. From this observatory strong German columns, composed of men of all arms, were signalled on the 11th of August at 4 p.m., advancing from Schiltigheim on the Lauterbourg road. They took up their positions on the north, a few miles from the advanced works, in the villages of Koenigshoffen, Oberhausbergen, Mittelhausbergen, and Schiltigheim, forming a circle of three miles. General Uhrich at once sent a strong force to occupy the outer works, and, in anticipation of the bombardment, he next day issued a proclamation calling in all remaining provisions, fuel, &c., ordering the closing of the gasworks, and cautioning the inhabitants to be prepared with baths of water on every floor, wet cloths, earth, and dry sand, to quench the first outbreaks of fire.

On the 14th of August, Lieutenant-general von Werder assumed the command of the besieging force, which consisted of the Baden division, the Prussian first reserve division, the Prussian landwehr guards division, and a detachment of artillery and technical troops, numbering in all about 60,000 men. Lieutenant-general von Decker and Major-general von Mertens were appointed commanders, respectively, of the artillery and the engineers. After the arrival of the two Prussian divisions the fortress was closely surrounded; General Werder's headquarters being established at the village of Lampertheim, some five or six miles north of the defences of Strassburg, and to the left of the railway leading thence to Werdenheim, from which it branched to Haguenau and Saverne. The left of the army of the besiegers rested on the Ill, and was thus protected from flank attack, while between the Ill and the Rhine were marshes unfavourable for the movements of troops. At the same time the headquarters were concealed from the fire of the place by the heights of Oberhausbergen. Hence the German fines encircled Strassburg till they met the river Ill again south of that town, near Illkirch, close to the famous Canal Monsieur, which connects the Ill with the Rhone.

For general defence, the *perimeter* of the town was divided by Governor Uhrich into four districts, under the command of General Moseno, Admiral Excelmans, and two colonels. The provisional regiments were sent to occupy the fortifications; the mobiles were designed to help in the operations. The ambulances, under Intendants Brisac and Milon of the Intendance, were immediately organized, and the students aided the direction of the medical service. On the 12th, the Prussians from their positions at the north-west, in the rear of the villages, commenced hostilities by sending a few shells against the fortifications, which were answered by the garrison; and on the following day, to ascertain the real strength of the besiegers, General Uhrich ordered a reconnoitering sortie by two squadrons of cavalry and two companies of infantry, who advanced on the villages of Neuhaff and Altkirch, captured 100 oxen and some supplies, and returned without meeting with any serious encounter.

On the night from the 13th to the 14th the cannonade and discharge of musketry gave the inhabitants a foreshadowing of the evils which were about to befall their unfortunate city. At daylight the placing of a Prussian battery and of three howitzers between the lines of railway to Saverne and Bale was signalled from the observatory. The firing of the besiegers became stronger, and from the range of their large guns, and the skilful aiming of their artillerymen, its effects were at once felt, while the shot from the forts scarcely reached them.

In the afternoon of the 14th General Uhrich sent Moritz, the colonel of engineers, on a second reconnoitering excursion on the left bank of the Ill. With 900 men of the line, fifty of cavalry, and two field-guns, he attacked the besiegers, and after a sharp engagement retreated on the town. The same day General Barral, who, as the chief of artillery, aided so materially in the defence of Strassburg, succeeded in finding his way into it under the disguise of a workman.

The 15th of August was the *fête* of the emperor, and a *Te Deum* was sung in the cathedral. On the same day the Prussians brought their guns to bear upon the second district of defence, approached nearer the town, and increased the rapidity of their fire. The immense superiority of their artillery to that of the French was now apparent, and led the garrison and the inhabitants to augur the worst. During the night several of the inhabitants were killed, and the city was fired in several places. The following day brought fresh misfortunes.

General Uhrich, wishing to test the enemy's designs and to prevent the construction of new batteries, ordered another reconnaissance to be made by two battalions, two squadrons, and a battery of artillery. The column advanced to the north-west, and an important engagement took place in which the French were repulsed, leaving in the hands of the Prussians three guns and numerous prisoners and wounded.

On the 17th, from the cathedral tower masses of German troops were seen advancing in the direction of Wolfisheim, about three miles from the fortified works of Strassburg. The 87th regiment of the line was sent to reconnoitre, and to protect 400 workmen busy in cutting the trees and clearing the ground near La Porte Blanche, in front of the second district of defence. The soldiers, under the command of their colonel, advanced to the village of Schiltigheim, which they found barricaded and well defended; and after a vain attempt to dislodge its occupants, they were compelled to retreat, having sustained considerable loss. The fire of the besiegers continued on the 18th, and on the 19th the bombardment with the heavy guns began in right earnest.

Hitherto the firing upon the town had been the result rather of accident than of deliberate intention on the part of the Germans. Notwithstanding the strength of Strassburg, its system of defence was old-fashioned. There were no detached forts, and the ramparts inclosed the inhabited parts of the town within so narrow a circle, that many of the houses necessarily suffered when the works were attacked. The garrison being comparatively weak, and the inhabitants very numerous, the German commander assumed that menacing the town would certainly induce them to supplicate the French general to surrender. General Werder, first of all, offered to allow a number of the women, children, and infirm to leave the city; but Uhrich declined, ostensibly on the ground that it would be difficult to choose from a population of 80,000. On the 21st of August, therefore, the bombardment was opened upon the town, after due warning had been given to the commandant, who does not appear to have communicated it to the citizens, probably fearing its effect upon the more timid part of the population. For six days were the inhabitants exposed to the pitiless fiery storm. Notwithstanding every precaution, the destruction of life and property was enormous, the proportion of civilians killed and wounded, of course, far exceeding that of the military. Uhrich, stern and unbending as he appeared, was compelled on the 24th to ask a favour of his enemy. He sent out a *parlementaire* with the request that General Werder would spare lint and bandages for six hundred wounded citizens of Strassburg, now lying in agony within the town, their injuries having been mostly sustained in the streets during the last three days' bombardment. The general at once sent in an ample store of both, and it was noticed that the fierceness of the besieger's fire visibly slackened from this time.

To lessen the damage caused by falling shells within the city, the squares and places were covered deeply with loose earth; and the inhabitants, having closed up their windows with mattresses, retired to what often proved to be a vain security in the cellars; for frequently would a falling shell pierce through roof and floors, and burst in the crowded basement, killing or wounding the whole of its occupants. On the 25th of August a shell from one of the giant mortars penetrated a house of six stories, and exploding in the cellar, killed sixteen persons. The bombardment, however, so far from scaring the citizens into a craven submission, roused a spirit of indignation, and a stronger determination than ever to support General Uhrich in resistance.

On the 26th, at four a.m., the firing was suspended till noon at the intercession of the aged and venerable bishop of Strassburg, who came over to the Prussian outposts, and asked for an interview with the general commanding-in-chief (Werder), stating that it was his earnest desire to intercede with his excellency on behalf of the minster in particular and the non-military part of the town in general. The bishop's request was communicated in due course to the general, who, however, declined to receive him, but informed him, through an aide-de-camp, that every possible precaution would be taken by the German army to avoid injuring the cathedral, and that no more harm than could be helped would be done to the town. His lordship was escorted back to the gate of the city, and at the same time a *parlementaire* was sent in to General Uhrich, conveying to that officer a full and detailed account of the reverses sustained by the French army before Metz, and urging upon him the surrender of the fortress upon the ground that further resistance would only be spilling blood to no purpose, the defence of Strassburg against the foes gathered round it being absolutely hopeless. To this communication the general only condescended to return the verbal message that "he meant to hold Strassburg as long as he had a man under his orders;" and the French fire was at once resumed by way of post-dictum. The bombardment was resumed at the expiry of the respite, and continued till the 27th, when the German commander, abandoning the hope of intimidating the city into surrender, gave orders to discontinue firing upon it, and commenced a regular siege. A vast quantity of additional artillery had in the meantime arrived, and on the 29th of August numerous siege batteries were commenced to enfilade and batter the guns of the place. In the following night the first parallel was opened against the north-western front of the fortress, at a distance of from 600 to 800 paces from the walls. In the night of the 31st the approaches to the second parallel were dug, and in the ensuing night the second parallel itself, distant 300 paces from the fortress. To accomplish this a detachment was called out from the Rupprechtsan, and led by roundabout ways in a zig-zag direction, so as to disguise the design, up to a field behind Reichstett, where they halted to await sunset and the arrival of the engineers. When it became dark they started again. Without speaking a word, they marched along the road through the three neighbouring villages of Höhenheim, Bischheim, and Schiltigheim. Armed with hatchets and spades, the iron turned upwards to avoid noise, they proceeded through the streets between the shut-up houses, over the doors of which small lanterns were glimmering. At last the spot was reached. Posted at arm's length from each other, the men began to dig, eagerly, noiselessly, indefatigably. A trench three feet broad and three deep was the task for each. The night was dark. The fortress was 300 steps before them, but they saw nothing either of it or of the battalions placed in front to protect them. Close behind a battery launched shells ceaselessly into the city. The loud yelling of dogs, disturbed by the proximity of the enemy, resounded from Schiltigheim. The work lasted almost the whole night. The men were wetted and chilled by the falling dew, and they had not a morsel of bread. Hunger and thirst spoiled their tempers. At last the task was done, and cheered by their success they retired at break of day to their quarters, to occupy immediately the small island of Watte.

One great mystery of the siege, to most of the scientific officers belonging to the German army, was the character of the French defence, so far as concerned the construction of the parallels and their communications by the besieging forces. From the night when these first broke ground, till the completion of the fourth parallel, the pioneers were scarcely ever molested in their task from the walls or outworks; but as soon as their work was finished, and they were well sheltered by six or seven feet of earth, a *feu d'enfer* was invariably opened upon the newly completed trench and the villages behind the approaches, which did very little damage to the parallels, and inflicted only slight loss on their occupants, but destroyed a vast amount of property owned by French subjects. The amount of work done in the construction of the parallels may be judged by the fact that the trenches before Strassburg were eight feet deep, and wide enough for three or four men abreast. Part of the second parallel was driven through the churchyard of Ste. Hélène, between Koenigshoffen and Schiltigheim, and skeletons and partly decayed corpses were turned up, to the great discomposure of the soldiers. The ground before the city was clay, and difficult to work either in dry or wet weather. In addition to the parallels, batteries were built, and in their neighbourhood powder magazines arranged, which had to be protected against even shells dropping from the heights. These batteries evinced the singular perfection to which the Germans had brought all the details of their organization. Not only were they so arranged as to inflict the greatest damage on the enemy with the least possible danger to themselves, but also to insure a degree of comfort which could have been little expected under the circumstances. Good solid platforms were erected for the guns, and wooden traverses between each gun gave house accommodation to both officers and men. Garden seats beside the guns for the men to sit upon, and small gardens at the end of each traverse, with flowers and a border of cannon-balls, presented something of the aspect of a summer residence, in spite of the grim realities of war. British officers who remembered the trenches before Sebastopol would have been surprised to find in the same kind of works before Strassburg, roomy apartments, tables with cloth covers, arm chairs, books, maps, walnuts, and an ample supply of beer at command. Each battery was furnished with a large plan of the city and fortifications, upon which was indicated the points specially to be operated upon; and as an instance of care and accuracy it may be stated, that when a fire was directed to be opened on particular public buildings, although these were not to be seen, so correct were the information and aim, as was afterwards ascertained, the doomed structures were destroyed without the least injury to buildings immediately adjoining. Life in these trench batteries, however, was frequently anything but safe or agreeable. Sorties from the garrison, and the mud produced by sixty hours of almost continuous rainfall, rendered the trenches so unpleasant that the men would have preferred the risk of half a dozen battles in the open to their twenty-four hours turn of duty under ground. Besides this, the latter parallels approached so near the city walls that the splinters caused by the German guns sometimes wounded their own artillerymen.

The most important sortie during the siege was made on the 2nd of September, when both wings of the German army were attacked at the same time. Owing to the incompleteness of the parallels, which did not as yet form continuous lines, or rather curves, surrounding the fortifications, but were dug at considerable intervals, and not uniformly in connection with one another, the French contrived, in the darkness of a cloudy and stormy night, to get between the first and second parallels, and succeeded in surprising a battery established near the extramural railway goods station. This battery, and the trench containing its infantry supports, were, for a few minutes after they became aware of their assailants' proximity, restrained from firing upon the latter by the impression that they were some of their own people—German soldiers retiring from the second parallel before a superior force of the enemy. This misapprehension was soon dispelled by the French attack, made with great resolution and fierceness; but the consequence of the untoward hesitation caused by the natural desire of the Prussians to avoid injuring their friends was an unusually heavy loss in killed and wounded. The men behaved with admirable steadiness, recovering themselves from their surprise almost immediately, and delivering so deadly a fire upon the Frenchmen that, after a desperate attempt to disable some of the guns in the battery known as No. 3, the latter fell back in disorder, and despite the exhortations of their officers, fled to the glacis, pursued by the Prussian soldiers, leaving between sixty and seventy of their number dead between the parallels. Their retreat, as usual, was covered by a furious cannonade from the walls, which was distinctly heard at Rastatt. Nothing was gained by the sortie, beyond ascertaining the position of the beleaguering forces, for which a heavy price in killed and wounded was paid. The attack was repulsed by the thirtieth Prussian infantry, and the second Baden grenadiers.

The spirits of the garrison had in the morning of the same day been revived by a report which, by some means, found its way into the city. Instead of the news of the battle of Sedan, which would have been received in the ordinary course, the following despatch appeared:—"France saved! Victory at Douancourt and at Raucourt. Great victory at Toul: 49,000 killed, 35,000 wounded, 700 cannons taken from the Prussians. Steinmetz's corps in full retreat, routed by Generals Douay and De Failly. MacMahon at Châlons-sur-Marne, with 400,000 men. Alsace saved in two days. MacMahon to the minister of the Interior. The French soldiers are making ramparts of the Prussian dead. From a despatch given by an emissary to Colonel Rollert."

The first intimation conveyed to the Strassburgers of the victory of Sedan was not understood. It came to them in the form of a salute of twenty-one guns, concerning which the *Courrier du Bas Rhin* said, on the following day:—"Yesterday the enemy's batteries threw, at regular intervals, twenty shells into the town" (the reporter had miscounted—there were twenty-one). "Our batteries made a vigorous reply, but after the twentieth shell had been fired the Prussian guns were silent."

During a two hours' truce, agreed to upon his request for the burial of those who had fallen in the sortie, the commandant of Strassburg was made acquainted with the crowning disaster that had befallen his imperial master. But he refused to lend the slightest credence to the telegrams shown him or the statements of the superior German officers, saying that they were all Prussian lies, made up to induce him to yield, and that he was not to be deceived by such shallow contrivances. A few days afterwards, however, the news of Sedan was confirmed by the same newspaper which had noticed the salute, the *Courrier du Bas Rhin*, the only one which appeared regularly throughout the siege.

The news of the revolution in Paris was first brought to Strassburg on the 12th September by the Swiss delegates. The Republic was proclaimed, and a new mayor elected, who issued a proclamation strongly condemnatory of the Bonaparte family—"that disgraceful family which three times in half a century has brought upon France the horrors of an invasion."

The Republican government appointed M. Valentin, who represented Strassburg in 1848, prefect of the department of the Lower Rhine, and urged him to obtain admission to Strassburg with the least possible delay. He obeyed, and entered the city by an indirect and difficult road. Disguised as a peasant, and availing himself of his acquaintance with the German tongue, he made friends with Prussian soldiers quartered in Bischeim. From them he obtained full particulars regarding the position and character of the works erected between that village and the city. He remarked that at one o'clock the fire of the besiegers was weakest, and the vigilance of their sentries most relaxed, as the soldiers then dined. Passing through the Prussian lines, between one and two o'clock on the 22nd of September, he arrived in safety at the ditch, across which he swam. The French soldiers fired at him repeatedly, but their bullets missed him. At last he reached a spot near one of the gates, where he was sheltered from the fire directed from the walls. Again and again he begged the soldiers to take him prisoner, and carry him before Governor Uhrich. Finally, they consented. When brought before the governor, he presented the official document containing his appointment as prefect. Its validity was at once recognized, and on the evening of the same day he issued a proclamation formally announcing his assumption of the post, and the establishment of the Republic. He was, however, little more than a week in office.

The Swiss delegates were the bearers not only of good news, but also of kind propositions. Switzerland, mindful of its old relations with Strassburg, made the generous offer to receive and provide refuge for its unfortunate citizens, should General von Werder permit them to emigrate en masse. As many as 4000 applications were addressed to General Uhrich for permission to quit. He sent the full list of names, with a notification of the age and condition of each applicant, to General von Werder, who began by granting safe-conducts to 400, either aged persons or who had been burned out. The first departure of emigrants was on the 17th of September, the second a few days after, and the third was fixed for the 27th, the very day on which the white flag was hoisted. Altogether, 1400 men, women, and children left Strassburg for Switzerland, who were hospitably received.

From a strictly military point of view it might be doubted whether General von Werder was justified in thus authorizing so numerous an exodus from the city. If he erred in exercising the virtue of mercy, however, it was on the right side. The delegates from the cantons of Basle, Zurich, and Berne took a practical and humane view of the bombardment. It may or may not, they thought, be justifiable in a military view to burn private homes, throw shells into girls' schools, and slaughter inoffensive men, women, and children indiscriminately. Setting aside this question, and without considering their own personal risk, the Swiss only saw that there was suffering in Strassburg, such as, fortunately, had not been known in Europe for half a century, and determined to relieve it. They first applied to General von Werder, with whose permission they sent in a letter, under a flag of truce, to General Uhrich. His answer was as follows:—"The work you have undertaken, gentlemen, is so honourable that it insures for you the eternal gratitude of the whole population of this city, as well as of its civil and military authorities. For my own part, I cannot find words in which to express my appreciation of your noble and generous initiative. But I feel it my duty to tell you how much I am touched by the step you have taken. A flag of truce shall be sent to Eckbolsheim to-morrow about eleven o'clock, and the bearer will have orders to accompany you here."

When the first band of emigrants, 400 in number, left, they were accompanied by General Uhrich to some distance beyond the gates, the bombardment being suspended for the time. At the first fine of German outposts there was a barricade, which it was necessary to take down to let the emigrants pass. Great hesitation was shown by the officers and men in charge, which, however, was ultimately overcome by General Uhrich promising to allow two hours for reconstructing the barricade, during which the outpost should not be interfered with. Further on the delegates and their charges were met by Prussian officers, who made a liberal distribution amongst them of such small comforts and necessaries as could be readily spared. The second convoy, a few days later, was much larger, and still more singular. Every description of vehicle was made available for the transport of goods and human beings, furniture, and families. Cabs, carts, hotel and railway omnibuses, huge market waggons, one-horse buggies, nondescript traps, seemingly made up of coachbuilders' odds and ends, followed each other in slow and solemn procession, laden with household stuff of the most incongruous description—mattresses and canary birds in cages, kitchen utensils and bonnet boxes, wardrobes and watering pots, all huddled together, without order or coherence, as if their owners had snatched them up just as they came to hand, irrespective of their value or utility. The number of men, women, and children in this long train of a hundred and twenty vehicles was over a thousand, one-third of whom consisted of well-to-do people, and the remainder mostly of the lower middle class. The feelings displayed by them were of a mixed kind—despondency on account of being driven into exile, the heavy losses they had sustained by the siege, and the reverses of French arms; joy at being so fortunate as to get away from the doomed city, and, in some cases, at the proclamation of a republic; for the Alsatians were by no means ardent imperialists. Amongst the carmen and cabdrivers permitted to convey the fugitives out of the town, and to return after performing that duty, might have been detected some gentlemanly-looking, intelligent faces, which unmistakably belonged to French officers, travestied for the nonce, who would doubtless have an interesting tale to tell of the German positions and dispositions when they presented themselves to General Uhrich a few hours later; though their reports could do no great harm to their enemies, who had Strassburg so tightly within their grasp, and whose strength was so overwhelming, that they could afford to tolerate and laugh at such small espionage.

It is a curious fact, which tells its own tale, that the avowedly vicious portion of the female population begged for permission to leave Strassburg under a flag of truce, the morning after the first bombardment, whereas the nuns and sisters of charity remained to the end. To the petition addressed to General von Werder by the members of the former class, his excellency replied that they might go where they pleased, provided they kept clear of his army, and did not attempt to enter the Grand Duchy of Baden.

The exit of the inhabitants caused but a momentary cessation of the bombardment. Day and night, with relentless activity, deadly projectiles from more than 240 heavy guns poured upon the doomed fortress, whose reply daily became more feeble. The guns were in reality insufficiently manned, General Uhrich having principally to depend upon some two or three hundred marine artillerists, originally intended for Rhine gunboats. Of these a large number were now killed or wounded; and although many of the line and mobile garde had been in some degree trained to take their places, they were next to useless for the professional operations of sighting, elevation, &c., so that in numerous instances one man had practically to serve several guns. Owing to this the French fire was sometimes suspended for several hours, and then broke out in a spasm of salvos, all along the line, which, after a few minutes, was again followed by another long interval of silence. Fortunate indeed were those whom German humanity permitted to fly from the precincts of the miserable town. The prices of provisions, notwithstanding the diminution in the number of consumers, rose enormously, and hunger was added to the horrors of the bombardment. The soldiery, grown impatient of control, gave themselves up to drunkenness and debauchery; whilst, despite all the endeavours of the besiegers to restrict their fire to the fortifications and purely military establishments, the town was frequently on fire in a dozen places at once, and burnt for days and nights together.

Several monster mortars were established near the fortress; and the projectiles they threw, weighing each two hundred pounds, caused fresh ruin and devastation with every discharge. While the German batteries were fast reducing the fortifications to heaps of battered and shapeless rubbish, riflemen were day and night firing at one another with Chassepot and needle gun, at distances ranging between one and two hundred yards; the patter and rattle of the musketry filling up the short intervals between the roar and crash of the great siege guns and mortars. The town was begirt with a semicircle of white smoke which melted into pale blue vapour as it rose from the trenches, whilst over-head hung a cloud of brown, gloomy fog, proceeding from the burning houses of its faubourgs.

Amidst all the carnage and destruction the Strassburgers bore themselves like men. Every day the municipal council met, not to trouble General Uhrich with their complaints, but to consider of measures for the public safety. An extra service of fire-engines was organized; a project for constructing bomb-proof places of shelter was discussed; refuges were publicly notified for those who had been burnt out of their houses, some of whom slept in churches, close to the entrance, where the architecture was most solid, some behind parapets on the quays of the canals, and some in the theatre, where nearly 200 poor persons were lying the night it took fire, and was burned to the ground. Many of the leading burghers helped to man the walls, to work the guns, to repair the damages caused to the works, and gave their money and their lives freely in a hopeless cause. They also exerted their influence over their poorer fellow citizens to prevent any attempt at pressure upon the military governor in favour of surrender. And throughout the German army, from the general downwards, all justly admired and honoured General Uhrich for the brilliant and heroic defence which he made against forces whom he knew to be overwhelming.

On September 21 and 22 the terrible grasp of the enemy upon the fortress was further strengthened by the capture of three of the lunettes, known as Nos. 53, 52, and 51 respectively. The two lunettes first taken were small detached works, lying several hundred feet in advance of the main rampart, surrounded by wide inundations. After they had been battered with the heaviest guns for a fortnight, mines were ultimately sunk under the water up to these islet strongholds. Their explosion destroyed a portion of the walls and laid them open to attack from without. A way had to be made across the water. In the case of one of the lunettes, which was protected on one side by only a broad ditch, a dyke was improvised of stones, sandbags, fascines, &c.; a work which, as the French had evacuated the place beforehand, was completed without much delay. Another lunette, with a sheet of water in front 180 feet wide, and a still larger one in its rear, gave more trouble. Under cover of night a bridge was made of a string of beer barrels, overlaid with boards, and placed between what may be called the mainland and the fortified isle. Though the French had been forced to clear out of this lunette also, the greatest caution was required in making this makeshift bridge, as the slightest sound would have attracted the attention of the sentinels on the main rampart in the rear, and spread the alarm. But so well had everything been prepared, and so noiselessly was the work carried on, that not a shot was fired on the French side until the first 100 men had got over, and with spades and axes were making themselves at home in the dilapidated shell of the deserted work. The next 100 crossed under a rattling fire; and as the shot now began to pour into the lunette, the greatest despatch had to be used in throwing up the breastwork which eventually sheltered the bold adventurers. Into the commanding positions thus obtained the Germans quickly conveyed artillery, which assisted materially in the formation of two breaches, one of them sixty feet wide, preparatory to the intended storming.

As General Uhrich yet showed no sign of yielding, the German commander now contemplated this final act of the fearful drama. It had been hoped that so excellent an officer as the governor of Strassburg had in everything proved himself, would have made a virtue of necessity, and by yielding up a charge he could no longer keep, avoided the dreadful alternative of having the fortress and town taken by storm. The time had arrived when a successful assault was clearly practicable, although it was calculated that the passage of the water defences alone would cost the Germans 2000 men; and wide as was the breach which had been made, the steep slope down to the water's edge, caused by the fallen débris, was still formidable enough to startle the boldest forlorn hope.

From the captured lunettes there ran a narrow dam across the intermediate lake up to the bastions of the main rampart. Along this dam, and up the breach, was the only way open to the assaulting party, with fire above and water below. It was, however, with aversion and horror that the German commanders contemplated the necessity of the extreme measure, both on account of the tremendous loss of fife that would certainly ensue to their own troops, should they be compelled to adopt it, and on account of the additional misery to which the inhabitants would be exposed during the state of furious excitement invariably experienced by the soldiery immediately after a successful assault. The men who composed the army before Strassburg were of an exceptionally humane temper as a rule; the large majority of them belonged to landwehr regiments, every second man in which was married and the father of a young family. Such troops were less likely to commit excesses in a conquered town than regular liners—mostly lads from twenty to twenty-three years of age, inexperienced in the cares of life and grave family responsibilities. But even German troops and landwehr, obedient as they were to their officers, and superior in civilization to the soldiers of any other army, might not easily be restrained from excesses when their blood was fevered with the fury of a successful but hardly-contested storm.

General Werder, however, determined, on the breaches being effected, to force the capture of the place. Accordingly, on the 27th September, a demand for surrender was made, with the alternative of an immediate assault. The German soldiers looked forward to the enterprise, although perilous, with anything but feelings of aversion. Trench duty had become tedious and harassing, and all were eager in the expression of their hope that it might soon come "zum Stürmen," and that they might be led out against the fortress to take it by assault, instead of being pent up in small country hamlets or kept crouching night after night in damp trenches. A soldier had written a new war song to the old popular tune of" Ich hatte einen Camerad," to be sung by the troops as they marched into Strassburg, and the camp now frequently resounded with the chorus, chanted by stalwart Baden grenadiers. Possessing a special interest, from its having been composed in the midst of this memorable siege, we reproduce it here:—

SONG OF THE GERMAN SOLDIERS IN ALSACE.

> In Alsace, over the Rhine,
> There lives a brother of mine;
> > It grieves my soul to say
> > He hath forgot the day
> We were one land and line.
> Dear brother, torn apart,
> Is't true that changed thou art?
> > The French have clapped on thee
> > Red breeches, as we see;
> Have they Frenchified thy heart?
> Hark! that's the Prussian drum,
> And it tells the time has come.
> > We have made one "Germany,"
> > One "Deutschland," firm and free;

>   And our civil strifes are dumb.
>   Thee also, fighting sore,
>   Ankle-deep in German gore,
>   We have won. Ah, brother, dear!
>   Thou art German—dost thou hear?
>   They shall never part us more.
>   Who made this song of mine?
>   Two comrades by the Rhine;—
>   A Suabian man began it,
>   And a Pomeranian sang it,
>   In Alsace, on the Rhine.

Shortly after the siege began, General Uhrich received a deputation from the council formed for the defence of the city, between whom and the governor opinions were freely and frankly interchanged. The result was a unanimous resolution by the council to strain every nerve to prevent the city from falling into the hands of the besiegers. General Uhrich, on his part, pledged himself to avert from the city the horrors of an assault, but reserved to himself the sole right of determining when the critical moment had arrived. Enough, he now felt, had been done for honour; hunger would soon reduce the city to the last extremity, even if spared immediate capture by the Germans; the garrison was fast becoming disorganized and mutinous; the threatened entrance of the Germans could not be successfully opposed; and to avert the sacrifice of many thousand lives which the assault would inevitably cause, the governor determined to capitulate. At five o'clock the white flag waved from the minster tower, and the air ceased to resound with the fatal thunder of artillery. The capitulation was announced in the following proclamation:

"Inhabitants of Strassburg,—As I have to-day perceived that the defence of the fortress of Strassburg is no longer possible, and as the council of defence unanimously shared my opinion, I have been obliged to resort to the lamentable necessity of entering into negotiations with the commander of the besieging army. Your manly attitude during these long and painful trials has enabled me to defer the fall of your town as much as possible; the honour of the citizens and of the soldiers is, thank God, unimpaired. Thanks also are due to you, the prefect of the Lower Rhine, and the municipal authorities, who, by your activity and unanimity, have given me such valuable co-operation, and have known how to assist the unfortunate population and maintain their dependence on our common fatherland. Thanks to you, officers and soldiers! To you, too, especially, members of my council of defence, who have always been so united, so energetic, so devoted to the great task which we had to accomplish; who have supported me in moments of hesitation, the consequence of the heavy responsibility which rested upon me, and of the sight of the public misfortunes which surrounded me. Thanks to you, representatives of our marine force, who have made your small numbers forgotten by the force of your deeds. Thanks, finally, to you, children of Alsace, to you, mobile national guards, to you, francs-tireurs and volunteer companies, to you, artillerymen of the national guard, who have so nobly paid your tribute of blood to the great cause which to-day is lost, and to you, custom-house officers, who have also given proofs of courage and devotion. I owe the same thanks to the *Intendance* for the zeal with which they knew how to satisfy the demands of a difficult position, as well with regard to the supply of provisions as to hospital service. How can I find language to express my sense of the services of the civil and military surgeons who have devoted themselves to the care of our wounded and sick, and of those noble young men of the medical school who have undertaken with so much enthusiasm the dangerous posts of the ambulances in the outworks and at the gates? How can I sufficiently thank the benevolent persons, the ecclesiastical and public authorities, who have opened their houses to the wounded, have shown them such attentions, and have rescued many from death? To my last day I shall retain the recollection of the two last months, and the feeling of gratitude and admiration which you have excited in me will only be extinguished with my life. Do you on your part remember without bitterness your old general, who would have thought himself happy could he have spared you the sufferings and dangers which have befallen you, but who was forced to close his heart to his feelings, for the sake of the duty he owed to that country which is mourning its children. Let us, if we can, close our eyes to the sorrowful and painful interest, and turn our looks to the future; there we still find the solace of the unfortunate—hope. Long live France for ever.—Given at headquarters, 27th of September, 1870. The divisional general, commandant of the sixth military division,

"UHRICH."

The mayor's proclamation, issued on the following day, stated that the surrender was inevitable, on account of two breaches and a threatened storm, which would involve frightful loss. The general, he said, would save Strassburg from the payment of a war ransom, and would insure it mild treatment. He exhorted the people to abstain from any hostile demonstration towards the enemy, as the least act of hostility would entail severe reprisals on the entire population. The laws of war decreed that any house from which a shot was fired should be demolished and its inhabitants shot down. "Let everybody," said the mayor, "remember this, and if there are people among you who could forget what they owe to their fellow-citizens by thinking of useless attempts at resistance, prevent them from so doing. The hour for resistance is past. Let us accept the unavoidable."

Immediately after the hanging out of the white flag firing ceased on both sides. Not a single gun was discharged from the walls or the trenches after half-past five o'clock. About eleven Lieutenant-colonel von Lesczynski and Captain Count Leo Donnersmarck rode out through Koenigshoffen, and asked of the French sentinels to see the general commanding the fortress. Their request was sent into the town; and, after waiting an hour sitting on the stumps of felled trees, close by the Porte Nationale, a field-officer came to them, saying that the general was "gone out," that he lodged at a great distance, and that the officer did not know where to find him. With considerable coolness under the circumstances he then inquired—"What *did ces messieurs* want?" *Ces messieurs* explained that they desired to know what was meant by the exhibition of the white flag, and to see the general, or some person duly authorized by him to communicate with them. The officer returned into the fortress, and the German plenipotentiaries went to Koenigshoffen, where they set about preparing a place to receive the expected Frenchmen. They fixed upon a small tent on the railway, hard by a detached first-class carriage which had for some weeks served as a resting-place for the officers belonging to covering parties stationed round a 24-pound battery. Over the table which had been brought into this tent was hung a portrait of MacMahon, in compliment to French military gallantry. Outside was stationed half a company of Prussian infantry and a few drummers. These preparations completed, the German plenipotentiaries waited the coming of the French delegates; but it was not till past one o'clock that the approach of the second commandant and the artillery director of the fortress was signified to Colonel von Lesczynski. The drums were immediately beaten, and the half company paraded before the tent. The delegates appeared much gratified at being received with military honours, and proceeded at once to fulfil their mission by making an unconditional surrender of the fortress. The treaty of capitulation, framed on the basis or model of that of Sedan, was drawn up, read, and finally signed at half-past two in the morning. The four commissioners took leave of one another with great courtesy, and Strassburg ceased to be a French fortress. At eight o'clock the French guards were relieved by Germans, who took possession of the gates and all other important posts. The garrison surrendered at eleven o'clock. The German army was paraded on an open ground, abutting on the glacis between the Portes Nationale and De Saverne, General Werder at its head, surrounded by a brilliant staff in full uniform (*de gala*). As the clock struck eleven, General Uhrich, followed by his staff, emerged from the former gate, and advanced towards the German commander, who, alighting from his horse, and holding out his hand, stepped forward to meet him. Next came Admiral Excelmans, Brigadier-general de Barral, and the other superior officers; then the regulars, marines, douaniers, and mobiles, numbering in all 15,347 men and 451 officers, with flags flying and arms shouldered. With the exception of the marines and douaniers, who made an excellent appearance, the troops behaved disgracefully, contravening the terms of the capitulation in a way that too plainly showed the state of utter insubordination into which they had fallen. At least two-thirds of the men were drunk; hundreds, as they stumbled through the ruined gateway, dashed their rifles to pieces against the walls or the paving stones, and flung their sword-bayonets into the moat; from one battalion alone came cheers of "Vive la Republique!" "Vive la Prusse!" "Vive l'Empereur!" The officers made no attempt to keep the men in order, or prevent them from destroying the arms which the signers of the capitulation had engaged to deliver up to the victors. Many of the men even danced to the music of the Prussian and Baden bands; some rolled about on the grass, uttering inarticulate cries; others made ludicrous attempts to embrace the grave German legionaries, who repulsed them in disgust at their unworthy bearing. The whole scene was calculated to bring the French army into contempt, and to extinguish the small remnants of respect for *les militaires français* that still survived in the breasts of a few of the foreign bystanders. In the course of the afternoon the whole were sent off under an escort, as prisoners of war, to the fortress of Rastatt, in Baden, the officers having the option of liberty on parole.

After the surrender the Germans entered, about 3000 strong, with banners flying, drums beating, and bands playing the "Watch on the Rhine." Although it was half-past eleven, and the inhabitants must have heard of the capitulation some hours previously, there were few people in the streets to witness the martial procession. It seemed as if they felt uncertain whether the bombardment they had endured so long might not begin again, or as if they preferred looking at their conquerors from the windows before trusting themselves to a nearer acquaintance. They had been living for six weeks in cellars and other underground localities, and could not at once realize that their dreaded enemies might now be safely met. By degrees they emerged from their retreats. The manure and mattresses with which the cellar windows had been protected against bullets were removed; the doors of the subterranean abodes were thrown open to admit light and air, and one by one, pale men and women, sickly by confinement, crept up into the sunshine they had missed for weeks; children, timid and emaciated, slowly came 'out into the open air, to be rewarded for their temerity by the sight of fresh uniforms and the sound of military music. Many afflicted parents went to the spot in the courtyard, where, in default of a more sacred resting-place, one of their beloved ones had been laid during the siege; the way to the cemetery, which was at some distance, having been too dangerous to admit of burial there. Having ventured so far, people, or, at any rate, as many as had their houses left standing, went up stairs to enjoy the long missed luxury of a room, and the everyday comforts it brings with it. At last, after the Germans had been in the town for hours, people came abroad to acquaint themselves with the new order of things, and to visit the relations and friends from whom they had been separated while cannon balls were flying about. What joyful embracings when those they sought were found alive! What pangs when they were found to have died a premature and violent death!

With one exception the inhabitants treated their conquerors with great consideration. On the evening of the 28th a Baden soldier was shot in a by-street near the cathedral, and another wounded. The assassin fled, but was captured by several citizens, and immediately shot by the German soldiers. As soon as General Werder heard the tidings, he ordered the city to pay a heavy contribution, and threatened to humiliate the inhabitants by making a triumphal entry into the town with his whole army. But being ultimately convinced that the act was entirely attributable to isolated ruffians, he cancelled the orders, and relieved the city from the onerous contribution of four millions of francs. The next day the Prussian commandant issued the following; notice:—

"The state of siege still continues. Crimes and offences will be punished by martial law. All weapons are immediately to be given up. All newspapers and publications are forbidden till further orders. Public houses to be closed at 9 p.m.; after that hour every civilian must carry a lantern. The municipal authorities have to provide quarters, without food, for all good men.

"MERTENS."

No salute was fired when Strassburg fell. The 28th and 29th of September passed without any signs of rejoicing; and it was not till the 30th—the same day on which, 189 years before, Louis XIV. by fraud and treachery became master of the town—that the joy of the Germans at regaining possession of a place which they looked upon as their indisputable property, was expressed in the form of thanksgiving; a Protestant service being performed on one side of the Orangerie Gardens, a Catholic service on the other. The officiating pastor in the Prussian religious camp was the chaplain of the 34th regiment. The troops were formed into a hollow square, in the middle of which stood a group of officers. The chaplain took his place on one side of the square, beside an improvised altar composed of drums built up against a tree, and nothing could be more simple or impressive than the whole service. He took for his text the opening verses of the 105th Psalm, and gave thanks to God for the recovery of Strassburg from the hands of the foreigner and its restoration to the German race, from whom, for nearly two centuries, it had been unjustly kept. The 30th of September, instead of being associated with the loss of Strassburg, would now, he said, be regarded as the happiest day in its history, the second birthday of the ancient German city.

After the services in the Orangerie a thanksgiving was celebrated in the Protestant church of St. Thomas, at which General von Werder and his staff were present. The general was received at the door by the clergy. The principal pastor delivered an address, in which he assured General von Werder that the "immense majority" of the population of Strassburg were German in feeling. There is no doubt that the Protestants of the city were well disposed towards Germany, and this, perhaps, the speaker chiefly meant. It is possible that General Werder, remembering the desperate resistance of the Strassburgers, and the 150 lb. shells which he had lately been throwing into their houses, may have doubted the accuracy of the statement that the "immense majority "were glad to see him. Be that as it may, he kept his eyes firmly fixed on those of the much-protesting pastor, held him all the time, as if affectionately, by the hand, and having heard him to the close, without altering his gaze or relaxing his grasp, replied. His answer, simple enough in itself, was delivered very impressively, and had a great effect on all who heard it. Still standing on the threshhold, he said:—"I am obliged to you for the manner in which you receive me. One thing ought to reassure you—my first visit in Strassburg is to the church. I am pained at the manner in which I have been forced to enter this German city; and, believe me, I shall do my utmost to heal its wounds. From my soldiers you have nothing whatever to fear. Their order and discipline are perfect; but do not forget that the same order will be expected and required on the part of the civil population. Once more I thank you for your expressions of good-will."

The service then began. The body of the church was full of troops, the general and his staff occupying seats in front of the pulpit. The sermon was preached by Emil Frommel, royal garrison chaplain of Berlin, and field-division chaplain of the guard landwehr division. The discourse was founded on 1 Samuel vii. 12, and was a fair sample of the military field preaching in the German armies. Pitched in the key of exultation which at the time found an echo in all German hearts and households, it had the ring of the song of Deborah and of Barak, or of those drumhead discourses to which Cromwell's grim Ironsides listened after Marston Moor and Dunbar.

The redoubts and other fortifications constructed by the besieged, as they appeared on the day after the surrender of Strassburg, betrayed the tremendous effects of the German artillery fire. The parapets and epaulements were knocked into hopeless masses of loose earth. Most of the embrasures had been closed with sand-bags; and the earthen tops of the stone-built magazines, in some cases forming the epaulements, had sandbags added to preserve them, and to aid their power of arresting the flanking fire of the besiegers. The fire from the Prussian batteries was so well directed that most of the shells struck the top of these epaulements, and bursting at the same moment, sent destruction to the men and guns underneath. There was not a gun but bore evidence that the flying fragments of shell had left their mark. Many of the guns were knocked over; wheels and carriages were smashed beyond repair; broken guns and fragments of carriages lay in and behind the batteries. In the two principal redoubts attacked, the appearances tended to indicate that the guns had not been replaced for some time, and that the garrison had ceased also to repair the embrasures and parapets.

Amongst the private property of the town nothing was more striking in the ravages of the bombardment than its searching character. It was a fiery furnace, under the scorching flames of which all constructive shams and artifices perished. No traces were left of paperhanging, cornices, mouldings, or ornamentation; the walls, after the ordeal, wore an aspect not far different from that they would exhibit if left to bleach in the rain and sunshine of centuries. The suburbs immediately exposed to the German fire were literally a heap of ruins, scarcely a house being left standing.

The devastation was greatest in the Jews' quarter, the fishermen's quarter, St. Nicholas, Finkenmatt, Broglie, and the neighbourhood of the Stein Strasse—all of them wearing exactly the aspect of the exhumed remains of Pompeii and Herculaneum. In the town itself nearly all the principal buildings were reduced to ashes. The prefecture, the Protestant church, the theatre, the museum, the artillery school, infantry barracks, military magazine, railway station, and, worst of all, the library, with its invaluable contents, were entirely destroyed. In the immediate neighbourhood of the public buildings many inhabited houses escaped with comparatively little damage; the reason assigned being that, in the public buildings, there was no one at hand to extinguish the first flames, and when these were seen ascending into the ah, they served as a mark for the enemy's guns. At night (and the severe bombardments were always at night) flames made a tempting target for the besiegers. The hotel de la Ville de Paris received forty shells during the siege, but engines and water-buckets were kept in readiness on all the floors, and fires in this building were no sooner kindled than they were extinguished.

The numerous handsome bridges which spanned the canal existed so far as their roadways were concerned, but scarcely a vestige of parapet remained, while the canal itself was almost choked—quite choked towards its southern extremity—with barges and boats of every kind smashed and sunken with everything they contained.

All that remained of the citadel, at one time deemed by its possessors almost impregnable, was huge masses of rubbish produced by the incessant fire from the batteries of Kehl on the one side, and the bombs thrown from those near Schiltigheim on the other.

One of the first acts of Lous XIV. on taking the city in 1681, was to dislodge the Protestants from the cathedral, which they had occupied from the period of the Reformation. The Dominican church, which had long been secularized, was allotted to them instead, and had its name changed to that of the Temple Neuf. It had one of the most famous organs of Silbermann. In the choir, divided from the nave, was lodged the special glory of Alsace—its library, the finest on the Rhine, in which the archives, antiquities, topography, and early printing collections were treasured. All perished. Since the apocryphal burning of the library of Alexandria, perhaps no equally irreparable loss has occurred. Unfortunately no catalogue of its many treasures exists. An elaborate one in MS. had been prepared by the librarian, but that also perished. A very fine work, the "Alsace Antiquary," perished among them—sixteen folio vols, of MS. upon Strassburg. Greatest loss of all was that of the most precious record connected with the discovery of printing—the documents of the legal process instituted by Gutenberg against the heirs of his partner Dreisehn, to establish his right as the inventor of typography. Among the early specimens of typography there was a copy of the first German Bible, printed by Mentelin about 1466, but undated; also three early Latin Bibles by Mentelin, Jenson, and Eggestein, the last bearing the manuscript date 1468. There was, besides, a rare copy of Virgil by Mentelin, a still rarer Commentary of Servius upon that poet, printed by the celebrated Valdarfer; a Jerome's "Epistles," by Schoeffer, 1470; and about 4000 other books printed before the beginning of the sixteenth century.

The inner part of the town, although it escaped the measure of devastation inflicted upon the fringe of suburbs and outer circle of buildings adjoining them, but belonging properly to the city within the Ill, suffered heavily. The stately picture gallery in the Klèberplatz was gutted from basement to roof; the archiepiscopal and imperial palaces, as well as other fine mansions near the minster, were much damaged; and bridges over the canals were entirely smashed, and the houses in the Quai des Bateliers, Quai des Pêcheurs, Place de Broglie, &c., were all greatly injured. The cathedral was to all external appearance uninjured. The spire, though it had been struck in more places than one, was as attractive a spectacle as ever. The cross on its summit appeared to have been touched by a projectile, as it leaned to one side. Some of the ornamental work had been carried away, and a portion of the stone stair in one of the side towers destroyed. The outer roof of the nave had been burned, and the windows here and there pierced with balls; but the famous clock escaped, and the cathedral was on the whole in excellent condition, owing to the orders of the Prussian commander, who would not permit a single bullet to be fired against it, except at the commencement of the siege, when the French used it as an observatory. In the promenade, where the bands were wont in times of peace to play of afternoons, trees and lamp-posts were lying about amongst Louis Quatorze chairs and all sorts of old fashioned furniture saved from burning houses; whilst even the little orchestra, struck by a shell, was partly smashed and partly burnt. No less than 448 private houses were entirely destroyed, and out of the 5150 in the town and suburbs nearly 3000 were more or less injured; 1700 civilians were killed or wounded, and 10,000 persons made houseless. The estimate of the total damage to the city was nearly £8,000,000.

Immediately after the capitulation, subscriptions were opened in Berlin and Frankfort to relieve the suffering Strassburgers, and restore the town; but towards the latter object little was raised, as the magnitude of the ruins seemed to render the efforts of private charity utterly inadequate.

In the narrow space of the botanic gardens, hardly exceeding an acre, the anguish of the siege was epitomized. At its commencement the city had three cemeteries, one of which was occupied for its defence; another was overflowed; the third was in the hands of the enemy, whose parallels were driven through it. As the only space available, the botanic garden, adjoining the arsenal and citadel, was turned into a burying-ground. After the siege it wore, as did, in fact, all the garden-ground for miles round, the aspect of a neglected overgrown wilderness. Along its eastern side a trench, much deeper and broader than that of the parallel, had been driven in two rows; and in piles, four and five above each other, the dead of the last six weeks had there been crowded. In this dense mass of mortality it was painful to witness the anxiety displayed by survivors not to lose sight of the remains of their relatives. Wooden crosses, with brief inscriptions, immortelles, bead wreaths, statuary, floral bouquets, crowded each other.

The open town of Kehl, opposite Strassburg, met with an even worse fate than the latter. It was bombarded early in the siege of Strassburg, an act considered by the Germans a piece of wanton and unjustifiable destruction, as its utter uselessness was apparent. By reducing Kehl to ashes the French did not retard by one day the progress of the besiegers, nor cripple them in the slightest degree. The batteries on either side of the town were as effective, after the inhabitants had been driven forth by showers of shells from their burning houses, as they were before. Pitiable as the destruction in Strassburg appeared, the streets and dwellings of Kehl presented a spectacle even more saddening. Not above five houses remained intact; and the only object which indicated that the ruins in the main street had once been habitable dwellings was a porcelain stove, standing erect amid the heaps of charred rubbish.

The catalogue of the guns employed and the shot fired in the siege of Strassburg deserves to be mentioned. There were 241 pieces placed in battery outside the walls. During the thirty-one days over which the regular operations extended these fired 193,722 rounds, or, on an average, 6249 per day, 269 per hour, or between four and five per minute. Of the total of the rounds, 45,000 shells were fired from the rifled 12-pounders, 28,000 shells from the long rifled 24-pounders; 23,000 7-pound bombs, 20,000 25-pound bombs, and 15,000 50-pound bombs from smooth-bore mortars; 11,000 shrapnels from the rifled 12pounders, 8000 shells from the rifled 6-pounders, 5000 shrapnels from the rifled 24-pounders, 4000 shrapnels from the rifled 6-pounders, 3000 long shells from the 15 centimetre guns, and 600 long shells from the 21 centimetre guns.

A valuable prize fell into the hands of Germany through the surrender of Strassburg. No fewer than 2000 cannon were found in the fortifications, arsenal, and foundry: 1200 of them were bronze guns of various calibre, mostly rifled, and the large majority new, having been made in 1862, 1863, and 1864, and never fired; 800 were iron, some of them very large, smooth-bored and rifled. One hundred and fifty tons of powder made up in cartridges, and four hundred and fifty tons in bulk, were discovered in store; besides many thousand stand of arms, including hosts of excellent Chassepots, although the mobiles and sédentaires were armed only with "tabatières." Clothing also was found, enough for a very large body of men. The military authorities estimated the value of the *matériel*, which by the capitulation legitimately became the property of Germany, at more than two millions and a half sterling. In hard cash they took 10,000,000 of francs (£400,000) deposited in the military chest of the garrison.

Subsequently a commission was appointed by the Tours delegate government to investigate the reasons for the surrender of Strassburg. It is needless to say that no imputation on the courage and patriotism of its defenders could be for a moment sustained.

The fortress, which was not taken either in 1814 or in 1815, made on this occasion a most heroic defence against an overwhelming force, furnished with tremendous artillery; and it is hard to say whether the inhabitants or the garrison should be held as entitled to most praise. The endurance of the citizens was certainly not less conspicuous than the bravery of the troops; and perhaps the truest symptom of patriotic feeling which the French nation showed during the days of adversity in the late war, was exhibited in the hearty loyalty with which the Parisians laid their laurel wreaths at the base of the civic statue of Strassburg. General Uhrich undoubtedly "made himself an everlasting name" by his defence of the Alsatian city, which will be narrated by Frenchmen in future generations as one of the few bright spots in a singularly gloomy period of the national history.

The siege of Toul is chiefly remarkable for the bravery and endurance with which its small garrison held out for six weeks against a force of 20,000 Prussians under the duke of Mecklenburg, and thus deprived the German armies during that time of the advantage of direct railway communication from the Rhine at Coblentz and Mayence via Nancy to Paris. The town lies in the valley of the Moselle, and its stout and prolonged resistance has led many to suppose that it occupied an elevated position. On the contrary, it stands in a sort of basin formed by an abrupt curve of the Moselle, and may be said to be completely commanded by the surrounding heights, inasmuch as the two hills St. Michel and St. Maurice overlook it at a distance of about 4000 yards. It is regularly fortified on Vauban's system; and has excellent walls, six bastions, and deep fosses filled with water. It was formerly deemed a very strong fortress; but as it possessed no outworks or detached forts, it proved to be untenable for any lengthened period before new long-range siege artillery. The most conspicuous object seen on approaching the town is the fine old cathedral, one of the most famous Gothic edifices of the sixteenth century. Orders were given by the German commander to spare it as much as possible; but injuries to the external walls were unavoidable, and a large window was destroyed. The public building that suffered most severely by the bombardment was the stately residence of the mayor, which was pierced in every part. It seems, however, that for five weeks the besiegers had only ordinary field-guns in use, against which the fortress held out stoutly, and had evidently no intention to give in. It capitulated only when the regular siege artillery of the Germans, heavy rifled breechloaders, came up. On the 20th, the besiegers advanced a battery within range of the bastions, and some well directed rounds drove the French from the walls, whence they had kept up a vigorous musketry-fire. Six Bavarian batteries planted on the heights made terrible havoc, 2000 bombs and grenades being fired daily at the fortress. By the fearful bombardment of the 22nd and 23rd September, when the town was on fire in twenty-three places at once, whole streets were destroyed, and the barracks, hospital, and chapel, situate on the plateau of the rock forming the fortress, became a heap of ruins. As the German armies around Paris were suffering serious inconvenience from the railway being held by Toul, the grand-duke had determined to storm the place. Before, however, the siege had been begun in earnest, and the first parallel dug out, on the 23rd September, while the bombardment was proceeding on all sides, suddenly a large white flag was exhibited from the Cathedral tower. All the batteries at the grand-duke's command were immediately silent, and a Prussian *parlementaire* rode into the town, who soon returned with the commandant of Toul, Colonel Hück. After long negotiations, the capitulation was agreed to; and as darkness had meanwhile set in, the commandant and the chief of the grand-duke's staff appended their signatures by the dim light of a stable lantern. The en the garrison of about 2500, including 500 infantry and artillerymen, the others being mobile guards, surrendered as prisoners of war. The terms of the capitulation were that the fortress, war material, and soldiers should be given up, with the exception of those mobile and national guards who were inhabitants of the place prior to the outbreak of the war. In consideration of the gallant defence of the fortress, all officers and officials having the rank of officers, who gave their word of honour in writing not to bear arms against Germany, nor to act contrary to her interests in any other way, had their liberty, and were allowed to retain their swords, horses, and other property. An inventory of the war material, consisting of eagles, guns, swords, horses, war chests, and articles of military equipment, was to be given to the Prussians. The convention thus far was similar to that of Sedan; but there was another article which said:—"In view of the lamentable accident which occurred on the occasion of the capitulation of Laon, it is agreed that if a similar thing should happen on the entry of the German troops into the fortress of Toul, the entire garrison shall be at the mercy of the grand-duke of Mecklenburg."

Some eighty officers, including all those belonging to the mobile guards, chose to give their parole and remain in France. Seventeen superior officers, including Commandant Hück, who was complimented on his bravery by the grand-duke, preferred Prussian captivity. The reasons given by the commandant for capitulating were, that he had only ammunition for three or four days, when he would have been forced to surrender, after all Toul had possibly been destroyed; and that the mobile guards were undisciplined and not sufficiently practised in arms to offer a long defence or to repulse a storming attack. The same evening the French garrison marched out and bivouacked in a meadow under guard. The next day they were sent by railway to Prussia, and the Mecklenburg troops occupied the place, which was entered by the grand-duke with a brilliant staff at the head of some regiments.

After the surrender Toul presented a scene very different from what is usually seen on such occasions. Instead of the bitter feeling on the one side and the exultation on the other, which are commonly exhibited, both parties, when the gate was opened, seemed to meet like the best of friends. The French garrison were delighted to be out, and the German besiegers no less so to find their work at an end. As there were many Alsatians among the garrison, besiegers and besieged at once entered into conversation, shared the contents of their flasks with each other, and but for the stringent rules separating prisoner from conqueror, would doubtless have made a jovial night of it. The anxious families had passed the last days chiefly in their cellars, the windows of their houses being thickly covered with manure. All now came creeping out, sunning themselves, and spreading out their beds everywhere to dry and air, as they had become damp in the underground abodes. Pale faces were visible everywhere, and loud lamentations were heard; but the habitual French elasticity and cheerfulness were soon manifested, the inhabitants being gladdened by the thought that the siege was ended, and life and health were no longer endangered. Excursions into the country were immediately undertaken, and civilians, with officers released on parole, were seen driving about and inspecting the positions which had so recently menaced them.

The following officers, men, arms, and munitions of war, &c., were captured at the surrender of Toul:—109 officers, 2240 men, 120 horses, one eagle of the garde mobile, 197 bronze guns, including 48 pieces of rifled ordnance, 3000 rifles, 3000 sabres, 500 cuirasses, and a considerable quantity of munitions and articles of equipment. Soldiers' pay for 143,025 days, and rations for 51,949 days, also fell into the hands of the Prussians.

It is no idle phrase that Strassburg and Toul "deserved well" of their country. Citizens, as well as regular soldiers, appear to have conducted the defence of the two cities. All that could be done was done. Among the incidents of a campaign prolific in startling illustrations of the collapse of the military system of France, it must ever be remembered, as a redeeming fact, that a fourth-rate fortress, defended by a garrison consisting almost entirely of civilians, held out for six weeks against the invading force, and blocked up for that time the direct communications between Germany and the bulk of her army.

CHAPTER XIX.

The Position of the German Armies in the beginning of October—Their Depot Battalions of the Line serving as Cadres—The great importance in Modern Warfare of Large Intrenched Camps, with a Fortress for their Nucleus—Count von Moltke's Plans—Occupation of Beauvais by General Manteuffel—The duty of General von Werder's Army—Levée en Masse ordered by the French Government—Formation of New Armies—Sad want of Discipline and Good Officers—The Franc-Tireurs—Severe Treatment of them by the Germans—Burning of Ablis and other Places—Inconsistency of Prussia in attempting to put down Irregular Warfare—Decree of the French Government with the view of protecting the Franc-Tireurs—More Prudence than Courage shown by the French in many Places—Panic at Orleans—Confusion in both the Military and Political System of France—Great Want of a Real General—M. Gambetta leaves Paris for Tours in a Balloon—Biographical Sketch of Him—Narrow Escape on his Aerial Journey—Address presented to him at Rouen—His Arrival at Tours, and his First Impressions of the State of Affairs—Important Proclamation issued by Him—Arrival of Garibaldi at Tours—He is despatched to the East to take Command of a Body of Irregular Troops—The Extraordinary Energy of M. Gambetta—Engagement between the French and Germans at Toury—Easy Victory of the French—Uneasiness at the German Headquarters, and Despatch of the First Bavarian Corps Southwards—The French are completely surprised at Artenay and easily overcome—Gross Neglect of the French Commanders—Obstinate Encounter near Orleans—Panic amongst the Franc-Tireurs and Terror in the City of Orleans itself—Disgraceful Conduct of the Troops—The City is entered by the Germans—Proclamation of the German Commander to the Inhabitants—The French Army of the Loire retire to Bourges—General d'Aurelles de Paladines appointed to command it—His First Order of the Day—Importance of the Capture of Orleans to the Germans in two ways—The Franc-Tireurs in the Forests around the City prove a great annoyance to them—Chartres and Châteandun fortified—Determined Resistance at the Latter Town—Chartres capitulates on Favourable Terms—The Military Operations in Eastern France—German Victory between Raon l'Etape and St. Diey—Capture of Epinal, by which Lorraine is cut off from the rest of France—Arrival of Garibaldi on the Scene, and Proclamation to his Irregular Troops—No Combined Action between him and the French General Cambriels, who is actively pursued by General von Werder—Another German Victory—Resignation of General Cambriels—The dislike of the Catholics to Garibaldi, and the obstacles placed in his way—Appointment of General Michel in the room of Cambriels—Surrender of Schlestadt—Siege and Bombardment of Soissons—Acquisition of a Second Line of Railway to Paris—Gallant defence of St. Quentin—Final occupation of it and other Towns in the North of France—The Excitement in Rouen and Amiens—General Bourbaki appointed to the command of the French Army of the North—Short Sketch of his Career—First Proclamation issued by him—Preparations for defence in Brittany under Count de Keratry—A Company of Volunteer Engineers formed in Eastern France to operate on the German Lines of Communication—Plan of their Operations—The Germans compel the most respected Inhabitants in the District to accompany the Trains or Locomotives—The Great Mistake of the French in not establishing suitable Cavalry Corps to harass the German Line of Communication—The Prospects for France brighter at the close of October than at the beginning, chiefly owing to the energy of M. Gambetta—Martial Law Established in all the Departments within Seventy Miles of the Enemy's Forces—Formation of Camps and adoption of Severe Measures in various parts of the Country—The extreme Republicans alone devoid of Patriotic Feeling—A Loan of £10,000,000 contracted—Appeals from France to England and other Countries for Intervention and Assistance—A Negotiation with the view to an Armistice is agreed on—Interview between M. Thiers and Count von Bismarck—Great mistake of the French in breaking off the Negotiations on the Question of Re-victualling Paris—The General Feeling in France when the Failure of the Negotiations became known—The Germans disappointed at the Prolongation of the War, but determined to support their Political and Military Leaders until Alsace and Lorraine had been recovered—Manufacture of the Pen with which to sign the Treaty of Peace—Count von Bismarck's Reply on receiving it—The serious Consequences of the War in France—The advantage, both in France and Germany, of the Women being able to undertake Agricultural Operations.

DURING the sieges of Metz and Paris, the chief interest of the war, of course, centered in those two cities. But while France watched with pride the endurance and determination displayed by her greatest fortress and her magnificent capital, the beleaguered garrisons and citizens in each case were anxiously looking for the armies of the provinces to come to their rescue, and assist in dispersing the besieging hosts. In the present chapter we propose to review the state of France, and the military operations of both the French and Germans elsewhere than at Paris and Metz, during the month of October.

It is a remarkable fact that, even after the fall of Strassburg, nearly the whole of the immense German army in France was fully employed, although not one-sixth of the territory of the country was held by the invaders. Metz, with Bazaine's army inclosed within its line of forts, found occupation for eight army corps (the first, second, third, seventh, eighth, ninth, tenth, the division of Hessians, and General Kummer's division of landwehr), in all, sixteen divisions of infantry. Paris engaged seventeen divisions of infantry (the guards, fourth, fifth, sixth, eleventh, twelfth North German, first and second Bavarian corps, and the Würtemburg division). The newly formed thirteenth and fourteenth corps, mostly landwehr, and some detachments from the corps already named, occupied the conquered country, and observed, blockaded, or besieged the places which, within it, still belonged to the French. The fifteenth corps, the Baden division, and one division of landwehr, set free by the capitulation of Strassburg, were alone disposable for active operations.

These forces comprised almost all the organized troops of which Germany disposed. In accordance with their original purpose, the depôt battalions served as cadres for the drill and organization of the men intended to fill up the gaps which battles and disease caused in the ranks of their respective regiments. Proportionately as the thousand men forming the battalion were sufficiently broken in to do duty before the enemy, they were sent off by detachments to join the three field battalions of the regiment; this was done on a large scale after the severe fighting before Metz in the middle of August. But the officers and non-commissioned officers of the battalion remained at home, ready to receive and prepare for the field a fresh batch of 1000 men, taken from the recruits called out in due course. This measure was absolutely necessary in a war as bloody as the present one, and the end of which was not to be foreseen with certainty; but it deprived the Germans of the active services for the time being of 114 battalions, and a corresponding force of cavalry and artillery, representing in all fully 200,000 men. With the exception of these, the occupation of scarcely one-sixth of France and the reduction of the two large fortresses in this territory—Metz and Paris—kept the whole of the German forces so fully employed that they had barely 60,000 men to spare for further operations beyond the territory already conquered. And this, while there was not anywhere a French army in the field to oppose serious resistance!

If ever there was needed a proof of the immense importance, in modern warfare, of large intrenched camps with a fortress for their nucleus, here that proof was furnished. The two intrenched camps in question were not at all made use of to the best advantage, for Metz had for a garrison too many troops for its size and importance, and Paris had of real troops fit for the field scarcely any at all. Still, the first of these places held at least 200,000, the second 250,000 enemies in check; and if France had only had 200,000 real soldiers behind the Loire, the siege of Paris would have been an impossibility. As it was, however, France was virtually at the mercy of a conqueror who held possession of barely one-sixth of her territory.

Count von Moltke's plan of operations embraced not only the siege of the capital, but also the occupation of the northern and eastern departments as far as was possible with the forces at his disposal, thus pressing at once on Paris and the provinces, and rendering each unable to assist the other.

On September 29 Beauvais, the capital of the department of the Oise, was occupied by the first Prussian corps, under General Manteuffel, who, with a portion of the army which had been engaged at Sedan, was commissioned to carry the war into the north-west of France; from this point threatening Rouen on the west and Amiens on the north. The fall of Toul and Strassburg in the last week of September liberated 80,000 German troops, part of whom were sent to assist in the investment of Paris, while the remainder, about 70,000, were formed into an army under General von Werder, to be employed in operations over southern Alsace and the south-eastern districts of France. It was to seize any points at which it might be attempted to form military organizations, to disperse the corps, break up depôts, and destroy stores. It was, further, to levy contributions upon towns which had not as yet felt the pressure of the war, and which expressed a desire for its continuance. It was hoped that in this way accurate conceptions of the state of the country and the helplessness of its government would be communicated to that part of the French public which had hitherto derived its impressions from the bulletins published at Paris and Tours.

On October 1 the Tours government issued a decree for a *levée en masse* of all Frenchmen of the military age—from twenty-one to forty—to be organized into a mobilized national guard. Had this decree been carried out, it would have supplied at least three millions of men, for not one in three, even of those liable to serve, had been as yet enrolled. The larger towns had done their part, but the country districts were surprisingly apathetic, and those who possessed any means and desired exemption from service obtained it with little trouble.

From this date, however, commenced the formation of new armies in the north, south, east, and west of France. Indeed, immediately after the events of the 2nd September, the government had adopted vigorous measures to raise fresh troops by means of a forced conscription, embracing soldiers whose term of service had long since expired, and youths not yet arrived at the legal age; and by calling out all the retired, invalided, and pensioned general and other officers, with all the depôt and garrison troops, gardes mobiles, marines, and gendarmes. The result was that, early in October, there were, in various parts of France, an immense number of men ready for service when provincial armies should be organized. This was especially the case in the district of the Loire, where a very well-defined nucleus of an army had already been got together. Its headquarters were about fifty-five miles south of Orleans, at Bourges, a place containing a large cannon foundry, and of strategical importance owing to its being situated within the loop formed by the Loire, and at the junction of the different roads leading to Tours, Blois, Orleans, and Nevers, all commanding passages over the river. The force numbered, on October 1, about 60,000 men, well armed, but greatly deficient in artillery. The regulars, mostly fugitives from Sedan, were in the proportion of one in nine; but even out of this unpromising material a very formidable army might have been obtained with a fair amount of discipline. There was, however, a strong republican feeling amongst them; they did not yield a willing obedience to superiors; they thoroughly distrusted those in command; and this, coupled with the want of good officers, went far to neutralize the efforts of the government.

Simultaneously with the formation of armies, irregular corps of volunteers, or franc-tireurs, began to spring up all over the country. Many of these were expert marksmen, and caused great annoyance to the Germans by cutting off their convoys, carrying out night surprises, and lying in wait and falling unexpectedly on their outposts or rearguard. Many others were merely highwaymen under a different title, who shot and plundered friend and foe alike. On the ground that these franc-tireurs wore no distinctive uniform, and had no regular officers, the Germans claimed the right, under the laws of war, of treating them as unrecognized combatants, trying them by drum-head court-martial, and shooting them as soon as captured. In fact, the whole policy of the Germans, at this time, seems to have been marked by extreme although necessary severity. Their rule was that every town or village where one or more of the inhabitants fired upon their troops, or took part in the defence, should be burned down; that every man taken in arms who was not, according to their notion, a regular soldier, should be shot at once; that where there was reason to believe that any considerable portion of the population of a town actively sided against them, all able-bodied men should be treated with merciless severity. A squadron of German cavalry and a company of infantry took up their quarters in Ablis, a village of 900 inhabitants, just off the railway from Paris to Tours. During the night the inhabitants, giving way to a patriotic impulse, with the aid of franc-tireurs attacked the sleeping men, killed several, and captured or dispersed the rest. The next day the German general sent a force which burnt Ablis to the ground, and a neighbouring village from which the franc-tireurs had come. The threat, by the French, of reprisals upon the captured hussars, alone prevented more of the able-bodied men of the place from being shot. This was but one of numberless instances. A Bavarian detachment in the neighbourhood of Orleans burned down five villages in twelve days. Thus the mode of warfare which was pursued in the days of Louis XIV. and Frederick II., in 1870 was again found necessary. The Prussian armies should have been the last in the world to treat with severity irregular warfare; for in 1806 Prussia collapsed from the absence of that spirit of national resistance which in 1807 those at the head of affairs, both in the civil and military departments, did everything in their power to revive. At that time Spain showed a sagacious example of resistance to an invasion, which the military leaders of Prussia—Scharnhorst, Gneisenau, Clausewitz—all urged their countrymen to emulate.

Gneisenau even went to Spain to fight against Napoleon. The new military system, then inaugurated in Prussia, was an attempt to organize popular resistance to the enemy, as far as this was possible in an absolute monarchy. Every able-bodied man was to pass through the army, and to serve in the landwehr up to his fortieth year; the lads between seventeen and twenty, and the men between forty and sixty, were to form part of the "landsturm," or *levée en masse*, which was to rise in the rear and on the flanks of the enemy, to harass his movements, intercept his supplies and couriers, and to employ whatever arms it could find, and whatever means were at hand to annoy him. "The more effective these means the better." Above all, they were to *"wear no uniform of any kind,"* so that the landsturmers might at any time *resume their character of civilians,* and remain unknown to the enemy." It was proposed more than once that the Prussian "landsturm ordinary" should be printed and issued to each franc-tireur as his guide-book, by which, upon his capture, he could at least show the Prussians that he had only been acting upon the instructions issued by their own king.

With the view of protecting these guerilla troops as much as possible, on the 1st of November it was decreed by the French government, that from that date every corps of franc-tireurs, or volunteers, should be attached to an army corps on active service, or to a territorial division; and they were strictly prohibited acting independently or beyond the assigned limits, under penalty of being disarmed and dissolved.

By the imposition of a fine of a million francs upon any department in which bands of franc-tireurs should be met with, the German authorities strove to keep down the perilous annoyance. On every town which fell into their hands after resistance offered, they also made heavy requisitions in money. Under these circumstances, and remembering what had happened at Ablis and elsewhere, it is not surprising that the local municipalities sometimes evinced more prudence than courage.

In the night of the 26th to the 27th September, General Polhès, the commandant of the military division of Orleans, suddenly turned out the garrison, and in hot haste took his departure southwards. The Prussians were coming. Next day it was discovered that they were not coming; that there were only a very few of them in the neighbourhood, who certainly were not advancing on Orleans. So General Polhès came back. A couple of hours after his departure, however, two regiments of French cuirassiers had arrived in Orleans from Blois, who, finding no one to give them orders, and hearing that the commander had retreated, also returned. In the forest of Orleans about 800 men, apparently forgotten, had been left without any orders. All this evidence of haste naturally spread alarm: the consequence was that the railway authorities went off with their rolling stock towards La Ferté and Beaugency, and those connected with the telegraph carried off their apparatus. The prefect, thus deprived of the means of recalling the runaway garrison, managed at last to press a one-horse chaise into the service of the state, to convey to the general letters informing him that a spontaneous deputation was about to start for Tours to ask of the government a general able and willing to defend the forest of Orleans and its environs. Meanwhile the money in the banks and public money-chests had all been removed; the municipal council had met and protested against the abandonment of the city; and all was confusion and fear.

The whole military and political system of France was in fact at this time in a state of hopeless confusion, without a directing head to set it right. The arrangement which gave the prefects the military command of their respective departments, was producing its natural results in disconnected and useless efforts and conflicting authority. Marseilles and Lyons were threatened with a red republican insurrection, which was only prevented by the good sense and patriotism of the masses. At Grenoble, General Monnet, a Crimean veteran, was, at the instigation of a few riotous citizens, deposed from his command of the garrison and imprisoned. The prefect of Lyons, without a shadow of justification, arrested General Mazure, in command of the troops in the city, and because the senseless act was approved by his colleagues of the government delegation at Tours, Admiral Fourichon resigned the portfolio of War. On the other hand, thirteen departments banded together to demand the nomination of a general of independent authority, to organize the defence of the western provinces. Here and there might be heard murmurs of revenge, and in certain districts corps were formed which the government would fain have dignified with the name of armies. But there was no man to stir up popular enthusiasm, or turn it to account; and France merely waited, every day increasing her peril. With an enemy 700,000 strong in their country, the French forces were without a commander-in-chief! No energetic man fit to be endowed with supreme authority, and capable of reducing the chaos to order, was forthcoming. Bazaine, the only man thought to be equal to the present emergency, was closely besieged in Metz, and with him were Canrobert, L'Admirault, Jarras, Coffinières, Leboeuf, and Bour baki. MacMahon was a prisoner at Wiesbaden, Uhrich was bound down by his parole, while Trochu, Vinoy, and Ducrot were busy defending Paris. Large forces were being concentrated both on the Loire and the Rhône, but no one had been yet appointed, or even nominated to command them. The ministry of war, by Fourichon's resignation, was vacant, and M. Cremieux, an amiable, easy lawyer, minister of justice in the Provisional Government, was acting war minister. His appointment, at such a crisis, was very unsuitable, and there were loud demands for transferring the war administration to a commission composed of MM. Glais-Bizoin, Laurier, Steenackers, Frayssinet, Le Cesne, and Alphonse Gent. The nation was becoming absolutely frantic with impatience and despair at the inaptitude of those who had the direction of affairs, and at the utter demoralization, both civil and military, which was spreading through every department.

In these circumstances M. Laurier, the acting manager for the department of the Interior, a man of considerable capacity, devoted to the cause of the nation, and faithful to the trust reposed in him by M. Gambetta, his chief, thought that the moment had come when the government of Paris should be informed of the serious state of things. Two words, translated "Come at once," were addressed by him to Gambetta, and intrusted to the carriage of a "pigeon traveller." The minister of the Interior knew his agent well. Without delay he consulted with his colleagues, who all felt convinced that his presence at Tours was indispensable, and that he ought to proceed thither immediately.

M. Léon Gambetta, the young barrister who was thus destined to play such an important part in the struggles of his country, won a seat in the Chamber of Deputies in 1869, as one of the members for Paris, and distinguished himself by his bold attacks on the imperial policy, and his advocacy of democratic principles. A native of the south of France, but of Genoese family, he was endowed with all the ardent physical and moral qualities of that passionate Italian race. His eloquence and capacity for business were proved by many successes at the French bar, achieved by the time he was thirty-two years of age; but he came first into public note as counsel for some of the accused under the government prosecutions of 1868, against the promoters of the subscription for a monument to Baudin, one of the members of the National Assembly killed in the street-fighting after the *coup d'état* of December, 1851.

For fully a week did this energetic young statesman have to wait in Paris for a favourable opportunity of starting. Morning after morning the Place de Saint-Pierre at Montmartre was thronged by people eager to witness his departure, and morning after morning pilot-balloons were sent up, in order to ascertain the direction of the aerial currents; but the wind kept persistently in the west, and would probably have carried the balloon into the parts of France occupied by the enemy, and possibly into Germany itself, had the attempt been made to ascend. At length it changed to the south-east; and at eleven o'clock on the morning of Thursday, October 7, M. Gambetta, accompanied by his secretary and the aeronaut Trichet, ascended in the *Armand Barbès*, carrying with him an immense quantity of letters and several pigeons. During the night, however, a contrary breeze sprung up. On Friday morning the aeronaut in charge of the balloon, believing they were not far from Tours, allowed the machine to descend—but only to find out that they were hovering over Metz, two hundred miles away to the east. The Prussian troops fired volley after volley at the travellers. The balloon was made to rise again, but not a moment too soon, for already some half dozen balls had pierced the car; and even one of the cords which attached it to the balloon was cut, and had to be spliced by the minister himself, who was slightly wounded in the hand. All through Friday the travellers made little or no progress, but on Saturday, at daylight, they descended in the neighbourhood of Montdidier, a small town about four leagues from Amiens, and one league off the railway between it and Paris. M. Gambetta was here met by a gentleman who conveyed him in his carriage to Amiens, whence he shortly after departed for Rouen, where a great demonstration was made by the national guard and the populace, and at the railway station the following address was presented to him:—"Illustrious Citoyen Gambetta; self-sacrifice is everywhere, but energy, foresight, and management are wanting. Raise up these, and the enemy will be driven forth, France saved, and the republic founded definitively and for ever. Vive la France! Vive la Republique!" M. Gambetta made a stirring reply, addressed specially to the people of Normandy, and concluding with the words, "If we cannot make a compact with victory, let us make a compact with death." Immediately after he left for Tours. Here the enthusiastic republican was unpleasantly impressed with the aspect of the place, the number of officers and soldiers idling about the cafés, and the absence of that stern concentration of thought on one object which he left behind him in Paris. He also found that little had been done, that there was a lack of resource and vigour ill befitting the gravity of the crisis; and it was with ill-concealed displeasure that he appeared at the Prefecture window in answer to the clamorous crowd below. In a few brief words he acknowledged the honour done him and, deprecating demonstrations, concluded as follows:—"Let us work and fight. I bring you the instructions and decisions of the Paris government. As I cannot speak to you all, I have written. In an hour's time you will be able to read the object of my mission. Once more, gentlemen, let us work and fight, for we have not a minute to spare. Everyone to his post. 'Vive la Republique!' " He at once held a council with his colleagues, and at night a decree was published, postponing the intended elections for a National Assembly, chiefly because twenty-three departments were more or less in the hands of the invader. Simultaneously with the decree, he issued the following circular:—

"By order of the republican government I have left Paris to convey to you the hopes of the Parisian people, and the instructions and orders of those who accepted the mission of delivering France from the foreigner. For seventeen days Paris has been invested, and offers the spectacle of two millions of men who, forgetting all differences to range themselves around the republican flag, will disappoint the expectations of the invader, who reckoned upon civil discord. The revolution found Paris without cannon and without arms. Now 400,000 national guards are armed, 100,000 mobiles have been summoned, and 60,000 regular troops are assembled. The foundries cast cannon, the women make 1,000,000 cartridges daily. The national guard have two mitrailleuses for each battalion. Field-pieces are being made for sorties against the besiegers. The forts are manned by marines, and are furnished with marvellous artillery, served by the first gunners in the world. Up till now their fire has prevented the enemy from establishing the smallest work. The enceinte, which on the 4th of September had only 500 cannons, has now 3800, with 400 rounds of ammunition for each. The casting of projectiles continues with ardour. Every one is at the post assigned to him for fighting. The enceinte is uninterruptedly covered by the national guard, who from morning until night drill for the war with patriotism and steadiness. The experience of these improvised soldiers increases daily. Behind the enceinte there is a third line of defence formed of barricades, behind which the Parisians are found to defend the republic—the genius of street fighting. All this has been executed with calmness and order by the concurrence and enthusiasm of all. It is not a vain illusion that Paris is impregnable. It cannot be captured nor surprised. Two other means remain to the Prussians—sedition and famine. But sedition will not arise, nor famine either. Paris, by placing herself on rations, has enough to defy the enemy for long months, thanks to the provisions which have been accumulated, and will bear restraint and scarcity with manly constancy, in order to afford her brothers in the departments time to gather. Such is without disguise the state of Paris. This state imposes great duties upon you. The first is to have no other occupation than the war; the second is to accept fraternally the supremacy of the republican power, emanating from necessity and right, which will serve no ambition. It has no other passion than to rescue France from the abyss into which monarchy has plunged her. This done, the republic will be founded, sheltered against conspirators and reactionists. Therefore, I have the order, without taking into account difficulties or opposition, to remedy and, although time fails, to make up by activity the shortcomings caused by delay. Men are not wanting. What has failed us has been a decisive resolution and the consecutive execution of our plans. That which failed us after the shameful capitulation at Sedan was arms. All supplies of this nature had been sent on to Sedan, Metz, and Strassburg, as if, one would think, the authors of our disaster, by a last criminal combination, had desired, at their fall, to deprive us of all means of repairing our ruin. Steps have now been taken to obtain rifles and equipments from all parts of the world. Neither workmen nor money are wanting. We must bring to bear all our resources, which are immense; we must make the provinces shake off their torpor, react against foolish panics, multiply our partizans, offer traps and ambushes to harass the enemy, and inaugurate a national war. The republic demands the cooperation of all; it will utilize the courage of all its citizens, employ the capabilities of each, and according to its traditional policy will make young men its chiefs. Heaven itself will cease to favour our adversaries; the autumn rains will come, and detained and held in check by the capital, far from their homes, and troubled and anxious for the future, the Prussians will be decimated one by one by our arms, by hunger, and by nature. No, it is not possible that the genius of France should be for evermore obscured; it cannot be that a great nation shall let its place in the world be taken from it by an invasion of 500,000 men! Up then in a mass, and let us die rather than suffer the shame of dismemberment! In the midst of our disasters we have still the sentiment left of French unity, and the indivisibility of the Republic. Paris, surrounded by the enemy, affirms more loudly and more gloriously than ever the immortal device which is dictated to the whole of France:—'Long live the Republic! Long live France! Long live the Republic, one and indivisible.'"

While the minister of the new French republic was careering through the clouds in a balloon, another and more celebrated republican was hastening from an opposite direction to meet him. Till lately Garibaldi had been virtually a prisoner in his island home, the Italian government keeping a vigilant eye on him. Ever since the fall of the empire, however, it had been his anxious desire to come to the assistance of the newly declared republic. His services in the field were at once offered, but the reply of the delegate government to his offer had been delayed. A brief but characteristic letter to his son-in-law, M. Canzio, explains his position in the meantime:—

"CAPRERA, *September* 13, 1870.

"My dear son—From the French government I have not received any reply, and that rubbish (*quella robàccia*) which calls itself the government of Italy, holds me prisoner."

"G. GARIBALDI."

The pope's temporal power, however, had fallen before the soldiers of Victor Emmanuel. Rome had become the Italian capital; and if the Italian cruisers still hovered round Caprera, at least Garibaldi found no great difficulty in eluding their vigilance, and escaping to France in what was there known as a *yack*. He arrived in Tours the same day as Gambetta (October 9), and so unexpectedly, that no preparations had been made for his reception. On the news of his arrival becoming known, however, a large number of franc-tireurs assembled before the prefecture window, at which the general presented himself, and in reply to the enthusiastic cheers with which he was greeted, said:—"My children, your welcome and that of your brothers overwhelms me. I am only a soldier like yourselves. I come to place myself among you, to fight for the holy republic!"

Garibaldi brought with him a name, but little more, to the aid of the republic he loved. The liberator of Italy, whose kindly face, loose grey cloak, and scarlet shirt, were familiar to every child in Christendom, more fitly represented the idea of a republic than any other man in Europe; and it was hoped that his presence in France at this time would give to the popular rising throughout the country an impetus, such as the appeals and proclamations of the new government had failed to impart. The state of his health, however, totally unfitted him for regular warfare; he knew little of the duties of a general in command of a large army; and he was looked on as the most dangerous and wicked of men by a large portion of the French, and by such persons as Colonel Charette and the pontifical zouaves, whose aid in this moment of need had also been tendered to and accepted by the French government. Singularly enough, Colonel Charette was also at Tours on this memorable day, exercising his troops, fresh from the defence of the pope.

To General Cambriels, who commanded in the east, Garibaldi was despatched to Besançon, to take command of the free corps and of a brigade of mobiles in the Vosges. He carried a strong letter of recommendation from Gambetta, and he seems to have been received with the utmost consideration by the civil and military authorities, as well as with great enthusiasm by the people.

M. Gambetta at the head of affairs, issuing commissions to parties so antagonistic as Garibaldi and the champions of the temporal power, offered to the imagination a strange, if not grotesque, combination of circumstances. But although he and his curious allies or subordinates were all animated with the most intense desire to benefit France, it seemed impossible that elements so discordant should long cohere, unless welded together for a time by a success which they shared in common. At present a bright spot in the fortunes of France was nowhere visible; but the courage and resources of her people were great, and their feelings of hatred against the invaders intense; and in these circumstances it was impossible to say what change to the better might not yet take place. Even a small advantage gained over a German force in a fair fight, might have the effect of reviving the confidence of the French, and inciting them to put forth the great power they undoubtedly possessed. With all the energy of which he was capable, M. Gambetta set about organizing armies in all the provinces of France, admonishing prefects, displacing and appointing generals, and showing himself whereever his presence could stimulate flagging patriotism or remove the depression caused by reverses. He issued a decree, establishing four military *régions*: 1, the Northern, to be commanded by Bourbaki, at Lille; 2, the Western, with General Fiereck commander, and Le Mans for headquarters; 3, the Central, commanded by General Polhès, at Bourges; 4, the Eastern, commanded by General Cambriels, at Besançon. Besides these, General La Motte Rouge on the Loire, General Esterhazy at Lyons, Count Keratry in the west, and Garibaldi in the east held distinct commissions; eight in all, acting independently of each other. The wonderful energy thus displayed by M.

Gambetta had a very inspiriting effect on the country, and the despair almost universally depicted on the countenance of French patriots shortly before gave way to hope.

Meanwhile the Prussians, on their part, were carrying out a preconcerted programme in their movements to the north and south of Paris, and in the east of France. The whole district between Paris and Orleans was daily scoured by them for requisitions. At Toury a large force under Prince Albert of Prussia protected the operations for supplying the army of Paris, and an immense quantity of provisions, sheep, and cattle had been collected here from the plains of La Beauce.

Early in October the efforts of the French to raise an army behind the Loire had produced some little result; and on the 5th General Reyan, having re-occupied Orleans, which General Polhès had abandoned so hastily some ten days before, pushed northwards to Arthenay and Toury with 10,000 men against the German foraging forces. An engagement took place at Toury, which lasted from seven a.m. till twelve. The German artillery dismounted several of the French guns, but by his great superiority of numbers General Reyan obtained an easy victory, and pursued the enemy for several hours. About fifty prisoners were taken, and a number of cattle and sheep, which the Germans were unable to carry with them.

Such a sign of life on the part of the army of the Loire gave some little uneasiness to the German commander at Paris; and to extinguish this first gleam of success, which was already exciting new enthusiasm in the country, the first corps of Bavarians under Von der Tann, which had arrived last at Paris from Sedan and had been purposely held in reserve, was now therefore ordered to march southwards to discover the movements of the enemy. It was strengthened by half the infantry of the twenty-second Prussian division, and by the cavalry divisions of Prince Albert and Count Stolberg, which were already in the district.

There was a more direct line of railroad than that through Orleans to Tours, diverging to the westward of it at Bretigny, and running through Châteaudun and Vendôme. This line it was necessary to watch with cavalry, in order to cover the right of Der Tann. It was the advanced guard of a column sent for this purpose which, on the night of the 7th, was surprised and cut up by the franc-tireurs at Ablis, about thirty-three miles from Paris, and which led to the destruction of that village on the following day, as stated in the early part of the chapter.

Von der Tann marched from his late quarters about Longjumeau on the 6th, and on the 8th gained Etampes, which had been held for some days previously by the foraging party driven out from Toury, twenty miles further off, by General Eeyan, on the 5th. The latter had fallen back a day's march from Toury, after the trifling success reported, and left his advanced guard of a brigade of troops at Artenay, the next large village to the south. The officer in command, General de Longuerue, seems to have kept no better look-out than those who suffered for their carelessness at Wissembourg and Beaumont. Early on the morning of the 10th the Bavarians were close upon him, and soon began to drive his troops southwards. Ignorant of the enemy's strength, he hastened to support his advanced guard with about 10,000 men, all that he had ready to his hands. Probably Der Tann's advance was mistaken for a separate and isolated detachment. At any rate, the raw French troops were soon engaged with a body of Germans of immensely superior strength, and although they fought desperately for several hours, they were of course overcome, and, with the loss of many prisoners and some guns, forced back towards Orleans, twelve miles from the scene of the morning's action. General Longuerue and a large body of the fugitives gained the forest of Orleans, where, awaiting reinforcements, they resolved to defend themselves.

The army of the Loire, now under the chief command of General La Motte Rouge, numbered at least 60,000 men. Of these, 15,000 had been left the whole of this day to withstand a force three times their numerical strength, and possessing six times their effective value as a military body, while 45,000 were idle, within easy reach of the battle-field. Although it was well known that the Germans were coming southwards by forced marches, no measures seem to have been taken to signal their approach, or to assemble reinforcements on any particular spot. The roar of the artillery in the battle of the 10th was distinctly heard in Orleans, and to bring out the mobile guard the tocsin was rung all day. In the course of the afternoon and throughout the night La Motte Rouge arranged to get together about 40,000 troops of all descriptions, including regulars, garde mobile, the foreign legion, and the pontifical zouaves; and with these he determined to prevent, if possible, the further advance of the enemy.

The renewed engagement began early on the morning of the 11th, and lasted nearly all day. The occupation by the French of the forest of Orleans, by which they obtained the cover of the wood, proved some compensation against the superior artillery of the Germans, and towards evening gave the affair the character of a skirmish rather than of a battle. At eleven o'clock the Prussian vanguard was in position at La-Croix-Briquet, between Artenay and Chevilly, close to the railway line and the main road, which passes through the village. The other corps were placed towards Artenay, facing the borders of the forest of Orleans.

The French, advancing from Chevilly and Cercottes, took up a line to cover their retreat on the forest, and extending in the direction of Orleans. They occupied the villages of Le Vieux, Cercottes, Salan, and the château of Les Quatre-cheminées and that of La Vallée, nearly reaching Orleans.

The two armies were soon engaged along theü whole line, and the fighting was well sustained by both. The Bavarians, however, gradually gained ground. Their artillery, the arm in which the French were deplorably weak, approached nearer and nearer, and occupied the best positions. The woods between Cercottes and Chartan and the village of Salan were fiercely contested, but ultimately captured. The bloodiest part of the day was the afternoon. About 3 p.m. the French were giving way on all sides towards Orleans, but at St. Jean de la Ruelle, a far-stretching suburb on the north, they made a last and desperate stand. From four till seven the fighting went on; and it can only be compared to the storming of Bazeilles. The German troops were fired on from the interior and the roofs of all the dwellings, and from the church tower; and several houses at different points were set on fire. While the great body of the Bavarians now advanced in front, the Prussian infantry division undertook a flank movement, supported by the cavalry, who could not, however, get speedily through the vineyards and narrow roads. When the bulk of the French, mobiles and franc-tireurs, saw the danger they were in of being outflanked, most of them discharged their guns at haphazard, and a panic set in, during which 3000 prisoners were made, and three guns taken.

As the conflict drew close to the city of Orleans, the shells reached the houses, and the confusion and terror was extreme. Soldiers and artillerymen crossed the Boulevards close to the railway. Their route was stopped by mobiles, but they continued their retreat, and the terrified inhabitants ran in all directions, exclaiming, "Les Prussiens! Les Prussiens!" Reinforcements arrived in the town while the battle was going on; but instead of proceeding to the field, they idled in the streets and cafés, the officers playing cards and the men roaming at discretion. When the flying army began to pass, those men hastened to join the rout, flung away their arms or broke them, and crossed the bridge over the Loire. Fortunately the principal columns of the French force had already retreated without confusion on La Ferté St. Aubin, at Olivet, on the little river Loiret. During the battle the regulars behaved very ill, throwing away their weapons and scampering off as if in panic; the mobiles, the foreign legion, and the pontifical zouaves fought nobly, having contended for nine hours continuously with forces in every way superior.

At eight o'clock the Germans entered the city. The municipal council was sitting at the Hôtel de Ville, intent on taking some decisive steps; the prefect Pereira, and the bishop, Monseigneur Dupanloup, met the Germans at the Faubourg Bannier, and tried to arrange a basis for negotiations. All the works of defence prepared during the last few days had now been abandoned at the approach of the enemy, and it was evident that peaceful arrangements alone could save the place from devastation.

On the 13th, the morning after the occupation, General von der Tann demanded from the mayor a contribution of 1,000,000 francs in specie, to be paid in twenty-four hours, but subsequently consented to accept provisionally 600,000 francs. Monseigneur Dupanloup wrote to the king of Prussia, praying for the remission of the remaining 400,000, in which, however, the prelate was not successful. Another demand was made of 600 cattle, 300,000 cigars, and all the horses in the town. The soldiers were billeted on the inhabitants, and the jewellers' shops and *objets de luxe* were strictly respected.

On the following day the German commander issued the following proclamation:—

"French Citizens,—As I wish to alleviate as far as in my power the fate of the population visited with the evils of war, I appeal to their good sense, in the hope that the sincerity of my words will not fail to open their eyes to the existing state of things, and determine them to range themselves on the side of the reasonable party, desirous of making peace. Your late government declared war against Germany. Never was a declaration of war more frivolous. The German armies could do nothing else than reply to it by crossing the frontier. Another government succeeded. It was hoped that it would restore peace. It has done nothing of the kind. And why? It feared to render itself impossible, and under the pretence that the conditions proposed by the German army were not acceptable, it preferred to continue a war which can only lead to the ruin of France. And what are the conditions of the victorious army, which it was deemed impossible to accept? The restitution of provinces which belonged to Germany, and in which the German language still prevails, in the towns as well as in the country, viz., Alsace and German Lorraine. Is this claim an exaggerated one?

What claims would victorious France have made? You have been told that the aim of the operations of the German armies was to degrade France. This is simply a lie, invented in order to excite the passions of the masses. It is, on the contrary, your government which, by its way of acting, brings the German armies necessarily into the heart of France, brings ruin thither, and will succeed, if it persists, in really degrading *La Belle France*, which might be the best friend of the very nation whom she has forced to fight her.

"The General of Infantry,

"BARON VON DER TANN.

"Orleans, *October* 13, 1870."

With quickness and energy the German general had thus struck the only force that could venture to the relief of the capital, and inflicted on the army of the Loire a severe, though not fatal blow. Its commander would seem to have been insensible to the lessons of experience, which should have taught him that the Prussian tactics were not to rest on a defeat, trifling perhaps, as in the case of Toury on the 6th; and that after a repulse or disadvantage large bodies would certainly be moved up, to take a decisive revenge. And yet, instead of a combined advance of the whole army on and beyond Orleans, isolated columns were sent, and a few brigades left to sustain for a whole day an overpowering attack. General La Motte Rouge was now relieved of his command, and the army of the Loire looked forward to a brighter future under D'Aurelles des Paladines, a general on the retired list, but with the reputation of a resolute soldier and stern disciplinarian, qualities much needed at the time, and of the possession of which he soon gave proof.

At Orleans, the Germans had reached the line usually regarded as marking the boundaries between northern and southern France. The provinces bounding on the Loire—Touraine, Orleanois, Anjou, Poitou—have been styled the garden of France. "C'est le pays de rire et de no rien faire;" but Orleans is a comparatively poor and decaying city, notwithstanding its historic fame and its fifty thousand inhabitants.

The army of the Loire retired into comparative obscurity after its misfortunes at Orleans, and removed its headquarters to Bourges, which, as a great depôt and foundry for artillery, possessed special advantages for strengthening the French in this most essential arm. Large reinforcements were also daily coming in, which General d'Aurelles des Paladines was energetically preparing for offensive operations. His first order of the day to his troops was in substance as follows:—"Soldiers, what I ask of you, above all things, is discipline and firmness. I am, moreover, thoroughly determined to shoot any one who hesitates before the enemy; and should I myself fail to do my duty, I tell you to shoot me."

A short time after the investment of Paris was completed, the German commanders seemed disposed to abandon the system of "requisitions," which was better suited for an advancing army than for one needing regular supplies. The first steps in this direction, however, called forth proclamations forbidding the sale of food to the Germans upon any terms; and the prefect of the Eure announced that any one found disposing of corn, hay, or provisions to the enemy, would be liable to be tried by court-martial and sentenced to death. As the enemy, however, were not inclined to starve while there was anything to eat, they helped themselves to what they needed. The region north of Orleans, the so-called

Beauce, was the most fertile district they had as yet entered. It supplied Paris with enormous quantities of excellent wheat, and abounded in steam and water mills. Of oats also, there was a large supply, a great acquisition for the German cavalry. The conquest of Orleans, therefore, served a very important double purpose for the Prussians. It not only relieved the army investing Paris on the south from any fear of being molested, but the rich provinces now occupied furnished such an abundance of provision as to materially relieve the railway from Germany, which the invader was now able to use more exclusively for bringing up to Paris additional troops, siege guns, and all kinds of war *matériel*.

Von der Tann did not follow up his successes with the rapidity which might have been looked for. He lay at Orleans for some days after it was captured, the main body of his army occupying a fine of about thirty miles from Jargeau to Beaugency, while his cavalry scoured the valley of the Loire for provisions.

Between Châteaudun and the capital were the large forests of Rambouillet, Batonneau, Gazeleau, and Bienonvienne. Extending to the very neighbourhood of Versailles, these immense woods had been haunted from the first by franc-tireurs, who constantly harassed the German patrols, and from their leafy retreats had in the course of the last few weeks shot at and killed many a solitary vedette. Emboldened by impunity, these bands gradually attracted strong reinforcements from the south, until the whole district was infested by them. A small army was thus collected in the rear of the besiegers, not dangerous, indeed, but numerous and active enough to cause serious annoyance. General von Moltke had recently taken vigorous means to clear the country of them near Paris, in consequence of which they fell back from the neighbourhood of Versailles to the southern outskirts of the forest, where they partially fortified some of the towns, especially Chartres and Châteaudun. To prevent renewed annoyance to the besieging army of Paris, Von der Tann sent General Wittich from Orleans with 7000 infantry, a detachment of cavalry, and three batteries of artillery towards these towns, which had now become the headquarters of the franc-tireurs.

On the morning of the 18th of October the Prussians appeared before Châteaudun, which, though defended by only irregular troops, gave proof of the determined stuff of which these were made, and of what might have been done by them had they been combined under good leadership, instead of being scattered in petty bands over the whole country. About 4000 strong, they had blocked up every entrance to the town, and so skilfully posted themselves behind cover, that the Germans had to bombard the place for eight hours before they could venture on a more direct and effective attack. It was nine p.m. ere the thirty guns that had opened the work of destruction were ordered off to make way for the storming columns; but the progress of the assaulting parties was stopped by the most solid barricades yet encountered in this war of sieges. Behind a thick layer of fascines, a wall of earth was heaped up five feet high and three wide. The earth was backed by stones and felled trees, to give additional solidity to the whole, and to form a sort of breastwork on the top. This formidable obstruction, lined with dense rows of Chassepots, proved impregnable to the infantry who advanced, drums beating, with levelled bayonets. After one or two vain attempts to get at the defenders, the artillery was set to work again, with like results; its shells bursting in the earthworks and doing comparatively little injury. Orders were then given by General Wittich to beat in the side walls of the houses, and thus penetrating from one dwelling to another, to take the barricades in the rear. But even this did not discourage the French, who disputed the possession of each house, and did tremendous execution among the engineers, as with pickaxe in hand they smashed in the walls. By this time nearly half the town was in flames, and the defenders fought with the fury of despair. At eleven o'clock the combat seems to have ceased by mutual consent. The Prussians drew off their troops, and camped outside the town; the French, collecting their forces and the inhabitants, retreated unmolested and in good order, a fact which shows the deep impression which the desperate defence must have made upon the Prussians.

The loss of the French in killed and wounded was about 300; that of the Germans probably more, including Pastor Schwabe, chaplain to the 22nd Prussian division, who, while in attendance on the wounded, was killed in the streets of Châteaudun. The gallant defence was duly recognized by the Tours government, which declared in a decree of the 21st that Châteaudun deserved well of the country, and granted 100,000 francs in aid of the houseless inhabitants.

Chartres, the capital of the department of the Eure and Loire, and having one of the largest corn markets in France, was invested on the morning of the 21st by the Prussian division which had attacked Châteaudun, and detachments arriving from Rambouillet, Etampes, Angerville, and Patay. On finding that the German artillery had been planted before the city, the cure of Morancy begged permission to enter it in order to persuade the authorities to capitulate. General Wittich consented to grant a respite till 1 p.m., but the investment of the place was meanwhile proceeded with. Happily, the authorities agreed to a capitulation, by which half the garrison were allowed to retire; only 2000 mobiles being disarmed. The terms, more favourable than those obtained by any other place since the commencement of the war, showed that the Germans were not unwilling to avoid a repetition of the Châteaudun street fighting. The Prussian troops entered and enthusiastically cheered Prince Albrecht, before whom they defiled. It had been stipulated that all the shops should be kept open, and that the town should be exempt from requisitions. The streets were lighted up, and the inhabitants, who collected in considerable numbers, were perfectly quiet. On the following day the troops, whose demeanour was very becoming, mustered in the famous crypt of the cathedral, and by lamp-light inspected every part of that elaborate structure.

The principal military operations during October, other than those between Paris and Orleans, were connected with the eastern department of France. Along with another army, which entered French territory across the Upper Rhine about Freiburg, General von Werder, with the Prussian and Baden troops released from Strassburg, co-operated in occupying upper Alsace, and in besieging Belfort, Schlestadt, and Neu-Breisach. From an early period of the war a very considerable force, alternately known as the army of Lyons and the army of the Rhône, was said to be forming in the south and south-eastern departments. According to French reports this army now numbered 100,000 men, and was stationed between Belfort and Langres. To disperse such a force, if it really existed, the

German operations in this quarter were pushed forward with considerable energy. On October 6 the Baden troops, under General von Degenfeld, fell in with a French army under General Dupré, in the Vosges mountains between Raon l'Etape and St. Diey, about thirty miles south-east of Luneville. An engagement ensued, which lasted from 9 a.m. till 4 p.m., when the French were defeated and driven back on Rambervillers. Their force consisted of a few regular troops and a large number of franc-tireurs, altogether about 14,000 men. The Germans were only about 7000 strong, but their superior *morale* and the cavalry and artillery in which they vastly excelled gave them immense advantages. General Dupré was wounded, and lost 1500 in killed and disabled, and 660 prisoners; the Germans lost about 450. The villages of St. Rémy and Nompatelize and the wood of Jumelles were carried at the point of the bayonet by the Baden troops, but their victory was by no means easy, as the French fought gallantly and made three vigorous onslaughts.

The beaten army retreated to Epinal, the principal town of the department of the Vosges, but was driven out on the 12th; and the capture of Epinal cut off Lorraine from the rest of France. The franc-tireurs ran away, and the national guards made the best resistance they could after the mass of the army had abandoned the town. General von Werder then turned southward and gained Vesoul, from which he drove the French so rapidly as to cut them in two, sending part on to Besançon and Dijon, and part to Belfort, in the opposite direction.

General Cambriels, recently appointed by the Tours government to the command of the French army of the east, now advanced with what miscellaneous forces he could obtain, as far as Belfort. Fearing, however, to be cut off, he fell back on Besançon, where he met with Garibaldi, who had been appointed to the command of the irregular troops of the east. Garibaldi shortly afterwards removed his headquarters to Dole, where he issued a proclamation reminding those under his command, that "in the country occupied by the foreigner, every bush, every tree, should threaten him with a shot, so that his men may fear to leave their column or cantonments. Numerous guerillas would render very difficult, if not impossible, those requisitions which hitherto a simple enemy's corporal has presumed to make wherever he sets his foot." The Italian hero recalled, in conclusion, the defence of Monte Video for nine years against 28,000 men inured to war, although that town had then but 30,000 inhabitants. "Monte Video sold its palaces, its temples, its customs rights, present and to come, unearthed the old cannon which served as boundaries in the streets, forged lances to supply the place of missing guns; while the women gave to the country their last jewel. A. village of France has more resources than Monte Video had then. Can we doubt of the success of the national defence?"

There was no combined action between Garibaldi and Cambriels, whose forces the German general still pursued with relentless activity. Indeed, so far from acting in concert, after his first interview with Garibaldi, General Cambriels tendered his resignation, which was declined by Gambetta; but the government now accepted it. The appointment of the Italian leader to a command so important and apparently rival, was viewed by Cambriels as equivalent to superseding him, and he was certainly not alone in regarding Garibaldi with disfavour. The acceptance of his services by the government was looked upon by all good Catholics, especially those of Brittany, as the last bitter dregs of France's humiliation.

It is clear that momentary impulse rather than love or admiration had prompted the shouts of "*Vive* Garibaldi!" for, from his first arrival in the east, all manner of obstacles were placed in his way by those who should have assisted him. French officers viewed him with extreme jealousy, and even his own Breton auxiliaries thwarted him on every opportunity. There was no doubt that General Cambriels stood his ground as well as was possible with the material at his command; but he doubtless thought that, had the forces of Garibaldi, which had done nothing at all, been with him, his position would have been better. He shared largely, moreover, in the peculiar feelings of the Catholics towards Garibaldi, whose appointment, indeed, was soon found to be far more hurtful than advantageous to the French cause.

The successor of General Cambriels was, however, a more congenial colleague to the great guerilla chief. General Michel, who was now appointed to the command of the French forces in the east, was in sentiment a republican and a freethinker, and was one of the superior officers who managed to evade the capitulation of Sedan, by cutting his way through the Prussian lines at the head of 2000 horsemen.

Part of the Baden corps which had driven the French before them at St. Rémy on the 6th, next proceeded to invest Schlestadt, which was then subjected to a regular siege. After it had been vigorously bombarded several times, preparations were made for taking it by assault. For this purpose the south-west side was selected, as the water from the Ill could be diverted from the fosses, the ditches laid dry, and the town more effectively cannonaded. On the night of the 22nd the first parallels were easily raised at a distance of only 500 to 700 paces from the fortress, and the guns brought into position. But when the commandant saw the number of guns constantly increasing, new troops coming up, and no chance of relief, the avoiding of useless sacrifices became the subject of imperative consideration. Like his colleague at Strassburg, he had no engineer detachment, the artillerymen only sufficed for the manning of the guns; and he therefore capitulated on Monday afternoon, October 24, surrendering 2400 prisoners and 120 guns, with abundance of provisions and war material.

The siege of Neu-Breisach was commenced early in the month; but as there was some apprehension that all the disposable German force might be needed in the field by General von Werder, operations were not pushed forward against the little fortress with much vigour.

The chief interest of the war in the north centered round the two towns of Soissons and St. Quentin. Soissons occupies a strategic position of the first importance, and its value, in a military point of view, as commanding a passage over the Aisne, is shown by its fortunes in the campaign of 1814, when it was besieged three times. On the 13th of February, the Prussian General Chernicheff took it by a *coup de main*, when General Rusca, its governor, was killed by a cannon-shot on its antiquated ramparts. But on the same day the French retook it, and Chernicheff was compelled to withdraw. Napoleon, who attached the greatest importance to the possession of it, urged its garrison to hold out to the last; and if the French governor had been an Uhrich, Marshal Blucher and the army of Silesia, pursued by Napoleon across the Marne, would probably have been annihilated. But the governor capitulated, Blucher escaped, all the emperor's plans were overthrown, and the surrender decided his fall. Owing to what it has suffered by wars, Soissons has a modern look, although it is one of the oldest towns in France. It was here that Clovis established the throne of the Franks, and his successors were called kings of Soissons. The town and fortress were dominated by heights which formerly would have given no advantage to an assailant, but from which an enemy with rifled cannon could now destroy the whole place. When Toul fell, a number of the heavy guns which had been employed there were sent to Soissons; but though invested, it was not seriously bombarded until the 12th of October. The garrison made a stout resistance, sacrificing everything to the defence of the city. As one of the suburbs, the Faubourg of Rheims, covered the position of the Prussians, it was resolved to burn it, an operation which was effected on two successive evenings. The guns of the place protected the march of the incendiaries, who suddenly invested the high street of the faubourg. Amid a shower of bullets, the houses occupied by the Prussians were set on fire, and the French, in order to dislodge the enemy, were obliged to break open the doors with the butt-ends of their muskets. At length an enormous column of smoke shot up, and in less than an hour were destroyed more than 200 dwelling-houses, a large sugar refinery, a foundry, a mill, and the houses of the Sisters of Mercy, besides many fashionable villas. Several of the inhabitants lost their lives. On October 12 the heavy guns of the Germans opened in full force on the unfortunate city, and for four days and nights poured an incessant and furious stream of deadly missiles into it. The havoc done to the people and their houses was greater than to the fortifications, in which not more than one hundred men were killed during the bombardment. On the 16th the fortress capitulated, as two breaches opened on the previous day, and the threat of an assault by the Prussians, accompanied with the offer of honourable terms, gave resistless force to the entreaties of the population for immediate surrender. By its fall, 4700 prisoners, 130 guns, 70,000 rounds of ammunition, and a considerable sum in the military chest, passed into the hands of the Germans. A still more important acquisition by the surrender was the opening of a second line of railway from Châlons to Paris, as the direct line along the valley of the Marne was interrupted beyond Meaux by the destruction of the tunnels and bridges. Of the 22,000 Germans under the duke of Mecklenburg, which formed the besieging force, the greater number marched at once to Paris.

To St. Quentin, a town of some 40,000 inhabitants on the line between Paris and Lille, within ten miles of the fortress of Ham, in which the ex-emperor of the French had been a prisoner for six years, the Prussians sent a considerable party to obtain provisions. On Saturday, October 8, they were announced to be at a few kilomètres' distance from the town, on the road to La Fère. The drums beat to arms. The national guards hastened to their posts. The prefect, M. Anatole de la Forge, wearing a plain uniform of the national guard, appeared in the chief square of the town with a broadsword in one hand and a revolver in the other, and urged the population to fight. Four formidable barricades had been constructed during the previous fortnight in the Rue d'Isle—one on the banks of the canal; two at 200 mètres' distance from each other, in the interior of the town; and the fourth closing the road from La Fere to the top of the Faubourg d'Isle. Ten men could defend this barricade for a brief space. At the entrance of the town, close to the Grand

Canal barricade, which formed, indeed, a very strong position, the fight began, and while it lasted the prefect remained in the first post of danger. The Prussians, numbering about 750, intrenched themselves in the railway station. Taking advantage of the angles of the houses, and of the openings in the railway balustrades, they endeavoured to deploy as sharpshooters, but failed to reach the national guard, and suffered rather serious losses, every man who showed himself being shot. The struggle lasted from half-past ten until about two o'clock, when the Prussians retreated, taking the road to Marie. On October 21 they returned, at least 5000 strong, and with twelve field-guns they for half-an-hour cannonaded the town. No resistance being offered, they entered, and demanded 2,000,000 francs, 1,500,000 of which (£60,000) was paid—an exaction which, the Germans said, would have been very much less had not the town defended itself on the first occasion.

Clermont was captured, after a brief resistance, in the end of September. Beauvais, Breteuil, Montdidier, Vernon, Gisors, and Gournay were also occupied, and from these points the Prussians scoured the country for provisions for the army around Paris. Here and there the national guard showed in force; but in these cases a requisition was made that all arms should be given up, under penalty of death, and the result generally was that, a few hours afterwards, waggon-loads of muskets poured into the German camp. In Rouen, Amiens, and the larger towns, the inhabitants were kept in a feverish state of excitement by the frequent raids made in the places around. The national guards were called out, equipped, and drilled, and throughout all the northern departments very large enrolments of garde mobile took place, who displayed a better spirit than was shown in many parts of the country; but it needed a responsible master-hand to introduce organization and discipline amongst them. Considerable spirit was shown by the irregular troops of the northern departments, who on every opportunity harassed the Germans, and caused them the loss of a gun—the first sacrificed by them in the campaign—in an attempt to cut the railroad between Amiens and Rouen. Early in the month General Bourbaki, the able commander of the imperial guard, and right hand of Bazaine, as we shall see in the next chapter, found his way out of Metz and through the Prussian lines, in connection with a mysterious intrigue, the exact nature and object of which did not at the time transpire. Suffice it here to relate that he came over to England, to visit the empress at Chiselhurst, who, as it turned out, had not expected him, and had nothing to say to him. He recrossed into France, hoping that the Prussian staff would allow him to rejoin Bazaine; but as they threw obstacles in his way, he repaired to Tours, and placed his sword at the disposal of the Provisional Government, by which he was at once appointed to the command of the army of the north.

This general is of Greek origin, and his father, a staunch imperialist, rendered important services to Napoleon I. It was he who, in the Egyptian campaign of 1798—99, went over from France in a felucca, and aided by his nationality, succeeded in duping the English cruisers and entering Egypt. He brought Napoleon such news as decided him on returning immediately to Paris, to which circumstance he owed his throne. Seventeen years later the same faithful adherent was sent to inform Bonaparte of the decision of the Allies, that he should be transferred to St. Helena.

General Bourbaki especially distinguished himself by his cool and determined courage in that training-ground of all modern French generals—Algeria. In the Crimean war he served as general of brigade, and his gallantry at the Alma, Inkerman, the Malakoff, and the taking of Sebastopol, is too well known to be dwelt upon here. General of division in 1857, he took no mean part in the Italian war, and in 1870 was nominated commander of the second camp at Châlons. At the beginning of the war he was appointed to the command of the imperial guard, joined Marshal Bazaine, and was forced with him into Metz, where he remained until his extraordinary release. He was one of the French generals who received a decoration from the king of Prussia in 1864. No name was better calculated to restore confidence and inspire energy into the newly-enrolled troops throughout the North, to whom, on his appointment, he issued the following proclamation:—

"FRENCH REPUBLIC.

"Citizens, national guards, soldiers, and mobile guards,—I have been called by the minister of War to the military command of the region of the North. The task which devolves on me is a great one, and I should think it above my strength were I not sustained by the feelings of patriotism which animate you. All my endeavours tend to the creation, as speedily as possible, of an active army corps, which, provided with a war *matériel*, can take the field and proceed to the assistance of the fortresses, which I hasten to place in a good state of defence. As to me, who have loyally offered my sword to the government of the national defence, my endeavours and my life belong to the common work which it prosecutes together with yourselves, and in the moment of danger you will see me at the head of the troops who will soon be organized. To fulfil this difficult task, and to make our implacable enemy pay dear for each step on our territory, concord and confidence must reign among us, and our hearts must be animated with only one wish—to save and avenge our unhappy France. You may rely upon the most energetic co-operation and the most absolute devotedness on my part, just as I rely upon your courage and patriotism.

    (Signed)   "BOURBAKI.
"LILLE, *October* 29, 1870."

Brittany and the district west of Paris began in October to show signs of activity in contributing towards the national defence. Early in the month the command of the western levies was intrusted by the government to Count de Keratry, a Breton noble, who forthwith issued a proclamation urging his compatriots to emulate the noble example of their brethren of Brittany who at that moment manned the ramparts of Paris. The army of the West had not, it is true, assumed large proportions as yet; but with good organization it was sufficiently numerous to be no mean auxiliary to the army of the Loire, in any attempt for the relief of the capital. Before Count de Keratry took the command of the army of the West it had been a continued source of misfortune to the district, by its ill-disciplined and scattered bands offering resistance to the German requisition columns, which, while utterly ineffectual, brought down severe vengeance upon unoffending villages, several of which were ruthlessly destroyed. The count soon afterwards assumed the command of the irregular forces of the West, franc-tireurs, &c., for the organization of which he was well fitted by his influence and experience. General Fiereck was appointed over the western regular army.

Besides the several field armies organizing in the provinces in October, a corps of volunteer engineers was formed, to operate upon the German lines of communication. These companies—known as "The Wild Boars of the Ardennes," "The Railway Destroyers," &c.—were composed of artisans of all classes, and carried picks, crowbars, mining tools, hatchets, powder petards and cases, for pulling up rails, blowing up bridges, felling trees, and mining roads. Two companies were specially designed to guard them when at work, and one to collect provisions and attend generally to the commissariat. In at least one instance the operations of this corps were eminently successful, and several railway accidents were caused to the German trains. To stop these proceedings, however, the Prussians issued an order that the trains should "be accompanied by inhabitants who are well known and generally respected, and who shall be placed on the locomotive, so that it may be made known that every accident caused by the hostility of the inhabitants will, in the first place, injure their countrymen." At Nancy the first hostage was M. Leclair, the venerable president of the Court of Appeal. On another occasion, Procureur-general Isard was "invited" to make an involuntary journey. Escorted by two Prussian gendarmes, he had to mount the tender and travel to Luneville, where his colleague in that town took his place. The president of the Chamber of Commerce, a judge, and a barrister, also occupied in turn the post of danger.

While speaking of the "railway destroyers," it may be remarked that, although the war we are now reviewing gives no actual examples of the working of the well-known theory of Marmont, that mounted infantry should play a striking part in the warfare of the future, we see at least that the German cavalry would have found their movements in the interior of France paralyzed by the hostility of the armed bands which Lurked in every covert, had they not fallen upon the device of attaching to each brigade a detachment of riflemen, to assist in dispersing these secret enemies. The clearing and occupation of the country south of Paris was accomplished mainly by the aid of the Bavarian riflemen who were employed with the fourth and sixth cavalry divisions; and when, after the fall of Metz, Manteuffel advanced to occupy the north of France with the first army, his flank and front were kept clear by the first division under Göben, who carried similar small parties of riflemen with each of his brigades, and used them constantly in his occupation of villages and other inclosed posts. Such infantry, however active, would of necessity have been a heavy clog upon the movements of the horse, had they not been repeatedly hurried forward in country carts or other wheeled carriages. Indeed, the device was simply a rude expedient to meet an emergency for which the Germans were not prepared. Had the events of 1870 been fully foreseen, some such scheme would doubtless have been fallen upon as raising bodies of mounted riflemen for the express purpose of ridding the advanced guards from lurking franc-tireurs. There is the highest authority—that of the most successful of the generals who have used this modified form of cavalry on a great scale—for asserting that, had the French early in this war trained up a mass of horsemen such as those that followed Sheridan during the American civil war, instead of devoting their whole efforts to the collection of masses of raw infantry and artillerymen, they might have so threatened the line of railroad which fed the German host before Paris as to render a continued investment impossible. Few at least will doubt that such a body, acting upon the communications of the Germans, would have done more to hinder the conquest of the country than tenfold their numbers sent on foot to be fresh food for the enemy's powder.

That the month of October closed with far brighter prospects for France than it opened, was due mainly to the energy and indefatigable activity of M. Gambetta. From the date of his arrival at Tours he had virtually been *the* government of national defence. Indeed the various proclamations and decrees issued rarely bore even the signatures of his colleagues, MM. Cremieux, Glais-Bizoin, and Fourichon. That some of these decrees were in spirit extremely revolutionary there is no doubt; but it is equally certain that under the exceptional circumstances of the country they offered the best remedies for its misfortunes. They did not result in the salvation of France, because in the hour of need no great military genius arose to enforce them. Could the minister have relied upon a colleague in the field of equal daring and energy with himself, it would have fared hard even with the magnificent armies of Germany. The first decree of October, for a *levée en masse* of all men between twenty-one and forty years, ought in a month to have been answered by a number several times larger than any trained army which Germany could bring into the country; and with very moderate organization, numerical strength so vastly superior should have had a proportionate effect on the fortunes of the war. October, however, closed with at least 700,000 German soldiers on French territory, to oppose which there were not 250,000 organized forces outside Paris and Metz. Twelve fortresses of France—namely, Strassburg, Toul, Marsal, Vitry, Sedan, Laon, Lutzelstein, Lichtenberg, Weissemburg, Soissons, Schlestadt, and Metz—had been captured by the enemy; and Phalsburg, Bitsche, Paris, Thionville, Mézières, Montmèdy, Verdun, Longwy, and Neu Breisach were besieged.

One of the earliest and most questionable of Gambetta's decrees was that which abolished the laws of regular promotion in the army, and opened every grade to civil talent. With the most orderly army, such an experiment would be dangerous in the most favourable circumstances; it was especially so in the midst of such confusion. M. Gambetta thought, however, that the only hope of France was in the creation of entirely new armies out of the civil population; and while he betrayed no little distrust of the regulars, he lost no opportunity of praising and encouraging the new levies, upon whom he imagined all the hopes of his country now rested.

All provinces within a hundred kilomètres (about seventy miles) of the enemy's forces were placed under martial law, and in each a commission of defence was appointed to concoct plans of defence, to fortify the points most suitable for defensive purposes, and to direct the local forces. It was further decreed that camps should be formed at a distance of not less than two miles from each town where the troops of all arms mustered over 2000, and that officers and men alike, taking up their abode there, should not return to town without a special permission. In these camps they were to undergo severe drill, and other discipline, to fit them in every way for service. Another decree enjoined on the prefects of invaded or threatened provinces to see that the country was laid waste, and all carts, horses, cattle, and sheep removed to a distance. Soldiers quitting their posts, or flying before the enemy, were to be brought before a court-martial, and shot. Any commanding officer whose troops should be surprised by the enemy, or who should have advanced upon a position "without suspecting the hostile presence," was also to be brought before a court-martial. The authorities of every town were to defend the place, or to show sufficient reason for not doing so.

Another edict was issued for the purpose of establishing proper systems of information. Hitherto the authorities had literally been acting in absolute ignorance of the movements and intentions of the enemy, while the Prussians, by their widely-spread system of espionage and their innumerable cavalry scouts, kept themselves perfectly informed of the position and intentions of the French. The government now ordered every maire to employ throughout his commune gardes champêtres, workmen, &c., who should instantly report to him the approach and direction of any body of the enemy, with an approximate estimate of their force and composition; and that this information should be immediately despatched to the prefect, to be telegraphed to the government. Every maire who failed in these details was to be tried by court-martial.

In the earlier part of the month the conduct of the extreme republicans, who alone of all the French nation showed themselves devoid of patriotic feelings, paralyzed the efforts of the large towns. Imperialists, Legitimists, Orleanists, alike laid aside their partialities and prejudices, and combined with the government for the national defence. The extreme republicans alone preferred party to patriotism, caused dissension, sacrificed France, under pretence of saving her, and thus gave a dim presentiment of the terrible scenes which, in Paris, were to aggravate the horrors of the war at its close. Paris, Bordeaux, Rouen, Lille, Havre, all great centres of industry, nobly allowed nothing to interfere with the national defence; while Lyons, Marseilles, Toulouse, and Toulon were sources of weakness, rather than of strength, to the country. The establishment of communal institutions and of the extremest forms of republicanism were deemed matters of greater importance than the expulsion of the invader. Ardent republican though he was, so ashamed was Gambetta of the conduct of the Lyons republicans, that on receiving the delegates of a committee from that city he exclaimed, "Your commune of Lyons is a disgrace to France and a laughingstock to Europe. Out with you at once!"

To meet immediate claims, and supply articles necessary for the purposes of the war, the Tours government, on the 26th of October, contracted a loan of £10,000,000. The result of the subscription to it proved that if France was doomed to succumb in the war it would not be for want of means to fight, nor of the spirit to use them. In her then critical situation, with the capital invested, and over a score of rich departments terror-struck by Prussian legions, it was thought that a loan of this extent must be a failure. For the first time, therefore, a French loan was opened in a foreign country—England. Subscriptions were, nevertheless, invited in France, and in less than three days the result was an amount equal, in round numbers, to £3,750,000. When it is remembered that a large proportion of the country, the metropolis included, could take no share in the subscriptions, and that local loans to an enormous amount had been contracted in all quarters for purposes of defence, such a result was a striking proof of the internal resources of France, and of confidence in the credit of the state.

Throughout October the French government continually appealed to England and the various European cabinets for interposition or assistance. In an important interview with Lord Lyons on the 15th, the French delegate minister of Foreign Affairs suggested that England, either singly or in concert with other neutrals, should request Prussia to state the conditions of peace which she would accept; that France should then submit her views; and that the neutral powers should in a conference, or by exchanging notes, give out with authority what in their opinion were equitable terms of peace, and call upon both belligerents to accept them. M. de Chandordy seemed to think that both must of course listen to the voice of Europe; but as this was by no means probable, his suggestion was not adopted.

Count von Bismarck had indeed pretty plainly intimated already the extent of the German territorial claims; for in a short despatch to Count Bernstorff on the 1st October, in which he combated the statement of M. Favre, that "Prussia means to continue the war and to bring France back to the position of a power of the second rank," he said:—"The cession of Strassburg and Metz, which we seek in territorial connection, implies a reduction of French territory equal in area to the increase through Savoy and Nice, while the population of these provinces obtained from Italy is about 750,000 larger. When it is considered that France, according to the census of 1866, numbers 38,000,000 of inhabitants without Algiers, and with Algiers now furnishing an essential part of the French war forces, 42,000,000, it is palpable that a decrease therein of 750,000 effects no change in the importance of France as against foreign countries."

M. de Chandordy represented to Lord Lyons that, to these claims of Prussia, France could never submit. He added, that "he felt he was entitled to appeal to the rest of Europe for support. The time for good offices had passed. The powers should now speak to Prussia in a tone which could not be mistaken, and take measures to insure their being listened to." Lord Granville, however, replied that England was not prepared to support by force any representations they might make to Prussia; and further instructed Lord Lyons, should opportunity arise, to point out that her Majesty's government thought the rigid determination expressed by M. Favre, not to yield an inch of territory nor one stone of a fortress, was a great obstacle to peace.

But though the English government could not yield to the appeals of France, they took advantage of a circular of Count von Bismarck's respecting the danger of famine with which Paris was threatened, to make a formal suggestion that both belligerents should agree upon an armistice for the convocation of a French constituent assembly, which might decide the question of peace or war. This proposal Lord Granville pressed with great energy, and informed Count Bernstorff that M. Thiers, backed by the personal intervention of the emperor of Russia, had proposed to undertake the negotiation. Russia, Austria, Italy, and Spain joined in urging the armistice; Italy, indeed, appeared to desire even more decided intervention. M. Tissot again pressed Lord Granville to call on Prussia to state her terms of peace, "bring them within fair limits, and then communicate them to the French government." All the principal powers, however, were agreed in restricting the proposed negotiations to the question of an armistice.

In virtue of these proceedings, M. Thiers had his first interview with Count von Bismarck, at Versailles, on November 1, when the general arrangements for an armistice of twenty-four or twenty-eight days were agreed to. The main difficulty arose out of the revictualling of Paris, to which the Prussian chancellor ultimately consented, on condition that, as a "military equivalent," the Germans should have at least one of the Paris forts. The veteran French statesman had not expected this, and with considerable warmth he replied: "It is Paris that you ask from us; for to deny us the revictualling during the armistice is to take from us one month of our resistance; to require from us one or several of our forts is to ask for our ramparts. It is, in fact, to demand Paris, while we should give you the means of starving or bombarding her. In treating with us for an armistice you could never suppose its condition to be that we should give up Paris herself to you—Paris, our chief strength, our great hope, and for you the great difficulty, which, after fifty days of siege, you have not been able to overcome." M. Thiers then left to consult with M. Favre, who, in turn, took counsel with his colleagues of the government in the city. The result was, that on the following day, November 6, M. Thiers received instructions to break off the negotiations, and at once left the German headquarters. For a third time, therefore, the hopes of peace were frustrated, and both parties girded themselves for a war *à outrance*.

Considered in the light of subsequent events, the French committed a grave diplomatic blunder in refusing the terms offered by the Germans, and allowing the negotiations to be broken off on the question of revictualling Paris. The king of Prussia and his advisers consented to the armistice under the mistaken idea that there was no prospect of an efficient force being formed in any quarter for the relief of the capital. The French had up to that time been everywhere beaten, and were therefore supposed to be incapable of again showing any head in the field. On the contrary, the several armies forming in the provinces only needed time to render them, both in number and organization, extremely formidable to the Germans. With regard especially to the army of the Loire, twenty-eight days would have enabled D'Aurelles to complete his cavalry and artillery, to establish discipline, and to concentrate his army in a state of readiness for an immediate advance. The Breton levies would have been prepared to operate from the west in force, and aid in a simultaneous march to the capital. In order to keep the truce, Prince Frederick Charles, who was now on the way from Metz, would have been arrested at full twelve days' march from Orleans, so that whatever French forces could have been collected within one hundred miles of Paris during the armistice would have been free from immediate danger of the overwhelming German reinforcements which presently proved their ruin. We cannot see how the revictualling of Paris would have affected matters at all. The inhabitants would not have been any worse off at the end of the armistice, supposing they had obtained no new supplies, since there was at any rate plenty of food to last them for that time. If, therefore, the German armies would have been compelled to raise the siege in December at all, after an armistice, they would have been forced to abandon it whether Paris were revictualled or not.

The news of the failure of the negotiations produced a momentary feeling of regret and disappointment in most parts of France. On November 10, however, there occurred the first German reverse of any magnitude during the war, resulting in the defeat of Von der Tann and the retreat of the Bavarians from Orleans. This raised the hopes of the nation, gave a new light to the failure of M. Thiers' mission, and England and the neutral powers generally were bitterly denounced for having suggested a temporary cessation of hostilities. Many of the journals and prefects, especially of southern France, repudiated with scorn the idea of peace, or even of an armistice, until satisfaction had been obtained from Prussia for the injuries she had inflicted upon their country. Thus the *Progrès* of Lyons said that the idea of an armistice could only enter into the skull of a Prussian, and could only have been proposed by an Englishman. "It is only when the Prussian hordes are hunting for their food like wolves in our provinces that our felon ally (England) dares to dash her bucket of water upon the brasier of our patriotism. Now that the French nation is upon the point of turning the victories of our enemies into unprecedented disaster, the quaking thrones of this supreme resurrection are trembling upon their bases, and seek, by means of an armistice, to smother the threatening flame." The prefect of the Haute Garonne was equally opposed to a cessation of hostilities, and stated in a proclamation that "we will establish the republic upon the corpse of the last Prussian and the body of the last monopolist." The prefect of the Ain declared that, "whether the traitors are Prussians, or still dare to call themselves Frenchmen, the bullet and the axe shall render equal justice to both."

Lord Granville's despatch, urging the arrangement of an armistice, was, in the first instance, met on the part of Count von Bismarck by the intimation that any overtures for negotiations must be made by France; and that the benevolent offices of England were regarded with no less coldness by Germany may be gathered from the following remarks of the *Cologne Gazette*:—"The Gladstone-Bright ministry, and especially the Foreign Secretary, Lord Granville, unfortunately did not do its utmost to prevent the outbreak of this great war. Indeed, one may say not its least—viz., the public declaration that France had no right to commence this wanton war. This sin of omission is now, alas, too late admitted even by the English. We carry on this war in a certain degree for England, for had imperial France conquered in it, Napoleon would certainly have seized on Belgium, which he coveted more than the left bank of the Rhine. It would then have been seen how England defended Belgium, after formally assuming the protection of it; and Napoleon III. would certainly have gained what was his ultimate object in his powerful naval armaments—the humiliation of England, the revenge for Waterloo of which the French are always thinking. We willingly do justice to the considerations on which England now seeks to arrest the destruction of Paris. It is only a pity that England's prestige suffered so grievously through its cowardly attitude at the commencement of the affair. Per se, we should regret as much as anybody the destruction of a city inhabited by more than a million of women and children, and in which so many treasures of art and science, which can never be made good, are collected. The entry into Paris, however, is a necessity for the German army, and an event which cannot now be averted, especially after the fall of Metz. May the Parisians therefore come to their senses, and by the acceptance of reasonable conditions of an armistice and peace, release us from that lamentable necessity!"

The feeling throughout Germany during October was one of extreme disappointment at the prolongation of the war, which every one expected would have ended soon after Sedan. But it would have been erroneous to mistake this wish of a speedy cessation of hostilities for a disinclination to continue it, should that appear imperative. Notwithstanding that the military system of the country made war sensibly felt, yet such was the general confidence in the military and political leaders that, as these held the objects of the campaign were not yet attained, the people were willing to support them to the end. If the generals had not declared the recovery of Alsace and Lorraine to be necessary for the protection of the German frontiers, the vast majority in the country would have been in favour of concluding peace at once, and on the terms proposed by M. Favre; but as the German generals were, and indeed had been for the last hundred years, of the opposite opinion, the nation was determined to profit by the opportunity, and acquire the territory which was to enable them to ward off future invasions with a greater chance of success than hitherto. Count von Bismarck was but too accurate an interpreter of the thoughts of his countrymen when, in his negotiations with M. Thiers, he spoke of the probability of future collisions with France, and of the duty the Germans owed to themselves to prepare for coming attacks of the fiery Gaul. The French were now reaping the fruits of the treatment they had accorded Germany for centuries both in word and deed. The people were but too keenly aware how frequently they had been invaded in the past, and could not help remembering with what intense hostility they had been spoken of by nearly every political celebrity in France up to the very outbreak of the war. It was the knowledge of the inveteracy of this feeling on the other side of the frontier, coupled with the observation that the French even now deemed themselves invincible, which led popular feeling in Germany to look forward to another war in the wake of the one in which they were then engaged. Had the French admitted that they were beaten, and that they had better give up battling with Germany for the mere sake of *prestige*, they would perhaps not have been suspected of a design to resume the fray as soon as they could after the conclusion of peace. But with M. Gambetta declaring the final victory of France a matter of course, and indispensable to civilization to boot, the Germans asked—"What can we expect but to see them come down upon us whenever the opportunity occurs? And the contingency being so very probable a one, ought we not to guard against it by securing those military and territorial advantages commended by the generals, whose experience and judgment we have every reason to confide in? Is not every peace with the French merely an armistice while they do not renounce their old ambition; and should we not be actually encouraging them to attack us again were we to permit them to repeat the thing under the same favourable conditions as formerly?"

An extract from the Bremen *Weser Zeitung* is subjoined as illustrative of this state of popular feeling:—"It is remarkable what an important influence a single trait in the national character of the French exercises upon the destinies of Europe. The constitutional vanity of the French, their inability to realize and recognize unpleasant facts, becomes as terrible a scourge to themselves as to the nations around them. Vanity has stirred them up to a frivolous war, vanity prevents the restoration of peace. Very characteristic in this respect is that passage in M. Favre's last circular, in which he depicts the ravishing aspect France will wear when perishing amid the flaring halo of glory and renown. The consciousness of playing an imposing *rôle* before the world to a certain extent consoles him for the ruin of his country. But is ruin likely to follow the acceptance of the German terms? Will not the French remain a powerful, gallant, rich, and highly-gifted nation even after the forfeiture of their German provinces? And, instead of revelling in the prospect of fine tragical catastrophes, had they not better look realities in the face, consider the common-sense question how to get out of a bad job, and extricate themselves at as cheap a price as possible? All the statesmen of Europe have had to do this occasionally, and history mentions even some French ministers who capitulated when there was nothing left but to capitulate. But it is quite true, while other nations praise those of their statesmen who in the hour of defeat averted greater evils by timely concessions, the French have always called Talleyrand a traitor for procuring them the best terms possible after the discomfiture of 1815. Though Talleyrand saved all he could for them, the French, in their uncontrollable conceit, only look to what he was compelled to sign away, and therefore insist upon regarding him as a rascal. They have no Talleyrand now, no man sufficiently courageous to bend to the inevitable. Sheer compulsion alone can terminate the war. We know it, and are prepared for it."

About the same time the Prussian government issued an important manifesto in the semi-official *Provincial Correspondenz*. Considerable impatience was exhibited in Germany at the delay in the siege operations before Paris. After ascribing this delay to purely military reasons, the article went on to speak generally of the prospects of the war in these terms:—

"Natural as it is to wish for a prompt termination of the war, we are perhaps not wrong in seeing the finger of Providence in the retribution which the French are thus bringing in full measure upon themselves. It seems to be decreed that they are to empty the cup of bitterness to the dregs, and, by having their insolence thoroughly chastised, be weaned from their bellicose propensities and converted into better neighbours for the future.

"All of us would have been delighted had the last shot in this sanguinary contest been fired on the heights of Sedan. Yet there is no denying that had peace been concluded then and there, the idea of holding universal supremacy, so firmly rooted in the French mind, would have regained irresistible ascendancy the moment we left the country. Even now the majority of the French deem themselves unconquerable, and, indeed, unconquered. They have heard of nothing but of victories, with, perhaps, a few insignificant reverses now and then. They have accustomed themselves to pooh-pooh the fancy that their armies have been subdued, and tell you, with the most implicit confidence, that if he liked Bazaine might easily get out of Metz and crush the forces besieging it. They smile at the thought of Paris ever falling into our hands when it is defended by hundreds of thousands of mobiles, and attacked only by German soldiers. Last, not least, they will swear that Europe will come to the rescue of their holy city, and save what they are pleased to call the 'metropolis of the world.' With these hallucinations the French are consoling themselves in the present disastrous period of their history. Were peace to be re-established before they have been cured of their self-sufficiency, they would doubtless flatter themselves that they have not been vanquished at all—that the war might have been continued, and that if it has not been, its premature conclusion is mainly owing to the pusillanimity and treachery of those in power. With these intoxicating illusions filling their brains, so arrogant a people as the French would not wait long before they attempted to win back what they had lost.

"Only after the Parisians, and with them the entire population of France, have been humbled to the dust; only when the military strength of their country has been entirely broken, and the hope of creating fresh armies is everywhere annihilated—will they become conscious of the magnitude of their defeat, and perhaps perceive and remember that to invade a neighbour may be attended with unpleasant consequences to themselves."

That at this period (October) the Germans were sanguine of a speedy conclusion of peace, is shown by the fact that the pen with which Count von Bismarck was to sign the treaty was already prepared. Herr Bissinger, jeweller, of Pforzheim, manufactured out of massive gold an imitation of an ordinary stout goosequill. The quill itself was polished, in order that it might be more conveniently handled, but the feather closely resembled a real quill, every fibre being represented, while the back of the feather was thickly studded with brilliants, and below them a count's coronet and Bismarck's monogram were engraved. Besides the engraver and maker, two goldsmiths were engaged on it for five weeks. The gold used was of eighteen carats, and that part in which the brilliants were set was of twenty-one carats.

In acknowledging its receipt Count von Bismarck wrote:—"Your beautiful and very artistic present has been delivered to me by Herr Jolly. I feel some difficulty in knowing how to express my thanks for it. At a time when the sword of the German nation has performed such illustrious feats, you render the pen almost too much honour in making it so costly. I can only hope that the use to which you have destined the pen in the service of our country may conduce to its permanent welfare in a fortunate peace, and I can promise you that, with God's help, it shall in my hand subscribe nothing unworthy of German feeling and of the German sword."

Serious as were the consequences of the war for Germany, under a military system by which almost all the able-bodied male population were liable to be called away from their occupations, its effects upon the French were far more serious. A policy of prolonged though apparently hopeless resistance might, indeed, in the end have caused extreme perplexity to the Germans; but, on the other hand, it seemed as if the king of Prussia was not far wrong in his assertion that the social system of France was falling to pieces under the enormous pressure of disorderly war. It is not too much to say that no words could be too strong to describe the critical condition of the French cities and great towns, seeing that all the familiar phenomena (save one) of the first French revolution were showing themselves at Rouen, Lyons, Dijon, and Marseilles. The clubs, the mobs, the municipalities claiming to be supreme over every other authority, the wholesale imprisonment of priests and so-called reactionists, the rumours of conspiracy, and specially of conspiracy in the prisons, the popularity of newspapers of the class of the *Père Duchesne*, seemed a prelude to another reign of terror. One thing only was wanting. There was an almost complete absence of clamour for civil blood, and when all the rest was so like, it was natural to wonder at the difference. Had the humanitarian spirit which when nations are at peace shows itself in effeminate reluctance to inflict painful punishment, but which when they are at war fails to save them one drop of blood, at least achieved this? Were French mobs less murderous because they had grown to be more humane? or was it that attacks on life had been exchanged for attacks on property? In Lyons the manufactories were still at work, and the workmen were receiving the highest wages required by the rules of the International Union. But the manufacture was only continued through fear of the consequences of stopping it; and it appeared as if general bankruptcy must sooner or later show what strain socialist theories were capable of bearing. Lyons doubtless spun and wove silk for the whole world, and thus, in spite of the impoverishment of all foreign customers indirectly caused by the war, may have been better able than other manufacturing towns to bear up against the loss of the home market, so long as its commodities found access to sea. But some of the cities most seriously threatened by revolutionary fury were wholly engaged in manufacturing goods to be consumed within France itself. In this condition was the great city of Rouen, which, with its surrounding villages, barely maintained itself against the competition of Manchester in the best of times, with the assistance of duties still largely protective. Certain political economists, distinguished for peculiar tenderness to all the heresies of the working class, have argued that the share of profit which workmen associated in trade unions may wring from their employers, is greater than an older generation of economical teachers had supposed. But the new doctrine is at best only intended for times of prosperity, and we have yet to learn how an arbitrary rate of wages can be long exacted from a manufacturer deprived of customers. The moment at which calamitous war and socialist convictions are found in presence of one another in any country, may well be regarded with terror.

Deplorable as was the case of both France and Germany in an agricultural point of view, it would have been incalculably worse if the women had not been trained to do much of the farm work which in England devolves on men alone. Every tourist in Rhineland and the south of France has noticed, and deplored, the extent to which female labour is there employed—not only for the fighter tasks of weeding and hoeing, as with us, but for ploughing, reaping, and all the more important branches of husbandry. It was now seen that such a condition of things renders the country far better able to sustain the requirements of war than otherwise it could be. With us the sudden demand on so large a proportion of our male population would almost suspend all agricultural operations; for steam, although it reduces the number of hands employed, throws the work more than ever upon the men. We notice these facts from no desire to see the women of Great Britain converted into farm drudges; but merely to show that soil, climate, and social habits abroad have combined with custom to render southern countries less dependent upon male labour than can be the case with us.

CHAPTER XX.

The Great Strength of Metz—Complete Blockade the surest means of Capturing it—Treble Cordon thrown around it, and other Measures taken by the Germans—Detailed description of their Positions, and of those occupied by the French—Genial Feeling between the Foreposts for some time—The completeness of the Prussian Forepost System—Repose in the City in the first days of September—Excitement in the German Army when the victory of Sedan became known—The Disastrous News conveyed into Metz by General Wimpffen, and a Request made to Bazaine to Surrender the City—His Reply, and general disbelief of the News in Metz for some days—Proclamation of General Coffinières urging Resistance to the uttermost—Bazaine, at last, compelled to admit the Unwelcome News relating to Sedan to his Troops—Establishment of a Balloon Service for Postal Purposes—Novel Contrivances in their Manufacture—The "Spy" Mania in Metz—Capture and Execution of a real Spy—The "Intelligence Department" organized by the Germans to remove the stigma attached to a Spy—Efforts of the Metz Newspapers to keep alive the spirits of the Inhabitants—Chief Events in the City in September—The Relative Positions of General Coffinières and Marshal Bazaine—Organization of a Corps of Sharpshooters for Dangerous Service by the French—The Legion of Honour refused on Two Occasions—Life in the Besieger's Camp—General absence of Excitement— Burning of Nonilly by the Germans—Daring of Lieutenant Hosius and Fifteen Men—Discovery of Underground Electric Wires by the Prussians—General von Steinmetz relieved of his Command, and Prince Frederick Charles appointed sole commander of the Besieging Forces— Sortie and obstinate contest on September 22—Complete Victory of the Germans—More serious Sortie on the 24th—Severe fighting—Fruitless attempt of the French to Capture the village of Noisseville—Coolness of the Germans under Fire—Successful Foraging Expedition by the French on September 27—Fearful Scene in a Convent—The Monotonous Life within the City and its depressing effects on the Inhabitants—Review of the National Guard—Dissatisfaction at no real attempt to break through the Besieging Army being made—Bazaine thereupon determines upon a vigorous Sortie—The Battle of Maizières—Ruse of the Germans at the Château of Ladonchamps—Description of the Country and of the German Positions between Maizières and Metz—The French advance under the cover of a dense fog, and succeed in capturing several Villages—Fearful slaughter in the ranks of two German Landwehr Regiments, who would neither Retreat nor Surrender—The French succeed in carrying off a large quantity of Forage, but are unable to maintain their Positions—Desperate and Bloody Encounter in Storming the Villages by the Germans—Gallant Cavalry Charge—Another Desperate Fight at Norroy—The Results of the Battle and the Losses on both Sides—Particulars of an Intrigue attempted with the view of restoring the Imperial Dynasty—General Bourbaki leaves Metz on a visit to the Empress—The Inhabitants of Metz anxious to Garrison the Forts, so that all the Military Forces should attempt a Sortie on a Gigantic Scale—Marshal Bazaine declines to accede to the Request—The Provisions becoming exhausted—Starvation or Surrender?—The Measures taken to prevent such a Calamity are too Late—Domestic Life and Prices in the City in October—Horse-flesh the chief food—Suppression of Newspapers and Retaliation of the Editors—"The Beginning of the End"—Wholesale Desertions from the French Army—A Large Number of the Inhabitants also make a fruitless attempt to get through the German Lines—Proposals for Capitulation—Important Interview between General Boyer and Count von Bismarck—General Coffinières declines to give up the Fortress—Meeting of General Changarnier and Prince Frederick Charles—An Unconditional Surrender demanded by the Germans—Settlement of the Terms of Capitulation, and Departure of part of the German Troops for Paris—Proclamation of General Coffinières and General Order of Marshal Bazaine—Excitement and Scenes in the City when the truth became known—Meeting of the Municipal Council for the Last Time and Manifesto to their Fellow Citizens—General description of the Scene presented by the French laying down their arms and marching into Captivity, and of the Triumphant Entry of the Germans into Metz—Proclamation of General von

Kummer, the new German Commandant—The terrible calamity to France involved in the loss of Metz—Feeling in the German Army at the Result—Proclamation of Prince Frederick Charles and Dispatch from the King of Prussia—Reception of the News throughout France—Proclamation of M. Gambetta—Bazaine unfairly denounced as a Traitor—An Impartial Estimate of his Conduct and Proceedings during the Siege.

THE SIEGE AND CAPITULATION OF METZ.

IN previous chapters we have given a description of the city of Metz and its fortifications, of the retreat of the French army thither after the great battles of August 16 and 18, and of the sortie made on the 31st, with the view of assisting the movements of MacMahon in his attempt to relieve Marshal Bazaine. In the present chapter it is proposed to relate the chief incidents of the siege, from the close of August to the date of the capitulation of the city on October 27.

As the record of the siege of Strassburg shows, the German armies were exceedingly well supplied with all the necessary means for carrying on such operations, and their superior officers excelled in scientific and professional attainments. But, even with the immense *matériel* and resources at their command, they could not repeat before the great Moselle stronghold the process by which Strassburg was reduced. The fortifications of Metz were of enormous extent and strength, and on the outbreak of war its natural position, so admirably fitted for resistance, had been further strengthened by trenches, new forts, bastions, and earthworks. To such extent, indeed, had the fortress been rendered impregnable, that to attempt to storm it would have been madness. The actual works of Metz could not be attacked, nor the city approached sufficiently near to render bombardment possible, without first carrying strong detached works, which were protected by heavy guns on the heights, and could not be held or even passed without a heavy sacrifice of lives. The frightful price at which the recent victories of Vionville and Gravelotte were won, had induced the king to issue an order that further effusion of blood should be spared; and as it was considered that the complete blockade of Metz must, sooner or later, answer the purpose of the Germans, it was resolved so to invest the city as to render any further sortie from the fortress a forlorn hope indeed.

For this purpose a treble cordon of investment was thrown around the place; every village through which these lines passed being strongly fortified, its streets barricaded, its houses loopholed, and every wall that could shelter a man or gun converted into a rough and ready fortification. At intervals in the first line were earthwork batteries, surrounded by rifle-pits and trenches, each battery having ten 12-pounder brass guns, capable of throwing shells of between twenty-three and twenty-four German pounds weight. The batteries in the second line, laid out in the same manner, commanded the several military roads. Beyond as well as between these lines, the trees were felled and the fields lined with rifle-pits and trenches. Outposts and sentries were placed so closely, that it was hardly possible to escape without notice; and strong patrols passing from point to point kept up constant communication. The foreposts, forming the first line, lay either in single houses well fortified by entrenchments and barricades, or in the field, behind earthworks of no inconsiderable magnitude. The next line, the *feldwachts* ("fieldwatches"), occupied woods or the gardens of chateaux, and comprised about two companies each, which rested, arms in hand, ready for a sortie at any moment. In front of these, and within easy shot of a Chassepot from the French ramparts, were the single sentries. The soldiers remained a week in the most advanced line; then they retired, and the line behind took their places, thus giving a change of position, and at the same time a change of duties. In the third line the qui vive, or look out, was easy, and the men got more rest. Near the foreposts, at intervals, were the Prussian beacons, made of bitumen, placed on long poles and covered with straw, so that they looked not unlike poplar trees, which are so common in France. All round the Prussian lines, at almost every half mile or so, two of these were placed; and their purpose was to give an alarm in case of a night attack. By lighting one, the exact direction of the attack could be indicated to the troops around, and it would serve as a guide by which they could move forward to the rescue. There were guards at each beacon, and a small wooden hut, in which were kept the means of lighting up.

Two observatories were erected: one at Mercy le-Haut, the other, which was the principal, near Corny, the German headquarters. A very favourable point for the purpose was here obtained in St. Blaise, an old ruin situate on the top of a hill, nearly facing Fort St. Quentin, and having to its left Fort St. Privat, the village of Jouy, and the Moselle at the foot of the hill. From this point a magnificent view could be had of the picturesque valley of the Upper Moselle, everywhere dotted with rich vineyards, sheltering woods, villages and hamlets, suggestive of anything rather than of war. Yet each of these quiet, dreamy-looking villages was but a link in the fatal chain drawn around the maiden fortress;-all nooks and corners being filled with troops who turned everything to account in strengthening their defensive position. The walls of each house were pierced with several rows of loopholes for musketry; and the garden walls, likewise, were "crenellated," or notched with indentations at the top, like battlements, through which the barrel of a rifle could be pointed at the foe outside. All the trees and bushes around the houses were cut down to deprive the approaching enemy of cover; the roads were barricaded with trunks and branches of trees, to prevent cavalry or artillery from coming near; and trenches were dug to form a covered way for the defenders of the post, from house to house, and from village to village.

From St. Blaise the besiegers had a view of the entire town and environs of Metz, and, by a powerful telescope mounted in the observatory, could see every movement of the French army. Concentrated here were the telegraphic wires, which ran in an unbroken circle round the beleaguered town, and by which the Germans could at a moment's notice convey intelligence to any army corps, or order movements of concentration on any threatened point from a score of different directions. They could thus in fifteen minutes collect 8000 men upon any spot, and on more than one occasion, when the assembly was sounded, a force of 22,000, consisting of every branch of the service, was, within twenty-eight minutes, in full marching order, ready to proceed to the front. In every village notices were issued that the German authorities would hold the inhabitants responsible for damage done to the telegraphic wires; and that this was no idle threat is attested by the fact, that the people of one of them were fined in the sum of 200,000 francs for the destruction of the wires in its vicinity.

From the commanding position of St. Blaise the line of French outposts could easily be traced. Starting from Bevoye, Magny, in front of Montigny, and from Moulin-les-Metz, on the other side of the Moselle, it ran in the direction of St. Hubert, between St. Ruffine and Chazells; from this point, in front of Sey, right under Mont St. Quentin, as far as Lessy; then taking a bend northwards by Plappeville to Devant les Ponts, and thence to Vigneulles and Woippy. The first German forepost on the right of the observatory was in the village of Peltre; next to that, La Papetrie; nearer to the Moselle and closer to Metz was the outpost of Frescaty. From Frescaty the line ran backward slightly to the Moselle, a little in front of Ars-sur-Moselle. On the slope on the western side of the river there was a forepost at Vaux, a village in the middle of that gloomy forest the glades of which were checkered with so many graves of the dead who fell at Gravelotte. Thence for a space the foreposts lay among the mementoes of the slaughter of that day. That at Chatel St. Germain was on the fringe of the plateau which was the closing scene of that desperate struggle on the 18th of August. From St. Germain the intrenched line ran across the plateau to Saulny, thence by Semecourt down into the alluvial plain on the west of the Moselle to the north of Fort St. Eloy, and thence due east to the river's brink. Not only was it possible from Mont St. Blaise to see the positions of the respective foreposts and their supports, but also the lines where Bazaine's army, as distinguished from the garrison proper of the fortress of Metz, in divers camps was disposed. These occupied the suburbs in every direction, under the protection of the outworks of St. Quentin, Plappeville, St. Julien, Queleu, and Montigny. In the space so environed, and outside Metz, the French had in all four great lagers or camps. The first and probably the largest was on the slope of Mont St. Quentin, looking toward St. Blaise, where the rows of tents athwart the slope, and past the village of Sey, stretched almost down to Chazells. Another, beginning at Longeville, a village on the west bank of the Moselle, in a line between St. Quentin and Metz, straggled up the river margin, first to St. Martin, where Bazaine had his headquarters, and on to the north as far as Devant les Ponts. A third great camp was in front of St. Julien, towards Vauloux, Vallieres; and the fourth was around Borny and Grigy. Besides these camps, there were two great collections of sick—one on the esplanade in front of the cathedral at Metz, and along the river brink, and the other on the island of Saulcy.

Between the foreposts of the two armies a tolerably genial feeling prevailed until September 28, when, after a small engagement, a wounded Prussian officer was found robbed and mutilated in a most barbarous way. On one occasion a note was left under a stone, addressed to the French officer in command of the foreposts, and requesting a bottle of champagne for the Prussian forepost officer. At the next round the Prussian patrol found the bottle of champagne, along with a request for a small piece of salt, which, of course, was granted. The completeness of the forepost system was a marked feature of the Prussian army, and one of the leading causes of its success. At night the *feldwacht* advanced to the post occupied during the day by the furthest outlying sentry. Here it broke right and left into small pickets, leaving a strong nucleus in the centre. The front, at a distance of two or three hundred yards, was occasionally traversed by cavalry patrols, who sometimes rode right in among sleeping Frenchmen, whose system of night vigilance was far from perfect.

Then there was a pistol shot and round of bootless Chassepot firing in the dark; the daring horseman dashing out through the French back to his supports. At times, and especially after the incident above alluded to, considerable asperity was shown between the respective advanced parties. A strict order was issued by the Prussian authorities against firing at small detached groups; but a single man could not show himself without a volley from the French. Not an uncommon amusement of the besiegers was to expose a hat, which was speedily riddled. The long range of the Chassepot gave the French a decided advantage in this kind of play; but ere long the Prussian foreposts were also supplied with those weapons, a considerable number of which had fallen into German hands; indeed, one regiment (the thirty-fifth) was entirely armed with them.

During the first days of September there was absolute repose in Metz. The marshal and the army, ignorant of the doings without, knew nothing of the fate of MacMahon. For his army, however, they confidently anticipated success, and daily expected to see their brothers in arms, victorious over the foe, approaching towards the walls, with the welcome message of relief. But on the 4th September the German camp and villages around became more than commonly animated. The Prussian soldier seemed to have thrown off his usually stolid air; stout sergeants were ardently embracing one another; privates throwing their caps into the air, and shouting like maniacs; Frenchmen, gathered together in little knots, talked and gesticulated vehemently; and hussars and mounted officers were galloping about in every direction. All this extraordinary excitement was caused by the following official bulletin from the king of Prussia, which was here and there read aloud from newspapers to astonished groups:—"This day, September 1, in the neighbourhood of Sedan, Marshal MacMahon has surrendered himself and the French army of 80,000 men to the Crown Prince. His Majesty the Emperor of the French has also given himself up as a prisoner of war." A few days later a flag of truce, accompanied by General Wimpffen, who had assumed the command of the army when MacMahon was disabled by his wounds, conveyed into Metz the disastrous news of the annihilation of the forces which had been destined for its relief. A request was at the same time made to Bazaine to surrender the city without further bloodshed. His answer was that he did not believe the report, that he should hold Metz to the last, and that, if the Prussians wanted it, they must come and take it. The news was indeed regarded as a device of the Germans for obtaining easy possession of the greatest stronghold of France, and was not believed, even when both French and German newspapers were received, containing detailed accounts of the capitulation. The hopes thus cherished, however, soon received a crushing blow. In the August battles around Metz the French had captured about 750 Prussians; but judging that he might require all the provender of Metz for his own army, Bazaine turned out those prisoners directly after the failure of the sortie of August 31. The courtesy of war demanded that a like number of French should be returned, but just then Prince Frederick Charles had no prisoners, having sent them all off to Germany. On September 9, however, 750 men, chosen from different regiments taken at Sedan, were sent into the town, bearing only too palpable evidence to the tale of France's humiliation. With such corroboration there were few French soldiers or citizens in Metz so sceptical as not to believe, or so light-hearted as not to mourn, the dismal tidings. The Orleanist sympathies of portions of the army, and the republican leanings of others, were soon made manifest, while the guards appeared to be the only troops who were decidedly imperialist. Bazaine counselled and maintained a dead silence; but General Coffinières issued within the city the following proclamation:—

"Inhabitants of Metz,—We have read in a German journal—the *Gazette de la Croix*—the very sad news of the fate of a French army crushed by the numbers of its enemies after a three days' struggle under the walls of Sedan. This journal also announces the establishment of a new government by the representatives of the country. We have no other evidence of these events; but we are not able to contradict this.

"In these very grave circumstances our only thoughts should be for France. The duty of each one of us, whether as simple citizens or as officers, is to remain at our posts, and to vie with each other in defending Metz. In this solemn moment, France, our country, is summed up for each one of us in the word Metz! that city which has so many times before successfully resisted our country's foe.

"Your patriotism, of which you have already given such proofs by your care for our wounded soldiers, will never fail. By your resistance you will make yourselves honoured and respected, even by your enemies. The memory of the deeds of your ancestors will sustain you in the coming struggle.

"The army which is about our walls, and which has already shown its valour and its heroism in the combats of Borny, Gravelotte, and Servigny, will not leave you. With you it will resist the enemy which surrounds us, and this resistance will give the government time to create the means of saving France—of saving our country.

"L. COFFINIERES,
"General of Division, Commandant of Metz.
"PAUL ODENT,
"Prefect of the Moselle.
"FELIX MARECHAL,
"Mayor of Metz.

"METZ, *September* 13, 1870."

The result of Bazaine's persistent silence was that the army felt angry at not receiving any official information of that with respect to which the town was informed; and on the 16th the marshal felt compelled to issue an order of the day, stating that, according to two French journals brought in by a prisoner who had made his escape, the emperor had been interned in Germany after the battle of Sedan, that the empress and the prince imperial had quitted Paris on the 4th, and that "an executive power, under the title of the Government for National Defence," had "constituted itself" in Paris. The names of its members were then given, and the marshal continued:—"Generals, officers, and soldiers of the army of the Rhine, our military obligation towards the country in danger remains the same. Let us continue then to serve it with devotion, and with equal energy defend its territory from the stranger and social order against evil passions. I am convinced that your morale, of which you have already given such proof, will rise to the height of the circumstances, and that you will add new claims to the admiration of France." The announcement was a good deal criticized, and political factions of all shades of opinion started up, and reviled each other with the utmost heartiness from day to day. In other respects within the town the days passed wearily by, cold and wet, and signalized by few events. The gates of the town were only opened two hours in the morning, between six and eight, and two in the evening, between five and seven. If any of the beleaguered inhabitants got out within three or four miles in any direction they reached the Prussian outpost, which cut off the chance either of return or of further progress, and such outside rambles were, therefore, generally avoided. One event which occurred, however, gave unfeigned delight to the citizens, namely, the establishment of a means of communication with the outer world. The discovery of an old balloon, which had done the French good service eighty years before, suggested to Mr. Robinson, the besieged correspondent of the *Manchester Guardian* (and to whose "Fall of Metz" we are indebted for many incidents in this chapter), that balloons might be used for communicating with the provinces on the present occasion. Mr. Robinson soon found himself installed as balloon manufacturer-in-chief, assisted, and sometimes hampered, by Colonel Goulier, of the Military Engineering College, and Captain Schultz, the inventor of the mitrailleuse. An "aerostatic post" was opened, and the first balloon manufactured after a world of pains. It was fashioned out of the ordinary white lining paper used by paper stainers, and on being experimentally inflated with lighted straw, after the primitive method of Montgolfier (for the stock of coal in the city was too small to allow of gas being used), was found to succeed extremely well. Admiration at its graceful proportions was being expressed on all hands, when one of the workmen, in his delight at the success, shouldered a ladder in a manner rather more triumphant than usual, and accidentally sent the end of it straight through into the machine, which of course collapsed. It therefore became necessary to produce another, and on the 15th of September the first balloon was launched. It carried 8000 letters, fastened in an india-rubber cloth, and accompanied by a notice, promising a reward of 100 francs to any one who, finding the packet, and taking it to the nearest post-office, or to the mayor of the commune, should there obtain a receipt for it. The balloon first went nearly due south, in the direction of Vesoul and Besançon, at the rate of about nearly thirty miles an hour. Several others were then made, either of thin paper lined with muslin, or of cotton cloth, the ordinary "Manchester goods," of which there was then a fair stock in Metz. Both were inflated with atmospheric air, by means of a huge fan bellows. The cloth balloon was made by Captain Schultz. It was heavier and stronger than those made of paper, and could therefore carry a greater number of letters. It took up a freight of 45,000 letters; but, after rising to an immense height, it slowly descended, was fired at by the Prussians, and fell within their lines. The cause of this failure was never ascertained; but it had the effect of discrediting the captain, who was not allowed to make another trial, though, according to Mr. Robinson, his idea was a very good one.

Nevertheless, the aerostatic plan was not abandoned. The worthy Englishman and his assistants still kept working away, building paper balloons, improving each one, and ended by adding an hydraulic apparatus to serve as an automatic ballast, and so correct the too rapid ascent and the loss of gas by the sudden expansion thus created. This hydraulic ballast consisted of a flask holding about two litres of water; its neck was corked and turned downwards, and two glass tubes, a long one and a short one, were inserted in it. The long one admitted the air, the short one emitted the water, and the gradual leakage thus created corrected the sudden ascensional power of the balloons. To one balloon was appended a couple of carrier pigeons, with a notice attached to their cage offering a supplementary reward of another 100 francs for any one who would send them back with news of the outer world. Poor birds! their fate was a pie. The balloon was captured by a distant band of Prussians, who ate the pigeons, and sent word back by a *parlementaire* that they were both welcome and tender.

The spy mania reached Metz, and arrests were of every-day occurrence, but as they generally turned out mistakes they ceased to excite attention. That a large number of spies entered and left the city with impunity there is no doubt, for it subsequently appeared that Prince Frederick Charles was kept thoroughly informed of everything that passed, even to the deliberations of the French councils of war. On one occasion a spy rode right through the place in the uniform of a sous-intendant, asking all sorts of questions about the supplies, and only betraying himself by inquiring where the bread for the army was baked. Such a question on the part of a commissariat officer so utterly astonished the gendarme to whom it was put, that before he could reply the clever Prussian saw the tell-tale mistake he had made, and decamped. Orders were sent round to all the gates to let no sous-intendant out that night without strict examination, and those of them who happened to be in the town had to prove that they were what they professed to be, before they were permitted to join their quarters; but the spy was a great deal too clever for the gendarmes, and probably rode out as a mounted gendarme, perhaps arresting an actual sous-intendant on the way. Early in August, one real spy was caught and shot in the fosse, a more honourable fate than he deserved; for he took pay from both sides, and probably served neither. The French, indeed, attributed their disaster at Woerth to the intelligence he gave the Prussians; but every disaster was attributed to a like cause. This man, named Nicholas Schull, would seem to have been a person of intelligence and fortitude. A Hungarian by birth, a scion of the noble house of Degelmann, educated in Vienna, a naturalized American, who had long dwelt in Mexico as a partisan of the Emperor Maximilian, from whom he received the decorations of the order of Guadaloupe, he had seen much of the world and its ways. He was captured on the night of the 10th of August, on the railway, while surveying the new earthworks which were in course of being raised in every direction to strengthen the already strong fortress of Metz. It seemed that about the 19th of July he was presented to General Ducrot at Strassburg, announcing himself as the sworn enemy of Prussia, and as equally the sworn friend of France. Without much hesitation or inquiry his services were accepted. On the 21st he left Strassburg and returned on the 26th, with an amount of information which induced the general to give him 800 francs, in German cash, with which to enter the Prussian camp and carry out his object. From that time until his arrest the French military authorities saw nothing of him. That he did visit the Prussian camp is certain; for on his arrest there was found on him a *laisser passer* from Soleski, the quartermaster general of the Prussian army at Mayence, and dated the 6th of August, requiring all military authorities to let him go where and when he would. With his appointment from General Ducrot, and this from General Soleski, he had the entire run of both armies. With characteristic sagacity the Prussian army had organized an "intelligence department," with different grades, promotions, and good pay. By this means the reproach associated with espionage was taken away, and a man of patriotic enthusiasm and a taste for adventure might enter such service without necessarily exposing himself to the contempt with which the spy is commonly regarded. When arrested, there was found on Schull the medal carried by all the Prussian spies, to be produced as a voucher of their being enrolled in the intelligence department. This and 1000 francs in gold were quite enough to convict him without the *laisser passer*, which, strange to say, was written, not in German, but in French. The council of war, after a few minutes' deliberation, condemned him to death. Half an hour's walk through the town amidst a drizzling rain, at five o'clock in the morning, brought him to the fosse of the citadel, where in a few minutes he stoically met his fate.

The Metz newspapers did their best to keep alive the spark of hope in the breasts of the citizens, by informing them that the latest arrivals from Prussia were the landsturm, old men more affected by rheumatism than by desire of military glory; that in the ranks around the town dysentery prevailed; and in a few more days the besiegers would cry for quarter. For publishing the effective of the army of Metz one journal was suppressed on September 6. Three days after another informed the public that "Italy, Austria, and Denmark, for reasons easy to comprehend, are hastening to our side, in order to profit by our certain victory." There followed an urgent appeal to stop the church bells, which were tolling all day in honour of the dead, and terrifying the living. On the 10th there were 13,500 wounded and sick in the hospitals, and 1500 in private houses. On the 11th an order was issued by Marshal Bazaine that private persons should reserve from their stores thirty days' forage, and give up the surplus, to be paid for. On the 13th the water of the fountain upon the Esplanade became corrupted by washing in it the dirty linen of the wounded; a circumstance the more unfortunate as the inhabitants were now compelled to drink veritable Eau de Moselle, the Prussians having cut off the water supply at Gorze. On the 15th all the grain in the city was ordered to be brought into a common stock. On the 15th *l'Independant* reported a decree of the town council for extracting salt from the tanneries. Horseflesh was now rising to a degree which caused anxiety, although the military administration undertook to deliver some horses to the city daily. Prices were fixed at from sixpence to one shilling and threepence the kilogramme. A line of rails was carried from the station into the Place Royale, the area of which was turned to account by railway carriages being converted into ambulances. Later in the month a saline spring was found, from which the inhabitants were allowed to fetch water, and vine tendrils were recommended for forage. Mock telegrams were issued from time to time, one of which, from King William to the queen, may serve as a specimen:—"Thank God for our astonishing victory; our losses are enormous; the enemy displays prodigies of valour; two regiments have twice, like a hurricane, traversed the ranks of our army." Among other grim facetiousness at times attempted in the same paper, the cattle market report of September 19 bristled with columns of ciphers, the only animals for sale being nineteen pigs. The Prussians, having opened depôts in the surrounding villages to supply the inhabitants, were requested to open some in Metz, where they would get good prices. On September 28 appeared an order from General Coffinières, prohibiting the sale of the new vintage as unwholesome, and announcing a distribution three days a week of horseflesh for the poor. Early in September the papers published an address from Bazaine to his army, telling them not to be downcast, still less to give way to disaffection, as in a few weeks he would turn the tables on the Prussians by taking the larger proportion of their guns and great store of their provisions. In the meantime he enjoined vigilance and alertness, and instructed his officers to study the writings of the Archduke Charles and Frederick the Great, and the History of the Thirty Years' War, to learn how to conduct the defence of a fortress. It is impossible to avoid thinking that, had the officers received a proper military education, there would have been little need for counselling them to "read up" now when the pinch had come.

Considerable unpleasantness sometimes arose from the relative positions of Bazaine, as the commander-in-chief of the army, and General Coffinières, as commandant-in-chief of the town of Metz. Their functions often clashed, and they were divided in their opinions. This they had in common, that both knew the city well, Bazaine having been born on the hills which surround it, and Coffinières having not only been a pupil of the *Ecole d'Application du Genie à l'Artillerie* in the town—the one great military engineering school of France—but also for many years a resident in Metz itself. General Coffinières was about some sixty-three or sixty-four years of age, a large-built, kind-hearted man, but of no great vigour of mind. Like most officers of engineers and artillery, his political proclivities were towards republicanism rather than imperialism. Under the imperial rule artillery and engineering officers in France were not generally intrusted with high commands, and many of them were thus of republican tendencies. General Coffinières presented no exception to the rule, save that promotion had naturally modified his dissatisfaction with the imperial *régime*. Appointed commandant by the emperor himself, and responsible only to him, he was supreme within the town and the detached forts, but beyond that he had no power. Strictly speaking, Bazaine had nothing to do with the defence of Metz. No legislator on military matters could ever suppose that a commander-in-chief would exhibit so little knowledge of the art of war as to leave permanently inactive before a fortified town a large army, whose active force neutralized the passive force of the fortifications. This strong fortress, instead of serving as the refuge for a small body of men, who by the aid of scientific engineering multiplied their force, became smothered by the number of friends which surrounded it, and who consumed those provisions in a few weeks which would have sustained an ample garrison for many months. Under these circumstances no provision had been made for the presence of a commanderin-chief of an army in the field at the council of defence, which, as stated in chapter xxx. of the "Réglement du 13 October, 1863," the last statutes of war of the French army, consisted of the commandant-in-chief of the place (*commandant supérieur*), the commandant of the place, the commandant of artillery, the chief of the engineers, and some other officers of minor grade. Not being included under the law, Marshal Bazaine would almost seem to have considered himself above it; and thus, taking advantage of General Coffinières' easy disposition, he ruled to a certain extent in Metz as well as out of it, very little being done without his opinion and consent.

The affairs with Prussian outposts at times furnished plenty of excitement. One of the most daring leaders of the French guerillas was a man of the name of Hitter. He was a good shot, and brought down the Prussian videttes and sentinels with deadly skill. He used also to intercept convoys of provisions and forage, and ultimately he organized a regular body of sharpshooters for night service. A great deal of execution was done on a small scale, and Hitter became so popular in Metz that Marshal Bazaine offered to decorate him. The blunt patriot, however, said that if he was forced to accept the decoration he would wear it on his back, and very far down too; and the marshal, of course, thereupon ceased to insist. The Legion of Honour was given away by Marshal Bazaine rather freely during the siege, but was subsequently refused in another instance besides the one just mentioned. A certain M. Bouchotte was to receive this order for his eminent qualities displayed in the service of the town during its investment. He, however, declined the honour with the following remarks: "I will not receive a decoration signed with the hand which has signed the capitulation of Metz." There was indeed no lack in Metz of those who were willing to undertake extraordinary and dangerous service, which well merited more than ordinary reward. It was thus that the French were generally kept well informed of the exact position and strength of the Prussian batteries. They had plans of all of them, and these they obtained by the daring of men who devoted themselves to the task of observing the works of the enemy. Night after night they went forth, bearing a pocket compass, a pistol, and a poignard, and in secrecy and danger they did the work that was required of them.

Save that it was possible to hear of everything going on in the country, and keep up communications with home and the outer world, fife in the camp of the besiegers was as devoid of incident as among the besieged. There was nothing of the excitement of the Strassburg siege, as the work was very much of the nature of a blockade; and instead of opening parallels and breaching fortresses, a strict though tedious guard against approach of help from without or of exit from within the doomed city was all that was required. Now and then a small skirmish or forepost engagement relieved the monotony; but it seemed as if Bazaine had given up all idea of troubling his gaolers by any endeavour to regain his freedom.

A little excitement was caused in the camp for one night by the burning of Nouilly, a village which had been regarded as neutral ground, from its being situated between the foreposts of the respective armies, and directly under the fire of Fort St. Julien and Les Bottes. Considerable stores of provisions were known to have been secreted by the villagers, who were now inside Metz. These stores the Prussians could not succeed in unearthing; but the peasants revealed to their countrymen the place where they had been deposited, and it was believed the French had more than once stolen in at night and conveyed some of them away. To prevent a repetition of this, the Prussian commandant resolved to burn the village, with the secret stores it contained, and issued a commission to that effect to Lieutenant von Hosius, of the fifth regiment. Out of quite a company who clamoured to be sent on the expedition, fifteen were selected who had not left wives in the Fatherland; for in truth the dangerous undertaking partook not a little of the nature of a forlorn hope. A few hundred yards in the rear of Nouilly the Prussians, it is true, had a *feldwacht*; but the French were nearer it on the other side, by Mey and the Bois de Grimont, and had strong temptations for entering it by night. Hosius might possibly encounter a force of French inside the village, and in that case, of what service would be his fifteen volunteers? It was, indeed, almost certain that the party would meet with fierce resistance in the execution of their task, and would probably on their return be shelled both by St. Julien and Les Bottes. But as it was now close upon nine o'clock, the hour appointed for starting, there was little time for these considerations. Supper was hastily disposed of, the lieutenant thrust his "Adams'" revolver into his belt, and sallied out to the spot where his little band was drawn up. In a few minutes was heard the measured tread of the party, marching at the Prussian quick step, which is quicker than that of most armies; and after a parting salute to their comrades, they disappeared in the darkness. For a while the crash of feet through the vines fell on the ear; then came the hoarse challenge of the *feldwacht* rear sentry, after which all was quiet.

An anxious and excited group, comprising nearly all the officers of the battalion, soon gathered round the bright watch-fire, where everybody tried to appear unconcerned, though it was certain that none was. The regiment, it was known, had never failed in any duty assigned it, and the chance of its failure now, though apparent in the minds of all, was a subject which no one cared to broach. Von Hosius was in no hurry to relieve the suspense. An hour had gone—Nouilly was but ten minutes' distance from Noisseville, and the colonel's nervousness was ill-concealed as he hacked at the burning log with his naked sword, and drove his spur into the leg of his chair.

A smothered shout from the lieutenant of the post caused all to spring to their feet. Flame-coloured smoke at last, and plenty of it; but it surely could not be so far away! It was indeed a false alarm, for the lowering smoke was on the other side of the Bois de Grimont, and arose from a private bonfire of the French. The dead silence that reigned in the valley, however, was favourable. Von Hosius had evidently encountered no French in the place, else the rattle of the musketry would have been heard long ere now, and the battalion, which was standing to its arms at the various company posts, would have been lining the entrenchment with the needle-guns poked over the earthwork. Another half-hour of suspense, and then a loud "Ha!" simultaneously from the lieutenant on duty and the sentry. This time it was no mistake. Von Hosius had taken his time, that he might do his work thoroughly. From six places at once belched out the long streaks of flame against the darkness above, and the separate fires speedily met. In ten minutes the whole place was in a blaze; the church steeple, standing out in the midst of the sea of flame, calling to mind the old motto of the Scottish Kirk, "*Nec tamen consumebatur.*" But the steeple, after all, was not the burning bush; for a fierce shower of sparks bore testimony to its fall. Here and there against the flame could be seen a human figure in frantic flight, and on a bluff, just outside the village, stood in the strong light a woman wringing her hands. These were the innocent victims of war!

Presently was heard again the crashing through the vinebrake, and the Prussian outpost sentry challenge. The watchword was returned in the hearty voice of Von Hosius, and in five minutes more the little party was inside the entrenchment of the *replie*. The affair was singularly successful. The duty had been executed without the exchange of a single shot. The village burnt till five the next morning; whatever stores were in it must have been consumed; and so coolly had the enterprise been gone about, that a respectable old horse, found in one of the stables of the village, was led back in triumph as a trophy. The French held their fire simply because they did not know whither to direct it. To have shelled Nouilly would only have been playing into the hands of the Prussians. The party which wrought the destruction might have come from Servigny, Noisseville, the Brasserie, or Montoy; and as the line of their retreat was not known, to have fired at haphazard would have been a useless waste of ammunition.

It was rumoured that, notwithstanding the strict investment, Bazaine contrived by some means to maintain communications with parties outside Metz. With apparent reason, the Prussian authorities doubted the statement, until, about the middle of September, it was corroborated by the discovery of underground insulated wires, leading, on one side of Metz, to Strassburg, on the other to Thionville, Longwy, Montmèdy, and Sedan. That a mode of communication so obvious, though invisible, should have escaped such engineers and electricians as the Prussian officers appears incredible. When the French besieged Sebastopol, they cut short, shallow trenches in all the directions from which they thought the batteries could communicate. When they stormed the Malakoff they had a picked corps of 200 men with sharp spades, who cut behind it when they got possession, and severed the wires supposed to communicate with the mines under the work, which were afterwards actually found. In this the French did not show their usual sagacity, nor the Russians their usual alertness. The wires were actually there, passed under the harbour across the Star Fort, and had the Russian electrician got any intimation, even by signal, he might in the moment of triumph have blown the French corps d'armée into the air, and, with the English defeat at the Redan, have changed the whole current of the war.

On the 21st of September General von Steinmetz, who till then had played a most important part in the war, was removed from the command of the first army round Metz, and appointed to the governorship of Posen. To him is due the credit of many of the brilliant and resolute attacks which issued in Prussian victories during the war; but he sometimes erred in attacking too rashly, and permitting his battalions to advance too far unsupported. Where, however, there was danger, or the army received a check, the first man in the breach or at his post was General von Steinmetz. He left the first army commanding the respect of every one—the friendship of but few.

The command-in-chief of the besieging forces, which hitherto had been somewhat divided, now devolved entirely upon Prince Frederick Charles; and it would seem as if Bazaine at once resolved to put his abilities to the test. On the 22nd of September, the day after the removal of General Steinmetz, there occurred the first sortie in any considerable force which had been attempted since the memorable one of August 31. The operations of the French, however, though not conducted on a vast scale, had sufficed to keep the German troops actively occupied, for at several points of the siege circle the men were frequently under arms for thirty-six hours at once, with but short intervals for rest and food. The object of the present movement was to harass the investing forces while ascertaining by strong armed reconnaissances the strength of the German positions. Under cover of a heavy cannonade from Fort Queleu, preceded by a shower of shells—some of which struck the Grange, and others fell as far behind as Ars-Laquenexy, and did considerable damage to the church—a strong division of French troops, composed of artillery, cavalry, and infantry, advanced in the direction of La Grange-aux-Bois. From an excellent point of observation they had previously been reconnoitred by the Germans, who knew their composition, strength, and direction, and were therefore at once prepared to meet them and to avoid at the same time a useless sacrifice of lives at their outposts. The French infantry were thrown into the woods round the village in skirmishing order and in large force, occupying a line which extended for about one mile to the Prussian right. This, of course, rendered the position of the Prussian outposts at La Grange-aux-Bois untenable. The Prussians in retiring availed themselves of every tree and knoll, and from behind a series of breastworks, which they had thrown up to strengthen their position, fired steadily upon the advancing enemy, and inflicted some severe losses. In order to reach the point at which their main supports were concentrated they had to pass over about half-a-mile of ground, every inch of which was gallantly contested. It was now about three o'clock. The French, in advancing, lost the advantage of the support of their artillery and cavalry; for the Germans had so obstructed the roads by frequent and strong barricades, constructed of hewn trees which lined the military road to Metz, and the nature of the ground, covered with dense woods, was so unfavourable, that mounted forces could not act, and guns could not be brought forward. All this time, however, a heavy and continuous rain of shells of great weight was poured upon Mercy-le-Haut and Ars-Laquenexy from Forts Queleu and St. Julien. At the junction of the roads leading from Mercy and Ars—which meet nearly at right angles—the Germans met their supports. A large body of troops of all arms had been concentrated here, and were posted in strong positions. The Germans at once assumed the offensive, and rushing impetuously to the attack, fairly drove back the French at a more rapid pace than that at which they advanced. All the German troops engaged carried their knapsacks, messtins, and cloaks. The fashion of having the cloak slung crosswise over the shoulder, round the knapsack, and under the opposite arm, turned many a bullet and saved many a soldier's life in this and other engagements. So equipped, they poured upon the French infantry so heavy and close a fire that they could not hold their ground. Already in advancing thus far they had found how effective a resistance could be made by a small body of men, fighting with vigour and handled with skill, on ground whose natural strength had been increased by every available means. The German troops, after having cleared the woods, drove the French back through the open, with considerable loss. La Grange-aux-Bois was speedily re-occupied, and by five o'clock the French had been forced to retire within their lines. The affair lasted altogether about four hours. This village had now the second time been taken by the French, but in both instances their occupation of it had been brief. Their attacking force was principally composed of Marshal Leboeuf's corps, and the regiment which bore the brunt of the onset on the German side was the thirteenth of the first Westphalian infantry division. The loss of the Prussians was one officer and fifteen men in all, wounded, and one killed. The French losses in killed and wounded were considerable, besides numerous prisoners left in the enemy's hands.

The sortie of the 22nd was but the prelude to a more serious attack on the 24th. Rightly guessing that, on the previous occasion, the observatory at Mercy-le-Haut had enabled their enemy to provide so warm a reception for them, the utmost efforts of the French were used on the 23rd to render it untenable. A large number of the projectiles with which it was continuously shelled took effect, and made far more holes in the roof than were needed for the purposes of observation. The shelling was continued on the morning of the 24th, but from the position, nevertheless, strong bodies of troops were observed gathering under the walls of Fort St. Julien, which presently poured out along the road leading from the fort, and extending towards the Prussian right. They advanced in marching order, the infantry well supported by artillery and cavalry. Despatches by orderlies and telegraph carried information of all the movements of the French, and the threatened points received timely warning, while preparations were made for immediate concentration. It was now two o'clock, and presently the fire began. The guns of Fort Queleu opened a heavy fire, and the shells dropped fast among the woods immediately to the left and below the chateau where the Prussian troops were hidden. For the first time, too, the guns from Fort les Bottes, the strong earthwork recently constructed immediately in front of the chateau and below the fort, delivered a maiden fire. The majority of the shells, however, pitched too high, passed over the woods, and fell into the meadows. There was a continuous roar of cannon on the right and left flanks, and volleys from both Prussian and French infantry in the *chaussées* showed that sharp fighting was going on at close quarters. Some mitrailleuses then opened fire with a hoarse grating sound, as if a ship had let go her cable and the chain was scraping out through the hawsehole. For some time the French advanced far into the enemy's lines; but as the dusk fell the vivid flashes breaking from the now gray woods, and the louder roar of cannon, told that the Prussians had once more held their own, and were driving back their adversaries under shelter of the forts, by this time ablaze with signal lights.

The most exciting part of the day's encounters occurred during an attempt on the village of Noisseville, which had already changed hands several times. The attack was conducted with the greatest caution, as a French company had, only an hour or two before, been severely cut up in advancing on a chateau out of which they imagined the enemy had been driven, but where he suddenly appeared in great force. The place, however, was ultimately taken, and, that it might not be the occasion of another surprise, was set fire to and burnt. Making this house a turning point, a considerable number of skirmishers advanced towards the little village, which had been so drenched with French and German blood. They could not tell if it was occupied. Not a blue coat was to be seen; all was perfectly still. A shell or two from field-pieces was tried; not a shot was returned. St. Julien sent in one of its long twenty-four shells at it, which went crash into the first house on the left, and made a great hole in it. Still not a movement. Another shell from St. Julien struck the house on the right side of the street with the same result. Still no sign. The French praised the admirable practice of St. Julien, but after the ruse of the little house they knew not what to expect from the big village. Meanwhile the men crept steadily on. Crack went the Chassepot whenever any one thought he saw something worth firing at. Still no reply. Were the enemy there or were they not? Just then, from the other side of the hill, was noticed a column of Prussian cavalry crawling out of the woods of Failly, like a big black snake, half a mile long. The officer in command gave orders to sound a retreat, and the men drew back again. Then began the fire. Noisseville was not empty now. Out of every loophole, from behind every wall, from every little hedge, sprang up armed men, who fired with an impetuosity that made up for their previous patience; but luckily the French were not quite near enough, and the Prussians thought it wise not to pursue. Under cover of their artillery, which went to the front, the French gradually got again within the shelter of the guns of St. Julien.

On the 27th of September another sortie in considerable force, intended as a great foraging expedition, was made with even more success in a military view than those a few days before. Peltre was the nearest railway station to Metz on the line which connected it with Prussia, and was therefore the great commissariat station for the Prussian camp to the westward, as the stations of Courcelles and Rémilly were for the eastern portion. The French had therefore a double object, to destroy the German provisions and get some for themselves, and to seize the opportunity, should any occur, of sending a few men through with despatches. All being ready, very early in the morning, before the sun was up, the French set out. To effect a greater confusion, simultaneous demonstrations were made in the direction of Borny and Ladonchamps; but the main line of attack was Peltre. The force consisted principally of the seventieth and eighty-fourth regiments of the line, supported by a battalion of chasseurs, and accompanied as before by cavalry and guns. The early hour, the suddenness of the attack, and the sallying out at different points, if they did not surprise the Prussians, at all events rendered them less prepared than usual to make any effectual resistance. The railway was still available for some considerable distance of the road, and the French troops were placed in the carriages, a field-piece or two mounted on some vans in front, and the engine placed behind the train. Alongside the line marched the rest of the troops, and a battery of mitrailleuses took up their position above the wood of Basse Bevoye. Quietly round towards the castle of Crepy crept the infantry, and the affray began. Hitherto the Prussians had but little notice of the approach of the troops; but now it became earnest hard work. Rattle after rattle of musketry fire rang out from one side or the other. At last the Prussians were overcome, captured, and their rifles broken, after which they were set free again. Meanwhile, another portion of the French force pushed on rapidly to the villages of Peltre and Mercy-le-Haut, which they occupied and fired, completely razing the observatory. In one part of their retreat the Germans entered a convent—called the Sisters of Providence—whose walls were already loop-holed; but under a deadly fire an entrance was forced, and now commenced a horrible sight for those poor peace-loving sisters. Their church became a charnel-house; the very sanctuary was stained with blood; and the house of mercy was turned into the house of vengeance. The Prussians craved, the French gave, no quarter, and flight there was none. The railway station close by was carried; men were killed at every step; but there were here some patient looking quadrupeds which must be saved, whatever became of the bipeds. The order of the day was to take care of the cows and sheep. Cattle trucks were broken open, sheep pens invaded; the cows were driven up the line, and the sheep tucked under the arm, or borne on the shoulder. Sugar, coffee, hay, straw, all needed, were found there, and the railway carriages were filled and sent back again. The German forces first assailed had fallen back as far as Ars-Laquenexy, on the road to Courcelles, which they supposed to be the point of the French attack. Meanwhile another corps, the first corps of the second army, prepared to attack the French in flank, and to cut them off from retreat to Metz. They, however, saw their danger in time and withdrew, carrying with them their dead and wounded, the captured provisions, and a hundred prisoners. The guns of Fort Queleu kept up a heavy fire during the whole affair, and Forts St. Quentin and St. Julien also vigorously cannonaded the Prussian positions opposite to them. In driving back the French, the Prussian field-guns, which opened a heavy fire on them, caused severe loss, and set fire to the villages of Colombey and La Grange-aux-Bois, both of which were wholly destroyed. So rapid and well-executed was the sortie, that at 11.30 a.m. all was again comparatively quiet, and, save the burning villages, little trace appeared of an affray in which about 8000 men on each side had been engaged.

Bazaine had been blamed for giving up the advanced position of Peltre, which for a time was in French hands; but the sortie was not made with a view of escaping from Metz, so much as obtaining food for his army and provender for his horses, both of which were getting exceedingly scarce in the town. So far, therefore, the object of the sortie was attained, and the measure of success which attended it encouraged the French on the following day to make a similar effort, on a smaller scale, in nearly the same direction. The Prussian foreposts occupied in no great strength the village of Colombey, where were three large châteaux, in the upper stories of which a considerable store of grain had been left by the original occupants, who had taken refuge in Metz, and probably gave information of the existence of these stores. At all events, in the afternoon of the 28th, the French, in large numbers, and covered by the artillery of St. Julien, made a dash at Colombey, their advance followed by a number of empty waggons. Once more they surprised the comparatively weak Prussian foreposts, and drove them out of the village. Covering their operations by throwing forward tirailleurs into the woods to the front and towards La Planchette, they filled the waggons with the grain, and started on the return journey. In the meantime, however, the Prussian artillery had come to the front, and the shells fell thick among the Frenchmen in Colombey and the convoy on the road. The former fell back in great haste under the guns of St. Julien, and the waggons went on at a gallop, but out of thirty-six only fourteen succeeded in getting safe off. The others were arrested *in transitu*, in consequence of the animals which drew them being disabled by the Prussian shells. Among the men the loss in killed or wounded was not great on either side.

But while outside the city walls the monotony of life was varied by these occasional sorties, within Metz the autumn wore on heavily. There was much to be feared. To calculate the duration of the food supply; to speculate on what Bazaine was doing, or meant to do; to build frail anticipations on the prospect of a relieving army, and to find them crumble into ruins; to make paper balloons, which, with their freight of letters, frequently fell into the hands of the enemy; to split into coteries, and wrangle about the future of France; to hunt down spies, to vex the Prussian outposts, and occasionally to engage in sorties—these were now the sole resources of the beleaguered citizens and army. The weather was often rainy and cold, and the spirits of the people were depressed by the sense of confinement and the monotony of existence. The Prussians were in no hurry; they could very well afford to let the Metzers wear themselves out. The Metzers fretted against the manacles that bound them, but fretted in vain. Every day brought the end nearer; yet still the way seemed long and wearisome. The citizens felt that they were shut up in a large prison, under sentence of being slowly starved; and they knew that their fate had been decreed by a power which never faltered in its will or failed in its resources. A little excitement was caused on Sunday, September 25, by a grand review of the national guards in the Place d'Armes in front of the cathedral. They numbered four corps, and, together with the volunteer artillery, mustered about 7000 men. They were clad in blouses, but with distinctive marks, giving roughly the character of a uniform to the dress. Their arms were old-fashioned percussion muzzle-loaders, of various patterns, and very ineffective. Not that there were not plenty of Chassepots in store; but the national guards were suspected of republicanism, and were therefore neglected and discouraged by the military authorities, though popular with the townsfolk.

The sorties we have referred to, of course, occupied comparatively few of the large army now encamped around Metz; and although a circle of defence extending over nearly thirty miles afforded ample employment for a still larger number, the fact that no determined effort was made to break away from the town, whose provisions were being rapidly diminished by those outside, created great dissatisfaction in it, and caused considerable relaxation of discipline among the troops themselves, great numbers of whom had taken no active part in the war since the engagement of August 31; indeed, the imperial guard had not fired a shot, or ever moved from their encampment, since August 18. Bazaine, therefore, notwithstanding the almost hopeless nature of the attempt, determined, early in October, to make a vigorous endeavour to break out in the direction of Thionville, about half way between Metz and Luxembourg. Thionville was at this time besieged by a large force under General Zastrow, but was extremely well supplied with provisions, the obtaining of which would have been of immense advantage to the marshal and his army. And even if this scheme could not be fully carried out, it was thought that a large part of the army might possibly reach the Dutch frontier, thus leaving Metz with so many the less mouths to fill, and by surrendering to a neutral save the ignominy of capitulating to the enemy. The foggy morning of the 7th October was therefore appointed to usher in what turned out to be the most important and determined sortie made by Bazaine since the failure of the 31st August. The Germans recognized it as the "Schlacht bei Mezie"res." Battles there were in plenty in this bloody campaign that showed a larger total of killed and wounded; but the "Battle of Mézières" made widows and orphans in the Fatherland far beyond proportion, for the men who bore the brunt of it were husbands and fathers—the stout landwehr men of the Division Kummer.

At an early stage of the blockade the Prussians seized upon the fine old chateau of Ladonchamps, which had often played an important part in the history of Metz. As it was necessary the French should carry the position, a field-battery was brought against it; but though there were the guns and the sentinel, not a shot was returned from it. Presently volumes of smoke rose up from behind the chateau. The farm was evidently burnt, and a rush was made to save the house. After a few musket shots had been fired the Prussians evacuated, and the French entered the place to find that the guns they had so much feared were simply portions of poplar trees neatly mounted on the wheels of broken carts, and that the "sentinel" was a man of straw. Such ruses, which were not uncommon during the war, caused many a mirthful moment, and relieved the weary tediousness of the siege.

Ladonchamps was taken by the chasseurs, who held it, with some few intervals, up to the day of the surrender of Metz, and it formed the *avant garde* of the French lines. To the right of it were Great and Little Maxe, and in front the two large farms of Great and Little Tapes. It was felt by the Prussians that it was dangerous to allow the French to continue in possession of Ladonchamps, as from it their batteries enfiladed the whole of the besiegers' front across the valley. On October 6, therefore, it was subjected to a most severe bombardment, resulting in the retirement of its garrison towards Metz. The Prussians then threw forward troops, establishing their *replis* in its rear, and sent sergeants' parties to occupy it and Grandes and Petites Tapes villages, which formed the key to its possession. St. Rémy constituted the chief support, and here lay the fifty-ninth regiment of the landwehr. Maxe, close to the river and considerably in advance, was occupied by outposts sent forward by the tenth army corps, on the other side of the Moselle. The two divisions of the landwehr stretched right across the valley from the bridge at Argancy, where they touched the tenth army corps, to near Marange, where they met the fifth, and to them was confided the keeping of the flat alluvial tract on the western side of the Moselle.

From Metz to Mézières, which was now the headquarters of General von Kummer, commanding the landwehr, there is a long trough with a flat bottom, the alluvial margin of the Moselle. This tract, which is about four English miles wide, is bounded on the west by the heights of Le Horiment, and nearer Metz by Norroy and Saulny. On the east it is bounded by a lower series of bluffs, on which stand the villages of Olgy and Malroy; but between them and the bottom runs the Moselle, infringing considerably on the flat expanse just opposite Olgy. Across this bottom, at the narrowest part, lies a series of villages—the two Tapes and St. Rémy, with Maxe and Ladonchamps, respectively, slightly to the east and west front. In all of them there were more or fewer Prussian troops.

About one o'clock on the 7th the Prussian batteries at Semecourt were heard delivering a vigorous fire, which was supposed to be caused by the tardy evacuation of Ladonchamps by the French. Over the valley hung a mist, which prevented any extended observation; but little importance was attached to the firing, although it grew louder and louder, until an aide-de-camp galloped up, spreading the alarm in every direction, and dashing on to General Kummer's quarters for instructions to guide the front.

Covered by the dense fog, Bazaine had made his dispositions with such adroitness, that when it cleared away a little past one his arrangements were already all but complete. The imperial guard came down from the hills of Plappeville and defiled into the valley of the Moselle. Several regiments of infantry, under the direction of General L'Admirault, pushed their way through the woods to the left in the direction of Nassoy and Feves. The sixth corps sent some few regiments to assist the guards, and together they marched into the valley. A strong assault was first directed against Ladonchamps, which the landwehr outpost held as if they had been 10,000 instead of 100 men, and the French infantry swarmed into it while their artillery played upon it. On went the French infantry, shell after shell falling thick amongst them, but they knew the nearer they got the less likely they were to be stopped. They encountered a very determined resistance. In addition to several fixed batteries, the Prussians brought on the ground a large number of field pieces, all converging on the French fine of advance. The brave General Gibon, who that day for the first time carried his *galon* as a general in the field, cried out, "Never fear, my lads, I'll serve as a bastion for you;" and, placing himself at the head of his brigade, on he went. But his career was brief; he fell in the affray mortally wounded. On rushed the guards, unchecked by the bullets which, like a storm of hail, assailed them. The shock of exploding shells made the ground tremble. Fire succeeded fire. The smoke of the sacrifice rose not to heaven, but hung over the earth. Inch by inch the ground was won, and Les Grandes Tapes was at length reached. Twice round the outworks a picked body of seventy-five guards went; at last, espying a "coign of vantage," they with a shout leapt the trenches, followed by their comrades, and Les Grandes Tapes was theirs. Suddenly, also, the villages of Petites Tapes, St. Rémy, and Maxe were overwhelmed by a rush of Frenchmen. The fifty-ninth landwehr in St. Rémy would not fall back, as in common prudence it should have done, but stood in the street till the French, having played upon it with their artillery, and rained on it Chassepot and mitrailleuse bullets, finally, by sheer numbers, pushed backward the shattered remnant on to the *chaussé*. The fusilier battalion of the fifty-eighth occupied Grandes Tapes before, and occupied it now, but with the dead and the wounded. The battalion would not give ground, and may be said to have been annihilated, as the men stood with their backs to the wall and their faces to the foe. The other battalions of the same regiment also suffered severely. As soon as they had gained possession of Les Grandes Tapes, the French began loading their wagons with forage; and, though the Prussians shelled them vigorously, they did not cease until they had got all they wanted.

So far, then, Bazaine had succeeded. He had re-occupied the chain of villages athwart the valley, and had got a few batteries of artillery out to their front to reply to the Prussian fire. But the *status quo* he neither wished nor had the ability to retain, prevented as he was by the Prussian artillery throwing its projectiles from three sides of the parallelogram. It seemed clear, however, that Bazaine would not have done what he did had he not contemplated something more; and that, there could be no doubt, was a sortie to establish connections with Thionville. His tactics were well conceived. From St. Rémy and the two Tapes he kept the Prussian fire engrossed, both musketry and artillery. He sent forward from Grandes Tapes swarms of tirailleurs, who fared very ill at the hands of the landwehr.

He massed nearly 30,000 men on the bank of the Moselle, under cover of the houses of Maxe, with the design of cutting through the Prussian environment where it was weakest, close to the river. The moment was critical. The landwehr had all been sent forward against the villages, with the exception of one brigade that was in reserve. But the tenth army corps had been crossing the pontoon bridge, and massing between the river and Amelange; General von Voigt Rhetz, who was in command of the day's operations, gave the order for several regiments to advance. It was a sight never to be forgotten. First came the fusiliers, extending at a rapid run into skirmishing order, and covering the whole plain with their thin long lines. Then the dense columns of companies of the grenadiers, with their bands playing and their colours unfurled. But all the work was not left to the infantry. The artillery, letting the villages alone, concentrated their fire on the advancing columns of the French by the Moselle. Want of fodder, which caused many of his horses to die of starvation, and the demand for horse flesh as food, both in the camp and town, had left Bazaine singularly weak in field artillery, and the only reply to the enemy was from the fort of St. Julien or from the ramparts of St. Eloy. But the mitrailleuse sounded its angry whirr; making the skirmishers recoil as they crossed the line of fire, and tearing chasms in the fronts of the solid masses of which they were the forerunners. The dense columns of the French staggered and then broke, and a *sauve qui peut* ensued into the village of Maxe. Once within shelter, they obstinately refused to go further. In vain the Prussian artillery, advancing closer and closer in alternate order of batteries, fired on the villages, with a precision and rapidity that could not have been exceeded on Woolwich Common. That obstinate battery in front of Grandes Tapes would not cease, and the French tirailleurs still lined the front of the *chaussée*. It was now nearly four o'clock, and the German columns halted, as if for breathing time, before storming the enemy's position. A shell from St. Julien, falling near a captain of cavalry, blew him and his horse into fragments; disturbing at the same time a hare, which bounded from its form, and scampered across the battle-field right in a line with the gun fire. As the landwehr stood in suspense, a staff officer galloped along the front line with orders for a general advance to take the villages by storm. The advance was to consist of four brigades of the landwehr, supported by two of the tenth army corps. In a few minutes the command came sounding along the line, and the men, springing from their cover, went forward with that steady, quick step so characteristic of the Prussian marching. The shells from the battery in front of Grandes Tapes tore through the line, the mitrailleuse and Chassepot poured against it their bullets; but still the landwehr, silent and stern, went steadily to the front. Those who had been in many engagements had never experienced a more furious fire than that to which the centre of this line was exposed. General von Brandenstein, commanding the third brigade of the landwehr, was shot down as he rode, and several of his staff were wounded. At length the entrenchments were reached, behind which were lying the shattered remnants of the fifty-ninth and fifty-eighth landwehr. The fraternization consisted in the cry of "Hurrah Preussen," and then "Vorwärts—immer vorwärts," and the line threw itself to its front in a run. The gunners from the battery, brave men and stubborn, had barely time to get round the corner before the landwehr were upon them. The guns they left perforce. In the villages the French made a last stand, but it was at serious cost. The landwehr, with less of the conventional warrior in them than the line, were not so much inclined to give quarter. Many a Frenchman that afternoon had for a shrift a bayonet thrust. They fought furiously in the narrow ways of the villages, and used the mitrailleuses with rare judgment and effect. But then came the steady, resolute stride of the landwehr, who by the lusty use of the bayonet soon cleared Les Tapes and Maxe of all save victors, dead, and wounded. The village of St. Rémy was also taken in the same way by the eighty-first regiment at nine o'clock in the evening, with a loss to the Prussians of five officers and over one hundred men. The end of the day found the French, though dislodged from the neighbouring villages, still in possession of the old chateau of Ladonchamps, to the shelter of which and its barricades they retired after the determined charge of landwehr, which had proved as resistless as that of the imperial guard at an earlier hour. From this shelter after dark a large body of troops sallied out, under the impression that a regiment of their comrades were still outside, and near the Prussian lines. A dim outline in the distance was supposed to be that of the absentees. On a closer inspection, however, the outline was resolved into a body of Prussian cavalry, who, for the purpose of disguise, were singing a French chanson. The French officer hesitated a moment or two, when all at once the charge was sounded. There was no disguise then. Horses' hoofs ploughed the ground, as, shouting now in German, the riders came on. A scamper was made by the French, which the Prussians hastened by a roll of carbine fire. Up to the very barricades they went, but the French were ready, and many a riderless horse dashed on almost into the outworks. The infantry having reformed, a stream of fire from Chassepots ran all along the front, which after a while caused the Prussians to retire, leaving the enemy in undisturbed possession of the chateau.

In another part of the field, westward of St. Rémy, and the two hotly-contested villages of Les Tapes, the position held by the Prussians on the wooded and hilly ground in the neighbourhood of Norroy and Semecourt, formed from the peculiarity of the situation a natural fortress. It had, however, been strengthened by art. The ground in front and facing Woippy had been cut up into a regular honeycomb of "Schutzengraben," whilst behind every wall a bank had been carefully erected, and the masonry pierced for rifles. The Prussians had become so accustomed to fortifying the small villages they occupied, and had besides so many opportunities of observing the dexterity with which the French made such places tenable, that in a very short time a battalion would convert a farmhouse, a garden-wall, or a hamlet, into a fortification from which generally nothing but artillery could dislodge them. In the present instance, however, all this elaborate defence proved of little avail, for the wellconducted steady advance of the French guard was irresistible. They carried the village of Norroy, and were moving on Semecourt and Fèves, with the intention, apparently, of penetrating towards Thionville by way of Marange, when they were attacked in flank by the troops lying at Amanvillers, St. Privat-la-Montagne, and Roncourt. The fire from Plappeville assisted them so long as they were in the neighbourhood of Saulny; but that assistance failed as soon as they got clear of their own outworks and carried Norroy. Here an obstinate fight continued for many hours; but the Prussians having been reinforced, the French fell back towards Saulny and Woippy, contesting every inch of the road. With the light of a brilliant moon, the big guns had no difficulty in opening fire. Plappeville, the works in Devant-les-Ponts, and some heavy pieces of the town itself, now took part in the action; but the Prussians seemed determined to take Woippy, which they eventually did at nine o'clock. They could not, however, hold it for any length of time, and when about eleven p.m. the action ceased, the French had regained Woippy, and the Prussian troops held Saulny.

This battle, the severest and most important which had taken place before Metz since the 31st of August, was without positive benefit to either side, as both lost heavily without gaining any advantages. The sortie only demonstrated to Marshal Bazaine the utter hopelessness of any attempt to break the bars of his iron cage, while the Prussians found it impossible to follow up their victory by penetrating into the immediate vicinity of the fortress. The French losses in killed and wounded were stated to be 1100. The estimate was published in Metz as, in some sort, a reply to the clamour for another sortie, which Bazaine was reluctant to risk. There is, therefore, every reason to believe this total correct. If so, the French losses were far less than those of their enemy. Eighteen hundred killed and wounded, and sixty-five officers, were the fearful sum-total of these few hours, among the landwehr alone—who, indeed, bore the brunt of the fray, and checked the rush of the French advance, by holding the villages while they had a man that could stand upright and fire the needle-gun. To them also was intrusted the grand final advance which swept the French out of the villages. The Prussian force engaged consisted of the nineteenth, fifty-eighth, and fifty-ninth landwehr regiments, forming the Posen and West Prussian brigades; the first army corps, the twenty-eighth, twenty-ninth, eighth, and seventh line regiments, and a portion of the seventh army corps. The number of French engaged exceeded 45,000. The roar of the artillery, mingling with the deadly clatter of the mitrailleuse, was indescribable; for not only were the French and Prussian field and horse-artillery engaged, but during the whole battle the forts kept up a continual blaze from their garrison guns. Singularly enough, this fire was fiercest about nine o'clock, as if the French feared an attempt upon the fortress, to follow up the day's success.

During the time when these important events were occurring, the imperialist cause, though unpopular, had not been quite forgotten by some of its former supporters. At least one intrigue had been attempted with the view of restoring the Napoleonic dynasty; and as it was partly carried on in the city of Metz, it may be right to notice it here.

M. Regnier was a landed proprietor in France, and the Prussians were but a few leagues from his residence when he and his family took flight for England, which they reached on the 31st of August. On the 4th of September the Empress Eugenie quitted Paris. On the 11th he knew she was at Hastings, and on the 12th wrote to Madame Lebreton a letter, which he requested should be communicated to her Majesty, apprising her of his intention to submit proposals to the emperor at Wilhelmshöhe for the preservation of the Napoleonic dynasty. The first of these proposals rested on the assumption that the regent ought not to quit French territory, of which the imperial fleet was a part, and that a portion of the fleet ought, therefore, to be occupied by her as the seat of government.

Madame Lebreton gave an interview to M. Regnier at the Marine Hôtel, Hastings, when she told him that the empress had read his letter, but that she felt that the interests of France should take precedence of those of the dynasty, and that she had the greatest horror of any step likely to bring about a civil war. M. Regnier then addressed another letter to Madame Lebreton, and subsequently saw three officers of the imperial household, who told him that the empress would not stir in the matter. He then proposed that certain photographs of Hastings, which he had bought for the purpose, might be inscribed by the prince imperial to the emperor. On the 17th of September, M. Regnier got back his photographs, on one of which was a note running thus:—"My dear papa,—I send you these views of Hastings, hoping they will please you.—Louis Napoleon." The empress, through M. Fillion, told M. Regnier that there would be great danger in carrying out his project, and begged him not to attempt it. Of course, M. Regnier made light of the caution; and on the 20th of September, the very day of Jules Favre's interview with Count von Bismarck, he was standing in the presence of the North German chancellor. From him he requested a pass permitting him free access to the emperor at Wilhelmshöhe, at the same time hinting that his object was to give peace to France by restoring Napoleon to power. On seeing the photographic view inscribed by the prince imperial, Count von Bismarck seemed disposed to attach a little importance to M. Regnier's mission, and explained to him the extremely embarrassing position in which the Prussian government found itself by not having a definite government in France with which to treat. He also expressed his regret that the emperor and his advisers had not accepted his suggestion, and signed a peace on Prussian terms after Sedan; adding, that as the self-constituted government of France also refused to treat on those terms, Germany had no alternative but to continue the war until a disposition was shown to concede the indispensable alteration of frontier.

Later in the day, after the famous conversation with M. Favre, in which the latter refused to yield a "stone of the fortresses or an inch of territory," Bismarck saw M. Regnier again, and the latter expressed his determination to go at once to Metz and Strassburg, to see the commander-in-chief of each place, and to make an agreement that those towns should only be surrendered in the emperor's name. Count von Bismarck's answer was:—Sir,—Fate has already decided; to blind yourselves to that fact is the action not of an indomitable, but of an undecided nature. Nothing can prevent what is from being as it is. Do what you can to bring before us some one with power to treat with us, and you will render a great service to your country. I will give orders for a "general safeconduct" which will allow of your travelling in all German possessions, and everywhere in the places occupied by our troops. A telegram shall precede you to Metz, which will facilitate your entrance there.

Disguised, and aided by Count von Bismarck's safe-conduct, M. Regnier proceeded to Metz, which he entered on the 23rd of September, and made his way to the presence of Marshal Bazaine, who told him that his position was excellent, and that he had hope of holding out for a long period. Afterwards, however, he changed his tone, and said it would be as much as he could do to keep his ground till October 18, and that only by living on the flesh of the officers' horses. The marshal hailed with evident satisfaction a proposal that he should be allowed a free passage for himself and army, with their colours, artillery, ammunition, &c., through the enemy's lines, on strict parole not to fight against the Germans during the remainder of the campaign; it being moreover understood, first of all, that he and his army would put themselves at the disposal of the Chamber and the imperial government, which would then be, *de facto*, the only legal one.

To explain all this to the empress, and pave the way for a treaty of peace and the return of the emperor, it was arranged that General Bourbaki should leave Metz for Chislehurst; travelling, however, in strict incognito, and not allowing the real object of his mission to transpire. Though one of the bravest of French generals, Bourbaki was little skilled in diplomacy; and as soon as he found himself outside Metz his one feeling was that of regret that he had left it. Meeting a comrade on his way through Belgium, who taunted him with treason in flying from France, he indignantly produced the authorization of Marshal Bazaine, and in maintaining his military honour exposed the whole intrigue. He presented himself before the empress at Chislehurst, on the understanding that he was there by her orders, and was of course surprised and chagrined to find that he had been made the tool of imperialist manoeuvres. Bazaine signed his name under that of the prince imperial on the stereoscopic view of Hastings, as a proof to Count von Bismarck that he had authorized M. Regnier to treat. On the 28th of September, when the latter again saw the German chancellor, he was told that his powers were not sufficiently defined, and that there could be no further communication between them. Nevertheless, Count von Bismarck sent a telegram to Bazaine, asking whether he authorized M. Regnier to treat for the surrender of Metz, and received for answer, "I cannot reply in the affirmative to these questions. I have told M. Regnier that I cannot arrange for the capitulation of the city of Metz." Here the whole scheme of the latter appears to have broken up. He reached Chislehurst on the 4th of October, to find that General Bourbaki had done absolutely nothing in the affair committed to his charge, and that he had left en route for Tours to offer his military services to the provisional government. M. Regnier laboured to persuade the empress to persist in endeavouring to re-establish the dynasty. He told her of the fearful misery he had witnessed in the country; village after village entirely deserted, the inhabitants seeking refuge in the woods, and camping there without shelter or knowing where to find food, and that on the approach of winter famine would certainly overtake them, threatening to involve all in destruction. All was, however, in vain. He could not alter the opinions of the imperial exile, who feared that posterity would only see in her yielding a proof of dynastic selfishness; and that dishonour would attach to the name of anyone who should sign a treaty based upon a cession of territory. Thus M. Regnier's scheme, which had been effected with much trouble and danger, ended, and with it the hopes of those who saw in the imperial restoration the only chance of maintaining future order in France.

The failure of the sorties did not much depress the people of Metz. On the contrary, they wished to make common cause with the army, and memorialized the governor to be allowed to garrison the forts while the whole disposable military force made another sortie on a gigantic scale. The expression of this wish they conveyed to him through General Coffinières. At the same time energetic attempts were made to effect a fraternization with the army, and a spirited address, signed by numbers of the citizens and national guards, was circulated in the camps. "We will shed with you," it said, "our last drop of blood; we will share with you our last crust. Let us rise as one man, and victory is ours. Long live our brothers of the army! Long live France, one and indivisible!"

The marshal, however, who had accompanied his men to the hottest part of the fight on the memorable 7th October, and who knew the utter inutility of the fearful sacrifice of life which another sortie must occasion, declined for the present to accede to the citizens' request. He was deterred also by a consideration of the state of his army, which was suffering exceedingly from the exposure of their camps and the privations to which they were subjected. About the 13th, the date of the memorial, there were, of soldiers alone, 23,000 in ambulances and private houses. There was also an enormous increase of sickness amongst the civilians, as might be expected in a place crowded with double the ordinary number of inhabitants; the surplus largely consisting of the poorer class of agricultural labourers, who naturally soon fell ill in a town abounding in hospitals fitted only to be human abattoirs, surrounded by huge camps where all sanitary rules were utterly neglected. It was, indeed, a marvel that Metz was not one huge lazar-house; but except amongst infants and the aged, the death-rate was by no means excessive, and the dead were buried without murmuring.

We have already said that as a fortification Metz might well have been deemed impregnable. It was handed down to the present generation, by Cormontaigne and other great engineers of the last century, as a very strong fortress—strong in its defensive works. The Second Empire added to these a circle of seven very large detached forts at distances of from two and a half to three miles from the centre of the town, so as to secure it from bombardment even with rifled guns, and to transform the whole into a large entrenched camp second to Paris only. With an army, however, of about 180,000 men added to the usual population of 60,000, and whole villages of country people who had sought shelter behind the forts, it was evident that the stock of provisions, however large, must soon be exhausted, and the terrible alternative of starvation or surrender arise. This moment of grief appeared now to have arrived. Whispered at first, with bated breath, in quiet corners; then talked of amongst twos and threes; then murmured in coteries and *cafés*; and at last the general commanding the town called the municipal council together and told them that the bread was done, and the city must capitulate. "Capitulate—never! not whilst a boot remains to be eaten," was the response. Measures were now taken to at least postpone it. But they came too late. Not a pastry cook was allowed to bake a bun for luxury, bran was mixed with the flour already existing, and no more white flour was allowed to be made. Other expedients were adopted, and good brown bread was daily to be had. All were placed on rations; if any went out to dinner they had to take with them their own bread; but generally indeed, dining out simply meant a feast of reason, with an interlude of horse flesh. In the early part of October a leg of mutton fetched eight francs the pound. Potatoes rose to one or one and a half franc the pound, and then disappeared altogether. Salad vegetables existed, but the places in which they were kept were very hard to find. Fowls fetched almost any price, and the lucky *avant poste* who could kill a rabbit under the pretext of firing at a Prussian was a wealthy man; forty francs being the least he might expect as a reward for his dexterity, plus the rabbit. Eggs rose to one franc each, and sugar sold at five francs and even at nine francs the pound. Coals there were none, and the supply of gas was almost exhausted when the end came. But the greatest privation was salt; nine francs had been paid for a pound, and he who could give a pinch of it was regarded as a valued friend; for the only absolute suffering arose from the want of it. Horse flesh required some seasoning to make it palatable. All sauces had disappeared, and food was equine in the extreme: horse-flesh soup usually excellent; boiled horse flesh by no means bad, often very good; horse beans as a *legume*, varied by lentils occasionally and a *roti* of horse, often tough beyond mastication—made the unvarying round. Such rations were unsatisfying and far from nutritious, as the animal had generally lived as long as possible, and was only killed to prevent his dying. The army was often worse off than the town, frequently from want of direction rather than of food. The *avant postes* were often forty-eight hours without victuals through the carelessness and neglect of the intendance; and as no additional means of grinding corn had been adopted, grain alone was often served out instead of bread. Of this the soldiers had to make the best use they could, bruising rather than grinding it in coffee mills, and boiling or baking the crushed mass.

The tedium of the siege to the inhabitants was increased at this time by the rather arbitrary suppression of several journals; and a curious feature of the siege was the excessive tenderness of the authorities towards the enemy. One newspaper, the *Indépendant*, was even suppressed for inserting an article severely condemning the Prussian proclamation which described the franc-tireurs as traitors, and threatened them with death whenever captured. The author of the article indignantly protested against the suppression, declined writing again under such liabilities, and threatened that, in a day not far distant, he would once more use his pen "to write history." To refer with any amount of respect to the republic also procured the exclusion of the article—for all articles had now to undergo a preliminary inspection. At length the journals retorted by suppressing anything that came to them from the military authorities, or by refusing to insert any communication with the word "capitulation" in it. Numberless sly hits were made at the marshal, with that adroitness of inuendo in which the French are always so felicitous; and the town swarmed with secretly printed pamphlets, not very complimentary to the powers that were. There was a great scarcity of paper in Metz at the time, and the journals came out in all shades of colour, from the brightest red to the deepest blue. The people, however, considered themselves lucky when they could get anything at all to read; and were equally compelled to be satisfied if they could obtain a meal of horse-flesh and a ration of brown bread.

With such a state of things existing in the town and camp,, it was impossible not to see that the end was fast approaching. Other indications were not wanting. From about the 15th October neither besieged nor besiegers fired a shot, and a feeling of cordiality again grew up between the outposts. The officers bowed to each other, and the men took off their caps in sign of friendship, and talked together. Sorties indeed continued, but their character was wofully changed. Instead of brilliant and impetuous battalions, they consisted first of tens, then forties, fifties, and even hundreds, of wretched, haggard, half-starved deserters. For a time these were received by the Prussians; but on a body of 800 presenting themselves, they were told they must go back and endure their troubles a little longer. Another day, through the driving sleet which flew like a thick mist across the plain, a black mass was descried advancing towards the Prussian lines, which at first was supposed to indicate a last desperate effort, and the alarm was at once given. As the shower passed there stood before the Germans, not soldiers, but thousands of men, women, and children, the civil inhabitants of Metz. The officer at once despatched orderlies in all directions, with orders to the foreposts to allow no individual to pass, and to fire upon any who should persist in the attempt. One man, sent as advance guard of this band, advanced a little too near, and was shot. The unfortunate citizens came to a standstill; but a woman advanced with a white pocket-handkerchief fastened on the point of a stick. The Prussians by this time were keeping up a sharp fire over the heads of this jaded crowd, who took the warning, and in a short time went back to Metz. The female kept advancing, but, on looking round and seeing herself deserted, she also turned and fled.

But if military operations were for a time suspended, diplomacy was not idle. On the 17th of October Marshal Bazaine's aide-de-camp, General Boyer, passed blindfolded through the German military lines to the headquarters of Prince Frederick Charles. On the 18th he went to Versailles and was conducted to Count von Bismarck. His appearance created such a sensation among the French inhabitants, that a guard had to be sent for to keep an open space in front of the count's windows. According to an apparently trustworthy account of their interview, published in the *Debats* in June, 1871, and when there had thus been ample time to obtain correct information, the general, after a few formal remarks, asked Count von Bismarck what were his aims and objects; in a word, what he desired as the result of the war. To this Count von Bismarck replied very frankly, that his policy was most simple; that the French might do as they please, that as for themselves (the Germans) they were sure of Paris, its fall being merely a question of time. "The French took Rome without injuring its monuments; the Germans will do the same with Paris, which is a city of art in which nothing shall be destroyed. I have nothing to say to the various considerations that you lay before me. You tell me that your Metz army is the sole element of order remaining in France, and that it is alone capable of establishing and upholding a government in the country. If this is the case, constitute this government; we will offer no opposition, and we will even render you some assistance. The marshal will repair to some town to be named with his army, and summon the empress thither. In our eyes the sole legal government of the country is still that of the plebiscitum of the 8th of May; it is the only one we recognize. You speak to me of the necessity for putting an end to a war such as this one; but whom am I to treat with? There is no Chamber. I had proposed to let the elections be held on the 2nd of October; the departments occupied by the Prussian troops would have had full liberty in the selection of their deputies. This offer was not taken advantage of. I then suggested the date of the 18th of October, with no better success." Count von Bismarck, entering into another train of ideas, then said with no little warmth, "I cannot say what will befall France, nor what is the future that awaits her; but I do know this, that it will redound to her shame, to her eternal shame in all time, in all ages, and in all tongues, to have abandoned her emperor as she did after Sedan. The stain which she will never wash out is the revolution of the 4th of September." Finally, returning to what was peculiarly the object of the interview, the chancellor repeated that he would offer no opposition to the reconstitution of a government by Marshal Bazaine and his army.

General Boyer stayed two days at Versailles, had two interviews with the count, and then returned to the neighbourhood of Metz, before entering which, however, he visited Wilhelmshöhe. On the 23rd he once more repaired to Versailles. From his statement it appeared that Bazaine was now quite willing to surrender with his array, but the commandant of Metz, General Coffinières, would not consent to give up the fortress. Prince Frederick Charles very naturally objected to take charge of 80,000 or 90,000 soldiers, hampered with the condition of having the same battle to fight for the city, and his answer simply was, "Metz, or nothing at all." Meanwhile, so confident were the German authorities of the early surrender, that a château at Frescati was prepared for the expected negotiations. Morning after morning every eye was turned anxiously in the direction of the town and outworks, until, on the 25th, a flag of truce appeared with a despatch to Prince Frederick Charles, intimating that General Changarnier would wait upon him at twelve o'clock that day.

Marshal Bazaine had received, almost at the same moment, a despatch from General Boyer, and another from Count von Bismarck, in which the latter declined all negotiations save on the basis of unconditional surrender. On receipt of these documents, which destroyed the marshal's hopes and plans, he immediately convoked his council of war. The council decided unanimously, with one exception, that the capitulation was necessary. Almost up to the last moment General Coffinières desired to make another attempt to break through the Prussian investment. By seven o'clock in the evening, however, Bazaine had succeeded in convincing Coffinières that, even if successful, such an attempt would only postpone the capitulation for a few weeks, at a great sacrifice of life; and accordingly a messenger was sent to Prince Frederick Charles, intimating an intention to surrender. This was the first proposition which included both the fortress and the army of Bazaine encamped outside. In expectation of an outbreak on the 24th, Bazaine, whether rightly or wrongly, had fully made up his mind that further sorties were useless, and that Metz must speedily succumb. The Viscount de Valcourt contrived to escape in disguise through the Prussian lines, with a despatch in a hollow tooth, covered with a top dressing of gutta percha. This was addressed to the authorities at Tours, and ran thus:—"I must give up Metz in a day or two. Make peace as soon as you can.—Bazaine, Marshal," &c. On the 25th October the marshal communicated to the council of war that he had received a despatch from General Boyer, stating that the empress would not accept the regency. Bazaine added, that as Bismarck had now refused to separate the fate of the town from that of the army, nothing remained to be done but to endeavour to get the best terms possible, and to accustom both soldier and civilian to the idea of capitulation.

General Cissy was then sent to arrange a meeting between the headquarters of the two armies, and, as we have just stated, General Changarnier subsequently had an interview with Prince Frederick Charles. It was hoped that the veteran soldier of France now sent to negotiate would be able to obtain exceptionally honourable terms for a valiant army, which had held the Prussians in check for three months and a half, after having been beaten by them several times. The prince gave the general an affable and cordial reception, but told him, that as he did not form part of the active army, he could not treat with him regarding the conditions of the capitulation; and that their conversation must be confined to pure and simple details respecting local events. He said, he knew well that Metz had victuals for only three days, and showing Changarnier a train in the railway station crammed with different kinds of provisions, he added: "That is for the city of Metz and for your army, which is in want of everything. We wish to put an end to your suffering!" Changarnier, however, proved to the prince that, although holding no separate command, he was nevertheless officially attached to Bazaine, and was acting in this matter with his authority. He pleaded hard to obtain for the soldiers the privilege of returning to their homes and families; but of course such a request could not be granted, and it is almost surprising that so old and experienced an officer should have thought of making it. At the conclusion of the interview he was almost heartbroken, and said, with a flood of tears, "We shall fall, but with honour. I wish, gentlemen, that neither you nor any brave soldier may ever experience this." Changarnier was then conducted back, as he had been brought, blindfolded, through the Prussian camp, and General Cissy was once more sent to continue the negotiation. He urged that though the army capitulated, that was no reason why Metz should surrender. The prince replied: "Before the declaration of war, we knew as well as you, down to the most minute details, the state of the defences of the town. Then the forts were scarcely sketched out, and the town could only make a feeble resistance. It is since the presence of the French army under its walls that Metz has become what it is. Through your exertions it has been converted into a fortress of the first class, and must accept, as a consequence, all the conditions of a capitulation which will make no distinction between the town and the army." As no mitigation of the humiliating terms thus seemed possible, submission only remained, and General Jarras, of the marshal's staff, was sent to arrange the clauses of the capitulation.

The discussion of these details was long, obstinate, and often warm, the terms demanded by the Germans appearing to their adversaries extremely and needlessly severe. The evening of the 25th, the whole of the 26th and the 27th, was occupied before the clauses were finally settled. So certain, however, were the Germans of the ultimate issue of whatever negotiations were carried on, that their second corps received marching orders for Paris at noon on the 25th, and was on its way early in the evening. On the 26th the interview became very stormy on the part of the French commissioners. They insisted on the officers retaining their side arms, and it was found necessary to telegraph to the Prussian king at Versailles for specific instructions. The king conceded the privilege in a telegraphic despatch which arrived at three a.m. on the next day. Early on the morning of that day the commissioners again met, there being present General Jarras, Marshal Bazaine's chief of the staff, and Colonel Fay and Major Samucle on the part of General Coffinières, the commandant of the fortress. The German commissioners were Generals Stiehle and Wartensleben. The conference lasted until eight o'clock at night, when a draught was signed for the absolute surrender of Metz and all its fortifications, armaments, stores, and munitions, together with the garrison and the whole of Bazaine's army.

In addition to the leading points of the surrender, the draught stipulated that the French troops should be conducted, without arms, by regiments or regimental corps, in military order, to some place to be afterwards indicated by the Prussians; that the French officers in command of the men should, after their arrival at this place, be at liberty to return to the entrenched camps, or to Metz, on giving their word of honour not to quit either place without an order of permission from the German commandant; that the troops, after surrender, should be marched to bivouac, retaining their personal effects, cooking utensils, &c.; that the French generals, officers, and military employés ranking as commissioned officers, who should engage by written promise not to bear arms against Germany, or to agitate against Prussian interests during the war, should not be made prisoners, but should be permitted to retain their arms, and to keep their personal property, in recognition of the courage displayed by them during the campaign. It was also agreed that all questions of detail, such as might concern the commercial rights of the town of Metz, and the interests and rights of civilians and non-combatants, should be considered and treated subsequently in an appendix to the military paper of capitulation; and that any clause, sentence, or word which might present a doubt as to its exact meaning, should be interpreted in favour of the French people.

The Metz municipal council, wrought up to the highest pitch of excitement by the reticence of the military authorities, went on the 24th to General Coffinières and demanded to be informed how matters stood. The governor told them he had no information to give, either as to the position of affairs in the rest of France or of those more immediately outside Metz; and advised them to apply to the marshal, which they agreed to do. The result of the inquiry confirmed their worst fears, that a capitulation was in course of arrangement. A thrill of rage and consternation passed through the city as the truth flashed upon it. The town council now met daily, and in answer to their persistent demand for a true statement of the situation, General Coffinières, on the morning of the 27th, issued the following official proclamation:—

"Inhabitants of Metz,—It is my duty to faithfully state to you our situation, well persuaded that your manly and courageous souls will rise to the height of this grave occasion. Pound us is an army which has never been conquered, which has stood firm before the fire of the foe, and withstood the rudest shocks. This army, interposed between our city and her besiegers, has given us time to put our forts in a complete state of defence, to mount upon our walls more than 600 pieces of cannon, and has held in check an army of more than 200,000 men. Within our walls we have a population full of energy and patriotism, firmly determined to defend itself to the last extremity. I have already informed the municipal council that, notwithstanding the reduction of rations, notwithstanding the perquisitions made by the civil and military authorities, we have no more food than will serve till to-morrow. Further than this, our brave army, tried already by the fire of the enemy, has lust 42,000 men, after horrible sufferings from the inclemency of the season and privations of every kind. The council of war has proof of these facts, and the marshal commanding in chief has given formal orders, as he had the right, to direct a portion of our provisions for the purposes of the army. With all this, thanks to our economy, we can still resist up to the 30th inst., but then our situation will not be sensibly modified. Never in the annals of military history has a place resisted until its resources have been so completely exhausted as this has, and none has ever been so encumbered with sick and wounded. We are, then, condemned to succumb; but it will be with honour, and when we find ourselves conquered by famine. The enemy, who has so closely invested us for more than seventy days, knows that he has almost attained the end of his efforts. He demands the town and the army, and will not permit the severance of the interests of the one from that of the other. Four or five days' desperate resistance would only place the inhabitants in a worse position. Rest assured that your private interests will be defended with the most lively solicitude. Seek to support stoically this great misfortune, and cherish the firm hope that Metz, this grand and patriotic city, will remain to France.

"F. COFFINIERES,"<br>"the General, &c."

"METZ, 27th October, 1870."

This proclamation, though full of kindly feeling, did not satisfy the people. The old question was asked and re-asked—Why were we not told of the shortness of provisions before? Why were not some means taken to prevent waste? Waste indeed there had been. On the retreat from the battle of Gravelotte, coffee, sugar, and biscuits, to the value of more than 100,000 francs, were burnt because they encumbered the roads. More than seventy carriages, which had been in the morning full of provisions, entered Metz empty. The roadside ditches were choked with boxes of biscuit bearing the English weight, and with the familiar inscription, in large black letters, "Navy biscuit." Soldiers filled their sacks with sugar, which they sold in town, or returned with a sugar loaf on each shoulder as a trophy of the maladministration of the army and the weakness of their generals. "How was it," it was inquired, "that in the early days of the siege officers were allowed to draw their double rations in camp, and then to come into the town and eat and drink as though no allowance had been made them! There were for three-quarters of the time an average of 8000 officers, with double rations for at least fifty days of the blockade, giving a total of 800,000 single rations, and who, meanwhile, fed upon the provisions of the town. All this, if you knew we had not sufficient provisions for a lengthened time, you should have prevented."

There seems to have been some truth in this, but expostulation came too late to serve any good purpose; already upon the walls was the proclamation of Marshal Bazaine, announcing the dreaded event in even plainer terms than that of the commandant. It ran as follows:—

"GENERAL ORDER. No. 12.

"To the Army of the Rhine.

"Conquered by famine, we are compelled to submit to the laws of war by constituting ourselves prisoners. At various epochs in our military history brave troops, commanded by Massena, Klèber, Gouvion St. Cyr, have experienced the same fate, which does not in any way tarnish military honour when, like you, their duty has been so gloriously accomplished to the extremity of human limits.

"All that was loyally possible to be done in order to avoid this end has been attempted, and could not succeed.

"As to renewing a supreme attempt to break through the fortified lines of the enemy, in spite of your gallantry and the sacrifice of thousands of lives, which may still be useful to the country, it would have been unavailing, on account of the armament and of the overwhelming forces which guard and support those lines: a disaster would have been the consequence.

"Let us be dignified in adversity. Let us respect the honourable conventions which have been stipulated, if we wish to be respected as we deserve to be.

"Let us, above all, for the reputation of our army, shun acts of indiscipline, such as the destruction of arms and *matériel*, since, according to military usages, places and armament will be restored to France when peace is signed.

"In leaving the command I make it a duty to express to generals, officers, and soldiers all, my gratitude for their loyal co-operation, their brilliant valour on the battle-field, their resignation in privations, and it is with broken heart that I separate from you.

"The Marshal of France, Commander-in-Chief,
                "(Signed)   BAZAINE."

It is almost impossible to describe the excitement which prevailed when this order was issued. The bewildered citizens ran to and fro in the streets, seeking a leader but finding none. The national guard refused to give up its arms, and assembled in the Place d'Armes. Some few officers of different regiments would have placed themselves at their head, but they were without any plan or point of union, and ran about like ants in an invaded ant-hill. The door leading to the clock-tower was broken in with the butts of muskets; the staircase was carried, and the great alarm bell of Metz was rung for the first time since 1812. The population streamed into the square from all quarters, and the streets were crowded with angry citizens. In the caserne of the engineers, a huge building on the esplanade, a band of officers of artillery and engineers, who had long been discontented with their enforced inactivity, were gathered together, and 8000 officers and men, divided into bodies, hidden in different parts of the town, were ready to put themselves under a general who had promised to lead them; but at the last moment he failed, and consternation and disorder were the result.

Now was exhibited a ridiculous feature of the outbreak. Foolish men crept in, and wise men crept out. An editor of one of the Metz newspapers, who had before achieved glory by entering the ante-chamber of General Coffinières and breaking down the harmless bust of the ex-emperor, preserving the whip with which he had done it as a trophy of his prowess, mounted his horse armed with a revolver, which he fired repeatedly in the air. He was attended by a young lady, the daughter of a gunsmith, who, mounted on one of her father's horses, and armed with one of his pistols, having a pocket handkerchief tied to it, bore aloft her standard, like a second Joan of Arc, through the streets of Metz. Ridicule speedily put an end to the silly movement; but it had the effect of defeating the seriously-entertained design of spiking the guns which yet remained in position, breaking the small arms contained in the arsenal, and finally blowing up the forts. Men were willing to brave death, but they feared being laughed at. The voltigeurs of the imperial guard, accompanied by the half of a regiment of the line, quickly suppressed the disorderly demonstration. The arms of the national guard were taken from them, and the few officers who could fled in sorrow from their last hope. Some of them managed to steal through the gates of the town, and tramped along the muddy road to Grigy, joined here and there by a few stragglers. They crept through the dark wood, but there all hope was lost. At four mètres apart stood the Prussian outposts; to proceed was death, to go back shame. They chose the shame, and the last night they entered Metz was one of weeping and tears.

Once more, and for the last time, the municipal council of the French city of Metz assembled, and, as if ashamed of the childish display of their fellow-townsmen, addressed to them a manifesto as follows:—

"Dear Fellow-citizens,—True courage consists in supporting an evil without those agitations which but serve to aggravate it. Afflicted as we all are by that which has fallen upon us to-day, not one of us can reproach himself with having failed, even for a single day, to do his duty. Let us not present the wretched spectacle of intestine strife, nor furnish any pretext for future violence, or for new and worse misfortunes. The thought that this trial will only be a transient one, and that we have assumed none of the responsibility to the country or to history attached to it, should be in such a moment our consolation. We confide the common security to the wisdom of the population."

This proclamation was signed by the mayor and all the council, but it had no date. The date was, in fact, sufficiently fixed by the circumstances. That black Friday—a day henceforth doubly unlucky in the history of the city of Metz—needed no formal date.

At one o'clock on the 28th it was ordered that the French army should formally lay down its arms within the city. There was no set ceremony, yet the affair was imposing from its very simplicity. Each corps, in order, laid down its arms in the neighbourhood of its own station. The third army corps—that of Leboeuf—began the movement, and the marshal himself came first, with a scowl upon his swarthy features. He wheeled to one side, and stood by the single Prussian officer whose duty it was to superintend the stacking of the arms. Regiment after regiment, the men defiled past, piling their arms in great heaps at the word of command from their own officers, who gave their parole, and were allowed to retain their swords. Some, however, declined accepting the terms, and preferring to go into captivity in Prussia, laid down their swords as the men did their Chassepots. The disarmed troops then returned into their bivouacs, which they occupied for one night more, before quitting for others round which should stand Prussian sentries.

The weather on the 29th of October was as dismal as the day was a dark one in the history of unhappy France. Thick masses of black clouds rolled overhead, and the rain poured down in torrents as the Frenchmen came forth and rendered themselves to their captors. Prince Frederick Charles, with his staff and officers, had posted themselves behind Jouy, on the Frescati road. Bazaine appeared first of all; he rode at the head of his officers to the prince, to whom he simply said: "Monseigneur, I have the honour to present myself."

The prince motioned him to his side, and then began the march of the officers and the army, partly classified according to their arms, partly pell-mell. Those who had a command were on horseback; the others had their arms in the state in which they afterwards laid them down in the town. Each corps, as it marched out, was received by the Prussians covering the respective section of the environment. They were led by their own officers, who formally handed them over to those of Prussia, after which those who had given their parole were at liberty to quit the ranks and return to Metz. The men were then marched out to the bivouac places, where wood for fires had been collected, and a supply of provisions was ready for distribution. The demeanour of the French troops was on the whole becoming, though here and there was evidence of considerable demoralization, the men being in a state of intoxication, and their clothes disarranged in utter disregard of decency. The officers, however, were taciturn and downcast. The reception of the prisoners, in the meadows near the Jouy road, lasted from 1 till 9. The last corps that finished the procession as evening closed in was the finest of all—the grenadiers of the guard, and they, as they parted from their officers, in many instances embraced them, kissing them on both cheeks. Never was seen more quiet, soldier-like demeanour than that exhibited by this splendid body of men as they marched past in perfect silence. Not a word was spoken. All that could be heard was the measured tread of thousands of feet as they splashed along the muddy road. The Prussian officers gazed with surprise and no little admiration, as regiment after regiment filed past, and congratulated themselves that they had no longer to fight such men.

At the same hour that the French commenced leaving the city, a battalion of the seventh army corps marched forward and took possession of La Porte Serpenoise, one of the gates of Metz, and another battalion from the same corps occupied the Porte Moselle. Two hours before the occupation of the fortress, an artillery officer and a small body of under-officers, accompanied by engineers, had been sent forward from each of the occupying detachments, to take over the powder-magazines and the respective forts, and not till they had reported that all was in order were the troops allowed to march in. This precaution was no doubt dictated by a recollection of the catastrophe at Laon. As the party approached the gate their wonderful discipline revealed the secret of their victory. Steady, resolute, unimpassioned, not a sign of exultation was visible on their faces. At a word they scaled the slippery glacis, and ranged themselves with mathematical precision along the rampart's crest. Their officers marched in front, keenly scanning the fosse, and guarding against every possibility of surprise; possession of the town was taken with as much caution as though its occupants had formed the grand guard of an impending battle-field. First the *tête du pont* was passed, the ravelin was reached, and the same minute surveillance was used. Lastly, the town's gate was entered with even greater precaution, and at twenty minutes past one o'clock the first Prussian foot fell within the city of Metz-la-Pucelle. Possession was quietly taken of the Place Moselle, and at four o'clock in the afternoon the battalion marched through the sad and silent streets (in some of which the houses were completely shut up), playing victorious German tunes. They entered the Place d'Armes, where the first object they saw was the black-draped statue of the gallant Marshal Fabert, who, as the inscription on the pedestal recalled, would, "rather than yield up a place intrusted to him by his sovereign, place in the breach himself, his family, his goods, and all he had, and never hesitate a moment." Four bodies of infantry, whose burnished helmets glistened in the fading light, marched and counter-marched in the square, speedily clearing it of the few idle gazers of the lower classes who had gathered in it.

General von Kummer was appointed provisional German commandant of Metz, and on the day after his entry he issued the following proclamation:—

"The fortress of Metz was occupied yesterday by the Prussian troops, and the undersigned is provisionally commandant of the place. I would wish to maintain among the Prussian troops their known discipline, the liberty of the person, and the security of property. Difficulties may occur at first to the inhabitants before all affairs are properly regulated; but they ought to be brought to me, and I shall know how to appreciate the circumstances under which the difficulties have occurred. If I encounter disobedience or resistance, I shall act with all severity and according to the laws of war; whoever shall place in danger the German troops, or shall cause prejudice by perfidy, will be brought before a council of war; whoever shall act as a spy to the French troops, or shall lodge or give them assistance; whoever shows the roads to the French troops voluntarily; whoever shall kill or wound the German troops, or the persons belonging to their suite; whoever shall destroy the canals, railways, or telegraph wires; whoever shall render the roads impracticable; whoever shall burn munitions and provisions of war; and, lastly, whoever shall take up arms against the German troops, will be punished by death.

"It is also declared that, (1) the houses in which, or from out of which, any one commits acts of hostilities towards the German troops will be used as barracks; (2) no more than ten persons will be allowed to assemble in the streets or public places; (3) the inhabitants must deliver up all arms by four o'clock on Monday, the 31st of October, at the Palais, rue de la Princerie; (4) all windows are to be lighted up during the night in case of an alarm.

"VON KUMMER.

"METZ, *October* 30, 1870."

By the capitulation of Metz a terrible blow, indeed, was inflicted on the French nation. Metz the invincible, Metz which was always French in tongue and race, even when it was a city of the holy Roman empire, Metz which had been incorporated in France for more than three hundred years—indeed, from before the English lost Calais—Metz had fallen, and three marshals of France and a vast army had surrendered with it to the enemy. To the victorious Prussians the Sedan prize of an emperor was of little use. But the great stronghold and the beautiful city that the French loved, along with the very flower and front of the army of France, and a mass of munitions of war, among which were 400 pieces of artillery, 100 mitrailleuses, and 53 eagles—all these formed a trophy which the German armies looked upon as shedding a new brilliancy on their victorious banners. The material gains indeed were past calculation. The strongest fortress in France, surrounded by works so extensive and formidable that the army of Bazaine could take refuge behind them without fear of a direct attack, was now in the hands of the Germans. On French territory they held a place from which all the armies of France, if France had armies, could not drive them. It was easily accessible from their own frontier, connected with North and South Germany by lines of railway, and possessed of it they could, even if they held nothing else, command the north-east of France up to the Argonne. Nor was this all. Metz was an arsenal as well as a fortress; to the guns on its fortifications must be added those which were found inside, as well as a vast machinery ready for the fabrication of arms and munitions of war. The spoils of the greatest army that had ever laid down its arms within historical times were in the hands of the victors. The entire army of the Rhine was armed with the Chassepot, and every weapon, except those which the French soldiers destroyed in their rage and despair, would be available to arm the German levies; while such was the quantity of field artillery, both of guns and mitrailleuses, which now fell into German hands, that it would be in the power of the king of Prussia to equip a first-rate army with the spoils of a single day. As to Metz itself, the French were, as we have said, intensely proud of their, till now, virgin city—proud of her historical fame, proud of her great strength, proud of her gardens, and bridges, and promenades that made her the queen of the valley of the Moselle. Her cathedral, if less renowned than that of Strassburg, was yet a noble and stately building; and there was this further point in her favour, when contrasted with Strassburg, that she was a French city, and had never belonged to Germany. It is true that she was once, as a free town, under the protection of the German empire; but then, as now, Metz was French in all her ways and habits, her speech and costume. And in her present days of bitter distress France had never ceased to look towards Metz for some faint gleam of consolation and hope. The sunlight that touched the grey forts of the capital of Lorraine, seemed to shed from thence a vague warmth and light of comfort through the gloom that lay dark over the nation. The hope of France was with Bazaine. Bazaine was to do this and that; the army of the Rhine was suddenly to appear in the rear of the Germans besieging Paris. Wild stories and rumours grew and flourished amid these eager anticipations. Bazaine could get away if he wished. Bazaine was amply provisioned for three months. Bazaine was lying inactive only that he might delude his foes, and strike hard and sharp when the moment came for his co-operation with the nebulous armies which, from over the whole of France, were supposed to be floating like clouds towards him. Nay, Bazaine had already broken through, and was at Thionville. Such were some of the delusions which the French people, following the example of their rulers, had invented for each other to believe. Long anticipated as it had been, the capitulation of Metz came upon the German army with a strange suddenness. It had been announced but a day or two before that the negotiations had been definitively closed; and men prepared themselves as they best could for another tedious period of on waiting, diversified with fighting. It was not till the following proclamation of Prince Frederick Charles was issued, that the men could fully comprehend the extent of the victory their patient courage had achieved:—

"Soldiers of the First and Second Armies,—You have fought and invested in Metz an enemy whom you had vanquished, for seventy days, seventy long days, which have made most of your regiments the richer in fame and honour, and have made none poorer. You allowed no egress to the brave enemy until he would lay down his arms. This has been done. To-day at last this army, still 173,000 men strong, the best in France, consisting of more than five entire army corps, including the imperial guard, with three marshals of France, with more than fifty generals, and above 6000 officers, has capitulated, and with it Metz, never before taken. With this bulwark, which we restore to Germany, innumerable stores of cannons, arms, and war material have fallen to the conqueror. Besides these bloody laurels, you have defeated him by your bravery in the two days' battle at Noisseville and in the engagements round Metz, which are more numerous than the surrounding villages after which you name these combats. I acknowledge your bravery gladly and gratefully, but not it alone. I estimate almost higher your obedience and your composure, cheerfulness, and resignation in enduring difficulties of many kinds. All this distinguishes the good soldier. To-day's great and memorable success was prepared by the battles which we fought before we invested Metz, and—as we should remember in gratitude to him—by the king himself, by the corps then marching with him, and by all those dear comrades who died on the battle-field or through maladies here. All this previously rendered possible the great work which, by God's blessing, you to-day see completed—viz., the collapse of the power of France. The importance of to-day's event is incalculable. You soldiers, who were assembled under my orders for this object, are about to proceed to various destinations. My farewell, therefore, to the generals, officers, and soldiers of the first army and Kummer's division, and a God speed to further successes.

"(Signed) The General of Cavalry,

"FREDERICK CHARLES."

"HEAD-QUARTERS, CORNY BEFORE METZ,
  "*October* 27, 1870."

On hearing at Versailles of the fall of Metz, the king of Prussia telegraphed to Queen Augusta as follows:—

"This morning the army of Marshal Bazaine and the fortress of Metz capitulated, with 173,000 prisoners, including 20,000 sick and wounded.

"This afternoon the army and the garrison will lay down their arms.

"This is one of the most important, events of the month.

"Providence be thanked!"

There was at the time a general disposition to sneer at his Majesty's way of describing a military catastrophe of unprecedented magnitude as the "most important event of the month." And yet a very slight effort of memory will show that the language was as strictly warrantable as simple. July had the declaration of war and the arming of Germany; August the triumphs of Woerth and Spichern, of Vionville and Gravelotte; September the capitulation of Napoleon's army at Sedan; and October, ere its close, gave into the hands of the monarch of an united Germany the maiden fortress which in other times Charles Quint beleaguered in vain! On the 28th the king conferred the dignity of field-marshal on the Crown Prince and Prince Frederick Charles; and it was about this time that rumour first began to speak of a restored empire of Germany in the person of the Prussian monarch—a project which was carried into effect not many months later, and to which the extraordinary successes of the war were manifestly leading the thoughts, and probably the desires of the German people.

On the 3rd of November the event was further alluded to in the following order of the day:—

"Soldiers of the Confederate Armies!—When we took the field, three months ago, I expressed my confidence that God would be with our just cause. This confidence has been realized. I recall to you Woerth, Saarbrück, and the bloody battles before Metz, Sedan, Beaumont, and Strassburg—each engagement was a victory for us. You are worthy of glory. You have maintained all the virtues which especially distinguish soldiers. By the capitulation of Metz the last army of the enemy is destroyed. I take advantage of this moment to express my thanks to all of you, from the general to the soldier. Whatever the future may still bring to us, I look forward to it with calmness, because I know that with such soldiers victory cannot fail!

"WILHELM."

That King William did not overrate the importance of the great event of October 27, was abundantly shown by the way in which the news was received throughout France. Her armies might be defeated, her emperor made prisoner, her fortresses of minor rank, or even Strassburg, fall into the hands of the enemy; but that Metz, her virgin and greatest stronghold, should share the same fate, seemed never to have entered the minds of Frenchmen. At Lyons, some persons who repeated the rumour of the capitulation were assaulted and taken to the police station. Several days after the *Journal de Genéve* ventured to intimate that Bazaine had surrendered, but the Lyonnais set upon the vendors, tore their papers, and threatened to drown all who should be found reading them; while the copies which had been supplied to the public establishments of the city were publicly burned. In Marseilles, and several other large towns, the news was received with a feeling of grief and depression befitting the greatness of the calamity. Immense crowds of workmen, displaying flags draped in mourning, but crowned with immortelles, marched bareheaded and in silence to the prefectures. When rumours of the capitulation reached Tours, the delegate government were besieged with crowds of excited citizens eager to know the truth, and the following official notice appeared in the *Moniteur* on the evening of the 28th:—

"Grave news, concerning the origin and veracity of which, in spite of my active researches, I have no sort of official information, reach me from all sides. The rumour of the capitulation of Metz circulates. It is good that you should know what the government thinks on the announcement of such a disaster. Such an event could only be the result of a crime, whose authors would deserve to be outlawed. I will keep you informed of what occurs; but be convinced, whatever may happen, that we will not allow ourselves to be cast down even by the most frightful misfortunes. In these days of vile (*scélerates*) capitulations there is one thing that cannot, and must not capitulate, and that is the French Republic.

"LEON GAMBETTA."

As the unwelcome truth was gradually confirmed, those of the French papers formerly published in Paris, but which now appeared at Tours, Poitiers, and Bordeaux, all commented upon the fall of Metz in terms expressive of pungent sorrow, and more or less of indignation. The *Français* referred "with deep grief to this great catastrophe. But before judging and denouncing we feel bound to wait for an explanation of the cruel necessities which induced Marshal Bazaine to take that fatal step, and also for a statement of the clauses of the capitulation. The disaster of Sedan struck us down; that of Metz overwhelms us. It is now a time to repeat, with supplications and tearful eyes, 'May God protect France!' " The *Gazette de France* recorded the fact "with a broken heart. It is almost impossible to believe that such a thing is possible. What curse is it that weighs upon France? 150,000 men formerly sufficed to gain victories over 400,000 enemies, but now they only serve to hasten the capitulation of a fortress. What a melancholy history is this! Strassburg fell because it had not a sufficient number of defenders, while Metz, in whose walls the enemy's cannon had made no breach, succumbed because it had too many soldiers shut up within its defences."

The fall of Metz was an event so grave as to justify a little caution in making it known to the French nation, in the excited state in which it then was. Anxious, however, to account for the event in such a way as to save the credit of the country, and at the same time, to detract from the triumph of their enemy, the Tours government scrupled not to heap upon the head of Bazaine charges of the vilest treachery. The gallant Uhrich of Strassburg, after having his praises sung throughout France for weeks, was at last accused of treason; and after making a surrender on a far greater scale, Bazaine could never have hoped to escape the same fate. M. de Valcourt, the officer of his staff who had escaped from Metz and arrived at Tours as the bearer of a despatch, drew up a long indictment against his chief, according to which Bazaine never seriously attempted to make an exit from Metz, from the 18th of August, when he was first driven under its walls. With a view to his own aggrandisement, he first of all deeply involved himself in imperialist intrigues, and proposed to the king of Prussia that the army of Metz should, after being neutralized for a time, return to France to "insure the liberty of elections;" his real design being to establish himself as regent during the minority of the prince imperial. But when his majesty declined to listen to any overtures except those of unconditional surrender, and Bazaine became convinced that he could only bring France and the Prussians to adopt the idea of a Bonapartist restoration, by adding to the other misfortunes which were already weighing down the unhappy country that of the capitulation of Metz, then, said M. de Valcourt, the marshal made it his business to hasten it; and to secure his own ambitious ends, delivered to the Prussians the town and fortress of Metz, with the army of 120,000 men encamped in the intrenched enceinte.

Unless they could be fully established, charges such as these against a soldier who had served his country with distinction for forty years, came with little grace from the delegate government. There is no doubt that, for at least eight days after the defeat at Gravelotte and retreat to Metz, Bazaine gave way to a culpable inactivity. This time was invaluable to the Germans; it gave them the means of counter-intrenching their army so strongly as to make egress from Metz very difficult, and enabled them to withdraw the three corps forming their new fourth army, to occupy the line of the Meuse, and frustrate the effort of MacMahon to relieve his brother marshal. The latter waited for his coming, and at his supposed approach attempted his one real sortie, that of the 31st of August, which opened the Prussian line eastward of Metz at the time. But this attack was so feebly followed up that at daybreak on the 1st the enemy recovered easily the positions he had lost. Strategically, indeed, it was so ill-directed that for the time its success would have carried Bazaine towards the Sarre, and left the first and second armies between his own and that of MacMahon which he had expected.

As to the later stages of the investment, when we examine the French and the German accounts, and compare with them the narrative already alluded to of Mr. Robinson of the Manchester Guardian, who spent the ill-fated seventy days with the army in Metz, we find the most perfect agreement on one point. No sortie after the 1st September ever showed the slightest indication of a real design to break out of the German lines. That of the 7th October, the most important, was conducted on a scale which sufficed to draw the attention of both armies to it, and to convince the French soldiers of the difficulty of the undertaking; but it was plainly not a serious attempt. It is perhaps possible that loyalty to the Empire, the political state of France, and the supposed prospect of an imperialist restoration influenced Bazaine's conduct; chiming in, as it does, with his direct communication with Versailles and Chislehurst, and with all that is known of his movements during the seven weeks in question. With this may possibly have been mixed up the idea, that in case of the tide of the Prussian success being stayed in some other quarter, France would have been better served by her intact army within the Metz lines than by its disorganized remains, after a long and fiercely contested retreat in open field. To those who witnessed the events transpiring outside, it was clear that in detaining a German army of more than 200,000 men around Metz, Marshal Bazaine was rendering his country a signal service, to the value of which every day added greatly. Thus, had he held out until the French victory of Coulmiers, that is, just fifteen days longer, the Germans must have raised the siege of Paris. The fact of his capitulating at the end of October, was, for France, the most calamitous event of the war; as, just when a gleam of success seemed to dawn on her struggling arms, it released an immense army to sweep down upon her and stifle for ever her newly-born hopes.

That a retreat was very difficult it is extremely easy to see. Of course there would have been a severe sacrifice. But it is doubtful whether this sacrifice would have achieved this just result. It was not only his army which the French marshal must force through the German intrenchments, but all the transport stores and provisions necessary to keep that army in a state fit to march. When we remember that the necessary transport for Bazaine's army would have covered 120 miles of road, if arranged along one road; that this line would have been perpetually assaulted in flank and rear by the German forces; and that no resting-place nor basis of operations offered him a friendly aid—we may well stand aghast at the boldness of the criticisms which have been so frequently indulged in in the siege of Metz. Undoubtedly there was great sickness among the troops, and it is said that one marshal, twenty-four generals, 2140 officers, and 42,350 men had been struck down by the enemy's fire. The statement of Marshal Bazaine, if correct, and there is no reason to doubt it, that when he surrendered he had only 65,000 men available for offensive operations, supplies, when collated with the numbers comprised in the capitulation, at once the strongest condemnation of the soldiery, and an undeniable excuse for their commander's inaction.

A calm investigation of all the circumstances inclines us to believe that Marshal Bazaine was forced to capitulate by the immediate prospect of starvation which threatened both his army and the city. But on the other hand, there is no doubt that the early exhaustion of food was the result of the grossest waste and mismanagement, and that no self-denial or restraint was practised by the French officers, such as might have been expected under the circumstances. Had the Metz supplies been properly husbanded, and every one placed upon rations at an earlier period, the place could have held out for the few days then so inestimably precious to France. But who at the commencement could have foretold this?

CHAPTER XXI.

The Early Days of the Investment of Paris—The National Guards and their New Duties—General Trochu's Plan of Action according to his own Explanation—The German Lines of Investment strengthened and lengthened—Proclamation of M. Gambetta, to raise the Spirits of the People after the fall of Strassburg and Toul—Extraordinary Precautions taken to prevent the Enemy from obtaining access to the City through the Sewers or Subterranean Passages—Surgeon-major Wyatt's Report on the Condition and Prospects of Paris at this time—The Rothschilds serve on the Ramparts—Reconnaissances from the City—Payment of Rent postponed—Demands of the Extreme Republican Gardes Mobiles, especially as to the Election of a Municipal Commune—Exciting Scene at the Hôtel de Ville—Speech of Jules Favre—Count von Bismarck and the Diplomatic Corps in Paris—Fruitless Visits of General Burnside to Paris in the hope of securing Peace—The Headquarters of the King of Prussia established in the Palace of Versailles—Description of his Triumphal Entry into the Town—Distribution of the Order of the Iron Cross—The Extensive Preparations being made inside Paris—Firing of the First Shell by the Besiegers—-Sortie of the Garrison—Defeat of the French, but Great Improvement observable in their Troops—Burning of the Palace of St. Cloud by the French—Sketch of its History—Proclamation of General Trochu as to the Mobilization of the National Guard—His wish to obtain good Artillery before attempting Sorties on a large scale, and determination to pursue to the end the Plan he had traced out to himself—The System pursued by the Germans in resisting Sorties—-The Country around the City very unfavourable for such Operations—The Germans massed in the largest numbers at some distance from the City, so that a Sortie was like "Pressure against a Spring"—All Troops for outpost duty changed every Four Days—Great Sortie from Mont Valérien on October 21—General Description of the Engagement which ensued—Improved Behaviour of the French Troops—General Ducrot and his parole—The Germans prepared to raise the Siege if necessary—The Investing Circle widened—Attack on Le Bourget by the French—The Prussians completely surprised, and the French thoroughly successful—Orders of Von Moltke to retake the Village at any cost—Very severe fighting on October 30—Incidents of the Engagement—Complete Victory of the Prussians, who captured 30 officers and 1200 men—The Great Loss amongst the Francs Tireurs—Depressing Influence of the Engagement on the Parisians, and Disturbances in the Capital on receipt of the News of the Fall of Metz—Attack on Félix Pyat for asserting that Bazaine was in treaty for the Surrender of that City—Arrival of M. Thiers in Paris on October 30, confirming the News and bearing Proposals for an Armistice—Riots in the City—The Commune demanded—The Rioters form themselves into a Committee of Public Safety, and arrest the Members of the Provisional Government—Energy of M. Picard on behalf of his Colleagues—The Rioters' Feast and Disgraceful Conduct at the Hôtel de Ville—Their Attempts to obtain possession of the Government Offices defeated—Liberation of the Members of the Government without Loss of Life on either side—Proclamation from General Trochu to the National Guard, explaining the real state of affairs—Plebiscite in the City—Enormous Majority in favour of the Government—The hopes of the Germans that the Disturbances in the City would lead to its speedy capture not realized—The Position of the Government much strengthened by the result of the Plebiscite.

IN a previous chapter we have described the course of events in Paris up to the time of its final investment by the Germans, and have shown how fully alive the Parisians were to the imminent danger of their capital, and with what earnestness and energy they set about defending it. The last communications received from it by the ordinary channels stated that the authorities were doing their utmost in organizing troops, in manufacturing arms and munitions of war, in strengthening the weak points of their defences, in connecting the outlying forts with chains of earthworks, and in husbanding their commissariat in view of a lengthened siege. The *morale* of the troops engaged during the early days of the investment indicated an undoubted source of weakness. The governor and his generals were therefore unceasing in their efforts to raise the standard of discipline; and by accustoming the soldiery to the military duties of the ramparts, to the manning of the forts, to meet the exigencies of the outposts, and to occasional reconnaissances of the enemy's position, laboured to familiarize them with the perils of actual warfare. This latter phase of General Trochu's duties was a most important task. The Parisian national guards formed a large part of the army of defence. Thousands of those, before the outbreak of the war, were indolent and pleasure-loving, the *petits crevés* of the boulevards, inveterate loungers, "who would have thought it preposterous to rise at nine, and would have been horrified at getting their feet wet." The hardships and fatigues of the siege were weighty matters to such luxurious citizens, although they passed their twenty-four hours' duty, often in the cold and rain, without a murmur. Each division of the national guard did duty by rotation on the ramparts, when it was the object of every one to make himself as cheerful and as comfortable as possible. Besides his usual accoutrements he provided himself with a store of personal comforts, by which, amid the vivacious conversation of his comrades, the duty was lightened, and often regarded more as a pleasure than a necessity. During the chilly nights, however, the uncomfortable arrangements of their tents awakened the guards to tantalizing recollections of their warm cafés and comfortable beds, and rendered welcome the sound of the *réveille*, at which they turned out in the most fantastic costumes, smoked their cigarettes, drank their morning coffee, greeted with cheers the relieving company, and then marched to their quarters in the city.

Of the real business of a siege, however, the Parisians for some time remained ignorant. The main body of the armed defenders of the city had hardly seen a German soldier. Even the garrison of the forts, the regular troops, and the *élite* of the provincial mobiles, who were stationed permanently without the *enceinte*, knew as yet but very little of their assailants.

A dangerous feature of the case, according to the statement made by General Trochu in the National Assembly in June, 1871, was that, in the quota of National Guards returned by certain quarters of the capital, there were some 6000 revolutionists, and 25,000 returned convicts, whose influence was often felt during the siege, and told with terrible effect after the capitulation.

General Trochu, in conjunction with General Ducrot, had formed a plan for encountering the invasion, which was at once intelligent and bold, and under more favourable conditions would most probably have insured success. It was not, however, as generally supposed at the time, founded upon the principle of making Paris the great centre and rallying point of national resistance; of detaining the Germans around its walls until formidable armies organized throughout the country should move to the relief of the capital, and, by co-operating with the armed masses inside, should compel the invaders to raise the siege. The project, as subsequently explained by General Trochu before the National Assembly, was rather to utilize the forces under his command, to break through the enemy's lines at a point the least expected, to force a passage to Rouen, there to establish a base of operations, and provision Paris by the Lower Seine. Unlike the majority of his countrymen, General Trochu did not depend on the assistance of the army of the Loire, which he knew could render none. A hastily got up and undisciplined army, such as that was, could never prevail in the field against a regular organized force. The general wished that the army of the Loire should confine itself to amusing: the enemy, by defending to the best of its power such towns as might be attacked, while he was preparing his troops and field artillery for active operations. Circumstances, however, did not favour the development of the scheme, which was never seriously attempted, as will be seen in succeeding chapters.

It is, perhaps, not a matter of surprise that no important sorties were attempted in the early days of the siege, although the red republican party in the capital were inclined to clamour for more offensive proceedings against the enemy. The disciplinary operations above alluded to were, however, continued with vigour, until the ramparts bristled with artillery, and a constant fire was kept up which interfered in a considerable degree with the works of the besiegers, who on their side were most active in securing their positions around the capital, until their lines of investment began to assume formidable proportions. The outer circle formed a huge chain of nearly seventy miles, the inner line extending over fifty; and day by day their grasp of the beleaguered city became more tight and rigid. As soon as it was seen that Paris would make a stubborn resistance, the invaders applied themselves to strengthen their communications, increase their forces, and accumulate stores and supplies for a regular siege. In this work they were very greatly assisted by the surrender of Toul on the 23rd, and the fall of Strassburg on the 28th of September, which gave them a line of railway and main road of communication. These facilities were immediately taken advantage of for the transport of heavy siege guns and munitions of war, while detachments were told off to keep open the communications, and flying columns organized to collect provisions and other necessaries. The German army, in fact, took the place of the population of Paris. The fertile country within a radius of some thirty miles from the capital, which in time of peace supplied the inhabitants with a large percentage of their daily food, now yielded its supplies to the invader, usually on payment, sometimes on compulsion. The whole region had become an immense camp of armed men, and with some degree of complacency a German writer avowed himself unable to guess how, after the departure of the German troops, the population of what was once the richest and most luxurious district of Europe would find subsistence in a region which would be as devoid of provisions as the Desert of Sahara. While collecting supplies, the foraging parties served at tire same time as a sort of observing force, intended to baffle any attempt to disturb the operations of the besiegers.

The great extent and immense strength of the fortifications, of which we have treated fully in a previous chapter, presented obstacles to the approach of the besiegers which would have deterred a less resolute enemy. On reconnoitring the neighbourhood of St. Denis, to the north of the capital, where four distinct and formidable fortresses formed a square, the Germans found that it would have to be reduced by a regular siege before Paris could be touched. The west side, between Mont Valérien and St. Denis, was the next point selected as most vulnerable. Between these two great fortresses there is a space of seven miles, partly protected by the river Seine, which, after skirting Paris on the west, runs midway between them. To fill up this gap the French had been hastily constructing a redoubt at Gennevilliers, half-way betwixt Valérien and St. Denis. This, however, like other projected defences, was so incomplete when the siege commenced that it had to be abandoned. Again, the east side of Paris, as being the most exposed, was fortified with almost superfluous precaution, with a number of detached forts lying close together, and enfilading the approaches to each other, at Aubervilliers, Romainville, Noisy, Rosny, and Nogent, with Vincennes and Charenton on the south. This rendered attack very difficult, although the Germans diverted the water of the Ourcq Canal in order to strengthen the position of the Prussian guards. Due south the same system of forts was kept up by Ivry, Bicêtre, Montrouge, and Vanves. The Germans therefore resolved on attacking the south-west side. A concentration of forces accordingly took place around Versailles, and their first attentions were paid to Fort Issy. When, however, the commandant was summoned to capitulate, he replied that he would not, "as long as breath remained in his body." Shortly after the commencement of the siege the villages of Sévres and St. Cloud were occupied by the enemy, who erected batteries opposite the Bois de Boulogne. The terraces of Meudon, the heights about St. Cloud, and the works at Montretout, were also all occupied by the German artillery. Thus the beginning of October found Paris so completely blockaded that its only means of communication with the outer world was by carrier pigeons or balloons, which sometimes fell into the hands of the Prussians.

The discovery that the difficulties of the siege would be greater than had at first been anticipated, did not for one moment deter the German commanders from facing them. Their unshaken confidence was the more remarkable, when it is remembered that General Trochu had 500,000 men under his command, half of whom were employed as the garrison of Paris, and the remainder formed into two armies intended for operations outside.

A momentary gloom was cast over Paris by the the surrender of Toul and Strassburg—especially Strassburg, the defence of which the Parisians had followed with intense interest. Their demeanour, however, was quiet and dignified, and the minister of the Interior issued a stirring and patriotic proclamation, which did much to raise the spirits of both soldiers and people. "Citizens," wrote M. Gambetta, "the increasing strokes of bad fortune can no longer disconcert your minds nor lower your courage. You wait for France, but you depend upon yourselves—ready for all things. Toul and Strassburg have just succumbed. During fifty days these two heroic cities have been exposed to veritable showers of bullets and shells. In want of ammunition and of provisions, they still defied the enemy. They have only capitulated after having seen their walls crumble under the fire of the assailants. In falling they have cast a look towards Paris, to declare once more the unity and integrity of *La Patrie*. The indivisibility of the republic devolves on us the duty of delivering them, with the honour of avenging them. *Vive la France! Vive la Republique!*" General Trochu likewise issued a short but re-assuring proclamation to the troops. The elections for a National Assembly were further deferred till, as was said, they could be freely held throughout the entire country.

As yet there had been no military demonstrations of an important character, but great activity prevailed within the capital. A peculiar feature of the defence was the armed vigilance of the *égoutiers*, employed in the main sewers of the capital. These labourers were placed on guard lest the enemy should attempt to debouch from the outlets of those subterranean passages on the banks of the Seine, into the very heart of Paris. The engineers also fortified the interior both of the sewers and aqueducts, while they blocked up the shafts entering the catacombs and underground quarries, and walled up every gallery that might give access from the outside to the inside of the circle of defences.

Besides the various journalists, whose communications furnished much valuable information respecting the daily progress of events, Surgeon-major Wyatt, of the Coldstream Guards, who had arrived a day or two before the final investment, on a mission from the British government to observe and report on matters of sanitary hygiene and military surgery in connection with the French medical staff, reported very favourably on the condition of Paris with respect to provisions. During the first weeks of the siege he expressed a firm conviction that the capture of the fortresses would prove a very difficult undertaking. "The zealous patriotism of all ranks," he said, "is remarkable, and no exceptions are asked for, the Rothschilds taking their turn of duty on the ramparts, equally with all the other citizens, as privates in the garde mobile. The Prussians have now certainly lost all chance of success by assault, for delay has rendered the place almost impregnable."

The forts continued to throw shells into the enemy's works, and reconnaissances were made in several directions—a party from the Fort de Noisy dislodging the Prussians from a post at Bondy. A series of such movements was continued in conjunction with the fire of the forts, but generally with little result beyond disturbing the operations of the enemy. For instance, in front of Fort de Nogent, three companies of mobiles and a detachment of spahis drove back the advanced posts of the Prussians, but falling into an ambush, were compelled to retire after placing some twenty men *hors de combat*. Reconnoitring parties were also despatched towards Clamart and Creteil, Malmaison and Gennevilliers, and on the route of the Lyons railway; but on each occasion they were driven back, the Germans having been seasonably reinforced.

Decrees were published by the government postponing the payment of the Michaelmas quarter's rent, and ordering the reproduction, in bronze, of the statue of the city of Strassburg in the Place de la Concorde. On the 3rd of October General Guilham, killed in the engagement of the 30th September, was buried with military honours, when General Trochu briefly addressed the troops. In the afternoon of this day some 10,000 armed national guards, under the command of M. Gustave Flourens, marched to the headquarters, and demanded of the government that the levy *en masse* of the entire nation should be decreed; that an immediate appeal should be made to republican Europe; that all suspected government functionaries, in a position to betray the republic, should be discharged; and that a municipal commune should be speedily elected, through which distribution should be made of all articles of subsistence existing in the capital. Once again during the week Flourens headed five battalions of national guards at the Hôtel de Ville, demanding to be armed with Chassepots, which it was not in the power of the government to supply. A day or two later a still more serious demonstration was made, organized by the central republican committee, in conjunction with citizens Ledru Rollin, Félix Pyat, Blanqui, Delescluze, and Flourens, at the Hôtel de Ville, with the view of forcing the government to consent to the immediate election of a municipal commune. Many thousands of people assembled, including a considerable number of national guards; and in front of the open windows of the Hôtel de Ville, where several members of the government were seated, shouts of Vive la Commune were raised. The only response to this appeal was the display of an armed battalion of national guards drawn up in line in front of the building, behind which numerous companies of gardes mobiles, with fixed bayonets, were posted. Some delegates were eventually admitted, who were told by M. Jules Ferry that the government would not entertain their demand. Gradually the crowd had enormously increased, when General Trochu appeared, and rode unattended round three sides of the Place, assailed with cries of *La Commune! La Commune!* uttered in a menacing tone, to which, however, he made no response. The gates of the Hôtel de Ville were closed, and the rappel beaten, which brought other armed national guards on the scene, prepared to support the government. The commander-in-chief of the national guards rode from group to group, haranguing the more violent among the crowd, but to no purpose. They demanded, and would have, the commune of Paris; and not until the place became completely occupied by national guards who were friendly to the provisional government, and pronounced emphatically against the election of the commune, were the agitators quieted. At this moment the members of the government appeared on the scene, and passed the national guards drawn up in line in review. The warm reception they met with from these citizen soldiers, and the great majority of the people massed around the three sides of the Place, furnished a convincing proof that the demands made by the more violent demagogues were entirely out of favour with nine-tenths of the Parisians. Shouts of *Vive la France! Vive la Republique! Vive le Gouvernement! Pas de Commune!* arose on all sides, and were prolonged until the members of the government retired in front of the entrance to the Hôtel de Ville. There M. Jules Favre made an eloquent speech to the officers of the national guard, congratulating them upon the attitude of their corps and the union that had been shown to prevail, and urging them not to harbour any feelings of animosity in reference to what had transpired that day. "We have no enemies," said he; "I do not think we can call them adversaries. They have been led astray, but let us bring them back by means of our patriotism." Such demonstrations oft-repeated during the siege were a source of constant embarrassment to the authorities, who, however, generally pursued a conciliatory course, combined with firmness sufficient to prevent an actual outbreak.

As before stated, diplomatic agents of various states determined to remain in Paris during the siege. But difficulties speedily arose. In the first place, a request in their name by M. Jules Favre that Count von Bismarck should give a week's notice before opening the bombardment, and that there should be a weekly courier for the passage of despatches to their respective governments, was refused, though permission was granted for the passage of open letters expressing no opinion on the subject of the war. Against this, however, the diplomatists protested, in a document signed by the papal nuncio, the ministers of Switzerland, Sweden and Norway, Denmark, Belgium, Honduras and Salvador, the Netherlands, Brazil, Portugal, the United States, Monaco and San-Marino, Hawaii, the Dominican Republic, Bolivia, and Peru. But the German chancellor was inexorable. After reminding them of his previous warning that diplomatic intercourse must be subordinate to military exigencies, he further said:—"The present French authorities have thought proper to fix the seat of their government within the fortifications of Paris, and to select that city and its suburbs as the theatre of war. If members of the diplomatic body, accredited to the former government, have decided to share with the government of the national defence the privations inseparable from residence in a beleaguered fortress, the responsibility for this does not rest with the Prussian government."

Several journeys, to and from the besieged capital, which the German authorities permitted the American General Burnside to make at this time, naturally excited considerable attention, but their significance was in many quarters over-estimated. The first visit had exclusive reference to the diplomatists just alluded to; but General Burnside had at no time any official authority. It was simply from yielding to a generous impulse, that he endeavoured, without any commission, to effect some conciliatory arrangement between the hostile parties. All the communications he carried to the Provisional Government from the Germans related to the cession of Alsace and Lorraine, and an indemnity of £80,000,000, which it was hinted at this early stage of the siege Count von Bismarck also demanded. These terms the French government would not listen to, and his visits thus led to no diplomatic result.

Outside the city the besiegers continued very active. On the 5th of October the king of Prussia left Meaux for his future headquarters in the old palace at Versailles, and was met near that place by the Crown Prince, attended by General von Blumenthal and a portion of his staff. The inhabitants of the town also turned out in considerable numbers to see King William establish himself in the heart of France, and re-occupy the historical palace of their kings. The streets were lined with German troops; and awaiting his arrival were General von Kirchbach, General von Voigts-Rhetz, commandant of the city, and their staff, the duke of Coburg, the duke of Augustenburg, two dukes of Würtemburg, the Prince Hereditary of Würtemburg, Prince Leopold of Hohenzollern, the Prince Hereditary of Mecklenburg Strelitz, with their officers in waiting.

At half past five in the afternoon the king, accompanied by the Crown Prince, arrived in an open carriage, amid the vehement cheers of the officers and troops, and the triumphal sound of drums and trumpets. Count von Bismarck and General von Moltke had been looked for with scarcely less eagerness, but neither the one nor the other was recognized by the crowds of soldiers or citizens, and they passed unobserved to their quarters.

Nothing could have brought home more vividly to the French nation the true nature of the crisis, than this undisturbed possession of Versailles by the Germans. On the day following the entry of the king, he and his generals paraded the grounds amid the cheers of the invading army. The German colours waved over the palace, wounded Germans were tended in the hospitals of the town, and a little later the ceremony was gone through of distributing the order of the Iron Cross to the German soldiers who had distinguished themselves in the campaign. The order of merit was distributed by the Crown Prince, who referred in glowing terms to the acts of heroism which had entitled the recipients to the honour.

Inside Paris the spirit of the people was now thoroughly roused. The iron-masters of the city were turning out immense siege guns and batteries of field artillery and mitrailleuses, while the women were making a million cartridges daily. General Trochu was likewise rapidly arming the immense levies called to the defence of the capital. He had already upwards of 200,000 breechloading rifles, more than sufficient for his regulars and the mobiles; while M. Dorian was busily engaged in manufacturing similar weapons for the national guards.

On the 11th of October the first shells were fired from the besiegers' works, one of which lodged in Fort Ivry, and called forth a tremendous reply from the southern line of forts, which was taken up by the entire series of batteries. Owing to this incident, probably, and to the agitation of the Socialistic section of the populace for more active efforts, the garrison made a second sortie on the 13th of October. The attacking force, consisting of General Blanchard's division, issued from the French lines in three columns, against the besiegers' works on the heights of Clamart, Châtillon, and Bagneux, southward of the city. To clear the way for the troops the guns of Montrouge, Issy, and Vanves opened a heavy fire in the early morning, and the brigade of General Lusbielle attacked with considerable intrepidity the barricaded villages in their front. After a severe hand-to-hand contest the enemy was dislodged and driven out of his advanced positions; the French, elated by this success, somewhat recklessly exposed themselves, and Prussian reinforcements having arrived on the ground, they were forced to fall back with considerable loss, including the *chef de bataillon*, Count Dampierre. In this action, however, the besieged showed great improvement in the manner of handling and serving the field-guns, as well as in the manoeuvring of their troops. The guns of the forts commanded the ground occupied by the Germans, and it is clear from the fact of their subsequently demanding an armistice to take away their dead, that their loss was heavy, including some fifty prisoners.

Nor was this action the only notable event of the day. The French regarded with a jealous eye the occupation of St. Cloud by the Prussians, who used it as an outpost, and had previously poured a heavy fire in the supposed direction of their works. The Duke Max of Würtemburg had also been wounded there by a French tirailleur. To prevent the chateau being turned to account by the enemy, the guns of Mont Valérien now opened fire upon the palace, and struck it with shell after shell. Speedily a sheet of flame shot upwards from it, as the batteries of Mortemart and Issy joined those of Mont Valérien; and a few hours sufficed to render the elegant chateau a smouldering ruin. The village of St. Cloud was also made a desolation by the French guns. The history of St. Cloud is peculiarly interesting. As early as 533, some sailors, intrusted with a little child for the purpose of its destruction, deposited it on the banks of the Seine in order to save its life. Thus providentially preserved, Clodoald became a monk, and founded a monastery, whence the district derived its name of St. Cloud. Being one of the prettiest environs of Paris, it was always a favourite summer residence, and the old French kings often stayed there. The village was burnt by the English in 1358; and it was there that Henri III. was assassinated in 1589. In 1658 Louis XIV. presented the place to his brother, the duke of Orleans, in whose family it remained for more than a century, when it again became a royal residence. It was at St. Cloud where Napoleon Bonaparte discussed and settled the arrangements which made him master of France, and it afterwards became his favourite residence. After witnessing various other historic evolutions, it fell into the possession of Napoleon III., who with the Empress Eugenie were its frequent occupants, and it was from it that the emperor started on the disastrous campaign of 1870.

On the 16th October General Trochu issued a proclamation to the mayors of Paris concerning the mobilization of the national guards. From this document he appears to have taken an exact measure both of the exigencies of his position and of his resources for meeting them. After referring to the difficulties and delays which had taken place in the matter, and the "very animated and legitimately impatient patriotism" of the public mind, he said:—"It is my duty to enlighten it while resisting its enthusiasm, and to prove to it that no one has more than I at heart the honour of the national guard of Paris, and the care of the great interests which will be at stake the day that that guard carries its efforts beyond the enceinte. When I undertook the defence of Paris, with the co-operation of devoted fellow-workers whose names will one day be remembered by the public gratitude, I had to face a sentiment vastly different from the one I am now discussing. It was believed and asserted that a city like our capital, governed by such various interests, passions, and requirements, was incapable of being defended. It was hard to believe that its enceinte and its forts, constructed in other times and under very different military circumstances to those which prevail at present, could be prepared in such a manner as to offer, unsupported by an army operating from without, a serious and durable resistance to the efforts of a victorious enemy. Still less was it admitted that the inhabitants could reconcile themselves to the sacrifices of every kind, to the habits of resignation, which a siege of any duration implies. Now that this great trial has been made, that is to say, that the placing of the city in a state of defence has reached a degree of perfection which renders the enceinte unassailable, the outer fortifications being at a great distance; now that the inhabitants have manifested their patriotism, and of their own accord reduced to silence the small number of men whose culpable views subserved the enemy's projects; now that the enemy himself, halting before these formidable defensive preparations, has confined himself to surrounding them with his masses, without venturing upon an attack, the public mind has changed, and shows now but one preoccupation—the desire to throw out in turn masses of soldiers beyond the enceinte and to attack the Prussian army. The government of the national defence cannot but encourage this enthusiasm of the population, but it belongs to the commander-in-chief to direct it, because with this right are connected, for him, unlimited responsibilities. In this respect it is necessary to be guided solely by the rules of the general experience of war, and by those of the special experience which we owe to the painful events that have overwhelmed the army of the Rhine. These rules demonstrate that no infantry, however steady it may be, can be safely brought face to face with the Prussian army unless it be accompanied by an artillery equal to that which the enemy has at his disposal; and it is to the formation of this artillery that I am applying all my attention. In the next place, our percussion guns are excellent arms behind a rampart, where there is no need to fire quickly. But troops who with such arms engage others provided with rapidly-firing rifles, would expose themselves to a disaster that neither bravery nor moral superiority could avert. As regards the appeal made to the patriotism of the companies destined for outside service, the government cannot address itself exclusively to the battalions provided with rapidly-firing arms; hence the absolute necessity for a friendly exchange of arms, effected by the mayor of each arrondissement, so that the volunteers destined for war service shall be armed with the best rifles of their battalion."

After giving directions for recruiting and equipping the mobilized battalions, and intimating that the battalions taking the field would be placed exclusively under the orders of generals commanding the active divisions of the army, and subject to military laws and regulations, the document concluded as follows:—

"In the month of July last the French army, in all the splendour of its strength, passed through Paris amid shouts of *à Berlin! à Berlin!* I was far from sharing their confidence, and alone, perhaps, among all the general officers, I ventured to tell the marshal-minister of "War that I perceived in this noisy manner of entering upon a campaign, as well as in the means brought into requisition, the elements of a great disaster. The will which at this period I placed in the hands of M. Ducloux, a notary of Paris, will one day testify to the painful and too well-grounded presentiments with which my soul was filled. To-day, in presence of the fever which has rightly taken possession of the public mind, I meet with difficulties which present a most striking analogy with those that showed themselves in the past. I now declare that, impressed with the most complete faith in a return of fortune, which will be due to the great work of resistance summed up in the siege of Paris, I will not cede to the pressure of the public impatience. Animating myself with the sense of the duties which are common to us all, and of the responsibilities which no one shares with me, I shall pursue to the end the plan which I have traced out without revealing it; and I only demand of the population of Paris, in exchange for my efforts, the continuance of that confidence with which it has hitherto honoured me."

On the 21st of October occurred a vigorous sortie m the direction of Malmaison; and as it was made under almost exactly similar conditions to those of Chevilly and Châtillon, previously narrated, it may be as well to notice the system of investment by which the Germans so successfully resisted these repeated attacks.

It must be observed that the country around Paris was not favourable for making sorties on a large scale. The first difficulty was the river. It was impossible to lay the bridges without the movement being observed by the enemy, and to inarch a large force across pontoons required a considerable time. Again, on those sides of Paris which are most open to attack—those not naturally guarded by the Seine—the defences are so close together as not to leave sufficient room for the manoeuvring of troops. A third obstacle existed in the natural formation of the ground, which is hilly and broken, except in close proximity to the river; and in the immense number of villages, hamlets, and detached houses existing in all directions.

The Germans did not form a fixed or continuous line round Paris, but were massed in the villages and hamlets; and the further behind the advanced posts the more numerous were the troops. The besieging army surrounded the city in three concentric zones. In the inner belt were the outposts and the rifle-pits, where the advanced guards were sheltered; behind these were the infantry of the army corps, with a large proportion of the horse, and a smaller division of artillery; and outside of all, the great mass of the field batteries, supported by the reserves of the infantry and cavalry. The pickets and advanced posts were generally within easy communication with each other, their supports, and the regiments from which they were drawn, being placed as near as circumstances would permit; but all the heavy bodies of men were massed at a considerable distance from the front. In consequence of this arrangement, any sortie in force sufficed to drive in the outposts; but, as has been well remarked by an English writer, it was like pressure exerted against a spring. The Germans had to retire to a distance proportionate to the pressure. But as they retired they gathered strength, until at last, the momentum and impetus of the opposing force being overcome, the spring expanded, and the French were driven back within shelter of the forts.

To the comfort of the men occupied in the dangerous and arduous work of the German outposts every attention was paid. Great care was taken that they should be well and warmly clothed, and the very best provision obtainable was supplied them by the commissariat. Those at Versailles lived in comparative security and luxury; and all regiments and detachments were therefore changed every four days, so that the entire army might share the privileges as well as the privations incidental to their position.

The preparations for the sortie of the 21st were made with great discretion and secrecy, and it was the nearest approach to a surprise by the French that had yet occurred. The attacking force was under the command of General Ducrot, who massed his troops in the rear of forts Mont Valérien and Issy. On the night of the 20th a feint was directed against the southern front of the investing lines, and on the morning of the 21st Mont Valérien opened a heavy fire on the supposed positions of the enemy. Shortly afterwards General Ducrot led out some 12,000 men, well supported by artillery, and a strong force in reserve. The alarm was soon taken at Versailles, and the troops were immediately called to arms and thrown towards the front, while the boom of the guns could already be heard in the distance. The king of Prussia, with his staff, hastened towards St. Germains, and in company with the Crown Prince watched the proceedings from the top of the aqueduct of Marly, which commanded a fine view of the scene of battle.

The French made a spirited advance under cover of their guns, throwing out long lines of skirmishers to ascertain the situation of the enemy. The attack was directed against the high ground in front of La Celle, St. Cloud, and the strong position which the Prussians had taken up at Bougival. The French were well led by their officers, who could be seen at the head of their regiments waving their swords and encouraging the men. The most vigorous attack was made upon the heights of Berene; but it made no impression upon the Prussians, who had fallen back into the woods, from which they could not be driven. As the French advanced across the open they caught sight of the spiked helmets of the enemy, who, commanded by General Kirchbach, were stationed along the vine-clad ridges in front of La Jonchère, awaiting the attack. The French were constantly strengthened from their reserves, and threw forward a battery of their field artillery, which incessantly shelled the woods in their front; but the Prussians held their ground, and their assailants appeared to contemplate a dash at them. The fire of the needle-guns, however, was rapid and constant from the cover; and although Ducrot gallantly rode in front of his troops, and a couple of guns were detached from the foremost batteries to fire on the German position, the French could not be induced to advance across the open ground. The critical moment had now arrived; reinforcements appeared in the rear of the Germans, and speedily some battalions of the landwehr of the guard, headed by their skirmishers, caused the French to falter, and eventually to give way, leaving their two advanced guns to fall into the hands of the enemy, while four battalions of zouaves narrowly escaped capture. The Germans then pushed forward, and among the vines a fierce hand-to-hand fight ensued, in which bayonets were crossed and a heavy fire of musketry maintained for a considerable time. The French were ultimately forced to retire, but their retreat was covered by reinforcements which arrived, and prevented the further approach of the enemy. The Prussians, however, had held their ground; and from that circumstance, coupled with the fact of their having, as before stated, taken two guns and above a hundred prisoners, they considered their success complete. The official list of killed, wounded, and missing on the French side was given at 443, while the German loss was estimated at 380. In this action the French behaved well; but the force engaged was insufficient to effect any important practical purpose, and led to little more than the casualties mentioned.

It may here be stated that General Ducrot, who commanded on this occasion, and whose services throughout the siege of Paris were highly valued by General Trochu, was especially obnoxious to the Germans, who officially accused him of having broken his parole after the catastrophe at Sedan, and of having returned to Paris to take a high command in the army. But in a letter to the governor, which was forwarded to the German headquarters, he indignantly denied the charge of a breach of honour, and showed that he had escaped the Prussian sentries disguised as a workman, after he had surrendered himself prisoner at the appointed rendezvous. "The German press," replied the general, "doubtless inspired by competent authorities, accuses me of having made my escape while a prisoner on parole, of having committed a breach of honour, and of thus having placed myself outside the pale of the law, and thereby of having given to an enemy the right to shoot me, should I again fall into his hands. I heed the threat but little. Whether I am shot by Prussian bullets on the field of battle, or when leaving a prison, the result is always the same. I am conscious of having done my duty to the last, both as a soldier and a citizen, and failing other inheritance, I shall leave to my children a memory honoured by all good men, both friends and enemies." That his version was substantially correct was shown by the subsequent withdrawal of the charges by the Germans.

The operations of the besieged which have been detailed produced one result which might have been serious for the Germans, had not the backward state of General Trochu's immense levies prevented him from making more effective diversions. The investing circle, although not broken through, was widened, and the guns of the forts swept the country in every direction to an extent so considerable as to render an actual attack by the besieging army very difficult. It is also probable that at this period the investing army was at its lowest point in numbers judged by the German strategists to be safe, and the result of the sortie of the 21st was awaited with considerable anxiety. In the event of a reverse the Germans, ever prepared for eventualities, had arranged for the immediate removal of their headquarters, and even for the raising of the siege of Paris, had it transpired that the immense forces of General Trochu were strong enough to break through their lines, and defeat them in the open field. The practical failure of these first sorties from the capital, however, tended to render the Germans confident of ultimate success, and from this time the belief was general that no assault would be necessary. They considered that they held Paris as in a trap, as in the case of Sedan, and that little else was required than to starve it into surrender.

The month of October, however, did not pass without another sortie, which was of the most sanguinary character, although again resulting in no practical advantage to the French. The hamlet of Le Bourget, situated on a small rivulet that runs into the Seine on the north-eastern side of Paris, lay in the middle of a considerable plain midway between the French and Prussian outposts. The rivulet had been dammed up by the enemy, and the country flooded. The village was occupied by a company of Prussian guards to prevent its being used for offensive purposes against them. The attack on it on October 28 was planned with great secrecy by General Bellemare, who ordered Commander Rolland, of the "Franctireurs of the Press," to make a night assault, supported by a part of the thirty-fourth regiment and the fourteenth battalion of the mobiles of the Seine. Taken by surprise, and not knowing the strength of the attacking force, the Prussians gave way, and retired in disorder, leaving knapsacks and helmets behind. The French continued their advance on the village. As the Prussians made a show of defending the church, with the design of taking them in flank the supports were ordered up, and several guns and a mitrailleuse were thrown forward, while a couple of heavy guns were posted in front of Courneuve. On this the Prussians were compelled to retreat, and on the arrival of General Bellemare at eleven o'clock the French were in complete possession of the village. Orders were then given to strengthen the position; provisions were brought up; the sixteenth mobiles and twenty-eighth regiment of the line appeared to relieve and support their successful comrades; and engineers and sappers worked unremittingly in making communications, crenellating houses, and erecting barricades. The loss of the French amounted to some twenty wounded and four or five killed, while the Prussians appear to have suffered considerably. The capture of Le Bourget, said General Bellemare's report, "enlarges the circle of our occupation beyond the forts, gives confidence to our troops, and increases the supply of vegetables for the Parisian population."

The Prussians, however, were not disposed to bear their defeat with indifference. Throughout the 29th they battered the village with their artillery, and at one time a deadly combat raged between the outposts of the combatants, in which the bayonet was freely used.

The result of the attack had been at once communicated to the German headquarters, and Count von Moltke issued orders to the general commanding the second division of guards to retake the place at any cost—an order which they were not slow to obey. General Budritzki, early on the morning of the 30th, in turn surprised the French with seven battalions of guards, and a bloody fight ensued, in which the Prussians displayed great exasperation of feeling, but were met with most obstinate resistance. The French having barricaded the streets, and made the most of every available means of defence, it required a desperate effort to force them out of their stronghold. At the moment when the fight was at the hottest, and the Prussians appeared in danger of getting the worst of it, General Budritzki rode to the front of the Elizabeth regiment on their advance, and, dismounting, seized the standard in order to lead them to the storm. With heavy sacrifices a firm foot was at last planted in the village. The Queen Augusta regiment had also reached Le Bourget. A detachment was about to advance, when the colonel, Count Waldersee, who had so far recovered from a wound at Gravelotte that he rejoined his regiment ten days previously, was struck by a ball which killed him on the spot. An officer was hastening to catch the falling leader in his arms when he too was shot. Colonel Zaluskowski of the Elizabeth regiment, and Count von Keller, were also killed. These losses appear to have roused the vengeful feelings of the Germans, and shouting fiercely, they made an irresistible onslaught, and swept the French out of the village at the point of the bayonet, to within a short distance of St. Denis; and so closely pursued them, that some 30 officers and 1200 men were captured, including a whole company of mobiles, stationed to the north of Le Bourget, who had not fired a shot. The franc-tireurs were so cut up that, out of 380 men, only 150 remained; and being all Parisians, their fate caused great mourning to their friends in the city, who had lately rejoiced at their success. The fourteenth mobiles also suffered fearfully. Out of a strength of 800 men, 200 only answered the roll call after the retreat. The Prussians also paid dearly for their victory, for besides those whose names have been already mentioned, the Augusta and Elizabeth regiments lost at least 30 officers killed and wounded, and upwards of 400 men. Gallantly as the French acted in this affair, it was altogether an unfortunate mistake, undertaken without the authority of General Trochu, and executed without any of that forethought and pre-arrangement which were necessary in order to turn the temporary advantage to account. Supposing it had been desirable to leave a small French force in so advanced a position as Le Bourget, it should have been solidly supported.

The result of the engagement had a very depressing influence upon the Parisians, and coupled with the unexpected news of another and far more serious disaster, caused considerable disturbances in the capital. On the 26th October a paper published in Paris by the notorious communist Félix Pyat, announced that Bazaine had been negotiating with the Prussians for the surrender of Metz. On the 27th the *Journal Officiel* contained a very emphatic contradiction, which read strangely enough in the light of subsequent events. After arraigning the "odious lines" before the tribunal of public opinion, the official organ said, "The author of these malignant calumnies has not dared to sign his name; he has signed *Le Combat*—surely, the *combat* of Prussia against France; for in lieu of a bullet which could reach the heart of the country, he levels against its defenders a double accusation equally false and infamous. He asserts that the government deceives the public by concealing from it important news, and that the glorious soldier of Metz is disgracing his sword and turning traitor. We give these two figments the most emphatic contradiction. Officially brought under the notice of a court-martial, they would expose their inventor to the most severe punishment. We think the sentence of public opinion will prove more effectual. It will stigmatize with just severity those sham patriots whose trade it is to sow distrust with the enemy at our gates, and undermine by their lies the authority of those who fight him." The punishment of Félix Pyat, however, was not left entirely to public opinion; for on the afternoon of the same day, the 27th, he was mobbed and hustled on the boulevards, and ran a narrow risk of falling a victim to the indignation of the crowd. On the following day his office was invaded by national guards, who, abusing him for vending false news, hauled him to the Hôtel de Ville before M. Jules Ferry and M. Henri Rochefort, who, after hearing what he had to say for himself, dismissed him with the assurance that he must have been hoaxed.

As has been related, however, in the previous chapter, the "hoax" was an accomplished fact at the moment when M. Pyat was being mobbed in Paris for hinting at its possibility—a fact which, much as the Parisians might be indisposed to believe it, was soon forced upon them by evidence that could not be gainsaid. On the 30th of October M. Thiers arrived in Paris with a safe-conduct, confirming the surrender of Bazaine and the fall of Metz, and bringing proposals of an armistice by England, Russia, Austria, and Italy, with the view of arranging for the convocation of a National Assembly. These proposals, as we have seen in Chapter XVII., led to no result, owing to the French insisting on the victualling of Paris as a condition of the armistice.

Thus a three-fold humiliation was inflicted upon the Parisians. In the affair at Le Bourget they were robbed of the first success, small enough in itself, which had attended the military operations of the siege; by the fall of Metz the last barrier was removed to the full outpouring upon their capital of all the warlike resources of Germany; and to add to their mortification, their rulers were actually willing to treat for an armistice with the victors. It is therefore little surprising that the temper of the revolutionary section of Paris was inflamed, and their rage indiscriminating. Bazaine was at Wilhelmshöhe, beyond their reach, but the government of defence was at hand, and daring to suggest terms of agreement with the Prussians. *Jamais! A l'ennemi! La guerre à la mort! A bas les traitres!* cried the infuriated populace; and by noon on the last day of October the Place de l'Hotel de Ville and its approaches were densely crowded by an excited mass from all parts of Paris, demanding the resignation of the government and the election of the commune. In the crowd were many national guards, armed and unarmed, including a considerable number from the neighbourhood of Belleville and other communist quarters, some of whom carried placards inscribed "No peace!" or "No armistice!" and "The commune for ever!" General Trochu, Jules Simon, and others, attempted at intervals to address the insurgents, but their voices were drowned by shouts of *Pas d'armistice! Guerre a outrance!* During the tumult a shot was fired by an individual in the crowd, when immediately a tremendous uproar ensued, accompanied with cries that the citizens were being fired upon. Some of the mob, calling themselves a delegation from the people, a number of ultra-democrats, having previously assembled in the hall of St. John, forced their way into the Hôtel de Ville, and in an insolent and threatening manner demanded explanations from the government on the Bourget affair, the capitulation of Metz, and the proposed armistice. This self-styled delegation brought with them the following decree:—"In the name of the people, the provisional government of national defence is dissolved. The armistice is refused. The election' to the commune will take place within forty-eight hours. The provisional committee is composed of the members whose names are affixed. The delegation will signify the purport of this decree to the members of the former government, who remain always confined 'to the hall of their deliberations.'"

The delegation was received, in the first instance, by M. Jules Ferry, speedily joined by General Trochu and Jules Favre. Respecting Le Bourget, General Trochu stated the facts which have just been detailed. As to the capitulation of Metz, he assured the delegates on oath that the government knew nothing of it, and disbelieved it on the morning of the 26th, when it was announced in the *Combat*. With regard to the obnoxious armistice, he assured them that nothing was decided, nor would be, without first consulting the popular wishes. The latter part of his discourse was drowned by tumultuous cries of "Down with the government!" "No armistice!" "The commune!" A scene of indescribable confusion followed; all the ill-disposed battalions of the national guard surrounded the Hôtel de Ville. Hundreds of them, following the delegation, and headed by M. Flourens, forced their way into the apartment where the government were deliberating, and proceeded to form themselves into a committee of public safety. Flourens, mounting the table at which the government were sitting, intimated to them that they were under arrest. General Trochu and his colleagues, who in the critical circumstances acted with calmness and dignity, were called upon to sign their resignation, and otherwise grossly insulted. A little later a red flag was hoisted from one of the windows of the Hôtel de Ville, and in the balcony underneath appeared MM. Blanqui, Flourens, Ledru Rollin, Pyat, Mottu, Greppo, Delescluze, Victor Hugo, and Louis Blanc, who proclaimed themselves the government, and that M. Dorian had been nominated president, which post, however, the minister of Public Works prudently declined. The announcement was received with loud applause by the revolutionary section below, and the name of M. Rochefort was added to the list.

But the success of the commune on this occasion was short-lived. M. Ernest Picard had succeeded in making his escape from the Hôtel de Ville, and hastened to the ministry of Finance, where he took the speediest possible measures to counteract the movements of the revolutionists, and release his colleagues from their hands. He wrote to the staff of the governor and the staff of the national guard, ordering the call to arms to be made in all the quarters of Paris. He had the national printing office occupied by troops, and prohibited the

Official Journal from printing anything not sanctioned by the governor. He also sent word to the different ministries to hold themselves ready for defence. In these conservative measures he was assisted by the characteristic doings of the revolutionary party themselves, who, instead of immediately securing the various ministries, fell upon the provisions stored in the Hôtel de Ville, devouring the dinner prepared for the government, distributing the other viands, and broaching innumerable casks of wine, of which they freely partook. They then set about amusing themselves by destroying the furniture, breaking the mirrors, and injuring the pictures in the palace, and defiling the sofas and the painted walls and wainscots. One of their partizans, however, did not forget the "sinews of war." A messenger from the Hôtel de Ville was sent to the ministry of Finance, with an order signed by Blanqui for 15,000,000 francs, payable to bearer, who was, however, immediately arrested, while M. Picard retained possession of the order, as proof of Blanqui's participation in the events of the day. Another communist, Citizen Millière, thinking to steal a march on his colleagues, left them at the dinner table and went to instal himself as minister of Finance, but he, too, was checkmated and missed his aim. An officer of Blanqui's battalion, who repaired to the *état major* of the national guard to give orders, was also placed under arrest. The prefecture of police was surrounded by 300 or 400 persons demanding admission, but M. Adam, the prefect, resolutely refused to yield to their demands.

After having lasted several hours, the tumult was rapidly suppressed. A meeting of officers was held at the Bourse, the assembly was sounded, and Admirals de la Roncière and De la Chaille placed themselves at the service of M. Picard, who throughout the disturbance acted with a coolness and presence of mind worthy of the highest commendation. At nine o'clock he arrived at the Hôtel de Ville with the 106th battalion of the national guards, who immediately ascended the staircase, forced their way through the commune guard, and having released General Trochu and M. Jules Favre, compelled the insurgents to lay down their arms and quit the building. The governor, as soon as liberated, proceeded to the Louvre, and being joined by M. Picard, General Ducrot, and other officers, organized active measures for the restoration of order, and the deliverance of his colleagues who still remained in the hands of M. Flourens and his party. Under Trochu's orders several battalions of mobiles quickly assembled, and the national guard at the same time collected in the Place Vendôme. Just before midnight parties of these troops defiled in the direction of the Hôtel de Ville, where MM. Garnier Pages, Jules Simon, and Magnin were still kept in confinement as hostages by two battalions from Belleville. M. Jules Favre had shown great firmness with the rioters, telling them that, as he had been chosen by the whole population, he would only retire at the bidding of his constituents. The agitators who surrounded Flourens demanded that the members of the government should be sent to Vincennes; some made even more menacing proposals. About half-past twelve seven battalions of mobile guards concentrated behind the Hôtel de Ville, where those from Belleville had barricaded themselves. A company of the mobiles now succeeded in effecting an entrance by a subterranean passage from an adjoining barracks, and proceeded to open one of the large gates, by which they admitted a goodly number of their comrades, who gradually drove back the rioters to the upper stories. At the same time numerous battalions of the national guard arrived on the spot, shouting, "Long live the Republic! Long live Trochu!" The mobiles, once masters of the Hôtel de Ville, shut the rioters up in the cellars, from which they subsequently brought them out, disarmed them, and set them at liberty. Their leaders were also treated with great leniency, and freely allowed to depart, although the Citizen Blanqui subsequently complained of rough usage at the hands of the troops. The mairies of the first and eleventh arrondissements had been taken possession of by the rioters. The former was occupied by a Dr. Pillot, who was ejected at two o'clock on the following morning by the commander of the eleventh battalion of national guards, and carried off in custody to the hotel of General Trochu. The other mairie was seized by the ex-mayor, Citizen Mottu, who had been dismissed a week or two before for forbidding all kinds of religious instruction at the schools in his district, and even interdicting the masters and mistresses from taking their pupils to church. He was, however, apprised of the order given for his arrest, and thought it prudent to decamp in the course of the night. At three a.m. all was quiet. The movement was merely a surprise, and the national guard, by their behaviour in the course of the evening, showed that it met with no sympathy from them. The riot might have been suppressed much sooner, but for the wish to avoid bloodshed; and happily the proceedings of the 31st of October, as well as those of the 4th of September, terminated without loss of life on either side.

On the following day General Trochu issued the subjoined proclamation to the national guards:—

"Your firm attitude has preserved the republic from a great political humiliation, possibly from a great social danger, certainly from the ruin of our forces for the defence. The disaster of Metz, foreseen though it was, but deeply to be lamented, has very naturally disturbed the public mind, and doubled the anguish of the public. In connection with that sad event the government of the national defence has been insulted by the supposition that it was aware of it, but kept it concealed from the population of Paris, when, I affirm it, we only heard of it for the first time on the evening of the 30th. It is true that the rumour was circulated by the Prussian outposts for the two days previous, but we are so used to false statements of the enemy, that we had refused to believe it. The painful accident which happened at Le Bourget, through a force which had surprised the enemy allowing itself to be surprised in its turn by its utter want of vigilance, had also deeply affected public opinion. Finally, the proposal for an armistice unexpectedly proposed by the neutral powers has been construed, in utter disregard of truth and justice, as the prelude to a capitulation, when in reality it is a tribute to the attitude and firmness of the population of Paris. That proposal was honourable for us. The government itself arranged its conditions in terms which it considered firm and dignified; it stipulated a suspension of hostilities for twenty-five days at least, the revictualling of Paris during that period, and the right of voting for the election of a National Assembly for every citizen in all the French departments. There was a wide difference between these conditions and those previously offered by the enemy—to wit, 48 hours' truce, very limited intercourse with the provinces to prepare the elections, no revictualling, a fortress to be given up by way of guarantee, and the exclusion of the citizens of Alsace and Lorraine from any participation in the elections. The armistice now proposed has other advantages to recommend it which Paris can fully appreciate, without its being necessary to enumerate them; and this is what is reproached to the government as a weakness, nay, rank treason. An insignificant minority, which cannot pretend to represent the feelings of the population of Paris, has availed itself of the public excitement to try and substitute itself by violence in the place of the government. The government, on the other hand, is anxious to have protected interests which no government ever had the duty of watching over simultaneously—the interests of a besieged city of two millions of souls, the interests of absolutely unlimited liberty. You have co-operated in the discharge of that duty, and the support you have afforded the government will for the future give it strength to put down our enemies from within, as well as to oppose our enemies without."

After the above episode in the history of the siege, the conduct of the government of national defence became somewhat dubious and vacillating. Early on the morning of the 1st of November the walls of Paris were found covered with a notice, signed by MM. Arago, Dorian, Schoelcher, and other officials, apprising the inhabitants that they were to elect on that day four representatives in each arrondissement. An ambiguous notice, intended as a disavowal of the one signed by the mayor and the minister of Public Works, appeared later in the day; and later still, fresh intimations were posted up all over Paris, intimating that the people would have an opportunity afforded them of saying whether they desired the commune or not. Again, on the 2nd November, the *Journal Officiel* published a decree, to the effect that, on the day following, they would be called upon to vote Yes or No, whether they wished to maintain the government of national defence, and that on Saturday the elections of the mayors and adjoints of the different arrondissements would be proceeded with. Decrees were also published revoking the commands of numerous *chefs de bataillons* of national guards, including that of M. Flourens, compromised in the proceedings of the 31st; and announcing that any battalion going out armed without superior orders would be forthwith disarmed and dissolved, and the commander brought before a court-martial. By these proceedings the position of M. Rochefort in the government of national defence was rendered untenable, and his resignation was forthwith announced, avowedly in consequence of the postponement of the municipal elections.

Notwithstanding that the plebiscite was ordered immediately after the tumult caused by the communists, the actual voting took place amidst the utmost order and quietude. The machinery for the working of the ballot in France is simple and complete, and very easily put into operation. The 3rd of November, therefore, passed off much as any ordinary day; the only difference observable being some small crowds collected in front of the various mairies and other places where the votes had been appointed to be taken. In the evening it was commonly known that the government had obtained an enormous majority; and at ten o'clock a proclamation of the result, so far as then ascertained, was made by torchlight, on the Place de l'Hotel de Ville, by M. Etienne Arago, the mayor, in presence of an immense assemblage, composed principally of national guards. The crowd next proceeded to the hotel of General Trochu, and with enthusiastic cheers saluted the members of the government who were there assembled. They, in turn, all made their appearance on the steps of the entrance doorway, from which General Trocliu and M. Jules Favre addressed short speeches to the populace, thanking them for the confidence they had shown in them by that day's voting. On the following morning the official announcement of the result of the plebiscitum showed that 321,373 had voted Yes, against 53,585 No. The voting of the army, which was not included in the above, was subsequently published, with the following results: 236,623 Yes, against 9053 No; giving a general total of 557,996 Yes, against 62,618 No, being as nearly as possible at the rate of nine to one. By order of the government, in the course of the day about a dozen of the leaders in the proceedings of the 31st were arrested, amongst them Citizen Félix Pyat, who was at once conducted to the Conciergerie. Citizens Flourens and Blanqui succeeded in concealing themselves. A decree appeared in the *Journal Officiel* appointing General Clément Thomas commander-in-chief of the national guard, in place of General Tamisier, who had been severely injured in the tumult of the 31st.

The news of the proceedings which have just been related reached the besiegers in an exaggerated and distorted form, and raised their expectations of a speedy capture of the city. Internal discord had from the first been reckoned upon by Count von Bismarck as a powerful ally; and it may therefore be easily understood that the intelligence of the outbreak after the surrender of Metz was received with great satisfaction, which was, however, followed by disappointment when the actual truth came to be known.

To the great bulk of the French community this futile attempt at open rebellion brought a positive relief. The fact of its utter failure secured them to a certain extent against the efforts of the disaffected, and by means of the plebiscite afforded an opportunity of placing General Trochu and his colleagues more firmly in their seats. Backed by the universal suffrages of the citizens, the provisional government had now real claims to general respect, and was enabled to proclaim that henceforth it would not permit "a minority to attack the rights of the majority, and by defying the laws, to become the effective allies of Prussia."

CHAPTER XXII.

The Provisional Government at Tours and the Fall of Metz—Imprudent Proclamation charging Marshal Bazaine with Treason—Bad Feeling caused by it in the Army—Protest of the Moniteur against the Proclamation and its Reasons for the "betrayal" of France—Reception of the News of the Capitulation in other parts of France—General Feeling in the North that it was useless to attempt to continue the Struggle after such a Disaster, and Efforts made there to bring about Peace—The Actual Position of Affairs at this Time—Patriotic Addresses and Promises of Resistance from other parts of France—Strange Proceedings of the "League of the South"—Divisions, and Distrust of the Republic in many Quarters—The Energetic Exertions of M. Gambetta—The Capitulation of Metz most fortunate for the Germans—Improvement in the French Troops and slight Successes on their Side—The German Commander arranges for raising the Siege of Paris if necessary—Capture of Dijon by Von Werder—The German Mistake as to Jhe Strength of the French Army of the Loire—Hesitation of its Commander—The Actual Condition of that Army at this time—Its strange medley of Uniforms and Arms—Qualifications of General d'Aurelles de Paladine for its Command—His Strict Discipline and its Beneficial Results—He resolves to attempt to annihilate the Bavarian Force in and around Orleans—Repulse of a Bavarian Reconnoitring Party on November 6—The French prepare to assume the Offensive—Retreat of Von der Tann from Orleans—The Battle of Coulmiers—General Description of the Engagement—Fierceness of the German resistance at Baccon—They are at last compelled to retreat and leave the French Masters of the Field—General Review of the Engagement and its Results—Energetic Measures of Von Moltke to prevent the expected March of the French on Paris—M. Gambetta visits the French Camp and issues a Proclamation of Thanks to the Troops—The Mistake of the French in not following up their Victory—General Paladine's Reasons for refusing to Advance—Temporary Alarm of the German Headquarters—The Operations in the North of France under General Manteuffel—Capture of Verdun after a Prolonged and Determined Resistance—Bombardment and Capitulation of Thionville and La Fere—The Germans advance to Amiens—Great Battle near the City on November 27—Defeat of the French after a most Obstinate Struggle—Retreat of the French from Amiens and the Entry of the Germans—Vain Attempt to defend the City by the Commandant of the Citadel.

ON receipt of intelligence of the fall of Metz, the Provisional Government at Tours seem to have been lost in rage and humiliation. Assuming that Metz could have held out, and that Bazaine had betrayed it to the enemy, they issued an imprudent proclamation, declaring that he had "committed treason," had made himself the accomplice of the "man of Sedan," had been guilty of a "crime beyond the reach even of the chastisements of justice;" and that the "army of France, deprived of its national character, had unknowingly become the instrument of a reign of servitude." So great was the irritation created among officers by this proclamation, that on the following day the Tours government issued another to the effect, that the soldiers were "deceived, not dishonoured;" that "those who called them accomplices were calumniators;" that "their brothers of the army of the Rhine have already protested against the cowardly attempt, and have withdrawn their hands with horror from the accursed capitulation"—which, considering they were not asked to sign, but only to submit to it, and did submit, was not very intelligible. Altogether, the conduct of this government at Tours was not fitted to reassure the public. M. Gambetta and his companions, in fact, forgot at the time that they occupied the position of ministers of

France, and that language and behaviour which might be pardonable in a demagogue holding no office, and without any feeling of responsibility, were inexcusable in the leaders of a great nation. It would seem, indeed, as if the government were eager to accuse, lest they should themselves be accused. It was of them that France had a right to demand why, during their six weeks' tenure of power, nothing whatever had been done or attempted to relieve Metz. They had allowed the enemy to go where they liked outside Paris, and to besiege and capture such towns as seemed best to them. Not a single victory or success of importance had the republic yet obtained; and fearing lest it should be asked of them why Metz had been allowed to fall unaided, after a siege of ten weeks, the government apparently hastened to throw the blame upon the generals who commanded. Their accusation succeeded with the mass, whose favourite cry was ever treachery, but it lost them much of the respect and confidence of intelligent France.

The effect of the proclamation on the army was pernicious. The serious difficulties which the several commanders had to encounter in maintaining discipline, proved that the soldiers were not so well disposed to obey and confide in their chiefs that the minister of War could afford thus to inspire them with mistrust. Admiral Fourichon refused to sign the proclamation. A triumvirate of three civilians it was that brought the accusation against Bazaine—the soldier who had fought the battles most honourable to France during the campaign, who gave breathing time to Paris to fortify itself, who had occupied 250,000 of the enemy's troops for two months and a half, who had held out until forced by famine to surrender—and that accusation was recklessly urged without inquiry and without knowledge. The army was indignant that no efforts, no bravery, no sacrifices were accounted of in the moment of a reverse, and that the men who were trumpeted as heroes one day should be denounced as traitors the next. The *Moniteur*, without mentioning the proclamation itself, indignantly protested against this cry of "treason" being raised upon the occasion of every misfortune. We have been betrayed, indeed, it said, but not as the multitude imply, by one or more individuals, who have sold us to the enemy for some pieces of money, but by the incapacity and carelessness of most of those who have exercised an influence upon the success of the war, either in declaring it, or preparing for it, or conducting it. The sovereign first was betrayed, a little by the reports of his ambassadors and marshals, much by his own blindness, his obstinacy before the hostilities had commenced, and his indecision afterwards. The generals have been betrayed by their incapacity, and by the disorganization of the administration, and by the negligence of their subordinates. The inferior officers have been betrayed by the vices of an organization, which doubtless it was not their place to reform; but they have been betrayed also by their too great confidence, by the insufficiency of their military knowledge and preparatory studies. The soldiers, in their turn, have been betrayed by the bad tactics of their chiefs; but they have betrayed themselves frequently by their insubordination and undiscipline. Let us examine and correct ourselves, and we shall be no longer betrayed.

Throughout the country the news of the fall of Metz was variously received, and to many Frenchmen, chiefly in the northern departments, it appeared hopeless to continue the war after so terrible a misfortune, following on the crushing blows that had descended on the nation. Almost the last regular army of any importance which France possessed had been handed over to the enemy, with weapons and munitions of war that could not easily be replaced. Of the fighting men who remained the majority were raw troops, hastily raised, imperfectly drilled and armed, whom it seemed vain, as well as cruel, to send against the tried and successful warriors of Prussia; and many who had been hopeful till then now cried for peace. Winter was approaching, which would tell, indeed, against the invader, but would also aggravate the sufferings of the poorer classes of Frenchmen. The harvest had been bad, the fields in many places cut up by the struggles of embattled hosts; trade and commerce were almost destroyed; rinderpest was spreading with alarming rapidity among the cattle; and the requisitions of the Germans became more onerous every day. In the north of France, where this feeling of apprehension especially prevailed, an appeal to the members of the provincial councils was circulated in favour of peace. This document stated that, as the ministry had postponed the elections till the retreat of the enemy, while Prussia would only conclude peace with a government empowered by the nation; and that as these conflicting views might prolong the war, it behoved men of influence, such as those composing the councils, to meet, and send a petition or deputation to the government, urging the importance of taking immediate steps to enable the nation to declare either for peace, or for the continuation of the war, if the Prussian conditions should be deemed unacceptable. "One must place justice higher even than patriotism," the circular proceeded, "and must confess that it was France which, badly influenced, declared war against Prussia, and that, had the fortune of war been so favourable to it that its armies had penetrated to Berlin, it would scarcely have made peace except on a rectification of frontier at the expense of Germany. France, therefore, should not deem it unreasonable if Prussia to-day makes the same demand, as long as it restricts it within reasonable limits. They will not be humbled who submit to a peace, but rather those senseless people who, in their mad pride and presumptuous patriotism, approved the war, and contributed to its being declared."

The tone of several of the northern papers was in somewhat similar strain. The *Courrier du Havre* exclaimed: "Peace! That is the cry which at this moment millions of voices raise in all quarters of the earth, as well as in down-trodden France; in Germany, intoxicated with unexpected triumph, in intelligent England, in practical America, in far-sighted Russia, in loyal Spain, and in Italy, where war is still fresh in people's recollection. Everywhere this cry is raised to the Almighty, and seeks to make heaven gracious, seeing that the leaders of the peoples are without mercy." The *Journal de Fécamp*, commenting on this article, said: "Yes; conquered and humbled France desires and demands peace. All resistance is for the future unavailing. It will only add new hecatombs of a million of corpses to the million of corpses mouldering on the fields of Wissembourg, Reichshofen, Jaumont, and Sedan. We are conquered, scattered, as a nation has never been before. Let us cease to delude ourselves with new hopes, and to calculate on an impossible resistance. We are honourably conquered. Our army, which is no more, has made heroic exertions. It has even won the respect of the victor. Honour is saved. We are conquered. Let us humble ourselves. Let us assume the dignity of misfortune. Silent and modest, let us submit. Peace, peace alone, which is everywhere demanded by all France, can save the country's future, by its men and resources being spared. In view of the country's misfortune, we must at this hour have the courage to bow our necks, and sue for peace."

Looking to the heroic efforts subsequently put forth by Frenchmen on the Loire, or even by those in the northern departments themselves, such language appears craven and unpatriotic; but a calm review of the situation at this time could hardly fail to excite the most anxious fear for the future of France. The war had been begun with 400,000 men, ready for service, with some 1200 field-pieces, and with two first-class fortresses on the frontier to support the operations: 100,000 men killed and wounded had fallen, and 300,000 were prisoners. The 1200 field guns had nearly all been captured, and the fortresses had surrendered; the emperor and his imperial guard were in the enemy's hands, the most experienced officers wounded or prisoners; and would France, with a third of its territory occupied, be able with raw levies to turn the tide which had swept away its veteran army? The loss of men sustained by the Germans in actual fighting was not greater than that of the French, while the balance of prisoners was enormously in their favour. It would be next to a miracle if the raw levies of France could chase away the invader, or even long hold him in check.

In spite, however, of such discouraging prospects, from almost every part of France except the north addresses were sent to Tours, assuring the government of support, and declaring that the population were ready to die rather than surrender, or accept a dishonourable peace. At Marseilles the body styling itself the League of the South issued a manifesto; concluding with a decree that, in all the departments which have adhered to the League, all citizens must hold themselves in readiness to quit their homes at the first summons, and to march under the standards of the republic against Prussian and monarchical despotism. "The point of rendezvous for the national forces will be the city of Valence and the surrounding plains. The delegates of the co-operating departments are designated as general commissioners of the League of the South. They will traverse the departments to preach a holy war, to call together republican committees in the various localities, and to act in concert with them in order to effect, by all possible means, a general uprising." The expense of equipping the forces of the League was to be met by public subscription, and the general commissioners were to arrange with the republicans of each department for the election of cantonal delegates, who should attend the general assembly of the League of the South at Marseilles, on November 5. The document concluded by saying, that "In the name of the republic, one and indivisible, the members of municipal and administrative bodies owe the most energetic assistance, as citizens, to the members of the League of the South, created for the defence of the republic, and to their representatives. Done at Marseilles, October, 1870."

It would have been better for France had these southern republicans seen, that the safety of their country at this painful crisis depended not so much upon the promulgation of the republic, as upon unity of co-operation with the government of "National Defence," and the sinking of all political predilections until the common enemy had been overthrown. M. Gambetta himself, however, had set the example of so mixing up republicanism with his measures for national defence that, of the two, he frequently appeared to be holding up rather the banner of the revolution than that of France; which led one of the most influential papers, referring to his proclamation after the surrender of Metz, to remark, "It is the republic, one and indivisible, that must be greeted before everything. One and indivisible! And how are you to avoid the division of the territory when you scatter broadcast divisions in hearts and minds, by charging with treason all those who do not bow the knee before you, or who destroy, even unintentionally, your calculations and your lies?" The article went on to observe that, while Gambetta was stigmatizing Bazaine as a traitor, a Marseilles club was condemning Gambetta as a scoundrel. "How," it was asked, "could any new form of government be permanently established in the midst of such revolting confusion? or what chance existed of the struggle being effectively carried on against the invasion?" A French clerical paper, the Union, also speaking of the sarcasm implied in the words "one and indivisible," when compared with the distracted state of the country, said that "at this moment it would be betraying our country not to tell the truth. Every day which is passing is only deepening the abyss into which we are plunged. Resistance to the enemy is weak; the Prussian flood is still rising, and anarchy is extending its ravages more and more. There are two governments, one at Paris, the other at Tours. The investment of the capital renders concert impossible, and the official bulletin is exposed to registering contradictory decisions. There exists at Marseilles a revolutionary power, which is self-constituted, and oppresses a noble city; Lyons has again become a free town in this sense, that as the violent administration of that great city only breathes demagogic ardour, it is free from everything which restrained it. In almost all our departments there is a tendency among the prefects to obey Paris or Tours as little as possible. The country is on the way to being covered with governments, and all this being developed alongside the Prussian invasion. These are frightful complications which have no name in political language."

There was a great deal of truth in all this, though it is difficult to say that any one in particular was responsible for the state of semi-anarchy that prevailed. In fact, when it is considered that France had now been two months without any definite ruling power, and that nowhere in the world is faction so general, it seems almost a wonder to find order or unity of action present at all. As a rule, the artizans supported a republic, while the peasantry and trading classes were in favour of some form of monarchy. The republic, however, though not generally loved for itself, was accepted as representing, for the time being, the principle of nationality and the determination to fight; and with the majority the Provisional Government, up to the present time (November), had gained rather than lost in popularity by its determination not to lower the national flag. Men argued that France was lost if she permitted herself to be disheartened, even by such a succession of defeats as those she had endured; and no people that values its own historic reputation can blame them for so thinking. M. Gambetta became the most influential man in the Provisional Government, because he was the most earnest in devising means for continuing the war. Being minister of the Interior as well as of the department of "War he had, by the authority of the government in Paris, been invested with two votes in the Ministerial Council of Tours. He thus acquired nearly dictatorial powers; for unless all the other three voted against him—a not very likely circumstance—his will would be law. The present and succeeding chapters will show with what almost frantic energy he used this power. The national defence during the autumn and winter was mainly due to him; and though the prolonged and agonizing struggle was destined to fail, the endeavour cannot be said to have been utterly vain, for, as we shall presently show, France was never so near victory during the whole course of the war, as in the autumn months that followed the capitulation of Metz.

The internal state of the country being so unsettled, the prospects of France in entering on another stage of the war, were thus far from cheering. On the one side were the hosts of Germany, by this time flushed with their unbroken successes, and, confident in their skilful generals, their splendid organization, their enormous resources, and their perfect discipline and equipment, regarding themselves as invincible. On the other side were the half-formed armies of France, consisting for the most part of men who knew nothing of actual war, who had never been under fire, who had little confidence in themselves and less in their leaders; who in many instances were poorly furnished with the necessary weapons, and some of whom seemed to think that little more was needed in meeting the enemy than to cry "Long live the Republic." As we shall see, however, in their future struggles they displayed in many instances heroic courage and self-sacrifice; and they more than once inflicted most serious blows on their enemy.

For the German armies the capitulation of Metz on October 28 came in very good time. Although the enormous forces around Paris, and those on the Loire, on the Saone, on the Somme, and elsewhere, had hitherto held their ground with unshaken firmness, still it was no wonder if they began to feel the strain which the task before them put upon their energies. And there were not wanting signs that the hastily-gathered levies of France were beginning to gain the necessary martial confidence and discipline that would enable them to hold their own before the well-drilled soldiers of Germany. In an engagement between the Prussian royal guards and some of the Paris garrison, General Trochu's raw levies did not fly in "wild confusion," as they were wont to do on former occasions. At Le Bourget, near St. Denis, on October 21, the German outposts were driven in by a sortie of the French, who proceeded to entrench themselves on the spot, from which they were not dislodged by the guards till the 23rd; and then only after a well-contested engagement, in which the Prussians took more than 1200 prisoners, and among them thirty officers, but not without sustaining "heavy losses themselves." In the north, on the 21st October, at Formerie, a town of the Oise, between Amiens and Eouen, an attempt made by the Prussians to cut the railway line was frustrated by a party of French regular infantry and mobiles, who were left masters of the position.

These, indeed, were trifling advantages, only to be noticed as slight breaks in that uniform run of ill fortune which had so long attended the French. But, independently of such incidents, there was undeniable evidence that, on the one hand, the German line around Paris had been somewhat inconveniently thinned to strengthen the detached forces under General von der Tann and Prince Albrecht; and on the other, that the Paris garrison had been making the most of the respite allowed to it in acquiring that steadiness, the lack of which had hitherto proved a bar to its success. Besides, Von der Tann, though apparently equal to maintaining his position at Orleans and on the Loire, seemed to evince some hesitation as to any further advance, and awaited the onset of the French army under Aurelles de Paladine; who, it was supposed, would soon muster up strength and courage either to force the Prussian general's position at Orleans, or to turn its flank and steal a march upon it on the way to Paris. In the north, again, the invasion seemed to have abated in activity, and people wondered how long it would be ere Bourbaki had collected, out of the various frontier garrisons and the solid populations of those districts, a force large enough to embolden him to take the offensive; while, again, Bazaine's army at Metz, exhausted and dispirited though it was said to be, hung in the rear of the German forces, and created some apprehension of danger, however indefinite and remote, that it might break loose and throw itself upon their lines of communication.

Bazaine's capitulation put an end to these apprehensions, and rendered Germany stronger, almost to the full extent of the forces by which she protected herself against danger from that quarter; for, besides placing 173,000 men, four marshals of France, 6000 officers, and one of the strongest places in Europe in the hands of the victors, it set free nearly 200,000 of them for new efforts and triumphs. The general importance of this event was, of course, apparent from the first; but not until some weeks afterwards did it fully appear how seriously its occurrence at this particular time affected the fortunes of the war. Had Bazaine been able to prolong the defence for another month, a relieving army, of which even the existence had come to be doubted, would almost certainly have made its way to the neighbourhood of Paris. In view of this contingency, indeed, as we explained near the end of Chapter XX., the German commander had actually arranged for raising the siege.

Of the immense force now liberated, one part remained to garrison Metz; another, nearly 50,000 strong, was despatched against the French army of the north; a third, comprising a single corps, was sent to Paris to aid the besiegers; and the remainder, about 75,000 men, under the command of Prince Frederick Charles, was directed to the south and east of France, to occupy the Upper Loire, and to co-operate with the army under Werder. For it must be remembered that, besides the campaigns on the Loire and the Somme, there had been for some time in the east of France another struggle, which had resulted in the advance of a German army, under this general, into the departments of the Vosges, the Upper Saône, and the Doubs, to Epinal, Vesoul, and Besançon; at which latter place he seemed to pause, fearing, it was said, the opposition of General Cambriels, at the head of the so-called army of the Vosges. Cambriels had recently reported that he had checked the enemy on the Ognon, compelled him to fall back upon Gray, and relieved from uneasiness not only Besançon and Dôle—his own and Garibaldi's headquarters—but also Belfort and Dijon. As a practical reply to this boast, Von Werder, who had gone back to the Saone at Gray, followed the course of that river to Pontailler, and struck across the country to Dijon, due north of Lyons and almost due east of Bourges, at about 100 miles' distance from either place. He appeared before it on October 29, and took it after a short cannonade.

It will thus be seen that no portion of the German forces liberated by the capitulation of Metz was moved, in the first instance, against the French massed on the Lower Loire, whom, indeed, a combination of circumstances had caused the German commanders, with less than their wonted caution, to disregard. As stated in a previous chapter, one corps of that army had been defeated with great ease, in the middle of October, by a Bavarian detachment, which had captured Orleans and still held it; and as the entire body had since made no sign, its real strength was not known, and it was supposed to be worthless.

To serve a purpose, no doubt, there had indeed been an immense amount of mystification about this army, especially a statement that it had been sent off northwards. Reports varied from day to day regarding its discipline, proficiency in drill, numbers, armament, equipment, artillery, transport. All that was known with any degree of certainty respecting it was that it wanted officers, arms, horses, all kinds of *matériel*, and especially time. It had its origin in a collection of companies, of squadrons of regiments, where the lancers mingled with the chasseurs, the dragoon with the Turco, the chasseurs de Vincennes with the zouave, a battalion of infantry with a battery of artillery, gardes mobiles with franc-tireurs. The large admixture of the latter corps gave an extremely picturesque aspect to the miscellaneous aggregate. Obedient to the summons, they had flocked together in larger or smaller bodies from every province of France, from the colonies, from the United States and Canada, from Algeria and Greece, from Italy and Spain, from Rio Janeiro and Monte Video. Almost all wore the short tunic or thick woollen blouse, generally of dark colours, black, green, blue, and brown, while some few corps adopted the grays and buffs in favour among English volunteers. There were Tyrolese and wide-awake hats of every description, with cockades of all sizes and feathers of every tint. The brigand was largely represented, reminding the stranger of Fra Diavola and Massaroni, and other well-known types and theatrical celebrities. The South American corps was got up with a particular eye to effect. Its chief, M. de Friés, received the name of D'Artagnan, after Alexandre Dumas' hero, and Mélingue himself never looked the part better. He and his men wore the South American poncho as an overcoat, carried the lasso, and could noose a horse at full speed and bring him to the ground. The Basque battalion, composed of hardy mountaineers used to toil up Pyrenean steeps, and wearing their national head-dress, the flat *bèret*, red, blue, or white, with a tassel pendant from its centre, presented a good appearance. Then there was the mysterious company of the Gers, consisting of fifty picked men, in black costume, with skull and cross-bone facings, and who never spoke. The arming of the troops was various. Those worst provided had the old Minie, but for this the Remington or Chassepot was substituted as soon as obtainable. Numbers of them carried revolvers and poniards. The "Foreign Legion," which, it is only just to say, was always cheerfully in the front when the greatest danger and hardest fighting were to be met, comprised among others about a score of finely-built, soldierly-looking Englishmen, and several Irishmen, lured to France at this juncture either by zeal for the cause or by a love of adventure. Not the least picturesque feature was the Arab cavalry, formed in the colony of Algiers, of volunteers recruited in the great tribes of the desert. The original design was that every province should supply a contingent; but it is doubtful if the total number of these Spahi warriors in the Loire army ever exceeded 600 men. Their presence was generally heralded by a clang of barbaric trumpets, and a chief with a face like a bronze statue headed the rather straggling columns of fiery little Arab horses. The men wore their native dress, their heads, as usual, being wrapped up as if they had all been afflicted with toothache, and they sat perched high up on their peculiar Moorish saddles. The chasseurs d'Afrique, the hussars, and the chasseurs à cheval, mustered largely, but it could not escape notice how absurdly overweighted the whole cavalry force was, by having to carry all sorts of cooking pots, *tentes d'abri*, and other *impedimenta*, which rendered them utterly useless in a charge. Smartness, cleanliness of horses, and pride of corps, as known in the English service, seemed not to exist in the cavalry of this army; and the men, seen on the march, always gave one the idea that their first and last business in life was to make their soup, not to fight. Besides their sabres, which they were hardly taught how to use, they were armed with a long, lumbering carbine, which was slung at their backs, and greatly hindered the use of the sword-arm.

Such was some of the rather unpromising material, gathered from every quarter of the globe, which, in the hope that it might be welded into something like an army, was intrusted to the command of General d'Aurelles de Paladine, a soldier who had seen hard service in the field, and had come out of his well-earned retirement to organize the forces of his country. By birth he was of an Auvergnat house. At an early age he entered the army, and in 1843 served in a campaign against Abd-el-Kader, under the Duc d'Aumale, who was then governor of Algeria. At that time d'Aurelles was *chef de bataillon* of the sixty-fourth infantry, and considered an excellent officer. He had the reputation of being a strict disciplinarian; and his passion for order and prompt obedience specially qualified him for reducing into shape the loose mass of regulars, gardes mobiles, foreigners, and franctireurs, dignified with the name of the Army of the Loire, which he found little better than a mob, and succeeded in rendering almost a match for the best troops of Prussia. The mutinous spirit which prevailed when he took the command he put down by offering the alternative of obedience or death; and before firing a shot at the Germans he shot down several score of his own men. General d'Aurelles de Paladine in several respects was like General Trochu. Both were strongly imbued with a religious spirit; both had lived in retirement for years—the one unknown, the other known only to strategists; and on the exertions of both seemed now to depend the last hopes of France.

As may be imagined, the task of D'Aurelles was not an easy one. For several weeks the troops were kept in the open air, exposed to all vicissitudes of weather, and engaged incessantly in the varied exercises which were necessary to accustom them to the tactics of war. To enforce good discipline amongst them proved for a time most difficult. Their idea of subordination seemed to be extinguished—a spirit which could be overcome only by a rigorous discipline, like that maintained in the Prussian army, in which insubordination is always punished by death. There were many loud and bitter complaints of D'Aurelles' severity; but the good fruits of the hardy training were soon seen in improved solidity and promptitude in manoeuvring, in the excellent health of the troops, and in their renewed hope and confidence.

The most ardent hopes of the French government, therefore, now centred in this army of the Loire. Should it have the fortune to gain a considerable victory, the effect throughout France, it was felt, would be incalculable in putting down resistance to the government, and in converting into soldiers, inspired with some confidence in their leaders and some respect for themselves, those hordes of armed men by courtesy styled armies.

The forces under General d'Aurelles de Paladine, early in November, amounted to 180,000 men, with 400 gun3, and nearly 15,000 cavalry. Since the disaster of Metz the authorities waited with intense anxiety for some serious movement on the part of this army before the victorious legions of Prince Frederick Charles should have time to approach. Although composed, as we have seen, of such heterogeneous masses, it was from its numbers by no means despicable; and at this conjuncture an opportunity was afforded its leader of striking a blow of which the results might have been momentous. At the beginning of November it was separated by a few miles only from a single Bavarian corps of not more than 25,000, scattered somewhat disorderly between Orleans and Châteaudun, and virtually forming the only German force between Orleans and the lines round Paris. General d'Aurelles de Paladine saw the favourable opportunity, and laid his plans for cutting off, and if possible annihilating, the small hostile corps which lay temptingly in his front. For this purpose he resolved to cross the Loire below and above Orleans, thus, by a converging movement, to close in completely on his foe; and in case he should succeed in sweeping away this only obstacle in his path, he intended to march straight on Paris, and endeavour to relieve it.

It thus happened that the 9th of November, which witnessed the surrender of Verdun, brought to the French, as a compensation in another quarter, their first gleam of success. After the battles before Orleans, Von der Tann, reduced to his own corps by the recall of the twenty-second division to Paris and the detachment of Prince Albrecht's cavalry to Chartres, remained inactive on the Loire. A force of 20,000, including Prince Albrecht's horsemen, was at Chartres about the end of October, to hold in check the army of Brittany; and Von der Tann's right flank was covered by a detachment at Châteaudun. Columns of various strength, detached from the investment on the different roads, occasionally suffering a reverse, formed a large semicircle round the rest of Paris from Compiégne on the north, by Montdidier, Breteuil, Beauvais, Evreux, Chartres, and Châteaudun, to Orleans on the south.

The occupation of Orleans, indeed, had proved scarcely less difficult than its capture. For more than a month the Bavarian general had kept the French constantly employed and himself informed of their movements, by a system of reconnaissances and patrols, which extended over a comparatively wide area, and necessarily exposed those engaged in them to the constant attacks of franc-tireurs concentrated at Tours, whose most energetic efforts were directed to harassing the troops in the occupation of Orleans, while the larger army was forming below the Loire to attack the comparatively small force at the disposal of General von der Tann. The occupation of Chartres and Châteaudun by General Wittich weakened the army at Orleans, which, receiving no reinforcement from other quarters, and reduced to a force of about 15,000 men, began to find itself in a somewhat critical position. The position, in fact, of the Prussian garrison of Orleans was one of even greater danger than Von der Tann suspected, for by about the end of October General d'Aurelles' army had assumed a form which enabled him to act, and it was agreed that he should begin to move forward from Blois on the morning of the 29th, with the intention of driving back the Bavarians, and then trying to reach Paris. But at the last moment D'Aurelles changed his mind; he telegraphed to Tours on the night of the 28th, to say that the roads were bad, the equipment of part of the garde mobile very insufficient, and that it was consequently imprudent to attempt an action.

It transpired subsequently that the news of the capitulation of Metz had become known to General d'Aurelles that very afternoon, some hours before the Tours government heard of it; and this was the main cause of his resolution not to move. His decision caused great disappointment at Tours, where it was immediately recognized that the Ked Prince's army, suddenly set free, would come westward as fast as possible, and that it was indispensable to relieve Paris before its arrival, which was expected to take place about the 16th or 18th of November. But instead of hastening forward, the Loire army was delayed by various circumstances which it is difficult to determine with precision, amongst which, however, the current reports that an armistice had been concluded appear to have had much influence on General d'Aurelles, and to have disposed him to stop where he was. The despatches afterwards made public, and a work published at the close of the war by M. de Freycinet, M. Gambetta's delegate to the ministry of War, show that the hesitations of the commander-in-chief were the object of continual correspondence between that officer and the ministry of War; but however strong may have been the pressure employed, it was not till the 6th November, more than a week after the date originally fixed, that the French army at last marched forward.

While this was going forward along the Loire, the Prussians had decided to send reinforcements to General Von der Tann. Some 30,000 men had therefore been detached from the army before Paris, and had been sent towards him under the orders of the duke of Mecklenburg. The arrangement was made too late; for on the same day (the 11th November) that the duke reached Toury en route for Orleans, Von der Tann entered the same town with the remnant of his valiant but thoroughly beaten troops, who, swept forward by the masses of D'Aurelles, had escaped entire capture only by a kind of miracle. We will, however, revert to the first dispositions of the French commander, which had resulted in this signal reverse for the German arms.

On November 6, leaving one corps at Mer, on the north bank of the Loire, to cover Tours, three others, moving from their headquarters at La Ferté (twelve miles south of Orleans), crossed the river at Beaugency and formed, with the corps from Mer, a general line extending from the Loire, on the right, to Marchenoir, behind the forest of that name, on the left. To ascertain the real nature of this movement, which appeared to threaten the Bavarian communications with Paris, Von der Tann, on November 7, ordered a reconnaissance, which, led by Count Stolberg, was pushed as far as Autainville, in the direction of Vendôme. This showed that the French were massed in the forest of Marchenoir, in that neighbourhood, in a force estimated at 60,000 men. The reconnoitring party consisted of 6000 men, with cavalry and artillery, and had been despatched with the further object of dislodging the French, if possible, from the wood. The Bavarians, however, had seriously under-estimated the number of their enemies, and were repulsed with loss.

The French, elated with their success, on the following day assumed the offensive, marched forward to occupy various positions, with the view of cutting off the communications of the Bavarian army, and by interposing between Orleans and the base of operations, render their escape impossible. De Paladine had carefully studied the situation, and a curious chance had furnished him with the most reliable and precise information. A paper, torn into the smallest pieces, was found lying on a table in a chateau which had been the headquarters of General von der Tann. It proved to be the rough draft of his orders to his officers, with a plan for the dispositions of the troops. The pieces were carefully pasted together by a person in Orleans, who obtained a translation of their contents into French, and sent them to the minister of War at Tours. This paper, containing the exact number of troops to be engaged, precise instructions as to their disposition, and even the place of each gun, was transcribed with fear and trembling, in a house actually filled with Bavarians; it proved of incalculable use to the French troops, who, as the Germans owned, had never before been so well directed as now. The French army of Beaugency was ordered to advance towards Orleans; the right wing to halt on the side of Ormes; but the centre and left wing, pivoting on the right, were to proceed in the direction of Gemigny, St. Péravy, Boulay, and Briey, to meet the cavalry corps which General Martin des Palliéres, stationed a few leagues above Orleans, at St. Benoit-sur-Loire, was bringing towards Cercottes.

As soon as General von der Tann perceived this design, he ordered the immediate retreat of the baggage and heavy material of the army by the direct road towards Paris; and, compelled to leave about 1000 sick and wounded in the hospitals of Orleans, he put himself at the head of the fifteen battalions which still remained to him, and marched directly to meet the enemy. Wishing to extricate himself from the maze of woods and vineyards, and to reach the open plain, where his cavalry and artillery would tell, he moved in a north-westerly direction. For a day or two previously there had been some excitement, the cause of which the French inhabitants of Orleans could not make out. It was supposed that a battle was going on, but where no one knew. On the night of the evacuation, however, all became clear. At about ten p.m. there was a general running in the streets, into which the inhabitants were not allowed to go; but the greater the running of the Germans, and the driving of all sorts of carriages, the stronger was the temptation of Frenchmen to learn the cause of the stir. At midnight the Place du Martroi, the Rue Royale, the Hue Bannier, and all the adjacent streets were blocked with gun, provision, and ammunition carriages, and in the morning the regiment of Bavarian guards were all that remained to tell of a German occupation. About noon on the 9th these filed off, with drums beating and colours flying, by the Rue Jeanne d'Arc and Rue Bannier, as though they had been going out for a *promenade militaire*. The townspeople were naturally delighted when, at the close of the day, they saw troops advancing towards the town under the tricolor instead of the abhorred black and white. Their exultation was natural, though, judging from the following notice issued by the municipality, it was rather overstrained:—"The mayor of the city of Orleans appeals to the generous feeling of the population; he is sure that the German wounded and prisoners will be treated by his fellow townsmen in conformity with the dictates of humanity. The mayor warns those of his fellow citizens who may have in their possession arms and ammunition, consequent on the disarming of the German soldiers, that they must immediately lodge them at the Hôtel de Ville. They belong to the state, and those detaining them will be prosecuted according to law.—ORLEANS, *November* 10."

There is no doubt that there was some haste in the retreat of the Bavarians; and that they were followed up pretty closely, is proved by the capture of Von der Tann's carriage and other articles of his property, by the leaving of the sick and wounded, and by the fact that many of the inhabitants made prisoners of the soldiers who had been billeted upon them. It was these accidental captures to whose "disarming" the notice pointed.

Early on the morning of November 9 the two armies became aware of each other's presence near Coulmiers, between that place and Baccon, a small village about fourteen miles to the west of Orleans. About ten o'clock the engagement began. The spot had already been rendered classic as the scene of a battle in 1409, in which the French, under the Maid of Orleans, defeated the English under Sir John Fastolf.

In the present instance, also, and for the first time in the history of this war, the tide of victory turned in favour of the French, who outnumbered the Germans in the proportion of four to one, and could not have been fewer than 90,000 men, with 120 field guns. The most that General von der Tann could hope to accomplish against such overwhelming odds, was to make good his retreat in the direction of Paris with the least possible loss of men and material. The nature of the country was such as to render cavalry operations impracticable, and for more than seven hours his small force, of little more than 12,000 infantry, succeeded in holding the whole French army in check. The action commenced by a well-sustained attack on the German centre and right wing, forcing the latter to give way, until General Orff, with the second Bavarian brigade, wheeled round the left wing to its support, and for a moment almost seemed about to change the fortunes of the day. The French, however, brought up strong reinforcements, and were supported by an admirably served marine artillery; an arm hitherto little feared in their hands, but which was now employed with a precision and efficiency which were the theme of universal remark among the German officers, who perhaps, considering their past experience, had begun to fall into the not unnatural error of underrating their enemy.

From this time the French continued to advance steadily towards Baccon, i.e., from the south-west to the north-east. The Bavarians had taken up a position which formed an acute angle with the French line, their line of battle being nearly parallel with the range of woods extending from Chaingy to some distance beyond Bucy St. Siphard. To deploy their forces they availed themselves of the ground between the farm of La Renardière, the fields of Huisseau, the farms and plantations of Coulmiers on the one hand, to Rosieres and the fields around Gemigny. At Baccon the French met with a stubborn resistance. The Germans had loopholed the houses, constructed barriers, and taken advantage of every wall and every hedge for cover. The village of Baccon is built on a hillock, on which the houses rise in tiers; the lowest being scattered about the plain at its foot. From that culminating point the Germans kept up a murderous fire on the French troops, who promptly responded to the orders of their officers to move forward. After a brief but desperate struggle, Baccon was carried by storm, and the Germans gave way. The French, even to the mobiles, most of whom were in this action for the first time under fire, behaved with great bravery and steadiness in the heat of the fight; but to the marine infantry and artillery, previously alluded to, D'Aurelles subsequently awarded the highest praise.

Notwithstanding, however, the repeated and furious assaults of the French, and the fearful loss they managed to inflict upon their opponents, they could not force them from the position they had occupied during the day, and night closed in, leaving the Germans worn out and decimated by the fight, but not vanquished. They had already marched all the preceding night; they had fought during the whole day of the 9th; and now their only chance of escape was to make another night march on Artenay. Leaving about 700 of their comrades, including 42 officers, dead and wounded, in the hands of the enemy, they turned their backs on the bloody field of Baccon as soon as the darkness set in, and under a fall of sleet and snow tramped their weary way to Artenay, having for thirty-six hours scarcely tasted a mouthful of food. It is said that, when Prince Frederick Charles asked Marshal Bazaine why the French army did not follow up their partial success on the 16th of August, and escape from their critical position before Metz during the night, he replied, "On ne marche pas la nuit." The Germans under Von der Tann, eschewing this comfortable principle, succeeded in reaching Artenay on the following morning in perfect order, and without much loss of material. The Bavarian life guards, who, it will be remembered, had been left at Orleans, and who quitted that city on the 9th, found themselves separated from the main body of the army by the events of that day, and came into unexpected proximity to the enemy, from whom they only escaped by a forced and arduous night march of fifteen hours, during which they were compelled to pass almost within earshot of the French position. Finally, the morning of the 10th found the gallant little army of Von der Tann united at Artenay, where, by having outmarched the enemy, they were enabled to enjoy a day's rest after their brilliant retreat, and take up a defensive attitude.

The result of the engagement was made known to the government at Tours by the following despatch on the 10th:—"The army of the Loire, under the command of General d'Aurelles de Paladine, carried Orleans yesterday after two days' fighting. Our losses in killed and wounded do not reach 2000; those of the enemy are more considerable. We have taken more than 1000 prisoners, and this number is being increased by the pursuit. We have also captured two guns of Prussian make, more than twenty powder and munition waggons with their horses, and a large quantity of fourgons and provision waggons. The principal seat of the action was round Coulmiers, and the ardour of the troops was admirable, notwithstanding the bad weather."

While the French thus acknowledged a loss of 2000, the official report of the German commander gave that of the Bavarians, in killed and wounded, at 42 officers and 667 men. The 1000 prisoners were the sick and wounded left at Orleans, and the two guns were two small unlimbered useless cannon which the Germans abandoned, as encumbering their movements. The despatches and report of General d'Aurelles de Paladine respecting the battle of Baccon were, however, written with a fairness and modesty which were new to the French, and the advantages he gained were not overstated. Had he claimed to have reduced the effective strength of the Bavarian corps by at least 4000 men, he would have been quite within the truth. Nor was this the only advantage gained. The *morale* of both men and officers was much improved. Cheered by a victory after continuous defeat, they did their duty better and more smartly; and all believed that the day had at last come when they would be able to beat back the invader, and re-assert their old standing amongst the warriors of Europe. Under their commander the new army had learned the very important lesson of light infantry duty, which the first French armies seemed to have quite forgotten—the art of protecting flanks and rear from surprise, of feeling for the enemy, surprising his detachments, procuring information, and taking prisoners. It was at length the Germans who had to grope in the dark in order to ascertain the position of the enemy.

But the energetic measures which General von Moltke took to meet its expected march upon Paris, furnished the most remarkable proof of the respect which the army of the Loire now inspired. As we have before remarked, so well had the preparations of this army been concealed that its very existence was doubted amongst the Germans. Now, however, even at the risk of actually raising the investment of Paris, the Prussian strategist found it necessary to hold in readiness against it the greater portion of the blockading forces on the south side of the city. He changed at once the direction of march of the two armies arriving from Metz, so as to draw them closer to Paris, that thus the whole of the German forces might be concentrated around it; and steps were also taken to surround the siege park with defensive works.

M. Gambetta was not slow to congratulate the army on its success. He at once visited the camp, and published the following proclamation to the troops:—

"Soldiers! Your courage and your efforts have brought back victory. To you France owes her first consolation, her first ray of hope. I am happy to convey to you the expression of the public gratitude, and the praises and recompenses which the government awards to success. Led by chiefs vigilant, faithful, and worthy of you, you have recovered discipline and strength, you have retaken Orleans with the ardour of old troops accustomed to conquer, and have proved that France, far from being overwhelmed by reverses which have no precedent in history, intends to assume in her turn a vigorous and general offensive. The advanced guard of the country, you are on the road to Paris! Let us not forget that Paris awaits us. Our honour is staked upon our succeeding in loosening the grasp of the barbarians who threaten her with fire and pillage. Redouble your constancy and your ardour. You now know the enemy. Their superiority consists in the number of their cannon. Recover the French dash and the fury which ought to help to save the country. With such soldiers the republic will issue victorious from the struggle."

The army of the Loire, however, had yet to prove its mettle in a general engagement with the "barbarians "in numbers more nearly equal; and as subsequent events showed that it was unequal to this task, we are confirmed in the opinion that it was a fatal error its success at Baccon was not at once followed up.

It is impossible for Frenchmen to recall the important phase of their great struggle which we have just described, without a pang of bitter regret that the successes of D'Aurelles at Baccon were not promptly followed up, presenting, as they did, by far the fairest and most promising opportunity during the war for reversing the ill-fortune of France. The Germans themselves admitted that if they had been pursued, every one of them, from the general to the last camp-follower, would inevitably have been taken prisoner. Having marched all night to come into action, they had to march all the next night to get away from it; and it was with the most intense astonishment that the exhausted Bavarians discovered on the 10th that General d'Aurelles was not attempting to come after them. And this was not their only surprise. On the 11th the duke of Mecklenburg met Von der Tann at Toury; and the latter was proposing arrangements to unite their two armies, so as to make a stand against the victorious French and cover Paris, when to his bewilderment instructions were telegraphed from Versailles to abandon the direct line of defence, and to immediately march north-west to Dreux (leaving D'Aurelles to do what he liked), in order to stop another French army which was said to be marching straight on Versailles from Argentan and Laigle. Looking back at all this in the light of what subsequently transpired, it seems incredible that the clever Prussians should have been so utterly taken in by the fear of an army which really did not exist, that they left the road to Paris wide open before D'Aurelles; and, more incredible still, that the Tours government should have failed to profit by the prodigious opportunity which was offered to them by this mistake of General von Moltke. The altogether insignificant character of what the German commander imagined to be an army approaching from the west is explained in the following chapter, and the explanations of General Chanzy and M. de Freycinet afterwards enlightened the world as to why the opportunity of capturing the defeated Bavarian army and of raising the siege of Paris was not utilized.

It appears that, when the fight began on the morning of the 9th, General Reyan, with ten regiments of cavalry and some batteries of horse-artillery, was ordered to cover the French left wing and turn the German right. General Reyan had been at some distance from the scene of action, and on the morning of November 9, after a long and tiresome march of fourteen hours, he came within view of German batteries. Instead of hastening on to the battle-field and executing the manoeuvre ordered, he opened fire on the batteries alluded to, and at two o'clock reported to D'Aurelles that his artillery had lost heavily in men and horses, and had no more ammunition, and that his cavalry had met with serious resistance everywhere. He added that he feared the enemy would outflank him, and he thought he should have to fall back. At five o'clock General Reyan again sent word that a column of infantry was now appearing before him at Villamblain, and he considered it indispensable to return to his encampment of the previous night. It was soon discovered that the column in question was composed of French franc-tireurs; but, unfortunately, the cavalry had already fallen back, night was coming on, and exhausted as they were with continuous marching, it was impossible to get the regiments forward again. The force, therefore, which was effectually to have cut off the retreat of the Bavarians, did not come into the engagement at all; and when the battle was won by the centre and right no cavalry was up to pursue the victory, or to ascertain the movements of the retiring Germans. The French slept on the field, but it began to rain and snow; the night was bad, there was no wood for fires, and the supplies of food and ammunition were got to the front with much difficulty. When day broke Admiral Jaureguiberry sent his own escort, forty-five men, in pursuit of the Bavarians, and they took two guns, 130 prisoners, and quantities of baggage and ammunition. If forty-five hussars could do this, what would General Reyan's ten regiments have effected? General d'Aurelles does not seem, however, to have thought of following up his victory, though he must have had at least 80,000 men still in good fighting condition, against about half that number under Mecklenburg and Von der Tann, supposing, indeed, the two latter to have united and made a stand. The days following the 9th were occupied in organizing convoys, in completing the artillery, and in procuring clothes for the soldiers, arrangements which it seems a singular lack of foresight to have left till a time like this. Day followed day, and the French did not move; their outposts advanced, but the army remained inactive. Von der Tann left a few troops at Etampes, and marched away with the rest to join the Duke of Mecklenburg at Chartres; so that, by the 14th, there were not more than 3000 Germans between D'Aurelles and Paris.

With these facts before us, it is easy to understand the alarm which we have described in Chapter XXIV. as prevailing at Versailles at this time. General von Moltke knew that nothing would stop D'Aurelles if he marched resolutely on by Etampes to the Seine; he feared that Mecklenburg would not get into position between Chartres and Dreux in time to paralyze the other imaginary army, which was supposed to be driving on Versailles in that direction; so that on the 14th and 15th November the German headquarters expected to be attacked behind from Rambouillet and to be cut off from their line of communications eastward by D'Aurelles. It is not strange, therefore, that they should have packed up their boxes, as was actually the case; it seemed impossible to the energetic Prussians that their enemy should not rush at them instantly, and make a desperate attempt to break the line of investment south of Paris, before Prince Frederick Charles could reach it. But when they learnt, on the night of the 15th, that D'Aurelles had made no sign, that the Red Prince's outposts had reached, the line of which Montargis is the centre, and that no French army had shown itself beyond Dreux, they took courage, stopped where they were, and so evaded the grave moral consequences which would have ensued on an evacuation of Versailles.

While the German headquarters were in this critical position, a conference had taken place, on November 12, between the French generals and M. Gambetta, who had come up from Tours to congratulate the troops on the victory of Coulmiers. General Borel, a very able officer, afterwards chief of the staff of Marshal MacMahon during the Communist siege of Paris, proposed to march straight to the Seine, but General D'Aurelles would not have that at all; not only did it seem to him impossible to continue the offensive, but he considered it was dangerous even to remain at Orleans. M. Thiers, who, as described in a previous chapter, had been endeavouring to arrange with the Prussians for an armistice, had just returned from Versailles, and reported that he had come through an army of 80,000 men; his imagination, in fact, having more than doubled the force, which was none other than that of the duke of Mecklenburg, now off to the west. To D'Aurelles, however, this was sufficient reason for not advancing. He said the enemy would be back on him directly; that an indisputable eye-witness had seen 80,000 Prussians marching down from Paris; that he was certain to be attacked in a day or two, and that his army was unfit to stand the shock. Finally, he proposed to immediately evacuate Orleans, and to return to his old position at Salbris. M. Gambetta, M. de Freycinet, and General Borel energetically opposed these arguments; but all they could obtain from D'Aurelles was, that instead of abandoning Orleans, the army should intrench itself round the town: no forward movement should be made, for the moment at least; but it was admitted that Paris should still be considered to be the destination of the army. A fortified camp was immediately formed round Orleans, new troops arrived, and in a few days the French had more than 200,000 men in position.

Leaving for the present the army of the Loire, we will glance at the events then transpiring in the north of France, which, next to those south of Paris, were the most important that occurred during the month of November.

Of the large force detached to operate in the north under General Manteuffel, a considerable portion was sent to assist in reducing several fortresses which had hitherto been rather invested than besieged, but whose fall, on the release of the immense siege *matériel* from around Metz, might now be counted on in a few days. The first place which followed the fate of the great Moselle stronghold was Verdun, a fortress of the second class, standing on the Meuse, where it begins to be navigable, about 150 miles east of Paris, 120 west of the Rhine, 30 north-west of Bar-le-Duc, and 40 from Metz. It has 13,000 inhabitants; and although partly fortified by Vauban, its strength is not great against modern artillery, as it is commanded by the adjacent bills, and the river is fordable in several places near the works. Its fortifications consist of a citadel, separated from the town by an esplanade, and of an *enceinte* of ten bastioned fronts. The place had been the object of much attention ever since the German armies crossed the Moselle. In the attempt to gain it, the army of the Rhine had fought the great battles of Vionville and Gravelotte; an immense store of provisions having been accumulated here as soon as Bazaine's retreat was contemplated.

Verdun was first invested on September 25, but not so strictly as to prevent the garrison from being subsequently largely increased. Early in October the place was completely closed in, and the usual summons to surrender made. Baron Guerin de Waldersback, the commandant, replied by expressing to the Prussian envoy his resolution to hold out as long as one stone remained on another; adding, "We shall meet in the breach." The breach, however, was precisely the place where, in this war of sieges, no German and French officers ever did meet. The bombardment from the German artillery was terrific, and was effected from two strong batteries, the one situated due north, the other east, of the place. On the 13th and 14th of October a perfect hurricane of shells was poured upon the devoted town, but without shaking the determination of the garrison. The brave General Marnier, sub-commandant of Verdun, putting himself at the head of some 3000 men, made a sortie in a north-easterly direction on the 28th. Without firing a shot, at the point of the bayonet he drove back the German advanced posts. He then attacked the batteries, and carried them by assault, destroying the works, dismounting and spiking the guns, and returning safe to Verdun. The conduct of the civilians, like that of their fellow-countrymen at Strassburg, Toul, and elsewhere, was honourable and spirited. From the first they were anxious to make the best possible defence, irrespective of personal losses. During the furious bombardment they took refuge in the cellars, where some of the more timid remained during almost the whole of the siege, while their houses were burning over their heads. This state of things could not, of course, continue long. Disease—small-pox especially—was adding its ravages to those of the enemy's cannon, and the mortality increased rapidly from day to day. Prospect of relief there was none. So long as Metz stood, and there was a possibility of Bazaine's army, or any portion of it, forcing its way through Prince Frederick Charles' lines, and throwing itself upon Verdun, there might have been a propriety in continued resistance. But the fall of Metz changed the whole position of affairs, and it then became simply a question whether the barren honour of holding out to no purpose for a few days longer was worth the penalty that must be incurred in the demolition of the remains of the town, and the slaughter of a great portion, at all events, of the surviving garrison and inhabitants.

At this point, too, the severely-tried endurance of the townspeople began in some measure to fail them. So long as their sufferings were of any use to France they had borne them with exemplary patience, and had shown as little desire to yield as General Guerin himself. But they now felt that nothing was to be gained by prolonging the struggle. The devastation wrought was greater even than at Strassburg, as the German guns easily dominated the entire town. It was this almost complete destruction that led to the ultimate surrender of the place, which was coerced into submission without having had to endure any very serious want of food, the supplies of which would, at the time of the surrender, have enabled the inhabitants to hold out for a while longer. The 9th of November, which, as we have seen, brought the first and most considerable victory of the war to the French arms, witnessed the capitulation of Verdun, when two generals, 160 officers, and 4000 men were made prisoners, and 136 guns and 23,000 rifles, with a considerable store of material of war, were taken.

As soon as Metz had fallen, Thionville also was very soon vigorously bombarded, and set on fire. Until the surrender of Metz the position of Thionville gave it an importance in the war with which no other fortress of its size and strength, except Toul, could compare. At the end of July it supported the left wing of the French army of the Rhine. During the operations before Metz its proximity was a cause of extreme annoyance to Prince Frederick Charles, as its abundant supplies presented a constant temptation to the hungry garrison of the larger fortress to endeavour to establish a communication with it, in which they once nearly succeeded. The town has between 7000 and 8000 inhabitants. The fortress is built almost entirely on the left or western bank of the Moselle; that part of it which stands on the right bank consisting of a fort of modern construction, containing magazines and fine cavalry barracks. It was formerly the residence of the Merovingian and Carlovingian kings, has been a fortified place since the thirteenth century, and has sustained numerous sieges, from that of 1643, when the prince of Condé took it, until 1814, when General Hugo, father of Victor Hugo, successfully defended it against the Prussians. When besieged by the allies in 1792, the citizens hung the figure of an ass over the wall with a bundle of hay at its mouth, and the inscription, "When the ass eats the hay you will take Thionville." The story illustrates the short range of artillery eighty years ago. Besiegers and besieged must have been very close together, or the placard could not have been legible. From 1815 Thionville was the advanced post of the north-east of France, between Metz and Luxemburg and Sarrelouis. Its fortifications belong to different epochs and systems of engineering. The *corps de la place* consists of an irregular heptagon, with demilunes, contregardes, and lunettes. The fort of the Double Crown is on the right bank. The full complement of the garrison of Thionville is 8000 men, but at the time of its investment there were not more than half this number. The fortress, however, held out until November 24, and was expected, from the boastful declaration of its commandant, to resist much longer. Less than three day's experience of the German artillery, however, was enough for him; and with a great part of the town in flames, a capitulation was signed, which gave the Prussians 4000 more prisoners and an additional 200 cannon.

In the course of General Manteuffel's progress towards Amiens, the only other fortified place which had not yet surrendered was that of La Fère, near the confluence of the Oise and the Serre, fourteen miles north-west of Laon, and on the road from that town to Amiens. It was invested about the middle of November, and on the 20th a courageous attempt to relieve it was made by a French force, which, however, was repulsed with heavy loss. On the 27th La Fère capitulated after two days' bombardment, yielding 2000 prisoners and 70 guns.

By a ministerial decision of November 18, General Bourbaki was summoned to take command of the newly-formed eighteenth French corps d'armée at Nevers; General Farre being intrusted provisionally with his charge in the north. It would seem from this that M. Gambetta, now the presiding genius of France outside Paris, had underrated the danger which menaced the wealthy and populous cities of the north from the advance of Manteuffel. So little, indeed, had been heard of the movements of this commander, that it was generally supposed he was hesitating to venture into a district where the brilliant fame of General Bourbaki had in a short time made him the rallying point for a French army of no mean pretensions. The fact was, that the advance of the first German army had been halted on the receipt of the news of the French movements about Orleans on the 9th, and its dispositions then seemed to indicate an intention to remove southward. This, however, was not the case. General Manteuffel left Rheims on November 17, and at this time his troops were reported as never having been in better case to meet an enemy, or to encounter the exigencies of a campaign. The artillery and cavalry horses were in splendid condition. Dysentery and other sickness, which prevailed around Metz, had gradually disappeared through change of air, exercise, and a good commissariat, and every thing was hopeful. Soissons was reached on the 19th, Compiegne—where the German commander occupied the emperor's chateau—on the 21st, and from this date little more was heard of Manteuffel's advance until the 24th, when a detachment forming his advanced guard was defeated in a smart skirmish with a large body of French, mostly mobiles. This occurred in the Santerre district, the eastern part of the Somme, and at the same time Prussian scouts were signalled in the neighbourhood of Amiens, plainly indicating an early advance upon the city.

Afraid to defend the slight intrenchments thrown up just outside the place, and reluctant to bring a battle so near their chief northern city, the French army moved out and took up positions extending from Boves to Villers-Bretonneux, about twelve miles east of Amiens. Here were constructed strong earthworks and batteries, which early on Sunday morning, November 27, were assailed by a vigorous fire from the German artillery. The division of General von Göben had come to the front, and a battle along the whole line shortly commenced. The French army of the north, numbering about 50,000 men, were divided into three corps—at Villers Bretonneux, a large manufacturing village commanding the road to Fergnier, at the entrance of the plains of Santerre; at Boves, which commands the road to Paris; and at a little village called Dury, commanding that to Breteuil. The artillery force was largely composed of seamen, who came very prominently into notice during the later phases of the war, and on all occasions bore themselves with signal bravery. In the present instance they sustained the heaviest brunt of the fight, and were almost all killed or wounded, only three officers escaping with their lives. The mobiles also showed great steadiness and resolution, and were the last to leave the field when the fortunes of the day proved decisive against them. The battle was to a large extent an artillery contest. The most serious engagement took place in front of Villers. At Boves the chief event was a charge of the ninth Prussian hussars upon a battery of marine volunteers, who were completely cut to pieces, though with considerable loss to the Germans, including Prince Hatzfeld, who was killed. Later in the day the thirty-third regiment advanced to the ravine between St. Nicholas and Boves, to storm the village and the French position; whilst a battery of artillery stationed themselves at a distance of 2000 yards, about a quarter of a mile in front of the farm at Cambos. No sooner had the thirty-third deployed, and, covered by half a company of skirmishers, advanced to the attack, than the French opened the most determined fire. They, however, were weak in artillery, and after about half an hour were driven from their position, the thirty-third storming the village of Boves, and taking 300 prisoners.

The French right rested in Hebecourt, a village in front of Dury; and the sixteenth division was sent to oust them from their positions, and drive them back upon Amiens. This done, Dury was stormed. Both these hamlets lie on the Amiens and Dunkirk road. About three-quarters of a mile beyond Dury were the French works, with a battery of four heavy guns placed upon the road itself. Immediately in front of these works, at a distance of 300 yards to the left of the road, was a small graveyard, surrounded by a hedge. For upwards of two hours this graveyard was held by two companies of the seventieth regiment, in face of the French battery, and of the long line of rifle-pits lying right and left of it. The only cover the men had was the gravestones, of which there were very few, the greater portion of the monuments being iron crosses. A display of more determined courage the campaign did not present. The Prussian batteries at Dury took up a position at 1200 yards, and although they lost five officers and half their horses, nothing would induce the commandant to retire to 2000 yards. It was principally owing to their fire that the French were ultimately driven out of the works and retired into Amiens. The final storming of the village was witnessed from a neighbouring church tower by an English officer, who, fascinated by the splendid advance of the thirty-third regiment, and forgetful of the elevation on which he stood, enthusiastically threw up his hat into the air, and incurred the penalty of having afterwards to trudge a long distance bareheaded.

Around Villers-Bretonneux a fierce battle raged between the main portion of the two contending armies for several hours. Between Boves and Villers is a wood, under cover of which the Prussians advanced, debouching about noon, with eighteen guns, which immediately opened on the French, who were massed on the plateau of Villers. After awhile they showed signs of wavering, but at this critical juncture reinforcements, principally in artillery, came up from Amiens, and roused the sinking spirit of the French troops; at every point their enemies now seemed to be giving way, until, at half past four o'clock, they had been driven some three kilomètres from Villers-Bretonneux. The Germans, like history, seem fond of repeating themselves; as, indeed, is also the case with the French. In several engagements, the moment at which the invaders appeared ready to yield was precisely that when they were preparing a last great effort to advance. When, on the other hand, the French troops had gained a slight advantage, they—forgetting that the lull among the enemy foreboded a storm—fell too speedily into the mistake of congratulating themselves. At half past four o'clock the Prussians seemed defeated; but from that hour they made a determined advance, and swept the enemy before them. The firing having for a time ceased, the French assumed that they were masters of the field, and had begun to establish themselves, when a murderous fire was suddenly opened upon them from positions where no enemies were supposed to be. Altogether taken by surprise, they at once fled. Fortunately for them, night came to their assistance; and before the sun of the next morning had arisen they were many miles away from the scene of conflict. Following up their advantage, the Prussians entered Villers, causing no small panic among the inhabitants. The women with children in arms shrieked and rushed wildly about. A number of them heedlessly ran in the line of fire, and were killed by shot and shell, and many more were drowned in the marshes about the city. Finding further resistance hopeless, General Farre ordered a retreat along the whole line; and great was the disappointment of the good citizens of Amiens to see approaching the disorderly remnants of that army of the north which it was expected should turn the fortunes of France, and drive back the Prussian veterans of Gravelotte in confusion.

On arriving at Amiens a council of war was hurriedly convened, at which it was resolved not to make any further stand behind the entrenchments around the city. The retreat was therefore continued, headed by General Farre and brought up in the rear by the prefect of the Somme. Before leaving the town, the following proclamation was addressed by the latter to the inhabitants:—

"Citizens,—The day of trial has come. In spite of the incessant efforts made by me for three months, to the feeble extent of my means of action, the chief town of the department falls, in its turn, into the hands of the enemy. The council of superior officers has just determined on the retreat of the army of the north and the disarmament of the national guard. I am absolutely obliged to leave you, but in the firmest hope of an early return. Calmness and confidence!—France will be saved. Vive la France! Vive la Republique!"

The mayor, left to his own devices, immediately followed with another:—"The generals intrusted with the defence of Amiens have suddenly departed with the troops, and, considering them too feeble, have abandoned us. The military committee has not been consulted. The prefect quitted Amiens to-night. As for me, I remain with my municipal council in despair, but without forces against the enemy: devoted to my fellow-citizens, and ready for all sacrifices in their behalf."

As it was well known to the German commanders that the forces opposed to them greatly outnumbered their own, it was deemed unwise to follow the pursuit too far, and orders were accordingly given to remain on the defensive. Very early on the morning of the 28th there was an unusual stillness, and no sentries were visible in front of the spot where the French were supposed to be. The commanding officer, therefore, sent forward a patrol the distance of some 300 yards to reconnoitre; and great was the surprise when, entering the works, they found nothing but the cannon and the dead bodies of those slain in the recent combat. Intelligence was immediately sent to General von Göben, who at once ordered an advance of the troops. Taking the road through Hebecourt and Dury, over a course thickly strewn with military accoutrements and the bodies of dead men and horses, the victorious army soon came upon an undulating plain, bounded by the town of Amiens. On the highest ridge of the plain the French had thrown up long lines of rifle pits; and the road was defended by a battery mounting two howitzers and two 16-pounder rifled guns, all of which remained in the hands of the victors. Right and left of the road the barracks of the troops came into view—plain wooden huts, on each side of which were raised platforms covered by straw mattresses. Half way between these lines and the town were two *emplacements* for guns, one to the right, the other to the left. The position was strong, and if resolutely defended would have been no easy matter to take. After some little delay Amiens was entered by three battalions of the 40th regiment, and two batteries of artillery, which filed past the general in the principal part of the town. The 45,000 Frenchmen that should have held it were in rapid retreat upon Arras, Doullens, and Rouen. The citadel had not, however, surrendered, and the commandant refused to give in upon any terms.

The mayor of Amiens took an early opportunity of waiting upon General von Göben, and with tears begged him to persuade Captain Fogel, the old line officer who commanded the citadel, to capitulate, and thus to set free 300 gentlemen belonging to the best families in the city, who were only increasing the general misery by a useless resistance. So far, however, from complying, the officer caused the citadel to open fire upon the town, the "gentlemen of the best families" thus doing all they could to destroy their own homes and kinsfolk. Two companies, therefore, of the 40th regiment took possession of the houses in the immediate neighbourhood of the glacis, and opened a small-arm fire upon the place, which was returned by the garrison with artillery and Chassepot fire. All day long this sort of guerilla warfare continued. On the evening of the 29th it was determined to shell the earthwork, and eight batteries marched out at three in the morning, taking up their positions right and left of the citadel at 2000 yards. But, as day dawned, the white emblem of submission was seen waving from the ramparts; the commandant having been killed during the night.

The citadel was much stronger than had been supposed. The garrison was composed of 400 men and twelve officers, with thirty pieces of ordnance. The height of the *revêtement* was 80 feet from the bottom of the ditch, so that to capture the place would have taken some little time, and occasioned no small loss; but the death of the commandant—killed while superintending the training of a gun—put an end to farther resistance.

The loss of the defenders was four killed and thirteen wounded. Within the citadel were found one officer and sixteen men of the fourth Prussian regiment, who had been taken prisoners a day or two previously in the fight before the town, and who were agreeably surprised when their countrymen knocked in the door of the room in which they were confined.

In the end, the city of Amiens had to pay dearly for its resistance, and the possession of the citadel enabled the general to take far more troops with him in his farther progress than he could have otherwise done. Very speedily a German prefect and sub-prefect were appointed, under whose auspicious rule, much to the astonishment of the mayor, affairs soon assumed their ordinary aspect.

CHAPTER XXIII.

Gambetta the Real Governor of France early in November—The French Position after their Victory at Baccon—Mistake of General D'Aurelles in not advancing at once on Paris—Military Reasons for his remaining inactive—Determination of the French to march on Paris at all Costs—The worst time possible chosen by them for this purpose—What might have happened had they made their way to the German Lines—The new Disposition of the German Forces in consequence of Von der Tann's Defeat, and the celerity with which they were carried out—Difference of the French Prospects on November 10 and November 19—The Cause of the False Alarm at Versailles—General D'Aurelles made Commander-in-Chief of the whole of the French Armies South and East of Paris—His Dispositions of his Troops—The Duke of Mecklenburg withdrawn from Le Mans and other Reinforcements sent to Von der Tann—Positions of both Armies on November 26—The Advantage still on the Side of the French—Reluctance of General D'Aurelles to Advance—Battle of Beaune-la-Rollande on November 28—Incidents of the Fight—Critical Position of Affairs for the Germans—Great Bravery and Determination of the Hanoverians—Arrival of Prince Frederick Charles, who turns the Fortunes of the day—The French compelled to Retreat—Losses on both Sides—Another Fatal Delay on the part of D'Aurelles taken Advantage of by the Enemy—A Plan of Combined Action arranged between D'Aurelles and Trochu—Battle at Patay between the French, under General Chanzy, and the Bavarians, on December 1—Another hard-earned German Victory—Arrival of Balloon Despatches from Paris, and Great Excitement at Tours—Further Engagement on December 2 and Retreat of the French—The Germans assume the Offensive on December 3, bring on the Battle of Chevilly, and achieve another Victory—Scene on the Battle Field at Night—Resumption of the Engagement at Cercottes on December 4, and ultimate Recapture of Orleans by the Germans—Difference between D'Aurelles and Gambetta as to Defending the City—Narrow Escape of If. Gambetta—The Scene in Orleans on December 4—Complete defeat of the Loire Army and Loss of 15,000 Prisoners—General Review of the Operations on both Sides from November 28 to December 4—Superior Strategy of the Germans—Operations in the Eastern Departments of France—Fighting on the river Ognon—Bombardment and Capitulation of Dijon—The Proceedings of Garibaldi—His Animosity to the Clergy, and Desire to establish the "Universal Republic"—Victory of Ricciotti Garibaldi over the Germans at Châtillon—Garibaldi himself advances to the Relief of Dijon—Extraordinary Panic amongst his Troops, who are compelled to beat a hasty Retreat—Ill-feeling between Garibaldi and the French Generals and the Priesthood—The Composition of his Army—Capture of Neu Breisach by the Germans—Proceedings in Brittany—A Common Plan of Defence agreed on for the South of France—Unpopular Decree of the French Government annulling the Exemption of Married Men and Widowers from Military Service—Formation of Camps for the Instruction and Concentration of National Guards—The Bells of the Churches offered for Cannon—The Triduum, or Exposition of the Real Presence, celebrated throughout France—Exports of Guns and War Matériel from the United States to France—The Friendly Feeling between America and Prussia nevertheless continued—Contrast with the Feeling manifested towards England—Important Circular of the Russian Government repudiating part of the Treaty of Paris of 1856—Reply of Lord Granville—General Indignation in England and Expectation of War—Count von Bismarck's Proposal for a Conference adopted—The Pros and Cons on the side of Prussia—Change of Feeling in England with regard to Germany and much Sympathy shown for France—Celebrated Letter from Mr. Carlyle on the German side.

WE have shown in the preceding chapter that, early in November, the operations of the French on the south and south-west of Paris were no longer those of incoherent bodies of timid recruits, but those of a regular army under a general in whom it had confidence; and that they were conducted on a most extensive scale. M. Gambetta, too, had established himself as the temporary dictator of France. His efforts to revive the spirit and draw out the military resources of the country had been equally unremitting and successful. He made and unmade generals, and nothing was heard of his colleagues. The fiery, thorough Frenchman of the southern type, in fact, alone governed, and his government was recognized. In the east of France he appointed several new generals, and those deposed could only offer piteous protests against his misconstruction of their conduct. He ordered Bourbaki to give up the command of the army of the north, and Bourbaki obeyed. France, outside Paris, had a government once more; it had a large army; it kept the enemy in check. At Paris the Germans made apparently no progress in the direct operations of the siege. They seemed unable to take the forts; and had probably been led to abandon all thought of an assault as too dangerous and costly, by the immense preparations made against it since the investment of the city. The boast of General Trochu that Paris was impregnable, seemed so far justified; while the provinces were not merely doing their best, but doing a very great deal, to relieve it. The news of the French victory at Baccon had given new life and spirit to the city population. It appeared, as M. About put it, that after all there was such a thing as provincial France; and the Parisians, who thought themselves deserted, were now ready to co-operate with their deliverers as soon as they saw a fair chance. The successes of General d'Aurelles de Paladine on November 9 had, in fact, given to France a new soul as well as a new army, which was designed for the relief of Paris; and in the opinion of every one except De Paladine himself, the auspicious day of hope and of triumph had at last dawned.

There are moments in almost every campaign when a single bold stroke, well aimed and delivered, will gain extraordinary results from fortune. Had General D'Aurelles, after his success at Baccon, pushed forward rapidly, either by the roads which lead straight from Toury to Paris or by the more circuitous route by Chartres, he could scarcely have failed to overwhelm the small force in his front, or at least to compel it to retreat with loss; in which case he would have found his way to the German lines open. When the news of the combats of the 9th and 10th arrived, the great general on whom devolved the direction of the German operations, alive to the extreme danger of a possible attack from without and within, had, as already stated, made preparations for removing his headquarters and raising the siege should it turn out that D'Aurelles was advancing on the French capital. But at this critical hour the latter was found wanting in genius and determination. He shrank from following up his success, and instead of making at once for Paris, he fell back on Arthenay and Orleans in order to obtain reinforcements and to form an entrenched camp under the screen of the forest, intended as a base for future operations. This was unquestionably a most unhappy resolve; but in justice to a veteran officer, who possessed no common organizing skill, it is fair to say that military reasons of a plausible kind may be assigned for it. There is no evidence to show that General Trochu, who communicated frequently with the provinces by balloons, pigeons, and other devices, expected relief at this moment; and if he had been unprepared to attack as soon as D'Aurelles appeared outside, the army of the Loire would perhaps have found itself in a dangerous position. In one respect General Paladine was, by what appeared a good authority, entirely misled as to the military obstacles in his path to Paris. M. Thiers had alarmed the French commander-in-chief by his report of having witnessed 80,000 Prussians on the way to Orleans; although this force, as explained in the previous chapter, was less than half the strength attributed to it by the veteran statesman. And whatever this army may have amounted to, it was quite diverted from the Orleans direction a day or two after M. Thiers had seen it, by being sent westward to Dreux, to cover the investing circle from the expected attack in that direction. The road from Orleans to Paris was thus left wholly undefended; for Prince Frederick Charles, although known to be coming, did not arrive from Metz till a fortnight later. It is true that the army of the Loire was as yet imperfectly trained, that its commissariat and ammunition service was but very indifferently organized, and that the depression caused by appalling reverses hung like a spell on the French commanders; and this may help us to understand why D'Aurelles hesitated to attempt the course which a bolder captain would have taken. The fact, however, remains, that this was the one golden opportunity of the war, and the responsibility of neglecting it must rest with the commander-in-chief, whose extreme caution led to his ultimate removal. When at last the patience of the minister of War was exhausted, and a letter by balloon from General Trochu, which unfortunately fell in Norway, informed Gambetta of the intended sortie by Ducrot, he allowed the generals near Orleans no further discretion in the matter. Accordingly, from November 28 to December 2, the operations of the army of the Loire took place which we shall presently describe; but unfortunately they were carried out by D'Aurelles at the most unfavourable moment that could have been chosen, whereas a fortnight earlier would have been the best. In the words of an anonymous, but very able military critic in the *Times*, to whom we have been greatly indebted, and whose impartial *resumé* of the events of the campaign has since been republished, "It is useless, perhaps, to speculate on what would have been the probable result, had D'Aurelles made good his way to the German lines in the middle of November. We do not agree with those who think that the Germans, caught between two fires, would have suffered a terrible reverse; Von Moltke would have certainly drawn off in time, as Napoleon did before Mantua when he became aware of the approach of Wurmser; and it may be assumed that the army of the Loire would before long have been compelled to retreat. Nevertheless, the siege would have been raised; the armies of Paris, now in fair order, would have marched out and made the renewal of the investment in winter almost impossible; and it is difficult to imagine what the effect would have been on a brave and emotional race like the French. This indicates what a misfortune to France was the fall of Metz at the close of October; how, in the words of one in the German camp, the capitulation 'came in the nick of time.' Had the fortress held out ten days longer no additional corps could have been moved to Paris; in all probability the Grand-duke of Mecklenburg could not have been detached from the besieger's lines; no apparition of Prince Frederick Charles could have alarmed the chief of the army of the Loire—and, in these events, we can hardly doubt that D'Aurelles, who had already defeated, would have overwhelmed Von der Tann, and marched with his whole force to Paris."

General von Moltke, alive to the danger with which he had been threatened in consequence of Von der Tann's defeat, made a new disposition of the German forces without the delay of an instant. While the grand-duke of Mecklenburg and Von der Tann were kept on the arc between Dreux and Toury, observing D'Aurelles and the French army of the west, the corps intended to march northwards were placed on an interior line from Laon in the direction of Rouen. Prince Frederick Charles received orders to suspend his movement towards the Upper Loire, to send a detachment to co-operate with the besiegers to the south of their lines, and to push "by forced marches "past the Upper Yonne, and take up positions in which he could communicate with Von der Tann and the grand-duke, and menace the right flank of the army of the Loire should it venture to make a move northwards. These movements were executed with the precision and celerity of well-commanded armies. Within a week after D'Aurelles had fallen back to his camp near Orleans, Manteuffel had formed a covering force against any incursion from the north; and the advanced guard of Prince Frederick Charles, reaching Fontainebleau, Nemours, and Pithiviers, and approaching the extreme left of Von der Tann, had almost closed the vast semicircle designed to oppose an iron barrier to the French armies of the Loire and west. Thus, the prospects of France, which on the 10th of November would have been really full of hope had a great commander wielded her forces, were overclouded by the 19th, and an opportunity equally favourable for repairing her disasters did not again occur.

Meanwhile great uneasiness had been caused at Versailles by the appearance of bodies of French troops on the roads leading to Paris from Rouen, Evreux, and Dreux. It was believed that the French armies of the north, and especially of Brittany, were about to make a convergent movement on Paris in combination with that of the Loire, and the French movements at Dreux seemed to confirm the belief. Detachments of the fifth and twelfth corps were therefore ordered from the neighbourhood of Versailles to support the grand-duke of Mecklenburg in meeting the anticipated attempt along the roads to Chartres and Dreux. This commotion proved, however, to have been caused chiefly by mere detachments of the forces of Brittany, which, upon the news of Von der Tann's retreat, had been pushed towards Paris. Dreux was held by about 6000 mobiles and marines, who, on the appearance of the duke of Mecklenburg, fought well; but as the opposing forces numbered more than 30,000 men, the French retired in great confusion towards Nonancourt. Here they rested for the night, and were preparing the inevitable coffee early the following morning, when the alarm spread that the Prussians were coming. The headlong flight was resumed in the direction of Le Mans. For thirty leagues they were harassed by their pursuers, whose tread they could still hear while traversing with difficulty the woods under cover of a fog. It was this handful of Breton mobiles and of marines which had thus, perhaps unintentionally, given to their comrades of the Loire the immense opportunity to which we have alluded. General von Moltke had been completely deceived as to its numbers, and in order to disperse it he had left the road from Orleans to Paris entirely undefended, and sent westward an army beyond all proportion to the danger he had to fear.

After the victory of the 9th, M. Gambetta, who showed much of real greatness and capacity at this crisis, determined that at any rate divided counsels should be no impediment to vigour of action. General Reyan, who on the 9th had not been successful in outflanking Von der Tann, was civilly got rid of by an order removing all retired generals lately appointed to the staff; an order construed by Gambetta as applying to those only whom it was not considered desirable to retain, for General D'Aurelles stood in the same list with the officer thus superseded. Longuerue, who had been under Reyan at the first, succeeded him, and D'Aurelles was promoted to the command-in-chief of the whole Loire army, having at the time of the battle had charge of only two corps, his own and the fifteenth. The former was handed over to General Pallières, one of the officers promoted by Gambetta after the battle, in recognition of the first success obtained by a French army in the war. Bourbaki was removed from his separate charge in the north to serve more immediately under D'Aurelles in the command of the eighteenth corps, and the independent command of General Fiereck and Count Keratry were also abolished. These arrangements were readily acquiesced in by all except Count Keratry, who hastily resigned his command, in a letter betraying a feeling of injured dignity.

Thus constituted generalissimo of the entire French forces south and east of Paris, General d'Aurelles de Paladine disposed of the army of the Loire as follows:—On the extreme left the seventeenth corps, under General Sonnis, was placed at Châteaudun, between which and Artenay, on the left also, was General Chanzy, with the sixteenth corps. The fifteenth corps, under General Martin des Pallières, was in the centre, with the headquarters behind Artenay; the twentieth, known hitherto as the army of the East, now under General Creuzot, was placed on the right about Ladon, nine miles due west from Montargis, and seven southeast from Beaune-la-Rollande; the extreme right, formed by the eighteenth corps under General Bourbaki, took up a position near Montargis. The united strength of the army thus brought into line amounted to 200,000 men, with about 14,000 cavalry, and between 500 and 600 guns.

After the false alarm at Versailles of a movement on Paris by Dreux was dissipated by the duke of Mecklenburg's successes over the petty levies which had created it, his triumphant progress towards Le Mans was suddenly checked by orders directing him to return and close in upon the right of Von der Tann, who lay isolated in front of the French camp. It had been discovered that D'Aurelles had not really moved; and it was either known or conjectured that behind his screen of wood he was receiving large reinforcements, to enable him to make a direct advance in overwhelming strength.

Whilst the duke of Mecklenburg drew in from the vicinity of Le Mans, and marched due eastward on Châteaudun, still more important reinforcements were on their way towards the other flank of Von der Tann. The march of Prince Frederick Charles with the three corps set free from Metz, was reported from day to day to be directed steadily on the passages of the Yonne, which crossed, he would be able to cover all the country between Fontainebleau and the Loire with the head of his columns. By November 24 these various corps had arrived, and the united armies of the grand-duke of Mecklenburg, Von der Tann, and Prince Frederick Charles now stretched away in a great arc of some 130 miles, trending nearly east and west, from Mamers by Chartres and Pithiviers to Montargis. The duke of Mecklenburg commanded on the western side of the arc, Von der Tann under him in the centre, and Prince Frederick Charles, whose headquarters were at Pithiviers, on the east. The principal forces of the Germans were on a line curving round from Senonches, eighteen miles south-west of Dreux on the left of Beaune-la-Rollande. Von der Tann's corps was between Bonneval, nine miles north from Châteaudun, and the Paris and Orleans road. The ninth Prussian corps was across that road in front of Toury; the third corps was in front of Pithiviers, and the tenth, forming the extreme left, was at Beaune-la-Rollande.

Such, about the 25th and 26th of November, were the positions of the armies intended to relieve and cover the siege of Paris. A glance at the map will show that, strategically, the French had a great advantage; from Marchenoir by Orleans to the road to Montargis, they had possession of the chord of the arc from Nogent-le-Rotrou, Chartres, Toury, to the left of Prince Frederick Charles, still somewhat to the east of Montargis; they held the principal roads to Paris, and could concentrate by shorter lines and more quickly than the enemy in front. United, they were in the proportion of nearly two to one to the Germans, for Prince Frederick Charles had not more than from 55,000 to 60,000 men, after the detachment he had made to the besieger's lines; Von der Tann and the grand-duke of Mecklenburg had probably not more than 45,000; and though the French troops, as a whole, were not to be compared with their foes, one half of them certainly were very fair soldiers. The arrangements did great credit to the military skill of D'Aurelles, and the zeal and patriotism of the French people; they showed either that the German commanders underrated the strength of the army of the Loire, or were still exceedingly hard pressed; and though they did not present a prospect of success equal to that of the 9th and 10th November, a great commander would have known how to turn them to good account. In fact, with this difference, that his numerical strength was not half, but double, that of his foes, D'Aurelles was in a position similar to that of Napoleon when he invaded Belgium in 1815.

During all this time Prince Frederick Charles had been marching with extraordinary speed. His brigades advanced separately, by various roads, to their general rendezvous at Pithiviers; but D'Aurelles let them come without attempting to attack them, though General des Pallières asked to be allowed to march against them with his division, and though M. Gambetta wrote a despatch on the subject on the 13th November. General D'Aurelles, however, invoked the old arguments of bad weather, bad roads, and ill-clothed troops; and time passed uselessly until the 19th November, when M. Gambetta seems to have lost patience. On that day he wrote to the general as follows:—"We cannot stop eternally at Orleans. Paris is hungry, and calls for us. Prepare a plan which will enable us to reach Trochu, who will come out to meet us." General D'Aurelles declined, however, to prepare a plan, on the ground that he could not do so without knowing what General Trochu meant to do. It was not till about the 23rd November that orders were at last given to get ready to march, and to send forward a few divisions to open the road.

The first movement of D'Aurelles, judged by strategic principles, apart from its eventual failure, cannot be said to have been the wisest or most promising operation. He threw forward his right wing by Ladon, Maizières, and Montargis, without any similar advance of his centre and left; and on November 28 he attacked with two corps, more than 60,000 strong, the tenth Hanoverian corps of General Voigts-Rhetz, which held the left of the Prussian line, and lay in position between the towns of Corbeille and Beaune-la-Rollande, across the road to Fontainebleau and Melun. The attack was begun on the outposts, early in the morning, by the advanced guards of several French columns which debouched from the wooded country in front. They showed in such force that the Prussian pickets were obliged to retire hastily on their supports, which took up a position between Beaune and the Montargis Railway, covered in front by a small brook, and withdrew from Corbeille altogether. The French advanced rapidly, and soon after eleven a.m. drew up in a parallel line, their main columns being concealed in the hollows of the undulating ground. Swarms of their skirmishers opened a biting fire on the position of the Prussians, who replied as warmly, and obstinately held Beaune. The French artillery advanced at a gallop and crowned a high mound or hill which almost overlooks the town; while several heavy columns of infantry prepared to storm it under their fire. The artillery actually came within 500 yards of Beaune and seemed to riddle it, as well as the barricades at its entrance, with their shell splinters. Bullets came thick in return from these barricades and through the loopholed walls; but General Voigts-Rhetz could only hold his own. The French, who were in far superior numbers, began to extend their left, and enveloping the Prussian right, threatened to cut it off from Pithiviers, whence Prince Frederick Charles was bringing up supports in person. And sorely were they needed. The French left gradually closed round more and more. At one o'clock a mitrailleuse battery was established on the very road to Pithiviers. It opened on the rear of the hard-set Prussians, while the shell and mitrailleuse batteries on the hill referred to above tore their front; and on three sides they were assailed by a continuous fire of musketry from the infantry, which Hartmann's cavalry in vain tried to check by frequent demonstrations on the flanks. The position was most critical. It was only the courage and constancy of the men which rendered it tenable at all. General Voigts-Rhetz, seemingly with a presentiment of the desperate work the defence would involve, had issued orders for the corps to hold the village to the last man, and above all not to be made prisoners, even if surrounded. The corps was Hanoverian, and had never yet been beaten, even during the war of 1866, in the course of which, indeed, they had seen the backs of their Prussian foes. General Wedel, who commanded in Beaune, responded to the order of Voigts-Rhetz by expressing his determination to hold the place as long as he had a man left. The French General Creuzot had been bombarding the place for several hours, his troops throwing ball and shell into the dwellings of their own countrymen, whose severe sufferings caused them to fly into the surrounding woods for shelter from the fire of their defenders. The town was on fire, but through smoke and flame the white jets of the musketry fire spurted out continuously with the roar of the artillery and the fitful grunts of the mitrailleuse. Meantime a sustained action was going on between the two other brigades of Voigts-Rhetz's corps and a French force which exceeded them in number; but for this the superiority of the Prussian artillery in open ground compensated.

The tenth corps, unsupported, had now held their position against overwhelming odds for nearly six hours. They were entirely surrounded by three French divisions, but refused to yield to a summons to surrender; on which the French suddenly pushed forward a great column to the assault of Beaune-la-Rollande, down the road to the main street. Men fell fast, but the column went on till it reached the barricade, where it was greeted with glistening bayonets, and soon melted away beneath a rolling fire. Long lines of dead and dying marked its path, thickest where the crossing of the brook caused a momentary delay and gave a steadier aim to their enemy. General Voigts-Rhetz, however, was very dangerously pressed, and his ammunition was expended almost to the last cartridge, when he received the welcome news that the "Red Prince" was close at hand, who, with his troops, began to show in the rear along the Pithiviers road. With steadiness and coolness, as if on parade, the columns drew up and formed in order of battle across the road, while thirty guns dashing forward covered a ridge north of Beaune, and opened fire on the French left. The arrival of these troops turned the day. Before they had formed up, the French began to withdraw their left, and D'Aurelles' took up a position in a line on the front of those troops who were fighting beyond the brook. But rapidly and skilfully as the French left retired, it could not avoid the attack directed against it by Stulpnagel, who drove straight at the heights over Beaune, and captured more than 1000 prisoners, who had held the various farmhouses. Voigts-Rhetz, thus relieved, at once assumed the offensive; but it was now dark, and pursuit was not possible, except in such charges as, by the light of the blazing town, Hartmann's cavalry could make on detached parties. The French artillery covered their retreat, and they drew off unmolested; but they left behind them their dead and wounded, and lost in all nearly 7000, including prisoners and missing; while the Prussians estimated their loss at only 1000 in that desperate fight.

At the time it was thought that this attack of the 28th was concerted with General Trochu in Paris, and that it threw a clear light on the object proposed by the latter in his sorties of the 29th, when Ducrot's attack on Villiers, postponed to the 30th on account of the rising of the Marne, was to have been made simultaneously with the demonstrations against Choisy and other points of the investing circle. It is now known, however, that the attack of the 28th was made in compliance with the urging of the Tours government, rather than as the result of any arrangement between D'Aurelles and Paris. A combined movement was certainly proposed by General Trochu, but, as we shall presently explain, it did not come to the knowledge of the commander of the Loire army until after the battle of Beaune la Rollande. Trochu's plan was limited to effecting a lodgment on the further side of the Marne, close to the besiegers' lines, and holding it until the arrival of a French army from the south, which he looked for on the 1st of December. As will be shown in the next chapter, he entirely performed his part of the plan; and it is obvious that, had an attack been made on the rear of the Würtemburgers by the troops coming from Beaune, at the same time that Ducrot assailed them in front, the Germans, obliged to concentrate their forces for a great battle, must have raised the investment. How nearly the only half-arranged plan succeeded is clear from the fact that, had the arrival of Prince Frederick Charles been delayed only one hour, he would in all likelihood have met the tenth corps in full retreat, and the two victorious French corps might then have marched to Paris by Fontainebleau. D'Aurelles, who in this operation had committed the grave strategical error of first striking at the strongest part of his enemy's line, now fell back towards his camp at Orleans, and remained inactive for two days, a delay which his adversaries turned to fatal account against him.

On the 13th November M. Gambetta had sent a pigeon-telegram to General Trochu, informing him of the victory of Coulmiers, and proposing joint action between the Loire and

Paris armies. A balloon reply was received, agreeing to the proposal, although Trochu himself had previously contemplated a great sortie in the direction of Rouen, and was rather disconcerted than otherwise at the success at Coulmiers. Another balloon left Paris on the 24th November, carrying word to D'Aurelles that a sortie on a large scale would be made on the 29th, in the hope of breaking the investing lines, and of effecting a junction with the army of the Loire. Most unfortunately, however, this balloon was carried into Norway, and it was not till the 30th that its intelligence reached Tours by telegraph. Such a definitive announcement from Paris was of course of the highest importance, and M. de Freycinet, M. Gambetta's delegate, was instantly sent up from Tours to General D'Aurelles, with instructions to send the whole army forward next morning towards Pithiviers, where the Red Prince's troops were supposed to be massed by this time. A council of war was called to meet M. de Freycinet, whose arrival was announced by telegraph; and though a march forward under such hasty circumstances was considered to be dangerous, and was objected to by the generals present, M. Gambetta's will prevailed. It was decided to attempt to form a junction with General Ducrot from Paris at Fontainebleau, and the details of the operation were discussed and settled. A large stock of food, representing eight days' rations for 300,000 men, had been prepared, and was to be sent after the army directly Pithiviers was taken.

These arrangements were made in the two Jays which followed the engagement of the 28th November. In the meantime, however, Prince Frederick Charles, warned by the affair of Beaune-la-Rollande, and having learnt, perhaps for the first time, the real strength of the French, perceived at a glance the disadvantageous position of the German forces, and issued orders for their concentration upon a narrower front, taking care, especially, to close the interval between Von der Tann and the grand-duke of Mecklenburg. Before this could be effected, however, the sixteenth and seventeenth French corps, under Chanzy and Sonnis, on December 1st attacked the Bavarians at Patay. Isolated as the Bavarians were, they were unable to withstand the impetuosity of a force nearly three times their strength; and for the greater part of a short winter's day a gleam of success warmed the hearts of the ill-fed and ill-supplied legions of General Paladine. Von der Tann's brigade was driven back with heavy loss; but it was almost immediately supported by two other brigades, and after a bloody fight the French were, by night-time, repulsed, though not until they had inflicted upon their adversaries losses amounting to above 400 in killed and wounded, of which the proportion of officers was unusually great. Had they been able to follow up their first advantage, and to push on somewhat further, the communication would have been severed between Von der Tann and the duke of Mecklenburg.

On the same day, December 1, another balloon reached Belle Isle, bringing news of the first day's sortie from Paris, announcing a victory, and stating that the battle would go on next day. Thereupon General D'Aurelles issued a proclamation to his men, saying, "Paris, by a sublime effort of courage and patriotism, has broken the Prussian lines. General Ducrot, at the head of his army, is marching toward us; let us march towards him with a vigour equal to that of the Paris army." Despatches were sent to Generals Briand at Rouen, and Faidherbe at Lille, begging them to support the movement by a concentric march on

Paris, so as to occupy the Germans at all points. M. Gambetta telegraphed all over France that the hour of success had come at last, and in the course of a speech delivered at Tours the same day, said, "Thanks to the efforts of the entire country, victory returns to us, as if to make us forget the long series of our misfortunes. It favours us from every point. In effect, our army of the Loire has for three weeks disconcerted all the plans of the Prussians, and repulsed all their attacks. Their tactics have been powerless against the solidity of our troops, who have now vigorously launched themselves in advance. Our two great armies march to meet each other. In their ranks each officer and soldier knows that he holds in his hands the fate of the country itself. That alone renders them invincible. Who then would doubt henceforth the final issue of this gigantic struggle? The Prussians can appreciate to-day the difference between a despot who fights to satisfy his personal ambition, and an armed people which refuses to perish. It will be the everlasting honour of the republic to have given back to France the sentiment of herself, and, having found her in the depths of abasement, her armies betrayed, her soil occupied by the stranger, to have brought back to her military honour, the discipline of her armies, and victory. The invader is now upon the route where he is awaited by the fire of our population raised in his rear. Behold, citizens, what can be done by a great nation which wishes to preserve intact the glory of its name, and to assert the triumph of right and of justice in the world! France and the universe will never forget that Paris first of all has given that example, has inculcated that policy, and has thus established her moral supremacy in remaining faithful to the heroic spirit of the Revolution."

Alas, that such fair prospects should be doomed to be so speedily extinguished! In the night following the battle of the 1st Von der Tann and the duke of Mecklenburg effected a junction with their respective forces, and on the morrow a more difficult task lay before the army of D'Aurelles. His troops, however, nothing daunted, resumed their attack on the 2nd, and a desperate conflict ensued, known afterwards as the battle of Bazoche-des-Hautes, which raged most fiercely round the chateau of Goury, a position which the French would certainly have captured but for the timely arrival of the Hanseatic brigade. Shortly afterwards, Prince Albrecht's cavalry also arrived, and the French retired to the village of Poupry, where for a time they made a gallant resistance. But though reinforced, they were unable to resist the steady wave of opposition which rolled upon them from nearly every side. The most they could hope to do was to retire as slowly as possible, and in this they succeeded, fighting well, and showing far more *élan*, the German officers said, than had been displayed by any of the troops they had already conquered. The village of Poupry was stormed soon after the middle of the day, and resulted in the capture of several coveted positions, sixteen guns, and about 2000 prisoners. The cost to the Germans was serious, but the result enabled them to interpose between the two French corps engaged (the sixteenth and seventeenth) and Pallières' fifteenth corps, which in consequence of the exposure of its left flank fell back before the enemy to Chevilly.

Prince Frederick Charles by this time had the whole German army nearly in hand, and resolved in turn to deal a decisive blow at the enemy now extended before him. Directing one of his corps to Beaumont, he restrained and paralyzed the whole French right wing, and struck rapidly at the comparatively scattered left and centre with the rest of his forces. On the 3rd he directed his ninth corps against Pallières' (fifteenth French corps) at Chevilly, and his third from Pithiviers, against Creuzot's twentieth corps at Chilleurs-aux-bois (due east from Artenay on the road from Orleans to Pithiviers). His tenth corps was advanced from Beaumont so as to interpose between the French eighteenth corps at Ladon and the twentieth at Chilleurs.

The engagements of December 3 were not of the sanguinary character of those of the two preceding days. The vast plain between Artenay and Orleans affords ample scope for the manoeuvres of immense masses of troops, and as there could not have been fewer than 150,000 men visible at one time in battle array, the spectacle was unrivalled. Here large bodies of cavalry scoured the plain; there artillery dashed to the front, and opened suddenly on the enemy, as any fresh points were exposed in his retreat; while dense masses of troops steadily advanced to the attack of new positions. The main point of assault was Chevilly. The troops looked well in spite of the searching severity of the weather, and of their having, for the most part, bivouacked unprotected under wintry skies and on the cold ground. The landscape, of broken woodland, somewhat resembling the neighbourhood of Strathfieldsaye, was slightly covered with snow. Forage was difficult to get, for the country, thrice fought over in six weeks, had been eaten bare. But Prince Frederick Charles' commissariat had done its duty, and the men went into action with the full stomach that so remarkably ministers to courage. The snow was not deep enough as yet to muffle their tread, and the roads, hard as iron, gave out a ringing sound under every galloping hoof. Once in the day the French made a desperate attempt to turn the grand-duke's right flank, but the Bavarians gallantly baffled it, and got round south as far as Giday. For the most part, however, the tactics of the French were defensive; and assisted by the heavy batteries of position so well served by the marines, they made the work of the assailants arduous and costly. At one time a dexterous and bold charge was made by a regiment of hussars, who crept round a French battery, rapidly charged it from the rear, and simply escorted it off with everyhorse, gun, man, sponge, and stick belonging to it; a few hours afterwards the Germans had all, beautifully complete, exposed to view just behind the Great Louis' statue in front of the château near Orleans. Night, however, which came so early at that season of the year, and which might well fall upon drawn battles, saw the French line abandoned. Five villages blazing in unison, the fair result of deadly and mutual fire, shed a lovely, if lurid, light over the snowy prospect; and by their assistant flames the victors read in deserted entrenchments and surrendered guns the measures of that day's success.

The troops bivouacked on the ground won, and the scene was as full of picturesque interest as that of the day. The night of the 3rd found at least 50,000 men of the German army sleeping *"unter freiem Himmel."* Huge fires of unthrashed wheat straw added their quota of blaze to the burning villages, and the heavens were aglow with ruddy lights. Around these fires were grouped crowds of soldiers unable to do more than take brief naps on account of the cold, and constantly making short pilgrimages between the straw in which they tried to bury themselves when asleep, and that straw at which they warmed themselves when awake. It was melancholy to see the amount of food thus necessarily burnt. In the two miserable farmhouses which compose Beaugency, were quartered the grand-duke of Mecklenburg and his train, including more than one other royal personage, all of whom had to content themselves with straw to lie upon and short rations; for the column which contained the army provisions had not arrived, and the men had to put up with such as might happen to be in their pockets. But the morrow—after a darkness not too long for rest or respite—brought them face to face with another iron line. Chevilly had been won; but behind it stood Cercottes, and behind Cercottes were the lunettes and batteries of Montjoie If ever a hard day's work was set for an army flushed, yet fatigued, with victory, it would seem to be the work of that unsabbath-like Sabbath. Would Orleans be reached before the frosty stars once more glittered upon their weakened ranks? There were eighteen marine pieces in position at Cercottes, six to the right and twelve to the left; another twelve stood ready to defend Montjoie; whilst the intersection of four railways immediately north of Orleans itself was known to have been turned to very important account. Yet with all the excellence of their position and its adjuncts, the French fought but ill. Their guns were admirably served, but there was no heart in the infantry; and when an entire battery was triumphantly carried by a battalion of jagers at the point of the bayonet, there were no serried lines ambitious to retake it. The troops, once finding themselves hurrying to the rear, though they did not actually run away, were not sufficiently disciplined to obey their commanders blindly; and, like a horse who has taken the bit between his teeth, moved steadily backwards, fighting as they went, but refusing to wait anywhere long enough permanently to arrest the advance of the enemy. The latter, finding them in this mood, and feeling sure of their object, did not press them unduly, and hence, perhaps, the comparatively small loss on their part, and the order with which the retreat was conducted. It seemed almost as though it had been arranged that the one party should recede, and the other advance, at a given pace. There is no doubt that the Germans saved a great many lives by this policy; but it is not the less certain that, had they pressed the enemy as severely as they might have done, the enormous stores and materials of all sorts collected in Orleans for Paris would have fallen into their hands. These the French succeeded afterwards in carrying away in safety. Before twelve o'clock on the 4th Cercottes had been carried, and late in the afternoon, Montjoie ceased to resist. At five o'clock darkness descended upon victors and vanquished; the latter still keeping up a sullen fire as they retreated. The darkness, however, was not for long. At seven the moon rose, not quite full, but clear, and brightening the frosty air; and with it came the cry of "Forward."

The fifteenth French corps had fallen back, routed, on Orleans; the twentieth, prevented from gaining that city by the turning of its left, retreated across the Loire at Jargeau towards Vierzon. The eighteenth, thus isolated, retired to Sully on the Loire (about midway between Jargeau and Gien), and thence by Gien towards Bourges. These two corps then pursued their retreat separately, and were ultimately united at Bourges, with the fifteenth corps coming direct from Orleans, under Bourbaki. On the other flank, the sixteenth and seventeenth French corps, forming the right wing, had been cut off from all communication with the centre; and thus the fifteenth corps under Pallières was alone available for the defence of Orleans, which was supposed to be intrenched. In reality, a few earthen batteries had been thrown up, but unconnected with each other: while nothing effectual had been done towards clearing their line of fire in front, or for connecting them with each other, so that the position could be got through at almost any point by the enemy's skirmishers. With the large amount of labour available after the reoccupation of Orleans, there was apparently ample time to have constructed a really strong intrenched position, behind which D'Aurelles might have made an effective stand with the whole French army. As it was, these imperfect works were quite insufficient to reassure the young levies under his command, demoralized by defeat and hardship. If ever a lesson was to be learnt of the importance of the spade in war, it was here.

General D'Aurelles having sent word to Tours that he considered it impossible to defend Orleans successfully, Gambetta instantly replied by telegraph: "Your despatch of to-night causes the most painful stupefaction. I can see nothing in the facts it communicates to justify the desperate resolution with which it concludes. Thus far you have managed badly, and have got yourself beaten in detail; but you still have 200,000 men in a state to fight, provided their leaders set them the example of courage and patriotism. The evacuation you propose would be, irrespective of its military consequences, an immense disaster. It is not at the very moment when the heroic Ducrot is fighting his way to us that we can withdraw from him; the moment for such an extremity is not yet come. I see nothing to change for the present in the instructions which I sent you last evening. Operate a general movement of concentration, as I have ordered." The greater part of D'Aurelles' army had by this time been beaten and scattered; and to Gambetta's telegram he replied at eight on the morning of the 4th: "I am on the spot, and am more able than you are to judge the situation. It gives me as much grief as you to adopt this extreme resolution. Orleans is surrounded, and can no longer be defended by troops exhausted by three days of fatigue and battle, and demoralized by the heavy losses they have sustained. The enemy's forces exceed all my expectations, and all the estimates which you have given me. The city will fall into the enemy's hands to-night or to-morrow. That will be a great misfortune; but the only way to avoid a still greater catastrophe, is to have the courage to make a sacrifice while it is yet time. I therefore maintain the orders which I have given." This brought back, two hours later, another angry protest from Tours, leaving, however, to General d'Aurelles the power to retreat on his own responsibility. This despatch left Tours at 11 a.m. on the 4th, and at noon D'Aurelles wrote from Orleans as follows:—"I change my plans. I send to Orleans the sixteenth and seventeenth corps. I have summoned the eighteenth and twentieth corps. I am organizing the defence. I am at Orleans, at my post."

The Prussians, however, arrived near the city before either of these corps could be brought up, and from three p.m. till after dark the fifteenth corps sustained a severe onset, which resulted in their retreat on the town. M. Gambetta came up by special train from Tours in the afternoon, with the idea that his presence might produce some effect; but on getting within about ten miles of Orleans his train ran into a barricade, which had been hastily thrown across the line by the enemy. At the same time some uhlans lying in ambush fired upon him, and he escaped almost by a miracle. Severely shaken though he was by the shock of the collision, the minister got back on foot to Beaugency, where he took a carriage to Ecouis, in the hope of there getting some news from Orleans, but he could find none. He then made his way to Blois, where at nine in the evening he received, through Tours, from D'Aurelles the disheartening despatch:—"I had hoped up to the last moment not to evacuate Orleans; but all my efforts were useless. I shall evacuate to-night."

The general belief in the efficient state of the army of the Loire, the news about Ducrot, the success on the 1st of December, followed by the decoration of Chanzy with the grand cross of the Legion of Honour, and certain intimations of the archbishop while conducting a special divine service, had not prepared the people of Orleans to expect the reverse which had already occurred. But the vague rumours which began to circulate on the 3rd, and which were considerably strengthened by the arrival of fractions of the defeated regular regiments, had begun to excite fears among the inhabitants that they might once more fall into the hands of the Germans. Many wealthy families, therefore, who, since the reoccupation of Orleans by the French, had returned to their homes, again began to prepare for leaving. Saturday night (the 3rd) saw the beginning of the flow of emigration, which was then ascribed mainly to timidity and exaggerated fears. Circumstances which occurred on the 4th, however, justified these apprehensions. A fearful noise of military carriages and waggons driving towards the bridge of the Loire had been heard through the whole night; all the stores of provisions intended to be carried into Paris as soon as an opportunity should occur, were sent to the southern bank of the river; and this, coupled with the further fact that in the morning, about seven o'clock, some ammunition carriages were observed taking the same direction, and blocking up the street by attempting to go three abreast—clearly indicative, not of precautionary measures, but of an intention to retreat—placed the unpleasant truth beyond further doubt.

In the afternoon and evening of the 4th the panic spread to the troops, who in retreating resembled more a flying mob than retiring columns. Men, horses, and waggons were jammed in the struggles to cross the bridge, as if the enemy had been at their heels. At a later hour quiet was restored, as it was generally supposed that the Germans would not enter the town until the following morning. The hotels were full of French officers carousing, as usual, and who were captured in great numbers, most of them in their beds. The reason of the midnight evacuation of the town was the sudden arrival of the duke of Mecklenburg's army, about nine o'clock, from the direction of Chartres, of the Bavarians by a road a little further to the west, while the third army corps was arriving from the east. Finding himself thus encompassed on all sides, General Pallières proposed to the grand-duke that his troops should be allowed three hours' grace to get across the bridge; threatening at the same time to blow it up and continue the defence of the town, should the proposal be rejected. As the Loire was then full of ice, and it would have been the work of some days to throw across a pontoon bridge, the grand-duke consented; thus probably saving much bloodshed. The retreat was then hurriedly effected, and when, at midnight, the Bavarians once more poured into the city, only a few isolated detachments remained to swell their already long roll of prisoners. The fifteenth corps, after crossing the river at Orleans, retreated on Vierzon.

The army of the Loire was thus broken to pieces, with a loss, including prisoners, of more than 15,000 men. All the heavy naval guns in the entrenched camp around the city fell into the hands of the enemy, with four gun boats, which had also been designed to assist in the defence. The attempt to relieve Paris had resulted in complete failure; but that the retreat was conducted with more than usual order, with the exception of the panic in getting away from Orleans, is proved by the fact that the loss of field artillery was comparatively small: eighty guns only were claimed, about forty-five of which were those of the entrenched camp. The French, during four days, disputed every available point, and retired as slowly as was practicable, consistently with their knowledge that two German corps d'armée were marching rapidly from opposite directions to get at their rear. "Talent in a general," said Napoleon, "is nothing without vigour and strength of character; and few men are able to direct an army 150,000 strong"—a remark which forms a fitting commentary on the conduct of D'Aurelles during these days. He had arranged his troops with much ability, but he failed in moving them so as to improve the advantage which his great superiority in numbers gave him. In his advance on Beaune-la-Rollande he had struck at his enemy at the strongest side, entirely neglecting that which was weak—the uncovered gap between Chartres and Toury; and though he was in the proportion of two to one, he had struck feebly and partially. He might have attacked with at least 20,000 more men, in which case he would probably have won, ill-planned as we may think his scheme to have been. If so, it would have been difficult to have intercepted him on the way to Paris, and what might the result have been if, in place of assailing Prince Frederick Charles, he had pushed in between Von der Tann and the grand-duke of Mecklenburg with a force which, on the 28th and 29th, the Germans certainly could not have withstood; or had he even thrown his whole line forward instead of advancing a single army? In truth, his movements on the 28th were vacillating, tentative, doubtful, and weak; and they not only led to defeat, but enabled his antagonists to form their plans. His hesitation, too, on the 1st of December, on which day his principal attack was not made till past noon, allowed Prince Frederick Charles to collect his comparatively small and ill-united army within menacing distance of the French, who were superior in numbers and better concentrated; and the feeble efforts he then made, and the remissness with which he saw his enemy close upon his centre and crush it, between his disseminated wings, are proofs of incompetence for high command. Contrast with this his enemy's movements. The German army was dangerously divided at first; and the single corps of Prince Frederick Charles was seriously threatened on the 28th of November. But the peril once seen, with what clear insight he averted it, and plucked from it safety! How skilfully he took advantage of the slackness of his foe, and held one of the French wings in check with a force probably not a third its numbers, while he collected the mass which he rightly calculated would suffice to overwhelm D'Aurelles' centre, and render his own army irresistible at the decisive point! The more these operations of the combatants are studied, the more it will appear that the French were defeated rather by superior strategy than because of the bad quality of their troops. Events, indeed, were quickly to show how a fragment of the army of the Loire, under another commander, could contend with honour against a victorious enemy; but this we leave for the more detailed narrative of December events.

In the eastern departments the German army under General Werder, after investing Schlestadt, Neu Breisach, and Belfort, and clearing the southern Vosges, advanced to within ten miles of Besançon, a fortress of the first-class and the headquarters of the so-called French army of the east. Here detachments of troops were found in outpost on all the roads leading to the Ognon; behind which river they drew into position, apparently determined to dispute the passages which the Germans broke into several columns to make. The principal fighting was on October 22, at Cussey, where the stone bridge, though neither destroyed nor barricaded, was defended by a sharp fire from the village beyond, which the French occupied in force. General Degenfeld, the German commander, after letting his guns play for some time on the houses, suddenly ordered the leading battalion, formed in column, to storm at a double; and the order was so well carried out that the Prussians, crossing the bridge at a rush, carried the village beyond with the bayonet, taking more than 200 of the defenders prisoners, and driving the rest into a wood—a feat on the achievement of which General Werder, who witnessed it, personally congratulated the troops. The brigade, having lost only twenty-seven men in the assault, now ascended the hill beyond, which divides the valley of the Ognon from that of the Doubs, in which Besançon lies. The other columns crossed the Ognon at various passages, and closed in. They soon found the French posted in a strong position, flanked by heavy field guns, from which, however, the reserve artillery of the Germans, which Werder ordered to be brought into action, dislodged them without further fighting. The cavalry followed up the retreat, but were soon repulsed by the fire from skirmishers in woods on the flank; and on a support of infantry being sent to dislodge these, it was found that they had fallen back finally on a line of earthworks, constructed with some pains to cover the approaches to Besançon on this side. The flanking columns had lost about sixty killed and wounded. General Werder estimated the French now concentrated before him at about 12,000 strong; but he had no intention of attacking them further, having already accomplished his object, which was to clear his way thoroughly before turning westward to make the flank march on Dijon. On the 24th he began to file off by his right towards Gray, a change of direction which he effected without being disturbed. On the 27th two petty actions were fought during the advance beyond this place, where the columns, meeting separately, found the roads barricaded and preparations made for resistance. In each of these affairs the French stood just long enough to enable the column they encountered to turn one flank and take a number of prisoners, among them several armed peasants, who were tried next day by a court-martial and shot, in accordance with the severe policy which the German authorities had adopted with regard to persons of this class. On the 28th Gray was left by the headquarters, and in the evening advanced posts were in sight of Dijon: they had come up so rapidly as to capture the French mail on its way into the town.

The comparative inaction of the Germans, for the week or ten days prior to these events, had led to the belief amongst the French that the presence of Garibaldi and their army of the east had so scared General Werder as to deter him from any further advance in that quarter. Reports, indeed, ascribed several victories to the Garibaldians, who were popularly supposed to have captured many. This naturally produced considerable confusion in the ranks, which was not lessened by their clumsily repeating the infliction in rising. Some were wounded in the feet, others in the legs, others in the hands and arms, and others in the back. Once up, however, they brought their rifles to their shoulders and fired, although they had been expressly ordered to use their bayonets only. A large portion of the French troops, who were some distance ahead, of course received the volley, which caused amongst them indescribable confusion. The Italians and franc-tireurs. who up to the present had sustained the German fire with coolness, imagined that they were attacked by the enemy in the rear. Many thought that they were cut off from the other portion of the army, and did their best to reach it. The mobiles, seeing men coming towards them, turned and fled, and neither persuasion nor menace availed to bring them back. The retreat now became general, and Garibaldi and his staff were left almost alone, surrounded only by the seventh chasseurs d'Afrique and the Italians. Had 500 horsemen been sent at this moment in pursuit, half of the army would have been either made prisoners or cut to pieces. Fortunately for the Garibaldians, the Germans appeared contented with having driven them back, and did not seem to be aware of the advantage they had

Save those under the immediate orders of Garibaldi and his sons, there were no large bands of franc-tireurs in the Vosges and eastern districts generally. This was principally owing to the unfavourable light in which the general was regarded, and was the more to be regretted by the French, as no other part of the country offered such opportunities for the tactics of well-organized free-shooters. The French generals of the regular army would neither serve under him nor give him any assistance, and they derided the orders of the government at Tours when it tried to compel them to do so. General Cambriels was superseded chiefly because he entirely ignored him, and would not even take the trouble to read his reports and orders. General Michel, Cambriels' successor, was at bottom of the same disposition, though he cloaked it with outward civility. Garibaldi, it was remembered, had fought against the French army in 1849 and 1868, and had so habitually abused them that sympathy with him from their superior officers was hardly to be expected. He had also a very dangerous enemy in the entire Catholic priesthood, whose influence with the people was unlimited. The French peasant, especially in the Vosges and in the Jura, can seldom read, and in all political matters follows blindly the leading of his priest. The village priests, with few exceptions, bitterly disliked Garibaldi as the pope's most dangerous enemy. Some, indeed, confessed that as Frenchmen they hated all Prussians intensely; but as good Catholics they hated Garibaldi still more, and refused absolution to any of their flock who dared to assist or serve under him. Thus the largest following which ever assembled under his command in the Vosges was about 8000 badly-armed and undisciplined men; 3000 of whom were Italians, 1500 Hungarians, Poles, Americans, &c., and scarcely 3000 Frenchmen. These last were chiefly youths from Lyons and other large towns, enthusiastic but undisciplined, and all expecting to be speedily made officers. They had only twelve guns and 300 cavalry, and the whole corps must have been scattered to the winds on the first encounter with a well-commanded Prussian division.

The various fortresses which were either regularly besieged or invested in this portion of France, became an easier prey to the enemy in consequence of the withdrawal in November of General Michel and his army of the east, to form part of the left wing of the great army of the Loire under D'Aurelles de Paladine, designed to advance on the besiegers of Paris. Early in October commenced the siege of Neu Breisach, a place constructed on the plan which Vauban almost uniformly followed in erecting his small fortresses. It is in the form of a regular octagon, the *enceinte* of which is pierced with four gates; it has also barracks and a tolerably spacious arsenal. Louis XIV., having been obliged to cede Alt Breisach to Austria by the treaty of Ryswick, built the new fortress two years afterwards on the left bank of the Rhine. Fort Mortier, an outwork at a distance of about a mile, was subjected to a severe bombardment, and captured after a gallant defence on November 9. For eleven days succeeding, Neu Breisach itself was fiercely and continuously bombarded. The engineer officer in command, Captain Marsal, was killed by a shell on the 19th, and his death had a very discouraging effect on the garrison. Most of the guns having been rendered totally useless, it was seen that further resistance would only occasion unnecessary bloodshed. A council of war was therefore held, which assented to a proposition for capitulation. The garrison, numbering 5000 men, were conveyed as prisoners of war to Rastadt. his made the twelfth French fortress captured by the Germans, and there were at the same time six others in a state of siege or investment.

Brittany and most of the western departments had as yet escaped the raids of enterprising uhlans. It was rumoured that 60,000 Prussians had been told off after the siege of Metz to overrun the west, but the Bretons themselves were little alarmed. The natural defences of the province are stronger than in any part of France. The mountains, rivers, and bridges are very numerous; and all the land under cultivation is divided into small fields of from four to eight acres, each surrounded by a bank seven or eight feet high, and six feet thick. No detachment of the enemy could have marched through a region so protected without serious risk. Here, as in some other parts of the country, the call to arms was responded to with an alacrity and self-sacrifice unprecedented. The greater number of the garde mobile were already before the enemy; and the remainder, who were ready to start at an hour's notice, might be seen drilling every morning with the garde sedentaire, from seven o'clock till nine. The calling out of the latter class would appear to have been a great mistake; for there was not the least probability of their services ever being required. Many of the Breton peasants, also, complained bitterly of the decree which called out all men up to forty years of age. It was found to be particularly oppressive at a time when they were employed on their farms in sowing corn for the next year's consumption; and as the days at that season are short, three hours taken from them daily to military exercises, seriously diminished the time required for agricultural pursuits. The people justly argued that this and a few other favoured departments, not likely to be laid waste by the victorious armies of King William, would be the only ones that could grow corn for the next year's consumption, and that their time would therefore be better employed in raising bread for the survivors of their country, than in going to drill for the amusement of M. Gambetta.

In the more southern departments nothing of importance occurred beyond the desperate attempts of bands of socialists to establish in Marseilles and Lyons those communal institutions, which subsequently at Paris brought additional disaster and confusion upon the country, after the Franco-German war terminated.

The delegate government at Tours was not so profuse in its issue of decrees, during November, as in the previous month. Among the most important was one to the effect, that the departments situated in the valley of the Rhône, between Lyons and the sea, should, from their geographical position, have a common plan of defence. To organize such a plan a superior committee was appointed, composed of the general commanding the eighth military division, the director of fortifications and engineers at Lyons, Marseilles, Grenoble, and Nimes, two civilian managers of ironworks, two engineers of mines and bridges, and an inspector of telegraphs. They had power, in concert with the departmental committees of defence, to execute works, to find artillery, and to transport and place in position heavy guns. The fortified posts were to be united by a special line of telegraph wire.

An extremely unpopular decree, already incidentally alluded to, was issued early in November, that married men and widowers were no longer to be exempt from military service during the war. In many parts the decree was resented by the peasantry, who openly refused to obey it, saying that they would rather be shot for disobedience near home, than killed by the enemy at a distance. The decree was ill-advised, as France had already far more volunteers than she could find arms for, and it was certainly against her established law and custom that a married man or widower with children dependent on him should be forced to take service. The measure was one proof among others of M. Gambetta's determination to war to the death, and to provide that the defence should increase in strength and obstinacy with the onward march of the Prussians. The intense ill feeling, however, provoked throughout the country by this unpopular decree, led, shortly after, to its recall.

An order was also issued to the various departments to provide a battery of artillery for every 100,000 of their population, with 200 projectiles for every cannon. Had M. Gambetta's various decrees been carried out, France, by the end of December, would have been in possession of 2000 field pieces and 3,000,000 soldiers, irrespective of the army of the Loire.

Another decree, on the 26th November, ordered the immediate formation of camps for instructing and concentrating mobilized national guards called out by the decree of the 2nd. Mobile guards, free corps, and contingents of the regular army, were also to be admitted into these camps, which were to be formed at St. Omer, Cherbourg, Conlie, Nevers, La Rochelle, Bordeaux, Clermont-Ferrand, Toulouse, Pas des Lanciers, Bouches du Rhône, and Lyons. Those at St. Omer, Cherbourg, La Rochelle, and Pas des Lanciers, were specially intended for strategical purposes, and were to be put in a fit state to receive 250,000 men. The others were to be capable of containing 60,000 men, and to be only camps of instruction. The artillery demanded of the provinces was to be delivered at these camps.

The happy liberty insured by a republic was exemplified by the somewhat peremptory manner in which M. Gambetta's prefects carried out his instructions. He had ordered that the *Bulletin of the Republic* should be read at certain times to "educate" the people in republican principles. Some of the newly-appointed prefects, enthusiastic disciples of the creed, went the length of attaching to disobedience of the order all sorts of pains and penalties. One of them, the prefect of Vienne, tearing probably that the immoral stories in which the *Bulletin* abounds might be slurred over, issued instructions that the schoolmasters should read in a loud and solemn voice, that they should enter into explanations, and that those who showed any lack of zeal in this service should be dismissed from their offices. In many of the districts the prefects forbade all religious instruction whatever, and some teachers, male and female, resigned their posts rather than submit to such a prohibition.

Early in the month many of the clergy patriotically united in offering the bells of their churches to be cast into cannon, an offer which M. Gambetta, on behalf of the government, accepted. Some of the newspapers remarked at the time, that the next step would be to seize those which had not been offered, and in one or two places this anticipation was actually realized. The prefect of Perpignan asked the various parishes in his district for a return of the size and weight of their bells, which he stated, however, would be taken only as required. The country people, however, very strongly objected to part with them; nor was there the slightest occasion why they should. During the war of the old republic, when France was blockaded by sea, and had no means of obtaining copper, it was absolutely necessary to seize the church bells. But she could now get, without difficulty, as much of it from abroad as she pleased. Besides, she had in one arsenal alone 2,000,000 kilos, of it; and in case of urgent necessity, every household in France could, if asked, have contributed at least one copper utensil, all the cooking apparatus there being made of that metal.

The evening of November 23 witnessed in every church throughout France the closing ceremonial of the Triduum. The gravity of events and the continued suffering of the people led the bishops to summon a special general council, in which it was decreed that a Triduum, or, in other words, the exposition of the real presence—the most solemn act of devotion in the Catholic Church—should be celebrated for three consecutive days in every diocese and parish in the kingdom. Whatever the religion of a country, there is nothing more solemn or touching than the spectacle of an entire nation, and that nation in mourning, lifting up its voice in united supplication to Heaven for deliverance from a cruel and heavy scourge. The response furnished a striking proof that Frenchmen fully realized the unprecedented danger of their position, and that they would neglect no means, human or divine, to avert the awful calamity impending over them.

The collateral evils and dangers arising from the war must have convinced the most obstinate believers in a policy of isolation, how universally the security of Europe is affected by a conflict between two of its greatest powers. The general sympathy of England with a just cause failed to conciliate the goodwill of the Prussian government or of the German army and nation. During the Crimean struggle arms and munitions of war had been freely exported from Prussia to Russia; and in the present contest the following rifled cannon and ammunition were furnished to the French from the United States within a period of about two months:—*Pereire*, date of shipment, September 3, 2500 guns and carbines; *Lafayette*, September 20, 6000 guns and carbines, and 3,000,000 cartridges; *Ville de Paris*, October 8,

90,000 guns and carbines, and 8,000,000 cartridges; *St. Lawrence*, October 20, 60,000 guns and carbines, and 7,000,000 cartridges; *Pereire*, October 29, 50,000 guns and carbines, and 9,000,000 cartridges; *Avon*, November 2, 80,000 guns and carbines, 11,000 boxes of cartridges, five Gatling batteries, and 2000 pistols; *Ontario*, November 7, 90,000 guns and carbines, 18,000.000 cartridges, and fifty-five cannon; total, 378,500 guns and carbines, 45,000,000 and 11,000 boxes cartridges, fifty-five cannon, five Gatling batteries, and 2000 pistols.

The North German government expressly forbade its consul at New York to interfere with the traffic in arms, and the relations of the confederation with the United States were friendly and even intimate; yet, as we have seen in a previous chapter, a comparatively insignificant exportation of arms from England to France served as a pretext for repeated protests. In his first complaint Count Bernstorff, conscious of the legal weakness of his case, invented a new doctrine of benevolent neutrality which ought, as he contended, to have been observed by England. Lord Granville, in a despatch equally courteous and conclusive, showed that, as benevolence to one belligerent could only be exercised at the expense of the other, Count Bernstorff's proposed rule for the conduct of neutrals involved a contradiction in terms. The new paradox was retracted, but the complaint was repeated in stronger language; and it was difficult at the time to avoid a suspicion that Count von Bismarck was actuated by political motives in displaying coldness to England. The suspicion seemed to be confirmed when, in the middle of November, the Russian government suddenly issued a circular repudiating a principal clause in the Paris treaty of 1856. Prince Gortschakoff stated that recent events affecting the balance of power had compelled the czar to reconsider the position of his empire, to which he found the neutralization of the Black Sea was injurious. Turkey could keep fleets in the Archipelago and the Straits. England and France could keep fleets in the Mediterranean; while the southern coasts of Russia were undefended. Written international law was no longer held in respect; the principalities of Moldavia and Wallachia bad been united; the Black Sea had been entered by whole squadrons; in fact, the treaty bad been violated in its essential provisions, and the emperor, therefore, "bids his envoys declare that he can no longer consider himself as being bound ('ne saurait se considerer plus longtemps comme liée') by the obligations of the treaty of 1856." He withdrew also from the convention with Turkey limiting the fleet of each power in the Black Sea, and permitted Turkey to do the same. Otherwise, he entirely adhered to the treaty, and did not wish to re-open the eastern question.

Lord Granville's reply was very firm, though courteous in tone. He pointed out that, though Russia did not profess to release herself at present from *all* the engagements of the treaty, "yet the assumption of a right to renounce any one of its terms involves the assumption of a right to renounce the whole." Prince Gortschakoff had indeed professed the intention of the Russian government to respect certain of these terms while it proposed to set aside others; but "however satisfactory this may be in itself, it is obviously an expression of the free-will of that power, which it might at any time alter or withdraw, and in this it is thus open to the same objections as the other portions of the communication, because it implies the right of Russia to annul the treaty on the ground of allegations of which she constitutes herself the only judge. Her Majesty's government have received this communication with deep regret, because it opens a discussion which might unsettle the cordial understanding it has been their earnest endeavour to maintain with the Russian government." Had Russia invited a congress to reconsider the provisions to which she now objected, her Majesty's government would not have refused to examine the question, in concert with the co-signataries to the treaty; and by that means "a risk of future complications and a very dangerous precedent as to the validity of international obligations would have been avoided." Lord Granville's language was felt to be very grave, perhaps not the less grave for its studious self-restraint and reserve. The great question now seemed to be whether the struggle in which it appeared almost certain that England must be involved, was to be with Russia alone, or with Russia and Prussia together, a secret understanding between these two powers being strongly suspected. Mr. Odo Russell was accordingly sent to the king of Prussia's headquarters at Versailles to ascertain, if possible, whether the North German government had been privy to the offensive menace of Russia. Prince Gortschakoff's circular had been issued when it might have been thought that the war was practically ended by the surrender of Metz, and its publication while the German armies still lay outside the walls of Paris was inopportune and unwelcome. The envoy of England was received with profuse courtesy at Versailles; the German government repudiated the idea of any secret agreement with Russia, and the immediate risk of collision was staved off by the general adoption of Count von Bismarck's proposal of a conference.

The circular of Prince Gortschakoff excited in England universal indignation, all classes and nearly all journals contending that, unless Russia receded from her position, there must be a declaration of war. The effect on Changé was nearly as great as that of the Duc de Gramont's declaration, ill securities falling 2 per cent., and the weaker continental stocks from 2 to 5; while Turkish securities dropped 9 per cent, in two days. The panic in Frankfort was even greater, the tone of the Viennese press being most warlike, while that of Berlin affected to make light of the whole subject. The Turkish government at once commenced arming, and in the English War Office an unusual bustle and excitement prevailed. There seems little doubt that, but for the adoption of Count von Bismarck's amicable suggestion, Great Britain, Turkey, and Austria would have declared war against Russia, and proceeded to immediate operations.

The repudiation of the treaty was received throughout Russia with immense enthusiasm, and considerably smoothed the way for the execution of a decree, already issued, introducing the Prussian system of a compulsory three years' service binding on the whole population. The reply of Prince Gortschakoff, in which he accepted the proposal of a conference, was couched in extremely courteous and conciliatory terms; but still it was clearly the intention of Russia to insist, forcibly if necessary, on being relieved from the treaty. Studiously polite as Gortschakoff's despatch was, it said—"It was impossible that Russia should agree to remain the only power bound indefinitely by an arrangement which, onerous as it was at the time when it was concluded, became daily weaker in its guarantees. Our august master has too deep a sense of what he owes to his country, to force it to submit any longer to an obligation against which the national sentiment protests."

Opinions may very much differ as to the wisdom and policy of imposing, even after the most successful war, on a great power like Russia conditions at once humiliating to its dignity and very difficult to enforce. It was easy to see that Russia would tolerate these conditions only so long as she was compelled, and that she would seize the first opportunity to free herself from them. Indeed, the wonder is that she so long conscientiously kept, instead of eluding them, as she might easily have done. Had she been so inclined, she might have built a whole fleet of ironclads and monitors, without incurring any serious risk that the powers who signed the treaty of 1856 would undertake another war on that account. It was also said that the Russian government, by limiting its action to the one offensive point, and seeking a settlement of it in a way that would satisfy her people, proved that it had been unjustly accused of harbouring sinister designs against Turkey, and wishing to bring about complications in the East. It, on the contrary, wanted to avoid them. Had Russia wished for such complications, she had abundant means of bringing them about in an indirect way. She might, for instance, had her wish been to complicate matters, have asked back the territory which she had given up at the mouth of the Danube. But she merely withdrew from the limitation of her sovereign rights in the Black Sea, by which a feeling of humiliation and heartburning was kept awake amongst her people, that time would certainly increase instead of diminishing. Besides, Russia, as the note said, was quite ready to confirm anew all the other stipulations of the treaty, or to amend them, in concert with the other powers, as might be thought necessary.

The conference, which assembled in London in February, 1871, resulted in a decision favourable to Russia, the objectionable provision of the treaty being removed, and the Black Sea deneutralized.

A very great change had come over English opinion regarding the respective combatants in the war since the battle of Sedan and the capture of the emperor and his army. Many who up to that time had been against France, now warmly sympathized with her, believing the war to be continued by the Germans merely for territorial aggrandisement. Some, on the other hand, remained firm to the German side, the most notable amongst them being Thomas Carlyle, who, in a celebrated letter in the *Times* of November 18, energetically pleaded the German cause against the "cheap pity and newspaper lamentation over fallen and afflicted France." An amiable trait of human nature probably, but a very idle, dangerous, and misguided feeling as applied to the cession of Alsace and Lorraine by France to her conquerors, Mr. Carlyle accounted that same pity and lamentation. The question for the Germans in this crisis was not one of "magnanimity," of "heroic pity and forgiveness to a fallen foe," but of prudence and consideration as to what the fallen foe would, in all likelihood, do when once again on his feet.

Germany had 400 years of dismal experience for her guidance in this matter, which Mr. Carlyle proceeded to summarize in his graphic way. First, there was Louis XI.'s behaviour to Kaiser Max, which was not unlike the behaviour of the younger Louis: "You accursed Head of Germany, you have been prospering in the world lately, and I not; have at you, then, with fire and sword!" The end was that opulent, noble Burgundy did not get reunited to her old Teutonic mother, but to France, her grasping stepmother, and remains French to this day. Max's grandson and successor, Charles V., suffered similarly from Francis I., whose life was spent in the violation of treaties and ever-recurring war and injury to Germany, against whom his most Christian Majesty did not scruple to commit the atrocity of covenanting with Sultan Soliman—"that is to say, letting loose the then quasi-infernal roaring-lion of a Turk, *then* in the height of his sanguinary fury and fanaticism, not sunk to *caput mortuum* and a torpid nuisance as now." Richelieu carried on the game of plundering, weakening, thwarting, and in every way tormenting the German empire. No French ruler, not even Napoleon I., was a feller or crueller enemy to Germany, or half so pernicious to it (to its very soul as well as to its body); and Germany had done him no injury, except that of existing beside him.

So, of Louis XIV.'s "four grand plunderings and incendiarisms of Europe;" of Louis XV.'s "fine scheme to cut Germany into four little kingdoms, and have them dance and fence to the piping of Versailles;" and of the treatment of Germany by the revolution and Napoleon I., Mr. Carlyle spoke by turns.

"No nation," said he, "ever had so bad a neighbour as Germany has had in France for the last 400 years; bad in all manner of ways; insolent, rapacious, insatiable, unappeasable, continually aggressive. And now, furthermore, in all history there is no insolent, unjust neighbour that ever got so complete, instantaneous, and ignominious a smashing down as France has now got from Germany. Germany, after 400 years of ill-usage, and generally ill-fortune, from that neighbour, has had at last the great happiness to see its enemy fairly down in this manner; and Germany, I do clearly believe, would be a foolish nation not to think of raising up some secure boundary-fence between herself and such a neighbour now that she has the chance.

"There is no law of nature that I know of, no Heaven's Act of Parliament, whereby France, alone of terrestrial beings, shall not restore any portion of her plundered goods when the owners they were wrenched from have an opportunity upon them. To nobody, except France herself for the moment, can it be credible that there is such a law of nature. Alsace and Lorraine were not got, either of them, in so divine a manner as to render that a probability. The cunning of Richelieu, the grandiose long-sword of Louis XIV., these are the only titles of France to those German countries. There was also a good deal of extortionate law practice, what we may fairly call violently sharp attorneyism, put in use. Nay, as to Strassburg, it was not even attorneyism, much less a long sword, that did the feat; it was a housebreaker's *jemmy* on the part of the *Grand Monarque*. Strassburg was got in time of profound peace by bribing of the magistrate to do treason, on his part, and admit his garrison one night. Nor as to Metz la Pucelle, nor any of these three bishoprics, was it force of war that brought them over to France; rather it was force of fraudulent pawnbroking. King Henry II. (year 1552) got these places—Protestants, applying to him in their extreme need—as we may say, in the way of pledge. Henri entered there with banners spread and drums beating, 'solely in defence of German liberty, as God shall witness;' did nothing for Protestantism or German liberty (German liberty managing rapidly to help itself in this instance); and then, like a brazen-faced, unjust pawnbroker, refused to give the places back—had ancient rights over them, extremely indubitable to him, and could not give them back."

As to the complaint by France of threatened "loss of honour," Mr. Carlyle asked whether it would save the honour of France to refuse paying for the glass she had voluntarily broken in her neighbour's windows? "The attack upon the windows was her dishonour. Signally disgraceful to any nation was her late assault on Germany; equally signal has been the ignominy of its execution on the part of France. The honour of France can be saved only by the deep repentance of France, and by the serious determination never to do so again—to do the reverse of so for ever henceforth. In that way may the honour of France again gradually brighten to the height of its old splendour, far beyond the *First* Napoleonic, much more the *Third*, or any recent sort, and offer again to our voluntary love and grateful estimation all the fine and graceful qualities nature has implanted in the French. For the present, I must say France looks more and more delirious, miserable, blameable, pitiable, and even contemptible. She refuses to see the facts that are lying palpable before her face, and the penalties she has brought upon herself. A France scattered into anarchic ruin, without recognizable head; *head*, or chief, indistinguishable from *feet*, or rabble; ministers flying up in balloons ballasted with nothing but outrageous public lies, proclamations of victories that were creatures of the fancy; a government subsisting altogether on mendacity, willing that horrid bloodshed should continue and increase rather than that *they*, beautiful republican creatures, should cease to have the guidance of it: I know not when or where there was seen a nation so covering itself with *dis*honour."

True friendship, Mr. Carlyle considered, would counsel France to face the facts and recognize that they came by invitation of her own. "She—a mass of gilded, proudly varnished anarchy—has wilfully insulted and defied to mortal duel a neighbour not anarchic, but still in a quietly human, sober, and governed state, and has prospered accordingly—prospered as an array of sanguinary mountebanks *versus* a Macedonian phalanx must needs do—and now lies smitten down into hideous wreck and impotence, testifying to gods and men what extent of rottenness, anarchy, and hidden vileness lay in her." That Bismarck, and Germany along with him, should now at this propitious juncture demand Alsace and Lorraine was, Mr. Carlyle declared, no surprise to him. After such provocation, and after such a victory, the resolution was rational, just, and even modest. "I believe Bismarck will get his Alsace and what he wants of Lorraine; and likewise that it will do him and us, and all the world, and even France itself by-and-by, a great deal of good. Anarchic France gets her first stern lesson there (a terribly drastic dose of physic to sick France!); and well will it be for her if she can learn her lesson honestly. If she cannot, she will get another, and ever another; learnt the lesson must be."

Finally Mr. Carlyle asserted:—"Considerable misconception as to Herr von Bismarck is still prevalent in England. The English newspapers, nearly all of them, seem to me to be only getting towards a true knowledge of Bismarck, but not yet got to it. "Bismarck, as I read him, is not a person of Napoleonic ideas, but of ideas quite superior to Napoleonic; shows no invincible lust of territory, nor is tormented with vulgar ambition, &c.; but has aims very far beyond that sphere; and in fact seems to me to be striving with strong faculty, by patient, grand, and successful steps, towards an object beneficial to Germans and to all other men. That noble, patient, deep, pious, and solid Germany should be at length welded into a nation and become queen of the Continent, instead of vapouring, vain-glorious, gesticulating, quarrelsome, restless, and over-sensitive France, seems to me the hopefullest public fact that has occurred in my time."

CHAPTER XXIV.

Feeling in Paris at the Commencement of November—Several Newspapers suggest a Capitulation, but the Government determine to continue tie Defence—Measures adopted with that Object in View—The Last Foreigners leave the Capital on November 7—Circular of the French Government as to the Position of Affairs, and blaming Prussia for the Continuance of the War—Critical Position of Affairs at the German Headquarters after the French Victory at Coulmiers, on November 10—Excitement at Versailles at the expected Departure of the Germans—Despondency in Paris prior to the Reception of the News of the Victory—Important Proclamation of General Trochu—New Life infused into the City on the Receipt of the News of the recapture of Orleans by the French—The General Rejoicing not shared by General Trochu—Suspension of the Siege Operations—Amenities between the Combatants at the Outposts—Order of the Day by General Trochu on the Subject—Troubles in the Turbulent Quarters of Paris—The Condition of the Forts—Gallantry and Ability of the Sailors—The French advance their Works towards the Prussian Lines—The Skill displayed by the Germans in erecting New Works—Stores of Food collected in Anticipation of the Expected Surrender of the City—Preparations for a Great Sortie—General Trochu's Original Plan obliged to be set aside—Communications between him and M. Gambetta—The New Plan of Operations—Inspiring Address of General Ducrot to his Troops—He resolves not to re-enter Paris unless "Dead or Victorious"—Successful Feint of the French at L'Hay and Choisy—The Bridges on the Marne having been carried away delays the Serious Operations in that Direction for a Day—Pontoon Bridges thrown across and the Attack commenced in earnest on November 30—The Peculiar Course of the Marne and the Scene of the Battle—Bravery of the Saxons and the Würtemburgers—The French, greatly assisted by the Forts, succeed in capturing Champigné, Brie, and Villiers—Serious Position of Affairs tor the Germans—Dreadful Struggle to drive the French out of the Village of Villiers—General Results of the Day's Fighting—The French again remain inactive at the Critical Moment—Preparations on the German Side for a renewal of the Engagement—A Council of War decides that Champigné and Brie must be retaken—The Dispositions of the Troops on both Sides on the morning of December 2—The French again taken by Surprise and Brie easily recaptured—The Outposts at Champigné also retaken—Panic amongst the French—Fearful and Destructive Fire from the French Forts—The Saxons fairly shelled out of Brie—Their Great Losses in attempting to secure the Bridges over the Marne—The French again occupy Brie and part of Champigné—Despatch from General Trochu to the Governor of Paris during the Battle—Review of the General Result of the Sortie—The French retreat across the Marne—Order of the Day by General Ducrot—The Journal Officiel's Explanation of the French retreat—Letter from the Provisional Government to General Trochu—The Losses on both Sides—An Impartial Critic's estimate of General Trochu's Operations—Ought he not to have resumed the Struggle on December 3, and have forced a Passage through the German Lines at any Cost?

AFTER the result of the plebiscite of November had been made known in Paris, and the negotiations for an armistice had failed, the capital assumed an attitude of calm preparation for future eventualities. The military operations were confined to mere outpost encounters, and the persevering bombardment of the German positions by the various forts and redoubts; but the less sanguine among the Parisians, and the higher class of journalists, looking at the facts, were beginning to question the possibility of breaking through the living wall which encompassed them, and the wisdom of the government in further exposing the defenceless millions of the city to the horrors of a prolonged siege. "It is time," said the *Journal des Debats*, "for illusions to cease; now or never is the hour boldly to look the reality in the face. We are vanquished. We are expiating the blunders of that government which, falling to pieces, has involved us in its fate. The surrender of Metz is the unhappy counterpart of Sedan. In this terrible duel between two nations, fought out under the eyes of all the European powers, France lies prostrate, beaten, and wounded. Can it, while its wounds are still open, prescribe absolute conditions? Can it speak as if it were the victorious party? No, that is impossible. Paris has resolutely equipped itself for its defence; it has become impregnable; it may be so. Our enemies will not coerce us with arms; but, alas! they will overpower us by famine. . . . We must not delude ourselves; the provinces are but little in a position to help us; they are themselves a prey to the invasion, and the enemy's requisitions bring upon them ruin and desolation. What will happen, then, if Paris, the beleaguered city, is confined to its own resources? It will succumb. Prussia in 1806 was in a still more desperate position than ours; it knew how to resign itself to it, and afterwards to raise itself up again. Let us then act as reasonable people; let us make a painful but temporary sacrifice; and when by peace we regain our freedom of action, let us, with energy and patriotism, set to work to redeem our lost dignity." Other Parisian journals followed in a similar strain; but the government considered that a continuance of the defence of the city was the only way of escaping honourably from the acknowledged dangers of the situation. The measures for the defence of the capital were therefore pushed on with increased activity. Fresh earthworks, redoubts, and rifle-pits were formed. Trees were cut down for construction and for fuel. The space between the ramparts and the forts became a zone of desolation. Destruction was a work congenial to the spirit of the young mobiles, some of them mischief-loving Parisians, some hardy striplings from the provinces, and they were not slack in performing this part of their duty.

The government, too, continued its exertions in organizing the army, and in forming, equipping, and drilling the war battalions of the national guard. From each of the 250 battalions of which it was composed, General Trochu had, in the first instance, called for 150 men as volunteers; but only some 12,000 had responded; and subsequently a draft was ordered, which legally mobilized the battalions, taking from the ranks, first, the volunteers, who had inscribed their names in the "offices of glory," and been honoured with a roll of the drum; then the unmarried men, or widowers without children, from twenty to thirty-five years of age; next, unmarried men or widowers from thirty-five to forty-five; fourth, fathers from twenty to thirty-five; fifth, fathers from thirty-five to forty. This law fell much more heavily on the old, respectable regiments of the quiet and wealthy quarters of Paris, in which nearly all the men were married, than on the newly-formed battalions raised in the turbulent districts of Belleville, where the unmarried were in a large majority, and from which the minimum of volunteers had been forthcoming.

On the 7th of November permission was given to a considerable number of foreigners to pass the French and Prussian lines; but an order was immediately afterwards issued that no one should be allowed either to enter or quit Paris. Among those who availed themselves of the permission to leave on the above day, were many English residents, who left by the gate of Charenton *en route* for Versailles, accompanied by Mr. Woodhouse, of the British embassy. Colonel Claremont, the military, and Captain Hore, the naval attaché to the embassy, still remained for the protection of the few British subjects who held by the besieged city.

A further disclosure of the plans of the government was made in a circular of the foreign minister, issued at this period to the French diplomatic agents abroad, regarding the nature of the negotiations for an armistice. This document set forth that the war was continued solely to gratify the ambition of the men at the head of affairs in Prussia; that, although the enemy's forces had been besieging Paris for fifty days, its inhabitants showed no signs of weakness; and that, in spite of some seditious attempts, the powers of the government of National Defence had been confirmed by the votes of an overwhelming majority of the population. After insisting that the revictualling of the capital was necessarily assumed as a consequence in any suspension of hostilities, M. Jules Favre concluded—"By refusing our demand to be allowed to revictual Paris, Prussia rejected the armistice. It is not only the French army, but the French nation, that she seeks to annihilate, when she proposes to reduce Paris by the horrors of famine. Let it be well understood that up to the last moment the government of National Defence, absorbed by the immense interests confided to it, will do everything in its power to render an honourable peace possible. The means of consulting France were refused to it, and it thereupon interrogated Paris. All Paris, in reply, rises to arms to show France and the world what a great people can do when it defends its honour, its homes, and the independence of its country."

While the government were thus engaged, the events to the south of Paris, as we have already seen in Chapter XXII., caused the Germans considerable uneasiness. On the 9th and 10th of November General D'Aurelles de Paladine, with the army of the Loire, obtained a victory over General von der Tann, which resulted in the recapture of Orleans by the French, and rendered the position of the besieging force around Paris very precarious. On the morning of the 14th a wild rumour spread through Versailles to the effect that "the Prussians were going away." By mid-day a crowd had assembled near the Prefecture, waiting eagerly for the announcement that the conqueror had departed. The enthusiasm of the city grew from hour to hour, as details of the royal preparations began to be generally known. The mayor informed his friends that the king of Prussia's boxes were loaded in the *fourgons*; spies came in haste from the Ombrages, with the news that the baggage of the Crown Prince was being brought out to the carriage drive; while inhabitants of the Rue de Provence and the Rue Neuve hurried up with the intelligence that they had seen Count von Bismarck and Generals von Moltke and Von Roon clearing out their papers. And these statements were facts. It had been determined that the German headquarters should be removed to a safer place—to Ferrières or Lagny. The besiegers, not pleased with the situation westward, though they kept the reason a profound secret, had decided to evacuate Versailles. The day wore on, however, and they did not go. The mob which had lined the pavement of the Rue des Chantiers, waiting to see the royal staff disappear, went home. Night came, and the next day, but the black and white flag still waved over the Prefecture.

The 15th was also an anxious day; the Prussians themselves did not know what was going to happen, beyond the fact that all the staffs were ordered to be in readiness to leave, and that the baggage was loaded in the vans. No officer could give one word of information, but observed gloomily, "There must be something wrong with Von der Tann." By the 16th, however, the crisis had passed; joy filled the hearts of the Germans, and dismay those of the French. Orders were given to unpack; boxes were returned to their quarters; and once more the besiegers settled down to their work.

It will be thus seen that for a moment the possibility of failure was contemplated at the German headquarters, and that they practically acknowledged the danger of their situation in the event of a powerful and victorious force marching to the rescue of the capital. They had evidently underrated the capabilities of Paris and the power of France to reappear in the field after the destruction of her regular armies. As a rule they professed to make light of the attempts of General Trochu's ill-disciplined levies to break through their lines of investment; but they well knew the inspiriting influence that a fair prospect of relief would have upon the besieged, and dreaded a sortie *en masse* while assaulted in the rear. When, however, it was ascertained that General D'Aurelles de Paladine was resting on his laurels, and in no condition to take the field in the direction of Versailles, the Germans proceeded to the disposition of their immense forces described in a previous chapter, in order to secure the protection of their investing lines.

For some days before the news of the recapture of Orleans reached Paris, the tone of the press and the spirit of the people was despondent, and by some peace was earnestly desired. Communication with the provinces had become exceedingly difficult; and as no carrier pigeon, almost the only means of information, had arrived for several days, the Parisians began to feel that they were likely to be thrown upon their own resources. One military writer frankly gave it as his opinion that to break the Prussian lines was impossible. "No man," said he, "who is thoroughly acquainted with the position of affairs, and possesses any knowledge of the progress of contemporary strategical science, will entertain such an idea. If the three corps d'armée, the cadres of which were set forth the other day in the *Journal Officiel* (even supposing them five times as numerous, and had they at their disposal an artillery ten-fold more powerful), were to make any offensive movement against the enemy, it would be a most unpardonable fault." A day or two later this document was copied into the Prussian *Moniteur Officiel* published at Versailles. The *Journal de Paris* followed in the same strain, treating the relieving army as a myth, and ridiculing the idea that a force consisting of the raw material of Paris would succeed in doing what Bazaine was unable to accomplish with the flower of the French troops—beating an enemy invigorated by his victories.

Several journals also reproached the government with imitating the example of their predecessors, in concealing from the public the disagreeable intelligence they received. The answer in the *Official Journal* was unfortunately too easy. In common with the rest of Paris, the government had to bear the consequences of an investment, which, notwithstanding repeated efforts, it had not yet been able to break through. It regularly sent off its despatches. During the first few weeks of the siege it had received some replies, which it immediately published. Since the 26th of October no information had reached it—a fact which it was unable to explain. But the ignorance which was an unavoidable result of the siege, could not justly be imputed to it as a crime. During this period, too, General Trochu prepared a proclamation, calm, truthful, and manly, but which, though intended to encourage, gave little indication of confidence in the ultimate result of the defence, as may be seen from the following sentence at its close:—"We have not done all we desired; we have done what we could in a series of extemporizations, the object of which had enormous proportions, amid the most grievous impression which can afflict the patriotism of a great nation. "Well, the future still demands of us a greater effort, for time presses. But time presses the enemy also, and his interests, the public feeling of Germany, and the European public conscience, press him still more. It would be unworthy of Franco, and the world would not understand it, if the people and army of Paris, after having so energetically prepared themselves for all sacrifices, did not know how to go further, viz., to suffer and fight until they can no longer suffer and fight. Let us, then, close our ranks around the republic and lift up our hearts. I have told you the truth, such as I see it. I wished to show that our duty was to look our difficulties and perils in the face, to approach them without alarm, to cling to every form of resistance and struggle. If we triumph, we shall have deserved well of our country by giving it a great example; if we succumb, we shall have bequeathed to Prussia, which will have succeeded the first empire in the sanguinary annals of conquest and violence, a work impossible to realize, a heritage of malediction and hatreds, under which it will succumb in its turn."

"What might have been the effect of this proclamation under the ordinary aspect of affairs it is impossible to tell; but a day or two before, a rumour had obtained currency in the *Journal des Debats* of the victory of the army of the Loire and the defeat of Von der Tann. The rumour was not generally believed, but immediately after the proclamation had been issued, the governor received a despatch from M. Gambetta, reporting the recapture of Orleans, and detailing the success of the French troops. New life ran through the city, the hopes of the populace revived under the influence of the reassuring message; and on the following morning M. Favre reproduced the news in the *Official Journal* "with inexpressible joy." The press followed suit; newspapers which with bated breath were whispering peace a few days before, enlarged in glowing terms upon the victory gained by the army of the Loire, and declared that all ideas of an armistice must be abandoned, in presence of this happy augury. Was it not at Orleans, said they, that four centuries and a half before, Jeanne d'Arc gained a victory which gave the first blow to the English dominion in France? and might not the same city again begin the movement which should rid France of the hated presence of the Prussians? Groups of people assembled to rejoice over the victory, almost all of whom drew sanguine parallels between the deliverance of France by Jeanne d'Arc and this new turn in the fortune of war, which came from the same propitious quarter. By some, D'Aurelles was honoured with the nom de plume of "Jean d'Arc," or "le Garcon d'Orleans." It was also thought by wiser observers than the volatile Parisians, that a change for the better had indeed taken place in the disastrous fortunes of France.

The effect of the news was to prolong the resistance of Paris, although, as we shall see afterwards, it was bitterly repented by General Trochu, whose celebrated "plan "it disconcerted by turning attention to the army of the Loire, and seriously shifting the scene of his intended operations.

For some days following, the operations of the siege were suspended both inside and outside the French capital; and during this pause a scene occurred at the outposts of the combatants, which was at utter variance with military discipline, but illustrated the triumph of humanity over national animosity. At some points of the line of investment the French and Germans approached so closely, that to the north-east of the city a degree of intimacy sprang up between them, and exchanges of tobacco and spirits were effected. On one occasion, indeed, several officers of a mobile regiment accepted an invitation by German officers to breakfast in the chateau of Stains. The festivities were somewhat prolonged, and the absence of the Frenchmen was reported to their superiors. These military escapades had in fact now become matter of public scandal, and General Trochu issued an order of the day intimating that they could not be tolerated in the presence of the enemy. "Such a state of things," he said, "very seriously compromises the reputation and dignity of the troops, and has been a source of danger to the cause of the defence. The enemy fails not to take advantage of disorders which occur before their eyes; and the government has learnt, with equal indignation and surprise, that an intercourse, the effect of which cannot be comprehended either by the troops or their officers, is occasionally established between our advanced posts and those of the Prussians. My severity will be exercised to its fullest extent to recall to a sense of duty those who may fail to observe its dictates."

This caution, of General Trochu had the desired effect; but another source of anxiety to the governor arose from marauders, who scoured the country within the circle of investment, plundering houses and estates outside Paris, and for whose suppression bodies of national guards had to be organized. Some trouble was also occasioned by large parties of peasants, including women and children, who, in search of potatoes and other vegetables, sometimes came close to the German outposts, which led to their being fired upon by the besiegers. Many of these people were killed, and more wounded, by the Prussian bullets. General Trochu therefore issued warnings against these explorations, unless the parties were defended by bodies of troops, which were accordingly detailed for the purpose.

Reverting to the internal life of the city at this time, we catch a glimpse of a social and political undercurrent which had eventually a most disastrous issue. The turbulent quarters of the city swarmed with democratic clubs, in which indignant citizens denounced the incompetency of the authorities, and vented their spleen against the king of Prussia and his retainers. Bombs, too, of a violently explosive kind were manufactured, and stored away in the city, evidently intended for use in other directions than against the besieging army. Attempts were also made by these democrats to organize bodies of "Amazons," which, although at the time they tended to excite only laughter and ridicule, undoubtedly formed the basis of subsequent outbursts of feminine fury. It was, besides, most difficult to bring the national guards of these quarters to face the common enemy. General Trochu's decree to form war companies proved almost a nullity; and while the required quota for active operations in the field could not be got, a disposition was shown to secrete arms and ammunition for a possible opportunity of internecine warfare and of plunder.

But amidst all these difficulties and discouragements, the governor and his generals were unceasing in their activity, and the general spirit both of troops and people was a steady source of strength. The conduct of the artillerists of the forts especially was truly admirable; nor was that of the French sailors who took part in the operations of the siege less deserving of praise. The only section of their country's defenders undaunted by defeat, they maintained a manly, cheerful bearing, the moral effect of which was highly valuable. The condition of the forts displayed the most systematic order and cleanliness, and the splendid and almost unceasing practice of these marine *pointeurs* won the admiration of beholders, and served effectually to check the operations of the most skilful engineers and strategists which have arisen in Europe since the days of the First Napoleon. "The marine," observed an able French writer, "has given all for the defence of Paris—admirals, officers, and sailors, an admirable system of signals, and an incomparable artillery. Six of the forts are commanded by naval officers. All the semaphores at Montmartre, Mont Valérien, Passy, Issy, and the Opera have been intrusted to them. These gunners have become famous for the accuracy of their fire, and after the siege people will speak of them as, after Sebastopol and Solferino, they spoke of the zouaves."

Not content with strengthening their defences inside the forts and ramparts, the Paris garrison, as the siege went on, also pushed out fresh works towards the Prussian outposts, and in a manner besieged the lines of the besiegers, as the Russians had done at Sebastopol in 1855.

These facts were taken into due consideration by the besiegers in the careful arrangement of their investing lines. The Germans worked unceasingly in strengthening their hold upon the capital, but their advanced lines were meant simply to guard them against surprises, and were most skilfully concealed; for many weeks their really dangerous works did not make a near approach, and their true positions were established beyond the reach of the guns of the forts. Their works were admirably constructed for defence; but up to the period of which we are writing it was only from the fire of the guns of the redoubts originally erected at Châtillon, Montretout, and other points, and which had fallen into the hands of the enemy at the beginning of the siege, that danger was really to be apprehended.

In anticipation of the surrender, stores of food were already being collected by the investing forces, to allay the agonies of hunger, which it was believed the inhabitants would suffer before that crowning humiliation should take place; but, as we shall see, the provisions proved to be more abundant than was anticipated by those who formed their conclusions outside the walls of the blockaded city.

THE GREAT SORTIE FROM PARIS.

Towards the latter end of November indications were not wanting that the brief pause in the actual warfare of the siege was about to end. On the 24th there was fighting at Pierrefitte; and on the 29th, while the important events narrated in the preceding chapter were occurring north and south of Orleans, the army of Paris began its mightiest effort to break through the German troops which hemmed it in on every side, in the hope of effecting a junction with the army of the Loire at Fontainebleau, and so compelling their enemies to raise the siege. To insure this result, it was of course necessary that each should succeed in its separate enterprize; but we have already shown how D'Aurelles de Paladine was prevented from carrying out his part of the arrangement, and we shall now see that, notwithstanding some important temporary successes, the great sortie from Paris also utterly failed to accomplish the purpose intended by it.

General Trochu, the "patient governor," had brought the armies within the walls of the city to as high a state of efficiency and discipline as he could, but only about 150,000 of them could fairly be classed as even tolerable soldiers. His purpose originally was to make his way through the peninsula of Gennevilliers to Corneille, and so on to Rouen and Havre; but, as he afterwards asserted in his celebrated defence speech before the National Assembly at Versailles, "when the news of the unfortunate, because delusive, success at Coulmiers became known in Paris, his plan was defeated. The works had been constructed for an attempt by way of Rouen; but the press and the government immediately demanded that a sortie should be made to meet the army which (they said) was coming from the Loire, a demand so impetuously urged by the public that it could not be resisted." He accordingly had to renounce all his preparations for a movement towards Rouen, and to prepare for a sortie in the direction of Orleans, although he confesses he had no hope of success when he undertook the task. However, being "summoned" in peremptory terms by his colleagues and by Gambetta (who had previously reproached him for his "persistent inaction") to join the combined movement, he concealed his misgivings and gave directions to mass the troops on the eastern fortresses and ramparts.

From official documents which have since been published, it appears that in November M. Gambetta had sent a pigeon-telegram to General Trochu, informing him of the victory of Coulmiers, and proposing joint action between the Loire and Paris armies. General Trochu replied on the 18th, by balloon: "Your telegram excites my interest and my zeal to the utmost; but it has been five days coming, and we shall want a week to get ready. I will not lose one instant. We have ample food till the end of the year, but perhaps the population will not wait till then, and we must solve the problem long before that." On the 24th another balloon was sent out with the news that a great sortie would be made on the 29th, in the hope of breaking the investing lines and effecting a junction with D'Aurelles. But, most unluckily, this balloon was carried into Norway, and it was not till the 30th that its intelligence reached Tours by telegraph. Of course it created an immense sensation; for though it was expected, the definitive announcement of a great sortie was an event of the gravest importance. The telegram was as follows: "The news received from the Loire army has decided me to go out on the southern side, and to march towards that army at any cost. On Monday, 28th November, my preparations will be finished. I am carrying them on day and night. On Tuesday, the 29th, an army commanded by General Ducrot, the most energetic of us all, will attack the enemy's positions, and if they are carried, will push onwards towards the Loire in the direction of Gien. I suppose that if your army is turned on its left flank" (an allusion to the duke of Mecklenburg, who, General Trochu thought, would move down from Chartres), "it will pass the Loire, and will withdraw on Bourges." It has just been stated that this important despatch, which announced the Paris sortie for the 29th, was not received at Tours till the 30th.

The first sign to the Parisians that the long inaction was to be broken was given on the night of Friday, the 25th of November, when it was announced by posters all over the city that from the evening of the next day all the gates would be rigorously closed, and no one would be allowed to pass in or out, except troops and such as had a special order from headquarters. On Monday, the 28th, an order was issued requiring tradesmen to surrender to the government bacon, hams, sausages, and provisions of all kinds—the stores of fresh meat having been entirely consumed in supplying rations for the army. Each man was provided with a loaf of bread, a bottle of wine, and two lbs. of bacon or meat, as they might be out of the way of obtaining supplies for a day or two. The same day it was announced that on the morrow the great effort for the deliverance of Paris would commence. All the ambulances had orders to get ready, and to send their waggons and appliances to certain places at certain hours. During the whole of the 28th the streets were filled with armed men marching towards the south and south-eastern quarters of the city. The plan of operations was to make a real attack by the second army, under General Ducrot, against the position held by the Würtemburgers and Saxons, between Bonneuil and Noisy-le-Grand; at the same time demonstrations, more or less serious, were to be made on the south side by General Vinoy against L'Hay and Choisy; on the west from Valérien, against Bougival, and on the north from St. Denis.

General Ducrot prepared his troops for the "supreme effort" by the following stirring address:—"Soldiers of the Second Army of Paris,—The moment has arrived to break the iron circle which has too long inclosed you, and threatened to stifle you by a slow and dreadful agony. Upon you has devolved the honour of attempting this great undertaking. That you will prove yourselves worthy of it I am convinced. Doubtless, at first, our task will be difficult, and we shall have to overcome serious obstacles. We must face them with calmness and resolution, without exaggeration, as well as without weakness. Here is the truth. At the outset, touching our advanced posts, we shall find implacable enemies, rendered confident and audacious by too frequent success. A vigorous effort will, therefore, be required, but it will not be beyond your powers. In order to prepare for your action, the foresight of him who holds the chief command over us has accumulated more than 400 pieces of artillery, of which at least two-thirds are of the largest calibre. No material obstacle can resist it, and in order to enable you to cut a way out, you will be more than 150,000 men, well armed and well equipped, abundantly provided with ammunition, and, I venture to hope, all animated by an irresistible ardour. Victorious in the first period of the struggle, your success is assured, for the enemy has directed to the banks of the Loire the greater number and the best of his soldiers. The heroic and successful efforts of your brothers detain them there. Courage, then, and confidence! Remember that in this supreme struggle we fight for our honour, for our liberty, for the salvation of our dear and unhappy country; and if this motive suffice not to inflame your hearts, think of your fields, which are devastated; of your families, which are ruined; of your sisters, your wives, and your

mothers, who are desolate. May these thoughts lead you to share in the thirst for vengeance, the intense rage which fills my soul, and may it inspire you to contempt of danger. For me, I have fully resolved—and I swear it before you, before the whole nation—I will not re-enter Paris unless dead or victorious. You may see me fall, but you shall not see me recoil. Then halt not, but avenge me! Forward! forward! and may God be your shield!
"The General-in-chief of the Second Army of Paris,

"A. DUCROT.

"PARIS, *November* 28.

It is difficult to imagine an English general addressing his army in such terms, but it is stated that this language was exactly suited to the occasion, and that, "going straight to the heart of the discouraged French soldier, it had a tremendous effect on the army and the people of Paris."

At eleven o'clock on the night of the 28th a fearful fire, opened by forts Charenton and Ivry, was caught up by Bicêtre, Montrouge, Vanves, and Issy, aided by gunboats, which, from a position above Pont a l' Anglais on the Seine, joined in the infernal concert. At the appointed hour on the following morning (November 29) a strong force, sallying from Valérien, threatened the German position west of that fortress; while two columns, issuing from behind Bicêtre and Ivry, under General Vinoy, made a vigorous attack on L'Hay and Choisy. This operation was a mere feint, intended to distract the attention of the Germans, and was effected with comparative ease, as the whole road between Sceaux and Choisy, passing by L'Hay and Chevilly, was untenable by the besiegers, on account of the fire from two formidable redoubts constructed by the French at Hautes Bruyères and Moulin-Saquet. The attacking force succeeded in driving the Germans from L'Hay and Choisy; but just as fresh troops were coming up to retake these positions, the French retired to the forts in obedience, to an order from General Ducrot, who, as we shall see below, had found it impossible to execute the more difficult part of the plan. The Prussian reserves, on approaching L'Hay and Choisy, suffered great loss from the two redoubts already mentioned, as well as from the gunboats on the Seine, and from a new kind of battery, consisting of guns mounted on iron-clad carriages, run out on the Orleans railroad towards Choisy.

To reach the points destined for the most serious attack the French had to cross the Marne, and march through the loop formed by that river just before its fall into the Seine; but on reaching their allotted posts early on the morning of the 29th, they found that a sudden rise of the waters had carried away the bridges over which they had intended to pass, so that they were compelled to remain idle for that day at least. The Marne doubles on itself several times in the neighbourhood of Paris; and its waters, together with those of the canal, have to be carefully managed by sluices, which had been neglected by the persons whose duty it was to attend to them for the previous two months, from fear of the German army. In consequence of the recent heavy rains, the water flowed over the gates, so that the river suddenly rose to nearly four feet above its ordinary level, forming, of course, an impassable barrier. During the night eight pontoon bridges were thrown across the Marne at Joinville—close under the guns of the double redoubt of Gravelle and La Faisanderie—

and at Nogent; and the water having somewhat subsided, the attack was begun in earnest on the following morning, Wednesday, November 30. A second sortie, in which he succeeded, was also made on this morning by General Vinoy against L'Hay and Choisy, for the purpose of alarming the Prussians in that quarter. At the same time the French, sallying forth from St. Denis on the north, gained possession of the villages of Le Bourget, Stains, and Epinay, in the attack on which they were aided by gunboats on the Seine. Reserve troops of the fourth Prussian corps were soon brought up; and the French retired, having effected their object of preventing the Germans from weakening that part of their lines by the detachment of forces to the other side of the city.

Meanwhile the extremely formidable attack was being made by General Ducrot upon the German intrenchments on the east of Paris. Before joining the Seine the course of the Marne forms an immense S, the upper or northern bend approaching Paris, and the lower receding from it. Both are commanded by the fire from the forts; but while the upper or advancing bend favours a sortie by its configuration, the lower or receding one is completely commanded by the ground on the left bank as well as by the forts; and here the river, also, both from the line it takes and from its many branches, is unfavourable to the construction of bridges under fire. Hence the greater part of this bend remained a kind of neutral ground, on each side of which the real fighting took place. The line of battle extended for about four English miles, from Noisy to Bonneuil; but the severity of the conflict was confined almost entirely to the end of the horse-shoe formed by the Marne, between Brie and Champigné, about a mile and a quarter in length. It was a cold but brilliant winter's day; and as early as half-past seven o'clock in the morning—indeed as soon as it was light— bodies of French troops, infantry, cavalry, and artillery, were seen descending the sloping ground from Fort Nogent, while others were advancing on Champigné from Chennevières, where they had crossed the Marne during the night. The main body of Ducrot's troops, with their artillery, passed over the river on the pontoon bridges at Joinville and Nogent, R'enault's second corps being in front; and soon there were three corps, numbering from 50,000 to 60,000 men, below the fortifications. As they descended into the plateau, forts Charenton, Nogent, Rosny, and the formidable batteries recently erected in front of Mont Avron, directed a constant fire on the outposts of the Würtemburgers and Saxons at Champigné, Villiers, Brie, and Noisy. The points thus selected for attack were the weakest in all the investing circle, and the sortie was made at the very moment when they were even weaker than ordinary; for Moltke, perceiving indications of the intention of the French to advance down the triangle, had given instructions for the line to be strengthened. The Würtemburgers were accordingly ordered to fall back from the front of their position to its second line; and the ground thus left vacant by them was to be occupied by the sixth (Saxon) corps. Thus it happened that the Germans were caught In a transition state: for the Würtemburgers retired rather early, and the troops intended for their relief came rather late; and it was precisely at this moment—when the ground that had been left empty by one had not been filled by another portion of the investing forces—that the French made their attack. At first the German outposts had to bear the brunt of the fighting, but before mid-day there were three regiments of Saxons on the field (104th, 106th, and 107th), all under the command of General de Nehrhof, and a brigade of Würtemburgers, commanded by Brigadier-general Reitzenstein. The Saxons had two regiments of cavalry and six of artillery, their entire force amounting to about 11,000 men. The Würtemburg brigade was about 7000, so that the whole of the German force in position to resist the sortie was only 18,000 men. The French advanced in excellent order under the guns of their forts, and it soon became evident that they intended to make a most serious attempt to break through the German intrenchments. The troops on that side accordingly sallied forth into the plateau, in order to meet their attack; and now came a murderous cross-fire from Nogent and Mont Avron. High into the air rose shells, that were literally vomited forth from both the fort and the batteries. They shot through the atmosphere like blazing comets, and fell in showers among the German soldiers, causing death and destruction all around the places where they exploded. The Saxons and Würtemburgers fought gallantly, but they were overwhelmed by superior numbers; and after a brief, though murderous struggle, they were compelled to retreat, and the French at once seized upon Champigné and Brie, the fire from the forts being discontinued the moment they got close to those places. A third French column had in the meantime marched up the Marne as far as Neuilly, there crossed the river, and now proceeded to cooperate with their comrades from Brie in an attack on Villiers, an important post in the investing circle, which was also captured after a fierce contest. Noisy-le-Grand, too, was seriously threatened; and indeed the assailants had a decided advantage along the whole battle-field for several hours, their force being too great to resist, although, owing to the nature of the ground, it was impossible fully to deploy their columns, and to make the whole power of their fire felt. Matters were now looking extremely serious for the German troops, but operations were suspended for a short time. The Würtemburgers were reinforced by detachments from the Saxon, Pomeranian, and Silesian corps; and then a change in the situation of affairs was made by Colonel Abendorth, who acted as brigadier-general in the room of General Schultz, wounded at Sedan. Placing himself at the head of a body of Saxons, he called on them to follow him into the village of Villiers. They responded with a loud "Hurrah," and rushed upon the French who held it. A dreadful struggle ensued. It was then that the only firing at very close quarters took place, because on the plateau the French, while using the Chassepot, kept at a long distance from the enemy, to avoid coming under the fire of their own forts. In the village it was necessarily otherwise; but neither during this fight, nor at any other time in the day, was there a bayonet charge. After an obstinate resistance the French were driven out of Villiers: many of them were made prisoners, and the rest had now to defend themselves in the open field. While Colonel Abendorth was leading an attack on them in the plateau, a battery of mitrailleuses placed right opposite Villiers was worked with great rapidity. Four mitrailleuse balls entered the chest of the colonel's horse, which dropped dead. An officer galloped up to him with another; and again he was in the saddle, and leading his men, who followed him impetuously with another loud "Hurrah." This was a most exciting moment. They had only proceeded a hundred yards when the second horse was killed by a rifle shot, and, with its rider, came to the ground. Though hurt by the fall, the colonel got to his feet and called on his men to continue the charge. They did so, and actually took some prisoners on the plateau. There was now a fierce cannonading on both sides, and the artillery did terrific execution. Some of the German troops stationed themselves behind a wall to fire upon the French with the advantage of that cover; but the shells smashed the wall, and annihilated several of the men behind. The Germans captured two field-guns, but such a shower of shot, shell, and grenades was poured upon the troops who attempted to remove them, that they were obliged to leave them on the field. The fighting gradually ceased, and soon after four o'clock the French retired, leaving strong garrisons in Champigné and Brie; but it was nearly five, and quite dark, before the guns of the forts were entirely silent.

While the contest was raging in this quarter, a column of French troops was directed eastwards towards Chelles, along the right bank of the Marne, in order to keep off the twelfth (Saxon) corps; and another army, debouching by Fort Charenton, advanced in the direction of Mesly and Bonneuil, in front of Creteil. They succeeded in obtaining possession of Mont Mesly, and with it the villages at its foot, about noon; and could they have held and entrenched it, a very important point would have been gained; but the Germans having been reinforced in the after part of the day by the seventh brigade of the second corps, the lost positions were reconquered, and the French driven back under the shelter of Fort Charenton.

At the close of the day the Saxons stood fast in Villiers, in spite of all that the French troops and forts could do to dislodge them; while the army of Ducrot solidly held the villages of Champigné and Brie, which in the morning had been German posts; and which, in the possession of the French, were a standing menace to the safety of the main line of investment, only 2000 yards distant. Their success was therefore real, though incomplete, for they had won positions which might prove of much value for ulterior operations. The French brought fourteen batteries across the Marne; but owing to the nature of the ground they could not get their guns on a height, at a fair range from the enemy's infantry, so that they did not make much use of them. The cavalry on either side took no part in the battle. Though the French had displayed unquestionable bravery and steadiness in these engagements, and though they had fought well and manoeuvred fairly, showing that the governor of Paris had created out of rude masses a disciplined and tolerably efficient army, yet they were unequal to their German foes, who were strung to the height of daring by continual success. The French had not as yet reached the besieger's lines: they had only won advanced posts from which they could gather and attack in force; still these made their position very threatening, and it is hard to say what the result might have been if Ducrot, sacrificing every consideration to the primary object of breaking out, had called in his reserves during the night, and, advancing from Brie and Champigné, had endeavoured to storm the German intrenchments the next day. He would certainly have had the superiority of numbers, and would have begun with some advantages of ground; and even those who can fully appreciate the obstacles he would have had to overcome will, at least, doubt whether he might not have triumphed. The French, however, as on so many previous occasions in the war, remained inactive at the critical moment, and their opportunity was lost for ever.

Instead of resuming the attack, the French army remained perfectly quiet during the whole of the next day, December 1, repairing losses and collecting supplies; and though it still held its ground beyond the Marne, it was not reinforced to any great extent; neither was much advantage taken of the day's rest to fortify the captured positions. On the German side, artillery and ammunition were brought up by various roads, followed by regiment after regiment of infantry. The second army corps was ordered to assist in the operations, for it was expected that the French, from Champigné and Brie, with reinforcements from Paris, would attack the German lines, and a second day's fighting was regarded as certain. Not a moment was lost, for by halfpast seven o'clock in the morning the infantry and artillery had taken up their positions for resisting any movement either from Brie or against Villiers. It was bitterly cold all day, and it was consequently a severe duty for officers and men to rest there inactively, while exposed to the shot and shell from Fort Nogent and the battery at Avron; from both of which there was firing, though only now and then was it very frequent, and it did no damage. During the day a truce was agreed upon for some hours, at the request of the French, to enable them to bury their dead and collect the wounded; unfortunately not an easy task, for owing to the severity of the conflict the losses on both sides had been fearfully heavy. Late in the evening the German leaders held a council of war at the Prefecture at Versailles, at which it was decided that Champigné and Brie must be retaken. General von Moltke held that it was essential; though the other generals expressed great doubts as to the advantage of an attack in which the lives of their soldiers must be so freely sacrificed. However, orders were given to regain possession of these two villages "at any cost," and to drive the French behind the Marne. For this purpose as many men as could be spared were to be massed together; and all night troops were marching in the direction of Brie and Villiers. It was arranged that the Saxons should attack Brie, and the Würtemburgers Champigné. The troops engaged consisted of the second division of the royal Saxon army (the twenty-fourth division of the German host), under General von Nehroff, and comprising the 104th, 105th, 106th, 107th, and 108th regiments. Taking each regiment at its full strength of three battalions, these would represent fifteen battalions, or about 12,000 men; but as more than one battalion was naturally employed elsewhere on outpost duty, it may be outside the exact number to put down the Saxon force at 10,000 men. Before the commencement of operations these splendid troops occupied positions in Cournay, Champs, Noisy, Villiers, and the vicinity. The division of the Würtemburgers was commanded by General von Obernitz, a Prussian officer, and they were posted at La Queue Noiseau, Ormesson, Chennevières, and the surrounding country. A contingent made up of contributions from various portions of the second army corps, supported and co-operated with the Würtemburgers; so that altogether the Germans engaged, or immediately supporting, must not have been less than 25,000. The troops belonging to the second army corps were commanded by General von Fransecki, who in virtue of his seniority had the nominal direction of all the operations, which were, however, supervised generally as regarded the Saxons by Prince George of Saxony in person. To oppose these veterans the entire second army of Paris had been assembled on the plateau between Brie and Champigné. The first and second corps (of three divisions each) commanded respectively by Generals Blanchard and Renault, occupied the centre and right; while the third corps (D'Exea's) was *à cheval* on the Marne, opposite Nogent—the first division (Bellemare's) holding Brie, and the second, or reserve (Mattat's), lying on the rising ground forming the watershed at the other side. In all there were over 100,000 French bayonets in the elbow of the Marne, though probably not quite half that number were actively engaged at any time. The third army (seven divisions, or about 110,000 rank and file), under General Vinoy, were stationed right and left of General Ducrot, all round the city; but their orders were merely to harass the enemy as much as possible, without making a serious attack at any point.

Friday morning (December 2), was again bitterly cold and frosty; and the German soldiers who had bivouacked in the fields lay crouched around huge fires of green wood, which they had cut from the trees. Soon after seven o'clock the 107th Saxon regiment inarched directly on Brie, a portion of them advancing from the direction of Noisy, and the rest coming up from Villiers. It is a notable fact that, although the French had every reason to expect an attack, they were taken completely by surprise; there were only about 100 of them in front of the village—the greater number being in the houses, some asleep, others composedly drinking their coffee. The Saxons rushed on the outposts, who commenced rifle-firing, and a fight, carried on from one end of the village to the other, at once ensued, in which some French reinforcements, who had already crossed the Marne with the intention of marching on Villiers and Noisy, took part. The attack was so sudden and impetuous that—unaided by the artillery of their forts, which could not be brought to bear on the position without destroying their own men—the French were unable to withstand it. Amid wild "hurrahs!" from the Saxons Brie was retaken, and about 300 prisoners were captured, including eight officers.

Just before eight o'clock the Würtemburgers, coming up from their posts on the south, assaulted Champigné with rapid discharges from their needle-guns: the French replied; but after a struggle, vigorously maintained on both sides, the Würtemburgers repossessed themselves of the outposts they lost on the 30th. This proved a critical moment for the French troops. In the plain below Champigné some hundreds of panic-stricken men were flying from the front, and the German shells began to fall among them, hastening their flight and increasing their confusion. The promptitude of the French commanders, however, prevented a terrible disaster. The bridges across the Marne were burned; gendarmes galloped to and fro, and belaboured the fugitives with the flat of their swords; batteries of artillery trotted into the plain and wheeled into position, and the heavy guns posted in the redoubt of St. Maur poured a murderous fire into the opposing German batteries, and in half-an-hour had silenced them. The heavy artillery of the French forts also continued to fire on Noisy; and about nine o'clock Nogent, Rosny, and Avron commenced shelling Brie, which had the effect of changing the whole aspect of affairs. During the preceding day the neighbouring forts and batteries had received many additional guns, and the rain of shot and shell which they now began to pour into the devoted German ranks, has been described by experienced soldiers as more tremendous than they had ever before witnessed. The French troops now rallied and reformed, and were moved to the front again, where they resisted and finally repulsed the German attack. The correspondent of the *Times*, who was present, gave the following graphic description of the scene:—"There was the direct and the vertical fire. Avron and Rosny fired their shells right across. One of the batteries on Nogent fired in that way, while the other threw its shells high up in the air, and they descended from a point directly over the place in which they were intended to explode. No shelter could be found from Noisy down to the near end of Champigné. Houses were battered into ruins, trees were smashed into fragments, and men fell dead and wounded everywhere. It was simply impossible for any troops to live under such a fire as was then descending on Brie, and the Saxons were fairly shelled out . of it. After an immense loss of men and officers, they evacuated it at ten o'clock. While this terrible and persistent discharge of shot and shell was going on, some of the Saxon regiments attempted to make their way to the bridges by which the French had crossed the Marne, while the latter were coming out by thousands in column after column from under Rosny and Nogent. I saw, I should think, not fewer than 20,000 of them in one long column on the sloping ground between those two forts. The attempts to get at the bridges were repeated over and over again, not only under the shelling from the forts, but in face of two batteries of mitrailleuses, the fire from which was scarcely less dreadful. In the distance were French infantry, scattered here and there, who kept up a continuous fusillade from their Chassepots. The *Schutzen* or chasseur regiment of Saxons replied to them. One line of this regiment was on a slope, and was so completely exposed to a combined fire, that an aide-de-camp was sent to tell it to retire. As he was approaching it, a ball struck him in the breast, and he fell dead. Colonel Hausen, of the *Schutzen* regiment, and thirty-four of its other officers were also killed, and the men were shot down like deer in a *battue*. Attempts were made by the Germans to bring their artillery into play, but such was the unfavourable nature of the ground that the guns could only be placed in positions where the shells from the forts would have knocked them to pieces in five minutes. Only one or two batteries fired, and that under circumstances which prevented their being of much service. There was cavalry on both sides, but they again took no part in the engagement. The Germans had to depend entirely on their infantry, which behaved admirably, and inflicted very great loss on the enemy. The lines of French were constantly thinned, but they were replaced by others, who kept up the Chassepot practice at just such a distance as enabled them to be safe from the fire of their own forts. There was a lull now and then in the rifle slaughter as the Germans retreated from the near approaches to the bridges over the Marne, but the shelling never for a moment ceased; and the mitrailleuses and Chassepots again performed their work of destruction, and again lines of Frenchmen fell dead and wounded from the fire of the needle-gun, as often as the Germans renewed the attempt to get at and destroy the bridges. All this time the wounded were being carried off the field by both parties; while some unfortunate soldiers, who though maimed were able to rise, fell dead from another ball, or the fragment of a shell, as they endeavoured to hobble off the ground. For miles round the whole earth seemed to shake from the thunder of the forts, while shells were passing over the battlefield and exploding in the woods and highways. Some of the projectiles reached a distance of 7000 yards from the batteries whence they were discharged. Ultimately the Germans were obliged to desist from the attempt on the bridges, though it was nearly three o'clock in the afternoon when they did so." Another eye-witness said:—"As the Germans advanced and the French retired, a most tremendous fire burst on the attacking columns. In vain, exulting in the pride of success, did the Germans press forward with shouts of defiance; in vain did officers break from their ranks and cheer them on against the receding enemy: whole files were literally swept away, until, at last, after a heroic effort, the retreat was sounded, and the German front fell back." Then the tide of battle turned again; the French pressed forward in dense masses, and the tricolor was once more seen in Brie and Champigné, although the Würtemburgers still continued to hold several outposts at their extreme end of the latter village. That portion of the French army who had not crossed the Marne then retired, and after a few parting shots the forts became silent. So ended this second engagement.

While the battle was still raging, General Trochu forwarded the following despatch to the chief of the general staff in Paris:—

"The Governor of Paris to General Schmitz.

"December 2.

"PLATEAU BETWEEN CHAMPIGNÉ AND VILLIERS, 1.15 p.m.

"Attacked this morning by enormous forces at break of day. We have been fighting for nearly seven hours. At the moment I write to you the enemy is retiring along the whole line, giving up the heights to us once more. Traversing the lines of riflemen from Champigné to Brie, I received the honour and the unspeakable pleasure of being cheered by the troops, exposed to the most violent fire. We shall doubtless have dreadful returns, and this second battle, like the first, will last the whole day. I do not know what future is reserved for these generous efforts of the troops of the republic; but I owe this justice to them, that in the midst of trials of all kinds they have deserved well of the country. I must add that to General Ducrot belongs the honour of these two days.

"GENERAL TROCHU."

The actual result of these two days of slaughter bore no proportion to the fearful loss of life; for while nothing had been gained by either party, both had lost much. The desperate action on Friday pretty clearly showed that, notwithstanding their overwhelming superiority of numbers, and the bravery of the greater portion of the French troops, they could not defeat their enemies in the open field. It will be noticed that on the second day the Germans acted on the offensive; and it was only by the aid of the heavy guns of the forts that the French were able to maintain the positions they carried on Wednesday. Giving them full credit for the bravery and heroism displayed by those of them who fought, it must still be said that, with all their valour, they were not equal to the task before them; for they could gain no ground against enemies over whom they had the advantage of numbers, of position, and of weapons. Considering the intention with which the sortie was made, it had proved a grievous failure. Its object, on the part of the French, was not merely a trial of strength between the two armies, or even to gain certain positions (in which case they might have had reason to congratulate themselves); but they wished to force a passage through the Prussian lines, and as they were no nearer the attainment of this end than they had been a week before, they could not be said to have gained anything. On the other hand, they had lost nothing, for the troops were encouraged by finding they could cope on equal terms with the Prussians in a protracted engagement on a large scale, rather than dispirited by the failure of their object.

The Germans made every preparation for a renewal of the murderous conflict on the following morning, and before daybreak troops to reinforce their army were pouring from all sides into Champs (the headquarters of the Saxon corps): the Bavarians were marched up from Lagny, and the roads bristled with bayonets. These precautions, however, proved unnecessary; for on the afternoon of December 3 the mass of the French retired across the Marne, unmolested, to the shelter of Vincennes, leaving garrisons in the villages which had been the occasion of so much slaughter. These garrisons also were finally withdrawn on the evening of the 4th, after which General Ducrot issued the following order of the day:— "Soldiers! After two days' glorious battles I have made you recross the Marne, because I was convinced that further efforts would be fruitless in the direction in which the enemy had time to concentrate his forces, and to prepare means of action. Had we persisted in that way, I should have uselessly sacrificed thousands of brave men. Far from aiding the work of deliverance I should have seriously compromised it, and at the same time have led you to an irreparable disaster. But the conflict has only ceased for a moment; let us resume it with courage. Be ready! Complete with speed your ammunition and your provisions. Above all, raise your hearts to the height of the sacrifice which is demanded by the holy cause for which we must not hesitate to lay down our lives."

True to the French characteristic of never admitting a defeat, the *Journal Officiel* of December 5, after announcing that the troops had recrossed the Maine and were encamped in the wood of Vincennes, gave to the Parisians the following elaborate explanation of this backward "strategical movement:"—"The plan, the execution of which has been for the last four days so vigorously earned out, now enters upon a new phase. In broad daylight our troops came down again in excellent order towards the Marne, while the enemy did not dare to molest them. The forts kept good watch. The fatigues so courageously endured by the young army of Paris required a short rest. The cold is much more severe and piercing on the hills than in the open country or inside Paris. The fight had lasted the whole day, and strict vigilance was necessary to avoid an unexpected attack, as was the case on the morning of the 2nd. Therefore no sleep was possible; added to which any one indulging in sleep on the hard ground in such a temperature would have risked being frozen to death. These, and strategical reasons, caused the movement, which will lead to fresh engagements, as announced in the order of the day of General Ducrot, the true meaning and import of which has been perfectly understood by the Parisian population. Some papers suppose that we have abandoned Champigné. This is not the case; on the contrary, we are assured that our troops remain strongly established in those positions. The number of German prisoners taken from the battlefield now amounts to more than 800; many of them are detained in the forts. No serious affair has occurred since the 2nd, but that does not prevent our generals preparing for the new stage of the struggle upon which we are now about to enter. The Prussian staff is reported to show uneasiness at the prospect. The enemy, who has in all directions to go over enormous distances before facing us, begins indeed to feel that he will soon be exhausted by marches and countermarches if we continue ever so little successively to attack him on several opposite points. The immense circle round which he has to manoeuvre grows daily more extended, in consequence of our conquering advanced positions after each engagement, and therefore the increasing difficulties of quickly concentrating troops which threaten General von Moltke's plans, must be contemplated at Versailles with some legitimate fear. Paris, on the contrary, perfectly understanding what is going on, co-operates by all the means at her disposal with the views of her skilful and gallant governor. The business of general organization, equipment, and the artillery works, is pushed on with fresh efficiency and vigour. The military resources placed at the disposal of battalions armed by private industry are, so to say, inexhaustible."

In order to show the intense delight inspired by the French successes, (?) the following letter was addressed by the members of the Provisional Government to their president, General Trochu:—

"General and Dear President,—For three days we have been with you in mind upon the field of battle, where the destinies of the country are being decided. We would wish to share that danger while leaving you that glory which so justly belongs to you, of having prepared and assured by your noble devotion the success of our valiant army. No one has a greater right to be proud of it than you. No one can more worthily pronounce its eulogium. You are only unmindful of yourself, but you withdraw yourself from the acclamations of your companions in arms, electrified by your example. It would have been agreeable to us to add our own, but permit us at least to express to you our hearty sentiments of gratitude and affection. Say to the brave General Ducrot and his gallant soldiers that we admire them. Republican France recognizes in them the noble and pure heroism which already has saved it. France now knows that she rests her hopes of safety on them and on you. We, your colleagues, acquainted with your ideas, hail with joy those grand and noble days in which you completely revealed yourself, and which we are convinced are the commencement of our deliverance." Neither then, nor at any subsequent period, did the true state of affairs justify the use of this highly inflated language.

As may be supposed, the list of casualties for the two days was on both sides frightfully heavy. On the 30th of November the French suffered equally with their enemies, for then they were the assailants, and it was only the fire from their forts which restored the balance of loss that must otherwise have been against them. But on the 2nd of December the German casualties far exceeded those of the French. The *Schutzen* and the 108th regiments, especially, were dreadfully cut up. The latter, after going into action, returned at the end of twenty minutes with the loss of thirty-five out of forty-five officers. The former covered themselves with immortal honour, but at a terrible sacrifice. They went into action about 2000 strong, and lost 760 men and 36 officers—more than a third of their entire strength. One company which began the fight with 170 men, came out with 70, and in another every one of the lieutenants was killed. The total loss on the French side was officially stated to be 1008 killed and 5082 wounded, who strewed the plateau in front of the villages of Champigné, Brie, and Villiers; and there is reason to fear that a great many of the deaths were owing to the want of attention during the severe weather. On one night the thermometer was twelve degrees, and the next nine degrees, below zero (Fahr.)—the cold being intensified by a cutting wind which pierced through the very bones, and transferred many of the poor fellows from the list of the wounded to that of the dead. The French superior officers also were very unfortunate: General de la Charriere was killed; General Renaud had to undergo amputation of the leg, and General Falherbe of the arm; and Colonel de Talhouet was also severely wounded: On the German side nearly 8000 officers and men were placed *hors de combat* by the two days' hostilities—a heavy total, which was chiefly due to the gallantry of the regiments engaged, "for they fought like lions." Perhaps no men were ever called upon to oppose by rifles alone such a cannonade and rifle fire as the Saxons, in particular, were subjected to; and they well deserved the congratulations and thanks which the king of Saxony sent them. It has been stated that the French army was principally composed of raw recruits: no doubt thousands of them were new to the service; but there were present zouaves brought from Algeria after the battle of Sedan, and the great majority of the men who fought on the two days had the bearing of seasoned soldiers. As an instance of the privations caused by the siege, some of them cut up the dead horses with their swords, and proceeded to cook and eat portions on the battlefield.

In his general review of this sortie, and of the last engagement in particular, the able writer of the "Campaign of 1870-71," in the *Times* (since collected and republished), says:— The governor of Paris had witnessed the vicissitudes of this memorable day, and he had seen his enemy, frightfully thinned, recoil baffled, if not routed. Nevertheless, rigidly adhering to his plan, he did not attempt to improve his advantage, and contented himself with maintaining his hold on the valuable outposts he had regained. That these tactics were in accordance with the general rules of the art of war, which almost assume that the garrison of a fortress cannot, when once invested, escape unless aided by a relieving army, will be hardly denied by competent critics. Still, Trochu may have considered the question from too narrow a point of view; and possibly he had then an opportunity of severing the circle around Paris, even without any external assistance. The whole German force on the French front on the 2nd of December was 25,000 men; this had been reduced at least a fifth; and though it had retired in good order, the extraordinary losses of its officers induce us to think that it had suffered some abatement from its high martial courage. On the other hand, the French were not less, certainly, than 55,000 strong; these could have been raised to 100,000 by immediate reinforcements from Paris; they were full of confidence, and the terrible execution done by the forts had inspired them with exulting hope. It may be, therefore, that had Trochu combined the troops he could have made available for a great effort on the 3rd of December, he might possibly have cleared a passage. Such was the opinion of eye-witnesses writing from the German camp after the war had ended; and, had he done so, and marched boldly on the great German depôt of Lagny, on the main line of the hostile communications, he might have caused the siege to have been raised, and have practically gained a base for his army. Such an attempt certainly would have been perilous, but there were strong arguments, we think, in its favour. The force inside Paris was not a mere garrison; a large and far from despicable army had been formed for active operations; and as Trochu ought to have been aware that, in the actual circumstances of the war, the arrival of a relieving army was an event he could not fully rely on, he ought, perhaps, to have made up his mind to act decisively with the means in his hands; and had he done so, he certainly had a favourable opportunity at this moment. Instead, however, of making the effort, the governor of Paris remained immovable. Without seeking to blame Trochu, we shall only remark that he never found so good an opportunity again, and that possibly genius and daring might at this moment have led to fortune.

CHAPTER XXV.

Scenes on the re-occupation of Orleans by the Germans—Difficulty of disposing of the large number of Prisoners—Important Proclamation of the King of Prussia, stating that another Crisis of the War had been reached—The French Seat of Government transferred from Tours to Bordeaux—Panic in the former City on the decision of the Government being made known—Visit of If. Gambetta to the French Army, and issue of a Stirring and Hopeful Manifesto by him—Results of the Capture of Orleans to the French—New Arrangements made by them—General D'Aurelles removed from the Chief Command, and General Chanzy appointed in his stead—Good Reasons for the Step—Chanzy's Skill and Energy—Position occupied by his Army on the right bank of the Loire—Battle of Beaugency on December 7—Timely Arrival of the Bavarians, and the French driven back after a very Gallant Resistance—Resumption of the Engagement by them on the following morning, and continued Obstinate Fighting on both Sides during the day—The Germans finally again Victorious—Capture of 400 Prisoners by them at Midnight without firing a shot or losing a Man—Fearful Scenes in Beaugency—Another Battle on the 9th, in which the Germans are again Successful—The French, however, commence another Engagement on the 10th, and are again defeated after a Severe Struggle—The Scenes in the Villages around in consequence of there having been no time to attend to the Dead and Wounded—Skilful Movement of General Chanzy, who takes up a very Strong Position near Fréteval, on the road to Paris—Timely Arrival of Reinforcements to the Grand-duke of Mecklenburg, and the French ultimately compelled to retreat to Le Mans—General Review of the Strategy on both Sides during this period—The Fearful Losses amongst the Bavarians—Letter from the King of Prussia specially thanking them—Attack on Tours by the Germans—Capture of Rouen after an unavailing attempt at Defence—Panic amongst the French Troops and Inhabitants of the City—The Germans actually invited to enter to protect the Citizens from the Mob—The Strategical Importance of the City to the Germans—Visit of the Germans to Dieppe, they having thus crossed France from the Rhine to the British Channel—Scenes in the Town—Blockade of their own Seaports by the French—Second Occupation of Dieppe—The Prussian Garrison at Ham surprised and taken Prisoners—Surrender of Phalsbourg and Montmédy by the French—Contrast between Châteaudun and Chartres—New Levy of Germans Troops, and unabated Enthusiasm throughout the Country—Severe Decree of the French Government as to Desertion—Abolition of the General Councils of Departments by M. Gambetta—Great Dissatisfaction throughout the Country at the Measure—Repudiation of the Treaty of 1867 for the Neutrality of Luxemburg by the Germans—Reasons for such a Step, and Reply of the Luxemburg Government—Sinking of English Vessels by the Germans on the Seine—Remonstrance of the British Government, and Prompt Reply by Count von Bismarck, guaranteeing Compensation to the Owners and Crews.

OUR last review of the events upon the Loire closed with the fall, for the second time, of Orleans before the victorious enemy. The entry of the Germans into the city, on the morning of Sunday, December 5, was a scene fitted to impress deeply both the victors and the vanquished. The rattle of the artillery trains, the roll of drums, the jingle of the trotting cavalry, the shouts of officers, the tramp of battalions, the hopeless "jams" of the baggage trains, the squads of prisoners arriving from different directions, the cowering, stray civilians, crushed by this din of war, and the weeping women—all combined to form a picture full of strong and striking contrast. If nations, like individuals, must pass through humiliation and suffering to rise to a higher and purer standard of virtue, the French were at this time draining the bitter cup to the dregs; while their opponents had the difficult lesson to learn of triumphing in a spirit of gentleness and moderation. The fact that the Germans had already once bombarded the town and driven out the enemy; and that, after occupying it for four weeks and being driven out in turn, they were now once more victorious over an army, the raising of which for her own defence had taxed the energies of Republican France to the utmost, naturally caused a high degree of exultation, and invested the second capture of Orleans with an interest peculiar to itself. The intensity of feeling arising out of these special circumstances was observable on both sides, and the proud elated air of the regiments which, with colours flying and bands playing, followed each other along the street, finally leading into the centre of the town, was in striking contrast with the dejected appearance of the inhabitants. At one point had been a barricade which raked the whole length of the street by which the city was entered, and along which the French had, during the night, kept up a storm of rifle bullets which, for a time, held their enemies at bay. Passing along this street the German troops finally debouched upon the Place du Martroy, in the centre of which, upon her bronze charger, and waving her sword, rode "The Maid," surrounded now by a dense throng of French prisoners captured in course of the night. As the whole army came pouring into the city, street after street began to resound with the strains of martial music and the tramp of armed men; and at every lattice, over which the blinds were kept closed for the most part, excepting some little chink left as a peep-hole, inquisitive and anxious eyes looked out. There must have been something appalling to the inhabitants in the numbers of the hostile army, as, in seemingly never-ending columns, regiment after regiment marched to the position assigned to it. On the balcony of the Hôtel d'Orleans stood the grand-duke of Mecklenburg returning the salute of his men, who looked for the most part as fresh and clean as if they had just turned out for parade, instead of having had three days of hard fighting in mid-winter. The jäger battalions, each man with a sprig of pine in his shako, were especially gallant-looking; and when the inhabitants came to compare the numbers and aspect of the conquerors, with their own troops huddled together and shivering in the middle of the square, they must have ceased to wonder at the result.

As usual, the number of prisoners was enormous, and considerable difficulty was felt by their captors in disposing of them. As many thousands as could possibly be crammed into it passed the night in the magnificent cathedral, which presented a very remarkable scene.

Considering all the circumstances under which Orleans was captured, and that for several hours its streets were actually defended by riflemen, it must in justice be said that the German troops displayed considerable moderation at a moment when, according to the rules of war, a certain amount of licence is supposed to be permitted to soldiers who may almost be said to have taken by storm a besieged town. This might possibly be owing to the fact that the Bavarians, who were among the first to enter, had during their former month's stay in the place made many friends, who now from motives of policy, if from no other sentiment, received them warmly as old acquaintances. No additional contributions were exacted from the city until, a few days after its occupation, the driver of a Prussian provision column was killed. He had asked a Frenchman in a blouse the way to the bivouac outside the town, where his waggon was standing. The Frenchman pointed in the direction he was to take; but the unfortunate waggoner, thanking him, had hardly turned away when a bullet passed through his back and entered his lungs. As the offender could not be discovered, a fine of £24,000 was imposed. Half the money was paid down in cash, and plate and other articles were offered in liquidation of the second moiety. The Bavarian officer, however, replied that he was commandant, and not a storekeeper; and that the amount would be increased by £4000 a day until the fine was paid. On the same or following day the money was forthcoming.

Numerous events following each other closely up to the present time, point to the early days of December as marking an important stage in the operations of the war. Not only had the army of the Loire been a second time defeated and Orleans reoccupied, but in the east Dijon had been captured; in the north the French army raised there had been shattered and dispersed, the large cities of Amiens and Rouen had been taken; and at Paris sorties on a great scale had been victoriously repulsed. The king of Prussia therefore issued the following important proclamation:—

"Soldiers of the Confederate German Armies!—We have again arrived at a crisis of the war. When I last addressed you the last of the hostile armies which at the commencement of the campaign confronted us had, by the capitulation of Metz, been destroyed. The enemy has since, by extraordinary exertions, opposed to us newly-formed troops, and a large portion of the inhabitants of France have forsaken their peaceful, and by us unhindered, vocations in order to take up arms. The enemy was frequently superior to us in numbers, but you have nevertheless again defeated him, for valour and discipline and confidence in a righteous cause are worth more than numerical preponderance. All attempts of the enemy to break through the investment lines of Paris have been firmly repulsed, often, indeed, with many bloody sacrifices, as at Champigné and at Le Bourget, but with a heroism such as you have everywhere displayed towards him. The armies of the enemy, which were advancing in every direction to the relief of Paris, have all been defeated. Our troops, some of whom only a few weeks ago stood before Metz and Strassburg, have to-day advanced as far as Rouen, Orleans, and Dijon, and among many smaller victorious engagements, two new important battles—those of Amiens and the several days' fight at Orleans—have been added to our former triumphs. Several fortresses have been conquered, and much war material has been taken. I have reason, therefore, for the greatest satisfaction, and it is to me a gratification and a duty to express this to you. I thank you all, from the general to the common soldier. Should the enemy persist in a further prosecution of the war, I know you will continue to show that exertion of all your powers to which we owe our great success hitherto, until we wring from him an honourable peace, worthy of the great sacrifices of blood and life which have been offered up.

"WILLIAM

"HEADQUARTERS, VERSAILLES, *Dec.* 6, 1870."

With the defeat of the Loire army a general impression prevailed that the entry of the enemy into Tours was simply a question of time. Whether this feeling was or was not shared by M. Gambetta and his colleagues, they doubtless judged that the victorious

Prussians would at once make for the city which, since the investment of Paris, had been the second capital of France. A proclamation was therefore issued by the ministers, in which they announced the abandonment of Tours as the seat of the delegate government, as under the circumstances of the hour it was of the utmost importance to prevent the freedom of the army from being impeded in any way by political or administrative considerations. As, therefore, the proximity of the seat of government at Tours might hinder the military operations, it had been decided that the whole of the government offices should be transferred to Bordeaux; which, owing to the facilities of communication which it offered both by land and sea with the rest of France, afforded peculiar advantages for the organization of the army and the continuance of the work of the national defence. Often during the campaign there might have been witnessed the sudden flight of a whole population before the dreaded Germans, but never was there seen a spectacle of the kind so general, or a terror so universal, as that which reigned in Tours when the decision of the government became known. The city has a population of 41,000 inhabitants; and after the government had made it their headquarters, at least 20,000 persons who had nothing to do with the place itself had taken up their residence there. All these had to move, or felt themselves bound to move in accordance with their own interests, when the authorities had decided on flying southwards. Many of course were obliged, by considerations other than selfish, to follow the fortunes of the emigrating ministers. Besides the different embassies, various official and semi-official newspaper establishments, a large body who had obtained, and who were trying to obtain, contracts for every conceivable article which the soldier could eat, drink, wear, or use in fighting, there were a vast number of persons who, living more or less on their own means, had fled from Paris, and were now anxious to escape again from the Germans, supposed to be in full march on Tours. It may therefore be easily understood how huge the exodus became when it was known the government had positively decided upon going south. The inhabitants of the place, French as well as foreigners, had been one and all so greatly deceived by the falsehoods told, and the greater falsehoods insinuated, regarding the doings and prospects of the army of the Loire, that in spite of themselves they read every official document in a sense almost exactly contrary to that which it bore. That the military situation was good, and that the government was departing merely to leave greater freedom of action to the army of the Loire, might have been credited after the battle of Coulmiers and the re-occupation of Orleans by the French; but it would not go down after the disastrous fight at Patay, the return of the Prussians to Orleans, the removal of D'Aurelles from the command, and the arrival in Tours of a host of wounded and of fugitives, both officers and men, from the beaten forces which had struggled with more or less valour, but with very little success, to stem the ever-advancing Prussian tide. The persistent misrepresentations of the French government had demoralized the public, and no good news was now credited until actually proved to be true. So everybody believed the worst to have happened, when it was known that the government was going. Meanwhile the railway terminus was besieged by multitudes of fugitives, waiting all day and all night for opportunities of departure.

But although the delegate government was supposed to have removed to Bordeaux, the course of events led its chief member to take an opposite direction, and proceed to the right bank of the Loire, between Meaux and Beaugency. Ever anxious to be where his personal presence might inspire new life and lead to renewed efforts for his country, M. Gambetta had, as already stated, narrowly escaped falling into German hands in his endeavour to reach Orleans on the 4th; and leaving his colleagues to manage the details of government at Bordeaux, he now, regardless of danger, hastened to where a portion of the lately-beaten army was fighting so as to deserve his commendation, and to justify the hope that, under favourable circumstances, they would be able once more to resume their forward march. The events of the first few days of December had, indeed, sorely tried the faith of those who were still sanguine as to the ultimate prospects of France; but whoever else might, Gambetta certainly was not disposed to give way to despair. His most cherished and loudly proclaimed anticipations had been rudely thwarted; the army which at such infinite pains he had collected, and which was to provide a grave for the enemies of France, had been defeated and dispersed: but all this failed to damp his ardent enthusiasm. In a manifesto, issued only a day or two after the proclamation of King William, he wrote—"Have no apprehensions. . . . The military situation, notwithstanding the evacuation of Orleans, is good. . . . Our enemies regard their situation as critical; I have proof of that. Patience and courage! We shall get through the work. Show energy, guard against panic, distrust all false rumours, and believe in the good star of France!" The succeeding narrative of events upon the Loire will show the grounds upon which M. Gambetta's renewed hopes were founded.

By the capture of Orleans the army of the Loire had been cut in two. General Chanzy, with the sixteenth and seventeenth corps, composing the left wing, had been cut off from Orleans on the 2nd, and fell back along the north side of the river, towards Meung, on the road to Blois. The right wing, consisting of Bourbaki's eighteenth and Crouzat's twentieth corps, crossing the river at Jargeau, retreated up its left or southern bank towards Gien; and the centre, comprising the fifteenth and nineteenth corps, which had been driven back through Orleans, subsequently separated, the former making its way for Blois in concert with General Chanzy, and the latter moving eastward to effect a junction with Bourbaki. The involuntary situation was accepted by M. Gambetta with characteristic promptitude. A decree was issued on the 6th, announcing that, in consequence of the recent military events on the Loire and the evacuation of Orleans, the government had decided on the formation of two distinct armies, to operate in the two regions separated by the course of the river, "thus preserving means of effecting a junction with Paris, which was the immediate and supreme object in view." The decree further announced the appointment of D'Aurelles de Paladine to the command of the camp of instruction at Cherbourg, and of Generals Bourbaki and Chanzy to the command of the first and second armies respectively. The new appointment of D'Aurelles was, of course, equivalent to dismissal from his position as commander-in-chief of the Loire forces. We have shown in Chapters XXII. and XXIII. that the generalissimo of the Loire army was vacillating throughout between the offensive operations for which M. Gambetta was urgent, and the more Fabian policy to which he was himself inclined; and it is certain that discouragement caused by his vacillation spread rapidly among the troops. What might have been expected from the whole Loire army had he been inspired with some of the boldness and intrepidity of M. Gambetta himself, was shown by the splendid rally of the left under General Chanzy, as contrasted with the wretched behaviour of the French centre when driven within the defensive works around Orleans. An impartial view of the events of the first few days of December, forces on us the conviction that Gambetta was justified, not in interfering from a distance with the details of the operations of D'Aurelles, but in removing him after it became clear that he had not the requisite power over his men for holding them together, and that he had suffered his army, in its chosen position, to be dissevered by the attack of a force not more than half its numerical strength. It would have been more prudent to have drawn in the French corps, spread out like the circumference of an open fan across the different roads centering on Orleans, so as to cover that city on a shorter line, and thus bring the several corps into closer communication, and prevent that separation which proved fatal to the defence of Orleans. The fact that the eighteenth corps on the right was obliged to retire eccentrically across the Loire without striking a blow, seems an instance of bad generalship on the part of D'Aurelles, which from his antecedents could not have been looked for. He bad, too, managed to lose much influence with his generally republican and freethinking soldiers, by having gone to venerate some relics in the Orleans cathedral, on an altar before which Joan of Arc had seen a vision of the Virgin Mary. The gratitude of France was, however, due to him for having formed, from an undisciplined mob, the first army which withstood the Germans in the field; and although M. Gambetta exercised a wise discretion in assigning the Loire army to younger and bolder men, he only paid a just tribute to his merits in offering him the command (declined on the ground of ill-health) of the new camp of instruction at Cherbourg.

When it was decided to remove General d'Aurelles from the charge of the army, it was generally acknowledged that M. Gambetta made a good choice of a successor, for there was no doubt that Chanzy had shown more military capacity than any general as yet tried on the Loire. It was he who really won the battle of Coulmiers on the 9th of November; it was the left wing, under his command, which had fought—at Patay, on the 1st December—the only creditable engagement of the Loire army in the several days previous to its retreat from before Orleans; and of all the undistinguished crowd of worn-out veterans, naval officers, and hastily-promoted colonels under whom that army was first brought together from its scattered depôts, Chanzy was the only general who had shone out conspicuously for vigour and military capacity in the field.

Even before the Bordeaux government had settled itself in its new home, General Chanzy had thoroughly justified his title to the most important military command M. Gambetta had to confer. We have seen how he was cut off from Orleans on the 2nd and 3rd of December, with his own (sixteenth) corps and the seventeenth. These, reinforced on the following week by the twenty-first corps, sent to him from Tours, constituted the new active army of the Loire, with which he was to endeavour to fulfil the hopes which General D'Aurelles had failed to realize. M. Gambetta had pledged himself to support the new commander with all the forces of the west; but as yet these were only in a rudimentary condition, and weeks must elapse before they could with any certainty be drawn upon. Meanwhile, it was most important to present the best possible face to the enemy.

The sixteenth corps, after the defeats of the 3rd and 4th of December, had retreated down the river as far as Mer, within fourteen miles of Blois. General Chanzy ordered its columns to re-form at Beaugency, seven miles nearer to Orleans. With marvellous rapidity he established a new system of defence, presented himself, much to the astonishment of his enemy, at the head of at least 100,000 men, and offered a resistance which forms one of the most interesting episodes of the war. The newly-organized army was posted between the two railway lines, one coming from Paris and Orleans, along the banks of the Loire, to Blois and Tours, the other from Paris direct to Tours by Châteaudun and Vendôme. Between Beaugency, on the first line, and Fréteval, a few miles north of Vendôme, on the second, extends the forest of Marchenoir—a region chosen by the French at an early period in the campaign as well adapted for defensive operations.

Up to the evening of the 8th, Prince Frederick Charles, with the tenth corps, remained at Orleans, while the rest of the German forces spread themselves out like a fan, along the roads which the retreating enemy had taken. Not at all expecting to meet with any serious opposition, the prince sent the duke of Mecklenburg, with about 40,000 troops, comprising the seventeenth division, and the remnant of Von der Tann's Bavarians, to follow up those who had taken the right bank of the river. It did not seem probable that the advance upon Tours would be impeded by only a portion of that French army which, as a whole, had already been beaten and dispersed. On the 6th of December the cavalry, who were sent to clear the way to Blois, were, on entering the town of Meung, fired upon by a body of 1200 foot gendarmes, who after a short resistance disappeared, and the road was reported clear for the advance of the army. Accordingly the leading columns passed through the town, unmolested and without suspicion, about ten o'clock on the morning of the 7th; but no sooner did they debouch upon the plain covered with vineyards, on the side towards Beaugency, than they were received with a hot artillery and Chassepot fire, which compelled them to fall back behind the extreme houses of Meung, which they rapidly loopholed and defended. After a short delay the artillery came to the front, the Mecklenburgers again advanced, and the battle became general. The French army was in position along the road which runs at right angles to the Loire by Ouzouer-le-Marché. Some brigades had been pushed along in echelon towards Meung, but the main body extended from Villorceau on the right to Cravant on the left, the village of Beaumont forming the centre of the position. A slightly undulating plain separated the two armies, and owing to the hard frost, the country was in admirable condition for the passage of artillery and cavalry. But the precaution taken by the French commander of causing the vine stakes to be left in the ground, paralyzed to a great extent the latter arm, in which the Germans were exceedingly strong. The seventeenth division, which found itself thus suddenly engaged with an enemy in very superior force, was for a time obliged to bear alone the whole brunt of the attack, and the seventy-sixth and ninetieth regiments of Mecklenburgers suffered severely both in men and officers. Cavalry operations, as we have said, were impracticable;

but the country was very favourable for riflemen and skirmishers. The German artillery, however, by their excellent range and practice, prevented anything like a forward movement on the part of the French, until the Bavarians, who were at some distance in the rear when the fight began, by an extraordinary feat in marching came up on the right of the Mecklenburgers late in the afternoon, and by their dash and impetuosity carried all before them. At dark the French, who had made a gallant fight throughout the day, found themselves driven back at all points, and the German army camped upon their hardly-won field.

During the night the duke of Mecklenburg was strengthened by the arrival of the twenty-second Prussian division. General Chanzy also received reinforcements, and early on the morning of the 8th commenced a vigorous attack, which might have seriously altered the German position but for the timely arrival mentioned. At first the form of the battle-field was very nearly that of a horse-shoe halved into pieces, separated at some distance from each other. One end of the shoe rested upon the village of Baulle, about half way between Meung and Beaugency, and the other upon Tavers, a village beyond Beaugency, on a ridge at the bottom of which a small stream flows into the Loire. On this ridge the French were posted; their position extending in a curve as if to complete the horse-shoe, which it was prevented from doing by the German position occupying the corresponding curve. The strength of the French position was on the ridge near the end of the straight part of the shoe; that of the Germans at the curve. In other words, the force of the attack of both armies was from their respective right wings. Between Baulle and Beaugency, a little to the right of the main road, was the village of Messas; in the same direction, and a little in rear of it, lay Villeneuve. Yet further back, and more to the right, was Langlochere, the centre of the battle-field of the 7th. Still further round the curve, but far more to the front, was Beaumont, and beyond that, at the broken end of the German part of the horse-shoe, Cravant. These villages were generally from a mile to a mile and a half distant from each other. The twenty-second Prussian division, which formed the German right wing, was to have commenced the attack, but was anticipated by the French. The Bavarians, who as usual had to sustain the brunt of the action, occupied the centre; and the seventeenth division, forming the left wing, held the high road leading to Beaugency at Baulle, a little in rear of Messas, which with Cravant had not yet been taken. For a long time the battle lay with the artillery of the respective armies, and this arm of the French force did much to retrieve its character. About one o'clock the Germans endeavoured to storm several of the villages in their front, but found the work by no means easy; mobiles as well as the more seasoned troops contesting gallantly every inch of ground. Messas, Cravant, and Beaumont were, however, ultimately taken, though after severe loss. Batteries on the left bank of the Loire commenced bombarding Beaugency in the afternoon, and painful havoc was committed among the wounded soldiers, with whom many of the houses and public buildings were crowded.

Towards evening a storming party pushed forward, and after severe fighting managed to occupy the town and capture a battery of six guns and 1100 prisoners. The day thus closed favourably on the whole for the Germans, who had slowly gained ground. The resistance of the enemy, however, had been as obstinate as it was unexpected, and throughout the camp an unpleasant sense of disappointment prevailed. It was, therefore, resolved that something further should be done to augment the acquisitions of the day; and about midnight two Hanseatic regiments who were occupying Messas, finding that the village of Vernon, immediately in front of them, was still occupied by the French, determined on surprising it; and rushing suddenly in, captured 400 prisoners without firing a shot or losing a man. The Bavarians were equally successful in a night sortie from Beaumont upon the neighbouring village of La Mee, which they also took by surprise and without loss.

The scenes in Beaugency, immediately after its precaution taken by the French commander of causing the vine stakes to be left in the ground, paralyzed to a great extent the latter arm, in which the Germans were exceedingly strong. The seventeenth division, which found itself thus suddenly engaged with an enemy in very superior force, was for a time obliged to bear alone the whole brunt of the attack, and the seventy-sixth and ninetieth regiments of Mecklenburgers suffered severely both in men and officers. Cavalry operations, as we have said, were impracticable; but the country was very favourable for riflemen and skirmishers. The German artillery, however, by their excellent range and practice, prevented anything like a forward movement on the part of the French, until the Bavarians, who were at some distance in the rear when the fight began, by an extraordinary feat in marching came up on the right of the Mecklenburgers late in the afternoon, and by their dash and impetuosity carried all before them. At dark the French, who had made a gallant fight throughout the day, found themselves driven back at all points, and the German army camped upon their hardly-won field.

During the night the duke of Mecklenburg was strengthened by the arrival of the twenty-second Prussian division. General Chanzy also received reinforcements, and early on the morning of the 8th commenced a vigorous attack, which might have seriously altered the German position but for the timely arrival mentioned. At first the form of the battle-field was very nearly that of a horse-shoe halved into pieces, separated at some distance from each other. One end of the shoe rested upon the village of Baulle, about half way between Meung and Beaugency, and the other upon Tavers, a village beyond Beaugency, on a ridge at the bottom of which a small stream flows into the Loire. On this ridge the French were posted; their position extending in a curve as if to complete the horse-shoe, which it was prevented from doing by the German position occupying the corresponding curve. The strength of the French position was on the ridge near the end of the straight part of the shoe; that of the Germans at the curve. In other words, the force of the attack of both armies was from their respective right wings. Between Baulle and Beaugency, a little to the right of the main road, was the village of Messas; in the same direction, and a little in rear of it, lay Villeneuve. Yet further back, and more to the right, was Langclochere, the centre of the battle-field of the 7th. Still further round the curve, but far more to the front, was Beaumont, and beyond that, at the broken end of the German part of the horse-shoe, Cravant. These villages were generally from a mile to a mile and a half distant from each other. The twenty-second Prussian division, which formed the German right wing, was to have commenced the attack, but was anticipated by the French. The Bavarians, who as usual had to sustain the brunt of the action, occupied the centre; and the seventeenth division, forming the left wing, held the high road leading to Beaugency at Baulle, a little in rear of Messas, which with Cravant had not yet been taken. For a long time the battle lay with the artillery of the respective armies, and this arm of the French force did much to retrieve its character. About one o'clock the Germans endeavoured to storm several of the villages in their front, but found the work by no means easy; mobiles as well as the more seasoned troops contesting gallantly every inch of ground. Messas, Cravant, and Beaumont were, however, ultimately taken, though after severe loss. Batteries on the left bank of the Loire commenced bombarding Beaugency in the afternoon, and painful havoc was committed among the wounded soldiers, with whom many of the houses and public buildings were crowded.

Towards evening a storming party pushed forward, and after severe fighting managed to occupy the town and capture a battery of six guns and 1100 prisoners. The day thus closed favourably on the whole for the Germans, who had slowly gained ground. The resistance of the enemy, however, had been as obstinate as it was unexpected, and throughout the camp an unpleasant sense of disappointment prevailed. It was, therefore, resolved that something further should be done to augment the acquisitions of the day; and about midnight two Hanseatic regiments who were occupying Messas, finding that the village of Vernon, immediately in front of them, was still occupied by the French, determined on surprising it; and rushing suddenly in, captured 400 prisoners without firing a shot or losing a man. The Bavarians were equally successful in a night sortie from Beaumont upon the neighbouring village of La Mee, which they also took by surprise and without loss.

The scenes in Beaugency, immediately after its capture, were painfully memorable. The night was very starry, and the rattle of the musketry never quite ceased. There was also a good deal of desultory firing about the streets by Prussian patrols, who sometimes caught sight of the uniforms of French soldiers who had brought in wounded comrades, and were endeavouring to rejoin their corps. The whole town was a vast hospital, and there was only one doctor capable of performing amputations! In the theatre alone were upwards of 200 desperately wounded men, forming a scene which those who speak lightly of war, or who hold in their hands the power of making it, should have witnessed. For many hours there was no medical man in the place. The cold was intense, and many a man's life slipped away because there was no one sufficiently skilled to bind up his wounds. The dead lay thick among the dying; and as the former were dragged out their places were instantly filled. Miserable objects, with broken jaws or faces half shot away, wandered about, pointing to their wounds, and making piteous signals for water which they could not swallow. Officers and men, veterans and boys, all lay in one indistinguisable mass of misery, from which the cries of "Water! For the love of God, water! A doctor! A doctor! "never ceased to come. It was indeed a relief when the surgeon arrived from other similar scenes, and calling out loudly, "Voyons, où sont les gravement blessés? où sont les amputations?" set to work with determined but kindly energy. It will always be a satisfaction to the subscribers to the great English fund for the sick and wounded to know, that numbers of the French were spared unutterable torture, and owed their lives to the supply of English chloroform, blankets, bandages, and wine which was fortunately forthcoming on that fearful night, and called forth many blessings on our nation.

On the 9th cannonading began at daybreak, and both sides were soon engaged along their whole lines. The German position had been improved, the grand-duke's army occupying almost the exact front of the French on the previous day. The shape of the half horse-shoe was still preserved, but the French half was now occupied by the Germans, who were slowly pushing their enemy back in every direction, though the latter still pertinaciously strove to hold their ground, and replied furiously to the German batteries. The village of Villorceau was taken by the Bavarians early in the day, and Cernay about the same time by some regiments of the twenty-second division. Both villages were the scene of desperate engagements; and at the close of the day the dead Bavarians and French around Villorceau lay thicker than pheasants after the hottest *battue* in England. It was noticed towards the afternoon that General Chanzy was concentrating strongly on the German right: he was in reality falling back on the forest of Marchenoir. About three o'clock the order was given for a general advance; and as the artillery went to the front, and the sharpshooters began to feel the enemy along the whole line, the firing became terrific. The rifles seemed endeavouring to rival the mitrailleuse in loudness and rapidity, and the two, combined with the bursting of the shells and the fire of some heavy naval guns which the French had in position, made four distinct sounds, which between four and five o'clock blended in a roar fierce beyond description. At this time, immediately under the blaze of the setting sun, might be seen long lines of French troops apparently retreating rapidly northwards, and their opponents had clearly the best of the fight. The day before it might have been considered a drawn game, but it could not be doubted who were the victors this evening; and the shade of anxiety which clouded all countenances the previous night and this morning, at the unexpected check which the German armies received, had now disappeared. Still the French were spoken of in far higher terms than at any time since the commencement of the war, and general admiration was expressed for the commander who, out of a beaten and flying army, could have got together material to present so bold and determined a front. In the course of the day the grand-duke was strengthened by the arrival of the tenth corps from Orleans, and the army once more camped among the frozen bodies of friends and foes, the interment of which had been prevented by long-continued fighting on almost the same area of operations. The duke of Mecklenburg, in imitation of his illustrious master, telegraphed to his wife with reference to this engagement of the 9th: "The enemy attacked us violently, but was victoriously repulsed by the advance of the seventeenth and twenty-second divisions. God was with us. Our losses were smaller than yesterday."

As if by signal the firing ceased at dusk on the 9th, and it might have been inferred that both sides were utterly exhausted by the three days' carnage. Quiet was therefore expected on the 10th, and by a few hours of much needed repose the grand-duke of Mecklenburg hoped to prepare his troops for the decisive battle, which it was thought might be looked for on the 11th. There were two parties, however, to this arrangement, and the irrepressible French seemed little disposed to enjoy the luxury of rest. On the 10th they hastened to commence an attack upon the twenty-second division, which was holding Cernay and Cravant, and bombarded those villages furiously for two hours. The Germans quickly brought their artillery into position, and an engagement became general along a line extending from Villorceau to L'Hay, a little eastward of Cravant. The two armies were now in almost parallel lines, from northwest to south-east, the French right resting on Josnes and the left on Villermain and Montigny. The attack made by the French in the early part of the day ceased, after having been replied to for a while; and the German army was too much in need of rest to court a struggle which would in all probability have to be renewed on the morrow. Only one incident of special note occurred during the day. The Prussians had taken the village of Villejouan, but the French in considerable force attacked and retook it, making more than 100 prisoners. A couple of German regiments came to the rescue, and, after losing very severely, again took the village; but their comrades had been passed to the rear in time to prevent their liberation. The French still swarmed around the village, and the Germans found themselves without ammunition. A number of the enemy, however, were made prisoners, whose cartouche boxes were still well supplied; and the Germans, seizing their Chassepots, returned the French fire with their own weapons. While still hotly engaged, the ammunition waggon on its way to their relief was suddenly brought to a standstill by three of its horses being shot, on which a party ran out under a heavy fire, brought in the waggon in safety, and finally succeeded in repelling the French attempt to retake the village. As all the superior officers had been previously killed, the battalion was commanded by a captain, who for this brilliant feat of arms received thanks from the grand-duke in person, and a promise of the iron cross. Along the whole of the now very extended line, however, the chief characteristic of the day was caution. With this one exception there were no brilliant dashes, no furious fusillades of small arms, and after a time even the artillery fire languished; but the day being remarkably clear, the scene, as a military spectacle, was perfect.

The incessant fighting of the last four days over almost the same few acres, rendered it extremely difficult to administer the usual alleviations to the sufferings of the wounded and dying. The scenes occurring in Villorceau might have been witnessed in almost every one of the numerous hamlets in and about which the work of slaughter had been done. The chief house in the place was a Pension de Jeunes Filles, and it is doubtful if any of the horrors of war depicted by the truthful pens of Erckmann-Chatrian equal those which that house exhibited. Every room (and there were many), from the cellar to the roof, was crowded with dead and starving men, lying so thick that it was impossible to move among them. Some had been there since Tuesday evening, many of them since Wednesday. It was now Saturday, and not one drop of water, not one atom of food, had yet passed their lips. Many were desperately wounded, although still alive. Among them were several officers. The house contained no furniture; the windows had been broken; and all these days and nights of almost arctic cold had the men been lying on the bare floor with their wounds undressed. The stench was fearful. Every house in the village was in the same state. In some rooms were twelve or fourteen men—many of them corpses! That night a kind uhlan doctor volunteered to bind up a few of the worst wounds, to enable the men to be transported, but he had nothing with him but a pair of scissors and some pins. Fortunately the resources of the English society did not fail, and most of the sufferers were removed during the night of the 10th or on the following day to the Couvent des Ursulines at Beaugency. Many were too near their end to bear being moved, and an excellent French abbé—himself a martyr to consumption—spent the night with them in prayer, and in dispensing, with the assistance of an English Protestant soldier, the last sacraments of the church.

On December 11 the two armies remained inactive, and on the 12th it was found that the French had mysteriously disappeared. It was evident that the attack of the 10th was designed to mask a movement of retreat, for General Chanzy had retired in perfect order, leaving not the slightest trace behind. The army of the grandduke of Mecklenburg immediately set out by crossroads, in full pursuit. Chanzy, however, eluded his pursuers, and while they were thinking of driving him upon Tours, he moved to take up a position, stronger than that which he had abandoned, on the direct road to Paris, and where he could receive reinforcements from the west.

Running almost parallel with the Loire is the Loir, upon which are the towns of Châteaudun and Vendôme, about midway between which the river traverses a range of hills—winding round the spur of one, and passing through a narrow valley, scarcely abrupt enough to be called a gorge, in the hollow of which lies the little town of Fréteval. From the left bank of the Loir the extensive forest of Marchenoir runs back in the direction of Beaugency, for a distance of twenty miles or more; while on the right bank the forest of Fréteval extends westward to almost an equal distance. The French had taken up a position on the spur on the right bank of the river, with the wood of Fréteval on the left and in rear, the wood of Marchenoir on the right, and the river Loir, which there makes a bend, in front. To strengthen the immense natural facilities for defence offered by his new position, General Chanzy planted batteries wherever any advantage of ground was to be had, and filled the wooded slopes with sharpshooters. The village of Fréteval was taken by the Germans at the point of the bayonet after some fighting on the 14th, but could not be held on account of its exposed position; and on the morning of the 15th the state of affairs was critical for them, and singularly creditable to the tactics of General Chanzy. The duke of Mecklenburg had been sent to drive farther away from Paris the army of the Loire, and now by a skilful movement it had not only placed itself on the road to the capital, but had got the start and left its pursuers in the rear. It will be remembered that on the 9th of the previous month the small Bavarian force under the command of General von der Tann, after making a gallant stand at Coulmiers, was obliged to retreat before the French army of the Loire. Now, after the lapse of five weeks, after marching incessantly and fighting eight battles, the Germans found themselves in sight of the wood on the other side of which the battle of the 9th was fought, with the same army before them, and in a stronger position than it had ever previously occupied! No German army was now between General Chanzy's and that which was investing the capital, and only an inferior force was behind. As Chanzy was in communication with Le Mans and the west, he might at any time become strong enough to advance, and might then, indeed, be advancing upon Paris by Châteaudun. The position of the French at Fréteval was too strong to be stormed with the force at the grand-duke's disposal; but, fortunately for him, a direct attack became unnecessary.

Prince Frederick Charles had sent the ninth corps down the Loire (a different river, it must be remembered, from the Loir), which had appeared in the rear of Blois, on the east bank of the river, on the 12th; but as the bridge was broken the corps could not enter Blois until the tenth corps, marching to that city, held out a hand to it by throwing up hastily a bridge of boats, by which it passed over. The tenth corps was sent to Vendôme, and by threatening the right of General Chanzy, succeeded in compelling the French to abandon their strong position at Fréteval, higher up the river. The French were posted in front of Vendôme, which they held on the 14th and 15th; but having been beaten in an artillery duel, they, on the evening of the latter day, evacuated the town, which the Germans entered on the 16th. The German line was now formed, the duke of Mecklenburg occupying Cloyes and Morde, the tenth army corps being at Vendôme, and the ninth at Blois. On the 17th Chanzy had another rear-guard action with Von der Tann at Epuisay, where the roads from Vendôme and Morée to St. Calais meet, and then withdrew to Le Mans, which he entered on the 21st.

The French had throughout been fighting a losing battle, but their commander felt that anything was better than the continued retreats by which the soldiers had been disheartened. A peculiar character was given to these daily encounters by the stern determination with which the French renewed the struggle, day after day, refusing to consider themselves as beaten, even after a series of undeniable defeats. Again and again the Germans in the morning found themselves occupying the positions held by their opponents in the evening; but the French held others in the immediate neighbourhood—every village serving as a fortress. When dislodged from one, they took up their stand in another, and so on from sunrise to sunset. Each battle was a mere series of skirmishes, in which, though the Germans were victorious, both armies left a vast tract of country strewed with their dead, who lay unheeded day after day.

Had the movements of General Chanzy since the evacuation of Orleans been dictated by the most profound strategy, instead of by necessity or accident, they could not have been executed more skilfully, or in a manner more harassing to his foes. The vast quantity of stores which had been accumulated in Orleans were sent across to the left bank of the Loire, with a comparatively small force to protect them, and to deceive the Germans as to the position of the main body of the army, which waited on the right bank, and fell upon the flank of the inferior German force at Meung. Here, for four successive days, Chanzy fought so hard that the Germans gained very little ground, and had to send for heavy reinforcements; when they expected him to rest he attacked them; and when they expected him to attack, he was gone, no one at first knew whither. He thus forced the duke of Mecklenburg to change his front and follow the retreating enemy to the almost impregnable position he had taken up at Fréteval, and in the vast forests upon the right and left banks of the Loir; where there seemed to be nothing to prevent his keeping the Germans at bay, while the bulk of his army might by forced marches have moved in four days, by Châteaudun and Chartres, upon Versailles. As it was, the French held their opponents in front of Fréteval for four days, till their position being turned by the tenth and third army corps, directed by Prince Frederick Charles upon Vendôme, Chanzy was forced to choose between retreating upon Le Mans or upon Paris. The former town, with the great naval fortresses in its rear, offered important advantages to a retiring army wearied with constant fighting; and once reached, a junction with the French army of the west would be effected, and large reinforcements obtained. Chanzy, therefore, directed his march thither, making admirable use of many defensive positions, and on the 21st of December reached Le Mans, having saved his army and joined his supports. Although his troops had suffered terribly, he had lost only seven or eight guns.

These operations reflected high credit from every point of view on the French commander, and proved what a part, at least, of the army of the Loire could do in untoward circumstances. Prince Frederick Charles apparently calculated that Von der Tann and the grand duke of Mecklenburg were in sufficient force to destroy Chanzy; but he baffled these expectations, and his vigorous stand at Beaugency and Marchenoir not only weakened his foes, but by drawing a detachment against his right perhaps saved the rest of the army of the Loire. In falling back on Le Mans, and retreating upon his reinforcements when his wing was menaced, eye-witnesses told with what foresight he availed himself of natural obstacles to baffle and impede his pursuers.

Though the retreat had been trying in the extreme, and many hundreds had disbanded, the great majority of the French troops had contended not without honour against their veteran and well-seasoned foes. That they should have been fighting in the open field at all, considering the helpless condition of France after Sedan, is not a little surprising. But that they should have fought, within thirteen days, ten such battles as Beaune-la-Rollande, Patay, Bazoches, Chevilly, Chilleure, Orleans, and the four about Beaugency, on terms so nearly equal, sometimes superior, against the best German troops, effecting their retreat on almost all occasions without any disastrous loss or confusion—is an achievement which reflects the highest honour on the generals who organized and commanded the army of the Loire. The weather had throughout been dreadful. As described by General Chanzy himself at one place in his valuable and concise work, "La Deuxieme Armée de la Loire," "A torrent of rain since the morning had melted the snow and produced a thaw. The roads were everywhere exceedingly slippery, and the fields were too muddy for the passage of horses and carriages. In point of fatigue to men and cattle, this day (12th December) was one of the most distressing of the campaign. Nevertheless, the march was effected with a reasonable degree of regularity, and by night all the corps were established precisely in the positions assigned to them."

In fact, the sufferings of the troops can have been but little less severe while they lasted than what was endured in the retreat from Russia. To fight all through a short winter's day, the fingers almost too cold to handle a rifle, and to find oneself at nightfall on a bare frozen plain, or, even worse, a muddy field, with no supplies at hand, and often even no fuel, shivering the long night through in a furrow, or wandering about in a vain search for food—a night of this sort, followed by another day of hopeless fighting, was, during the first fortnight of this dreary December, the condition of the soldiers of the French army, in which the sufferings of the sound were only surpassed by those of the miserable wounded, who crawled unaided into the nearest ditch to die. Notwithstanding all these disadvantages, the methodical way in which the business of the headquarters was conducted during this time was most admirable. Night after night, when the troops were getting such fragments of rest as their condition made possible, was passed by Chanzy in writing long despatches to the provisional government, and dictating orders for the following day. Promotions were made, casualties filled up, and the business of the army generally carried on with the greatest detail and precision. To read General Chanzy's orders of the day at this time, one might suppose that they were issued by the commander of a confident, well-conditioned army, making war in ordinary fashion, in regular campaigning weather. The whole episode is a remarkable instance of the effect of character in war. With a less determined and obstinate commander, it is hardly doubtful that this army would have gone to pieces. As it was, Chanzy's determined attitude, and the spirit he succeeded in infusing into those around him, had the effect of keeping the Germans, who were also of course suffering very much from the weather, on very respectful terms. Altogether, the retreat from Orleans to the Loire during the first half of December was perhaps as creditable to French arms as anything that occurred during the whole war.

It must in justice be remarked, however, that if the French had thus fought with heroic steadiness and courage, the Germans also bore up against their great hardships and heavy losses with their wonted fortitude; not excepting the Bavarians, about whose demoralization idle tales had been in circulation ever since their first mishap at Coulmiers. These troops had, indeed, suffered so severely, that they were reduced to about one-fifth of their original force; yet to the last they exhibited the utmost gallantry. Each corps d'armée left Germany 30,000 strong; before any of the fighting round Beaugency, the first was in sixteen battles, without reinforcements, and General von der Tann could not number more than 5000 effective bayonets. Some reserves arrived from Germany on the 7th December, and the active part they took in the engagements of that and the two following days may be judged by the fact that the corps sustained an additional loss of 1200 men and forty-eight officers. On the 12th the corps was ordered back to Orleans to enjoy a season of well-merited repose, and a very complimentary letter was addressed by the king of Prussia to General von der Tann.

Not deeming it prudent to pursue their enemy further for the present, the armies of Prince Frederick Charles and the duke of Mecklenburg remained in the country between Orleans, Vendôme, and Blois; and with the exception of an expedition to Tours by Voigts-Ehetz and part of the tenth corps, no further encounter took place between the combatants until the winter campaign in January, the events of which will be related in a future chapter. When the Germans reached Blois and Vendôme they were at less than two day's march from Tours, on the two railways converging on that town, the one from Orleans, and the other from Châteaudun. After the government delegation left for Bordeaux, General Sol, who had the command of the Tours military division, seeing himself exposed to attack from these two lines, and also from Vierzon, immediately retreated. M. Gambetta, deeming the evacuation of Tours precipitate, removed him from active service, and appointed

General Pisani in his place. The force of Voigts-Rhetz having been signalled in the immediate neighbourhood, General Chanzy sent a despatch to Pisani ordering him, with the 6000 troops under his command, to harass the enemy as much as possible, but by no means to risk a defeat. Accordingly, on December 20, he, with his little army, attacked the Prussians at Monnaie, and after inflicting on them no little damage and taking sixty prisoners, retreated with considerable loss. Pisani, watching the course of events, lingered for some time about the vicinity of Tours, before which the Prussians appeared the next morning. Thinking that, as the garrison had left, the town would make no resistance, they sent forward a squadron of cavalry to take possession. The towns-people, however, had made up their minds to attempt a defence, and when the hostile cuirassiers came within easy range, the Tours national guards fired on them, and forced them to retreat at full gallop. The Prussians then determined to try the effect of a bombardment, unlimbered a battery of artillery on the edge of the lofty plateau rising at only a few hundred yards to the north, and began shelling the town. As Tours was perfectly open and totally unprovided with the means of defence, this mode of attack soon began to tell. Several were killed by the shells, and amongst them M. Beurtheret, the editor of the *Union Liberale*. Fearing that the town might be totally destroyed, M. Eugène Gouiz, the mayor, accompanied by his adjuncts and an interpreter, went to the Prussian commander with a flag of truce, and asked for a cessation of the bombardment, which was at once and unconditionally accorded. The Prussians did not occupy the town, but, probably supposing that considerable French forces were in the neighbourhood, retired soon afterwards to Blois. Tours was thus again left in peace, and was re-occupied by General Pisani and his troops as soon as the enemy disappeared.

Dropping for the present the subject of the operations of the armies on the several zones around Paris, we will glance briefly at the principal towns and fortresses captured by the Germans during December, taking them in chronological order. After the first battle of Amiens, which took place on the 26th and 27th November, and which resulted in the destruction of what was then called the French army of the north, some remnants of that force were said to have fled in the direction of Caen. General von Göben, with the first corps, was despatched to pursue these, with instructions also to make a reconnaissance upon the Rouen road, but not to attack the enemy there if in positions behind earthworks. At a meeting of the principal inhabitants and the military and civil authorities, it was determined not to defend Rouen, as in consequence of the incomplete state of the lines of defence any attempt at resistance would be useless. But changing their minds, an address was issued by the municipal council, intimating that the enemy was approaching nearer and nearer, that the military were concentrating for defence, and exciting the citizens to make an effort equal to the sacrifices the country required of them. The available forces of the town were accordingly sent to Buchy to arrest the course of the enemy, and the result' closely resembled the memorable battle of Bull's Run.

Buchy is a village, very insignificant in itself, but strategically of no small importance, as there the road and railway from Amiens to Rouen bifurcates, the northern branch going on to Clères and St. Victor (on the way from Rouen to Dieppe), thus forming the apex of a triangle, of which the lines to Rouen and to Clères form the sides, and the railway from Rouen to the Clères station of the Dieppe Railway, the base. The French force consisted of undisciplined mobiles and mobilized national guards, from several departments, of a corps of franc-tireurs, a provisional regiment of the line (*regiment de marche*), and a small detachment of cavalry. The Prussians advanced on Buchy from St. Saens, and about five o'clock on the morning of 3rd December sent some shells into the French positions. The first discharge dismounted one of the *three* guns with which the French attempted to open fire against a Prussian battery of from thirty to forty. The mobiles, who were drawn up to protect them, no sooner heard a shell bursting than they fled across country, and paused not until they reached Rouen in the evening. There they scattered all over the place, filled every *café* and wine shop, drank very freely, confessed that they had retired, but boasted loudly of what they would have done in other circumstances, and gave exaggerated accounts of the enemy's numbers. A panic spread throughout the city. The treasure and notes in the Bank of France and in the receveur-général's hands were embarked on board the *Protectrice*, a powerful ironclad floating battery, supposed to have been moved to Rouen for the defence of the city; but she now got up steam and was soon out of sight. The various French merchantmen in the river also dropped down with the tide. Early next morning, which was very cold, the *rappel* was sounded for the muster of the national guard, who turned out with readiness. They were kept waiting for nearly six hours in the cold, and were then marched to the railway station for conveyance to Clères. Ultimately, however, the authorities again changed their minds, and the guards remained, to be disarmed and disbanded by the Prussians. A number of siege guns, which had been landed on the quay only two days before, were spiked and thrown into the river. The town, meanwhile, was seemingly emptied of its male population, and the sad, anxious faces of the women expressed the fears by which they were agitated.

In the meantime, the strange manner in which the French troops, evidently strong in numbers, had abandoned position after position from Gaille-fontaine along the road to Rouen, induced General von Göben to make one of those rapid advances which had so often led to triumph. The forces under his command received with their usual enthusiasm the order to advance upon the road to Rouen; and notwithstanding the severe marching and fighting of the last few days, all strode along seemingly as fresh as when they left the banks of the Rhine. They anticipated a battle before Rouen; believing that the French were strong in numbers, well armed, and provided with artillery, with the advantage of occupying a fortified position.

A halt was made at Buchy, where the precipitate retreat of the French took place to which we have already alluded. Little knowing the terror they had caused, the Prussians concluded the force they had dispersed was but the outpost of a more formidable body. But on their arrival at Quincampoix, on the morning of December 5, the advanced guard brought in an elderly gentleman, taken prisoner as he drove from Rouen in his gig, and who turned out to be the mayor of Quincampoix. From him the Prussians learned that 35,000 troops had camped at Quincampoix the previous night, but had only remained for an hour, and then continued their retreat upon Rouen, which intended to make no resistance. The intelligence was so astounding, that it was at first believed to be a ruse to induce the somewhat wearied Germans to advance upon a strong position defended by fresh troops. But after a short consultation with Colonel von Witzendorff, the chief of his staff, and Major Bomki, General von Göben ordered the troops to advance. Just at this moment the omnibus from Rouen arrived, with intelligence to the general which seemed almost incredible. In the morning the French troops had all retreated upon Havre. The town had subscribed 10,000,000 francs as a contribution, which General von Göben was invited to come and take. Everything was now boot and saddle; the fortieth and seventieth regiments, forming the thirty-first brigade, with the ninth hussars and two batteries of artillery, pushed along the road to Isneauville, and the staff waited in Quincampoix, to let the infantry advance.

Arrived at Isneauville, the Germans came upon the first lines of the French works. In the middle of the road lay two heavy ship guns, 24-pounders, which it was clear that the French had not had time to put into position. Everything betokened a hasty retreat. The batteries were unfinished; while, on either side of the road, the Prussian troops actually marched among the still burning camp-fires of their opponents. The question naturally arose, what had the French general at Rouen been doing for the last two months? He had more than ample time, money, and material, to say nothing of his close proximity to Havre, Dieppe, and Boulogne, to establish a line of defence before the city that might have very greatly altered the face of matters. He had done nothing but abandon every position which, with immense labour, his troops had constructed between Isneauville and Gaillefontaine, where every village might have been made a fortress; all the more easily because his army, instead of being made up entirely of mobiles, included several line regiments, and the fifth hussars, with thirty-five guns.

Rouen lies in a basin, surrounded by high hills, from which Von Göben's army quickly had a view of the famous city. A patrol of hussars was sent forward to arrange for the entry of the troops; but in the meantime a magistrate appeared, a thin old man, with the ribbon of the Legion of Honour on his coat, asking the general to send some troops into the town as quickly as possible? The square of the Hôtel de Ville was in the hands of the *gamins*, who, armed with the weapons thrown away by the national guard, were trying their best to shoot the mayor. In that drunken, reckless style in which a French mob delights, they were firing upon the Hôtel de Ville, the façade of which was pitted with bullets, the windows broken, and the members of the commune, huddled together in a back room, in despair. Fortunately for the mayor and the town, the German troops were soon upon the spot, when one battalion of the fortieth, with two guns, took up its position in the Place Cauchoise; while the other two battalions, with the seventieth regiment, filed in different directions through the town. The general then rode to the Place de l'Hôtel de Ville, where, beside the statue of Napoleon I., he saw the sixteenth division, with bands playing and colours flying, march past.

Great indignation was expressed in other parts of France at the capitulation of Rouen without resistance; but it was only one of a large number of instances in the course of the war, in which every one cried "forward" to his neighbour without moving a foot in advance himself. Nancy and Rheims were pronounced cowards because they offered no resistance to the enemy, having indeed neither arms nor men. Châteaudun was, in fact, the single open town which defended itself; for with this exception every other in France, so defiant when the enemy was distant, learned prudence at its near approach.

A "mild invasion" is almost a contradiction in terms; yet if ever a city was mildly invaded it was Rouen. Not one shop was closed, nor, as far as an ordinary observer could judge, was the petty commerce of the place interfered with. But capital was too sensitive not to take the alarm. Nearly all the great factories and printworks, on whose operations Rouen depended, were closed, and the distress of the workpeople was soon obviously very great. Some ingenious speculators in the locality had formed a special insurance company for guaranteeing subscribers against the various evils of war; but among these evils the occupation of Rouen by the enemy had not been foreseen, and the company, too severely tested at the very outset of its enterprise, collapsed.

In Rouen the German army of the north found many of its wants abundantly met. Among other things obtained was a supply of fresh horses, 40,000 pairs of boots, 10,000 blankets, 2000 shirts, 20,000 pairs of socks, and 100,000 cigars, and the city could, if needful, have furnished a considerable amount of specie. Here the army was in secure and comfortable winter quarters, in direct communication with the Crown Prince of Saxony and the army of Paris; and from this point, unless the communication by way of Amiens should be disturbed, a great military movement might be organized. The cost of all these advantages to the army of the north was eleven men killed and fifty wounded, without the loss of a single officer. The French had lost five officers killed and eighteen wounded, forty-five rank and file killed, 100 wounded, 600 prisoners, and twenty-seven pieces of heavy marine artillery, together with the wealthiest city of Western France.

Apparently from a desire to reach the sea, and thus be able to say that the Prussians had crossed France from the Rhine to the British Channel, a detachment of Manteuffel's army visited Dieppe from Amiens. The much dreaded occupation had been for weeks past the nightmare of the worthy Dieppois, who had spent much time in making defensive preparations. In spite, however, of wooden barricades and innumerable drillings of the national guards, when the inhabitants heard of the near approach of the enemy, the guns were spiked, the arms and ammunition were shipped to Havre, the brave nationales and *douaniers* doffed their uniforms, and all prepared to receive the invader as amicably and cordially as dignity would permit. On the morning of December 9 the usual advanced guard of uhlans gave the customary warning of a large body of troops being behind them, who would require unlimited food, board, and lodging. Accordingly, a few hours afterwards, in marched the main body, with bands playing and colours flying, as if they were returning from a victory into one of their own towns. Many of the houses had been dressed out with flags of various nationalities, the English strongly predominating; hung out to show that the occupants were not French, and therefore not liable to the obligation of billeting the enemy. Every house, however, on which the lot fell had to receive its soldier guests; and the English residences were apparently at a premium—perhaps a delicate though unwelcome compliment to proverbial British hospitality. The troops behaved with great moderation, and all passed off quietly. As no resistance was offered, the Prussians levied no contribution. There were even less than the usual requisitions, though 25,000 cigars were demanded at the manufactory, and the authorities had to supply large quantities of provisions, wine, and brandy. Shortly after their entry into the town the uhlans rode to the Plage, where many of them for the first time saw with admiration the broad expanse of the ocean, and gave three hurrahs for the king and Vaterland. Orders were issued towards nightfall that no lights should be exhibited at the entrance of the port. Frenchmen were stationed at the pierhead to warn off every vessel that should attempt to force an entrance, under the penalty of being fired upon by the enemy. This measure seemed hard; but a man-of-war had been seen cruising in the offing in the latter part of the afternoon, and measures had to be adopted to thwart a night attack from the seaboard, should such be attempted. The departure of the troops, which took place the day after their arrival, was regretted by those of the inhabitants who were engaged in commerce, and who had realized no small harvest. As the Prussians seemed to intend making Dieppe a provision depôt for themselves, both this port, and Fécamp and Havre, were shortly afterwards declared by the French government in a state of blockade, and men-of-war were stationed near to enforce its observance.

On December 19 Dieppe was occupied a second time by the Prussians, and as the little army quartered there were in want of boots and horses, all residents and visitors, not being foreigners, were called upon to send their horses to the marketplace, where a Prussian officer selected a certain number, and, according to the custom in such cases, bought them at his own valuation, paying for them in paper redeemable at the end of the war. As nearly all the good horses at Dieppe belonged to Englishmen, the Prussians, out of many hundreds brought forward, found very few worth taking—altogether, not more than a dozen. In the matter of boots they were more successful; the dealers in these articles having been required to send to an appointed place all the ready made goods they had on hand, on assurance that whatever was taken from them would be paid for at its full value.

Of course, too, there was a little money transaction. No contribution was levied. But Dieppe possessed a tobacco manufactory, which, like all such establishments in France, belonged to the state; and General von Göben explained to the municipality that, as state property, the tobacco manufactory passed from the hands of the French to those of the Prussian government. As the representative of that government he could not work the manufactory, neither could he carry it away with him, and he had no wish to burn it. He therefore proposed to sell it, and (making a good guess) fixed the value at the round sum of 100,000 francs. The municipality protested against the exorbitancy of the demand, which was ultimately reduced to 75,000 francs. Part of the money was paid down at once, and the rest in a day or two after.

On the 9th of December, the same day on which Dieppe was occupied the first time by the Prussians, a somewhat compensating advantage was achieved by a band of active and daring Lille mobiles, who surprised the Prussian garrison at Ham, the fortress where Napoleon III. was once imprisoned. At six o'clock in the evening the detachment of French arriving before the town, which is protected by a strong castle, first fell on the sentries, and then sounded the Prussian signal for a general march. About 200 of the garrison, mostly belonging to the field railway detachment, hastily collected, and were caught as in a trap. Others fled to the fort, pursued by the French with levelled bayonets. At midnight a *parlementaire*, accompanied by a lieutenant, appeared before the fort; but they were fired upon, when the flag-bearer was killed and the lieutenant wounded. At one o'clock in the morning the French captain, accompanied by a Prussian officer who had been made prisoner, presented himself as a *parlementaire*, when in an interview with the commandant it was agreed that the place should be surrendered at six o'clock, and that officers who were prisoners on either side should be exchanged. At the appointed hour the French entered the fortress and found the Prussians, seventy-six in number, drawn up in line and disarmed.

Of all the towns besieged by the Prussians during the war, none held out more gallantly than Vauban's virgin fortress of Phalsbourg, a description of which is given in Chapter X.

Phalsbourg was closely invested on the 9th of August, and on the evening of the 10th it was bombarded for an hour and a half by two batteries, under the command of General Gersdorff, with four and six pounder shell guns. In that brief space 3000 projectiles are computed to have been thrown into the fortress; but only one house was seriously injured. On the 14th, at seven in the morning, the bombardment was renewed, and raged until four in the afternoon, along the side of Phalsbourg which runs parallel with the Port de France. In the conflagration which it occasioned, few of the houses of the town escaped without more or less injury, while forty, including the church, were burnt. Towards the close of the day a summons to surrender was sent to the governor, General Talhouet, who returned a firm refusal. The siege was soon after changed into a blockade. The beleaguering troops were relieved from time to time on their march westward, no week passing without *parlementaires* knocking at the gates. The garrison consisted of about 1000 regular troops and 800 gardes mobiles. The investing force varied; at the close it numbered 5000 infantry, with artillery, and a squadron of Bavarian cavalry. On November 24 there was another smart bombardment, but famine at the last compelled the garrison to open the gates. The fortress was not well provisioned. Very early in October they began to eat horse flesh. Salt, tobacco, coffee, and sugar rapidly failed, and latterly wine. Towards the close, every other day, the rations of the garrison consisted of a water soup, whose only nutritive properties were derived from the fat of cattle and horses. The population of Phalsbourg is set down in gazetteers at 4000, but nearly half that number had quitted the town, or been turned out of it at the commencement of the siege. Those who remained suffered the same privations as the garrison, and to scarcity of food was added want of water, a Prussian spy having cut the conduit which supplied it. After the rout of Woerth the wreck of MacMahon's army was rallied upon Phalsbourg, when 35,000 kilogrammes of its provisions were drawn upon, and there was not sufficient time to revictual. The earlier sorties of the garrison, for collecting supplies, were often successful; but in the later the villages were found cleared bare by the besiegers.

An enormous quantity of powder had been stored at Phalsbourg, at the beginning of the war, for the use of the army of the Rhine. For some days previous to the surrender volumes of smoke ascending from the place told that these stores were being gradually burnt, that they might not fall into the hands of the enemy. Before the gates were thrown open to the besiegers, 12,000 rifles, with 9,600,000 rounds of cartridge, were destroyed, and 12,000,000 lbs. of powder were flung into the moat, all the cannon spiked, and their wheels and carriages broken. On December 12, after sustaining a siege of five months, the fortress capitulated unconditionally; and fifty-two officers, 1839 men, and sixty-five guns, fell into the hands of the captors.

The only fortress in German Lorraine which now remained in French hands was Bitsche. This place also had been besieged since August; but its natural position was so strong that it was unlikely to yield except to famine, and there had for some time been a tacit understanding on both sides to suspend firing, and thus avoid useless bloodshed.

On the 14th December Montmèdy capitulated, yielding to the Germans an additional sixty-five guns and 3000 prisoners. The fortress had been bombarded by about seventy heavy guns, throwing balls of the average weight of 150 lbs., which did frightful execution. The upper town was almost destroyed, while the lower suffered but little. The iron roof of the powder magazine had been struck, and the commandant, seeing that the fortress and both the towns were likely to be blown up, called a council of war, which unanimously decided on capitulation. Thirty or forty persons were killed during the siege, and sixty wounded. The Germans lost only a few, as their guns were beyond the range of those in the fortress. The surrender released nearly 400 German soldiers, principally landwehr, who had been imprisoned here for several months. Negotiations for an exchange failed on account of the commandant demanding two Frenchmen for one German, a demand which provoked the retort that one German soldier was worth much more than two Frenchmen.

Montmèdy did not possess much strategic importance for the Germans, as it was too remote from the real scene of operations; but it had long been a favourite rendezvous for the franc-tireurs of the Ardennes, and its possession was necessary to prevent the communications of detachments operating along the Belgian frontier against Mézières, Longwy, &c., with Metz and Thionville, being exposed to the chances of a guerilla war.

We have spoken of Châteaudun as affording the only instance of an open town which in the whole course of the war made a vigorous stand against the enemy. A visit to that and the neighbouring town of Chartres afforded reflection for the moralist, and ample explanation of the non-resistance of open towns. Châteaudun, with the hand of war resting heavily upon it, was continually experiencing a change of garrison, and every change brought a pang of some sort. One day came the Germans, and left after staying a week; then came the French, taking what the Germans had left, scolding the inhabitants for giving these Germans anything, and going; back came the Germans the same evening, squeezed the sponge for the last drop, lived upon the inhabitants until it was a mystery how anybody in the wretched place lived at all, only to make way once more for the French, and so on. For weeks after the memorable fight, for which Châteaudun was voted to have "deserved well of its country," there might have been seen groups of men and women gloomily huddled together among the ruins of their burnt houses, the picture of misery and woe, and who seemed to pass their existence in brooding over their misfortunes, or in watching the ingress and egress of the various troops. It was a pleasing contrast to leave such a scene, and arrive in the sleek, well-preserved town where the mayor had made friends with the enemy the moment he presented himself at his gates, so that Chartres scarcely suffered perceptibly from the war. The Châteaudun church was riddled with shot and shell, and showed great gaps in its walls and roof. The gigantic Chartres cathedral, towering above every surrounding object, and visible for leagues from every quarter of the landscape, stood intact. The narrow winding streets of the picturesque and historic old town were always alive and animated; all the shops open and well stocked, and even the market-place well supplied with provisions. No sign of plunder or pillage here; people received payment for everything, and in consequence of their good behaviour escaped heavy requisitions. Certainly, alack of patriotism was attended with great advantages both to conquerors and conquered; and it was astonishing how well all seemed to get on together, and how few bitter recollections the Germans left behind them in places where from the beginning they had been humbly received and systematically well treated.

We have pointed out in a previous chapter that the desperate attempt of D'Aurelles on December 1 to push his army towards Paris, was part of a scheme arranged with General Trochu to break up the besieging forces. The defeat of the army of the Loire, therefore, and the retirement of Ducrot from across the Marne, marked the failure of the first combined attempt on a great scale to raise the siege of Paris. The Germans were on all points triumphant; and yet their able and experienced chiefs did not share in the exultation of the camp. No one knew better than the great strategist who directed the movements of the invading host, how perilous is a miscalculation in war, how insecure the German position had been made, and how success was even yet possible, if not prevented by mighty exertions. Victorious, too, as the Germans had been, their losses round Paris, and especially in the protracted struggle with Chanzy's army, had been severe; and as Paris still held out resolutely, and the winter was extremely rigorous, it was obvious that new and immense demands on the German resources were required. It had become necessary to strengthen considerably the barrier to the armies intended to relieve the capital, to fill up the gaps caused by the prolonged contest, and to increase the efficiency of the means employed to reduce the besieged city. For this purpose reinforcements, numbering not less than 200,000 men, were in the course of December marched into France. The new levy consisted partly of a portion of the supplementary (*ersatz*) reserve; men who had been passed over year by year, from the practice in Prussia of absorbing into the line less than one-half of the young men qualified and legally bound to serve. Citizens of all classes and occupations, who never dreamed of being again called upon for military service, received a peremptory summons to start, after a short drill, for the seat of war. There was, however, no grumbling, for the persistency with which it was believed the French had for many years contemplated the invasion of Germany, and the recklessness with which they entered upon it at what appeared to them a favourable moment, created and sustained a degree of indignation which nothing hitherto had been able to allay. This feeling was not confined to the towns and centres of culture, but penetrated even to the remotest villages, and promised a supply of willing and ardent reserves quite as long as the patriotic zeal of the French was likely to fill the ranks of M. Gambetta. The new comers occupied the captured towns and the extensive line of communication, while the more seasoned troops whom they relieved were sent to the front. With them the shrunken battalions of Prince Frederick Charles and the grand-duke of Mecklenburg were replenished, the armies of Manteuffel in the north, and Werder in the east, were augmented, and the sphere of their operations extended; the hold on the communications was tightened, the siege of new fortresses undertaken, whilst at Paris every nerve was strained to accelerate the attack, and lessen the difficulties of a mere investment.

Two decrees of special importance were issued by the French during the month, the first referring to the numerous desertions from the army, which were now of daily occurrence. It was notorious that by far the greater part of the prisoners "captured" in the fighting at and around Orleans, were men who delivered themselves up to the enemy, preferring a temporary sojourn in Germany to the chances of Prussian steel or bullets. The ill-success of the armies, also, was largely ascribed to panics raised by troops who, terrified at the approach of danger, fled from the enemy. To prevent these scandals, M. Gambetta decreed that to all the armies of the republic should be attached a regiment of mounted *gendarmes*, the officer in command of which was to preside over a permanent court-martial, to be established in the rear of each army, with the following instructions:—"To follow the army, and to dispose his men in such a manner as to watch and close all the issues from it. To arrest fugitives, and hand them over to a troop in due formation. They will regard as fugitives every soldier, every officer, or group of soldiers, found retreating without a written order, or without being placed under the command of a superior officer. Every soldier, not being wounded, found in the rear of the army without arms or equipment, will immediately be brought before the court-martial. Any one who shall raise a cry of '*Sauve qui peut*,' or of 'We are pursued,' will be taken before the court-martial. Exercise the greatest rigour and the greatest vigilance in the performance of these duties"

On the 25th of December a far more unpopular, and in every way unjustifiable, decree was issued, abolishing the councils general of departments, as well as the councils of arrondissements; and it proved that the "government of the three lawyers," as it was frequently called, or to speak more correctly, the Gambetta dictatorship, was every whit as absolute, and when occasion arose much more tyrannical, than was ever that of the much-reviled "man of Sedan." The act can only be compared to a ministerial warrant of the Home office in this country, which should abolish all boards of magistrates and municipal councils, and hand over the county property and the control of county rates to a band of hungry adventurers and government adherents. The councils general sat regularly in the month of August, and for many years their meetings had been looked forward to with strong interest, as presenting one of the few opportunities that remained for the expression of public opinion. They had the almost absolute control of financial contributions, expenditure, receipts, and local taxes; they created resources, and contracted loans.

Such a provincial representation was peculiarly dear to the nation, and there were not wanting loud and vigorous protests against the decree. The patriotic portion ol the country, however, saw that the time would be equally ill-chosen on their part for domestic discords; and after the first feeling of indignation the decree was admitted, and agitation left over for the future. It may be here remarked that not long after the conclusion of peace it was deemed advisable to rescind the decree of M. Gambetta and his co-delegates, and the councils general were re-established.

As in November, when Russia repudiated the treaty of 1855, so in December another danger burst upon Europe, in consequence of Count von Bismarck repudiating the treaty of 1867 for maintaining the neutrality of Luxemburg, on the alleged ground that she had not preserved her neutrality during the war. In his note to the government of the grand-duchy he declared, that "the hostile sentiments of the population have manifested themselves in the maltreatment of German officials in the duchy; but Prussia does not hold the government of Luxemburg responsible for the bad conduct of individuals, although more might have been done to repress it. The provisioning of Thionville, however, by trains run from Luxemburg, was a flagrant breach of the laws of neutrality, which could not have taken place without the connivance of the officials. The Prussian government at the time lodged a complaint with the government of the grand-duchy, and pointed out the consequences to which proceedings of the kind must inevitably lead. The warning was disregarded. After the fall of Metz numbers of French officers and soldiers, escaping from the captured fortress, passed through the territory of Luxemburg to evade the German troops, and to rejoin the French army of the north. In the city of Luxemburg itself the resident French vice-consul had an office at the railway station, designed to assist the French fugitives in reaching their own country; and at least 2000 soldiers had in this manner reinforced the French army. The government of Luxemburg did nothing to prevent these acts; and the fact undoubtedly constitutes a gross violation of neutrality. The conditions upon which Prussia had based her neutrality have, therefore, ceased to exist; and, consequently, Prussia declares that on her part she no longer considers herself, in the conduct of her military operations, bound by any regard for the neutrality of Luxemburg, and reserves to herself the right of claiming compensation from the grand-ducal government for the German losses arising through the non-observance of neutrality, and of taking the necessary steps to secure herself against the repetition of similar proceedings."

The note was answered by M. Servais, minister of State and president of the Luxemburg government, in a long and elaborate document, disputing the truth of some of the Prussian chancellor's statements, and diminishing the significance of others. The Luxemburg government had evidently not been sufficiently vigilant in preventing breaches of neutrality; but it was equally clear that Count von Bismarck had been to some extent misled by the exaggerations of persons who, as M. Servais remarked, "never tired of lightly reporting things calculated to endanger and cast suspicion on the grand-duchy, while keeping themselves out of all responsibility." Fearing absorption into Germany by the Prussian chancellor, the inhabitants hastened to testify their attachment to their legitimate rulers by numerous addresses; but the matter was at length amicably settled by a special Prussian officer being sent to Luxemburg to confer with the grand-ducal government with a view to the prevention of any similar ground of complaint.

It was impossible that, when our nearest neighbours were fighting, we should not in a vast variety of ways be inconvenienced, and run the risk of being involved in the broil—an illustration of which occurred on the 21st December. Six English colliers, returning from

Rouen, were stopped at Duclair, twelve miles lower down the Seine; some shots were fired, and the vessels themselves were sunk to bar the navigation. The incident was readily seized on by that numerous section of Englishmen who, without any real intention of forcing the country into a war with Germany, caught at an opportunity of showing sympathy with France by a paper quarrel with Count von Bismarck.

The facts were that six small sailing colliers had been discharging coals at Rouen, by permission of the Prussian authorities; and after unloading had received, through the British consul there, a permit to return to England. Following the usual course, they dropped down the river to a village called Duclair, about twenty-eight miles below Rouen, where ballast is taken in for the homeward run. When the crews had finished ballasting, the ships were seized by the Prussians, towed into position across the fair-way channel, scuttled, and sunk. The British consul, informed of what was going on, started from Rouen by land, reached Duclair at the moment the soldiers were about to sink the vessels, and entered a vigorous protest, of course without effect. He then undertook the negotiations for the bonds of indemnity, which the officer in command of the Prussians was willing enough to furnish.

In considering the question involved in this attack upon neutral property, it must be borne in mind that it occurred in time of war, and in waters which, after the expulsion of the French, were subject to the German military authorities. Trading vessels have not, like men-of-war, the exceptional property of being extra-territorial; and there is, therefore, a great difference between the confiscation of an English man-of-war and that of an English collier. In this case the act was a kind of military necessity. French men-of-war had frequently steamed up the river, landed troops, and caused loss to the German forces by firing upon them. Hence the determination of the Prussians to have the Seine blocked up; and as this could not immediately be done by means of batteries or torpedoes, they seized and sunk, off Duclair, eleven vessels, of which six were English.

Lord Granville, on hearing of the seizure, sent a remonstrance to the Prussian authorities, and Count von Bismarck at once wrote as follows to the representative of Germany in London:—

"VERSAILLES, *Jan.* 8, 1871.

"The report of the commander of that part of our army by which the English collier-ships were sunk in the Seine has not yet arrived; but as far as our intelligence goes, the general outline of the facts is known.

"You are authorized , in consequence, to say to Lord Granville, that we sincerely regret that our troops, in order to avert immediate danger, were obliged to seize ships which belonged to British subjects.

"We admit their claim to indemnification, and shall pay to the owners the value of the ships, according to equitable estimation, without keeping them waiting for the decision of the question who is finally to indemnify them. Should it be proved that excesses have been committed which were not justified by the necessity of defence, we should regret it still more, and call the guilty persons to account."

The reply of the Prussian chancellor was considered satisfactory, and the fullest compensation was shortly after made to the owners and crews of the vessels.

CHAPTER XXVI.

The German Plan of Campaign in the North of France—Alarm in the town of Havre—Singular Treatment of a Government Order—Appointment of General Faidherbe to the Command of the French Army of the North—The Germans lose an Opportunity—Advance of Faidherbe on Amiens—Von Göben despatched to accept the Challenge—The Positions of the respective Armies—Battle of Pont Noyelles—The Struggle around Querrieux—Gallant Conduct of the French—Ingenious Device of General Faidherbe to secure an Unmolested Retreat—By an Incautious Advance Von Göben provokes another Attack from the French—The Battle of Bapaume—Positions of the Armies—Excellence of the French Artillery—The Prussians forced back into Bapaume—Critical Position of Von Göben's Troops—General Faidherbe claims the Victory, but omits to follow up the Advantages—Incident of the Pursuit—Von Göben retires from Bapaume—Fall of Péronne—Sharp Engagement near Havre—Siege and Capitulation of Mézières—France in very Serious Circumstances—M. Gambetta conceives a last desperate Effort against the Invader—Prompt Consent of General Faidherbe for the Army of the North to do its Share—The French descend in force upon St. Quentin—Characteristics of Von Göben—The Battle of St. Quentin—Position of the Town and of the respective Combatants—Fatal Separation of the French Army—Fearful Charge of Prussian Cavalry—The French obliged to give way, and finally retreat in disorder—Imposing Advance of the German Army—Storming of St. Quentin—An Opportune Railway Trip—The Siege and Fall of the Fortress of Longwy.

THE plan of campaign adopted by the Germans in the north, after the capture of Amiens on November 27, was considered as pointing to immediate operations against Havre. The greatest excitement, therefore, prevailed there on news being brought that Rouen had been occupied; and the excitement was by no means allayed by the further intelligence that on the same day the Prussians had succeeded in recapturing Orleans. The commandant-in-chief of Havre and the mayor at once issued the following proclamation to the inhabitants:—"By a rapid march the enemy has arrived at the gates of Rouen. Havre, more menaced than ever, but long prepared, is determined to offer the most energetic defence. At the approach of danger we make a new appeal to the patriotism of the population. No sacrifice will be too great to repulse the enemy, and preserve our rich and valiant city from pillage and the inroads of the foreigner. Supported by its energetic cooperation, we answer for the safety of Havre." The inhabitants of the neighbouring communes were invited to take refuge within the town, large stores of cattle and fodder were collected, and such things as could not be received, but which might have been serviceable to the enemy, were destroyed. The situation of Havre was especially favourable for defence. There was no lack of men, arms, and ammunition. The fortified works around the town were formidable; and as it could not be entirely surrounded by the Germans, it could evidently stand a very protracted siege. General Briand, with the forces which had evacuated Rouen, shortly came in, together with a large number of franc-tireurs and moblots. Almost simultaneously came an order from the Tours government for 4000 of the troops, and a proper complement of guns, to be embarked for Cherbourg. This created a furious scene of riot and disorder. Vast crowds paraded the town, protesting against the order, which the authorities were about to carry into effect. The guns had been shipped, but the mob proceeded to the harbour and compelled the commander of the transport vessel to unship them. Finding that no other course would appease the populace, both the civil and military authorities resolved to disobey M. Gambetta's order, and issued all over the town a proclamation to the effect, that in their opinion he was not in so good a position as themselves to judge of the local necessities of the defence. "In presence, therefore, of circumstances the gravity of which hourly increases, and the legitimate emotion of the population, the superior commandant and the sub-prefect have replied to the government that the departure of troops from Havre was inexpedient just now." The proclamation afforded a curious illustration of the state of discipline prevailing in the country at this time. There have been instances of disobedience of orders in all countries; but the conduct of the authorities of an unruly town in informing the mob, under whose pressure they acted, that they had disobeyed because they knew better, was unprecedented even in the history of France.

After the battle of Villers-Bretonneux and the capture of Amiens, the remnants of the French army of the north fell back behind the formidable network of fortresses by which France is defended on her Flemish frontier.

The three northernmost departments, from the Somme to the Belgian frontier, hold about twenty-fortresses of various sizes, which, though wholly useless nowadays against a large invasion from Belgium, formed a most welcome and almost unattackable basis of operations in this case. When Vauban planned them nearly 200 years before, he could not have foreseen that they would serve as a great entrenched camp, a sort of multiplied quadrilateral, to a French army against an enemy advancing from the heart of France! But so it was; and small as this piece of territory is, it was for the nonce impregnable, as well as important on account of its manufacturing resources, and its dense, hardy, and patriotic population.

The army of the north first assembled under the command of General Bourbaki; and when the ex-commander of the imperial guard was summoned to take charge of part of the Loire army, the northern forces were left for a time under the direction of General Farre. It was during this interval that the battle of Villers-Bretonneux was fought and Amiens captured. On the 3rd December M. Gambetta replaced General Farre by the appointment of General Faidherbe, one of the most competent commanders the war produced. He was a native of the provinces he was called to defend, having been born at Lille on June 3, 1818, and had greatly distinguished himself in Algeria and Senegal.

Opposed to Faidherbe was probably the least dangerous of the German military leaders, as was evidenced by the fact that, had the advantages secured by the battles before Amiens on the 26th and 27th November been promptly followed up, the greater part of the beaten French army would undoubtedly have been captured. So great was the panic that whole regiments of the French lay concealed for days in the woods adjoining Amiens, not daring, in the presence of the dreaded German troops, to retire on the open field. But when, much to their surprise, they found they were not pursued, they collected their scattered forces and retired behind their northern fortresses, while the main body of the Germans went off towards Rouen. Had General Manteuffel, instead of taking this course, made a bold effort to cut off the retreat, it seems certain that French operations in the north would have been permanently paralyzed. As it was, the number who escaped to the triangle protected by Arras, Cambrai, and Lille was so large that, with the addition of some mobiles and drafts from various neighbouring garrisons, they formed for General Faidherbe an army of about 50,000 men and 70 guns.

The 20th of December was fast approaching when Manteuffel, while engaged in the comparatively sentimental work of capturing open towns and taking seaside trips to Dieppe, received intelligence that a new French army of the north was descending upon Amiens, and Von Göben was hastily despatched back to the scene of his encounters of November 27. General Faidherbe had advanced much sooner than was originally intended, in consequence of a rumour that the Germans were preparing an attack upon Havre. He had gathered together a large number of men, and in his safe northern retreat would gladly have had a little longer time for reorganizing them. The fact, however, that the second seaport of the country was threatened hastened his movements, and he advanced on St. Quentin, a detachment capturing Ham in passing; reconnoitred La Fère; and on the 14th December commenced demonstrations in the direction of Amiens. The German commander had been too well aware of the strength of Havre to lightly attempt an attack upon it; and the fears of the inhabitants, for which, indeed, there had been no real cause, were dispelled by the manoeuvres of General Faidherbe; in consequence of which large detachments of Manteuffel's army were at once recalled, and a series of closely-contested engagements ensued, the most serious commencing on December 23 and ending on January 3.

At a little distance from Amiens General Faidherbe found that nature had supplied him with defences much superior to those of the best engineer. From Querrieux to Bussy, on the summit of a hill, or kind of elevated plateau, about three miles in length, the French army was posted, with its artillery, ready for action. Near the foot of this hill ran a small river, the L'Hallu, skirted by a long narrow line of wood, beyond which were numerous small villages—Daours, Pont Noyelles, Querrieux, Bavelincourt, &c. The French right wing rested on a wood on the brow of the hill overlooking Contay and Vadencourt; the centre was at Pont Noyelles and Querrieux, and the left at Daours.

The great festive season of the year had come, and throughout England bright faces, blazing fires, groaning tables, mirth and laughter were to be seen on every side. It was far different, however, with our nearest neighbours, who, especially here in the north, were busily preparing again to defy their enemies to mortal combat. The morning of December 23 was bitterly cold and the frost most intense, as the army of General von Göben assembled on a vast plain near Querrieux, before marching to accept the challenge of the French. The fifteenth division, under General Kummer, crossed the Somme by some pontoon bridges near Carnon, and, leaving Rivery to the left, formed on the plateau in front of Allonville, with the cavalry of General Count Göben on the right. The sixteenth division, under General Barnakow, marched up the road to Rainneville and Pierregôt to the north of Amiens, whilst a brigade proceeded along the Somme from La Motte upon Vecquemont. General von Göben's plan was to advance upon the French position of Allonville and Querrieux, and to make a strong demonstration on their centre and left flank; whilst General Barnakow, with the sixteenth division, after arriving at Rubempré, was to wheel round, and, having first taken the villages along the extreme right, to advance upon the French position, and endeavour to turn their right flank, thus encircling them so as to shut them up to a retreat on the Somne, which it was thought would be fatal.

Having ridden some distance out upon the Albert road, the general and his staff dismounted, and, sending their horses to the rear, awaited the advance of the troops upon Allonville. This little village is situated upon one of those ridges of hills that lie along the east side of the valley which stretches from Frèchencourt past Querrieux to Corbie. A magnificent sight was presented by the advance of the troops. The twenty-ninth brigade, commanded by Colonel von Bock, and composed of the thirty-third and sixty-fifth regiments, with artillery, and one squadron of the king's hussars, marched forward to the right of the farm of Les-Alençons; the thirtieth brigade, with the seventieth and twenty-eighth regiments, and two batteries of artillery, advanced upon the left of Allonville, covered by a regiment of lancers; whilst Count Groben's dragoons rode along the crest of the hill, looking across to the heights on the other side, above Corbie. Steadily, as if on parade, marched the compact masses of infantry; the skirmishers in front, with their supports to the right and left of the Albert road. They took possession of the woods beside Allonville, and in a moment the village was occupied, while as yet not a French soldier was to be seen. But an orderly galloped up to say that the village of Querrieux in the front was strongly held by French troops. At Les-Alençons a road leads off to the left through the village of Cardonette, and on to the Pierregôt road. Along this galloped Captain Allborn with orders from General von Göben to the sixteenth division to change front to their right flank, and, marching across between Molliens-aux-Bois and Mirvaux, to storm the French positions in the villages of Bavelincourt, Behencourt, and Frèchencourt. From the chateau of Bengerie the French tirailleurs were seen retiring upon Querrieux. The twenty-ninth brigade then brought their left shoulders forward, and two batteries of artillery took up position on the right. At ten minutes past eleven the first shot was fired by the French infantry from a windmill to the right of Querrieux, and the battle of Querrieux—or of Pont Noyelles, as it was called by the French—commenced. By twelve (noon) the village was stormed, and the French had retreated upon the well-nigh impregnable position already referred to. The considerable village forming the centre of their line of battle was thus taken; but the position of the Germans was anything but pleasant, as the ridge and village they occupied were easily commanded by Faidherbe's artillery from the elevated plateau opposite; and the French batteries all along the height, especially that to the right of the villages of La Houssoye, kept up a determined and well-directed fire upon it. Meantime, to the right the Prussians had taken the villages of Daours, Vecquemont, and Bussy, the French retiring upon their intrenched position in front of Corbie. Here both sides fought hard, appealing to the bayonet to settle the disputed possession of the villages, whose capture in fact formed one of the most remarkable incidents of the battle, as it was accomplished by the Rhenish rifle battalion against a whole division of the French army. With only about 800 men, Major Bronikowski waited till the heavy columns of the enemy who came to attack him were within ninety paces. The Germans had every one been waiting at this point with the eye on their enemy and the finger on the trigger; and when their commander gave the word, "Nun!

Kinder, schnell Feuer!" they sent such a volley into the ranks of the French as to leave upwards of forty dead in one place. The Germans had in the meantime been reinforced, but they had not more than 2500 men in all at this point; and with this inferior number the French left was forced back upon Corbie, the villages of Bussy, Daours, and Vecquemont were taken, and, still more surprising, held against repeated assaults.

At two p.m. the French, under a heavy fire of artillery, endeavoured to retake the village of Querrieux. Hard, indeed, was the struggle between the combatants here. For nearly twenty minutes they fought, actually looking into each other's eyes. But the French again retired, and again their five batteries of thirty guns opened a crushing fire upon the Prussian line. Every eye was now anxiously turned to the left flank, but as yet there were no signs of Barnakow's division. The Prussians were very weak before Querrieux, and the reserve was ordered to move up to the left of that village. The thirtieth brigade deployed in the valley and took a small village, into which the French poured a shower of shell and shrapnel from their batteries to the right of the Albert Road. And now the space between Querrieux and Bengerie began to be filled with those telltales of an action—carts and carriages of all descriptions, bearing ghastly burdens to the rear. Fortunate it was that the waggons of the British Society were there, for they supplied blankets to cover the poor suffering soldiers, the pain of whose wounds was increased by the biting frost and intensely cold winds. About this time—half-past two p.m.—the French made a strong demonstration between La-Neuville and Daours. With their guns planted to the left of La Houssoye they opened a heavy fire upon the Prussian right flank, a considerable body of troops at the same time advancing as if to retake Bussy. But Captain Fuchius' battery of horse artillery galloped to the right, unlimbered, and opened such a hot fire upon them that first of all the infantry halted, then faced to the right about, and eventually doubled to the rear in a most orderly manner, the artillery quickly following their example.

About three o'clock the welcome sound of General Barnakow's artillery was heard, and his troops were shortly seen advancing on Frèchencourt from the Contay road. At four p.m. the sixteenth division had stormed the villages of Bavelincourt, Behencourt, and Frèchencourt; but their further advance was stopped by the same formidable position which had brought the fifteenth division to a halt. Now, however, the Germans held the line of villages in the valley through which the small river L'Hallu flows, and which now formed the line of demarcation between the two armies. On the other side of this stream a natural glacis extended to the summit of the ridge of hills occupied by the French. Up this glacis, with 50,000 troops at the top, and fifty or sixty guns, it was both too late and too dangerous to advance; but the artillery on both sides continued firing, as did also the skirmishers, some of whom were at a distance of but 300 yards apart.

Meantime the village of Querrieux was held by two battalions of the thirty-third and the sixty-fifth regiment. Again and again had the French unsuccessfully tried to retake it. Thus far all had gone well for the Germans throughout the day, and as darkness set in it was hoped the French would give up the contest. Suddenly, however, a fire was opened from the hill, far exceeding in intensity and deadliness the artillery play at Gravelotte. It was dusk, and the spectacle was indescribably grand. To this fire the Germans responded but feebly, as the men had expended their ammunition, which encouraged the French to come down the hill and renew their attack on Querrieux. The sixty-fifth were obliged to fall back, and as they did so the dark uniforms of the French chasseurs were seen advancing at the other end of the principal thoroughfare. They had not proceeded far, however, before they were received by a murderous fire from the thirty-third, who advanced upon them from the cross streets with the bayonet, and once more drove them back pell-mell out of the village. The thirty-third and sixty-fifth were now nearly without ammunition, but the gallant fellows would not give up the position so dearly bought; and there they stood, each man in his place, determined to make cold steel do the work of ball-cartridge. It was now dark. The Prussian artillery had ceased firing, and the village of Querrieux was burning in four places, the flames throwing their light far and wide over the surrounding country. Six companies of the thirty-third regiment determined to avenge the last attack of the French. In the dark they stole out of the village, formed line, and at the point of the bayonet charged up to the French battery on the right of the Albert Road. They had spiked two guns and taken the horses when they were attacked by five French battalions, before whom they were forced to retire into Querrieux, followed so closely that at one moment it was thought the village was lost. By this time, however, the sixty-fifth had received ammunition, and drove the French back with a withering fire. It was now nearly six o'clock, and the battle of Pont Noyelles was over, in which the Germans had taken seven villages, 900 prisoners, a lieutenant-colonel, and a post-captain in the navy, who was jocosely asked why he had not brought his ship with him. The day had witnessed one of the severest actions of the campaign, but had resulted in no real gain to either party. The Germans had captured the villages and numerous prisoners, but the French still held the formidable position just beyond them, across the little stream. For that reason General Faidherbe claimed the victory, and in support of his claim made his men bivouac on the ground, with the thermometer marking 8° below zero, impressing on them, with the susceptibility of a French general, that the hardship was absolutely necessary to show that the day was theirs. That they fought stoutly there is not the least question, and great credit was due to their artillery, which was well served; but from the course their general felt compelled to take almost directly afterwards, it is difficult to see how he could fairly claim to have obtained any advantage.

As night closed in each army could observe the position of the other, clearly marked by the lines of bivouac fires, which burnt brightly in the intensely frosty atmosphere at intervals of 1500 to 2000 yards. Early next morning Generals von Göben and Manteuffel visited the field of battle, and witnessed the curious sight of nearly 60,000 French troops, with at least seventy cannon, looking down upon 24,000 Prussians with forty guns. There stood the heavy masses of the French infantry, drawn up along the brow of the hill, with their batteries right and left of the brigades, covered by cavalry; there stretched a long line of tirailleurs covering the whole front, keeping up a constant fire, wherever there was a chance, upon the valley below. On the German side all was still. The troops stood to their arms, the artillery was unlimbered, the cavalry kept their bridles over their arms; but not a shot was fired. They felt that they were too weak to attack the powerful force opposed to them, by which every moment they expected to be assailed. The day, however, wore on; General Faidherbe declined to follow up his "victory;" and the two armies stood still, silently confronting each other. Their weakness in numbers had been apparent to the German commanders early on the 23rd, and Manteuffel had telegraphed for reinforcements. About midday on the 24th, intelligence was received that Prince Albrecht was coming from Paris with a cavalry division of the guard, and that General Schüler von Senden, with a division, was advancing in the direction of Corbie from St. Quentin. Meanwhile, General Barnakow had been detached to the French right, in order, if possible, to turn their position; and the Germans now commenced such dispositions of their troops as would enable them to avoid making an assault on the Franvillers heights. Towards the afternoon a heavy cannonade, intermingled with the discharge of rifles, was opened from the hill, the reason of which was soon after apparent. The French, witnessing the movements of their enemies, had seen at once the great peril they would be in should the Germans succeed in completing their tactics, which must have led to a repetition of the manoeuvre at Sedan. They peopled, therefore, the top of the hill with soldiers, and feigned an intention to continue the battle. For that purpose they discharged cannons and rifles, galloped to and fro along the line, and showed themselves exceedingly busy. But in the rear, behind the hill, was going on the very different movement of conveying men, horses, and cannon to the railway train. This completed, the dummies on the summit suddenly disappeared, and when the sixteenth German division had completed their arrangements for attack, they found that the French had abandoned the most magnificent position nature could give them, and were in full retreat upon Arras and Lille. General Faidherbe admitted the loss of 1400 in killed and wounded, while that of the Germans was officially returned as 800, including twenty-six officers. The brunt of the day's action was borne, on the German side, by the forces under Von Göben, who from this, time became general of the army of the Somne, while Bentheim, at the same time, took command of the army of the Seine, with headquarters at Rouen, General Manteuffel still holding the command-in-chief.

With only one of his divisions—the fifteenth, with which he had fought at Pont Noyelles— and with the younger Prince Albrecht's flying column, of about the strength of a brigade, Von Göben followed Faidherbe to Bapaume, sending the sixteenth division to invest Péronne, and keep the communications; a disposition of his army which could only be justified by the event, and which could not fail to tempt the French commander to attack him before he could concentrate his forces. He very speedily had reason to recall the sixteenth division, and to leave the besieging of Péronne to General von Senden, with what forces and material he could collect from St. Quentin and Amiens, which the result proved to be sufficient.

Faidherbe gave as an excuse for his retreat on the 24th the failure of his commissariat and train; experience, apparently, not having yet taught the French the value of these services, to the shortcomings of which their earliest disasters of the campaign were to a great extent due. This, however, was doubtless only part of his reason for retreating behind his fortresses. Here he received intelligence of the somewhat incautious advance of Von Göben to Bapaume, and perceiving his chances, determined at once to resume the offensive.

On Friday, the 30th December, the country round Arras was swept by the division Lecointe, which on the following day proceeded to advance, with its left wing resting on La Scarpe, and its right on the heights of Beaumont-les-Loges. The front of the army, slightly convex in shape, extended for about a league before Arras. On the 2nd January the advanced guard attacked the Prussian post before Bapaume, but, owing to the failure of a subordinate general, without serious effect. Some detachments made a reconnaissance on the Arras and Douai roads, and came so near to a battery of artillery that, had it not been for Count Portalais and his squadron of king's hussars, the French might have recorded the capture of some Prussian guns. When, however, they were within 200 yards of the battery, it was saved by the hussars, who rushed upon them, cutting them down where they stood, and making 200 prisoners. Having thoroughly felt his way on the German left flank, General Faidherbe determined to attack at Bapaume the next morning. Accordingly, at nine a.m. on the 3rd January, just as General von Göben with his staff arrived at Le Transloy, half way on the Péronne road between Combles and Bapaume, the French commenced the action.

Bapaume, with the villages of Avesnes-les-Bapaume, Ligny-Tilloy, and Grevillers, were held by the fifteenth division, under General Kummer. The twenty-ninth brigade consisted of the battalions of the thirty-third and the sixty-fifth regiment. Two battalions of the thirty-third held the villages of Avesnes and Grevillers; the sixty-fifth regiment the suburb of Bapaume, called the Faubourg d'Arras. The thirtieth brigade, consisting of the twenty-eighth regiment and the second battalion of the sixty-eighth, made ground towards the Arras road and the wooded heights of Sapignies. Bapaume and its environs were consequently held by about eight battalions, with six batteries of artillery. As at this moment, with the exception of those of the nineteenth regiment, no battalion could bring more than 600 men into action, the Prussian force at Bapaume may be put down at 5000 infantry, with thirty-six guns. To their left was the brigade of General Count Groben, who lay at Miraumont, on the Arras and Amiens Railway. The Prussian right was commanded by Prince Albrecht, the younger, with the fortieth regiment, three batteries of horse artillery, and the division of the cavalry of the guard, whose headquarters were in Equancourt, at the juncture of the Cambrai, Bapaume, and Péronne roads. The reserve consisted of the eighth jager battalion, one battalion of the thirty-third regiment, one battalion of the sixty-eighth, and the artillery reserve. These lay upon the Bapaume and Péronne road, between the villages of Beaulincourt and Le Transloy. The position of the Prussian troops was, therefore, with their left at Miraumont, centre at Bapaume, and right at Equancourt. The French right extended beyond Achiet-le-Petit, and lay in the villages of Bihucourt, Achiet-le-Grand, and Gomiecourt; their centre was in Behagnies and Sapignies; whilst their left rested upon Vaulx and Lagnicourt.

The French began with an attack upon the Faubourg d'Arras, and by an attempt to drive the thirty-third regiment out of the village of Grevillers. In this they failed, being driven back and pursued by the thirty-third into the village of Biefvillers, which the Prussians stormed and took possession of, but were soon obliged to evacuate. Heavy masses of infantry came on to attack the gallant little band, amongst whom the French artillery was making sad havoc. Slowly, and with their faces to the enemy, they retreated upon the suburb of Bapaume, where they found the sixty-fifth regiment at their backs, and whence a quick and uninterrupted fire was soon opened upon the French troops. Meantime the Prussian artillery posted on the Arras road swept the plateau beneath, and poured a plunging fire of shell into the heavy French masses as they struggled across to gain the Faubourg d'Arras. The French artillery was never better served than on this occasion, both for rapidity and precision. Besides having excellent cannon, and knowing how to use them, the soldiers of the army of the north behaved most admirably under fire, although composed mainly of recruits, and without skilled leaders. Numerous bayonet charges were executed with creditable courage and gallantry against old and well-trained Prussian warriors. During one of those charges one battalion had to pass battalions of Prussians hidden at about five yards' distance. A full charge was given from the needle-guns with such terrible effect, that it seemed as if little more than fifty men of that battalion remained alive or unwounded.

In the course of the morning the thirty-third regiment, now fearfully reduced, was obliged to retire from the suburb it had held so bravely, and took possession of the old citadel of Bapaume, situated on the Albert road, and of the windmill to the left. The sixty-fifth still held a part of the Faubourg d'Arras, while two horse-artillery batteries were sent forward to the left, and, taking up a position at Ligny, opened fire upon the French right.

The action now became general and Bapaume was in a circle of fire and smoke. The Prussian centre, overwhelmed by the numbers of the enemy and the hot artillery fire, was beginning slowly to give ground, when the Rhenish jägers, with two fresh batteries, deployed to their left and went into action. Meantime Prince Albrecht had marched upon Baucourt from Equancourt, and had detached two batteries with some cavalry in the direction of Beugny-le-Château, whilst he himself, with the fortieth regiment and the remainder of his command, excepting the hussars of the guard, engaged the French left from Fremicourt. The hussars of the guard were sent along the road to Cambrai, to make sure that no troops were advancing on the Prussian right from that place. At the village of Boursies two regiments of French infantry, with a squadron of cavalry, were reported as advancing on the Cambrai road upon the German right flank. The officer in command was equal to the emergency. A squadron was dismounted, and took possession of the buildings and outhouses of the village. The hussars with their carabines opened a heavy fire upon the French as soon as they were within range; who, thinking that the village was held by infantry, made a hasty retreat. While matters were going on thus on the centre and right of the Prussian army, General Count Groben marched from Miraumout against the French right. Making a slight *détour* to his left flank, he suddenly appeared on the enemy's rear, and, opening fire from his artillery, made them imagine he was about to attack them in reverse, which speedily had the effect of compelling the French centre to draw off some of their forces, and gave a little breathing time to the gallant defenders of Bapaume.

There, in the meantime, confusion reigned supreme. The inhabitants were rushing off pell-mell in all directions. Shells went hurtling into the houses, bullets smashed the windows, and the town was set on fire in several places. On the road outside Bapaume, leading towards Beaulincourt, could be heard the sound of the heavy guns playing upon

Péronne; and anxious must have been the commander of that fortress for news of those who were trying to relieve him, and whose fire he could distinctly recognize. Towards halfpast one things had a serious aspect for the Germans. The heavy fire and superior numbers of the French had told so effectually, that the whole of the suburb of Arras was relinquished, and the twenty-ninth brigade, under Colonel von Bock, retired into Bapaume. The thirtieth brigade formed up in rear of the town on the Péronne road, and for a brief period the French suspended operations, except on the right flank, where Prince Albrecht was hotly engaged, but where neither side gained any advantage for a time. By sunset, however, the French had not only entered the suburb of Arras, where they at once erected strong barricades, but, after desperate fighting, had taken most of the villages around Bapaume, and even had their posts in some of the streets of the town itself, at only about thirty yards from the German outposts. The sixty-fifth regiment accordingly began to prepare for a fight in the streets by building barricades at every corner, and turning every window into a loop-hole. The terrified inhabitants fled into the cellars, and even the soldiers were not without apprehension, in consequence of the very superior strength of the French. Fortunately for them, the battle did not extend into Bapaume, and the day closed upon a sanguinary fight, which again produced little or no real advantage to either party.

General Faidherbe subsequently issued a proclamation, expressing the greatest indignation at the pretensions put forward by the Prussians of having had the advantage in the action, and claimed to have won a "complete victory;" which, he asserted, was proved by the fact that his army slept in the villages it had taken. He had not, be said, followed up his victory, because of the failure of his commissariat, and his fear that an advance would involve the destruction of Bapaume. The battle may, indeed, be fairly said to have been won by the French, but a fatality seemed to attend their movements even when they were successful. Faidherbe's army had behaved with the greatest gallantry, and their repeated attacks so exhausted the Germans—the thirty-third regiment, for instance, having less than half its strength and only three officers left—that at six p.m. General von Göben gave the order to retreat across the Somme. The heavy baggage trains were already in motion when it was discovered that the French commander, whether unaware of his victory, or dismayed by his own losses, or alarmed by the prospect of wanting food, retreated, and the German movement was stayed. Had he only advanced, or even maintained his position till morning, he would have secured an unmistakable victory, which might possibly have given new life to France. It would, at the least, have enabled him to relieve Péronne, and to partially clear the left bank of the Somme; and this would have had much more effect in inspiring his troops with ardour and energy than a paper assertion of victory while in full retreat before the enemy. It was this want of vigour, rather than of capacity or courage, in the French generals, which on more than one occasion made their greatest efforts of so little avail.

The real fruits of the victory remained, of course, with the Germans, though dearly purchased by the loss of nearly 1000 killed and wounded. If the French slept in the captured positions, their nap must have been brief indeed, for by midnight a movement of retreat was commenced along their whole line. The proof of a victory is in its results: and

General Faidherbe would have furnished the best evidence of having gained it if, instead of wasting time in undignified discussions with General Manteuffel, he had by advancing made the most of it: for he must have known that every day which passed added to the difficulties, the dangers, the agony of Paris. The allegation that the object of the fighting at Bapaume was frustrated by the shortcomings of the French commissariat, acquitted the soldiers at the expense of their commander, who had full time for the organization of the service in the north, and should therefore have seen that his army was in a condition to keep the field. As to his other reason for stopping short before Bapaume, "lest an attack upon that place might involve its destruction," he ought to have considered that between him and Paris there were many such places, within which the Germans might have chosen to await his onset, and that if he were equally scrupulous about the safety of all of them, he would never achieve the deliverance of the capital. Pursued to within about four miles of Arras by the Prussian cavalry—who, however, captured no guns and but few prisoners—the army of the north again found itself under the friendly shelter of their fortresses.

The principal cavalry intrusted with the pursuit were the eighth Rheinischer cuirassiers, commanded by Captain von Marées, who, just beyond the village of Sapignies—between it and Mory—came upon two retreating battalions of French infantry, one a chasseur regiment, the other consisting of gardes mobiles. At the moment he discovered them he was riding exactly parallel to them, the undulating country having hitherto hidden them from his view. He at once determined upon attacking them. The greater part of the country in the neighbourhood of Bapaume is arable land, most of which had been ploughed, and the furrows, from the severe frost of the previous ten days, were frozen as hard as bars of iron. Every one can see how serious were the difficulties which a heavy cavalry regiment would have to encounter in an attack over such ground. After some deliberation a spot was, however, chosen upon which to attack.

No sooner did the French infantry perceive the approach of the Prussian cuirassiers than they formed two squares. The foremost square, which was first attacked, waited until the cavalry came within 300 yards before it opened fire. Then, however, a perfect shower of bullets rang against and pierced the cuirasses of the advancing horsemen. The captain was shot through the knee, and his charger through the head; the lieutenant was unhorsed, and suffered a severe concussion; and the squadron sergeant-major received a bullet through the heart. Undaunted by the fall of their officers and sergeant-major, the men rode boldly at and right through the square, scattering their foes on all sides, and sabring and trampling down many. Having thus pierced their way to the other side of the French, they immediately spread to avoid any concentrated fire. Had they been supported, which unfortunately for them they were not, in all probability the regiment of infantry would have been cut to pieces; but a ravine of great depth separated them from their comrades, who were unable to cross in time to take part in this gallant action. The remains of the shattered French square were thus able to gain the shelter of a village, against which it was of course impossible to advance with cavalry.

Von Göben did not consider it wise to hold Bapaume, and soon after the battle of the 3rd retired to Domprere. The retrograde movement was carried out along the whole German line; General Kummer, who with the fifteenth division was at Albert, withdrawing upon Bray-sur-Somme, and Prince Albrecht retiring upon Combles. Considerable detachments of men and siege material were despatched to Péronne, which, under the fearful artillery fire poured upon it, speedily became a mass of ruins, and on January 10 capitulated unconditionally, with its garrison of 2000 men, to General von Senden.

The same day on which the severe action at Bapaume was fought General von Bentheim, on the Seine, had a somewhat sharp engagement with the French troops from Havre; to which place a new commander had been recently appointed, who had won considerable popularity by encouraging and organizing a scheme for attacking the Prussian forces in the neighbourhood. For several days the Prussian commander had heard that large numbers of French were massing upon the left bank of the Seine, threatening Rouen. To prevent the completion of these movements Von Bentheim, with a strong division, on the 3rd of January, at five a.m., surprised the French army in their quarters. The attack was short, sharp, and decisive; four standards, 500 prisoners, and two rifled guns falling into the hands of the Prussians. Not satisfied with the result, a company of infantry were immediately placed upon waggons, and, with two horse-artillery guns and two squadrons of cavalry, under the command of Major Preinezer, of the artillery, went in pursuit of the flying enemy, and captured two more guns and many additional prisoners, before they could ensconce themselves behind the earthworks of Havre.

Besides Péronne, two other fortresses fell early in the new year; namely, Mézières on January 2, and Rocroi on January 4. The former had undergone a tedious process of investment, almost since the capitulation of Sedan; for as it could give little annoyance to the Germans, its reduction by siege guns was deferred. Like almost all the other fortresses besieged, it speedily yielded to powerful artillery, which in a bombardment of about three days caused a vast amount of damage to life and property. The wreck, indeed, baffles description; terrible as was the scene presented by Bazeilles after being fired by the Bavarians, it was not so fearful as that which met the eye in some parts of Mézières. At Bazeilles the walls of most of the houses were left standing, and the streets were free of *débris*; but at Mézières, in many places, the houses were a mere waste, and not a stone of the front walls was left standing. The narrow streets were so choked up with fallen stones, that it was often difficult to get along. The church was also much injured. The 2nd of January witnessed the capitulation of the fortress and the surrender of the garrison, numbering 2000 men.

Part of the force which had reduced Mézières at once marched north-west to Rocroi, on the Belgian frontier. Early on the morning of January 4 some cavalry appeared suddenly at the gate, and demanded an immediate surrender, threatening bombardment in case of refusal. The commandant, believing that the enemy were unprovided with siege guns, returned a firm reply in the negative. The effective garrison consisted of 150 mobiles and 120 artillerymen and engineers. The guns were old-fashioned pieces, and the fortifications antique. A dense fog prevailed, when at noon the sound of a cannon was heard and a hissing shell fell within the fort. It appears that about thirty-six German guns were ranged in batteries against the town, and a fierce fire was at once opened from them. A number of long-range guns were placed further in the rear, and the whole were supported by a force of several thousand men. On the other hand, the fort of Rocroi possessed only four guns of serviceable range. When the first shell fell the mobiles rushed towards the ramparts on the side away from the fire, climbed over them, and fled in all directions. The 120 men who kept their ground, for five and a half hours bore an unrelenting bombardment, of which every shot told, and which crushed the town by the weight of 2000 projectiles. Fires broke out in several places, and a dozen houses were in flames. The four French pieces which were available fired as rapidly as possible against an enemy who could not be seen, and their balls fell at random. The powder magazine was so much damaged that there was imminent danger of its explosion. At half-past five another *parlementaire* appeared, stating that it was useless to prolong the resistance, and that only from respect to the valour displayed had the Germans been induced to take the unusual course of sending a second summons. The town continued to burn, and no assistance was to be looked for. The commandant, therefore, consented to capitulate, and the Germans entered and extinguished the fires, which, owing to a violent wind, threatened to destroy the whole place. Of the 120 men, nearly one-half managed to escape after the capitulation; the remainder, together with the officers, were sent to Germany.

While General Faidherbe was, as we have seen, availing himself of all opportunities of annoying and injuring his enemies in the north, things in other parts of the country were beginning to look extremely serious for France. Paris, patient and resolute, still kept at bay the hosts encompassing it, but only by submitting to privations so severe that it was easily seen they must soon issue in starvation or submission. The army of the Loire, at one time so full of promise to the nation, had been obliged to retire, defeated and scattered, upon Le Mans; and already the Germans were concentrating to deal it the last crushing blow. Seeing that his chances depended upon the hazard of one last desperate throw, M. Gambetta conceived the idea of a simultaneous offensive movement throughout the country. Paris was to make a formidable sortie in force, Faidherbe was to advance from the north, and Chanzy from the south, while Bourbaki was to put forth all his strength to cut the Prussian communications, and even push his way into Germany. M. Gambetta accordingly telegraphed to General Faidherbe that the moment for the supreme effort had come, and directed him to draw upon himself as many of the Germans as could be diverted from Paris. Promptly obeying, he eluded the troops who were watching him, and by forced marches arrived on the south of St. Quentin, threatening his enemy's lines of communication. It was thought advisable, however, to conceal if possible the extent and object of this movement. In a despatch to Bordeaux published on the 18th January, General Faidherbe therefore stated that, "having learnt that the Prussians at St. Quentin demanded of the inhabitants a sum of 548,000 francs, he had resolved to put an end to their exactions, and sent a flying column for that purpose under the orders of Colonel Isnard. That officer encountered the enemy at Catelet Bellicourt, and pursued him, killing and wounding thirty men. Colonel Isnard subsequently entered St. Quentin on the 16th, the enemy flying in great disorder, and abandoning 130 prisoners, as well as a considerable store of provisions. The inhabitants of the town received the troops with great enthusiasm."

Though somewhat coloured as to the "great disorder," &c., the despatch was correct in stating that St. Quentin was evacuated by the Germans. No artifice, however, could conceal from the well-informed Von Göben that the French had really advanced in great force; and promptly gathering together his little army, he gave orders for an immediate attack. The remarkable feature in the conduct of this commander was the great exactness with which he carried out his plans, and the care taken by him of all parts: none were neglected by him, even while each was working for itself for a certain time, and scarcely knowing it was connected with another until the moment came when all acted together as a whole. He cared comparatively little how many perished on the march, provided it was completed in the given time; and in the operations around St. Quentin on the 19th were seen the results of his exact method. Every one was in his right place at the right time. The officers of the Prussian army attributed to Manteuffel's slowness the fact that Faidherbe had not been more decisively beaten on previous occasions, while the confidence of the common soldiers in Von Göben's talent was great. On the fatiguing march through snow and mud, from morning till evening, they might often be heard saying, "Well, Göben knows that all this is necessary," and they held on as merrily as ever.

The fighting commenced by some skirmishes on Wednesday, the 18th of January. On the previous day General Faidherbe had established his quartier-general at St. Quentin, and early the following morning despatched a brigade of the twenty-second corps in advance of the main army, which shortly after followed, in a southerly direction towards Mézières on the Oise. The French being very deficient in cavalry, his reconnaisances were too limited to enable him to know for certain the direction occupied by the enemy, and in consequence a portion of General Faidherbe's men came unexpectedly upon advanced posts near the village of Roupy. They were suddenly attacked by a Prussian battery, and compelled to fly with severe loss. Several other skirmishes of a similar nature and with like result occurred in the course of the 18th, showing clearly the proximity of very numerous hostile forces, and giving some indication of the severity of the battle next day.

About nine o'clock on the morning of the 19th the principal engagement commenced by an attack of the Prussians, from some heights overlooking the villages of Grugis and Castres, upon the twenty-third French corps, commanded by General Gislin. The unceasing fire of the Chassepots was not to be mistaken, and served to point out distinctly the French position. To understand this fully the reader must picture St. Quentin situated in a hollow, inclosed by hills, the hilly circle being separated by a valley from a second similar circumvallation. Eastward of this natural fortress, about 5000 paces from the second height, between St. Quentin and Savy, a small village to the south of it, is a thick forest of considerable length, separated by a plain of about 500 paces from a second forest, less extensive than the former, still more westward, towards the road to Péronne, near Vermand. The French army was so posted on the second height as to have its left wing eastward of St. Quentin, the right beyond the second forest, and the bulk behind both forests, which were lined with soldiers. Two batteries were, in a masterly fashion, placed behind the height separating the two forests, and so concealed that their existence became known only by the smoke after the discharge. On the Prussian side the sixteenth division was on the right, the third cavalry division on the left wing, and the fifteenth division in the centre. The respective batteries were with their divisions, and the artillery corps kept in reserve.

At Savy orders were given to the Prussian infantry to take the forests; and to help them, three batteries were mounted near a windmill behind the village, which threw their shells partly into the forests, and partly amidst those troops who were posted on the height connecting them. The French batteries, likewise, began to roar from behind the hill, and aimed well. So long was the range of the Chassepots, that at a distance of 1000 yards the advancing infantry had already several wounded.

So early as ten o'clock the French had to abandon several of their positions, and a powerful attack was then made upon their lines by the Prussians with a large artillery force. The twenty-second French corps, however, held its ground well for a time, but the twenty-third soon began to give way. The two corps had unfortunately become separated by the Canal Crozat, too broad and deep to be crossed but by bridges, and consequently could not aid each other. The twenty-third corps, therefore, soon began to yield, and by three o'clock made a disorderly retreat—in fact, "ran away" would more correctly describe the conduct of those who had not become prisoners. General Faidherbe endeavoured to restore confidence by directing some battalions of the twenty-second corps to go to their aid; but before this movement could be accomplished the panic was too great.

The cavalry fared no better. Immediately behind Savy several squadrons of French dragoons were drawn up in line against about an equal number of the king's hussars. The former were extremely nice and clean; their horses well tended; saddles and bridles apparently a few days only in use; their white cloaks as if put on for the occasion. The hussars, on the other hand, as well as their horses, were covered with mud; their uniforms, usually so neat and shiny, were all soiled from the long and toilsome marches of the last few days. Suddenly, and without a moment's warning, the hussars dashed forward like lightning against the enemy, and fairly overrode him. The first shock dismounted half of the French dragoons; their white cloaks covered the ground, or were trodden into the earth; while the other half fell under the strokes of the hussars' sharp sabres, or were made prisoners. When brought in it transpired that they had entered the army only three weeks before, and had never previously been on horseback.

At noon the Prussian artillery, having no means of estimating the effect of their shells on the concealed batteries of the enemy, left off firing. They resumed it only when the French batteries, pressed hard by the German cavalry division, had changed their front towards their right flank, and continued it until they had compelled General Faidherbe to give up his excellent position. The twenty-third French corps having given way, the forests were already in possession of the Prussian infantry. About three o'clock two light and one heavy battery advanced in columns in the direction of St. Quentin, leaving the first forest to their left. Before that forest they were drawn up in line against the artillery of the French, who, being in retreat, had taken position on the first height around St. Quentin. Nearly at the same time four batteries of the corps artillery were summoned to the battlefield, and placed themselves at the right of the former three. Thus, on the west side of St. Quentin, seven batteries came into action, and the grandeur of their roaring, and the whistling of their shells, were indescribable. The cavalry division continued to exercise the utmost pressure on the French right, as the sixteenth division did on the left, and General Faidherbe had no other course but to abandon the last heights, and to fall back into the town.

From the time the twenty-third French corps had commenced their early retreat, the twentysecond, under Generals Deroja and Paulze d'Ivoy, sustained the brunt of the fight. Even among them some mobiles gave way, but were again rallied and placed in front of the regiment of zouaves of the north. These latter were as fine and daring a body of troops as the French had; but by four o'clock General Paulze d'Ivoy, being unable any longer to continue the defence, the retreat was sounded; and under a tremendous fire from the augmented Prussian batteries, the disheartened French set out for St. Quentin, but only en route for a farther distance still; for, determined to repossess the town they had evacuated three days before, the Germans were gathering fast for the pursuit. Thus, when evening was falling, the weary men—almost dead with several days' marching to and fro, first upon Albert, next tacking westward upon Fins—were trudging several kilomètres to Cambrai, in the dreary darkness, knowing they had lost an important day, and that their conquerors were pressing forward to occupy the town they held the night before.

One of the grandest war pictures ever witnessed was now displayed. The full light of day had already disappeared; the wide plain on which a fierce battle had raged was silent; but on the right and left wing were heard the cries of victorious troops. When the enemy was driven from his last position, the whole long line of German infantry and cavalry, followed by the artillery, began to march on St. Quentin, with drums beating and banners fluttering in the air; and amidst the shouts of "Hurrah!" advanced until they reached the heights just abandoned by the French. The batteries were then mounted in a semicircle around the town, which the fifteenth division now took by storm, assisted by the sixteenth, which attacked it on the east. To defend the place successfully was impossible; to remain within it was either to become victims to the pitiless rain of Prussian shells, or be taken prisoners. The majority of the French, therefore, after some slight show of resistance, fled in utter confusion, some to Guise, but most to Cambrai, the Prussian cavalry making about 4000 prisoners at St. Quentin alone. They had previously taken an equal number, and, in all, the battle finally resulted in the capture of more than 12,000. Had not night retarded the pursuit, it is probable that few, indeed, would have been left to France of its army of the north.

Thus, within ten days, a second French army, upon which high hopes had been built, was shattered and dispersed beyond recovery. In a report to the minister of War, General Faidherbe stated that at this battle his troops amounted to only 25,000, his four divisions having been reduced during six weeks' operations to 6000 or 7000 men each; and that, resolved to sacrifice his own army in order to assist the sortie from Paris, he had gone forward certain of meeting an overwhelming force. If the army of the north was indeed reduced to a strength of 25,000 men, France and Paris, which had been led to believe that it had at least three times that number, had been shamefully deceived.

In a pamphlet published by him at the close of the war, General Faidherbe also remarked somewhat complainingly respecting this battle, "How could we withstand indefinitely the fresh troops brought continuously by rail on the field of battle, even from Paris?" That no very great force was despatched from among the besiegers of Paris might be inferred from the fact that they themselves had serious work on hand just at this time, the sortie on Montretout having taken place on the same day as the battle of St. Quentin. It is doubtful, however, if the whole war affords a more striking example of the military genius of Von Moltke than an opportune railway trip he ordered for the sixteenth brigade, forming part of the beleaguering army. As the result of calculation he had found that Von Göben would make his mark at St. Quentin all the deeper if he were strengthened with 4000 or 5000 men and a few guns; by calculation and good information together, he had even learnt the hour at which this help would be most useful. The brigade quietly went away for the fight, just as a lawyer goes down to a provincial town for the circuit; and, the work done, it returned immediately to its quarters before Paris, just as the lawyer returns to his cases in the Queen's Bench. The device had simply for the time converted 5000 men into 10,000. Of all Von Moltke's predecessors, Napoleon I. perhaps most effectively utilized his soldiery by means of rapid movements; but he had not the locomotive and the *militär-zug*. General Faidherbe had carried out M. Gambetta's instructions to the letter; he had drawn upon himself as many of the Prussians from around Paris as could be spared, but by doing so he had effectually insured his own irremediable defeat. The victory had cost the Germans 94 officers and 3000 men.

The only other matter of any importance which occurred during the war in the north of France, was the siege and fall of the fortress of Longwy, the strict investment of which was not undertaken by the Germans until after the fall of Mézières. It is situated on the Belgian frontier, thirty-three miles north-north-west of Metz. Its citadel stands on a steep rock, below which extends the town, hospital, military prison, &c. Longwy, which has been termed the "Iron Gate of France," was taken by the Prussians in 1792, and again by the allies in 1815. The details of the siege of 1871 prove that the defence of the place was in no way exceptional as compared with that of similar crowded fortresses in north-eastern France, and that it was given up owing to the same causes which led to the surrender of Thionville, Mézières, and Péronn. The working parties, with the siege train, were brought into the vicinity on the 18th of January, concealed in distant villages during the daytime, and in the evening advanced to begin the work of throwing up the usual concentric batteries which the Germans had found so effectual in like cases, and which were placed at points averaging 1500 yards from the town. Their construction was attended with unusual difficulties, owing to the severe frost which prevailed, and in consequence they were not completed until the night of January 21. There were nine of them in all; eight armed each with four rifled German 12-pounders or 24-pounders, and one with four French mortars, the same as at Thionville. Fire was opened at seven a.m. on the 22nd, and was hotly replied to by the fortress at first, the French causing a good many casualties, and dismounting three of the guns in one Prussian battery (No. 6), on which they directed their chief fire. This, however, soon slackened, from the effects of the constant shower of missiles thrown into the bastions, and then the German artillery began to direct their shots against the public buildings and barracks. Their fire was kept up at the usual measured intervals during the night, and resumed continuously next morning. At ten a.m. of the 24th the church tower fell with a mighty crash, audible above the din of the firing; and at four p.m., after thirty-three hours' bombardment, Colonel Massaroli hoisted the white flag and sent out a *parlementaire* to treat for terms, which Von Krenski readily granted. Nearly all the houses in the town were more or less damaged, some, however, very slightly; but the public buildings had been set on fire by the shells, and were wholly destroyed. It needed not this fresh proof to show how untenable the second-rate Vauban fortresses of France had become in the face of modern artillery, before which they inevitably fell without even causing the besiegers the trouble of opening approaches, unless the inhabitants had consented to be wholly sacrificed to the defence.

CHAPTER XXVII.

The State of France at the Close of 1870—The Accumulated Misfortunes of the Country— German Strategy and its Object—Activity of Chanzy—An Expedition to St. Calais and its Results—A Warm Protest—German Preparation for the Winter Campaign—The Progress towards Le Mans—"Beating up" the Enemy in a Fog—"Only an Incident"—Closing in upon General Chanzy—Great Strength of Le Mans—The Utility of a Map in War—The Battle of Changé—Audacity serving the Purpose of Numbers—The Wisdom of Secrecy in War—Gallant Behaviour of the Third Corps—Carrying the Heights of Champigné—A Brave Officer not to be Deserted—The Beginning of the End—The Army of General Chanzy in Full Retreat—Capture of Le Mans—The Takings of the Victors—The German Losses.

HOW many years must pass before a Frenchman shall have forgotten the closing scenes of 1870? Christmas and the new year was fast approaching, but men's minds were oppressed from day to day with thoughts contrasting sadly with the associations of the season. Not a single rift could be seen in the clouds which hung over the fairest part of Europe. From every quarter came distressing reports of the misery already inflicted by the war, and gloomy anticipations of the future. The bitter severity of the weather intensified the agonies of the wounded, whose sufferings were too horrible to relate; while in rural parts a distressing solitude, only broken by the occasional appearance of women or old men, reigned along the roads and around farm-houses and hamlets. Ploughs rusted in untilled fields, and the only sign of life in connection with farming affairs, was the sight now and then of a woman tending sheep or goats, as in some barren mountain district. The young and middle-aged men had been drained away to such fields as now surrounded Beaugency. Thousands of wounded constantly passed southwards, until there was scarcely a town in France without a military hospital; and yet the prospect of a decisive issue to the war seemed as faint as ever. Throughout the United Kingdom there prevailed a strong feeling of sympathy with France in her misfortunes, and an impression that Germany could now well afford to show a generosity which would encourage the French to entertain the idea of concession and peace. It could not be denied that the Germans had been driven into a war of defence, and that the disasters they had inflicted on the French were justly merited; but the punishment had already been exemplary beyond any recorded in history. They had taken prisoner the emperor who menaced them and the statesmen who joined with him in his schemes were driven into exile. They had destroyed or led into captivity his whole army, with nearly all its marshals and most renowned commanders. They had taken Strassburg and Metz, with a number of minor fortresses; they had overrun France and laid her provinces under contribution from the Rhine to the Channel; they threatened her beautiful capital with fire and famine; the ruler of Germany had occupied for three months the palace of the man who was his greatest enemy, and "all the glories of France" were humbled under his flag. Was not such a punishment enough for justice? Would it not be a cruelty akin to that practised by the Roman on the Gaul if Germany, with her veteran army and her incomparable organization, continued to crush the gallant but undisciplined bands who were now fighting in desperation to save some shreds of the honour of France?

To such reasoning the impassive Bismarck still had but one answer. His royal, and soon to become imperial, master was quite willing to listen to overtures from France, but would not surrender his claim to a solid security for the future, and a substantial compensation for the thousands of precious lives he had been compelled to sacrifice. On the other hand, M. Gambetta's answer to this demand for a "solid security" was the organization of new armies and defences on every side.

We have shown in previous chapters that the great object of the German commander was to cover the army investing Paris. Every movement was necessarily subordinate to the siege of the capital. D'Aurelles de Paladine, strongly posted at Orleans, constituted a danger which it was requisite to remove. But that object attained, it was questionable whether success in that direction need be much further pursued. The one essential point was, that no French army in the provinces should be suffered to acquire sufficient consistency to threaten the rear of the Germans before Paris. To secure this object General von Moltke required as much caution as boldness. It was necessary that his base of operations should not be so widened as to weaken it. His armies away from Paris must be like an outer suit of armour to his army around it: they must stop every gap, and make fast every link and joint in defence of the inner panoply. At first the German flying columns merely threatened Orleans, Chartres, Dreux, Nantes, Beauvais, and Soissons; but after subduing this first zone, their excursions extended towards Bourges and Tours, Evreux and Rouen, Amiens and St. Quentin. The advancing tide had been here and there momentarily stemmed, but hardly ever forced permanently backwards. It mattered very little whether or not Prince Frederick Charles entered Bourges, or the grand-duke of Mecklenburg, Tours, or Manteuffel, Havre. The important point was that neither Chanzy from Vendôme, nor Bourbaki from Gien, nor Faidherbe from St. Quentin, should have a chance of marching to the relief of Paris.

Bearing these strategical motives in mind, it will be readily seen why, after General Chanzy's brilliant and gallantly defended retreat to Le Mans, fully described in Chapter XXV., the German commanders stopped short in the pursuit at Vendôme. They were undoubtedly weary of the continual strife; but apart from this, further sacrifice in following Chanzy was needless, as the besiegers of Paris were relieved from present anxiety, and it was hoped that the speedy fall of the capital would be the signal for a cessation of hostilities. Such, however, was not Chanzy's opinion. Once behind the fortifications of Le Mans, he, though almost under his enemy's eye, set to work with immense energy to reorganize his shattered forces. The camp of Conlie was broken up; the best of its recruits were drafted to Le Mans; and with these and other reinforcements he soon found himself again at the head of about 150,000 men, thoroughly armed with Remington or Chassepot rifles, and provided with a field train of at least 300 guns. But the result of all these preparations will abundantly prove that armed men do not, strictly speaking, constitute armies.

From the 15th of December, the day on which the last serious fighting occurred, to the first few days of January, the army of Prince Frederick Charles was comparatively inactive; the men, save in a few reconnoitring expeditions, enjoying a period of well-earned rest. One of these expeditions threw a little light upon the question, often suggested, but never fully tried, as to how the invariably victorious Germans would behave in a retreat. In retaliation for the doings of some franc-tireurs, a small column of troops was ordered to sweep the country from Vendôme as far as Sougé, on the bank of the Braye, and levy requisitions. The orders were to advance as far as Montoire on December 26, to push on through Les Roches on the 27th, remain the unbidden guests of the villagers at Sougé, and return on the 28th. The advanced guard reached Troo on the 27th, and here met with determined opposition from the French, who, from the shelter of houses and walled gardens, poured forth such a fire as checked the advance. After a two hours' conflict the French were thrust out, and leaving a company to hold the village the column pushed on to Sougé. This was found filled with troops, and another fight ensued, during which it was observed that the heights in the rear were being crowded with Frenchmen bent on cutting off the retreat of their diminutive enemies. It was seen that the only chance was at once to fight their way back to Vendôme; and relinquishing the idea of passing the night at Sougé, Colonel Boltenstern ordered a hasty retreat, the thundering of artillery and Chassepots on all sides now telling him only too plainly into what a hornet's nest he had fallen. The men marched rapidly, and had well nigh gained the shelter of Montoire, when a row of armed men appeared in their front, blocking up the entire retreat. Shells fell fast among the little band from the sides and behind; rifle bullets whistled through the air from the foe in front; and many a spiked helmet sank from its place. Still before them rolled the icy waters of the Loir, bridgeless until that fine in front could be passed. Scattering four companies into skirmishing order, the colonel took the rest of his men in hand, and sent them full at the French. The line barring the passage hesitated, wavered, and broke; too soon for success, too late for safety. There was no time to count the killed and wounded, nor the prisoners whom the Germans took and drove before them as they went, for the increasing fire told of an enemy gathering in strength for pursuit. Steadily the little column trimmed their ranks and crossed to the left bank of the river, carrying their prisoners, uncounted as yet, with them. For some time hostile infantry pursued along the road; then all was quiet, and on the Germans marched in the twilight and the darkness, driving their herd of prisoners, until, having accomplished his orders, the colonel reported himself at Vendôme about an hour before midnight. He had lost in round numbers 100 men; but when the unwounded prisoners came to be counted, it was found there were ten officers and 230 men.

Another expedition was followed by such important events that a brief mention of it cannot be omitted. At St. Calais, a little town of 4000 inhabitants, lying between Le Mans and Blois, some franc-tireurs and French dragoons lodging there saw a small Prussian force approaching on the morning of December 25, and took the opportunity of firing upon it from some houses. The Germans vigorously replied; the franc-tireurs retired; and the mayor went out and endeavoured to explain to the Prussians that the inhabitants were not responsible for the resistance offered. He was, however, rather rudely repulsed, and the unfortunate town ordered to pay 20,000 francs immediately. The sum was afterwards reduced to 15,000 francs, and the town was asserted to have been given over to pillage for an hour. This, however, has been as loudly denied; but the report exasperated General

Chanzy, and induced him to write a warm protest to the Prussian commandant at Vendôme. The protest was embodied in an order of the day, and read three times to the French troops on parade; General Chanzy expressing confidence that every one would share his indignation, and his desire to take revenge for the insults heaped upon the French nation. The following is the text of the protest:—

"To the Prussian Commandant at Vendôme,—I am informed that violence, for which I can find no language suitable to express my indignation, has been resorted to by the troops under your command against an innocent population at St. Calais, notwithstanding their good treatment of your sick and wounded. Your officers have extorted money and authorized pillage. This is an abuse of power which will weigh upon your conscience, though patriotism may enable our countrymen to bear it. But it cannot be permitted that you should add to this injury a gratuitous insult. You have alleged that we are defeated. This is false. We have fought and held you in check since the 4th of December. You have dared to treat as cowards men who could not answer you, pretending that they submitted to the will of the government of National Defence in resisting when they really wished for peace. I am justified in protesting against this statement by the resistance of the army, which up to the present time you have not been able to conquer. We reassert what our struggle has already taught you; we shall struggle on, conscious of our good right, and determined to triumph at any cost. We shall struggle on *à outrance*, without truce or mercy. It is no longer a question of fighting against a loyal enemy, but against devastating hordes, whose sole object is the ruin and humiliation of a nation fighting for the preservation of its honour, its independence, and the maintenance of its rank. You reply to the generosity with which we treat your prisoners and wounded by insolence, by arson, and by pillage. I protest with indignation, in the name of humanity and the law of nations, which you trample under foot."

General Voigts-Rhetz sent the letter to his chief at Orleans, saying that he knew not what answer to give to such a document, which differed strangely from all that he had read in the history of warfare. Meantime he bid his men hold fast to their posts, and guard patiently the line of the Loir. At Orleans the letter was regarded as a challenge to a renewal of fighting, and confirmed the suspicion as to the mischief which had been brewing around Le Mans. General Chanzy was doubtless about to commence some new movement for the relief of Paris, and severe as the weather was, Prince Frederick Charles resolved to take the initiative, and march out to meet him. Two main circumstances contributed to this resolution. In the first place, by his eccentric movement eastward (described in the succeeding chapter), General Bourbaki had removed all apprehension the prince might have entertained on his account, and enabled him to take with him the bulk of his force to the west without any uneasiness as to the safety of his position on the Loire at Orleans. In the second place, Von Moltke had determined on resorting to extreme measures against Paris; and as he was about to use his heavy guns, he was able to spare bayonets and sabres for the armies in the provinces. Accordingly, dispositions were made for a gradual concentration towards Vendôme, and for the first three days of the new year the roads from Orleans leading in that direction were covered, as far as the eye could reach, with infantry, cavalry, and train, all advancing with the regularity of a well-directed machine to their respective starting points. The tenth German corps (Hanoverians) guarded the advanced positions on the Loir, occupying Blois and Vendôme, and the country between. Von der Tann s Bavarians were resting near Orleans. The ninth corps (Schleswig-Holsteiners and Hessians) held Orleans, with detachments before it and higher up the Loire. The third corps (Brandenburgers) were higher up the river towards Gien. It was intended that these various corps should advance by different roads towards the line of the Loir, drive back the French before Vendôme, find out and overthrow the army of Chanzy, and by taking Le Mans relieve the investing army before Paris of all fear for its safety. The eighteenth division (ninth corps) was to reach the Loir at Morée, and having cleared the way, prepare to act as a reserve. The third corps were to cross the river near Vendôme, while the tenth were to march to La Chartre, and be ready to turn Chanzy's right, and then join the other corps in the battle before Le Mans. The duke of Mecklenburg, who was at Chartres, was to advance and drive in Chanzy's left. Duke William of Mecklenburg, with the sixth cavalry division, was to keep on the left of the prince's forces; the second cavalry division was to maintain the communication between the ninth corps, which formed the prince's right, and the left of the duke of Mecklenburg's army. The fourth cavalry division was to protect the grand-duke's right, and the fifth was sent to keep watch in the country north of his line of march.

For the success which eventually resulted from these movements the Germans were indebted in no small degree to the masterly strategy of their commander. Prince Frederick Charles, as will be seen from the various movements we are about to relate, put in practice against Chanzy the principles which had succeeded so well against Benedek in the Bohemian campaign—a double attack was made upon his opponent, the one line at right angles to the other. The grand-duke of Mecklenburg's corps were not moved up directly against Le Mans from Chartres, but were required to make a detour, so as to descend in a northerly direction, and compel Chanzy's army to present two fronts—a mode of operation implying a certain contempt for the enemy, inasmuch as it offends against the rule of attacking with superior numbers. But the capacity of a commander is shown by his knowing when a rule must be observed, and when it may safely be set aside.

On the 4th of January Prince Frederick Charles moved his headquarters to Beaugency, the grand-duke of Mecklenburg being still at Chartres. The third corps was by that time concentrated in and around Marchenoir, the eighteenth division was near Orleans, the nineteenth at Blois, and the twentieth at Vendôme.

On the 5th the prince moved to Oucques, where the third corps had their headquarters. The eighteenth division moved up from Orleans to Ouzouer-le-Marché, and took its place on the right of the force, under the immediate command of the prince. The twentieth was still before Vendôme, skirmishing with General Chanzy's advanced posts, and the nineteenth moved up from Blois towards St. Amand. The grand-duke advanced from Chartres southwards to Illiers.

On the 6th Prince Frederick Charles marched from Oucques to Vendôme, close on the other side of which the tenth corps was seriously engaged with the French before the forest of Vendôme, supported by the third corps, which had advanced that day from Marchenoir. The opposition was greater than the Germans had expected, as the French fought better than usual. The fire of musketry was hot in the front, but the Hanoverians and Brandenburgers pressed on until their artillery and needle guns had borne down all opposition, and their leading division, the fifth, had reached a rivulet between Azay and Villiers. It subsequently transpired that General Chanzy had determined upon forcing his way towards Paris at whatever cost, and with this view had arranged for his army to move in several columns, every man being furnished with four or five days' provisions. It was one of these columns, on its way to attack Vendôme on the 6th, which came in contact with the fifth division (third corps), and for a time resisted all the efforts of the Germans to continue their advance. Night, however, found the French forced back beyond the Azay-Villiers line, where the Prussians halted, after taking 500 prisoners. On the right the eighteenth division reached Morée, on the Loire, north of Vendôme. While this engagement was going on, Duke William of Mecklenburg fell in with considerable forces of the French on the left, near Villerporcher, and was unable to proceed. General Hartmann was therefore sent with a cavalry division and a brigade of infantry from the tenth corps, in the direction of St. Amand, which caused the French troops in that quarter to fall back towards Tours, whence they were transported by railway to Le Mans. On the same day the grand-duke marched with the seventeenth division to Brou, and the twenty-second advanced to La Loupe and La Fourche.

All the marches from Orleans had been made in bitter weather. Three or four inches of snow lay upon the hard frozen ground, and a piercing wind blew. The moisture exhaled from the lungs or skin froze instantly, and covered hair, beards, and greatcoats with rime. Icicles hung from moustaches and formed curious frames for the indispensable pipes or cigars which protruded from all mouths.

On the 7th a thaw set in; the roads were covered with melting snow, the ditches were fast turning to running streams, and the rivers were more impassable than usual. A dark fog, sometimes concealing all objects at a distance of 100 yards, obliged the Germans to advance with caution. The tenth corps was delayed by the attack on Duke William, and not till next day, when the French had retreated towards Tours, was its march resumed. The fifth, sixth, and eighteenth divisions, however, advanced steadily, occasionally coming in contact with the rear-guards of the French columns. By night-fall the first two of the three divisions had reached the line of the Braye, at Savigny and Sargé, and the last was at Epinay. The grand-duke of Mecklenburg moved his headquarters to Beaumont les Autels; the seventeenth division being at Authon and the twenty-second at Nogent-le-Rotrou.

The doings of the Prussian army during these first few days of January thus consisted principally in a well-devised concentration; and no part of the strategy of the war better showed how thoroughly both officers and men had been trained by a system of peace manoeuvres to act together in war with the greatest intelligence. The sagacity displayed by the Prussian soldiers, indeed, is worthy of admiration. A description of the advance of one of the columns on the seventh will give a fair idea of the progress of the army generally. Imagine a straight road leading over a succession of round hills; on either side of it a rich country, dotted with farm-houses, cottages, orchards and walled gardens, hedges, (exactly like those of England), and occasional woods. In fact, Kent and Surrey combined, with vineyards instead of hop-gardens, would be an exact picture of the country through which the Germans were pushing on, under all the disadvantage of the fog, in a land never seen before.

The column was led by a small detachment of cuirassiers. After these came three infantry soldiers, two of them about 150 yards in front of the column, and one behind to connect these foremost men with the detachment of infantry which followed. The three foremost soldiers of the German army in face of the enemy were accompanied by four pet dogs, trotting quickly along beside them. After the infantry detachment came a squadron of cuirassiers, then more infantry, all of the same regiment, and followed by the light battery of the advanced guard. Owing to the thick mist the troops moved cautiously, for they knew that the enemy might appear at any moment. The pace was a moderate walk, about three miles an hour, with occasional halts, to examine a farm or a group of cottages near the road. Right and left of the road were cavalry and infantry marching in pairs, searching like dogs for game. They were generally concealed by the fog, but now and then a small party would peep out from a lane or cottage garden, and vanish again into the mist, when they saw that all was going smoothly, and that they had not lost their place beside the column. The troops marching along the undulating road had no reason to take thought for anything, save in front, as they had perfect confidence in the sagacity of their comrades, who, sometimes walking quickly, sometimes with rifle at the charge, were pushing on as well as they could over vineyards and gardens, ploughed fields and stubble, walls and fences, peering into every tree and bush for any enemy who might possibly be concealed by a copse, a garden wall, or a cottage. Occasionally one would run to the road and report something that had a suspicious look, when instantly some of his comrades were sent in the direction named to see whether any Frenchmen might be concealed there. All this was done so quickly as scarcely to interrupt the march of the column.

After a time there was a halt. The red trowsers had been seen to the right for a moment, and had immediately disappeared in the fog. Quest was made with increased numbers and redoubled caution among the small fields and hedges, but no sign of the enemy. The march was resumed, and continued until the few horsemen in front rode back to the head of the column, reporting something like men on the road. Slowly the infantry advanced, straining their eyes to ascertain the nature of the obstacle. The fog became thicker, and closed in the view to within a few paces. The foot soldiers, with outstretched necks, felt their way onwards. The fog became gradually lighter, when dim figures assembled together, and above the group an appearance like the erect quills of a porcupine—soldiers, probably, with bayonets. Instantly there is a murmur, "Are they ours?" Has one of the searching parties gone a little too much to the front? Nay. The figures remain still, and seem to block the way. "Cuirassiers to the front!" In a sort of good-humoured growl, some one says, "Yes, it is always cuirassiers here, cuirassiers there." But the order has been given, and the cuirassiers know no other obligation but the call to duty. The men, who had been brought in behind the infantry detachment, draw their swords, set their helmets firmly on their brows, press their knees firmly to their horses, and file past the infantry once more to the front. "Trot!" The fog comes down again, and the dim figures with the spikes become once more invisible, but not unheard. The horses have not gone more than half the 400 or 500 yards uphill in the direction given to the riders, when the air is filled with a crackling, whizzing sound, as of innumerable heavy insects flying faster than insects ever flew before. Every horseman bends to his saddle-bow. The officer who leads them waves his sword, and gives a word of command. The cuirassiers who went at a trot return at a gallop, but always steadily and in order, followed by those swift hornets with the fierce stings. Like magic the foremost infantry soldiers dissolve, but not to retreat. They spring to the sides of the road into the ditch, full of half-melted ice, into the fields, and begin in their turn to creep forward. The enemy is still in the mist, though near: and as the hornets come thickly and fast, the squadron of cavalry now occupying the front seems inclined to follow the example of the infantry, and dive for shelter. But such is not their part in battle, and one simple "No," in an expostulatory tone, from their commander, recalls them to their steady attitude. One of them, and not the least steady, remarked quietly, "These French Chassepots . shoot so far that one gets killed without seeing them. A comrade of mine was shot yesterday through his heart, and I don't think he even heard the rifle."

Cavalry are of no use where these men stand, so their officer soon draws them off into a field at the side. On the left, behind a house a little removed from the road, cavalry patrols are calmly waiting under shelter. Along the strait road for miles is a column of infantry, artillery, and train. Now for the mitrailleuse at work in its proper place. Its horrible growl must have been expected by many, but it came not. The French always seem to do the wrong thing. Their shells burst high in the air, and they pit their mitrailleuses against field artillery at long ranges.

Meanwhile, the infantry soldiers work steadily forward, firing at the flashes of the enemy's rifles, and helping to create a denser cloud than ever, though the sun at that moment, half-past twelve o'clock, seemed striving to break through the fog. The fight is partly transferred to the fields, for the bullets fly more at the sides of the road, and strike the trees with a sound like the chopping of an axe. Several minutes go by, long minutes, when the hornets are whizzing past with their sharp stings. The firing increases in intensity, but there are several shots now for every bullet that comes down the road or at the sides. The report of the needle-gun, too, sounds farther off. It increases to a heavy fire as more men come up. Still the French hold their ground. Guns begin to press forward, but as they cannot be made to tell, they do not fire a single shell. The sounds grow faster and fiercer. The combatants approach each other. A loud hurrah makes the mist quiver again. The Prussians have skirmished enough; they bound forward, reckless of consequences, and carry the position by storm.

It was only an incident which checked the march for a few minutes. It is past, and the Prussians move on, looking sadly on the stretcher with its straw, and the fine young fellow with the pale face trying to support his broken arm and save it from the swing of the bearers; looking yet more seriously at those forms lying quietly by the side of the road, their faces covered decently from the light, which they will never see more.

On the 8th the ground was again frozen, and the prince moved his headquarters to St. Calais, where he had the fifth and sixth divisions not far in front of him, on each side of the high road; the eighteenth division being just behind Illiers. The tenth corps, in spite of the obstacles to its advance, was at La Chartre on the Loir, on its way to Le Mans. To connect La Chartre with St. Calais, a detachment of six squadrons of cavalry, one battalion of infantry, and six guns, was formed, and placed under the command of General Schmidt. On the same day (the 8th) the grand-duke of Mecklenburg reached La Ferté St. Bernard with his entire infantry corps; the fourth cavalry division marched down the Huisne to Belleme; the second kept up the communication between the grand-duke's and the prince's corps; and the fifth was on the grand-duke's right.

On the 9th the roads were once more hard as iron with frost, and covered with ice, which remained for days, and made the cavalry all but useless in the actions which were to result in the capture of Le Mans. A strange sight was presented by the army, as it struggled on over the icy roads. Even the prince had to dismount and walk; most of the staff and cavalry escort were also dismounted; others, mounted, forced their horses to stumble on in the ditch by the side of the road. The horses of the artillery and train were falling every instant, and ice nails became worth nearly their weight in gold. Still, however, the army pressed on, slipping and falling, but never halting, driving before it the French, who had hesitated too long to descend on Vendôme, and were now recoiling from the first shock of contact with the burly Brandenburgers on the hills above the Loir. The prince's headquarters were this day moved to Bouloire. Both divisions of the third corps were at Ardenay and along the line of the Narrais. The eighteenth-division was with the prince; the nineteenth about Vancé; the twentieth at Grand Lucé. The grand-duke moved with the seventeenth division to Le Luard, near Connerré the twenty-second occupying Sceaux, on the main road six miles in advance of La Ferté. The German army was now within fighting distance of Le Mans. The prince had in front of him an army numbering, according to telegrams from Bordeaux a week before, 200,000 men, but rated by the Germans at the time at 160,000, and afterwards said by English correspondents at General Chanzy's headquarters to have been 118,000. The armies of Prince Frederick Charles and the duke of Mecklenburg numbered only 85,000, although in telegrams sent to Bordeaux from Le Mans they were reported to reach a strength of 180,000. But both men and horses were in the finest condition, and the supply departments were admirably served. The ninth corps had very recently shown its marching powers by having advanced, on the 16th and 17th of December, more than fifty English miles in twenty-four hours! The men were much attached to the prince, their commander, who on the 9th marched with them for twelve miles with the greatest ease.

Le Mans, towards which the Germans were now hastening, is naturally a place of considerable strength, being situated just above the confluence of the two rivers, the Sarthe and the Huisne, the former flowing from north to south parallel to the railway line which, from Cherbourg and Caen, goes by Alençon and Le Mans to Tours; the latter following a north-westerly course parallel to the other line which, from Paris by Chartres, Nogent-le-Rotrou, and Le Mans, proceeds to Angers. The town lies on both banks of the Sarthe, and the Huisne winds round the hills which dominate the place on the east and south. To these natural advantages the French had for several weeks been adding earthworks of some magnitude, rendering the position one of extraordinary strength and security. In addition to these points in their favour General Chanzy's men were armed with breech-loading rifles from the United States, of a pattern far surpassing the needle-gun; and he was also well supplied with the Gatling gun—a mitrailleuse firing a heavier projectile than that used in the imperial army early in the campaign.

On the 10th Prince Frederick Charles had drawn so near the French position, that the question seemed to be how to get into Le Mans. This, however, was a problem, for the grand-duke was not coming up so quickly as had been expected. The tenth corps, delayed by the state of the roads, was still behind, though the brave Hanoverians were toiling and sliding along as best they could. Using the only force immediately at his disposal, the prince ordered General Alvensleben to lead the third corps (his Brandenburgers) from Ardenay, and clear the principal roads to Le Mans, nearly up to the Huisne, behind which the French had taken up their position. He accordingly ordered three of his brigades to advance by different forest tracks and meet at night at Changé, while the fourth was to push on and clear the woods to the right as far as Champigné. One of the three brigades, the ninth, met a French corps in the woods near Challes, and succeeded in driving them back towards Parigné, where a stand was made. The commander of the tenth brigade, General Schwerin, hearing the sound of firing at Challes, took at once a decided step, accepting the responsibility without hesitation. He saw by his map that there was a road leading behind the battle, where he might take the French in rear. He marched his men quickly towards the place, which he had never seen, but knew to be there, because a military map was as familiar to him and as easily read as a book, and the careful Prussian war office had supplied him with the means of knowing France better than Frenchmen themselves knew it. When the enemy began to retreat, therefore, they found the Germans barring the way beyond Parigné. Defeated, broken down, and bewildered, they surrendered themselves and two mitrailleuses, because General Schwerin had a map, could read it, and knew how to take on himself responsibility.

Parigné, behind Challes, the place thus taken by General Schwerin, did not surrender without a fight. It was strongly occupied by the French, and so built that several streets, slightly divergent, ran from the centre of the town in the direction of the German advance. It would have been hard to carry the place had it only been attacked in front; but the turning movement was irresistible, and Parigné soon fell into the hands of the Prussians.

The eleventh brigade, keeping more to the right, pressed on until it found itself close to Changé about four o'clock in the afternoon. Then the men were halted to take five minutes' rest, while the church bell rung out an alarm in their ears. The sound of the bell was soon drowned by the rolling fire of rifles and the explosion of bursting shrapnels. The men sang, mocked the hideous crash of the iron missiles, and speedily threw themselves into their work, like well-trained fox hounds in a cover. The French had no need of intrenchments, for every field had its banks and hedges. Along these the thirty-fifth regiment (Berliners), scattered into skirmishing order, crept or ran suddenly from bank to bank, across the fields, always driving back the French, but leaving many dead and wounded. At last they gathered together in groups, and dashing forward with a vociferous cheer, carried the hamlet Gué la Har, about 1000 yards short of Changé. Supposing their work to be over for the day, they must have felt disappointed in finding that there were many banks yet to be carried, and a natural wet ditch, now covered with ice, to be passed before their quarters for the night could be won. The evening closed in; the fight raged in the twilight and in the darkness, under the gloom of which it was hard to tell friends from foes. The Berliners doubted sometimes whether they should fire against some dark group visible against the snow, until, in measured accents, broke forth the war cry, "Brand-en-burg! hur-rah! "quickly answered in like fashion. The dead lay thickly, and the wounded must surely perish that bitter night unless room should be won for them in Changé. Still the Chassepot bullets, fired at random by Frenchmen who were comparatively safe behind banks or in houses, whizzed through the air in a fearful leaden storm. The Prussians were discouraged, but still constant, when they heard sudden firing in advance of them, and to the left of the village much crackling of Chassepots, and the well-known sound of the needle-gun, speedily followed by a "Hurrah," and they knew that Changé was theirs. The timely friend was again General Schwerin with the tenth brigade, who, by bringing his troops round in rear of Parigné, which they had taken, had now outflanked and turned the position of Changé. Still the ill-fed, thinly-clad soldiers of France, though startled, behaved well, maintaining a gallant defence in the streets for some time after the place was entered. All, however, was in vain; for when man met man at close quarters, the terrible Chassepot was no longer of advantage; and finding further resistance useless, the Frenchmen took refuge in the houses, only to be made prisoners. Eight hundred of them soon lay huddled together in heaps for warmth within the walls of the church, whence the tocsin had sounded that afternoon. The orders of General Alvensleben had been faithfully carried out, and the three brigades made their hardly-won quarters that night in the village. This action of the 10th was distinguished by the Germans as the Battle of Changé; those of the 11th and 12th being called the Battles of Le Mans.

On the morning of the 11th the French watched the enemy from a position which might well be deemed impregnable. A curving range of hills forms a vast natural parapet before Le Mans, the river Huisne forming its wet ditch. On this parapet guns and mitrailleuses, side by side, were more thickly planted than the Germans had ever seen before in the campaign. All the bridges over the river were also in the hands of the French. The grand chaussée from St. Calais and Vendôme was that by which the prince's eighteenth division was advancing; but the river is fenced off from the road by a range of hills which, running from the north-east towards Le Mans, meets the Huisne at Yvré. The prince had only three divisions with him—the fifth and sixth of the third corps, and the eighteenth of the ninth corps; for the grand-duke was still at some distance, and the tenth corps, detained at Montoire, had got no farther than Mulsanne and Ruaudin, on the south-westerly road from Le Mans. Across the Huisne the prince's three divisions had in front of them, at one time or another, almost the whole of the French army, and all the while the whole passages of the river were in their hands. Cautious and timid commanders would have hesitated, perhaps retired, before a danger so imminent. But neither Prince Frederick Charles nor Alvensleben of Mars-la-Tour were timid commanders. "The whole country is full of woods, right down to the Huisne," they said. "Let us attack, and the French will never know how weak we are." The wisdom of secrecy in war was, in fact, never more manifest than in the operations of this day; for had the French known the real number of the force opposed to them, they would certainly never have permitted their position to be taken. Their ignorance, or at least the possibility of deceiving them by an audacious movement, was one of the elements in the calculations of the German commander, who might have been attacked with a fair chance of success if the French had been well served by spies. The prince ordered the eighteenth division to carry the hills above Champigné, and sent the fifth and sixth divisions, forming the third corps, against the Huisne. The third received the order to advance on the 11th, in the middle of the day. Their numbers could not have exceeded 18,000 men, for they left Orleans only 22,000 strong, and had been fighting ever since. They advanced, however, against the great natural rampart held by 50,000 men, over ground covered with woods, and intersected by lanes separated from them by ditches and banks. The woods were filled by French riflemen, and beyond the river, in front, were their artillery and mitrailleuses. Alvensleben's brigades advanced, the tenth going northward to try and gain the road to Le Mans by Savigné; the eleventh marched upon Château-les-Noyers, about 500 yards from the Huisne; the twelfth was sent to attack Yvré; and the ninth was held in reserve. The eleventh, in executing its orders, soon found itself enveloped in a furious tempest of fire from the French batteries on the hill opposite Château-les-Arches. After the battle not a tree could be found that was not marked with balls. The eleventh was compelled to give way, and the twelfth, recalled from Yvré, was sent to its aid. The latter attacked Les Arches and drove the French out; but when the divisional artillery was brought up, it could not hold the position in face of the French fire. Towards evening the eighth regiment was sent forward from the reserves to its assistance, as a French force of 25,000 was pushing forward to secure, as was afterwards found, the road by which another French force, retreating from before the grand-duke of Mecklenburg, might enter Le Mans. This, however, was not known at the time; and had the French at this moment advanced boldly, they might very likely have swept away the small number of Germans opposed to them. But they were contented with simply holding the position, which the third corps was not strong enough to carry. Help had been hoped for from the tenth corps, but these were still toiling painfully along the slippery road from La Chartre; so on this, as on other occasions, the Germans had to multiply their numbers by audacity and quickness. They ran from hedge to hedge and from tree to tree, never exposing themselves unnecessarily, yet always ready for a charge and hurrah when a chance presented itself. But Chassepots innumerable crackled in front, the mitrailleuse snarled from its cover, and the perpetually recurring thump of the Gatling was met on every path. The third corps could do wonders, and on this fatal 11th it fought gallantly all day, and held its own against fearful odds; but it failed to accomplish the task assigned to it, and the face of General Alvensleben wore an anxious and unsatisfied expression, as he saw his men struggling in vain against superior numbers, and falling wounded or dying in the snow, while the mournful wind sane; dirges over them through the pine trees.

Meanwhile the action on the main road was progressing. The twelfth brigade, which had occupied Château-les-Arches, hard by the road, in the morning, then joined the rest of the third corps, and it came to the turn of the eighteenth division to carry the heights of Champigné, which tower above the road, not parallel to it, but converging from about a mile to the right of St. Hubert, and coming close to the highway not far from the river Huisne in the direction of Le Mans. The hills are steep, and the end nearest St. Hubert is broken by three ravines. The prince, who was at St. Hubert, ordered the attack to be made, and moved near to watch it. A road from St. Hubert leads towards the right to Champigné, at the foot of the heights nearest to where the Prussians were advancing. One brigade remained at St. Hubert. About four battalions marched along the main road towards Yvré, which lies in the rear of the heights and the river; nearly an equal force took a path through the woods leading to the village of Champigné. The former force, spreading out into company columns, covered by skirmishers, went at the heights in front, with its left towards the river, and took the hills before it in gallant style. The other four battalions, or three with some jägers, pushed through Champigné, and moved steadily at the flank of the hill. One battalion remained below in reserve; one company mounted the hill, upwards, onwards, driving the enemy before them, over one elevation, down into the ravine, up and down again, striving to gain the flank of the French, and assist their struggling friends who were attacking the hills in front. But on the last crest stood three mitrailleuses snarling defiance, and causing even the Germans to recoil. The fire was terrible, especially when artillery could not fire at it from long range. The small force lay down to save themselves as well as they could, and when the company rose afterwards it was short of thirteen men. The rest of the brigade cleared the back of the heights.

Then Captain Mauntz, of the eleventh infantry, chose a small body of picked men, determined that the prince's commands should not remain unfulfilled. Quietly they stole through the ravine, quietly gained the crest where stood the many-barrelled pieces belching forth volleys of bullets. The hill was so steep that the muzzles of the mitrailleuses could not be pointed low enough to meet them until the band of brave men had reached the summit. One moment's breath, and then with a wild hurrah they sprang forward, and carried everything before them. The road was cleared, the men on the other bank rose to their feet—all except the thirteen who never rose more—and the heights commanding the Huisne were in the hands of the Prussians, though not completely until the next day. While Captain Mauntz and his chosen comrades stood beside the pieces they had taken, a Prussian battery opened upon them, not knowing of the gallant deed they had accomplished; and either here, or a little later from the French, he received a wound, "light" in the vocabulary of soldiers, but heavy enough to prevent him from advancing further that day. He was reposing quietly in a little hamlet on the heights, when it was reoccupied by the French, who held it through the night. They would have carried him off as a prisoner, but a woman who had seen his gentleness to her wounded countrymen caused him to lie on her bed, and represented to the French that his wound was dangerous, so that they also pitied him and left him there. Night came, and the faithful few whom he had led so well, consulting how they might rescue him, moved silently out in the darkness and crept into the village, where the French were taking their rest after the battle. The Prussian *kinder*, who knew where their captain lay, stole quietly into the house with a stretcher, and saluting him with "Here, captain, now is your time," they set him on the canvas, and slipped out as they had come, unperceived.

By this time it must have been perceived by the gallant General Chanzy that his army was in sore peril. Before him were the advancing troops of Germany; on his left the duke of Mecklenburg was ceaselessly pressing, driving his outstretched wing so closely to the body as to cripple his powers of motion; behind him was the Sarthe. Another day and his army would be taken as in a net. There was only one chance for him. He had his railways, while the roads were in such a state that the Prussians could hardly move on them. Not unwisely, he began at once to retreat. The German cavalry saw with bitter disappointment trains moving towards Sillé, Le Guillaume, Sable, and La Flèche, while they were prevented from cutting the iron way by the ice on the roads and the closeness of the country, everywhere intersected by numerous small hedges, gardens, and farm inclosures. So the French lines became weaker, while the Germans were strengthened by the arrival at last of the tenth corps.

The night of the 11th was passed in some anxiety by General Alvensleben. When complimented in the evening on the behaviour of his men he remarked, "Yes, but I am not quite satisfied with what the third corps has done." Not satisfied, when he had shown so bold a front that the French must have believed they had a whole army before them! The Germans, indeed, disappointed as they were with their tactical achievements, did not know what advantages they had really gained this day. While Alvensleben was vexing himself in his quarters, General Chanzy was writing a despatch announcing his own defeat. In the course of the night he telegraphed from Le Mans to Bordeaux the following message to M. Gambetta:—"Our positions were good last night excepting at La Tuillerie, where the mobiles of Brittany disbanded themselves, thereby causing the abandonment of the positions we occupied on the right bank of the Huisne. Vice-admiral Jaureguiberry and the other generals think a retreat is necessary under these circumstances. I resign myself to it unwillingly." La Tuillerie was an important link of the positions stretching from Changé to Savigné l'Evêque, and upon its maintenance Chanzy calculated as the key to his whole plan of resistance. The Brittany mobiles who held it had been warmly praised for their behaviour under fire hitherto; but an attack of artillery opened upon them on the evening of the 11th completely disconcerted both officers and men. The officers were too astounded to give orders, and the men, thus left to themselves, in an evil moment determined upon instant flight. Horses were precipitately harnessed to the guns, and the column commenced a retreat which never paused till they reached Le Mans. A movement of retreat had been previously commenced by other parts of the army, but it was not until the abandonment of this essentially important position that General Chanzy became convinced of the utter hopelessness of further resistance. The possession of La Tuillerie would have enabled the Germans effectually to turn the French position and attack them in the rear, a manoeuvre which might have resulted in a worse misfortune than a retreat. Had La Tuillerie been held by such men as held the left bank of the Lisane—as in the next chapter we shall have occasion to show—the chances of Prince Frederick Charles entering Le Mans would have been exceedingly small.

On the 12th the grand-duke of Mecklenburg, who had fought a successful action at Connerre, was able to move his own headquarters to Montfort, his seventeenth division being at Corneille, and the twenty-second at La Croix. The French, as we have seen, were already in full retreat, and their guns had almost all disappeared from the hills; nevertheless, as a matter of prudence, General Chanzy ordered an attack on Les Noyers, which, in the prevailing uncertainty, and after the heavy loss of life on the previous day, caused some anxiety to the Germans. The attack, however, was repulsed; the sixth division took Yvré; while the tenth corps and General Schmidt's detachment, after some fighting at Château de la Paillerie, reached the heights above Le Mans, and threw some shells into the town on the retreating columns of the French. The fifth division followed in the same direction, and the Germans passed into Le Mans, not, however, without some opposition from the French, who fired upon them from houses, and maintained an obstinate contest in the streets and squares. It was not until the following day, January 13, that Prince Frederick Charles thought it prudent to remove his headquarters to the prefecture of the captured town. The grand-duke of Mecklenburg was sent towards Alençon, which in a few days experienced the fate of Le Mans. The eighteenth division pushed on, and occupied the entrenched camp at Conlie. The tenth corps was sent on towards Laval, but found the bridges broken up, and was not sufficiently strong to overcome such opposition as Chanzy's troops were still able to offer. At Le Mans and Conlie an enormous quantity of arms, ammunition, food, and what was even of more consequence, railway materials and rolling stock, fell into the hands of the Germans. On the 16th Prince Frederick Charles reported that, in the engagements from the 6th of January to that date, he and the grand-duke of Mecklenburg had taken from the enemy more than 22,000 unwounded prisoners, two colours, nineteen guns, and more than a thousand loaded ammunition conveyances, besides a large quantity of arms and other war material. The army of the Loire was in fact broken up, and with it Paris had lost its best hope of relief. The losses of the Germans in the fighting about Le Mans amounted, in killed, wounded, and prisoners, to 177 officers and 3203 men.

CHAPTER XXVIII.

The War protracted in the East—The Germans at Dijon—The Battle of Nuits—Evacuation of Dijon—The last Great Effort of France—Composition of the Loire Army—The Portion under the Command of Bourbaki—The Scheme of Colonel de Bigot—Vital Importance of the German Communications—Pro and Con of the proposed Eastern Expedition—Result of it as concerned Chanzy's Army—Errors in Bourbaki's Arrangements for marching—The confusion resulting—Arrival of General Werder at Vesoul—Battle of Villersexel—The German Position for covering the Besiegers of Belfort—Battle of Hericourt—Piteous Sufferings of the French from Defective Supplies—The attack on General Werder resumed—Temporary Success of General Cremer's Division—Repulse of the Second Attack—Deadly Precision of German fire—Third Day of the Battle, and Retreat of Bourbaki's Army—Criticism upon the Engagements—Von Moltke's Master-stroke—The Expedition of Manteuffel—Garibaldi hoodwinked—Fatal irresolution of Bourbaki—Exclusion of the East from the Armistice—The Horrors of the Moscow retreat renewed—The French Army driven into Switzerland—Gratitude of the Emperor to General Werder—An Extraordinary Feat of Marching—Exit Garibaldi—Siege of Belfort—Failure of the German Assault—Capitulation, with Honourable Terms.

WE now resume our narrative of the events which transpired in the east of France, and which will conclude our history of the war, apart from Paris. The struggle was practically closed in the south and west by the capture of Le Mans and the dispersion of Chanzy's army, just described; in the north by the defeat of Faidherbe at St. Quentin on January 19; and at Paris, by the capitulation, on January 28: but for several days a portion of eastern France was unfortunately excluded from the operation of the armistice concluded at Versailles, and the war was consequently prolonged there to a later date than in any other quarter.

Our last notice of affairs in the east was on the occasion of the expedition of Garibaldi for the relief of Dijon, an enterprise which resulted in almost disastrous, certainly ridiculous, failure. The motley assemblage of troops of all nations, generally known as "Garibaldini," was pursued by a Prussian detachment as far as Autun, where a smart fight took place, after which the Germans deemed it prudent to retire back to Dijon, being considerably harassed by the French on the way. At that town General Werder, with the Baden corps, remained, as it served as an advanced post of observation in case any serious movements were made by the French to interrupt the lines of German supply and communication from Strassburg, *via* Nancy, &c., to Paris. The great and important fortress of Belfort, which formed the key to central and southern France, had been for some time besieged by a force under General von Tresckow; and in addition to its other uses General Werder's position at Dijon afforded a safeguard against the approach of any relieving corps to this stronghold.

The position was held without any incident worthy of notice until the middle of December, when General Werder became unpleasantly aware of a concentration of French in his front, and he determined to ascertain, if possible, its proportions. Accordingly, on the 18th of December, the first and second Baden brigades, under General Glumer and Prince William of Baden, proceeded towards Beaune, and at Nuits, a small town about eight miles north-east of the former place, encountered a strong French force under General Cremer. A most desperate engagement ensued, which lasted for five hours, and issued in the Germans storming, with severe loss, the defensive position of the French. General Glumer and Prince William were both put *hors de combat*; and Colonel von Reutz, the officer upon whom the command then devolved, was himself soon after mortally wounded. Of the Germans fifty-four officers and 880 men, killed and wounded, covered the field, while the loss of the French was not less than 1000, besides sixteen officers and 700 men taken prisoners, and the capture of four gun-carriages, three ammunition waggons, and a large quantity of arms. But as the position thus won was considered too advanced and exposed to be held with any advantage, it was evacuated on the 20th by its conquerors, and at once reoccupied by the French.

The evacuation of Dijon by the Germans followed soon after the battle at Nuits. This step was taken in consequence of the very large concentration of French troops discovered not only at Beaune but at Besançon, the entire suspension of civilian traffic on the Lyons and Besançon Railway, the possibility of portions of the Loire army being despatched to the east, and the probability of those forces attempting the relief of Belfort or a movement on his flank. General Werder was accordingly directed to concentrate the Baden division on the line of Vesoul, Lure, and Montbéliard, to give up the advanced positions of Dijon and Langres, and to repel any attempt to relieve Belfort. The French ships of war had about this time captured several German merchant vessels, and detained the captains as prisoners of war. In retaliation the Prussians, a few days before leaving Dijon, summoned thirty of the "notables" of the place, and explained to them that they required forty hostages, who would be sent off to Germany, where, however, they were assured they would be well treated. Twenty were taken from Dijon, ten from Vesoul, and ten from Gray, and in spite of some strong protestations were at once despatched to Prussia. Dijon had been required, on the entry of the Germans, to deposit £20,000 as security for the good behaviour of its townsfolk; but at the entreaty of the mayor, who gave a touching description of the distressed condition of the working classes, the amount was reduced to £12,000. This was returned to the mayor by General Werder on his departure, with a letter complimenting the inhabitants on their exemplary conduct.

We now approach the last effort that could at all be regarded as formidable, made by the provincial armies to retrieve the disasters of France and checkmate the enemy, whose hitherto triumphant progress had been without a parallel. Our readers will remember that after the army of the Loire had been dispersed from Orleans on December 4, it was divided involuntarily into two main portions, and that M. Gambetta, accepting the situation, constituted the two halves respectively as the first and second armies. That which had fallen back along the upper, or left bank of the Loire, towards Bourges, now called the first army, was placed under the command of Bourbaki, the late chief of the imperial guard; while the other division, or second army, was confided to General Chanzy. The "great and paramount object" of the forces of both generals, as announced by M. Gambetta at the time, was the relief of Paris; and in order to effect this the two armies were each reinforced, reorganized, and thoroughly equipped, as far as was possible whilst under the surveillance of a vigilant enemy. In all, including the forces operating in the east and north, there could not at this time (about the end of December) have been less than 450,000 Frenchmen, with from 700 to 800 guns, under arms, exclusive of the garrison and army of Paris—a marvellous spectacle, considering the circumstances; but unfortunately, as Napoleon has observed, there is a wide difference between men and soldiers. The great bulk of these troops were unformed levies; and as most of what was best in the force originally under D'Aurelles had fallen in the terrible struggle of the previous two months, it may be affirmed that the real strength of the principal armies in the field, under Chanzy and Bourbaki, was not nearly equal, even if united, to that of the first army of the Loire. The organization of the new corps was pitiable, and there was such a lamentable want of officers, that their proportion to the men was wholly inadequate. Thus, while the victorious armies of Germany, as we have seen in the previous chapter, had been largely and formidably strengthened, there was nothing like a corresponding increase in the forces of France.

So far, however, as comparative numbers could constitute strength, the forces of Bourbaki and Chanzy were strong indeed, considerably outnumbering the united forces of Prince Frederick Charles and the duke of Mecklenburg, who were thus exposed to an overwhelming onset, had both branches of the Loire army resolved upon closing in upon them. Though Bourbaki had remained inactive for several weeks, he with such good effect held in check the German army occupying the line of the Loire, under the command of Prince Frederick Charles, that, enterprising and adventurous as the prince was known to be, he seemed reluctant either to attack Bourbaki or to withdraw from his position in front of him. The prince's duty was to cover Paris on the southern side; and he co-operated with the grand-duke of Mecklenburg, who, with his army at Chartres, was almost daily awaiting Chanzy's attack from Le Mans. If at this juncture any important event of the war could have been confidently anticipated, it was a combined movement by the two French generals against the prince and the grand-duke. The courage and firmness with which Chanzy held every position from Vendôme to Le Mans, although he fought single-handed and stood on the defensive, may be taken as an earnest of what he might have achieved had he been seconded by Bourbaki and acted on the offensive, as best suits French soldiers. That he had by far the best disciplined half of the Loire army may be inferred from the fact that, while his troops performed prodigies of valour at Beaugency, and stubbornly contested every inch of their retreat, those under Bourbaki had fallen back along the Upper Loire without firing a shot. Bourbaki's soldiers, however, if properly provisioned, were by no means unfit to take the field; and, such as it was, his army was sufficient to paralyze all German movements. To withdraw it, therefore, from Bourges, till it was demonstrated either that Chanzy could raise the siege of Paris without Bourbaki's help, or that he could not raise it even with his help, would appear to be the height of folly.

Not so, however, thought Lieutenant-colonel de Bigot, a staff officer of the regular army, and attached to the seventh division at Besançon. It was natural that the mind of this intelligent officer should dwell especially on the best means of striking an effective blow in the part of his country in which he was, or had been, more immediately interested. He saw that Belfort was invested by some divisions of Werder's army, while Werder himself was operating generally in Franche Comté. His forces, however, were inconsiderable, numbering perhaps 40,000 or 50,000 in the field. They were, withal, occupied in reducing or holding the northern towns of the province, and in guarding the railway lines that from Dijon and Vesoul converged on Paris; they were already kept somewhat in check by Garibaldi and the French army of the east, and had even suffered some slight reverses. Bourbaki, however, and his numerous army were in force at Bourges and Nevers—that is, at no great distance to the west; and Colonel Bigot thought an opportunity was thus presented to strike a sudden and decisive blow which, if successful, would completely change the position of France in the east, and might lead to the relief of Paris. If Bourbaki, with 90,000 out of his 120,000 troops, were to unite with a part of the army of the east, he might, by a rapid attack, isolate and overwhelm Werder, and cause the siege of Belfort to be raised. This done, he could not only master the German communications by Dijon and Vesoul, but a few marches would place him upon the leading railway line which, from Strassburg to Paris, via the great depôts at Nancy, was the mainstay of the besieging army, and essential to its safe existence. A move of this kind, vigorously executed, might compel the invaders to relax their gripe on the invested capital; nor was it necessarily attended with peril to the operations of the French as a whole. True, the withdrawal of Bourbaki might subject Chanzy to the necessity of fighting single-handed with Prince Frederick Charles and the grand-duke of Mecklenburg, who were now extended from Chartres to Orleans, with detachments pointing towards Le Mans; but having been largely reinforced, he could, it might be expected, hold his own; nor was it likely that a combined movement of this kind would be made against him. On the contrary, it was reasonable to suppose that, when informed of Bourbaki's march, Prince Frederick Charles would detach against him the whole or a large part of his troops, or would pause, hesitate, and delay at Orleans. In either case Chanzy would be safe, and might perhaps be able, by a bold advance, to defeat the enemies in his front in detail, and so open a way to Paris. Nor would the operations of Bourbaki be marred even were he followed by Prince Frederick Charles; for he would have greatly the start of him; and a French corps could be left in his rear to observe and retard the prince's movements.

Such was the scheme for the last effort of the provincial armies in behalf of Paris; and although it is unfair to judge of strategy by the event, yet looking at the relative condition and strength of the belligerents, the project from the first might have been pronounced desperate. No doubt the communications of the Germans formed their most vulnerable point, and a few facts will suffice to show their vital importance. Experience had shown that "requisitioning" was of but trifling use in providing for the wants of an army. Only upon the first occupation of a district did it supply any considerable amount of food. If the enemy remained for any length of time the provisions of the inhabitants were either exhausted or concealed, and were not to be had for love or money. Throughout the siege of Metz the troops engaged in that undertaking had to be fed by Germany; and although the army besieging Paris, and those in the several zones around, resorted at first to extensive requisitions, the supplies from this source ultimately proved so precarious as hardly to be worth the danger incurred by the detachments told off to gather them in. Throughout the war, therefore, Germany was the main base of supplies for her armies, whose enormous requirements may be conceived when we remember that, in the course of twenty-four hours, each corps d'armée consumed 1800 loaves of 3 lbs. each; 120 cwts. of rice or pearl barley; either 70 oxen, 120 cwts. of bacon, or a proportionate amount of prepared sausage; 18 cwts. of salt; 30 cwts. of coffee; 12 cwts. of oats; 3 cwts. of hay; 35,000 quarts of spirits and 3500 ounces of orange essence, or some other bitter tincture, to mix with the spirits. To this gigantic repast must be added 60 cwts. of tobacco, 1,100,000 ordinary cigars, and 50,000 officers' cigars for each ten days. Multiply these figures by twenty-five, and we have the sum total of the consumption in one day, or as regards tobacco in ten days, of the German troops in France. The difficulties of bringing up such gigantic stores were often aggravated by the usual disasters incidental to warfare. Sometimes a large number of the oxen, having become infected with the cattle plague, had to be destroyed; and frequently stores would arrive in such a condition that they had to be thrown away and replaced by fresh cargoes. The wear and tear of the war in a rainy autumn and an unusually cold winter, moreover, required the continuous forwarding of an incalculably large stock of every article of clothing. Several times during the campaign each corps had distributed among them woollen shirts, flannel bandages, woollen comforters, woollen plaids, woollen stockings, boots, &c. The field-post, too, in an army where everybody could read and write, took up no inconsiderable amount of rolling stock. From the 16th of July to the 31st of December, 1870, no fewer than 67,600,000 letters and 1,536,000 newspapers—in other words, about 400,000 letters and 9090 papers per day—were despatched from and to the army. In the same period 41,000,000 thalers and 58,000 parcels of all sizes and weights were sent by the War Office to the German military authorities in France. The soldiers received from or sent to their friends and relatives at home 13,000,000 thalers and 1,219,533 parcels, or 22,173 of the latter per day. A large number of sick and wounded were constantly being conveyed back to Germany, besides prisoners, the number of whom was unprecedentedly large. Add to all this that, towards the close of 1870, from 180,000 to 200,000 new troops were brought up to the seat of war, and that the transport of guns, shell, and every variety of ammunition never ceased for one day until peace was declared, and we can then form some idea of the extreme importance of having secure command of the various roads and railways of German communications. Colonel de Bigot rightly judged, therefore, that if the transport of such vast and necessary supplies could be effectually stopped, German armies in France must soon cease to exist, and they would fall an easy prey to levies of men who, however raw, were well armed, and operating in their own country.

The scheme of isolating the Germans from their base of supplies, after defeating them in Franche Comte, would have been feasible, and even promising, had Bourbaki had a trained and well-organized army of 150,000 men, and could the forces of Chanzy have been counted on to cope successfully with Prince Frederick Charles and the grandduke of Mecklenburg, on the supposition of thenacting together. But even on these hypotheses it is doubtful whether it would not have been more prudent to attack the communications of the Germans at points considerably nearer Paris than a few marches to the west of Belfort; and in the actual state of the combatants the whole project was, we think, desperate. Bourbaki's army, even if reinforced to 150,000 men, was known to be raw and ill provided; its movements would have to be conducted in an exceedingly intricate and mountainous country, in the depths of a severe winter; it was, therefore, by no means certain that it would overpower Werder and raise the siege of Belfort, and far from probable that it could master, at least for a sufficiently long time, the great line of the German communications, already not without protection, and which reinforcements could easily reach. Success, therefore was far from assured, even where it appeared most promising; and even success, unless extraordinary, would leave the rest of the forces of France exposed to defeat and disaster. The march of Bourbaki from Bourges and Nevers would obviously set Prince Frederick Charles, in conjunction with the grandduke, free to move against and attack Chanzy; and how could he, with an unorganized and inefficient army, contend against masses of veteran troops, who could, moreover, speedily receive additions? The notion that Prince Frederick Charles would follow Bourbaki, and leave Chanzy to deal separately with the grand-duke, was a mere assumption; and it was absurd to imagine that the prince, a really great commander, would halt, irresolute where to strike, and allow his enemies to elude him. Thus, while the operations of Bourbaki were not very promising in themselves, and would expose Chanzy to defeat and ruin, their failure would not only mar the prospect of raising the siege of Paris, but bring down disaster on his own army.

Properly considered, the project, in truth, was simply a series of eccentric movements, to be executed by inadequate forces, against an enemy vastly superior and in a formidable central position; and those who admire it overlook the decisive fact of the immense disparity between the combatants. There seems very little doubt that at this conjuncture it had become impossible to relieve Paris; the German commanders had rectified the miscalculation they had made, and the barrier of the covering armies, which in consequence of the bombardment could now be reinforced from within, had become too formidable to be broken. Nevertheless, one chance there perhaps was; and had it been seized by the French generals, they would at least have averted a frightful catastrophe. Had Bourbaki vigorously attacked Prince Frederick Charles, instead of going off to the east, he would certainly have detained a very large part of the prince's forces. By that means, although the operation might not have succeeded, Chanzy might have defeated the grand-duke and any other divisions in his front, and at least have endeavoured to reach Paris. In any case the French armies would have had their lines of retreat open, and would have followed the rules of prudent strategy. The contrary course, however, was adopted. A scheme which *might* be attended with results so dazzling seized on the imagination of the ardent Gambetta; and in the last days of December Bourbaki, leaving one corps under Le Comte at Bourges, to observe the movements of Prince Frederick Charles, set off with three corps from his headquarters to effect a junction with the army of the east, a portion of which was to co-operate with him.

The result was what might have been expected by those familiar with the German strategy. Prince Frederick Charles no sooner saw that the enemy, who at Bourges and Nevers had compelled him to remain in force at Orleans, had gone away, than he instantly prepared to turn upon Chanzy, his nearest antagonist, and if possible to overwhelm him.

For this purpose he directed a general movement of his whole troops, in concert with those of the grand-duke, against Le Mans; and as he had three well-recruited corps, with more than 300 guns, and the grand-duke had perhaps 60,000 men, with probably detachments from the besiegers' lines, it was certain that this splendid force would suffice to crush a French army composed chiefly of raw levies, and hardly, if at all, superior in numbers. By the first days of January the broad German line, extending from Chartres to Beaugency, was in full march on the positions of the enemy; and in the preceding chapter we have traced the disastrous fate of the best half of one of the largest and most patriotic French armies the campaign produced.

The command of the proposed expedition to the east was, in the first instance, offered by M. Gambetta to the staff officer who had devised it. The reason why he declined it, and the manner in which it was ultimately carried out, reveals with fearful significance the concurrence of causes which contributed to the misfortunes of France. Colonel de Bigot refused to accept the command, "because he would not serve under a revolutionary government!" and the choice of M. Gambetta then naturally enough, but unfortunately, fell on Bourbaki, who did not thoroughly apprehend the plan he was commissioned to execute. Rightly appreciating the necessity of rapid movements and good lines of retreat, Colonel Bigot had proposed that the French army should advance in four or five columns at least, and should especially hold in force the passages along the Swiss frontier. For this purpose he had insisted that the march to Belfort should be made by a number of converging routes, and that the roads by Montbéliard and Pontarlier should be occupied by several divisions. Instead of this, Bourbaki chose to move with the great mass of his men in a single column through the rugged defiles in the valley between the Ognon and the Doubs, throwing out only very feeble wings. The result was, of course, to retard his progress, and to confine him almost to one line of operations. His force consisted of four corps of three divisions each and a reserve division, and numbered altogether 133,000 men and 332 guns and mitrailleuses. The cavalry were hardly worth taking into account, being composed of the *débris* of all sorts of regiments, and, as a rule, badly mounted. The infantry, on the other hand, taken altogether, were good: the mobiles especially were strong and young; the regiments *de marche* were indifferent, but they were blest with officers worthy to command, whereas eighty per cent, of the officers of mobiles were not fit to be corporals. Though the greater number were supposed to have had four months' training, they were incapable of carrying out the orders issued, and in many instances, under the fire of the enemy, had to be shown how to execute the simplest movements. In general, however, they were not wanting in courage. It is due to General Bourbaki to say, that the expedition was undertaken in spite of his protest that his troops were not equipped and supplied for an arduous campaign; though, had the original plan of different routes been adhered to, much of the misery that ensued would doubtless have been avoided. As it was, the march was heart-rending; the troops were half famished for want of food, without shoes, and starved by the cold; the few staff officers, knowing nothing, were continually giving wrong orders, and the artillery and trains were in hopeless confusion. One instance will suffice. On the very day of the first attack on Von Werder, when it might be supposed moments were of priceless importance, the division of General Cremer, while marching to take the Germans in rear at Frahier, were actually cut in two by the eighteenth corps of 30,000 men and seventy-two guns marching on Chagey. A delay of three hours took place before the two corps got disentangled, and the contemplated rear attack on the enemy never took place.

As already mentioned, General Werder retired from Dijon on December 27, to Vesoul, where he arrived on the 30th. Several strategic movements were made from the town, with the intention of deceiving the French, and gaining time for reinforcements to arrive. Twice the whole army left Vesoul, bag and baggage, but returned the same evening, after a promenade of four or five hours. This lured the French general to approach within a couple of leagues of Vesoul; but as it was a strong position, he retreated without hazarding an attack. Finding this, on the 9th of January General von Werder quitted Vesoul to take up a strong position before Belfort, at Brevilliers. On his way he met a part of Bourbaki's army at Villersexel, and a desperate struggle ensued for the place, from which an active general might easily have outflanked the Germans. Werder won the position, capturing some 1000 prisoners, but gave the enemy an apparent claim to victory by immediately evacuating it. The truth was that a part of his forces had fought the action to detain the French and give time to the main body to fall back to strong positions before Belfort, along the east side of the little river Lisane, a tributary of the Doubs, from Montbéliard by Hericourt to Chenebier. On the 12th January Werder reached his goal, his army was completely concentrated and strongly entrenched; and with reinforcements of heavy guns from the lines around Belfort, he confidently awaited the arrival of the French. Villersexel was only about twenty miles from the Prussian position at Hericourt, and it took Bourbaki five days—from the 9th to the 14th—to bring his troops up in front of that position, so as to be able to attack it next morning! To meet the 133,000 Frenchmen now before him General Werder had less than 40,000 men, of whom 4000 were cavalry, so that in round numbers the French were nearly four to one. The original plan of Colonel de Bigot embraced a simultaneous attack upon the front and rear of the Germans, which, with the immense preponderance of men, might easily have been effected. But the time lost by the French was an important gain to their enemy, whose dispositions now rendered such a movement extremely difficult, and the attack was mainly confined to the front at Hericourt.

At eight o'clock a.m. on the morning of Sunday, January 15, General Bourbaki commenced the attack with artillery, which kept up a continual fire until dusk. The small-arms, which did not come into play until a couple of hours later in the morning, never ceased throughout the day, and at about four o'clock the roar of all arms was fearful. The Germans kept steadily the position they had taken, and when night put an end to the conflict they bivouacked, along the whole fine, on the same spot on which they were attacked in the morning. The frost was about twenty-five degrees below the freezing point, and no adequate idea can be formed of the horrible sufferings which resulted on this night from the defectiveness of the French arrangements. To General Cremer's corps was intrusted the operations against the extreme right of the Prussian position, near Chenebier, and of all Bourbaki's army no portion had made such energetic efforts in getting to the scene of action. It had been detained at Dijon till January 9 by a piteous call from

Garibaldi, who mistook the appearance of a few uhlans at Flavigny and Semur for an advance of the whole Prussian army on the capital of Côte d'Or. By forced marches the corps reached Lure on the 14th, cold and hungry, and wearied with a march of twenty-five miles in the snow. Wearied, as may be imagined when it is remembered that the French soldier carried sixty pounds; and cold, because shoe leather had failed, and in many instances the men were barefooted. Pushing rapidly on, the gallant corps reached Etoban at half-past three on the 15th, and did excellent service with their artillery on the Prussian position at Chenebier. Neither officers nor men had anything to eat from seven a.m. on the 14th till six p.m. on the 15th, although during that time they had marched over forty miles, and been for several hours under fire of the enemy. Night closed in, the hardest the French had yet known, and the Prussians were but 800 yards distant from the main body. The only thought, however, was how to fight against the cold, and contrary to all military rule fires were lit, round which there huddled, without distinction of rank, generals, officers, and men, ay, and even horses, to avoid being frozen to death. A strong cutting wind swept across the plateau, carrying before it blinding clouds of snow, and drifting into small mounds that buried the men up to the knee. Sitting on their knapsacks they passed the night with their feet almost in the fires, in the hope of retaining the vital heat. Their craving for food was forgotten in the torpor that gradually stole over the camp, and the rest so anxiously looked forward to was found by many in that "sleep which knows no waking."

Next morning, the 16th, General Bourbaki renewed the attack, principally on the right wing, against which immense masses of troops were thrown in a vain endeavour to break the German line. Had that object been accomplished at this point, and the advantage actively pursued, the French would have obtained the considerable siege material before Belfort; the investment of that place would have been raised; fresh troops would have been thrown into the garrison, and a further supply of victuals into the town; the army of General von Werder, if not beaten, must have retired, and it would then have been possible at once to cross the Rhine and carry the war into German territory at Baden. On the second day, as on the first, however, along the whole line the inflexible German troops remained almost unshaken in their position: almost, for the divisions under General Cremer, by far the best of Bourbaki's force, succeeded in an attack on Chenebier, and a bold, well-supported flank movement at this crisis would have enabled the assailants to reach Belfort. As, however, on so many other occasions during the war, the French success was not followed up, and the Germans were allowed to take up a still stronger position at Frahier. In the attack the French sustained a very heavy loss, and that of the Germans was much greater than on the first day, when it was only from 200 to 300. On the second it was nearly 1200, principally at Chenebier and Champney. In killed, wounded, and taken prisoners, the French lost a far greater number; while the waste of ammunition may be conceived from the fact that on one acre of ground, where there was not a single man, about a thousand shells were thrown. The mitrailleuses made a fearful uproar, but either they were difficult to manage or were ill served, for they did comparatively little damage. When they did strike, however, the result was murderous; twenty-one men were killed and wounded by one volley. The fire of the Germans on this occasion was marked by a precision perhaps never before equalled. Near Bussurel an attack was made on a battalion of landwehr by 600 French, who were allowed to come within 150 paces, when the Germans fired and killed or wounded the whole 600, with the exception of forty-two, who, panic-stricken, were made prisoners. Again, the second day, the German army bivouacked on the ground they had taken up in the morning.

The third day, January 17, the attack was renewed, but faintly. Bourbaki's orders clearly showed that he had lost all confidence, not only in his men but in himself; and in the afternoon he directed a retreat along his whole line, having failed to attain even his first object, much more to reach the German communications. The luckless commander retreated by the narrow valley through which he had advanced, and it was not until the 22nd that his army, a beaten and disbanded mass, found a temporary shelter under the guns of Besançon.

In this three days' battle 133,000 Frenchmen fought against 35,000 to 40,000 Germans, and could not force their entrenched position. With such a numerical superiority, the boldest flank movements were possible. Fifty thousand men resolutely thrown upon the rear of the Germans, while the rest occupied them in front, could scarcely have failed to force them from their position. But merely its entrenched front was attacked, with immense loss as the result. The flank attacks were carried out so weakly that a single brigade (Keller's,) not only sufficed to counteract that on the German right, but to hold Frahier, and ultimately Chenebier, so as in turn to outflank the French. Bourbaki's young troops were thus put to the severest task which can be found for a soldier in battle; while their superior numbers would have rendered it easier to carry the position by manoeuvring.

Though successful, the troops of Von Werder were sorely tried in the engagements; and not until the 20th, two days after Bourbaki's retreat, were they able to commence the pursuit. For three nights in severe frost, and a fourth under a complete thaw, the Germans had bivouacked on the field, and had made efforts which perhaps have never been surpassed, if equalled, in the long roll of battles. When it is considered that this defence was made between two hostile fortresses (Belfort on the north, not four miles distant, and Besançon, from two to three days' march to the south-west), against an enemy very nearly four times as numerous, who never once shook the German position, the brilliancy of such a defence and the heroism of the troops will remain one of the greatest achievements of the war.

On the 20th General Werder began his southward march, and found everywhere traces of an army not only demoralized but starving. The road as far as Rougemont was strewn with knapsacks, broken Chassepots and swords, cartouche pouches, caps, cooking utensils, and indescribable refuse. Dead horses abounded, from which the flesh had been hacked as they lay. By the 23rd 12,000 prisoners had been taken. The French army, in fact, was in a state of dissolution, when a new enemy descended on its path.

The French operations had been arranged with the greatest possible secrecy; but Von Moltke seems from the first to have divined Bourbaki's mission, and set himself to baffle, and, if fortune favoured, to defeat and crush him. The stage which the siege of Paris had reached enabled the great strategist to diminish the force of the investing army, and a whole corps (the second) was directed from the capital to watch from Troyes and Châtillon-sur-Seine the operations of Bourbaki's army. This corps, supported by some divisions from Metz and the German army of the north, was placed under the command of Manteuffel, with orders to push forward rapidly, as soon as Bourbaki had begun his march to Belfort, and fall on his flank and rear. Disregarding all obstacles, the Germans, not more than 50,000 strong, but well provided, in perfect order, and in the highest state of efficiency for war, were soon, therefore, closing in upon him. The four divisions comprising the expedition were concentrated about Châtillon on the 12th of January, when Manteuffel arrived from Versailles to take personal command. To move rapidly to Werder's aid it was necessary to cross the hills as directly as possible, and the chief routes were closed by the French holding Dijon and Langres. The march was, however, commenced without delay on the three cross-roads between those places which debouched at Selongey, Pranthoy, and Longueau, into the great valley which runs north and south between the Côte d'Or and the Vosges and Jura ranges. The second corps, being to the right or south on the march, detached Kettler's brigade on Dijon to keep Garibaldi occupied. The roads, naturally bad, were rendered almost impassable for artillery by the frost; but large working parties dragged the guns up the slippery inclines; and through the untiring exertions of men and officers the main body of the army was debouching from the hills by the 18th, undiscovered by the French on either side. On the 19th the advance reached the valley of the Saone. At this time it was intended to continue the movement eastward on Belfort; but news of Werder's successes before that place, and of the retreat of Bourbaki, now reached Manteuffel, who swung round to his right, and turned southwards to intercept the French.

For several days the detachment left at Dijon furnished ample employment for Garibaldi, who imagined himself and his troops to be hemmed in by a besieging host. To sustain this idea some attacks were made by his opponents, and as they were "victoriously repulsed," the old general published flaming proclamations, congratulating his men upon having "conquered the most experienced troops in the world." "In an obstinate two days' struggle," he added, "you have written a glorious page in the annals of the republic, and the oppressors of the great human family will once more recognize in you the noble champions of right and justice." In a defence of his military conduct afterwards published in the Italian papers, it transpired that General Garibaldi was all this time utterly ignorant of the manoeuvres of the Germans which were going on around him. The detachment from Manteuffel's force thus effectually hoodwinked him, while the main body of the army moved past his position to accumulate upon Bourbaki's rear. Manteuffel reached Dole on the 24th, and here captured 230 railway waggons loaded with provisions, forage, and clothing—an irreparable disaster under the circumstances to the now hardly-pressed French. From Dole the Germans crossed the Doubs, and rapidly marched to seize the defiles along the Swiss frontier, and thus hem in their intended victim.

Bourbaki reached Besançon on the 22nd, where with fatal irresolution he halted until the 26th, issuing orders, meanwhile, which can only be explained on the supposition of his utter bewilderment. The ex-commander of the imperial guard may have been a dashing officer at the head of a division; but the nerve required to brace oneself up to a bold resolution in a decisive moment is very different from that which enables one to command a division with *éclat* under fire; and like many men of undoubted personal bravery, Bourbaki seemed deficient in the moral courage so necessary to decision of character and promptitude in action. From the moment when he saw that he could not pierce Werder's lines, his mind ought to have been made up as to the course he should take. He must have known that Prussian reinforcements were approaching his line of retreat from the north-west; that his position, with a victorious enemy in his front and a long line of retreat, close to a neutral frontier, in his rear, was extremely dangerous; that in regard to its object this expedition had irretrievably failed; and that his most pressing, nay, his only duty, under the circumstances, was to save his army by retiring as hastily as he could. But the resolution to retire, involving as it did a practical confession that he had failed in his expedition, appears to have been too much for him. He dallied about as if loath to quit the scene of his last battles, unable to advance, unwilling to retreat, and thus gave Manteuffel the time to cut off his retreat. After four days of inactivity a reckless order for a retreat southwards towards Lons-le-Saulnier was given; but at that very time the Germans at Mouchard and Salins were nearer the Swiss frontier than the fugitives, and their retreat was virtually cut off. It was no longer a race; for the Germans could occupy leisurely the outlets of all the valleys by which escape was possible, while Von Werder pressed on the French rear. The unhappy Bourbaki, frenzied by finding his enemies thus closing in upon him, madly shot himself, and his ruined army rushed forth from Besançon almost literally without a commander. The horrors of that flight were like those of the retreat from Moscow; cold, hunger, and terror soon breaking up the mass into a horde of pitiful fugitives.

Such was the situation of military affairs in the east of France when Paris capitulated and M. Jules Favre negotiated the armistice. Count von Bismarck, desirous that Belfort should be in German hands when terms of peace were discussed, demanded that the fortress should be surrendered. As he must have expected, this demand was refused, and he therefore declared that the siege operations must go on. M. Jules Favre had been for months past shut up in the besieged capital, and if he knew aught of the operations in the east, it was only through the medium of a sanguine despatch from M. Gambetta, conveyed through the precarious pigeon post. Having, therefore, no definite idea of the real state of matters, he actually stipulated that if Werder were left at liberty to besiege Belfort, Bourbaki should be free to endeavour to raise the siege. The stipulation was acceded to, and the consequence of M. Favre's ignorance was that the army of the east, of which, since the incapacity of Bourbaki, General Clinchamp had taken the command, was given over to the last horrors of defeat. Driven like a flock of sheep into a mountainous country, where skilful leading alone could have saved even well-formed and well-disciplined troops; hemmed in upon the Swiss frontier without hope of escape; pressed closer and ever closer by a relentless enemy—the army lost provision waggons by the hundred, and the men walked they hardly knew whither, over icy roads or through the deep snow, day after day. General Clinchamp made a last effort to escape by the only route which he could now hope might be open; but in anticipation of this the narrow strip of country along the Neufchâtel frontier was already blocked by the columns of Manteuffel. A series of running fights ensued near

Pontarlier, which ended in the French being fairly driven over the frontier. A convention was signed between General Clinchamp and the Swiss General Herzog, who with a large force had been guarding the neutral line; and on the 1st of February the relics of what had once been an army of 133,000 men crossed that line and laid down their arms. The Germans had captured about 15,000 men, with 19 guns, before their escape to neutral territory could be effected; while 84,000 surrendered to the Swiss. Most of these unfortunate men—surely the most to be pitied of any of the victims of the war—arrived in Switzerland in a state which defies description. Their clothes were rent, and dropping off them in tatters; their feet and hands were frost-bitten. While the shrunk features and crouching gait told of gnawing hunger, the deep cough and hoarse voice bore witness to long nights spent on snow and frozen ground. Some had bits of wood under their bare feet to protect them from the stones; others wore wooden sabots; hundreds had merely thin cotton socks, and many none at all; others who appeared well shod would show a boot without sole or heel—the exposed part of the foot, once frozen, now presenting a wound crusted with dirt. For weeks none had washed or changed their clothes, or put off their boots. Their hands were blacker than any African's. Some had lost their toes; the limbs of others were so frozen that every movement was agony. The men stated that for three days they had neither food nor fodder served out to them, and that even prior to that period of absolute famine one loaf was often shared between eight of them. One corps, the twenty-fourth, escaped, and regained Lyons; but with this exception, such was the melancholy fate of the army led by the brave and brilliant Bourbaki. It was ill organized, ill formed, and execrably led; for the officers of the general's staff proved themselves ignorant of the very roads of their own country, and continually compromised the safety of the corps by their mistakes. Yet such as it was, its capabilities, or what were deemed such, caused for the first fortnight of the year much anxiety at Versailles; and the German emperor celebrated its defeat in the battles of January 15, 16, and 17, by the bestowal of preeminent honours and rewards upon General Werder, the commander. On the 18th of January the emperor sent the oak-leaf for the Order of Merit, which General Werder had already received. On the 20th he issued 150 Orders of the Iron Cross for distribution among the army, accompanied with the following telegram:—

"VERSAILLES, *January* 20.

"General von Werder,—Your heroic three days victorious defence of your position, in the rear of a besieged fortress, is one of the greatest feats of arms in all history.

"I express my royal thanks, my deepest acknowledgments, and bestow upon you the Grand Cross of the Red Eagle, with the Sword, as a proof of this acknowledgment.
"Your grateful king,

"WILLIAM."

The catastrophe of Bourbaki's army was the Sedan of the war in its second phase. In a purely military point of view it was as heavy a blow as the fall of Paris, for it deprived France of the only force available to defend the east and centre. Though not necessarily the result of the false strategy we have described, it must, in a good measure, be ascribed to it;

though doubtless the main causes were the disorganized state of Bourbaki's troops, his own incapacity, and the great ability with which Manteuffel's movements against him were directed. If Von Moltke had never done anything else, this single operation would mark him out as one of the master spirits of war; nor less admirable were the precision, the intelligence, and the promptitude with which the Germans went down on their foe. The march of Manteuffel has, perhaps, not a parallel in modern war, and formed a most striking proof of the perfection of the Prussian administration of supplies upon the march. In sixteen days his force, with all its trains of necessaries and other impediments, crossed two ranges of mountains over byroads; and, leaving enemies on each flank, and passing through the heart of one poor and hostile district, plunged directly into another equally poor and hostile, to intercept and finally destroy an army numerically twice as large. On the other hand, the uselessness of attempting great combinations with undisciplined troops and an inefficient commissariat, was shown at every stage of the miserable failure in which Bourbaki's career well-nigh ended.

As soon as possible after the news of Bourbaki's reverses reached him, Garibaldi withdrew, comparatively unmolested, into a department protected by the armistice, and Dijon was immediately reoccupied by the Germans. The part which he played in the war, although doubtless well-meant, will always form one of the most singular and humiliating features of the struggle. To the dire necessities of the nation alone he owed his position in France. The fanciful garb and swaggering mien of the foreign adventurers who followed him, caused them to be sneered at as "Franconi's circus;" but in the anguish of her defeat France was loath to part with even the least chance of deliverance, and Ricciotti's success at Châtillon, and the capture of the one Prussian flag at Dijon on January 23, reconciled many Frenchmen to the presence of the Garibaldini. But unfortunately for himself, the general was loudly blowing his own trumpet at Dijon, and claiming a great victory, at the very time when he was duped by Manteuffel and prevented from rendering any aid to Bourbaki. Scarcely troubling himself to inquire how it was that, in the midst of his fancied triumph, he found himself in full retreat, Garibaldi heard of his return as a member of the National Assembly, and leaving his disorderly army to take care of itself, he made his way to Bordeaux. He had on his arrival his programme all ready; he would vote for a republic, and for a peace on the conditions of the *status quo ante bellum,* allowing the Germans only a pecuniary indemnity, *to be paid by the partisans of the empire and by the priests.* On the following day he resigned both his seat in the Chamber and his command in the army; and asserting that his duty was at an end and his mission concluded, he retired to Caprera.

Of all sieges during the war that of Belfort was the most prolonged, and the most trying equally to victors and vanquished. The fortress was invested on the 3rd of November, but not until the 3rd of December was a formal bombardment opened, which down to the 18th of February was kept up almost continuously night and day. For seventy-three days without interruption the civil population lived in the vaults and cellars of the town. At the moment of investment the population, usually 8000, numbered about 6000. There was a garrison of 16,000 troops, composed of gardes mobiles, with a fair proportion of line, artillery, and 457 officers. These at the close were reduced, by wounds, disease, and some slight desertions, to 13,500, and 400 of the population perished during the siege.

The besieging force seized early upon the position occupied by the Prussians in 1814—that is, the villages of Danjoutin and Bauvilliers—the south or Swiss side raking the town and forts in profile, and intercepting the approach of a relieving army from the east; but the heights to the right and left, those of the two Perches and of Bellevue, from which in 1814 the town was bombarded, were crowned with recently constructed forts, with which an incessant contest had to be maintained. The most noticeable incident of the siege occurred on the night of January 26, by which time the besiegers' parallels were within thirty yards of the two forts. Then the assault was delivered. Through the Bois des Perches, the trees of which had been cut to spikes, pressed the heavy German columns, to be received by a murderous fire. That night, in killed, wounded, and prisoners, they lost nearly 1000 men. The assault failed, but the next day the French vacated the two forts. The tidings of their abandonment were communicated by some deserters, and the besiegers lost no time in occupying them and placing guns in position. From this moment the fate of Belfort was decided. The fort of Bellevue opposite, at a lower altitude, was speedily silenced. The population were notified by M. Denfert Rocherau, the commandant, that beyond a certain point no fortress was defensible; and its condition having been communicated to the Paris government, their despatch authorizing surrender relieved the garrison from hopeless resistance, and the town from imminent destruction. Belfort passed through a somewhat similar ordeal in 1814, when it was bombarded by the Allies, and from the very heights which now were French forts; but the power of the artillery, though at a longer distance, was so much greater now than then that it did much more injury. Then, as on the present occasion, the town surrendered only in consequence of negotiations preliminary to peace. The troops were allowed to quit with the honours of war the place they had so well defended, and the garrison marched out with arms and baggage, taking with them also their papers and archives. The town was originally included in the territory demanded by the Prussians preliminary to peace; but Count von Bismarck ultimately offered to yield it on condition of the German occupation of Paris; and to save a position of such importance, M. Thiers consented to this last act of humiliation for the capital.

CHAPTER XXIX.

Feeling in Paris after the Sortie on November 30 and December 2—Communications between Count von Moltke and General Trochu as to the Fall of Orleans—Paris Determines to Resist to the Last—Disbandment of some of the Republican National Guards—Difficulties of the Government with the Democratic Clubs, which advocate most Extreme Measures—Irritation amongst the Germans at the Long Continuance of the Struggle, and Preparations for the Bombardment of the City—Presentation of an Address to the King of Prussia on the Unification of Germany, and His Majesty's Reply—Proclamation of General Trochu to the Army, and Reception of Encouraging News from M. Gambetta—Great Sortie at Three Different Points on December 21—Description of the Engagements and their Results—Severity of the Cold, and Sufferings of the French in Consequence—Christmas Inside and Outside the City—Commencement of Active Siege Operations, and Capture of Fort Avron by the Germans—The Last Days of 1870 in Paris—Want of Food and Fuel—Bombardment of the City—Renewed Determination to resist on the part of the Inhabitants—Results of the German Fire—Remonstrances of M. Jules Favre and the Diplomatic Agents against the Destruction of Hospitals, Churches, and Schools, and Count von Moltke's Reply—Installation of the King of Prussia as Emperor of Germany at Versailles—Description of the Ceremony, and Address of the King—Bloody Sortie on January 21—The Germans at first surprised, and Desperate Fighting on both Sides—The French unable to maintain their First Successes—Excited State of Public Feeling in the City during the Fight, and Despair when the Soldiers returned—Military Reflections on the Engagement.

ALTHOUGH the result of the great sortie on November 30 and December 2, described at the close of Chapter XXIV., failed to secure any advantage to the besieged, the Parisians were fain to believe that the retrograde movement of their troops on that occasion had only been undertaken with a view to future and more effective operations. In fact, the prevailing opinion was that the retreat was purely strategical, and that the army encamped in the Bois de Vincennes was yet destined to retrieve the fortunes of the capital. It was even currently reported in the city that the Prussians had evacuated Versailles, and crowds assembled in the public places, hoping to find the information officially confirmed. These illusions, however, were rapidly dispelled. The German successes at Orleans on December 4 were immediately communicated to General Trochu by General von Moltke; with an offer that, if he deemed it expedient to receive confirmation of the fact through one of his own officers, a safe conduct to come and return should be provided for him. This intelligence was, of course, forwarded in the hope that the government of Defence would see from it the desperate character of their position, and be induced to capitulate; and when the document was discussed at a council of ministers, the minister of Finance, M. Ernest Picard, seemed disposed to embrace the opportunity of considering whether a cessation of hostilities were possible. Whatever impression his counsels might have made upon his colleagues, was speedily nullified by the determined course of the governor of Paris, whose conduct on this occasion was certainly not that of a man who thought himself engaged in a hopeless cause. General Trochu contended that the overtures of the enemy went to prove their critical position in the heart of a hostile country in midwinter; that the victory at Orleans might not be so conclusive as was represented; and that everything was to be gained by continuing the struggle until help came from the provinces, as Paris could still hold out, and victories might follow reverses. Accordingly, yielding to his eloquence and enthusiasm, the council decided unanimously on the continuance of the war, and the German *parlementaire* was despatched with a reply declining Count von Moltke's offer.

The Parisians were immediately informed of this interchange of correspondence by a note sent to the press, in which the members of the government again expressed their determination to prosecute the defence with vigour. "This news," said they, "which reaches us through the enemy, supposing it to be accurate, does not deprive us of our right to rely on the great movement of France rushing to our relief. It changes nothing either in our resolutions or our duties. A single word sums them up—to fight! Long live France! Long live the Republic!"

A profound impression was, however, produced in the city by the intelligence. The question as to the truth and importance of General von Moltke's communication was freely discussed, and led to the expression of very conflicting opinions; but at best the tidings were unwelcome, and confirmed the misgiving which now prevailed respecting the possibility of averting the fall of the capital.

On December 8 a decree was published disbanding the tirailleurs of Belleville, consisting chiefly of red republicans. They had repeatedly demanded to be led against the enemy, but on the only occasion on which they were called to encounter the least danger they had behaved in the most cowardly and disgraceful manner; many of them afterwards deserted, and it was next to impossible to maintain even the appearance of discipline amongst the remainder, either officers or men. In fact, they were useless for service, and were, moreover, on such bad terms with the battalion of La Villette, that a barricade had been erected in the trenches to separate them, and prevent collision! A day or two later another order of the day was published, dissolving the battalion known as the volunteers of the 147th. It had received orders to proceed to Posny, but mustered only 100 men, half of whom presented themselves without arms. The battalion refused to march, on the plea that their wives had not been paid the allowance which, by order of the government, they were to receive while their husbands were in the field.

While these extreme military measures were required to preserve discipline in the ranks of the disaffected national guards, the government experienced no small difficulty through democratic clubs inside the city. At most of these gatherings the authorities were loudly denounced as betrayers of the republic; and at one of them a motion was proposed, signed by M. Ledru-Rollin, calling on them to renounce the idea of capitulation, and to make a sortie *en masse*, so as to force the Prussian lines and deliver Paris with the least possible delay! It was urged, with somewhat more reason than was displayed in the discussion of other matters, that battle should be given to the enemy before famine had weakened the bodies and damped the courage of the people. Eight days—a space which was considerably reduced by the more enthusiastic—were allowed the government to raise the siege. If they failed to do anything within that period, they were threatened with another demonstration at the Hôtel de Ville and the proclamation of the Commune.

On the other hand, the prolongation of the struggle was causing irritation, not only in the besieging camp but throughout Germany, and in some quarters a change of tactics was warmly urged, to bring about the capitulation of the city. Preparations for bombardment were therefore carried on, but the plan of "waiting and watching" was still continued. The weak points of the German investment were also strengthened, although the general feeling was that the delay in striking a successful blow from inside the city had rendered General Trochu's operations comparatively hopeless. The promised relief had failed; the army by which it was to be achieved had been hurled back beyond the Loire; and although the besieged garrison might make a gallant effort, the Germans entertained little apprehension of their succeeding in breaking through the lines of investment.

On the afternoon of December 16 a deputation of thirty members from the North German Reichstag, headed by the president, Herr Simson, arrived at Versailles with an address from the legislature to King William, and to congratulate him on the decision of the South German princes to offer him the imperial crown of Germany. On the 18th the deputation was received at the headquarters in the prefecture of Versailles. Herr Simson read the address, setting forth that, by means of treaties with the South German states and by making two alterations in the constitution, titles were secured to the future (German) state and to its most exalted head, which had been revered for long centuries, and to the restoration of which the yearning of the German people had never ceased to be directed. The address then continued:—"Your Majesty receives the deputies of the Reichstag in a city in which more than one destructive armed incursion against our country has been considered and put into execution. Near it, under the pressure of foreign force, were concluded the treaties in immediate consequence of which the German empire collapsed. To-day, however, the nation may from this very spot console itself with the assurance that emperor and empire are again erected in the spirit of a new and living present, and that, with the further assistance and the blessing of God, it will secure in both the certainty of unity and might, of right and law, of freedom and peace." In his reply, after referring to the wonderful dispensations of Providence which had brought them together in that "old French royal residence," and to the support he had received from the German provinces, the king said:—"The victorious German armies, among which you have sought me, have found in the self-sacrificing spirit of the country, in the loyal sympathy and ministering care of the people at home, and in its unanimity with the army, that encouragement which has supported them in the midst of battles and privations. The grant of the means for the continuation of the war which the governments of the North German Confederation have asked for in the session of the Diet that is just concluded, has given me a new proof that the nation is determined to exert all its energies to secure that the great and painful sacrifices, which touch my heart as they do yours, shall not have been made in vain, and not to lay aside its arms until German frontier shall have been secured against future attacks. The North German Diet, whose greetings and congratulations you bring me, has been called upon before its close to cooperate by its decision in the work of the unification of Germany. I feel grateful to it for the readiness with which it has almost unanimously pronounced its assent to the treaties which will give an organic expression to the unity of the nation. The

Diet, like the allied governments, has assented to these treaties in the conviction that the common political life of the Germans will develop itself with the more beneficial results, inasmuch as the basis which has been obtained for it has been measured and offered by our South German allies of their own free choice, and in agreement with their own estimate of the national requirements."

In the evening the deputies dined with the king, and the following morning (Sunday) were taken to the front to obtain a glimpse of the beleaguered city. They then attended divine service at the chapel of Louis XIV. in the palace of Versailles, where King William was attended by a large number of illustrious personages.

Returning to Paris at this period, there were evident indications that another sortie was in active preparation. On the 17th of December General Trochu issued an address to the army, in which, after giving them credit for having made efforts on behalf of the country which had been of good service to their sacred cause, he proceeded:—"Our companions in arms of the army of the Loire—improvized by the patriotism of the departments, as the patriotism of Paris has improvized the army of Paris—set us an admirable example. They recruit themselves under fire, as we do, at the price of heroic sacrifices, in a combat which astonishes the enemy, who staggers under the magnitude of his losses and the indomitable energy of our defence. May these noble examples strengthen you; may the touching spectacle of the citizens of Paris become soldiers like yourselves, and fighting with you in the close bonds of duty and peril, raise you to the high level of all duties and dangers; and may your commander succeed in instilling into your souls the sentiments, the hopes, and the firm resolutions which animate him."

On the following morning the *Official Journal* contained a despatch from M. Gambetta, to the effect that the army of the Loire, far from being annihilated, "according to the lies of the Prussians," had been divided, and that now two armies, instead of one, were marching upon Paris from the south. A hopeful view was likewise taken of General Faidherbe's operations in the north. "The Prussian retreat," continued M. Gambetta, "is a movement concerning which there can be no mistake. If we can only hold out, and we can if we have only the will, we shall beat them. They have suffered enormous losses, and experience the greatest difficulty in obtaining supplies of food. But to triumph we must resign ourselves to supreme sacrifices without murmuring, and fight even unto death." Most of the Parisian journals received the announcement with exultation, and began to speculate upon the German retreat.

In preparing for the approaching sortie orders were given that the gates of the city should be closed; the marching companies of the national guard, provided with 120 rounds of ammunition per man, had their posts assigned them; battalions of sappers and miners were despatched to the front with materials for the construction of bridges; and trains of artillery waggons proceeded to the scene of the proposed operations.

The action commenced about eight o'clock on the morning of the 21st, and extended over an area reaching from Mont Valérien to Nogent-sur-Marne, or half round the city. On their right the French, commanded by Generals Malroy and Blaise, acting under the orders of General Vinoy, attacked the village of Neuilly-sur-Marne, the Villa Evrard, a lunatic asylum in advance of Neuilly, and the Maison Blanche, a farmhouse near the Strassburg railway. The attack was opened and maintained with great vigour, but the fighting was carried on almost exclusively by artillery. The French soon gained a decided advantage, the superiority of their new heavy guns being speedily established. The Prussian batteries at Noisy-le-Grand maintained a stubborn ordnance duel with theirs on the plateau of Avron, and somewhat checked the advance for a time; but although in one redoubt alone they had placed a battery of twenty pieces of artillery, the guns of Avron, assisted by the Fort de Nogent, dismounted every one of them and destroyed the work. After this the French succeeded, in spite of a vigorous defence by the Prussians, in successively taking and occupying Neuilly-sur-Marne, La Maison Blanche, and Villa Evrard, which had been occupied as the headquarters of the Prince-royal of Saxony. Meanwhile Fort Nogent kept silent the Prussian batteries of Noisyle-Grand and Villiers.

The centre of the movement, and that which sustained the heaviest of the fighting, was commanded by Admiral la Roncière, under General Ducrot, whose troops consisted of soldiers of the line, a brigade of sailors, and the mobiles of the Seine. Preliminary to the attack on Le Bourget, which was the centre of the action, the Forts Aubervilliers and L'Est directed a vigorous fire on the village, as did also a couple of batteries stationed at Courneuve. Pieces of flying artillery were likewise moved up, and on the Soissons Railway a novel mode of attack was made by a couple of cuirassed locomotives, which were used to considerable advantage. Steaming forward to the most favourable point with comparative impunity, these formidable batteries of cannon and mitrailleuses poured a destructive fire into the German positions. At eight o'clock there was a lull in the fire from the forts, and the infantry were thrown forward to the attack. An attempt to take the village by storm was made by a battalion of marines, commanded by M. Lamothe Heuet, and the 138th regiment of the line, supported by the tenth and twelfth battalions of the mobiles of the Seine. The marines, at the head of the column, went into action hatchets in hand, and rifles slung at their backs, and had a desperate hand-to-hand struggle with the men of the Prussian royal guard at the entrance of the village. The marines, however, succeeded in getting into some houses, and took ninety-seven prisoners, who were immediately sent to the rear. The northern part of Le Bourget was held for three hours, but the fierce and stubborn resistance made by the Prussian guard caused it to be abandoned. The French had lost very heavily. Of 600 who went forward to the assault, 279 were wanting at its close. Of fourteen marine officers engaged, four were killed, and four others seriously wounded. The tenth mobiles had its lieutenant-colonel, the commandant, the captain-adjutant-major, a captain, and a lieutenant, put *hors de combat* almost at the first fire.

While this column was engaged on the left of the village, another attack was directed on it from the south by a second column, composed of the franc-tireurs of the press (300 strong), and the 134th regiment of the line, under the leadership of General la Voignet. The first and second companies of franc-tireurs extended in skirmishing order and advanced at the *pas gymnastique*, with the intention of entering the village by the left; the third company entered by the right; and the fourth advanced on the full front. The Prussians were admirably protected by barricades and breastworks; every house was a small fortress, and from every window, roof, and cellar a formidable fusillade kept the assailants at bay. The French, however, showed great coolness and courage; but the attack failed. At two o'clock the fire of the small arms ceased; the baffled columns retired, carrying some of their wounded with them; and the forts renewed their cannonade. Generals Trochu and Ducrot were on this part of the field, and ordered up three batteries of field-guns, which opened on the enemy's position. His guns at the Pont Iblon and Blanc-Mesnil were silenced, and a portion of Ducrot's army was enabled to advance on the farm of Groslay and Drancy, to the south of Bourget. A diversion was also made during the attack on this quarter, on the village of Epinay, by mobiles of the Seine and national guards of St. Denis.

On the west, and simultaneously with the attack upon Le Bourget, General Noel also made a demonstration against Montretout on the left, Busanval and Longboyau in the centre, and on the right against L'Ile du Chiard; the latter under the direction of the *chef de bataillon* Faure, commandant of the engineers at Mont Valérien, who was grievously wounded at the head of a company of the Paris freeshooters. The only purpose of this movement was to distract the attention of the besiegers.

During the general attack the weather was intensely cold, and although a large number of Frenchmen had been provided with pickaxes and spades to intrench the troops as soon as an advantage had been gained, the ground was frozen so hard that they could not carry out their purpose. To this excessive cold the French attributed their want of success, and certainly it told very much against their movements.

At the close of the day the French right still held the positions they had gained, but the main body of the troops was withdrawn to the trenches, a sufficient force being left to hold Neuilly, Villa Evrard, and Maison Blanche. At Villa Evrard a somewhat remarkable incident occurred. When the action was over the French prepared to encamp, and lighted their bivouac fires. General Blaise and some officers of his staff were warming themselves round one of these, and discussing the incidents of the day, when suddenly a Prussian bugle was heard, followed in an instant by a discharge of musketry. General Blaise was killed on the spot, and several of his staff were severely wounded. The enemy who had done this turned out to be some Saxons who had remained in the cellars of Villa Evrard, and had crept out of their place of concealment when all was quiet. Few of them, however, escaped.

In this sortie it will be seen that the French had obtained considerable advantages, and occupied several positions which they had taken from the Prussians; but contrary to expectation the movement was not followed up, avowedly owing to the cold, which, as already stated, was exceptionally severe for the French climate. In one of the outposts on the night of the 23rd, 125 men were frost-bitten, and several instances occurred of others who were frozen to death.

This state of affairs continued until the morning of the 25th ushered in Christmas, which found the besieged capital undergoing fearful hardships, but still determined to hold out against the invader. Hardly a cannon shot, however, disturbed the hours of the Christmas festival, such as it was. Rations of beef, with a small portion of butter per head, were served out instead of horseflesh. On the German side it was made as comfortable as circumstances would permit, and although the fear of renewed sorties required the strictest watch to be kept, there were many very successful merrymakings and much joviality.

Almost immediately after Christmas active siege operations were commenced by the German commanders. The French position on the plateau of Avron was first selected as the object of attack. One of the results of the sortie of November 30 was the occupation by the French of a broad spur of land lying along the front of Fort Rosny, and reaching from Drancy to Neuilly-sur-Marne. On this ground, which included the plateau of Avron, the besieged had established batteries, amounting in the aggregate to 100 guns, some of which were powerful marine artillery, supported by a large infantry force. From this *point d'appui*, which bulged out into the lines of the besiegers, much trouble and annoyance had been caused to them.

On the 21st December, when the French advanced to the capture of Villa Evrard and Maison Blanche, they made this excellent position their starting point, and were materially supported by the fire of the guns from the redoubt. This finally determined the Germans to destroy it, although their engineers had been for some time previous selecting their points of attack, and working parties had been engaged during the nights in making preparations. The works were completed with great rapidity after the sortie, and on December 26 the Germans had established twelve batteries of heavy guns brought from Strassburg, Toul, La Ferté, and Soissons—three at Raincy, three at Gagny, three at Noisy-le-Grand, and three at the bridge of Gournay. Lieutenant-general von Kameke was appointed chief engineer, and Major-general Prince Hohenloe commanded the batteries, with Colonels Reeff and Bartsch as chief assistants.

The positions, which were admirably chosen, completely enfiladed the plateau of Avron, and also covered the Forts Noisy, Rosny, and Nogent. During the night of the 26th the German pioneers were busy cutting down the trees which had masked their works, and met with considerable attention from the French forts, which had awakened to the dangers of the situation. On the following morning the weather was intensely cold, and the snow was falling quickly, but the German guns opened a tremendous fire upon the plateau, which was continued with systematic steadiness throughout the day, and was only partially suspended when far into the night. Some of the shells from the batteries of Raincy actually fell within the district of Belleville. The besiegers made a vigorous reply, although their discharge was less regular and their aim less accurate. The troops, however, stood firm, and although some 3000 shells were thrown from the German batteries the entire casualties were less than sixty. On the morning of the 28th the cannonade recommenced, and continued during the day at the rate of about five to eight shots per minute.

General Trochu rode out early to the plateau, and visited the trenches, addressing some words of encouragement to the troops. During the afternoon the Prussians brought up some field batteries, and pelted most furiously at the French positions on the plateau, which was completely furrowed by the fire of eight converging batteries. During this fierce cannonade, the French troops sought concealment in the trenches, but the ground, hard as granite through the frost, opposed a resistance which caused almost every shell to burst. The French batteries, the parapets of which were almost as brittle as glass, were also struck full in front by shots from Chelles, right and left by the enfilading fire of Raincy and Gagny, and pounded at in the rear from Noisy. The powerful artillery of the French was unable to cope with the Krupp cannon; the plateau became untenable; and orders were consequently given to the troops occupying it to retire. The retreat commenced at six o'clock in the evening; but as there were about 100 guns, many of them of large calibre, to carry off along the slippery roads and in darkness—for the camp fires were extinguished, so that they might not attract the enemy's fire—it was three o'clock on the following morning before the mitrailleuses which had remained behind to protect the retreat were enabled to quit the plateau. The gardes mobiles, exposed in the trenches for six and thirty hours to the Prussian cannonade, lost about 300 in killed and wounded. One shell alone laid six low out of a party of nine gathered round the breakfast table of a commander of mobiles, who, together with his wife, was wounded, while only a single one of his guests escaped scathless.

The Germans, however, were surprised at their own success, and not until the afternoon of the 29th did their patrols, who groped their way up the sides of the plateau, discover that the position had been evacuated. The same evening the villages of Bondy and Villemonble were found deserted, and at midnight the German advance came upon the late French positions on the crest of Avron, amidst an awful scene of devastation.

The military bulletin announcing the abandonment of the plateau had a most depressing effect upon the Parisians, whom no consoling news now reached from outside, and who were without fuel and almost without food. The document intimated that the conditions of the defence would have to be changed, although its means and its energy would not be affected by the bombardment. During the whole of the 29th the Germans continued to bombard Forts Noisy, Rosny, and Nogent. In the course of five hours 155 shells fell on the barracks in Fort Rosny; casemates believed to be impenetrable to every kind of missile were rent and torn away; and from eight o'clock in the morning till six in the evening nearly 2000 shells fell within the enceinte and on the scarp and counterscarp of Fort Rosny alone; yet very few of the naval gunners were injured, and "the men stood to their pieces firm, resolute, vigilant, and undauntable." In the adjacent village only a few houses were damaged, and yet the road between Rosny and Avron was so ploughed up by the number of projectiles which had struck it, as to be impassable. The military report stated that altogether between 5000 and 6000 shells were thrown against the three forts in the course of the 29th. The closing days of the year 1870 proved a trying time indeed to the beleaguered city. While the German guns were pounding away at the eastern forts, the inhabitants were suffering not only from the want of food but also from the bitter cold. The price of fuel in consequence rose immensely, and the government had been unable to obtain a supply for the wants of the people. They therefore resolved to cut down the woods of Vincennes and Boulogne, and the trees on the boulevards; but the necessary preparations consumed time, in which the poorer classes were perishing. An indiscriminate onslaught was consequently made upon trees, palings, and trellis-work, without distinction of public or private property. These proceedings led the authorities to speedily accumulate a sufficient supply.

Thus closed the year 1870 in and around the capital of France. Provisions were getting dearer and dearer. The death rate had doubled. The "Red" party were showing signs of uneasiness. The popular voice bespoke impatience with the feebleness of the government operations; and the Prussians were thundering at their very doors. But no one dared to whisper the word "surrender!"

The new year was ushered in by the booming of the guns from the Paris forts, while the German sentinels stood to their posts in the biting cold which prevailed. The besiegers, strengthened by their easy success at Mont Avron, had the fullest confidence in their ultimate triumph; and the besieged, amidst hardship, disease, and death, appeared equally determined to prolong the struggle. The gloom of the city, as on the emperor's fete day, when the army of the Rhine was grappling with the invader, was increased by its contrast with the usual festivities of the season, and by a growing apprehension that the energies of the provisional government were not equal to the duties which the emergency imposed on them.

The morning of the 5th of January commenced a fresh era in the history of the siege, for on that day the bombardment of the city itself really commenced. The months spent in watching an enemy who contented himself with remaining passive, not even answering the fire of the forts, combined with the growing scarcity of food, had told heavily on the Parisians, whose martial ardour was fading fast under the ever-present shadow of the Germans. The bombardment came like a ray of light to restore energy and give the required excitement.

The Germans directed their shells on the city from the south, and continued their fire from day to day with great severity. Their projectiles fell in the quarters of Grenelle, Vaugirard, and Montrouge, reaching even to the gardens of the Luxembourg, killing and wounding men, women, and children, and striking alike public buildings, private dwellings, and military hospitals. Some 40,000 deadly missiles were hurled upon the forts alone before the general bombardment commenced; but after the 5th of January 10,000 shells on the average were daily fired from the German batteries, of which 500 fell within the city proper. The French, however, replied with considerable effect, and caused much damage to the enemy's batteries; many of their naval guns being superior in weight to any that the Germans could bring against them.

The bombardment has been described as "the one mistake made by the Germans during the war," and very probably it prolonged the defence of the city. That it was commenced without the previous warning usually given by civilized nations where the fate of non-combatants is at stake, excited the just indignation of the French government, as well as of the various diplomatic agents within the city; and this bitter feeling was intensified by the presumed peculiar direction given to the Prussian fire. In one night five shells struck the Hospital of the Infant Jesus, where 600 sick children were domiciled. On the night of the 8th, a poor woman was slain in the Hospital de la Pitie; men were killed and wounded in the Military Hospital of Val de Grace; and five little children asleep in their beds at the school of St. Nicholas fell victims to a shell, which also wounded many others. Nor was any respect shown by the besiegers to associations connected with scientific research. The garden of Medical Botany, founded in 1626 by Louis XIII., and associated with the greatest names among the *savants* of the nation, was vigorously assailed, and a greenhouse filled with rare tropical plants was totally destroyed. These occurrences roused the faltering spirits of the people; and the government issued an indignant protest, in which they deprecated the fact that "Prussian shells had been wantonly launched against hospitals, ambulances, churches, schools, and prisons, and that the exigencies of war could never be an excuse for the shelling of private buildings, the massacre of peaceful citizens, and the destruction of hospitals and asylums. The government of National Defence, therefore," continued the document, "protest loudly, in the face of the whole world, against this useless act of barbarism." Notwithstanding protests of this nature, however, the bombardment continued with great violence, and spread death and dismay throughout the more exposed quarters of Paris. Count von Moltke, in reply to the French complaints, said that the striking of hospitals and ambulances was purely accidental, owing chiefly to the long range and the fog. "When the batteries are approached nearer the city," said the general, "the gunners will be able to take better aim."

During this time also, much internal uneasiness prevailed in the capital. Rumours of treachery and espionage were rife, and suspicion was openly expressed against the households of those high in position. The members of the government of Defence had hitherto worked harmoniously; and although the confidence of the populace in General Trochu had at times wavered, it was not till late in the history of the siege that there appeared reason to believe the other members of the cabinet doubted his ability to offer effective resistance to the German army.

Beyond the bombardment, almost the only movement among the opposing armies consisted in casual engagements between outposts and patrols. In some of these skirmishes, which were secretly planned, the French obtained slight advantages, taking and killing some of the enemy. The range of the French operations embraced demonstrations against the bloody ground around Le Bourget and Mont Avron; and the Saxons put out a feeler to test the capacities of Fort Noisy, but only to discover the impossibility of a successful assault. Thus while cold, hunger, and death prevailed in the French capital, the besiegers also were subjected to a heavy penalty, and had to encounter much hardship and danger as they closed their grip upon the city.

But there is perhaps nothing more remarkable in the history of the war than the scene which was witnessed in the palace of Versailles on the 18th of January. After having long lain in abeyance, the title of Emperor of Germany was to be restored to the Prussian king in the midst of an enemy's country! Could any event more forcibly illustrate the astounding victories of the German arms and the humiliation of their opponents? The previous day witnessed a great "gathering of the clans," and the ceremony of formally proclaiming William Emperor was made the occasion of a grand military display. The Galerie des Glaces had been prepared, delegates from all the regiments of the third army with their colours had been summoned, the Bavarian regiments also sending their colours. The flags were arranged in a semicircle in the order in which their regiments lay before Paris, the place of honour being given to those of the landwehr guard, which, placed in the centre on a raised platform, were protected by the gardes du corps. An altar had been erected on the side of the gallery facing the park, and here stood the army chaplains, conspicuous among whom was the king's favourite preacher, Chaplain Rügger. On the right of the altar were ranged the military choristers and musicians, to the left the delegates from the various regiments, decorated with the Iron Cross. At twelve o'clock the king arrived, followed by a host of grand-dukes, princes, counts, and generals. After prayers and a consecration sermon by Rügger, the king from the steps of the altar made a short speech, and commanded the chancellor to read aloud his address to the German people, as follows:—

We, William, by God's grace king of Prussia, hereby announce that, the German princes and free towns having addressed to us a unanimous call to renew and undertake with the re-establishment of the German empire the dignity of emperor, which now for sixty years has been in abeyance, and the requisite provisions having been inserted in the constitution of the German Confederation, we regard it as a duty we owe to the entire Fatherland to comply with this call of the united German princes and free towns, and to accept the dignity of emperor. Accordingly, we and our successors to the crown of Prussia henceforth shall use the imperial title in all our relations and affairs of the German empire, and we hope to God that it may be vouchsafed to the German nation to lead the Fatherland on to a blessed future under the auspices of its ancient splendour. We undertake the imperial dignity, conscious of the duty to protect with German loyalty the rights of the empire and its members, to preserve peace, to maintain the independence of Germany, and to strengthen the power of the people. We accept it in the hope that it will be granted to the German people to enjoy in lasting peace the reward of its arduous and heroic struggles, within boundaries which will give to the Fatherland that security against renewed French attacks which it has lacked for centuries. May God grant to us and our successors to the imperial crown that we may be the defenders of the German empire at all times, not in martial conquests, but in works of peace, in the sphere of national prosperity, freedom, and civilisation."

Count von Bismarck read the proclamation, and the grand-duke of Baden advancing, cried, "Es lebe Seine Majestat der Deutsche Kaiser Wilhelm, hoch!" The assembly cheered, and the German princes did homage to their new suzerain. In the evening a dinner was given to the emperor, to which all the German princes were invited, and at which Mr. Odo Russell represented England.

On the same day, at home in Prussia, Count Itzenplitz had read the proclamation of the king relative to the imperial dignity in both houses of the Prussian Diet, when a call for cheers for Germany's emperor, King William, was responded to amidst great enthusiasm.

While these important historical events were taking place at the German headquarters, the interior of Paris was busied with preparations for a great military movement—the last and most bloody which took place under the walls of the capital. It was felt that the time for the final great effort had arrived. All promises of help from the provinces had collapsed, and there was nothing for it but that General Trochu should silence his detractors, and play his last card by making a great sortie on the besiegers' lines. All through the day troops marched merrily along towards the western gates of the city, singing the "Marseillaise" and the "Chant du Départ." The populace assembled in the principal thoroughfares to see them pass, and great anxiety was shown by many of their relatives. The troops consisted of regulars, mobile guards, and mobilized national guards; and on the night of the 18th they encamped without the walls, behind Mont Valérien and in the Bois de Boulogne, so that they were ready for action early on the following morning. The plan of the sortie had been carefully prepared by a council of war under the presidency of the governor of Paris, the base of operations being Mont Valérien. The army of operation was composed of 100,000 men, formed in three main columns, and supported by 300 guns. The movement was directed by General Trochu in person, who had left General le Flo in Paris as governor *ad interim*.

The column of the left, under the command of General Vinoy, was ordered to carry the redoubt at Montretout and the villas of Beam, Pozzo di Borgo, Armagand, and Ermenonneuve; the centre, under General Bellemare, was to proceed to the east of the Bergerie. The column of the right, commanded by General Ducrot, was to operate against the west of the park of Busanval.

The line of front from Montretout to Ruel extended, as will be seen by reference to the map, about three English miles across. The task of bringing together and handling a force so large, and most of them novices, in such a narrow compass, was difficult and delicate; and their concentration was not effected without immense trouble. The night was dark, and the morning of the 19th enveloped in a curtain of thick fog.

The preparations, however, had been carried out with great secrecy, and in the earlier period of the action the Germans were taken completely by surprise. But the positions attacked had been selected by the besiegers from the natural difficulties which they presented to the enemy, and every accident of the ground had been turned to profitable account. There were a series of intrenchments and crenellated walls and barricades, in addition to a most formidable abattis created by the felling of the woods. The trees had been all made to fall with their branches towards Paris, and the base of each trunk served as a cover for a marksman to fire over as his opponent was struggling to get at him.

Daybreak found each division of the French troops under arms, but considerable delay occurred through difficulties encountered by the right, under General Ducrot. About ten a.m. General Vinoy advanced against Montretout, defended by a single company, before any general alarm had been raised in the German camp. This division pushed on from behind Mont Valérien by the road parallel to the Seine, hidden for a space by the hillock of La Fouilleuse. The column of assault consisted of the zouaves, the 106th of the line, and several battalions of the national guard. The French rapidly swept into the village, and thence enveloping the earthwork rushed upon the little garrison. The Germans fought stubbornly, and a bloody hand-to-hand struggle ensued; but they were speedily overpowered by numbers. Those who were not killed were taken prisoners. Following up their success, Vinoy's army descended upon the village of St. Cloud, which they quickly took, together with many prisoners. The Germans then began to fall back upon the woods, followed by a host of skirmishers, who kept up a brisk fire, which made much noise but did little damage, as the Prussians took advantage of every object that offered cover.

Meantime General Bellemare, who commanded the French centre, attacked the château of Busanval and the height of La Bergerie. These positions were held by a force far superior to that with which the French left had to contend. The first obstacle met with was the farm of La Fouilleuse, whence a withering fire of small-arms was poured in upon the French advance. Twice were they driven back, but still persisting and trusting to a rapid advance, they, at a third effort, carried the farm with a rush and cheer. Still pressing onwards with undaunted courage, another spirited charge rendered them masters of that portion of the German position which lies between La Fouilleuse and St. Cloud. Having thus effected a junction with the right of Vinoy's corps, and the right of Bellemare's corps having captured the château of Busanval and the heights of La Bergerie, they were insensibly broken up into detached masses, and the fight subsided into a number of isolated combats, in which the French wasted much ammunition, and in return were shot down by the Germans, who fired steadily and securely from the cover of trenches and stone walls. The heavy force thrown into the park of Busanval was permitted by the Prussians to approach within less than 200 yards of a loopholed wall which they held at the top of a slope, when presently a terrible discharge of musketry from their infantry within an incredibly short space of time covered the ground with dead and wounded Frenchmen. As the French troops were struggling in the forest, General Vinoy had massed some regiments of mobilized national guards to act as reserves, and to support the attacking forces. The only Prussian shells thrown at this point during the day fell among these guards; and although some of them had fought splendidly in the earlier part of the engagement, these terrible missiles so scared them that they broke and ran amidst the wildest confusion. In the garrison at La Bergerie were two companies of the garde landwehr, who, when the French advanced, lined the park walls of that place, and held the whole column in check by a murderous fire, which piled the front with dead. Again and again the French tried to carry the position, but failed. The Prussians fought till mid-day, when a detachment of the fifth corps came to their help, at the sight of whom the men who were left gave a tremendous cheer; but at eleven o'clock the French, coming on in force against Garches, once more occupied the heights and carried the village.

The weak point of the attack, however, was the French right under General Ducrot. This division had received orders to march from St. Denis, a distance of ten miles, during the night. The route lay along a defective line of rail, and on a road encumbered by a column of artillery which had lost its way in the dark. The district, besides, was swept by a Prussian battery at the Carriéres de St. Denis, which took the advancing troops in flank. From these causes the march of the French was greatly delayed, and their passage secured only by a cuirassed locomotive mounting a couple of guns, which General Trochu sent along the St. Germains Railway to their assistance. Eventually the troops under General Ducrot formed into line of battle; but at the very outset his right, established at Rueil, was fiercely cannonaded by formidable German batteries from the other side of the Seine. His late arrival proved disastrous. The Germans had taken the alarm; and although the right rushed bravely on and stormed and took Busanval, when they reached La Jonchere and the Porte de Longboyau they encountered, equally with the left and centre, a deadly fire from behind loopholed walls and crenellated houses, so that here too the bodies of the slain were literally piled in heaps. Again and again General Ducrot led his troops to the attack, and at a fearful cost succeeded in taking La Jonchere; but their utmost efforts failed to obtain the desired object of forcing a way to Celle St. Cloud and joining hands with General Bellemare to the south of La Bergerie.

The tactics of the besiegers on the 19th January were identical with those previously pursued; and although, as has been stated, the Germans were taken by surprise, the probability of attack had been foreseen. A rumour to that effect, indeed, had nearly a fortnight before reached General von Blumenthal, who then made dispositions which were nearly identical with those of the 19th. When the sortie was developed General Kirchbach sent word to the emperor "not to be uneasy; he could promise his Majesty the enemy should never pass his lines." He kept his word; but it proved a hard task. A hotter fire was never perhaps maintained than during part of the day.

The rush of the French at first carried the foremost positions of the Germans; but the supports were coming quickly from every quarter, and the artillery poured in a fire of great precision, which caused much havoc. The seventh grenadiers and the forty-seventh battalion marched to Vaucresson, formed for attack, and at twelve o'clock came down on Garches with great impetuosity, driving out the French, who still, however, hung about the position till two o'clock. The fusilier battalion of the seventh being ordered to attack and take the place, made a grand advance, sustained by the jägers and the rest of the fifty-ninth. Reserving their fire till they were within 200 feet of the French, they then literally destroyed them.

When the full force of the Prussian attack was brought to bear, the effect was deadly. The Germans made a fierce onslaught on the centre and left of the French position, which caused them to fall back; but a little later they moved forward again, and the summit of the plateau was once more recaptured. As night set in, however, it was impossible to bring up artillery to secure the position; and the French troops, fatigued by twelve hours' fighting, and by the marching on the preceding nights, were ordered to retreat. Montretout, however, the first position captured in the morning, was the last to be retaken by the Germans, who at half-past ten p.m. drove out the enemy by a splendid dash; but a French regiment of mobiles, notwithstanding, actually held out in St. Cloud until the following day. Even then they persistently refused to surrender; but at length such a force of artillery was brought to bear on the village from the heights above, that further resistance was seen to be useless. Of this regiment only 300 remained to lay down their arms. The Germans, profiting by this incident, at once completed the destruction of the village of St. Cloud, so that it could offer no further shelter to the troops of the besieged.

During the progress of the sortie great anxiety was felt in the French capital. Every available point of observation was eagerly seized, and the people waited in hope of favourable news. About six o'clock in the evening a cheering bulletin was issued by General Trochu. But the arrival of ambulances filled with wounded men told of terrible slaughter at the front; and the truth became partially known at half-past nine, when another bulletin from General Trochu was issued, stating that the enterprise so happily commenced had not resulted so favourably as might have been hoped, as the enemy, who had been surprised in the morning, brought up towards the latter part of the day immense masses of artillery, with infantry of reserve.

On the morning of the 20th the presentiment of coming evil was fully verified. The army had retired within the line of forts, every house in Neuilly and Courbevoie was full of troops, and regiments were camping out in the fields, where they had passed the night without tents. Many of the men were so tired that they threw themselves down with their muskets at their sides, and fell asleep in the mud, which was almost knee-deep. Bitter were the complaints of the commissariat. Bread and *eau de vie* were at a high premium. During the fight many of the men had thrown away their knapsacks, with their loaves strapped to them, which now became the property of the Prussians. Some of the regiments, chiefly those which had not been in the action, kept well together; but a vast number of stragglers were wandering about looking for their battalions and their companies. About twelve o'clock it became known that the troops were to re-enter Paris, and that the battle was not to be renewed. About one the march through the gate of Neuilly commenced. Most of the onlookers appeared to be in blank despair, so fully had they been impressed with the conviction that the great sortie must end in a decisive victory. Their loss was estimated at between 6000 and 7000 in killed and wounded. General Trochu requested of the German commanders an armistice of a couple of days, in which to collect the wounded and bury the dead. The request was refused; but an interval of a couple of hours was granted, during which the artillery ceased, and the work of mercy was heartily engaged in, while a large portion of the dead which had been left within the Prussian lines were buried by the German *krankentragers*.

On reviewing the results of the sortie, it would seem that the concentration of a large army between the forts and the *enceinte* of Paris demanded too much time; that the French troops were not sufficiently organized for extensive manoeuvres; and that the object of the action was not sufficiently important to warrant the sacrifices made. The details of the affair and of the minor sallies that preceded it show beyond doubt, that Trochu's troops had attained just so much discipline as enabled him to bring them out from cover under fire, but that neither he nor his lieutenants could get them to advance when the fire was fairly opened on them. The strength of the German intrenchments and the excellence of the German batteries was indeed great; but no one can suppose that, had the besiegers and besieged been compelled to change places for forty-eight hours, the former, with their accumulated moral fighting power to back them, would not have found a way through the miles of circuit round their army. Nor can it fail to be observed that on this occasion the energy shown for a brief space, in the attempts of General Ducrot to seize the loops of the Marne seven weeks before, was almost wholly absent. The causes of this depression were the ruin of the French. General Trochu, though obeyed, did not lead to victory; and as he thus failed to inspire his troops with confidence in his generalship, Paris was doomed to the heavy fate before her.

CHAPTER XXX.

Irritation against General Trochu—He is compelled to retire and is succeeded by General Vinoy—Bad News from the Provinces—The Government compelled to ration Bread—Revolutionary Rising on January 21—Liberation of Gustave Flourens from Prison—An Attack on the Hôtel de Ville completely frustrated, and several Insurgents killed and wounded in the Streets—Opening of new Siege Batteries and Continuation of the Bombardment—Error as to the Amount of Food in the City—Interview between M. Jules Favre and Count von Bismarck—Feeling in the City—The Capitulation and its Terms—Occupation of the Forts by the Germans—The Return of the French Soldiers and Sailors into the City—Revictualling of Paris—Munificence of England—The Effect of the Capitulation at Bordeaux—Magnificent Proclamation of M. Gambetta—He forbids the Election of Adherents of the Empire—Despatch from Count von Bismarck on the Matter, and Reply of M. Gambetta—Action of the Paris Government and Resignation of M. Gambetta—Election of the National Assembly and its Meeting at Bordeaux—Resignation of their Powers by the Government of National Defence—M. Thiers chosen as Chief of the Executive Power—Declaration from the Departments to be annexed to Germany declaring their Unalterable Attachment to France—Action of the Assembly thereupon—Negotiations for Peace at Versailles—The Great Struggle with regard to the Cession of Metz—Peace at Last—Important Telegram to the Emperor of Russia announcing the Fact—The German Plan of Operations in case Peace had not been concluded—Scenes in the National Assembly when the Terms were discussed—Large Majority in Favour of their Adoption—Action of England with regard to the Reduction of the Indemnity—Letter from the King of Italy against the Hard Terms imposed on the French—Occupation of Paris by the Germans—Last Telegram from the Emperor King—Reception of the News of the Conclusion of Peace at Berlin.

THE failure of the sortie of the 19th January produced a greater effect on Paris than any other incident had caused since the beginning of the siege, and excited violent public irritation against General Trochu. Several members of the government resolved on appointing another military commander, and the mayors of Paris also called on him to give in his resignation. His position had, in fact, become untenable; but, according to his own statement in his "Defence Speech" before the National Assembly at Versailles, he determined not to resign, believing that to do so would be an act of cowardice; and not until he was actually compelled to do so by the government did he retire. He, however, retained his post as president. His successor as commander-in-chief was the old comrade of Lord Clyde, General Vinoy, who had specially distinguished himself in the Crimean War. He was very popular in the city for having saved his division from the catastrophe of Sedan, and brought it back to Paris.

But Paris had by this time two other great causes of alarm. The utter defeat of Chanzy had become known, and although fabulous reports of the success of Bourbaki were current, he was a very long way off; and then bread was getting short. Some time previously the government promised that it should not be rationed; but it had been rationed, and the ration consisted of a piece the size of a penny roll, made of rye, bran, hay, and a very little wheat. Even this miserable pittance was not always to be had, so that many who went for rations had to return without any. The thoughts of the Parisian populace, however, pointed not to capitulation, but to revolution. The wild spirits of Belleville thought the sure way to save the capital was to turn out the government, instal the Commune, and place all the forces under some unknown young officer, whose military aptitude might be doubtful, but who could be trusted to show himself the reddest of red republicans. Accordingly on Saturday, January 21, a number of these agitators combining went to the prison of Mazas, where M. Gustave Flourens, a leader of the ultra-democratic faction, had been confined since the former attempt, early in November, to upset the government at the Hôtel de Ville. Five or six hundred men, armed with Chassepots, among whom were many of the mutinous battalion of national guards that M. Flourens had commanded, arrived at the prison about midnight, and, through the vacillation of the superintendent, they were enabled to rush in and liberate M. Flourens and five of his political friends, whom they at once conducted in triumph, with drums beating, to Belleville. Next day a party of 200 or 300 insurgents, mostly wearing the uniform of the national guard, proceeded to the Hôtel de Ville, shouting "Vive la Commune!" and in the true spirit of cowards shot at two officers who came out to speak to them. Upon this the gardes mobiles in the building fired steadily and deliberately from the windows at the most active and forward of the assailants, who, returning the fire as they fled, made off, some taking refuge behind the lamp-posts, some crouching or lying down behind the heaps of earth in the Place de l'Hotel de Ville, others entering the nearest houses and continuing to fire out of the windows, or from their roofs and balconies. The conflict lasted half an hour, when the insurgents, who had collected in the Avenue Victoria, hoisted a white handkerchief in token of submission. About thirty of them were overtaken and arrested. Nearly a hundred persons lay prostrate on the ground; but when the firing ceased, many of them who had escaped scatheless at once got up and sneaked away. A dozen were severely wounded, and five or six killed. On the following day the clubs were extinguished in which certain ranters had nightly spouted sedition; and the *Combat* and the *Reveil*, the two newspapers which—the one in the morning, the other in the evening—had daily stirred up the people to rebellion, were suppressed.

While these lamentable occurrences were taking place inside the city, and Frenchmen were shedding the blood of their brethren, the bombardment was vigorously pressed by the Germans outside. The siege batteries on the north, in the construction of which little opposition had been encountered, and which were armed with the heavy artillery which had reduced Mézières, opened fire on Saturday the 21st, after a summons to St. Denis to surrender had been refused. They continued to ply as vigorously as their companions on the east, during the few remaining days of the siege. The forts of La Briche, La Double Couronne, and De l'Est were, however, very strong, and responded vigorously to the German attack. The bombardment of the capital during the last week of the siege presented, however, few points of interest. The shells which fell within the *enceinte* caused little loss of life, and still less alarm. The citizens made up parties to watch their descent on Auteuil and Vaugirard, and the gamins applauded when an "obus" ever and anon splashed in the ice of the still half-frozen Seine.

General Vinoy's appointment as commander-in-chief had been hailed as giving promise of renewed efforts; but on Tuesday, January 24, it began to be whispered about that an error of several days had been made in the calculation of the period that provisions would last, and that, between Paris and actual starvation, there remained barely sufficient time to collect and bring in supplies of food. That the government must therefore, and at once, treat for terms of capitulation, was evident to all who knew the facts of the case. The newspapers had up to this time been silent on the subject, but by degrees the truth percolated through the well informed, and by the evening half Paris knew that Jules Favre had actually left that morning for Versailles to ask for terms. The news came first as a great surprise, then as a great disappointment, and lastly, as a considerable relief—except in the tumultuous district of Belleville, where some serious signs of insubordination were shown, which were, however, instantly suppressed; General Vinoy having guaranteed to maintain order there at all costs during the negotiations. Not only had Chanzy's collapse become generally known in the city, but also that Bourbaki had been defeated; and as the last chances of Paris were thus exhausted, there was no reason for any longer holding out. The government was, indeed, very much blamed for allowing itself to be driven into a corner by not having discovered sooner the actual state of the provisions, and above all, for not having replaced Trochu by Vinoy three months earlier. But these censures apart, the idea of capitulation was accepted as a melancholy necessity, relieved greatly by the reflection that Paris had, at least, made a splendid defence, and that it had yielded, not to arms, but to hunger.

The negotiations, between M. Favre and Count von Bismarck were continued daily till the 28th, when a general armistice for twenty-one days was agreed on, and the bombardment of the city ceased and was not afterwards renewed. The war may thus be said to have lasted exactly half a year; for on the very day six months that the Emperor Napoleon left St. Cloud for Metz, the capitulation was signed. With one exception, the terms of the capitulation were comparatively light. The exception was a fine of £8,000,000, which was levied on the Parisians. The city itself was not to be occupied, and even its name did not occur in the articles of capitulation, which professed to treat only of the surrender of the forts. The troops in these were to be disarmed and confined in Paris; but the national guard and one division of the line, deputed to keep order in the city, were to receive *tabatières* and muzzle-loaders in exchange for Chassepots. No public property was to be removed, but all munitions of war were to come into the possession of the captors. The general armistice included the revictualling of the city, and the convocation of a freely-elected Assembly which should authorize either the conditions of peace or the continuance of the war.

Thus the prize for which the German army had watched and waited for more than four weary months (the siege having lasted 131 days and the bombardment twenty-three), was at length within their grasp, and, as may be naturally supposed, they lost no time in entering upon the possession of the forts they had so hardly won. That of Valérien was the first occupied, and was visited by the king of Prussia—now emperor of Germany—on January 29. Altogether 602 field-pieces belonging to the army of Paris were handed over to the Germans, and 1357 guns in perfect condition were found in the forts.

In striking contrast to the exultation of the Germans was the state of affairs in the city. On the same day that Valérien was occupied, the French troops who had been camped outside during the siege—mobiles, sailors, linesmen, and franc-tireurs—came within the walls. They were without their arms, dirty, tired, many of them so ill that they could scarcely walk, and with that dead, despairing look which the beaten soldier always wears.

The most pressing matter after the capitulation was, of course, the revictualling of the city, which was indeed within not many hours of actual famine when the armistice was agreed to, and neither any government nor any charitable societies could, by the most strenuous efforts, have prevented thousands of human beings dying of hunger, had the siege continued another week.

On February 4 the supplies included a very large quantity of provisions from England, under the care of Colonel Stuart Wortley and Mr. George Moore, which had been purchased with subscriptions received by the Mansion House Committee, and consisted chiefly of concentrated milk, cheese, bacon, biscuits, flour, Liebig's extract of meat, and preserved soup. These supplies were distributed among the twenty arrondissements of the city, according to their respective population. On the arrival of Colonel Stuart Wortley and Mr. Moore, they were received by M. Jules Favre, who, in the name of the people of Paris, expressed his heartfelt thanks to them for the efforts made in England to relieve the distress in the capital. The English cabinet, on February 1, had also placed all the stores of the administration at the joint service of the French and German governments for the purpose of revictualling the city; and when the fact was announced in the House of Commons, the general cheering which it elicited showed the warm and universal approbation with which it was received by the representatives of the people. Food to the value of £50,000 was forwarded in the first government despatch. The energy and zeal thus shown on all hands prevented any deaths occurring from actual starvation, and in a few days there were supplies of everything in abundance.

The intelligence of the capitulation of Paris fell upon Bordeaux like a peal of thunder. Tidings of the negotiations arrived in the city from England, before M. Jules Favre's despatch could reach the Delegate Government. M. Gambetta at first refused to credit the report; and when the official news was received, he published a magnificent proclamation, which was really worthy of the occasion. He assumed, indeed, with more of French vanity than truth, that though, overpowered by famine, she had been compelled to surrender her forts, "Paris remained still intact, as a last homage which had been wrested by the power of moral grandeur from the barbarians." To the determination of Paris, and the value of the delay her resistance had caused, he did ample justice, but insisted eloquently on the misfortune entailed on the eastern armies by the armistice which M. Favre had negotiated without taking counsel of the Bordeaux government, and without really understanding its drift. He, however, accepted the armistice, and urged the duty of turning it to account as a war measure. "Instead of a reactionary and cowardly Assembly, of which the foreigner dreams, let us summon a really national and republican one, which desires peace, if peace secures honour, rank, and integrity to our country, but would also be determined to wage war and be ready for everything rather than assist at the assassination of France. Frenchmen! let us think of our fathers who bequeathed to us France, compact and indivisible. Let us not alienate our inheritance into the hands of barbarians. Who would sign it? Not you, Legitimists, who have so boldly fought beneath the banners of the republic to defend the territory of the ancient kingdom of France. Nor you, descendants of the citizens of 1789, whose masterpiece it was to seal the old provinces into an indissoluble union; and it is not we, the working men of the towns, whose intelligence and generous patriotism have always been the representatives of France in her strength and unity, as a people initiating modern liberties; nor you, labouring men of the country, who have never withheld your blood in defence of the revolution to which you owe your property in land and the dignity of citizens. No! not one Frenchman will be found to sign this infamous pact. The foreigner will be deceived. He will be compelled to relinquish the idea of mutilating France, because we are all inspired by the same love for our mother country, and we are unmoved by defeats. We shall again become strong, and we shall expel the foreigner. To achieve this sacred object we must devote our hearts, our wills, and our lives. We must all rally round the republic, and above all prove our calmness and firmness of soul. Let us have neither passions nor weaknesses. Let us simply swear, as free men, to defend before and against everybody, France and the republic. To arms! To arms! Long live France! Long live the republic, one and indivisible!

"LEON GAMBETTA."

On the same day M. Gambetta issued a decree forbidding the election to the Constituent Assembly of any who had been councillors of state, ministers, senators, members of departmental councils-general, or government candidates for the Corps Législatif under the empire.

A great meeting of the republican party was held at Bordeaux in the evening, when resolutions were passed declaring that the capitulation of Paris was not binding on the provinces, and requesting M. Gambetta to become president of a committee of public safety, to act independently of the Paris government. This step he hesitated to take; having received from the diplomatic representatives of Austria, Spain, and Italy, who were sojourning at Bordeaux, a communication stating that they were accredited to the Paris government, and that if he separated himself from it they would leave. But fresh cause of irritation was furnished by a telegraphic despatch to him from Count von Bismarck, protesting against his decree concerning the elections, as irreconcilable with the freedom of choice stipulated by the armistice. The decree was stigmatized as an "arbitrary and oppressive" act of M. Gambetta himself. This despatch he immediately published, with an indignant comment, exposing the "insolent pretension" of Prussia to interfere with the constitution of a French Assembly; and declaring that its object was to obtain the support of "accomplices and flatterers of the fallen dynasty and allies of Count von Bismarck." The Paris government, however, met the remonstrance in a very different spirit. M. Jules Favre, in replying to it, assured Count von Bismarck that, as the country wished free election, there should be no restriction upon the right of voting, and promised that the decree of M. Gambetta should be rescinded; though, with the ingrained intolerance of French politicians, this was afterwards qualified by withholding from members of the families who had reigned over France the right to a seat in the Assembly. To prevent any confusion which might arise from M. Gambetta's decree, the elections were adjourned from Sunday to Wednesday; and M. Jules Simon, a member of the Paris government, was sent to

Bordeaux with instructions for their management. These were rejected by M. Gambetta and his colleagues, who published a note in the *Moniteur*, stating that they felt it their duty to maintain their own decree, for the sake of the national interest and honour, despite "the interference of Bismarck in the internal affairs of France." The Paris government then resolved to put an end to the authority of the delegation government in the provinces; but to avoid further complication M. Gambetta resigned on the 8th of February, and along with his resignation sent to the prefects a despatch characterized by extreme moderation and good sense, recommending them not to resign, but to carry out the elections of February 8, a course by which they would "render to the republic a supreme service."

The elections, considering the state of the country, were conducted with facility and good order not a little remarkable, and an Assembly was returned which was Conservative, Orleanist, Legitimist, Republican, or anything but Imperialist. In Paris the extreme Radicals, to the surprise of every one, gained the day; but this was partly explained by the fact that the more moderate Parisians had abstained from voting, and by the exodus of 140,000 whose means had allowed them to quit the city. The candidate chosen by the largest number of constituencies was M. Thiers, who was elected in no fewer than eighteen departments.

The National Assembly met at Bordeaux for a preliminary sitting on the 12th of February, and immediately constituted itself, although its members were not nearly all present. On the following day it held its first public sitting, when M. Jules Favre, in the name of his colleagues both at Bordeaux and Paris, resigned their powers as the government for National Defence into the hands of the representatives. He said—"We have borne the burden of government, but we have no other desire, under existing circumstances, than to be able to place our temporary plans in the hands of the National Assembly. Thanks to your patriotism and reunion, we hope that the country, having been taught by misfortune, will know how to heal her wounds and to reconstitute the national existence. We no longer hold any power. We depend entirely upon your decision. We confidently expect the constitution of the new and legitimate powers." M. Favre then announced that he and his colleagues would remain at their post, to maintain respect for the laws, until the establishment of the new government.

On the 16th the Assembly, by an immense majority, elected as its president M. Grèvy, a moderate republican of long experience in public life. Next day it proceeded to the most important duty which it had to perform prior to the negotiations for peace, and chose M. Thiers chief of the executive power, who the same evening received the congratulations of the ministers of England, Austria, and Italy, and was immediately called to enter upon the duties of his office. At the sitting of the Assembly the next day (February 18), M. Keller, a deputy, laid on the table a declaration, signed by the deputies of the Lower and Upper Rhine, Meurthe, and Moselle departments, in which lay the territories understood to be required by Germany. The declaration expressed in the strongest terms the unalterable attachment of these departments to France, and earnestly entreated the Assembly not to abandon them to the enemy. The document was very well framed, and the pathetic spirit which it breathed must have gone to the hearts of many who heard it. In reality, however, it virtually called on the Assembly to abide by the famous declaration that "France would never cede an inch of her soil or a stone of her fortresses;" and that, of course, was now impossible. There was immense republican applause when the declaration was read, and M. Rochefort demanded that it should be immediately referred to the bureaux, so that the Assembly might give to the negotiators of peace either imperative orders not to agree to the cession, or full freedom. M. Thiers, instead of proposing delay, boldly and unexpectedly supported the motion, as he evidently saw that its presentation furnished an opportunity of making the Assembly itself a party to the retraction of the vow that no territory should be ceded. He said, from the bottom of his heart he fully shared M. Keller's feelings, and urged that, after so affecting and grave a document had been read, the Assembly, without loss of a moment, must in honour deal with it, and order its bureaux to report instantly on the proper answer to give to it. In two hours the Assembly received and adopted a report to the effect, that the petition of Alsace and Lorraine must be referred to the negotiators to deal with as they thought best. Thus quietly and unmistakably, though indirectly, the negotiators were empowered to make a cession of territory the basis of negotiation. In times of sudden and rapid change a whole line of policy is often abandoned, simply because at a particular moment it ceases to be insisted on. The policy of carrying on the war *à outrance* was tested and abandoned, without one word being said about it when the report of the bureaux was received by the Assembly. No voice was lifted up to propose that Alsace and Lorraine must remain French at all hazards.

At the same sitting M. Jules Favre astutely proposed that the government should be supported in its negotiation by a committee of fifteen members of the Assembly, who should be in constant communication with the actual negotiators, and would, of course, be pledged to support the treaty of peace when finally referred to the Assembly for ratification. The precaution was not unnecessary, as it was possible that very severe terms of peace might cause in the Bordeaux Assembly some sudden revulsion of feeling against the negotiators. But twenty men of great influence, all supporting each other, would be more than likely to prevent such a turn of the tide.

M. Thiers arrived at Versailles early on Tuesday, February 21, and spent the whole day in conference with Count von Bismarck. He fought gallantly to the last, but could not, of course, either by argument or entreaty shake the fixed resolution of the Germans, which imposed conditions more onerous than France had been prepared to expect. The indemnity which the Germans demanded was resisted as one without precedent in history, the very attempt to comply with which would derange the finances of the entire world. France had been weighed down with German requisitions for seven months; Paris had just paid a war contribution of £8,000,000 sterling, and had, besides, her own war debt to provide for. The interest of the loan that would be necessary to provide such an indemnity as that demanded would utterly crush the great body of the tax-payers of the country, make their position intolerable, and lead them to prefer war at any risk to life under such burdens. The imperial chancellor was, however, inexorable. France had caused the expenditure incurred by the Germans, and she must defray it. In the end, M. Thiers consented that France should bind herself to furnish the sum named.

The territorial surrender gave more trouble. It was known that Alsace, with Strassburg, must be sacrificed, but it was hoped, even against hope, that Metz might be saved to France; and M. Thiers exerted his utmost efforts to retain it, even though it should be without fortifications if necessary. Count von Bismarck urged that the Germans must have Metz as a security against invasion. M. Thiers pleaded the nationality of the inhabitants; but he was reminded that those among them who did not like to become Germans had been promised ample time in which to wind up their affairs, sell their property, and retire to France. So strongly did M. Thiers feel on this point, that at one time he seemed determined to withdraw rather than incur the responsibility of ceding it; and he personally waited on the emperor and the imperial prince of Germany to lay his appeal with regard to it before them. Those august personages received him with politeness, but finally remitted him again to Count von Bismarck. At last, after eight hours and a half of discussion on Friday, five hours and a half on Saturday, and five hours on Sunday, the name of M. Thiers was affixed to the treaty of peace on February 26. All that time had to be added to the hours spent in previous conversation, negotiation, and exposition, which, as we have said, M. Thiers managed with consummate ability and address, but without material result. At the close of the last day's interview there was a stormy scene. Count von Bismarck, who was not very well at this time, became impatient of delay, and insisted on the signature of the treaty on the close of the discussion, which would be the signal for the German troops recommencing the war. M. Thiers was consequently obliged to sign. When all was over the emperor sent for the Crown Prince, and the father and son, tenderly embracing, wept for joy and thankfulness. The gratifying news was immediately telegraphed to the empress, at Berlin; to the emperor of Russia, and to the king of Bavaria. The telegram to the emperor of Russia concluded as follows, and excited considerable interest at the time:—"We have thus arrived at the end of the glorious and bloody war which has been forced upon us by the frivolity of the French. Prussia will never forget that she owes it to you that the war did not enter upon extreme dimensions. May God bless you for it!—Yours till death,

"WILLIAM."

The threat of Count von Bismarck, that the German armies would immediately resume offensive operations in case the treaty was not agreed to, was not a mere formal one, for during the whole period of the armistice the Germans were as active as if war was inevitable; and those military men who were in the secret spoke with the utmost enthusiasm of the grand plan of attack on all the French positions which General von Moltke had prepared for the opening of hostilities, if necessary. In two days the Germans would have been engaged in sweeping away the levies which had been collected to oppose them at every point where they stood in force; and an advance on five great fronts, converging at certain points, would have led to the most complete discomfiture yet seen of the armies of France. The country would, in fact, have been overrun from the Mediterranean to the Pyrenees, and the disasters of January repeated on a larger scale.

M. Thiers arrived at Bordeaux on February 28, when a sitting of the Assembly was at once held, at which, in the midst of the most profound silence, he rose and said: "We have accepted a painful mission; and after having used all possible endeavours we come with regret to submit for your approval a bill for which we ask urgency. 'Art. 1. The National Assembly, forced by necessity, and not being therefore responsible, adopts the preliminaries of peace signed at Versailles on the 26th February.'"

At this point M. Thiers, overpowered by his feelings, was obliged to leave the hall. His old friend, M. Barthélemy St. Hilaire, therefore continued to read the preliminaries:—

"1. France renounces in favour of the German empire the following rights:—The fifth part of Lorraine, including Metz and Thionville; and Alsace, less Belfort.

"2. France will pay the sum of five milliards of francs, of which one milliard is to be paid in 1871, and the remaining four milliards by instalments extending over three years.

"3. The German troops will begin to evacuate the French territory so soon as the treaty is ratified. They will then evacuate the interior of Paris, and some departments lying in the western region. The evacuation of the other departments will take place gradually, after payment of the first milliard, and proportionally to the payment of the other four milliards. Interest at the rate of 5 per cent, will be paid on the amount remaining due from the date of the ratification of the treaty.

"4. The German troops will not levy any requisitions in the departments occupied by them, but will be maintained at the cost of France.

"5. A delay will be granted to the inhabitants of the territories annexed to choose between the two nationalities.

"6. Prisoners of war will be immediately set at liberty.

"7. Negotiations for a definitive treaty of peace will be opened at Brussels after the ratification of the treaty.

"8. The administration of the departments occupied by the German troops will be intrusted to French officials, but under the control of the chiefs of the German corps of occupation.

"9. The present treaty confers upon the Germans no rights whatever in the portion of territory not occupied.

"10. The treaty will have to be ratified by the National Assembly of France."

The government asked the Assembly to declare the urgency of the discussion of the treaty, and Mi Thiers made a touching and passionate appeal to its patriotism, in the painful situation in which the country was placed.

Several deputies for Paris, supported by M. Gambetta, proposed motions in favour of delay, on which M. Thiers said: "We, like you, are the victims of a state of things which we have not created, but must submit to. We entreat you not to lose a moment. I implore you to lose no time. In doing so you may perhaps spare Paris a great grief. I have engaged my responsibility, my colleagues have engaged theirs, you must engage yours. There must be no abstention from voting. We must all take our share in the responsibility." M. Thiers concluded by expressing the wish that the committee would meet that evening at nine o'clock, and that a public sitting of the Assembly would be held next day at noon, which accordingly took place. At this sitting M. Victor Lefranc read the report of the committee on the preliminaries of peace, which recommended their immediate acceptance by the Assembly, as their refusal would involve the occupation of Paris, the invasion of the whole of France, and occasion terrible calamities. The committee earnestly urged the meeting not to take a step fraught with such consequences, and expressed confidence that no member would, in the circumstances, fail of his duty. The Assembly was much agitated. M. Edgar Quinet protested strongly against the acceptance of the preliminaries, which would, he said, destroy the present and future of France. M. Bamberger, a deputy from the department of the Moselle, followed in the same course; and concluded by condemning Napoleon III., saying he was the person who ought to be compelled to sign the treaty. When M. Conti, the late chief of the emperor's cabinet, rose and attempted to justify the empire, the Assembly almost unanimously (there being only five dissentients) voted by acclamation a resolution confirming the fall of the empire, and stigmatizing Napoleon III. as responsible for the heavy misfortunes of France. M. Louis Blanc spoke against ratifying the preliminaries of peace, believing it possible to continue the struggle by substituting partizan warfare for hostilities on a large scale. He also made an appeal to Europe, declaring that if she did not arrest the arms of Prussia, she would sign her own death-warrant. M. Victor Hugo made a most impressive speech on the same side; but the bill for ratifying the preliminaries was carried by 546 against 107—a majority of fully five to one.

After the vote, M. Keller, in name of the deputies for Alsace, the Meuse, and the Moselle, renewed the protest proclaiming the cession of territory to be null and void, and declaring that, one and all, they reserved to themselves the right of claiming to be united with France, which would always keep a place in their hearts. M. Keller further stated that, in the circumstances created by the vote, they could no longer retain their seats in the Assembly, as they could not represent a country ceded to the enemy.

Thus peace came at last, and France, burning with shame and heartbroken by sufferings, showed by the votes of her representatives that she was glad to have got it on any terms. In fact, her only choice lay between the acceptance of peace on the terms offered and ruin. However dearly the purchase had been made, it would buy the invaders out of the country. To Frenchmen the terms must, of course, have seemed oppressive, and what a pang must have shot through the hearts of all the deputies when, after the vote of ratification, the representatives of Alsace and German Lorraine bade their brethren farewell, on the ground that, the departments from which they came having ceased to be French, they could no longer sit in the Assembly!

The negotiations for peace were throughout carried on entirely between the principals, and the intervention of neutrals was avowedly discarded. The only approach to it was on the part of England. M. Thiers had seen fit to communicate the most important article of the conditions, that relating to the cession of territory, to no one, not even to M. Jules Favre. He took the entire responsibility of dealing with Count von Bismarck on that head, and England had therefore no room to say a word in the matter. But M. Thiers having informed the new French ambassador to England (the duke of Broglie) that the indemnity was fixed at six milliards, and that this was more than France could pay, he called on Lord Granville on the morning of February 24, and asked him to interfere in order to obtain a reduction. Lord Granville immediately presented him to the queen, a cabinet council was held, and in the evening his lordship telegraphed to Mr. Odo Russell, stating that England advocated a reduction of the amount demanded. By the time that Mr. Russell received the telegram the demand had been reduced by £40,000,000 sterling, and to this final arrangement M. Thiers agreed. Lord Granville had, however, sent early in the day through Count Bernstorff to Count von Bismarck a telegram of the same import as that which had been forwarded to Mr. Odo Russell; and Mr. Russell, in his reply, expressed a hope that this telegram might have had something to do with the reduction in the amount of the indemnity. Lord Granville stated to the French ambassador, that he thought the confining of the negotiation to the representatives of the belligerents was the wisest and best course, and the most likely to be beneficial to France; and the French ambassador had nothing to do but to assent to it, as it had been adopted by the head of his government. The king of Italy wrote to the German emperor, expressing his surprise and disappointment at the hard terms exacted from the French, especially with regard to the cession of territory; but hard as they were, there is no reason to suppose that the active intervention of neutrals would have led to their modification, while it would almost certainly have issued in a rupture of the negotiations, and in a renewal of the war.

One of the conditions on which the armistice was renewed at Versailles was, that 30,000 German troops should enter Paris and occupy the Champs Elysées and the Place de la Concorde. Such triumphs have been the reward of victory ever since war began, and will probably be claimed so long as it exists. In the present instance the feeling amongst the Germans on the subject, officers as well as men, was so strong, that even Count von Bismarck would scarcely have dared to refuse them the gratification, and such a refusal on the part of the new emperor would have made him unpopular where he most desired to be venerated. The feeling was also unquestionably strengthened by the arrogant tone in which the Parisian press spoke of the victorious army while under the walls of the city. "The German hordes," they said, "had not ventured to pollute Paris with their presence, so imposing was the Holy City even in her great distress." Such sayings were pleasing to the Parisian public, and, not without success, they tried to believe them. It was pleasant to think that the "barbarians," like that awe-stricken slave who dared not slay Caius Marius, seized with respect on the threshold of Paris, would not presume to enter. It was pleasant to read and to write to that effect, but certainly not very prudent as regarded the conquerors, by whom it was felt that the actual occupation of the city would be the most effectual means of putting an end to these vain and boastful exaggerations. It was a curious proof of the ascendancy which Paris exercised over French feeling, as well as imagination, that all Frenchmen seemed to regard this occupation in the light of an inexpiable insult—though they have entered every capital in Europe except London. The Prussian *Moniteur Officiel* at Versailles sarcastically published the description of Napoleon's triumphal entry into Berlin in 1806, after the battle of Jena, from the "History of the Consulate and the Empire," by M. Thiers. Yet M. Thiers himself was on the present occasion very much affected by the occupation; and General Trochu, a moderate man if ever one existed, was driven by grief and irritation into writing a silly letter, advising the Parisians to close their gates and let them be blown open by German cannon—in other words, to risk an absolutely purposeless massacre.

When the determination of the Germans became positively known on Monday, February 27, the agitation in the city was indescribable. Groups of excited civilians assembled on the boulevards, vociferating for *guerre à outrance*, and several companies of the national guard declared their intention of opposing the Prussian entrance. A proclamation issued by MM. Thiers, Favre, and Picard, stating that they had done all in their power to secure good terms, somewhat calmed the excitement, and the more moderate admitted that it was absolutely necessary to conclude peace. Even the temperate *Journal des Debats*, however, said, "Our conquerors have used their victory cruelly; their demands, financial and territorial, have been such that in the conferences with M. Bismarck our negotiators, M. Thiers and M. Jules Favre, have several times been on the point of breaking off, even at the risk of seeing the war recommence. The commission of the National Assembly partook of the emotion of the negotiators when the conditions were communicated to them. It is death at heart and the having nothing more to hope, except in the justice of God, that have forced them to submit to the frightful yoke of necessity." Patience and abstention from all attempt at disorder were, however, advocated on all hands, and even the radical journals exhorted the people to be calm. On Tuesday, General Vinoy issued an order of the day condemning the disorderly conduct of the national guard, who had beaten the rappel the previous evening. M. Picard also published a manifesto declaring that Belfort had been saved by giving way to the entry, reminding the population that the safety of Paris, and indeed the whole of France, was now in their hands, and imploring them to remain calm, united, and dignified in their misfortune. Still considerable agitation prevailed. Many of the Belleville and La Villette Beds loudly proclaimed their dissatisfaction at the treaty, and vented their indignation by tearing down the ministerial proclamations. A large meeting of national guards was also held, at which it was decided that the entry of the Germans should be energetically resisted, and that the Hôtel de Ville should be attacked. Accordingly, on Tuesday morning an attempt was made to seize that building; but the government was prepared, and the rioters had to beat a retreat. They then went to the Place de la Bastille, and established a formidable park of artillery. The *enceinte* at Belleville and Montmartre had also been refortified, and sentries were placed on the ramparts. The *Vengeur*, however, a journal of the most ultra opinions, published an article strongly protesting against any resistance being offered to the entrance of the enemy.

The "occupation" commenced on Wednesday, March 1, when the German legions made their entry along the broad Avenue de la Grande Armée; and skirted or passed beneath the lofty Arc de Triomphe, inscribed from summit to base with the names of victories gained by the French over their present conquerors and others. For two days the Champs Elysées and the Place de la Concorde were German military parade-grounds and camps. Martial music resounded from morn till night, generals caroused in the palaces of the Elysée and of Queen Christine of Spain, hussars stalled their horses in the Palais de l'Industrie, artillery kindled their bivouac fires around the Arc de l'Etoile, cavalry paraded the Cours la Reine, infantry manoeuvred in the side walks of the Champs Elysées, and uhlans slept by moonlight beside their horses under the trees. On Wednesday, when the troops entered, the Parisians looked angry and reserved, and the Prussian quarter, as it was styled, was far from thronged; but by the afternoon of the following day the Champs Elysées presented the aspect of a fair. The assemblage, of course, consisted chiefly of the lowest classes, but amongst them were also some well dressed persons, who had come out to listen to the music and to take a look at those "Goths and Vandals" of whom they had heard so much.

Owing to the quarter where the German troops were installed being inclosed by barricades at all its principal entrances, and to the subordinate thoroughfares being strictly guarded by both French and German sentinels, the most complete order was observed. Neither French soldier nor national guard was permitted there in uniform; sections of the mob were at times unruly and more or less insulting towards their conquerors, whose admirable forbearance, however, prevented any outbreak. The greatest humiliation they inflicted on the Parisians was performing martial airs, long after sunset on the Thursday, under the Arc de Triomphe, that cherished souvenir of French military renown. All the shops in the city were closed, as were all the cafés and restaurants; no papers were published; every blind was drawn down; the city was sad and solemn, even in those remote districts where no Prussians were; so that this seclusion was no parade of tribulation before the enemy, but was the real expression of the national sorrow. Nothing, in fact, could be more dignified or becoming than the bearing of the people in general. There can, however, be no doubt that the main reason why the occupation passed off so quietly was, that two days had been allowed to elapse between the time when it was known that it was to take place, and that of its actual occurrence. In those two days the excited population had time to calm down, and to calculate all the consequences of offering violence to an enemy within the gates, and while every gun of the forts pointed towards the city.

Throughout the whole of the occupation the Germans behaved in a manner worthy of themselves and of their country. The Bavarians, who had suffered so severely and fought so gallantly in the war, were assigned a place of especial honour; and portions of the Prussian corps who had done most hard work were allowed the honour of entering the city. But there was no air of triumph or parade. It was looked on as a mere military operation which had to be got through in a business-like, unpretending way. Neither the Emperor William nor his son entered the city. Count von Bismarck rode up to witness the scene as the Prussian regiments passed in; but he turned his horse's head and did not enter. The soldiers were good-humoured and grave, and impassive to the petty insults of the mob that stared at them; and nowhere did the army of occupation or its leaders exhibit any of that flaunting arrogance with which the first Napoleon and his marshals and soldiers used to ride through the cities they had captured.

As early as six o'clock on Thursday morning M. Jules Favre went to Versailles with the news of the vote at Bordeaux, ratifying the treaty of peace, and demanding the immediate evacuation of Paris. This was refused until the French foreign minister could show official documents. This difficulty, however, had been foreseen, and a special messenger was despatched from Bordeaux with an official, account of the sitting in the chamber as soon as the vote had taken place. At eleven a.m. the courier reached Paris, and at once started for Versailles. Arrangements were then entered into between the French and Prussian generals for the immediate evacuation of the city, which was commenced on Friday at an early hour, and terminated about noon. The exit of the Germans was even more imposing than their entry. The road under the Arc de Triomphe, which had been purposely blocked up by the Parisians before the entry, was carefully levelled, and regiment after regiment passed through, cheering as they marked the names of the various German towns once conquered by that great enemy of their ancestors, Napoleon I.

On the previous day (Thursday, March 2), the emperor king sent the following characteristic telegram to his queen at Berlin:—"I have just ratified the conclusion of peace, it having been accepted yesterday by the National Assembly in Bordeaux. Thus far is the great work complete, which through seven months' victorious battles has been achieved, thanks to the valour, devotion, and endurance of our incomparable army in all its parts, and the willing sacrifices of the whole Fatherland. The Lord of Hosts has everywhere visibly blessed our enterprizes, and therefore, by his mercy, has permitted this honourable peace to be achieved. To him be the honour; to the army and the Fatherland I render thanks from a heart deeply moved."

This telegram was publicly read at Berlin on Friday amid salvos of artillery and peals from the church bells, and the city was brilliantly illuminated at night in honour of the peace.

CHAPTER XXXI.

Naval Operations—Projected Sea and Land Attack on Germany—Danish Feeling in favour of France—Total want of Preparation in the French Navy as well as in the Army—Part of the intended Fleet only despatched—Conflicting and Absurd Orders to the Admiral—Precautions taken by the Germans to prevent a Landing on their Coast—The Blockade of their Ports more Nominal than Real—Discouragement in the French Fleet and Return Home—Final Resumé of the Events of the War—Contrast in the Preparation for War in France and Germany—The Reports of Baron Stoffel to the French Government on the German Military System—The hopelessness of the Struggle in France after the Collapse of her Regular Army—Military Opinion of the Siege of Paris and its Bombardment—Conduct of the Germans in France—Chronological List of the German Victories—The Spoils of the War and the Extraordinary Number of French Prisoners—Total Losses on both Sides—Territorial Alterations made by the War—Prince Bismarck's Reasons for Annexation—The Military Positions of France and Germany entirely reversed—Official Publications issued after the War—The True History of the Secret Treaty contemplating the Annexation of Belgium by France—The Mission of M. Thiers and the Influence of M. Gambetta—English Benevolent Operations during the War.

NATAL OPERATIONS OF THE WAR.

FROM a statement on the subject in Chapters IV. and V., it will be seen that the naval strength of Prussia was in power and extent only about one-third of that of France, which had, in fact, a maritime armament only second to that of England. With such a preponderance of ships and guns, it was natural that France should at the outset count upon achievements at sea even more completely triumphant than the victories anticipated with such certainty on land. Unfortunately for her, whatever has been said of want of preparation and of blundering with respect to the army, applies equally to the navy, though in the case of the latter it was not attended with such disastrous results. The plan of attack meditated by France when war was declared included a joint advance by the army into Germany, by both its western and northern frontier. The main advance was of course entirely by land; but a large force was at the same time to be conveyed by ships of war to the Baltic coasts, and by an invasion of Hanover and Holstein to embarrass the Germans with an attack in rear. An air of feasibility was given to the scheme by the popular feeling in Denmark, which was at first so extremely warlike and anti-German, that it was thought probable the Danes would seize the opportunity of rising, and, by joining the French side, endeavour to pay off the scores of 1864. A subscription for the French wounded was set on foot in Denmark, and speedily reached the sum of 80,000 francs, while one opened for the Germans only amounted to 1800 francs in the same time. The Danish press vehemently advocated war and revenge on the Germans, and stated that the appearance of a French fleet in the Baltic would command a ready ally. As Denmark could have at once assembled 40,000 men, to co-operate with the proposed 30,000 from France, Prussia would have been menaced in the north by an army of 70,000, which would have compelled her to concentrate 200,000 men in that part alone, besides the garrisons of the different towns, which could not be withdrawn with an enemy threatening her coasts.

After war was declared several days of uncertainty passed respecting the appointment to the command of the important Baltic expedition, when on the 22nd of July Vice-admiral Count Bouet-Villaumez was suddenly informed of his nomination to this duty by the emperor. The fleet was to consist of fourteen ironclads, a large number of corvettes, and other vessels necessary for the expedition. A second fleet, commanded by Vice-admiral La Roncière le Noury, was to follow shortly, made up of gunboats, floating batteries, and large transport steamers, with the 30,000 troops on board, under General Bourbaki. Cherbourg, however, had been stripped to foster Brest and Toulon, till there were neither fire-arms, victuals, nor sailors, and the fleet at last consisted of only seven ironclads and one corvette. Especially was it without the American ram the *Rochambeau*, the only vessel capable of encountering the *King William*, but so disliked by the French builders as an American vessel, that they had hidden her up under pretence of repairs. The admiral, however, considered he could at least neutralize the great Prussian ship, by smashing in its iron sides with the ram of his flagship the *Surveillante*; and thus elate with hope, and determined to make the best of the first instalment of his promised fleet, Villaumez set sail on the 24th July, all his fears allayed by a ministerial despatch promising that more vessels should speedily follow in his wake.

The admiral's orders were to direct his first operations against Jahde, near which he hoped to surprise the Prussian admiral, Prince Adalbert, in the open sea and compel him to fight. The prince, however, was not to be found; and finding his fleet was insufficiently supplied with coal, Villaumez was obliged to make for a port in Denmark. Here he received a verbal order from the French minister to sail for the Baltic. As this, however, was at variance with his first and more definite instructions, a telegram was sent for fresh orders, which had scarcely gone when a despatch from Paris arrived advising him to choose "some point of observation," whence, while respecting Danish neutrality, he could still watch the enemy's shores and supply his ships with everything they needed. The necessity was at the same time impressed strongly upon him, of leaving a powerful force at Jahde to take note of the enemy's movements.

Here was a fair specimen of orders, counter orders, and messages without aim or purpose. Where should this point of observation be? In the North Sea or the Baltic? But how was it possible to watch the Hanoverian coast from the Baltic, or to exert any influence at the North Sea upon what was going on along the Pomeranian shores? Could this double task be accomplished with seven ships? A German philosopher long since reproached the French with total ignorance of geography; and whether the taunt was just or not, it is certain that a more insane contempt was never shown for it than when Admiral Villaumez' fleet was sent, *entirely unprovided with maps*, to cruise about the Danish coast. The intricate straits through which the Baltic is reached are difficult enough to navigate in fair weather; but for ships of the heavy draught of French ironclads, with stormy seas, and no maps, it would be a miracle if they escaped the fate of the armada. It would seem as if the ministry of Marine at Paris had been equally ignorant of geography, for on no other supposition can the despatches to the admiral be explained. A glance at the map would have shown that from Jahde to Kiel was a distance of 900 miles, and as it was difficult to see how seven ships could prove an effectual patrol over this extent of coast, Admiral Bouet determined to wait for the answer to his telegram. An order to proceed to the Baltic soon arrived, and, indefinite as it was, the commander hesitated no longer. Skilful Danish pilots were procured, by whose help the Great Belt was passed, and after reconnoitring Kiel and Femern, the admiral pursued his route for the purpose of discovering a suitable landing-place for the promised and long-expected troops. This enterprise was one of no little difficulty, for all the lighthouse lights and beacons along the coast had been purposely extinguished, the buoys taken up, and an abundance of torpedoes laid near any place favourable for observation. If any spot or harbour was pitched upon as fit for attack and effecting a landing, it was generally the case as with Kiel. A large ship would be lying athwart the harbour mouth ready to be sunk at a moment's notice, with three rows of stakes, several rows of torpedoes, and a regular hedge of fishing nets ranged behind her. To commence operations against any such place gunboats, floating batteries, and troops to secure the ground gained were indispensable; and with all these the fleet was totally unprovided. The admiral sent off to apprise the minister of his difficulties, and on the same day received three despatches, the first dated 6th August, commanding his instant return to France; another, dated a day later, bade him remain where he was. Another, later still, but written on the same day, informed him that the army had suffered reverses, and reminded him that it was the duty of the fleet to strain every nerve and lose no opportunity to do the enemy an injury. Distracted with contradictory orders and bad news, the admiral determined to form a committee, consisting of the six principal officers of the squadron, who should report upon the most attackable part of the sea-board. The committee came to the conclusion that of all points on the Prussian coast Colberg and Dantzic alone could be attacked, but the slight impression likely to be made would only weaken the *prestige* of the French fleet. To do any good, ships of a peculiar construction would be required, and, above all, a respectable force for landing. Just as this rather despairing report was presented Admiral Villaumez heard that the Prussian fleet had left Jahde Bay, and was making for the Baltic. Delighted with the prospect of at least doing *something*, he hastily collected his ships and made for the Great Belt, there to dispute the passage of the enemy's vessels and offer battle. But the Prussian fleet had not left Jahde at all. On the contrary, it was closely blockaded there by Admiral Fourichon. Finding little chance of accomplishing anything else, Admiral Bouet now declared the Prussian harbours of Kiel, Lubeck, Neustadt, Stettin, Stralsund, and Rugen, to be in a state of blockade, and caused official notices to be issued accordingly. Having only large ships, however, the blockade was more nominal than real; for the light German craft could always creep along the coast and elude the utmost vigilance of the French. More than this, whenever an opportunity offered, in thick weather or on dark nights, the small, fast-sailing Prussian corvettes would steal out, and gliding quietly along the coast, would take the huge French frigates by surprise, fire at them, thrust torpedoes under their keels, and make off, without the possibility of pursuing them. It is easy to imagine the discouragement of both officers and crews when they plainly perceived that, notwithstanding their patriotic efforts, they must give up all hope of being rewarded by victory. All the intelligence from France told only of fresh misfortune, while they themselves were condemned to a fatal and humiliating inactivity.

While Vice-admiral Bouet made the best of a bad matter in the Baltic, Vice-admiral Fourichon entered the North Sea upon an even more useless cruise along the shores of Schleswig and Hanover. An ordinary map will show the reader why cuirassed vessels can effect nothing in these waters. Having been ordered to watch the mouths of the Weser, Elbe, and Jahde, Admiral Fourichon found himself, about the middle of August, in a boisterous sea washing a shallow coast, without a harbour of refuge for many leagues around. The English island of Heligoland was closed against him, and all other harbours being distant, he had to take in coals and provisions when out on the high seas. With storms almost constantly blowing from the south-west—that is, away from the land—as is usual in those latitudes, he was expected to blockade one of the most dangerous and inaccessible coasts known to navigators. Thus circumstanced, the chief thing he had to guard against was injury to mast and engine. If seriously damaged in either of these particulars, any frigate would be hopelessly lost on the Hanoverian shores.

Unfortunately, the weather soon became extremely bad, and storm following storm, the provisioning on the high seas was very difficult. Though the frigates themselves might hold out against the weather, the ships that brought them coals and victuals had to tack about for days before they could come alongside. Not a few were lost. As the season advanced, the more dangerous became the equinoctial gales, and the fuel diminishing, the situation of the squadron began to be critical. In this extremity, on September 12, Admiral Fourichon determined to return to Cherbourg, where he was met by the yacht *Hirondelle*, which had been looking out for him for several days. The *Hirondelle* was charged with despatches informing him of the overthrow of the Imperial government and his appointment to the ministry of Marine. Leaving his squadron under the command of the rear-admirals, and informing Admiral Bouet that he had quitted the North Sea, Admiral Fourichon left for Paris, and for him and his second in command, Admiral Jaureguiberry, a more distinguished part in the war now remained. As minister of Marine, Fourichon was colleague and companion of M. Gambetta after his balloon exit from Paris, and was as conspicuous for his wisdom and moderation as was the minister of War for his impetuosity. Jaureguiberry was appointed to high command in the army of the Loire, and fought with extraordinary talent and bravery in the various engagements with which General Chanzy was connected, from December 2 to the final dispersion of the Loire army at Le Mans about the middle of January, 1871. The whole French fleet was subsequently ordered again to the Baltic, but returned to the North Sea, and ultimately to France. It had driven the Prussian fleet into harbour, where, if it gained nothing, it suffered as little. During a blockade of four months, maintained along 700 miles of coast, twenty small German merchant craft were captured; but beyond these trifling items the French navy achieved literally nothing.

At home a more remarkable use was found for the fleet, and a more curious phase of war is not to be found. The Germans had invaded France from the Rhine to the Channel, and fearing lest Dieppe, Rouen, and Havre should be made by them bases of operations or of supplies, the French government stationed several vessels of war off each of these places;

and the singular spectacle was presented of a French fleet blockading its own ports, a task it performed far more effectually than it had been able to do with those of the enemy. A large number of the sailors and men of the marine were drafted into land corps, and at Paris, Orleans, Le Mans, in the north under General Faidherbe, and in many other parts of France, did excellent service in manning the artillery, and not unfrequently bore a part in the thickest of the numerous sanguinary actions of the campaign.

FINAL RESUME OF THE EVENTS OF THE WAR, AND MLTJTARY OPINION OF THE SIEGE OF PARIS.

In Chapters IV. and V. of this work we described in detail the various features of the military systems of France and Germany respectively. A number of books and pamphlets published after the war threw additional light upon these characteristics, and their influence upon the singular course of the events of the campaign. Any one conversant with the systems of the two nations would naturally suppose, from the readiness with which Napoleon III. plunged into the struggle, either that he was ignorant of the immense superiority of the German organization, or that he believed the war would bring into relief in the French military machine decisive reforms, which Marshal Niel was supposed to have carried out into law. The reforms, however, proved to have been only upon paper, and the writings of the emperor himself show that he was quite familiar with the numerical and other disadvantages of his army as compared with that of Germany; but his dependence was upon a somewhat desperate and rapidly executed strategy, which proved to be utterly impracticable. What the war, even within a week or two from the time when it was declared, did bring into prominent and terrible relief, was a monstrous imperfection in the French organization, of which the War office was grossly and unpardonably ignorant; and this ignorance forms the key to the overwhelming misfortunes we have narrated.

Considerable indignation was at first vented against Colonel Stoffel, the French military attaché at Berlin, for not having more fully apprised his government of the immense resources and preparations for hostilities throughout Germany. Immediately after the war, however, Baron Stoffel published the reports on these subjects which he had made from 1866 to 1870, many of which it transpired *had never so much as been opened*. These reports not only described most fully the formidable nature of the German organization, but pointed out in contrast the feebleness and inefficiency of the French system; and had the Imperial government studied them, it would have been more fully alive to the madness of the enterprise entered upon on the dark and calamitous 15th July, 1870.

According to a calculation of Baron Stoffel made some months before hostilities broke out, and essentially corresponding with that of the Emperor Napoleon in January, 1871, the standing army of France consisted of 372,558 men and 72,600 horses, whereas that of Northern and Southern Germany, when united, amounted to about 429,000 men, and from 80,000 to 90,000 horses. Thus, even in the single particular in which it was generally believed in Europe that she would possess a decided advantage—a regular army ready for the field—France was considerably overmatched; but this disproportion gives no idea of her immense inferiority in military power to her enemy. Apart from an unknown number of discharged soldiers and worn-out veterans, and from the practically worthless national guard, the whole reserves of France were composed of about 320,000 men, the residue of seven contingents of conscripts who had never actually joined the colours, and of the garde mobile, who on paper numbered rather more than half a million of men, but who had not yet been even embodied. The numerically imposing reserves of France, therefore, were simply a collection of "men with muskets;" and, good as might be their natural qualities, this circumstance was decisive against her in the contest in which she was engaged. On the other hand, the reserves of Germany, comprising the landwehr and the reserve proper, formed, in round numbers, about 800,000 men, all practised soldiers, in the flower of their age, and though separated for a time from their colours, all disciplined by long military service, and maintained in their martial bearing and spirit by frequent exercises even during peace.

After the events of the war, it would be useless to comment on the worth of this colossal force; but we may observe that, although its real qualities were never understood in France, Baron Stoffel had furnished the emperor with the fullest information respecting it. A report presented in 1869, after showing with remarkable clearness the homogeneous character of the German regular army and reserves, declared that a war even with Prussia alone could, humanly speaking, have no chance of success:—"Prussia, or more accurately, the North German Confederation, can dispose of a million of soldiers, well trained, well disciplined, and admirably organized, whereas France possesses only between 300,000 and 400,000."

Yet even these figures do not furnish anything like the real measure of the strength of the belligerent powers for military operations. The principle of local preparation for war was utterly disregarded in France; the elements required to form her armies were scattered over all parts of the country. In one place there was an immense material, in another a vast aggregation of soldiers; and a disunited regimental system was the most striking feature of her military organization. Moreover, even in her regimental units, local association was never the rule; each regiment was composed of men collected indifferently throughout the empire; and owing to a singular regulation, which required recruits under all circumstances to proceed to their depôts in the first instance, the increasing the force of any given regiment always consumed no little time. This system obviously threw great difficulties in the way of rapidly combining troops and forming them into well-appointed armies—a vital point in modern warfare. When the reserves of regiments were separated from each other by great and irregular distances, and when, in order to take the field, it was necessary to draw from remote points the materials of each corps d'armée and to fashion into organic masses men, horses, guns, and other *impedimenta*, delay and confusion were the inevitable result, and the arraying the armies of France was a tedious, uncertain, and cumbrous process. On the other hand, in Prussia and throughout Germany the principle of military organization was local; the empire was parcelled out into districts, each of which could furnish a separate army, complete in every appliance of war; and these distinct units of the mighty array which made up the collective national force were locally recruited, administered, and commanded. In a corrupt, an unwarlike, or a divided state, such a system might be very dangerous; but in the actual condition of Germany it enabled her to put forth her strength with extraordinary facility and despatch; it being obviously comparatively easy to combine troops collected from no great distances and already organized, and to expand them into even the largest armies. The result was that the "mobilization" of the forces of Germany, immense as they were, was swiftly, surely, and thoroughly accomplished, and under the conditions of modern warfare this feature of her military organization augmented her power in a wonderful degree, and largely multiplied the advantages she possessed already over her weaker antagonist.

Nor in this vital point of preparation for war did the difference end here. In France power over the military machine was centralized in the highest degree; the minister of War had complete control over every department of the service; hardly any arrangements could be made without his orders and supervision, and local subordinates were deprived of almost all direct authority. This system had its good side; but it threw an undue and intolerable burden at the outbreak of war on a single person. It thus caused responsibility to be ill divided, and tended to complication, to delay, and to irreparable mistakes. In Germany, on the contrary, power is localized in the army to the widest extent; the commanders of the different corps d'armée have an ample range of control, and the central authority seldom interferes. A system like this, in certain conceivable cases, might lead to great and dangerous abuses; but it worked well in the last campaign, and contributed to the precision and swiftness which characterized the German operations. The contrast between the two systems is thus presented in one of the numerous publications by actors in the war:—

"It became necessary to form into brigades, divisions, and corps d'armée the scattered elements of our military power. This important duty, which requires calm reflection and a profound knowledge of the means within reach, devolved, owing to our vicious system of centralization, upon the minister of War and his office, and had to be accomplished in a few days. In Prussia, on the other hand, the central authority does not pretend to do everything; it imposes on the commander of each corps d'armée the task of completing all needful preparations."

These opposite modes of setting in motion the antagonist armies led to moral results not unimportant. The hastily-collected French corps had little of the unity or cohesion which long and intimate association had given to the arrays of Germany. We should not, of course, lay too much stress on a mere circumstance of organization, but the "Officer of the Army of the Rhine" is probably correct in saying:—"Confusion and slowness in the earlier operations were not the only unfortunate results of this system of mobilization; it produced even more decisive effects throughout the entire campaign. By throwing together elements not previously united, by giving the troops commanders whom they did not know, and the commanders forces and means not familiar to them, the unity and mutual confidence which ought to connect the soldier with his superiors of every grade were seriously diminished in the French army."

The general result of the utter inferiority of France in force and military organization was that, though the first to draw the sword, she had not, probably, set in motion more than 220,000 men when the battles of Woerth and Forbach were fought, and that less than 120,000 were added during the crisis which ended in the capture of Sedan, when her fate may be said to have been virtually sealed. On the other hand, though the German commanders were taken somewhat by surprise—a point on which Baron Stoffel insisted in the preface to his reports—they were, nevertheless, able to bring into the field, within three weeks after war was declared, armies of which the aggregate numbers were over 500,000 men, and to add enormous reserves to these.

Independently, too, of inherent defects, the French army had felt the pernicious influence of the political and social state of the country. Too much is not to be made of this; for it must be remembered that French armies have marched to victory under an order of things essentially similar to that which existed in France in 1870. Nor can it be fairly asserted that the institutions of Germany must necessarily produce an excellent military instrument: one has only to read the remarkable preface to the "Military Memorial" of Prince Frederick Charles, and the observations of the gifted author of the "Prussian Infantry in 1869," to see that German officers of a high order of mind regard the autocratic system of Prussia as having a bad effect on the German soldier, and believe that the natural dash of the French is largely due to the usages of the country. But the evils at the root of society in France had in 1870 a peculiar tendency to injure and demoralize the army, whereas those which existed in Germany were not felt in her military service. The French generals were, in too many instances, the mere favourites of a sovereign who was, from the nature of his position, compelled to consider devotion to himself before merit. The venal corruption of an age of revolutions had found its way into the ranks of the French officers, and had made them dissolute, ambitious, and selfish; and the fortune which had long smiled on their arms had filled them with self-conceit and vanity. Above all, the constant agitation and changes of society in France had spread insubordination throughout the army and seriously impaired its discipline; and the dangers had been much aggravated which seem inseparable from its democratic organization. On the other hand, the energies of the Prussian government had been concentrated for years upon the creation of a formidable army; the discernment of the king and the skill and integrity of Von Moltke and Von Roon had neutralized the ordinary evils of an aristocratic military system, by making promotion depend upon merit; and the national movement which was stirring Germany had given her soldiers the energy and impulse which the institutions under which they live are not in themselves calculated to encourage. The subordination, the discipline, the order which naturally belong to the German army were seconded in 1870 by science, ability in command, and fervent patriotic enthusiasm, and this rare combination proved irresistible.

Such, then, or nearly so, were the forces of France and Germany at the beginning of the campaign. Overmatched in numbers, and very inferior in organization, in efficiency, and in military qualities, the French army was directed against an enemy in overwhelming strength and in a state of complete preparation for war. France, humanly speaking, could not have triumphed; but this is no reason why her army should have suffered disasters almost unparalleled, or why the country should have been overrun and conquered. Errors in command which have never been surpassed, and a fatal sacrifice of military considerations to the exigencies of a political situation, were the causes why the ruin was so overwhelming; for, notwithstanding all that has been written to the contrary, the French army in this calamitous struggle was not devoid of the high qualities which had justly gained for it glory and renown.

Our brief retrospective remarks have thus far had special reference to the war as carried on between the regular armies of the two nations. As to that great phase of the campaign subsequent to Sedan, which closed in the overthrow of Chanzy, Faidherbe, and Bourbaki, if the lesson is not to be taken home, that trained soldiers cannot be met with untrained levies, however gallant and patriotic, then are the lessons of history written to no purpose. Well would it have been if, in September, 1870, the French had consented to put an end to the war. The terms they would have had to accept then might have been onerous, but they were sure to be aggravated by the continuance of a struggle to which he must have been sanguine indeed who should have predicted a happy issue. Still, "France was bound to fight on for honour's sake," it was said. It is doubtful, however, if there is any honour to be reaped in enterprises absolutely hopeless; and suicide, in either nations or individuals, is a very questionable proof of courage. The struggle, as we have shown, was unequal from the outset, and subsequently, when the French army was so utterly prostrated in the field as no other within historical record had ever been, the condition of France became infinitely worse; because it was impossible that she should supply a second army equal in efficiency to that which had been lost, and no less impossible that, had the second even been as good, it would have proved itself equal to the exigency. For a better one the elements were nowhere to be found. The men, however, into whose hands power had fallen could not be made to see the true position of the case, or brought to acknowledge it. France in their hands apparently had ceased to be capable of acting rationally, and her measures were as those of a man in a dream or delirium. Orators appealing to frenzied mobs, and substituting for political facts the impressions of an assembly, a market place, and a single hour, collected crowds of men and boys, called them armies, gave them officers like themselves, and then dashed them in the face of a foe who was, in fact, what they could only pretend to be. On the one side it was history; on the other, a theatrical performance redeemed from ridicule only by the sacrifice of the miserable actors. The contrast was greatest where it was most dangerous. Men who could only talk of war as of a thousand other subjects waged it against those who lived for it alone, and who were warriors, if nothing else. On the one side were trading politicians, republican *préfets*, jealous of military command, and soldiers who had served, if at all, only against half savages; on the other side, men who lived, thought, and felt by act and rule of war, deeply imbued with its subtle skill, its hard sway, its cruel logic, and its fell liberties, enforcing its rights to the letter. The result was almost always and everywhere the same, and it is hard to say whether the incapacity of the commanders, the inadequacy of the preparations, or the unsoldierlike quality of the men, most contributed to it. The French troops, as might have been expected with raw and untrained levies, were invariably found incapable of holding positions, maintaining advances, supporting one another, or converting into a reality some momentary semblance of success. The enormous disasters with which the campaign opened were repeated, with variations of circumstances, over a third of France, and for half a year. Crowds of fighting men were surrounded and caught like shoals of fish. The only result of their courage was that after heaps fell under the fire of batteries never reached, and often not even seen, they surrendered or fled. The Great Napoleon long since told the French in the plainest terms, that it was one of their national delusions to believe that the revolutionary levies of 1793 saved France from the Allies; and the wisdom of his views has been recently even more strikingly illustrated. It is vain to think that collecting mobs of armed men in uniform, whether under the name of mobiles, sedentary guards, or volunteers, or county militia, will avail to defend a country that is seriously attacked. Massed together by the hundred thousand, as before Orleans, such a body becomes too unwieldy to move with effect, and a panic ruins it at once. Divided, as before Le Mans, it is simply exposed to be cut up in detail. Scattered out by a march over a long distance, as near Belfort, it is at the mercy of any small regular force that manoeuvres boldly against it.

With regard to the siege of Paris, that a population so vast should have held out for such a lengthened period, and have willingly endured such hardships and privations, said much for the government arrangements, and did infinite credit to the patriotism of the people themselves; but, looked at from a purely military point of view, the general opinion amongst those best qualified to judge—and which was well expressed by a very able military critic in the *Saturday Review*—is, that the defence of the city was tame and passive; and that, had different weapons been adopted, the world could not have beheld the singular spectacle of 500,000 men compelled to lay down their arms and surrender their scarcely injured forts to an army less than half their number, which had, in the open field, hemmed them in till their resources failed. Had General Trochu had as much constructive power as he undoubtedly had critical genius, the result might have been very different. From the first he seemed to have overlooked those engineering resources at his command, which might have sufficed to render the siege impracticable to the moderate number of Germans which finally triumphed over him.

Supposing there really was not sufficient time, before the Prussians came up from Sedan, to destroy thoroughly the huge belt of shelter which afterwards saved their army from being paralyzed by the frost, it would certainly have been quite possible to remove wholly the timber which they used so freely during the siege. As to the villages and detached buildings, there will probably be different opinions, and many will think that the cheapest and safest defence in the end would have been such wholesale demolition as would have deprived the Prussian corps allotted to the investment, of any ready made means of covering the continuous lines which they held throughout it in comfort. But the difficulties in the way of adopting this course were no doubt appalling; and we therefore pass from this part of the question to look at the investment completed, as it was in September, with but trifling opposition, and the outlying villages in the enemy's hands. Let us then suppose that Trochu's plans had been guided by a general of such constructive genius as Todleben, who, in view of the manifest uncertainty of relief, was prepared from the first to use all the resources at his command in an active and vigorous defence, instead of maintaining the passive attitude which was actually assumed.

Early in the siege there was at the governor's command such a supply of labour as no commander had ever before collected on one spot; nor were the other means wanting, both for strengthening the existing defences and for carrying on outside them a system of intrenchments, which would have mightily enhanced the difficulties of the problem placed before the German staff. Tools there must have been in abundance, since the resources of that vast metropolis were at the command of a firm and decided governor. There was a good supply of brushwood for fascine works in the Bois de Boulogne, and the stocks might have been largely supplemented by rough and ready expedients. Timber was plentiful, stacked in the builders' yards; and, above all, the sandbags, for rapid construction of shelter the handiest of all means, might have been made to any extent required. In short, it would have been easier to organize vast bodies of improvized pioneers with their tools, than to create out of the chaos inclosed that active army which promised so much and did so little. And in methodically fighting from the first under cover, the most irregular troops that Ducrot or Vinoy could put in line would have been almost as formidable—in a finished work certainly—as the best soldiers France had sent into the field to be slaughtered under MacMahon or entrapped with Bazaine. Such a system would have gone far to put the ill-matched forces upon an equality, even if it had not restored to the defenders the natural advantage of superior numbers.

If it be asked how the hundred thousand armed workmen, that might have been at once organized, could have been employed more profitably than the large parties which actually laboured in the later stages of the siege, we turn to the facts recorded, and point, as a single example, to what happened with regard to Mont Avron. The work thrown up on this hill was the only serious attempt made, from first to last, to extend the limits of the defence. Its mere occupation caused the Germans to erect against it a dozen batteries in a semicircle five miles long, protected by a parallel, covered by strong guards, and giving work to a whole corps. But Mont Avron was occupied by a redoubt quite detached, left destitute of bombproof shelter, and, above all, placed there nearly three months too late, when the enemy's siege train had arrived. Had Trochu been fortunate enough to have had for chief engineer an officer of such intelligence and energy as Todleben, or he to whom Belgium owes the strength of Antwerp, what could have hindered a number of such redoubts appearing early in the siege, their works pushed gradually forward, connected by cover with the place, supplied with rough bombproofs that would have made them safe from distant bombardment, and well manned by guards regularly relieved every twenty-four hours? Of course the Germans would have attacked them; the nature of the circumstances would have impelled them to do so t since otherwise their lines would have had to recede bit by bit, and must have grown longer and weaker in receding. Let any one who wishes to understand the necessities of the supposed case remember what anxieties the first occupation of Le Bourget gave Count von Moltke, the hasty order which came to Prince Augustus, that the guards must retake it at all costs, and the heavy lists of killed and wounded to which the execution of the order led. Yet Le Bourget was merely an ordinary walled village, taken by a young brigadier, and occupied without even the care to loophole it properly before it was re-attacked. A strong work thrown out there early in the siege would have cost the Germans ten times as many men to take it as the village did at the end of October; and as their heavy guns were not then up, a similar front of offence might have been pushed forward in half-a-dozen different places simultaneously. To erect such works would have been slow and toilsome; but to prevent their advance altogether would have overtaxed the siege materials of the Germans, and by forcing them to assault would have caused a constant drain on their limited supplies of men, even in case of success; whilst one or two serious failures would have stimulated the zeal and energy of the defenders to put forth redoubled exertions, to the proportional cost of the enemy.

Had a Todleben or a Brialmont been present to advise Trochu, such a series of defences could, no doubt, have been started before the end of September; and if conducted with the vigour and skill which either of those renowned engineers would have infused, would soon have driven the Germans so far off, at more than one point, as practically to cut their circle into isolated segments; or, had the Germans effectually restrained them, it must have been at such an expense of life as of itself would have raised the siege, or at the least drawn in their detachments from all other quarters, and left their rear and communications dangerously weak. Their headquarters at Versailles might have been threatened, their depôts on the railroad driven further off, and, above all, the first decided advantage gained in this manner would have given that moral impulse to the defenders which from first to last no step taken by their chiefs ever evoked among them. The effect of the most rousing proclamation, or of the most carefully coloured intelligence, is but transient; but to have held a mile or two of ground fairly won from their foes would have stimulated every soldier in the garrison to new efforts by a definite and tangible object. The battalions that wasted their time in purposeless drilling for a field they never entered would here have found useful scope for their services; and their officers, raw to their duties at first, would with practice have come to display the well-known ingenuity of their nation, so often exhibited in defences on a smaller scale.

In consequence of the tactics adopted by the French, the Germans had time to so strongly entrench their positions, and so dispose their numerous field artillery, as to enable them to hold securely any point suddenly attacked, even against very superior numbers. Yet their own forces at any given point were of necessity comparatively weak. The extent of their inner line of investment was fifty miles; that of the outer circle, occupied by the headquarters of the two besieging armies, was at least sixty-six miles. Taking fifty miles as the basis, and estimating the German force at 200,000, the average strength at any given point was only in the proportion of 4000 men to one mile. Under these circumstances, good soldiers, led by well-instructed officers, could not have been held in so long; but Trochu's army did not consist of good soldiers, and it may reasonably be doubted whether he would at any time have been justified in attempting to break clean through the German lines of investment, having no promise of assistance from without. To have done so for the mere purpose of carrying into the field beyond an army of raw soldiers of the strength just mentioned, short of provisions, short of horses, would have been to weaken the defence without gaining any corresponding advantage, save that of diminishing the number of mouths which remained inclosed. Without the requisite accessories such an army could not have sustained a campaign; and in order to subsist it would have had, even if not pressed by the Germans, to break up into separate fragments and hasten from the district near the capital. A number of recruits might possibly thus have been gained for Bourbaki and D'Aurelles; but they could have no effect upon the investment, unless the Germans had given it up for a time, and changed it into such an unremitting pursuit of their new enemy as, under the conditions supposed, would have insured his destruction. No real attempt was, in fact, ever made to carry the army through the lines, except on the one occasion when Trochu's information led him to suppose that D'Aurelles was approaching Fontainebleau in November, with the vast train of supplies known to have been gathered behind his intrenched camp at Orleans. A junction with him thus provided would have put matters on altogether a different footing from the mere escape of 100,000 or 150,000 men out of the lines with three days' rations in their haversacks; and the position assigned for the meeting would have planted the French so threateningly on the flank of the German communications, as to have caused the instant and complete abandonment of the investment. This was the only practical attempt at strategic combination shown during the four months' siege; but it was foiled doubly in its execution, by the superiority in tactical power of Prince Frederick Charles' army to that of the army of the Loire, and by the failure of Ducrot to win sufficient ground beyond the loops of the Marne to enable him to develop his masses of men on a broad front, and so make some decisive use of his superiority of numbers.

Yet admitting that Trochu was probably right in determining not to risk bodies of his troops in the open field without supplies and unsupported, even supposing they could force a passage by surprise, his plan of waiting for relief from without, and holding his defences passively until it came, stands self-condemned by the results. The intermediate course of an active and vigorous resistance, so active and vigorous as to have placed the besiegers, with their inferior numbers, practically on the defensive, was, as we have said, hardly thought of, and rejected as too difficult and laborious. At least, no systematic effort was made to carry it out.

With regard to the bombardment of the city by the Germans, that is also now admitted to have been a mistake and failure. In the words of the able and very impartial military correspondent of the Times, "There was nothing gained by it; not a single day sooner did Paris yield. No practicable breach was formed except one, very small, in the rear of Fort Montrouge. There was, in fact, no military effect whatever from the bombardment of Paris."

The final German triumph at Paris was undoubtedly somewhat marred by the thought, that another month of the same patience which they had shown till the new year opened would have given them uninjured the prize they sought. The very works surrendered into their hands to save the lives of the starving multitude within, must have seemed to reproach silently the hasty counsels of those who led the emperor-king from his original plan to adopt sharper measures, which proved abortive and fruitless. The conquest so won was stained by what was then plainly seen to have been a superfluous use of the resources of war. For more than three months the German staff held to the resolve to reduce Paris by starvation, and there is no reason to doubt that they could have maintained their lines throughout intact for that purpose. After suddenly changing their minds and beginning a direct double attack by bombardment and approach, the capital fell, before either of these methods had in any way affected its powers of resistance, under the inevitable pressure of coming famine. In using the other modes the Germans were not, of course, going beyond their rights. A capital which, for strategic ends, has been deliberately turned into a fortress, is beyond dispute liable to be treated as a fortress.

A great deal of angry recrimination passed between Count von Bismarck and M. de Chandordy, delegate of the French Foreign minister, respecting the general conduct of the war by the respective belligerents. The Frenchman accused the Germans of committing needless and unjustifiable atrocities while overrunning his country; and the Count retorted by counter-charges of using explosive bullets, barbarities committed by Turcos, burning and scuttling of German merchantmen, and systematic disregard of the Geneva convention. None of the despatches, however, drawn up under the influence inspired by war, can be looked upon as impartial or altogether reliable. They all naturally took their tone from exaggerated statements, and from reports and testimony distorted by passion or by suffering.

The concurrent testimony of all observers was that, at the opening of the campaign, the conduct of the German troops was excellent; they were not more remarkable for courage and discipline than for honourable treatment of the invaded country. The picture was subsequently darkened; complaints were made that the German leaders acted like Tilly and Wallenstein; and dreadful stories were told of murdered free-shooters, of villages burnt by way of reprisals, of barbarous executions, of innocent citizens made hostages, of devastation carried out on system, as if by the savage hordes of Attila. According to the remark of the old Greek, that human nature in the same circumstances is usually pretty nearly the same, we can easily account for these things, without imputing any peculiar guilt, or even ferocity, to the German armies. In the first place—and this unhappily is attested throughout the history of our race—prolonged war makes men indifferent to the sight of suffering; the soldier who knows he may die to-morrow becomes reckless of the miseries of others; and we cannot doubt that a change like this passed over the character of the invaders of France as the contest went on and deepened. In the second place, the system of requisitions pursued by the German commanders—a system, it must be said with regret, perhaps necessary in a campaign conducted on such an enormous scale—has invariably been attended with the consequences before mentioned. Forced contributions generate resistance among the non-combatant population; this leads to a guerilla warfare, which compels the generals of the invading army to exercise severities of all kinds, unhappily often without discrimination; for no officer will allow his men to be destroyed, and his army perhaps endangered, by irregular bands of armed peasants.

In the course of a letter addressed to his daughter by an officer of high rank at the German headquarters, the following passages occurred:—"I have now been for four months in the thick of the war. You know that I am just to friend and foe, and have a feeling heart for any suffering on whatever side. This much premised, I can assert with a good conscience that so great and sanguinary a war has never been conducted with so little suffering or hardship. That in isolated cases things happen on both sides which, without exact information and inquiry, might be denounced as barbarities, is quite conceivable in a struggle in which unchained passions are so powerfully excited. Never before, however, have three-fourths of all wanted by the troops been supplied from the victor's country, or bought for ready money from the enemy, in order to spare the country visited by the war. *It has never come to my ears or those of my many acquaintances that a German soldier has ill-treated a French woman.* The entire contributions hitherto(December, 1870) levied by our armies, do not reach the sum exacted by the French under Napoleon from many a large town in Germany, although money was worth much more then than now. As evidence of the discipline of our troops, I may mention that while in France, with the exception of a single case at Nancy, I have not seen a drunken German soldier. In numberless cases our troops have, at the request of officials or communities, protected private property against attacks by Frenchmen—*e.g.*, the champagne vineyards."

We give these extracts as only fair statements, especially in regard to the treatment of French women; and we may remark that many alleged atrocities, the subject of comment all over Europe at the time—such, for instance, as the reported roasting alive of a franc-tireur near Dijon—appeared in quite a different light upon closer inquiry. Whatever wrongs may have been committed under the excitement of the war, the authorities of both sides willingly rendered homage to the leading international principles of civilization, and in their despatches earnestly endeavoured to justify themselves in the eyes of Europe for any violation of the sacred duties of humanity.

LIST OF THE GERMAN VICTORIES; THE TOTAL LOSSES ON BOTH SIDES; AND THE TERRITORIAL ALTERATIONS MADE BY THE WAR.

In a previous part of this chapter we have pointed out the disastrous consequences to France of her unpreparedness for the war, and we will here present a summary of the results accruing to Germany through her superior mobility, organization, and numbers. War was declared on July 15, 1870, and terminated February 16, 1871, after lasting 210 days. In the first week after the declaration of war the German troops were mobilized, their despatch to the west and disposition along the Trèves-Landau line requiring nearly a fortnight. The troops sent to the frontier amounted to over 500,000 men, and to bring the whole mass up in a fortnight about 42,000 had to be conveyed by rail per day. The transport was effected on five lines, two of which, however, were but little used. Besides the men, there were horses, guns, carriages, ammunition, and provisions to be sent. Four Prussian corps d'armée, to get to the French frontier, had to travel a distance of from 400 to 600 miles, and had to be fed on the way. As in the first few days of the campaign, and during the last period, there were no engagements, the war was practically reduced to 180 days. In the course of these there were considerably more than 100 engagements, besides twenty-one great battles, the chronological order of the latter being—Wissembourg, Woerth, Spicheren, Courcelles, Vionville, Gravelotte, Beaumont, Sedan, Noisseville (before Metz), Beaune-la-Rollande, the three battles round Orleans, Amiens, Champigné and Brie (before Paris), Beaugency, Bapaume, Vendôme, Le Mans, Belfort, St. Quentin, and the great sortie against St. Cloud. Twenty-six fortresses were taken, namely, Lutzelstein, Lichtenberg, Marsal, Vitry, Sedan, Laon, Toul, Strassburg, Soissons, Schlestadt, Metz, Verdun,

Montbéliard, Neu-Breisach, Ham, Thionville, La Fére, the citadel of Amiens, Phalsbourg, Montmèdy, Mézières, Rocroi, Péronne, Longwy, Paris, and Belfort. Reckoning only those actually transported to German fortresses and towns, 11,650 officers and 363,000 rank and file were made prisoners. The prisoners at the capitulation of Paris amounted to nearly 500,000, that being the number actually engaged in the defence of the city. Had not the war closed with the fall of the capital, these also would most likely have been transferred to Germany. Of the ill-fated army under Bourbaki 84,900 were driven across the frontier and compelled to lay down their arms in Switzerland, and fully 20,000 fled into Belgium after the battles of Metz and Sedan. The total number of prisoners and of fugitives interned in neighbouring states thus amounts to the extraordinary total of nearly one million. The quantity of arms and other warlike material captured was equally remarkable, and altogether unprecedented in any former war. Thus at the Alma the Allies took two colours and two guns, at Inkermann they lost three guns, and at the storming of the Malakoff one standard and thirty-one guns were captured. The number of prisoners in the campaign did not exceed 6000. The entire spoils of the French in 1859 consisted of three colours, twenty-six guns, and 16,000 prisoners. The Prussians, on the other hand, took at Düppel nineteen colours, 119 guns, and 3400 prisoners; at Alsen, thirteen colours, ninety-nine guns, and 2494 prisoners; at Königgrätz, seven colours, 161 guns, and 19,800 prisoners; altogether in 1866, thirteen colours, 208 guns, and 49,000 prisoners. The more formidable total of 1870-71 consisted of 6700 guns (including mitrailleuses), 120 eagles and colours, and sufficient chassepots to equip the entire German army. Such large stores of cloth were captured at Metz and Le Mans as sufficed to renew the whole of the uniforms required; and notwithstanding the great number of horses which perished, the end of the war found Germany richer than before in this description of live stock—Sedan and other battlefields having yielded far more than the number lost.

The losses of both combatants were in proportion to the magnitude and fierceness of the operations of the campaign. Considering the hasty and confused manner in which the French forces were collected after Sedan, it is doubtful if accurate returns of their loss can ever be forthcoming. Some months after the campaign closed the numbers were returned as 89,000 "killed;" and if this is to be taken as including wounded and missing, the German loss far exceeded it, for the entire loss of Germany has been ascertained to have been about 180,000—rather more than half of whom are invalided.

The most costly fight to the Germans was that of Vionville, on August 16, 1870, when, in order to prevent the escape of Marshal Bazaine's army, more than 17,000 men were sacrificed. There was a great disparity of numbers in the battle, as 45,000 Prussians fought from 8 a.m. till 4 p.m., at first against 160,000 and by noon against nearly 200,000 French. Another instance of similar disparity was at Belfort, where about 36,000 Prussians and Badeners maintained a three days' battle against Bourbaki's army of nearly 130,000. There were instances, on the other hand, in which the disparity was reversed—notably at Wissembourg and Woerth, where, although the fortune of the day was in the end against them, the French undoubtedly made a most gallant and heroic stand. Gravelotte, also, was a most costly and hardly-won victory, although full 270,000 Germans confronted less than 210,000 French—including, however, the élite of the army.

Losses in men and warlike material to a certain extent were what France must have laid her account with in entering upon the campaign. That the loss should have been far beyond all precedent was what she might in time have become reconciled to, had even a small measure of success attended her arms. Unfortunately, the terms of peace which she was eventually obliged to accept involved sacrifices inflicting a rankling wound, which it is to be feared time alone will never heal. Alison observes that, "The policy of the Allies, when dictating terms to France in 1814, was founded on a noble spirit—it rested on the principle of eradicating hostility by generosity, and avenging injury by forgiveness. The result proved that, in doing so, they proceeded on too exalted an estimate of human nature." The Germans of 1871 comfort themselves by reflecting, that they profited by the teachings of history and avoided the errors of their forefathers. Without seeking to eradicate hostility by generosity, they calculated on France nursing the spirit of vengeance and retaliation; and their one aim in dictating the terms of peace was to make her enter on any future war with Germany with the odds heavily against her. The population of Alsace and Lorraine had so conclusively shown their wish to be united to France, as to satisfy their conquerors that, in spite of their common language, they would have to treat them as vanquished aliens. There was therefore no pretence of moderation, nor any further talk of uniting to Germany the lands torn from her in past ages. By a turn of events as surprising to the conquerors as to the rest of the world, France had in a few months been so utterly crushed that Germany could ask of her what she liked. That which she asked was safety, as absolute and complete as possible. She might perhaps have had more, but she obtained all she wanted; and the maximum of military defence with the minimum of disaffected population, sufficiently explains why the demand was made for only a fifth of Lorraine with Metz, and the other four-fifths were allowed to remain French.

Had no loss of territory been involved, peace might doubtless have been arranged after the collapse of the empire and army at Sedan; and many deeply sympathized with France in the agony of dismemberment she had struggled so heroically but vainly to resist. The Germans, however, listened neither to the counsels of neutrals in the matter, nor to pleadings urged in the name of the civilization of the nineteenth century. One idea filled their minds, that France would seize the earliest opportunity of making war upon them again. The Allies, they said, in 1814 were very moderate towards France, and Prussia especially failed in her desire to obtain a good military frontier on the French side, because, it was said, the way to keep France quiet was to treat her generously. Since then one generation of her people after another, almost every statesman, and every political chief, had been hungering for the Rhenish provinces and threatening Germany with war. Government after government had arisen in the country, some of them upholding social order, some singing the paeans of humanity and rushing into the arms of universal brotherhood; but all alike, royalist, imperial, or republican, good or bad, liberal or illiberal, thirsting for the left bank of the Rhine. In a moment of profound peace war had been made upon Germany, on a pretext so frivolous that the warmest partizans of France were scandalized. There was now a chance of making the French see that war with Germany would henceforth be a very serious thing, and the opportunity was used to the full. The Germans were told that to cripple and humiliate France unduly could not be for the good of Europe. They replied that they had first to think of themselves; and that in July, 1870, a strong military frontier would have been of much more use to them than any preservation of the balance of power. They were taunted with forcing men into citizenship with them by tearing them from France, and with thus violating the unwritten laws of advancing civilization. But they closed their ears, like deaf adders, to all this, and listened only to the voice that bade them think of their own safety. Of course there were many who thought that the policy of Germany was due simply to a greedy and relentless extortion, which had always been one of her principal characteristics—a view on which we here pronounce no judgment. We have merely endeavoured to give as faithfully as possible the reasons in support of the territorial claim advanced by the government and by the principal organs of public opinion throughout Germany.

Were the terms of peace to be judged apart from any political or national aspect, and solely in the highest interests of mankind, it could perhaps be wished that Germany had displayed a magnanimity unparalleled in history, by declining to take any French territory, and resolving to abide the consequences. She might have suffered for her magnanimity, but a magnanimity that counts the risk it runs is the highest and most ennobling of virtues. The world would have been a better world had Germany, relying on her own strength, refused additional guarantees for her security. The Germans, however, in their intense horror of the miseries of war, and under the irritation caused by the constant restlessness and aggressiveness of France, could not bring themselves to set before mankind so elevating a spectacle. They were bent upon security; and so far as that is possible, to all human views they attained their object.

The territory conceded is 5580 square miles in area, or about equal in extent to that of the three departments of the Haut Rhin, Bas Rhin, and Moselle. It is inhabited by 1,597,219 people, 200,000 of whom are French, the rest German, or mixed, in race and language, but all strongly French in feeling. The new frontier line begins at Cattenom, near Longwy, on the borders of the duchy of Luxemburg, and takes a southern course, having Thionville, Metz, Château-Salins, on the east (all of which therefore now belong to Germany); and Verdun, Toul, Nancy, and Luneville, on the west. After cutting a corner off the department of the Vosges, the line then coincides with the western boundary of the department of the Haut Rhin as far as the canton of Belfort, which it leaves to France by striking off to the canton of Delle, between which town and Joncherey it terminates on the Swiss frontier. Germany is thus advanced about 100 miles nearer Paris, and comes into possession of a long line of forts invaluable for defensive purposes. The principal are Metz la Pucelle, Thionville, Strassburg, Schlestadt, Bitsche, Marsal, Neu Breisach, Phalsbourg, and Hagenau; while amongst the towns are Colmar, Mulhausen, Guebwiller, Molsheim, Saverne, Château-Salins, Sarreguemines, and Forbach. Thus the whole department of the Bas Rhin, the greater portion of the Moselle, the Meurthe, and the Haut Rhin, and a small corner of the Vosges, are comprised in the concession, which may be more briefly described as the whole of Alsace (minus Belfort) and about a fifth of Lorraine.

The annexation of this strip of land, narrow as it looks upon the map, entirely reverses the relative military positions of France and Germany. Up to July, 1870, France had the aggressive position. Metz, with its recently built forts, was her sally-port towards the German left bank of the Rhine, as Strassburg was towards South Germany. Either of these places was important enough to serve as a base of operations for a large field army; while on the German side the nearest base opposed to Metz was Mayence, opposed to Strassburg, Ulm—both places a long way to the rear. By its geographical configuration, the ground on the German side does not furnish any nearer positions of sufficient strategical importance to make it worth while turning them into large fortresses, and thus the whole of the German left bank of the Rhine, and a large portion of Southern Germany, including all Baden and Würtemburg, were always open to French invasion. There was only one way to meet this danger—the way made use of in this war—that the Germans, ready before the French, should concentrate the whole of their force on the border line between the Moselle and the Rhine, and invade France in their turn. In that case, however, a lost battle would have driven them back to Mayence and across the Rhine, and laid open all Baden and Würtemburg.

Thus the German Rhine fortresses, Germersheim, Mayence, Coblenz, and Cologne, though forming a strong line in themselves, were a protection only to the country behind them—that is to say, to the country east of the Rhine and north of the Main. The fortresses situated in advance of the Rhine, Landau, Saarlouis, and even Luxemburg, were of no great importance; at most, they closed bines of railway, but none of them could arrest the march of an army.

In his speech on the government of the newly-acquired territory in the German Parliament in May, 1872, Prince Bismarck said that Germany could not permit the state of things we have described to continue, and it would have been suicidal on her part not to have availed herself of the opportunity offered by the war to amend it. He regretted to say that some other powers had not been of that opinion. These powers had not been particularly gratified by the determination of Germany to recover her lost provinces; and when they found her firm bad proposed that the affair should be compromised either by a dismantling of the Alsace and Lorraine fortresses, or by the formation of Alsace and Lorraine into an independent and neutralized state, protected by a European guarantee. For Germany it had been quite impossible to entertain either of these suggestions. A joint guarantee might be valuable enough, had not some states been latterly in the habit of explaining it away the moment after acceding to it. Besides, even if honestly enforced, no guarantee could have prevented France from attacking the German shores, while Germany, with a small fleet and cut off from France by an intermediate barrier of neutralized states, would have been powerless to reciprocate. As to trie idea of razing the fortresses, this would have inflicted upon France a more severe humiliation than the mere loss of territory. It would have deprived France of the right to exercise her sovereignty in a portion of her own territory—a penalty which no great state is likely to submit to long. Add to this that the

Alsatians would not have been very good neutrals, and it was clear that there remained nothing but to solve the difficulty by downright annexation.

The treaty of peace completely reversed the military position of the two countries. By the possession of Strassburg and all Alsace, the whole line of the Rhine, up to Basel, became German property; and Strassburg, flanked to the south by Schlestadt and Neu Breisach, from a sally-port against South Germany, becomes its chief and central bulwark, the Vosges range forming the first fine of defence. North of Strassburg, even the western slopes of these hills belong to Germany, and with them the small places of Phalsbourg, Petite Pierre, Lichtenberg, and Bitsche, which more or less effectively command the passes. Thus South Germany received not only a powerful barrier against French aggression, but also a strong basis of operation, with the roads prepared and secured, for attack against France.

But this is only the least important point. The transfer of Metz gave the Germans a power of attacking France such as she would obtain against Germany by the possession of the whole left bank of the Rhine, with all its fortresses and their bridge-heads on the right bank. If the French had Coblenz with Ehrenbreitstein and Mayence with Castel, then Germany would be in the same weak strategical position relatively to France that she is now in with regard to Germany. The possession of Metz advanced the German base of attack against France by fully 120 miles. It gave them a stronghold superior in natural position, engineering strength, and extent, to any one they had before, situated exactly where they must wish such a powerful outpost of their Rhenish system of fortification to be—flanked, moreover, to the north by Thionville and by Luxemburg. And, just as beyond the Rhine, in the interior of Germany, there are scarcely any points naturally adapted for large fortresses to bar the road to Berlin, so there is, west of the Moselle, the same dearth of strategical positions capable of being turned to account in keeping the enemy at a distance from Paris. With the Germans in Metz, the road to Paris is open to them, as soon as the French army in the field shall have lost one great battle. Verdun and Toul, with Frouard or Nancy, might hereafter be formed into a system of fortifications, but they could never counterbalance or replace Metz; and between the Meuse and Paris there appears to be no position, were it ever so much fortified, where a defeated army could arrest the conquerors.

On the other hand, were the German army to be beaten before Metz, the garrison of that fortress (unless the whole army blundered into it, as was done in August, 1870) would hold in check more than twice its numbers, and the whole territory between the Moselle and the Rhine would remain disputed ground until Metz were again reduced by the French. No army will like to undertake the reduction of two such places as Metz and Mayence at one and the same time, unless the enemy repeat the Bonapartist campaign of 1870, which is not to be expected. Thus the possession of Metz enables the Germans, in case of defeat, to carry on the campaign for at least a couple of months on the left bank of the Rhine, and to weaken a successful enemy to a serious extent before he arrives on that river, their main line of defence.

In the same spirit in which the Germans claimed Metz and the line of the Vosges, they further insisted on making France pay the largest indemnity it could afford. The terms as to money, no less than as to territory, appeared merciless. Eminent financiers were solemnly summoned to consider how much could be squeezed out of France; and the sum of two hundred millions was by them scientifically ascertained to be the extremest burden the camel could bear without breaking its back. The Germans, of course, liked the money for its own sake, and no nation on earth was more likely to prize a windfall of £200,000,000 sterling. But perhaps their main idea was not the mere pocketing of this magnificent prize, but to obtain a guarantee of safety. A very heavily taxed nation shrinks from war, and France for the next quarter of a century will be most severely taxed in proportion to her resources and population. Altogether she will be fortunate if, in 1874, when the indemnity is paid, she has a debt of less than £1,200,000,000 sterling, and a mortgage of less than £40,000,000 a year upon her industry. For many years she will thus be exposed to all the disorders which heavy taxes, constant deficits, and revolutionary finance experiments bring in their train. It is true that in course of time peace and industry may make the augmented debt felt as little as that of 1870. This, however, must be a slow process, and meanwhile France, under the penalty of risking national bankruptcy, will be bound over to keep the peace towards Germany; while the latter, with £200,000,000 to make good its losses, and enriched by the industry and commerce of Alsace, may count on keeping ahead in the race, and entering on a future war with a sounder financial system and a more solid credit than France can hope for.

OFFICIAL PUBLICATIONS ISSUED AFTER THE WAR.

After the conclusion of the war most of the leading actors on the French side published defences or explanations of the various parts they had taken in it. In fact, so great was the flood of publications on the subject, that such a profusion of information, instead of enlightening the reader, only bewildered him. It seems necessary, however, in dealing with the consequences and results of the war, to notice a few of the works which bear very specially on some of the chief events narrated, and which, in one or two instances, throw a little additional light upon them, without, however, on any material point affecting the truth of our original statements with regard to them.

Perhaps the most historically important and remarkable work of all was that of Count Benedetti, explaining the relations between France and Prussia from 1864 to 1871, and especially with regard to the celebrated secret treaty, as to the annexation of Belgium by France, which caused so much consternation in England, and which is fully described in Chapter III. Soon after the secret treaty was divulged, Count Benedetti took occasion to publish a letter to the effect that, although the treaty was in his handwriting, it was written by him *purely at the suggestion and dictation* of Prince Bismarck. This statement might possibly have been allowed to stand unchallenged, had not Count Benedetti, at the close of the war, become infected with the prevailing mania of rushing into print in further justification of his conduct. In his work, "Ma Mission en Prusse," he stated that when the negotiation as to Belgium was going on, he communicated solely with M. Rouher, and as his correspondence was not official, he could not refer his readers to any official record of it; but so extremely scrupulous was he, that he *would not write a line the accuracy of which could not be verified.* Thus all that passed between him and the French government, while the negotiations were in progress, was necessarily buried in darkness. Still he could give his readers the general tenor of this buried correspondence, and he particularly requested them to treasure in their minds two great truths—that the proposal for the annexation of Belgium to France was, in his words, a purely Prussian conception, as he merely embodied in the famous draught treaty the suggestions of Count von Bismarck; and secondly, *that the emperor would have nothing to do with the annexation of Belgium, and would only take Luxemburg*, whereas Count von Bismarck offered, in return for Prussia being allowed to consolidate its power from the Baltic to the Alps, that France should first get Luxemburg and then Belgium.

The luckless diplomatist was not aware that the French government, to aggravate the humiliation they had brought upon themselves, had left the most important state papers to be seized by the invader at St. Cloud. The fact, however, was that while, in honour of himself and the imperial government, M. Benedetti was printing the above version of what had happened, his enemies were in possession of the documents which he supposed were for ever safe in the custody of M. Rouher, and of which they availed themselves as soon as M. Benedetti's work appeared. According to these documents, what really happened in the latter half of August, 1866, with regard to Belgium, seems to have been as follows:—On the 12th the emperor wrote to M. Benedetti to say that he finally abandoned all claim to Mayence and to the left bank of the Rhine. It is acknowledged by both parties, that the emperor's reasons for doing so were, that Count von Bismarck had plainly told M. Benedetti a week before that to persist in such a demand meant instant war. On August 16 a diplomatic messenger was sent from Paris with a letter of instructions to M. Benedetti to make new demands; and these instructions Count von Bismarck used as the weapon to annihilate the pretensions of M. Benedetti after the publication of his volume. After a caution as to the strictly confidential character of the negotiations, the letter proceeded, "In proportion to the chance of success our demands will have to be graduated as follows:—In the first place, you will have to combine into one proposition the recovery of the frontiers of 1814 and the *annexation of Belgium*. You have, therefore, to ask for the extradition, by formal treaty, of Landau, Saarlouis, Saarbrück, and the duchy of Luxemburg; and you have to aim at the annexation of Belgium, by the conclusion of an offensive and defensive treaty *which is to be kept secret*. Secondly, should this basis appear to promise no result, you will resign Saarlouis, Saarbrück, and even Landau, which, after all, is but a dilapidated nest of a place, the occupation of which might excite German national feeling against us. In this eventuality your public agreement will be confined to the duchy of Luxemburg, and your secret treaty to the reunion of Belgium with France. Thirdly, supposing a clear and unmistakable reference to the incorporation of Belgium is found unpalatable, you are authorized to assent to a clause in which, to obviate the intervention of England, Antwerp is declared a free city. In no case, however, are you to permit the reunion of Antwerp with Holland, or the incorporation of Maestricht with Prussia.

"Should Herr von Bismarck put the question, what advantage would accrue to him from such a treaty, the simple reply would be, that he would thereby secure a powerful ally; that he would consolidate his recent acquisitions; that he was only desired to consent to the cession of what does not belong to him; and that he makes no sacrifice at all to be compared to his gains. To sum up, the *minimum* we require is an ostensible treaty which gives us Luxemburg, and a secret treaty, which, stipulating for an offensive and defensive alliance, *leaves us the chance of annexing Belgium at the right moment*, Prussia engaging to assist us, if necessary, by force of arms, in carrying out this purpose."

These instructions of August 16 were answered by Count Benedetti in a letter dated Berlin, August 23, and commenting upon it, in replying to his book, published in 1871, Prince Bismarck drily observed that "this letter, which is entirely in his own hand, like so many other interesting documents of the same kind, is at this moment in the possession of the German Foreign Office." In the letter Count Benedetti told his correspondent that he had received his communication, and would conform as closely as possible to the principles laid down in it. He inclosed a draught treaty, explaining that he preferred one treaty to two; that he found Landau and Saarbrück unattainable, and that he had accordingly kept to Luxemburg and Belgium. The Germans had also got hold of the reply to Count Benedetti's letter from the French government. A general approval was given to his draught; but whereas the fourth article contemplated the extension of Prussian supremacy south of the Main, and the fifth provided for the annexation of Belgium, the French government wished it to be made clear that the latter article was not to be regarded as only binding if the former had been carried out. "It is obvious that the extension of the supremacy of Prussia across the Main will, as a matter of course, compel us to seize Belgium. But the same necessity may be brought on by other events, on which subject we must reserve to ourselves exclusively the right to judge."

Amendments to carry out the views of the French government were added on the margin of M. Benedetti's draught treaty, and as thus amended, it also fell into the hands of the German government. On the receipt of his revised draught, Count Benedetti presented to Count von Bismarck a draught treaty incorporating the amendments with his original handiwork, and this was the treaty which Count von Bismarck published to the world in 1870. When, however, M. Benedetti came to discuss the project he was disappointed at the reception he met with; and he wrote home on the 29th of August, expressing for the first time a doubt whether France could count on the sincerity of Prussia, which, according to his belief, had succeeded in establishing an alliance with Russia, that might lead to the co-operation of France being refused. The whole matter, for the time at least, thus dropped, and secret negotiations were suspended for several months.

These documents entirely disposed of M. Benedetti's case, which was that the suggestion for the annexation of Belgium came solely from Count von Bismarck, at whose dictation the draught treaty had been written; and that the treaty was at once rejected by the French government, which would have nothing to do with the annexation of Belgium. In short, Count Benedetti's story was shown by the documents of his own government to be entirely untrue.

In so far as regards France, there is the clearest evidence of her determined design upon Belgium, and the French government had actually condescended to calculate what it might be necessary to provide as a sop to appease England. It is more difficult to say what was the true history of the part played by Count von Bismarck and Prussia in the matter. A part of M. Benedetti's book is proved to have been utterly false, but other parts the Prussian minister by no means explained. All that is really proved by the emperor's instructions of August 16 to Count Benedetti is, that the French government was plotting to seize Belgium, while he—anxious to put his government forth as a paragon of virtue—endeavoured to make the world believe that France would not have Belgium, even if offered. Prince Bismarck's revelations would have us infer that the proposal to lay hands on Belgium originated with her, but this by no means follows. Louis Napoleon had manifested considerable uneasiness at the growing power of Prussia, and could not but see that it was quite possible for him to prevent the easy subjugation of Austria in the war of 1866. He thought it reasonable, therefore, to inquire of Count von Bismarck, what compensation he might expect in return for allowing Prussia unmolested to absorb German territory on all hands. The idea of French interference evidently caused great uneasiness in Prussia; and on the 6th of June (more than two months prior to the letter of instructions above quoted) M. Benedetti wrote to his government that Count von Bismarck had told him that the compensation France might require in consideration of any future territorial aggrandizement of Prussia must be sought in a French-speaking district. This, it appears to us, was the first intimation of the secret treaty business. Count von Bismarck wished to disarm the hostility of Napoleon III., and in order to this he chose to keep dangling before him the prospect of an accession of territory to France at no risk or cost to himself. By this device he was completely taken in, and confirmed in his intention of maintaining an absolute neutrality between Prussia and Austria. On the 16th of July M. Benedetti wrote that Count von Bismarck had pressed on him the advantages of an alliance between the two countries. On his objection that to take the compensation offered would involve a breach of international treaties, Bismarck replied that if France and Prussia were united they need not fear armed resistance either from Russia or England. On the 26th of July M. Benedetti wrote again, that he should be telling the French Foreign minister nothing new in saying that Count von Bismarck "is of opinion that we ought to seek compensation in Belgium, and has offered to come to an understanding with France on this head." All these letters, written from time to time by M. Benedetti, in the ordinary course of his business, for the exclusive and private information of his own government, were published in his book, and their accuracy was certainly not impugned by anything Prince Bismarck afterwards published.

Putting all the accounts together, therefore, we think it is not very difficult to guess what really happened. Prince Bismarck was, in June and July, 1866, very much afraid of France helping Austria, and thought it expedient to agree that the former should have some makeweight to counterpoise the increased power of Prussia. As he did not wish to give up German soil, he suggested that France should take Belgium. France did not at all approve of this. She did not wish to get into a great international quarrel, and held that, as it was Prussia that was winning, she it was that ought to pay. France demanded Mayence and the left bank of the Rhine. Count von Bismarck rejoined that, rather than agree, he would prefer war. France backed out of the demand, but immediately caught at his suggestion for the annexation of Belgium, with, however, a demand for Luxemburg and a slice of Germany. Count von Bismarck would consent to no infraction of German territory, but was quite open to discuss what compensation he was to receive for Luxemburg and Belgium. During all this time that he was keeping France and M. Benedetti in play, he was arranging a Russian alliance; and no sooner had that point been gained than he threw M. Benedetti and his draught treaty to the winds, and vowed that he could never have the heart to do anything distasteful to England.

Under the title of "A Ministry of War for Twenty-four Days," Count de Palikao endeavoured to shuffle all the responsibility of the march to Sedan off his shoulders, and to justify the other acts of his administration. He admitted having been the author of the plan which proved so disastrous to MacMahon, but endeavoured to show that it was founded upon military considerations suggested by a former well-known campaign of Dumouriez in the Argonne. Dumouriez marched from Sedan southwards and won the decisive battle of Valmy; therefore Count de Palikao thought if MacMahon marched northward towards Sedan he too would win a great battle over the sons of those who were defeated at Valmy. "When I conceived the march of the army of Châlons on Metz, in order to operate its junction with that of Marshal Bazaine," says the War minister of twenty-four days, "I understood that Dumouriez's plan could be executed in an inverse sense, that is to say, by a rapid march from the valley of the Marne to the valley of the Meuse." In Chapter X. of this work we have expressed our opinion that the sending of MacMahon northwards in the attempt to relieve Bazaine was one of the most striking examples in all history in which military were sacrificed to political considerations; and notwithstanding Count Palikao's explanations, to that opinion we still adhere.

From M. J. Valfrey's "History of French Diplomacy since the 6th September," and the official documents published by M. Jules Favre, we obtain a clear insight into the extraordinary part played by M. Gambetta in the misfortunes of France, and some very interesting details respecting the mission of M. Thiers to this and other countries in September, 1871. The mission intrusted to M. Thiers was the opening of a series of illusions destined to be dispelled by a terribly painful experience; and the manoeuvres of M. Gambetta to paralyze the small results of the mission inaugurated what may be called the "era of patriotic falsehoods." It was an understood thing that, with M. Gambetta, "country" was synonymous with "republic;" if no republic there was no country; to save the country, therefore, it was necessary to save the republic. But if the republic signed a disastrous peace it was lost. This was the reason why, after the 4th of September, M. Gambetta was ever found impeding all attempts at a peace, or even an armistice. Before leaving Paris by balloon he was hostile to the pacific projects of M. Jules Favre, and he found a powerful auxiliary in the famous "plan "of General Trochu; at the end of October he resisted in his despatches the attempts at an armistice made by M. Thiers; in February, at Bordeaux, he voted against peace. His conduct was consistent, and from his own point of view irreproachable.

M. Thiers had been charged by the government of the 4th September with a mission to all the great powers, the main object of which was, if possible, to draw them into alliances with

France, so as to continue the war and expel the Germans from French territory. Where, however, the Emperor Napoleon in the fulness of his power, and his cousin Prince Napoleon, had, after a first disaster, been unsuccessful, there could be little chance for the representative of a country without an army and without a government. Besides, these projects of coalition "against the common enemy" were little likely to be favourably entertained by cabinets accustomed to look upon France as "the common enemy." In case of the failure of these projects M. Thiers was to induce the various powers to remonstrate strongly with Germany upon the exorbitancy of her demands. But to extort from Germany better terms than she deemed equitable was a task which would have required the combined efforts of Europe—a task, withal, in which it was doubtful whether Russia would, or Austria could, co-operate. It would be hard to say what England alone, or even England with Italy, could have done for France after Sedan; and M. Thiers should have considered how little influenced France herself would have been by the mere remonstrances of Europe, had the Prussian armies been overpowered in two pitched battles, Mayence and Coblenz besieged, and the French van-guard in sight of Berlin.

In spite of his quick intelligence, M. Thiers did not at once perceive how difficult it would be to turn the opinion of Europe in favour of France, or instead of listening to his fears, he obeyed only the promptings of his devotion to his country. He went to London, and there proved in lengthy conversations, to his own satisfaction at least, how necessary France was to the equilibrium of Europe and to the happiness of mankind. He was listened to, as he always had been, with deference, with sympathy, and even with pleasure; but Lord Granville answered that England "did not mean to go to war; that by interfering in behalf of the neutral powers she might run a risk of offending Prussia, who would not put up with her intervention; and that such an intervention might do more harm than good." He added, that England had already paid the penalty sure to fall on all neutrality; that she had given offence to both belligerents, and the Germans complained of her too great partiality to France. M. Thiers insisted that the course England had followed, and was bent on following, would cause her to fall from her rank among nations, and that her inaction, under present circumstances, amounted to connivance with Prussia, as it would necessarily turn to her advantage.

The English minister had, however, made up his mind not to compromise his country on any account. Her Majesty's government were fully aware of the futility of offering mediation between two belligerents who could not agree upon a basis of negotiation. They had brought the two plenipotentiaries face to face at Ferrières, and there left them to do the best they could together.

M. Thiers next went to Vienna, charmed Count Beust, thought that he had won him over, and went on to St. Petersburg. There all was cordiality and goodwill; the Emperor Alexander was understood to renew his promise that the French territory should be spared; this was much. Returning to Vienna, M. Thiers was received with good words, but it was necessary to make sure of Italy. King Victor Emmanuel was frankness itself; he acceded to everything asked by him, provided that his cabinet consented, but the cabinet did not consent. These great armies, this general rising announced by M. Gambetta, were they indeed real? M. Thiers, speaking officially, had no doubt about them, but when he spoke in his own name he was full of anxieties. His sad pilgrimage over, he returned to the government of the Delegation, bringing with him, besides the fair words which he everywhere received, a telegram from the Emperor Alexander to the king of Prussia, the object of which was to arrange for the entrance of M. Thiers into Paris, and to facilitate overtures for an armistice. If the Delegation approved, the telegram would be sent. At Tours the proposal was met by a similar proposal from the British cabinet. The combination decided their acceptance; for fear of showing unreasonable stubbornness, M. Gambetta yielded. While apparently joining in the opinion of his colleagues, however, he drew up privately for the government of Defence a long despatch, intended to precede M. Thiers and to destroy beforehand the effect of his speeches and his advice. This despatch may be said to throw a full light upon the character of M. Gambetta, as well as upon this episode of a very dark story. Overpowered by the authority of M. Thiers, M. Gambetta gave his vote for peace, but by underhand means he endeavoured to make it impossible. He put the government of Paris on its guard against the very objectionable views of the negotiator; the country was not so exhausted as he thought, men abounded, the staff of officers was being reformed. There existed in reality an army of the Loire of 110,000 men, well armed and equipped. The general who commanded them was not a great captain, but he was fully competent for his task. Another army was forming in the east; the west was getting ready; the north would stand firm; the franc-tireurs were the terror of the enemy; with Keratry and Garibaldi to command them they formed important resources. In a word, the military position was excellent, and as Paris would hold out long enough for all these forces to come into action, the state of affairs, from being critical, would become favourable; the flight of time, the rigours of winter, were so many auxiliaries which might be counted on.

This picture was drawn with the view of rendering the government remaining in Paris more exacting with regard to the conditions and even the acceptance of the armistice. To give additional effect to the picture, M. Gambetta furnished a highly coloured description of the state of people's minds in France. According to him elections were demanded only by a minority in the country. All the towns were "passionately republican and warlike;" even the provinces began to show their teeth. The Legitimists and the Orleanists alone, enemies to the supremacy of the capital, demanded new elections. There were no disturbances in the large towns. Lyons and Marseilles recognized the authority of the central government; leagues had been formed, but a little firmness and plain dealing sufficed to disperse them. Besides the republican party, "with the exception of two or three ultramoderate individuals, are unanimous in considering the elections as a perilous diversion from the necessities of the war." If an armistice was to be concluded, it must serve to reinforce the defence and not to weaken it. There must, therefore, be laid down as absolute conditions the revictualling of besieged places.

"Far from weakening the spirit of resistance," says he, "we ought to excite it still more; we ought only to accept the truce proposed to us if it is advantageous from a military point of view, and only to make use of it from a political point of view if we are resolved to hold really republican elections." The eloquence of Gambetta had the most disastrous influence upon those who read his fatal despatch; it persuaded them that the armies from the outside were hastening towards them, that the enemy was about to raise the siege, was imploring quarter, and must be made to pay for it. The armistice, as we know, was rejected, because the Germans would not consent to the re-victualling of Paris, and ultimately France had to pay three milliards more than would probably then have satisfied her enemy, and to lose, besides Strassburg and Metz, the whole of Alsace and a portion of Lorraine.

A singular feature of the war publications was the complaisance with which all the French generals sang their own praises. General Faidherbe was always victorious, and General Chanzy would have ultimately triumphed had the war continued. In our account of the operations in the north of France we have already alluded to M. Faidherbe's work, "Campagne de l'Armee du Nord en 1870-71 ," and see no reason to modify the opinions then expressed. The object of successful war is not to fight battles, or win them, for their own sakes, but as means to certain desired ends; and the whole question of a general's alleged victories turns on the degree in which he approached to or attained his object. Now, if Faidherbe in December wished merely to fight a defensive action and then move off, or in January to fight a defensive action and then move off, he certainly succeeded. But if the battle of Pont-a-Noyelles came out of an attempt to recover Amiens, as is generally supposed, or that of Bapaume of the desire to save Péronne, as Faidherbe himself tells us, then it is certain that he failed on each occasion, and can claim no success merely because he was not re-attacked or pursued.

ENGLISH BENEVOLENT OPERATIONS DURING THE WAR.

We have more than once, in the course of this history, alluded to the difficult part which England, as a neutral nation, had to play during the war. We were regarded by the belligerents as cold-blooded and lukewarm, for not taking an active share in a contest which stirred up the fiercest passions of both countries, and which each worked itself up to consider could only be rightfully regarded from its own point of view. Many Frenchmen felt more disposed to forgive Germany the invasion of their country than to forgive England for "permitting" it; while on the other hand, many German newspapers demanded a "bloody reckoning" of us for allowing the export of arms; forgetful that Prussia supplied Russia with them in the Crimean war, and that her jurists maintained that it was *then* both legal and expedient.

There is, however, one field where the much-maligned neutral is allowed fair play—the hospital and the ambulance. Here, at least, the United Kingdom showed that its neutrality was owing to no indifference, and that it is possible for outsiders to feel that there is a certain amount of truth and right on both sides, which the eager combatants overlook in the heat of the fearful strife—

> "Where furious Frank and fiery Hun
> Charge 'neath their sulph'rous canopy."

In these days of close intercourse and free trade among nations, England must suffer by all the misfortunes of its neighbours; a truth which, it may be hoped, will in time bring about a more charitable spirit towards us. Commerce is a sensitive plant, which shrivels up immediately under any cold chill, and our commerce, as the greatest in the world, is the most quickly affected. Yet the British contributions on behalf of the sufferers by the war exceeded those for any former object, and were larger by far than for our own Patriotic Fund, in the Crimean distress, in the same time. Such aid by neutral nations is regarded by some as an indirect subsidy for the carrying on of war; but a little reflection as to the circumstances of the recent contest will show that such was not the case in 1870—71. Under ordinary circumstances it is an admitted fact that any provision which a government can maintain for the service of the sick and wounded in time of peace, is invariably inadequate to meet the enormously increased demands which instantly spring up at the commencement of war. While the French arrangements in this respect were found on almost every occasion to be very greatly defective, the abundant provision made by Germany often seemed equally shortcoming. For the reason of this we have not far to seek. The campaign was one of unprecedented mutilation and slaughter; but in addition to this, and as a natural result of the extraordinary success of the Germans, a battle invariably threw upon their hands the sick and wounded of both sides; and the enormous strain under which they laboured may be gathered from the fact that the three first battles, Wissembourg, Woerth, and Forbach, left with them no less than 20,000 wounded. Vast as were the efforts made, the utmost that one side could do proved a very inadequate provision for such an excessive mass of suffering; and the object of the British National Society for aid to the sick and wounded in war was to supplement the overtaxed exertions of the military surgeons, and provide some few comforts for the sufferers beyond those allowed by the somewhat Spartan practice of military hospitals.

Subscriptions were opened in August, 1870. In six weeks a sum of £145,000 had been raised, vast stores of every description were being judiciously distributed, and fifty thoroughly qualified surgeons bad been despatched to the scene of conflict. The total sum ultimately received by the society in voluntary, and even unsolicited, subscriptions was £296,928—sent by 899 auxiliary committees, 317 bankers, 30 masonic lodges, 139 managers of concerts, lectures, &c.; the employés of 100 firms, 65 servants' halls, 257 schools, 172 regiments, including militia and volunteers; 30 ships of war, 5824 congregations and parishes, and 11,832 individuals. The value of the stores, no less important than the money, contributed by the public was estimated at £45,000; and a classification of the donors showed that stores of various kinds had been received from 224 branch committees, 252 parochial, congregational, and other collections, 69 schools and asylums, and 4354 individual contributions, of whom 380 sent their gifts anonymously. The stores embraced every conceivable article of hospital utility—bedding, clothing, medicines and surgeons' stores, food, and surgical instruments. As the war progressed the supplies of the last-named were especially acceptable, none being procurable in either of the belligerent countries, as German makers were in the army, and Paris, the regular source of French supply, was besieged. Large supplies of chloroform were also sent, and in addition to its use in the ambulance hospitals, permission was given by the king of Prussia for its conveyance into Metz, Strassburg, and Phalsbourg, some time before their surrender—the first instance of such mitigation of the horrors of a siege. The final report of the society showed that £20,000 was given to the German military at Versailles, and £20,000 to General Trochu in Paris, under a promise in both cases that it should be used purely for extra comforts, additional to the usual hospital allowance of each army; that £27,472 was spent in food, wines, spirits, and medical comforts for the disabled soldiers; that £28,971 was devoted to the purchase of clothing and bedding, £8090 to the purchase of surgical instruments, and £7866 to that of medical stores, disinfectants, &c. Besides these amounts we find an entry of £2111 expended in buildings for hospitals and stores, £21,705 on the transport service, including the purchase and hire of horses, vehicles, and forage, stable expenses, repairs, and packing and carriage of stores; and £23,845 on staff allowances and expenses abroad, including the pay of surgeons, dressers, nurses, lay-agents, infirmiers, drivers, grooms, porters, messengers, &c. Different other aid societies and ambulances, whose members by their local knowledge proved the best almoners that the committee could employ, were subsidized by the British society to the extent of £89,898.

At the close of the war the large sum of about £70,000 was still in the hands of the bankers, and it was resolved to apply for a charter of incorporation for the society, so as to insure permanence to its operations; the money being invested in the joint names of Prince Arthur, Lord Shaftesbury, and Colonel Lloyd Lindsay, as trustees, in order to form the nucleus of a fund for future use should occasion arise. One of the greatest difficulties of the committee was to allay the jealousies of the different military and medical authorities of both armies, who, though the system of distribution was rigidly impartial, were always complaining that they did not get their share of good things. In the course of their report the committee observed:—"We know that we have saved lives, mitigated the sufferings, and carried assistance and comfort, which could not otherwise have reached them, to thousands of sick and wounded in every stage and degree of their misery." "We simply administer the funds which the public intrusts to us, never having solicited subscriptions, remembering that our legitimate function is only to assist the government and people of Germany and France to do their own work, and is only of a supplementary nature."

Some agreeable proofs were received that, in spite of small misunderstandings, our efforts to mitigate the sufferings of the wounded on both sides were received by the two belligerents in the same spirit with which the help was offered. The Crown Prince of Germany, whose wife, our princess, conducted an admirable war hospital at Homburg, wrote to Colonel Lloyd Lindsay:—

"HEADQUARTERS, VERSAILLES,
"*November* 2, 1870.

"The noble contributions brought by Colonel Lloyd Lindsay, for the use of the sick and wounded, from the English society of which he is the director, deserves somewhat more than a simple acknowledgment.

"On this, as on other occasions of distress, the help of the English public has been poured out with a liberal and impartial hand.

"The gifts which have been offered, in a truly Christian spirit, have excited a feeling of heart-felt gratitude amongst those in whose name I speak. In doing so, I am repeating the feelings of the whole of my country people, in this instance represented by those for whose special benefit these gifts are destined."

"(Signed), FREDERICK WILLIAM."

The queen of Prussia also sent word to the committee, that she had observed with sincere admiration the generous manner in which the English nation endeavoured to alleviate the fearful sufferings of the present war, and to participate in the care of the numerous wounded, by supporting the existing societies and hospitals, by the erection of their own hospitals, establishment of depôts, and the distribution of gifts. "In my relations with the German societies, I feel it an urgent obligation to express this to the English committee for aid to wounded and sick soldiers which directs this benevolent activity, and in their name, as well as in the name of my countrymen far and near whom this assistance has benefited, to offer the most sincere and deep-felt thanks. By such proofs of true humanity the nation does honour to itself, and preserves its old reputation of maintaining the interests of humanity as everywhere the first consideration. It may likewise rest assured that with us in Germany what we owe to it in this respect is most warmly acknowledged and felt.

AUGUSTA.

"Homburg, *Nov.* 8, 1870."

The minister of War in France, General Le Flo, in acknowledging the gift of half a million of francs (£20,000), said that he understood the wish of the English subscribers to be, that the sum should be specially devoted to procuring for our sick and wounded, such additions to the regular hospital allowances as may enable them to feel that a friendly hand has been extended for the relief of their sufferings. "Allow me to express, in the name of the army and of our whole country, the sentiment of profound gratitude with which this brilliant manifestation of the sympathy of your generous nation inspires me. In happier and still recent times, it was granted to the soldiers of our two countries to fight side by side for a common cause, and the deed which you this day perform is a proof of the esteem with which you still regard us. I am deeply touched by it, as the interpreter of the grateful feelings of my nation."

Large, however, as was the sum received by the British National Society, it by no means represented the whole amount subscribed for the same or similar objects in Great Britain and its colonies. The Society of Friends raised a sum of no less than £75,681, known as the "War Victims' Fund," which was disbursed by members of the worthy community, who at their own expense visited the scenes of the war, and distributed help in the most judicious manner among the French civilian population suffering from its consequences. A large portion of the money was devoted to providing seed corn and vegetables for the impoverished inhabitants, who were thus relieved from the fearful contingency of a severe famine in addition to the other horrors of the war.

To carry out more fully the view of the Society of Friends in providing seed corn, a special subscription was commenced among the farmers and agricultural interest generally of England and Scotland. The "French Peasant Farmers' Seed Fund" which was thus raised, amounted to £51,582, and was distributed, without almost any cost to the fund, by gentlemen whose practical experience insured the certainty of the money being expended to the greatest possible advantage.

The *Daily News'* Fund, a subscription received entirely through the office of the popular newspaper of that name, amounted to £21,679, and was gratuitously distributed by several gentlemen—principally by Mr. W. H. Bullock, who for six months devoted the whole of his time, and not a little severe labour, to the task.

When the siege of Paris was evidently drawing to the only end to which it could come, it occurred to Mr. Knowles and some other gentlemen in London, that if the French capital stood out until the food within the city was exhausted, there would be the terrible likelihood of 2,000,000 of their fellow-creatures starving within twelve hours of our own shores. The sympathies of the great British capital for its sister city were aroused by such a prospect. A meeting was held at the Mansion House without delay, a committee was formed of representative men of all creeds and classes, and with the view of accumulating large supplies of food, to be sent into Paris as soon as the gates should be opened, the sum of £130,000 was subscribed in an incredibly short space of time. The British government also came handsomely to the help of the committee, and supplied it with the means of transport, and with large donations of provisions from the Admiralty victualling yards. The work of distribution was confided to Lieutenant-colonel Stuart Wortley and Mr. George Moore, two gentlemen enjoying universal esteem and confidence, and both well acquainted with Paris and with the means best suited to the pressing emergency. To food, fuel, garden seeds, and to setting free from pledge tools and implements, to enable the population of Paris to resume its industry, £70,000 was devoted by the committee; and the immediate relief of the city being effected, attention was turned to the suffering districts outside its walls. Large sums were distributed to relieve the distressed inhabitants of the circle of investment; and considerable grants were made to committees appointed to inquire into the cases of those who, in the various departments around Paris, had been entirely deprived of their homes and means of livelihood. To the Peasant Farmers' Seed Fund a sum of £13,000 was granted; and many of our fellow-countrymen in Paris, impoverished by the continuance of the siege, were assisted in leaving the city, or received temporary aid within it. During the siege the English residents had been supported mainly by the munificence of Richard Wallace, Esq., whose liberality was also amply extended to the poor of the city generally. Through Lord Granville, Mr. Wallace received the thanks of the British government, and he was shortly after created a baronet. The French authorities also showed their sense of his generosity by re-naming one of the Paris streets the Rue de Wallace.

Whatever form of government ultimately prevails in France, among all sober minds and honest hearts the memory of the proofs of generous friendship shown by England towards that country, and more particularly towards the city of Paris, will not be easily effaced. Those Frenchmen who, during the war, sought an asylum across the channel, the wives and daughters of those husbands and fathers in Paris who desired to save them from the dangers and severe privations of the siege, know what a kind, sometimes almost enthusiastic, reception was given them; they witnessed the wide sympathetic movement which sprang up on all sides; they saw the solicitude with which high and low in our great metropolis went to the succour of their besieged city, to save it from the horrors of famine. London was more concerned with the care of revictualling exhausted Paris than was the French government, and succeeded better. The report of a commission of inquiry upon markets, subsequently revealed the extent of the services rendered by the English to Paris; and judging by this, it is fearful to think what would have become of a population of two millions of souls had not the English waggons arrived almost as soon as the gates were opened, whilst the provisions bought by the French government were waited for in vain for weeks.

When, after the new disasters caused to Paris by the Commune, regular authority had resumed its sway, and a legal municipality had been established, one of the first acts of the authorities was to show to England that there still existed in Paris grateful spirits, and that the recollection of her bounty was not effaced. A medal was struck; a bronze model of the Hôtel de Ville, the symbol of the town itself, was added to the medal; the insignia of the Legion of Honour were given by the government, and a Parisian deputation, composed of the prefect of the Seine, M. Léon Say, and the president of the Elective Municipal Council, M. Vautrain, was commissioned to carry to London these souvenirs, and to tell in that city what true Parisians had been thinking and saying for months. The mission was well fulfilled; the reception given to the French representatives was such as to enhance the value of the services already rendered; and a return visit by the lord mayor of London tended to strengthen the ties between the two nations.

PARIS, BEFORE, DURING, AND AFTER THE SIEGE:

WITH AN ACCOUNT OF THE

RISE AND FALL OF THE COMMUNE,

B Y   A   R E S I D E N

CHAPTER I.

Convulsions of Nature and of States—Paris the Metropolis of Brilliancy—The Boulevards and their Cost—Rebuilding of Paris, and a Delusion caused thereby—The first Reverses of the War, and their Effect upon the Capital—The News of Sedan and approaching Imprisonment of the Parisians—Energy and Self-denial of the People aroused—Great Want of a Controlling Head at this Crisis—Difficulties arising in consequence—Paris previous to the War—The Contrast when the National Disasters began—The Boulevards invaded—Enormous Victualling Supplies, and the Hopes excited thereby—"Many a true word spoken in jest"—Failure of Dairy Produce—Vegetables at a Premium—The Dawn of Horse-beef—Exorbitant Prices of all Provisions—Hopes founded upon Delusions—"All Lost, except Honour"—Cats, Dogs, and Rats in the Market—"Ordinary" Prices for Delicacies—Elephant Steaks—Disappearance of Fish—Unpleasant Substitutes for Butter and Fat—Articles of Drink, Coffee, Chocolate, &c.—The Policy and Necessity of High Prices—Failure of Official Interference with Prices, except in the case of Meat—Conduct of Purveyors generally—Consternation respecting Bread—How Corn-mills were improvised—Bread rationed at last—The Quality of the Bread supplied, and its Composition—The Effect of the Interdict upon Flour—Siege Fare and Siege Flavour—Distressing Monotony—The Greatest Sufferers—Mendacious Newspaper Statements—Restaurant Customers notified to "bring their own Bread"—The Sufferings from the Scarcity of Fuel—Not so bad after all as things might have been—Water Supply—The Consumption of Wines, Spirits, Alcoholic Drinks, and Tobacco—General Effect of the Diet and other Circumstances—A Calamity which might have been a Catastrophe—Uncontrollable Yearning for Fresh Food when the Gates were opened—Arrival of Provisions from England, and Changé of Feeling in the City towards Great Britain—Markets immediately established under German Supervision—The Return of the Sailors to the City—Distressing Incident at Mont Valérien—General Condition of Society under the Siege—Lights put out and Places of Amusement closed—The Theatres and Actors in Siege-time—Paris the Brilliant becomes Paris the Dull—Efforts to keep up Communication with the Outside World—Balloon Experiments—The Torture of Suspense—The Pigeon-post and Marvels of Photography—Deciphering Despatches—Sensation caused by the Arrival of the First Post—Escape from the City and its Difficulties.

CONVULSIONS of all kinds naturally attract more attention than the phenomena, however grand and important, which are the fruit of nature and progress. The dismemberment of an old kingdom causes more surprise than the creation of a new one out of a desert, although the latter is the more important event; but this is the natural result of the progress of civilization, while the former is unexpected, violent, extraordinary. Again, great social convulsions appeal far more directly to the mind than mere material ones, however startling and horrible; the latter affect our senses and call forth our sympathies, but the former appeal to every feeling, and set in vibration every chord of our system. The world is deeply moved by the news of earthquakes that bury thousands of human beings . beneath the ruins of their dwellings; it shudders at the progress of epidemics that fill the land with desolation, and at wars which devour the flower of the manhood of nations, break up kingdoms, and snap old associations, but the effects soon pass away; the alteration of the arbitrary or imaginary "Balance of Power," that ill-defined theorem of diplomacy, leaves society almost as little affected by it as is the rotation of the earth or the precession of the equinoxes. But when we see an old, and once great, nation utterly ruined, its government and institutions all swept away like chaff before the wind, and its whole social system, political, material, and intellectual, reduced to chaos, surprise and sympathy give way to astonishment and dismay. We feel for the moment that all laws and principles are set aside, that human nature is suffering shipwreck, and that all our philosophy, all our learning, all our art and science, are built upon sand, and may be engulfed should the terrible storm extend to our own land. The situation is one of fearful interest, of sublime horror; and the wonder is, not that all the world should be so deeply moved as it is, but rather, that even the pressing necessities of life and the demands of duty should allow of its being for an instant absent from our minds. Great kingdoms and empires have been subverted, and will doubtless be so again; the sceptre has passed from one hand to another like a harlequin's wand; powers and landmarks have disappeared, after the world has been familiar with them for ages; great states have slipped down from their stations, or new ones have grown up and overtopped them: but the spectacle of a nation of forty millions of people reduced, in a few months, from a condition of apparent prosperity to the verge of bankruptcy, material and social, surpasses all that is recorded in history, or that the most imaginative mind could have conjured up in the way of convulsion. Such a saturnalia of bloodshed, revolution, famine, and ruin, such a subversion of powers, military, political, and social, has never before been presented to the bewildered senses of the civilized world, and the eye strains itself painfully and hopelessly to see the *finale* of the terrible drama.

The struggle between France and Germany, and the fortunes of the former especially, will supply future historians with an inexhaustible theme; and we hope to contribute a page or two of materials by recording our own impressions of Paris, after a residence of many years, received before, during, and after the siege.

Gay, beautiful, splendid, brilliant, all the adjectives of admiration have been lavished on Paris, and many of them were deserved. The atmosphere, the out-of-door life, art, fashion, and fancy, have always rendered Paris a kind of paradise to the visitor from gigantic, magnificent, but gloomy London; and during the last twenty years so much had been done to make Paris more attractive, more *coquet,* as our neighbours say, cleaner, more beautiful and brilliant, that it is not surprising that the great mass of foreigners should have accepted Paris, at the valuation of the Parisians, as the queen of cities, the great capital of the world. Visitors bent on pleasure, and even residents in search of elegance and ease, took no note of politics and economics; they did not calculate the cost, they had not to consider the future; and as this state of mind exactly suited the great majority of the natives also, Paris was declared, pretty generally, to be not only pleasant, but prosperous and glorious in the highest degree.

The skill of the engineer and gardener had done wonders for Paris. The Bois de Boulogne, the public promenades, the great new boulevards and avenues, the public squares or gardens, the profusion of fountains and flowers, even the sewers themselves, had been the subjects of fashionable gossip, and of enthusiastic admiration and laudation, not only from journalists and sketchers, but from practical men of the world, from ministers of state downwards; while those who counted the cost too carefully were set down as belonging to that unamiable class of individuals who would point out the incipient wrinkles on the brow of beauty, or search for flaws in a precious gem.

Beyond all question, the new boulevards and houses of Paris are stately, airy, and gay, the promenades and pleasure grounds are charmingly planted, and they are, or rather were, tended and garnished and watered and lighted in the most admirable manner, and, which deserves special notice, by highly scientific and economical means. Those who are curious on these subjects should read the "Pares et Promenades de Paris," by M. Alphaud, under whose management the Bois de Boulogne, the Bois de Vincennes, and all the pleasure grounds of Paris were laid out and kept in order. Side by side with the description of these extensive works will be found detailed accounts of the expenses, not only of the original operations, but also of the whole of their maintenance; and this portion supplies many most valuable hints for all who have to manage public places and municipal affairs. It would have been well for the city of Paris and for France, had the demolition and reconstruction in the capital and other towns been conducted with like economy.

The rebuilding of Paris, as the alterations of the city were called, was principally caused by the necessity which the government felt for protecting itself against revolutionary attacks; but it was warmly advocated, on the other hand, on the score of salubrity, which was a well-founded argument, and as making Paris the central attraction and mart of luxury of continental Europe; and the swarm of visitors and customers which new Paris attracted warranted this argument also, in the opinion of those who only looked upon the surface of affairs. On the other hand, the discontent was great, as there was a strong feeling that all that was being done for the capital was done at the cost of the rest of the country; and this feeling, as we shall see, bore poisonous fruit in the jealousy and mistrust which split the nation into many parties, and threatened to replace centralization by isolation under the name of federalism.

The enormous expenditure of the government and of the municipality of Paris gave rise, naturally, to enormous extravagance and speculation; the monied aristocracy, and indeed all classes, vied with each other in luxury and show; the Bois was filled with carriages and horses of the most costly and elegant description, in rivalry of the wealthy aristocracy of England; balls and entertainments assumed a pretentious and costly character, out of keeping with the old habits of Paris; and thus a fictitious appearance of great wealth was produced, which deceived the general world. But the most marked effect of the governmental and civic extravagance was a system of ingenious yet heedless speculation, which enriched the few and ruined thousands; immense gambling was taken for great financial prosperity, and until the greater part of the brilliant bubbles burst, Paris claimed to have assumed the first place in the monetary as well as in the artistic and fashionable world. We know now how hollow was the claim, how complete the delusion! Before the Into fatal war was declared the financial position of the government, as well as of the city of Paris, was disastrous, while extravagance, public and private, had rendered all the necessaries of life inordinately dear; visitors became less numerous, and natives as well as foreigners were compelled to fly from a city where rent, food, and fuel, in fact, all articles of common consumption, were ruinously dear.

It was just as the truth was breaking upon the most unthinking, when the means of public and private life were becoming almost impossible, that the declaration of war burst upon astonished Europe, and terrified the thinking portion of the French people. The cry, *à Berlin*, was naturally taken up by the army and by the least trustworthy portion of the population, and was certainly not discouraged by the government in its inconceivable blindness; and whilst the Marseillaise was being roared in the streets and theatres in the hope of coming victories, it fell upon the ears of thousands like the knell of the sad disasters which were so soon to arrive.

With the war itself we have nothing to do in this chapter, but only with its effects on Paris. At first, by means of shamefully deceitful information, Paris was led to believe that a new era of glory had actually set in; but this deception was of short duration, and the effect of the disasters that followed each other with such appalling force and rapidity is indescribable. Paris was stunned at first, then almost driven to madness; her usual life was suspended as if by catalepsy; the gay throng seemed to have melted into air; art, literature, science, even frivolity and glaring vice, were at once quenched; theatres and other places of amusement were closed; the detested police, which had swept the streets fortunately of thousands of vagabonds of both sexes, was, in its turn, swept away; and Paris, left to itself, ceased to be gay, and, instead of rushing into excesses, sank into lethargy.

The disgrace of Sedan fell like a thunderbolt upon the people of Paris. Deception, whether from without or within, could not gloze over that dreadful capitulation; it could not be converted even into a glorious failure; there was not a single extenuating circumstance surrounding it; all the glory and prestige of French arms seemed extinguished for ever, and the leaders were openly denounced as cowards and imbeciles. The only consolation was that he who proclaimed and directed the war had succumbed in the catastrophe. Democracy again raised its head, and calling upon the people to rise as one man and defend the fatherland, awoke them from the torpor that looked like death. For a time again hope revived, and the nation seemed roused to action; but promise after promise proved delusive, and at length, when it was known that the enemy was marching with calm but decided steps towards Paris, the agony of the people became almost insupportable. The apathy with which the great mass of the population waited for the moment when we were all to be made prisoners within the walls, can only be accounted for by the total absence of political life and individual action which had been imposed upon the population by an absolute government, working on the weaknesses of the national character.

When General Trochu and others at the head of affairs commenced the preparations for the defences of the city, able assistance was offered on every side; engineers, architects, and scientific men of all classes, not only organized, but helped to carry out with great energy the necessary works; members of the Institute, with the weight of sixty and more years upon their shoulders, laboured side by side with the pupils of the schools, literary men, and *ouvriers*, and the amount of work that was done was prodigious. On every side and in every form individual devotion and self-negation were common, the absence of it in fact was quite exceptional; every one's powers and capabilities were freely placed at the disposition of the chiefs, or were employed in auxiliary work, amongst which the establishment of temporary hospitals and ambulances occupied a prominent place. This was work in which all could contribute, and it was executed generously and ardently; Sisters of Mercy and Sisters of Charity, high-born dames and famous actresses, doctors and priests, *frères* and nuns of all classes, in cloister, tent, theatre, saloon, and hotel, devoted themselves day and night, uncomplainingly, to their sad labour, while those who had the means filled the cellars with wines and cordials, the store-rooms with linen, and the wards with beds and bedding. Amongst the few bright points in the siege of Paris, the most prominent are the devotion and the sacrifices that were made in aid of the wounded and the suffering. Many strangers aided greatly in the work, but none to the same extent as our own countryman, Mr. Richard Wallace, whose name has in consequence been given to the street formerly known as the Rue de Berlin.

In the midst of all this individual activity and devotion there was one great want—peculiarly patent to the eye of an Englishman, and characteristic of Paris—the city was a great agglomeration of individuals without a head; there was no general action, no public life. It is true that a number of clubs were opened, and that speech was free, but, with one or two memorable exceptions, the discussions there exhibited nothing but ignorance and violence. Population, like children, cannot be expected to perform at a moment's notice acts for which they have not been trained. Accustomed to look to government for everything; shut out from all the rights, though not from the duties and obligations of citizens; accustomed to be led or driven, as the case might be, by the agents of authority, just as flocks of sheep are conducted by the shepherds and their dogs—the disappearance of the directing powers reduced the population of Paris to a helpless, excited, and sometimes a mischievous crowd. Here and there men of commanding talent, such as Professor Wolowski, M. Desmarest. one of the ornaments of the Parisian bar, and the Protestant ministers, Coquereland Pressensé, produced considerable effect on crowded audiences; but, speaking generally, nearly all who should have been the leaders and directors of the people were dumb, or wasted their words. The silence of the clergy of France, almost absolute, was one of the most marked and extraordinary facts during the whole period of which we are speaking. The archbishop of Paris issued one admirable address, touching the duty of the people under the circumstances, calling upon the clergy and the laity to lay aside all animosity, and be charitable and considerate towards each other, to respect the powers that were, and thus to aid in the re-establishment of order; but this and one or two other rare examples were more than counterbalanced by the violence of a well-known religious journal, which even surpassed the lowest club in the virulence of its personal abuse. Generally, the clergy felt it could not safely interfere; it knew it had not the slightest hold on the masses in Paris; and the editor of the journal in question had the incredible folly and wickedness to seize on the fact of a shot being fired on a flag of truce, to declare that "it was probably aimed at a priest who was present, as the democrats would rather kill a French priest or *frère* than a Prussian."

The government of the national defence suffered seriously from this state of things. While the work of preparation was new the people generally supported and individually helped it, and, with few exceptions, the press showed a most friendly spirit; but the new government, like that which had preceded, was utterly isolated from the people; it had neither the aid of aristocracy, middle classy or the masses; it could not call around it, or obtain the opinion of any one class or party; it could gain no moral support anywhere, and consequently, having been compelled to act unaided during the early and more hopeful days of the siege, it had the whole of Paris against it when faint hope was converted into blank despair. Nor was it in a political sense only that it was isolated. The founders, the engineers, the railway companies, and others, gave most valuable aid in the armament of the city; but the mercantile and shopkeeping classes seemed to have been paralyzed in all their members by the loss of their old directing heads. The consequence was, that the management of the food and other supplies, and nearly all the ordinary business of a city that then contained more than 2,000,000 of souls, was left to advocates and others, as ignorant of trade and its thousand requirements as grocers and others of the law of evidence. The result was a violent breach between the government and nearly all the wholesale and retail tradesmen of the city, the complete disorganization of the whole of the ordinary modes of supply, a frightful waste of provisions, an amount of suffering and a mortality which are frightful to look back upon. It is only when such facts as these are laid before us, and their effects are considered, that the causes of the difficulties of France in general can be traced. Louis XIV. and XV. broke down the influence and ruined the character of the old aristocracy, the first Empire reduced the whole nation politically to the condition of slaves, the second Empire completed the work of destruction, first by its overweening pretension and extravagance, and finally by the utter incompetency of its chief and instruments. Where is the man, or where are the men, the assemblies, the representatives, to lay the foundations of a new France, able and worthy to hold its own? Who will make the French understand that the time for domination, false glory, and pretension is past, and that France must be content to take her own proper place amongst the nations and keep it, or follow the fate of the fallen empires of the ancient world? Time alone can show. The grand characteristic of new Paris when the word for war was given at the Tuileries was spruceness. If the greater part of the new structures had too much the air of barracks, if the new boulevards were fatiguing on account of their length and monotony, if the Bois de Boulogne had somewhat of a cockney, theatrical, over-wrought appearance, if the banishment of every natural element in favour of an artificial one, wherever possible, produced something of a vulgar, *parvenu air*, still the exquisite cleanliness of the streets in the better parts of the city—not the inferior portions—the care with which the capital was swept and garnished, planted and watered, and decorated in every way, made it an attractive place; and especially so for those who were satisfied while they themselves were comfortable, cared nothing about principles of government, the rights of humanity, or the progress of civilization.

With the destruction at once of the army and the empire the aspect of Paris underwent an extraordinary change; the police and nearly all the other agents of the late government disappeared, the whole municipal organization fell at one blow, and dirt and disorder assumed universal sway. It would be difficult to conceive the rapidity and completeness of the change that took place; smiling frivolous Paris became at once a dirty camp. In the first place lodgings had to be found for 80,000 *mobiles*, besides the national guards from the districts just outside of Paris; they were billeted on the inhabitants while huts were being provided for them. These were erected in the centre of what used to be the outer boulevards of the city, following the line of the old *octroi* wall, demolished when the city was extended to the fortifications, and on the unoccupied ground in the new districts. During the day the new and least frequented boulevards were continually occupied by troops drilling, marching, skirmishing, cooking, or eating. Quiet, "genteel" squares and places in the new districts were converted into *places d'armes*, and a large portion of the Avenue Wagram was converted into a park for the artillery of the national guard, the staff of the corps being established in the very house in which about ten years since the emperor was entertained at a collation upon the occasion of the opening of the magnificent Boulevard Malesherbes. All the unoccupied apartments in the handsome *hôtels*, or private residences, whether furnished or not, were taken possession of and converted into staff quarters, stations, and ambulances; and from break of day, and even earlier, all the prominent corners were occupied by coffee and other stalls, superintended by neat, coquettish, or brazen, slatternly *vivandières*, or, as they are commonly called in France, *cantinières*. Every scrap of waste ground in the neighbourhood of the huts and *places* referred to was seized upon as sites for refreshment booths and shanties, which were generally constructed of old boards and window frames brought in by the suburban population on the approach of the German army. *Bifteks* and *côtelettes*, soup and bouilli, coffee, wine, and brandy were offered, and very freely accepted, at prices alarmingly low. Some of these establishments were of a curious character: near the *Parc Monceaux* an adventurous caterer for the thousands of mouths set up a *café-restaurant* in two old omnibuses, and seemed to have plenty of customers. The *mobiles* received their rations in the streets and boulevards, set up their soup kettles, and fried their potatoes on the side walks, and ate, drank, smoked, sang, and talked, when off duty, as if they were perfectly at home; the *patois* of Alsace, Normandy, Brittany, and Provence mingling curiously with the Parisian tongue. In very bad weather the shops and ground floors of untenanted houses served as refuges to those who could not afford to frequent *cafés* and wine shops; but, generally speaking, from the first streak of daylight to late in the evening, the whole of the boulevards and broad streets were thronged with soldiers and recruits in the most varied costumes, from the common *blouse* of the workman to the gay uniform of the citizen soldier. The national guard included men nearly of all ages and of all classes of society; and it was a curious sight to see highly respectable citizens, often "with fair round belly with good capon lined," fling themselves flat on the ground, in dust or mud, at the word of command of the drill serjeant who was busy converting them into sharpshooters.

The military were not the only invaders of the boulevards; the great mass of the washing of the city is usually carried on in the outskirts of Paris, and when the *blanchisseurs* and *blanchisseuses* were compelled to retreat within the walls, they also seized upon the boulevards as their ground; and the trees which the other day were watched with such sharp eyes by the police that scarcely any one dared touch them with his finger, now served as supports for clothes' lines, and in many parts these were covered continually with masses of linen that would have made Falstaff's army mad with delight. Still another class took advantage of the occasion; those who could manage to bring in from their own or somebody else's garden outside, any kind of vegetable or green meat, from a few cabbages and cauliflowers to a bag of potatoes, a few handfuls of onions, leeks, garlic, or salad, planted themselves where they thought best; and the corners of many of the boulevards were converted into regular, or rather, irregular markets, for the sale of every conceivable article of consumption, except those of a superior kind. To complete the picture, the *chiffoniers* and *chiffonières*, male and female rag and bone collectors, had disappeared, and the refuse from the houses lay continually before the doors till dissipated by the traffic or the wind; and when the gates of the city were finally closed, the dung and litter from all the stables in Paris was collected here and there on vacant bits of ground, and added greatly to the general metamorphosis. At first this threatened to be the source of serious mischief, for the weather was extremely hot, and the number of flies was incredible; in houses near the stations of the omnibus company they hung in great black clusters in every corner and attractive spot, and pestered us in the house abominably. At length the frost fell upon us, which banished the flies and subdued the effluvia, but which brought terrible evils of other kinds in its train.

It was a curious sight for the Parisians, usually so regularly and systematically supplied with the necessaries of life, to have the whole system of supply laid open before their eyes. In ordinary times no cattle are seen in the streets of Paris, few heavy waggons laden with hay and straw; and the supplies of wheat, vegetables, fish, &c., come to the markets in the small hours, when Paris generally is asleep. The *abattoirs*, where the cattle are slaughtered, are on the outskirts of the city, and the meat is brought to the butchers in great covered carts; the sides of beef, &c., being curtained over generally by means of white cloths. Now all was changed! Every railway station was choked up with corn, hay, straw, cattle, sheep, pigs, and provisions; the streets were blocked up by huge carts, military waggons, trucks, and vehicles of all kinds; the wine merchants were bringing in thousands and thousands of barrels of wine and pieces of spirits from their cellars beyond the *octroi* circle; droves of bullocks, sheep, and pigs crowded every boulevard; the little farmers and dairymen brought in their cows and poultry with their children and household goods; here a poor woman had several cocks and hens in each hand; now a man brought in a barrow with half a dozen white geese sitting with all gravity and grace, their necks erect, their eyes wide open and gazing curious on the novel scene, with nothing to indicate the fact of their feet being imprisoned beneath them. Pigs, goats, and rabbits came in at every gate, and had to take up their abode in empty shop, cellar, or elsewhere. One landlord who had given shelter to a farmer and his family, was not a little astonished a month afterwards to find a magnificent suite of rooms converted into a menagerie; a litter of pigs grunted around Mama Sow in one room, flocks of pigeons flitted and cooed in a second, while a third was occupied by a large family of ducks, who were revelling in the delights of a bath standing in the centre of the drawing-room floor.

The cattle and sheep were collected together in the Champ de Mars and other open spaces, on the green slopes of the fortifications and all around between the ramparts and the forts, under the protection of the latter. The flour market, the military storehouses, the cellars of the great central *Halles*, or market of Paris, and many buildings, including amongst others the new opera house, which it was little supposed would ever be turned to such use, were crammed with flour, corn, hay and straw, biscuits, salt beef, pork, and fish, preserved meats, cheese, butter, potatoes, and provisions of all kinds. Paris was amply victualled; the siege could not last more than a few weeks, the forts were impregnable, the enemy would soon find himself between two fires, and in the meantime there was no fear of famine, or even scarcity, except of green vegetables! Such was the tenor of nearly all that was said and printed in Paris in September, 1870; those who had laid in stocks of provisions on their own account kept the fact secret for fear of being laughed at, and in some cases, perhaps, as a precaution against exciting envy in their neighbours' bosoms. The government assured the people that the provisions were ample, that the stock of meat was good, and that of breadstuffs inexhaustible; and this we are assured was said in all good faith. Some doubters joked upon the subject, said that horse was capital eating, and that the omnibus *cavalerie* would feed all the population of Paris for weeks, that when the horses were gone we should relish cats and rats; the dubbing of a rat by the name of the "future partridge" was pronounced a capital joke. We little dreamed of the grim reality that was to come upon us before the waning year should have finished its course!

We very soon found to our cost what a serious matter was the feeding of 2,000,000 of people, and how miserably helpless was a great city cut off from the rest of the world; the thousands of sheep and hundreds of other animals required for such a carnivorous monster as Paris were reckoned up, and various calculations made as to how long our meat would last at the rate of the fifth of a pound per head *per diem*, the quantity fixed by the first rationment of the authorities. We had not to trust long to guesses or calculations, for we soon learnt that the "salutary precaution of rationing the amount of food" was nothing more than a euphonistic phrase for scarcity and approaching famine.

No sooner was Paris invested than we began to feel our helplessness. Dairy produce was the first to fail us; a large number of cows had been brought into the city, but the supply of milk was far below the average; even during the first month it was allowed by law to be mixed with water to the amount of forty per cent.: a great error, not only on account of its deterioration, but also it was found impossible to prevent the dose of water being increased, and the consequence was, that while we paid more than double the usual price, the milk was almost worthless. Before long the fodder began to fail, numbers of the cows were killed and eaten, no one being allowed to retain them unless he could show that he had plenty of food to give them. Concentrated milk was largely used, but the stock was soon exhausted, and the small tins that sold usually for tenpence became worth five or six francs, and even more. The value of asses' milk is rated very high in Paris, and previous to the siege many of those animals might be seen, or heard, for they wore bells round their necks, trotting into the city in' the morning to the various markets; one person living in the neighbourhood of Paris kept some hundreds of asses, and we saw them come in just before the actual closing of the city. The proprietor generously placed the whole of the milk gratuitously at the disposition of the medical profession for the use of the sick and infirm; but like the cows, the poor asses also disappeared, and it is more than probable that not one of them ever saw their fields and stables again. Goats helped our supply for some time, for these creatures are always numerous in and around. Paris, and as they live and thrive where almost any other animal would starve, they held out till fresh meat of any kind became worth almost its weight in gold. Eggs were of course scarce at the very commencement of the siege, and when a fowl, young or old, became worth forty or even fifty shillings, and corn of all kinds was wanted for bread, eggs were almost unattainable, and fetched one, two, and finally three francs each!

The disappearance of butter was a terrible deprivation to the Parisians, who consume immense quantities of it in all forms, but especially in cookery; the commonest salt butter soon became worth ten francs a pound, and finally even four times that price, while the small quantity of fresh butter made in Paris rose gradually to forty, fifty, and even sixty francs; the first pastry cooks and provision shops in the city sold little pats of it at a franc or more each, and ladies carried these precious morsels away with more delight than at another time they would have exhibited over a brilliant ring or bracelet. Cheese disappeared at a very early period; Gruyère, which generally sells for tenpence or a shilling a pound, was worth at least five-and-twenty shillings. On the first day of the new year, when every gentleman calls and presents each of his lady friends with a bouquet, sweetmeats, costly jewels or trinkets, a pound of fresh butter or cheese or half-a-dozen new-laid eggs formed a princely offering, far above rubies. Those who spent the New-year's Day of 1871 in Paris are not likely to forget it as long as they live; rich as well as poor, with few exceptions, learnt then, if they never knew before, what cold and hunger, or at any rate the craving for wholesome food, were like!

Vegetables were of course dear, and very soon excessively scarce; cauliflowers and cabbages rose in price rapidly, from one to fifteen francs a-piece; carrots, turnips, and wretched heads of green celery fetched two and three francs each; beetroot reached eight francs a pound; a clove of garlic or a leek was worth a franc, and at last even double that sum; and onions, without which cooks are badly off indeed, were amongst the rarest of provisions, and rose in price from one to seven francs the *litre*, which holds a pint and three-quarters. All this was bad enough, but worse still was the failure of potatoes. The season had been bad for them; they were dug up before they were thoroughly ripe, and stored anywhere; the consequence was the price soon rose from sixpence and eightpence the *boisseau*, a measure containing less than a peck, to three, four, and five francs, and finally they were quoted at the market at *fifty francs*, or two pounds! The deprivation was felt severely, and some time before the end of the siege placards appeared in various parts of the town offering thirty-five francs the *boisseau*, but without producing any results. Nor were there any substitutes to be found, when the haricot beans and lentils, of which there is an enormous consumption in France, had been all eaten up; rice, dried peas, and even dried Windsor beans, were sought after with avidity, and each in its turn became exhausted, as macaroni, vermicelli, and the other *pâtes d'Italie* had previously. The prices which some of these articles had attained in the month of January will show at once how rare they had become:—Rice, two francs a pound; small tins of preserved peas, ordinarily sold for one or two francs, became worth seven and eight francs, and then disappeared altogether; tins of preserved haricot beans were equally dear and scarce; and at the last period of the siege we were asked eight francs a pound for the remainder of a jar of the commonest dried peas!

When the quantity of meat to be sold to each family was fixed by the municipal authorities, that is to say, when the *rationnement* commenced, and horse and other meat took their places beside that of beeves, we came to understand fully what a state of real siege meant. At first the allowance was the fifth of a pound per head per diem; this was soon reduced to two ounces, and finally and for many weeks the quantity to be obtained did not equal one ounce of raw meat per head daily. The prices of beef and horse flesh were fixed, and not high; but pork, veal, and mutton had almost entirely disappeared when the first *rationnement* took place. Very soon there remained nothing but horse flesh, the small supply of beef being reserved for the sick and the aged. It is needless to dwell on the condition of the population, reduced to an ounce of horse flesh a day, without fish or poultry, except at enormous, prices, butter, eggs, potatoes, or other vegetables. But the smallness of the amount of animal food was not the only cause of suffering; the moment the *rationnement* commenced the whole system of supply was deranged, the butchers declared they could not keep their shops open with the prices fixed by the authorities; most of them were closed, and special places were opened for the sale of meat in each of the *arrondissements*, or sections of the city; the *maires* and other officials, with few exceptions, were utterly incapable of the management of the business, and the greatest possible confusion and suffering were the consequence. The poor women and the cooks in every family were compelled to stand for hours at the doors of the *boucheries*, waiting to purchase their morsels of meat; in many cases they took their places over night in order to reach the counter before the meat had all disappeared, and thus during the coldest weeks of one of the severest winters known, and frequently with masses of half-melted snow beneath their feet, five, six, and even eight hours did these poor women wait, and then often found the stock of meat exhausted; and as the distribution only took place once in three days, sometimes extended to four, the supply of meat really became insignificant. At first only beef was placed under requisition, and other kinds of meat were left free; then horse flesh was taxed, and the price fixed, and each person might purchase two ounces of that in place of one ounce of beef; mule and asses' meat was still free, and in great demand, especially the latter, at high prices; but it was found that horse was sold as mule flesh, and finally all kinds of meat were placed under the same regulations. By this time, however, very little but horse flesh remained, and much of that was execrable.

During the last three months of the siege small quantities of mutton, veal, cow-beef, mule and asses' flesh, that came few know from where, were sold at rates varying from six to twelve francs a pound, and purchasers almost fought for it. Coarse sausage, of horse flesh, fetched eight francs a pound, and that made from mule and asses' meat nearly twice as much; black-pudding composed of horse blood sold readily at six and eight francs a pound, and was pronounced capital eating, although there was little or no bacon or fat of any kind in it. For a time we were led to believe that there were large supplies of salt meat in store, but this ended in nothing but disappointment; once we obtained some wretched salt beef or horse, but only once, and we did not desire a repetition. It was said, we believe with some truth, that by the negligence or inexperience of the authorities, or by the unprincipled conduct of speculators, large quantities of meat salted down were quite uneatable; at any rate, the promised salt beef never reached our mouths.

Under such circumstances, it seems incredible that the population of Paris should have existed at all, or that the authorities were not forced to capitulate by popular clamour. In the first place, the feeling of honour was very lively; to propose capitulation at one of the clubs, or in any public place, would have been an act of the greatest temerity, and might have cost the author of it his life; secondly, the mass of the people and, we believe, the government also, deceived by the reports sent from Tours and Bordeaux, fully expected that, although detained, the new armies levied in the provinces would arrive to the rescue of the capital. We know now how utterly fallacious was that hope, but it was impossible for Paris to know the truth at the time. We heard of the victories of Chanzy and other generals, and the account came all dressed in glowing colours for our special ears; and we could not conceive that the whole organized power of a great country like France was at an end, or so near it as scarcely to form an element in the question between her and the enemy. We were starved, or nearly so, materially, but we were fed with false hopes, so that capitulation looked like the grossest cowardice; and France will be intensely thankful hereafter to the people of Paris, who in thus suffering, and still upholding the honour of the city, did so much to save the national pride. The people of Paris deserve to rank with the Old Guard at Waterloo; their leaders were incapable, their force was broken down by that of the enemy, everything around them was chaos, but they stood their ground as long as human nature was capable of enduring; and they may honestly adopt the words of the brave Francis I., "All is lost, except honour!" But when honour is saved, all is saved for the future; a nation whose honour is intact is only scotched, not killed. When France shall find worthy rulers, and cease to be the plaything of adventurers and revolutionists, she will, let us hope, again take a high place amongst nations, and commence another, brighter, and purer career than that already written against her name in the book of European civilization.

But even honour cannot exist upon air! How then were the people kept alive? At the time when an ounce of horse flesh a day first became the ordinary allowance, the quantity and quality of the bread were excellent and unlimited; there was an immense supply of biscuit, plenty of sugar, coffee, chocolate, and wine; the elements of life-sustaining diet were still present though unequal; the destitute were well supplied with soup, made from refuse meat, bones, and annual greases; as for the mass, they took kindly enough to horseflesh, and eked out the supply of meat from all sources. For a time, the accounts of the consumption of the flesh of cats and dogs were regarded as jokes, but they soon proved their veracity; dogs and cats were not only eaten, but declared by many to supply excellent food; and finally they appeared regularly in the markets, and ended by being actually in great demand, at prices ranging from four to six shillings a pound. Rats were strongly eulogized by the members of a somewhat fantastic club of naturalists, and were certainly eaten at last in large numbers, selling for two and three francs each; it was said that Paris was thereby cleared of rats. This is probably an exaggeration, but it was absolutely true that cats and dogs had almost entirely disappeared. The beautiful half-angoras, which used to be so common, were only to be found in houses where they were protected with the greatest possible care. When a cat came to be worth ten and even twenty francs, the pussy that ventured out alone was a "gone coon."

The affluent classes, and indeed all who had money at command, whether they could afford it or not, added to the common fare delicacies, which in the end rose to almost fabulous prices; a few of these, the result of personal experience and observation, will be interesting by way of record:—

Fowls.	40s. to 50s.
Turkeys and geese,	5l. to 6l.
A fine turkey stuffed with truffles,	8l.
Ducks,	30s.
Pigeons,	8s. to 15s.
Rooks,	5s.
Sparrows, or any other small birds,	1s. to 2s.
Hares,	2l. to 3l.
Rabbits,	30s. to 40s.
Ham,	40s. per lb.
Preserved beef,	15s. per lb.

The above were ordinary prices which ruled for weeks; special instances of still higher rates might be adduced.

The papers amused their readers considerably with accounts of the immense success of elephant and other meats which were sold at great prices; but these belong simply to the curiosities of the siege. The elephants killed were but two very small ones, and the whole of the rare animals and large birds killed for food were the property of the Acclimatization Society, which had not fodder enough to maintain them; none of the animals belonging to the Jardin des Plantes were slaughtered. A well-known butcher made a great show of these rare meats, and of *pâtés* and preparations made from them; and those who could find nothing better to do with their money paid exorbitant prices for elephant steaks, elan beef, roasted cassowary, and other delicacies, from which under ordinary circumstances they would have turned away with disgust.

Fish, of course, was almost unattainable; the appearance of a fine fresh salmon caused a positive sensation in the city; a small plate of Seine gudgeons was worth five shillings; and the few pike, carp, tench, eels, and other fish that appeared in the markets, sold almost for their weight in gold. It will give an idea of the absolute dearth of anything like fish to mention that the ordinary shilling box of sardines in oil became towards the end of the siege worth at least a dozen shillings.

Few articles attained such high prices relatively as oils and greases; the absence of butter and the want of fat was not only felt in cookery, but began to tell most seriously upon the health of the people; olive oil was almost exhausted, and was worth from ten to twenty shillings a pint, and rapeseed oil, which was used as a substitute, was not to be had under three or four shillings. The whole of the suet, and all the other fat, was melted and purified at the *abattoirs*, and sold for four to five shillings a pound; the very commonest grease, even cocoa butter, generally used only by the fine soapmakers, although declared detestable in flavour, was not to be had under eighteenpence a pound.

It may be remarked, that while almost every kind of meat was accepted and eaten with very little complaint, the substitution of grease for butter created general disgust. The Academy of Sciences tried to persuade the people that any kind of oil or grease, even tallow, might be easily purified and rendered tasteless; but the universal verdict was that none of the substitutes for oil and butter were fit for human consumption. The one article which supplied the place of fat in the food was chocolate, and its consumption was enormous; fortunately the supply was large, and although it at last became scarce, the price did not rise very high. Honey was also a useful auxiliary, but the stock was not great, and before the armistice was agreed to it was worth eight or ten francs a pound. Chocolate and sugar were used in enormous quantities, and although the raw material began to run low, and the refiners and manufacturers had great difficulty in obtaining fuel, and had to pay enormous prices for it, the supply held out to the end. At one moment the prices of these important articles threatened to increase seriously, and the authorities made an attempt to fix the price of sugar; but this attempt at controlling trade, like most others of the same kind, failed utterly: refiners refused, in fact were generally speaking unable, to sell large quantities at a loss, and retailers who had made heavy contracts refused to sell at less rates than they paid for the goods wholesale. At one moment we feared that chocolate and sugar were both all but exhausted, for the grocers almost universally refused to sell to one person more than half a pound of the former or a pound of the latter, so that the members of a family had to visit different shops in order to obtain sufficient quantities of these always useful, and now almost indispensable, articles of consumption. It seems extraordinary to lay so much stress upon an article like chocolate, which many persons, and the writer amongst the number, scarcely ever touch; but for a long time the only substantial aliment within common reach was chocolate, made without milk, or with an exceedingly small quantity, with dry bread; chocolate was used also largely with rice, while the latter held out, and a small quantity of rum. Coffee was plentiful, but the absence of milk made it of little use; a thimbleful of black coffee, made as strong as brandy, is much relished after a good dinner, but a large cup of black coffee fasting is anything but an agreeable beverage, and if persisted in would soon tell upon the health of the consumer. Had the siege occurred in hot weather coffee would have been invaluable, as it forms one of the most wholesome drinks possible for the summer, and is specially recommended to the army. This beverage is called *mazagrin*, and is made by pouring iced-water on strong cold coffee, and adding sugar and a small glass of brandy, according to taste; it never disorders the stomach, and therefore is invaluable in the dog-days. But although we led a dog's life of it during the latter portion of the siege, it was not the heat that troubled us; and our ounce of horseflesh did not produce that amount of oppression which demands large libations of any kind, except those which supplied warmth and comfort, and a feeling, if not the reality, of support.

The exorbitant prices of many articles of consumption have been referred to more than once, and there is no doubt that a number of persons traded largely on the scarcity of provisions, and demanded and obtained outrageous prices, but these did not in all cases represent great profits. The poulterers, for instance, who sold miserable fowls or small rabbits for thirty and forty shillings each, had immense trouble to obtain a supply, which, after all, was extremely limited; and the poor man or woman who sold the few fowls or rabbits that they possessed, could not certainly be blamed for selling them at high prices, when they themselves often wanted the means to obtain a dinner except by charity; moreover, had the prices been maintained at the usual rates all the poultry, and many other articles, would have been consumed long before they were, and even the sick and invalided would have been unable to obtain the slightest delicacy, or even change of diet. Some grocers and other tradesmen undoubtedly kept back provisions until almost famine prices were reached; but nothing proved that this was done on a large scale, and many respectable shops refused to buy of wholesale dealers who thus traded on the sufferings of others, and announced the fact by placards in their windows, somewhat in the following form:—

"We beg to inform our customers that our stock of——is exhausted, and that we refuse to purchase more of those wholesale dealers who have kept back their stocks until they could obtain exorbitant prices for it."

The great mass of retail dealers did not take undue advantage of the state of affairs, and we believe that the number of wholesale dealers who did so was very small. In many cases within our own experience respectable shopkeepers made no advance at all. They said, so long as our stock lasts we shall sell at the usual rates; and they kept their word. On the whole, the usual course of trade was not interfered with, and wherever an attempt was made to fix prices by authority utter failure was the result, the article generally disappearing at once from the public view. Official interference simply caused secret instead of open dealing. The case of meat was different; the supply was precisely known, and as all the animals are sold and killed in one place in Paris, under the eye of the municipal authorities, the requisition and rationing which were necessary, first, to limit the consumption, and, secondly, to keep down the prices, only interfered with the butchers' trade, and was fully justifiable on the score of necessity.

Manufacturers, dealers, shopkeepers, the mass of purveyors generally, acted, on the whole, admirably. Thousands of them were utterly ruined, and many of them met their ruin with truly noble courage, giving liberally, putting all considerations for the future out of sight, and turning all their attention to the defence of the city or the succour of the sick and wounded. The members of the literary professions also exhibited the most praiseworthy devotion.

We have not yet reached the culminating point in the alimentary view of the siege of Paris; meat we knew must very soon run short if the siege were prolonged, vegetables we knew we must be content to do without; many other articles of food we were aware would either vanish altogether or become very scarce, but up to a late period of the investment we were positively assured that there was no lack of flour or corn, and that there could be no necessity for restricting the consumption of bread. We believed this, as we believed the approach of the provincial armies to our relief, because we believed the members of the government to be honourable men; we came to know how utterly unfounded were both beliefs, yet the government could hardly be charged with deception; the sufficiency of bread depended on the length of the siege, that again on the arrival of the armies of the departments, while the knowledge that the government possessed respecting those armies reached it from sources in which it certainly had a full right to trust. It deceived the people because it was itself deceived, and bread only failed us because the hoped-for aid from the provinces turned out to be a mere will-o'-the-wisp. When it was whispered that bread was about to be rationed the dismay was extreme, but assurances were given that the measure was one of precaution only, that the supply of wheat was immense, only there was some difficulty in grinding it into flour. The task, in fact, was one of great difficulty; Paris possessed at the time of the investment no flour mills worth speaking of, with the exception of those belonging to the army; all had to be created. Fortunately large numbers of fine millstones had been brought in for safety, and numbers of millers had come in from the surrounding country; these, with the aid of engineers and others, set to work manfully; mills were established at railway stations, locomotives being used to supply power; numbers of small iron mills of improved construction were made and set to work at the large engineering establishment of MM. Cail & Co., and finally, nearly four hundred mills of different kinds were in operation. Unfortunately, just as the means for converting corn into flour were complete, it was discovered that the wheat was nearly all gone!

In spite of all the assurances that were put forth, the appearance of the decree fixing the quantity of bread to be purchased daily at 300 *grammes*, or little more than ten ounces per head per diem, caused universal consternation; and as the official arrangements—as a matter of course—broke down, certain quarters of the town were short of flour, no bread was to be had, and numbers of men paraded the streets declaring that the government was starving them; in other districts many persons, on the day before the decree appeared, bought up all the bread they could find, cut it up and dried it in ovens, storing it away for the last emergency. This gave rise, of course, also to general insufficiency, and increased the dismay of the people. Assurances were put forth that all these errors and accidents would be immediately corrected or avoided for the future, and that the population would be supplied with pure wheaten bread, not so white as usual, but more wholesome and economical; in other words, the flour was only sifted once, and consequently only the coarse bran was removed. The promised bread appeared and quite fulfilled the promise which had been given for it, and Paris was satisfied; when one morning the supply nearly failed altogether, thousands of families could not obtain a single crust of bread on that day, and stale pieces were worth almost their weight in gold. This state of things went on for a week or two, the supply always being below the amount fixed, and consequently people were turned away every day with empty hands from the bakers' doors, and women carrying loaves home were positively afraid to meet the gaze of their disappointed neighbours. Not only women and children, but soldiers and men in the vigour of life, would stop a person in the street and beg with tears in their eyes to be allowed to buy even a slice of the loaf he or she was carrying home—and who could refuse such a request, although he knew that at home every slice missed was a calamity? The condition and feelings of those unfortunate creatures who waited, frequently all night and always for hours, in the bitter frosty air, standing with aching feet in half-melted snow, and were told when they were in sight of the baker's shop that there was no more bread, may be imagined but cannot be described; this happened several times in the district where we lived. Still the bread, though short in quantity, was excellent in quality, appetizing and satisfactory; but it did not long remain so. It was announced that in order to economize the wheaten flour a certain quantity of rice would be mixed with it, and we were curious rather than anxious to know what would be the effect of such mixture; our consternation was extreme when the first sample of the new kind of bread appeared. It was a dark mass of heavy indigestible stuff, that not a single individual in Paris would have touched under ordinary circumstances. The bakers did not know how to manage the rice, said the *savans* of the *Académie des Sciences*; a day or two would suffice to teach them this, and then the bread would be good again! The day or two fled, and a week or two after them; the bread was certainly better made, but its composition became a subject of general curiosity. The fact was, that wheat flour formed a very minute portion of the whole; rice of the poorest quality, ground oats, haricot beans and lentils, bran, and as some declared, cut straw, were all called into requisition, and the result defies description, as it defied digestion. A hale, active man could manage with the aid of stimulants and exercise to turn the gritty, leaden mass into chyle, but for the sedentary, the sick, the delicate, such bread was almost entirely valueless; small as the quantity eaten was, the result was long sleepless nights and a continuous feeling of uneasiness, if not actual pain. A sort of specific disease was created, for which the prescribed remedies were ether, ginger, and peppermint, separate or mixed.

It is difficult to imagine the effect of scarcity of flour without having witnessed it; the decree, calling up all corn, flour, biscuit, and other breadstuffs, interdicted the application of flour to anything but breadmaking; none was to be obtained for culinary purposes, and no baker or confectioner was permitted to rebolt or sift the flour he received from the government mills. The consequence was, that the pastrycooks' shops, generally so well supplied in Paris, gradually became almost empty, and were finally closed one after the other. A very few, in the most conspicuous situations, managed to supply a certain number of *pâtés* to the end of the siege by the use of rice flour, or by some clever evasion of the law; these were excellent, the ability of the cooks, with the aid of mushrooms, converting horseflesh into a delicious compound—at least, it seemed delicious to us then. Those *pâtés* were of course very dear, but they were almost scrambled for, and ladies and gentlemen bore them off in triumph, dropping *sous* right and left into the hands of the half-famished creatures, or the cunning beggars that crowded around the doors and stared longingly at the tempting wares in the windows. A person endowed with any natural sensibility, although knowing that much of the appearance of starvation was assumed, felt almost ashamed to pass through the eager, watching groups, buy a pate, which the very children amongst them knew cost enough to keep a poor family for two or three days in ordinary times, and pass out again with the dainty morsel in his hand in presence of a hundred beseeching or envious eyes.

The stock of dry confectionery did not hold out long, and finally the commonest ship biscuit was worth several pence; the pieces of broken ones were laid carefully together on paper, and exhibited and sold at the best shops. Eating became so absorbing a matter, that jewellers, goldsmiths, shopkeepers of all kinds in the very best and most fashionable streets of Paris, became dealers in chocolate, or in poultry or other rarity attainable, including butter and eggs.

The above is an accurate account of the general state of food supplies, and those who had no reserves and who could not afford, that is to say, who positively had not the cash to purchase expensive additions to their ordinary fare, came fully to understand the true meaning of the words siege fare. Even those who were most fortunate could not escape altogether; they could not obtain good bread by any outlay whatever, and scarcely a morsel of fresh meat, except the diurnal ounce of horse flesh; while even the most extravagant comestibles were frequently more or less musty, and everything almost had an antiquated taste, which we designated amongst us as the "siege flavour." The positive physical deprivation was galling, but the greatest punishment of all was the dreadful monotony; the mind could never entirely free itself from considerations of the immediate wants of the day, and fears respecting the morrow; servants were almost always out seeking bread, meat, or some other necessary, the tradesmen ceased their calls, every one had to go to shop or market cash in hand and bring home his or her purchases; there were no errand boys, no vehicles, every one was at once his own purveyor and his own porter. Soldiers and single men who lived out were relatively better off; the latter got their rations like other people through the *restaurateurs*, to whom they transferred their meat tickets, and the soldiers cooked theirs with their comrades in the barracks, huts, or on the sides of the boulevards, or they ate it at the cheap canteens which were established in all quarters of the town. As to the very poorest of all, they were fed at the public soup kitchens, and were relatively as well, if not better off, than any one. The classes that suffered most were those which always suffer most, the lower ranks of the middle class, those who had scarcely anything to spend, and yet who were too independent to appeal to public charity. It was in those classes that the mortality was greatest; poor seamstresses, shop-girls thrown out of work, men too old for service, singers, dancers, actors and actresses, starved or fell into ill health in their garrets, with few to heed them or lend them a helping hand. Many a poor actress accustomed to lively society, played constantly for charitable objects, receiving nothing but a franc or two for the necessary gloves or other trifles, and returned home weary and famished, ready to fall a victim to the small-pox or other disease that predominated. The secret history of these poor creatures can never be written, or it would present one of the saddest records that a civilized society ever presented.

Certain newspaper correspondents and others have made light of the sufferings of the population during the siege, and some have declared that they dined at their restaurants as usual, only paying a somewhat higher rate for what they ate: such assertions are reckless and untruthful. It is true that a few of the best restaurants had wonderful supplies of preserved meat, and could obtain poultry and other things at exorbitant prices; but fresh meat was only to be found here and there, and a good wholesome dinner could only be obtained by the expenditure of three or four times the usual amount, and frequently much more. Speaking generally, the restaurants were closed, many houses famous for their *cuisine* put up their shutters at the very commencement of the scarcity; the best and most popular of the fixed price dining houses struggled manfully for a time, diminished their portions, doubled their prices, yet were compelled finally to shut up. The cheap restaurants, or *établissements de bouillon*, as they are called, were kept open by some arrangement of the authorities, as it would have been absolutely dangerous to have left thousands of single men and women without some such resource. We visited some of these more than once, and found them crowded, but the fare was limited to a few dishes of horse, dog, cat, or what not, while in the absence of butter and oil everything had a nasty tallowy taste, that disgusted all but the heartiest; omelettes and eggs in any form were out of the question; there were no vegetables but the commonest haricots and lentils, and these were very dear; few sweets and very rarely any cheese; when a morsel of the last-named article was to be had, it was worth almost any price, and we remember one instance amongst others when we were charged about seven pence for a morsel of bad Dutch cheese that certainly did not weigh half an ounce. Those who found the restaurants "the same as ever" must have been peculiarly lucky during the siege, or very unfortunate previously. To give another instance of the price of ordinary provisions, it may be mentioned that several shops made a special trade of providing little luncheons for men on duty; these consisted of a small round tin box about an inch high and two inches in diameter, containing a rough kind of potted horse flesh, and were purchased eagerly at a franc each.

The positive scarcity of bread, or rather the impossibility of obtaining an extra morsel of that which is eaten so lavishly in Paris by all classes in ordinary times, may be illustrated by the fact that all the restaurants and *cafés* were compelled to ask their customers to bring their own bread, and this was not a mere request, but an actual necessity, as we found on one occasion when entering a well-known restaurant on the boulevards without our slab of baked bran; we were compelled to consume what we could get without bread, potatoes, or other vegetables, except haricots. Even the clubs were compelled to act in the same manner; a rich man of title, on one occasion, talking to some ladies of our acquaintance on whom he had called, said, "I am going to dine at my club, and here is my bread," taking a slice out of his pocket. He did not find dining out "as usual!"

The excessive rigour of the weather was a fearful addition to the sufferings of the people; fuel is always a dear thing in Paris, coals twice the price they are in London, wood very expensive to burn, charcoal also dear; coke alone, which is coming much into use, is the only fuel to be had at a moderate rate. The coal was all requisitioned at an early part of the siege, the gasworks were soon stopped, and then there was no more coke to be had; charcoal was sold, when it could be found, at four times, and even more, the ordinary rates, and, finally, wood was requisitioned for baking and other purposes, and then we understood that it also was nearly exhausted. The authorities had already cut down a quantity of timber in the Bois de Boulogne, to prevent its forming a cover for the enemy; the axe was now called into requisition, not only there but in the Bois de Vincennes and in the outlying boulevards, and this green wood was the only fuel which the people had to depend upon for weeks; moreover, the quantity which each family could purchase was limited to half a hundredweight for five days, or about ten pounds in weight of green wood, which was half water, per diem! No matter how large was the family, unless it possessed a store of wood of its own, it was impossible to maintain more than one fire for all the purposes of cooking and warming; and this at a time when two coats, a railway rug, and thick woollen mittens scarcely kept the body warm enough for the fingers to manage a pen. Moreover, as in the case of the meat and the bread, this miserable modicum of wet wood that spluttered and smouldered, and finally shrunk up into something like a black sponge, was only to be obtained at a high price, and after spending hours with hundreds of others, exposed to cutting winds, or the feet buried in half-melted snow; and when obtained, the means of carrying it home rested with each purchaser. Under such circumstances, it is not surprising that everything wooden began to disappear; small trees on the boulevards were cut down and made off with, every atom of wooden railing disappeared bit by bit, unoccupied huts were robbed of their doors and planks, gardens were invaded and were denuded of their trees; there were no guardians but the national guards, and the national guards wanted firewood. At last the suffering from the want of fuel rendered people desperate, and depredations began to be effected in open daylight; in one case, close to our house, the remains of a fine old property, on which there was a grove and clumps of fine walnuts, elms, and other trees, was invaded by a number of men with axes and saws; in an incredibly short space of time every tree was brought to the ground, and all were soon reduced to logs, which were carried off by the men, while troops of women and children collected and carried off every twig that they could find. The authorities were utterly powerless, so they contented themselves by causing the roots to be grubbed up and sent to the public kitchens. The proprietor must have stared when he visited his land again, and would find some difficulty in getting any compensation for his lost timber.

So great was the want of fuel at last that all kinds of wood, whether for building or cabinet making, was put in requisition; little builders sold their scaffold poles, and almost everything they possessed that would burn, at exorbitant rates, and the flooring of a vast number of rooms doubtless met a similar fate to that of the furniture of the enthusiastic Palissy the Potter. A few more days of such paucity of fuel would have caused the furniture of Paris houses to begin to find its way into the stoves and grates.

Paris, however, escaped some of the worst features of a siege; water never ran short, although the enemy, according to the military custom of civilized nations, cut off one of the sources of supply, and salt, although dear, can hardly be said to have become scarce; on the other hand, the evils that commonly arise from the use of too much salt meat were happily escaped by the fact, that nearly all the provisions salted down at a great cost by the authorities and their contractors and agents turned out totally unfit for use. This was only one instance of fearful waste caused by the inexperience or carelessness of those who had the management of the provisions; tons of cheese, potatoes, and other commodities were forgotten or left to rot in cellars at the markets and elsewhere, while the population would have eagerly purchased them at exorbitant prices.

Wine and spirits, those highly-lauded and much-deprecated aids to diet, became of immense importance during the siege; their consumption was enormous, and doubtless their use ran frequently into abuse. Soldiers exposed for hours in the most inclement weather were not, as it may well be supposed, scrupulous about the number of *cannons*, or *petite verves*—the common name for the wine glass of the shops and the dram glass , intoxication was prevalent, and gave rise to constant complaints on the part of the military commanders, some of whom were themselves accused of going drunk upon duty; these were, however, officers of the national guard, to whom the duties of the camp were new, and whose habits were utterly subverted. With less sustaining food than usual at their command, and having much time on their hands, they flew to the *diva bouteille* as a resource against ennui. Every little *café* and coffee stall sold wine as well as brandy; and although this seems in ordinary times to produce no bad result, under the peculiar circumstances of the siege it doubtless held out unusual temptations to the young and the thoughtless. But wine and spirits in other ways were of immense service; in the absence of butter, fat, and oily substances they supplied the carbon which is so necessary a portion of diet that without it otherwise good food becomes unsatisfactory and unsustaining. Brandy, but more especially rum, was largely used in cookery; rice and rum was a common sweet dish while the rice held out; wine was employed in the stewing of horse flesh, and hot wine was strongly recommended by doctors even for females and young persons. The method of preparing it was similar to that adopted in France and elsewhere for punch; a considerable portion of the spirit was got rid of by setting the wine for some time over the fire, and then the latter was poured upon toast, and all eaten together like soup; the dish was, in fact, called *soup au vin*. Rum was also drunk in small quantities, burned, just as the Chinese drink thimbles' full of their rice spirit at meals; and ladies, who scarcely ever before drank a drop of spirit in their lives, found great benefit from it. They were not likely to have acquired a taste for it from their siege practice; on the contrary, the very smell of rum was afterwards, as far as our experience taught us, peculiarly repugnant in consequence.

Bread, haricot beans, soup, and wine, form the staple diet of the French *ouvriers*, and indeed of all classes except the wealthy; and there being no beans or potatoes, and but little bad bread to be had, the consumption of wine must have increased at least threefold. The consequence was, all the common wine was consumed, and the poor soldiers and others, instead of getting a *litre*, nearly a quart, for sixpence or sevenpence, had to pay tenpence or more for an ordinary bottle, which does not hold two-thirds of a *litre*.

The English residents in Paris, and many of the French, soon found out the value of good English porter, stout, and ale; and the stocks of the agents of the Burton and other brewers were soon exhausted, for unfortunately the siege happened just previously to the period for the importation of the new beer; and long before the gates of Paris were opened again, there was not a bottle of ale or stout to be obtained, except out of a private cellar. French beer, bad at all times, was almost undrinkable during the siege, and the Austrian and other foreign beer establishments were all quickly closed in consequence of the exhaustion of their stocks.

Tobacco, too, was a precious auxiliary; and when a report went abroad that it was likely to be rationed, the consternation was extreme. This dreaded necessity, however, never arose; and if the ordinary tobacco became a little worse than usual, the supply held out without stint.

The effect of the diet and other circumstances of the siege may be pictured in a few words. The mortality increased from less than 3000 to more than 5000 deaths per week, exclusive of those in the military hospitals and ambulances; in other words, the number increased to nearly the extent of 500 a day; add to this, first, the effect on the constitutions of thousands of survivors and upon their offspring, the deaths and sufferings of the army, to say nothing of property wasted, debts incurred, and consequent taxation, and we obtain a glimpse of the effects produced by the royal game of war.

The calamity which fell upon Paris was serious enough, but it narrowly escaped taking the form of a frightful catastrophe. The feeling of the people was so intensely opposed to capitulation, the hope of succour arriving was clung to naturally with so much tenacity, that the government put off to the last moment the hateful act of succumbing to the enemy; while the forts around the town were almost entirely uninjured, while men and arms and ammunition held out, while there was food enough to keep the population from starving, every man who had a spark of the hero within him naturally shuddered at the very idea of capitulation. But the time came when valour would have become crime; and had the armistice been deferred three days longer there is no saying what might have been the consequences. The moment the gates were opened the people were seized with an uncontrollable yearning for fresh food. The first who brought loaves of white bread, joints of fresh mutton, and vegetables into Paris, were regarded with as much curiosity as artists who had produced new forms of beauty, or searchers who had discovered hidden treasures. To obtain something different from siege fare seemed the sole object of the whole world. The arrival of quantities of provisions from England caused profound sensation, and Paris would certainly not have refused a vote of thanks, as the Bordeaux Assembly did; on the contrary, the papers the least friendly to Great Britain were loud in their praise, not only of the munificence of the British nation, but of the determination and rapidity with which the succour was brought to the doors of those who wanted it so visibly. There was sad delay in the distribution, but this was not the fault of the English committee, as the Parisians knew well enough. The people of Paris, always either kept in the dark or led with falsehood, were ignorant of the motives and acts of the English government, and the press, unfortunately, was either ignorant or malicious, and led the people, who were foolish enough to believe it, to think that the English nation rejoiced in the sufferings of its neighbour; but the gates once open, the falsehood was soon exposed, and the gratitude felt for the munificent aid sent to Paris and other parts of France was spontaneous and general.

The moment the gates were open the people flocked to the outposts of the enemy for provisions; regular markets were held at a dozen points around Paris, at the outposts of St. Denis, the bridge of Courbevoie, and elsewhere; it was an extraordinary sight to see, as we did, hundreds of Parisians around the barriers, which were kept by German soldiers and French gendarmes acting in concert, eagerly pressing for the chance of purchasing what the country people had brought in; the contents of waggons, carts, and trucks were swept away almost in the twinkling of an eye, the Germans keeping watch over the transactions, and suppressing any attempt at unusual extortion. In some cases, where exorbitant prices were demanded, the German officials fixed the prices and superintended the sales. Here and there were some unfortunate scenes, some very rough justice; but on the whole the management was better and the disorder less than could fairly be expected.

It took some time, of course, to revictual Paris; supplies came in fast, but not fast enough; prices fell, but not rapidly, on account of the eagerness of the purchasers; twice and three times the ordinary prices were cheerfully paid by those who had money for butter and many other articles; white bread reappeared almost immediately, but for some days a leg of mutton was worth twenty or more francs. It was no easy matter to stock the market of a city which required 400 to 500 head of cattle and 3000 sheep a day. Fuel, too, presented a great difficulty; the railways were encumbered, the river traffic interrupted by the breaking down of bridges and the removal of dams, but thanks to the re-establishment of the natural modes of trade, to the energy of philanthropists as well as of men of business, a few days sufficed to fill our cupboards, Paris became a civilized city once again, and its inhabitants were no longer reduced to the grovelling necessity of giving nearly their whole time and thought to the supply of merely animal wants. One must pass through a siege before he can estimate the value of a bit of wholesome mutton, a potato, and a slice of good bread, and understand the real difference between civilized society and that state of things which poets have often dwelt upon with much misplaced rapture, anent the noble savage and free fife in forest or prairie.

There was one terrible drawback to the sensation of relief which, in spite of the hard conditions, followed the armistice; the enemy was to occupy Paris, not in the ordinary fashion of conquerors, it is true, but almost by way of form. The whole of the Champs Elysées, from the Arc de Triomphe to the Tuileries, and thence to the river, was to be occupied by the Germans; all the side streets leading to the Champs Elysées were closed at the further end by French picquets, and the space marked out left entirely to the conquering army. The press and the clubs called upon the people to treat the days of occupation as days of mourning, and the appeal had its effect; the figures of the towns of France on the Place de la Concorde had their faces covered with crape, a puerile act, perhaps, but not without significance. With one solitary exception, every shop, *café*, restaurant, and garden was closed in the Champs Elysées; the same was the case in all the side streets, all along the parallel Faubourg Saint Honored the great boulevards, and in all the principal streets at the western part of the city. There were few but soldiers visible, and these parts of Paris seemed almost to belong to a city of the dead; at the ends of the Rue Rivoli and the Rue Royale, where they touch the Place de la Concorde, were lines of artillery waggons, drawn up under the charge of a few unarmed artillerymen.

In the Champs Elysées itself a certain number of persons went about amongst the German troops; these included a fair proportion of well-dressed people, some military men, inhabitants of the quarter, newspaper correspondents on duty, a sprinkling of ladies, and a number, not very large, of the lowest orders, principally boys. There were three or four slight disturbances during the two days of occupation; the people of the single *café* the door of which was open, and frequented by the Germans, were hooted, and finally the tables and contents destroyed; and if, as asserted, the Germans compelled the proprietor to serve them, this was against the stipulations of the convention, and very hard upon the cafe keeper. The *gamins* of Paris, the most insolent street boys in Europe, jeered and hooted a few German officers, and caused some little difficulty, and one or two women who gave offence were very roughly handled; but on the whole, the conduct of both the French and Germans was excellent, and it is difficult to imagine such a painful occurrence as the occupation of a portion of a city by a triumphant enemy giving rise to less disturbance. Fortunately, too, that occupation was suddenly shortened by the early payment of an instalment of the indemnity, and the Champs Elysées was cleared of the Germans.

Another painfully exciting scene was the return of the sailors into Paris from the forts, after these had been given up to the enemy. The sailors, or infantry and artillery of the marine, as they are called in France, behaved splendidly in the various sorties and in the manning of the forts; and the armistice was a bitter disappointment to them. The excitement of the men was so great that it was considered dangerous to attempt to disarm them, so they all came into Paris with their guns slung over their shoulders. Their appearance as they issued from the Paris terminus of the Western Railway will not easily be forgotten by those who witnessed it; the officers marched along calmly with compressed lips, the blue-jackets swarmed along the streets as if they were going to charge a redoubt; he would have been a bold man who should have dared to say a word to displease them; their step was far from steady, for it was evident enough that they had been allowed to seek solace for their injured feelings in the bottle. A terrible incident will show how the sailors fought and felt; when the armistice was made, five lieutenants had fallen as seconds in command at Mont Valérien, and when the sixth, who was then acting, heard of the capitulation, he cried:—"It shall never be said that the fort was delivered up while I was alive," and deliberately blew out his brains in the presence of the man. No wonder his brother officers and the brave fellows under them came into the city with knitted brows and flashing eyes. If the army of France had been made of the same stuff as these noble sailors, the history of the fearful struggle might have been strangely different. Officers and men, although somewhat slighter, looked so like English salts that it was difficult to imagine them belonging to another country. The sons of the ocean have a strong family likeness.

It must be difficult for any one who was not in Paris at the time of the siege to realize the condition of society at that time. It is almost needless to say that commerce was utterly at an end, for that was a natural result of communications interrupted, but nearly all business was at a stand-still, with the exception of that which had to do with the necessaries of life or the material of war; and even for the latter the supply of workmen was frequently very inadequate. Once taken away from the foundry or workshop, numbers of men preferred idleness and fifteen pence a day to hard work with three times that amount of pay; it was with great difficulty that hands enough were found for the casting of cannon, the transformation of muskets, the repair of arms, and the manufacture of ammunition of various kinds. As to money matters, few landlords, except the poor proprietors of single houses or grasping misers, asked their tenants for rent, and fewer still obtained it when they asked; and Paris, at the conclusion of the siege, presented the extraordinary condition of a city that owed three quarters' rent! All other payments were suspended, bills stood over by law, houses of undoubted stability declined to pay accounts until after the war, and, generally speaking, no one asked for what was due to him, and no one tendered what he owed. Pay as you go now, was the general cry; we must leave outstanding affairs till we have got rid of the Prussians. Many persons, doubtless, took care to place all the money and property they could in safety when the first news of the reverses arrived, but the great mass of the manufacturing and shopkeeping class, and many other classes, were utterly ruined.

The aspect of the Bois de Boulogne, the Champs Elysées, and the boulevards, was most extraordinary. In the busy central portions of the town the streets presented much the same aspect as usual, but in the fashionable and main streets the change was very remarkable. There were no carriages in the Bois, for most of the owners had fled the city and most of the horses were eaten. The splendid half-bred pair, purchased for hundreds of pounds a few months previously, and the poor cab hack, alike were requisitioned, paid for by the government at a fixed rate per pound, live weight, sent to the *abattoir*, and converted into "beef." Valuable horses thus fetched a tenth part of their value, while a good fat cab or omnibus horse fetched more than usual. Thirty to forty thousand horses were eaten. The reader may imagine the void that their absence created. There were no parties, few ladies were left in the city, people wanted all their cash for the supply of the cupboard; those who rode at all used the omnibuses, and the few cabs to be seen were only in demand by officers on duty, or luxurious national guards riding to their posts of duty. There were no carriages at the door of the jockey club, no crowd of *voitures* at the Grand Hôtel; all were reduced to the democratic omnibus, or the still more democratic Shanks' mare, or, as the Cockneys call it, the Marrowbone stage. The roads thus were left free to the national guards, who inhabited many of the boulevards almost in permanence, and the pavements were nearly as vacant as the carriage ways; many of the great *cafés* were closed, and, with very few exceptions, those which remained open were nearly deserted; even in the very heart of the town, where at midday, just before dinnertime, and all the evening, there used to be a continual throng of visitors and a flying crowd of waiters, was exhibited the spectacle of a superannuated attendant hovering over one or two equally superannuated customers. In one of the best *cafés* in Paris the chain of one of the three great iron shutters was broken by accident. The shutter remained closed for weeks. The waiter shrugged his shoulders, and said it didn't matter; half the room was three times as much as was required then—and it was perfectly true.

Paris the brilliant was not only dirty, but dull. All the theatres were closed by order of the prefect of police at the commencement of the siege; and the scenery and properties packed away in secure places against the danger of fire. The *cafés chantants*, *casinos*, and all other places of amusement, were also closed, and, with the exception of performances in aid of the funds for the ambulances and other charitable purposes, there were scarcely any means of relaxation in the city for the 80,000 provincial mobiles far away from family and home, and the thousands of national guards; and the poor fellows had no resource but drinking at the wine shops and *cafés*, or going to bed with the fowls. The streets were miserably dull; in place of two or three gaslights they were lighted with one small petroleum lamp, that looked more like a taper burning before a statue of the Virgin than a street light; and in the bitter, cold, dark nights of January few who had a home of their own troubled the pavements of Paris with their presence.

When performances took place at the theatres the scene was a curious one; whatever the play, it was acted without scenery or costumes. The actors of the Théâtre Français performed a classical play, some of them dressed in the uniform of the national guard, while the others wore evening dress and white gloves, and carried a crush hat; and a well-known actress of the same theatre played the mischievous page Cherubino in a black silk dress. The saloon of the theatre was converted into an ambulance, and sick and wounded men lay around the statues and busts of Voltaire, Molière, Corneille, Racine, and all the stars of past days, and the actresses superintended the ambulance with great assiduity and kindliness. On the evening in question Mlle. ——, who had just left the stage after an admirable performance of the page, and being the only one of the lady attendants present in the theatre, was summoned, all panting with excitement, to receive a patient who had been injured in the street. A few weeks later still M. Seveste, a clever young actor of the theatre, was brought to the ambulance there mortally wounded, and died in the arms of his sister artistes. Such were a few of the effects of the siege on the theatres and on the actors and actresses, a body often shamefully maligned, but which did its duty in every way during the siege with great devotion and gallantry, as did the artists of every class, writers, painters, sculptors, and others.

It was a melancholy sight to see the Theatre Français filled almost exclusively with dark-blue uniforms and black dresses, and lighted with a few lamps in place of chandeliers, lustres, and floatlights. The opera house, when it opened, resorted to the old method, and lighted up with wax candles, but at all the other theatres petroleum reigned alone, but shone with no imperial lustre.

At home the like dulness pressed upon all; scarcely a visitor rang the bell from one week's end to the other; the news that reached us was often disastrous, generally unsatisfactory; sickness and death, ruin and hopelessness, pressed upon all, and when common daily wants left the mind a few moments of repose, it was difficult to find any intellectual solace. As may be supposed, the publishers produced few works; in fact, the appearance of a single volume was an extraordinary event, a few pamphlets relative to passing events forming nearly the whole literature of the period. Nearly the whole of the scientific and literary periodicals ceased to appear; almost all engaged in them, writers, artists, publishers, and printers, were enrolled in the mobiles or the national guard; old men, women, and children were alone left to carry on most of the business of the city. At first the newspapers brought us daily budgets of most exciting news, and the accounts of the vast preparations which were being made for the defence of the city filled our minds; but the seal of secrecy was naturally affixed on many operations lest the enemy should benefit thereby. The result was, however, just what it always is in France, where publicity is never in favour with the authorities, the enemy knew everything, while the besieged population was only supplied with incomplete or false information. When the English and German papers were completely shut out, we in Paris scarcely knew more about what was going on within a mile or two of us than we did of the events in Timbuctoo.

The scarcity of paper, too, added to the difficulties of publishers; the numberless little political papers which made their appearance and sold for one or two *sous*, were printed on the most wretched paper that ever passed through the press, and were scarcely legible, and the established journals of large circulation were put to the greatest straits; large-sized paper was almost entirely exhausted, and the *Gaulois* and others, in order to print two copies at once, were compelled to paste two small sheets together and then cut them apart after they were printed. Towards the end of the siege the scarcity increased to such an extent, that four half sheets had to be pasted together to produce the double sheet.

When, on Sunday the 18th of September, we learnt that the railways were all cut, and that no more letters could be sent out or received, we began to understand what a state of real siege meant; we groaned over the prospect of being shut out from communication with the rest of the world for weeks. What would have been our feelings, had we known that our isolation was to last for more than five long miserable months!

The greatest efforts were made to maintain correspondence. Of course, the telegraph wires were cut at once by the enemy, and it is said that a cable laid in the bed of the Seine was found and severed; the director-general of the post and telegraphs, one of the few really capable men that the war brought forward, had light copper balls made in which letters were sent down the river, but the enemy soon discovered them, and by the simple expedient of a net across a bridge fished them all up. Numbers of men attached to the post office, tempted by large offers of reward, tried to make their way across the enemy's lines; a few succeeded, one or two even went out and returned more than once, but the majority were never heard of. These brave fellows underwent great hardships; one of them remained hidden for nearly a day in the icy waters of the Seine, and others were several days without food while exposed to the cold of an almost arctic winter, or struggling against snow drifts, in which some doubtless perished.

It remained to try the worth of balloons, and these turned out of the greatest value to us; an extensive manufactory was established at one of the railway termini, which eventually had to be moved to another on the arrival of German shells; all the gas that could be produced was reserved for the inflation, all the aeronauts were called into requisition, and a number of intelligent young sailors instructed in the art of aerial navigation. The departure of the first balloon, with half a ton of letters, was an event which created immense interest, which went on increasing with every successive departure; the balloons were named after the heroes of the day or the towns which had held out courageously against the enemy, and the privilege of being present at the departure of a balloon was sought for most eagerly. More than forty balloons were despatched, but not one came into Paris; several attempts at directing their course were made, but they were all fruitless. The fate of some of the aeronauts became known to us; one poor fellow perished in the ocean, but a portion of the letters in his charge were recovered; one or two fell into the hands of the enemy, and one reached his destination after having been carried to Christiania, in Sweden. For the rest, we hoped that they had arrived safely beyond the reach of the enemy, who fired upon them whenever they appeared, but only in one instance succeeded in bringing the balloon down; but when the siege was raised we were astonished at the success of the balloon post, and of the small number of mails that had been lost.

But the anxiety of the population for news from without soon arose to positive torture. Government and other messengers came in now and then, and spies and agents brought us small supplies of news and newspapers; but thousands of persons, separated from all whom they loved, were weeks and months without knowing where wives, children, and friends were, or whether they were alive or dead. The agony suffered may be conceived, but defies description. A single case, which came to our personal knowledge, will supply a striking instance. A lady whose husband was in Algeria received news of his dangerous illness; she started from Paris, but was soon met by the news of his death; she had left her daughter, a young wife, in Paris in a critical condition, but was unable to get back within the city, and after weeks of torture, heard of the confinement and death of her beloved child! Multiply such cases mentally by thousands, and you may attain to something like a conception of the sufferings entailed on millions of men, women, and children, utterly innocent of any share in the cause of this frightful war.

The employment of pigeons to bring us in news was naturally thought of at the first moment of the siege, and fortunately the supply of birds for the purpose was considerable, amounting, in fact, to more than four thousand. They were carried in cages attached to the balloon cars, and being taken to Tours, Orleans, and other places, were sent in with governmental and private despatches. The arrival of these winged postmen created the greatest excitement, but unfortunately they were few and rare; but they brought us more consolation than anything else did during the siege, and every one who was shut up in Paris will regard a carrier pigeon with affection, or at least with gratitude, as long as he lives, or his nature must be very hard and prosaic.

The poetic notion of a pigeon messenger, a beautiful bird with a *billet doux* suspended to its neck or tied beneath the wing, did not meet the requirements of Paris. Our wants were sentimental as the gentlest love passage, but large, pressing, absorbing as hunger or thirst; we yearned for news with the most intense longing; no traveller in the Arabian desert ever looked forward to the next oasis with more eagerness than we for the arrival of the next pigeon. An admirable system of despatches was conceived, and by successive improvements was carried to great perfection. This plan has been explained and illustrated in articles and lectures—the most complete account, perhaps, will be found in the London *Engineer* newspaper of the 7th of April, 1871; but an outline of the mode adopted and of the results will be interesting to all and sufficient for most readers.

The first despatches sent were written on the thinnest paper manufactured, in ordinary writing or cypher; secondly, photography was called in aid, and the manuscript despatches were reduced to a very small compass, so that one pigeon could carry an immense number of messages; next, the despatches were set up in type and printed, so that they could be still further reduced by photography, and yet be more legible than the former; and lastly, these microscopic photographs were sent on films of collodion, which were ten times lighter and thinner than the thinnest foreign post paper made. The despatches were placed in quills and attached in the usual manner to one of the central tail feathers of the pigeon. The photographic part of the operation was first executed in the ordinary way by means of apparatus existing at Tours, but superior instruments were afterwards sent off by balloon from Paris, part of which, after incurring great danger, reached its destination, and did valuable service. The fact of these instruments being made available seems almost miraculous, for the balloon in which they were, like another which left Paris at the same time, was fired at by platoons of infantry for an hour, and pierced by the enemy's balls. The latter was captured immediately, and the former also, after a portion of the instruments had been placed in safety.

The first photographic reductions on paper measured 2½ inches by 1½, and contained 240 ordinary despatches; the collodion films carried much more, each small page of print, containing 15,000 characters or about 200 despatches, being reduced to a mere speck, in fact, a parallelogram measuring superficially about *one twenty-fifth of a square inch*; on an average, a collodion film measuring $2\frac{1}{5}$ by $1\frac{1}{5}$ inches, and weighing the six-hundredth part of an ounce, carried sixteen of the small printed pages or 3200 despatches. Finally, 15,000 ordinary messages and 500 pages of official despatches were contained in a small quill attached to the tail feather of the pigeon; some carrying as many as twenty-three films of collodion. Numerous copies, sometimes as many as fifty, were sent by different birds. In all, nearly 100,000 despatches were sent to Paris, but the proportion received was very small; many of the birds had a long way to fly, and a great number were doubtless shot or killed by birds of prey.

The deciphering of the despatches when received in Paris was a matter of great difficulty, but after several improvements it was accomplished perfectly. The quill having been split open with a pen knife, the collodion films were placed in water containing a little ammonia, which caused them to unroll almost immediately; they were then dried, placed between sheets of glass, and the despatches transcribed by clerks, with the aid of powerful microscopes; the next step was to magnify the collodion despatch by means of the megaroscope, or microscope with the electric light, throwing the characters on a screen, and so large as to be read off with ease by hall a dozen transcribers at the same time; the last improvement was to reproduce the despatches of the original size on collodion, to separate the messages one from the other by scissors, and to send to each of the persons to whom they were addressed a perfect reproduction on collodion, stuck on a piece of gummed paper, of the original photographed despatch, thus avoiding all copying and transcription, and saving an immense amount of time.

The sensation caused by the arrival of the first parcel of letters and the first telegraphic despatches, after the armistice had been signed, was indescribable. In spite of pigeon posts there were thousands of families who had not received a scrap of news from without for more than five months; great was the excitement also of those who wished to fly to their wives, children, and friends, while the means of communication were limited on account of the necessity for the transport of provisions, the destruction of bridges, the want of horses, and the regulations of the German authorities.

People shuddered at the idea of encountering the victorious enemy, now masters of the whole district around Paris, with headquarters amid the ruins of Saint Denis and the cathedral, or rather abbey church (which is a prominent object from the western outskirt of Paris), and in complete command of the railways and of the whole country around; they dreaded the great cost of a journey which was sure to be extended to two or three times its usual length; they feared to face the dangers of the road, partly on account of the swarms of German soldiers, but still more on account of the numerous bands of marauders which it was known infested the country, laid every one under contribution, and feasted, like the horrible vulture, on what the war had left behind it. But the yearnings of affection, the cruel anxiety, the thirst for freedom from the unhappy city, so long a sad prison to its inhabitants, overcame in most cases all other feelings, and many thousands had but one thought—how they were to get out of Paris.

In the first place permission was necessary, and the prefecture of police was densely crowded from morning to night by applicants for passes to enable them to leave the city; and when, after many visits and tedious waitings, these had been obtained, the difficulties were far from overcome. The railway offices and stations were as densely thronged as the prefecture of police, but the officials could give little or no information about the trains; the German authorities had their own necessities to supply, and when the rails were left free by them the convoys of provisions and fuel blocked all the lines.

Young active men, and many women, trusting to their own physical powers, set out on foot, and walked till they could find some kind of conveyance; others who possessed, or could buy or hire vehicles at exorbitant rates, fared perhaps the best; but in several instances the travellers were stopped and robbed of all they possessed. When trains first began to leave Paris, passengers were only carried short distances, and then were dependent on the Germans for their further progress, which became inexpressibly tedious, and often extremely expensive, for the railways were destroyed in many places, and vehicles of any description very scarce. When the direct lines of railway were nominally open, travelling was far from being agreeable; and those who quitted Paris were compelled to carry nothing more with them than they could hold conveniently in their hands; for noble bridges over broad rivers were broken down, and at certain places the whole of the passengers had to descend from the carriages, shoulder their luggage, trudge a considerable distance on foot, cross the river by a temporary bridge of boats, and remount a long hill on the other side to regain the railway. No matter what was the weather, there was not the slightest shelter, not the faintest hope of assistance; all were compelled to tramp along amid masses of German soldiery, rough navvies, and peasants, with the fear haunting every one that the train on the other side would be chockfull before he reached it. Many, women especially, were unable to keep up with the throng, and were left behind to pass a miserable twenty-four hours before another train should appear. This state of things continued till the middle of the month of March, or later, by which time the greater portion of those who had connections abroad, or the means of escaping from the long-beleaguered city, had quitted the capital, little dreaming what would happen there ere they saw it again.

CHAPTER II. PARIS UNDER THE COMMUNE.

The State of Affairs in Paris after the Departure of the Germans—Origin and Real Meaning of the Term Commune—Ultimate Aims of the Communists—M. Jules Favre unfairly blamed for having agreed at the Capitulation that the National Guards should retain their Arms—Universal Delusion as to the Insignificance of the Communist Rebellion—The Mistake of not removing the Seat of Government to Paris Immediately after Peace had been agreed to—Sympathy of the Troops with the Rebels—The Government reduced to a State of Inactivity or compelled to besiege the City—Suppression of Revolutionary Newspapers in reality proves a Source of Strength to the Insurgents—Complete Absence of Agitation on March 16—Proclamation of the Government on the Following Day—The Attempt to put down the Rising on March 18 completely frustrated, and Two Generals brutally murdered by the Communists—Proclamation of the Communist Leaders and seizure of the Official Journal for their Purposes—Decree for a Municipal Election—Honourable Attitude assumed by the Parisian Press against the Assumptions of the Communists—Election of the most Violent Republicans as Mayors—An Attempt to stem the Torrent of Rebellion leads to a Massacre in the Streets—Terrible State of Affairs under the Communal Regime—Great Want of Money—Assassination openly advocated in the Official Journal—Seizure of some of the Forts by the Communists, and Preparations for Action against the Government at Versailles—Paris again cut off from the Outside World—Extraordinary Decrees of the Commune—The "Pales" and the "Reds"—Engagement between the Communists and the Versailles Troops—An Attempt on Versailles defeated and Flourens killed—Decrees of the Commune abolishing the Payment of Rent and other Interferences with Private Affairs—The Difficulties of Living in the City—Effects of the Commune on Trade—Formation of New Barricades and Mines within the City—Decrees handing over Workshops to the Workmen—The Artists and the Commune—The Commune and the Press—Suppression of Opposition Journals—Dissensions in the Commune—Seizure of the Archbishop of Paris and other Dignitaries of the Church—Letter from M. Thiers to the Archbishop denying that the Communists Prisoners were shot or ill treated, and offering a Pardon to all who would lay down their Arms—The Students at the Medical School decline to join the Commune—Important Letter of M. Louis Blanc—Marshal MacMahon placed in Command of the Versailles Troops—Continual Fighting—Curious Combination Outside Paris—Fearful Scenes at Les Ternes and Neuilly—Truce in order to allow the Inhabitants to leave.

THE occupation of a portion of Paris by the Germans—fortunately shortened by the activity of the government in making the first payment of the indemnity—had happily given rise to no disturbances of the slightest importance. The appeals of the press and of other bodies had a good effect; the great mass of the people had closed their shops, and regarded the day as one of mourning; but the public had been disturbed by rumours of the intention of some of the national guards to fire upon the Germans, and some fear was entertained that they would keep their word. This fear was increased by an act that occurred on the 27th of February. A portion of the Avenue Wagram, in which no houses have yet been built, although the avenue itself has been formed for nine or ten years, had been converted into an artillery park for the national guard; and at the conclusion of the armistice a large number of the new bronze pieces of eight had been placed there under the care of the artillery of the guard, whose quarters were in the wooden huts erected on a large space of ground close at hand. On the day mentioned, the inhabitants of the Place Wagram adjoining, of whom the writer was one, saw that the guns were being removed; at first four horses mounted by artillerymen of the national guard were brought for each gun, and the work went on in the most quiet and regular manner possible; presently no more horses appeared, but men and boys, and even women, attached themselves to the guns and trotted off with them. Still no suspicion was entertained that a rebellious act was being performed in broad daylight under our eyes, till, after seventy or more of the guns had been abstracted, we saw a squadron of cavalry enter the park and take charge of the remainder. Soon we found that the guards favourable to the Commune had arrived in considerable numbers at the park, and acting in spite of the artillerymen, who, however, offered very little resistance, had taken first the horses from the pickets in the rear, and finally the guns themselves from the park. The reason given out for the act was, that in spite of the assertions of the government the artillery of the national guard was to be given up at night to the enemy. Few people believed in such an act of deception; but it was not difficult to imagine, in the excited state of the popular mind, that the leaders of the Communist guards might truly believe what they asserted.

The principal fear which seized upon the authorities—who were totally unable by threats or otherwise to get the men to give up the guns—seems to have been that they would be used against the Germans entering Paris, and consequently the national guards that were still loyal were called out; cartridges were served out for the mitrailleuses belonging to those troops; and these and other guns were placed at many points commanding the great boulevards, and other places where *émeutes* were feared. The guards in opposition to the government made a demonstration against this movement, but happily no collision occurred. Squadrons of cavalry, principally gendarmerie, patrolled the streets in all directions at a trot. Fortunately the temporary occupation by the Germans did not give rise to any offensive act against them; in fact, the city was remarkably calm during the two days of the occupation. It was said that the conduct of General Vinoy had inspired confidence, and that the national guard had no intention of opposing the government.

When the conditions of peace, which had been agreed to at Bordeaux by the overwhelming majority of 546 against 107 votes of the Assembly, were known in Paris, the consternation was terrible. The war, which had commenced with the view to wrest the Rhenish provinces from the Germans, and throw a new halo of military glory around the dictature of the Napoleons, had ended in the loss of most important provinces, with an immense indemnity in addition to be paid to the conqueror; the cry of *à Berlin* had been converted into the dreadful reality of *à Paris*. The effect of the publication of the conditions in the *Official Journal* cannot be described; it was felt throughout Europe, though not of course in the same intensity. The terms seemed to the unfortunate people of Paris to include the utter ruin and prostration of the country; and the outcry against those who had negotiated such a contract of peace was general, except with the few who saw clearly enough that they had only done so in the utter impossibility of obtaining any better conditions. One effect of the action of the Assembly was the sudden termination of the German occupation, and this had naturally a tranquillizing effect, and the danger of an insurrection seemed to be passing away. The gendarmerie still paraded the streets, the abstracted guns were still in the hands of the recalcitrant national guards, who persistently declared that they held them to prevent their being given up to the enemy; yet when the Germans evacuated Paris in the morning of the 3rd of March, we fondly hoped that the poor city would return to something like its ordinary life. The weather became splendid, and people said that the sun of Paris was rising anew; the gas was lighted again in the streets on the departure of the enemy, and it was taken as a promising token of the return of industry and all the occupations of peace. These pleasant hopes were strengthened by the complete re-establishment of the postal service; letters began to reach us in due course from London, with many dated previously to the investment; even newspapers, which had been accumulating at the various ports and provincial towns, came in upon us in floods of twenties and thirties. It would be difficult to imagine what we, who had been shut up for nearly half a year, felt when the doors of our prison were fairly thrown open; we came back as it were to life, we believed at last that we were still of this world. Letters, old as well as new, were devoured with painful eagerness or tearful delight, and old newspapers were opened and arranged, and smoothed out, and cut with infinite care, and finally read as if they had been Sibylline leaves or Cupid's delightful literature. No wonder that we disbelieved in rumours of coming danger, or even difficulties; no wonder that we refused to believe that after all we were not at peace: and when at last the truth was forced upon our minds, when it became known that the rebellious national guards had established batteries on the heights of Montmartre and Belleville, and had taken and kept possession of many other important positions, we rather laughed at the folly and hopelessness of the insurrection than feared for the result. Barricades, it is true, were beginning to make their appearance, but 40,000 more soldiers had been sent for; the brave and experienced General Aurelles de Paladine was announced to take command of the national guard of Paris; the mounted gendarmerie kept order in the main streets and boulevards of the city; and it was almost universally felt by those not in the secrets of the Communists, that if the insurrectionists did not lay down their arms immediately, they would be quickly dispersed by the shells of Mont Valérien or the forces from Versailles. How we waked from our pleasing delusion is but too well known, and how Paris was a second time fortified, and a second time besieged within six months, is now matter of history.

Before entering upon the account of Paris under the Commune, it is necessary to say a few words about the term itself. When first it was uttered at the Hdtel de Ville, while the enemy was at the gates, very few had any notion of what it meant. "Cry *Vive la Commune!*" said a fellow to a passer by. "What is the Commune?" said the other. "Oh! I don't know!" was the rejoinder; "but I was told to cry, *Vive la Commune!* and to tell every, one else to do the same."

The word communism would naturally, at first sight, be taken in its old meaning of property divided in common, but this would be an error; the word is derived from the French word *commune*, a district or subdivision of a department which has a municipal council of its own. Each commune is supposed to elect its own council, and, with certain precautions, such is generally the case; but during the whole of the period of the reign of Louis Napoleon, Paris, Marseilles, and Lyons were utterly deprived of all municipal rights whatever; the government not only appointed the prefects and sub-prefects, but the municipal councillors, and even the *maires*, of whom there are twenty in Paris, their *adjoints*, or assistants, down to the lowest official. Thus these three great cities were deprived of all municipal freedom, and the inhabitants had no voice in the management of their local affairs. Such a state of things was anomalous in the nineteenth century, and the fact of its existence was proof positive that the government felt that it was opposed to the opinions and the desires of the most populous cities in the country. Unfortunately, M. Thiers and, perhaps, the Assembly were no more favourable to municipal liberty than former governments; and therefore the adoption of the *Commune*, and the term *Communist*, afterwards changed to *Communalist*, was a happy one; and had the object of the Communalists been merely to obtain for Paris—and consequently other great towns—municipal self-government, they would have deserved, and would have obtained, the support of all true liberals.

The Communalists had adopted a clever cry, and thus drew around them sufficient adherents to enable them to carry out their designs; but when once in power it was soon manifest that the commune, or municipal rights, was not their ultimate aim, but the complete destruction of all general government, and the establishment in its place of a federation of free communes somewhat after the model of the Swiss republic. It is impossible to say what may occur in the progress of political science and the growth of civilization; but in the present state of Europe such a splitting up of France into a mass of little independent states, which would be eternally jealous of and pulling against each other, would be nothing less than the annihilation of the nation proper, and the reduction of France to a third-rate power.

Another object of the Commune was the extinction of the church. The hatred of the people of Paris and other great towns in France for the clergy proves that the church has not been more fortunate than the government in acquiring the love, or even the respect, of the nation at large; and the Communalists aimed at overthrowing all religion as well as all general government.

It is but just, however, to say that the leaders of the Commune declared that had the Assembly listened to their appeals, and granted municipal liberty to Paris, the insurrection would have been put an end to on the instant.

Lamentable as such a programme as that of the Communalists was, extraordinary as it appears to Englishmen, accustomed to representative government and political as well as religious discussion, is it very surprising that ignorant men should be led by demagogues who preach such doctrines, when we consider how long the great cities of France have been completely deprived of municipal freedom, and that a well-known member of the present French Assembly did not hesitate to make in his place the ludicrously illogical assertion, that the "republic was above universal suffrage?" When would-be teachers of the people and sharp critics of others descend to clap-trap expressions like the above, which was equivalent to declaring that the tree was above its roots, or that the effect was totally independent of its cause, can we wonder at the madness, the folly, the criminality of the ignorant masses, or at the conduct of those who fancied they could reconstruct the government of a country according to their own childish notions?

The Communal insurrection was rendered possible by the fact of the national guards having been allowed, by the terms of the convention with the Prussian authorities, to retain their arms; and M. Jules Favre was blamed for not having taken the opportunity of getting the arms out of such dangerous hands, just as he was blamed for not having concluded a peace immediately after the disaster of Sedan. The conduct of those who so calmly utter their prophecies after the fact, calls to mind the stinging expression of the poet—

> "The juggling fiend, who never spoke before,
> But cries, 'I warned you,' when the mischief's o'er."

It is impossible to deny, we think, that if Jules Favre or any one else had accepted Count von Bismarck's conditions at that time, and thus put an end to the war, there would have been an indignant scream from one end of the nation to the other, and especially from the capital, that France had been sold, betrayed, disgraced; and that the miserable traitor must have known that the *grande nation* only required a few weeks to rally its forces, to place arms in the hands of every man and boy, and drive the enemy at the bayonet's point to the Rhine, and perhaps beyond it. Such language was in fact used, such hopes were nursed, and to those shut up in Paris, as well as to some other people, they did not seem absurd. It is equally impossible, we think, to deny that the condition that the national guard should retain not only their small arms, but also their artillery, was one for which M. Jules Favre deserves gratitude, and has been loaded with abuse. The national guard was greatly pleased at the time; its self-esteem was thus spared a deep wound; and to convert this into a reproach against the minister is surely an act that comes under the poet's lash.

France appears to have been the victim of every form of deception; every act seemed to turn against her. Her, or perhaps we should say, her late ruler's ambitious schemes, have turned to the glory of Germany; the snatch at the Rhenish Provinces has ended with the loss of Alsace and Lorraine, just as the dog in the fable lost his meat by snatching at its shadow; the honourable preservation of the arms of the national guard enabled the Commune to rebel against the government, which had prevented their being delivered to the enemy; and the government was kept at bay for six weeks by the very ramparts and forts which its chief, M. Thiers, erected at enormous expense against foreign enemies thirty years before.

When in March the heights of Montmartre and Belleville were crowned with revolutionary batteries, when numbers of the national guards were in arms against the government, even those who knew well the seething mass of discontent in Paris, made light of the fact; they were wrong, but they erred in good company; all the world, or nearly so, was of the same opinion. It was almost universally believed that the first shot from Mont Valérien would put to flight the rebellious artillery of Montmartre and Belleville; and that the only reason why that shot was not fired, was that the government knew perfectly well that it could put an end to the *émeute* whenever it pleased, and only held its hand because it felt confident in the good sense of the better portion of the population, and desired to spare bloodshed. As in every case from July, 1870, to the moment to which we refer, these views, though shared by nearly all who expressed any opinion, turned out erroneous.

The total absence of anything deserving the name of public opinion, of political life, left Paris, as usual, a prey to ignorance and mad fury. The press, occupied almost solely with the advocacy of party views or the vilification of opponents, took, as usual, no care to ascertain what was actually going on close around it; second-rate writers filled what are called newspapers, but which are really little more than satirical squibs in a daily form, with long frothy articles pretending to be political, but intended to be comic while they were simply weak and ridiculous, and the Commune was thus enabled to carry on its manoeuvres without the great mass of the people knowing anything about them. Rochefort, Pyat, and others put forth revolutionary arguments of the most atrocious character in their journals, managed to persuade the ignorant that the views of the Commune were full of wisdom and justice, and that the political millennium was really at hand, while the better informed passed over their lucubrations with confident contempt. The mistake was a serious one for Paris; it consisted in this, that no one understood how completely all classes were demoralized, high as well as low, civilians as well as soldiers. The proofs came with fearful rapidity, bearing upon their faces the unquestionable mark of authenticity.

Another mistake, in which nearly all the world participated, was brought to light at the same time: this was the removal of the seat of government from Paris. When the Assembly met at Bordeaux the expression of approval seemed all but universal, and when it was removed to Versailles there was scarcely a dissentient voice raised against it. Some deputies recommended Fontainebleau; but it is clear that that would have been no improvement. The absence of the government and of the army gave the Communalists the very opportunity they required; the effect of thus abandoning Paris was to frighten the timid out of it, and to give up the city to the revolutionists, who soon took advantage of the occasion thus offered to them.

This fact allowed the disorganization of society to appear in all its horrible nakedness. The Commune determined to have recourse to universal suffrage; it was far wiser than M. Louis Blanc, who had declared in public that the republic was above that and everything else; it knew, though he ignored the fact, that popular government must have a popular vote, or the appearance of it, for its base, and accordingly it determined to elect the *maires* of the twenty arrondissements, or districts, of Paris. Some few of the newspapers denounced the proposed election in bold terms, and at first nearly all the press declared the claims and the doings of the Communalists to be ridiculous and mischievous; and if at that moment there had been a spark of political life in Paris, it would have been easy to blow it into a flame and destroy the nascent revolutionary government. But the mass of the middle classes, the men of education and the men of substance, who might have stemmed the growing torrent, had either fled at its approach or cowered in helpless silence. The elections took place; no one had the courage of opposition: abstention, the proof of weakness, was the only weapon used, and of course it was utterly ineffectual. Two men, M. Desmarest and M. Albert Leroy, well-known liberals, but utterly opposed to Communalism of the Pyat-Blanqui pattern, had the courage to refuse to accept the mandate which the voters had attempted to force upon them, and we never heard that they suffered for their patriotism. Had other liberals taken a manly course, the shame of the Communist domination would have been spared to Paris. As it was, the Communalists were left to vote alone, and the result was the installation, as members of the government, of the most violent demagogues, men who were avowed opponents of all that was decent and holy. Such was the effect of the absence or the cowardice of the middle classes of the Parisian population. "When the elections had been accomplished, some of the respectable journals still wrote in opposition, and the Commune used against them the old means of punishment, suppression or suspension. Others, the *Siècle* amongst the number, turned towards the rising sun that was so soon to set in blood, and supported the Commune in equivocal though effective terms. These, like the men of the middle classes, bowed down before the demagogues.

This absence or disorganization of the middle classes left the ground clear to the Commune; there was neither government nor popular opinion to restrain it; there remained nothing to depend upon for its suppression but force of arms. The first attempt showed that the demoralization of the army, or of a portion of it, was more complete than even the experience of the previous months had led the world to suspect. Led against the rebels at Montmartre, one or more regiments, either sympathizing with the insurgents or cowed by their determination, threw up the butt end of their muskets in the air and shouted for the Commune. What was the government to do under such circumstances? To repeat the attempt was to run the risk of another disgraceful scene of the same kind, and to expose such of the regiments as might remain true to their colours to almost certain death. The consequence of this was that the government, forced to retire and reorganize its forces, to wait for reinforcements of soldiers upon whom they could depend, was shut out from Paris, and M. Thiers was placed in the predicament of doing nothing, or of besieging the forts and ramparts which he himself, nearly thirty years before, had erected against possible, but then not probable, enemies from abroad. He may probably infer from the difficulties which they gave him, that these fortifications deserve the admiration of the world. Although, in a previous chapter, the belief has been stated that they were of inestimable advantage to France, many think that much of her sufferings, and especially those of Paris, were caused by these very forts and walls; that but for them peace might have been made earlier and upon better terms; but for them the population of Paris could not have been starved into submission, its people decimated and its rising generation impoverished by disease and suffering; that the flight within the walls and the closing of the gates took the place of bold attempts at reorganization in the field, which might possibly have changed the course of events; and we know now from General Trochu's own admission, that not a hope existed of the garrison of the city triumphing over the enemy. During the existence of the Commune, the walls of Paris might have enabled the Versailles government to starve out the insurrection, as the Prussians had starved down the resistance (it is to the credit of M. Thiers that he did not resort to this atrocious expedient); but they certainly caused that same government to bombard the city, to rouse all the ferocity of the Communalists, to give them time to exhaust the resources of the place, to inflict enormous suffering upon the quiet portion of the population, and finally, cause the destruction of many of the finest monuments of the city, and of an immense amount of private property. To a population that has not the force to defend its country in the field, fortifications, with the present system of warfare, simply offer the chance of being starved into submission at enormous cost, which, eventually, the survivors have to defray. The fortifications that make a people strong against enemies from within, as well as from without, are freedom and self-dependence—forts of which M. Thiers, and all the emperors, kings, and presidents in France to the present time, have never been able to learn the value. The doings of the Commune were so atrocious, that most men looked upon the leaders as wild beasts; but had they simply demanded free municipal government they would have deserved and obtained the support of all liberal-minded men; for in that case they would simply have been asking for that which was their birthright, and of which they had been deprived for years by rulers for their own ends. The final acts of the Commune or of the mob were infamous, and infamously carried out; but the leaders of the Commune were not a set of thieves and bandits, any more than were the concocters and agents of the atrocious massacres of the *coup d'état* in 1852. The Commune was the natural child of governmental incapacity, and the selfishness of vulgar speculators, just as the crowd of vagabonds that fill our jails, infest our streets, and from time to time endanger the peace of our community, are the result of the culpable neglect of government, the indolence of wealth, and the selfish and vain squabbling of parties and sects. Perhaps now that such a fearful drama has been played before the world, we may pay more attention to the means of education and the demands of morality.

The course of events from the beginning of March to the end of May is extremely difficult to explain. We have already said something of the commencement of the insurrection. The following, taken from a journal published on the 9th of March, will give an idea of the small impression events had then made on the public mind:—

"Tranquillity is likely soon to be restored; sleep quietly, people of Paris.

"General d'Aurelles de Paladine (commandant of the national guard) met the officers, and the *maire* of Montmartre, at a private audience.

"The meeting was a long one, and the negotiations were well advanced by the discussion.

"M. Clémenceau especially exhibited great moderation, and we are happy to record the fact.

"The men of Montmartre admitted that they began to weary of their watch over the cannon in their possession.

"One more good movement to counteract a bad one, and all will go well."

The red flag of the insurrection had been placed in the hand of the figure at the top of the column of July. Admiral Pothueu went to the Place de la Bastille, and sent a young sailor up, who, after some hesitation, took down the hateful flag and replaced it by the tricolor.

An incident of a different kind occurred on the boulevards. A paper signed Blanqui had been stuck upon a column calling the people to rise, and attracted a crowd of idlers, when a man, one who truly deserved the name of *Citizen*, advanced and said—"Messieurs, I have too much respect for universal suffrage to stand by quietly, and see appeals made to violence in a country in which it is not legally permitted to appeal by any other means but the voting paper." Then quickly tearing down the placard, he went his way amid the surprise of all, and the acclamations of a portion of the bystanders. Had that man been a fair example, instead of an exception, of the people of Paris, the Commune might have been strangled in its birth. Unfortunately, the great mass of the writers and talkers were far too much occupied with abuse and ridicule of the existing government—which certainly deserved neither—to bestir themselves and stop the operations of the Commune, which at the outset had not the sympathy of the people.

At this very time M. Louis Blanc, in his place in the Assembly at Bordeaux, presented a proposition, signed by Victor Hugo and others, for the impeachment of the government of the National Defence. In this precious document the provisional government was charged with having brought about the capitulation of Paris, "which the heroism of the people, if left to their own inspirations, would, according to all probability, have saved." It is due to the Assembly to add that, while a few members applauded this nonsense, the great majority received it as it deserved to be received.

While the commander of the national guard was doing his best, by constant interviews with the officers under his command, to assure them that the government was true to the republic, and that he would never destroy it; while every one seemed convinced that an amicable arrangement would soon be brought about, the attention and time of the Assembly was diverted by the complaints of the extreme Left; while M. Victor Hugo found time to vilify all Europe as cowardly (*lâche*) in not rendering assistance to France during the war, and finding himself impatiently listened to gave in his resignation; while the Assembly itself was preoccupied with the question of its removal from Bordeaux to Versailles—the government had the unhappy idea, which generally crowns all difficulties in France, of suppressing half a dozen of the revolutionary papers. It could not have easily taken any step more calculated to aid the leaders of the insurrection, and to strengthen their cause with the masses. Prevented from acting in broad daylight through the press, the secret action became at once more energetic and more deadly. There was a review on the same day at the Champ de Mars—it was some time before another review took place there—and between the two reviews Paris had been besieged a second time, her palaces ruined, and her streets again sullied with the blood of Frenchmen.

On the 16th of March Paris was remarkably quiet; the government was praised for having met the difficulty with firmness, and the best writers in the journals were hopeful. The guns on Montmartre were only guarded by four national guards, and Belleville, the other stronghold of the insurrection, was almost as quiet. The crowd that had surrounded the column of July had dwindled down to forty or fifty idlers and hucksters, who were selling, or trying to sell, medals and biographies of Garibaldi; the cold was severe, snow was falling, and almost everybody kept within doors.

A simple incident will illustrate the condition, or rather, it should be said, the apparent condition, of Paris on the day in question. A small body of marines, about to quit Paris for the coast, marched up the Rue Rivoli to lay an offering at the base of the July column in the Place de la Bastille; they made no demonstration whatever, except placing a small flag and a wreath at the foot of the republican monument. No one took any notice of the act, there was no crowd; and when they had accomplished their patriotic act they marched straight to the railway station and set off on their journey.

This same week several of the rooms of the Museum of the Louvre were opened. The great mass of the works of the old masters were still absent, but those of the French school, the drawings and several other collections, were open as usual to the public; and this fact gave a feeling of security which can only be understood by those who know what an important position art occupies in Paris, and how completely the Louvre stands as its representative. To complete the picture, it may be mentioned that the opening of the school of the Beaux Arts was officially announced for the 20th of March, and the dates fixed for the competitions for the annual prizes.

By this time the Assembly had quitted Bordeaux; and the theatre in the Château of Versailles, where the brilliant throng of courtiers were accustomed, during the reigns of Louis XIV. and XV., to flutter round the sovereign, gay and buzzing as the insects that swarm about the rose, though far less innocent in their occupations, was being fitted to receive the deputies of the third French republic on the 20th of the month. The ministers had already arrived, and on the 17th M. Thiers had a formal reception of all the officers of state, civil and military. After the reception there was a council of ministers, and the report afterwards was that—"Decisions had finally been arrived at to put an end to the irregular state of things which existed at Montmartre and Belleville." Such was the aspect of affairs on the 17th of March. On the following morning appeared a proclamation, signed by all the members of the government, calling upon the population to support the authorities, and put an end to the state of anarchy caused by a handful of men who had coerced others and threatened to bring about a civil war; the government informed the people that it had taken means to put an end to the insurrection, and trusted that it would have the support of all well-disposed citizens. True to its promise, two forces were directed on that same morning, one against Montmartre, the other against Belleville. The exact truth respecting what took place there is known to few, and will never be known to the world at large; but we all know, and in Paris it was known in an hour or two, that the government had utterly failed, and that the Commune was master of the position. It would be impossible to describe the disappointment, the disgust, the terror, that seized upon the well-inclined portion of the people of Paris when the deplorable truth became known. The accounts were at first most contradictory, but all agreed as to the main point, namely, that the government had met with a very serious defeat. The most terrible facts that came to light at the very outset, were the refusal of more than one regiment to act against the insurgents, and the fraternization of a considerable number of the regulars with the rioters. One regiment seems positively to have refused to act; another gave way at the first attack of the rebels, who effectually prevented the guns which were in the possession of the soldiers from being carried off; while a third is said, apparently with truth, to have openly declared against the government, and to have gone over at once to the Commune.

An atrocious act, perpetrated at Montmartre, completed the horrors of the day. General Lécomte, who commanded the attack, was made prisoner, and taken, it is said, before a band of men called the central committee; at this moment General Thomas, a soldier of high reputation, who commanded the national guard during the siege, appeared in plain clothes, and was also made prisoner. What actually occurred is involved in some mystery, but the horrible truth remains, that about a hundred ruffians seized the generals, dragged them into a garden, and then having pinioned them, shot them, and afterwards mutilated their bodies with bayonet wounds. One of the unfortunate officers, at the moment the rifles were levelled at them, looked full in the faces of their murderers, and with his last breath, and throwing all his force into the expression, flung the word *lâches* (cowards) at the teeth of the miserable assassins. The two aides-de-camp of General Lécomte, very young men, were also about to be shot, but were saved by a brave young fellow of seventeen, who threw himself between the officers and the wretches who were prepared to murder them, declaring that what had already been done was infamous, and that nobody knew the men who had given orders for the execution of the generals. The central committee of the Commune declared afterwards that it had nothing whatever to do with the assassination of the generals, who were killed by an enraged group, headed by a serjeant. The rebels at the same time made prisoners of several officers and 130 gendarmes and gardiens de Paris enrolled as soldiers.

Complete was the victory of the Commune. Before the day had ended the whole of Paris was in its possession; the Hôtel de Ville, the Luxembourg, and all the barracks in its hands; barricades thrown up in all the principal streets; and the members of the government, the soldiery, and all the officials in flight. The defection of a portion of the army, the want of determination of the rest, the connivance of one part of the national guards, the indifference of the others, and the unaccountable absence of anything like public spirit, made the Communalists masters of the capital of France almost without a struggle. Paris has seen other revolutions; government has before now been overthrown in France: but never in the history of the world did a handful of men, scarcely three of whom were known to the Parisian public, vanquish the whole force that a government could bring against it in a few hours, and remain masters of the field.

On the day after their victory the leaders placarded Paris to the following effect:—

"Citizens,—The people of Paris have thrown off the yoke which it was attempted to fasten upon their necks.

"Calm and immovable in its strength, Paris awaited without fear as without provocation, the insolent fools who would have dared to touch the republic.

"This time our brothers of the army would not lay hands on the holy ark of our liberties. Our thanks to all! and may Paris and France together lay the foundation of a republic proclaimed with all its consequences, the only government which can for ever close the era of civil wars.

"The state of siege is raised.

"The people of Paris are convoked to elect communal representatives in the several sections.

"The safety of all citizens is assured by the co-operation of the national guard.

"The central committee of the national guard.

"(Signed), ASSI, BILLIORAY, FERRAT, BABICK, E. MOREAU, C. DUPONT, VARLIN, BOURSIER, MORTIER, GOUHIER, LAVALLETTE, FR. JOURDE, ROUSSEAU, CH. LULLIER, BLANCHET, J. GROLLARD, BARROUD; H. GERESME, FABRE, POUGERET.

"HÔTEL DE VILLE, PARIS, 19th *March*, 1871."

Another proclamation, signed by the same persons and issued on the same day, ran thus:—

"*To the National Guards of Paris.*

"You have intrusted us with the defence of Paris and of your rights.

"We feel that we have fulfilled that mission; aided by your generous assistance and admirable *sang froid*, we have driven out the government which betrayed us.

"We have fulfilled your mandate and we return it to you, for we have no pretension to take the place of those whom the popular breath has driven away.

"Prepare then your communal elections without delay, and make us the only recompense we have ever hoped for, that of seeing you establish a veritable republic.

"In the meantime, we retain the Hôtel de Ville in the name of the people."

It will be perceived that not a single fact is here stated proving, or even intended to prove, that the government and the Assembly had betrayed the republic; the proclamations of the Commune were not peculiar in their style; each reader was left to construe the meaning for himself. The arguments of the Commune were such as we have heard before: it had the power, and invented the offence to be punished.

On the 17th of March the Communalists had taken possession of a number of guns in the old Place Royal and other places, and carried them off to Belleville. It was stated that they had in their possession in all 448 cannons, mortars, and mitrailleuses; this formidable artillery consisted principally of breech-loading brass guns throwing a sixteen pound shell, subscribed for during the siege, and for the production of which all the skill, science, and energy of the military and civil engineers, the founders and machine-makers of Paris, had been called into play. A very small number of these pieces had ever been fired against the invading Germans.

In vain did the government make appeals by proclamations and in the *Official Journal*, to arouse the population against the rebels. Paris was fairly cowed, had no faith in itself or any body else, and the communal leaders had everything in their own hands. The central committee at once seized upon the *Official Journal*, appointed a delegate to superintend its publication, and thus communicated with the people.

On the 20th of March an announcement appeared in that *Journal*, to the effect that the election of the municipal and communal council of Paris would take place on the 22nd of that month; one representative was to be elected for every 20,000 inhabitants. The "new government of the republic" took possession of all the ministerial and other public offices; all political prisoners were released, and full amnesty granted for political offences. The Assembly, on the other hand, had removed all its ministries to Versailles, which was declared to be, *pro tem.*, the seat of government. The army had been withdrawn by General Vinoy; its force was announced, in a letter to the *maire* of Rouen by M. Thiers, to number

40,000 men, and to have arrived in good order at Versailles. The Commune put forth a proclamation, in which the demands of the people of Paris were thus set forth. Starting with the assertion that "Paris, since the 18th of March, had no other government but that of the people, the best of all," the document went on to declare Paris "a free city, in which every one had the right of freedom of speech," and to state that her demands were "the election of the *maires* and their assistants, as well as the municipal council," and "the election of all the chiefs of the national guard, without exception." "Paris," said this document, "has no intention to separate itself from the rest of France; far from it. It has borne for her the empire, the government of the National Defence, all kinds of treason and rascalities. It has no intention to abandon her now, but only to say, in the character of an elder sister, 'Support yourself, as I support myself; put down oppression, as I have put it down.'"

The former portion of this document, that which referred to the elections of the *maire* and municipal council, as well as of all the officers of the national guard, was echoed by the deputies representing the department of the Seine. A placard to that effect, signed by MM. Louis Blanc, Schoelcher, and ten other deputies, was posted in Paris, and some few days later a motion with the same object was made, without success, in the Assembly at Versailles.

The press at last assumed a very honourable attitude. A declaration, signed on behalf of thirty-four political journals, including nearly all the well-established journals and several new ones—the *Siècle* being one of the few exceptions—declared that the pseudo-government installed at the Hôtel de Ville had no right whatever to call upon the electors to vote for representatives; that the attempt to dominate was the act of a minority against universal suffrage; that it was not Paris acting against France, for the chiefs of the insurrection did not represent the capital any more than they did the nation; and called upon the population not to give any countenance to an anti-social usurpation. The *maires* of Paris also met and passed an address to the Assembly, urging that body to decide on the question of the municipal elections. At length, therefore, something like public spirit was evoked, but the act was all too late; the capital was in the hands of the Commune, which had no intention to listen to reason. If the press, the *maires*, and the majority of the people of Paris had always acted as they now did, unfortunately at too late a moment, no body of men, however powerful, reckless, and unscrupulous, no party, however violent, could have succeeded in trampling upon the rights of the people.

All protests and arguments were ineffective now; the ball had been fired from the gun, and neither voice nor declaration could arrest its progress. The Commune declared that, not being able to make a satisfactory arrangement for the elections with the *maires*—the only power left but itself—it had determined to proceed without, or in spite of them; and the elections accordingly took place on the 26th of March, nearly all the *maires* in the end aiding in the work. The warning of the press was effective in some parts of the city, but not in others. In some districts nearly two-thirds of the voters on the list went to the poll; in others not a quarter of the whole; the average was about half. But it must be remembered that a large number of the voters had left Paris by this time. The result is well known; men such as Pyat, Blanqui, Assi, Flourens, and Delescluze were carried with overwhelming majorities. Only two men belonging to the true liberal party were elected, without their cognizance, and they lost no time in sending in their resignations. What did that matter to the Commune? It had between eighty and ninety men returned by universal suffrage; and the new government was declared to be firmly established.

The efforts of the Left in the Assembly produced little effect. M. Thiers energetically opposed the project of allowing the people of Paris to elect their *maires* and the national guards their officers. The only concession made was that they should elect the municipal council. Had this been conceded a month earlier, the insurrection might have been prevented; for every one who has lived long in Paris knows that the appointment of the municipal council by the government was an arbitrary act of absolutism, which rankled most deeply in the breast of every one deserving the name of a politician. Now, the resolution of the Assembly, like nearly all its acts, was fatally too late! The condition of affairs at this moment was well expressed by a writer in the *Temps* of the 23rd March:— "With pain and discouragement in the soul we take up the pen. To the last moment we hoped that the conciliatory disposition of the government and the Assembly, and the courageous firmness of the *maires* of Paris, would have helped us to avoid the catastrophe. It seemed impossible that criminal hands could hurl the country into the abyss, upon the edge of which she was already struggling. We were mistaken: blood has flowed, and we dare not measure the extent of the misfortunes which overwhelm or which threaten us."

On the 21st March a number of private individuals, headed by a Russian gentleman long resident in Paris, made a most praiseworthy attempt to stem the torrent of rebellion. They met in front of the new opera house; one of their number, a soldier of the line, carrying a flag with the inscription, *Réunion des Amis d'Ordre*. Numbering not more than twenty persons at starting, the procession swelled as it passed along the main boulevards to a thousand or more. It was received by the people with acclamation, and no attempt was made to interrupt its course, except by a captain of the national guard at the head of his company at the Place de la Bourse; but the men saluted the flag of the friends of order, and the drummers beat the *rataplan*. In the Rue Drouot was stationed a battalion of the national guard attached to the Commune; there was some fear of collision, but none occurred; the men of the guard thronged to the doors and windows of the *mairie* and saluted the flag. Some one suggested that there was danger of the manifestation being looked upon as reactionary, so the words *Vive la République* were written with chalk beneath the inscription on the flag. The procession set out again on its way amid the acclamations of men, women, and children, and cries of Down with the Commune! *Vive l'Ordre! Vive l'Assemblée Nationale! Vive la République!* The procession entered the Place Vendôme, where the insurgent national guards had established their headquarters. A deputy of the Commune addressed it from the balcony; but when he pronounced the words "In the name of the central committee," the crowd hissed furiously and he disappeared, while the friends of order marched without opposition around the column—afterwards thrown down—and proceeding on its course, crossed the Seine into the revolutionary quarter of the schools, and returned to the Place de l'Opera still amid the cheers and friendly cries of the population. On the following day the friends met again at the same place, again paraded the boulevards, swelling in numbers as they went, and finally proceeded up the Rue de la Paix towards the Place Vendôme. Why it selected that place again for a visit is incomprehensible, and what happened to lead to the catastrophe that followed is not, and probably never will be, known; but suddenly firing was heard, the crowd rushed madly down the street, men and women fell killed or wounded, and the friends of order were dispersed never to reappear again.

The leaders declared that they were fired upon without notice or provocation; while the Communists asserted that the foremost men were armed with revolvers, and fired first. On the face of it this assertion is false; it is inconceivable that the leaders of such a movement could have committed the atrocious folly of attacking a mass of insurgent guards with a few revolvers. The probability is that some scoundrels fired a shot or two from the side of the procession, simply as a means of bringing about the conflict.

Like the government, the Assembly, and the *maires*, the friends of order were too late. Their success in the streets and boulevards was great, and had they pursued their object with judgment as well as energy, there is no telling what may have been the happy result. Had the respectable people of Paris acted as some of the national guards and the Breton mobile acted against the Communists on the 31st of October, and made a strong manifestation in the interest of order before the government had been driven out of Paris, there is little doubt about the result; but the population had been for nineteen years told, nay forced, to leave everything to the government; it had been terrified by imprisonment, persecution, and hosts of police spies; it had been constrained to act the part of the humble bee, and that only; and it felt perhaps that the fighting bees might be left to battle alone with the hornets that had come upon the scene. Besides, it is difficult for a population purposely retained in political ignorance to act like men accustomed to think and speak their thoughts, to take care of and to act for themselves; so the people stood by and looked on while the conflict was proceeding, and the friends of order did not make their appearance till all order, and all hope of it for the moment, had disappeared. The impression, that with a little more energy even at the last moment order might have been restored, is strengthened by the fact, that as the friends of order were marching along the boulevards, another procession, with a flag which bore the inscription "*Vive l'Assemblée Nationale,* met and joined it. If ten good stalwart standard-bearers had appeared in ten different parts of the city, and roused the sluggard population by a few energetic appeals, surely the organization of the Communal forces might have been nipped in its bud, and Paris spared the infliction and the disgrace of the second siege.

The discomfiture of the friends of order was final. No more attempts were made to arrest the Commune, which was now undisputed master of the field. The new terror had set in: a man dare scarcely speak to his neighbour for fear of being denounced as an enemy of the "new government." All the members of the national guard were summoned to join the ranks, and those who did not obey had to hide themselves with the utmost care: any one discovered in hiding was a lost man. The officials in their retreat to Versailles had carried off all the money and documents they could. The able director of the post office had cleverly sent away all the carts and vans belonging to the establishment, with the clerks and postmen. All the public services were thus abruptly put an end to, and the Commune had to reorganize everything, which, it must be admitted, it accomplished with much ability. But the re-establishment of the post office outside the walls was beyond its power; for fifteen or sixteen days no letters, or scarcely any, came in or went out of Paris, and for some days before, the only means of communication was by sending to Saint Denis, Versailles, or elsewhere. Milkwomen, washerwomen, and special messengers were employed to carry out and bring in letters, but for the great mass of the population the post was suppressed. Those who passed in and out did so at the risk of their lives, and had it not been for the fact that the Northern Railway was worked under the Prussian flag, ingress and egress would have been nearly impossible. The city was again almost a prison, and had not the Versailles government and the Germans allowed provisions to pass in, the famine of the siege might have been repeated; as it was, the supply of provisions was irregular, and sometimes these were dear and bad, but there was no actual scarcity; the Commune, fortunately, did not reduce Paris to sawdust bread and ounces of horse flesh.

The grand difficulty of the Commune was the want of money; in one or two instances it had not the means of paying the national guards their daily stipend of fifteen pence a head, and serious trouble seemed imminent. The Bank of France was in great danger; reports were set afloat that not a penny was left in the bank-cellars, and that all the notes had been destroyed. This was not the case; the bank was saved by the good generalship of one of the members of the Commune, M. Ch. Beslay, who, after the suppression of the revolt, was allowed to go free in consideration of the great services he thus rendered. The chiefs found a quantity of unissued bonds at the Hôtel de Ville; these they naturally put in circulation. They obtained two or more large sums from the bank and from the private bankers of Paris; they made large draughts on the railway companies; they forced the chests of the insurance and other offices, and of some notaries and private persons; and they were in consequence denounced as thieves and bandits—which they were not. Some of them were brutal and ferocious enough, but that was not their general character. Anything more deplorably wicked and foolish than the conduct of the Commune it is not easy to conceive; but there is no reason to believe that the leaders were actuated by any worse spirit than wild political fanaticism, the kind of madness that at various epochs of the world has seized upon the best, as well as the worst, of men, and that self-esteem which stands for patriotism, and in presence of which all considerations of danger and disgrace seem to be utterly set aside. And there was this excuse for the conduct of the leaders of the Commune, that other leaders, better known to the world, preached doctrines which almost naturally led to Communism, while very many more exhibited very moderate admiration indeed for true liberalism in government.

The tardy act of the Assembly in according the people of Paris the right of electing its municipal council, was a tacit admission that it had done wrong in not granting it before; and surely the claim to elect the *maires* cannot be considered very unreasonable. If the appointment of municipal officers cannot be accorded to the great towns, such as Paris,

Marseilles, and Lyons, it is a proof, as we have before said, that the government that withholds the right has not the sympathy of the people of those cities.

If the Commune did not seize upon private property for its own purposes, it certainly made improper requisitions in other ways. Men in power rarely pay much attention to the rights of individuals, when their own necessities are pressing; and the men of the Commune being often hard up, did as most men under the circumstances would have done, they helped themselves; in other words, they visited the restaurants and shops, took what they wanted, and paid in paper that certainly was not a legal tender, and would not be rated A 1 in any money market in the world.

In the *Official Journal* of the 28th of March there appeared a letter written by M. Ad. Vaillant, in which assassination was openly advocated. It was written in reference to the asserted appearance of the Duke d'Aumale at Versailles. "If this be true," says the writer, "the duke did not meet a *citizen* between Bordeaux and Versailles. We see by such facts how much the moral and civic sense is weakened with us. In the ancient republics tyrannicide was the law. Here pseudomorality calls this act of justice and necessity assassination. To the corrupt who are happy in monarchical rottenness, and the intriguants who live by them, is added the group of sentimental fools." The letter concludes with the following paragraph:—"Society has only one duty towards princes—Death. There is but one formality to be observed—Identification. The Orleanists are in France; the Bonapartists want to return: let good citizens be on the alert." The delegate of the Commune in command of the *Official Journal* says, in introducing the letter, that "it appears to meet satisfactorily the difficulties of the movement!"

It is true that acknowledged patriots, as well as many others, more or less honest, have joined and taken the horrible oaths of secret societies of assassins, and have afterwards moved in the world, and been accepted by honest, respectable men; but the crime of assassination, whether by plain "citizen" or prince, and whether of a single individual or of a thousand, or the incitement to it, should never be allowed to pass without the author being branded as he deserves. The Commune made a lame attempt to disown the act of one of its members in this case some days later.

Having secured the command of the city, the Communalists closed the gates of the fortifications, took possession of the forts on the south side of the town, and prepared for action against the government at Versailles; they also seized upon Vincennes, or rather it was given up to them by the disgraceful treachery of the artillerymen, who sawed through the bars of the windows and let down the drawbridge. The governor himself was made prisoner, and it was several days before he could escape and inform the government of what had happened. The insurgents of the southern forts now began to move to Clamart, Bagneux, and Châtillon, the site of so much bloodshed during the Prussian siege. Regular military establishments were formed, with tents and canteens, provisions being furnished from the stores of preserved meats, &c., found in the building of the new opera house. Every night reconnoitring parties were sent out in various directions, and on that of the 26th March one of these parties met an unpleasant surprise. General Ducrot, who was said to have been killed, appeared with the Marquis de Gallifet and a body of cavalry at Châtillon.

This appearance of the forces of the government so near the city cooled terribly the ardour of the Federals; and there was a report all over Paris that a conciliation was on the point of being effected. Admiral Saisset had put forth a proclamation which caused much satisfaction in the quarters of the insurgents; and even the women, who had exhibited the utmost rancour against the Assembly, and had done as much, if not more, than the men in maintaining the insurrectionary movement, appeared satisfied. It was said that the admiral had promised a complete amnesty, and that order would soon be restored. This, however, was evidently not the object of the ringleaders of the rebellion; and it was soon discovered that, while they had the power to influence a large portion of the national guards, and money and ammunition lasted, they had no intention of yielding; unless, indeed, they obtained their own terms, which it was not in the power, if it had the will, of the Assembly to accord. To adopt the absolute unity of Paris would have been to strike France out of the list of nations.

The result of the late elections gave the Commune new force; the leaders redoubled their activity, and those able to bear arms had the greatest difficulty to keep themselves out of the insurgent ranks; reconnoitring parties were multiplied day and night on all sides of the town, and particularly between Paris and Versailles; and it was evident that each party expected some important movement to take place on the part of the other. The appearance of the city itself was extraordinary: the Hôtel de Ville was completely encircled by barricades and artillery; the air of the Place Vendôme became more ferocious than ever; small reviews took place at Montmartre; the barricades were reconstructed and extended in the great quarter of the Batignolles; the Faubourg Saint Antoine was all up in arms; every gate of the city, or nearly so, was guarded by guns against the approach of the enemy; the railway stations were all in the power of the insurgents, who were enabled to overhaul every train, and arrest all whom they suspected. The obedience of the great mass to the Commune seemed all but absolute, and the few who attempted to escape from the disagreeable duty imposed upon them found themselves treated with small consideration.

On the 29th of March, after the election, the Commune put forth a characteristic proclamation, of which the following are the most remarkable passages:—"A cowardly aggressive power has seized you by the throat; you, in your legitimate defence, have repulsed this government, which would have dishonoured you by imposing a king upon you. Now the criminals, whom you disdained even to pursue, abusing your magnanimity, are organizing a monarchical conspiracy at the very gates of the city. They invoke civil war; they make use of all kinds of corruptions; they accept all the accomplices who offer their aid; they have even dared to make an appeal to the foreigner."

The impudent falsehood of the assertions in this precious proclamation is glaring; but the mass must be treated to some kind of reasoning, and the exhibition of the spectre of a king was sure to have its effect.

A string of decrees followed the above proclamation. The conscription was abolished; no military force but the national guard was ever again to enter Paris, and every hale citizen was to be enrolled in the civic corps; no rent was to be paid for the nine months ending with April; all sums paid within that period were to go to the future account; everybody was free to throw up his lease during the coming six months; and all notices to quit were to be void for three months. Finally, all the employés of the government who did not immediately adhere to the Commune were to be dismissed forthwith; fortunately for them, they had already dismissed themselves to Versailles.

The red flag waved over the palaces and public offices; the Commune was master of the situation, caused Paris to be effectually shut off from the rest of France, and seemed to be assured that all the other great towns would follow the example of the capital, and thus bring about the Communal dream of federation without a central government. The horror of the word government amongst the French republicans is almost ludicrous. A story is current of a hot-headed ultra in 1848, who, having visited the Hôtel de Ville and seen the new ministry at work, said to his friends afterwards—"Republic! why, that is not a republic; it is a *government!*" It must be admitted, on behalf of the republicans, that the governments which have successively ruled over France have done all in their power to give the word a bad name, and to produce the catastrophe that happens, proverbially, to the dog who is so treated. On the other hand, it cannot be denied that the Commune was amazingly like a government.

On the 1st of April Paris found herself fooled into the position of a beleaguered city; all communication, except what was winked at by the Versailles authorities, was cut off, and for sixteen days from that period the post did not bring in or take out any mails; the interruption was as complete as during the Prussian siege. "Why does not the army at Versailles put an end to such a state of things?" was now the indignant cry of those lukewarm friends of order who had stood with their hands in their pockets and lips sealed during the whole time that the Communalists were completing their work, trusting in Providence to deliver them; or rather, we should say, considering what must have been the quality of their minds, waiting like Mr. Micawber, in the hope that "something would turn up."

During the night of the 31st of March the following proclamation was posted all over Paris:—

"Ex-prefecture of Police.

"The greater part of the public services having been disorganized in consequence of the manoeuvres of the government of Versailles, the national guards are invited to send any information which may interest the committee of public safety, in writing, to the municipal police.

"(Signed) A. DUPONT,

"Chief of the Municipal Police."

The imperial government itself could not have penned a more diplomatic document—the allusion to the "manoeuvres of the Versailles government "is superb in its way!

On the morning of the 2nd of April the guns of Mont Valérien, the only one of the forts in the hands of the Versailles government, were thundering away for hours, and a report was spread that the Prussians were aiding the government, and that there would soon be an end of the Commune; the middle classes, who, however, scarce dared speak above a whisper, were in a state of great delight. Within the city the *rappel* was beaten everywhere; whole battalions in full marching order passed and repassed in all directions; while, on the other hand, numbers of *fuyards*, dirty and footsore, came in, and a report was current that a serious engagement had taken place near Montrctout. The omnibuses were crowded with national guards hurrying to or from the *enceinte*, and as there were scarcely any cabs in the streets and no carriages to be hired, he who had not a horse of his own had great difficulty in getting from one part of the city to another, to say nothing of the fact that every man and boy between the age of sixteen and fifty was liable to be arrested as a traitor unless he wore the uniform of the national guard.

One of the most disgraceful sights was that of the appearance of a considerable number of men of the regular infantry of the fine marching in the ranks of the Communists—marching under the red flag with music at their head. This is another and a striking instance of the utter demoralization of the mass of the people.

The reports of a conflict turned out to be correct, and the Communist accounts appeared in the *Official Journal*. The executive committee informed the national guards by proclamation, that "the royalist conspirators had commenced the attack. Yes! in spite of the moderation of our attitude they have attacked us! Not being able to count on the army of France, they have attacked us with pontifical zouaves and the imperial police" (incorporated in the army by the government of the National Defence). "Not content to cut off correspondence with the provinces, and with making vain efforts to reduce us to famine, these furies have dared to imitate the Prussians and bombard the capital. This morning the *chouans* of Charette, the Vendeans of Cathelineau . . . covered the inoffensive village of Neuilly with shot and shell, and commenced the civil war with our national guards. There were killed and wounded."

A little later we were told that Bergeret was at Neuilly; that the fire of the enemy had been silenced; that the spirits of the Communists were excellent; that soldiers of the line who had come in from the enemy declared that, with the exception of the superior officers, no one would fight. This was followed by another sensational paragraph, in which it was asserted that "a school of young girls, coming out of the church of Neuilly, had been literally cut to pieces by the bullets of the soldiers of Favre and Thiers."

It was soon found out that this cry of triumph covered the rage of defeat; and as to the destruction of the school, that was shown to be a deliberate and infamous invention. But the people must be kept in heart, the national guards must be kept in good spirits. The above announcements were followed by a string of decrees. The first of these declared that the crime of civil war had been committed, and soldiers, women, and children killed, with premeditation and snares, against all right and without provocation. MM. Thiers, Favre, Picard, Dufaure, Simon, and Pothuau were charged to appear before the justice of the people, and their property would be immediately seized and placed under sequestration, &c.

The Commune announced that it adopted the families of all citizens who should succumb in repulsing the "criminal aggression of the royalists," &c.

Following these came a series of decrees of another character, which are so characteristic that it is proper to give them in full, with the preamble which introduced them to public attention:—

"Considering that the first principle of the French republic is liberty; considering that liberty of conscience is the first of liberties; considering that the budget for the religious establishments is contrary to principle, because it lays a charge on the citizens against their faith; considering, in fact, that the clergy have been the accomplices of the crimes of monarchy against liberty—It is decreed,

"1. That the church is separated from the state.

"2. That the *budget des cultes* is suppressed.

"3. The property called mortmain belonging to religious congregations, whether real or personal, is declared to belong to the nation.

"4. An inquiry will be immediately made respecting this property, in order to ascertain its nature and place it at the disposition of the nation.

"(Signed) THE COMMUNE OF PARIS."

Long and passionate appeals were made to the people in Communal journals, intended to show how calm was the attitude of the Commune, and that the sole object of the "people at Versailles," was the defeat of the republic and the re-erection of some new and odious tyranny. These appeals were constant, and their object was to draw away the attention of the population from what was going on without the walls. They failed in that object; the unfortunate middle and decent classes, many of whom had been silly enough to believe in the Commune, and all of whom had been almost criminally neglectful of their duties, in remaining inactive and leaving the coast clear for demagogues and fanatics, now saw their error, but as usual, they saw it too late. The die was cast, they were again prisoners, and might again be brought to the verge of starvation as in January.

"Les Français peints par eux memes" was the title of a famous satirical book of sketches; the "Commune painted by itself" would make another curious work. A writer in the *Official Journal*, M. J. B. Clément, treated us with a long sketch of "Les Rouges et les Pales," which, of its kind, is a gem. M. Clément says, "The *Reds* are men of quiet and peaceful manners, who place themselves at the service of humanity when the affairs of the world are embroiled, and who return and take up the hammer, the pen, or the plough, without pride and without ambition. . . ." Veritable patriots every one! "The *Pale* are men of frivolous and noisy habits, who intrigue, accumulate offices, and embroil the affairs of the world. Inflated with pride and ambition, they wrap themselves in their infamy, and roll along on the soft cushions of emblazoned carriages, which transport them from the court of assize to the gaming house. They do not dress themselves because the weather and decency require them to do so; they *costume* themselves in order to dazzle you, and to make you believe that they are not flesh and bone like yourselves; their life is an eternal masquerade; they have knee-breeches for such and such a ball, pantaloons with gold bands for another; they have coats of apple-green cloth embroidered on all the seams, and cocked hats with plumes. I ask you whether all this is not pure comedy? . . ."

"They do not reside, they stay in hotels in which all is gold, marble, and velvet; all is gilt-edged. . . . Their horses are better dressed than you" (the *Reds*, whom M. Clément addresses in an affectionate way as *Misérables*! after Victor Hugo); "their dogs are better fed and taken more care of than your children" (not complimentary this to the *Reds*). "There are 100,000 poor in France, who would be happy to live in their stables and dog kennels. . . . The *Pale* do not eat to live; no! They are the gourmets for whom exist the Chabots, who are decorated for having found out the art of seasoning a truffle, and the Vatels, who blow out their brains because the sauce is not quite of the right golden colour." Poor Vatel, who fell like Cato on his own sword, to be accused of such a coarse conduct as blowing out his brains! But M. Clément knew his readers. What was fact to him in comparison with brutal sensation?

"The *Reds* will not have to pay taxes any longer to support others; they will have no more barracks full of soldiers, because not being the enemies of the people they have no fear of them; they know that the people will arm themselves when our frontiers are menaced." Then we have the fraternity and equality of Tom Paine tossed up afresh with Clément sauce, which is not too piquant.

"The *Pale* want their infants to come into the world with the look of a drop of milk fallen from the lips of the virgin, while yours should be but vulgar bales of flesh.

"They will not have equality, because of their little white hands and little rosy feet, which are not adapted for working and walking. I am astonished that these gentry do not place themselves in niches, and call upon us to fall down and adore them three or four times a day. . . .

"They oppose equality because they are the apostles of war, of despotism, of discord; because it is amidst our troubles and our calamities that they collect their parchments, cover their seams with gold, fabricate coronets, and cut out mantles of purple and ermine—colour of the blood and the innocence of their victims. . . ." Such is the kind of writing by means of which the silly people are led out to seek equality, and find misery and death. What is the exact nature of the crime an educated man commits who thus, as it were, flirts petroleum on the flames of revolution from his pen? Does it differ in kind from assassination and incendiarism?

Up to the last moment it was hoped that attempts would be made by prudent men within and without Paris to prevent actual civil war; but the hope proved delusive, blood had already flowed, and all Paris seemed up in arms; battalions tramped along the Champs Elysées and the Boulevards unceasingly; 50,000 men were reviewed in the Champ de Mars before going out to meet the hated Versaillais. The news that a conflict had taken place soon reached us, and was found to be only too true; but with it came that of the success of the Commune, which turned out to be utterly false. When the truth began to ooze out the fury of the insurgents was excessive; their leaders had lied to them and they would not be undeceived. Two youths arriving near the Place Vendôme were telling the people of the rout of the Communal guard, when they were pulled out of their chaise and in danger of their lives, which were saved by a vivandière, who at the same time expressed her indignation by spitting in their faces!

The fact of the failure of the first attempt of the Communal forces being known, there was a furious scene at the headquarters of the national guards; but the leaders acted with great energy, made light of the defeat, called all their forces to arms, and were answered with an amount of promptitude and determination that certainly were rarely exhibited by the national guards during the German siege. The sight struck terror into the souls of the friends of order, who saw in this obstinate determination nothing but the promise of enormous bloodshed and savage recrimination. When amid the din that arose just without the city, shells were seen to burst, at first at some distance, then nearer, and at last actually within Paris, till the great avenue leading from the Arc de Triomphe was rendered untenable, then the sad truth broke upon the unfortunate people of Paris that the capital was being bombarded for the second time within a few weeks—bombarded by Frenchmen fighting against Frenchmen!

But even danger did not inspire resolution. The friends of peace, all but the Communists, disappeared utterly from public view; thousands fled at the first report of the insurgent arms, and every day added to their number. As the respectable classes had abstained from voting at the municipal elections, and so left the government of Paris in the hands of the Communists, so afterwards they abstained from all the rest of their duties by carrying themselves off. Never was an unfortunate nation left so utterly a prey to demagogues and fanatics. A passage in Sir Henry Bulwer's "Life of Lord Palmerston" may perhaps throw light upon this national annihilation. In his journals dated 1829, Lord Palmerston says: "The difficulties are great from the dearth of eminent public men. Bonaparte crushed everybody both in politics and war; he allowed no one to think and act but himself, and has left, therefore, nothing but generals of division and heads of departments, no man fit to command an army and govern a country." Twenty years more of imperialism completed the work, and resulted in the state of things lately seen in France.

Mont Valérien astonished the Communists by a very warm cannonade, and killed and dispersed a large body of men. The Communist leaders had bought over, or thought they had bought over, the commandant; and when they found they had been out-tricked by the Versaillais their rage was terrible, and cries of "treason" arose as usual amongst them. This every-day charge of treason is very lamentable, and was lampooned most cleverly in a piece that was played some three or four years since at the Gymnase. A gambler being seen to secrete a pack of cards in his hat, the cards were adroitly exchanged for others, and the party sat down to play. In a few minutes the face of the would-be trickster began to exhibit the most lugubrious expression; in a few minutes more he had lost what little money he had, when, quitting the table and coming close to the foot-lights, he said to the house, "I am robbed!" The hit was palpable and most effective; but still, after the failure of every manoeuvre our friends here persist in exclaiming, "We are betrayed!"

The Communalist leaders were determined not to let the grass grow under their feet; they planned a regular attack on Versailles. The army was divided into two divisions, one commanded by Bergeret, a printer, the other by Flourens, the maddest Communalist of them all. They marched off with flying colours, persuaded that the men of the line would join them on the road, and that Mont Valérien would not fire upon them. They were "betrayed" as usual! Mont Valérien cut one of the corps up sadly; the men from Versailles did not join them: on the contrary, the two forces were allowed to advance, completely entrapped, Flourens killed, an immense number taken prisoners, the rest flying back to Paris, to find the gates shut against them by their own enraged comrades.

The news of this defeat brought joy to the hearts of the friends of order; but the joy was soon overcast, the hope which it raised sadly deferred. The sad drama was not nearly played out yet.

War was not the only difficulty with the Commune. It had, in the first place, the terribly onerous task of finding money to pay its 200,000 guards, and to keep up some necessary public services; it had, moreover, to meet the demands of its own supporters. It performed the last-named duty in a very trenchant manner. It declared all arrears of rent to be sponged out, and any sums paid on the old to go to the new account; it declared all leases void, if the tenant should desire it, and all landlords' notices to quit, null; and these decrees were acted upon. Instances came within our own knowledge of persons who moved out their goods in defiance of their landlords, and under the protection of Communist bayonets. Of course the proprietors of houses were placed in the greatest straits; they were compelled to pay taxes and cut off from their rents. One of these unfortunate small proprietors, a man who lived upon the rent of a small house in a poor neighbourhood, about £36 a year—there are lots of such *petits rentiers* in Paris—hit upon the happy idea of taking a stool and an accordion, seating himself on the bridge called the Pont des Arts, and soliciting alms as a man ruined by the Commune. The dodge told well, and the man became a public character; and capital tales were invented about him, of which the following is the most amusing:— "Fortunately one of the, now, beggar's tenants was a man well off, and possessed a grand and noble soul. He visited his landlord and said to him, I will not pay you your rent because Saint Commune has forbidden it, but I will pension you. He kept his word, and the following morning, on passing over the bridge, he paid the first instalment of the pension— one penny!"

The position now began to be extremely uncomfortable. Provisions, though not absolutely scarce, were often dear and generally bad; the streets and all waste ground were filthy in the extreme, and the danger of epidemics breaking out was considerable; and added to all this, the difficulty of escaping from the toils of the Commune were great, in the case of any one capable of bearing arms. The railways had been closed for a day or two, when the Prussians sent a message to the managers of the Eastern line to say, that if the service were not recommenced they would take possession of it; this was awkward, and the Commune was compelled to yield. A picket of guards was, however, placed at the terminus, and the "new government" revenged itself, not only by seizing any arms or provisions, but also by making itself very disagreeable to all who wanted to leave Paris. This was not, however, general, for there was scarcely any interruption of the Northern and Western lines, but great difficulty in procuring French passports. As to the chance of a man in the prime of life being allowed to pass the gates of the city, that was all but hopeless; hundreds tried it, but were turned back. Some of them at last hit upon the happy expedient of entering the service, going out with the battalions, and deserting on the first opportunity.

There is no doubt that this course was adopted in many cases, and such conduct may account for some of the noisy enthusiasm evinced on marching out of the city, and for the routs that followed.

As to correspondence, the only letters that got out of Paris for many days were taken, as already stated, by the milkwomen or other "special couriers," but none came in that we heard of; that business might have been regarded by the robust *laitières* as rather too dangerous.

It will give some idea of the effect of events on ordinary trade to state the following facts respecting one of the great ladies' shops in Paris. In the spring of 1870, 260 young men and women were employed there, and the receipts amounted to 40,000 francs, or £1600, a day; now there were but fifty persons to serve, and the takings had dwindled down to £60 a day. And yet this amount under the circumstances seems large, for nobody bought anything he could do without, and dress, instead of being sedulously cultivated, as usual, was as carefully avoided; the worst-dressed person was most secure against annoyance.

By the middle of April, when Marshal MacMahon had assumed the command, Paris began to hope that the reign of the Commune was nearly at an end, and the operations around gave fair ground for such hope; the roar of cannon and the crash of mitrailleuses were continuous, and being closer home, the noise was much louder than at any time during the siege. Every day engagements took place so near the city that the smoke and flash of musketry were distinctly seen from houses considerably within the circle of the fortifications; the constant shower of shot and shell came nearer and nearer, till the few inhabitants who resided on the outskirts of the city either fled into their cellars or to some less dangerous roof. Many people who had left Paris had placed their apartments at the disposal of their friends, who gladly availed themselves of them, and fled into the interior of the city. In many places the cellars were the only resort, and cases occurred in which whole families were confined to them for weeks, while the shells were flying almost without cessation over their heads.

The conflict went on perpetually; and the struggle was maintained with bravery by both sides. May-day came, and still there was little change in the aspect of affairs, although the end was evidently approaching.

One of the most curious combination of circumstances that could well be imagined was to be seen, just outside Paris, at this period. The Germans were in possession of St. Denis, as they had been long before; the Communists were in possession of Asnières and Bois-Colombes, and the Versailles troops of the little town of Colombes close at hand. Constant conflicts were going on between the Versailles and the federal forces, under the eyes of the Germans, who had adopted the island of St. Ouen, near St. Denis, as their observatory; and the bridge being broken down they had established a ferry boat, which carried them backwards and forwards for a few sous. From this spot they watched with their glasses the conflicts going on amongst their late opponents. To complete the picture, St. Denis, almost utterly ruined, and in possession of the enemy, is only seven miles from Paris, and many Parisians passed the day in Paris and went to St. Denis for safety for the night; here they were under the military police regulations of the German authorities, and were compelled to be within doors at ten o'clock; and if found infringing any of the regulations were clapped in the guard-house, and let out the next morning on paying ten francs for the smallest offence.

The destruction at St. Denis was terrible, and the isle of St. Ouen was cleared of everything that was on it, and now Asnières, Neuilly, and all the villages and hamlets around seemed doomed to destruction. There is but one consoling fact, namely, that, with the exception of Neuilly, they were amongst the ugliest and most uninteresting suburbs that ever lay around a chief city. While the poorest hamlet in England has its flower-gardens, and even the commonest inn has something of a rural and ornamental character, nearly all the French suburban villages consist of hideously ugly houses without an atom of forecourt, much less garden, and the rural inn is replaced by a miserable wineshop, and a *café* which can only be described as a dirty barn reeking with stale tobacco. St. Denis was a place of large business, and possessed one or two pretentious restaurants, but not one decent inn or *café*. The contrast between Paris and its immediate surroundings is one of the most curious that can be imagined.

In the winter we had watched the growth of the barricades within Paris; we had seen every open place and salient corner converted into a redoubt, and the railway within the walls fortified and crenelated throughout its entire length; we had seen some of these fortifications removed, wondering, as we watched them, what effect this grand lesson in barricade making might have upon the population at some future period of difficulty. We little thought how soon our speculations were to be carried into practice. The feelings of peaceful people in Paris may be imagined when a long official document appeared, of which the following is a very condensed analysis:—

"The barricade commission" (of which many have since obtained unenviable notoriety, and not a few have gone to their account) "met under the presidency of Citizen Rossel, delegate of war.

"The president laid the existing system of barricades before the meeting, and these, as well as the new plans, having been discussed at length, it was resolved that two lines of barricades should be formed along the whole line open to the attacks of the troops of Versailles, and that those lines should be continued around the whole town.

"Citizen Gaillard, senior, proposed that the sewers should be cut in the fosses of the fortifications, and mined in front of the barricades. He pointed out that the principal object of the latter was to show, both to the enemy and the population of Paris, that to take the city it must be destroyed house by house. It was necessary, therefore, to collect behind the barricades all the means of defence most likely to act on the *moral* of the enemy. It is not probable that they will require to be used, for the attack will not be energetic enough to reach so far; but with such an organization Paris may defy treason and surprises.

"The commission decided that the gas and water pipes should be preserved intact until the moment of attack, and also such sewers as were necessarily opened for mines.

"It resolved to abandon the construction of subterranean mines as too slow an undertaking, but decided that mines should be formed below and at the sides of sewers, and laid down the following rules on the subject:—The first series of mines to be twenty yards in advance of the fosses, and to be charged with 100 pounds of powder; the second series to be twelve yards beyond, and to contain 200 pounds of powder; the third series to be at the same distance further in advance, and to contain the same quantity of powder as the second; and so on, in addition where necessary. Each mine to have a separate train to fire it.

"The general plan to be made known to the public by placards and lithographic sketches.

"Lastly, every one of the gates of the *enceinte* was ordered to be barricaded on each side, and that all the roads leading thereto, and every corner house near a gate, should be barricaded and occupied by soldiers."

Such was the prospect laid open to us. As regards the barricades, they were immediately commenced and carried out with great rapidity and ingenuity; every one was forced to aid in the work, and two formidable rings of barricades were erected around the city. In important positions these barricades assumed the character of veritable redoubts, and were armed with the excellent new bronze breech-loaders in the possession of the Commune; never was an insurrection mounted on such a scale or provided with such means.

We know less about what was done with respect to the mines, but there is every reason to believe that the work was pretty thoroughly carried out; certainly wires were discovered in many places, and cut by the Versailles troops on entering Paris. Bands of men were told off for this dangerous duty, the men wearing bands round one arm to assure the inhabitants of their peaceful intentions. Some of these men fell by accidents in thus foiling the plans of the Federals; but no clear or trustworthy account of the whole expedients that were prepared for the last struggle has appeared.

Other matters also engaged the leaders of the Commune at this period, especially the means of carrying on necessary works, and a document to the following effect was issued:—

"Commune of Paris.

"Seeing that many workshops have been abandoned by those who directed them, who have escaped from their civic obligations without any consideration for the interest of the working classes; seeing that in consequence of this cowardly flight, many works essential to the ordinary life of the masses have been abandoned, and the existence of the workmen compromised—It is decreed:—

"That the synodical chambers of the workmen be convoked, in order to establish a commission of inquiry with the following objects:—

"1. To draw up a list of the works abandoned, with an account of the exact state of the machinery, tools, and plant which they contain.

"2. To present a report on the practical means of placing these workshops in condition for working, not by the deserters who have abandoned them, but by the co-operative association of the workmen who were employed there.

"3. To draw up a plan for the constitution of such co-operative associations.

"4. To form an arbitration jury, which shall, on the return of the employers, settle the conditions on which the workshops shall be definitely ceded to the workmen's associations, and upon the quotas of indemnity to be paid to such employers."

Doubtless some of the workshops referred to were taken possession of by the Communal authorities; but this wonderful decree can scarcely have come into anything like general operation. Arms and food were the principal requisites in demand; the former were found in large quantities, and the workshops in the Louvre established by the government of September supplied all the necessary means of repair; as to food, that existed, and when not to be had in the ordinary way, was simply requisitioned, and sometimes paid for in paper money of the Commune—I O Us of which the current value was about the same as that of a button top.

A commission of artists was formed, the objects of which were that artists should have the management of everything in the world of art; namely, the preservation of the works of the past, the bringing before the attention of the world the works of the present day, and the regeneration of the future by education: in short, the care of the public galleries of art, the management of the exhibitions of modern art, and the education of future artists—free trade in art, in its fullest acceptation. The publication, under the commission, of an official journal of art, formed one of the special objects mentioned.

Liberty of the press seems to be a plant that can not flourish in French soil. The Bourbons would not have it; the Orleanists liked it not, and gave it little chance. Imperialism detested it, fought against it in every way by repression, suspension, fine, and imprisonments without end; half the journalists were inmates of prisons during the reign of Napoleon III. Latterly the imperial government set steadily to circumvent what it could not absolutely eradicate, by starting at its own cost false liberal and opposition journals, and trying to corrupt existing ones; in which it succeeded to a certain extent, but with no practical result but the loss of its money and the ruin of the credit of the papers which listened to the charmer. The government of September could not bear such a power as the press near the democratic throne; it also tried its hand at suppression and coercion, and fairly burnt its fingers. The Commune adopted much the same course as most of its predecessors, and although it did not arrive at the slaughter of imperial times, it made its arm felt in like manner. It suspended and suppressed half a dozen or more journals; the *Bien Public* was absolutely suppressed on the 21st of April. M. Dubisson, who printed the *Figaro* and many other papers, was forbidden to use his type and presses, and an attempt was made by the Commune to take possession of them; but M. Dubisson's printers stood by their master, and although almost starved out, they refused to submit to the tyrannical demand. The printing office of the *Opinion Nationale*, an old liberal paper, the editors of which declined to accept the Commune, was forcibly taken possession of. All this was disgraceful, especially so in a government pretending to be founded on liberty, equality, and fraternity.

M. Rochefort cannot be quoted as having done much for his country, except adding fuel to the flames and aiding civil war by puerile violence; but in this case of the interference of the authorities with the press he behaved well, and deserves credit for it. In his paper, the *Mot d'Ordre*, he addressed stinging articles against a liberal government interfering with a liberal press; he said, the members of the Commune were editors of papers, and insulted honest republicans who could not use reprisals and suppress the Communal journals in their turn.

The *Affranchi*, which was edited by Paschal Grousset, caused bitter smiles by announcing that the Commune was well off for cash, and that the financial committee was in a position to pay a thousand millions of francs, or forty millions sterling, as the share of Paris in the Prussian indemnity, and to spread that sum over ten years, and still be able to diminish the octroi dues; these, adds the writer, are acts to which neither the empire nor the government of the 4th of September have habituated us.

This was all lamentably ridiculous; the Commune had money then, but how did it obtain it? By confiscating the bonds of the Hôtel de Ville and the cash of the bank to a certain extent, and by levying contributions on the railway companies, the insurance offices, the notaries, and others. After all, there remained the query: Was not the whole statement a mendacious tissue of absurdities? But the Commune's supporters must be kept in hope, and tickled and pleased; what mattered a few more falsehoods for such a purpose?

Amongst other decrees, the Commune issued one ordering all *cafés* to be closed at midnight; there was little cause for this, for there was scarcely any one in them long before that hour. Another decree caused some amusement; bakers were ordered not to work at night, because it was bad for the health of the men, and Paris can do very well, it said, with stale bread in the morning!

Reports were rife at this time, that the members of the Commune were all at sixes and sevens with one another. Cluseret was charged with all kinds of crimes and offences, and if his dear colleagues could have found any better, or worse, man to put in his place, he would soon have had a safe lodging. M. Cluseret demanded the arrest of M. Félix Pyat, which it is said was agreed to; and the latter attacked M. Vermorel violently in *Le Vengeur*, for having opposed him in the Communal councils. M. Pyat tendered his resignation, and this, like the rats quitting a ship, was looked upon as proof that the end was near. His resignation was based on an absurdity. He took his seat there at the end of March, when the law about the number of votes at an election was arbitrarily set aside; and now he would quit it on the ground that the same illegality was to be practised with respect to the election of supplementary members to fill vacancies. Logical M. Pyat! Three urgent appeals were, however, made to M. Pyat to withdraw his resignation; one from ladies, to whose decree the amiable Félix declared he must submit.

The court-martial established to judge all acts threatening the public safety, had been dissolved after a great row in the Communal council, by which General Cluseret was said to have been very rudely treated. M. Assi was arrested for the second time.

When the Commune was elected, the central committee of the national guard, the original revolutionary body, was to dissolve itself; but it had done nothing of the kind. It had adopted M. Louis Blanc's dictum, and maintained itself above and in spite of universal suffrage, and in spite of its own declaration to the contrary before the elections took place. What power it exercised actually, no one exactly knew; but it represented the 200,000 bayonets, and that was enough for a power to place itself "above universal suffrage." As might have been expected, these two conflicting bodies did not pull well together; like the Siamese twins, they were united, yet not of one mind. The schism between the two was becoming wider every day; and there was an idea abroad, that the central committee was not unlikely to arrest the whole of the members of the Commune, and then try to make terms with Versailles. All this showed that the Commune felt itself hopelessly lost, which few regretted, although a week or two before one was almost inclined to believe that nearly the whole population of the capital was with it.

Proposals for an amicable settlement were put forth on all bands, especially by the *Temps*, which journal declared that nothing could be settled by the victory of either party over the other. The *Temps* is a sensible, well-written, really liberal journal, which had never bowed down before the Commune; but in this case its judgment was not accepted by any one that we knew; on the contrary, the general opinion was that, painful as was the necessity, the government had no other course but to force the Communists to submission, or fight it out; and such proved to be the case.

The most infamous act of which the Commune was guilty, was the seizure of the archbishop of Paris and more than a hundred priests and dignitaries of the church; the excuse given was that prisoners taken by the government forces had been barbarously murdered, and that the priests and prelates were merely seized as hostages in case any such conduct should be pursued in future.

The archbishop of Paris wrote from his prison to M. Thiers, probably at the instigation, or in consequence of the declarations, of the Commune. The authenticity of this letter was not believed in, but M. Thiers has shown that it was perfectly authentic by the following reply:—

"VERSAILLES, *April* 14.

Monseigneur,—I have received the letter from you brought by the cure of Montmartre, and hasten to reply with that sincerity from which I shall never depart. The facts to which you call my attention are absolutely false, and I am really surprised that so enlightened a prelate as you, Monseigneur, should for a single instant have imagined them true. The army never has committed, and never will commit, the odious crimes imputed to it by men who are either calumniators or are misled by the atmosphere of lies which surrounds them. Our soldiers have never shot their prisoners, or sought to dispatch the wounded. That in the heat of combat they may have used their arms against men who assassinate their generals, and do not hesitate to accumulate the horrors of civil upon those of foreign war, is possible; but once the fighting over, they act with the generosity of the national character; and the proof of this is patent to everybody here in Versailles. The hospitals contain very many insurgent wounded, who are treated in precisely the same way as the defenders of order. This is not all. We have made in all 1600 prisoners, who have been transported to Belle Isle and other maritime stations, where they are treated just like ordinary prisoners, and much better than any of our men would be who might fall into the hands of the insurrection. I therefore, Monseigneur, repudiate altogether the calumnies which have been repeated to you. I affirm that our soldiers have never shot any prisoners; that all the victims of this wretched civil war have fallen in the heat of battle; that our soldiers have never ceased to be guided by those humane principles which animate all of us, and which are alone worthy of the freely elected government that I have the honour to represent. I have already declared, and I declare again, that all the misguided individuals who may repent of their errors and lay down their arms, will have their lives spared, unless they be judicially convicted of participation in those abominable assassinations which all honest men deplore; that necessitous workmen shall receive for some time yet to come the subsidy which enabled them to live during the siege, and that once order re-established, all shall be forgotten. Such are the declarations I have already made, which I renew, and to which I shall remain faithful whatever happens; and I give the most positive denial to everything contrary to these declarations. Receive, Monseigneur, the expression of my respect, and of the pain I feel at finding you a victim of this frightful system of hostages, borrowed from the reign of terror, and which we might have hoped would never re-appear amongst us.

"The President of the Council,

"A. THIERS."

The countless stories of the assassination of prisoners did much to inflame the minds of the Communistic national guards and the rabble against the government; but we were too much accustomed to deliberate falsehoods of this kind to be astonished at anything, and few doubted the sincerity of M. Thiers' express denial of any such atrocities having been committed. The letter produced a great impression, as it was calculated to do.

Of these unfortunate prisoners sixty were confined in the prison of the Conciergerie, and others at Mazas, La Roquette, and elsewhere. It is asserted that they were treated with the greatest rigour, fed on the commonest and scantiest prison diet, confined in cells which they were never allowed to quit; and as many of the prisoners were old men accustomed to every comfort, the punishment fell most severely upon them. But the torture of any one in a religious garb seemed to give intense pleasure to the Communists.

The "new government" commenced the manufacture of balloons; it formed a body of balloonists, with a captain and other officers. The object of the balloons was said to be, first, military observation, and secondly, correspondence with the departments. They also seized upon the arm-shop established at the Northern Railway Works, and finished a number of brass guns that were left in an imperfect state at the time of the armistice.

The want of money was, in spite of all the assertions to the contrary, pressing, and all means were tried to fill the exhausted coffers of the Commune. One day 600 national guards surrounded the offices of the great Paris gas company, and forcing the iron chest, took away 70,000 francs; the money was, however, afterwards returned with an apology.

An incident which told decidedly against the Commune occurred at the medical school. The students were convoked to appoint ten delegates to confer with the government on the reorganization of the medical schools; but by a majority of two-thirds they refused to go into the question with the Commune, and dispersed with cries of *Vive la République!* This incident was the more important, from the fact that the medical schools as a body are radical in the extreme. In September, when nearly all the world was content to write up "Liberty, Equality, Fraternity," the medical school added the words "or Death;" and within the walls on which this Robespierrean motto appeared, met one of the most violent clubs in Paris. The fact was, we believe, that many of the students hailed the Commune with great zeal at first, but that they had had enough of it. In our own country, the opinions of a school of young men and boys would not go for much; but in Paris, where almost every well-educated man seems to shrink from public life the moment he leaves college, it has decided importance. The Commune lost something by the defection of the radical medicals.

Another proof of the difficulties of the Commune was shown in the closing of a well-known *café* near the Bourse, on account of the too free conversation concerning the disastrous effects of the revolution.

M. Louis Blanc has filled an important place in the public mind, and in some respects deservedly so. We have felt obliged to say what we believe to be truth respecting the harm some of his acts and speeches have done, and we therefore think it right to let his own account of his views appear here, in the form of a letter addressed to M. Cernuschi, the editor of the *Siècle*.

"VERSAILLES, *April* 20, 1871.

"Sir,—You wish to know if I have remained a Socialist. Upon this point your curiosity must be very great, since this is the second time you have publicly asked me the question. Be assured, I have remained a Socialist. Permit me to add, that if you are ignorant of this it is not my fault, for in my letters to the *Temps* I have never missed an opportunity of declaring my political and social convictions; and again quite recently I explained, developed, and defended them in a book published in France under the title of 'The Revolution of February.' True, from the moment I returned from exile to shut myself up in besieged Paris, my thoughts and my mind were completely occupied by poignant anxiety for the misfortunes of my country. But what I was, I still am. At the present moment I feel myself drawn as powerfully as ever towards the study of the problem long since laid down in these terms: The moral, intellectual, and physical amelioration of the condition of the class the most numerous and the poorest, by the co-operation of efforts instead of their antagonism, and by association instead of conflict. If with regard to the practical means to be employed for arriving *gradually* at the solution of this great problem, twenty years of observation and sincere study had led me to modify my ideas, so far from concealing this, I should consider myself bound in honour to declare it. I have not this duty. Perhaps the reason is that the wrong means have been taken to convince me, my opinions having been calumniated or burlesqued rather than discussed. As to the reproach you address to me, of belonging to a party which, to quote your words 'fears to injure the millennial edifice of royal unity, and dreads the apparition of a federal constitution, by which the chain of the past would be broken,' let us come to an understanding. To break the chain of the past I believe to be neither desirable nor possible, for the simple and very well-known reason that the past is the parent of the present, which in its turn is the parent of the future. And I should deem it deplorable, provided that the chain of the past could be broken, that it should be broken for the profit of the federalism which you appear to wish for. If the only thing at issue were to 'injure the millennial edifice of royal unity,' an old republican like me would not be terrified by such a result. But the principle for which I will fight as long as I can hold a pen, is that which the Revolution proclaimed; that from which it derived the strength to crush the coalition of the kings; that expressed by these words, which explain so many victories and recall so many grand deeds—'Republic, one and indivisible!' France advancing united and compact to the pacific conquest of its liberty and that of the world, with Paris—the immortal Paris—for capital, is a prospect which tempts me more, I admit, than France reverting, after being torn in pieces, to that Italian federalism of the middle ages, which was the cause of continual intestine contentions in Italy, and which delivered her, lacerated by herself, to the blows of every foreign invader. Not that I am for centralization carried to extremes. Far from it. I consider that the commune represents the idea of unity not less truly than the state, although under another aspect. The state corresponds with the principle of nationality, the commune corresponds with the principle of association; if the state is the edifice, the commune is the foundation. Now, upon the solidity of the foundation that of the edifice depends. Hence it follows that in recognizing the right of the commune to govern itself, to elect its magistrates, beginning with the mayor, to control their office, to provide, in a word, for everything which constitutes its own life, for everything which its autonomy realizes, the cause of national unity is really served. But just as it is necessary that the municipalities should be free in their movements—in everything which specially concerns each of them—so is it necessary that the bond which unites them one to the other, and attaches them to a common centre, should be vigorously fastened. Just as decentralization is necessary in everything affecting local interests, so would it be dangerous if extended to general interests. Suffocation, no; unity, yes. Assuredly no one will deny that it is in conformity with good sense to attribute what is personal to the individual, what is communal to the commune, what is national to the nation. The difficulty would be to trace a well-defined line of demarcation between these various classes of interests, were not the means of distinguishing one from the other almost always furnished by the very nature of things, and inherent in the laws of evidence. Under any circumstances, this is a matter for free investigation and free discussion. But, alas! how distant the day seems still in which that maxim which so much sophistry has obscured will be received as an axiom—'Force founds nothing because it settles nothing.' What, in fact, is taking place? The cannon roars; the abyss opens; we slay; we die; and such is the fatality of the situation, that those within the Assembly, and those without, who would give their lives to see this sanguinary problem solved in a pacific manner, are condemned to the torture of being unable to perform a single act, to utter a cry, to say a word, without running the risk of provoking manifestations contrary to the object they propose, or without rendering themselves liable in this manner to irritate the malady, to envenom the wound. Was ever misery to be compared with this? And when the return of civil peace depends, on the one hand, upon the formal recognition of the sovereignty of the people which abides in universal suffrage, that will express it in a more and more intelligent manner in proportion as the organization is improved; and on the other hand, upon the ungrudging consecration of everything which constitutes municipal freedom, is it conceivable that, instead of seeking an issue from so many evils in a policy of pacification, of conciliation, and of forgetfulness, Frenchmen should continue to cut each other's throats under the eyes of the enemy, whom our discords strengthen, and of the world, which is scandalized? Oh, civil war, grafted so lamentably upon foreign war; frightful struggle pursued amid an intellectual night, that a single ray of thought ought of itself to dissipate, there is one thing which equals thy horrors, it is thy madness!

"LOUIS BLANC."

If the above letter does not show very clearly what M. Louis Blanc's exact opinions are—half the number of lines would have served that purpose, had he desired to have been explicit—it is quite clear that he repudiates the Communal notion of federation; but the blame, or rather the dissension, therein expressed is so mild, that it can scarcely be said to have shut the door in the face of the Commune, but rather to have kept it ajar, in case of possible eventualities.

With respect to the finance of the Commune, it was asserted that its daily expenses amounted to between 700,000 and 800,000 francs, or £28,000 to £32,000, while the receipts fell something like £8000 below that sum; the difficulty of making up such a deficit by means of loans, bills, &c., must have been great. It must be stated, however, that on other hands, such a deficit, or any deficit, was strenuously denied. One fact, however, is worth a hundred assertions, especially in Paris, and here is a striking one—the Commune demanded from the railway companies the payment of 2,000,000 francs, £80,000, within forty-eight hours. This was the sum of the arrears of taxes due by the companies to the government; they were also called upon to pay their dues regularly for the future.

The two adjoining quarters of Paris, Les Ternes and Neuilly, were reduced to a deplorable state. All the inhabitants not retained by force or a sense of duty had left; and the poor, who had nowhere else to go to, were living in the cellars, half starved, with shells from Valérien and Courbevoie falling incessantly. The stories that we heard were horrible; for example, a child's funeral was passing through a bye street, when a shell fell amongst the mournful party, all of whom fled but the father and mother of the deceased, who flung themselves on the ground: when they rose they found the coffin and remains cut to pieces. A poor woman in a cellar saw her husband dying of a wound and of starvation before her eyes; she begged for aid, for food, for a doctor, but all her appeals were useless; the poor man died. She implored the few passers-by to get the remains buried; but the shells threatened the living too seriously to allow them to think of the dead. The poor woman at length made a hole in the floor of the cellar and interred the body; but she could not bear the neighbourhood of the corpse, and becoming half frantic rushed out into the street, and declared that she would go out and meet her death at the hands of the enemy, rather than starve in a vault. The poor creature found at last some aid. This was only one of a hundred such cases, and the least miserable seem to be those whom a friendly shell or bullet snatched away from such fearful tortures.

At last a cessation of hostilities was agreed upon, in order that the miserable inhabitants of these districts might get away, and save their lives and what little else was left to them.

THE TRUCE.

The question of a truce with rebels was a difficult one for M. Thiers, but he agreed to it at the request of a masonic delegation which waited upon him under a flag of truce at Versailles. The delegates asked for an armistice for the poor inhabitants of Neuilly, to which M. Thiers agreed; but when they talked of conciliation with the Commune, and a recognition of the municipal franchise of Paris, the chief of the executive was adamant, and declared that for the present he adhered to the municipal law voted by the Assembly. No one can blame M. Thiers for not yielding to the demands cf a tyrannical rebellion; but sooner or later Paris will have municipal liberty, or the whole life will be crushed out of her in the struggle. The position of two millions of people without power over their own affairs, is only possible in presence of a forest of bayonets. This is the only document of the kind that passed between the "governments" of Paris and Versailles, and we therefore quote it entire as a curiosity:—

"An armistice for the benefit of Neuilly, Tuesday, 25th April, from nine o'clock in the morning until five o'clock in the evening, has been agreed to, subject to the following conditions:—

"The troops of Versailles and Paris will maintain their respective positions.

"Sufficient notice will be given to the people of Neuilly, during which they can abandon the scene of mutual conflict.

"In no case must they pass the bridge of Neuilly or the lines of the Versailles troops.

"Persons residing within the said lines, who may not be permitted to enter Paris, will go towards St. Ouen and St. Denis.

"The road will be made practicable by the cessation of fire on both sides from Neuilly to St. Ouen.

"During the armistice no movement, either of the Paris or Versailles troops, is to take place.

"Citizens Loiseau-Pinson and Armand Adam, present within the limits occupied by the troops of Versailles and Paris, will remain there during the armistice, and if necessary, be warned that all emigration is suspended and hostilities about to recommence.

"Citizens Bonvalet and Hippolyte Stupuy, present within the same limits occupied by the troops of Paris and Versailles, will in turn be warned by Citizens Loiseau-Pinson and Armand Adam.

"These conditions are approved and accepted by the generals commanding the first corps d'armée, and by the Commune of Paris."

[Here follow the signatures.]

"A system for supplying the starving inhabitants of Neuilly with food has been organized by the delegates, who will remain on the bridge of Neuilly throughout the whole duration of the armistice."

The armistice was announced for the 24th of April, but by some inexplicable blundering this was an error. The consequence was that crowds of people went down to the gates as near as they could without coming within range of the fire, to bring away their friends and such of their own property as was still undestroyed the moment the hostilities were suspended; but to their surprise and rage, at noon, when the armistice was to commence, the fire increased instead of ceasing. Shells fell in great numbers in reply to the fire of the insurgents, and then it came out that the Commune had not yet agreed to the terms proposed; if this were true, as it appears to have been, the conduct of General Cluseret in announcing the armistice was, to say the least of it, culpable. No suspension of hostilities took place on that day, and the whole of the people who went to Neuilly, in expectation of the armistice, were greatly enraged. The whole of the ground from Neuilly to the Arc de Triomphe was covered with shells, and no one could cross that quarter without running great danger; several persons, in fact, were killed, and more wounded.

The armistice really took place on the 25th; an immense collection of cabs, carts, and vehicles of all kinds were collected at the Palais de l'Industrie, the headquarters of the association in aid of the wounded during the siege, provided by the delegation to assist the unfortunate inhabitants and refugees to clear out of Neuilly—a considerate act which deserves notice. In spite of all this, many of the inhabitants remained, having probably no other place to go to, for they are the poorest of the poor. Still, it was difficult to imagine any one remaining to face almost certain death by projectiles, or what is far worse, starvation. Half Paris flocked to the spot on the occasion, many in order to see the devastation which had been caused in and around the village, which was even greater than that created at St. Cloud during the siege.

The suspension of arms was completely respected on both sides during the armistice. No firing took place from either the Versailles or Paris lines, but both sides proceeded with their barricades and redoubts almost in sight of each other. General Okolowicz afterwards made a formal complaint on the part of the Federals, that the Versailles troops broke the terms of the truce by carrying on their works during the armistice; but the charge is mendacious in the extreme, for trustworthy witnesses saw barricades and ditches being proceeded with on the insurgent side, and were even compelled to lend a hand to the works. So much for General Okolowicz's complaint!

The armistice ceased at one in the morning, and at about three Mont Valérien opened fire with great vigour, and the Versailles troops were in full activity on all sides. The damage done to this quarter is immense. As to the Avenue de la Grande Armée, there is not a house that has not been hit, and most of these fine new mansions are seriously injured, while the shells fell like hail all the way to the Champs Elysées. The smaller buildings in the avenues and streets leading to the two gates of Porte Maillot and Ternes are utterly ruined; not merely chipped and pierced, but roofs, corners, and walls shot away. To give an idea of the devastation, and of the number of projectiles which have fallen in this quarter, it may be mentioned that scarcely a tree or a lamp-post escaped, the former being cut to pieces, and the latter bent or snapt off. Add to this that the pavements or roads were ploughed up by the shells, or covered in many places with the rubbish of the fallen houses, and some idea may be formed of the condition of this quarter of the town, which a few months since was the favourite resort of the English residents and of many well-to-do Frenchmen, who were beginning to understand the benefit of the English arrangement, living away from the dusty, stifling, gas-polluted air of the city. The more remote parts of Neuilly are less injured, but it will be a long time before that favourite suburb can assume its tranquil umbrageous aspect, and its promenades become filled again with troops of laughing children under the charge of their white-capped French *bonnes*, or spruce English nursery governesses. The horrors of a foreign war are bad enough, but those of a fiendish conflict between members of the same nation surpass anything that misguided human nature brings upon its own head.

Some serious accidents happened through the eagerness of the poor people in trying to save their remaining goods; staircases and floors gave way under foot, and loss of life and serious injuries were the result; and amongst the very worst effects of this frightful conflict was the apathy with which such calamities were regarded. Death and suffering had become so common, that scarcely any one seemed to have any thought except for himself and those who were nearest and dearest to him. The French are noted for the transient effect produced upon them by disaster, but nothing more revolting can be imagined than the callousness with which the great mass regarded the scenes of havoc and the sufferings which were enacted hourly before their eyes. War may have, and assuredly has, at times a noble aspect and a worthy cause; but civil war is a crime against nature and a disgrace to mankind.

One had scarcely the heart to listen to anecdotes or trivial incidents at such a time, but they existed and formed the staple of much small talk. In this quarter of the town there was a man, an Englishman, famous for his breeds of dogs and other animals. Towards the end of the siege he had a litter of famous bull pups; a lady wanted one of the queer little balls of fat, and he asked her twenty pounds for it. Upon her exclamation at the price, he declared that in three months they would be worth double that sum each. Poor man, in much less than three months food and fuel had become almost worth their weight in gold; the half-mad starving people broke down his palings to warm themselves with, burst into his house, and all the dogs, including the little twenty pound puppies, were mercilessly gobbled up. The Commune finished what the siege marauders had commenced; his farm outside the walls, and his house just within them, were soon in ruins; his losses were so serious, that he may be excused for declaring that the French are the "stupidest, thickheadedest, and vain-gloriousest people as he ever knowed." Alas! that such should be said of a nation which calls, and believes itself, the most glorious, unselfish, and logical people on the face of the earth, and in a city which claims to be the very kernel of the universe, the admiration, the envy, and the despair of the civilised world!

CHAPTER III.

Advance of the Versailles Army—Severity of the Struggle in the Asnières Road—Destruction of the Villages of Mendon and Belleville—Life in the City and Suburbs during the Second Siege—Distress amongst the Market Gardeners—Case of Special Hardship—Dissensions within the Commune—Proclamation of M. Thiers strongly condemning the Proceedings of the Commune, but promising that the Lives of all who laid down their Arms should be spared, and asking for the Assistance of all Orderly Citizens—Small Effect produced by the Proclamation—Life in Paris towards the End of the Communal Regime—Absurd Legislation—Fruitless Acts of the Freemasons and others with the View of bringing about a Reconciliation—Violent Article of M. Rochefort against the Release of the Hostages—A Committee of Public Safety appointed—New Reign of Terror—Arrest of the Governor of the Invalides—Rumour of Prussian Intervention, and Feeling in the City on the Subject—State of the Provision Market and General Health of the City—Further Efforts to bring about a Truce—Grand Concert at the Tuileries—Horrible Scenes in Churches—Bombardment of the Forts and Western Part of the City—Extensive Conflagrations and Exciting Scenes—Appointment of Rossel as Communal Commander-in-Chief—Biographical Notice of him—Balance Sheet of the Commune and Ability of Jourde, the Finance Delegate—Construction of Inner Barricades—Summons to the Commander of Fort Issy to surrender, and Characteristic Reply of Rossel—Statement of the Communal Forces—Capture of Fort Issy and Attack on the Ramparts—Rossel's Indignation at the Acts of his Colleagues and Resignation—Appointment of a New Committee of Public Safety—Rossel proposed as Dictator by Rochefort—Counsel of Félix Pyat—Arrest of Rossel—Destruction of M. Thiers' Parisian Residence, by order of the Commune—State of the Press at this Period—Terror in the City—Desertions from the Communal Ranks—Financial Difficulties—Bombardment of the Gates, of the Fortifications, and the Barricades—Capture of Fort Vanves by the Government Troops—Wretched Appearance of the Garrison on their Return to Paris—Increasing Severity of the Attack on the City and Desperate Position of the Communists—Extraordinary Legislation by them—Determination to burn or blow up the City rather than Surrender—Demolition of the Vendôme Column—Disgraceful Scene—Proclamation of Marshal MacMahon on the Subject—Cowardice of some of the Communist Leaders.

DURING the week previous to the truce of Neuilly the Versailles army had been gradually making advances against the Communists. On the 17th April the chateau of Bécon was taken by a regiment of the brigade Lefebvre; the park was immediately placed in a state of defence and batteries constructed. On the following day the Versailles troops continued to advance, dislodged the insurgents from all the houses in the Asnières road, took the railway station, and established themselves there. The condition of the houses around after the fight showed how sharp was the struggle here: many of them were reduced to mere heaps of ruins; others had only the back walls left standing, with the staircases in some instances hanging suspended to them, nothing else remaining but the fireplaces in their niches, a clock, a lamp, or a few ornaments on the mantelpieces, and the paper-hangings on the wall, torn and blackened, making together as terrible a picture of the material ravages of war as could well be imagined. All around was desolation and ruin; the houses that were not utterly destroyed had their walls pierced in every direction, piers knocked away from between the windows, roofs destroyed, the floors in most cases burnt, or fallen in. The railway station suffered almost as much as the houses around.

On the same day a regiment of the Grémelin brigade, with a battalion of the brigade Pradier, took the village of Bois-Colombes, an important position. The attack was then continued against the blocks of houses which were occupied by the insurgents at Neuilly. At the same time General Cissey advanced against Fort Issy by parallels between Clamart and Châtillon, the insurgents making constant but ineffective attempts to prevent the advance. Batteries were also established on the heights at Châtillon, Meudon, and Belleville; and Bagneux, where the conflicts between the French and Prussians had been so sharp, was wrested from the insurgents.

On the 23rd of April it was decreed that two new corps d'armée should be formed, principally of prisoners returning home from Germany; this was immediately carried out, and the command of the new corps given to Generals Douay and Clinchant.

On the 25th the batteries on the right opened fire; those at Breteuil, Brimborion, Meudon, and Moulin de Pierre, covered Fort Issy with their shells, while those of Bagneux and Châtillon attacked Fort Vanves; these two forts were, however, well armed and manned, and replied vigorously, and were aided by the guns on the fortifications of the city at the Point du Jour. A quarry near the cemetery of Issy was taken from the insurgents, and a trench was cut all along the road from Clamart to Moulineaux to command the last-named village. Preparations were now made to carry out the approaches to the right and left of Fort Issy, and to isolate it as far as possible; for this purpose it was necessary to take Moulineaux, an advanced post of the insurgents, and this was effected in the evening of the 26th of April by General Vinoy. On the following day the village was fortified, and a second parallel established between Moulineaux and the road called the Voie-Verte to within 300 yards of the glacis of the fort, works being pushed forward at the same time in the direction of the railway station at Clainart. These operations enabled the government forces to debouch upon the positions which the Communists still held to the west of the fort, on the plateau, in the cemetery, on the slopes, and in the park, in advance of Issy; these positions were, however, strongly entrenched, and the insurgents maintained a vigorous and constant fusillade from redoubts, houses, and crenelated walls.

The taking of Issy was not such an easy matter as some people imagined; six hours was the time talked of by the governmental organs, but it really took twice that number of days, and the operations completed the destruction of the villages of Meudon and Belleville. All the slopes around these places were studded with little chateaux and cockney boxes, nestling in charming gardens and amongst noble trees, and commanding some of the most beautiful views around Paris; these were nearly all laid in ruins, and the appearance of the whole neighbourhood rendered desolate in the extreme. Within the fortifications on the city side of the river the destruction was equally or even more terrible. The Germans reduced the Point du Jour and parts of Auteuil to ruins; and as the insurgents were strongly entrenched there, the governmental batteries completed the work. Hundreds of houses were levelled with the ground, the railway station destroyed, and the beautiful compound bridge over the Seine, over which the railway passes on a viaduct, was seriously disfigured, although the structure was not materially injured.

It must be difficult for those who have not been within a besieged city to picture exactly to themselves the state of the case. So long as the conflict was confined to the outlying forts it was extremely difficult for one not engaged in the operations to see what was going on. Many persons, some from curiosity only, volunteered to aid the wounded within the forts, and they, of course, had good opportunities of seeing, and feeling, the effects of the Versailles artillery; but those who remained within the city, however near to the fortifications, or made their way to the outlying villages, saw nothing but smoke, with an occasional flash at night, and heard nothing but the thunder of the guns. From the plains lying between St. Denis and Versailles, however, all the scene of the conflict was visible, but of course at too great a distance to make out much more than rude outlines and smoke. In these plains the poor peasants continued their work in the fields, but all their labour brought them only a miserable pittance; their cottages had been destroyed; their cattle and horses, if they had any, eaten; their tools stolen, lost, or burnt; the usual means of conveyance being all cut off, it was always difficult and often impossible for them to get into the city, where their vegetables would have been most welcome. The people of the villages around were themselves too seriously impoverished to be good customers. They had no resource but to carry their products to Versailles, which compared to Paris was a very poor market for such a large tract of cultivated ground as that referred to. These difficulties, however, were not all with which they had to contend. The whole neighbourhood had become demoralized; the government was too much occupied to attend to police regulations; the gendarmes were all in the army: and consequently the unemployed workmen and labourers, together with vagabonds of all classes from the neighbouring villages, spent a part of the night generally in foraging on their own account. They went to gather wood in the forest of Saint Cloud, but on their road men, women, and children filled their pockets with whatever vegetables they could lay their hands on, and the' unfortunate gardeners had no remedy. As to the pillagers, they were shameless; shouted loudly for the Commune or for the Republic, according as they were near the troops or the insurgents, and made the whole district which they infested unsafe for any one but themselves.

It was not only the little cultivators and labourers who were reduced to the verge of starvation, but men formerly of considerable means, and many of the instances were most distressing; one case may be mentioned by way of illustration. A market gardener and proprietor of some houses at Bagneux, a respectable, well-educated man, fled like the rest of the inhabitants of that harassed village on the approach of the Germans, having been lucky enough to save some part of his property. His houses were destroyed during the siege, and a battery was erected on the site of his garden. He went with his family to Châteaudun, where his wife's family had some property and she herself possessed a few houses as her portion; these were completely destroyed when the Germans fired the town. Immediately after the armistice the person in question returned to Paris, and with the little money left them he and his brother-in-law settled at Neuilly, under the shadow and, as they supposed, the protection of Mont Valérien, and opened a shop. Here the house was half burnt, his stock in trade scattered by shells; some of his money had been taken by the Communists, and some had been stolen; his furniture was either destroyed or had to be abandoned; and he came into Paris with his wife and a troop of other fugitives, with all that was left to him, a bed, a few clothes, and a bag of valuable seed in a wheelbarrow. His case is doubtless but one amongst thousands equally lamentable.

Although Issy did not fall in six hours, or in six days, the government was making head, and the fact was evident in more ways than one. On the 29th April, in the evening, the cemetery, the trenches, and the park of Issy were taken by three columns of Versailles troops. The park was defended by barricades armed with mitrailleuses, but the conflict did not last long, and the loss on the side of government was not serious. A great many of the Communists, who fought bravely, were killed, and a number of prisoners were taken. At about the same time another small victory was gained near Fort Vanves.

The dissensions within the Commune itself, and the reluctance of the national guards to be killed for an idea, became now very evident. The central committee and the councils quarrelled amongst themselves and with each other; the decrees began to lose their importance, and were openly disobeyed. A court-martial was appointed to try prisoners or offenders. It tried one and passed sentence of death; the council first commuted the sentence, and then dissolved the court-martial. General Dombrowski on an important occasion asked for large reinforcements, and when the battalions were called upon for service, not a hundred men appeared in place of some thousands; whereupon a battalion was disbanded, and a number of men condemned to ignominious punishments. This proceeding created a very bad impression in Paris; yet it is difficult to see that a commander could have acted more leniently with troops that had voluntarily joined the Commune and afterwards refused to fight. The truth was, the rats were quitting the sinking ship.

On the last day of April it was declared that Fort Issy was in the hands of the Versailles government, but the rumour turned out to be incorrect. It appeared that there had been some sign of capitulation, but on a flag of truce being sent to the insurgents they refused to lay down their arms; and on the following day General Eudes reached the fort with reinforcements, and having taken the command, refused to listen to any propositions; the siege operations, which had for a moment been suspended, were therefore recommenced with renewed vigour. For another week the conflict was maintained with determination, the batteries opposite to Issy and Vanves continually pouring shot and shell into the two forts from seventy guns, and destroying all the buildings around them.

On the 8th of May a' proclamation, signed by M. Thiers, appeared in Paris; it was addressed to the Parisians, and opened with the declaration that "France, freely consulted by universal suffrage, had elected a government, which was the only legal one, the only one which could command obedience, unless universal suffrage were a vain expression." It then went on to say, this government had given to Paris the same rights which were enjoyed by Lyons, Marseilles, Toulouse, and Bordeaux, and that without offence to the principle of equality the Parisians could not ask for more rights than all the other towns of France possessed. This was a most unfortunate commencement; for all the world knew that the denial of municipal rights to Paris and the great towns was a breach of that very principle of equality, as such rights remained to all the smaller towns; a little concession on this head at that moment would have disarmed the Commune utterly, but that concession M. Thiers would not make. The document proceeded as follows:—

"In presence of this government, the Commune, that is to say, the minority which oppresses you, which dares to cover itself with the infamous red flag, has the pretension to impose its will upon France.

"By its acts you may judge of the *régime* it would impose upon you. It violates property, imprisons citizens as hostages, transforms your streets and public places, where the commerce of the world was installed, into deserts, suspends work in Paris, paralyzes it in the whole of France, arrests the prosperity which was ready to revive, retards the evacuation of the country by the Germans, and exposes you to a new attack on their part, which they declare themselves ready to effect without mercy, if we ourselves are unable to put down the insurrection. We have listened to all the delegations which have been sent to us, and not one of them has offered conditions which did not include the abasement of the national sovereignty before revolt, the sacrifice of all liberty and of all interests.

"We have repeated to these delegations that the lives of all who lay down their arms will be spared, and that we will continue the subsidies to distressed workmen. We have promised this, we promise it again; but the insurrection must cease, for France will perish if it be prolonged.

"The government which addresses you would have wished that you should have emancipated yourselves from a few tyrants who are playing with your liberties and lives. But as you cannot, it has collected an army before your walls, an army which comes, not to conquer, but to deliver you at the cost of its blood.

"Up to the present time it has confined its attack to the outer works; the moment is now arrived when, in order to abridge your sufferings, it must attack the *enceinte* itself. It will not bombard Paris, as the Commune and the Committee of Public Safety will not fail to assert.

"A bombardment menaces the whole city, renders it uninhabitable, and its object is to intimidate the citizens and force them to a capitulation.

"The government will not fire a cannon except to force one of your gates, and will do all in its power to limit to the point attacked the ravages of a war of which it is not the author.

"It knows, it would have known even if it had not heard so from all parts, that as soon as the soldiers have crossed the *enceinte* you will rally around the national flag, in order to aid our valiant army to destroy a sanguinary and cruel tyranny.

"It depends upon you to prevent the disasters which are inseparable from an assault. You are a hundred times more numerous than the supporters of the Commune. Be united; open for us the gates which are now closed against law and order, against your prosperity and that of France. Once the gates open the cannon's voice will cease to be heard; peace, order, and abundance will enter within your walls; the Germans will evacuate our territory, and the traces of your misfortunes will be rapidly effaced; but if you do not act, the government will be compelled to take the most prompt and surest methods for your deliverance. It is due to you, but it is above all due to France, on account of the evils which beset her, because the enforced idleness which is ruining you extends to her, and is ruining her also; because she has the right to save herself, if you do not know how to save yourselves.

"Parisians, reflect seriously that in a few days we shall be in Paris. France is determined to put an end to this civil war; she will, she ought, she can; she is marching to deliver you. You can contribute to your own deliverance by rendering assault unnecessary, and by taking your place, from the present moment, amongst your fellow-citizens and your brothers."

This proclamation did but little good, as far as appeared; the peaceably inclined citizens seemed to have been struck with apathy, to have no bond of union, no capacity for action; but it must be remembered that the Commune took all possible means to prevent the circulation of the document; that even those who were against the Commune were very lukewarm friends indeed of M. Thiers and the Assembly; and, lastly, that the press, with few exceptions, had not the courage to speak out boldly.

At the period at which we are now arrived it was evident to all the world, and, doubtless, recognized by the Commune itself, that its fall must occur shortly; and it is somewhat surprising that the quarrels which now were constant amongst the leaders did not lead in one way or other to capitulation. The mass was evidently only kept from declaring against further struggle by the severe measures which were put in force against offenders. People were seized in the streets, forced to enter the ranks, and in some cases sent off at once to the forts; an instance occurred in which a young man was sent to Fort Issy, although, or perhaps because, he had a brother in the Versailles army. Atrocious as was the conduct of many of the leaders, they exhibited wonderful personal courage and devotion to the cause they had espoused; and had all been like the leaders, the task of the government in putting down the Commune would have been far more difficult than it proved to be. In its administration the Commune often committed great absurdities, passing laws which were either ridiculous in themselves or impracticable for the time, and consequently were disregarded. One day a decree was issued that the *Official Journal*, which is private property, should be sold for one *sou* instead of three; but of course it continued to be sold at the old price. The most absurd decree of all, perhaps, was that in future no workman should be fined for arriving late at his work. In the first place, when this decree was issued there were scarcely any artizans at work anywhere; and, secondly, the whole nation is so wanting in punctuality, that business would be impossible but for fines and positive regulations. The idea of manufacturers and companies not being able to enforce the attendance of their workmen and assistants is absurd enough, in a general way, but amongst the Parisians half an hour would soon grow to an hour, and the hour perhaps to two; and the acme might at last be reached by the workmen merely looking in once a week for their wages, unless, indeed, they should insist on having the money sent home to them.

It was at this time that the proposal first appeared, for destroying the front portion of the Tuileries, so as to throw the inner court, known as the Place de Carrousel, open to the Place de la Concorde and the Champs Elysées. The effect of such an arrangement would be excellent; but it is very questionable whether the destruction of the old portion of the

Tuileries was not desired more on account of its royal history than with a picturesque view. The destruction, as is well known, afterwards took place, but the fire effected more than was contemplated in the above proposal; not only the front, but one side of the building being completely burnt out. It should be noted, however, that the portions burnt did not include any of the art galleries; the whole of the destroyed portion being devoted to government offices and official residences, with the exception of the library of the Louvre, which was rich in works on art.

The freemasons of Paris made an attempt to bring about a reconciliation, but they set about it in a very odd way. About 120 masons went outside with flags and ensigns, in spite of the fire from the guns of the batteries; they then proceeded in a body towards Versailles. Five of the number were killed, and nearly the whole of the rest turned back, only three being allowed to proceed to. Versailles and see M. Thiers. It appeared that the proposed plan of conciliation included the dismissal of all the ministers who formed part of the government during the siege of Paris; that Paris should elect not only its municipal council, but also its twenty maires; and that the police should be entirely under the orders of the municipal government. Of course such a proposal was not accepted. It is said that many of the venerables of the masons protested against this step, admitting that it was the duty of masons to strive for peace and goodwill, but that they had no right to join a political party. It never seems to have struck these freemasons, that their work should have begun earlier and at home; had they in March thrown all the influence they possessed into the scale of law and order, they might have done some good; but the notion that their banners and protests would stop the action of the government when the rebellion which they supported was in full force was certainly rather puerile. It appears that, as soon as the nature of the deputation was understood, the government batteries ceased firing; and, as already stated, the deputation was received by M. Thiers, so that there was no disinclination to receive proposals for terminating the conflict.

Other attempts were made with the same view. The republican union of Havre had the curious idea of sending a delegation, inviting M. Thiers and the Assembly to put an end to civil war by the recognition of the Commune! It is needless to say what was the reply in this case. Petitions were sent in from many other places with similar proposals, but they were unceremoniously shelved by the Assembly; and upon one occasion a tremendous sensation was produced by a deputy, who rose in his place and declared that, sooner or later, the Assembly would be forced to accept a compromise; and, strange to say, many journals and well-informed persons took the same view, even at this time, when the back of the Commune was nearly broken. This mistaken view of the case arose, as did most of the errors during the siege, and as, indeed, the majority of the popular errors in France and elsewhere do arise, namely, from false news and imperfect information. The Communists believed that all France would eventually rise and declare for the Commune; the freemasons of Paris believed that all the lodges in France would respond to their appeal; while, in truth, with few exceptions, France was waiting with much coolness to see whether Paris would succeed or not, and to act accordingly afterwards.

In spite of the critical situation of the Commune at this time, in spite of the financial difficulties with which they had to contend, which crippled their action and did not allow them to buy friends, it must not be supposed that the leaders maintained the rebellion by the force of their own talents and energy alone; they had the support of a large number of the Parisians then present in Paris. A monster meeting was held in the great court of the Louvre, when the unusual spectacle of public speaking in the open air was exhibited. A resolution was passed, without any dissentient voices, approving of the programme of the Commune. There is no doubt that the Communal party was kept together principally by the false statements and atrocious arguments of the Communal press; and to give an idea of these it may be mentioned that the moderate journals, having protested against the arrest of the archbishop of Paris and the other unfortunate hostages, Rochefort, in the *Mot d'Ordre*, wrote a violent article protesting against the proposed release of the prelate. There had been many reports current of the release of the hostages, which proved false; and this article in the *Mot d'Ordre* made the blood run cold in honest men's veins, though few believed that the threatened assassinations would ever be carried into effect.

It must also, in justice, not be forgotten that the friends of order were seriously menaced, and had little chance of expressing their opinions. In one day, at this period, the Commune suppressed one journal, the *Pays*, tried to arrest the editor, caused the disappearance of a second paper, the *Messager*, and attacked a third. On the next day the last-named paper, the *Soir*, and *La Paix*, were also suppressed. This was the work of Raoul Rigault, the procureur-général, one of the most violent of the Communists.

The difficulties of the Commune had now reached a climax, and the natural effect in such cases—internal quarrels—occurred constantly. When severe reverses are suffered generals are often charged with treason, and General Cluseret was no more fortunate than his colleagues. He was arrested, charged with being a Bonapartist, and with designs of making himself dictator. But the Commune did not stop there. It dismissed the whole cabinet, or rather the executive commission, which consisted of one delegate from each of the ministries, and handed the power over to a Committee of Public Safety, consisting of five members—Antoine Arnaud, Léo Meillet, Rauvier, Jules Girardin, and Félix Pyat.

The title of this new authority was alone enough to make people shudder. Committees of public safety have always characterized the most lawless and dangerous periods of revolution and tyranny. People felt and said that a new reign of terror had been inaugurated, and unfortunately the ill-sounding epithet turned out to be only too appropriate. The following sketch by an English correspondent who had an interview with Reynard, the second in power at the prefecture of police, supplies an illustration:—"He seemed to me the very embodiment of the legendary revolutionist—a tall, handsome man, with a pale face, long flowing hair, almost hanging over his shoulders, a menacing moustache, a determined frown, and hands which grasped nervously at any document or paper likely to assist the cause he loves. Round his waist he wore a broad band of blue silk, surmounted by a narrow scarf of red. The blue tunic of the national guard, and a collar embroidered with gold lace, completed the costume, which impressed me with the idea that the days of 1793 had returned."

The appointment of this Committee of Public Safety was not made without a violent conflict within the Commune, and twenty-three of its members voted against the proposal, so that the former commenced its career with a most dangerous body of enemies close at its elbow.

That a reign of terror had already set in was scarcely an exaggeration; the arrest and imprisonment of General Martimprey helped to prove it. The general was governor of the Invalides, and a man of ninety years of age, paralytic, and for some time almost bedridden; this poor man was brutally arrested and confined in a cell in the Conciergerie ("in a cold, damp cell," say the accounts, but that is doubtless a mere bit of newspaper phraseology), for the simple reason that he was the brother of General Martimprey who took an active part in the massacre of 2nd December, 1851. The destruction of a chapel erected to the memory of General Bréa, who was basely shot in 1848 when entreating a body of revolutionists already surrounded by the troops to lay down their arms, and whose fall created a great sensation at the time, is another instance of the violent spirit of the Commune. This chapel was declared to be a "permanent insult to the conquered of June, 1848, and to the men who fell for the cause of the people." The man who killed the general, a fellow named Nourri, who should have been shot, was sent to Cayenne, and the Commune said, "He has been kept there twenty-two years for the execution of the traitor Bréa," and ordered with characteristic swagger that he should be set at liberty as soon as possible. It was remarked at the time that some of the Commune were far more likely to join Nourri at Cayenne than to welcome him to Paris.

The relations of the Communist leaders are not badly illustrated by what is probably a mere newspaper story, namely, that when Cluseret arrived in his cell at Mazas he found the following inscription on the wall:—"Citizen Cluseret, you have confined me here; I expect you will follow me in a week.—General Bergeret." Another member of the Commune, Colonel Boursier, was also arrested. Amidst all the violence and recrimination it is pleasant to find one example of conscientiousness and liberality; all kinds of charges had been made against Cluseret, but his successor Colonel Rossel wrote to one of the papers clearing Cluseret of the imputation of having tried to provoke a rebellion against the Commune when he found he had lost popularity. This trait adds to the pain that one feels that such a man as Rossel should have thrown away his life in such a cause.

One of the most absurd, painfully comic announcements appeared about this time, to the effect that as soon as a convenient place of meeting could be found the sittings of the Commune would take place in public.

A rumour was afloat at this period that the Prussian General Fabrice had declared to M. Jules Favre that the prolonged occupation would add seriously to the German costs; and that Prussia would be compelled to enter Paris and put an end to the existing state of things, either with or without the concurrence of the French government. It does not appear that there was any truth in this rumour, but it was widely credited, and, strange to say, the great mass of respectable people seemed to regard the possibility of such an event with satisfaction rather than the reverse, so much had the feeling altered within a few weeks; so much worse than foreign occupation is intestine war! It must be remembered, however, that the peaceful portion of the population was worn out, impoverished, subdued; and no wonder, considering that it had been shut in, almost constantly, for seven months. It would have subdued, or maddened, almost any nation, and it was torture to the impatient Parisians; they had been half starved for months, and now, though provisions were not actually wanting, their means of life had been terribly diminished; there was little trade going on, no foreign or provincial money coming in, no gaiety, and no repose. No wonder if the entering Germans had even been hailed by all but the "reds" with gratitude, concealed, if not expressed.

Provisions were running rather scarce, and fears were at one time entertained that the supplies would be cut off altogether; the number of head of cattle at the market was not half the usual amount, and the entrance of 600 bullocks by the German lines created quite a sensation. There never was any actual scarcity during the Commune as during the siege, but vegetables and many other things were dear and sometimes scarce; milk failed early, the cows being few and fodder rare; the condensed milk was eagerly bought up, and the stock as quickly exhausted; it all went, Anglo-Swiss, Irish, and Aylesbury. It was the same in the case of preserved meats, *extractum carnis*, and all the preserved, potted, pickled meats and vegetables from all quarters of the world; and the siege and the Commune will have madi, more people acquainted with English, Scotch, and Irish stores than twenty years of free trade, free intercourse, and the freest puffing would have done: so true is it that the nearest way to a man's heart is through his stomach. Sheridan, or some other wit, said, "Give us our luxuries, and we will take care of the necessaries of life;" but in Paris the necessaries had become luxuries, and doubled the force of the demand. When the Commune was at an end, and we once more met at well-furnished tables, and could command any delicacy within our means, the sensation was quite curious. We had had a lesson in social science, which, let us hope, we may not soon forget. While on this phase of the subject, it may be remarked how little illness there was in Paris and Versailles, except in the military hospitals; we had been terrified by prophecies of pestilence after famine, but there was nothing of the kind; the health of the city was peculiarly good. There was, however, one painful explanation of the fact, namely, that the aged, the ailing, the weak, and the young had fallen during the last months of the siege at a frightful rate; disease had tougher materials to deal with than usual, and, moreover, when the incubus disappeared men were compelled to exert themselves, and exertion was positive recreation after the dull monotony of the past months.

We have spoken above of some of the absurd decrees of the Commune; let us in fairness note one of the follies of the government and the Assembly. M. Dufaure, the minister of Justice, introduced a bill for punishing as receivers of stolen goods any person who should purchase property confiscated by the Commune. Some few only of the deputies protested against what is equivalent to setting aside the orders of the House of Commons on the score of "urgency," on the ground that laws of exception passed on the spur of the moment were generally unjust; but the mass adopted the useless project almost unanimously. While the Assembly was passing the above law, the Commune on its part decreed the entire abolition of all political oaths.

About the same period General Rossel published an order that no horses should be allowed to leave Paris, except for military duty. The preceding acts of authority troubled few people, but Rossel's order produced a panic. "Are we to be rationed on horse flesh again?" was the universal inquiry.

Numerous appeals were now made both to the Assembly and the Commune for an armistice or truce. The Union Republican League sent addresses to both parties, imploring them to agree to a truce for twenty days, during which time arrangements might be made to put an end to the fratricidal struggle. The women of Paris placarded the streets to the same effect, and the freemasons of Havre and Fécamp drew up addresses to M. Thiers and the Commune, imploring them in the name of humanity to suspend hostilities and open negotiations. These appeals were supported by the most respectable journals in Paris, and even M. Félix Pyat wrote to M. Thiers, stating that he was ready for conciliatory steps. The only effect all this produced was a violent article in the *Official* (Communal) *Journal*, and a declaration of Paschal Grousset that it was high time for the Commune to have done with conciliation and conciliators, that it had had enough of both. As the temper of the government and the Assembly was much the same as that of the Commune and M. Grousset, the advocates of conciliation were silenced. This was effected in part by the suppression of more journals; the whole number put down by the Commune were said at this period to approach twenty.

It seems very curious to talk of a grand concert at the Tuileries amid such scenes as were going on around, yet such an entertainment really took place on Sunday, the 17th of May; and the state apartments, the court, and the gardens were thronged with a dense mass of people. The concert was not classical, far from it; but the music was lively, and the Parisians made a *fête* of the affair, which was for the benefit of the sufferers in the war. The proceeds amounted to nearly £500, which, under the circumstances, must be regarded as a grand success. It was a great thing for the Commune to find amusement for the people. The music was heard well in what used to be the emperor's private garden, and the thousands outside the building thus had their part in the concert. With the same view, the leaders of the Commune patronized the theatres, sat in the late imperial box, some dressed in irreproachable evening costume, others in republican finery, and others again in glaringly vulgar clothes, perhaps assumed for the sake of popularity. The Park of Monceaux and some other gardens, long closed, were also reopened, to the great delight of nurses, children, and old people. These were not all the amusements offered to the people; the churches of Saint Eustache and Saint Germain l'Auxerrois were devoted to public meetings, and from the pulpits of these two fine old edifices were uttered some of the most horribly blasphemous discourses that ever escaped from human lips, while amongst the most violent of the speakers, and the most turbulent in the audiences, were troops of women. The scenes in these churches surpassed description; hundreds of filthy, dissipated wretches of both sexes, smoking, singing, swearing, drinking, and sometimes dancing together, presenting orgies that could scarcely be surpassed by any of the descriptions of Eugène Sue, or other able delineator of the foulest assemblages of bygone times.

In order further to please the million, the Commune ordered that all pledges at the Mont de Piété—the governmental and only pawnshop in Paris—not exceeding twenty francs in amount, should be restored to the owners upon their proving their identity.

A very ominous announcement appeared in the *Official Journal* over the signature of the prefect of police, to the effect that no anonymous denunciations would be attended to. This went far to show that the infamous system of secret accusation had been resorted to, and it was well known that the prisons were crowded with "hostages "and "suspects," or, in other words, political opponents; but the announcement was read in the worst sense, as all official notices are in Paris, whether under Dictator, King, or Commune, and was construed into an invitation of signed accusations. Such a hint gave to the Committee of Public Safety a hideous resemblance to its predecessors, which were as inquisitorial as the secret council of Venice or the dreadful Spanish tribunal. It was asserted that General Cluseret had succeeded in obtaining the liberation of the unhappy archbishop of Paris; but this was found to be incorrect, and it was known that the number of so-called hostages had been increased, so that the significance of this notice assumed a very terrible character. In connection with the persecution of political opponents, it may be mentioned that at this period it was declared and pretty generally believed that the Commune had the intention of suppressing nil the political journals except the *Official*, which was in their hands. Such an act might be excusable under certain circumstances, and would be far less unjust than the suppression of opposition journals only; but the Commune, like all French governments, kept to the latter system to the end.

During the beginning of the month of May the Versailles generals gradually perfected their plans, and drew the line around the city tighter and closer. Failing to silence the forts of Issy and Vanves, and repulsed in an assault on the former, powerful batteries were formed on the heights commanding the forts, generally on the very spots selected by the Germans, and often partly constructed with the fascines and gabions, of which they had left an immense stock unused. Some of these batteries contained seventy and even eighty guns, many being ship guns of great calibre. As many as ten of these batteries poured their converging fires into the fort of Issy. In addition to this, several gun-boats made their appearance on the Seine. The Commune had also a few gun-boats on the river, and one of these was sunk by shells from a battery. The positions of the insurgents around Issy, as already stated, were taken at the end of April, and subsequently several other redoubts and positions were wrested from them, either by force or stratagem. In some cases considerable numbers of prisoners were secured, and it was declared on the part of the Commune that they were shot without mercy. Some cases of summary execution undoubtedly happened; but there is no reason to doubt the assertion officially made afterwards, that with the exception of acts committed in the heat of the moment, no prisoners were executed otherwise than by the order of properly constituted courts-martial. It is notorious, however, that masses of prisoners were marched to Versailles in the most lamentable condition, wounded, footsore, and without food, and that they were grossly insulted by ferocious crowds, who heaped all kinds of indignities upon them: but civil war is always the most horrible, and the exasperation of the people, although to be regretted, can scarcely be blamed severely. On the 1st of May the Versailles troops had advanced to within 200 yards of the entrenchments of Fort Issy, although at the same time they had suffered repulses at other points. Fort Issy was in a very dilapidated condition, the casemates and nearly all the constructions around destroyed, and half the guns, originally sixty in number, dismounted. The case, in fact, was so bad that the garrison, which numbered 300, was seized with panic, declared that it could no longer hold the fort, refused to obey the orders of the Commandant Mégy, spiked some of the guns, and quitted the place. Had this state of things been known to the government generals, they might at once have marched in and taken possession, but this was not to be. Mégy proceeded to Paris, and surrendered himself a prisoner. General Cluseret, advised of this state of things, sent fresh troops into the fort, and the firing recommenced. Strange to say, immediately after this occurrence Cluseret himself was arrested, as already stated, and the afterwards famous Rossel was appointed delegate for war, with La Cécilia as commandant of Fort Issy. One way of accounting for the fort not being assaulted as soon as the firing ceased was, that the Versaillais believed the place had been mined, and that the retreat of the Communists was only a trap; but this could hardly have been the case.

As Colonel Rossel from this time was the most prominent figure in the Commune, and in fact the only man of real mark that the insurrection produced, it will be well to give a few particulars respecting him. He was born at Saint Brieue in Brittany in 1844, and was consequently only twenty-seven years of age; his mother's maiden name was Campbell, so that he was half Scotch in blood. Rossel was a slight man of middle height, with fair hair and small beard, wore glasses, had a very deliberate, reserved, yet self-confident air, and had altogether far more the air of an English, Scotch, or Prussian officer than a French one; in fact, he was as unlike the common type of the last as possible. He had a hatred of show and ceremony, dressed in the simplest manner, and was altogether a man of decided mark. He spoke English perfectly, and was well acquainted with British history, habits, and opinions. About twelve years ago he graduated at the Ecole Polytechnique, being second in a long list of candidates for commissions, and on leaving that establishment joined the engineers, in which he obtained the rank of captain. When Gambetta became the virtual dictator of France, Rossel went to Tours and asked for a command. The delegate minister of War was pleased with Rossel's republican notions, and at once promoted him to the rank of colonel, intrusting him with an important and delicate mission on the Loire. When peace was proclaimed Rossel sought an interview with M. Thiers, and asked him for employment, offering to resign the rank he held as colonel if the new government would promote him to be *chef de bataillon*, or major, in his own corps. But those who had been favoured by Gambetta were not looked upon with much love by M. Thiers, and Kossel's request was refused. His pride was wounded at the idea of having to go back to the rank o: captain, so he resigned the service, and, happening to be in Paris on the 18th March, offered his sword to the Commune. He was accepted, and at once promoted to the rank of colonel.

The young Bonaparte once offered his sword to Great Britain; had it been accepted, what a change might have been produced in the history of Europe! Had M. Thiers accepted young Rossel's services the Commune would have lost, and the government gained, a well instructed and clever officer, and poor Rossel himself, perhaps, would have risen to an eminent position.

Had the Commune ever a chance of success this Committee of Public Safety would have ruined it. One of its acts was the appointment of one Moreau civil commissioner to the delegate of war, or, in other words, a person of their selection to look after Rossel, who, however, does not seem to have troubled himself about him.

Another member of the Commune who showed much ability was the delegate of finance, Jourde, whose balance sheet to the end of April showed that in forty days the expenditure had amounted to rather more than £1,000,000 sterling, or £28,000 a day. The revenue from octroi duties, tobacco, stamps, and other sources, was more than £300,000 less than the expenditure, and this deficiency was made up by loans from the Bank of France. The balance sheet only shows about £357 for seizures, all of which was taken from priests and religious bodies. After the 1st of May Jourde obtained more than £40,000 from the railway companies. The balance sheet surprised everybody, and certainly showed great ability on the part of the delegate Jourde. He showed his force of character by resigning his position on the appointment of the Committee of Public Safety, declaring that he would not consent to be the servant of that committee, as the finance minister was a member of, and only responsible to, the executive committee. The consequence was that his resignation was accepted, but he was immediately re-elected, almost unanimously, and assured that the new committee would have nothing to do with finance.

About this time batteries opened at Montmartre, and the cannonading became more terrible and continued than had before been witnessed. The thundering of the guns was constant night and day. The government, on its side, attacked the western portion of the city with great determination; half Neuilly was burnt, and all that part of Paris within reach of the Versailles batteries pelted with shot and shell without cessation; M. Thiers' promise not to bombard the city had been forgotten!

One of the terrible features of the second siege of Paris was the frequency of the fires caused by the shells from Versailles batteries. In the midst of the horrid monotony of the cannonading, suddenly the people would be startled by a noise of a different kind, or by the sky becoming vividly illuminated. The general impression was—that which was generally hoped for—namely, that the assault had taken place at last, and that delivery was at hand. Frequently these explosions and fires were the result of a shell having entered a powder magazine, but more often the lurid glare was caused by some large factory or other establishment being in a blaze. It was not uncommon to see two or more fires raging at once; in one case, at least, there were three large conflagrations going on at the same moment. When these occurrences took place the scene was terrible. As the flames mounted in the air dense masses of smoke would hang over the city, the smoke of one being lighted up most fantastically by the flames of another. Drums and bugles were heard to sound, the bells of the churches rang out the tocsin in discordant notes, masses of soldiers and firemen tramped past for the scene of the disaster; and amid all this, regardless of the accident, regardless of the danger to human life, as of day or night, week-day or Sunday, the cannon continued to roar, and the balls and shells to rain upon the devoted city. Horrible comment on the civilization of the nineteenth century of the Christian era! The month of May rose brightly on Paris, and such were the scenes with which the coming spring was welcomed!

The government forces having obtained possession of all the positions around Issy, set to work systematically to cut it off from Paris by means of a trench, while a second trench was formed for the assault. On one occasion the Communist soldiers surprised eighty of the sappers and miners, and made prisoners of them. Their fate was never known, but it is scarcely doubtful. It must be remembered with regard to the defence of Fort Issy, that the insurgents still possessed the next fort, that of Vanves, which constantly shelled the men employed in the trenches.

When Rossel assumed the chief military command, a decree was issued which divided the national guards into two armies, one commanded by 'General Dombrowski, the other by General Wroblowski, both Poles. From this moment a great change took place. Dombrowski ordered the rest of the inhabitants to quit Neuilly, and took up a strong position there; and Rossel immediately commenced the formation of the last lines of defence, inner barricades, which were constructed with singular ability and rapidity.

The following summons, with Rossel's reply, will serve to give a fair idea of the character of the man:—

"In the name and by order of the field-marshal commanding-in-chief, we summon the commandant of the insurgent forces at present in Fort Issy to surrender himself and all his troops in the fort. A delay of a quarter of an hour will be granted to answer the summons. If the commandant of the insurgent forces declares in writing for himself, and in the name of the entire garrison of Fort Issy, that he obeys the present summons, without other conditions than that of saving their lives and liberties on condition of not residing in Paris, this favour will be granted. If the commandant fails to reply in the space of time indicated, the whole garrison will be shot."

To which Rossel replied:—

"MY DEAR COMRADE,—Next time you permit yourself to send us a summons so insolent as that in your handwriting yesterday, I will have your parlementaire shot, in accordance with the usages of war.—Your devoted comrade,

"ROSSEL."

As an element in the history of the Commune, it will be well to state what was the force at its command at this period; the muster roll was published in the *Official Journal,* and included twenty-four marching and twenty-five sedentary legions; the real fact, however, was stated by a well-informed person to be that there were, except on paper, no more than twenty legions of each class. The marching legions consisted of 3655 commissioned officers, of whom only 3413 answered to the call; and 96,325 non-commissioned officers and privates, of whom only 84,986 answered the call at this time. The real force for duty outside the walls of Paris was therefore at this period, in round numbers, not much more than 88,000 in all. The total number of available sedentary guards was about 77,600. The value of these forces, except for service behind walls, was admitted by the Communists themselves to be very various; many of the corps were unsteady, while some who behaved well one day would exhibit great want of discipline on another; it was, however, recognized on all hands that the new commandant, Colonel Rossel, thoroughly understood the nature of the troops with which he had to deal, and was reorganizing the whole with extraordinary ability.

Issy fell at last into the hands of the government troops on the 9th of May, and on that same evening M. Thiers issued a circular on the subject, the purport of which was as follows:—The able direction of the army and bravery of the troops have obtained a brilliant result. After only eight days' attack Fort Issy was occupied by us. We found a quantity of ammunition and artillery. Fort Vanves cannot resist much longer; and, moreover, the conquest of Fort Issy is alone sufficient to assure the plan of attack laid down. Fort Vanves did, however, hold out for nearly another week.

In the same circular we have an account of the commencement of the actual attack of the fortifications. It appears that General Douay on the same night, under cover of the batteries of Montretout and the darkness, crossed the Seine and established himself in front of Boulogne, opposite the fortifications: 1400 men from several corps commenced a trench at ten o'clock and worked all night till daylight. At four in the morning they were covered from the fire of the enemy, and at a distance of only 300 yards from the fortifications, where, if necessary, a breaching battery could be established. M. Thiers completed his circular in the following terms, intended as a warning to the departments to which it was addressed:—

"Everything makes us hope that the cruel sufferings of the honest population of Paris are drawing to their close, and that the odious reign of the infamous faction which has taken the red flag for its emblem, will very soon cease to oppress and dishonour the capital of France.

"It is to be hoped that passing events will serve as a lesson to the miserable imitators of the Commune of Paris, and will prevent their exposing themselves to the legal severities which await them if they dare to push further their criminal and ridiculous enterprises."

When the attack on the ramparts commenced the guns of Mont Valérien and Montretout opened a tremendous bombardment on the Point du Jour and Auteuil; the guns on the ramparts answered sharply, until they were silenced by the superior weight of metal on the other side. The most fearful excitement now occurred; the inhabitants of Auteuil fled into Paris in the utmost consternation, with what little of their property they could carry, feeling convinced that the district would very shortly be in the hands of the government troops; at the same time many battalions of Communist guards were marched to the support of those on the ramparts. The scene was one of the direst confusion and terror, and everyone was surprised when the bombardment suddenly ceased; it was explained afterwards that the Versailles authorities caused the firing to be stopped, in order to see the effect on the Parisians of the proclamation addressed to them by M. Thiers on May 9, and which is given above. But there was no organization of the friends of peace and order; no one dared to bell the cat, and so the work of destruction recommenced and was carried on to its bitter end. It must be repeated also, in addition, that there were few in Paris who had any love for M. Thiers' government; the chief did not profess to be republican, and the acts of the Versailles authorities were generally regarded as neither liberal nor energetic, and as usual, party feeling shut out political common sense.

The Commune had apparently no fear of the effect of M. Thiers' address, for it published it in the *Official Journal*, and although copied into all the other papers, and backed by the fact of the taking of Fort Issy, it produced no impression but that of its own weakness and glaring misrepresentations.

When Issy fell the committee tried to deny the fact for a day or two; but Rossel wrote a letter to the Commune in which he denounced with the utmost bitterness the mischievous interference of different authorities, and tendered his resignation. He commenced by stating that he could not any longer endure the responsibility of commanding where every one discussed, but no one obeyed. Nothing was yet organized in the military services, and the management of the guns rested upon a few volunteers, the number of whom was insufficient. The central committee forced upon him its co-operation in the organization of the guards, which he accepted, but nothing had been done by it. He said he would have punished the enemy for his adventurous attacks upon Issy, had he had even the smallest force at his disposal. The garrison were bad and badly commanded, and the officers drove away Captain Dumont, an energetic man who had come to command them. He continued as follows:—"Yesterday, when every one ought to have been working or under fire, the chiefs of the legions were discussing the substitution of a new system of organization for mine. My indignation brought them to their senses, and they promised me that they would not again take a similar course. An organized force of 12,000 men with which I engaged to march against the enemy was to have been summoned at 11 a.m., and now 1.30 p.m. has come, and there are only about 1000 men ready. Thus, the incapacity of the committee has hindered the organization of artillery, the vacillation of the central committee stops the organization of men, and the petty preoccupations of the chiefs of the legions paralyze mobilization. I am not a man to recoil before repression; and yesterday, while the chiefs were discussing, an execution party awaited them in the yard. I have two lines to choose—to break through the obstacles impeding my course of action, or to retire. I cannot break through the obstacles, because the obstacles are your weakness. Nor will I attack the sovereignty of the people. I retire, and I have the honour to demand of you a cell in Mazas."

This is the language of a man; and every one applauded, except M. Félix Pyat, who declared in his paper, that if Rossel had not sufficient power to confine, nor intelligence to keep the central committee to its purely administrative functions, it was not the fault of the Committee of Public Safety. But M. Pyat was one of that very committee! All that can be deduced from the above is, that the whole of the affairs of the Commune, military and civil, were in a hopeless condition. One result of Rossel's letter was that the Committee of Public Safety was requested to resign, which it did, and a new one was elected, consisting of Jauvier, Antoine, Arnaud, Gambon, Eudes, and Delescluse.

On the other hand, Rochefort and others openly advocated the appointment of Rossel, or some other person, as dictator. The salvation of the Commune depended on it, they said, and there was not a day to lose. True enough: but what difference would the appointment of a dictator have made? Rochefort was one who was clever at destruction, but his advice and attempts at construction were always utterly worthless.

The League of the Republican Union still tried to bring about reconciliation. It asked the Commune to recognize the republic, and it implored the government to grant Paris full municipal rights. It was evident that the appeal was now too late, yet every approach towards, or exhibition of a desire for reconciliation, tended to appease the violence of party feeling and helped to break the fall; but M. Pyat, again, was of a different opinion, and in his paper denounced every attempt of the kind. Next to Rochefort, Pyat has perhaps contributed more than any other man to render liberal government almost impossible in France; but he exceeded even him, in the mischievous lolly which he exhibited during the last days of the Commune, when nothing was to be gained, and much injury could be and was done by such journals as that of Pyat's. They helped to blind the leaders as well as the Communists in general, and led them on to absolute destruction.

Rossel's resignation led to his arrest; he was accused of treachery to the Commune, in having publicly announced the capture of Fort Issy without the permission of the Committee of Public Safety. He was given in charge to Girardin, one of that very body; but strange to say, prisoner and keeper escaped together from the Hôtel de Ville. Bergeret was ordered to arrest them. Here we have an example of the extraordinary doings of the Commune. Bergeret, Cluseret, and Rossel, follow each other in command of the forces, and as prisoners; and the first is set to catch the last, who has run off with his keeper, who was formerly one of the very body against which he specially complained.

Rigault furnished his enemies with another proof, or at least good reason for believing, that the prisons had been filled in a very irregular manner, by the publication of an order to the effect that no one was to be confined unless an official report detailing the alleged offences of the accused, with the names and addresses of the witnesses, were lodged at the clerk's office of the prison by the citizen making the arrest. Such documents gave point to epigrams like the following: "The Commune consists of a number of violent persons who are always arresting one another."

The Committee of Public Safety was the body that ordered M. Thiers' house to be destroyed, and this act was drawn up in a perfectly regular manner. The precious document ran as follows: "The Committee of Public Safety, considering that the proclamation of M. Thiers declares that the army will not bombard Paris, while every day women and children fall victims to the fratricidal projectiles of Versailles, and that it makes an appeal to treason in order to enter Paris, feeling it to be impossible to vanquish its heroic population by force of arms, orders that the goods and property of M. Thiers be seized by the administration of the Domains, and his house in the Place St. Georges be razed to the ground. Citizens Fontaine, delegate of the Domains, and Andrieux, delegate of the Public Service, are charged with the immediate execution of the present decree." This order, as it is well known, was duly carried out. The property within the house was not destroyed. The books were conveyed to one of the public libraries; the collection of works of art, which was of considerable value, was housed at the Tuileries; the linen was handed over to the army surgeons to be used in the hospitals, and the furniture was ordered to be sold. As to the house itself, it was proposed to set fire to it; but as it did not stand alone the commissaire of the police of the quarter pointed out the danger of such a project in a rather dense part of the city, and accordingly it was systematically pulled down. Rochefort was one who saw the folly of this proceeding, and he said in his journal that the Assembly would of course compensate M. Thiers for the loss. But the Communists knew that the latter set great store by his collections—who at the age of seventy does not worship his *lares et penates?*—and that the destruction would give him and his wife, and her sister, who lived under the same roof, great pain; so the well-known modest hotel was destroyed. As to the treasures, they were, as we have said, deposited in the Tuileries, which fact would go towards proving that M. Courbet, the artist who had the charge of the artistic property, did not intend, although he had advocated it, to destroy the palace. When the fire happened there, these treasures were destroyed with the rest. Only one single object is known to be saved, and to that a curious interest attaches. It is a small Etruscan urn of terra-cotta, which in spite of its brittleness remains intact, and the surface of which has become glazed by the lead or other substance melted upon it during the conflagration. A curious relique of M. Thiers' collection of objects of art!

The condition of the press in Paris at this period was very curious. Only two or three of the old established journals continued to appear in their ordinary form, and some of these exhibited curious internal changes; but in spite of all the suppressions, in spite of the danger of saying a word against the grand philosophic government of the people, 'the Commune, the number of newspapers was not decreased; on the contrary, they seemed to multiply. Suppression became a farce in most cases. If you asked for one paper the newswoman presented you with a similar one, kindly informing you that the *Bien Public*, or some other paper, was suppressed, and that the one she offered you came from the same office; it was, in fact, the same paper with the title changed, and this went on for some time, the Commune having far too much else to attend to, to look sharply after the slippery journalists. It is always remarkable with what apparent ease new journals are started in Paris, and it was more than usually so during the siege and the Commune. It was simply a question of supply and demand. People had very little to do, were thirsty for news, and had little money to spend; so dozens of halfpenny journals sprang up and found tens of thousands of readers. These literary mushrooms will certainly form one of the most curious collections of materials for the history of France, such as they are, for future students. They will not add much to the reputation of the Paris press; but they will supply a collection of the most vituperative and scandalous libels and atrocious calumnies that have appeared in the present century.

It would be interesting to give a few extracts from these ephemeral journals, but they would lose half their character in an English dress, and many of the most characteristic are totally unfit for reproduction. The proposals of some of the writers would seem to have emanated from the brain of fiends rather than men. The *Père Duchesne*, a paper named after one of the most sanguinary of the old revolutionary prints, was foremost of its class. Its gods seem to have been Robespierre and Marat, the hideous wretch who fell by the hand of Charlotte Corday; and it recommended strongly the guillotine and reign of terror as the best means of bringing about liberty, equality, and fraternity! These incendiary writers took great care of their own carcases when the crash, or rather before the actual crash arrived, and many of them are now haunting the neighbourhood of Leicester Square and Soho, and vainly striving to earn bread and cheese, and at the same time to revolutionize England with their disgusting journals, in which honourable men, because they are of a different way of thinking to the writers, are stigmatized by the most filthy epithets in every article. These dirty little sheets will meet the fate they deserve, but they will do good during their short lives. They will make known the wretched *animus* of the scribes who hounded thousands on to their death or destruction, and were the first to fly from the dangers they had helped to create. To repress these wretched prints would indeed be a mistake, for they are of real value as mirrors to show people what class of men these would-be Marats of the nineteenth century are, and how they would construe liberty, equality, and fraternity.

The terror which is recommended by the writers above mentioned had actually begun to hover over Paris. The arrests had become numerous and constant, the search for members of the national guard who declined to serve the Commune was now pursued with energy, and every unfortunate man who was caught was immediately sent off to one of the forts or other dangerous position. Of course, all who could manage it deserted immediately, and thus the numbers of the Communal forces were constantly dwindling, in spite of the impressment. The deserters were not, however, confined to the pressed men; many others also went over to Versailles. One instance may be specially mentioned. A young officer was sent by Rossel with a flag of truce and a despatch. On delivering it he declared that he had no knowledge of the contents, and that he preferred being kept as a prisoner to being sent back to Paris. All this shows how near the cause of the Commune was to its end. In the meantime the terror was increased. Cournet, who had been at the head of the police, was found too easy, and therefore Ferré was appointed in his place. The ferocious character of this man is well known, and he has paid the penalty of his crimes. His great friend, the fierce Raoul Rigault, once gave proof of a less sanguinary nature than has been attributed to him. Schoelcher, one of the deputies of Paris, had been arrested, but was set free after two days' confinement; Rigault announcing to him in a letter that he was free, and adding that he had thought of detaining him as hostage against Edward Lockroy, who was in the hands of the Versailles authorities, but on second thoughts did not see that one absurdity could be properly answered by another. The unfortunate archbishop of Paris and the other hostages found no pity in the eyes of the Ferrés and the Rigaults.

Another act of the Commune was the establishment of a police. It was one of their grand principles that "the safety of the city was to be left for evermore in the hands of the national guards;" now they found out that a police was necessary, and a decree was issued in which it was stated that the Jews, the Athenians, the Spartans, and the Romans all found police necessary, and so the great French Federal Communal government must also have its police! In connection with police regulations, it may be mentioned that all citizens were obliged to provide themselves with cards, in imitation of the *cartes civiques* of 1790, on which was to be inscribed the name and address of the bearer, with full particulars, attested by the municipal authorities. Any national guard, or apparently, any one else, had the right to demand to see any one's card on any occasion. All this was said to be in consequence of a great secret conspiracy; but more probably it was simply the result of the terror of the Communists themselves, who felt that every honest man must be their enemy, and thoroughly mistrusted each other. Arrests were made in all directions. Colonel Masson, lately appointed chief of the staff of the war office, and dozens of other officials, were thrown into prison.

The financial question also began to press most seriously upon the Commune. The offices of more than one of the financial societies were invaded, and the seal of the Commune affixed to the safes in which the cash was deposited. It did not appear that any of the property was removed. Next the Bank of France was invaded by the national guards, in spite of all the efforts of M. Beslay, who was the Communist delegate to the bank, and who had very cleverly managed to prevent its treasuries being ransacked. No money was taken, but M. Beslay immediately gave in his resignation as a member of the Commune. The bank at this time contained three milliards (£120,000,000) in securities, a milliard in metal belonging to the state, a milliard composing the fortune of ninety families, and a milliard in bank-notes. M. Jourde, the Communist Finance Minister, also exercised the full weight of his influence to prevent the bank from being pillaged.

As soon as the government had got possession of Fort Issy, in which were a hundred guns and loads of ammunition, the guns were turned against its neighbour, Fort Vanves, which suffered greatly; rockets were also thrown into it and set the buildings on fire; the barracks were thus destroyed. A vigorous bombardment was then maintained all along the lines; not only were all the gates of the fortification shelled, but also the barricade in advance of the Arc de Triomphe. This and other barricades, such as one by the arch itself, and others in the Place Vendôme, the Rue de la Paix, by the Tuileries, &c., were constructed with uncommon care in the manner adopted by the engineers during the siege of Paris. They were composed of fascines and small sacks filled with sand, and everything was finished off in the most elaborate manner, giving the barricades almost a theatrical air. It must not, however, be understood from this that they were toy-works; it was only the outward appearance that was toy-like. On the contrary, they were admirable earthworks, designed and executed in the best manner; and armed as they were with beautiful breach-loading bronze guns and mitrailleuses, might have given the troops immense difficulty. But in a large city like Paris, at least on the outer circle, the number of such barricades, to be of any service, must be immense; the line must be almost continuous, or they are easily turned. When this is not the case the enemy can choose his mode of attack, and circumvent obstacles.

On the night of the 13th of May Fort Vanves was in the hands of the government troops. In the case of Fort Issy the insurgents had abandoned the place so secretly, that the Versailles generals were not aware of the fact until they approached and found it empty. The garrison of Vanves found its way back into Paris through subterranean passages leading to the Catacombs. A miserable spectacle they presented, worn-out with long service in the fort, having spent the night in their subterranean retreat, without arms or caps, their clothes torn, their hands and faces begrimed with dirt, frequently mixed with blood, foot-sore and famished, they were indeed objects of pity, and all the more so, from the fact that their escape was not to freedom, but into a trap; they merely dragged their wearied bodies from a lost fort into a barred city, with no prospect but death or imprisonment. As an instance of the tactics of the Commune, it may be mentioned that for two days the *Official Journal* tried to hide the fact of the fall of Vanves, and declared that the Versailles troops had made an attack and been repulsed with great loss, on the night after that in which it had been abandoned by the Communists! However, the Communists were not the inventors of false reports. Fort Vanves was boldly defended, but the shelling and burning of the buildings created a terrible panic, and it was said that all the garrison except 150 men abandoned the place; these fought gallantly for a long time, but were at last compelled to retire. When the Versailles troops succeeded in establishing themselves there, on the 14th of May, they found only a few insurgents and thirty corpses. There were in the fort fifty guns and eight mortars, some provisions, and an electric wire by which the fort was to have been blown up. A place called the Seminary, near Issy, was taken on the previous day, when a hundred of the insurgents were killed and several hundreds more taken prisoners.

As already stated, the shelling of the ramparts began as soon as Fort Issy was taken, and after Vanves fell and the trenches were opened around the Boisde Boulogne the effects soon became serious, and could no longer be concealed. The bastions at the Point du Jour and Auteuil had become untenable; the casemates were destroyed by shells, which also began to fall a mile within the fortifications, so that the neighbourhood was soon deserted by the Communists, as well as by the unfortunate inhabitants. The attack was carried on simultaneously on two sides of the city, by Auteuil and Passy, and by Clichy, where a pontoon bridge was thrown across the river; several of the barricades just outside Paris were also taken. Squadrons of cavalry had been stationed all round the city, and fighting was going on at a dozen points near the walls.

In order to meet this state of things the Communists formed more barricades. One behind the Arc de Triomphe was guarded by six cannons and four mortars; a large number of guns and mitrailleuses—more than sixty, it is said—were placed in battery on Montmartre. The most feverish excitement was evident everywhere. Detachments of guards paraded all the streets of Paris; and such was the distrust of the sedentary national guards, that the battalions were ordered to do duty at a point far away from the quarter of the city to which they belonged, lest they should desert, which they had commenced doing to a large extent. The quarters which were mistrusted were watched by franc-tireurs; every person was suspected; no one could pass into or out of Paris without being examined; and even omnibuses and cabs were stopped in the streets and their occupants interrogated. Never were distrust and anxiety more plainly evidenced. Numerous arrests took place every day; and although many of the prisoners were released on' examination, the prisons were filled to overflowing. The Commune itself was torn by intestine quarrels, and threatened to fly to pieces like one of its own bombs; the *prudent* were disappearing, the desperate were quarrelling, and men of a lower cast than most of the old members made their way to power, so sweet it seems to be, although on the verge of a precipice. Twenty of the most moderate and able men in the Commune protested against the existence of the Committee of Public Safety; but it was maintained that it was necessary that there should be some body above the ministers, in fact, an imperialism, so strangely do all extremes, all nonconstitutional governments, resemble each other in their modes of thought and action!

The Central Committee, which still existed in spite of the appointment of the Committee of Public Safety, and which seemed indeed to have set aside the general government of the Commune, now openly advocated and put in practice the plan of the old republic and the consulate, and appointed a civil commissary to watch over each military commander. A man named Dereure was appointed to be by the side of Dombrowski, one Johannan by that of La Cécilia, and one Milist by that of Wroblowski. Cluseret, who had escaped his persecutors, wrote a letter to Rochefort, in which he dwelt bitterly on the faults committed, and declared that nothing remained to be done but to make good their position by barricades. Newspapers that had supported the Commune all along now gave it up as a delusion, and wrote against it, showing the conviction of the writers that the hour of deliverance was very near.

Misfortunes are said never to come alone; in truth, they have fallen on Paris in crowds. Just it this moment a cartridge factory, in which 500 women were employed, near the Champ de Mars, exploded, and caused the destruction of a post of national guards close at hand. At least 200 of the poor women were killed, and a number of the guards. Of course, in the state of affairs at the period, no exact account could be obtained.

A movement having occurred at this time amongst the German troops, it was given out that they were about to join the French outside, storm the city, and massacre the people. It was evidently only a Communist trick, to arouse the spirit of the people and throw odium on the Assembly; but instead of producing the intended effect it simply terrified the timid nearly out of their senses, and did not certainly strengthen the Commune's hands. This rumour was made the occasion for the declaration that, in presence of such infamous conduct on the part of the Assembly, they would burn and destroy every public building in Paris. One man, who must have had a good deal more money than wit, offered a sum equal to £8000 to any man who should succeed in bringing M. Thiers into Paris. Certainly the chance of his having to pay the reward was a small one, so he obtained a day or two's cheap notoriety.

So desperate had the position become that the Committee of Public Safety having been blamed in a manifesto, threatened to imprison the minority, and carried out the threat in the case of one member named Clément. It also ordered that no one in prison should be released except by the express order of the committee itself. In spite of all the difficulties which surrounded the Commune, however, it could not refrain from playing at legislation; the love of power was so sweet, that even when all was crumbling beneath its feet, it devoted itself to reform the code for future generations; and as the time was evidently short, a vast deal of work was done on paper in the smallest possible time. Amongst the rest of the propositions, that of suppression of a part of the city *octroi* dues was sure to be most popular, and was made prominent. More than a hundred millions of francs were to be presented to the people under this head, to be made up by—1st, Saving thirty millions on police and religion, which was declared to be only another name for espionage; 2nd, By a tax amounting to fifteen millions on railways; 3rd, By the profits on assurance, which the city was to undertake on its own account. In addition to this, there was a proposition to declare at once all titles, arms, liveries, and privileges of nobility illegal, and consequently abolished; the Legion of Honour was to be suppressed; all children were to be considered legitimate; and every man and woman after the age of eighteen (a royal majority) were to be married by simply declaring the fact before the proper authority, without any parental or other consent being required. The Commune, however, could not agree on these and similar points; there was a tremendous scene in the council, and the minority seceded, and were not imprisoned. The Committee of Public Safety proceeded alone with its work, and issued its decrees in the *Official Journal*. One of these suppressed at a single blow ten journals, including the *Patrie*, the *Revue des Deux Mondes*, and, singularly enough, the *Commune*. Ominous fact! Another ordered that no new journal or review should be allowed to appear until after the war was ended; that all articles must be signed by the writers (the imperialist condition); that offences against the Commune should be submitted to a court-martial, and that printers contravening this decree should be tried, with their accomplices, and their presses seized! Such are the kindly and considerate feelings towards the press and its liberties left on record by the Committee of Public Safety of 1871.

The Commune seemed, in fact, as its last hour approached, to be endowed with supernatural powers of legislation and diabolical work, and amongst other matters it discussed the mode of dealing with the unfortunate hostages. Some proposed that the victims should be drawn by lots, others that the most culpable only should at first be shot, and the rest reserved for a later period. A well-known man named Wolff, formerly secretary to Mazzini and president of the Universal Republican Alliance of London, was accused of being a secret agent of M. Piétri, prefect of police under the empire, of receiving from him a salary of £20 a month, and of furnishing him with reports of the doings of the Commune; silver candelabra and other plate and ornaments in the churches were seized; and it was announced in many journals, and notably in the *Cri du Peuple*, that rather than capitulate the committee had resolved to blow up and burn the city. This fact is important, as it has been strenuously denied that the Commune caused the destruction that afterwards occurred; at any rate, they had recommended it in one of their favourite journals. As to the destruction itself, that commenced some days before the government troops had made their way into Paris. The demolition of the expiatory chapel, erected in memory of Louis XVI. and Marie Antoinette, was commenced though not accomplished; and every one knows of the demolition of the Column Vendôme, which was accomplished in a very systematic manner by a builder who undertook the job at a given sum. In the first place the column was sawn through just above the square base upon which it stood; an immense bed of dung covered with faggots was prepared in the place, so as to deaden the shock of the fall of such a huge mass; a mast had been erected to which were attached pulleys, through which ropes, fastened to the statue on the top of the column, passed and were tightened by a windlass, while other ropes were pulled by hundreds of shouting fiends until the proud memorial of Napoleon's victories tottered, fell, and broke into fragments, amid the shouts and mad rejoicings of all the scum of Paris, who crowded in thousands round the spot, and it is marvellous that no accident happened. In consequence of the preparations that had been made, the crowning statue was uninjured; but the bronze plates which surrounded the column and which were covered with bas reliefs commemorating Napoleon's greatest victories, were parted and some of them broken.

Marshal MacMahon made good use of the occasion in an address to the army, in which he said:—"The foreigner respected it—the Commune of Paris has overthrown it. Men calling themselves Frenchmen have dared to destroy, under the eyes of the Germans who saw the deed, this witness of the victories of our fathers against Europe in coalition. The Commune hoped thus to efface the memory of the military virtues of which the column was the glorious symbol. Soldiers! if the recollections which the column commemorated are no longer graven upon brass, they will remain in our hearts. Inspired by them, we know how to give France another proof of bravery, devotion, and patriotism."

By this time a large number of the Commune became terrified at their position, and twenty or more are said to have suddenly ceased to attend the meetings. We know now that these fierce leaders were, many of them, intent on their own safety only; and that having led thousands to destruction and shown the example of demolition, they exhibited their heroism by running away from their victims, and some of them succeeding are now exiles, trying to make the world believe that they are victims of their patriotism. The most honourable and brave of the Communists fell fighting in a hopeless cause or by the bullets of the victorious army.

While these latter events were passing in Paris, the bombardment of the city was proceeding with terrible intensity. The Versailles and Auteuil gates were the first that were demolished, and the bastions around, as well as the Point du Jour, were soon untenable: the bombardment of Porte Maillot and the Champs Elysées to the arch, and farther, was continuous and most violent; and the destruction of the houses from the gate in question to the arch was frightful. Few parts of Paris have suffered more. The Auteuil Railway passed across beneath the road, close to the Porte Maillot; not only was the station there utterly destroyed, but the tunnel was blown up, and the railway traffic stopped for a considerable time afterwards. Not a vestige remained of gate or station. Trees and lamp-posts had disappeared; and the whole quarter presented a scene of desolation which it is impossible to exaggerate. A severe struggle took place at Clichy, not far from Saint Denis, on the Seine: it was taken by the Versailles troops on the 17th of May. It was a very important point, as it covered the road to Neuilly; in fact, there was constant fighting and cannonading along the whole line, not only at the ramparts, but at many points outside, the Federals answering the Versailles batteries from Montmartre, the Trocadéro, the fort of Montrouge, and many sections of the ramparts. The fire was not, however, well sustained. On the 18th or 19th a breaching battery was opened in front of the village of Boulogne, which fired rapidly and continuously, and was replied to vigorously by the guns on the ramparts at Vaugirard; but on the latter day the gates of Auteuil and Point du Jour were completely destroyed, and this was the beginning of the end. At this time the Communists established a powder magazine in the palace of the Legion of Honour, and considering the short distance that this building is from the Louvre, and the fearful fires that raged in that quarter of the city afterwards, it is surprising that a greater catastrophe than any that occurred, namely, the burning of the

Louvre, with all its precious treasures in pictures, sculpture, engravings, and antiquities, did not crown the work of the Commune.

CHAPTER IV.

The Beginning of the End—False Communal Announcements—The Communists at bay—M. Rochefort attempts to escape, but is captured and taken to Versailles—Abominable Threat of the Communists—All Communication with Paris cut off—Condition of the Interior of the City—Perpetual Arrests, Domiciliary Visits, and Robberies—Entrance of the Versailles Troops—An Army of Amazons—Speech of M. Thiers in the Assembly on May 22—Fighting behind the Barricades—Description of the Barricades—The Communists set fire to the City—Continued and Severe Fighting—Use of Petroleum Bombs—Convoys of Prisoners to Versailles—Merciless Treatment of them—Circular of M. Thiers—Massacre of the Archbishop of Paris and other Hostages by the Communists—Reasons assigned by the Communists for arresting them—End of the Struggle—Severe Lesson for the Middle Classes—The Buildings partially or totally burnt—Were there any Pétroleuses?—Retribution—Fearful Scenes in the City and at the Camp of Satory, near Versailles—The Women of the Commune—Trials of the Prisoners—Sketches of the most Notorious and their Sentences—Rochefort and his Sentence—Trial of the Alleged Pétroleuses—Groundless Accusation as to the Number of Englishmen in the Communal Ranks—Ducatel the "Saviour of Paris," and his Reward—Estimates of Value of Buildings Destroyed—All the Registers of Births, Deaths, and Marriages Burnt—Proceedings of the Assembly after the Suppression of the Commune—Present Position of France, and her Prospects for the Future.

NOTWITHSTANDING its desperate position the Commune worked hard to keep up appearances. It declared in the *Official Journal* on the 20th of May that the position was in every respect good and strong; that their organization was much improved, and confidence was strengthened! At this very time crowds of Communists were flying into Paris in the most disorderly manner. It condemned to death four individuals found guilty of being concerned in the firing of the great cartridge factory in the Champs de Mars. General Cluseret was to be tried on the 22nd. On the 21st a decree appeared abolishing all the grants made to the theatres by the government, and all monopolies connected with the theatres, which were to be placed under the management of associations. On the same day the *Official Journal* contained accounts of successes of the Commune nearly all round Paris, repulses of the Versailles troops at half a dozen spots, successful reconnaissances here and there on the part of the Communists, "defeat of Versailles troops by Garibaldians at Petit Vanves," "everything going on well at Neuilly." The previous day's results had been "very satisfactory to the Commune; the battery at Montmartre had dismounted its opponent at Gennevilliers." The reports of Generals Dombrowski and Wroblewski confirmed all the pleasing reports of the Commune, and declared their belief that the approaches of the Versailles troops had been destroyed. La Cécilia had 12,000 men with him at Petit Vanves; the Central Committee had sent forward large reinforcements of troops, with *matériel*, to all the threatened points; seven times were the Versailles forces repulsed in attempting to storm the ramparts, and were compelled to give up the attempt; several members of the Commune had gone to the advanced posts among the troops—they must have taken the wrong way, for some ol them were found a good way off, and some found themselves in London not long afterwards—all the members who left the Commune had been replaced, &c., &c. Such were the announcements put forth to amuse the deluded followers of the Commune. It is true that the notices in the *Official Journal* were without date, vague, and to a careful reader significant. But the mask was cunningly worn to the end; it was often awry, to be sure, and the audience should have observed this, but did not. Thousands still allowed themselves to be led out to slaughter, and false reports of success laid the way for more bloodshed.

An order of the barricade commission put the true complexion on the state of things, by ordering the inhabitants of all the houses at the corners of the streets, in the neighbourhood of the ramparts on the south side of the city, to leave their houses, which would be occupied by the national guards, and the walls loopholed for defence. The Communists were at bay; and it is but just to say that some of the leaders behaved heroically, though the sacrifice of their own lives was but a poor recompense for the lives of thousands upon thousands that lay at their door.

The legislative farce was still being played with wondrous face. On the 19th or 20th of May the Commune decreed that a superior commission of accounts should be appointed, to consist of four members, who should report monthly; that all contractors and accountants guilty of theft or malversation should be punished with death; that all pluralities of salaries should be prohibited. Then, amongst a dozen other matters, we have a resolution to the effect that the corps of marines is to be dissolved! A report was ordered to be made on the reform of the prison system. One member of the Commune proposed the abolition of religious worship in all churches, which, he further proposed, should be devoted in future to lectures on atheism, the absurdity of old prejudices, &c. M. Pyat, in the *Vengeur*, said, in an article that bore his signature, that if the minority of the Commune should persist in abstaining, new elections should be ordered to replace them. About the same time M. Pyat disappeared! At almost the same moment as the above remarkable coincidence occurred, M. Henri Rochefort announced in the *Mot d'Ordre*, his journal, that in consequence of the measures taken by the Commune against the press the *Mot d'Ordre* would cease to appear. Curiously enough, on the same day or the day previously, M. Rochefort did not appear in Paris, but was found at Meaux, and conducted to Versailles in an omnibus guarded by chasseurs. Rochefort had tried to disguise himself by having his hair cut short and his beard shaved off, but his peculiar and well-known physiognomy gave him little chance of escape.

One by one the leaders of the rebellion disappeared from the scene. Several were lucky enough to escape into Belgium; others secreted themselves in Paris and were afterwards taken. But we must not forestall events, but confine ourselves at present to what was actually going on in Paris. The two following documents, the former issued on the night of the 20th and the latter published on the 21st of May, present a curious contrast. M. Thiers addressed a circular to the prefects of the departments, in which he says: "Those who have misgivings are wrong. Our troops are working at the approaches; we are breaking the walls with our batteries. At the moment I am writing never have we been nearer the end. The members of the Commune are occupied in saving themselves by flight. Henri Rochefort has been arrested at Meaux." The proclamation of the Commune says: "All inhabitants of Paris who are absent from the city must return to their houses within forty-eight hours, otherwise their stock, bonds, shares, and ledgers will be burnt." This abominable threat was all the more infamous from the fact that no one could at that time enter Paris, the Versailles troops having complete command of the gates, and having already stopped a number of persons, including English and Americans. It was said afterwards that the order was a mistake, and would be cancelled; but it formed a part of the system which we now know was attempted to be carried out, if not by the Commune, by individuals, of burning all the documents, public and private, that were deposited in the Hôtel de Ville and other edifices.

The preparations for what afterwards happened were now being made. The well-known bronze bas-relief of Henri IV., which was over the central door of the Hôtel de Ville, was taken down, and it was asserted, had been cut up into pieces and distributed. The truth was, however, that the bas-relief was taken down and stowed away, and afterwards found intact, that it might not be destroyed with the beautiful Hôtel de Ville, which it had so long decorated. This bas-relief was not, however, the original; that was destroyed at the first Revolution and replaced by a new one. When its place was laid bare there appeared a square hole in the wall, in which originally, it is supposed, were deposited the coins and other things placed there at the time of the building; but the hole was empty, and may now be seen in the vacant space of calcined stones.

On the 22nd of May all communication whatever with Paris was systematically cut off; on the north, the trains were stopped at St. Denis and none allowed to leave Paris; numberless arrests were made, Assi being amongst the number of prisoners.

The Germans, who had remained completely neutral, except when the conditions of the peace 'seemed in danger, now prevented the fugitives from quitting the city. The advanced corps were doubled and exercised the greatest vigilance; every one was driven back, no matter what was his condition; wounded officers and men, including one general, were forced to retrace their steps and return to the desolation they had helped to create.

The condition of the interior of Paris at this moment was wretched in the extreme; as usual, the cry of treason was up, and every one suspected his neighbour of being an agent of Versailles or of Louis Napoleon. Men, and women too, were arrested on the slightest pretence; *cafés* which exhibited more animation than the majority were constantly visited; cordons of soldiers would suddenly be drawn across a street or boulevard; a commissary of police would appear in the doorway of the establishment, and order every one within to remain there on pain of death. The visitors would be severely scrutinized, and generally a few suspected individuals would be arrested, and the rest dismissed. But on more than one occasion hundreds of men and women, old and young, respectable or otherwise, were thus entrapped in a mass, marched off to the Hôtel de Ville, and examined by police or other communal authorities. Most of them were released in a few hours, but the arrests were sufficient to fill all the prisons to overflowing.

Another cause of intense terror and suffering was the domiciliary visits of the national guards; these had a double object, the finding of arms, and also of national guards, or of any young able-bodied men, in hiding. Woe to any who were found, especially in uniform; they were immediately marched off to the forts or the advanced posts, and their chance of escape was small. Every kind of arm that was found was taken away; and when the house or apartment belonged to a late senator, or other marked Bonapartist, all the valuables were seized, and frequently the furniture and other things destroyed. In other instances there was not much mischief done, though of course, as in all such cases, there was a number of black sheep who took advantage of the state of things, and helped themselves to whatever came within their reach. When the Commune had fallen some curious scenes occurred; those who had helped themselves to their neighbours' goods began to feel uneasy, knowing that if discovered the retribution would be swift and heavy, and the conduct of every man in Paris would be known to his neighbours through the concierges. A single instance, which will serve as an example, came within our knowledge; a very handsomely furnished suite of rooms in the Place Wagram had been divested of every portable valuable, but it seemed that the possessors of some of the goods got uneasy; for one evening at a late hour a ring came at the gate, and a man called out, "Here are your clocks," and ran off. At the gate were found, not only six time-pieces, which had been stolen from the apartments referred to, but another which had doubtless been taken from some neighbouring house. A quantity of money and jewellery, stolen at the same time, was not returned with the clocks.

On the night of the 20th the siege batteries maintained an incessant fire for eight hours against Porte Maillot and Auteuil, and on the following day, Sunday—nearly all important military engagements seem to take place on Sunday—General Douay with his corps d'armée entered Paris by a breach in the walls, and occupied positions near Auteuil, whereupon a flag of truce was hoisted at the Saint Cloud gate, and the Versailles batteries immediately ceased, by signal, to fire on that part of the city. At the same time another corps d'armée, under General Dubarrail, had occupied Choisy-le-Roi, and a third had entered at Porte d'Issy; the first and third here joined, and the whole prepared to march against the Communist forces, who still held their ground with obstinacy. To meet the attack, one of the largest guns in Paris, a huge naval breech-loader, had been remounted on the ramparts, and on one day destroyed the roof of the barracks of Mont Valérien, and on another did great damage to the Château de Bécon. This gun, called Joséphine, was the same which during the siege sent a shell from the fortifications to Saint Germain, and caused the Germans to shift the position of then hospital. The insurgents placed twelve heavy guns on the bastions at Clichy and Gennevilliers, to prevent the troops crossing the Seine at that part. They also set up some large guns on the Arc de Triomphe, which caused the Versailles gunners to fire at that, the most beautiful of all the architectural monuments in Paris. Fortunately they did it but little harm; but the houses around were considerably injured, and many men and horses were killed in and around the Place de l'Etoile. This caused the shells to come further than ever into Paris. The Pont de Jéna was struck several times, and on one occasion a carriage close by the bridge was cut to pieces by two shells, which struck it at once, and three passengers were badly wounded.

The success of the government troops was not uniform; in the neighbourhood of Issy and Vanves, the insurgents were driven in, but at the Dauphine gate the attacking force was kept back by the steady fire of the mitrailleuses. In the evening of the same day, however, the Versailles troops, as already stated, entered Paris by the gates of Saint Cloud and Montrouge, the insurgents quitting the ramparts. The corps of fusiliers and marines, headed by a captain in the navy named Trèves, had the honour of first entering the city. They immediately cut the telegraph wires and stopped the communications of the Commune. The resistance on the road by Auteuil to Paris was not great. The Federalists fled into the city, generally in the wildest disorder—as most beaten armies do; and the shells from the Versailles batteries now falling well within the ramparts added to the confusion. The inhabitants were stricken with terror, and a large number of lives were lost amongst the civilians.

Even at this eleventh hour the Commune continued to arrest all the men capable of bearing arms, and on the very day before the entry of the government troops it was said that 2000 were impressed.

A sad smile was brought up on the face of those who were on the boulevards on the 20th of May, when a regiment, or rather a mass, of women, all armed and wearing something more or less military about them, and commanded by several grey-headed old men, appeared and marched along. This army of amazons never faced the enemy. Many women, however, exhibited the utmost courage, not to say ferocity; for instance, on the last day of the defence of the *enceinte* a vivandiére of one of the battalions, who had just joined,' and was not even equipped in the usual short skirt, trousers, and military cap, but who carried a Chassepot, sat down behind the ramparts by the Bois de Boulogne and deliberately fired twenty rounds at the enemy; preparing to fire her twenty-first cartridge, she was struck by a piece of a shell and her head shattered in the most frightful manner.

On the 21st and 22nd May two very short but important proclamations appeared with M. Thiers' signature; the first merely stated that "the Saint Cloud gate had been destroyed, that General Douay was entering with his troops, and that two other generals were hastening after him." The second was still more curt:—"Half the army is already in Paris. We have possession of the gates of Saint Cloud, Passy, and Auteuil, and we are masters of the Trocadéro."

The work went on fiercely on both sides; on the 22nd thousands of prisoners were taken, men, women, and children, and sent off to Versailles; the troops were pouring into Paris through the crushed gates and walls; the Saint Germain quarter was occupied by General Cissey with 20,000 men, and other corps reached the entrance of the Champs Elysées, and the barricades at the Place de la Concorde were now brought into play against them. In a few hours more there were 80,000 Versailles troops in Paris, and the barricades were being shelled by the forts and batteries. The army advanced towards the centre of Paris; they occupied on the 22nd, amongst other places, the Champ de Mars, the place in front of the new opera house, and the esplanade of the Invalides; but the insurgents had placed guns on the terrace of the Tuileries, and swept the whole of the Champs Elysées. The fighting was serious round about the terminus of the Western Railway, which is not very far from the Madeleine; conflagrations and explosions took place in a dozen places at once, and a funereal pall of smoke seemed to hang over the city. Few imagined how much more sombre and lurid that pall was to become before the Commune was entirely subdued!

On the 22nd of May M. Thiers made a statement in the Assembly, of which the following were the most important passages:—"The cause of justice, order, and civilization has triumphed, thanks to our brave army. The generals, officers, and soldiers, especially the latter, have all done their duty. I congratulate the army for having generously shed its blood to accomplish its duty." M. Thiers then alluded to the powerful effect of the Versailles artillery, which had enabled the engineers to advance rapidly with the works against the forts of Issy and Vanves, and subsequently against the *enceinte*. He then added: "We did not expect to enter Paris for two or three days, and then only at the cost of painful efforts and sacrifices. We have been spared this cruel task. Yesterday General Douay perceived that the gate of St. Cloud was approachable. His army soon penetrated into the interior of the city, and advanced as far as the Arc de Triomphe. General L'Admirault entered simultaneously on the left, and occupied the avenue of the Grand Army and the Arc de Triomphe; while General Vinoy communicates with General Cissey, who rests his left wing upon Mont Parnasse, and his right upon the Invalides. General Clinchant for his part has entered by the Faubourg St. Honored and reached the Opera House. Such was the position of affairs at two o'clock yesterday afternoon. We are disposed to believe that Paris will soon be restored to her rightful sovereign, namely France."

The Assembly at once voted thanks to M. Thiers and the army; and M. Jules Simon brought in a vote for the reconstruction of the Column Vendôme and the restoration of other public monuments. Alas! they little thought what a much longer list of restorations and reconstructions the morrow would give rise to!

During the course of the following day, the 23rd of May, the army made great progress; there were nearly 100,000 men in Paris; Generals Douay and Vinoy surrounded the Place Vendôme, the staff quarters of the Communists, Neuilly, the Northern Railway station, and Montmartre. The last-named hill had been armed with a large number of guns, and great fear was entertained of the mischief that they would do to the interior of the city; but they were silenced with comparatively little trouble, and by a sort of retributive justice, by batteries placed close to the spot where the artillery was seized and carried off by the Communists in March. The government troops arranged a number of guns on the Place Wagram, and those of Montmartre facing the other way, the batteries were taken in flank and rear and immediately silenced. Many thousands of the insurgents were taken prisoners and a large number killed, but the rest still fought behind the barricades with great energy, and kept the entering army at bay for a time; but it was soon found that barricades could be turned, as Montmartre had been, and thus the army took the Place de l'Etoile and obtained possession of the Elysées and all that neighbourhood. Thus one by one all these barricades fell, and the conflict was confined to the centre and the north-east side of the city. Here, however, the insurgents made a desperate stand, and held the army at bay for two days longer; the barricades were guarded with numerous guns and mitrailleuses, and in the streets of the centre of the city they could not be turned.

Of these barricades, those who have never seen a siege or a revolution can scarcely form an idea. They were not heterogeneous heaps formed of omnibuses, cabs, carts, furniture, and paving stones, but were very carefully constructed on military principles. The first of them was in fact a wall all round the city, at a very short distance from the fortifications, constructed of earth, about three feet thick and six feet high, and crowned with sand-bags. Behind this rampart was a ledge, also of earth, on which the men stood and fired over or between the sand-bags, so that those not actually engaged in firing, stepping down, were well covered. In forming this outer ring of barricades good advantage was taken of the circular railway which runs round just within the walls. In those parts where the railway is in a cutting, as it is during the greater portion of its length, the barricade was raised against the inner railings, which thus became themselves a portion of the work. Every station on the line in these parts was converted into a small fortress, the windows being built up with stones and mortar, or filled with sand-bags, and pierced everywhere. At the foot of the stairs at each station there was a second work of the same kind, in case of the former proving untenable. On the line itself, here and there, were strong oak gates, with numerous holes for riflemen, which could be shut and firmly fastened on the approach of the enemy; and lastly, the whole of the shrubs on the slopes of the cuttings, and they were thick and fine, were cut off at a foot or so from the ground, and every stump cut to a sharp point. In places where the railway cutting was interrupted by a tunnel, the street, boulevard, or place above was converted into a strong bastion, arranged for artillery as well as riflemen. Some of these were truly formidable works. In addition to all this, the road which skirts the railway along the entire length was protected by loopholed walls, built half across the road, and each alternately covering the space left open by the side of the preceding one. Thus an advancing army would at every point meet with a strong wall, behind which were dozens of riflemen. Where the railway dipped below the surface the same principle was followed; only, in the absence of the cutting and rails, the barricade being self-sustaining, had to be much more substantially constructed. The second ring of barricades being much nearer the centre of the city (the Arc de Triomphe was one of its links), was necessarily not continuous, but consisted of isolated barricades and redoubts across the streets and boulevards. Against infantry only they would have been extremely formidable, but the shells which fell upon and within them soon rendered the inner ring also untenable. When the army under the Versailles generals got within this inner ring, the strategic value of the great new boulevards was well demonstrated. Cannon and mitrailleuses were brought to the intersections of these broad thoroughfares, including the Champs Elysées (which were thus swept down their whole length, and the road cleared of the insurgents down to the very heart of Paris), the Rue Royale, the place in which the new opera house stands, and, finally, the Place Vendôme, the Place de la Concorde, the Place de la Bastille, and many other important positions. The artillery thus placed poured a crushing fire of time fuse shells on the barricades around the Tuileries, the Bourse, the Palais Royal, and the Hôtel de Ville, and on the boulevards, to which was added a murderous cannonading from batteries placed on the Trocadéro, a most commanding situation.

It was impossible for the insurgents to maintain their position after this. The men were demoralized, no generals were to be found; half-drunk and half-mad, their companions falling around at every instant, they raised the usual cries of "Treason!" "We are betrayed!"

&c; and then came the common street fighting, without order or hope. Barricades were now formed, or tried to be formed, of whatever could be seized upon—the military bedsteads and bedding of the barracks in the Louvre, goods out of private houses, vehicles, and whatever came to hand. The courage of many of the insurgents was beyond all question, but the carnage was frightful and the end was inevitable. The last stand in this central part of Paris was made whilst the public buildings around were blazing in the midst of, perhaps, the most fearful combat that even the streets of Paris have ever witnessed; for the Communists, now in utter despair, had carried out their threat as far as lay in their power, and had set fire to some of the most valuable public edifices.

At first it was impossible to ascertain the extent of the mischief. When the Tuileries were set on fire the Communist guards were in possession of the site, and kept off all who would have attempted to stop the conflagration, and it was believed, and the supposed fact, telegraphed all over Europe, that the Louvre was destroyed. This fortunately proved not to be the case. The army obtained possession of the spot before the ruin was consummated, and managed to stop the fire by isolating the buildings on both sides. The grand collections of pictures, sculpture, antiquities, and objects of art of all kinds, were saved. The truth, when known, was, however, sad enough.

The effect of the fire can never be described; the whole mass of the Tuileries, front and side, was in flames, as were the Palais Royal and the great building occupied by the ministry of Finance just opposite. On the island close at hand the fire was darting up from amidst the quaint old towers of the remains of the Palace of Charlemagne; the Palace of Justice, the Prefecture of Police, and the Sainte Chapelle, were all supposed to by doomed. On the opposite quay, the great buildings occupied by the Council of State and the Court of Accounts were blazing furiously; and somewhat later the fire appeared further east; the Hôtel de Ville was also in flames. Add to this that dozens of private houses and other buildings around these edifices were included in the conflagration, while fires, caused no one can say how, occurred in all parts of the city, and imagination may draw something like a picture of the scene. Over the city hung a huge canopy of smoke, almost shutting out the light of heaven; and this was illuminated in the most extraordinary manner by the flames, the pyramids of fire, which sprung up from the petroleum-saturated floors. Further on we shall speak of the actual damage done; for the present our object is to sketch as clearly as we can the progress of the Versailles army and the extinction of the Commune.

While this tremendous fire was raging, the fighting was furious around the Tuileries and the Hôtel de Ville, at Montmartre and Belleville: the Versailles batteries cannonaded the parts of the city still in the hands of the insurgents without cessation; while the Communists on their side bombarded the city from the southern forts, and threw petroleum bombs from batteries on the heights around. During the last struggle this was continued during the whole night, and it was in vain that firemen and others attempted to make their way through the serried masses of now infuriated Communists, who guarded every avenue. It is admitted that the insurgents fought in the streets with great bravery; while independent observers mostly agreed that the Versailles troops were remarkably cautious. The generals, or the soldiers, may have taken a lesson from the Germans, and have found out at last that rashness is far more likely to lead to reverses and panic than to success. In this terrible case of street fighting especially, discretion was the better part of valour, as the unfortunate population had to be considered. At every important point, by the Madeleine, the Bourse, the New Opera, the Rue Royale, and the Rue St. Honoré, the struggle was desperate; and as the Communists are proved to have fought like wild beasts at bay, the soldiers who conquered them must have had valour as well as discretion. Thousands of the insurgents fell, and many more escaped to hiding.

From the moment that the army made its way fairly into Paris, commenced one of the most painful phases of the insurrection, namely, the convoy of prisoners to Versailles. The resistance of the Commune and the burning of Paris seemed to have almost extirpated the sentiment of pity from the mind. The miserable prisoners (men, women, and children), sore-footed, half-starved, and often wounded, were driven like wild beasts. Their guards were, as a rule, utterly merciless, and only laughed at their sufferings; while the populace, even educated men and women, insulted the fallen wretches in the coarsest manner. Certainly one of the worst points in the French character is the savage bitterness exhibited towards an enemy, whether victorious or prostrate.

To give an idea of the treatment of the prisoners, it was said that Rochefort, although guarded by three detachments of gendarmes and chasseurs, was handcuffed, and in such a manner that one of his wrists was hurt. If a man fell out of the ranks from fatigue, he stood a good chance of being shot. Many instances are recorded of summary execution on the road. The following was related by an English correspondent:—"The whole way to Sévres the road was crowded with trains of waggons, ambulance vans, policemen, and cavalry escorting prisoners. To show the bitterness of feeling among military men at Versailles, I may mention that when one of four field-officers in conversation expressed a wish to see the prisoners handed over for the benefit of science to the professors of vivisection, the other three applauded the idea. While talking, a young captain entered the café to refresh himself with a glass of beer. He was in command of a convoy of prisoners going to Satory, and said he had ridded his country of some of the scoundrels. One from fatigue, one from weakness, and two who were sulky, had sat on a bank. He ordered them to get up directly if they did not want to be shot. 'Shoot us,' replied one of the prisoners. 'I will take you at your word, my good fellow,' the captain answered, 'and I shall consider those who do not get up directly to be of the same mind as you.' No one moved. The firing party was quickly told off, and the four men were corpses in another instant. The captain was highly commended by his brother officers for his firmness, and when he had gone all fell to praising him."

Amongst the prisoners were many women, "Amazons of the Seine," vivandiéres, and others. Many of these were wounded, some had children in place of knapsacks, nearly all were fatigued, famished, miserable; but they were compelled to march at a good quick pace by mounted gendarmes, who were evidently quite prepared to enforce obedience to their orders; and in their condition, and under a hot sun, they must have suffered horribly. When they arrived at Versailles the jokes and ribaldry of the spectators was enough to madden them; but generally they kept a firm and defiant countenance, and in some cases answered insult with its own coin. The women and the boys bore themselves far more bravely than the men; but then, they had not suffered so severely, and they had less to dread. As to the boys, many of them little imps of ten or eleven years of age, who were in some cases attached to battalions of national guards, and in others belonged to special corps, "Infants of the Commune," or something of the kind, but all either dressed in the uniform of the guard or wearing a scarf or belt over their blouse, they strutted along with their noses in the air, as if, to use the stereotyped phrase of French politicians, the "eyes of all Europe were upon them." To be a revolutionist is, as it were, a profession with numbers of Frenchmen. The number of old men amongst the prisoners was surprising. These were the patriarchs of Saint Antoine, the men of the Faubourgs, who had taken part in every revolution and *émeute* since they were children, who hailed a struggle against any authority as the highest treat in their lives; these men appeared under the Commune, as usual, in order to give courage to the younger, and threw the weight of their experience into the Federal scale. When there was an inclination towards panic it was they who stemmed it; and when the Commune was on its last legs they came out by hundreds, perhaps by thousands, and steadily blew the embers again into a fierce flame. These men marched like martyrs to their fate, and had they fought in a better cause they would have been true heroes. They are the rank and file of the army of which Blanqui and Pyat, and others, are the chiefs; but unlike these men they dared to fight, disdained to fly, and were ready for death; and many of them met the grim monster unflinchingly. It was principally due to the steadiness of these men, no doubt, that the last struggle was so severe; all hope had vanished, but the old revolutionary blood was at boiling point, and hundreds faced certain death with unflinching countenances.

On the 25th of May M. Thiers issued the following circular:—

"We are masters of Paris, with the exception of a very small portion, which will be occupied this evening. The Tuileries are in ashes, the Louvre is saved. That part of the Ministry of Finance which skirts the Rue de Rivoli is burnt, the Palais d'Orsay, where the Council of State and Cour des Comptes were lodged, is also burnt. Such is the state in which Paris is delivered to us by the wretches who oppressed and dishonoured it. They have left 12,000 prisoners in our hands, and we shall have 18,000 to 20,000; the ground is strewed with their dead. The fearful spectacle will serve as a lesson to those madmen who dared to declare themselves partizans of the Commune; justice will soon satisfy the outraged human conscience for the monstrous acts of which France and the whole world have been witnesses. The army has been admirable. We are happy in the midst of our misery to be able to state that, thanks to the wisdom of our generals, it has suffered but small loss."

When that circular was despatched the whole extent of the evil was not consummated; on the same day the Hôtel de Ville, with an immense building connected with it, but on the opposite side of the way, the Lyrique Theatre, and all their contents were destroyed, and the crowning horror of the Communists' crimes, the massacre of the hostages, was perpetrated.

The unfortunate men who were incarcerated as hostages consisted almost entirely of priests, monks, gendarmes, and municipal guards who had been *gardiens de ville* under the empire. The pretext for arresting them was, in the first place, that the Versailles authorities had put many Communists to death in cold blood, and that these hostages were seized in order to prevent, by the fear of retaliation, such summary executions in future. The precise truth of the accusation against the government will never be known. M. Thiers, or another influential member, declared in the National Assembly that no such executions had taken place; and that except those who had been sacrificed by the enraged soldiery on the field, no man had been executed except after a fair trial by court martial. This denial leaves the question much where it was; some very gross cases have undoubtedly been proved against officers, to say nothing of the soldiery, but whether the Commune had good ground for retaliation of the kind threatened, it is impossible to say. As stated in a previous chapter, the unfortunate archbishop wrote to M. Thiers from prison on the subject, and the latter denied the accusation.

Why so many ecclesiastics had been arrested was explained by a member of the Commune in this way, that all Catholic priests must be enemies of the Communal movement by profession; that they had kept up communication with the government at Versailles, and had done all they could against the Commune by their preaching and arguing; and that in time of war it was absolutely necessary to put down such intrigues. But another ground was alleged, namely, that it had been discovered that the priesthood had secreted large numbers of arms; 2000 it was declared had been found at Notre Dame, and a great many also in a Jesuit establishment; that it was evident that these, and many other arms, had been secreted in order to furnish their disciples with the most approved weapons against the Commune. These arms had come into their hands in the various ambulances under their charge, and should have been returned into the government stores, instead of being hidden away for future use. It was further declared that only in case of the Communal prisoners being shot would any harm be done to the hostages; and, lastly, that instead of being treated with severity, the archbishop received the greatest consideration. These statements cannot be accepted as of much value. The Communists may have had cause, or believed they had cause, for reprisals, and they seized as hostages the men whom they most hated, namely, ecclesiastics and policemen—the agents of the church and empire, which they detested.

The unfortunate hostages, 232 in number, were confined at Mazas; not like prisoners of war, but like felons in separate cells. About this there is no question. They were first taken to the Conciergerie, thence to Mazas, and finally to the criminal prison of La Roquette.

On the entrance of the Versailles troops into Paris the unfortunate hostages were ordered for execution; and on the 24th of May the unhappy archbishop, with the Abbé Deguerry, of the Madeleine, the apostolic protonotary, and other priests, two Jesuit fathers, M. Bonjean, the president of the Cours des Comptes, and senator under the empire; M. Jecker, the banker who was the agent for the Mexican loan, which was one of the causes of the war against that country; and some other victims not named—were butchered in the most cruel and insulting manner in the outer court of the prison, under the eye of a delegate of the Commune. Two days later thirty-eight gendarmes and sixteen priests were murdered at the cemetery of Père la Chaise. The unfortunate gendarmes, gardes de Paris, and gardiens de la paix left behind them a large number of widows and children without provision, and a public subscription in their favour was afterwards raised, and produced more than £.10,000.

When the government troops reached La Roquette they found there and saved 169, according to one account, and according to another, 132 other hostages, all of whom had been ordered for execution.

The archbishop of Paris is the third who, within a few years, has met a violent death. Archbishop Affre fell in 1848, when making an appeal to the insurgents; and Archbishop Sibour was assassinated in church by an unfrocked priest named Verger. The victim of the Commune, George Darboy, was a man of high attainments, and had held several professorships. In 1850 he was appointed bishop of Nancy; he attached himself to the empire, and in 1863 was made archbishop of Paris and grand chaplain to the empire, and senator, and thus was an object of popular hatred. It should be recorded of him, that during the siege he was one of the very few ecclesiastics who made any public appeal to the people in favour of order and toleration. He published an admirable letter, in which he implored the more violent polemical writers to set aside their discussions and party quarrels, and give all the assistance they could to the then government. His appeal was totally ineffectual, but the act should not be forgotten. M. Darboy had the misfortune of being too imperialist for the people, and too liberal in his views for the ultramontanes and the pope, with whom he was not in favour.

Unhappily, these were not the only victims of the Commune. It was reported that many of the gendarmes taken were shot on the instant; but there is no proof of this. One case, however, is beyond all question, that of a well-known liberal and republican journalist, named Chaudey, who was charged with intriguing with the Versailles authorities; He was shot in the prison yard without, as is asserted, any form of trial. M. Chaudey was a man much esteemed, and his execution—assassination we should rather say—created a deep sensation against the Commune.

After the army had possession of the central portion of the town, the eastern and other quarters, and several of the forts, were still in the hands of the Communists, and desperately though hopelessly they fought. A circular, signed by M. Thiers and issued on the evening of the 27th of May, tells how sharp was the conflict. After speaking of preceding events, and stating that the prisoners taken amounted at the above date to 25,000, the document narrates the proceedings outside the city, the taking of three of the forts, one, curiously enough, by cavalry, the attack and taking of the barricades on the left side of the Seine, and then proceeds:—"General Vinoy, following the course of the Seine, made his way towards the Place de la Bastille, which was defended by formidable intrenchments; took the position with the divisions Bruat and Faron, and made himself master of the Faubourg Saint Antoine to the Place du Trône. The efficacious and brilliant aid given to the troops by the flotilla of gunboats must not be forgotten. The troops have this day taken a strong barricade at the corner of the Avenue Philippe-Auguste and the Rue Montreuil. This has brought them to the foot of the heights of Belleville, the last asylum of this insurrection, which in its fall has committed its last act of monstrous vengeance in incendiarism.

"From the centre towards the east the corps of General Douay followed the line of the boulevards, resting its right on the Place de la Bastille, and its left on the Cirque Napoléon. The corps of General Clinchant, in joining that of General L'Admirault, met with violent resistance at the Magazins-Réunis, which it gallantly overcame; finally, the last-named corps, after having seized with great vigour the stations of the Northern and Eastern railways, proceeded to Villette, and took up a position at the foot of the Buttes-Chaumont.

"Thus two-thirds of the army, after having successfully conquered all the right bank of the Seine, are now stationed at the foot of Belleville, which they will attack to-morrow morning."

The circular concluded with a high eulogium on the army, and with regrets for the fall of General Leroy, and "the Commandant Seboyer of the chasseurs-aux-pied, who, having advanced too far, was taken by the scoundrels who defended the Bastille, and was shot against all the laws of war. This act was indeed in accordance with the conduct of those who burnt our cities and our monuments, and mixed liquids to poison our soldiers almost instantaneously."

This last passage seems to allude to an asserted fact, that in some of the forts poisoned wine or spirits were found.

Another circular, published on the following day, records the actual conclusion of the struggle. It states that during the night all difficulties were overcome. A young officer named Davoust took the barricades, and the corps of General L'Admirault occupied the heights of Belleville. At the same time General Vinoy took the cemetery of Père la Chaise, the *mairie* of the twentieth arrondissement, the headquarters of the insurgents of Belleville, and the prison of La Roquette, where, as already stated, the 169 hostages were found and set at liberty. The following passage concludes this, the last of the Versailles circulars relating to the insurrection:—"The remaining insurgents, now driven to the extremity of the city, between the French army and the Prussians, who have refused to let them pass, will expiate their crimes, having no choice but to surrender or die. The too guilty Delescluze was found dead; Millière, not less guilty, was shot for firing a revolver three times at a corporal who was ordered to arrest him. . . . The insurrection, confined to a space of a few hundred mètres, is now definitely crushed. Peace is established, but it cannot drive from honest breasts the grief which has so deeply penetrated them."

The last place in the hands of the insurgents was the fort of Vincennes, and the garrison surrendered on the morning of the 29th of May. "The army collected at Versailles," said an official summary, "has in six weeks vanquished the most formidable insurrection that France ever witnessed. The military works amounted to more than twenty miles of trenches, and eighty batteries armed with 350 guns. It had to take five forts, with formidable armaments and obstinately defended, besides numerous earthworks. The *enceinte* of the city was forced, and the army advanced to the heart of Paris, in spite of all obstacles, and after eight days' of incessant fighting the whole of the fortresses, redoubts, and barricades of the Commune fell into its hands. It took 25,000 prisoners, 1500 guns, and 400,000 Chassepots. Street fighting is generally excessively murderous for the assailants, but all the positions and barricades were turned, and the losses of the army were comparatively small." The following are the official numbers given:—Killed, 5 general and staff and 78 other officers; and wounded, 10 of the former and 420 of the latter. Privates: killed, 794; wounded, 6024; missing, 183. The casualties of the army amounted then, in all, to more than 7500, and the losses on the side of the insurgents must have been three or four times as numerous. This statement is from the report of Marshal MacMahon, commander-in-chief of the army.

The final struggle had brought the cannon into the heart of Paris, and taught the middle classes, and especially the proprietors of houses and shopkeepers, a fearful lesson, which it is to be hoped will not be lost upon them. During the siege they gave little encouragement to the government of the National Defence, but, on the contrary, criticized its every act, as though the position were not one of the greatest possible difficulty, with an enemy surrounding the city and famine within. When the Commune seized upon the Hôtel de Ville and installed itself master of Paris the population scarcely raised voice or hand against it; and when for a time there seemed to many a chance of success for the so-called Federal government, the conduct of the great mass was such as to give the idea that such a prospect was not disagreeable. After a few weeks of imprisonment, when private houses were searched for men and arms, when perquisitions were made in all directions, when goods were demanded and paid for with worthless scraps of paper, then they found out, too late as usual, the mistake they had made; and when the cannon and mitrailleuses began to roar and hiss in the fine new boulevards, the punishment fell directly upon their unthinking, irresolute heads. The Versailles gunners did not intentionally fire upon the houses, but barricades had to be demolished and streets cleared of the enemy; and when the shells and bullets were once let loose many of them took vagrant directions, and much destruction and suffering were the consequence.

Even now the marks are not obliterated; the front of the church of the Madeleine, although not materially injured, is one mass of blotches and spots, which mark the ravages by shot and shell; in the Rue Royale, which extends from the church to the Champs Elysées, several large houses were utterly destroyed, and the gaps are only now being gradually filled up. On the boulevards, especially near the new Grand Opera, hundreds of houses were struck by shell, and dozens of huge plate-glass windows, for some time after patched all over with paper, showed how freely the bullets flew about in that neighbourhood. Nor was the destruction of property the worst that occurred; in some of the streets strewed with corpses, the gutters actually ran blood. Death entered the houses in its most fearful aspect; a poor woman was sitting at the counter in her own shop, near the Porte Maillot, when a shell entered and severed her head from her body; an English publican was putting up his shutters in the Champs Elysées, when a soldier deliberately took aim at the man, whose little boy gave him warning when too late; he fell a corpse at his own door. These are but instances from hundreds of similar cases. There was scarcely a house or a shop in any part of Paris in which, at one moment or other, life was not in danger. Cases of extraordinary escapes were numerous. In one case the *dame de comptoir* of a *café* not far from the Arc de Triomphe had just quitted her seat at the marble table, where she superintended the service and took money, when a huge shell pierced the wall behind her chair and went crushing into the marble slab of the counter; in a private house in one of the new boulevards another shell entered through the front wall, passed across the first room, through a second wall, reducing the whole contents of a bookcase nearly to powder, and without exploding, half buried itself in the seat of an arm chair which the lady of the house occupied almost constantly. This will give some slight idea of the state of Paris during the last days of the Commune.

In the consternation which came over all at the outbreak of the fires, the exaggeration of the mischief was naturally great. It was supposed that the Louvre, with all its contents, was lost; this was happily not the case. The galleries of the Louvre, the beautiful water-side front built by Henri III., the old and the new squares, and even that part of the great gallery recently rebuilt, which connects the Louvre on that side with the Tuileries, are completely untouched; the only portion of the Louvre collections destroyed was the library, which contained some very rare manuscripts and books, and a valuable general collection of works relating to art (about 90,000 in number), the large majority of which may be replaced. The ruin of the Tuileries was, however, almost total; the old central portion, built by Catherine de' Médicis, with the wings and one of the corner pavilions, which completed the front towards the Champs Elysées, were utterly destroyed, the roofs and floors annihilated, and the bare walls calcined, and ready to crumble at the first shock. Never was devastation more complete. The pavilion at the corner by the river, which had lately been rebuilt, was scarcely injured. The side of the palace in the Rue Rivoli was in almost as bad a state as the front, the walls alone standing.

The injury done to the Palais Royal was far less than was at first supposed. This famous building, originally the palace of Cardinal Richelieu, afterwards the scene of the fearful orgies of the Regency and of the wild financial schemes of John Law, was composed of a palace, the front, and a square of houses in the rear, with a garden in the midst; the restaurants, jewellers' and other shops of the Palais Royal are known to all who have visited Paris. The palace alone was burnt, and principally that portion of it which was occupied by Prince Napoleon, who, seeming to have had a pretty clear presentiment of what was to happen, had removed his pictures and other valuables; he had, in fact, disposed of a portion of them by public auction some time previously.

The other public buildings destroyed in this portion of the city were the immense range of offices which belonged to the ministry of Finance, the front of which is in the Rue de Rivoli, and one side in the Rue Castellane. It was one of the largest public offices in Paris. Nothing remained of it but the walls, and not all of them. A larger and more stately building was, however, destroyed on the opposite side of the river. This was generally known as the Palais d'Orsay, being on the quay of that name. This building was the result of one of the whims of the Emperor Napoleon. It was constructed for the residence of all the foreign ambassadors in Paris, who the emperor was vain enough to suppose would live, as it were, in a kind of diplomatic barrack at his invitation. In the time of Louis Philippe the building was used for industrial exhibitions. Lately it was tenanted by the Council of State and the Cour des Comptes, or Board of Audit. Near this is a pretty little classic building, the Palace of the Legion of Honour, with a semicircular Corinthian front; this was only partially burnt.

The Prefecture of Police, which was burnt, was a handsome new building at the back of the Palais de Justice: the latter was but little injured. Immediately adjoining these buildings is one of the most elegant and curious edifices in France, the Sainte Chapelle, erected by Saint Louis to contain a mass of relics brought from Jerusalem. One or two shells would have reduced this architectural gem to a heap of ruins: but fortunately it escaped both bombardment and fire. The famous Gobelins manufactory, with its historic collection of tapestry, one of the great sights of Paris, was, however, completely destroyed.

But the crowning misfortune of all was the destruction of the Hôtel de Ville. This was one of the most beautiful examples of French Renaissance, and its historical reputation was even greater than its architectural beauty. From the time of the bold Henri Quatre it had been the scene of the most stirring incidents in French history; and lastly, it was the theatre of the civic festivities on every joyful occasion. A few statues and busts, a few battered pieces of plate, and a few mural paintings, were all that remained of this noble old edifice. Opposite to it was a very large auxiliary building, in which were other offices belonging to the city; this also was a complete ruin, together with a mass of houses around it.

The churches fared better. An attempt to burn Notre Dame was frustrated by the Versailles soldiery, who entered just in time to save this fine structure. The chairs, benches, and wood work had all been heaped around the high altar, and fire actually applied; but in this case the design of the destroyers was frustrated. Several other fine churches were injured by shot and shell, but none of them were destroyed. Two theatres, the Porte Saint Martin and the Théâtre Lyrique, were completely burnt, and some damage was done to two others. As to private buildings, the number destroyed was enormous. Some streets in the very heart of the town had huge gaps, which are now being filled up slowly; but in the distant quarters, where the shells from the Versailles batteries took most effect, and in those parts where the Communists made their last stand, the havoc was fearful. When forced to quit a position they generally tried to fire the houses, and in too many cases they succeeded. Much has been said about the use of petroleum, and there is no doubt that it was used in the case of the Tuileries and other large buildings. The smoke was of a most peculiarly suffocating description, and the burnt stone of the walls is of a red colour; but the stories relative to the women called *pétroleuses*, who were said to be employed by the Commune to throw the villainous stuff into the cellars of private houses, with lucifers or lighted rags, were probably pure invention—the French press being, unfortunately, far more celebrated for originality than accuracy. This petroleum pouring has not, we believe, been proved in any one case, and therefore it is but just to give the Commune the benefit of the doubt that hangs around the subject. The destruction of the public buildings was bad enough, but a systematic and general plan of destroying the whole city is too fiendish to be attributed to any one without far clearer evidence than we have in this case. Several women have been condemned to death, (though none executed), three of them for having used petroleum; but there was nothing in the evidence as printed to bear out the accusation.

A very prompt offer of assistance in extinguishing the fires was received from the chief officer of the London Fire Brigade. A force of 100 men and 12 engines—towards the expense of which the British government voted £1000—was on the point of starting from Dover, when a telegram was received from Jules Favre, thanking the brigade, but stating that, owing to the exertions of the Paris pompiers,. further help was not urgently needed.

During the previous twenty years the demolitions and constructions in Paris had formed a new wonder of the world—street after street and boulevard after boulevard of palaces had sprung up. Various were the views expressed concerning the policy of many of the changes made; but all expressed their astonishment at the amount of work done and the grandeur of some of the edifices; yet in three days more public buildings were destroyed by the Commune, and through its acts, than all those twenty years produced. So much more easy is it to destroy than to build up! As all the so-called glories of the empire ended in the loss of provinces wrested 200 years before from a neighbour, so the epoch of what was called the "rebuilding of Paris" closed with the destruction of the Tuileries and the Hôtel de Ville, its two most famous palaces and most renowned monuments.

We have already spoken of the fortunate accident by which the Sainte Chapelle escaped destruction. We may here mention another which is equally remarkable, although the building is far less important. Visitors to Paris will not have forgotten the expiatory chapel of St. Ferdinand, erected by order of Louis Philippe to the memory of his eldest son, the duke of Orleans, who was killed by a carriage accident. When the Germans drew their iron belt around Paris, the houses in the immediate vicinity of and outside the fortifications were demolished by thousands, lest they should afford cover for the enemy. It was proposed to take down the little chapel and mark the stones, so that it could be readily reconstructed. Other and more pressing matters caused this project to be set aside, and the chapel stood alone in a plain strewed with ruins. Towards the close of the Commune it was ordered to be destroyed, but it still stands, apparently untouched; and near it is a tree, the only one left amidst the desolation. This is a cypress which marks the spot where the prince met his death. In a country where fatalism is entertained by many minds, it would not be surprising were the Orleanists to look upon this lonely chapel and tree as omens of the future fortunes of the family.

The Commune was no more. It was estimated that more that 40,000 had been killed (of whom about 10,000 fell in Paris, after the Versailles troops had made their way into the city), and about 35,000 were made prisoners. The total number of insurgents in arms had been reckoned at about 165,000; but it is very questionable if so many actually took part in the conflict: but supposing the total to have been smaller, the carnage was almost, if not absolutely, unprecedented. Dombrowski, Delescluze, Gambon, and some other leaders, fell the heroes of a hopeless cause; but the great mass of them took to flight, or lay in hiding, hoping to escape the doom that hung over them. For those in power two balloons were provided, and although it was never known who went away in them, or where they fell, it is believed that they escaped capture. Rossel was discovered in the disguise of a railway engineer; Okolowitch was found in an ambulance, and shot in the Parc Monceaux; Pilotell, Napias Piquet, Brunei, Millière, and some others, met with summary execution by the troops. Piquet was shot in the presence of his daughter. Millière, it is said, had the day before his death caused thirty refractory Communists to be shot. The fate of many is unknown, and will probably never be discovered.

While some of the leaders—who, when real danger came had proved arrant cowards, and thought of nothing but their own safety—were doubtless laughing at their cleverness and luck, their poor deluded victims were being slaughtered in the streets of Paris, or driven like wild beasts into the prisons of Versailles; men, many of them probably innocent, were dragged out of shops and houses and shot like dogs. Several hundreds, it is declared on good authority, who had sought refuge in the church of the Madeleine, were bayoneted in sight of the altar. Not one came out alive! Men and women accused of pouring petroleum on the floors of public buildings, and of throwing petroleum bombs, were dragged into the streets and shot; or in some cases battered to death with the butt ends of guns. Human beings seemed to be turned to fiends, taking pleasure in denouncing each other. No one was safe, and it is dreadful to think how many innocent lives were thus sacrificed.

The stream of prisoners on the road to Versailles was continuous; men, women, and children driven by the swords of the cavalry or the bayonets of the infantry. A party of 1500 deserters from the army, about whose fate there could be no question, were greeted by the mob with fiendish derision. If a man stumbled or fell out of the ranks a bullet was the only argument. A woman tried to slip out of the ranks, when an officer drew his sword and inflicted a deep wound on her face and shoulder. At Satory, the camp near Versailles, the executions were incessant; the number was so great that after a day or two they attracted no attention. The name of Dereure, a leading member of the Commune, was one of the very few that transpired. The condition of the prisoners was frightful; the numbers were so great that the government scarcely knew what to do with them, half starved, many of them wounded, all worn out with fatigue. Men and women were huddled together like cattle in pens, with nothing but a little filthy straw, and at first not even that, to lie upon; and nothing but hunches of bread to sustain them. And hundreds of these were dismissed as soon as the first examination took place, as having been arrested by mistake!

The number of prisoners was at first far larger than that of their guards, and fears were entertained of an insurrection; so large numbers of the former were drafted off to Cherbourg, Brest, and Toulon, where the hulks are still crowded.

The number of deaths was naturally large; the two principal causes being the effects of previous intoxication and want of proper food.

As in the first revolution, the women played a hideous part in the insurrection; their leader was said to be a Russian, Olga Demitrieff, who, with a central committee, was installed at the *mairie* of the tenth arrondissement. Natalie Duval, of whom we shall have to speak presently, was one of the most active of the lieutenants. These women were enrolled in what was called a mystical warlike association; and on the 23rd of May fifty of them went to defend barricades which they themselves had erected in various parts. Several of these viragoes were killed and many more taken. It appears that they were exercised in the use of arms every day in the court yard of the *mairie*. It is said that there were originally in all 400 of these Amazons, most of whom were employed in hunting up and denouncing national guards in hiding to the prefects of police, a work which they performed with fiendish pleasure.

Amongst the women arrested were the sister of Delescluze, described as a most dangerous woman; Madame Colleuil, a hideous virago, who made herself conspicuous by her insane violence at certain clubs; Madame Jaclard and Madame André Leo, of the same class.

A pamphlet, published concerning the doings of *General* Eudes, a druggist's assistant who reigned for a time at the Palace of the Legion of Honour, brings a number of women forward. Eudes' wife, aged twenty-three, is accused of having carried off a number of clocks and a large quantity of linen. She had a carriage at her disposal, and constantly took away linen and other articles. The wife of Captain Hugo, an old soldier, is also accused of helping herself in like manner. Captain Mégy, long notorious, was one of Eudes' companions here. On the 22nd of May he caused a concierge to be assassinated, broke the mirrors with his revolver, and ordered the building to be set on fire, which was done. Colonel Collet and his wife were of the same party. He acted as judge of the court-martial, having formerly been a huckster. This fellow gloried in his crimes. He boasted of having had two gendarmes and a gardien shot in a convent at Vaugirard, having had them stripped naked first. He brought the horses of the gendarmes to the palace for his own use. Madame Collet acted as second in command of the household to Madame Eudes, had charge of the stables and of the kitchen, and rode out in her carriage every morning and evening. This precious family sent all the silver in the palace to the mint to be melted, while the crosses and medals they wore in derision. There were eighteen horses in the stables. The horses were named Thiers, Favre, Trochu, and so on; and over each stall there was a placard bearing the name of the horse and of his master. All the pictures, porcelain, and glass were destroyed.

Much has been said about the time allowed to elapse before the prisoners were brought to trial; but it is forgotten, in the first place, that this is quite the rule in France, where six or more weeks often elapse before a prisoner is brought before any tribunal, being interrogated in secret by a *juge d'instruction*—a custom which is the great blot in French jurisdiction; and in the second place, it is forgotten that the government had to deal with an unexpected mass of prisoners, while the duty of magistrates had to be performed by soldiers, who were new to the work. It was not till the 7th of August that the first trials commenced, under the presidency of Colonel Merlin, an engineer officer. The first list included Ferré, a clerk; Assi, working engineer; Urbain and Verdure, schoolmasters; Billioray and Courbet, artists; Rastoul, doctor, and Jourde, medical student; Trinquet, shoemaker; Champy, cutler; Régère, veterinary surgeon; Grousset and Lisbonne, writers; Lullier, formerly a naval officer; Clément, dyer; Parent, designer; and Deschamp, bronze worker. Of these Ferré, Assi, and Urbain were the most notorious.

Ferré, as the coadjutor of the infamous Raoul Rigault, was the instrument of the assassination of the archbishop and his unfortunate fellow-prisoners at La Roquette. He was a known man in 1868. At the funeral of Baudin he had tried to bring about an *émeute* by an address which commenced with the following expressions:—"*Vive la République!* The convention at the Tuileries! The goddess of reason at Notre Dame!" At the clubs he invariably called for the resuscitation of the revolution of 1793. He was included in the charges tried at Blois in connection with the death of Victor Noir at the hand of Pierre Bonaparte, but was acquitted, and he insulted the president in the grossest manner. On the present occasion he refused to answer any questions, or to have an advocate to defend him. He was accused of having caused the assassination of the two generals at Montmartre. As delegate of police he suppressed newspapers at his will. He was accused of superintending the execution of numbers of prisoners, and even of having himself fired the first shot from a revolver. A female witness declared that she heard him address his men in the following terms:—"All the sergents de ville, all the gendarmes, all the Bonapartist agents, will be shot immediately;" and we know that the threat was partially carried out. He seems to have been one of the principal instigators of the burning of the public buildings, and orders to that effect in his handwriting were produced. One of these related to the offices of the ministry of Finance. It was at the capture of six men of the Communist battalions that Ferré appeared at La Roquette and said: "Citizens, you know how many of ours have been taken. They have taken six. We have six to execute." And the archbishop of Paris, two abbes, two monks, and the Judge Bonjean were shot! This act was followed by other assassinations, especially those of the gendarmes, already alluded to in the letter of the cure of the Madeleine. Ferré denied none of the charges against him, and declared that the execution of the hostages and the burning of the public buildings were perfectly legitimate acts. He concluded a violent and characteristic address as follows:—"I was a member of the Commune of Paris, and I am now in the hands of my conquerors. They demand my head; let them take it. Free I have lived, and free I will die. I add but one word. Fortune is capricious. I confide to the future my memory and my vengeance." Ferré and Rigault were rather wild beasts than men. The latter met his death in the last struggle; the former was condemned and shot at Satory, and it must be admitted that his fate created little sympathy. If, however, the conduct of Ferré had alienated almost all feeling from him, who can read without a pang the following painful letter written by one of his brothers or sisters to the president of the court:—

"Sir,—My father, Laurent Ferré, is at present a prisoner in the citadel of Fouras; my brother, Théophile Ferré, is lying under sentence of death at the prison of Versailles; my mother, driven out of her mind by the efforts of the police to wring from her the address of my other brothers, now in exile, died a lunatic at the Hôpital Ste. Anne on the 14th of July last; I myself was arrested and kept a prisoner for eight days. A fresh misfortune has overtaken me. My second brother, Hippolyte, was transported on Thursday to the military hospital at Versailles suffering from brain fever, caused by cellular confinement for three months at Mazas, and afterwards at Versailles. My brother Hippolyte has never been tried. He is accused, but nothing more. I was denied access to the military hospital, but they told me my brother was in a cell. I ask your permission to see my brother, and next his release on bail. He is only twenty-four, and had no official employment under the Commune. Military justice will be only just by not showing itself merciless. —I am, &c.,

"A. FERRE."

What a fearful picture! Yet hundreds of families must have such sad stories to tell. One came within our own knowledge: a clever and respectable watchmaker's shop being closed after the fall of the Commune, we were told on inquiry that the man had been shot by the troops, that his three sons were prisoners, and that their mother was somewhere in a madhouse!

Urbain was one of the *maires* of Paris during the Commune; and, with a woman named Leroy, was accused of spending the public money and stealing jewellery. He was proved, moreover, to be one of the most urgent advocates of violence, and he completed his guilt by a demand, which appeared in the *Official Journal*, for the execution of the archbishop and the other hostages.

Assi's name is well known as the member of the *Internationale* who was the principal mover of the strikes at Creusot. After these events, not being able to find employment, he set up for himself as a maker of military equipments. During the siege he became lieutenant in a marching regiment of national guards; and finally, he was one of the central committee of the Commune. He was afterwards governor of the Hôtel de Ville, colonel of the national guard, and exhibited the greatest activity and much talent in organization; his ambition created enemies, and he was arrested, and passed some time in prison. He was soon, however, released, and became the director of the ammunition manufacture, in which he showed great ability. The petroleum bombs are attributed to his ingenuity; but he produced an immense sensation in court when he declared that these were made after a model which had been prepared to be used by the government against the Prussians.

Jourde, who acted as Finance minister, was admitted to have shown great ability. It appeared that he had received in all from the Bank of France more than £640,000; the rest of the treasure, which amounted to £120,000,000 sterling, was saved by the energy of the deputy-governor of the bank and the Communist Beslay, of whom we have already spoken. An attempt was made to show that Jourde helped himself largely, but it failed; and the general impression is that this man was an honest as he certainly was a capable minister of Finance: and yet he is a mere youth, and looked extremely weak. He very nearly effected his escape with a false passport, but was tripped up by a clever agent. Captain Ossud, who first examined Jourde, declared that he was the most truthful of all the prisoners, and that he believed he had spoken the whole truth.

Lullier, who was formerly in the navy, but was dismissed for striking his superior officer, and who was afterwards involved in several broils, must be set down as a madman. He belongs to a respectable family, but with the exception of Ferré, was the most forbidding and vulgar-looking man amongst the accused. He behaved in the most theatrical manner in court, declared that he had nothing to do with the fires or the assassinations, but explained how, "as a general," he had taken Paris, but that not agreeing with the Commune he had planned to make himself dictator. He admitted that he had placed himself in communication with Thiers, but that he did not mean to betray the Commune; only he meant to be dictator, and *in extremis* to negotiate with Versailles. He spoke for an hour and a half, drew a bacchanalian picture of the life of the Commune at the Hôtel de Ville, "where beautiful *vivandiéres* filled high in their glasses the wine of triumph," which another prisoner declared was an infamous falsehood, as they never even got a glass of wine and water there. Like Ferré, Lullier was condemned to death, but the sentence was afterwards commuted.

Clément, the dyer, received an excellent character from his employer, to whom he had been foreman for years. He had aided him greatly during the siege, had bought wine for the hospitals out of his own money, and when elected maire under the Commune he dined with his former employer, and said that he feared the Commune were a bad lot, a set of jacobins, and would do no good; and wished he were back in his wooden shoes again. Several witnesses proved that he had protected priests, nuns, and churches with extraordinary courage, and some priests spoke eloquently in his favour. When the Commune was overthrown he deposited the balance of the funds for the poor in his late master's hands, saying:—"Heaven knows what will become of me, but I know I can trust you to place the money in the hands of the proper authorities." The employer could only account for Clement's joining the Commune by supposing that his head had been turned by the socialist theories of Proudhon. Sad that such a man should be placed in a dock by his own imprudence!

Urbain and Trinquet were condemned to imprisonment for life, with hard labour; Assi and another to imprisonment in a fortress; Jourde, Grousset, and five others, to transportation for undefined periods, during pleasure; Clément escaped with three months' imprisonment; and Descamps and Parent were acquitted. Courbet was let off with six months' imprisonment and a fine of £20. This leniency is attributable to two causes; first, to the fact that Courbet acted as minister of the Beaux Arts, and did all he could to save the art treasures of the nation; and secondly, to the daring defence of his advocate, M. Lachaud, who, in his own impassioned manner, raised his client to the very pinnacle of greatness as an artist, and called him almost an idiot in politics. With indomitable visage he declared that Courbet's published letter, in which he recommended the taking to pieces of the Column Vendôme, meant its preservation, and not its destruction!

Two curious facts were brought out on the occasion of these trials, which will doubtless be new to English readers; first, that the costs are fixed by law, and did not exceed one pound for each prisoner; and secondly, that advocates receive no fees in political cases. What would British judges and barristers say to such regulations!

The prisoner who attracted the largest amount of sympathy was the Tin fortunate Rossel, whose conduct and talents have made him almost a martyr in the opinion of the world. Rossel was half a Scotchman, his mother being a Campbell. He was a highly-educated soldier, and had already made his name known as a military writer before the war between France and Germany. Of his bearing while acting as War delegate under the Commune we have already spoken; of his talents, his determination, his courtesy, and his dignity as president of the courts-martial, all who came across him spoke in the highest praise. Rossel was tried twice, and in each case condemned to death and military degradation, the first judgment having been quashed on a point of law. The second trial took place before a court martial, presided over by Colonel Boisdénemetz, whom the French reporters nicknamed "Lucifer box;" and who seemed determined to put the worst construction possible on all the prisoner's acts. Rossel's defence was that he only joined the Commune, in the hope that the

Parisians intended to renew the struggle against the Prussians. It was true that he very soon learned that the Commune had no intention of fighting the Germans, but he did not make the discovery until it was too late. "How could you hope," asked the President, "to defend Paris against the Prussians when they held the northern and eastern forts, and the Parisians had nothing to defend them but the dismantled *enceinte* of the city?" "The same *enceinte*" replied Colonel Rossel, "kept out the army of Versailles for two months; why should it not have repulsed the Prussians?" "But you know that the army of Versailles did not have recourse to radical measures "(*les grands moyens*). Those among us who had remained in Paris during the reign of the Commune, and who had witnessed the daily storm of shells in the Champs Elysées, to say nothing of the tremendous bombardment of Auteuil and Passy, could not help wondering what were the means which Colonel Boisdénemetz would have had the Versailles army employ against Paris. The president next asked Rossel how he could believe that it was possible to carry on the war against Prussia after the fall of Paris, and he called on the prisoner to point out the plan of campaign which he would have pursued. Rossel answered, modestly enough, that the time had not yet come to judge of the expediency of making peace with the Germans last February, but that he, as a matter of opinion, still held that French resistance might have been prolonged after the capitulation of Paris.

The result of the trial, as had been foreseen from the first, was a sentence of death; but so strong was the feeling in favour of Rossel that few thought it would be carried into effect. It did take place, however, on November 28, and was certainly one of the most unwise or unfortunate acts, as it greatly intensified the hatred of the existing Communists for the government; but it is admitted by most people, that neither by military nor civil law could he have been acquitted or sentenced differently. And M. Thiers, we presume, shrunk from the responsibility of commuting a sentence which had been confirmed by a second trial and a Commission of Pardons.

The following extracts from the unhappy Rossel's posthumous writings will have a melancholy interest, and should inculcate more than one useful lesson:—"There is one point on which I consider the Commune as a complete experiment; that is, the incompetence of the working classes for government. It is necessary, it is *necessary* that, until things are changed, the exercise of the functions of government should remain in the hands of the instructed classes; or rather it is necessary that the government should remain in the hands of the bourgeoisie, until the working classes are possessed of sufficient instruction. Let the people then acquire instruction, if they wish to have their legitimate share in the conduct of business and the distribution of fortunes. But, for the present, I will speak the word without mincing it—the people are too stupid to govern us. They have not sufficient sound ideas, and they have too many false ideas."

"The greater part of my time, when I was chief of Cluseret's staff, was certainly taken up by importunate and useless individuals, delegates of every origin, inquirers after information, inventors, and above all officers and guards, who left their posts to come and complain of their chiefs, or their weapons, or of the want of provisions and ammunition. There were also almost everywhere independent chiefs, who did not accept, or did not carry out, orders. Each district had a committee as useless, as quarrelsome, and as jealous as that of the 17th. The artillery was sequestered by an analogous committee, also dependent upon the federation, and who formed a rare collection of incapables. Every monument, every barrack, every guard-house, had a military commandant; that military commandant had his staff, and often his permanent guard. All those spontaneous productions of the revolution had no other title or rule than that of their own pleasure, the right of the first comer, and the pretension to retain the place without doing anything. You might see doctors promenading with a general's gold lace and escort; barrack door-keepers equipped like superior officers; and all those fellows had horses, rations, and money."

"There were in Paris, on the 18th of March, [this is an account for the accuracy of which I can vouch] sixty revolutionary battalions. The remainder were divided, and incapable of escorting a decisive action. The ninety conservative battalions were of older standing, better equipped, and better armed than the revolutionists; they were equally numerous, better commanded, and better disciplined. But those unworthy citizens are accustomed to trust entirely to the army and to the police, whose duty it is to get killed for the cause of order. But there are moments when the police is worn out, and when the army does not clearly understand on which side its duty lies, or whether it be not its duty to remain quiet. At those moments the streets of Paris are at the mercy of the first comer."

The trial of Henri Rochefort (Count Henri de Rochefort de Sercay is his full title) excited great interest; but he was ill, broken down, and said not a word in his own defence, so that the curiosity of the public was disappointed. The original charge made against him, of complicity in the assassination of the hostages, could not be supported, and was withdrawn; and it was clearly shown that he had protested against the execution of prisoners and incendiarism, in his paper, when it was very dangerous to do so. His attacks against the existing government were, however, violent in the extreme; and the judge advocate said it was necessary to enforce the utmost rigour of the law against Rochefort and his satellites, whom he designated as a pestilential race of young journalists, who made a trade of sedition. Rochefort was defended with great talent by the same advocate, M. Albert Joly, whose reputation was made by this and Rossel's trials; but the court had fully made up its mind, and sentenced the prisoner to transportation to a fortress. It should be remembered that Rochefort, violent as his writings were, was not a member of the Commune, and was not even charged with any overt act of sedition.

The trial of the *pétroleuses* was looked forward to as promising great excitement; but it only produced disgust in some minds and disappointment in others. The prisoners were five very common-looking women, who had been *vivandiéres*. Not a single case of the use of petroleum could be proved against them, and these miserable women were condemned to death for taking part in the Communal army, and "attempting to change the form of government." The sentence created a positive feeling of shame in the minds of honest Frenchmen; but happily it was not carried into execution.

The trial of Madame Leroy, a pretty young woman of light character, who had lived with Urbain, whose trial and conviction has been already mentioned, caused some interest. She had a clever counsel, and acted her part with much skill, escaping with a sentence of simple transportation.

The heroine of the Commune, however, was Mademoiselle Louise Michel, a schoolmistress of high attainments and position, thirty-five years old, and very handsome; who, when the insurrection commenced, had sixty pupils belonging to good families under her charge. She was tried as an accomplice in the acts of the Commune, as having fought in uniform, and as having written articles in the *Cri du Peuple* inciting to the assassination of the two generals.

Her manner was calm, modest, and unassuming; but she defied her judges, saying that she gloried in the social revolution; she respected the court more than the Committee of Pardons, which judged in secret. . She stood face to face, she said, with avowed enemies, who she knew must condemn her. She admitted that she attended and took part in almost every council of the Commune, which she declared was honest and innocent, and had no thought of murder or arson. She would have shot the two generals, Clément Thomas and Lécomte, with her own hand had she seen them on the scene of action, but she repudiated as a dastardly deed their execution when they were prisoners. She had proposed fire as a strategical means of opposing the advance of the Versaillists. She had exhorted Ferré to invade the Assembly, and regretted that he had not done so. *She meant two lives to be sacrificed at Versailles, that of M. Thiers and her own.*

M. Marchand, the counsel assigned to her, declined, by express order of the prisoner, to speak for the defence. She said, "All I ask of you is to send me to Satory. Shoot me there, and let me sleep by the side of my beloved Ferré. The public prosecutor is right; I have no place in this world, at a time when an ounce of lead is the portion of the lovers of liberty and right."

The president, Colonel Delaporte, stopped her harangue, and after a few minutes' deliberation the court sentenced her to transportation for life in a fortress.

The trial of a man who acted as jailor under the Commune, with others charged with the murder of the hostages, did not take place till January, 1872: one prisoner only was condemned to death.

On the 18th of February commenced the trial of the prisoners charged with the massacre of the Dominican monks at Arcueil. This act was marked by unusual atrocities; the unfortunate monks and some of the attendants having been tortured with such refined cruelty that the Father Guerny, a missionary, declared that no savages had ever treated missionary martyrs with greater cruelty than the Commune had treated its victims. The Dominicans had no fear from the Communists, for they had converted their house into an hospital, and had collected the wounded and dying even on the battlefield. But the 13th Communist legion was commanded by a man named Seresier, who been noted during the siege, when he commanded the 101st battalion, for his implacable hatred against the clergy, and for having profaned several churches. On the 17th May a fire broke out near the monastery at Arcueil, and the monks were accused of having set fire to the place by order of the Versailles government; and two days later the house of the Dominicans was surrounded by two companies of the national guards, under the command of Léo Meillet, who was then governor of the fort of Bicêtre. This man had escaped, but his accomplice Lucipia, who had given Seresier his orders, was one of the accused. After the pillage of the house the monks and their servitors, with a few pupils, were transferred to Fort Bicêtre, and afterwards taken to the *mairie* of the 13th arrondissement near the Port d'Italie, which was used as a military prison. A Communist captain demanded that the monks should be given up to them, and said that they should have their turn at the barricades. The Dominicans refused to bear arms, declaring that their duty was to succour the wounded and dying, and not to fight. "You promise to take care of the wounded," cried the captain. "Very well! then go away; you are free, but go out one at a time." The unfortunate Dominicans did as they were told, and the men under Seresier's orders shot down thirteen of the victims. This atrocious deed was committed at the moment of the entrance of the Versailles troops into Paris, and more lives would have been taken, had the insurgents not been forced to fly.

The council of war was presided over by Colonel Delaporte, and there were fourteen prisoners placed at the bar. The first on the list was the commandant Seresier, already mentioned, a currier by trade; the second, whose name was Boin, was also a currier; the third, Lucipia, a law student; the others were Quesnot, a mechanic; Gironée, an architectural draughtsman; Pascal, a miscellaneous dealer; Annat, a bookseller's assistant; Bouillac, a labourer; Grapin and Busquant, cobblers; Gambette, a labourer; Boudaille, a corporal in the line; Buffo, a stone mason, and wife. Seresier, the commander of the corps who assassinated the Dominicans, and Boin, who had been appointed by the former keeper of the prison, declared that they had nothing whatever to do with the massacre. The other prisoners declared that they had nothing to do with the assassination, and some laid the whole to the account of Meillet, who had escaped, and Seresier, who, they declared, was drunk and furious, threatening everyone around him with his revolver.

The evidence of one of the Dominicans, Father Rousselm, who had escaped the fate of his brethren, created a deep sensation. He is a fine energetic man, and dressed in the long white robe of the order, presented a commanding appearance. It appeared that he had exhibited great calmness and courage during his imprisonment. He recognized Seresier and several others amongst the prisoners, and said that the insurgents behaved well until the arrival of the 101st battalion, when the Dominicans were accused of showing lights and ringing bells as signals to the Versailles troops. Meillet took possession of the college. Seresier was also there, and said to the witness, "As to me, I believe in neither God nor devil; not even in confession." When taken to Bicêtre, the situation of the monks was described as horrible. There was a crowd of the lowest rabble, who insulted the prisoners in the grossest manner, and stripped them of everything of any value, as well as of all their clothing. The witness then described the manner in which the monks were told to leave one by one, and how they were shot down amid the grossest insults; the witness, who had been separated from the rest by accident, making his escape. A day or so later he saw the remains of his unfortunate brethren, and declared that the corpses were horribly mutilated. Another monk, who also had the good fortune to escape, gave similar evidence, and declared that he and another man were found by Seresier in a cellar, and were actually about to be executed, the pieces being pointed towards them, when they were saved by the arrival of the Versailles troops.

One of the most disgusting features of this and other acts of the Commune was that to which all the witnesses deposed; namely, that the women were the most violent, and constantly urged the men to greater atrocities, and heaped the grossest insults upon the prisoners.

Seresier, Boin, Lucipia, Boudaille, and Pascal were condemned to death; Léo Meillet, dialer, and Moreau were also condemned to death in their absence. The rest of the prisoners were sentenced to imprisonment and hard labour for life, with the exception of the old man Gambette, who escaped with two years' imprisonment, and the woman Buffo, who was acquitted. Gambette said as he left the court, "Is it possible? Two years' imprisonment for doing nothing but beating my drum!"

The trial of Blanqui, "the Nestor of revolution," as his friends delight to call him, caused great interest. The charge against him was in connection with the *émeutes* of the 31st October, 1870, and the 22nd of January, 1871. A number of persons had been tried and acquitted, a year before, when the responsibility seemed to be thrown on Blanqui, who was condemned to death in his absence. Ill luck had thrown him into the hands of the authorities.

Blanqui is a little spare man, sixty-seven years of age, with hair and beard white as snow, and a pair of small bead-like eyes, sunk deep in their orbits, but full of feverish energy. He has spent three-fourths of his life in Cayenne and other places of imprisonment, and has been four times condemned to death. He had refused to answer the *Juge d'Instruction*—that is to say, the interrogatories put to him in prison; and when the president of the court-martial, Colonel Robillard, called upon him to give explanations of his conduct with respect to the affair of La Villette, he replied politely but triumphantly, "*Pardon*, but I am not accused with respect to the affair of La Villette." The colonel admitted the awkward plea, but added, "That is true; but in virtue of our authority (*pouvoir*) we ask you for information respecting other facts than those which are included in the accusation." To this extraordinary ruling Blanqui answered coolly, "You have only to read my journal, *La Patrie en Danger*. You will find the affair in detail there, and much more complete than I can give it you." The colonel was not, however, to be turned from his course, and the following colloquy took place:—

"President—Nevertheless, speak about it yourself!

"Blanqui—Very well! The La Villette affair was the 4th of September, three weeks too early. It was an attempt to overturn the government. It was a 4th of September spoiled.

"President—But who gave you the right thus to change the form of government?

"Blanqui—It was in the name of the country in danger that we took it upon ourselves. You talk of right! Who gave any right to those of the 4th of September?

"President—At any rate they were the elected of the nation. . . ." But the colonel had had enough of La Villette, and, after some awkward hesitation, added, "Well, let us go to the affair of the 31st of October," (when the Hôtel de Ville was invaded). The colonel had better have stuck to the record, and commenced there.

Blanqui then went at length into the last-named affair. MM. Jules Ferry, Jules Simon, and other members of the September government were examined; but this portion of the inquiry is not in place here, and besides, the facts have already been given at sufficient length. Blanqui maintained that the affair ended with an understanding that there should be no prosecution, and this was certainly the understanding in Paris at the time; the fact of M. Jules Favre leaving the Hôtel de Ville, arm-in-arm with Blanqui, being universally asserted. The witnesses were not at all unanimous or clear upon this subject, and Blanqui certainly had the benefit of the doubt in the opinion of the public. M. Dorian, member of the Assembly, did not hesitate to declare that Blanqui was perfectly right upon this point.

The prisoner exhibited the most perfect coolness and presence of mind, and gave the court some sharp retorts. Amongst others, "I have noted," he said, "that the commissary of the government [who read in court a decree of M. Thiers, authorizing M. Jules Simon, as a minister, to give evidence], evoked against me principles which existed before our first revolution. For him the revolutions of 1789, of 1830, and of 1848, are so many crimes. Well! I retain this fact in my memory from to-day, that, under a government called republican, I have been prosecuted in the name of monarchial principles." And having no more to say, he calmly took up his cloak, threw it over his shoulders, and followed his guards out of the court, with more apparent unconcern than was shown by any one there.

The court only deliberated for half an hour, and sentenced Blanqui to transportation in a fortified place. When re-introduced, the prisoner heard his sentence read without exhibiting the slightest emotion; and it is said that, since he has been in prison, he has devoted himself principally to astronomy and mathematics.

There must surely be something rotten in our boasted civilization, when a man of such intelligence and self-reliant power can find no better occupation for his admitted talents than that of permanent conspiracy; or are we to attribute his extraordinary career to insanity, monomania, or mere idiosyncrasy?

The trial of a well-known young physician, named Goupil, created some sensation from the intelligence and respectability of his appearance, and in some measure also, from the fact that his young wife and two children appeared in court. There were two charges against Dr. Goupil; the first being that he had, on the 31st October, the day of the first communalist *émeute*, sequestrated a captain of the national guard, who was the bearer of an order from the government. The charge was proved to a certain extent, and the captain had been detained for about half an hour, but solely, as the prisoner said, because the order was believed to be a forgery. Strange to say, the accused was charged by the court with having had to do with a certain printed document, of which no mention was made in the charge against him; it appeared that this paper, an appeal to the people on the part of the maire, was very violently worded. Goupil made some alterations in the draft for the printer, and declared that he was thanked at the *mairie*, for having done so, and afterwards charged with the fact as a crime. Goupil was condemned to two years' imprisonment and costs. The second charge on which he was tried was far more serious; he was a member of the Commune, delegate to the minister of Public Instruction, and was charged with the arrest of a M. Magnabal, and the sequestration of two Lazarist monks. It was clearly proved that Goupil had always tried to protect the clergy, and had protested energetically against acts of brutality unworthy of intelligent men, and had declared that the clergy had done nothing to excuse the absurd and cowardly persecutions of the Commune. These declarations had made him suspected, and nearly caused his arrest, and when ordered to search religious houses for concealed arms, he was accompanied by agents of the police, to force him to act as ordered. He was so disgusted with the conduct of the Commune, that he gave in his resignation, and on the 6th of April managed to escape from Paris. The principal of the Lazarists, and others, bore testimony to the truth of Goupil's statement, and said that when Lagrange, the special agent of Goupil, searched the house, nothing was destroyed, broken, or damaged, and no one put to inconvenience. All the witnesses gave similar testimony; but Goupil was condemned to five years' imprisonment, by a majority of five against two in the council. The sympathy in favour of Dr. Goupil and his unfortunate family is very general, and it is not likely that such a severe sentence will be carried out to the full extent.

The French law allows of appeal in case of condemnation to death, and nearly all the prisoners sentenced have availed themselves of the privilege. Many cases stood over for weeks, and even months, in consequence, and because the sentences are finally deliberated upon by a council of mercy, and a long time generally elapses between sentence and execution.

On the 22nd of February the execution of Verdaguer, Herpin-Lacroix, and Lagrange—condemned for the assassination, or for complicity in the assassination, of Generals Lécomte and Clément Thomas at Montmartre—took place. The culprits were not informed of the decision until three o'clock of the morning of the execution. Verdaguer had been ill, and subject to violent convulsions, and was at first terribly affected at the idea of leaving his wife and children; but he soon rallied. This man and Lagrange were both deserters from the army, so that their case was doubly bad. The three men exhibited great calmness and resignation, declared their respect for the law and for their judges and all with whom they had come in contact in prison, and embraced the director and all the attendants, as well as each other, with emotion.

The execution took place in presence of a mass of troops, composed of detachments from all the corps in the army. At half-past six all was over, and the troops left the ground, according to custom in such cases, the band in advance playing gay music! The custom of quitting the grave of a hero with lively music, although it grates upon the feelings, is comprehensible from a military point of view: the deceased has died the death which, to a soldier, is glory; but music after such a scene as the above is horrible to 'think of!'

On the 14th of March commenced the trial of twenty-three prisoners implicated in the "affair of the Rue Haxo," which was the most considerable massacre under the Commune, no less than forty-seven hostages having been shot in that street on May 26. Some of the prisoners were old acquaintances of the frequenters of the Versailles Riding School since it became the theatre of bloody assizes. François, the Communal gaoler of La Roquette prison, already under sentence to hard labour for life for participation in the murder of the archbishop of Paris, again appeared in his old place. Next to him was Ramain, the turnkey, let off before with ten years' penal servitude, but now once more put upon trial for his life. Several of the other prisoners, officers of the Communal army, were respectable-looking men. One, describing himself as M. de Saint Omer, a lieutenant of the 74th federal battalion, says that he was a merchant in Cuba; another, named Benot, a journeyman butcher, who was one of General Bergeret's colonels, was accused of having insisted upon the execution of the prisoners, although he had received orders to the contrary from the then Communal delegate for war, M. Parent. The indictment, like many of its foregoers, lamented that justice had not laid hands upon the principal criminals. It accused François and Ramain only of having given up the forty-seven hostages, knowing that they were going to be executed, but anticipated that the defence to be made by these prisoners would be, that they obeyed the order of an officer who represented that for strategical reasons it was necessary to evacuate the prison. François knew the name and rank of this officer, but would not mention them. More than half of the indictment laboured to show that François must have known for what purpose the prisoners were taken away from La Roquette. Whatever may or may not have been the complicity of François, the facts were that forty-seven hostages, consisting of thirty-five gendarmes, ten priests, and two laymen, were marched in custody from the prison to the portals of the Père La Chaise cemetery, and then along the Boulevards Menilmontant and Belleville, and the Rue Puebla, to the mayoralty of the Rue Haxo, which was the headquarters of M. Ranvier, a member of the Commune. The officer (name still unknown) who was in command called upon a Major Devarennes, commandant of a battalion at a barricade, for a reinforcement of eight men; and then one of his captains, named Dalivon, and his lieutenant, St. Omer (both prisoners at the bar), came forward "with alacrity," and brought many more men with them than were asked for. The crowd which followed the cortége was at first only "curious" to see men "who, it was boasted, were prisoners taken from the Versailles army;" but gradually they became bloodthirsty, and cried, "Down with the priests!" Their "hideous ferocity" went on increasing till they got to the Rue Haxo. Here the war delegate, Parent, ironically (as the indictment alleged) harangued the members of the Central Committee, saying, "Now, gentlemen, is the time to show your influence, and prevent the Commune from being dishonoured." A federal officer got upon the top of a cab and made a speech. Then the hostages were brought out, one by one, upon a bit of waste land appointed for their execution, and shot down with the muzzles of the muskets almost close to them. The trial lasted several days, and ended with the following judgments:—Seven of the accused condemned to death; seven to forced labour for life; two to the same punishment for twenty years; three to transportation for life; and four others to slighter punishments.

On the 21st March a man named Rouilhac was condemned to death, another, named Roussion, to hard labour for life, and ten others to various degrees of punishment, for an infamous murder which was perpetrated on the 24th of May. A chemist named Dubois, who lived at the Buttes-aux-Cailles, had the hardihood to declare against the Commune, and when his house was about to be turned into a fortress against the troops he barricaded the door. A large body of the federals fired cannon at the house, then forced open the door, and finding the unfortunate Dubois in the garden, shot him, and exhibited the body for a whole day in the front balcony. The house was then sacked, 2000 francs stolen, the wine drunk, and the servant thrown into prison.

Captain Matusewitchz, who was formerly in the 134th regiment of the line, was condemned to death. He was colonel of a regiment of federals, but made his escape from Paris. He was found guilty of participation in the insurrection, and also of having stolen the money intended for his own men.

One ecclesiastic only was charged with Communism, the Abbé Perrin, found guilty by a Versailles court-martial of exciting to civil war, &c., and arresting some of his fellow-priests, was sentenced (extenuating circumstances being admitted) to two years' imprisonment. The prisoner, who was vicar of St. Eloi, in Paris, exclaimed in the course of the trial, "And only think that I once refused a bishopric!"

The military secretary of the unfortunate Rossel, an intelligent young man named Jules Renard, was tried by court-martial. He took honours a few years ago at the normal school, and afterwards became mathematical professor in a large school at Lagny. When the war broke out he enlisted as a private in the 17th chasseurs and, after the 18th March, came to Paris to take service with the Commune. Rossel made him a staff colonel. He escaped to Belgium after the entry of the Versailles troops into Paris, passed some time in England, where he was almost starving, and in September, 1871, returned to Paris, where he obtained a place in a school, and lived quite unsuspected by the police. But the news of Rossel's execution excited him so much, that he went to Versailles and gave himself up. The court-martial sentenced him to transportation for life in a fortified place.

An extraordinary scandal occurred at Versailles, before the sixth court-martial. An obscure Communist, named Michel, was tried for bearing arms under the Commune. He was too poor to pay an advocate, and at the last moment he wrote to M. Bigot, who acquired a certain celebrity as counsel for Assi, to defend him. M. Bigot came into court, knowing nothing whatever of the matter; and he asked the president to be good enough to hand him down the *dossier*, or brief of the case, to enable him to see what the charges against his client were. To his great astonishment he saw on a margin of one of the pages a minute, in the handwriting of the president, of the verdict which had been agreed upon before the defence was heard. Against every charge was written the words, "Guilty by a majority." M. Bigot said nothing of this in his speech, merely pleading that his client, who had been in charge of the powder magazine at the fort of Vanves, was not proved to have borne arms. But after Michel had been found guilty and sentenced, by a majority of five to two, to two years' imprisonment, M. Bigot rose and moved that the president should put upon record that the conviction and sentence had been agreed upon by the court-martial before the trial was over. The president, in an angry tone, refused to take official notice of the objection, and accused M. Bigot of an "abuse of confidence "in making it. The defence would doubtless be, that the sketch of the probable judgment made by the president was merely for his own guidance, and did not exclude revision if, subsequently to his memoranda, new light should be thrown upon the affair. But, making the best of it, the business was an extremely awkward one. It is impossible to deny that the judges ought to have been listening to the defence, instead of drawing up their judgment before the case was concluded.

M. Elisée Reclus was a lucky man; his scientific friends in England saved him. He writes:—"I am able at last to tell you that I am free. After having been kept for a long time in prisons, and sent from one prison to another, I left Paris for Pontarlier, escorted by two police agents, who left me on the free soil of Switzerland. While breathing and enjoying the pure air of liberty, I do not forget those to whom I am indebted for my freedom. Having been claimed by so many Englishmen as a student of science, I shall work on more than ever to show them my gratitude by my works and deeds."

A prominent member of the Commune, M. Grelier, who for a time filled the office of minister of the Interior, was arrested in a peculiar way. He succeeded for many months in eluding the search of the police, and was all the time a cook in the house of the Jesuit Fathers at Meudon. What an unlikely place for a Communist to have found a refuge in! The police had long had their eye upon a major of the Commune, who, disguised in rags as a beggar, made frequent visits to the Meudon monastery. The ostensible object of his appearance there was to get a share of the kitchen scraps, which the monks are in the habit of daily giving away; but in reality he went to talk politics with Grelier. The false beggar, when arrested, did not perhaps exactly betray Grelier, but gave the police information which led to his arrest. It appears that when it was all over with the Commune, Grelier bethought him of a cousin who was a servant in the house of the Jesuit Fathers. This relation recommended him successfully for a cook's place, which he took under a false name, and which he might in all probability have filled for a long while to come unmolested, had he not yielded to the temptation of keeping up political intercourse with old friends.

The council of war condemned to death Colonel Henry, who made a considerable figure at the commencement of the Commune till he was made prisoner, so that he was more than a year in prison. The prisoner was deeply moved at the trial, and pleaded hard for mercy. Five other prisoners, Girin, Félix, Leprince, Badinier and Lemare, were sentenced at the same time to various terms of imprisonment, and of hard labour for life.

The *Official Journal* says that during the week ending the 10th of February the councils of war tried 305 prisoners, while 598 others were set free for want of evidence against them; and also, that the total number tried to that date was 4242, and of those dismissed on the preliminary examination 20,704.

Of those found guilty, 36 were condemned to death; 86 to imprisonment with hard labour; 341 to transportation within a fortified place—which means Cayenne or New Caledonia; 1002 to simple transportation; 470 to imprisonment, and 21 to confinement in penitentiaries. All the above sentences of transportation and imprisonment are for life, or during pleasure. In addition, 184 were sentenced to imprisonment for three months or less, 584 to periods exceeding three months, and 425 for one year or more; 80 were condemned to banishment, and 1 to labour in public works—an unexplained singularity. Of those tried, 1012, or nearly one-fourth, were acquitted.

Of the whole mass tried, twenty-five per cent, are reported as having undergone previous punishment for some crime or other; and three to four per cent, are foreigners. This last phrase completely nullifies the assertion that the Commune was the work of foreigners, rather than Frenchmen. Eleven prisoners, one of whom had been condemned, are reported as having escaped from the prisons of Versailles, and three from hospitals; while 213 died in prison. The report concluded with the statement that all the prisoners' cases had undergone preliminary examination, and 6000 then awaited trial before the councils of war! These facts exhibit in a terrible light the frightful evils brought upon society by the acts of the Commune: 25,000 persons confined for periods varying from one to ten months; of whom more than 20,000 were discharged because nothing could be proved against them, 3230 sentenced to death and various degrees of punishment, and then, more than ten months after the end of the Commune, above 6000 remained to be tried. A later return, to the 30th of March, gave the following figures:—21,092 discharged, 6887 condemnations, and 4265 remaining to be tried. Add to the above the tens of thousands killed and wounded, the thousands widowed, rendered orphans, driven insane, and ruined, and you have before you one of the most frightful pictures of human folly and human suffering ever presented to the imagination.

The great majority of the female prisoners were at the outset transferred to the prisons of Amiens, Arras, and Rouen, and few of them had been tried by the middle of the month of February, when two captains were charged with what is called in France the instruction; that is to say, the preliminary examination in private, which stands in the place of the inquiry before a police magistrate in England. The result of this examination was the dismissal of the great majority, about 130 only being retained for trial.

The large number of prisoners who have been set at liberty from time to time create much uneasiness in the minds of many Parisians, and furnish others with arguments, honest or otherwise, in favour of severe measures; for it is urged that the spirit of the Commune is as lively as ever. It is asserted that, since the return of the discharged prisoners commenced, there have been many signs of projected revenge, which naturally terrify the peaceful portion of the population. At the commencement of February there were accounts afloat of bombs having been thrown and exploded in the Boulevard Malesherbes, and in some of the public squares. The only acts of the Communists that are beyond question are the posting of a few inflammatory placards here and there; and even this may have been the work of one or two fanatics, or, which would be perfectly consistent with the Parisian character, of mischievous *farceurs*, on whom a horse whip might have a salutary effect. Whatever truth there may be in the statements and views referred to, there is no question as to the effect which the violence of the Commune has had upon liberalism. The journals, remarkable formerly for their true liberalism and moderation, have lost all hope and confidence. The following short extract from such a journal now before us is a case in point:—"For our part, after the experience of 1871, we ardently hope that the political and moral sense of the nation will remount the revolutionary stream. The current destroys everything and reconstructs nothing; in the place of ideas and principles it produces baseness and cupidity. Never, then, was firmness, determination, more necessary on the part of the Assembly and the Government."

When the Commune broke down it was declared that there were masses of Englishmen in the ranks. Prince Bismarck asserted in public that they numbered 4000. Some of the Paris papers cleverly seized upon this fact, and on the names of three Polish generals, upon which to found an argument that the Commune was not French, but cosmopolitan. This was smart, but like many such arguments, too smart by half. The Commune was thoroughly Parisian, and the foreign element a mere item in it. As to the 4000 Englishmen, where Prince Bismarck got his information from is a curiosity. Lord Lyons tells us that only thirteen were arrested after the army had entered Paris; and all but one were discharged. This exceptional Englishman has the un-English name of Fabre de Lagrange; but he is a British subject, a native of Jersey. He was well known as an expert electrician, and was charged with having managed the lighthouse at Montmartre, and of drawing up an excellent plan of destroying or paralyzing the action of the army, by means of mines fired by electricity. He asserted that he merely obtained employment as he was without means, and only amused the Commune with plans that could not have been carried out.

The army entered Paris on the information of Ducatel, one of the keepers of the Bois de Boulogne, who at the risk of his life jumped down from the ramparts, and told Captain Trèves, a naval officer, that the ramparts were deserted. There is no doubt about the value of his services, for M. Thiers gave him the cross of the legion, and presented him with 30,000 francs, equal to £.1200. Ducatel was taken up by the Opposition, and a good subscription raised for him, so that he was provided with a capital of about £4000. The secret of this was, that his name was peculiarly unpleasing to the army, which desired people to believe that it forced the ramparts and rushed into 'the city with irresistible impetuosity; and the royalists and others took up Ducatel simply to annoy the government. A lucky man is Ducatel! But what shall be said of party tricks like these, at a time when France wanted the aid of all her sons to bind up her wounds and restore her vigour. If half the energy wasted in such unworthy manoeuvres as this had been employed in an honest direction, the case of France would never have been as bad as it is at present.

The debts, old and new, of the city of Paris, are fearfully heavy, and must for a long period remain a sad burden on the people; but the new prefect and municipal council do not exhibit a desponding feeling, and propose to devote a sum equal to nearly £1,000,000 sterling for urgent public works, including £120,000 towards the rebuilding of the Hôtel de Ville.

In addition to the immense debt which weighs upon the city, there are the results of the conflagration to be added. The destruction of buildings alone has been estimated at £5,250,000 sterling. The following are the chief items of this estimate:

Palace of the Tuileries,	£1,080,000
Hôtel de Ville,	1,200,000
Treasury,	480,000
Palais Royal,	120,000
Palais de Justice,	120,000

Prefecture of Police,	80,000
Conciergerie,	20,000
Public Granaries,	200,000
Arsenal,	60,000
The Gobelins,	40,000
Palace of the Legion of Honour,	40,000
Assistance Public,	80,000
Council of State, &c.,	356,000
Entrepôt at La Villette,	120,000
Two Public Tax Offices,	260,000
Barracks,	20,000

besides ninety-two houses in Paris proper, and many hundreds in the outlying districts. When in addition to the above we consider the enormous quantity of grain, wine, and spirits burnt in the public warehouses; the destruction caused by shot and shell; the works of art, furniture, plate glass, and merchandise burnt or otherwise destroyed, an estimate which places the total material losses caused by the insurrection at more than £10,000,000 sterling, is probably not exaggerated.

A commission has reported on the burning of the docks at La Villette; the total loss is set down at £1,200,000, of which sum rather less than half represents wine, brandy, and articles of food. The destruction of the great government corn stores, called the Grenier d'Abondance, has not been reported upon officially; but the loss in this case is estimated approximatively at nearly one million sterling.

The destruction of the entire registers of births, marriages, and deaths of any city, must cause immense inconvenience; but especially so in Paris, where the formalities respecting births, deaths, and marriages are so multitudinous and minute that it is a wonder any one ventures either to be born, to be married, or to die. No boy can enter any of the public schools, no man enter any public office, without producing the certificate of his birth; then every year all the youths of the age of twenty have to appear and draw lots for military service, when, of course, certificates of birth are required. This conscription gives rise sometimes to curious scenes; not to present yourself at the proper age for the conscription is a very serious offence, and the municipal officers take care to hunt up defaulters very sharply. A few years since an inhabitant of Paris received a peremptory summons to bring up his son to draw for the conscription. The reply was he had no son, but a daughter of that age was produced. The parents protested that they had nothing to do with the blundering of an official clerk (a blunder easily made, as the French words for son and daughter, *fils* and *fille*, are very like in writing and sound). The managers of the conscription declared, that as the child was described as a boy on the register *he* must draw a number out of the urn; therefore *she* did so, and fortunately drew a high one, which gave her exemption. Had it occurred otherwise, she would have been enrolled for a time amongst the recruits, and it is terrible to think of the formalities that would have been to go through to release the young lady from military service. Perhaps it would have ended in a compromise, and she would have been enrolled as a vivandière!

Now all these registers are burnt, any one who does not happen to have the certificates of his birth, &c., in his possession, is placed in a great difficulty. The authorities have appointed a commission to act in the matter, and every one is called upon to deposit all the certificates in his possession relating to himself or his relations, and all these certificates will become the property of the state. It is naturally objected to this arrangement that many people regard such documents with almost superstitious affection, and that therefore the authorities ought not to appropriate, but merely copy and return them. However the affair may be worked out, it is quite certain that out of the million and three quarters of inhabitants of Paris a very large proportion will never be able to prove, legally, that they were ever born at all; and how they are to get through life under such circumstances is a puzzle. It is proposed that in future duplicates of such registers shall always be deposited in other towns, so as to prevent such another accident. This suggestion is certainly applicable to other cases besides the registers of Paris.

This loss of documentary evidence had very nearly been accompanied by another, namely, the destruction of the *Grand Livre* of France, which like our national debt books consists of thousands of folio volumes. This, however, was in duplicate, and one if not both copies were saved, so that the holders of government stock are spared the inconvenience which might have fallen upon them.

Some of the acts of the Commune also are causing similar complications; thus all the marriages which took place between the 18th of March and the 22nd May are declared void, as having been solemnized in the presence of revolutionary functionaries. An inquiry has been made into the subject, and in cases where both parties are living, and act in good faith, there will be little difficulty; but an unprincipled man or woman may seize upon the opportunity to set aside the contract, and the other party would have no remedy.

But this is only one, though a very serious one, of a series of difficulties. When we reflect that from September, 1870, to the end of May, 1871, the entire life of the nation, and particularly of Paris, was as it were suspended, that trade and commerce were laid aside, engagements deferred, in too many cases *sine die*, and that everything had to be taken up and set going again, with obstacles of all kinds in the way, dearness of money, loss of machinery, plant, and stock, and what is still worse, a diminution by thousands and tens of thousands of workmen, who will never more labour or suffer, the prospect is indeed a sad one; and from it we obtain something like a notion of the miseries which ambition, war, and revolution are capable of inflicting on an unhappy nation.

It is well that history is imperfect; for a true summary of all the crimes and sufferings, the mental and bodily torture, the destruction and devastation which were crowded into that short space of time, would form one of the most dreadful accounts that was ever exhibited against poor human nature. May the events of 1870 and 1871 close the era of war and revolutions, and may Paris grow more prosperous and more glorious; richer and richer in art, literature, and industry; gayer, brighter, more beautiful than ever!

CHAPTER V.

Parliamentary Inquiry into the Facts of the Communist Insurrection—Evidence of M. Thiers with regard to it and Subsequent Events—Evidence of M. Cresson and the Communists of October, 1870—Extraordinary Leniency to Prisoners—Unpatriotic Conduct of a Paris Mayor—Evidence of General Trochu—Strange Opinions and Statements—M. Jules Favre's Views—Evidence and Opinions of Jules Ferry, Picard, General Aurelles des Paladine, Adam, General Le Flo, General Vinoy, Admiral Saisset, Marshal MacMahon, Marquis de Ploeuc, Corbon, General Cremer, and others.

A LONG report, occupying two volumes, and containing the evidence of a large number of important witnesses upon the events of the disastrous year 1871, furnishes the world with a mass of very important facts, and throws light upon many points in its history.

The testimony of M. Thiers occupies the first place. He said the government had no confidence in the success of the steps to retake the guns from Montmartre, but it was impossible to refrain from making the attempt. After the failure of this undertaking, M. Thiers says he did not for a moment hesitate about withdrawing the army from contact with the revolution. "On the 24th of February," he adds, "when matters had already taken a bad turn, the king of Prussia asked him what was to be done, and I answered that we must leave Paris, and return there with Marshal Bugeaud and 50,000 men." Attempts were made to get together such of the national guards as were still to be depended on, but all the drumbeating and exhortations only produced from 500 to 600.

All the forts except Mont Valérien had to be evacuated, because they would have required 8000 men, which the government could not furnish. M. Thiers went on to say that, during the first fortnight that he was at Versailles, he was anything but easy in his mind; for "had we been attacked by 70,000 to 80,000 men, I would not have answered for the stanchness of the army." The Communist leaders told the people of Paris something like this over and over again, but they were not believed; and they, by the accounts of their own generals, never could get together anything like that number of trustworthy troops.

The president of the republic naturally concluded with a few sentences relating to the subsequent state of affairs, and thus excused, or rather justified, the facts of the Assembly remaining at Versailles, and Paris being kept in a state of siege. "I continue to believe," he says, "that while standing upon our guard, and being always prepared for resistance, there should be constant moderation in the general conduct of the government, which, however, does not exclude either assiduous vigilance or invincible firmness."

One of the most important witnesses examined was M. Cresson, who was prefect of police from November, 1870; and having collected 1200 sergents de ville, or gardiens de la paix publique, as they were called, and having selected twenty-two commissaries, proceeded to arrest the Communists who had created the insurrection of the 31st October. A man named Châtelain, known as an agent of the *Internationale*, in whose possession were found some very important documents, was arrested in his own apartments; but M. Jules Ferry, a member of the Government, denied the political power of the *Internationale*, said that it was composed of very honest men, that he knew them, and that he had pleaded for them as advocate. Châtelain was therefore released. About the same time a man named Ranvier, a fanatic capable of anything, was also arrested. He had two interesting daughters, and begged the favour of going to see them. The *juge d'instruction* and the *procureur de la republic* gave him forty-eight hours' leave, but without informing the prefect of police of the fact. Ranvier departed, and appeared that very night at the Belleville clubs, at one of which he said: "They had not the courage to shoot me. We will have that courage, and shoot them." Of course he did not return to prison.

The history of Félix Pyat, as told by M. Cresson, is still more strange. He was taken prisoner, and immediately wrote to M. E. Arago, then minister of Justice, "What a misfortune I am your prisoner. You ought to be my advocate." M. Arago immediately called on M. Cresson, and demanded the liberation of Pyat as "one of the veterans of the democracy." M. Cresson refused to comply, but three days later the prisoner was released by an order, on the ground that there was no case against him.

M. Cresson gave it as his opinion that if, after the 31st October, the Communists had been taken before a court-martial, it would have been an act of justice, and would have given immense confidence to the majority of half a million who, on the 2nd of November, had voted the act of confidence in the government, and would have imposed silence on the 50,000 or 60,000 bandits—this is M. Cresson's exact expression—who were in opposition, and whom it was necessary to put down. Of the mayors of Paris, M. Cresson says some of these were good men, but a great many of them were animated by the most detestable spirit. It must be remembered that there are twenty mayors in the city, each powerful in his arrondissement, or district, so that their influence is considerable for good or evil. Bombs, he adds, were being manufactured at Montmartre, and the individual who specially interested himself in their fabrication was the mayor of Montmartre, M. Clémenceau! When this was discovered he at once gave up 600, but a still larger number was afterwards found in his possession!

M. Cresson demanded the closing of the clubs, but this measure was not carried out till after the 22nd of January, and they were soon opened again after the capitulation on account of the elections; during which time public meetings are legal. M. Cresson thinks the principal cause of the insurrection was the revolutionary spirit which had been engendered during the siege, by permitting "mayors and assistant mayors to be elected in Paris who did not recognize the government." Many people, on the contrary, think that the cause of the success, for a time, of a Commune, was the refusal of the government to give the Parisians the use of their municipal rights! Who shall judge between the advocates of arbitrary government and of free institutions?

General Trochu, the ex-governor of Paris, was re-examined before the commission, and his views of the causes of the insurrection were read with astonishment. He considered that one of the first causes of this insurrection was the relations of the empire with the demagogues. "For myself," he says, "politically speaking, the empire and the demagogy were *Siamese twin brothers*, although in reality enemies." The general is also convinced that the hand of Prussia was in all the difficulties that the government had to contend with in Paris, and that M. Bismarck had his allies and his accomplices in the clubs and the radical press. "The demagogues," he says, "organized themselves during the siege to the cry of *guerre à outrance*—war to the knife, as we should say; but once masters of Paris, in possession of 2000 pieces of artillery, with considerable provisions of all kinds, they hastened to come to an understanding with the Prussians, and were full of politeness and complaisance to them." The general further declared his belief that "Dombrowski was an agent in the pay of the enemy." The ex-governor added a good deal more in the same strain, but nothing sufficiently circumstantial to demand quotation.

General Trochu agreed with all the witnesses that to have disarmed the national guards at the time of, or after the capitulation, would have been impossible; and he added that had the army retained their arms Paris might have been kept quiet, but "in spite of all the arguments and pleadings of himself (the general) and M. Jules Favre, M. Bismarck persisted in disarming it. He only exhibited any consideration for the national guard."

When we remember the congratulations of the then government respecting the retention of the arms of the national guard, these revelations and assertions from the mouth of a member of that government fall strangely on the ear.

M. Jules Favre was the next witness, and said, that the government of September found itself in presence of a vast political conspiracy, better organized than could have been imagined; but he did not regard the members of the *Internationale* as the leaders in the insurrection of the Commune of the 18th of March. He believed the causes to be various; first, there were the fortifications, which rendered the resistance possible for a time; next to that, the moral condition of the city. During the siege the upper and intelligent classes behaved admirably, but towards the end of January their generous patriotism ran into extravagance. As to the intermediate classes, M. Jules Favre declared them to have been most ignorant and dangerous; and the working-classes, with some admirable exceptions, lost during the siege all ideas of morality and economy, and were prepared for anything that should change the face of society and satisfy their political and social passions. The monster that the government had to contend with was sketched with much vigour:—

"Every day new legions were organized in order to obtain the pay; the expense amounted to 600,000or 700,000 francs (£24,000 to£28,000) per day; the situation was horrible! I felt sure that if we should succeed in passing the crisis without, we should have to contend with the crisis within; you cannot place arms in the hands of so many vagabonds (*mauvais sujets*) without having to think some day how you are to get them out of them again."

M. Favre struck a right chord when he enumerated amongst the probable occasions of the insurrection the absence of the best men in the national guard. Fatigued with their five months' imprisonment and poor fare, eager to clasp again in their arms their loved ones, who had been sent all over Europe out of harm's way, those who had the means rushed out of Paris at the opening of the gates, little suspecting what would spring up and occupy the vacuum they had left behind them. Again, the entry of the Prussians exasperated people's minds; and here M. Jules Favre read his countrymen a lesson which they would do well to study carefully. He said, "A proclamation" (a placard would have been the proper word), "with the following sentence, 'the barbarians halt at the gates of the holy city,' furnished M. Bismarck with the last pretext for insisting on the occupation." It would be well to remember for the future that no one likes to be insulted, and that probably the Prussians argued, that if they did not enter Paris the French would at once have proclaimed that they were afraid to do so.

M. Jules Favre thought that "the *Internationale* was not first in the breach on the 18th of March, but that it organized the victory," and he did not agree with General Trochu with respect to the relations between the Prussians and the demagogues during the siege.

M. Jules Ferry, ex-mayor of Paris, whose correspondence has been published, proving that he was a good deal more clear-sighted than some of his colleagues, gave an extraordinary account of the Belleville men.

"At the end of September, or the commencement of October," he says, "we were much surprised to find superior arms in the hands of the Belleville battalion. We inquired into the matter, and learnt that it was Flourens who had purchased and paid for these arms, amongst which were some Chassepots." These arms, it is said, were purchased before the 4th of September—the end of the Empire.

M. Jules Ferry gave an account of his visit to Belleville with a flag; it appears that the flag had been asked for some time before, and evidently not given. Now, some one on the staff fancied that if it were sent it would be a mark of confidence and esteem to the tirailleurs of Flourens—for whom, it is added strangely enough, General Trochu had sympathy—and the government might thence draw some good soldiers for the defence; and so M. Ferry was deputed to deliver the flag into the hands of the *legionnaires* of Belleville. "But," says M. Ferry, "I was very ill received, I was mistrusted by this population. I saw there men who only thought of one thing, namely, to explain to me why they would not go out? One of them said to me, 'I cannot quit the city, for the reactionary party has become master of it,' and he went into his house. Do you know," said M. Ferry, "what was done with that flag? The guards tore it in pieces before reaching the trenches, saying, 'This flag which they have brought to us is intended to denounce us to the Prussians; they have given us a special flag to show where the Belleville men are, so that Bismarck may massacre us!' "

M. Picard exculpated the Communists from the crime of assassinating Generals Lécomte and Clément Thomas. "Bonapartist agents played a great part in the insurrection of Montmartre. The day Generals Lécomte and Clément Thomas were killed, a young naval officer whom I know intimately, and who had a narrow escape of being shot with them, came to tell me how they were assassinated. It was the regular soldiers who were the assassins. A person wearing the uniform of an officer of marines commanded the firing party. Had it not been for him, the generals would have been released. Nobody knows what has become of this officer. The naval officer of whom I speak remained in Paris, and sought in all directions to find out where the murderer was, but without success."

This is very horrible, but the following is not less so. It was admitted in the evidence before this commission, that the government was very anxious to prepare for a capitulation and guard against a civil war by getting the Bellevillites slaughtered. The ill-starred Clément Thomas entered into this patriotic scheme, which Ducrot discountenanced. This warrior told Trochu and his colleagues, when they asked his opinion, that they would find it harder than they supposed to get 10,000 Nationals slaughtered in battle.

General Aurelles des Paladine, a severe soldier, very accurate as to fact, and having a rare memory, made an excellent witness. He gave a sketch of the councils of the government of the National Defence, which will not easily be forgiven by those who are there shown up. He says:—"M. Thiers was at Bordeaux, where he arrived on the 15th March. M. Jules Favre, who remained in Paris, had the direction of the branch of government installed there. His colleagues were M. Picard, minister of the Interior, and M. Pouyer-Quertier, minister of Finance. All the other ministers were replaced by their first secretaries, or heads of sections. M. Jules Favre informed me that the cabinet council met every evening towards nine o'clock, and requested me to be present at its sittings. I went every evening on his invitation. The opinion that I formed from what I saw at the council-board was, that in the grave and difficult situation in which the country found itself little was to be hoped from the efforts of the ministers. Their meetings generally began at half-past nine. Sometimes the council only opened at eleven at night, because the members did not arrive sooner. The proceedings commenced by a few words about public business, or state affairs. The rest of the time was passed in gay conversation, M. Picard laying himself out to crack jokes and tell good stories. M. Jules Favre did not talk much, but his colleague of the Interior was hardly ever silent. If he could not keep up an amusing conversation with his neighbour on the right, he tried what he could do with the one on the left. I admit this was not businesslike; but what I say is literally true. The talk and fun went on till one o'clock in the morning. Occasionally a despatch was brought from the prefecture of the police, from a ministry, or from the staff, to keep us informed of the situation. General Vinoy often lost patience. He sat next me, and we used to say that it was pure loss of time for us to attend those ministerial councils. As commander of the national guard, I chiefly corresponded with M. Picard. I gave him a daily report of what was going on. His answer generally was, 'Oh, it's nothing. We're used to that sort of thing. You know of what curious stuff the population of Paris is made.' M. Picard was incredibly careless in business matters. Here is an instance. The officers of the national guard who were mobilized had been promised a rise of salary, and the same pecuniary advantages as the officers of the Line; that is to say, an indemnity for their outfit. These advantages were formally promised. But as the siege dragged on, the government began to repent of saddling the state with such a heavy expense. It was then decided that no allowance for outfits was to be made. However, a compensation of some sort was necessary, and it was finally arranged that two months' extra pay was to be given as a remuneration for the cost of uniforms, &c. The first month was paid in February, but not the second. When 1 took the command of the national guard, I was overwhelmed with demands and complaints. I understood nothing of the matter, and asked an explanation from a member of my staff, who gave me a very clear one. In consequence of what he told me I at once waited on M. Picard, to demand the entire fulfilment of the engagement made by the government. He received me in his gay, jaunty way, and when I told him on what errand I had come, he said, 'Make your mind easy, and pay them the other month.' 'But I must have the order.' 'Nothing easier, I shall give you one. Yes, I shall see that you are given one.' 'But,' I interrupted, 'it must be a written order.' 'You shall have one; go and tell those officers that the matter is all settled.' I went, as I was authorized, and thought the affair was arranged; but the complaints and demands, I found, went on. Numbers of officers came to claim what was due to them, and I put them off with quotations from M. Picard. At length I summoned my principal staff officer, Roger du Nord, and instructed him to prove to the duns that what was due to them would most certainly be paid. He objected, telling me that the shortest way was to pay the debt at once. I positively refused to do this, unless furnished with M. Picard's written order, for the sum total amounted to 900,000 francs. M. Roger du Nord then went to expostulate with the minister of the Interior, and to inform him of my determination. Pressed in this way, M. Picard turned round and refused plump to give any order. 'Since the money is not paid,' he said 'let them wait some time longer for their indemnity." The 18th of March came round a few days later, and from that day to this not a centime of the indemnity has been paid."

Mr. Adam, prefect of police under the government of the National Defence, together with MM. Favre, Ferry, and Arago, denied that there was any connection between the Communists and the enemy; but he gave the following sketch of the Bonapartist machinations:—"Before the 31st October my attention was called to the proceedings of the Bonapartists. I quietly attended to this matter, and did my best to follow the conspirators secretly. It was difficult to track them, owing to the Bonapartist composition of the police. The presence of General Fleury was reported to me. I am unable to prove it; but this much I know, that a very important member of the imperialist party entered Paris in October. It was only at a later period that I understood why he came. Towards the end of October the Bonapartists plucked up courage, and managed to send emissaries backwards and forwards through the Prussian lines in the direction of Reims. I cannot affirm in how far these movements were connected with the insurrection of the 31st October. Subsequent to this date, the Bonapartist agents who were introduced into Paris disappeared as if by enchantment. I quitted the prefecture shortly after, and it was only when I heard of the capitulation of Metz that I understood the gravity of the intrigues which had been signalized to me."

A very important witness, General Le Flô, minister of War during the siege, went to Bordeaux in February, and only entered Paris on the 17th of March, the day before the insurrection broke out openly. He found the government occupied with the plans of the attack on Belleville and Montmartre. The army then numbered about 40,000. After the failure of the above attack General Le Flo went to M. Thiers, and they together went to see General Vinoy. From that time the president of the council thought that if the situation did not improve in the afternoon, there was nothing to be done but to evacuate Paris. At six in the evening the minister of War and General Vinoy were of opinion that it was necessary to quit the Hôtel de Ville, the prefecture of police, the Luxembourg palace, and the Palais de l'Industrie in the Champs Elysées. The government was much opposed to such a course. A discussion then took place respecting the holding of the Ecole Militaire and the Trocadéro; but General Le Flô maintained that there must be no half measures, and that to remain twelve hours longer in Paris was running the risk of not taking one single regiment back to Versailles entire. Such, though General Le Flô did not say so in as many words, was the small confidence which the generals entertained towards the army. Finally, General Le Flô gave an order in writing to General Vinoy, to abandon all the points which the army then occupied in the interior of Paris. "It was I," says the general, "who gave this order; it is I who am responsible for it; I am glad of the opportunity of asserting the fact. . . Consequently, if there be any merit in the act, I am glad to claim it." It is added that M. Thiers had, at the time in question, already left Paris for Versailles.

With respect to leaving the arms in the hands of the national guards, General Le Flo was decidedly of opinion that it would have been impossible to have taken them from them:—"If we had attempted to disarm them at the moment of the capitulation, we should certainly have failed. We should have had to fight a battle in Paris which would have lasted, perhaps, three days, and we had but three days' provisions; the consequence would have been famine at the end of that period, with 250,000 Prussians encircling us." The general is, however, of opinion that while it would have been impossible to disarm the national guards, a great fault was committed in allowing the disarmed troops to re-enter Paris during the armistice; they became perverted, and thus aided the demagogues in arms to carry out their schemes. This supposed effect of an enraged and demoralized army sounds like truth.

The commission of inquiry then interrogated General Le Flo concerning the evacuation of the forts, and if he assumed the responsibility of it. The general replied:—"The forts were evacuated without my knowledge, and it was not until five or six days after the fact that I was informed of it. It had never entered my brain that such an act could have been committed." The fact of such a proceeding remaining unknown to the minister of War for nearly a week, shows what a state of disorganization must have existed everywhere.

In conclusion, General Le Flô attributed the insurrection of the 18th March principally to the discontent of the national guards. He considered "it was a grand mistake not to have employed them more, for they would have fought very well. I told General Trochu twenty times that he was wrong in making no use of them; that he would be forced to do so some day, and then he would not have the credit of the initiative. General Trochu was not disinclined to employ them; and I must add that the man who was absolutely opposed to it was General Ducrot."

General Vinoy who was commander-in-chief of the army of Paris at the time the insurrection broke out, was the next witness, and a very important one. M. Thiers, it appears, before quitting Paris for Versailles, had given a written order to the effect that all the troops then in the south forts should be collected at Versailles. The general said he was opposed to the attempt to take the cannon from Montmartre; he recommended instead that the payment of those who had them in their possession, the allowance of fifteen pence a day, should be stopped; but he could not get the government to agree to this, nor could he get the leaders Henry, Duval, Razoua, and others, arrested as he wished. The government declared that it had not the means, and suggested that the troops under him, the commander-in-chief, should do it; but he replied that with 12,000 in a city in which the national guards had 300,000 muskets in their hands, it was impossible. The commission asked the general whether the attempt to retake the guns was not compromised by the unfortunate delay in bringing up the necessary horses to take away the cannons; he admitted the delay, but said that there were 600 guns to be taken away, and that each required from four to eight horses. Seventy pieces were got away; but it would have taken three days to have removed them all, and the insurrectionists might have taken others from the ramparts during the time.

In connection with this question of removing the guns, it may be mentioned that the Communists took them away, and got them to the top of Montmartre with much less than eight, or even four, horses to each. We saw many of them taken from the Artillery Park in the Avenue Wagram, first by two or four horses, but afterwards by troops of men, women, and children, who made quite an amusement of the affair. It would seem almost as though General Vinoy desired to shield the ill will of the regulars as much as possible, which was not unnatural; for had there been the will, it does not appear that the way to get the guns down could not have been found.

Another important point mentioned by the general was the temporary vacation of Mont Valérien; he was aghast when he found that the order to withdraw the troops from the southern forts had been applied to Valérien, and he immediately went to see M. Thiers on the subject. This was in the morning of the 20th of March. The account of the interview is quite dramatic; the general says:—"I went at one o'clock in the morning to see M. Thiers. He was in bed, and I had an explanation with him. He said, 'But what troops will you put in Mont Valérien?' I answered: 'You know that I sent you the 119th of the Line to Versailles, to clean and take possession of the town; this regiment is well commanded, and it is that which should be sent to Mont Valérien, and that immediately.' M. Thiers agreed to sign the order which I asked for; I then went in search of the colonel of the 119th, and asked him where his men were. The answer was that they were distributed here and there all over the town." Three hundred men were soon got together and sent off with an escort of cavalry to Mont Valérien, which otherwise would doubtless have been occupied by the Communists, thus rendering the position of the government infinitely worse even than it was. It will not be forgotten that it was this fortress which afterwards destroyed the Communist forces marching towards Versailles under Flourens (who fell on the occasion) and other leaders; and that no second attempt was ever made in that direction.

With respect to the other forts, General Vinoy was of opinion that it was absolutely necessary to abandon them on account of the disorganized state of the army. Besides, it was impossible to revictual them without the means of transport; and, moreover, they were within reach of the fire from the cannon on the ramparts of the city.

The above evidence shows what a condition the army was reduced to! As to the condition at headquarters, it is shown by the evidence of Generals Le Flô and Vinoy, that the order to evacuate Paris emanated from the minister of War, and that for the evacuation of the forts from M. Thiers; but neither thought it worth while to consult the council of ministers on the subject, nor was the commander-in-chief informed of what M. Thiers had done; he left him and the minister of War to find it out for themselves!

Admiral de Saisset, who is known to be a brave old sailor, was one of the worst witnesses possible; his thoughts were confused, and his assertions loose and careless in the extreme; he contradicted those with whom he had acted, and was contradicted by them. He said that Dombrowski, Engel, and Veysset, all dead, were traitors in the Communist camp. He admitted against himself, that he was sent from Versailles to amuse the Parisians by promises, which he knew the government did not intend to keep; M. Thiers, said the Admiral, never had the slightest intention of making any compromise with the Commune. How the government could have chosen such an agent for such an employment is beyond understanding; and how it could venture to send him before the commission to be examined, is equally extraordinary.

Marshal MacMahon's evidence was, of course, almost entirely military; he had nothing to do with the conduct of matters in Paris previous to the Commune, as he only returned from Germany on the 17th of March, the very day before the outbreak. He was immediately offered the command of the government troops; he only accepted it on the 6th of April. The marshal's description of the second line of defence within the fortifications at Auteuil and Passy, to some extent confirms the charges of treachery made by others against Dombrowski. The insurgents had made themselves, he says, a position of immense strength, by crenelating the railway viaduct near Point du Jour, and loopholing all the houses and garden walls around; they, together, formed a kind of fortress extending from the Bois de Boulogne to the Seine. The evidence of the marshal seems to prove that the insurgent troops had been drawn by their leaders from this strong position, so that the marshal obtained easy access, through Auteuil and Passy, to the central portions of the city. But turning and carrying barricades afterwards, he lost 600 men, killed, and had 7000 wounded. He describes the struggle as far more serious than generally represented. The insurgents profited by all the defences thrown up against the Germans, to oppose the government troops, and cause the victory to be sanguinary. In the early part of the struggle, says the marshal, the insurgents were intensely excited, and numbers of them fought with great energy. The red bags on the barricades were, in some cases, defended to the last man. They appeared convinced that they were fighting in a sacred cause, and for the independence of Paris. Their enthusiasm the marshal believed to be genuine. Eight days after the commencement of the struggle, the case was altered, a moral collapse had occurred; the prisoners declared that they only took up arms because they could not help it, that they served the Commune in order to obtain bread, &c.

When Rossel was arrested, he was taken before Marshal MacMahon, who says that he denied he was Rossel; he seemed confused, broken, bewildered. After being questioned he became confused, and at length said—"Well, I am Col. Rossel, I am tired of concealing my name; I am at length delivered from the miserable life I have long been leading." From that moment he was himself again, and recovered his natural ease of manner and self-possession. He was under the impression that he would be shot on the instant, and said to the commissary of police charged to interrogate him, "All I ask is, that they will allow twenty-four hours to elapse before my execution."

The president asked, "Did the women participate in the wild excitement of the men?"

"Yes, near Montmartre especially, they insulted and reviled the soldiers."

"After the taking of Paris, were there many cases of assassination?"

"Very few. All the time I was in Paris, only four soldiers and an officer were fired at."

"Is it true that there were many cases of poisoning?"

"I only heard of one. I was told that a man was taken to the ambulance in the Champs Elysées, directed by Dr. Chenu. He had violent colics; and there was an idea that he had been poisoned. Doctors Chenu and Larrey, who examined him, were of this opinion. I heard that the man ultimately died, and that he had been poisoned by a woman, who offered him a drink. No other case of the kind ever came to my knowledge."

"Can you tell us the number of insurgents shot in Paris?"

"When men surrender their arms it is admitted that they should not be shot. Unhappily, in different places my instructions to this effect were forgotten. I believe, however, the number of executions in cold blood has been greatly exaggerated."

"How many were killed fighting?" "It is impossible for me to say. I don't know."

"A general tells me that 17,000 were killed fighting in the streets and on the barricades?"

"I don't know what data he has to go upon. But it appears to me that his estimate is exaggerated. All I can say is, that the insurgents lost a great many more than we did."

There are ample proofs on record that MacMahon's orders were disregarded. Major Garcia, on his own showing, was one of those who forgot Mac Mahon's orders not to shoot prisoners in cold blood. He gave a dramatic account of Millière's execution, at which he presided, on the steps of the Pantheon. "He (Millière) was brought to us while we were breakfasting in a restaurant in the Rue Tournon. He was surrounded by an infuriated crowd, which threatened to tear him in pieces. I said to him, 'You are Millière?' 'Yes,' he answered, 'but you are aware that I am a deputy.' 'Possibly. And it also happens that there is a deputy here to identify you. M. de Quinsonas cannot fail to recognize you.' I then told him that the general's orders were to shoot him. 'Why?' 'I don't know you personally, but I have read your articles with indignant loathing. You are a viper on whose head one likes to tread. You detest society.' He cut me short, saying, with a significant expression, 'Yes, I detest this society.' 'Very good. Society in her turn will cast you from her bosom. I am going to have you shot.' 'Your summary justice is barbarous and cruel.' 'And all your cruelties! Have you thought of them? At all events, you say you're Millière, and that's enough for us.' Orders were then given for him to be taken to the steps of the Pantheon (a church!), and there executed. He was commanded to go on his knees, and demand pardon of society for the evil he had done; but he refused to be shot kneeling. I then said to him, 'It's the order; you mustn't be shot in any other posture.' He attempted to go through the farce of opening his shirt and presenting his bare breast to the firing party, on which I called out, 'You want to show off. I suppose you wish it to be said in what way you met death. Die tranquilly, and it will be better for you.' 'I have a right in my own interest, and in the interest of my cause, to die as I have a mind.' 'With all my heart; but kneel, I command you.' 'Not unless I am forced by two men.' Two men were told off to put him on his knees. The firing party was drawn out; Millière cried out, *Vive l'humanité*. He was going to cry out something else when he fell."

The next witness examined by the commission was the marquis de Ploeuc, the under governor of the bank of France, who gave an interesting account of the difficulties of his position under the Commune. When the army left Paris on the 18th of March the bank had in its possession, in bullion, notes, deeds, shares, plate, and jewels, an amount equal to very nearly £97,000,000 sterling! The bank at this moment represented, more completely than it had ever done, the credit of the country; for had it been invaded and pillaged by the Commune, it is difficult to say what might not have happened, with one-third of France in the occupation of foreigners, and an enormous debt to be paid almost immediately. M. Rouland, the governor of the bank, went immediately to Versailles, and from the 23rd March M. de Ploeuc acted as governor. On the evening before the bank had paid 1,000,000 francs (£40,000) to Jourde, Varlin, and Billioray, to enable them to pay the national guard, and to assist their wives and children. It was impossible for the bank to transfer itself to Versailles, and it was determined to accede to all demands actually necessary, to prevent its being invaded by the Communists. But already a second 1,000,000 francs had been demanded by Jourde and Varlin, who talked about taking radical measures if their demands were not promptly complied with. The second million was paid. After the proclamation of the Commune, M. Beslay, who had first been named governor of the bank, but who finally declined that title, was named delegate of the Commune at the bank, and entered into possession. M. Beslay then rendered such services to the bank as obtained for him the means of passing into Switzerland without hinderance. The truth, says M. de Ploeuc, demands that it should be known that it was by the influence, energy, and acuteness of M. Beslay that the bank was enabled to maintain its battalion of guards, formed of its own officers and servants, for its defence. From the 6th of April there were fears that M. de Ploeuc would be arrested, so that he was compelled to abstain from regular attendance at the bank, and the council met at the house of one of the regents. The situation grew worse and worse. A paper fell into the hands of the Communal leaders which led them to suppose that the crown diamonds were deposited in the bank, and it required great determination and patience to prove to them that this was not the case. By about the 12th of May the difficulties became terrible. Jourde pretended that the bank was accused of being used as the resort of Versailles conspirators, and as a magazine for arms. It was with the greatest difficulty that the occupation of the establishment was prevented; but at last it was agreed that previous notice should be given to M. Beslay, the delegate. Had the Commune got possession, it is impossible to say at what cost they could have been satisfied. The dangers had risen to the highest pitch on the 23rd of May. The troops had been in Paris for forty-eight hours, but the bank was not protected, and the fires which sprang up on all sides approached nearer and nearer to the building. It was not till the morning of the 24th that General l'Hériller made his way to the bank, and there established his head-quarters.

The finale of this story is that the Bank of France managed to escape by paying over to the Communal leaders, in all, the amount of 7,290,000 francs or £291,600, not more than a three-hundredth part of its stores.

M. Corbon, another witness, gave an insight into a new matter; he was formerly one of the maires of Paris, and during the Commune period he was one of the principal members of the Republican Union League, which is mentioned in the early portion of our notice of the Commune, but about which it was next to impossible to get fill iher information.

The republican league must be regarded as representing the real grievances out of which the Commune sprang, but as opposed to the Communistic leaders; in other words, the league, according to M. Corbon, represented the ardent desire of the Parisian population for municipal franchise, and formed a sort of moral shelter for those citizens, who, although very ill pleased with the Versailles government, would not act with the Commune.

The first idea of the league was to act as intermediary between Paris and Versailles; a deputation from amongst its members placed itself in communication with M. Thiers to ascertain on what conditions he would consent to treat. These conditions were stated, and M. Corbon does not seem to consider that they were exaggerated. The next thing was to ascertain those of the Commune; the league therefore sent delegates to the Hôtel de Ville, but they were very ill received, the Committee of Public Safety declaring the members of the league to be its worst enemies, and that they were undermining the defence to the profit of Versailles. Some members of the Commune, however, Vermorel and others, took a different view of the matter, exhorted the League not to lose courage—"Continue your work," said Vermorel; "the league may yet save all, may save Paris, and may save us from ourselves and from this frightful war."

The last attempt of the league was on the 23rd of May, when the Commune was in dissolution, but the Central Committee still sitting at the Hôtel de Ville. The result of this appeal places the committee in the most ludicrously painful light. The *ultimatum* of these men, who must have known by this time that they were utterly defeated, was to the effect that the committee would consent to abdicate and resign its powers on the condition that the army should immediately retire far from Paris, that the assembly should be dissolved on the same day as the Communal government, and that until a constituent assembly could be formed the government should be carried on by the delegates (of whom is not stated) of the great towns. This ridiculous ultimatum was, of course, waste paper.

The last act of the league, if M. Corbon is to be credited, and we know no reason why he should not be, had, however, a most important effect. Three of the Committee of Public Safety, terrified at the state of affairs and at the ruin already caused, revoked the order that had been given to set on fire the Imperial Printing Establishment, the Archives, and the Library of the Arsenal; and these three public edifices were saved, with the mass of public records of the history of France, the valuable books, and the splendid founts of Oriental and other type for which the Imprimerie is famous all over the world.

This short account of the acts of the Republican Union proves the truth of the opinion advanced in a chapter on the Commune; namely, that had the mass of the well-disposed Parisians exhibited any kind of cohesive action, the Commune could never have gained its mischievous power. We have seen that the league in March bearded the Commune and exhibited considerable energy, finding favour with the people; that it was able to maintain itself and attempt to bring about a conciliation; and that at the last it was still in existence, and seems to have done some service. That it did not do more must be attributed to the absence of many of the most influential citizens after the siege, and to the culpable apathy of the remainder.

General Cremer, who obtained the liberation of General Chanzy, had an opportunity of seeing the famous central committee and the most conspicuous members of the Commune at their work, and gave a graphic description of them before the commission of inquiry. He found that there was no regular president; one member being in the chair one day, and another on another day. "It was a deplorable sight," he says, "to see the *salons* of the Hôtel de Ville full of drunken national guards. In the great hall there was a disgusting orgie of drunken men and women; the committee met in a room at the corner of the building by the quay, and here there was more order and decency. The attendance of the members of the committee was very irregular, and when a meeting was called all the cabarets had to be ransacked." General Cremer's account of the *deliberations* of the committee is singular; he says, "They quarrelled" (literally, 'took each other by the hair') "during the first five minutes of their sitting; no pot-house exhibits such scenes as did the meetings of the committee; all the eccentric doings of the minor theatres of our days were unsurpassed by what I saw in the committee. Had they not been horrible, they would have been irresistibly comic. There were never more than six or seven members present at once; some were constantly going out and others coming in; some were always intoxicated, and these were the most assiduous, because as they were it was not easy for them to leave the room. There was one of middle height, well built, with long greyish hair, ill-kept beard, who invariably had his Chassepot in hand; when he addressed you he pointed it at you, and when he had finished he shouldered it again."

The publication of the evidence taken before this commission caused considerable sensation, and one violent quarrel. It is understood that the various witnesses, or some of them at least, believed they were merely supplying private information for the use of the government, and were thunderstruck at seeing their revelations appear in print. This belief is in part supported by the very free and easy manner in which some of the witnesses spoke of acts and communications which were certainly and necessarily of a secret nature. The extraordinary part of the affair is that the book is supposed only to be distributed to members of the Assembly, and not to be sold by the booksellers; but any one can obtain it for about fifteen shillings, and it has sold largely. It is said that some one acting for the Count de Chambord has spent hundreds of pounds in distributing it in the large towns; the revelations contained in it, both as regards the imperialists and the republicans, being of course immensely interesting to the royalists.

Among the contradictions to the evidence that have appeared in print is a letter from the Communist General Cluseret, who denied the truth of Admiral Saisset's assertion that the former was an agent of Prussia. Admiral Saisset was, as we have said before, one of the most unhappy of witnesses; he gave evidence which did himself little credit, and his assertions respecting others have been strenuously denied, and in some cases disproved; all admit that his mind is of a curiously illogical mould. In reply to General Cluseret's letter, it is declared that, in 1870 at any rate, he was in relation with the German legation at Berne. This, however, is evidence as loose as that of the brave but blundering admiral, who was challenged by the ex-General Cremer for stating that the latter was paid heavily for securing the release of General Chanzy from the Communists. He was compelled to retract this, and General Cremer cleared himself of any such imputation.

CHAPTER VII. GERMANY AFTER THE WAR.

Return of the Emperor to Berlin—Contrast with the Arrival of the Emperor Napoleon as an Exile in England—Rewards and Honours to Counts von Moltke and Bismarck—Meeting of the First Reichstag of the New German Empire—History of the Union of Germany, and Full Description of the Constitution of the Empire, with its similarities to, and differences from, those of other States—The Ceremony at the Opening of the First Imperial Parliament—Speech of the Emperor and Address in Reply—Delay on the part of the French in concluding the definite Treaty of Peace—Sharp Speech of Prince Bismarck, and its Effect in France—Differences as to the Meaning of some of the Points Agreed to in the Preliminary Treaty—Feeling of Exasperation in Germany—Meeting of MM. Jules Favre and Rouyer-Quertier and Prince Bismarck at Frankfort, and Settlement of the Treaty—Its Terms, and the Slight Alterations made by it in the Original Draft—Reception of the News in Germany and France—Grand Military Festival at Berlin—Full Description of the Proceedings—Legislation of the New German Parliament—Special Act for the Government of Alsace and Lorraine—Resistance of the Population to the new order of things—Seditious Language Forbidden in the Pulpit—Severity of the German Regulations as to Nationality and the Conscription for the Army—Payment of part of the Indemnity anticipated by the French with Beneficial Results to both Countries—Arrangement as to the Customs' Duties of Alsace and Lorraine—Application of the War Indemnity in Germany—Increase of Pay to Disabled Soldiers—Burying of 40,000,000 thalers as a "War Treasury"—Military and Naval Preparations to provide against the Contingency of another War.

WHILST the terrible drama described in the previous pages was being enacted in Paris, very different had been the course of events in Germany.

His Majesty the emperor returned to Berlin on March 17, and met with a very hearty reception; but the demonstration from beginning to end bore a civilian impress, and in the most military capital of Europe there was no military show. It might almost be said, indeed, that there was little actual rejoicing, or rather that the joy of the people was dashed with the recollection of what the struggle had cost them. Many thousand German soldiers were still in France; many thousands more lay in French graves. The recollection of these losses, and the absence of so many countrymen and friends weighed upon the minds of the Prussians, and saddened even their looks of thanksgiving. Nevertheless they illuminated their capital, and received their sovereign with the grateful loyalty due to his achievements. They felt the magnitude of their success, and testified, though in a comparatively quiet way, the depth and sincerity of their emotions. The emperor-king met his wife and children once more after a separation of eight perilous months; and on re-entering his palace, with a peaceful promenade of the population under the lamps of welcome, the eventful day concluded.

Three days after the German sovereign re-entered his capital as a conqueror, the ex-emperor of the French landed as a refugee at Dover. Since the previous 10th of July the one sovereign had gained a new title and an exalted position in Europe; the other had lost his throne, and, after being for six months a prisoner of war, was now an exile in a foreign land.

The emperor of Germany took the earliest opportunity of showing his sense of obligation to his two invaluable servants—Counts von Moltke and Bismarck. The former was created a field-marshal, and received the grand cross of the Order of the Iron Cross; the latter was raised to the rank of a prince. Subsequently the estate of Schwarzenbeck, in Lauenburg, was conferred upon him by the emperor, in acknowledgment of his services to the country. It had a rent-roll of 40,000 thalers; the capital value, according to German calculations, being equal to 1,000,000 thalers—the very sum the emperor intended as a gift. That sum, however, by no means expressed the full extent of his Majesty's generosity. The lands had been crown lands; the rents, even at the time of their assessment many years before, had been fixed very low; the above sum therefore represented not more than about the third part of the real value; and it was considered that, on the expiry of the leases in a few years, the rents would easily bear to be tripled. The German chancellor thus practically received a gift of 3,000,000 thalers.

On March 21 the dream of generations was fulfilled, when the emperor opened the first Reichstag of the new German empire. For the first time since the beginning of the century, a parliament met representing all the states of Germany. It was no mere Constituent Assembly, like the one wrecked on revolutionary breakers twenty-two years before; nor was it restricted to the treatment of financial affairs, as was the Customs' Parliament, the makeshift devised in 1866. It was a recognized body established on the basis of a new constitution, ratified by all the local sovereigns and parliaments of the land; a supreme legislative corporation, whose jurisdiction included a large portion of the ordinary political business, and was sure in the natural course of things to extend.

And here, as we have hitherto only incidentally alluded to the growth of the "United States of Germany," it may be well to state briefly the circumstances under which the union was effected, and to glance at the leading features of the new constitution.

The original constitution of the North German Confederation, comprehending the Prussian monarchy and the small northern and central states, came into general operation on the 1st of July, 1867. It instituted a Federal Council of forty-three members, and an Imperial Parliament of 297, which bodies were to form the Legislature in all matters affecting the common interests of the united states—such as the civil rights of German subjects, the army and navy, matters of trade and finance, railways, posts, and telegraphs, and the administration of justice. The presidency was assigned to the king of Prussia, with power to declare war and make peace, to conclude treaties with foreign powers, and to send and receive diplomatic agents. Where such treaties affected matters reserved to the Legislature, they required the sanction of the Federal Council and of the Imperial Parliament.

The victorious progress of King William in the war with France could hardly fail to determine the waverers of the south to accede to the union. First came Baden and the southern portion of Hesse-Darmstadt, by a convention signed on the 15th of November, 1870. The treaty with Würtemburg was concluded on the 25th, that with Bavaria on the 23rd, of the same month; and they severally took effect on the 31st of December, just before the assumption of the imperial crown by the Prussian king.

Baden and Hesse adopted the federal constitution with very few alterations—Baden reserving to herself the taxes to be raised on brandy and beer. By the treaty Würtemburg reserved the same taxes, and also, for the present, the regulation of her own posts and telegraphs. Her military relations to the Confederation were settled by a separate convention bearing the same date, so that her army corps should form part of the federal army, under the supreme direction of the president of the Confederation.

The accession of Bavaria was not so easily effected. The Bavarian government reserved to itself the right of separate legislation in domestic matters, the settlement of political rights and of marriage, and the regulation of the laws of assurance and mortgage, as affecting landed property. It further reserved the administration of its own railways, posts, and telegraphs, subject to the control of the Confederation in so far as the general interests might be concerned, and to the normal principles which the Confederation might prescribe for railways to be used in the federal defences. A committee of the Federal Council was to be appointed for foreign affairs, consisting of Prussia, Bavaria, Saxony, and Würtemburg, with Bavaria as president. At those foreign courts where there were Bavarian envoys, they were to represent the federal body in case of the absence of its envoy, and at the courts where Bavaria might keep envoys the federal envoy should not be charged with affairs exclusively Bavarian; Bavaria, in the absence of Prussia, to have the presidency in the Federal Council. The taxation of Bavarian brandy and beer was reserved. Bavaria was to bear the costs of her army, as a corps belonging to the federal army, such corps to be regulated in time of peace by her own government. Her fortresses were to continue her own, subject, however, to federal supervision; and the important stipulation was made, that in the Federal Council fourteen adverse votes should suffice for the rejection of any measure affecting the constitution.

After the meeting of the Reichstag some trifling amendments were made, and, as finally agreed upon, the constitution of the German empire bears date April 16, 1871. By its terms all the states of Germany "form an eternal union, for the protection of the Confederation and the care and the welfare of the German people." The supreme direction of the military and political affairs of the empire is vested in the king of Prussia, who, as such, bears the title of Deutscher Kaiser (German Emperor). According to article two of the constitution, the Kaiser represents the empire internationally, and can declare war, if defensive, and make peace, as well as enter into treaties with other nations, and appoint and receive ambassadors. To declare war, if not merely defensive, the Kaiser must have the consent of the Bundesrath, or Federal Council, in which, together with the Reichstag, or Diet of the Realm, are vested the legislative functions of the empire. The Bundesrath represents the individual states of Germany, and the Reichstag the nation. The members of the Bundesrath, fifty-eight in number, are appointed by the governments of the individual states for each session, while the members of the Reichstag, 382 in number, are elected by universal suffrage and ballot for the term of three years.

The Bundesrath and Reichstag meet in annual session convoked by the Kaiser, and all laws for the empire must receive the votes of an absolute majority of both Chambers. The Bundesrath is presided over by the Reichskanzler, or Chancellor of the empire, appointed by the Kaiser, but the president of the Reichstag is elected by the deputies. The payment of any salary or compensation for expenses to the deputies is forbidden by article thirty-two of the constitution.

The Bundesrath, in addition to its legislative functions, forms a supreme administrative and consultative board. It prepares bills and issues such supplementary provisions as may be required to insure the enforcement of the federal laws. The better to superintend the administrative business of the empire, the Bundesrath is subdivided into eight standing committees, respectively for army and naval matters; tariff, excise, and taxes; trade and commerce; railways, posts, and telegraphs; civil and criminal law; and financial accounts and foreign affairs. Each committee consists of representatives of at least four states of the empire.

The common expenditure of the empire is defrayed from the revenues arising from customs, certain branches of excise, the profits of the post and telegraphs. Should the receipts from these various sources not be sufficient to cover the expenditure, the individual states of Germany may be assessed to make up the deficiency; each state to contribute in proportion to its population.

Viewed in connection with history, the new German Confederation is a curiosity. Though a confederation, it is not republican, but monarchic. Its chief is a hereditary king, who, by its constitution, is clothed with the rank of emperor; and its other members are mainly monarchies ruled by kings, dukes, or other princes: three only are free cities, whose constitutions are, of course, republican. Now for ages past the chief federal systems of the world, Achaia, Switzerland, and America, and a crowd of others of less fame, have all been republican. For a union of princes worthy to be called federal we shall look in vain in the pages of history, unless it be said that something of the kind is to be found in the days of the twelve kings of Egypt, the seven lords of the Philistines, or among the tetrarchs of Galilee. No doubt under the old German Bund the presidency was vested in Austria; but at that time the league was so much laxer, the powers which it gave to the federal president so much smaller, that the likeness it bears to the present is not great. The rank of German emperor, with the federal authority vested in that office, is attached by the constitution to the crown of Prussia; and the really novel and important point is that the hereditary chief of the empire is also the hereditary chief of one, and incomparably the greatest, of its states. It is as if the governor of the state of New York should be *ex officio* president of the United States. The absurdity of this arrangement would be apparent. Instead of seeking the good of the Union, the president so chosen would be almost sure to consult the interests of his own particular state, and would almost certainly be appointed for that express purpose, which would not the less consciously be followed that New York, though the greatest state in the Union, is by no means so much the greatest as Prussia is greatest among the German states. But hereditary succession, whatever may be said against it, is likely to do much to lessen evils of this kind. Succeeding by right of birth to the imperial crown, as well as to the crown of Prussia; brought up, it may be hoped, with a view to the greater post as well as to the smaller—a German emperor may easily learn to feel not merely as a Prussian, but as a German, and learn to make the interests of the lower office, should the two ever clash, yield to those of the higher; the interests of his kingdom to those of his empire.

The monarchic nature of the Confederation is again very apparent in the construction of the Bundesrath, or Federal Council. This body does not answer to the Swiss Bundesrath, which is the executive of the league, but to the Swiss Ständerath or the American Senate. All these bodies represent the states as states, while the other house of the Legislature in each case represents the Confederation as a nation. But the constitution of the German Bundesrath differs in two important points from that of the Ständerath and the Senate. In both the Swiss and the American systems the true federal idea is carried out; each state, great and small, has the same number of votes in the Upper House of the Federal Assembly. The American states and the Swiss cantons differ widely among themselves in extent and population. In one house of the Legislature, therefore, each has a number of representatives in proportion to its population; but in the other house, as independent and sovereign states united by a voluntary tie, they have all equal rights, powers, and dignity, the smallest state having the same number of representatives as the greatest. The Swiss and American confederations, however, were in their origin voluntary unions of independent states, which have since admitted others to the same rights as themselves. In Switzerland, indeed, the original cantons which formed the kernel of the League are now among the smallest of them all. The political equality of Berne and Uri, of New York and Rhode Island, is therefore among the first principles of the two confederations. It would be childish to expect the same sort of equality to be established between Prussia and the conquered enemies or dependent allies, out of which she formed a nominal confederation after her victories in 1866. The confederate nation, as a nation, might, just as much as Switzerland and America, have equality of representation throughout its extent; but it could not be expected that the states, as states, should have the same privilege, or that Prussia should have no greater voice in the federal body than Schaumburg-Lippe and Schwarzburg Sondershausen. Each state, therefore, of the North German League kept in the new Bundesrath the number of votes which it had held in the Plenum of the old German League, Prussia adding to its own number those of Hanover and the other states which it absolutely incorporated. As these did not amount to more than seventeen votes out of forty-three, the proportion could hardly be called unfair; and by the accession of the southern states it has been so reduced, that Prussia has now only seventeen votes out of fifty-eight.

Compared with the senates of the Swiss and the American confederations, there is another obvious difference in the Senate of the new Confederation, directly and necessarily arising out of the monarchic character of the German League. The Swiss constitution provides that the members of the Ständerath shall be chosen by the cantons; the American, that the senators shall be chosen by the legislatures of the several states. No one would have thought of making the Ständerath consist of the chief magistrates of the several cantons or their representatives. But in a confederation whose states are monarchies, it would hardly be possible to shut out entirely the executive governments of the several kingdoms or duchies from a direct place in the federal body. The German constitution, therefore, makes the Bundesrath consist of representatives of the several states, who may be either the princes themselves or their ambassadors. Each state may send as many representatives as it has votes, but these votes must be given as a whole. Bavaria, for instance, may send six representatives; it has in any case six votes, but these must all be given in the same way. This is going back to the arrangements of the ancient league of Lykia, and is unlike the system of America and Switzerland, where each member of the Senate or the Ständerath has an independent vote.

Yet another peculiarity of the new Confederation is an important provision in the constitution of the empire, which did not appear in that of the former North German League. In the latter the president—that is, the king of Prussia—had the absolute power of making war or peace. He had to obtain the consent of the Legislature only when the articles of a treaty concerned matters with which that body had to deal. By the new constitution, the emperor cannot declare war without the consent of the Bundesrath, except in cases of sudden invasion. His power with regard to war is thus much the same as that of the president of the United States with regard to peace; but the powers of the executive with regard to war and peace are quite different in the three confederations. In Switzerland these powers are vested wholly in the Federal Assembly. In America the Congress declares war, but peace is made by the president, with the assent of the Senate. In Germany the emperor makes peace, with the limitations above mentioned; but he can declare war only with the consent of the Bundesrath.

The constitution of the new German empire, with its elected but not elective emperor, its Upper House of princes reigning by divine right, and its Lower House of members chosen on principles the most democratic, thus appears one of the most remarkable ever accepted by a great people. The new Kaiser has kings among his subjects, and his prerogative is curiously limited by theirs; but still he is in a sense monarch of Germany, a centre round which all Germans may legally rally if they please. Although compelled to explain his foreign policy to the council of kings, as the president of the United States explains his to the Senate, the emperor still dictates that policy, appoints and receives all diplomatists, and is apparently in no way obliged to alter his course should his council disapprove. He cannot, indeed, declare a war without their consent, unless Germany is attacked; but then almost any war may be described as one of self-defence, and in extreme cases the Kaiser can exert a mighty pressure upon the councillors. He has, it is true, on behalf of his hereditary territories, only seventeen votes, while his prince vassals have forty-one; but half of these princes are independent only in name, and of the remainder the king of Bavaria alone retains anything like a solid or defensible position. Even he could not resist unless encouraged by foreign aid, which his people would in no case endure. Of the twenty-four sovereigns and free towns in council,. sixteen have only one vote each, and are in a military sense powerless, mere nobles or towns of Prussia; while the chance that Bavaria with her six votes, Saxony with her four, Würtemburg with her four, Baden and Hesse with their three, and Brunswick and Mecklenburg with their two each, should all unite and carry, moreover, half of the powerless princes with them, is so small as to be not worth taking into account. Besides, in the extreme and most improbable case of a vote on war being carried against the emperor, he could, as king of Prussia, declare war for himself—a separate right which he alone has as head of a great power—and thus compel his allies either to rise against him, which would be impossible, or to remain neutral and see the representative of German military honour defeated in battle with the foreigner. Except in Bavaria the emperor is commander-in-chief throughout Germany; appoints all general officers; is, in fact, military service being universal, master of all men from the princes downwards. Bavaria, it is true, retains her separate army, and may appoint diplomatists if she pleases; but that state excepted, the empire is for all military and diplomatic purposes one and indivisible.

Had the unionists secured only this much, they would have been very successful; but they secured a great deal more, and framed a Legislative Chamber, whose powers will very likely prove far more potent throughout the fatherland than any ardent patriot ever contemplated. The local parliaments of the separate kingdoms and states still exist, but they have absolutely no control, either in theory or fact, over external politics or military organization, and are sunk into mere provincial legislatures, with less power than belongs to each of the separate states of America. On the contrary, the Reichstag, elected by universal suffrage, and completely dominated by Prussia, which returns almost two-thirds of its members, has, when in harmony with the council, entire power over criminal legislation, tariffs, excise, coinage and paper issues, commercial and banking laws, copyright laws, navigation laws, laws of judicial procedure, hygienic laws, press laws, trades-union laws, and laws affecting intercommunication; with the two small exceptions, before-mentioned, that Bavaria and Würtemburg fix the taxes on their own beer and brandy, and Bavaria can still compel strangers from other provinces to sue for a permit of residence. It is scarcely conceivable that a Parliament, of which one house is so democratic in its mode of election, so closely bound up with the dominant member of the federation, and invested with such extensive powers, should not go beyond the paper limits of its authority, especially when its legal rivals anxiously wish that it should not remain within them. The Prussian Liberals would most gladly merge their Parliament in the central one, thus getting rid at once and for ever of their tiresome and conservative house of squires; and Hesse and Würtemburg are equally desirous of being freed from the pressure exercised by their courts. In fact, except in Bavaria, where the Ultramontanes are powerful, there is scarcely a party in the empire disposed to stand up for state rights. The drift of opinion, of events, and of material interests, is towards a sovereign Parliament seated in Berlin— towards a legislative unity which would in a year or two reduce the states to provinces with hereditary lord-lieutenants at their head, and municipal councils to manage local affairs, including, it may be, education and the control of religious establishments. Prussia alone can resist this tendency, and her interest is to profit to the uttermost by her numerical preponderance—to widen in every direction the attributes of the Legislature in which her children are supreme.

There are, however, weak points in the new constitution, which in course of time may possibly involve the empire in serious difficulties. In the first place, absolute power is not lodged anywhere, either in the Kaiser, or the Parliament, or the subordinate legislatures, or the mass of the people, while the necessity for such power is perpetually recurring. Had it existed anywhere in the American constitution, the civil war might very likely have been averted, or at all events the obvious illegality of the insurrection must have cost the seceders hosts of supporters. It may be needful yet, in unforeseen contingencies, to override the Kaiser, or a state, or a combination of states, even while acting on their legal rights; but nowhere within the constitution is it to be found. Nor is there any provision for the reception of new states which may yet come in, and may fatally derange a system carefully framed to give its natural ascendancy to the state which has made Germany.

Again, with respect to the Bundesrath, or Federal Council, it is to be observed that no House of Lords so powerful was ever yet constructed. It is a co-ordinate branch of the central legislature, and is filled by men who must be conservative, who cannot be without followings, who are all in high military command, who have prestige such as can never belong to mere nobles, who debate in secret, and whose number cannot be increased. Each member is protected by immunities such as no noble ever possessed—is, in fact, beyond the law, whether local or imperial, cannot be menaced without treason, or severely criticised without danger of incurring the penalty attached to insulting German sovereigns. The immense strength of the United States Senate, when opposed to the House of Representatives, is the most striking feature in American politics, and its power is derived from the fact that its members represent states instead of districts. So will the imperial councillors, while they will have the further advantages of their royal rank, and their influence, necessarily great, over local elections. Should they rally round their chief, instead of quarreling with him, as they are very likely to do, they will form a conservative power against which the tide of popular feeling may break for years in vain.

Considerable interest of course attached to the opening of the first imperial German Parliament; but though distinguished by somewhat more pomp and circumstance than previous openings of the Reichstag had been, the ceremony was, on the whole, imposing rather from its simplicity than its magnificence. The aristocracy of Prussia and the North, who in other circumstances would have flocked to Berlin on such an occasion, kept quiet in their country houses and provincial towns, as there were few who had not cause to mourn the loss of relatives in the war. The "Weisse Saal," or White Hall, in which the ceremony took place, is a magnificent apartment of white marble attached to the Schloss Chapel, and worthy of the great historical spectacle of March 21. The architecture and decoration display a blending of strength, austerity, wealth, and grace. Lighted from a row of deep-set windows on one side, the walls between and below these are merely whitewashed, and are plain almost to meanness. There is an utter absence of drapery; but the ceilings are richly chased and gilt, and the compartments of the roof and side panels filled with frescoes worthy of a city where poetry and high art conspire to adorn the very beer cellars. A more fitting apartment could not have been chosen to witness the culminating glory of the House of Hohenzollern, and the triumph of the Prussian ascendancy. Twelve electors of the line of Brandenburg look down in marble from the walls, and there are eight noble figures representing the older provinces of the Prussian state. The vast hall below was bare of all furniture, except for the canopy on the dais, and a few chairs arranged on either side of it for the ladies of the blood and the representatives of the foreign powers. One door opposite was kept by the dismounted cavalry of the guard—with the eagle fluttering open-winged, in old Norse fashion, over the golden helmet, the white tunic with the crimson back and front pieces, embroidered in enormous stars of black and white and crossed with broad silver bandoliers. At the other entrance were posted the foot guards of the palace, in the quaint costume they had worn on high ever since the days of the great Frederick—a long blue frock coat laced with cross bars of white, and the lofty triangular shield-like shako, faced with polished steel and backed with scarlet cloth. Gradually officers in multifarious uniforms, land and sea, horse and foot, foreign and native, came straggling in, slipped nervously on the polished floor, or withdrew modestly into the deep bay windows.

About the time the emperor was expected no little sensation was caused, amidst all this blaze of gold and colour, by the entrance of several working men in cloth caps and coarse fustian jackets. As the more respectable-looking mechanic of the number advanced to the imperial dais, he might have been taken for a Cromwell of the Prussian type, determined on outdoing "Old Noll" by ordering his satellites to "take away that throne." They at all events did take it away, and proceeded to open certain dingy bundles, when panels of rusty marble, somewhat like the compartments of an iron garden seat long exposed to the weather, fell out on the crimson velvet of the dais. Out of these materials they erected a very ancient-looking but substantial structure, supported by four cannon balls; and it afterwards transpired that this was the imperial throne of the Saxon emperors, just arrived by special train from Goslar.

Then the hall began to fill, first with uniforms, thickly sprinkled with the sombre black and white of the civilian members of the Reichsrath. But the impression which, though doubtless erroneous, might have been produced upon a stranger, was that this constitutional ceremony was a military pageant, in which arms, once in a way, condescended ostentatiously to the gown. It was natural, however, for the moment, that the martial element should be in the ascendant. Peace, with her attendant blessings, had just been obtained by the sword, and she had to bow in gratitude to the prestige of war.

A burst of distant music excited general expectation; and very soon the grand entrance was thrown open. As the guards presented arms the Emperor William and Empress Augusta entered, and moved slowly down the hall, bowing to the crowd in acknowledgment of the loyal shouts and waving of hats and handkerchiefs. The old monarch, in his stately yet homely dignity, looked every inch the soldier—a man of firm mind and fixed ideas, inheriting the force of character and arbitrary will of his ancestors, and bent on being lather of his people in his own way. The various great officers of the empire now took their places, according to rank, around the Kaiser. The Crown Prince, Prince Frederick Charles, Bismarck, Moltke, Von Roon, and others with whose names the events of the past few months had rendered the whole world familiar, occupied places immediately adjacent to the throne, and were each objects of special interest. The white banner of the empire was carried by Fieldmarshal Von Wrangel, who, though over ninety years of age, stayed at home from the war sorely against his will. Three vociferous cheers were given for German emperor, after which Prince Bismarck stept out, and bowing profoundly, handed the speech, printed in large letters in a bound volume, to his august master, who proceeded to read it. Repeatedly he faltered; once his voice broke altogether from emotion as the cheers rang out around him; but recovering himself he finished amid a tempest of cheering, and handed the book to an aide-de-camp. Taking his helmet, he bowed low to the assembly, and retired greeted by another chorus of cheering, called for by the Bavarian representatives in the Bund.

The speech congratulated the Reichstag upon the victorious termination of the glorious but trying struggle from which the nation had just emerged—a struggle which had resulted in that unity which, although veiled for a time, had always been present to the mind of Germans, who had now in indelible characters, on the battle-fields of France, marked their determination to be and to remain one united people. Against the abuse of the power thus obtained Germany would be guarded by that amicable spirit which pervaded the culture and morals of the people; and the emperor regarded with special satisfaction the fact that, in the midst of a terrible war, the voice of Germany had been raised in the interests of peace, and a London Conference for settling international questions had been brought about through the mediatory endeavours of the German Foreign office. The first task of the Reichstag would be to heal as far as possible the wounds inflicted by the war, and to mark the gratitude of the fatherland to those who had paid for the victory with their blood and their life. The war indemnity to be paid by France would, with the approval of the Reichstag, be disposed of in conformity with the requirements of the empire, and with the just claims of the confederate members. The speech indicated the leading measures which would have to be considered in the current session, the legislation required for the territories recovered by Germany, &c.; and concluded by expressing a hope that the German imperial war would be followed by an equally glorious and fruitful peace for the empire.

An address in reply to the speech was drawn up by members of all the various political parties in the Assembly, and one or two of its most remarkable passages we must present entire. After reciprocating the emperor's congratulations on the attainment of the goal so long desired by their ancestors, and so ardently hoped for by the present generation, the address proceeded:—"We beg your Majesty to accept the thanks due to the illustrious commander-in-chief of the German army, due to the bravery and devotion of our troops. We are fully sensible of the benefits conferred upon us by deeds which have not only averted present danger, but protected us from the recurrence of similar troubles in the future. Defeat, and still more the strength added to our frontiers, will henceforth restrain our neighbour.

"The dire misfortune France is suffering now, in addition to the calamities of the war, confirms a truth which, though often ignored, is never neglected with impunity. In the family of civilized nations, even the most powerful can remain happy only by prudently confining their action to the improvement of their own domestic affairs.

"In times past, when her rulers were governed by a doctrine imported from abroad, Germany, too, chose to meddle with the concerns of other nations, and by doing so undermined her own existence. The new empire is based upon our own views of national and political life, and, armed for defence, will be entirely devoted to works of peace. In her intercourse with foreign nations Germany claims no more for her citizens than that respect which right and international usage accord. Unmoved by hostility or friendship, she is well content to leave other nations to themselves, and will be happy to see them regulate their own affairs as they think fit. Interference with the internal arrangements of other nations will, we hope, never be resorted to again under any pretext or in any form.....

"The German people cherish the warmest feelings of brotherly sympathy for the inhabitants of the recovered territories. Alsace and Lorraine are studded with monuments commemorating the most glorious phases of German culture and national life. Although the vestiges of the past may in some cases have been obliterated by long estrangement, Alsace and Lorraine have been our own for a thousand years, and the majority of their inhabitants to this day retain our language and national characteristics. We hope that legislation and administration will unite in reviving the German nationality in those splendid provinces, and in strengthening the ties which bind them to us, by conciliating their feelings. In this spirit we shall undertake the work of ordering the rearrangements to be introduced in Alsace and Lorraine.

"Your imperial Majesty,—Germany, to be satisfied, and Europe, to be safe, required the establishment of the German Empire. Our national longings for unity have been fulfilled at last, and we have an empire protected by an emperor, and placed under the safeguard of its charter and its laws. After this, Germany has no more ardent wish than to achieve victory in the noble strife for peace and liberty and their attendant blessings.

"We are, the most faithfully devoted subjects of your imperial Majesty,

"DER DEUTSCHE REICHSTAG."

When, soon after the capitulation of Paris, the required preliminaries of peace were agreed to, it was expected that a definite treaty to the same effect would be arranged and signed with little delay. France, however, was plunged into fresh troubles by the Paris Commune; weeks, in fact, months, passed by, and up to the beginning of May there appeared no indication of a desire on the part of the French government to conclude the treaty. The inference which Prince Bismarck drew from this delay may be gathered from a speech made by him in the German Parliament. "I confess," said he, "I am compelled to assume that the French government are determined to gain time by unnecessary delays, and that they hope they will be able to obtain more favourable conditions some future day, when their power and authority have been re-established." The chancellor went on to say that the imperial government were determined not to entertain any proposals springing from such a motive. Consent had been given for the return of all the prisoners to France, but under these circumstances the transfer was at once stayed, and about 250,000 men were retained. The cost of this measure to Germany was all the larger, that the French government had not as yet been in a condition to defray the expense of provisioning the army of occupation, as stipulated in the preliminaries, and which alone amounted to 36,000,000 francs per month, besides a large sum due as interest upon the stipulated indemnity. Prince Bismarck expressed considerable surprise at the remissness of the French government; and said that, as the Germans could not be expected to go on advancing money in this way to the French exchequer, authority would be given to return to the practice of requisitioning, unless the amount over due were shortly forthcoming.

Respecting the policy of non-intervention which the Germans so strictly observed during the troubles of the Commune, Prince Bismarck made some remarks which will serve to show the chaotic condition into which France had by this time been plunged. "It has been observed," he said, "that if we had interfered promptly we might have prevented France from lapsing into her present lamentable condition. But, gentlemen, I shrank from the responsibility of advising his Majesty to meddle with the domestic concerns of our excitable neighbours. Had we offered to intercede, the contending parties would have probably shaken hands, and, turning round upon us in the French emotional fashion, embraced each other with the enthusiastic cry, 'Nous sommes Français; gare aux étrangers!' Besides, we have no wish to deviate from the programme solemnly announced by his Majesty, which renders nonintervention in the domestic concerns of other nations a principle of our policy. I admit that the interest we have in securing the payment of the indemnity, was a strong temptation to take an active part in the establishment of a solid government in France. I also allow that we might have succeeded in instituting some such government. But just consider what the position of such a government would have been. A government virtually appointed by the foreigner might have found it difficult to hold its own, the moment we withdrew our protection; even if strong enough to assert its authority, it might have thought its position so disagreeable as to resign incontinently, and leave the responsibility of settling with us to its successors. But is there any one in this Assembly who could tell me who their successors would be? Things might actually have come to such a pass that *we* should have had to look out for a successor to M. Thiers. With the like unpleasant prospect before us, I think I may hope for the approval of this Assembly and the nation at large, if I think it as well to abstain from all interference whatever. At the same time, I am not at liberty to give a promise to France to this effect. We must reserve to ourselves the right of protecting our interests, and while leaving the French to themselves, we must guard against guaranteeing them impunity should our just demands be ignored."

This speech had an immediate effect. Within a very short time France, having concluded a temporary loan, at seven and a half per cent, interest, with certain London and Frankfort bankers, paid the whole of the instalments for the provisioning of the troops due up to the 1st of May. Communications were also resumed with a view to the definite settling of the treaty, when it was found that the French put a very different construction from the German government upon certain important points in the preliminaries signed at Versailles. First, the French government contemplated paying the greater part of the indemnity in stock; secondly, they insisted upon charging Alsace and Lorraine with a portion of their national debt; thirdly, they raised certain pecuniary demands connected with the cession of railways in Alsace and Lorraine; and they claimed a larger strip of territory round Belfort than the Germans were disposed to concede.

Concerning the first of these disputed points, it will be remembered that France, in the preliminaries of peace, engaged to pay one milliard of francs in 1871, and the four remaining milliards within three years of the date of the ratification of the preliminaries. But no sooner were negotiations for the definite treaty opened at Brussels, than her representatives declared that it would be impossible to pay such an enormous amount in silver. The coin, they asserted, could not be collected in all Europe, at least not for this purpose, nor by them; and therefore they argued that the preliminaries must be understood to imply payment in stock. The German negotiators replied that there was a great difference between paper and bullion, and that as no paper had been allowed in the preliminaries, the natural inference was that cash was meant. Upon this the French negotiators somewhat modified their position, and submitted to their German colleagues a proposal to pay one milliard in cash and four milliards in stock. The cash would be handed over within three years from July 1, 1871; the date of the delivery of the stock—French Five per Cents.—being left to special agreement. The German plenipotentiaries, however, did not conceal that they looked upon this proposal as an attempt to violate the preliminaries ratified by the French government and National Assembly, and it was plainly intimated that Germany would insist upon her rights. She had just been compelled to raise another loan in consequence of the prolonged maintenance of her forces on the war footing, caused by the insurrectionary difficulties in France, and to meet the unforeseen necessity of retaining the prisoners of war in Germany. That under these circumstances the French should throw obstacles in the way of the final settlement, with the view, as was considered, of gaining time and strength to make better terms, excited in Germany a feeling approaching to exasperation; and to prevent the unpleasant complications which seemed impending the French ministers of Finance and Foreign Affairs, M. Pouyer-Quertier and M. Favre, were despatched to Frankfort, where they were shortly joined by Prince Bismarck.

Before going thither the imperial chancellor had determined that, if the result of his interview was not satisfactory, the German army should at once occupy Paris either by an arrangement with the Commune or by force; and that the French government should be required to withdraw its troops behind the Loire, and then resume negotiations. Perhaps there was some foreboding, in the minds of the two French ministers, that this was the alternative awaiting them if they adhered to the views they had formed. At all events, Prince Bismarck found little difficulty in inducing them to abandon their proposal respecting payment in French stock, or the handing over of French debts with the ceded territory. A perfect understanding having been arrived at with regard to these matters, it was further agreed to settle at once the terms of the treaty. With regard to the indemnity of five milliards, it was decided that the payment should be made either wholly in specie, or in notes of English, Dutch, Prussian, or Belgian banks, or in first-class bills. The first half milliard was to be paid within thirty days of the occupation of Paris by the Versailles army; a second payment of one milliard was to be made by the end of 1871, and the fourth half milliard by May 1, 1872. The French negotiators demanded 800,000,000 francs for the Alsatian and Lorraine railroads, which however, was reduced to 325,000,000 francs, and even that sum was allowed only on condition of the German government obtaining possession of the line from Thionville to Luxemburg. The purchase-money of the railways was to count as part payment of the first two milliards of the indemnity, and it was stipulated that the whole of the last three milliards should be paid by the 1st of March, 1874. Interest at the rate of five per cent, was to be paid upon the indemnity until its entire liquidation, and in the meantime the German army of occupation in eastern France, consisting of at least 50,000 men, was to be maintained at the cost of the French government. The East of France Railway Company received 2,000,000 francs for the portion of St. Louis and Basle line on Swiss territory.

With regard to the extended area demanded by the French round Belfort, Prince Bismarck offered to give up the whole arrondissement of Belfort on condition of his acquiring for Germany a strip of territory along the Luxemburg frontier, comprising the communes of Redingen and Moyeuvre, where German was almost entirely spoken; and this proposal was ultimately agreed to by the Assembly. Respecting commercial relations, it was agreed that Germany should be treated on the same footing as the most favoured nations— namely, England, Belgium, &c; and further, that the Germans who had been expelled from France should be restored to the possession of their property and to their rights of domicile on French territory. Permission was granted that the prisoners might return, and the garrison towns be again occupied; the force before Paris, however, was not to exceed 80,000, and the remainder of the army was to remain behind the Loire.

In Germany the news of the peace of Frankfort was received with enthusiasm, and was justly regarded as a new and brilliant jewel in the princely coronet with which the emperor had rewarded the services of his chancellor. The success of Prince Bismarck surpassed, in fact, the most sanguine expectations. While thousands of his countrymen were prepared to hear that he had made financial concessions in order to obtain guarantees for the punctual payment of the rest of the sum, and no one ventured to hope that the amount stipulated in the preliminaries would be exceeded—all were surprised by the news that a definite peace had been concluded, without any reduction having been made in the sum demanded; that the interval between the dates fixed for the payment of the instalments had been shortened; and that far better security had been obtained by Germany.

The reading of the treaty in the French Assembly at Versailles naturally caused very great emotion. It was proposed to receive and ratify it in silence, as a lamentable but inexorable necessity. To this the single dissentient was General Chanzy, who could not resist the temptation of pointing out the strategical advantages Germany obtained by the cession of the strip of Luxemburg frontier; and also of blaming the French negotiators for submitting to burdensome and humiliating conditions *while the Prussians might have been conquered, had it been wished.* Such language might have been understood had it come from a Communist, who, ready enough to fight his own government, could never be induced to face a Prussian; but it is rather surprising as coming from one who, having failed in spite of his preeminent courage and skill, had thus clearly exemplified the utter inutility of resistance. In announcing the signature of the treaty, M. Thiers dwelt mournfully upon the onerous conditions involved, but found comfort in the thought that "all Frenchmen will be. restored to their country, and we shall be able to fill up the ranks of our glorious and brave army in far greater numbers than we were at first permitted to do by the preliminaries of peace. Our army, besides, has again raised the high fame of the French name and the power of France in the eyes of Europe, and the world once more renders it justice." These observations were received with great applause by the Assembly; though, looking at the events of the previous twelve months, it is not easy to see on what grounds.

On May 20 the treaty was ratified at Frankfort amidst great public rejoicing, and immediate arrangements were made for disbanding the huge assemblage with which the conquest of France had been achieved. The celerity with which this was carried out was little less remarkable than the extraordinary rapidity with which the German armies were brought together at the commencement of the war. At that time a fortnight sufficed to place upon the war footing a force sufficient to take the initiative and carry the hostilities into French territory; and only about the same time was required to send back to their quiet dwellings army and corps' commanders whose names had become famous in history, and to restore to the peaceful avocations of the spade and mattock vast hosts who had proved themselves such adepts in the use of the sword and field-gun.

Previous, however, to the final disbandment of the troops, it was arranged that their return home and entry into Berlin should be the occasion of a grand war festival, a fitting celebration of the great achievements of the past few months. The triumphal entry was the seventh recorded in the history of the city, and those which preceded it mark well the gradual rise of the successful state. On the first occasion of the kind Berlin was only the capital of Brandenburg, the duchy of Prussia not having reverted to this dynasty. The Austro-German Emperor Ferdinand had summoned the Brandenburg Elector, Joachim I., to assist him against the Turks. The elector sent his son with a force of 6000 men from various parts of northern Germany, or Saxony, as it was then called. With these the prince defeated an army of 15,000 Turks, and was triumphantly received by his father on his return in May, 1532. Between this and the second entry there was an interval of nearly 150 years. In December, 1678, the great Elector, Frederick William, chased the Swedes from the island of Rugen, having effected a landing in 350 small vessels, only eleven of which belonged to the government. To commemorate this the Berliners erected triumphal arches, and placed two clumsy imitations of men-of-war on either side of the *via triumphalis*. The most extraordinary entry of all was that of Frederick the Great, after defeating Austria, in 1763. Though victorious in the end, the hero-king was so distressed by the terrible losses sustained in a seven years' war, that he slunk into the capital unseen by his citizens, who were awaiting his appearance with all due pomp and circumstance. The year 1814 witnessed the entry of King Frederick William III., the father of his reigning Majesty. So conscious was the king of having had no immediate share in the war which led to the fall of Napoleon I., and so strictly honest was he in word and deed, that when his subjects received him at the Brandenburg Gate he uttered these memorable words;—"Personally I have no right to accept your thanks. But if this honour is offered to Field-marshal Blucher, and to the guards and my sons, who alone deserve it, I shall be most happy to join them, and enter Berlin in their company." This was the first time that the procession passed along the Linden, and the culminating point of the day was the performance of divine service in the open square before the Old Palace. During the offering up of the Thanksgiving Prayer the king, the princes, and the entire army there assembled, knelt, and remained in this devout posture for nearly ten minutes. To his son, the Emperor William I., two triumphs were vouchsafed before the late crowning event. His first entry was made in December, 1864, after the defeat of the Danes; the second in September, 1866, when Austria had succumbed to his arms.

The troops detailed to take part in the triumphal procession in 1871 numbered more than 45,000 men, consisting of the Prussian guards, some southern detachments, a certain number out of every regiment that had taken part in the campaign, a "combined" artillery battery, and the second West Prussian regiment. The latter formed part of the corps which carried the heights of Weissenburg, captured the first French colour, and also specially distinguished itself at Woerth. It was, however, selected to accompany the procession, particularly as the regiment in which the emperor served his term before promotion to the rank of officer. Previous to their first appearance in Berlin the troops were quartered in various neighbouring towns and villages, each of which celebrated a triumphal entry of its own on a small scale, and treated the gallant warriors with profuse hospitality.

By the municipal authorities no expense or trouble was spared to render the capital itself, and the approaches by which the troops were to enter, worthy of the magnificent historical spectacle it was to witness. From the Halle Gate to the Schloss—about five miles—two rows of ornamental flagstaffs were placed, fifteen paces apart, on the top of each of which was fixed a Prussian standard, with two German flags suspended half-way up over the escutcheon of one or other Federal state. Occasionally amidst this armorial exhibition might be seen the quartering of the Austrian two-headed eagle—a graceful remembrance of former alliance, and of the many eventful years in which the two countries went hand in hand. All the flagstaffs were connected by a continuous garland of fir, the symbolical tree of Brandenburg, which furnished many miles of festoons for the occasion. Amidst these, at various intervals, were more imposing decorations, consisting of gigantic pictures (some allegorical, others representing different scenes in the war), and of immense trophies commemorative of the leading battles, generally surrounded by the artillery and other spoil captured in the engagements. The way on both sides from the Tempelhof Field to the Palace were also lined with captured cannon and mitrailleuses, each having inscribed upon it the name of the place at which it was taken. The mitrailleuses particularly were a source of endless curiosity to the youth of Berlin, who, by grinding their handles, extracted a faint echo of the reality of their grunting; rode on the top of them as if they had been ponies; or examined with wonderment the intricacies of the spirals.

The Unter den Linden of Berlin, with the magnificent squares touching it at each end, is a justly famous locality. Running from east to west, a fine avenue extends 3000 feet long and 70 feet wide. On each side is a paved way for horsemen, flanked by a broad carriage road with adjoining foot pavement. The houses on both sides are amongst the finest in the capital, and contain a brilliant row of shops. To do honour to the occasion the centre avenue was lined with French cannon, and pillars exhibiting the official war telegrams, connected by festoons and garlands of fresh flowers. At five points the line of captured artillery was broken by triumphal arches, equally simple and tasteful in style. Between two columns placed on each side of the avenue, was suspended a gigantic display of canvas, like an ornamental carpet, covered with choice paintings in wax colours. These exquisite hangings were twenty feet by fifteen; and on one of them, Germania, in the attitude of an exalted priestess leaning against the national oak, sword in hand, while lightning flashed from the lurid sky, called her people to arms. Bavarians, Prussians, and Saxons, were all thronging forward to obey the summons. On the painting were words taken from the emperor's first proclamation on the outbreak of the war; and lines from Becker's "Rhein-Lied," composed in 1840, when M. Thiers seemed inclined to do as Napoleon did in 1870, were inscribed upon the back of the canvas, which formed a splendid purple silk standard, vandyked at the bottom. A couple of hundred feet further on, the next painting, whose subject was again explained by extracts from the emperor's proclamations during the war, exhibited genii bridging over the Main, on the banks of which the Bavarian and Prussian at length united shaking hands. On the third picture, Germania, a blue-eyed virgin of mild maidenly type, standing erect in a gold chariot, rushed into battle, with her fierce stalwart sons crowding around her. While they were cutting their way through death and flame, the German eagle in the sky swooped down on her Napoleonic colleague. In the fourth and fifth pictures, devoted to the apotheosis of Peace, Germania was represented as advancing liberty, industry, and science, under the shadow of the Imperial crown. As another little by-play, the genii of Concord, at a vast elevation in the sky, were performing celestial music, and urging by their harmony, the scholar, the manufacturer, and the merchant to fresh efforts. The unfortunate sufferers through the war were not forgotten amid all the rejoicing. The roads on each side of the avenue were appropriated to the wounded and their attendants, and some thousands were here seated on the "tribunes" prepared for them.

At the western extremity of the Linden is the Paris Square, an open area nearly as large as Trafalgar Square, London, and surrounded by palatial mansions. The opposite end, in the direction of the Park, is closed by the Brandenburg Gate, that celebrated pile, so often called the Prussian Propylaea. It consists of six double columns connected by a flat ceiling, on the raised centre of which stands the celebrated Victory in her iron car. On this auspicious day Victory had her attendants; for hundreds of bold Prussians clambered to her aerial heights to see the entry under the auspices of the protecting divinity of their land. The colossal proportions of the gate were enlivened by a profusion of green garlands of fir and oak.

Where the Linden abuts on the monument of Frederick the Great the Opera Square begins. It is 2500 feet long, about 1500 feet wide, and one of the handsomest places in the world. The king's palace, the Crown Prince's palace, the university, the opera, the arsenal, and in the background the ancient castle, with the town-hall tower overlooking the whole, form a cluster of monumental buildings such as are rarely seen together anywhere. The way of the troops into the interior of the city lay through the Brandenburg Gate, along the central avenue of the Linden, and down the Opera Platz, where in front of Blücher's statue was held the concluding parade.

Most of the public buildings were decorated with festoons, flags, and pictures commemorative of events of the war, or with well-executed statuary designs; and every open space contained memorials, trophies, or allegorical representations in many forms. Perhaps the best and most significant of these were in the Opera Square and Potsdamer Platz. In the latter, on a lofty pedestal surrounded by a circular platform, a colossal statue of Victory—a jubilant angel in a short tunic—soared into the air to a height of seventy feet. The platform at the base was graced by about thirty French cannon, the substantial harvest of the conqueror; and the significant word "Sedan" shone forth in golden letters from the supporting pillar, itself a model of beauty and taste. In front of Cannon-hill, as this exhibition was jocularly termed, were seated two immense and rather morose-looking Amazons, the one on the right side representing Metz, the other on the left, Strassburg. Strassburg, lugubrious in mien, sank the torch with which she so long combated her countrymen; Metz, like a pert vixen, had one arm combatively akimbo, and seemed to look down defiantly upon her captors. That Herr Begus, the renowned artist to whom the city was indebted for these remarkable ornaments of the *via triumphalis*, should have modelled the two cities so true to things as they were, was one proof among others that the Germans had no wish to deceive themselves or others as to the nature of their position in the new provinces.

In the Opera Platz, close to the castle, was a gigantic group representing Germania with Alsace and Lorraine. On the circular base, sixty feet in circumference, appeared in alto-relievo no less than thirty figures the size of life, representing German soldiers hurrying to the strife. Bavarians mingled with Prussians, and the Würtemburg forage cap was conspicuous beside the landwehr shako of the north. Girls were taking leave of their sweethearts, and as the strong and the fair clung in mute embrace, boys threw up their caps, each contending who should carry his father's gun. A lower frieze allegorized the German rivers, and the whole, as a work of art, deserved to be executed in a more permanent substance than plaster of Paris. Between this group and the Museum, in the large area known as the Lustgarten, stood the statue of King Frederick William III., father of the emperor, the unveiling of which was to form the grand closing feature of the day's festivities.

To witness the spectacle Germans and representatives of nearly every other nationality crowded in immense numbers to Berlin, the population of which was for the time almost doubled. The aspect of the city, from an early hour on the morning of the 16th, may be compared to Fleetstreet and Holborn in London on the well-remembered Thanksgiving Day in February, 1872; and large as were the sums paid on that occasion for eligible windows from which to view the procession, it is doubtful if they exceeded those offered in Berlin on June 16, 1871, for sites commanding favourable views of the military triumph. Very early in the day the burgomaster received telegrams from the German societies at Vienna, Marburg, Graatz, and other Austrian towns, congratulating Berlin on her successes, and dwelling with significant emphasis upon the fact that the senders belonged to the nation of the fatherland, and regarded its victories as their own—a fact the more significant that, only a week or two before, a thousand Germans from Hungary had asked permission to take part in the entry and march behind the troops. From regard to their sovereign's feelings the request was refused, but many nevertheless came, and joined the gratified Berliners in drinking to fatherland.

The auspicious morning dawned with beautiful weather. Business was, of course, entirely suspended, and from the early hour of five o'clock the streets streamed with people, who, in a continuous line, crowded the road the troops were to take. Gradually rising from the level streets, and often reaching to a considerable height, they formed so many artificial slopes, gorgeously decked out with scarlet cloth and overtopped by banners and standards, like trees shooting up from a hill side. By eight o'clock the roads were crowded with a vast array of civilians awaiting the army of soldiers, who after many dangers and vicissitudes enjoyed the supreme blessing of seeing home once more. The citizens who had not the privilege of a tribune ticket, took time by the forelock in such portions of the thoroughfares as were open to them. The numerous city guilds paraded the streets in their quaint semi-military insignia and ensigns, each accompanied by its band; and had there been an individual in all the city not conversant with the "Watch on the Rhine," he would on that day have had the opportunity of thoroughly making its acquaintance.

The arrival of a long and melancholy file of wounded, who seated themselves on the tribunes along the Linden avenues, was the signal for the first grand outburst of cheering, while the guild bands struck up with renewed vigour. At length there were indications that the great event was about to take place. Like a herald announcing his master's approach, a vehement hurrah arose along the procession. There was reason for joy For the first time in history it was not a Prussian, but a Pan-Germanic army, that entered Berlin in triumph. For the first time for centuries, the nation had grounded its political unity upon the rock of a united army. To accomplish this end, many a disaster had to be endured, many a bitter draught swallowed; but the full time was now come, and victory and comparative safety were, to the great joy of the people, the reward of prejudices conquered and interests more firmly secured.

The first glimpse the townspeople caught of the procession was as it swept down Belle-Alliance Street, and through Königgrätz Street, towards the Halle Gate. "Belle Alliance" is the Prussian designation for Waterloo, and "Königgrätz" for Sadowa. The army which was now returning after accomplishing the crowning achievement of Sedan, were thus significantly reminded, by the route they followed, of the two other most important battles of the century, which had paved the way for German unity. At the Halle Gate a noble and gigantic statue of Berlin extended a cordial hand to the victors; and here the civic dignitaries stood to welcome them on their entrance into the capital. To remind them of Paris incidents a flight of diminutive balloons was let loose by an adept of the aeronautic art. Marching on to the Anhalt Gate the soldiers found themselves saluted by the lusty hurrahs of 3000 boys placed on a large platform, flanked by trophies. Proceeding between the flagstaff's marking its course, the gallant array reached the Potsdam Gate with its imposing embellishments. Here the statue of Victory looked down upon them from her terrace bristling with cannon. The two captured ladies, Strassburg and Metz, were seated at her feet. The king stopped his charger, and looked up admiringly at the beautiful group. Many a soldier as he passed along sadly remembered the sacrifices by which the two western fortresses of the enemy had been won, and how much more easy it was for the sculptor to represent them as they now were, than it proved for the army to reduce them to this position.

An expectant flutter pervaded the multitudes crowding Unter den Linden as the thunder of drums and clashing of brass bands, mingled with the lusty cheers, told that the brilliant cavalcade was drawing near the Brandenburg Gate. The national anthem was suddenly drowned by the deafening huzza which resounded from the square inside the portico, and told that the head of the army had entered the city. The gallant Marshal Wrangel led the van; and the veteran warrior, who won his spurs against Napoleon I., was in his place at the head of a generation whom he had taught the way to victory. Alone the old man rode, and was lustily cheered by the people. Behind him were his staff, composed of generals like himself superannuated from active work, or who from other causes were not in the war. Then came the officers of the central staff, and of the staffs of the various armies in the field—an intellectual *élite*, with many a famous name among them. Lieutenant-colonel Verdy, Moltke's assistant and another Prussian Clausewitz, rode close by Colonel Leszczynski, Werder's chief of the staff, and the hero of the three days' battle before Belfort; Blumenthal, who served under the Crown Prince at Woerth; Stosch, who assisted the grand-duke of Mecklenburg at Orleans and Le Mans: and Stiehle, who advised Prince Frederick Charles. These were followed by the leaders who had served as civil governors during the war—Bettenfeld, Falkenstein, Bonin, and Fabrice. Behind them rode the great generals of the campaign—the duke of Mecklenburg-Schwerin, Prince George of Saxony, Fieldmarshal Steinmetz, and Manteuffel, Werder, Von der Tann, Göben, Fransecki, Kamecke, &c.

After a slight interval there followed the illustrious trio who, under the emperor, had the direction of the war—Moltke, Roon, and Bismarck. As the three became visible the cheering rose to a tempest, and the shower of laurel wreaths, which had been pouring down all the while from the grand stand and the windows, became all but overpowering. They looked as characteristic as ever. Moltke was the abstracted sage, caring little for anything under his immediate observation, unless it happened to be a hostile army or two, and seemingly fighting out some imaginary battle in his own mind. Bismarck in his cuirass, taller than tall Moltke, and twice as stout, appeared the stern representative of sovereign common sense he had proved in his rare career. Neither he nor Roon, in whose grim warrior face every ploughed furrow pointed to administrative precision and energy, appeared to care much for the jubilant shouts.

Behind them, the solitary centre of the splendid picture, on his dark bay war-horse, rode the emperor and king—of truly royal aspect, beaming with dignity and good-nature. No welcome could be heartier than that given him; no acknowledgment more gracious. Behind him rode the field-marshals of the royal house—the Crown Prince of Germany, looking every inch a prince and a soldier, on a chestnut horse; and Prince Frederick Charles, heavy-browed, stalwart, and square, with his firm, strong seat on the bright bay charger. Following these came a great company of German sovereigns and princes, who had come to rally round their emperor as in days of yore. Immediately behind came nearly a hundred non-commissioned officers of varied German nationalities bearing the spoils of war—the eagles and the colours. As he wheeled under the gate Kaiser Wilhelm looked back significantly at these prizes, about to pass under a structure once despoiled by the armies of the nation from which they had been taken. Having bowed repeatedly to the stands encircling the square, his Majesty advanced towards a platform on which stood sixty young ladies, who had been selected to greet him by a poetical recitation, and the presentation of a laurel wreath—a time-honoured usage imperatively required by German custom on such occasions. As was the ceremony, so was the costume traditional. The fair band were clad in white, trimmed with blue—the colours of Innocence and Faith—with bare heads and beautiful bouquets. Two matrons chaperoned the girls, and Fraulein Blascr, the sculptor's daughter, advancing with six of her companions, had the honour of addressing an appropriate poem to the emperor—all about the war which had been so terrible, and the peace which was so soothing. Having received the laurel wreath, he placed it on the hilt of his sword, kissed the speaker, and thanked the blushing donors in fatherly terms. "It is very kind of you," he said, "to come and welcome me. But do not forget those who are coming behind me. I can assure you, they are more worthy of your notice than I am. Receive my reiterated thanks." The Crown Prince likewise accepted a wreath, which he kept in his right hand during the rest of the march. At the head of the Linden the emperor was received by the burgomaster and town council, who presented to him a municipal address, which having been duly responded to, the procession moved on.

And now for the troops. Horse, foot, and artillery, they came on—a glorious sight as they poured through the historical gate. With the brilliant sun reflected on their arms, and the air filled with martial music, eye and ear were alike gratified. With steady tramp came the laurel-crowned stalwart infantry men of the Prussian guard, followed by deputations from all other regiments of the united army—picked men, well fitted to be the representatives of a renowned force. Strong in limb, tall in stature, and manly in countenance, they were uncommonly fine and soldierly-looking troops. There was no very marked difference in type between Northerners and Southerners, only the Bavarians looked a little more elastic and had a rollicking dash in their gait, while the Prussians were somewhat more solid and precise. Heavy grenadiers and light fusiliers alternated in dark-blue columns. In the moving panorama brisk hussars in red tunics succeeded to gigantic cuirassiers in white uniforms. Of course the lancers were not absent, and the multitude of sight-seers had the pleasure of passing in review many a squadron of those ubiquitous uhlans whose swiftness and daring struck terror into the enemy. Every now and then the rumble of artillery was heard; and gunners, who, in keeping with their sombre work, wore the darkest blue of the service, passed in through the gate. The seemingly interminable current swept continuously along, in undiminished strength and rapidity.

The spectators shouted, and the soldiers reciprocated the greeting with hand and sword. If popular sympathy was more warmly expressed towards one part of the army than another, perhaps the Würtemburgers and Bavarians received a heartier welcome from their northern countrymen. Along the whole route the people studiously evinced their joy at the re-union at last effected between themselves and their brethren of the south. As may be imagined, the French colours, or rather their German bearers, likewise elicited a tribute of applause; and it was remarked that many of them were new, and had evidently seen little service. Artillery and commissariat waggons closed the warlike train, which included all branches of the service, the military clergy and *vivandiéres* not excepted. They were about 45,000 strong, and took three hours and a half to defile.

Having reached the Opera Platz, the emperor, with the princes, the royal guests, and generals, took up their station before the Blücher statue, the Reichstag rising in a bank behind. It is the point from which the kings of Prussia have witnessed festive reviews for the last fifty years. The troops formed in broad fronts as they arrived, and executed the ceremonial march of the Prussian service. As an exhibition of the precision and regularity attained by the first military nation in the world, this part of the day's proceedings, which occupied about two hours, was perhaps the most remarkable and interesting. Like a moving wall, the broad front stepped forward. Though extending over nearly the whole width of the wide square, there was a cohesive force in the ranks which made the living unit disappear in the one animated whole.

All being ready for the occasion, the emperor, with his suite of sovereigns and princes, entered the square, and took up a position under an awning between the two fountains. As the Kaiser advanced the troops presented arms, and the bearers of the trophies laid them down at the feet of the statue. As a loud and sustained roll of drums died away, the cathedral choir burst out into a hymn, after which the chaplain-general, standing on the steps of the monument, offered up a short prayer. Von Bismarck then approaching the emperor, asked and obtained his permission to unveil the statue. As the canvas fell from it, the drums rolled, the trumpets blared, the standards of the guards were lowered, the troops presented arms and cheered, a salute of 101 cannon was fired, and the church bells rang all over the town. The national air was performed, while the emperor, helmet in hand, approached his father's statue, walked slowly round it, and not without emotion addressed those around him as follows:—"What we projected amid the most profound peace is completed; what we had hoped to unveil in the profoundest peace—this statue—has now become a memorial of the close of one of the most glorious, though one of the most sanguinary, wars of modern times. If the king to whom we erect this statue could see us now, he would be well satisfied with his people and his army. May the peace which we have achieved by so many sacrifices be lasting. We must all do our part that it may be so. God grant it!" "Unn danket alle Got" was then played from the museum, the troops joining in the grand Te Deum of Germany; and the pageant of the day closed.

In the evening, beneath a sky of Italian clearness, a magnificent illumination took place. Everywhere a profusion of coloured lamps was ranged in symmetrical figures over the house fronts. Strings of Chinese balloons lined the Linden and other streets, shedding a soft lustre on the green boughs and leaves, and contrasting finely with the flaring torches above them. Crowns and eagles, adorning the exchange and many other buildings by coloured *lampions* placed inside a surrounding of gas, added to the general splendour. No jewel ever possessed a softer radiance than the variegated glass representing ruby and sapphire in these mimic crowns; while at intervals the warm effulgence of electric light burst forth at various points along the *via triumphalis*.

During the illuminations merrymaking in the old German style was carried on, and an *al fresco* entertainment was given to the soldiers in a square in the centre of the town. A portion of the Domhofs Platz, opposite the House of Parliament, had been inclosed and converted into an impromptu saloon, in which dancing was kept up until the dawn. All round the square refreshment tents were erected, and the wearing of a military cap gave a claim to unlimited beer and sausage. In nearly every other district of the city the inhabitants clubbed together to provide feasts for certain numbers of soldiers, and at most of these entertainments the various dishes were prepared and served up, not by hired attendants, but by young ladies of the middle class—an arrangement natural in a country where all classes indiscriminately are represented in the rank and file. For days and nights together were these entertainments and rejoicings kept up; the extraordinary nature of the occasion having roused the usually sober and impassive nature of German townspeople to such a festive pitch that it seemed difficult to reduce it to the work-a-day level. Amidst all the merrymaking, however, there was no drunkenness, no oaths, no indecorum of any kind. The general behaviour of the men indicated that they felt they had a real stake in their country; that the success which was being celebrated, and the results it had produced, could be maintained only by hard work, both of body and mind; and that the exciting influence of these festive days, should not be allowed to vitiate the moral resources of the nation. However mighty Germany may become, geographically placed as she is between three military powers, she will need all her energy to protect house and home; and this fact of her political life was felt, and served to modify many a triumphant speech and writing during the Berlin rejoicings.

As in the chief city of Prussia, but of course on a smaller scale, Bremen, Hamburg, Munich, Dresden, and other towns, in then: turn had a public holiday and festivities on the return of the soldiers of their respective states.

The legislation of the Parliament, the opening of which in March, 1871, we have already described, was devoted principally to questions directly raised by the new organization of Germany, to the disposal of claims upon the indemnity levied from France, and to the settlement of the new Alsace-Lorraine province. It is tolerably certain that immediately after Sedan the acquisition of Strassburg would have satisfied the territorial demands of the Germans; but when it was seen that the united armies could hold Paris with such a grasp that its fall was a mere question of time, the claims of the fatherland were, as a matter of course, extended to the restoration to Germany of the territory which by force or fraud had been wrested from her by Henry II., Louis XIV., and Louis XV The only matter of doubt was as to the party to whom the new province should revert, and the investment of Paris had not long been complete before Bavaria expressed a desire to appropriate a good share of the conquered territory. To her it seemed just that she should receive a special reward for supporting the North at a crisis when the defalcation of the South might have been fatal to all the fatherland. So strongly, indeed, was the desire of the Bavarian government expressed, that the Prussian cabinet deemed it injudicious to resist the demand of so important and faithful an ally. It was obvious, however, that if Bavaria had a right to claim a gratuity of this kind for adhering to treaty obligations, so had the other states; and it was equally certain that if unity was to be established on a firm basis, territorial acquisitions must not be portioned out amongst the allied states as in former centuries, but kept together and placed as a whole under the central government of the land. Public opinion, anxiously wishing to promote unity, at once pronounced against the scheme of the Munich ministry, and the Bavarian press rejected it even more decidedly than the Prussian. A considerable party in Prussia claimed the territory for themselves, on the plea of not further multiplying the divisions of Germany; but the voice of the nation pronounced unmistakably in favour of retaining the new province as a "monument of the common victory." Accordingly the Alsace bill, framed by the Federal Council, entirely ignored the claim of Bavaria and all other individual states, and made the central government paramount in the recovered lands. The bill provided that Alsace and Lorraine should become the common property of the various states forming the German empire, and should, until January 1, 1874, be governed by the emperor and minor sovereigns assembled in Federal Council; but their prerogative after that date was to be restricted by the German Parliament, which in addition to its other functions was to act as Legislative Assembly for Alsace and Lorraine. To reconcile the Alsatians to this plan and to the want of a local Parliament, they were to have the right to send deputies to the German Parliament as soon as it began to legislate for them.

For some time after the incorporation of the province, two classes of its population offered active resistance to the new state of things—the lower orders and the priests. The former frequently attacked the sentinels and soldiers sauntering about in the by-streets and public promenades of the larger towns; while the priests lost no opportunity of instilling French feeling into the minds of the country people. These manifestations of dissatisfaction were met by characteristic discretion. The civil and military authorities in Alsace were ordered to treat the people with the greatest leniency, and to take no notice of the petty provocations so frequently offered. In case, however, of open resistance or serious attack, the culprits were to undergo the full rigour of the law. Boys and mill-hands, for instance, might, without being called to account, indulge in the harmless diversion of saluting policemen with the favourite cry of *Vive la France, à bas la Prusse*; but if a blow was dealt, or even aimed at the representative of the law, prompt punishment was to follow. At the same time the people were given to understand, that any one opposing the rulers would not improve the chance of having his losses in the war made up to him—an announcement strictly in accordance with the law, which, while it empowered, did not oblige the government to accord damages to the new citizens of Alsace and Lorraine. With the priests there appeared great reluctance to interfere, and only the strongest reasons of expediency ultimately induced the government of Berlin to depart from its established policy of religious toleration. It was found, however, that the Ultramontane clergy were endeavouring to excite the utmost hostility to German unity as established under the supremacy of Prussia—a leading Protestant power. The Diet therefore passed a bill for the repression of seditious language in the pulpit, and the law was of course operative in Alsace, as well as throughout the other portions of Germany.

It was stipulated by the Treaty of Peace that an "option" should be accorded to the Alsace-Lorrainers as to their future nationality, and it has been charged against the German government that the rules which affect those who declined to become Germans were made tyrannically narrow and severe. Every Alsatian was compelled to make up his mind to accept German citizenship, with all its consequences, or part with the property and the civil rights which had been his inheritance. It was argued that, were concession made on this point, there would be nothing to prevent the whole population from remaining on the soil as aliens, and sheltering itself under its French nationality. This argument is no doubt logical, but to an impartial observer it would seem that German statesmen would have acted wisely in interpreting the "option" in the widest sense; that there should have been no attempt to force the people of Alsace and Lorraine into compulsory exile; that they should have been permitted to call themselves French subjects, and to have a French domicile, whilst quietly carrying on their usual business, and not urged—at all events till the breaking out of a fresh war—to strike their tents and go. But the German government not only refused to allow this intermediate state of affairs, and compelled all born Alsatians and Lorrainers to reside in whichever country they chose to abide by, but it added to the pain of this choice by making all who did not decide on going into France before the 30th of September, 1872, liable to the German law of conscription, unless they had already served in the French army and navy. In other words, before that date all inhabitants of Alsace-Lorraine had to choose either exile from their homes, or to see their sons and brothers incur the liability to be drafted into an army which will, in all probability, have to fight against the country of their birth and of all their traditions. These terms made the "option "a choice, on the one hand, between exile, and the sacrifice of all indemnity for the heavy private losses caused by the war (which the Germans promised to those who remained); and on the other, not merely alienation of nationality, but the bitterness of seeing sons and brothers pouring out their blood for what they regard as the wicked cause of the conqueror of their land. To many, of course, the choice was merely nominal, for they could not leave the little they possessed and go forth as outcasts; and in their case the acceptance of German nationality was, therefore, a necessity. The decree, however, resulted in a great and steady stream of middle-class emigration from the conquered provinces into France, including many war propagandists, who had the great advantage of pointing to their own sacrifices as guarantees of their sincerity. This rigour, as it seems to us, can scarcely fail to create even more bitterness in the hearts of those who stay than of those who go, for it will mingle with their grief the poison of a certain amount of humiliation and self-condemnation. If Prince Bismarck were bent on interpreting the "option" in this severe sense, we think he should have exempted Alsace-Lorraine for another five years from all military conscription. To impose on the inhabitants that liability as the immediate corollary of the option to stay in the province of their birth, was hard indeed; and the regulation by which minors were denied any choice, and were compelled to follow the decision of their parents, seems certain to produce much stubborn resistance on one side, and to necessitate a harsh discipline on the other. Conquest must always be hard and stern work; but there is such a thing as superfluous rigour. The French already abound in legends of German atrocities in Alsace, notable examples of which are to be found in MM. Erckmann-Chatrian's fiction "Le Plebiscite." Why lend colour to such stories, by pursuing a policy which will certainly furnish numbers of unoffending citizens with a far more reasonable ground for vindictiveness than the plunder of their cellars or the seizure of their cattle?

In the Treaty of Peace a passage had been introduced relative to the eventual substitution of financial guarantees for the right conceded to German troops to occupy a portion of French territory, as it had been anticipated that, under certain circumstances, such an arrangement might be for the advantage of both parties. The German army of occupation found it a most wearisome task to keep guard over a country in which they were universally hated, and had to protect their lives by stern measures, which in turn provoked new complaints and new plots of vengeance. In a short time the relations between the conquerors and conquered in the occupied provinces became very unpleasant; industry was greatly fettered by restrictions which the occupying force imposed on communication and exchange; and the dissatisfaction and irritation thus kept alive shook public confidence so profoundly, that M. Thiers, taking advantage of the financial provision in the treaty to which we have referred, conceived the idea of buying the Germans out of at least six departments. According to the treaty of Frankfort the departments of the Aisne, Aube, Côte d'Or, Haute Saone, Doubs, and Jura would in any case have been evacuated on the 1st of May, 1872, on payment of the half milliard then due; and had the payment been made at once, the evacuation might have been demanded directly. But France was at this time unable to meet such a draught on her resources. It was not that she was not rich enough to get credit for twenty millions more in the markets of the world, but she could not procure the specie requisite for so large and sudden a payment without producing a ruinous crisis in the money market. Trusting that a promise to pay in the May following, if backed by the guarantee of a number of great mercantile houses, might be satisfactory to the Germans, the French government made the proposal. Prince Bismarck agreed to it, but at the same time would not pledge himself not to discount the bills given him as guarantee; and as, by retaining the power of discounting bills of twenty millions sterling whenever he pleased, he would have been the financial master of Europe, the bankers to whom an appeal had been made refused to run the risk. The proposed arrangements thus appeared to have failed; but M. Thiers, persuaded that some other basis of negotiation might be devised, despatched M. Pouyer-Quertier on a tentative mission to Berlin.

Finding the French government thus anxious to come to a financial arrangement so as to release the six departments, Prince Bismarck speedily devised one. The bankers who had undertaken to guarantee the payments in May, were to have received a commission of 10,000,000 francs; and it occurred to the astute minister that if France was willing to pay such a commission, it were better it should go into the pocket of his imperial master. He accordingly agreed to accept the word of M. Pouyer-Quertier and M. Thiers on behalf of the French government, without any further guarantee. But as by the Frankfort treaty the twenty millions, or half milliard, was not due until May, nor the six millions interest on the unpaid portion of the indemnity until March, he proposed that the twenty-six millions should be paid by nine equal fortnightly instalments, beginning 15th January, 1872. On M. Pouyer-Quertier acceding to this arrangement, Prince Bismarck undertook that the German troops should at once evacuate the six departments; on the distinct stipulation, however, that they should not be occupied by the French, but should for the time be declared neutral ground, in which no French soldiery should appear, except such as might be necessary for police purposes. In other words, the departments, though evacuated, were really to be held in pawn by Germany, in case France failed in any of the money payments, when the Germans were immediately to re-enter—a course which their strong position on the borders of the departments would render extremely easy. Germany was clearly the gainer in every way by the transaction, as it was freed from the burden of providing an occupying force, and as considerable pecuniary advantage was secured by obtaining payment in advance. France, on the other hand, paid less money for the evacuation than she would have had to give the bankers in purchasing their good offices. That her own soldiers might not go into six French departments until a certain sum of money had been paid, was no doubt humiliating; but the only alternative was the presence of German troops. In another way the arrangement was beneficial to France. Stability to the government in the then unsettled state of the country, was of inestimable value; and there is no doubt that the very frank and respectful manner in which the Germans recognized in the cabinet of M. Thiers the centre of real power in France, tended largely to consolidate its authority. On the whole, therefore, the treaty of evacuation was not purchased at more than it was worth; but the Germans, as usual, took remarkably good care of themselves in the negotiations. Prince Bismarck saw, with his usual perspicacity, that provided he got all he really wanted, the more he strengthened the hands of the government of France, the greater would be the security that Germany would receive in due time, and that she would be paid even with some acceleration, the enormous sums to which she had become entitled by the fortunes of war.

When the time for payment of the first instalments of the half milliard arrived, the French minister of Finance declared himself ready to pay the whole amount at once, which, by an arrangement between him and the German ambassador, Count Arnim, was accordingly done. By this arrangement France obtained a discount of five per cent, on the amount, effected a saving of £800,000, and was relieved from any further payment till March 1, 1873. Whatever fault, indeed, may be found with the government of M. Thiers in other respects, it certainly set about the liquidation of the German indemnity with a singleness of purpose, a zeal and ability, above all praise.

In negotiating the terms of evacuation Prince Bismarck contended, that as France wanted something from Germany she must give something in return; and Germany required such a temporary arrangement as to Customs duties as would mitigate to Alsace and Lorraine the immediate evils of their separation from the French commercial system. It was therefore agreed that for eighteen months specific manufactures of Alsatian produce should be admitted into France at a very reduced duty. The National Assembly, not comprehending the nature of the agreement, voted as an amendment which seemed only fair, that the arrangement should be reciprocal, and that France should be permitted to export into Alsace and Lorraine on the same advantageous terms as these provinces might be allowed to export into France. The National Assembly failed to see that, while the beneficial concession claimed by Bismarck applied only to purely Alsatian produce, to throw Alsace open to the admission on similar terms of all French goods, would have been equivalent to the throwing open of all Germany, of which Alsace was now become a portion. As the only alternative, the Germans would have had to re-establish Custom-houses on the eastern frontier of the new province; but as this would clearly have constituted it a separate country which, commercially at least, would have belonged to France rather than to Germany, Prince Bismarck refused to admit the amendment of the French Assembly. At the instance of M. Thiers, M. Pouyer-Quertier agreed to set aside the vote if, to justify this course at home, Prince Bismarck would consent to the restoration of two or three small communes adjoining Luxemburg, which had been included in the recent transfer of territory, and to the reduction, from eighteen to twelve months, of the exceptional privileges allowed to Alsace. The concessions were granted, and some paltry slices of territory again reverted to France; but the minute care exercised by Prince Bismarck on behalf of his country did not fail him even here. The smallest details did not escape him, for like the Jew of story-books, he was equally at home whether selling seven oranges for sixpence, or arranging for a loan of millions sterling. He subsequently explained to the Reichstag that he gave up two parishes because, lying on the western slope of the Douron hills they were only accessible from the French side; the one thing valuable in them, the only one thing, was a forest, crown property: so he excepted the forest from the cession; the parishes were to belong to France, but the woods to Germany. In the other instance, the frontier line had been so drawn as to oblige the inhabitants of a petty place, in order to reach the quarter with which all their dealings were connected, to go from Germany into France. By conceding their small strip of land, Prince Bismarck allowed the inhabitants to remain French; but he made the French government undertake to build a new station at the point where the railway became German—an obligation which, imposed on a great power like France, furnishes a curious example of what the tempers of her statesmen had in this crisis to endure, and of the class of minute affairs to which Prince Bismarck found time to give his mind. It may be observed, however, that this matter was conceived exactly in the vein of German commerce, which seems destined to push its way over the world by attending to sixteenths, where other nations concern themselves with eighths per cent., and it was certain therefore to be highly relished and approved by the chancellor's audience.

M. Pouyer-Quertier, throughout his stay at Berlin, was treated in the most friendly manner by the emperor, and as the result of his negotiations there were signed on the 12th of October—first, a territorial convention, relating to certain ratifications of frontier; secondly, a financial convention, involving the evacuation of six departments in the east; and, thirdly, a convention bearing upon the temporary Customs system in Alsace and Lorraine.

A considerable portion of the war indemnity, 1,500,000,000 francs, having been paid by France, measures were taken by the Reichstag for the allotment of it. The total disposable sum was, however, less than a milliard and a half by 325,000,000 francs, the amount allowed for the purchase of the Alsatian railways. This left 1,175, 000,000 francs, or 313,000,000 thalers, of which sum 4,000,000 thalers were reserved to endow the generals, and another 4,000,000 to assist those members of the landwehr and reserve who had suffered in their pecuniary circumstances by the war. Towards indemnifying the Germans expelled from France 2,000,000 thalers were allotted; but it may be mentioned that these amounts mostly represented only the first instalments of what was intended to be devoted to the various objects, the full sums being made up as the indemnity flowed in. To indemnify expelled German subjects, for instance required, at least 15,000,000 thalers, to be made up by 8,000,000 out of the war indemnity, of which the 2,000,000 was the first allotment, and by 7,000,000 thalers previously levied in France. To shipowners whose vessels were seized or detained in harbour by the blockade 7,000,000 thalers were voted, and about 20,000,000 were set apart for the inhabitants of Alsace and Lorraine, for damages sustained and provisions supplied both to French and Germans in the course of the campaign. Add to this 5,000,000 thalers required for repairs and rolling stock of the Alsace-Lorraine railways, and there was a total of 42,000,000 thalers laid out in compensating some of the evils inflicted by the war, on parties who, according to old-world usages, would very generally have been left without any redress.

The very flourishing condition of the finances also enabled the government to pass a Military Pensions Bill, which rendered disabled German soldiers the best paid in Europe. Thus, whereas invalids who leave the service in consequence of their wounds, without being actually disabled for work, receive in Austria a monthly pay of $1\frac{1}{2}$ thaler, in Italy 7 thalers, in France $7\frac{1}{2}$, and in the United States $11\frac{1}{2}$, they were by this bill henceforth to receive 12 thalers in Germany. Invalids partially disabled receive in Austria $4\frac{2}{3}$, in France $10\frac{1}{3}$, in Italy 12, in England 15, in the United States 21, and in Germany from 15 to 18 thalers per month. Totally disabled men are paid $7\frac{1}{2}$ thalers per month in Austria, $13\frac{1}{2}$ in France, 15 in Italy, 15 to 25 in England, 28 to 35 in the United States, and 24 in Germany. The payment between 1866 and 1871 was rather below this standard, but still very liberal; and it must be remembered that a thaler goes much further in Germany than its equivalent does in England. To the provision made for invalids and compensation to widows and orphans, the Prussian authorities ascribed much of that readiness to brave the dangers of battle displayed by their reserves and landwehrmer in the late war.

This liberal measure of the government absorbed 31,000,000 of the 271,000,000 thalers remaining. They had the power to devote 240,000,000 thalers for the purpose; but as the whole sum was not required at once, and as the individual states desired to have a portion of their war expenditure reimbursed, only the above instalment was then set aside for the pension list, leaving exactly 240,000,000 thalers, which were divided according to the number of men supplied by each state. In other words, Prussia, or rather the late North German Confederacy, received five-sixths of the whole, the remaining sixth being portioned out between Bavaria, Würtemburg, Baden, and the southern half of Hesse, which before the war had a separate contingent. The 200,000,000 thalers thus accruing to North Germany were employed in replenishing the war treasury, and canceling a portion of the war debt.

The war treasury is one of the "peculiar institutions "of Prussia, and consists of a certain sum which is deposited in gold and silver in the cellars of a citadel, where it remains, without yielding interest, till the sound of the war trumpet again calls it into use. Previous to the war with France it consisted of 30,000,000 thalers; but when Southern Germany was included in the empire, it was proposed to augment the sum to 40,000,000. Some few members remonstrated against the burying alive, as it were, of such an enormous sum, and the Finance minister, Herr Camphausen did not deny that 40,000,000 thalers was a large sum to lock up, and a small one with which to carry on a war; but he insisted that in these times it was of the last importance not to be taken by surprise, and to be able to complete the national armaments with the least possible delay. "It was for the purpose of making these preliminary armaments with the greatest despatch that the government required the sum demanded; it was to prevent a fall in the price of public securities, which must result from large sales on the eve of war, that government wanted cash, not stock;" and he observed that if the rate of exchange on London sank only $2\frac{1}{2}d.$ after the declaration of war in 1870, it was owing mainly to the fact that Prussia was in possession of a war fund. The proposal was, of course, ultimately carried, and the 40,000,000 thalers were duly consigned to that dormancy in which we wish there were any good grounds for hoping they may lie, until the world becomes wise enough to justify their being brought forth to the light for a more beneficent purpose than that contemplated in their burial. We fear, however, that for the present such a hope is vain. Already the warlike preparations in France, described in the next Chapter, have produced a settled conviction in Germany that a "war of revenge "will be undertaken at the earliest favourable opportunity.

CHAPTER VIII. FRANCE AFTER THE COMMUNE.

The Question of the Future Constitution for France—Repeal of the Law exiling the Bourbons, in spite of the Opposition of M. Thiers—Failure of an Attempt to form a Coalition between the Monarchists in consequence of an Extraordinary Manifesto of the Comte de Chambord—Prolongation of the Executive Powers vested in M. Thiers for three years, and the Title of "President of the French Republic" conferred on him—The Duc d'Aumale takes his seat in the Assembly—The Financial Position of France and the Total Cost of the War—Peremptory Refusal of M. Thiers to impose an Income Tax—Wonderful Success of a Loan for £100,000,000—The Budget for 1872-73 and the Future Expenditure of the Country—Return to Protection in France and withdrawal from the Treaty of Commerce with England—Abolition of the Passport System—Reorganization of the French Army—Adoption of the Principle of Universal Military Service and Abolition of Substitutes—Full Explanation of the New System and Comparison of it with that of Germany.

AS soon as the Communist insurrection of Paris had been suppressed, and the first stern outcry for the punishment of its guilty authors had been appeased by reprisals of extreme severity, the question of the future constitution most suitable for the country excluded consideration of all others. The Assembly elected in February contained a large majority of members pledged to monarchical principles; and their first act would probably have been the proclamation of a monarchy, had not M. Thiers advised them to suspend all questions of internal reorganization until peace should be concluded. During the reign of the Commune, with the capital of the country in their hands, no steps could be taken in favour of monarchy. When the revolt was put down, M. Thiers, who had hitherto been regarded as the champion of constitutional monarchy, and who on May 11 demanded a vote of confidence from the Assembly, which was granted by 495 to 10, seemed ready to exert all his influence as head of the administration to secure the indefinite prolongation of the Republic, with himself as president.

The monarchists, on their part, were determined to bring the matter to an issue. On June 8 the Assembly, by 484 votes to 103, passed a resolution repealing the laws under which the House of Bourbon had been exiled, and another declaring valid the elections of the Duc d'Aumale and the Prince de Joinville, who had both been returned to the Assembly in the previous February. Knowing that resistance was vain, M. Thiers assented to the resolutions. But he professed no sympathy with the party by which they had been carried. On the contrary, he plainly told his audience that the act was not one of clemency to individuals, but of political intrigue. He insisted that a state had the right to exclude royal pretenders from its territory, and that there could be no injustice in maintaining a decree of exile against those who would return, not as French citizens, but with the avowed intention of conspiring against the government and subverting the commonwealth. "You think," he said to the Assembly, "that you are doing a great act of generosity. You are doing something quite different. The laws it is proposed to abrogate are not laws of proscription, but laws of precaution." He referred as an illustration to what he still deemed, as formerly, the mistaken clemency of the republicans of 1848, in allowing the Bonapartes to enter France. Louis Napoleon came, and the Republic was overthrown. M. Thiers thus cleared himself from the suspicion of complicity with the purposes of the Assembly, by avowing that, though he did not oppose, he yet did not approve, the act on which the majority had determined. He was, no doubt, sincerely of opinion that, under all the circumstances, the time was inopportune for changing the form of government and plunging the country into political controversy. He did not pretend to be a republican in principle, an opponent of every government which had an hereditary chief; he had striven, he said, for forty years to procure for France a constitutional monarchy after the English pattern, and he expressed a preference for English institutions over those of the United States. But this, he argued, was not the present question. The Republic existed, and could not be overthrown but by a revolution, and at the cost of political struggles which would inflict new calamity on France. He reminded the Assembly that it had been agreed at Bordeaux to set aside all questions which could divide the country. "I have," he said, "accepted the Republic as a deposit, and I will not betray the trust. The future does not concern me; I merely look at the present."

He also told his audience of the suspicions which the royalist tendencies of the Assembly had excited in the great towns. All the cities of France had sent deputations to complain that the Assembly wished to get rid of the Republic. He had presumed to deny the allegation, and to declare that though there were members who favoured monarchical principles, they had the wisdom to waive their preferences. But a royalist movement would convert these suspicions into certainty. The public mind was still excited; the insurrection was put down, but not extinguished. One of the great weapons of the Commune was the cry that the Republic was in danger. Could there be a worse time for changing the government? "I do not desire," said M. Thiers, "to discuss the possibility of a monarchy at some future time; but in order that it may be durable, it is necessary that it should not be said that the Republic had not had a fair trial." He further argued in favour of the political *states quo* from the necessity of dealing at once with the German occupation. "We have 500,000 Germans to feed. We have a deficiency of 400,000,000 francs in the revenue derived from taxation. We must have recourse to credit, and in order to this we require the confidence of Europe. No one doubts the resources of France, but it is feared that our union will be broken up." Speaking of the House of Orleans, he said he had been the minister of that House; he had been attached to it in exile, and he felt a warm friendship for it. But his friendship for his country was stronger still.

These powerful arguments might have been thought to have had considerable influence on the Assembly, and that the royalists would, at all events, have reckoned the cost before they attempted to carry into effect the plans which they had projected. Such, however, was not the case, for the different sections of the monarchical party—the Legitimists and Orleanists—agreed to support the candidature of Henri V. (the Comte de Chambord, grandson of Charles X.); and as he is childless, and upwards of fifty years of age, they also fixed upon his cousin, the Comte de Paris (grandson of Louis Philippe), as his natural successor. The Comte de Chambord returned to France for the first time since his boyhood; but the hopes of the coalition which had been agreed upon with the view of placing him upon the throne were dispelled by a manifesto, in which he avowed that he could only consent to be made king upon principles at variance with the ideas, associations, and prejudices of modern France. This document has such an historical importance, as it seems to have settled for ever the question of any future legitimist government in France, that we give it entire:—"Frenchmen! I am in the midst of you. You have opened the gates of France to me, and I could not renounce the happiness of again seeing my country. But I do not wish by a prolonged sojourn to give new pretexts to stir up men's minds, already so disturbed at this moment. I therefore leave this Chambord, which you gave me, and of which I have with pride borne the title for these last forty years in the land of exile. As I depart, I am anxious to tell you that I do not separate myself from you. France is aware that I belong to her. I cannot forget that the monarchical right is the patrimony of the nation, nor can I forget the duties which it lays upon me with respect to it. I will fulfil these duties, you may take my word as an honest man and as a king for it. By God's help we shall establish together, whenever you may wish it, on the broad basis of administrative decentralization and of local franchise, a government in harmony with the real wants of the country. We shall give, as a security for those public liberties to which every Christian people is entitled, universal suffrage, honestly exercised, and the control of the two Chambers, and we shall resume the national movement of the latter end of the eighteenth century, restoring to it its true character.

"A minority rebellious against the wishes of the country has taken that movement as the starting-point of a period of demoralization by falsehood, and of disorganization by violence. Its criminal excesses have forced a revolution on a nation which only asked for reforms, and have driven it towards the abyss in which it would lately have perished, had it not been for the heroic efforts of our army. And it is upon the labouring classes, upon the workmen in the fields and in the large cities, whose condition has been the subject of my most earnest solicitudes and of my dearest studies, that the evils of this social disorder have fallen most heavily. But France, cruelly disenchanted by unexampled disasters, will perceive that it is not by going from error to error that one can reach truth, that it is not by shifts that one can escape eternal necessities. She will call me, and I will come to her *tout entier* with my devotion, my principles, and my flag.

"With respect to this flag, conditions have been put forward to which I must not submit.

"Frenchmen! I am ready to do all in my power to lift up my country from its ruins, and to restore it to its proper rank in the world. The only sacrifice that cannot be expected from me is that of my honour. I am and wish to be the man of my own age. I sincerely do homage to all its greatness, and under whatever colours our soldiers marched I have admired their heroism, and given thanks to Heaven for all that their valour has added to the treasure of the glories of France. There must be no misunderstanding, no concealment or reticence, between us. Whatever charges about privileges, absolutism, and intolerance—or, what do I know?—about tithes, about feudal rights, the most audacious bad faith may lay against me, whatever phantoms it may conjure up to prejudice you against me, I shall not suffer the standard of Henry IV., of Francis I., and of Joan of Arc to be torn from my hands. It is by that flag that national unity was established, it is by it that your fathers, led by mine, have conquered that Alsace and that Lorraine whose fidelity will be the consolation of our misfortunes. It is that flag which conquered barbarism in that land of Africa which saw the earliest deeds of arms of the princes of my House: it is that flag which will overcome the new barbarism by which the world is threatened. I will intrust this flag with confidence to the bravery of our army. The army well knows that the white flag has never followed any other path than that which leads to honour. I received it as a sacred deposit from the old king, my grandfather, who died in exile. It has always been inseparably associated in my mind with the remembrance of my distant country. It has waved over my cradle, it will overshadow my grave. In the glorious folds of this stainless flag I will bring you order and freedom.

Frenchmen! Henry V. cannot forsake the white flag of Henry IV.

"HENRY.

"CHAMBORD, *July* 5, 1871."

The proclamation took the country completely by surprise, and, especially in the Chamber, did more to extinguish the aims of the legitimist party than could have been done by months of political indiscretion on their part. It is, however, due to the Comte de Chambord to say, that if he threw away his chances as a king, he stood higher, if possible, in the estimation of his countrymen as an honourable man; and with all the sharp criticism to which the proclamation gave rise in the newspapers, there was mingled a feeling of kindliness for him, and appreciation of the honesty and nobility of his character, which at the moment, when the cause which he represented was at such a discount, reflected credit on all.

Disappointed in the Comte de Chambord, the Assembly could not agree upon the choice of a monarch, and on August 12 a motion was made to prolong for three years the executive powers vested in M. Thiers. In the event of the National Assembly breaking up before that period, it was proposed that his powers should continue during the time necessary for constituting a new Assembly, which would then have to decide upon the question of the executive power.

M. Thiers, in reply, said he was deeply moved by the confidence reposed in him by the Assembly. The task laid upon him was heavy, but he was ready to submit to the will of the country. He believed all must acknowledge that the proposals had been made without any participation on his part, but since they had been brought forward, he must call upon the Chamber to decide upon them both with the briefest possible delay.

The matter was accordingly at once taken into consideration, and on August 31 the Assembly, with assent of the government and by a majority of 480 to 93, agreed to the following bill, by which it will be seen that M. Thiers exchanged the title of chief of the Executive Power for that of "President of the French Republic:"—"The Assembly, considering the necessity of acquiring for the government of France a degree of stability adapted to the present state of affairs, and strongly to unite together the public authorities by a fresh proof of confidence accorded to the chief of the Executive Power for the eminent services which he has rendered to the country, and for those which he may still render, decrees:—

"Art. I. M. Thiers shall continue, under the title of President of the Republic, to exercise those functions which were conferred upon him by the decree of the 17th of February, 1871.

"Art. II. The powers conferred upon M. Thiers shall have the same duration as those of the Assembly.

"Art. III. The President of the Republic shall be responsible for all his decrees, which are to be countersigned by a minister; and the president has the right to speak in the Assembly whenever he shall deem it expedient.

"The ministers will likewise be responsible, and render account of all their acts to the Assembly."

Notwithstanding the vote of the Assembly, already noticed, repealing the laws of proscription against the Bourbons, the Duc d'Aumale was warned that his appearance would embarrass the progress of public business, then in a most critical condition, and pledged himself to M. Thiers and a committee of the Assembly not to take his seat. This pledge he religiously observed until December, when, deeming circumstances much changed by the elevation of M. Thiers to the presidency, and hearing his own inaction ascribed to irresolution, he in a personal interview desired the president to release him from his engagement. M. Thiers, thinking that the moment the duke entered the Chamber the majority would regard him as the alternative man, but embarrassed perhaps by his old relation to the House, at first refused, then hesitated, and finally declared that the decision of such a matter rested with "a power above himself"—the "sovereign" Assembly. On this the duke, through one of his followers, requested an opinion from that body, and on December 18 the Chamber after a fierce debate decided, though in a very singular and hesitating manner, in his favour. The original mover, M. Desjardins, proposed that the Assembly should "invest the deputies for the Oise and Haute Marne—Prince de Joinville and the Duc d'Aumale—with the plenitude of their rights," and the government suggested, as a counter proposal, that it should pass on to the order of the day. This suggestion was rejected by 358 to 273, but the motion of M. Desjardins was also lost by 360 to 294; the majority shrinking, apparently, from a vote which would be interpreted in the country as distinctly monarchical. Before the vote was taken, M. Fresneau, moderate Orleanist, introduced another motion, that "the Assembly, considering that it has no responsibility to assume nor advice to offer on engagements in which it had no part, and of which it cannot be a judge, passes to the order of the day." As the words "of which it cannot be a judge "were distasteful to the personal supporters of the Duc d'Aumale, as implying a reproof, they were withdrawn by the mover; and the revised motion was then put and almost unanimously accepted by the Assembly, only two members, in a house of 648, opposing. The effect clearly was, that as the government claimed no pledge (a point strongly reaffirmed in debate by the minister of the interior, M. Casimir Perier), nor was any claimed by the Assembly, which even declined to consider whether there was one, the duke stood released from pledges and accordingly took his seat on December 19. The members in the train from Paris, by which he reached Versailles, fell back respectfully to allow him and his brother to walk on alone; in the Assembly he was received with considerable agitation.

The two other matters which have chiefly engrossed the attention of France since the war, are the state of her finances and the reorganization of her army.

On June 20, M. Thiers fully explained the financial position to his fellow-countrymen. He calculated that the war had cost France £340,000,000 in actual money, including the German indemnity, but excluding the loss sustained by the inhabitants of the departments ravaged by the enemy. Taking the most moderate estimate of the damage inflicted by requisitions and the destruction of property, the cost to France was about two millions sterling a day as long as the war lasted! a pecuniary expense unprecedented in history, besides the loss of two great provinces. M. Thiers severely condemned the dethroned emperor for having permitted Sadowa, and for having subsequently attempted to redress that error under circumstances which made success impossible; but foreign observers, anticipating as we may believe the judgment of posterity, cannot lay exclusively upon Napoleon III. the guilt of a war for which M. Thiers himself was, perhaps, more than any other man primarily responsible. He it was who revived the Napoleonic legend, who excited the people to demand the Rhine frontier, and who never ceased to heap reproaches upon the emperor for having assisted in the unification of Italy, and kept the peace while Prussia was engaged with Austria in 1866. M. Thiers was, unquestionably, the foremost apostle of that selfish policy which demanded that all the rest of Europe should be weak, in order that France might be the mistress of the Continent.

The actual expenditure of France itself in 1870 M. Thiers estimated at £132,000,000, of which about £47,000,000 was spent by the successive governments of the country in prosecuting the war up to the end of December. The balance of £85,000,000 represented the normal expenditure of France under the later years of the empire. The actual income from taxation was not above £70,000,000; but the loans authorised by the Corps Législatif before the revolution of the 4th of September, and the loan subsequently raised in England by M. Gambetta, added to the receipts from taxes, produced a total income of £106,240,000. This, compared with an expenditure of £132,000,000, left an uncovered balance of £25,760,000. The deficiency for 1871 was as great as that of 1870, for not only had the cost of the war to be met, but the receipts from taxes and the other sources of national income had very much declined. The excess of expenditure over income, independently of the German indemnity, was £39,440,000; and this, added to the uncovered balance of the previous year, made a total of £65,200,000 against the treasury.

In order to meet this deficiency and the payment of the portion of the indemnity due to Germany in 1871, a loan of £100,000,000 at five per cent, was proposed to be issued at eighty-three, which would give investors interest at the rate of six per cent. M. Thiers said, that after studying the subject he was fully persuaded that France was well able to meet the additional taxation which must be demanded of her; no country in the world possessed such recuperative power. No new loan would be required for three years, within which time France, if she acted wisely, might reorganize herself, and lay the foundation for future prosperity and glory. Referring to the new taxes proposed, he said he had been much pressed not to impose any on raw materials used by textile manufacturers. "But I," he added, amidst the laughter of the Assembly, "am an old protectionist, and with me anything old is not likely to change." He hoped that all classes would cheerfully submit to necessary sacrifices, and disclaimed any intention of levying fiscal duties to the extent of prohibition.

At the conclusion of M. Thiers' speech, M. Germain created much excitement by suggesting an income tax as the proper remedy in the present crisis. From the Left the proposal called forth applause; but it had a very different effect on the wealthy country gentlemen on the Right. The speaker in vain quoted the example of England, and urged with great vehemence that the best way to oppose Communism was voluntarily to tax themselves for their country's good.

M. Thiers replied with much warmth and energy, describing the income tax as a "disorderly tax." He had never in his life flattered popular passions, and would not now. The income tax was utterly unsuited to Frenchmen, who would never bear its inquisitorial nature. The attempt to impose it would set class against class and produce horrible disasters. He begged all who had any confidence in him to understand, once for all, that he would never consent to it. Now the Right in their turn vehemently applauded; the Left were silent.

The subscriptions for the loan were received on June 27, and in less than six hours amounted to more than double the sum required—a fact without parallel in history. A people crushed by a foreign invasion, with the enemy still on its territory, without settled institutions, torn by recent civil war, and still in dread of future disturbance, subscribed within a few hours for the largest sum ever borrowed by any government. The total amount raised in France was three and a half milliards—two and a half in Paris, and a milliard in the provinces. The hoarded bullion of the country was poured into the public treasury when the gates were opened, with a force like that of water seeking its level. There was as much eagerness to lend money to the government as there had been to obtain bread during the famine. Public loan offices were thronged like bakers' shops, and the clamorous multitude of capitalists swayed to and fro at the doors for the turn of each subscriber.

The success of the loan proved that, though industry was for the time disorganized, the actual savings of the country were sufficient to carry it through its most pressing difficulties. It is interesting to know from what class these immense sums of money were drawn, and in what form they were previously held. They came chiefly from those possessed of moderate fortunes, including numbers of subscribers from the country districts. This stratum of French society is essentially penurious. To the provinces economy degenerates into parsimony, and in the north especially the people are hard and griping. But niggardliness, though in itself an unamiable quality, is useful in a state; and it may be doubted whether among the more active and adventurous people in England half as many of the lower middle class would be found able to invest in a loan. Notwithstanding the extravagant style of living which prevailed in Paris under the Empire, it is estimated that in the country savings to the amount of £100,000,000 a year were put by; for the great mass of the middle class retained their old habits of prudence, economy, and regular, though not hard work. Small families, small establishments, small expenditure in entertainments, and hardly anything spent on travelling and junketing—such were the features of citizen life in town and country. The consequence was that the most enormous sum ever demanded by a government was speedily forthcoming from thousands of modest hoards. The little purse was the mainstay of France in her calamity. From every quarter, from the districts still occupied by the Prussians, as well as from those which the enemy had never trodden, money in abundance was placed at the service of the state. But perhaps the most remarkable feature of the transaction was not the amount of money contributed, but the promptitude with which it was given. The French people had evidently an absolute belief in the security of the state—a belief so manifestly universal as to expose the real numerical insignificance of those desperate factions which pretend to revolutionize society. The socialist members of the International were certainly not among the subscribers to the government loan, for one of their absurd doctrines is that there should be no public creditors; but we may be equally sure that the millions who came forward with their money had not the smallest fear of these fanatical conspirators. Confiding in the good faith and the permanence of society, they eagerly embraced the opportunity of lending their money on the security of the nation, especially on terms a little more favourable than before. The French really borrowed, all things considered, on very easy conditions. They did, for instance, materially better in the money market than the Americans, notwithstanding the superior resources of the United States. The Americans were unwise enough, not indeed to propose repudiation, but to talk about and discuss it as a political "question," whereas the public credit of France has never been suspected. That was the secret of her success, and when she offered to pay six per cent, for money, her own people were ready with it to any amount. A love of hoarding truly Asiatic was found compatible with an astonishing readiness to lend. One word from government unlocked all the little repositories of money in the country, turned every available franc into the coffers of the state, made the terrible spectre of finance disappear as M. Thiers approached it, and enabled him to proceed in all confidence to buy the Germans out, and to stop the drains caused by their protracted presence on French soil.

The manner in which this was done is described in the previous chapter, and in order to complete the picture of the financial condition of the country, it will here only be necessary to give some particulars of the budget proposed for 1872—73, which was submitted in December, 1871.

Of the £340,000,000 which the war cost, £213,649,000 had then been provided from the following sources:—

The war loan of August, 1870.	£32,183,000
The loan raised in England.	8,356,000
The sale of the Rentes belonging to the dotation of the army, of surplus stores for the supply of Paris, &c., ...	4,510,000
The advances made and to be made by the Bank of France, ...	61,200,000

The allowances made by Germany for the transfer of the part of the Eastern Railway which lies within the annexed territory . . .	13,000,000
The tax for the cost of the garde mobile.	5,400,000
The last loan, ...	89,000,000
Total.	£213,649,000

The balance remaining to provide was therefore £126,351,000.

The estimated receipts of 1872 amounted to £97,174,500, and the expenses to £96,613,400.

The budget consequently showed an expected surplus of £561,100. The receipts consisted of the product of taxes which existed before the war, £72,620,500, and of new taxes, £24,554,000. This latter sum does not, however, correctly represent the increase of annual expenditure brought about by the war; that increase really amounts to nearly £29,000,000, but the actual addition to the budget was reduced to £22,529,000 by the savings effected on other items. Notwithstanding the dryness of a long array of figures, it seems worth while, in a chapter dealing with the consequences of the war, to give the list of additions and diminutions, as otherwise the position could not be clearly understood.

The savings on the last budget of the Empire appear to have been as follows:—

The suppression of the civil list of the emperor and his family and of the dotation of the Senate, ...	£1,385,000
Ministry of Justice: reductions in the Council of State and suppression of several law courts, ...	100,600
Ministry of Foreign Affairs: suppression of legations and consulates and diminution of salaries, ...	33,200
Ministry of the Interior: diminution of salaries, &c., ...	110,500
Economies in Algeria, ...	31,400
Reductions in the cost of collecting taxes, ...	440,800
Reductions in the expenses of the Ministry of Finance, ...	24,400
Reductions in the cost of the Navy, ...	1,253,000
Reductions in subventions to theatres and various works dependent on the Ministry of Fine Arts, ...	79,800
Reductions in subventions to various institutions dependent on the Ministry of Commerce, including race prizes, ...	50,800
Public works, ...	2,809,800
Total of reductions, ...	£6,328,300

The augmentations were as follows:—

Interest on the loan of £30,000,000 issued in August, 1870, ...	£1,584,00

Interest on the English loan of £10,000,000,	600,000
Interest on the last loan of £80,000,000,	5,555,800
Interest on the £13,000,000 still due to Germany,	6,000,000
Interest on the £13,000,000 credited by Germany for the annexed portions of the Eastern Railway (the French government keeps the money and pays interest on it to the railway company)	650,000
Interest on the advances made by the Bank of France,	367,200
Repayment on account of the advances made by the Bank of France.	8,000,000
Increase on the budget of the Ministry of War, which stands for 1872 at £18,000,000,	3,025,100
Increase of soldiers' pensions,	148,000
Increase of civil pensions,	66,200
Increase of pensions to aged persons,	24,000
Dotation of the president of the Republic,	30,500
Cost of the present Assembly over and above that of the former Chamber,	127,200
Extra dotation of the Legion of Honour, in consequence of the large number of crosses distributed during the war,	106,900
Cost of naval pensioners, in consequence of the absorption of the special resources hitherto employed to pay them,	280,000
Sundries.	8,009
Augmentations in various Ministries, including repairs of damages, cost of collecting the new taxes, new telegraphs, rebuilding bridges, &c.,	756,500
Payment on account of the repayment to the Departments and Communes of the cost of the garde mobile,	1,288,000
War expenses incurred by the Ministry of the Interior,	240,000
Total of augmentations,	£28,857,400

In addition to the £96,613,400 of state expenditure, the budget showed a further sum of £12,825,000 for departmental outlay; the general total therefore amounted to £109,438,000, which was to be employed as follows:—

Interest and dotations,	£44,393,500
Ministry of War,	18,002,000
Ministry of Marine,	5,906,700
Ministry of Justice,	1,343,000
Ministry of Foreign Affairs,	499,400
Ministry of Interior,	5,975,300
Ministry of Finance,	811,600
Ministry of Public Instruction, Worship, and Fine Arts,	3,815,500
Ministry of Agriculture and Commerce,	642,400
Ministry of Public Works.	5,225,000
Cost of collecting taxes,	9,533,500
Deductions and repayments of taxes,	465,100
Departmental expenditure.	12,825,000
Total,	£109,438,000

This enormous budget, it must be admitted, represented the worst; there was nothing more behind. It included interest not only on the loans then brought out, but also on those to be afterwards raised: for £6,000,000 shown as interest at five per cent, on the £120,000,000 then due to Germany, will probably suffice to cover the cost of further issue of Rentes to the same amount. On the other hand, there does not seem to be any probability of reductions; the £8,000,000 payable annually to the bank of France will have to be maintained during nearly eight years; with the exception of the cost of the army, all the items of current expenditure were apparently cut down to the lowest point; the sum allotted to public works was insufficient; and even if any margin should arise, either from an increase of receipts above the estimates, or from diminutions of outlay on certain heads, there will be urgent employment for it. France must, therefore, look forward to a lasting annual taxation of £110,000,000, or £40,000,000 more than England!

In order to provide for this enormous expenditure many of the old imposts which correspond with the English excise duties, as well as the house, land, and other taxes, were increased, and the government proposed to obtain the balance by the augmentation of the existing import duties, and by imposing a tax on certain raw materials. A great number of French economists desired that for the latter proposal—which was truly regarded as a return to the old protective system—an income tax should be substituted; but the suggestion was again strongly opposed by M. Thiers, and rejected in the Assembly by a large majority.

Before any material alteration could be made in the import duties it was necessary to set aside the celebrated treaty of commerce, which was negotiated in 1860 by the late Mr. Cobden, M.P., and the Emperor Napoleon. By it the duties on silks and velvets and kid gloves imported into England were entirely repealed, and those on wines very much reduced; whilst, on their side, the French agreed to admit English manufactures at much lower rates than before, although still very high according to free-trade principles. In fact, the treaty was objected to by some in England on the ground that its advantages were chiefly on the side of France. In ten years it increased French exports to England by 175 per cent., and English exports to France by only 139 per cent. The so-called "balance of trade" was largely and constantly against England. Though the trade with England forms about one-fourth of the whole foreign trade of France, while English trade with France forms only about one-tenth of the whole foreign trade of England, no considerable agitation against the treaty ever prevailed in this country. But in France it was more than once "denounced," by M. Thiers and others, in the interests of those who were supposed to have been injured by it. When the treaty was negotiated it was hoped, that through the introduction of the leaven of free trade into the minds of the French people, they would ultimately be converted to the principle altogether. Every year, it was supposed, would show them more plainly the wisdom of the policy into which they had been forced by a ruler more clear-sighted in this respect than his subjects, and that complete and unconditional abolition of all remaining restrictions on commercial intercourse would follow. The treaty was, in fact, concluded at the desire of the emperor, in order that principles which he knew to be salutary might be recommended to his subjects by the example of foreign concessions.

The treaty might have had to sustain a very formidable attack, even had the imperial power not been overthrown. It was initiated when the authority of the emperor was at its height, within a few months after his splendid victories in Italy, and when the idea of uniting what are called the Latin nations under French leadership, maintaining a beneficial alliance with England, and thus constituting something like a confederation of Western Europe, opened the minds of Frenchmen for the time to larger political theories. But the chief movers in the treaty were, undoubtedly, the Emperor Napoleon himself, who had formed clear views in adversity and exile, and his personal followers, who entered readily into the ideas of their master. The treaty was negotiated and put in operation without resistance from the protectionists, but not without many murmurs, and a resolution on the part of that numerous and powerful class to fall back upon the old system as far as possible, whenever an opportunity should offer. That opportunity might have occurred, even if the Empire had lasted. As the emperor's energies declined, as the old companions who had stood by him in support of an English alliance and a free-trade system passed away, it is probable that the interests which were aggrieved in 1860 would have regained sufficient power to modify legislation. The argument that France could abrogate the treaty without losing the English trade which had grown up under it, dates from before the war. It was said, with some plausibility, that England would not retaliate by imposing high duties; that she wanted the wines and the silks and fancy goods of France, and must have them whether France took, or did not take, anything from her; in short, that these productions, by their special and unique character, were indispensable to England, as to all foreign nations, while France might be independent if she wished it, and had the greatest interest in becoming so.

The five milliards of indemnity hastened the consummation. No free-trader has ever disputed that duties may be imposed for the purpose of revenue; for though direct taxes may be theoretically preferable, it must also be admitted that they cause much irritation, are largely evaded, and cannot practically be increased beyond certain limits. If France be condemned for many years to raise a sum immensely larger than sufficed for her necessities in 1860, and if those acquainted with the feelings and habits of the people agree that direct taxes cannot be safely increased, it is not for us to blame the French government for desiring to regain absolute freedom in dealing with the national finance. It may indeed seem strange that a nation so acute and logical as the French should reject principles which in England are held proved to demonstration. Many will hardly believe that amongst a people who have produced some of the best and clearest expositors of free trade, and in whose literature its doctrines are even more popularly set forth than in our own, should still cling to the high duties, and even the prohibitions, which were in favour thirty years ago. The most eloquent speakers, and the writers most influential in their manner and style, are, as a rule, free traders; the notice to terminate the English treaty was almost universally condemned by the best part of the French press as a retrograde step; while the protectionists say little, and say it very indifferently. But late events have clearly proved that, after a quarter of a century of controversy—for the free-trade contest has been going on in France ever since the repeal of the English corn laws—the principles on which English legislation is based have not been cordially accepted in France.

There can be no doubt that, under any financial system, the country is in every way able enough to supply the wants of its government; but a wise policy may make all the difference between an easy and an oppressive taxation.

As early as August, 1871, M. Thiers told Lord Lyons that the treaty of commerce had always been regarded by his present colleagues and himself as disadvantageous, not to say disastrous, to France. He should prefer getting rid of the treaty altogether, as commercially it had been advantageous to England only. From her, as the most formidable competitor in commerce, concessions which might safely be made to other countries ought to be withheld. Nevertheless, apparently for political reasons, he did not wish to abrogate the treaty altogether, and should England consent to the modifications he desired the convention might be maintained. Giving in to these would not, he contended, be a retrograde step, or a departure from the principles of free trade; the really retrograde policy would be to reject them, thus abandoning the principle of the treaty and sacrificing the numerous liberal commercial arrangements which would remain. Lord Lyons told him that it would be a painful task to communicate these views to her Majesty's government; and it must have been painful to listen to them.

A long correspondence on the subject ensued between the two governments, and M. Thiers referred to it very pointedly in his message to the Assembly in December. The treaty, he complained, had been concluded without consulting the nation, and absolute free trade had been introduced without any preparation, causing deep injury to the trade in iron, woven fabrics, agricultural products, and the mercantile marine. He reported that the government proposed, as a basis of negotiation with England, an increase of from three to five per cent, in the duties on woven fabrics, with twelve or eighteen per cent, on mixed wool; that these overtures met with an unfavourable and dilatory response; that England objected to the change as a retrocession from free trade principles; and that the government therefore intended to give notice to terminate the treaty, continuing the negotiations during the twelve months which it had then to run. In any case, the existing friendly relations with England would remain unaffected, and the tariffs would be altered only on the points specified.

Official notice to terminate the treaty was given on March 15, 1872. The French government asserted to the last that it had no desire to effect an economic revolution of a nature tending to disturb the commercial relations of the two countries, but that it only wished to provide in the best manner for the pressing wants of French finance and industry. It recognized with satisfaction not only the courtesy manifested by Lord Granville in his communications on the subject, but also his acknowledgment of the difficulties against which France was struggling, as encouraging the hope that a resumption of negotiations might yet lead to a satisfactory compromise. Finally, it heartily reciprocated the declaration of her Majesty's government that, whatever might be the issue of the discussion, England would not regard it as a proof of hostility, or as affecting the *entente cordiale* which the commercial treaty was designed to strengthen.

The negotiations published in the Blue Book on the subject prove that the French government never exactly understood the English. Up to the last, M. Thiers did not believe we should go the length of accepting a "denunciation" of the treaty, but persuaded himself that it would be modified in the sense he desired. It was in vain Lord Granville again and again declared, that we could be party to no treaty involving an increase of protection, especially when it was stated on the other side that our consent was most earnestly sought for the purpose of inducing other nations to follow our example. M. Thiers was so convinced that, if he only held out long enough, he must lure us back, that at one time he proposed to send over M. Pouyer-Quertier to remove the slight difficulties in the way of a settlement; and he could hardly be persuaded that, without some preliminary agreement on principles, the visit of the finance minister would end in nothing but disappointment and vexation. M. de Remusat, the foreign minister, appears to have seen a little more clearly than his chief the bearing of Lord Granville's notes and the conversations of Lord Lyons; but even he could not be made to perceive that an import duty on wool or raw silk would be a protection to French producers of these articles, even though it were accompanied by import duties on cloths and manufactured silk. All that could be got from him when driven hard was, that if it were a protection it was very small; that Frenchmen were now heavily taxed; and, lastly, that small protective duties were not at variance with the spirit of the treaty. Correspondence thus conducted could end only in the "denunciation" of the treaty, and it is to be hoped that in future nothing will be done to enable him or any successor of his to allege afterwards that we have made a gain, and that France has suffered a loss, through a bargain between us.

With regard to another matter in which Englishmen took a special interest, M. Thiers adopted a much more satisfactory course. For many years Englishmen had been allowed to travel in France without any restriction whatever; but during the war the old system of passports was revived, and it was ultimately made more stringent than ever. Remonstrance from the English government was for some time useless, although it was clearly shown that the revival of the wanton and tyrannical restriction was quite inoperative for the purpose of preventing and detecting crime, and acted merely as an impediment to honest travellers.

At last, however, M. Thiers, somewhat unexpectedly, gave way on the subject, and the intercourse of the two countries was practically restored to the freedom which existed, to their common advantage, in the days of the Empire. It is not often that a veteran statesman, arrived at the height of power, and fixed in his own opinions by the deference he receives, is willing to abandon anything on which he has set his mind; but in the present instance M. Thiers wisely gave in to the views which he found to prevail among men younger and holding inferior places, and in so doing he gave a better proof of capacity to govern than would have been afforded by any display of successful obstinacy.

The other subject to which M. Thiers chiefly directed his energies after the suppression of the Communist insurrection, and to which he seemed to pay, if possible, even more attention than to the financial condition of the country, was the reorganization of the French army.

The war had been so disastrous to France that it had destroyed her military power, materially as well as morally. It emptied the arsenals, exhausted the stock of the arm manufactories, left vast stores in the enemy's hands, and shattered or dismantled such of the strongholds as were not irreparably lost. The first steps to be taken were, of course, with the men. It became necessary not only to reunite scattered fragments of regiments, to provide *cadres* for them, to re-arm, clothe, equip, and train them, and to re-establish the health of the returned prisoners, but to collect in the centre of the country a force strong in numbers and quality, capable of overawing disorder, and of exhibiting to Europe visible proof of the reconstitution of the French army with all its old merits. In his speech to the Assembly, in December, 1871, M. Thiers was able to state that this project had been almost completed, permitting the incorporation of 600,000 infantry into 150 regiments of 3000 in the field, and 1000 at the depôt, and securing the constant "feeding" of the acting army, whatever the ravages of battles, marches, and diseases. Under the Empire, there were only 128 or 129 regiments, including the guards and zouaves; but with 150 regiments thirty-seven to thirty-eight divisions could always be organized, dispensing with the appointment of new *cadres* at the moment of taking the field, when every one so made was worthless. The increase of pieces of artillery from scarcely two and a half to four per thousand men, would also remedy one of the principal causes of the recent disasters. The threatened feud between the old officers, owing their advancement to length or distinction of service, and the new, owing it in part to the course of events, had been prevented by a spirit of moderation and good sense, and the deference of the juniors, so that the reconciliation was complete in most of the regiments; experience and the spectacle of a rigorous obedience in Germany having shown, both to soldiers and officers, that discipline was the life of armies. Hence order and respect for superiors prevailed. Destroyed or dispersed *cadres*, owing to the return of a large number of prisoners, would soon be reorganized, the troops were well armed, but their equipment and clothing were less advanced. As to recruiting, too much stress had been laid on the numbers, instead of on the quality of soldiers, and the Prussian victories had been attributed to compulsory service. On this point M. Thiers said: "If by compulsory service it is meant that the French should be imbued with the patriotic thought that amid great perils they all owe their lives to the country, it is right, and we applaud it; but if it is meant that in peace, as in war, all Frenchmen should belong to the active army, this is pursuing the impossible, threatening the disorganization of civil society by the absolute ruin of the finances, and preparing an army, numerous without doubt, but incapable of really making war. There is, moreover, an impossibility of fact which you will at once appreciate. The class which every year attains, at twenty-one years, the age of service consists of 300,000 men. If these were enrolled there would be, with three years of service, three contingents, making about 900,000 men, which would constitute, doubtless, a very imposing force; but the budget, pushed to the utmost, could not pay more than 450,000, so that half would successively have to be relegated to their homes in the middle of their time of service, to give place to the new comers."

Urging that in eighteen months soldiers could not be formed, much less sub-officers, and that Prussia owed its success to the persistent struggle of the king and his principal minister for the prolongation of the period of training, the president proposed, as adequate to every necessity, to make service compulsory on all in time of war, but to enrol annually by lot during peace 90,000 men, clear of all deduction. The term of service would be eight years—five under the colours, and three in renewable furloughs; thus furnishing eight contingents of 90,000 each, which, added to the 120,000 otherwise recruited, would give a total of 840,000, or 800,000, making allowance for deaths, and the annual draught for the marine. A force would thus be secured which, in 1870, would certainly have won or disputed the victory, and saved provinces and milliards. Five years' active service would not be too heavy for the population, and the power of substituting one man for another would tend to mitigate it; while those not drawn could be intrusted with the protection of the towns, and in war with that of fortresses and frontiers.

This proposal of M. Thiers, which showed that, as in some other respects, he was yet untaught by the lessons of the past, and failed to see that the chief cause of the demoralization of the French army was the combination of conscription with paid substitutes—met with a firm and steady resistance from the National Assembly. The difference between him and them was fundamental. M. Thiers wanted an army formed on the same basis as that which capitulated at Sedan. He argued that the disasters which overtook the imperial troops reflected no discredit on the principles on which they were recruited and trained, but were due to the systematic neglect of those principles. Had the army been in fact what it was on paper, all might have gone well. What other motives M. Thiers might have had for wishing the principle maintained, or why he pronounced so decidedly against universal service, and in favour of a limited conscription, it is perhaps scarcely lair to surmise. But a general impression certainly existed that he was eager to hurry forward the day when France should be once more in a position to play an independent part in the affairs of Europe, and saw that a shorter time would suffice to put an existing system into thorough repair than to organize one entirely new. But his reasons, whether expressed or unexpressed, had no weight with the Assembly. They referred the matter to a well-selected committee, by whom it was most closely investigated, and through whose influence the government proposal was completely recast; while the shape in which it was presented showed how deep was the impression left by the war on the minds of Frenchmen. Both the Right and the Left in the Assembly would naturally be opposed to a large military establishment; but the desire to give France the power to measure herself again with Germany was stronger than any dread of domestic tyranny, and without a single dissentient vote the committee recommended as the basis of their scheme, that every Frenchman between the ages of twenty and forty should be not only liable to military service, but, with a few exceptions, should actually serve in the army or navy. The proposals of the committee were adopted by the Assembly, with very few alterations, June, 1872, and the new system will come into operation on the 1st of January, 1873. France will be divided into twelve military regions, each with a corps d'armée to which will be attached all soldiers found in the region, whether they have been liberated by anticipation, not having completed their period of active service, or belong to the reserve, or have been allowed to return home, on no matter what pretext.

A corps d'armée will comprise two divisions of infantry of three brigades, one brigade of cavalry of three regiments, two regiments of artillery of fourteen batteries, a battalion of engineers with military train, &c. Each brigade of infantry will be uniformly composed of two regiments; the battalions of chasseurs à pied will be abolished as a constituted body, and will reappear as companies d'élite; and the battalion of infantry will be composed of five companies, including one of chasseurs, recruited from among the best shots in the corps. One of the three regiments of the cavalry brigade will be parcelled out between the two divisions for divisional service, for furnishing escorts, estafettes, &c., and the commander of the corps d'armée will have only two regiments of cavalry at his disposal for reconnoitring. This is hardly considered sufficient, but in addition to these two regiments there will be the cavalry of the reserve.

Each of the regiments of artillery will comprise fourteen batteries—ten field batteries, two foot, and two in the depôt. Out of the ten field batteries there will be eight mounted, and two of horse artillery. The artillery o: a corps d'armée will thus be composed of twenty batteries—eight attached to each division, two to the cavalry brigade, and two in reserve.

Each corps d'armée will detach a brigade for service in Paris or Lyons, and the twelve brigades thus obtained will form two corps d'armée for Paris and one for Lyons. By this combination a garrison easily moved and renewed will be kept up in these two troublesome centres of France, without the normal condition of the corps d'armée in the interior being greatly affected. The brigades thus detached, though forming a variable corps as far as regards the source from which they are drawn, will be under the command of a permanent staff and permanent generals, and so be ready to march at once in the event of war. This combination has been rendered necessary by the impossibility of garrisoning Paris with Parisians and Lyons with Lyonese, on the principle of territorial recruitment. The normal force of a corps d'armée upon a war footing will therefore consist of only five brigades, as the sixth brigade will be detached for service in Paris and Lyons.

In Algeria a permanent corps d'armée will always remain, composed of three divisions, one for each province. In the event of war, there will therefore be ready for service the twelve regional corps d'armée, the three of Paris and Lyons, and, in addition, a division of marines and three brigades borrowed from Algeria; in all, sixteen corps d'armée.

Independently of the twenty-four regiments of regional artillery, there will be ten others for supplying Paris, Lyons, and Algeria, as well as the general reserves of the army.

Such is a brief sketch of the plans adopted by the Assembly for the distribution of the force of 1,200,000 men now considered requisite for the defence of the country, and which will be divided into an active army, reserve of the active army, a territorial army, and territorial reserve.

The new military law, as regards recruitment, is based on the following general dispositions. As before stated, it lays down the principle of personal military service, not allowing substitutes; and consequently every Frenchman from twenty to forty years of age will be forced to serve. It also modifies the provision by which certain citizens, such as eldest sons of widows, &c., used to be entirely exonerated.

Although the contingents will in future comprise all the young men capable of military service, the old *tirage au sort*, or drawing of lots, will be maintained; but the men who draw good numbers, instead of being exonerated as heretofore, will only escape service in the marines, and be placed in the second instead of the first part of the contingent of the active army.

Definite exemption will in future be accorded only to young men whose infirmities render them unfit for all active or auxiliary service.

The exemption for insufficient height is done away with, and the lads below the standard will be employed as auxiliary troops. The same law will be applied to youths of feeble constitution, who will have to present themselves three successive years before the Council of Revision before being told off to any special duty in hospitals, &c. The other cases of exemption specified in the law of 1832 will also be modified; in future the eldest son of a widow, the eldest lad of a family of orphans, and the young men who have brothers on active service, will not be exempted, but will receive a temporary dispensation, and be called upon to serve only in case of absolute necessity. In regard to youths destined for holy orders and for public instruction, the law of 1832 is very slightly changed, but the new law accords no special favour to young men carrying off the first prizes at the Institute and the University. In the case of young men studying for a profession at the time of being drawn, the authorities may allow them to postpone serving until their studies are completed. In all cases the ecclesiastical student must take orders before he is twenty-six years of age. The exemption of priests was one of the great grudges which the Communists had against the whole body of the ecclesiastics; and during the siege of Paris several attempts were made to force the government to call on the seminarists to fall into the ranks of the national guard. In the early days of French history the clergy were obliged to serve like other vassals. When a bishop or an abbot renounced the profession of arms, he was forced to place himself under the protection of an *advocate* or *vidame*, to whom he paid so much a year, and it was probably this mediaeval custom which the Communists wished to revive.

A certain number of men, deemed indispensable for the support of their families, will get temporary and renewable dispensations; but, as in most other cases, they will be called upon to serve in the event of danger.

The most important regulation in the new military law is, without doubt, the rendering it imperative that every Frenchman capable of bearing arms must form part of the active army for a period of five, and of the reserve of the active army for four years. On the expiration of these nine years' service the soldier will pass five years in the territorial army and six in the reserve of that army. In the marines, where the service is considered harder, its duration will not be so long, and exchanges will be permitted.

All the youth of the class called out, who are found fit for service, will be at once incorporated into one of the corps of the active army, but they will not all have to serve the same length of time in the effective. The minister of War will make known each year the number of men he requires, and those drafted into the active army to fill up its ranks will constitute the first portion of the contingent. The young men not comprised in that portion will only pass six months under the flag. It will be thus seen that when once the system comes into complete operation the reserve forces of France will be continually in process of recruitment through two distinct channels. Every year a certain number of troops who have served their full time with the colours will pass back into the civil population, and every year a certain percentage of the civil population will learn as much soldiering as six months in camp can teach them. When this system has been completely carried out, the active army can be reinforced in case of need by all the trained soldiers who have already served their full time, and by as many of the civil population who have served for six months as it proves necessary to call up.

The soldiers of the second portion of the contingent, though allowed to return home at the time stated, will be subjected to reviews and exercises; and so with the men of the reserve, who will be liable to be called out twice in the year, for four weeks at a time. Those belonging to these categories will be allowed to marry without authorization, and any man becoming the father of four living children will pass by right into the territorial army.

As regards volunteers, it is laid down that they must be able to read and write, and that in the event of hostilities any Frenchman, having completed his time in the active army and the reserve, will be allowed to volunteer for the duration of the war. Soldiers in the second portion of the contingent will be permitted to volunteer to complete their five years' service in the active army, and will have the right of objecting to being sent home before serving out their time.

On the subject of engagement and re-engagements, a large portion of the law of 1832 is unaltered; but one clause in the present law is an entire novelty in France (although a somewhat similar plan has been long in operation in Prussia), and will allow young men who have taken out diplomas—who are bachelors of letters, arts, or sciences, or who are following one of the faculties of the University, the Central School of Industry and Commerce, the School of Arts and Trades, the Conservatory of Music, the veterinary or agricultural schools, &c.—to contract a conditional engagement for one year. They will be required to pass a certain examination before the War minister, and will then be permitted to join the army for the short period stated, provided they equip and keep themselves. If at the expiration of a year they pass a military examination, they will be freed from service and allowed to retire with the grade of sous-offieier. Should a young man of this class desire to finish his studies before serving, he will be allowed to remain free until he is twenty-three years old, when he must pass his year in the ranks.

An important clause in the new law sets forth that any soldier who has passed twelve years under the flag, and has served as sous-officier for four years, will be entitled to a certificate giving him the right of claiming a civil or military employment, in accordance with his capacity. A special law is to settle the status of these employés in the public service.

As soon as the recommendations of the committee were made known, M. Thiers withdrew the opposition which he originally offered to the principle of universal service, and agreed to accept the increased strength of the army in the future as compensation for the greater delay in attaining it. The only point upon which any serious difference of opinion then existed was the question of substitutes. M. Thiers pleaded that, without allowing these, it would be impossible to satisfy the requirements of a civil career; but the committee replied that these were provided for by the clauses introduced into the bill to meet the case of students and young men preparing for professions. It is clear that the prohibition of substitutes is essential to the success of a system of compulsory service. So long as they are allowed, the army is not a really national force, but one composed of men who serve because they cannot help it, or who have been bribed by those who wish to avoid the duty which has devolved on them. The particular difficulty started by M. Thiers is disposed of as soon as service becomes really universal. It cannot be maintained that a year of camp life interposed between the preparatory study and the practice of a profession would be any real injury to a young man, unless it were exacted from him and not from his rivals. When it is imposed upon all alike, it simply interferes with the preparation for civil life by one year. M. Thiers would create a real, on the plea of doing away with an imaginary, hardship. Nothing could make military service more unpopular, or bring the government into greater discredit, than a provision allowing a student of law or medicine who could afford to buy a substitute, to set up as a barrister or a physician a year earlier than one of equal capacity and education, but by whom, from his limited circumstances, a substitute was unattainable.

Having thus given an outline of the French scheme, it may be interesting to compare it briefly with the military organization of Germany. The French Assembly has so fully adopted the principle of universal liability to military service without substitutes, that their system is even more thorough than that of Prussia, where anything beyond slight bodily defects disqualifies a man for enrolment, or even the Ersatz reserve.

It will be observed that in France the period of service extends from the age of twenty to forty, while in Prussia a man is free after he has attained the age of thirty-two, or has served twelve years. It is evident, there lore, that in France the service will press nearly twice as hard upon the nation as it does in Prussia. In Prussia also, in the case of the educated classes, the burden is much lightened by allowing young men to enter the army at seventeen, and to commute their three years' service with the colours and four years in the reserve, for one year with the colours and six years in the reserve, provided they give proof of their education, and consent to provide their own clothing, equipment, and subsistence. In France neither the educated nor the uneducated man can enter before he is twenty.

With regard to organization, the first point observable is, that the picked shots, instead of forming a third sub-division to each company, as in Prussia, are formed into a fifth company. There is something to be said for each arrangement, but on the whole the Prussian system seems preferable, as it renders each company an independent tactical sub-unit. In the English army the marksmen are mixed up with the worst shots, and of their superior skill no advantage whatever is taken. The abolition of the battalions of chasseurs is a measure the wisdom of which is not very clear, for it is always convenient to possess in each division or corps d'armée battalions trained for the special duties of the advanced guard. The distribution of the cavalry in the French system seems open to serious objections. In reconnoitring, a brigade of two regiments will not suffice to perform the duties of so large a body as a corps d'armée. Moreover, the employment of cavalry *en masse* is obsolete, and to withdraw them from the corps d'armée for the purpose of forming a grand reserve, is to ignore the progress of the science of war. In future, we conceive that on the battle-field cavalry will only be able to act in comparatively small bodies, such as a regiment, or, at most, a brigade of two regiments. To form a corps of two or three, or even of one division, would therefore seem to deny that arm all opportunity of combining effectually its action with that of infantry and artillery. Cavalry ought to be chiefly attached, but not chained, to the divisions of infantry, in order to be able to take prompt advantage of the quickly passing opportunities which offer themselves.

The completeness of the localization in the French scheme, and the principle of keeping every corps d'armée in a state of continual readiness for active service, cannot be too much praised. The great distinction between the two systems here compared is, that service with the colours is in France to be five years, while in Prussia it is only three. The French, from natural insubordination and want of education and intelligence, probably require longer military training than the Prussians. But even the Prussian authorities would prefer a longer period of service, did circumstances admit of its being introduced. We are not, therefore, disposed to find fault with that portion of the French plan. We do, however, think that two trainings yearly, each of four weeks, to which the French reserve man is to be subjected, will impose an unnecessary hardship on the nation What master will care to employ a workman liable to be called away so often, and for so long a time? Further, a person once thoroughly trained could well keep up his military proficiency by means of a much less time. In Prussia the men on furlough, corresponding to the army reserve of the French, are only liable in four years to take part in two manoeuvres, neither of them exceeding eight weeks. Practically they are not kept out for half that time.

As a whole, the French may be pronounced an exaggerated copy of the Prussian system, but it wants its practical character and its completeness. Imperfect, however, though it be in some respects, it is a great improvement on the old organization. It raises the status of the army, and adds enormously to the material strength of the country, while at the same time it promises to contribute largely to its moral regeneration.

Under the new system it is intended that France shall be able to bring into the field an army of 1,185,000, armed with the best weapons that science can invent and money procure. It is further designed that the fortifications of Paris shall be so extended as to embrace the heights which the Germans occupied in the late siege, and that the eastern frontier shall be covered with a line of fortresses.

The reform of the military schools also formed a part of the programme of the government and of the Assembly. The war brought out clearly the inadequacy and vices of the instruction given in them. The pupils of the Polytechnic were too often theorists, who retained in the colleges to which they were afterwards sent—the military engineer college, the artillery and staff colleges—the faults of their training. Over-instructed in some branches, ignorant in others which are indispensable, they showed themselves especially incompetent on the staff. Under the most favourable circumstances, however, it must take a considerable time and no little effort of administrative ingenuity, before the armed power of France can be considered materially a match for that of Germany.

On June 29 a new treaty was concluded between Germany and France, which was, on the whole, beneficial to the latter Under previous arrangements no more money was to have been paid until March 1, 1874, and the six departments were all to continue to be occupied till that time; £120,000,000, with interest, were then to be paid, and the Germans were forthwith to evacuate France Under the new arrangement £20,000,000 were to be paid within two months on the ratification of the treaty, and two departments, comprising the finest parts of Champagne, were to be evacuated It was also agreed that £20,000,000 more should be paid on February 1, 187'3, and £40,000,000 more on 1st March, 1874; and on these £80,000,000, or two milliards, being paid, two more departments, those of Ardennes and the Vosges, are to be evacuated. The last £40,000,000 are to be paid, with all interest then due, on March 1, 1875, and then the last of the six occupied departments, those of Meuse and Meurthe, are to be evacuated, and Belfort is to be handed over to France. The main features of this new treaty were, therefore, that by an immediate payment of £20,000,000 France purchased the liberation of two departments, and she had a year more given her before she made a final settlement with Germany. The French government tried hard to obtain the further concession, that in proportion as the area of occupation was diminished the numbers of the occupying army should be diminished also. But the Germans, for military reasons, would not agree to this. They insisted on being at liberty to keep 50,000 men in France, so long as they were there at all.

Immediately after this treaty had been ratified by the Assembly, preparations were made for contracting a new loan in order to carry its provisions into effect. The amount asked for was three and a half milliards, or £140,000.000, at five per cent., and as it was issued at eighty-three it promised investors about six per cent, interest. The success of this loan was almost beyond the power of imagination. More than twelve times the amount required was offered! Of this enormous sum France of course subscribed the greater part. The eagerness of the people there transcended everything which had been observed in connection with the imperial loans. Not fewer than 250 places for subscription were opened in Paris alone, and at all of them the tradesmen and workmen pressed to make their demands (in many cases they waited all night in order to obtain a good place), and to hand in the deposit which should entitle them to their allotment. Abroad the loan was hardly less attractive, and Germany alone more than covered the whole amount required. In England, too, the subscriptions were very large—far exceeding any which had ever been offered to any foreign country, or even to our own. Of course the offer was to some extent unreal, as many subscribers, anticipating that they would only be alloted a portion of the amount asked for, sent in requests for much larger sums than they would have been prepared to take. But the deposit required to guarantee good faith, the fourteen per cent, actually sent in to the Mairies and the Treasury in gold, silver, banknotes, and immediately available securities, was £240,000,000, or £100,000,000 more than the amount required—an amount nearly four times the sum ever asked for in a single loan in the whole history of finance.

The great moral lesson of this marvellous success was, as it seems to us, that it clearly proved that the people of France—the six or seven million male adults who plant and plough, and build and trade within her borders—are not disenchanted by her reverses, are not distrustful of her future, and are not fearful lest she should be eaten up by Communists, or should cease to be a state. All accounts testify alike that subscriptions came from the very lowest, that the *queue* of persons waiting to subscribe in Belleville, the Communist stronghold, was one of the longest in the capital. The conservative power of confidence such as this could scarcely be overrated, even were the possession of means to subscribe in itself not so conservative an influence; but as it is, the subscription was of itself, in our opinion, almost a guarantee for France. A nation in which industry, patience, self denial, and habits of saving arc so conspicuous as in France, and in which the masses so trust the state, cannot be dead or dying, or even weak. There must be vitality in it, even if misdirected; force, even if the force has not yet accumulated itself in the hand most competent to guide it. What nation, at any height of prosperity, could give a more decisive and unanswerable proof of its belief in itself, of its own intention to live, of that confidence in its own continuance which is, after all, the best security that it will continue, and continue great? Money is not all, either in war or peace, though both have been made so expensive; but the nation which, with the victorious foreigner camped on her soil, with an openly expressed determination to "revindicate" two of her provinces at the earliest opportunity, and with all her institutions to re-arrange, can, at a word, command £120,000,000 to be paid away in tribute to an invader, is and must remain, both for war and peace, one of the greatest of nations.

THE END.

PART III.

THE RHINE VALLEY.

> A thousand battles have assailed thy banks,
> But these and half their fame have passed away,
> And slaughter heaped on high his slaughtering ranks
> Their very graves are gone, and what are they?
> Thy tide washed down the blood of yesterday,
> And all was stainless; and on thy clear stream
> Glanced with its dancing light the sunny ray;
> But o'er the blackened memory's blighting dream,
> Thy waves would vainly roll, all sweeping as they seem.
> Adieu to thee, fair Rhine. . . .
> The negligently grand, the fruitful bloom
> Of coming ripeness, the white city's sheen,
> The rolling stream, the precipice's gloom,
> The forest's growth, and Gothic walls between
> The wild rocks shaped as they had turrets been.
> In mockery of man's art; and these withal,
> A race of faces happy as the scene,
> Whose fertile bounties here extend to all,
> Still springing o'er thy banks, though empires near them fall.
> <div align="right">Byron's <i>Childe Harold</i>.</div>

CHAPTER I.—Introductory.

FROM THE SOURCES OF THE RHINE TO STRASBURG.

WITH the exception of the Nile and the Jordan, there is no river in the world which has exercised so great an influence on the fortunes of nations, or produced so powerful an impression on the minds of men, as the Rhine. We know all that can be said in favour of the mighty Mississippi, and its turbid roll of waters; of the Amazon, and its forest-clad banks; of the "sacred Ganges," and its traditions dating far back into the twilight of human history; of the Indus, which marked at one time the frontiers of Western civilization; of the Thames, which, comparatively insignificant in its course and volume, has nevertheless gathered to its ample bosom the commercial navies of the world: but of none of them can so much be advanced to interest and astonish and attract the thinker, as of the "exultant and abounding" Rhine. The great German river possesses every charm which can fix our attention; it is rich in the graces of scenery, in historical associations, in those songs and legends which naturally spring from the fertility of the popular imagination. It flows through a succession of landscapes which vary from grave to gay, from the sublime to the beautiful; it is haunted by memories of heroes, of warriors, princes, and poets; by the shadows of terrible battles which have been fought upon its banks; by the immortal music of the Lorelei, who, as old poets tell us, frequents its liquid depths, and incessantly raises her sweet but melancholy strains. It is the river of the grand epic of the Nibelungen-lied; it is the river of the faithful Roland, of the two brothers of Liebenstein, of the white-bearded and imperial Charlemagne, of the mighty Barbarossa. From the earliest ages it has borne that singularly impressive character which is still its dower. Long before the Teuton settled on the slopes of its fertile hills it was called, as it is still called, the Rhine (*hren, rhenus*); and the word thrilled in the ears of the Celts of old, as it now thrills in the ears of Frank and German. Two thousand years ago, as now, it was "the river," the river of rivers, the king of rivers, for the great German race; and mailed warriors sang, as well-armed veterans sing to-day:—

"Am Rhein, am Rhein, du wachsen unsere Reben,
Gesegnet sie der Rhein!"

The people prayed on its banks—for it was as sacred to them as the Ganges to the Hindu—and lighted their tapers, and offered their offerings in honour of the noble river. And through the course of succeeding generations, the popular devotion has never failed, and you can stimulate the dullest brain and coldest heart into enthusiasm by whispering—the Rhine.

There are rivers, says a German writer, whose course is longer; there are rivers whose volume of water is greater: but no other unites in the same degree almost everything that can render an earthly object magnificent and attractive. As it descends from the remote ridges of the Alps, through fertile regions into the open sea, so it comes down from remote antiquity, associated in every age with momentous events in the history of the neighbouring nations. A river which presents so many historical recollections of Roman conquests and defeats, of the chivalrous exploits of the feudal age, of the wars and negotiations of modern times, of the coronations of emperors, whose bones repose by its side; on whose borders stand the two grandest monuments of the noble architecture of the mediaeval days; whose banks exhibit every variety of wild romantic rocks, dense forests, smiling plains, vineyards, sometimes gently sloping, sometimes perched among lofty erases, where industry has won a domain among the fortresses of nature; whose banks are ornamented with populous cities, flourishing towns and villages, castles and ruins, with which a thousand legends are connected, with beautiful and picturesque highways, and salutary mineral springs; a river whose waters offer choice fish, as its banks produce the choicest wines; which, in its course of 900 miles, affords 630 of uninterrupted navigation, from Bale to the sea, and enables the inhabitants of either side of its fertile valley to exchange its rich and luxurious products; whose cities, famous for commercial enterprise, science, and military strongholds which furnish protection to Germany, are also famous as the seats of Roman colonies and of ecclesiastical councils, and are associated with many of the most important events recorded in the history of mankind;—such a river, says our authority, it is not surprising that the Germans should regard with a kind of reverence, and frequently call it in poetry *Father*, or *King Rhine*.

GENERAL STATISTICS.

The Rhine, in its earliest stage, consists of three branches, the Front, the Middle, and the Back Rhine, and in these branches absorbs nearly all the drainage of the northern basin of the Alps.

Each branch has, of course, its own fountainhead.

The Front Rhine (*Vorder Rhein*) rises from the Toma Lake, which is 7460 feet above the sea level, and coated with ice for the greater part of the year, in a region of dreary rocks and steel-blue glaciers.

The Middle Rhine (*Mittel Rhein*) springs from the Cadclrhin glacier, and descends abruptly into the Medelsee valley.

The Back Rhine (*Hinter Rhein*) issues from the icy solitudes of the Rheinwald valley, at the base of the Moschelhorn, Adula, and Piz Vol Rhein, about six miles above the little village of Hinter Rhein (4800 feet above the sea), where it is crossed by a stone bridge with three arches; and thence traversing the Via Mala and Trou Perdu, swollen by thirty torrents, it winds through the fair valley of Domleschg, where it receives the Nolla, the Albula, the Davos, and the Rhine of Oberhalbstein."

The Front Rhine, near the pastoral hamlet of Chiamont, is augmented by two streams, one coming down from Crispalt and the other from the Corvera Valley. At Dissentis, where the traveller may see the remains of a fine old Benedictine abbey, it receives the Middle Rhine, and the united stream then proceeds to join the more important current of the Back Rhine at Reichenau.

Such is the origin of the great German river. Fed by the snows of the Swiss mountain glaciers, it strikes eastward from Reichenau to Coire. Then it takes a northerly direction, and flows through the beautiful valley which bears its name, as far as the Lake of Constanz. At Constanz it issues from the lake, and proceeding westward traverses a second lake, which it quits at Stein; then it runs to Schaffhausen, to form the magnificent cataract known as the Falls of the Rhine. From Schaffhausen to Bâle it keeps a westerly course. Near Waldshut it receives the Aar, which, with the Limmat and the Reuss, brings to it the waters of the Swiss cantons of Friburg, Lucerne, Unterwalden, Uri, Schwyz, Zug, and Glarus, and no inconsiderable portion of those of Vaud, Neuchatel, Berne, Soleure, Argovie, Zurich, and Saint-Gall; for its basin extends, west to east, from the Lake des Rousses to the frontier of the Grisons; and south to north, from the massive ridge of St. Gothard to its own borders.

Beyond Bâle, the Rhine, receding from rugged Helvetia, takes a northerly direction, and forms as far as Strasburg, one of the great fortresses in the French outer line of defence, the boundary line between the grand duchy of Baden (right bank) and the empire of France (left bank).

From Strasburg our river flows northward, or more correctly speaking north-eastward, to Mannheim, where it receives the Neckar. At Mainz it turns to the west, then to the north-west, and flows past Coblenz (where it is augmented by the Moselle), Bonn, Köln, and Dusseldorf, to Arnhem, where it strikes westward to Utrecht, and dividing into two channels, the Waal and the Lek, which again unite near Arnhem, sluggishly meanders through a flat and deltoid country, to empty its waters, amid shallows and mud banks, into the German Ocean at Catwyck, below Leyden.

Its length of course may be thus estimated: From its extreme source to the city of Constanz, 135 miles; from Constanz to Basel (Bâle), 80 miles; from Basel to Lauterberg, 110 miles; from Lauterberg to Bingen, 90 miles; from Bingen to its mouth, 270 miles: total, 685 miles. Its average velocity is ninety-one mètres, or 995 yards, per minute. Its basin includes an area of 82,000 square miles, inhabited probably by 18,000,000 inhabitants. Of this area a ninth part belongs to Switzerland, an eighth to France, a seventh to Belgium and Holland, and the remainder, with the exception of a small Austrian territory, to Germany, as represented by Prussia, Bavaria, Baden, and Würtemburg.

The breadth of the Rhine at the principal points on its banks is as follows:—

	English Feet
Near Reichenau,	250
At Stein,	280 to 330
Schaffhausen,	330
The Falls of the Rhine.	660
Rheinfelden,	750
Near Strasburg,.	1090
Mannheim,	1350
Mainz,	1350
Biberich,	1650
Eltville,	1950
Near Bingen,	1020
Near Coblenz,	1380
Near Neuwied,	1530
Bonn,	1360
Cologne (Köln),	1400
Hittorf,	1750
Dusseldorf,	1350
Kaiserswerth,	1510
Wesel,	1650
Below Wesel,	1950
Near Emmerich,	2350

The Rhine is navigable from its mouth to Schaffhausen, a distance of 500 miles. Its average depth, from the sea to Köln (160 miles), is ten to twelve feet; from Köln to Mainz, five to six feet; but the depth is affected by the character of the seasons, being greatest when a very warm and genial spring has largely melted the mountain snows.

The Rhine, says Victor Hugo, combines the characters of all other rivers. It is swift as the Rhône, broad as the Loire, shut in like the Meuse, tortuous as the Seine, green and lucent as the Somme, historic as the Tiber, regal as the Danube, mysterious as the Nile, gold-spangled as a river of America, haunted with fables and phantoms as a river of Asia.

TO REICHENAU.

Having furnished the reader with these general particulars—with an itinerary, as it were, of the district he has to traverse—we now proceed to a detailed description of the course of the great German river.

The fountains of the Back Rhine are romantically situated. They issue from the bosom of the Rheinwald glacier—a torrent of ice fully four and twenty miles in height—thirteen or fourteen in number, and fall over the ridge of the Moschelhorn into a dark blue pool at the base of the glacier, which is fed by inexhaustible but concealed streams. This pool is about four feet broad by one and a half deep. Receiving tributes of melted snow and ice on either hand, the infant river pours through a chasm or crevasse, called the Gulf of Hell; passing the spot where a "Temple of the Nymphs" once consecrated the silent mountain solitudes; and hurries onward to Reichenau, to receive, as we have already said, the united stream of the Front and Middle Rhine. The distance is about forty-five miles, and in this distance the river has a fall of nearly 4000 feet, a fact which attests the impetuosity of its current, and the steep rugged character of the valley, or succession of valleys, through which its hurrying waters swirl and foam.

The chief town in this wild and picturesque region is Splügen, lying in the shadow of the densely wooded mountain of that name. It boasts of a quaint little church and a grey old timber bridge, of a decent inn, and of several houses of such fantastic design, that they would delight the soul of an artist. Its chief importance lies in its position at the commencement of the great Splügen Pass, one of the main channels of communication between Switzerland and Lombardy.

We are now in the territory of the Grisons; a territory which comprehends within its limits the elements both of the grand and beautiful, the sublime and terrible. The Rhine traverses it from end to end, and in so doing traverses a series of landscapes wholly unequalled in Europe; landscapes which combine the rock and the torrent, the forest and the ravine, the pastoral meadow and the sylvan glen. We can well believe that they kindle an almost divine enthusiasm in the soul of the poet. Certain we are that not even the dullest can look upon them without an emotion of sympathy.

The territory of the Grisons, anciently forming the Republic of the Three Leagues in Rhaetia Superior, consists, in the main, of the upper valley of the Rhine, and occupies an area of 130 German square miles. It is the largest canton included in the Swiss Confederacy; but in point of population only the eighth, its inhabitants not exceeding 100,000 in number. These are divided between the Lutheran and Roman Catholic creeds in the proportion of 60,000 to 40,000, and are of German, Romansh, and Italian origin. The chief town is Chur, or Coire.

The character of the country, and especially of the Engadine, which is its most beautiful and pastoral portion, has been described with singular force and effect by Michelet, in his book on "The Mountain." But on its icy plains and snowy wastes, its broken masses of rock, its precipices, its wild awful ravines, its foaming torrents, its deep shadowy forests of murmurous pine, its bold mountain terraces, and its occasional bursts of Arcadian loveliness—where some crystal stream winds through a quiet and leafy vale, sheltered, tranquil, and genial, and enhanced in its still beauty by the mystic horror of the frowning heights beyond—we are forbidden to dwell. Nor can we speak of the 180 ruined castles, which, planted on their rocky eminences, form so curious an object in the most attractive landscapes, and of each of which some legend might be told, or some historical fact narrated.

After leaving Splügen, the Rhine increases in width, and its waters assume a blue-green tint, as they enter upon the dark and desolate ravine of the Rofla—*die Felsengallerie* (or tunnel gallery), *durch die Roffler*—and plunge under arching crags, and down steep descents, with a deafening din and a ceaseless whirl and eddy. The rocks on either hand are gaunt and precipitous, relieved only by the brushwood growing from their fissures, or the rows of tall spectral firs which stand like wardens on their summits. The Rofla defile is about half a league in length, and a road was first formed through it in 1470, at the same time that the Via Mala was constructed.

Into the dark deep gulf the Rhine plunges with a mighty bound. It is spanned by the Rofla bridge, 4140 feet above the level of the sea. Here it is joined from the south by the Averse water, or the Avner Rhine, the two streams meeting together with a wild clash and tumult, like two warrior-foes, and hurtling from rock to rock, and dashing from side to side, as if in the throes of a mortal combat, while the echoes resound with the din, and the living spray flashes far up the rugged precipices which confine and limit their struggles. He who gazes on the scene may understand the full force of Byron's powerful expression, "a hell of waters;" for the deep shadows, and the boiling currents, and the roar and crash that cease not day nor night, seem, in very truth, infernal!

But swift as the change in a child's heart from agony to joy, is the change which operates in the character of our river as it passes from the Rofla into the gentle valley of Schams, or Schons; so named, it is said, from the six mountain streams which here descend into the all-absorbing Rhine. It is the central of the three terraced basins through which the Back Rhine traces its course, and forms the natural transition between the snow-clad Rheinwald and the sunny Domleschg.

The transformation, says one authority, is magical; all at once we find ourselves in quite a different world. The blue sky is no longer hidden by lofty menacing rocks; the mountains on either side stretch down into the lowlands with a more gradual slope; the Rhine winds more tranquilly and deliberately through green meadows, studded with farm-house and cottage; while, on the wooded heights, the ancient ruins of many a deserted stronghold stand like the monuments of a bygone age.

The valley of Schams is nearly fourteen miles in length, from Thusis to the borders of the Rheinwald, that is, from north to south; but its central and inhabited portion, the vale within the valley, docs not exceed a couple of leagues in length. Its form is oval, and there are geological indications that it was once, like the other valleys of this romantic district, the bed of a lake.

The principal village in the valley is Andur, situated 3000 feet above the sea. Its inhabitants speak the Romansh language, and profess the Lutheran religion. They are chiefly employed in the iron furnaces and smelting-houses which fill this countryside at night with a score of blazing fires.

We next come to the bridge of Pigneu, (Pigné or Pignel), a place whose chief reputation is founded on its thermal springs, which have a temperature of 50° K., and are described as alkaline chalybeate waters.

The next village is Zillis or Ciraun, where there stands a large church, the oldest in the valley. In 540 it was bestowed by Otto I. on Bishop Waldo of Chur, to compensate for the injury the see had sustained by the invasion of the Saracens.

Two bridges are here thrown across the river, and lead up a gentle and pleasant ascent to the picturesquely situated villages of Donat, Pazen, Fardün, Casti, and Clugien. On the high ground above Donat, to the right, moulder the ruins of Fardun.

The rocky strongholds of the barons, says a judicious writer, were nearly all on the left bank of the Rhine, near the old high road which wound over the heights towards the Heinzenberg, before the defile of the Via Mala was opened, and that highway rendered available. Near the hamlet of Casti, and almost opposite Andur, is the castle of Castellatsch, from whose hoary height you can enjoy a superb panorama of the entire landscape. Both names indicate their derivation from the Roman Castellum, or from Castel.

Not far from the hamlet of Mathon, which is built on the table-land above Donat, one weather-beaten ruinous tower of the old castle of Oberstein overlooks the valley. Near the adjoining village of Bergenstein also stood a stronghold bearing the same name. And thus, as the eagles build their eyries among the rocks, so did the old feudal barons erect their towers on the difficult heights, prepared to swoop down on wealthy burgher or opulent priest as he passed unwarily beneath.

At Zillis a bold mountain-ridge, extending from the Piz Beverin to the Mutnerhorn, cuts across the fair meadow-valley of Schams, and separates it from the luxuriant Domleschg. Ages ago it undoubtedly blocked up the waters of the Rhine, and confined them within the hollow, which they converted into a silent lake; but in the course of generations these waters have broken through the barrier, assisted, perhaps, by some violent subterranean convulsion, and excavated the grand majestic defile of the *Via Mala*, or Evil Way.

The cliffs on either side of this defile rise from 400 to 500 feet in height, but approach so closely together that, in several places, the distance between them does not exceed thirty feet.

The lower part of the Via Mala is called the "Lost Hole." Here the road skirts the margin of an awful, brain-dizzying chasm, and enters a gallery 216 feet long, ten to fourteen feet high, and fifteen to eighteen wide, which it was found necessary to cut through the projecting mass of perpendicular rock.

The two banks of the river are here connected by bridges of bold and airy span. The first at which we arrive, 2622 feet above the sea, was erected in 1731. The second, built in 1739, lies 300 yards farther south. It is between the two that the traveller gazes, with mingled awe and admiration, on the most romantic and impressive portion of the great Via Mala. Grandly wild is the dark abyss, lying 400 feet deep in shadow, where, at the second bridge, the mad torrent foams, and boils, and rushes over crag and boulder. The rocky declivities start up so abrupt and sheer, that the width of the cleft at the top scarcely exceeds that at the bottom. So narrow is the gap, that huge fragments of rock, or trunks of venerable pines, hurled over the parapet of the bridge, never reach the water, but lie wedged between the sides. The mighty roar of the torrent; the ghastly white spray which mantles its darkling waves; and the rugged black acclivities, with their numerous projections and pinnacles rising far above the mist of the abyss, cannot but produce a strong impression on the mind which rightly appreciates the various features of the scene.

Close to the mouth of the Via Mala stands the gray old castle of Realt, on a precipitous rock 960 feet in height, and guarding the defile like some veteran knight of the "brave days of old." It occupies the site of the ancient Hohenrhaetien—the Hoch-Royalt, or Rhaetia alta—whose erection belongs to so remote an antiquity that the peasants are fain to connect it with one Rhaetus, the leader of the Etruscans in their war against the Gauls, 587 B.C.

From the early days of the Frank supremacy to the close of the eighth century, Realt belonged to a powerful Rhaetian family, the counts of Victorinz or Realt, who encouraged the diffusion of Christianity in their territory, and founded the convent of Katzis.

In the eleventh century the knights of Hochrealt again figure upon the scene, and one of them, Sir Heinrich, received the episcopal mitre in 1213. The castle continued to be inhabited down to the middle of the fifteenth century.

It must once have been of considerable size, to judge from the extent of its ruins; and of great strength, owing to its formidable and almost inaccessible position. The only pathway to the summit climbs the northern side; elsewhere, the cliff descends straight into the narrow gulf watered by the Rhine.

Here, according to an old legend, the last governor of Hohen-realt precipitated himself on horseback into the chasm. The fort was surrounded by a large body of malcontent peasantry; the servants and men-at-arms of its captain had been slain or put to death. Instead of surrendering, he set fire to the castle, mounted his steed, rode to the loftiest peak, and spurred the animal with a swift bound into air—and destruction; exclaiming, "Death, rather than the people's tyranny!"

The chivalrous spirit of the knight, mounted on a phantom white horse, is believed still to gallop to and fro among the mouldering ruins at "dark midnight."

After passing Hohen-realt, we enter the valley of the Domleschg, where the Rhine receives a turbid rivulet called the Nolla. The valley (vallis domestica) is a broad and fertile district, lying at an elevation of 2250 to 1870 feet above the sea, and running due north and south for about ten miles. The mountains on either side are from 7000 to 8000 feet high, and with their glittering crests of snow, and bare sides and bold rugged forms, present a striking contrast to the smiling scene through which the Back Rhine carries its emerald waters; a panorama of meadow, orchard, and vineyard, of green hills and rich deep forests, of gray old castles and church-spires, with villa, castle, and farm enlivening the whole. The vine is here met with for the first time on the banks of the Rhine, and the chestnut and mulberry thrive in the open air.

The mountains on the east are of a very rugged character, especially the Three League and the Malix. Not less formidable are the Mutterhorn and Piz Beverin to the south. But the terraced range of the Heinzenberg on the west bears a more genial aspect, and its amphitheatre is studded with numerous smiling villages.

The principal town in the Domleschg is Tosana, or Thusis, which lies sequestered in a kind of rocky hollow, overshadowed with walnut trees, chestnuts, and fruit trees, and pleasantly distinguished in the distance by its white church-steeple. Wolfgang Musculus, a scholar of the sixteenth century, was born here.

After crossing the limpid Albula, which empties itself into the Rhine near a toll-bridge, at an elevation of 2240 feet above the sea level, we come to Katzis, a small Romansh and Roman Catholic town, literally embowered in orchards. Its Dominican nunnery was founded in the seventh century by Paschalis, bishop of Chur.

On the opposite bank stands Flirstenau, and its Episcopal castle, built in 1270 by the bishop, Henry of Chur, to protect the surrounding country from the inroads of the robber knights. It is by no inharmonious consequence that it is now used as a prison.

The castles of the Domleschg are numerous. Near that of Fürstenau stands the fastness of the barons Von Planta. Close at hand may be seen the ruins of Husensprung; those of Campi remind the spectator of the gallant race of Campobello, or Campbell, to which belonged the historian and reformer Ulrich Campbell. On the opposite side of the valley is Baldenstein; Jagstein and Schauenstein may also be mentioned; and along the right bank of the river we arrive, in due succession, at the mouldering battlements of Paspelo, Alt-Sins, and Neu-Zinsenberg, which were once associated with many a hope and fear, many a proud ambition and dark despair and tender love, but are now desolate and silent, save for hooting owl and whirring bat. The reflections which yonder gray old walls awaken are necessarily trite, for what is more commonplace than the mutability of worldly things? Yet in such scenes as these they naturally rise to the mind, and demand expression; and, at all events, the traveller will do no harm if, sparing himself elaborate apostrophes and profound meditations, he chants the well-known lines of Coleridge—

"The old knights are dust,
Their swords are rust,
Their souls are with the saints, I trust."

They had God's work to do in their time, and nobly and loyally some of them did it.

The castle of Ortenstein is spoken of as in excellent preservation. Its position is so picturesque that whoever sees it once will remember it always; but it has no historical associations to seize upon the memory, and endow it with a vital interest. It is still inhabited by the descendants of its old lords, the Travers, who formerly played a considerable part in the affairs of the Grisons, though in no wise connected with European history. John Travers was one of the earliest of the Lutherans.

The castle of Rhäzüns, near the village of the same name, is the finest in the Domleschg, perhaps in the whole countryside of the Grisons. It lies romantically in the turbulent stream, says Gaspey, enthroned on a high rock, with its weather-beaten towers, still firm and strong, overlooking the valley whose entrance it commanded. According to a local tradition, it was formerly a Roman fort. In the earliest times a powerful family dwelt at

Rhäzüns; when, in the fourteenth century, it became extinct, the castle and lordship passed to the Baron of Brun, who was one of the earliest members of the Upper League.

In the year 1459 died Ulrich von Brun, the last of his race. The castle and lordship were inherited by the counts of Zollern, who sold them to the archducal house of Austria. The Hapsburgs bestowed them as a fief on the Von Marmels; next on the Von Plantas; and finally, on the Travers. Early in the eighteenth century it was the residence of the Austrian ambassadors in the Grisons, and of the stewards of the estate, who were entitled to a seat and vote in the conferences of the Upper League. By the peace of Vienna, in 1805, it was given to Bavaria; by that of Presburg, in 1805, to France; and in 1815, at the Congress of Vienna, Austria relinquished her claim on the castle in favour of the Grisons, though she took care to retain all the lands included in its seignory.

Traversing the rich corn-fields of Bonnaduz (Ponnad'oz = Pan-a-toto, or "Bread for all"), a Romansh village, built of stone, we reach at last the confluence of the two arms of our great river at Reichenau.

At the point of junction stood, six centuries ago, a watch-tower, like the border peels of southeastern Scotland, called La Punt; which was afterwards converted into a castle by one of the bishop of Chur, and re-named Reichenau—in compliment to the abbot of the island of Reichenau, in the Lake of Constanz, with whom the good bishop had frequently "crushed a cup of wine." It suffered terribly at successive epochs, and losing its castellated character, figured towards the close of the last century as a school, where no less a man than Heinrich Zschokke, the moralist, was tutor, and Benjamin Constant, afterwards so eminent a French savant, pupil.

With this educational establishment a curious incident is connected, not without interest at a time when the crown of imperial France has suddenly fallen from the astute brow which for so many years had worn it. We shall tell it nearly in the language employed by the author of "The Upper Rhine."

It was growing dark one afternoon in October, 1793—an epoch like the present, when Europe shook with the tread of armed men, and the spirit of Revolutionary France was all aflame—it was nearly dark when a young man, carrying a bundle over his shoulder at the end of a stick, and who, from his wayworn appearance, had evidently travelled far on foot, knocked at the door of the house. In indifferent German he inquired for the director, Herr von Jost, and on being ushered into his presence handed him a letter of introduction from General Montesquiou, which ran as follows:—

"Sir,—In the bearer of this note I bring you acquainted with a young man who, pursued by the French assassins, is anxious to obtain a secure asylum in your quiet Reichenau. He resided for awhile in Zug; afterwards with me in Bremgarten; and hopes now to meet with shelter for a longer period in the highlands of Rhaetia. His great acquirements in mathematics and in French render him eligible for the situation as teacher, which, as I perceive from the newspapers, is now vacant in your establishment.

"Receive him, brave fellow-soldier, who have valiantly fought in the Swiss guard, and in my army in Savoy. You will do so with the greatest satisfaction when I communicate the secret of his rank. He is the young duke of Chartres, the son of the duke of Orleans. As you are aware, he served honourably in the army of the Republic, under the name of the younger Egalité, but was forced to fly from the blood-thirsty Committee of Public Safety, and now seeks shelter in neutral Switzerland. I trust you will be able to afford it to him

"MONTESQUIOU."

After consulting his partner, Herrvon Tscharner, and his head-master, Professor Vesemann, the director willingly complied with General Montesquiou's request, and under the assumed name of Chabaud the young duke of Chartres entered the establishment as an usher. For eight months he taught mathematics with patience and success, boarding at the common table with the pupils and other teachers, none of whom suspected that a Bourbon was among them.

Here the duke learned of the execution of his father, who, instead of swimming with the fierce current of the revolution, as he had hoped, was overwhelmed by its violence. Here, too, he heard of his mother's exile to Madagascar. At length he ventured from his concealment to make a tour in the north of Europe, and finally, in 1796, to sail to America.

Years passed away. The star of the first Napoleon rose above the horizon like a terrible meteor, portending ruin to nations, and sunk in blood and ruin on the well-remembered field of Waterloo. The Bourbons regained the throne of their ancestors, to prove that they had forgotten everything, and learned nothing. Charles X., in 1830, was driven into exile, and the former teacher of mathematics at Reichenau became Louis Philippe, king of the French.

In his prosperity he was not unmindful of his days of adversity, and he caused a painting to be executed in which he was represented, surrounded by his pupils.

In 1847 it was announced that the grandson of his old director, Herr von Jost, who through political troubles had been driven from Switzerland, had been appointed to a lieutenancy in the French army, and presented with a handsome outfit by King Louis Philippe. A twelvemonth later, and under the assumed name of Mr. Smith the monarch was hurrying to a safe retreat in England; leaving his throne to be occupied, after a brief interval, by the third Napoleon, who, after twenty years of rule, has been compelled to surrender himself to a Prussian king. Such are the vagaries of Fortune! May we not learn a lesson from them?

There are two timber bridges at Reichenau: one over the Front Rhine, of comparatively small dimensions; the other below the junction of the stream, 237 feet long, and 80 feet above the surface of the water. It was constructed by a self-taught architect.

The valley of the Front Rhine is usually called the Oberland, and is deservedly famous for the bold and romantic character of its scenery. It is forty-eight miles in length, and the descent from Chiamict to Reichenau is 3420 feet. Besides the Middle or Medelser Rhine, the Front Rhine receives about sixty brooks and mountain torrents, of which the Somvix, the Glenner, and the Savien are the chief. It therefore contributes no inconsiderable augmentation to the volume of the Back Rhine. The principal points of interest are:—

Ilanz, or Ylim, 2240 feet above the sea; a picturesque but decayed little town, embosomed among the mountains. It seems shut out from the world, and wholly unconnected with the living present; but the artist would find in its vicinity many of those things of beauty which, from the thoughts they inspire and the emotions they awaken, are so much more precious than the most coveted idols of society.

Dissentis is scarcely less remarkable for the infinite romance of its isolated position. Its Benedictine abbey was formerly one of great influence, as well as of high antiquity. It is said to have been erected about 614 by the devout and enthusiastic St. Sigisbert, a disciple of the Irish apostle, St. Columbanus. Here was buried the body of the martyr Placidus.

The Devil's Bridge (*die Teufelsbrucke*) lies away from the beaten route, but is worth a visit. It spans the mountain torrent of the Reuss, which roars and welters in a rugged defile, 100 feet beneath its mossy arches.

Another place to which the traveller may make a detour, on his way to Reichenau, is the beautiful little village of Andermatt. It is situated 4446 feet above the sea, at the mouth of the fair valley of Unsem, and at the foot of the St. Anna mountain, whose piny slopes are rich in living verdure, while its crest is crowned with a diadem of snow and ice.

FROM REICHENAU TO CHUR.

"We shall henceforth follow the united stream of the Rhine, and as we trace its winding course, shall traverse a country widely differing in the character of its scenery from that which has hitherto engaged us.

But it cannot be said that any great change occurs in the six miles between Reichenau and Chur: Chur, or Coire, the time-honoured capital of the Grisons. On either side the mountains rear then black wooded acclivities, whose summits, for several months in the year, are covered with glittering snow. The valley between is sufficiently iertile, and romantic little glens descend to the green bank of the Rhine, which now sweeps onward with a moderately rapid current, now dashes, hurries, foams, and thunders over a bed of rugged rock.

On the left runs the long bold ridge of the Kalanda, with the quaintly shaped and quaintly named peaks of the Men's Saddle and the Women's Saddle towering in its rear. On the right, the mountain of the Three Leagues, and the Spontiskopfen, present an admirable diversity both of form and colour.

This part of the Rhine Valley, that is, from Reichenau to Chur, varies in elevation above the sea level from 1550 to 1850 feet. Its fertility is considerable; and agriculture on the Swiss method, which possesses a certain undeniable simplicity, is carried on with some success. It contains two towns and eleven villages, and the population exceeds 20,000.

Of the villages Ems is, perhaps, the largest and wealthiest; the inhabitants are Catholics. The appearance of Ems is squalid-looking and dirty. This, indeed, is the character of many of the villages of the Grisons; while, on the other hand, the traveller is not less struck with the cleanliness and orderliness by which others of them are distinguished.

Felsberg is situated on the lower bank of the Rhine, nearly two miles lower down, and at the foot of the Kalanda, which hangs above the village a stupendous piece of overhanging rock, threatening at some not far distant time to crush into shapeless ruin the houses and church below. It is an awful "sword of Damocles," which no stranger can regard without an emotion of terror. Its downfall, says a German writer, will occur sooner or later, for the water flowing in the gaping clefts undermines the foundation, and must inevitably provoke the destruction of the entire mass. Aware of this fact, the Felsenbergers have of late years founded a new settlement near the margin of the Rhine; where, indeed, they are not liable to be crushed, but run the hazard of being drowned in the frequent inundations of the river.

It is possible from Felsberg to ascend the Kalanda; but as its summit is only 7877 feet above the sea, and its sides are not broken up with any fathomless chasms or frightful precipices, it would certainly be despised by the most timorous member of the Alpine Club. The view from its white crest, however, is very beautiful and extensive; one of those views which make the joy of the spectator's later life. Who can conceive of aught more beautiful than a fairy ring of snowy peaks, whose sides are richly diversified with masses of forest, and at whose base the green pastures smile with an inexhaustible verdure?

CHUR, OR COIRE.

Chur, the ancient capital of the Grisons, is the Curia Rhaetorum of the Romans. It is situated at an angle of the Rhine, where the river abruptly strikes to the northward, and the plateau on which its high-gabled houses, and grotesque spires and steeples cluster, is hemmed in on three sides by the ranges of the Three League Mountains, the Parpfran Highlands, and the Hochwang. At the foot of the heights, and at the mouth of a ravine from which the Plessaur brings down its glacier waters, it takes its stand, like a venerable monument of ancient civilization; and far across the valley it seems to cast its gaze, until bounded in the blue distance by the "silver-glancing ice peaks" of the Oberland.

Chur is fully 1800 feet above the sea. It is distant ninety-seven miles east from Bern, and fifty-eight miles east-south-east from Luzern. As it lies on the high road to the great Alpine passes of the Splugen and Bernardin, it still retains a considerable trade. Surrounded by lofty walls, which are strengthened with massive towers, and divided into close narrow alleys and streets, whose houses bear the venerable impress of antiquity, Chur presents peculiar attractions for the traveller. It is divided into an Upper and a Lower Town. The former contains the Episcopal palace and its appendages, a canonry, a Capuchin monastery, the ancient convent of St. Lucius, and the cathedral, a Byzantine edifice of the seventh century. In the Lower are to be found the government house, the Schwarz house, St. Margaret's castle, and St. Martin's church.

The population of Chur numbers about 5500, who are nearly all Calvinists. The doctrines of the Reformation were early and enthusiastically embraced here, and have been maintained with steadfastness. They were first preached by John Comander, from the old wooden pulpit of St. Martin's.

Chur can boast of one artistic celebrity, Angelica Kaufmann, born on the 30th of October, 1741. She once enjoyed some reputation as a portrait painter, but her works have long passed into comparative oblivion.

Having thus briefly specified the general character of the town, we may proceed to notice some of its more interesting details. Let us pass, then, into the Bishop's Quarter.

The Emperor Maximilian was accustomed to describe the bishoprics which formerly ruled all-powerful over the valley of the Rhine in some such epigrammatic terms as these:

Constanz was the largest, Basel the blithest, Strasburg the noblest, Speyer the devoutest, Mainz the most dignified, Worms the poorest, and Köln the richest. He might have added that Chur was the oldest. It is certain that the see was in existence as early as 452, and ecclesiastical tradition asserts that St. Asimo was its first occupant. However small its beginnings, it soon rose into importance, and waxed fat and wealthy. Its territories were enlarged by the gifts of the pious, no less than by judicious exchanges; and the bishop of Chur became a power in the Grisons, helping to make the history of that remarkable province. Though shorn of his ancient privileges, he is still a considerable prelate, and since 1824 has been the clerical administrator of the cantons of Uri, Schwyz, and Unterwalden. He is elected by a chapter, consisting of twelve prebendaries, six of whom live at Chur. His country seat, Molinara, is situated near Zizers, where there is a railway station.

The bishop's palace, or hof, is an ancient edifice, crowning a steep hill in the Roman Catholic quarter of the town. Its staircase and halls are quaintly decorated with devices in stucco. The private chapel is located in an old Roman tower called Marsol (corrupted, it is said, from *Mars in oculis*), attached to the north-east side of the palace. In this tower St. Lucius suffered martyrdom. In another wing is a much mutilated fresco of a "Dance of Death." A second Roman tower, Spinöl (*Spina in oculis*), strengthens the southwestern angle of the walls.

In the rear of the palace runs an abrupt hollow, planted with vineyards, and leading by a picturesque winding path to the Roman Catholic seminary. From this point a fine view of the town, the Rhine, and the Schalfik-thal, may be obtained.

The church of St. Lucius, or the Dom, is a noteworthy example of the early Gothic, including some fragments of an earlier building, erected by Bishop Tello in the eighth century. The outer gate is flanked by the statues of the four evangelists, resting upon lions. Their position at the outer gate, according to Beda, indicates that they point the way to our Saviour, while the principal gate is the symbol of Christ himself, who leads the devout worshipper to the Father and the communion of saints.

The choir is raised upon steps, leaving open to the nave the crypt beneath, whose roof rests upon a single pillar. The high altar is enriched with quaint old timber carving, supposed to have been executed by Holbein the elder. In the sacristy are preserved the bones of St. Lucius, a British king, and the supposed founder of St. Peter's church, Cornhill. There are also an episcopal crozier, a chasuble with raised work, a fourteenth century pyx, and several other curiosities and relics.

The paintings are numerous and interesting. The names of their artists being unknown, they are freely attributed to Holbein or Albert Dürer, Nor are old monuments wanting. A sarcophagus of red marble is that of the Bishop Ortlieb of Brandis; and in an adjacent vault lies the dust of many of the bishops of Chur.

On entering the nave you will do well to look attentively at the first pillar on the left, in which, according to an old tradition, some huge bones are built up; reputed to be those of a certain gigantic robber, named Long Kuhn, or Long Conrad of Schwyz, who, after plundering the Grisons in 1251, was overtaken and slain by the inhabitants near Tavanusa on the Upper Rhine.

> "I know not if the tale be true,
> As told to me I tell it you."

Chur, or Coire, is the terminus of the United Swiss Railway, which leads to Rorschach on the Lake of Constanz, with branches to Glarus, St. Gall, Winterthur, Rapperschwyl, and Zurich. The distance to Rorschach is sixty-two miles.

From Coire the traveller may visit Samaden, and the grand and romantic Julier Pass, opening up the finest scenery of the Engadine. Or he may proceed to Splügen by the Via Mala, or to Chiavenna by the Splügen. Klosters, in one direction, and Süs in another, are also accessible from this point. The traveller will find Michelet's "La Montagne" an excellent guide to this part of Switzerland. He has described the Engadine with remarkable fervour and brilliancy.

FROM COIRE TO RAGATZ.

After quitting Coire, we continue to traverse a rich and ample valley, inclosed between the Kalanda, or Galanda-berg, on the west, and the Falkniss, on the north-east. Almost every ridge and projecting crag are crowned by the ruins of "chiefless castles," so gray and weather-worn that they can scarcely be distinguished from the rock on which they stand; while the sides of the mountains are marked with the deep furrows of the winter torrents.

Of one of these ruined fortalices, that of Ober-Ruchenberg, the following legend is told. It is all that men seem to know or imagine about it:—

When the fairy queen, who dwelt in the silent heart of the great mountains, was giving birth to one of her elfin progeny, she was generously assisted by the then lady of Ruchenberg. As a reward, the dame received a set of golden ninepins, with which she could at all times obtain the faithful service of the mountain sprites. They were handed down as precious heirlooms to her descendants; one of whom, a great grandson, and a turbulent dissolute rake, abused the fairy gift by lavishing on unworthy objects the treasures it placed at his disposal. At last his summons was answered by nine living giants, who suddenly rose from the earth with a sound as of thunder, and as they rose the castle crumbled into ruin, and its profligate lord was carried off from the eyes of men. This evil man, however, had a daughter who was as devout as he was blasphemous. The fairies saved her from the general desolation, and thenceforth she spent her life in the haunted caverns of the mountains. Once every hundred years she is permitted to revisit the glimpses of the moon, and standing on the shattered ramparts of the old baronial stronghold, she waits the coming of the fortunate knight who is to restore her to her kind, and, at the same time, to win from the fairy queen the dangerous but valuable gift of the golden ninepins.

Nearly opposite Coire stands the castle of Haldenstein, with a village of the same name. The castle, sumptuously rebuilt by the French ambassador to the Grisons, in 1548, suffered severely from fire on several occasions, but was restored in the last century by the family Von Salis, to whose posterity it still belongs. The ruins of the ancient fortress are situated on a rocky height at some distance from the more modern erection.

To the north of the village some shattered walls mark the site of the ancient castle of Lichtenstein.

After passing the point where the Landguart, nr Langaurs, rolling down from the valley of Prättigau, pours its noisy waters into the Rhine, we diverge a little from the right bank of the river to visit the old and tranquil town of Mayenfeld, said to be the Roman Lupinum. Its modern name is probably derived from the "May-fields," or May courts of jurisdiction, held here under the spreading boughs of a lime tree during the Carlovingian era. It boasts of a Roman tower, erected by the Emperor Constantius about 340; and of an excellent wine made from prolific vineyards of modern growth. The valley of the Rhine from this point presents a noble prospect, in which the peak of the Falkniss, rising on the north-east to an elevation of 7824 feet, is necessarily a conspicuous and impressive object. The view also comprehends the summits of "the Seven Electors," and the villages of Malans, Jenins, and Sargans.

From Mayenfeld we may visit the fortified Lucian pass, named after the martyr, St. Lucius, and 2180 feet high, which commands the road from Germany to Italy. Territorially it is included in the old principality of Lichtenstein-Vaduz.

Continuing our route along the valley, we call at the romantic town of Malans, lying at the foot of the Augustenberg (7356 feet.) Here, at Castle Bodmer, was born the poet Von Salis, whose lyrics breathe so tender and melancholy a spirit. "The Silent Land," one of his most pathetic strains, is well known in England by Professor Longfellow's admirable translation of it.

At fourteen miles from Coire the traveller reaches Ragatz, a village of between 600 and 700 inhabitants, situated at the mouth of the gorge (*tobel*) through which the foaming waters of the Tamina rush down to join the Rhine. It depends for its prosperity on its vicinity to the hot mineral springs of Pfeffers, and its position at the junction of the great roads from Zürich, St. Gall, Feldkirch, Coire, and Milan. It contains a small English chapel.

At Ragatz a victory was gained by the Swiss confederates, under Itel von Reding and Fortunatus Tschudi, over the partizans of Hans von Rechberg (March 6, 1446).

A road tunnelled through the rugged defile of the Tamina, for about two miles and a half, leads to the old baths of Pfeffers (or Pfäffers), one of the most remarkable and wildly romantic spots in Switzerland. The walk thither is undoubtedly picturesque and impressive. "At the edge of the narrow path, which ascends gradually and not too abruptly, and which occasionally passes under the tunnelled rocks, the foaming torrent rushes onward, bounding impetuously over every impediment, and scarcely deigning to greet the melancholy rocks in its rapid course. After a walk of three miles, a narrow slope, clothed with pine trees, is seen wedged in under the face of the rock, only a few feet above the raging Tamina, on which is built a tolerably large and straggling massive edifice. Nothing more dreary can be conceived than its situation in the cool dark glen, almost buried beneath the rocks that tower above it to the height of six or seven hundred feet; in the height of summer, in the months of July and August, the sun manages to find his way into this singular retreat from about ten o'clock in the morning till four in the afternoon. This is 'Bad Pfäffers.'"

The hot springs of Pfeffers were not known to the Romans. The story runs that they were discovered by a hunter, Karl von Hofenhausen, who, having penetrated into the gorge of the

Tamina in the pursuit of game, was attracted by the columns of vapour rising from them. In authentic documents they are first mentioned in 1050, when they were conferred by the Emperor Henry III. on the monks of Pfeffers. Centuries passed, however, and nothing was done to facilitate access to their wonder-working waters. Patients who had faith in their curative properties were let down to the spring from the cliffs above by ropes; and with an admirable desire to benefit by them as much as possible, were wont to spend a week together, both day and night; not only eating and drinking, but sleeping, "under hot water instead of blankets." In 1629, however, the ravine was enlarged, and a bathing-house, on the site now occupied by the present establishment, was erected by the Abbot Jodvens. The healing waters were conveyed from the spring in wooden conduits, and the work duly celebrated at Whitsuntide, in 1630, by a service of thanksgiving. The present baths were completed in 1716, but are now very scantily patronized; most visitors preferring the conveniences and liveliness of Ragatz.

An excursion to the source of the waters (whose temperature is 97° to 98°), has a perilous air about it, well calculated to terrify weak nerves.

Proceeding through the bath-house, you cross the Tamina on a bridge of planks, which, in the shape of a scaffolding, is prolonged into the dark dim gorge above the contracted but noisy torrent. It is carried all along the abyss as far as the hot spring, and furnishes the only means of access to it, as the sides of the gorge are vertical, and there is not an inch of space between them and the Tamina for the sole of the foot to rest. A few yards from the entrance the air is darkened by an overhanging mass of rock. "The sudden chill," says a writer, "of an atmosphere never visited by the sun's rays, the rushing and roaring of the torrent thirty or forty feet below, the threatening position of the rocks above, have a grand and striking effect; but this has been diminished by modern improvements, which have deprived the visit to the gorge of even the semblance of danger. In parts it is almost dark, where the sides of the ravine overlap one another, and actually meet overhead, so as to form a natural arch. The rocks in many places show evident marks of having been ground away, and scooped out by the rushing river, and by the stones brought down with it. For several hundred yards the river pursues an almost subterranean course, the roof of the chasm being the floor, as it were, of the valley. In some places the roots of the trees are seen dangling through the crevice above your head, and at one particular spot you find yourself under the arch of the natural bridge leading to the staircase mentioned further on. Had Virgil or Dante been aware of this spot, they would certainly have conducted their heroes through it to the jaws of the infernal regions.

"After emerging from the gorge at the bathhouse, the traveller may ascend the valley above it by a well-marked track; ascending the steep left bank, and then keeping to the left, and descending a little, he will in about half a mile cross by a natural bridge of rock, beneath which the Tamina, out of sight, and heaving from above, forces its way into the gorge of the hot springs. A steep path or staircase (*steige*), formed of trunks or roots of trees, on the right bank, is then met with, ascending which you reach an upper stage of the valley, formed of gentle slopes, and covered with verdant pasture on one side, and with thick woods on the other. The two sides are separated by the deep gash and narrow gorge along the bottom of which the Tamina forces its way. This is, perhaps, the best point for obtaining a general view of the baths, and the singular spot in which they are sunken. On looking over the verge of the precipice you perceive, at the bottom of the ravine, at the depth of 300 feet below, the roofs of the two large buildings, like cotton factories in size and structure. The upper valley, also, with its carpet of bright green, its woods, and the bare limestone cliffs which border it on either hand, and above all, the huge peak of the Falkniss, rising on the opposite side of the Rhine, form a magnificent landscape."

The traveller's attention will next be directed to the convent of Pfeffers, an edifice of considerable extent, but by no means remarkable for architectural excellence. As in all Benedictine convents, a church occupies the centre of its enceinte. The position is admirable: from its lofty mountain-platform it looks out, in one direction, on the rich Rhine valley, backed by the lofty summit of the Falkniss; in another, it commands the lake of Wallenstadt, and the peaks of the Seven Electors (*Sieben Kurfurster*.)

The foundation of the convent dates from 713, when its erection was commenced by S. Pirminius, bishop of Meaux, on the left bank of the Landguart. While felling timber for the building a carpenter accidentally wounded himself. Some drops of blood fell on a chip, which was straitly picked up by a white dove, and carried across the Rhine to the forest on the opposite heights. On seeing the dove let fall the chip from the top of a larch tree, S. Pirminius exclaimed, "There the Lord wills that his house should be built." And thus the convent came to be raised on its present site, and to assume for its device a flying dove with a chip in its beak.

The convent lasted for ten centuries, but its financial affairs becoming hopelessly involved, a majority of the brethren requested the government of the canton (St. Gall) to suppress it, and it was therefore abolished in 1838. The building has since been converted into a lunatic asylum.

We continue our route to Rorschach by way of Sargans; Sevelen (where, on the left, across the Rhine, lies Vaduz, capital of the miniature principality of Lichtenstein); Werdenberg, formerly the seat of a patriotic line of nobles of the same name; Sennvald, a village at the foot of the Kamor; Altstetten, a town of 7000 inhabitants, in a fertile country; S. Margarethen, near the Austrian ferry, an English-like village surrounded by groves and orchards; and Rheineck, a hamlet at the foot of vine-clad hills.

Between Rorschach and Rheineck the Rhine enters the Boden See, or Lake of Constanz. The flat delta is covered with morass, and presents no beauty to attract the traveller's eye. Rorschach (inns: Hirsch, and Post) is a quiet town, the principal station of the lake steamers, and a large corn market. The grain required for the supply of the Alpine district of North Switzerland is imported from Suabia in boats across the lake, and temporarily stored in spacious warehouses. There are several thriving muslin manufactories.

The only noteworthy buildings are the ruined keep of the castle of St. Anne, and the dilapidated palace of the abbots of St. Gall, now known as the Statthalterz.

LAKE OF CONSTANZ, OR BODEN SEE.

Steamers navigate the lake between Constanz, Schaffhausen, Ueberlingen, Meersburg, Friedrichshafen, Rorschach, Ludwigshaien, Romanshorn, Lindau, and Bregentz. The voyage from Rorschach to Constanz occupies three hours, and from Constanz to Lindau about five hours. Printed bills of fares, hours, and places of starting will be found at all the principal inns in the above-named towns.

The Lake of Constanz, called by the Germans *Boden See*, and known to the Romans under the name *Lacus Brigantinus* (from Brigantia, the modern Bregentz), is bounded by the territories of five different states, Baden, Würtemberg, Switzerland, Bavaria, and Austria. A portion of its shores belong to each state. Its elevation above the sea is estimated at 1385 feet. Its length is about forty-four miles from Bregentz to Constanz, and thirty miles from Bregentz to Friedrichshafen. Its maximum width is nine miles; its maximum depth, 964 feet. It is full of fish, and as many as twenty-five species have been distinguished. Locally it is divided into four sections: the Lake of Bregentz, the Lake of Constanz, the Lake of Ueberlingen, and the Lower Lake. Its waters are clear, of a greenish tint, and an agreeable flavour. Their surface is never smooth; a ripple is always upon it, even when no breath of air is felt in the "blue serene;" this constant agitation is probably due to some under-currents.

Its main tributary is the Rhine, which enters at its eastern extremity; but it also receives upwards of fifty brooks and torrents. It is frequently visited by storms, when its billows roll with crested heads, like those of a tempest-stricken sea. Though its shores present no very attractive panorama of scenery, they are exuberantly fertile; and on the south the landscape assumes a certain picturesqueness of character from the numerous ruined forts which crown each conspicuous height.

On an average the waters of the lake are lowest in February, and highest in June and July, when the snows, melting on the distant mountains, swell every brook and torrent which flows into its basin.

The lower section of the lake is generally frozen every winter, but only a small part of the upper is ever "bound in chains of ice." The Swiss chroniclers, however, record several occasions when, if they may be credited, nearly the whole of the lake was frozen; as in 1277, 1435, 1560, 1573, 1587, 1695, 1785, 1788, and 1830. But the entire surface was not iced over in the three last-named years; navigation was still possible in the centre.

The following tradition is connected with the freezing of the lake in the sixteenth century (1587):—

During the winter, which was one of extraordinary severity, a horseman, bent on visiting the lake, descended from the rugged mountains and rode forth into the deep snowy plains. Wherever he gazed, the hard whiteness met his eye; not a tree, not a house, relieved the monotony before him. For leagues he pressed forward his weary horse, hearing no sounds but the screams of the wild water-fowl, or the shrieks of the wind across the echoing waste. At length, as the darkness of night spread over the sky, he descried in the distance the faint glimmer of a taper; trees sprang out of the low creeping mist; the welcome sound of dogs broke on his ear; and the wanderer stopped his horse before a farm-house. He saw a fair maiden at the window, and courteously inquired how far it might yet be to the lake.

"The lake is behind you," she answered in exceeding surprise.

"Nay, not so, for I have just ridden across yonder plain."

"Mary, Mary, save us! You have ridden across the lake, and the ice has not yielded under you!"

The villagers had by this time gathered round the stranger horseman, and uttering loud exclamations of surprise and wonder, they bade him be thankful for the great mercy Heaven had vouchsafed him. But they spoke to ears that could not hear. When he realized the full extent of the peril he had so narrowly escaped, both brain and heart gave way, and he fell from his horse lifeless.

CIRCUIT OF THE LAKE.

We now propose to notice briefly the interesting points on either shore of the Boden See.

On the west, two leagues from Rorschach, lies the ancient town of Arbon (the Arbor Félix of the Romans), a quiet little settlement of some 750 inhabitants. The Romans built a fort here, which, in the fifth century, they were compelled to abandon to the Allemanni. On its site, in 1510, were reared the present castle (except the tower, which is three or four centuries older) and the church, which dates from the same epoch. Its belfry is detached, and boarded, not walled, on the side nearest the castle, in order that no besiegers might be able to use it as a point of vantage.

From Arbon to Constanz the south shore of the lake is occupied by the canton of Thurgovia, one of the most fruitful districts in Switzerland. Gardens, orchards, and villages remind the traveller of some of the midland scenery of England.

Following the sweep of a noble bay for eight or nine miles we arrive at Romanshorn or Romishorn, which clusters somewhat irregularly on the low peninsula forming the northern boundary of the bay. The peninsula curves like a horn; hence the name of the village, which is populous and thriving, and stands in a land of vines. A fine view of the lake, and of the white peaks of the distant Alps, may be obtained from this point.

At Romanshorn is the terminus of the North Eastern Railway. It is fifty-one miles distant from Zurich. The steamers from Bregentz, Lindau, and Friedrichshafen call here.

Of the valleys of Utwyl and Kuswyl we have nothing to record, nor of Güttingen, except that it possesses an ancient castle, pleasantly situated on a little promontory. Soon after passing the latter, the industrious traveller reaches the Benedictine nunnery of Münsterlingen, founded, it is said, by Angela, the daughter of Edward I. of England, in commemoration of her escape from a great storm on the Lake of Constanz. Whether this be true or not, it is certain that the convent was largely endowed by Queen Agnes of Hungary, and that the Emperor Sigismund and the outlawed duke of Austria were reconciled here in 1418. A new building was erected for the nuns in 1715, but in 1838 the nunnery was converted into an hospital.

Just before entering Constanz we reach the Augustinian abbey of Kreuzlingen, now suppressed, like the nunnery, and adapted to the purposes of an agricultural school, with between ninety and one hundred pupils. The foundation dates from 1120, when it was established by Bishop Ulrich I.; but the ancient monastery, standing near the city gate, was frequently exposed to the hazards of war, as in 1450, when it was set on fire, and during the Thirty Years' War, when the Swedes plundered and destroyed it. A new convent was therefore erected on its present site, at a greater distance from the city. When the famous Council of Constanz was held in 1414, Pope John XXIII., on his way thither, spent the night at the abbey of Kreuzlingen, and was so well pleased with his reception that he presented the abbot with a superb vest richly set with pearls. The papal donation is still preserved at the abbey, along with a curious piece of wood carving, by a Tyrolese artist, which represents our Saviour's Passion, and consists of several hundreds of well-executed figures.

Our survey of the lake has thus conducted us to the old, decayed, but historical city of

CONSTANZ,

Nine miles from Schaffhausen, twenty-six miles from Rorschach. Population, 4500. Inns: Brochet, Post, and Hôtel Delisle.

The most interesting associations connected with Constanz are those of its great council, held in 1414-18, and the martyrdom of the Bohemian reformers, John Huss and Jerome of Prague, the apostles and heirs of Wycliffism; and who, in spite of the safe-conduct granted to the former by the Emperor Sigismund as president of the assembly, were seized, accused of heresy, tried, condemned, and executed.

The avowed object of the Council of Constanz was the reformation of the church; but the question which secretly agitated the minds of its members was, the supremacy of a general council over the pope, or of the pope over a general council. It was the first council which had represented Latin Christianity; and it was called, not by the papal volition, but at the instigation, or rather by the command, of the Emperor Sigismund. The pope, John XXIII., had made it a condition that it should not be held within the dominions of the emperor; but when the latter named Constanz as the place of meeting, he was compelled to yield. And in truth no city could have been better suited for such a purpose. It was pleasantly and healthily situated at the foot of the Alps; accessible from Italy and from all parts of Christendom; on the fertile shores of a spacious lake, so that an abundant supply of provisions might be readily obtained; and inhabited by an orderly and peaceful population.

To Constanz, therefore, in the summer of 1414, bishops and princes, patriarchs and professors, abbots and priors, laymen and clerics, began to make their way from every country in Europe; and with these were mingled merchants and traders of every kind and degree, and every sort of wild and strange vehicle. It was to be, apparently, not only a solemn Christian council, but an European congress; a vast central fair, where every kind of commerce was to be conducted on the largest scale, and where chivalrous, histrionic, or other common amusements, were provided for the idle hours of idle people. In its conception it was a grand concentrated outburst of mediaeval devotion, mediaeval splendour, mediaeval diversions: all ranks, all orders, all pursuits, all professions, all trades, all artizans, with their various attire, habits, manners, language, crowded to one single city.

Down the steep slope of the Alps wound the rich cavalcades of the cardinals, the prelates, the princes of Italy, each with their martial guard or their ecclesiastical retinue. The blue waters of the ample lake were studded with boats and barks, conveying the bishops and abbots, the knights and burghers of the Tyrol, of eastern and northern Germany, Hungary, and from the Black Forest and Thuringia. Along the whole course of the Rhine, from Köln, even from Brabant, Flanders, or the furthest north, from England and from France, inarched prelates, abbots, doctors of law, celebrated schoolmen, following the upward course of the stream, and gathering as they advanced new hosts from the provinces and cities to the east or west. Day after day the air was alive with the standards of princes, and the banners emblazoned with the armorial bearings of sovereigns, nobles, knights, imperial cities; or glittered with the silver crosier borne before some magnificent bishop or mitred abbot. Night after night the silence was broken by the pursuivants and trumpeters announcing the arrival of each high and mighty count or duke, or the tinkling mule-bells of some lowlier caravan. The streets were crowded with curious spectators, eager to behold some splendid prince or ambassador, some churchman famous in the pulpit, in the school, in the council, it might be in the battle-field, or even some renowned minnesinger or popular jongleur. Yet with all these multitudes perfect order was maintained, so admirable had been the arrangements of the magistrates. Constanz worthily supported her dignity, as for a time the chosen capital of Christendom.

And the pope, who had some cause to fear the council, was received with every outward sign of respect and spiritual loyalty. The magistrates and clergy attended him through the streets, and to the venerable Minster (October 28). Nine cardinals and about six hundred followers formed his retinue. But on the 3rd of December another arrival caused still greater excitement. There entered the city a pale thin man, in mean attire, yet escorted by three nobles of his country, with a great troop of other followers from attachment or curiosity. He came under a special safe conduct from the emperor, which guaranteed in the fullest terms his safe entrance into and safe departure from the imperial city. This was the famous Bohemian "heretic," John Huss.

In these pages any chronicle of the proceedings of the great council would be out of place. But we must briefly trace its dealings with the Bohemian reformer, from the imperishable association of his name with the city whose history we are sketching. He appeared before the council not so much as a preacher of dogmas as a reformer of abuses. He was provided with the imperial safe-conduct, with testimonials to his orthodoxy from the highest authorities; yet he did not enter Constanz without dark misgivings. In a farewell address to his followers he said, "I expect to meet as many enemies at Constanz as our Lord at Jerusalem; the wicked clergy, and even some secular princes, and those Pharisees the monks."

His misgivings were speedily justified. A charge of heresy was brought against him. The emperor abandoned him, and basely consented to violate his royal word. It was soon understood that he was to be tried by the council, condemned by the council, and that whatever might be the sentence of the council it would be carried into execution by the secular arm. Huss was thrown, a prisoner, into the castle of Gottlieben, outside the city walls. He was called upon to retract his errors. "I will retract," he answered, "when convinced of them." On the 5th of June, 1416, he was brought before the council; again on the 7th and the 9th; but in the presence of his many accusers he maintained a calm and unmoved composure, and the serenity of a mind at ease. On the 9th, after he had been carried back to prison, the emperor rose, and addressed the council:—"You have heard the charges against Huss proved by trustworthy witnesses, some confessed by himself. In my judgment each of these crimes is deserving of death. If he does not forswear all his errors, he must be burned. If he submits, he must be stripped of his preacher's office, and banished from Bohemia; there he would only disseminate more dangerous errors. The evil must be extirpated, root and branch. If any of his followers are in Constanz, they must be proceeded against with the utmost severity, especially his disciple, Jerome of Prague."

Huss calmly refused the recantation demanded from him; and on the 1st of July was led forth from his prison to undergo the sentence which had been passed upon him as having swerved from the true Catholic faith. Having been degraded from the priesthood in the sacred shades of the cathedral, he was delivered over to the secular arm. The emperor gave him up to Louis, Elector Palatine, the imperial vicar; the elector to the magistrates of Constanz; the magistrates to the executioners.

With two of the headsman's servants before him, and two behind, he went forth to the place of execution. Eight hundred horsemen followed, and the city poured out its whole population. The bridge was narrow and frail; so they went in single file, lest it should break beneath their weight. They paused before the episcopal palace, that Huss might see the pile on which his books lay burning. He only smiled, for he knew that the right or wrong in matters of belief cannot be determined by brute force. As he went along he addressed the people in German, protesting against the injustice of his sentence; his enemies, he said, had failed to convince him of error.

The place of execution was a meadow outside the city walls. Here he knelt, and, kneeling, recited several psalms, with the perpetual burthen, "Lord Jesus, have mercy upon me. Into thy hands I commend my spirit." "We know not," exclaimed the people, "what this man may have done, but we do know that his prayers to God are excellent." His attendants demanded if he would have a confessor. A priest, mounted on a stately horse, and richly clad, declared that no confessor should be accorded to a heretic. But others were more charitable, and one Ulric Schorand, a man of piety and wisdom, was summoned from the crowd.

Ulric insisted first that Huss should acknowledge the errors for which he was condemned. Unawed by the prospect before him, he refused to confess. "I have no need of confession," he said; "I am guilty of no mortal sin." He turned round, and made an effort to address the people in German, but the elector caused him to be interrupted. Then he prayed aloud, "Lord Jesus, for thy sake I endure with patience this cruel death. I beseech thee to forgive mine enemies." As he spoke the paper mitre with which his head had been crowned in derision fell to the ground. The rude soldiery replaced it, saying, "He shall be burned with all his devils!" In reply he said gently, but firmly, "I trust that I shall reign with Christ, since I die for his holy gospel."

With an old rusty chain he was now bound to the fatal stake. The Elector Palatine and another again urged him to recant; but firm in faith and hope, Huss assured them that the testimony he had borne was true, and that he was willing to seal its truth with his blood. All he had taught and written was with the view of saving the souls of men from Satan's snares, and from the power of sin. The fire blazed up; an aged crone busied herself in piling up the wood: *O sancta simplicitas!*—"holy simplicity!" cried Huss, in the spirit of tenderness and compassion. Then the flames crackled, and the smoke went up in thick wreathing clouds, while he, with his last gasping breath, continued to pray to the Saviour, and to commend his spirit into his hands. All the remains of his body were torn in pieces; even his clothes were flung upon the fire; the ashes were gathered and cast into the lake, lest his disciples should make reliques of them. But their loyalty defied this precaution; they scraped together the earth around the pile, and carried it to Bohemia.

Huss was born in 1369, or, according to other accounts, in 1373, at Husinec in Bohemia, and studied philosophy and theology at the university of Prague. He became bachelor of theology in 1394, and in 1396, master of arts. He commenced teaching in the university in 1398; and the year following he took part in a public academic disputation, in which he defended several of the tenets of Wickliffe, with whose writings he had, so early as 1391, become acquainted. Along with the office of teacher in the University, he had held that of preacher in the Bethlehem chapel at Prague.

A few months after the death of Huss, Jerome of Prague, his follower and companion, expiated his deviation from the doctrines or the spirit of the Catholic faith, by undergoing a similar fate. Like Cranmer, he at first recanted; but like Cranmer he grew ashamed of his recantation, and his soul rose to the fiery heights of martyrdom. In spite of the earnest protest of Robert Hallam, bishop Salisbury, that God willeth not the death of a sinner, but that he should be converted and live, Jerome was condemned to be burnt alive, and the sentence was carried into effect on the 1st of June, 1416.

It is said of him that at the place of execution his countenance was not only composed, but cheerful. When bound, and bound naked, to the stake, he sang his hymns of thanksgiving, with a voice whose clear loud accents never trembled. The executioner offered to light the fire behind him, that he might not see it. "Light it before my face," he exclaimed; "were I the least afraid, I should not be standing here."

Constanz is full of memorials of the two martyrs, but more especially of the elder and more famous one, John Huss. The house in which he lodged on first reaching the city stands in the Paul's Strasse, near the Schnetzthor, and is distinguished by a rude stone bust. He was afterwards confined in the Dominican convent (December 6, 1414, to March 24, 1415), which is now a cotton manufactory. Its church, a thirteenth century building, is in ruins, and these ruins are picturesque, while the adjacent cloisters will attract the visitor's attention from their singular character. The chapter-house is probably older than the church. The little island occupied by this interesting edifice was formerly fortified by the Romans, and a portion of the wall, towards the lake, still bears witness to the solidity of Roman masonry.

The council, to whose zeal for the Catholic faith Huss and Jerome fell victims, held its sittings in the Hall of the Kaufhaus, which was built in 1388 as a warehouse, but afterwards used as the town-hall. The council was composed of thirty cardinals, four patriarchs, twenty archbishops, two hundred professors of universities and doctors of theology, besides princes, ambassadors, ecclesiastical dignitaries, abbots, priors, and distinguished civilians. The place of meeting was a large room, divided by two rows of wooden pillars into three aisles.

In a small apartment at the north extremity of the building are shown some curious relics, more or less interesting according as they are more or less authentic. The principal are:—1st. The ancient fauteuil of Pope Martin V., whom the council elected in place of John XXIII., and the throne of the Emperor Sigismund. 2nd. On a platform in front of the throne, the three effigies of Huss, Jerome of Prague, and Father Celestine. 3rd. A model, and some original fragments, of the dungeon in which John Huss was imprisoned at the Dominican convent. 4th. The beautiful gilded casket, ornamented with bas-reliefs, in which were deposited, in 1417, the votes for the election of Pope Martin V. 5th. The Gothic altar, the gilded and illuminated parchment missal, and the cross of the same pope. 6th. A life-size statue of Abraham, which supported the cathedral pulpit, and being mistaken by the populace for a figure of Huss, was grievously defaced. 7th. An old Germanic urn, with a patera, and images of idols. 8th. A stone idol of great antiquity, worshipped, it may be, by one of the old Teutonic tribes. 9th. Small statues of stone and metal discovered in the neighbourhood. 10th. A collection of painted glass. 11th. A collection of various sculptured objects. 12th. A collection of indifferent oil paintings. 13th. A well-executed view upon the lake.

Another memorial of the martyrs is the field outside the town, in the suburb of Brühl, where they passed through their fiery trial. Rude images of Huss and Jerome, moulded in clay excavated from this very spot, are here offered for sale to the much-enduring stranger.

The ancient bishopric of Constanz, occupied in due succession by eighty-seven bishops, was abolished in 1802. Happily, the noble cathedral in which they played their part has survived the ravages of time, the storms of war, and the changes from the old order to the new, of which Constanz has witnessed so many. It is true that it has suffered from the "pestilent heresy" of "restoration;" but its main features remain unaltered.

It was begun in 1052; but the work of completion was very protracted, and occupied from early in the thirteenth to the middle of the sixteenth century. The ground plan is cruciform, with very beautiful open-work turrets at the west end. The tower, rebuilt in 1511, after the destruction of an earlier one by fire, was crowned (1850-1857) by an open spire of limestone, under the direction of Herbsch. The doors of the main portal are of oak, and quaintly carved with a representation of our Lord's passion, executed in 1470 by one Simon Baider. The workmanship is admirable for boldness and decision. The nave is supported by sixteen pillars, each of a single block, and dates from the thirteenth century. Here, at sixteen paces from the entrance, you may see the stone on which Huss stood, while undergoing the ceremonial of "degradation."

In front of the high altar stands the tomb of Robert Hallam, bishop of Salisbury, who died at Constanz on the 4th of September, 1417. He was a man of great ability and moderation, and as the head of the English deputation to the great council secured the confidence of the Emperor Sigismund. It further deserves to be remembered that he alone, or almost alone, protested against the sentence of death delivered upon John Huss. His tomb, as the workmanship proves, is of English brass, and was probably sent over from England by his executors.

The organ dates from 1520, but was restored in 1680 in the style of the Renaissance.

In a chapel on the south side may be seen a carving of the Entombment of Christ, by the sculptor, Hans Morinz; in a chapel on the north, the tombs of the Weller family, and of Bishop Otto von Sonnenberg. In one to the left of the choir are some striking half-length figures, the size of life, grouped round a dying Virgin, sculptured in sand-stone, and painted; apparently the work of a fifteenth century sculptor. The elegant winding staircase, close at hand, is ornamented with sculptures and statues. In a chapel to the east may be seen the tomb of Bishop Otto III., margrave of Hochberg-Roetaln, who died in 1432, and above it an altar picture on glass of six of the apostles. The tombs of bishops Burkhard and Henry von Ho wen are situated in the transept.

The sacristy contains some curious relics; an old painting of The Crucifixion, date 1524, erroneously ascribed to Holbein; and the armorial shields of all the prelates who have occupied the episcopal throne of Constanz. In the vestry room above it is shown a range of curious cupboards, or presses of carved oak, none of a later date than the fifteenth century.

Two sides of the ancient cloisters, with their richly sculptured arches, are still standing. Attached to them is a chapter-room of the fourteenth century, in whose centre rests a thirteenth century work, in the Italian Gothic style, representing the Holy Sepulchre; it consists of an open rotunda, decorated by arches resting on small columns. Externally are placed, against the piedroits, certain finely executed statues, half human size, representing the Annunciation, the Birth of Christ, the Adoration of the Magi, and, underneath, the twelve Apostles. In the interior is quite a cluster of statues—an angel, and the three holy women visiting the tomb of our Lord; two groups of Roman soldiers sleeping, and a man attired in the dress of a physician, seated at a table, with two vessels before him, in one of which he is stirring some drug or potion; in his left hand he holds a large round spoon, on his head he wears a kind of square cap. Next comes a female pointing with her finger to two others, who carry a couple of vases. All these figures, like those on the outside of the structure, are half the size of nature.

There is little else to be seen in Constanz. St. Stephen's church, however, is not without interest. It was founded in the ninth century, rebuilt in the thirteenth, and completed in the fifteenth by Bishop Otto III. von Hochberg. It contains some good ancient coloured glass, and some new (in the choir) by Dr. Stanz, of Berne. The high altar-piece is by Memberger. The sculpture of the choir, of the door of the sacristy, and the tomb of his own wife, is by Hans Morinz (1560-1610), and well worthy of a careful examination. You can see that the artist wrought at his work with a conscientious devotion to his art; the execution is everywhere honest, careful, and vigorous.

Some portions of the old walls and towers are still extant. The bridge across the Rhine, which here flows from the Upper into the Lower Lake, is roofed over, and protected by some military defences dating from the fifteenth century. The moats may also be traced by the inquisitive stranger.

EXCURSIONS FROM CONSTABZ: REICHENAU.

The Isle of Reichenau is worth a visit. It lies in the broad part of the Rhine, where the river still retains something of a lacustrine character, and contains the church and treasury of a Benedictine abbey founded by Charlemagne.

The island is low but pleasing, and from its highest point, the Hochwacht, commands a fine view of the river, and of the upper and lower lakes. It measures one league and a quarter in length, and about half a league in breadth. The principal villages are Reichenau, or Mittelzell, Oberzell, Niederzell, and Unterzell. The population (1500) are chiefly occupied in the cultivation of the vine.

We have spoken of the abbey as founded by Charlemagne. More strictly speaking it originated in an ecclesiastical colony planted by St. Pirminius, which the great emperor of the Franks afterwards endowed with ten towns. It throve mightily, and met with numerous wealthy and liberal benefactors. Thus, Genla, duke of Suabia, conferred upon it Tuttlingen, Wangen, Stettin, and five and twenty villages. It obtained from King Carloman four towns on the lake of Como; from Charles III., Zurxach; from Louis the Pious, Altheim, Riedlingen, and five villages; and from Duke Berthold of Suabia, thirty villages. It must be confessed that the monks, if at all grateful, had good reason to celebrate masses continually for the repose of the souls of men so generous and devout! The abbey had upwards of 300 noble vassals, 1600 dependent monks and priests, and of its superior it was proverbially said, that he could ride to Rome and yet dine and sleep every day on his own land. Hence came the present name of the island, Reichenau.

Rapid and astounding as was the rise of this celebrated foundation, not less rapid and astounding was its fall. In the tenth century it had already begun to decline. In 1175 its annual revenue had sunk from 60,000 to 1600 florins; in 1384 it had decreased to three silver marks; and the abbot was so poor that, instead of entertaining princes and nobles at his table like his predecessors, he was compelled to ride on his white pony, every morning and evening, to sit at the frugal board of the priest of Niederzell. It was the old story; profusion and ostentation and luxurious living had wasted the resources of the monastery, and as might have been anticipated, the result was, that those ecclesiastics who had kept a court equalling a king's in splendour, were succeeded by others, who lived upon the scanty alms of the charitable.

In the course of time the abbey was incorporated with the see of Constanz (1541), whose bishops assumed the title of abbots of Reichenau, and restored its former glories. Since 1799 the services of the church have been conducted by three secular priests.

Of the various conventual edifices, once so celebrated for their extent and magnificence, the church and the treasury, as already stated, are all that remain.

The church was built in 806 by Abbot Hatto, but was thrice destroyed. The tower is probably a portion of Abbot Hatto's work, and is Romanesque in style. Here was buried Charles the Fat, in 887, as an inscription, carved in 1728, duly records. His grave, however, can no longer be recognized. The treasury contains some remarkable relics, such as the silver-gilt shrine of St. Fortunatus, an ivory ciborium, a cope, a crozier, a missal of the tenth century; a so-called emerald, weighing twenty-eight pounds, which is, however, only coloured glass; and the waterpot used by our Lord in his miracle at the marriage of Cana— a marble urn of simple design, presented to the convent by Simon Wardo, the general of Leo the Byzantine emperor.

The valuable manuscripts which the convent formerly possessed have been removed to the libraries of Carlsruhe and Heidelberg.

At Niederzell the church has two small towers in the Byzantine style. It was built in the ninth century by Bishop Egino, of Verona, who lies buried here. Persons suffering from fever were accustomed, down to a very recent date, to offer up their prayers in this quaint old church, and then lie down on the grass which covers the good bishop's grave, in the hope or belief their devotion would be rewarded by a cure.

At Oberzell the Byzantine crypt of its little but ancient church is spoken of as a remarkable monument in an architectural point of view.

Near this village moulder the ivy-clad rums of an ancient castle, that of Schoppeln, which formerly belonged to the abbots of Reichenau, but was destroyed in a popular insurrection in 1382. The abbot Mangold, who was also bishop of Constanz, had arrested some Constanz fishermen for casting their nets within the limits of his jurisdiction, and had deprived them of sight with his own hands. The fishermen then rose in open revolt, invaded the island, set fire to several farms, and demolished Schoppeln.

THE ISLAND OF MEINAU.

The island of Meinau, situated about four miles north of Constanz, is of a more attractive appearance than that of Reichenau, and with its terraces and vine-clad hills, its groves and gardens, might be held to realize a poet's dream of an enchanted isle, frequented by wood-nymphs, and haunted by celestial music. "Nature," says a topographical writer who does not ordinarily grow enthusiastic, "nature has lent it every charm (and lent them apparently in *perpetuo*), and all the sweet sunny visions of blest isles and floating gardens, of which the poets sing, are here realized. It rises from the smiling lake in the form of terraces. The gently sloping green banks are decked with fruit trees, gardens, vineyards, and meadows; old masonry looks picturesquely forth from the green foliage, and the summit is crowned with a stately castle, from whose terrace a most splendid view is afforded of the lake and the surrounding landscape. Its loveliness gave rise to the name of *Maien-aue*, or 'May-meadow.'" It is connected with the mainland by a wooden bridge, 630 paces long, and by the bridge belonging to the railway. Its circumference is estimated at forty-three miles.

Anciently the island belonged to the barons of Langenstein, and they erected a castle on it, which, with the island, was handed over to the Teutonic order, in 1282, by Arnold von Langenstein and his four sons, the five chivalrous knights having taken upon themselves the Teutonic vows. A commandery was then established here, and Herz von Langenstein, one of Arnold's sons, was the first of a series of sixty-five "commanders," who maintained the repute of the order in this beautiful island. He seems to have been the beau-ideal of a knight; not only a warrior but a poet, for a collection of his poems has been discovered—one of which, dated 1293, and devoted to a glorification of the life of St. Martina, consists of 30,000 verses. We may be permitted to hope he did not compel his knights to listen to their recital.

On the 11th of February, 1647, the Swedes, under their great general, Wrangel, landed in the island a detachment of 1000 musketeers, with four cannon, and drove out the imperialist garrison. It is said that they found a great booty here, valued at 5,000,000 florins. When the Swedish army, and the French under Turenne, retired from the shores of the lake, the imperialists made a bold attempt to recover Meinau; but the attack was defeated by the Swedes, who held possession of the island until September 30, 1648, when they evacuated it in compliance with the provisions of the treaty of Westphalia.

In 1805 the island was annexed to the grand duchy of Baden. Afterwards it was sold to a natural son of Prince Esterhazy, who in his turn sold it in 1839 to the Countess von Langenstein, the morganatic wife of the Grand Duke Louis of Baden. In 1854 it was purchased by Prince Frederick, regent of Baden. The castle is an eighteenth century building, and uninteresting.

PETERSHAUSEN.

Petershausen skirts the right bank of the Rhine, nearly opposite Meinau, and forms a village suburb of Constanz. It derives its name from the old Benedictine abbey, *Domus Petri*, or Peter's House, and is inhabited by about 250 to 300 Catholics, who depend for their support on the breeding of cattle and the cultivation of the vine.

The founder of the *Domus Petri* was Gebhard, bishop of Constanz, and the work was begun in 983. The following legend is connected with it:—The bishop, who himself superintended the erection of the abbey, happened on one occasion, while the interior was in course of decoration, to be absent. The knavish painters seized the opportunity to bury their best colours in the neighbouring forest, and on the bishop's return demanded a fresh supply of materials. But the holy prelate was fully equal to the task of coping with dishonest workmen. Endowed with the gift of second sight, or some faculty not less useful and wonderful, he conducted them to the wood, and said, "Let us see if the grace of the Lord will not furnish us with what we require!" Striking his staff in the ground he exclaimed, "Dig!" They dug, and the hidden treasures were revealed. "Now, my dear children," said the bishop, slily smiling, "let this miracle strengthen your energies, and I pray ye resume your work." On the following day, however, the deceitful painters suddenly fell to the ground as if they were dead. The bishop touched them with his pastoral staff and said, "I will not reward you by permitting you to lie here and take your rest. Up, up, and persevere in well-doing." The dead then arose, and by their redoubled industry showed the miraculous character of the episcopal exhortation.

So, at length, the abbey was completed. The church was dedicated to St. Gregory, whose bones were sent hither from Rome by the pontiff; and the new foundation was richly endowed by its founder, and afterwards by Otho III. and the Duchess Hadewig.

For some centuries it prospered exceedingly, but about 1489 a cloud came over its fortunes; it fell into a wretched poverty, and all its monks deserted it, except John Meek of Lindau, who in 1518 became abbot, and energetically laboured to effect its restoration. When the people of Constanz embraced the doctrines of Luther, its then ruler, Gebhard III., took to flight, and the abbey was destroyed. On the success of the Catholic league, however, the city was compelled to rebuild it, the monks returned, and it regained much of its ancient prosperity. In 1803 the convent was finally dissolved.

We must now return to Rorschach, in order to complete our circuit of the Lake of Constanz, by exploring its north-eastern shore.

LINDAU

From Rorschach we may proceed by rail to Lindau, passing Bregentz.

Lindau, with the villages of Nonnenhorn and Wassenburg, constitutes nearly the whole of the Bavarian territory on the shore of the lake. It is the terminus of the Bavarian Railway, and distant about five hours' journey from Augsburg. Built on three islands, it has sometimes been called the "Bavarian Venice," but the points of resemblance are not visible to the unprejudiced eye of the stranger. It contains about 4000 inhabitants, has two good inns, is quiet and orderly, and wholly destitute of animation, except when the pilgrimages to Einsiedeln commence. It has a considerable transit trade and a good fishery, which might easily be made better if the Lindauers were less inclined to take things easily.

Lindau is agreeably situated: exactly opposite it may be seen the broad extensive valley through which the Rhine descending from the Rhaetian Alps, hurries to the lake. The rocky mountain chain of Switzerland runs along the whole of the right side of this valley as far as the lake, and then, extending along the same in a chain of fertile hills, forms its southern shore. The left side of the valley is bounded by the sterile summits of the Vorarlberg, which, continuing towards the east, terminate in a range of steep and lofty cliffs, washed by the dark-blue waters of the Boden See. All that portion of the latter which lies to the east of Lindau forms a fine large oval basin, two leagues wide, and nearly as long, at whose western extremity stands the little town of Bregentz. Towards the west and north the lake stretches out into a bright and magnificent expanse. From Lindau to Constanz, as the crow flies, measures thirty-three miles, and to the end of the Upper Lake, forty-eight miles. The western and northern shores, though much indented, preserve on the whole a straight line, and the eye is therefore enabled to range unobstructed over a sheet of water, whose area is not less than forty German square miles. When the atmosphere is not too transparent, the views are bounded only by the horizon, and it is easy to understand why the lake was once called the Suabian Sea.

The three islands on which our Bavarian Venice takes its stand boast of an area of 102 acres. The foremost is the largest, and communicates with the mainland by a timber bridge, 290 paces in length. The principal part of the town is erected on this island; the second, connected with it by drawbridges, is given over to fishermen and vinegrowers. The third, called the *Burg*, is linked to Lindau by a stone bridge. It contains the old church of St. James, and some remains of ancient walls, supposed to be Roman. The town itself is strongly fortified.

In its earlier history the great enemy of Lindau seems to have been fire, and we read of conflagrations destroying it in 948, 1264, 1339, and 1347. Its position, however, was admirably adapted for defence in time of war, and commercial enterprise in time of peace. Thus, it rose again from its ashes with unabated vigour, and in 1496 had acquired so much importance that the Emperor Maximilian I. selected it as the seat of the Imperial Diet. It may further be mentioned, that it was one of the first towns which embraced the doctrines of Luther; with the cities of Constanz, Strasburg, and Memmingen, it was represented at Schmalkalden when the great Protestant League was formed, and subscribed to the famous Confession of Augsburg.

When, at the beginning of the Thirty Years' War, a crusade was preached against the German Protestants, the gallant burghers of Lindau prepared to defend their principles with the sword. They fortified their town, under the superintendence of the count of Solms, but were unable to resist the overwhelming force sent against them by the emperor; and as a punishment for their disaffection a garrison was quartered upon them for twenty years.

In 1647 Lindau was unsuccessfully besieged by the Swedes under Wrangel. After the French Revolution it several times changed masters; but, by the Peace of Presburg in 1806, was finally given to Bavaria, to which it still belongs.

Its public buildings are unimportant. St. Mary's church formerly belonged to the nunnery of Lindau, which consisted of an abbess and twelve nuns, all of noble family. The abbess possessed a singular privilege; namely, she was allowed to rescue a criminal from the gallows by cutting the rope from his neck with her own hands. "This act of mercy took place at the corner of the so-called 'Kerwatzen;' the knife destined to sever the cord was borne after the abbess in solemn procession on a silver salver. The individual delivered from the executioner was then regaled in the convent, and the rope tied about his middle, to remind him of his fortunate escape. Each abbess exercised the privilege *once* only; it was actually carried into effect in the years 1578, 1615, 1692, and as late as 1780."

In Trinity church, which once belonged to the Franciscans, but has been disused for many years, the town library is preserved. It contains two manuscript chronicles of the town, some blackletter bibles, block-books, and interesting ancient MSS. The Lutheran church is of great antiquity.

From Lindau we proceed to Friedrichshafen, the terminus of the Stuttgard and Ulm Railway. Langenargen and Friedrichshafen are in the lake territory of Würtemburg; the former a small market town, which formerly belonged to the Counts de Montfort, and contains the ruins of a strong castle, built on a jutting peninsula by Count William in 1332; the latter a busy and thriving port, with a harbour constructed by Frederick, king of Würtemburg. The imperial town of Buchhorn, to the north-west, and the convent of Hofen, now converted into a royal chateau, are situated within its boundaries, and are connected by a long street which skirts the shore of the lake. The views from the palace are very beautiful and extensive.

From 1632 to 1634 Buchhorn was occupied by the Swedes under General Horn, who successfully resisted an imperialist attack, delivered both by land and water.

MARSBURG.

Soon after entering the Baden territory we reach the ancient town of Marsburg, clustering on the slope of a considerable hill, under the protection of the castle which crowns the summit. It is surrounded by vineyards and orchards, and its inhabitants deal in wine, fruit, cider, corn, and fish. Its history is crowded with episodes of strife and turbulence, so that one would be tempted to believe its burghers lived in armour, and slept with sword and crossbow by their side. Its inhabitants evinced a disposition, at an early date, to embrace Lutheran opinions; and by way of warning the bishop of Constanz burnt an heretical priest here, on the 10th of May, 1527. John Hüyli, the victim, died with a courage which the fear of torture and death could not shake. Having arrived at the place of execution, he publicly thanked the bishop for the indulgence shown to him during his imprisonment. As the pile was lighted, he exclaimed, "Alas, my good people, may God forgive ye, for ye know not what ye do 1" And while the flames wreathed around him, he continued to sing aloud, "Gloria in excel sis Deo! Te Deum laudamus!" His death did not arrest the spread of his opinions; the cause for which he died thenceforward progressed rapidly in Constanz and Lindau.

The old castle of Marsburg is an interesting specimen of mediaeval military architecture. The main building, flanked by four circular turrets, was erected in 1508 by Hugo von Breitenlandenburg, bishop of Constanz. The outer wall is more ancient, and probably of Frankish architecture. A new castle, separated from the old by an artificial ravine, was built by Bishop Antony von Siggingen of Hohenburg, and continued to be occupied as a residence by the prelates of Constanz until their see was suppressed. It commands a magnificent prospect from its stately terrace.

In the cemetery chapel of Marsburg lies the dust of that extraordinary man, half-enthusiast, half-impostor—Antony von Mesmer, the inventor of Mesmerism. He was born in 1734 at Itznang, on the Lower Lake, and died at Marsburg in 1815. His monument was erected at the cost of the Society of Naturalists of Berlin.

UEBERLINGEN.

Passing New Bernau and its picturesque chapel, which lies embowered in vineyards, and the chateau of Maurach, we arrive at the ancient imperial town of Ueberlingen, situated on a creek or narrow bay of the lake, which is named after it the Ueberlingen See, or Lake of Ueberlingen. "The place has a venerable appearance, looking precisely as it did after its recovery from the ravages of the Thirty Years' War in the middle of the seventeenth century. It is situated close to the lake, which is here very deep, on a rocky soil, surrounded by vineyards and corn-fields; it still boasts of walls and moats, has eight gates, sixteen towers, an old minster, and four other churches. It is particularly animated in the suburb, where there are many fishermen's cottages. A considerable corn market is held here every week."

The following summary of events is borrowed from Dr. Gaspey:—

As early as the commencement of the seventh century the place (then called Ibriungae, not being mentioned as Ueberlingen till 1257) was a central point of the Frankish dominion, and a nursery of Christianity. Gunzo, a Christian Frankish duke of Allemannia, had his seat here. Frideburg, the beautiful and only daughter of the duke, was the betrothed of the Frankish king Sigebert, Theodoric's son; she was smitten, however, with severe illness, so that her father and all the people believed her possessed of an evil spirit. She was restored by the prayers of St. Gallus, who, at her desire, was fetched from the wilderness, but had at first refused to obey the mandate of the prince, and had fled into the valley of the Rhine. According to an old tradition, the evil spirit departed from Frideburg in the form of a black raven, which flew out of her mouth. The duke, grateful for his assistance, was desirous of conferring on him the episcopal dignity, the see of Constanz being just then vacant; St. Gallus, however, declined the proffered favour, and desired it might be awarded to the dean of Juaradaves, named John, who had been instructed by him in the word of God.

In the middle of the fourteenth century, when the country was devastated by the great plague of the so-called "Black Death," and certain zealots wandered from place to place, pursuing the Jews with fire and sword, many of the Hebrew persuasion were also sacrificed here. The mutilated corpse of a boy who had been missed by his parents was found in a brook; as the body was borne past the houses of the Jews the wounds broke out afresh. In accordance with the old superstition that the wounds of a murdered man bled in the presence of his murderer, this circumstance was held to be a satisfactory proof of their guilt. Under the pretence of rescuing them, the terrified Jews were removed to a tall stone house, in the lower story of which a quantity of faggots had been collected. As soon as the victims, over 300 in number, had been enticed into this supposed retreat, the faggots were lighted. The hapless Jews were driven by the flames from story to story, and, at last, got out upon the roof. But there was no chance of escape. The whole house was consumed, and with it every living creature. In their desperation, the Jews hurled down knives and stones and burning rafters on the crowd of persecutors who stood below and mocked at their agonies; some precipitated themselves from the windows, but were quickly seized and massacred.

As a reward for its heroic conduct in the Peasants' War, Charles V. bestowed upon it many privileges. It suffered greatly during the Thirty Years' War; was besieged by the Swedes in 1634, but forced them to retire. Five years later it was attacked by the Bavarians, and after an obstinate resistance compelled to capitulate. In 1802 Ueberlingen was attached to the grand duchy of Baden.

The only public edifice in the town worthy of notice is the Minster, or Cathedral, which presents some Gothic features, and whose interior is both spacious and majestic. The tower is upwards of 200 feet in height.

The mineral springs of Ueberlingen seem, of late years, to have risen in repute.

The northern section of the Lake of Constanz is divided into two basins, as a glance at a map will show the reader, by a long narrow peninsula jutting out from the mainland in a south-westerly direction, and terminating opposite Constanz. Here, at its extremity, is situated the suburb-village of Petershausen, connected with Constanz and the left shore of the lake by the bridge of the Strasburg Railway. The island of Meinau, already described, lies between this peninsula and the right shore of the lake; that of Reichenau, between the peninsula and the left shore of the lake, in the northwestern basin (or *Unter See*), which strikes inland as far as Rudolfzell.

In our preceding descriptions we have been as brief as was consistent with our duty to the reader, because the upper course of the Rhine, however beautiful may be its scenery, is not much visited by the British tourist; nor has it proved of any great strategic importance in the principal European wars. Moreover, with the exception of Constanz, we have met with no city of eminent historical importance, nor with any of those exquisite landscapes which song and fable have endowed with undying attractions. But now we enter upon "hallowed ground." The river whose descending wave we accompany will carry us past cities and towns indissolubly associated with the great men and deeds of bygone times, and with the stirring events of the present epoch; as well as through scenes of the highest interest and the most admirable beauty. We must proceed, therefore, at a slower pace; but not, we trust, to the dissatisfaction of the reader, who will find food for meditation and objects of curiosity abundantly supplied in every page.

CHAPTER II. THE RHINE, FROM CONSTANZ TO STRASBURG.

> Backward, in rapid evanescence, wheels
> The venerable pageantry of Time,
> Each beetling rampart, and each town sublime,
> And what the dell unwillingly reveals
> Of lurking cloistral arch, through trees espied
> Near the bright river's edge.—*Wordsworth.*

RIGHT BANK OF THE RIVER TO SCHAFFHAUSEN.

THE Rhine issues from the Boden See in a westerly direction, between the towns of Stein, on the right bank, and Steckhorn, on the left.

Stein, on the right bank, is in German territory, and picturesquely situated among vine-clad hills. A wooden bridge, forty-four mètres in length, connects it with a suburb on the left bank. It contains a population of 1500.

In the eighth century it was already a considerable village. In 945 it was raised to the rank and privileges of a town by Duke Burckhardt II., of Suabia; and in 1005 a further impetus was given to its prosperity by the removal hither of the Benedictine abbey of St. George, from Hohentwiel. The barons of Klingen, lords of the abbey, gradually crept into possession of the town; one moiety of which, in 1359, they sold to the duke of Austria, and receiving it again as a fief in 1415, sold it a second time, with the other moiety, to the barons of Klingenberg. From the latter the town succeeded in purchasing its freedom, in 1459, for 1500 florins, and it then entered into an alliance offensive and defensive with the towns of Zurich and Schaffhausen. In 1484 its heavy debts, and the exactions of the abbot of St. George, compelled it to place itself under the protection of Zurich, then a powerful and influential city; and so it remained until 1798, when it was formally incorporated with the canton of Schaffhausen. The abbey of St. George had previously been suppressed, having fallen before the sweeping whirlwind of the Reformation.

The artist will find in the town many old houses well worth a place in his sketch-book, such as the Red Ox and the White Eagle. Near the bridge is a mansion of venerable antiquity, bearing the sign "Zum Klu," and reputed to have been formerly the house of assembly for the nobles. It is enriched with some very fine specimens of the best painted glass, perfectly wonderful in their depth and glow of colour. In the town hall hangs the portrait of a citizen of Stein, Rudolph Schydt, Baron von Schwarzenhorn, born in 1590, who after having been carried into slavery by the Turks, was, by a strange revolution of the wheel of fortune, to become Austrian ambassador at the Turkish court. The large and profusely ornamented silver goblet is shown which he presented to his native town, and which, on the occasion of a wedding, figures always among the decorations of the feast.

In the old abbey of St. George the visitor will find a really noble hall, profusely ornamented with quaint frescoes and some good wood-carving.

On the rocky height above the town stands what time has left of the ancient castle of Hohenklingen, or the Steiner Klinge. To the family which formerly occupied this fortress belonged Walter von Klingen, a minnesinger of great celebrity, and the friend of Rudolph of Hapsburg, whose future greatness he predicted. He lies interred, with Iris three daughters, near Bale, in the convent of Klingenthal, which was founded by his pious generosity. From the topmost roof of Hohenklingen was precipitated the burgomaster Ezweiler, in 1758, for having treacherously plotted to deliver up the town to the Austrians.

About three miles to the east, at an elevation of 650 feet above the Rhine, and on the southern slope of the Schienenberg, are situated the quarries of Œhningen, remarkable for their abundant store of fossil remains of terrestrial and fresh-water animals, as well as plants, discovered in their marl and limestone rocks. The most curious discovery was that of a fossil fox, made by Sir Roderick Murchison. The strata lie immediately above the formation called Molasse, and in their organic contents differ from all fresh-water beds previously discovered.

Continuing our course along the left bank of the river we next reach Hemmishofen, lying in a pleasant gap or hollow between the hills. Then we come to the mouth of the little river Biber, which winds past the château of Ramson, and in the shadow of luxuriant "beechen groves "make our way to Gailingen, a hamlet embowered among vines, and chiefly inhabited by Jews. Near this point the French army, on the 1st of May, 1800, effected that passage of the Rhine which enabled Moreau to gain his great victory of Hohenlinden.

Passing through the glades of the Schaechenwald we next arrive at Büsingen; and soon afterwards, at Paradies, a nunnery of the order of St. Clara (*Clarisses*), founded in 1214 at Constanz, and thence transferred to its present site. In the neighbouring marshes many rare plants are found.

The imperial army, under the archduke Charles, crossed the Rhine at Paradies in 1799.

LEFT BANK OF THE RIVER TO SCHAFFHAUSEN.

On the left bank of the river, after leaving Constanz, the first point of interest at which the traveller arrives is Gottlieben, and here he will regard the hoary castle with curious eyes, from its imperishable associations. It was the temporary prison in 1414 of John Huss and Jerome of Prague, who were confined in its dungeons, in gross violation of the imperial safe-conduct, at the instigation of Pope John XXII. By a strange turn of fortune, the latter, a few months later, was himself a prisoner at Gottlieben, by order of the Council of Constanz, and was here compelled to sign the bull by which he virtually abdicated the papal throne. In 1454 Félix Hämmerlin, the canon of Zurich, better known by his Latinized name of Malleolus, the most learned scholar and generous philanthropist which Switzerland in the fifteenth century could boast of, was also imprisoned here. He was afterwards removed to the convent of Luzern, where he was buried alive.

During the siege of Constanz, in 1633, the Swedish general, Horn, established here his headquarters. The castle was purchased in 1837 by Prince Louis Napoleon Bonaparte—now Napoleon III.—who demolished a part of it, and reconstructed it on a more extensive scale.

The Rhine now broadens into the north-western section of Lake Constanz—an ample basin, known as the Zeller See north of Reichenau, and the Unter See south of that island. The shores of the Zeller See are studded with several picturesquely situated villages— Heyne, Allensbach, Markelfingen, Rudolfzell (already mentioned), Moos, Itznang, Weiler, Horn, and Gaienhofen. The Baden Railway skirts its north-western shore from Rudolfzell to Petershausen, where, as before stated, it crosses the Rhine and enters Constanz.

On the left or southern shore, our exploration brings us to Ermatingen, a small town of 1500 inhabitants—agriculturists, traders, and fishermen—dominated by the castles of Hind and Wolfsberg, the latter belonging to an English family.

The château of Arenenberg (formery Narrenberg) we regard with peculiar interest as the residence and death-place of the duchess of St. Leu, ex-queen of Holland—Hortense Beauharnais, daughter of Josephine, and the mother of Napoleon III., who purchased and restored the chateau in 1855. The emperor resided here previous to his mock-heroic descent upon Strasburg.

In this neighbourhood, to the south of the village of Maunenbach, are situated the chateau of Solmstein, built in the twelfth and rebuilt in the fourteenth centuries; and nearer the village, that of Eugensberg, which was inhabited for a time by Queen Hortense.

The castle of Sandegg, which belonged to Count Eugene de Leuchtenberg, was destroyed by fire in 1834.

Passing Berlingen, we next arrive at Steckhorn, an ancient town of about 1500 inhabitants, situated at the point where the Rhine issues from the lake-like expanse of the Zeller Zee. The old castle has been converted into a manufactory.

On a promontory covered with fruit trees stands the Cistercian monastery of Feldbach, founded in 1252. Its chapel contains a statue of Walter von Klingen, the feudal superior of the lords of Feldbach, and a bounteous benefactor to the abbey.

The chateau of Clansegg is comparatively uninteresting. Through a broken and picturesque country, and passing the chateau of Neufturg, we proceed to the village of Mammern, occupying a tongue of land which juts boldly into the river. On the opposite bank are Wangen and Oehringen.

The chateau of Oberstad has undergone that process of transformation which so signally marks the rise of a "new order" of things upon the ruins of the old. It has been converted, like that of Steckhorn, into a factory. Strigen and Kattenhorn are still famous for their vines.

At Eschenz the tourist, if he have time, may reasonably spend a few hours in examining the Roman and Germanic antiquities which render its neighbourhood so full of interest. On the hills above are planted the châteaux of Frendenfels and Liebenfels, the latter recently restored.

The channel of the Rhine has considerably narrowed at Burg, where it is divided into two contracted branches by the small island of Woerd. The chapel so conspicuous on this little islet—which was anciently connected with Burg by a Roman bridge, whose piles were visible as late as 1766—was erected in memory of Sidonius, bishop of St. Gall. He was for some time confined here a prisoner, and perished, in 759, the victim of a false accusation.

The small hamlet of Rheinklingen need not delay our progress. Diessenhofen is a town of 1650 inhabitants. From 1640, when it was conquered by the Leaguers, until 1798, it formed a small republic under the protection of Schaffhausen and the eight ancient cantons of Switzerland. The Rhine is here spanned by a substantial bridge. The town has some large tanneries, and a considerable fair, especially for cattle.

St. Katharinenthal is a Dominican convent, founded in the thirteenth century, and still inhabited by a prioress and four nuns.

We now enter the town of

SCHAFFHAUSEN.

Population, 8711. Sixty-four miles from Bale; twenty-nine miles from Constanz. Hotels in the town, Falke, Krone, Loewe; and at the Falls, Schweizerhof and Bellevue. On the left bank, Schloss-hauffen, Witzig, and Schiff.

Schaffhausen, the chief town of a canton of the same name, has a population of 8711 inhabitants, and stands on the right bank of the Rhine, at an elevation of 1270 feet above the sea, in the valley of Durach or Taunerbach. It is situated just above the commencement of the falls or rapids which render the Rhine unnavigable as far as Basel. Anciently it was a landing-place and customs-town, where all goods brought from the south or north had to be embarked for conveyance up the river; and it owes its name to the *boat* or *skiff-houses* erected for this purpose. But the introduction of railways has year by year diminished its importance, and it chiefly depends at present on its limited manufactures of soap, candles, silk, cotton, iron; its tanneries, potteries, and breweries; and the influx of tourists attracted by its vicinity to the celebrated Falls.

Though it does not merit a long visit, yet it possesses many features of interest for the cultivated traveller. No other town in Switzerland—perhaps none in Germany, with the single exception of Nuremberg—has so faithfully preserved a mediaeval character and physiognomy. If, like Pompeii, it had been buried under the ashes of a volcanic eruption, and only recently exhumed, it could not more thoroughly have retained the sentiment and aspect of antiquity. It is an old-world place, and in passing through its streets you feel suddenly transported back to the sixteenth century, when it was a city of influence, wealth, and power. Many of its houses are remarkable for their antique architecture, for the turrets and projecting oriel windows which relieve their facades, and for the quaint carvings and mouldings in wood and stucco with which they are embellished. It is unfortunate that few of them now exhibit any traces of the fresco paintings with which they were originally covered; and the antiquary will regret, though the sanitary reformer will rejoice, that the muncipality have of late years been inspired with a spirit of improvement, and have begun to widen the ancient streets and to substitute blooming gardens for grim but useless fortifications. The wall and six turreted gateways of the town are, however, as yet extant, and will furnish the artist with many picturesque subjects for his pencil. The house called Zum Ritter, opposite the Krone Hôtel, is a "bit" worthy of Prout.

The celebrated wooden bridge, which was formerly the glory of Schaffhausen, and the most perfect specimen of that species of architecture in the world, was burned by the

French, under Oudinot, in 1799, after their defeat by the Austrians at Stockach. It consisted of a single arch, 365 feet in span, and was built by a carpenter from Appenzell, named Grubenmann. A model of it is preserved in the town library (20,000 vols.), which also contains the collection of books made by the great Swiss historian, Johannes Müller, a native of Schaffhausen (1752-1809).

"At Schaffhausen," wrote Montaigne, on passing through the town in 1580, "we saw nothing rare;" and nothing rare is to be seen there to-day. On the hill above it, the Emmersberg, however, is planted the singular fort or castle called Annoth (that is, *ohne Noth*, or "the Needless "), because it was erected in order to provide the poor of the town with food. It was built in 1560. The walls are upwards of eighteen feet thick, and its vaults are bomb-proof. There are subterranean passages under it. From the summit of the tower may be enjoyed a prospect of singular beauty and variety.

Frederick duke of Austria, in 1415, having assisted Pope John XXIII. in his escape from Constanz, provided him with an asylum in the castle of Schaffhausen. To effect his purpose, he had proclaimed a splendid tournament without the gates of Constanz. All the city poured forth to the spectacle; the streets were wholly deserted. Pope John, in the dress of a groom, with a gray cloak, and a kerchief wrapped closely over his face, then mounted a sorry and ill-accoutred steed, with a cross-bow on the pommel of his saddle (March 20). Unperceived and unchallenged he passed the gates, and in about two hours reached Ermatingen. A boat was ready, he glided down the rapid stream to Schaffhausen, and took refuge in the ducal castle.

The emperor and the Council of Constanz were quick in their punishment of the pope's abettor and assistant. The ban of the empire, and the excommunication of the council, were both launched against him on the 7th of April. "All his vassals," says Milman, "were released from their sworn fealty; all treaties, contracts, oaths, vows, concerning the man excommunicated alike by the church and the empire, were declared null and void. Whoever could conquer, might possess the territory, the towns, the castles of the outlaw.

The Swabian princes fell on his possessions in Alsace; the Swiss Cantons (they only with some reluctance to violate solemn treaties) seized his hereditary dominions, even Hapsburg itself. Before the month had expired this powerful duke was hardly permitted to humble himself in person before the emperor, whose insatiate revenge spared nothing that could abase his ancient foe. It was a suppliant entreating pardon in the most abject terms, a sovereign granting it with the most hard and haughty condescension. Frederick surrendered all his lands and possessions to be held at the will of the empire, until he should deign to reinvest the duke with them under the most degrading tenure of allegiance and fealty. The pope then fled from Schaffhausen to Fribourg, and thence to Brisach; but he was quickly pursued, overtaken, and thrown into prison in the strong castle of Gottlieben."

The Minster, anciently the abbey of All Saints (Allerheiligen), was founded in 1052, and completed in 1101. In 1753 it was restored, but with a pitiful want of taste. It retains, however, the principal features of its ancient style, the Romanesque, and its round arches and massive construction will interest the stranger. The arches of the nave rest upon single circular pillars; those of the central transept on square columns of such solidity that they seem intended to outlast the world. Prior to the Reformation, the great boast of the minster was a colossal figure, called the "Great Good God," which attracted numerous pilgrims. It was a figure of Christ twenty-two feet in height, and occupied the site of the present pulpit. The story runs that an irreverent jester, boasting that he was the brother of the Madonna of Einsiedeln, was cast into prison for blasphemy. On being brought next day before the magistrate, he said, "Yes, the Madonna at Einsiedeln is my sister, and what is more, the Devil at Constanz and the Great God at Schaffhausen are my brothers; for my father, who is a sculptor, made them all three, and therefore we must be akin."

The great bell of the cathedral, founded in 1486, bears the celebrated inscription which suggested to Schiller his "Song of the Bell:"

"Vivos voco, mortuos plango, fulgura frango."

The Gothic cloister contains numerous whitewashed and plaster-daubed monuments of the magistrates and principal families of Schaffhausen.

The church of St. John is the largest in Switzerland; but its spaciousness is its sole distinction. It was built in 1120.

On the public promenade near the casino garden, a well-executed marble bust on a pedestal of gray marble, which is enriched with some bas-reliefs in bronze, perpetuates the memory of Schaffhausen's most famous citizen. The inscription on it runs as follows:—

"JOHANNES VON MULLER,
Von Schaffhausen,
Geb. 8 Jan. 1752. Gest. 29 May, 1809.
Nie war ich von Einer Partie,
Sondern für Wahrheit unci Recht
Wo ich's erkannte."

That is, "I was never of any particular party, but for Truth and Light, wherever I recognized them."

Schaffhausen is a place of great antiquity. Annual fairs were held in the village, which then belonged to Count Ebenhard III., of Nellenburg, as early as the eleventh century. It increased so rapidly, that in the next century it claimed the rank and enjoyed the privileges of a town, and was taken by the Emperor Henry VI. under his protection and that of the Empire. The neighbouring nobility thought it an honour to obtain its freedom, and Schaffhausen having thrown off the supremacy of its abbot was received, in 1246, among the number of free cities. Its burghers having been greatly favoured by the house of Hapsburg, always loyally supported it, and at the battle of Morgarten fought bravely in the Austrian ranks. It attained the climax of its prosperity early in the fifteenth century, when it had a population of 12,000, and was the great commercial depôt of Upper Swabia. Its administration was then in the hands of an elective burgomaster, and its citizens were mustered in twelve guilds, one of which was restricted exclusively to persons of noble birth.

When Duke Frederick the Penniless was placed under the Imperial ban in 1415, for his share in the escape of Pope John XXIII., Schaffhausen found itself in a position of extreme peril, and only escaped the vengeance of the emperor by payment of a fine of 30,000 ducats.

The duke, who had deserted it in its difficulties, then attempted to recover possession of it; but the burghers gallantly maintained the independence they had so dearly purchased. For this purpose they concluded an alliance with the Swiss, who nobly came to their aid when, in 1451, the Austrian forces under Von Hendorf had nearly succeeded in their investment of the town. In return for such loyal service, Schaffhausen supported the League, of which it became a member in 1501, in its wars with Burgundy and Swabia. Meantime, it continued to increase its territory by buying up the lands of the neighbouring nobles, whose profligacy forced them to raise money at any cost.

In 1529 Schaffhausen declared itself Protestant. It was afterwards somewhat disturbed by the outbreaks of the Anabaptists; but the course of its history ran with tolerable smoothness until the European convulsions caused by the French Revolution. In the great struggle between revolutionary France and Austria it was ultimately occupied by both armies; and from the 7th to the 10th of October by the Russians.

The canton of which it is the capital lies on the right bank of the Rhine, occupies a superficial area of 117 square miles, and has a population of 37,000, of whom 34,000 are Protestants and 3000 Roman Catholics. The surface is hilly and irregular, with many picturesque valleys, one of which, the Klettgau, is famous for its vineyards.

The principal products are grain, flax, hemp, and fruits. The canton contains the two small towns of Neunkirch and Stein, the latter, in reality, a suburb of Schaffhausen; the five market towns of Unter-Hallau, Schleitheim, Wilchingen, Thüingen, and Ramsen; twenty-eight to thirty villages; and about forty castles and farms.

THE FALLS OF SCHAFFHAUSEN.

The course of the Rhine from the suburb of Stein to the little village of Obernid, where it quits the canton of Schaffhausen, measures about nine Swiss leagues. In this distance it descends 210 feet; and such is the rapidity of its current that in the severest winter it never freezes. Nowhere, in the whole extent of its manifold windings, is the river brighter or more transparent; its deep blue waters, with their emerald gleam, flow onward with many a crest of pearly foam, but are never unclean or turbid. The depth varies, but between Stein and the Falls attains a maximum of thirty feet.

About a mile and a half below Schaffhausen the river, for a distance of 1000 feet, whirls and foams and eddies over a succession of broken calcareous rocks. It is here called the "Lachen," or "Pools," from the countless basins into which the waters are pent up. On the left, just below these pools, a huge crag juts forward like a promontory, and contracts the channel of the river into a space of one hundred and twenty feet. With a fall of eight or ten feet, the current dashes headlong through this narrow throat, and then suddenly expands to a breadth of 560 feet, darts off at a right angle towards the south, and for half a league is content to mitigate its fury, and flow with some degree of moderation through sloping banks covered with luxuriant vineyards. But the shores gradually grow steeper, and draw nearer together; and the river, confined between the heights of Bohnenberg on the one hand, and of Kohlfurt on the other, and broken up into three channels by two isolated masses of projecting rock, leaps a descent of forty-five to sixty feet with indescribable violence and boundless fury.

In *front* of the Falls, on the right bank, stands the castle of Woerth, and nearly opposite it, on the left, the chateau of Lauffen (*i.e.*, the "rapids"), from either of which a fine view of the "hell of waters" may be obtained. Immediately *above* the Falls the river is spanned by the stone bridge of the Schaffhausen and Zurich Railway, and the rocks on the right bank are occupied by some iron-works, whose hammers are worked by the waters, but whose dingy buildings considerably detract from the beauty of the scene.

Perhaps, after all, the best point of view is from the chateau of Lauffen. Here a wooden gallery projects to the very edge of the rapids, so that you can touch the water with your hand. You see the emerald-tinted, azure-shining mass swirling impetuously downward, almost over your head, with a roar like the thunder of battle. Hurled against the rocks, like a stone from a catapult, part rises in a cloud of dense and flashing spray, part sweeps onward in a boiling rush of foam, while the main volume of water, descending into the semi circular basin beneath, again is partly dissipated into foam and spray. But the great charm of the picture is its variety. At times it is dark and dim, and then the heart of the spectator is troubled with its infinite suggestions of terror; but when the sun shines it is lit up with a myriad shifting hues, and brightened into beauty by an endless succession of rainbows.

No ancient or classical writer mentions these rapids. The first author who refers to them is the Florentine Poggio:—"The river," he says, "precipitates itself among the rocks with so much fury and so terrible a roar, that one might almost say it bewailed its fall."

They are thus described by Montaigne:—"Beneath Schaffhausen the Rhine encounters a hollow full of great rocks, where it breaks up into many streams, and further on, among these same rocks, it meets with a declivity about two pike-staves in height, where it makes a huge leap, foaming and roaring wildly. This arrests the progress of the boats, and interrupts the navigation of the river." In such cold and passionless language does the great essayist describe one of the most beautiful scenes in Europe!

Madame Roland is more enthusiastic:—"Figure to yourself," she says, "the river in all its majesty sweeping headlong like a sea of leaping foam; until the rocks, crowned with verdure, interrupt the course of its vast sheet of water, of this torrent of snow. The irritated river lashes its inclosing banks in furious wrath, undermines them, encroaches upon them, and multiplies its falls by the gaps it cleaves in them; it crashes down with a turmoil which spreads horror on every side, with which the whole valley re-echoes, and the shattered billows soar aloft in vapours richly adorned by shining rainbows."

Dr. Forbes speaks of the scene as being singularly impressive by moonlight. No sound is then heard but the one continuous roar of the water, softened by the distance, and seeming to fill the whole air, like the moonshine itself. There is something both wild and delightful in the hour and its accompaniments. The mind yields passively to the impressions made on the senses. A host of half-formed, vague, and visionary thoughts crowd into it at the same time, giving rise to feelings at once tender and pathetic, accompanied with a sort of objectless sympathy or yearning after something unknown. The ideas and emotions most definite and constant are those of Power and Perpetuity, Wonder and Awe.

But we must be careful to avoid exaggeration in our pictures of natural phenomena. The language in which some writers speak of the Falls of the Rhine is grotesque in its extravagance. Dr. Forbes honestly confesses that, after all, they impress the intellect much less than the feelings. The first view, in truth, is somewhat disappointing, particularly as to the dimensions of the Falls, both in breadth and height; and as you gaze, you feel a sort of critical calculating spirit rising within you; but this is speedily subdued by something in the inner mind above reasoning, and you are overpowered by a rush of conflicting emotions. Milton makes his Adam and Eve tell us that they "feel they are happier than they know:" the spectator of the Rhine Falls feels they are grander than he thinks.

For the convenience of the tourist we may add that the distance between Constanz and Schaffhausen is three posts and a quarter, or twenty-nine one-fourth English miles.

	Posts	Eng. Miles.
Constanz,		
Steckhorn,	1	1
Diessenhofen,	1⅜	12½
Schaffhausen,	⅞	7¾

From Constanz to Lauffen is three miles. The tourist can take the railway if he pleases, stopping at Dachsen station; or he may go down by boat, or travel by road.

DESCENT OF THE RHINE CONTINUED: SCHAFFHAUSEN TO BASEL.
(Railway from Schnjfhnusen.)

Schaffhausen to Waldshut, ...	29	miles
Waldshut to Lauffenburg, ...	9	"
Lauffenburg to Sackingen, ...	6	"
Sackingen to Kheinfelden, ...	10	"
Rheinfelden to Basel, ...	10	"
Total distance, ...	64	miles

We shall first pursue the right bank of the Rhine from Schaffhausen to Basel, and then, returning to Schaffhausen, follow up the left bank.

Below the Falls, the Rhine "nobly foams and flows" through a fertile and attractive country. At first it takes a southerly direction; then it strikes towards the west and north; and, after awhile, bends round with a southerly inclination. Here two narrow tongues of land confine the channel of the river, which is further impeded by a little islet. On one of these tongues, or peninsulas, stands the small town of Rheinau, belonging to the canton of Zurich; and on the island, connected with the mainland by a substantial stone bridge, stands the Benedictine abbey of the same name, conspicuous with its towers. It was founded in 778, and contains the marble tomb of its supposed founder, an Allemannic prince, named Wolfhard.

Just above Rheinau our river receives the Thur, and just below it the Toss. Neither rivulet contributes any great augmentation of volume. A more considerable tribute is furnished by the Aar, which flows into the Rhine opposite Waldshut, and near the little village of Coblence (Confluentia). The Aar rises in the two huge glaciers of the Ober and Unter-Aar Gletscher, near the Hospice of the Grimsel. The Unter-Aar glacier divides into two branches, the Lauter Aar and the Finster Aar; and from these the river draws its ice-cold emerald waters, which, swollen by their transit through various Swiss lakes, and by the junction of the Reuss and the Limmat, wind through valley and glen to feed the great German river.

It was near this point of junction, and on the deltoid tongue of land between the Aar and the Reuss, that the Romans raised their mighty fortress of Vindomissa, the most important settlement they had in Helvetia. Its name is preserved in the little modern village of Windisch, but notwithstanding the immense extent of the Roman settlement, which stretched twelve miles from north to south, its remains are inconsiderable. In the Bärlisgrube vestiges of an amphitheatre have been discovered, and on the road from Brauneck-berg to Königsfelden the ruins of an aqueduct.

When Christianity was introduced into Helvetia, Vindomissa became the seat of the first bishopric, which was afterwards removed to Constanz. In the third and fourth centuries the town was ravaged by the Vandals and Allemanni, and in the sixth it was destroyed by Childebert, king of the Franks.

Near its ancient site was erected the monastery of Königsfeld, and about two miles westward, on a wooded height, moulder the ruins of the castle of Habsburg or Habrichtsburg (Hawk's Castle), the cradle of the imperial house of Austria. The town of Bruegg, or Bruck, lies further to the south.

"Thus," as Gibbon says, "within the ancient walls of Vindomissa, the castle of Habsburg, the abbey of Königsfeld, and the town of Bruck have successively arisen." The philosophic traveller may compare the monuments of Roman conquests, of feudal or Austrian tyranny, of mediaeval monasticism, and of industrious freedom. "If he be truly a philosopher," says Gibbon, "he will applaud the merit and happiness of his own time."

If he be truly a philosopher, we may add, he will certainly contemplate with interest the ruined castle which witnessed the dawn of the fortunes of the Hapsburgs; of the great family—often defeated but never wholly crushed—who wore so long the imperial crown of Germany, the inheritance of Roman empire, and maintained for centuries so bitter a struggle with the rising Hohenzollerns for the retention of the imperial power. At last they seem to have been worsted in the fight, and the fatal field of Sadowa has handed over the supremacy of Germany to the Prussian dynasty.

The castle of Hapsburg was built by Werner, bishop of Strasburg, son of Kanzeline, count of Altenburg, early in the eleventh century. His successors increased their family inheritance by marriages, donations from the emperors, and by becoming prefects, advocates, or administrators of the neighbouring abbeys, towns, or districts. His great grandson, Albert III., was owner of ample territories in Suabia, Alsace, and that part of Switzerland which is now called the Aargau, and, moreover, held the landgraviate of Upper Alsace.

Albert's son, Rudolph, was the true founder of the family. The emperor bestowed upon him the town and district of Lauffenberg, and his astuteness and perseverance gained him great influence in Uri, Schwytz, and Unterwalden. Dying in 1232, his two sons, Albert and Rodolph, divided their inheritance. The former obtained Aargau and Alsace, with the castle of Hapsburg; the latter Cleggow, the Brisgau, and the counties of Rheinfelden and Lauffenberg. He fixed his residence in the latter city, and thus established the branch of Hapsburg-Lauffenberg.

Albert married Hedwige, daughter of Alice, countess of Baden, and by her had three sons, Rudolph, Albert, and Hartinau. The former, born in 1218, displayed a surprising sagacity and heroic prowess, and after a stirring career was elected emperor of Germany, and successor of the Caesars, in 1273.

From this point, as Dr. Bryce remarks, a new era begins in European history. In A.D. 800 the Roman empire was revived by a prince whose vast dominions gave ground to his claim of universal monarchy; it was again erected, in A.D. 962, on the narrower but firmer basis of the German kingdom. During the three following centuries Otto the Great and his successors, a line of monarchs of unrivalled vigour and abilities, strained every nerve to make good the pretensions of their office against the rebels in Italy and the ecclesiastical power. Those efforts failed signally and hopelessly. Each successive emperor continued the strife with resources scantier than his predecessors; each was more decisively vanquished by the pope, the cities, and the princes. Still, in the house of Hapsburg the Roman empire lived on 600 years more; and the crown of the Caesars and of Charlemagne and of Otto was transmitted from generation to generation of the descendants who sprang from the loins of Werner, the founder of the castle of Hapsburg.

That castle is now in ruins. The keep, tall, square, and built of rough stones, with walls eight feet in thickness, is the only portion entire. The view from its summit is justly described as both picturesque and interesting; picturesque from the variety it includes of wood, and savage glen, and mountain height, and rolling rivers; interesting, because it sweeps, as it were, over a wide historic field. Yonder lie the ruins of Vindomissa; yonder, those of Königsfelden: to the south rises the desolate keep of Braunegg, which formerly belonged to the sons of the tyrant Gessler; below it, in the quiet shades of Beir, Pestalozzi, the educational reformer, died and lies buried. But more; at a glance you take in the entire Swiss patrimony of the Hapsburgs—an estate inferior in size to that of many an English peer—from which Rudolph was called to wield the sceptre of Charlemagne. The house of Austria, 130 years later, were deprived by Papal ban of their ancient Swiss domains; but the ruined castle, the cradle of that house, was purchased not long ago by the present occupant of the Austrian throne.

The abbey of Königsfelden ("King'sfield") was founded in 1310 by the Empress Elizabeth and Agnes queen of Hungary, in memory of the murder of the husband of the one and the father of the other, the Emperor Albert, just two years previously. The convent, "a group of gloomy piles," was suppressed in 1528. Parts of it have been occupied successively as a farm-house, an hospital, and a lunatic asylum; a portion now serves as a magazine, but divine service is still celebrated in the choir. Other parts are falling rapidly into a decay which threatens to be irretrievable. There is much excellent painted glass in the church; and the visitor will not fail to gaze with compassionate interest on the sculptured stones which mark the last resting-places of a long train of knights and nobles slain in the fatal field of Sempach (1386)—Austria's "Sadowa" of the fourteenth century.

The high altar, it is said, indicates the spot where the Emperor Albert fell beneath the swords of his murderers.

The emperor at the time was preparing to lead a formidable army into Switzerland, with the view of suppressing the revolt which had broken out in the cantons of Uri, Schwytz, and Unterwalden. His nephew John, having attained his nineteenth year, had demanded the possession of his inheritance, which the emperor had seized during his minority. Angered by repeated denials, and instigated by some discontented nobles of Aargau and Kyburg, he entered into a conspiracy against his uncle with four confidential adherents of illustrious birth, namely, his governor, Walter von Eschenbach, Rudolph von. Wart, Rudolph von Balne, and Conrad von Tegelfeldt.

The emperor, accompanied by his family and a numerous train, among whom were the conspirators, set out on the road to Rheinfelden, where his consort, Elizabeth, had gathered a considerable force. As he rested at Baden for the purpose of refreshment, the young prince once more demanded to be installed in his estates and dignities; but Albert flung to him a wreath of flowers, observing that it better became his youthful years than the cares of government. Stung by the insulting jest, John burst into tears, threw the chaplet on the ground, and retired to concoct a scheme of immediate vengeance.

Arriving on the banks of the Reuss, opposite Windisch, the conspirators were the first to pass the ferry, and were followed by the emperor with a single attendant, his son Leopold and the remainder of the suite waiting on the other side of the river. As he rode slowly through the meadows which lay at the foot of the bold rock crowned by the frowning towers of Hapsburg, conversing familiarly with his nephew, he was suddenly attacked by the conspirators, one of whom seized the bridle of his horse. His nephew, exclaiming, "Will you now restore my inheritance?" wounded him in the neck with his lance. Balne ran him through with his sword, and Walter von Eschenbach clove his head at one tremendous blow. Wart, the other conspirator, stood aghast, unwilling at the last to share, yet afraid to prevent the terrible crime; the attendant fled, and the emperor, falling from his horse, lay weltering in his blood.

The atrocious deed was witnessed by his son Leopold and all his suite, but they were unable to cross the river in time to arrest the murderers. Their conduct, in truth, is inexplicable, for they left their dying master to breathe his last in the arms of a compassionate peasant woman, who chanced to appear on the scene.

"A peasant-girl that royal head upon her hosom laid,
And, shrinking not for woman's dread, the face of death survey'd:
Alone she sate. From hill and wood low sunk the mournful sun;
Fast gushed the fonnt of noble blood, Treason his worst had done.
With her long hair she vainly pressed the wounds to staunch their tide,
Unknown, on that meek humble breast, imperial Albert died."

—Mrs. Hemans.

Near the mouth of the Aar occur the rapids of the Rhine known as the "Little Lauffen." A ridge of rocks is thrown across like a weir; but a gap in the centre, eighteen feet wide, admits of the passage of small vessels. When the waters are high they overflow the ridge, and produce a miniature fall; when low, the rocks lie bare and exposed, and with the help of a plank you might cross the river dryshod from the Swiss bank to the Baden.

Swollen by the accession of the glacier-born Aar, onward flows the Rhine with a bold and impetuous current, passing Waldshut on the left, and near Lauffenberg executing another abrupt descent of about twenty feet. Here a bridge, 306 feet in length, connects Lauffenberg with Klein Lauffenberg; the two containing, perhaps, a population of 1000. On the hill above the former town are the ruins of the stronghold of the Lauffenberg branch of the Hapsburgs.

We pass onward to Rheinfelden, a picturesque place, with a pleasant, suggestive name. It has high hills at its back, and open meadows on either side, and a foaming river in its front; so that an artist will be glad to enshrine its principal features in the amber of his memory. And the archaeologist will be pleased to know that it occupies the site of the Roman station *Augusta Rauracorum*, which was founded by Munatius Plancus in the reign of Augustus, and destroyed by the Huns in 450; while the historian will recollect that Rheinfelden itself has many associations of storm and strife. Did it not stand on the debatable frontier-line of the Holy Roman empire, and was it not frequently fought for by contending armies? Especially was this the case in the Thirty Years' War, when the celebrated Lutheran leader, good Duke Bernard of Saxe Weimar, sheltered his battalions under its massive battlements and defeated Johann von Werth and the Catholic army. In 1744 it was captured and razed to the ground by the French, under Marshal Belleisle; but it contrived to raise its head again from the ashes, and its future safety was secured in 1801 by its annexation to neutralized Switzerland.

Its prosperity now depends upon its extensive salt-works, and on the visitors who seek relief in its saline baths from some of the many ills which "flesh is heir to."

It was in descending these rapids in a small boat that Lord Montague, the las', of his line, was drowned. On the same day his family mansion, Cowdray, in Sussex, was burned to the ground.

Here, almost in the centre of the river, lies a large mass of rock, precipitous on either side, but with a sufficiently level area on its summit for the erection of a strong fortress. This, we are told, is the celebrated "Stone of Rheinfelden;" anciently occupied by a formidable castle, but now by nothing more terrific than the house of a customs officer.

At this point occur the *Hollenhallen* rapids, where the seething and swirling river, and the rugged rocks, form a spectacle of singular and romantic interest.

Between Rheinfelden and Basel (Basle, or Bale), only two villages remain to be noticed, on the right bank of the Rhine, those of Basel-Augst and Kaiser-Augst. The Roman ruins in their vicinity mark the westward limits of the once wealthy and powerful Augusta Rauracorum. An encampment at Kaiser-Augst, of which some remains exist, was probably the outwork or advanced post, designed to protect the city from any sudden incursion of the turbulent Germans.

RIGHT BANK OF THE RHINE.

Returning to Schaffhausen, we cross to the right bank of the river, which is traversed by the Baden Railway, and proceed to indicate its points of interest as far as Basel.

The first town of importance is Eglisau, where the river is crossed by a timber bridge. The valley here is narrow but fertile, and blossoms with orchards and vineyards.

Opposite Eglisau the Glatt, which rises at the foot of the Almann, pays its tribute to the Rhine.

A broad rock, just below Kaiserstuhl (the ancient *Tribunal Caesaris*), is crowned by a graceful chateau, fancifully named Schwarz-Wassertels ("Black Water-Wagtail"). Weiss-Wassertels, on the Baden bank, is in ruins.

Waldshut, situated on the slope of the Black Forest, is a walled town, small but pleasant, with a population of 1200. It lies at a considerable elevation above the river, and commands some magnificent prospects, bright, varied, and romantic. It owes its foundation to Rudolph of Hapsburg; was unsuccesfully besieged by the Swiss in 1462; at the epoch of the Reformation became the headquarters of the Anabaptist leader, Balthasar Hubmeier; and on his flight was captured by the Austrians.

About two miles to the north is situated Höchenschward, 3314 feet above the sea-level, and the highest village in the Black Forest. It is unnecessary to say, that the tourist who climbs to this natural watch-tower will be able to satisfy himself with some of the finest pictures in all this romantic region. How grand they are may be inferred from the fact that a great part of the snow-covered chain of the Alps, with their bold peaks, like a combination of colossal spires, towers, and pyramids, sharply defined against the azure sky, may be seen from this point. For an Alpine panorama it can hardly be surpassed.

Passing the mouth of the Meng we arrive at Sückingen, a considerable town, traditionally celebrated as "the first seat of Christianity on the Upper Rhine." Here a chapel, monastery, and nunnery were founded by St. Fridolin in the seventh century. The bones of the saint are preserved in the ancient abbey-church, a quaint edifice distinguished by two towers.

Between Säckingen and Basel there is nothing to interest; but if we travel by rail we pass through a fertile country, and pause at the stations of Breunet, Rheinfelden, Wyhlen, and Grenzach. The Rhine here flows through a narrow but deep valley.

BASEL, BASLE, OR BALE.

Population, 45,000 (of whom 19,697 are Roman Catholics). Hotels: Three Kings, Schweizerhof, Cigogne, Sauvage, Couronne, Kopf, and Hôtel de la Poste. The Central Railway station is on the south side of the town; the Baden station in Klein (or Little) Basel, on the right bank of the river. Post and Telegraph offices in the Freien Strasse. English Church service in the church of St. Martin.

Basel is happily situated on the left bank of the Rhine, at an elevation above the sea of 730 feet, in an open and sunny plain, surrounded at a sufficient distance by verdurous hills and wooded mountain slopes. It is the point of junction of three very different countries— France, Germany, and Switzerland—a circumstance to which its proverbial wealth and prosperity are undoubtedly due; and of each it seems to exhibit some characteristic feature. It is connected with its suburb, Klein Basel, on the right bank of the river, by a wooden bridge 840 feet in length, which was originally constructed in 1285. Basel is the chief town of the old canton of the same name, and of the new canton of Bâle-Ville.

"The first thing which strikes the stranger on entering Basel," says Emile Souvestre, "is the expression of melancholy and solitude which everywhere encounters his eye. At the sound of carriage-wheels the shutters fly forward, the doors are closed, and the women hide themselves. All is dead and desolate. It looks like a town to let. You must not think, however, that the voluntary imprisonment of the good people of Basel denotes any want of curiosity; for they have found a means of satisfying both that and their primitive savageness. Mirrors fixed to hinges of iron, and skilfully arranged at the windows, enable them to descry, from the shades of their apartment, everything which transpires without, while sparing themselves the annoyance of being scrutinized in their turn.

"But if there is a certain gloom in the appearance of the streets of Basel, we must own that their cleanliness is exquisite. Every house looks as if it had been finished off last evening, and was waiting for its first tenant. Not a cranny, not a scratch, not a spot on all those oil-painted walls; not a crack in all those marvellously wrought railings which protect the lower windows. The summer benches, placed near the threshold, are carefully raised, and let into the wall, to shelter them from the sun and rain. If the street be on too abrupt a descent, hand-ropes, fixed to the walls, arrest the tottering steps of old age, or of the peasant, bowed beneath his heavy burden. Everywhere you meet with this minute thoughtfulness, this anxiety, this attention, which is that of the proprietor, and, at the same time, of the head of a family."

It is some years ago since this graceful sketch was written, and Basel, while retaining its cleanliness, has lost much of its sadness. Its hotels are conducted with as much vivacity and politeness as the best in France; its inhabitants are as frank and honourable as those of an unadulterated German town. There are few cities on the Rhine where an English tourist can more pleasantly spend a summer holiday.

Basel is the ancient Basilia, which is first mentioned by Ammianus Marcellinus in a passage of much perplexity to antiquaries. He speaks of a fortress, Robur, as erected near Basilia by the Emperor Valentinian I. The exact site of this ancient fortress is an archaeological puzzle which has had a strong attraction for many inquisitive Dryasdusts, but scarcely seems worth our formal discussion. When Robur disappeared we know not, but it is certain that Basilia, though not mentioned in any of the Itineraries, became a town of considerable importance; and after the ruin of Augusta Rauracorum it would seem to have been the chief town in this part of Switzerland (Rauracia). The episcopal seat was removed to it; an episcopal palace was erected; and houses rapidly sprang up in the shelter of the ecclesiastical power.

Though plundered by the Barbarians in the fourth and fifth centuries, and by the Huns in the tenth (A.D. 917), it rose on each occasion with renewed vigour. In 1032 it was transferred from the kingdom of Burgundy to the sovereignty of the Holy Roman Empire; but it still continued under the immediate control of its bishops, whom Charlemagne had elevated to the rank of *princeps aulae nostrae*. For this reason it ranked as a tree town, like Ratisbon or Worms, and never laboured under the incubus of a provincial governor. But as it waxed strong and wealthy it grew impatient even of episcopal jurisdiction, and from 1200 the efforts of its citizens to throw off the yoke were resolute and unceasing.

Meanwhile, churches, palaces, and convents had multiplied in the prosperous town. A cathedral was built, and richly endowed, by the Emperor Henry II. in 1010-1019. In 1061 it was the seat of a general council, where the anti-pope, Honorius II., was elected, and Henry IV. crowned by Roman ambassadors. To protect it from Rudolph of Suabia it was fortified with walls and ditches in 1080. In 1247, relying on its virtual independence, it joined the League of the Rhenish Towns.

In the thirteenth century its tranquillity was greatly disturbed by the quarrels of its patrician families, as was Florence by the feuds of Guelph and Ghibelline, and Rome by those of the Colonnas and Orsinis. The two great families of Schaler and Monche were accustomed to meet and carouse at the hostelry of the "Sigh," and as they carried a banner emblazoned with the figure of a parrot ("Psittich"), they were known as the Psitticher. Another company of knights and burghers held their revels at the "Fly," and bore a star as their emblem. All the town in due time was divided into two houses, like ancient Verona; and every inhabitant belonged to either the Stars or the Psitticher. The two factions were constantly engaged in open warfare, which became more serious still when Count Rudolph of Hapsburg and the bishops intervened in it; the former siding with the Stars, the latter with the Psitticher. Count Rudolph, assisted by the Stars, was laying siege to the town, when he received the news of his election as king of Rome. The siege was immediately raised; and the bishop threw open the gates of Basel without demur to the successor of Charlemagne. This prompt obedience led to the entire reconciliation of the two parties. The emperor frequently visited the faithful town, and both he and his successors endowed it with many privileges. The wife and two of the sons of Rudolph were interred in the cathedral.

The history of Basel is curious in many respects, and especially in the illustrations it affords of the surprising vitality of a great town. Its tenacity of life was truly wonderful. In 1312 it was literally desolated by the "Black Death," which carried off on this one occasion 14,000 persons; and each time that it visited Basel, which it too frequently did during the next three centuries, it was not satisfied except it counted its victims by tens of hundreds. In 1356, on the 18th of October, the town was overwhelmed in ruins by a terrible shock of earthquake. Not a tower or spire escaped, and scarcely one hundred houses, while upwards of 300 lives were lost, and the whole neighbourhood, for miles around, was fearfully ravaged. Yet it survived these disasters. In a few years it was populous and prosperous again. It rebuilt its cathedral, reared anew its churches and public edifices, purchased the village of Klein Basel, on the opposite bank of the river, and the lordships of Liestal, Waldenburg, and Homburg.

Meantime its burghers grew more and more sensible of their power. They defied Austria, and they defied the church. The patricians retaining some privileges dangerous to the commonwealth, they were summarily deprived of them; and the clergy launching the bolts of excommunication, were bidden to sing and pray, or remove themselves from the town. They entered into a confederacy with other cities, and surrounded their own with new walls. They were active in trade and commerce, encouraged mechanics, and established the first paper mills of Germany.

The great (Ecumenical Council of Basel was held from 1431 to 1438. It commenced on the 14th of December, 1431, and consisted of eleven cardinals, three patriarchs, twelve archbishops, one hundred and ten bishops, six temporal princes, and a large number of doctors, besides ambassadors from England, Scotland, France, Arragon, Portugal, Sicily, and Denmark, from the princes, cities, and universities of Germany. It was presided over by the emperor, who submitted for the consideration of the Fathers the all-important question of the marriage of the clergy. John of Lubeck, says Milman, was authorized to demand in the emperor's name, the abrogation of celibacy. John of Lubeck is described as a man of wit, who jested on every occasion. But on this subject jesting was impossible; it was of a nature so grave and important that a serious treatment of it was imperative. The celibacy of the clergy is practically so interwoven with the framework of Catholicism, that the question of abandoning the system could not be expected even by its advocates to obtain from the council a unanimous response to it. It furnished, indeed, the subject of no small debate, and facts and reasons, for and against it, were urged and rebutted by the spokesmen in the council, in accordance with the views which reflection and observation had led them to espouse. The Greek Church, it was urged, admitted marriage. The priests of the Old and New Testaments were married. It is said that the greater part of the council were favourable to the change; but the question, as unsuited to the time, was "eluded, postponed, and dropped."

The most important act of the council was the deposition of Pope Eugenius IV., and the election of Duke Amadeus of Savoy, under the title of Félix V. (1440). In the interval Basel was again visited by the Black Death. The mortality was terrible. The ordinary cemeteries were wholly insufficient; huge charnel-pits were dug to receive the dead. The Fathers, however, stood nobly to their post, and refused to quit the blighted and sorrowing city. When the plague passed the pope was solemnly crowned at Basel, his two sons, the duke of Savoy and the count of Geneva (an unusual spectacle at a papal inauguration), standing by his side; 50,000 persons were witnesses of the magnificent ceremony. The train worn by the new duke-pope was of surpassing splendour, and worth, it is said, 30,000 crowns.

After this event the influence of the council gradually declined, and they had the good sense to consummate their own dissolution, at the instigation of Æneas Sylvius Piccolomini, afterwards Pius II. He officiated as secretary to the council, and has left on record a graphic description of the coronation of Félix V. He speaks in enthusiastic terms of the pope's gravity, majesty, and ecclesiastical demeanour; "the demeanour of him who had been called of God to the rule of his universal church." Of the 50,000 spectators many, he says, wept for joy; all were excited. Nor does Æneas forget his own part in the ceremonial. "The cardinal of Santa Susanna chanted the service; the responses were given by the advocates and notaries in such a dissonant bray that the congregation burst into roars of laughter. They were heartily ashamed of themselves. But the next day, when the preachers were to make the responses, Æneas, though quite ignorant of music (which requires long study), sung out his part with unblushing courage (*cantilare meum carmen non erubui*). Æneas does not forget the tiara with 30,000 pieces of gold, the processions, the supper or dinner to 1000 guests. He is as full and minute as a herald, manifestly triumphing in the ceremonial as equalling the magnificence, as well as imitating to the smallest point, that of Rome."

In 1444, on the 26th of August, the battle of St. Jacob was fought beneath the walls of Basel; and 1400 Swiss, who had hastened to protect the city from the Armagnacs, were slain after a desperate defence of ten hours against 30,000 enemies.

In 1460 Pope Pius II. granted Basel a bull for the foundation of an university, which was solemnly opened in the same year, and rapidly rose into high repute. In 1501 the thriving, busy, opulent, learned city, was received as a member into the Swiss confederacy. No sooner was the treaty of alliance signed than the good burghers of Basel immediately threw open their gates. Hitherto, the dangers to which they had been incessantly exposed from the neighbouring nobility, had not only compelled the citizens to guard them day and night, but also to keep them constantly closed. From this date, instead of an armed guard, they stationed there a single woman with a distaff to levy the toll.

In the early part of the sixteenth century Basel reached the climax of its prosperity, and its fame as a centre of learning spread over all Europe. It was the rendezvous of men of science and letters, the gathering place of a host of scholars, empirics, professors, physicians, philosophers, and fools. Not one of the least famous was that singular character, half-impostor, half-philosopher, Aureolus Philippus Theophrastus Paracelsus. He was not a native of Basel, he had not studied at its university, but on his arrival there was warmly welcomed. For the learned of that age formed a compact, freemason-like guild, whose sympathies were not with the world, and whom the world hated as well as feared. At first, therefore, the much-travelled philosopher, who shook off the dust of Italy and Denmark, Hungary and Muscovy, at the gates of Basel; who had visited the rose gardens of Persia, fallen a prisoner to the Tartars, and been despatched by their Cham on a mission to

Constantinople, was well received by the Illuminati of Basel. But Paracelsus was a man of original intellect and aggressive character. Almost immediately on his arrival he provoked the jealousy of his brothers in science by a bold stroke of medical practice. The celebrated printer of Basel, Jacob Froben, had long suffered from an intense pain in the right foot, which not all the doctors of Basel could relieve, and which permitted its victim neither to eat nor sleep. He summoned to his aid this new physician as a last desperate chance; for as Paracelsus boasted that he had turned over the leaves of Europe, Asia, and Africa, it might reasonably be supposed that he had gathered some useful hints out of so vast a volume.

Paracelsus obeyed the summons, prescribed fomentations, and administered a specific which he had brought back from the East in the shape of three black pills (*tres pilulas nigras*); the said specific being opium, previously unknown in Europe. The printer quickly tasted that luxury of repose which had so long been denied to him. Sleep restored strength and energy to worn-out nature. He speedily recovered, and everywhere sounded the praises of his able physician, who was soon afterwards unanimously elected to the chair of medicine at the Basel University (A.D. 1526).

As a professor, Paracelsus attained the very summit of popularity, and from all parts of Christendom students flocked to attend his lectures. They were characterized by much originality, no little talent, an unconscionable amount of self-praise, and an uncompromising denunciation of all other teachers but himself. "There is more knowledge," he would say, "in my shoe-strings than in the writings of all the physicians who have preceded me! I am the great reformer of medical science. You must all adopt my new and original system—you, Avicenna, Galen, Rhazes, Montagnana, Miseri; you must and shall follow me, gentlemen of Paris, of Montpelier, of Vienna, and Köln! All you who dwell on the banks of the Rhine or the Danube, who inhabit the islands of the seas—you, too, Italians, Turks, Sarmatians, Greeks, Arabs, Jews—you shall follow me! If you do not freely enlist under my banner, it is because you are but as the stones which the very dogs defile! Rally, then, to me as your leader; for the kingdom shall be mine, and sooner or later you must swallow the bitter draught of obedience!"

Then the splendid charlatan brought forward a vase of fire, upon which he flung handfuls of nitre and sulphur. And as the lurid flames shot upwards, he flung into them the ponderous tomes of Galen and Avicenna, and while his audience gazed in astonishment at this novel act of incremation, he exclaimed:—"Thus, ye doctors, shall ye burn in everlasting fire! Get thee behind me, Sathanas! Get ye behind me, Greek, Latin, Arab! ye have taught nothing but absurdities; the secret of nature is known only to myself!"

It is no wonder that the cordiality with which Paracelsus had been received by the learned of Basel, was soon replaced by jealousy, suspicion, and dislike. It may be that his ability and success, quite as much as his ostentatious vanity, worked his downfall; but it must be owned that his mode of life, intemperate and licentious, was calculated to disgust his friends and embolden his enemies. His pupil, Oporinus, says of him, that he never put off his clothes at night for the two years he was with him, but with his sword hanging by his side, would fling himself on his bed, filled with wine, towards the hour of dawn. And in the darkness of night he would start up suddenly, and deal blows all around him with his naked sword; now striking the floor, the bed, the doorposts, and striking so furiously that Oporinus often trembled lest he should be unwittingly decapitated.

Meanwhile he effected numerous cures, and, at length, one of so brilliant a description that it ought to have consummated his fortune. Unhappily, it cut short his career at Basel.

One of the canons residentiary lay, as was supposed, at the point of death. In his extremity he had recourse to Paracelsus, promising him a splendid recompense if his treatment should be successful. Paracelsus, like Caesar, *venit, vidit, vicit*. He administered his favourite specific, and the canon recovered. But with a shameful ingratitude he then refused to fulfil his contract, asserting that his illness could not have been serious if it could be so easily cured. Paracelsus summoned him before the magistrates, but they decided that the patient could only be required to pay the usual fee. In a tempest of rage the discomfited philosopher poured out his indignation on the heads of the purveyors of the law, and the next morning secretly quitted Basel to avoid being thrown into prison.

A man of greater eminence, the celebrated Erasmus, whose work in promoting the Reformation was scarcely inferior to that of Luther himself, lodged with the printer Froben, in the house "Zum Luft," from 1521 to 1529, and again in 1536, in which year he expired at Basel. It was here he undertook and carried out his "enormous labour" of editing and translating selections from the writings of the Fathers. While the art of printing was young, the New Testament was little known by the body of the people; all that they knew of the Gospels and the Epistles were the passages more immediately connected with the services of the church. Erasmus published the text, and with it a series of paraphrases containing bold innovations on the system of doctrine which had previously been maintained, and thus subjected himself to the censures of the ecclesiastical authorities. Erasmus, however, had little of the spirit of the martyr. He courted fame; but he held not his opinions with such earnestness as to prompt him to expose himself to suffering for their sake, and, indeed, was not fully trusted by either Catholics or Lutherans.

It should be noted that this was the earliest published New Testament, and the printing press of Basel had the honour of giving it to the world.

Here, too, appeared, in 1524, his "Colloquies," a book of keen and lively satire, in which he ridiculed many of the tenets and observances of the Romish Church. Here he made his attack on Luther, in his treatise "De Libero Arbitrio" (on Free Will), which led to a controversy between them; indeed, he went so far as to write to the elector of Saxony, urging bun to punish Luther for his opinions. In 1529 he left Basel and retired to Freiberg in the Brisgau; but the quiet and learned city on the Rhine, with its literary circle and university and printing-office, had an overmastering attraction for him, and he returned to it in August, 1535.

His edition of "Ecclesiastes" was printed at Basel, and here he commenced his edition of Origen. Confined to his house by an attack of gout, he employed his leisure in writing a commentary on the 15th Psalm, "De Puritate Tabernaculi." It was the last effort of his clear and vigorous intellect. An attack of dysentery brought him to the verge of the grave, and he prepared to meet his end with firmness. Without absolution or extreme unction, or any sacerdotal ceremonies, but with the words "Lieber Gott" on his lips, he died, on the 12th of

July, 1636, at the age of seventy. He was buried with great pomp in the cathedral, where his tomb is as a sacred shrine to every lover of learning.

A contemporary of Erasmus, and a man whose fame is inseparably associated with Basel, Hans Holbein the younger, deserves a longer notice than our limited space permits us to dedicate to his memory. Whether he was born at Basel is uncertain; most probably his birth-place was Augsburg; but he must have come to this city at a very early age, as his father was engaged in decorating its town-house in 1499, and the year of Hans' birth is invariably stated to have been 1498. His great artistic capacity showed itself in his youth, and at fourteen he painted two admirable portraits of his father and himself. About 1523 he became acquainted with Erasmus, whose portrait he painted, and for whose works he executed many splendid wood-engravings. The scholar recommended him to visit England, and thither the artist repaired in 1526, with a letter of introduction to Sir Thomas More, who welcomed him with the most delicate and generous kindness. The chancellor having embellished his apartments with Holbein's pictures, became anxious to introduce him to Henry VIII. in the manner best adapted to secure the royal favour and protection. Accordingly, he arranged his pictures in the most advantageous order in the great hall, and invited the king to an entertainment. When the latter entered, he was delighted with the excellence of the artist's works, and so warmly expressed his admiration that Sir Thomas begged him to accept of the one he most affected. But the king inquired anxiously after the artist, and when the latter was introduced, received him graciously, observing, "that now he had got the painter, Sir Thomas might keep his pictures." Holbein died in England in 1554, of the plague.

Some of the houses were formerly adorned with his frescoes, but these were unhappily destroyed when the edifices were rebuilt. A well-known anecdote is related in connection with a painting which formerly "glorified" the house of an apothecary in the Fishmarket. When Holbein was employed upon this task it was summer time, and the days were so hot that he found himself compelled to resort very frequently to the "Flower" inn. A merry company of roysterers was wont to assemble there, and a shady room with a bottle of sparkling wine, to say nothing of lively jest and joyous song, proved so much more attractive than a hot scaffolding, that Master Hans spent almost the whole day at the hostelry. His employer remonstrated with him for his idleness:—"I do not pay you to drink," he said, "but to paint my house. You must leave off revelling and drinking, or I will have none of you." The artist promised amendment, and thenceforth, whenever the owner of tire house took up his watch, he found Hans Holbein at work. But alas, on one occasion after convincing himself of the painter's diligence, he chanced to cross over to the tavern. What was his surprise to find him seated at the table with his glass and his long pipe! Hastily returning home and ascending the scaffold, he found that what he had supposed to be Holbein was only *a pair of legs* which he had painted with the most wonderful exactness to imitate the real limbs.

It is said that Holbein's wife was a shrew, and that he went to England, not so much to please his friend Erasmus, as to escape her vixenish tongue. But as Mrs. Jameson remarks, those who look upon the portraits of Holbein and his wife at Hampton Court, will reasonably doubt whether the former black-whiskered, bull-necked, resolute, almost fierce-looking personage could have had much to endure, or would have permitted much, from the poor broken-spirited and meek-visaged woman opposite to him, and will give the story a different interpretation.

Among the mediaeval celebrities of the old city we may mention John Wessel; Sebastian Brunel; the scholar and reformer Reuchlin, who taught Latin and Greek at Basel from 1474 to 1478; and Johannes Hussgen, or Œcolampadius, one of the supporters of the Reformation. The latter was born at Weinsburg in 1482. His father was a merchant in moderate circumstances, who destined him for his own vocation; but his mother, a woman of energy and talent, recognizing the abundant promise of her son's childhood, succeeded in obtaining for him the boon of a superior education. He learned Latin in the grammar-school of Heilbronn; studied law in the university of Bologna; but not liking the law, betook himself to Heidelburg in 1499, where he studied theology and the *literae humaniores*, acquiring such a reputation for scholarship that the Elector Palatine Philip appointed him tutor to his son. His heart, however, was in his theological studies, and returning to Weinsburg, he entered zealously and perseveringly on the duties of a parish priest. His sermons on the "Seven Words of the Cross," published in 1512, are remarkable for their earnestness, and show that his energies were all enlisted in his Master's service.

To improve his knowledge of Greek he visited Tubingen and Stuttgard, availing himself of the lessons of Melanchthon at the one place, and of those of Reuchlin at the other, and imbibing from both a strong sympathy with the scheme of doctrine proclaimed by Luther. In 1519 we find him studying Hebrew at Heidelburg; and soon afterwards the bishop of Basel invited him to become a preacher in its cathedral. There he made the acquaintance of Erasmus—whom he assisted to prepare his edition of the "New Testament"—and of the other men of letters who, in the first half of the sixteenth century, shed so great a lustre upon the ancient Swiss city.

In 1519 he published some writings of a decided Lutheran tendency; but the doubts which possessed him were so strong, and the struggle between the traditions of his youth and the new sympathies which had risen in his mind became so violent, that he suddenly took refuge in a monastery near Augsburg in 1520. Carrying on his studies in tranquillity, his views gradually underwent such a change that he resolved to abandon the church with which he had hitherto been connected; and returning to Basel openly appeared as a teacher of the doctrines of the Reformation. Having been appointed by the municipality in 1523 to a lectureship in the university on biblical criticism, he chose the prophecies of Isaiah for his theme, and denounced the doctrines of Romanism with a degree of vehemence which had a stirring effect on the minds of the citizens. It is needless to trace any further his career; the work which he had set himself to do, he did uncompromisingly. In 1529 the Reformation was formally adopted in Basel, and two years later he closed in peace a life of unceasing labour.

Basel, however, was slow in the adoption of new ideas and new practices; and, as Mr Mayhew remarks, it stoutly resisted, throughout the Middle Ages, every attempted innovation in the manners and customs of its citizens. It was called in these days "the reverend city of Basel," and its councillors were honoured with the title of "the noble, dread, pious, resolute, prudent, wise, and honourable lords." Whether they always deserved these epithets may reasonably be doubted; assuredly they could not often be applied to the members of municipalities nearer home! They were so "resolute" in the maintenance of their dignities, that in 1501 the council issued a decree, declaring, that if it so happened that, either through scorn or through envy, any person should curtail their civic title in any manner whatsoever, and neglect to address them as their ancestors had been always addressed, every letter and message would be incontinently dismissed without receiving the slightest notice.

Even as late as the end of the last century, it was the custom in the city of Basel for the clocks to be set one hour in advance of all others in Europe. Tradition explains this practice by ascribing the deliverance of the town from a conspiracy to surrender it to the enemy at midnight, to the circumstance that the minster clock struck one instead of twelve. We do not ask the reader to accept this tradition as authentic; but to the practice, at all events, the citizens clung so pertinaciously, that when in 1778 the "noble, dread, pious, resolute, prudent, wise, and honourable lords" of the corporation issued an edict to the effect that all the clocks of Basel should, after the 1st day of January next ensuing, be regulated by solar time, the alteration was so unfavourably received, that the town council was compelled, a fortnight afterwards, to issue a second decree repealing the first. And the clocks of Basel were kept one hour before the sun until the present century began.

After the Reformation, a singular rigidity of spirit took possession of the town, which became as violently fanatical as the straitest of Scotch sects during the most flourishing times of Calvinistic supremacy. The burgomasters regulated the dress and viands of their fellow-citizens by the severest sumptuary edicts, and enforced upon all a sober economy in table and wardrobe. They would not allow women to have their hair dressed by males, nor a dinner-party to take place whose bill of fare had not been revised by the civic authorities. All persons going to church were compelled to wear black; and no carriage was allowed to pass through the gates during Sunday morning service—a rule still enforced, or at all events enforced down to a very recent period.

This rigid devotion is too frequently unaccompanied by a spirit of Christian charity; and Mr. Mayhew points out that for years a violent feud prevailed between the two quarters of the town—Basel east and Basel west, Klein Basel and Grosse Basel. A curious memorial of this antipathy existed in the image called *Lallen König*, or the "Stuttering King." A tower on the left bank of the Rhine was so situated as to command the bridge which connects the two towns. Here, near the summit, was placed a clock, with a giant's head skilfully carved in wood projecting from the wall above. A long tongue was thrust from the open mouth of this monstrous figure at every beat of the pendulum, and made to roll about derisively in the face of the people of the Klein Stadt on the opposite bank. To avenge this insult, the people of Klein Basel also set up a wooden image at their end of the bridge: a huge carved dummy, which turned its back on the Lallen Konig in a manner more significant than graceful. This singular specimen of local humour was not removed until 1830.

The later history of Basel does not present many features of interest. Yet in 1795 the Lutheran city was associated with an event which the tragic drama that has recently passed before our eyes renders peculiarly significant. The coalition which had been formed against revolutionary France had been shaken to its foundation by the vast successes of her arms; and Prussia, deserting her allies, opened conferences at Basel with the representatives of the French government, and in January, 1795, concluded a peace. It was a fatal step on the part of Prussia, and opened the way to those changes in Europe which brought humiliation and disaster on her head. By signing the treaty of Basel, says Prince Hendenberg, the Prussian king abandoned the house of Orange, sacrificed Holland, and laid open the empire to French invasion. Accident alone prevented the treaty of Basel from being followed by a general revolution in Europe.

Had Frederick William possessed the genius and resolution of Frederick the Great, he would have protected Holland against the arms of France, and included it in the line of military defence of Prussia.

By the treaty of Basel he entered upon a policy of neutrality, which alienated from Prussia every European power, so that when she was compelled to descend into the arena to fight for her national existence she fought alone, and was prostrated on the field of Jena. Eighty years have passed away, and Jena is at length avenged. In 1795 Prussia concluded with a French Republic a peace which involved her in dishonour and disgrace; in 1871 she may again be called upon to sign a treaty with another French Republic, but on this occasion, under very different conditions, and with very different aims. The next treaty at Paris, under whatever form of government, will rest on other principles than those of the treaty of Basel in 1795.

In 1830 the democratic spirit of the second French Revolution made itself felt in Basel, and fierce and even sanguinary struggles took place between the peasantry who adhered to the old constitution, and the townsmen, who sought to establish a socialistic and communistic republic. The townsmen having been defeated near the village of Prattelen, on the 3rd of August, 1833, Basel was occupied by Federal troops for eleven weeks, and until the peace of the town was fully insured. The result was the division of the canton of Basel into two independent cantons, Basel-town and Basel-country; the former retaining only three communes, or rural districts, on the right bank of the Rhine. Each canton has its separate constitution.

In addition to the literary worthies already mentioned, Basel can boast of an ecclesiastical historian of great merit, Karl Rudolf Hagenbach, born in 1801, and of two illustrious mathematicians, Leonard Euler and John Bernoulli. It is worth noting that the latter came of a family which produced, in all, eight distinguished mathematicians. The first of the series was James Bernoulli, 1654-1705, professor of mathematics in the university of Basel. His brother was the celebrated John Bernoulli, born at Basel in 1667; he was the friend and correspondent of Leibnitz: died in 1748. Nicholas, the nephew of the two brothers, was born at Basel in 1687, and died in 1759. Another Nicholas, the eldest son of John, born in 1695, was not only an eminent mathematician, but an able jurist and an expert linguist; he died in 1726. Daniel, the second son of John, and the most distinguished of the family, was born at Groningen, but he was educated at Basel, did the best of his work at Basel, and died at Basel in 1782.

John, the third and youngest son of John Bernoulli, succeeded his father as professor of mathematics at Basel, and held that position until his death, in his eighty-first year, in July, 1790. He was a foreign associate of the French Academy of Sciences; and it should be noted, that from the election of his father and uncle to that body in 1699, to his own death in 1790, the name of Bernoulli continued in the list of members for one and ninety years.

John, elder son of the foregoing, born in 1744, worthily maintained the reputation of this remarkable family. He obtained the degree of doctor of philosophy at the age of thirteen; and at nineteen was appointed astronomer-royal at Berlin. He died in 1807.

We close this extraordinary list, which affords so strong a proof of Mr. Galton's theory of hereditary genius, with James Bernoulli, brother of the preceding, who was born at Basel in 1759, and died at the premature age of thirty, in 1789.

Thus much have we thought it necessary to say of the historical associations and literary glories of Basel. Now,

> "Let us satisfy our eyes
> With the memorials and things of fame
> That do renown this city."

Foremost amongst these stands the Cathedral or Münster, the former cathedral-church of the bishopric of Basel. It is built of red sandstone, with two towers, one 200, the other 205 feet high; and though not magnificent in aspect, nor chaste in style, is eminently picturesque, and pleases, if it docs not promptly attract, the spectator's eye. It was begun in 1010 by the Emperor Henry; consecrated in 1019; greatly injured by fire in 1185; almost destroyed by an earthquake in 1356; rebuilt immediately, and completed to the very top of the towers in 1500. Its architecture is a mixture of the Romanesque and Pointed styles, the latter prevailing. The interior was restored in 1859, and restored with much care; though the zealous archaeologist will, perhaps, regret that the chisel was so freely used. Externally, the most striking features are the porch of St. Gallus, in the north transept (thirteenth century), with its curious, very curious, statues of Christ, John the Baptist, the Evangelists, and the Ten Virgins; and the western part, with its tower and carving, and its figures of the Virgin and Holy child; the emperor Henry I. (or Conrad II.?); the empress (Helena or Cunigunda?), and their two daughters; and the equestrian statues of St. Martin and St. George.

Within, the objects of interest are not very numerous, but the artist may find some entertainment in studying the fantastic masks which terminate the corbels. The stone pulpit, dating from the fifteenth century, is also worth examination; the font (1465) is curious; and he must not omit to notice the four columns of the choir, which are formed of groups of detached pillars. Observe, too, the tomb of the Empress Anne (1281), wife of Rudolph of Hapsburg, from whom the imperial house of Austria sprang; and that of Erasmus (dated 1536), in red marble. The stone carvings inserted in the wall are peculiarly mediaeval in character.

The windows are filled with modern stained glass, which lacks depth and delicacy of colour.

A staircase leading out of the choir conducts us to the chapter-house, or Concilium's Saal, a small low Gothic chamber, with four windows, which remains in the same condition as when the Council of Basel held some of its seances here, between 1436 and 1444. Two clepsydra;, or water-clocks, which the princes and prelates will often have gazed upon during the tedious harangue of some merciless orator, are still suspended to the wall; and the room also contains several plaster casts, more or less interesting, the famous Lallen König (removed here in 1837), some pieces of mediaeval furniture reported to have belonged to Erasmus, a few quaint old chests, and the six remaining fresco fragments of the original "Dance of Death" (Danse Macabre), which once enriched the walls of the Dominican church, and a set of coloured drawings of the whole series of figures.

From the researches made by certain archaeologists it seems evident that the custom of painting on the walls of the cloisters and churches a succession of images illustrative of Death wheeling away in a mad wild dance persons of all "sorts and conditions," existed before the fourteenth century. Some authorities are of opinion that the idea of these paintings was suggested by the puppet-shows; others, by the terrible depopulation of Europe through the frequent visitations of the plague. Fabricius asserts that they received the name of the "Danse Macabre" from the poet Macaber, who was the first to treat this fantastic subject in some German verses, translated into Latin by Desrey de Troyes, in 1460. The Latin version is still frequently reprinted, with the blocks of the ancient woodcuts, under the title of "La grande Danse Macabre des Hommes et des Femmes." The "Dance of the Dead" at Basel was painted, it is said, by order of the council, to commemorate the mortality occasioned by a pestilence in 1439.

As the elder D'Israeli observes, the prevailing character of all these works is unquestionably grotesque and ludicrous; not, indeed, that genius, however barbarous, could refrain in so large a picture of human life from inventing scenes often characterized by great delicacy of feeling and depth of pathos. Such, says D'Israeli, is the newly-married couple, whom Death is leading, beating a drum, and in the rapture of the hour the bride seems with a melancholy look not insensible of his presence; a Death is seen issuing from the cottage of the widow with her youngest child, who waves his hand sorrowfully, while the mother and the sister vainly answer; or the old man, to whom Death is playing on a psaltery, seems anxious that his withered fingers should once more touch the strings, while he is carried off in calm tranquillity.

The majority of the subjects, however, are purely ludicrous, and could only awaken risible emotions in the minds of their spectators. There is no question of teaching or impressing; they amuse, and nothing more. What was their object? To excite a contempt of death? We think not. Life was but little valued in the middle ages, for the conditions under which the millions lived were so harsh and rigid, that the grave must have appeared to them in the light of a place of blessed repose and felicity. We believe that these Dances of Death, like so many of the carved caricatures in church and cathedral, were a kind of protest on the part of the weak against the strong; the silent yet significant satire by which the oppressed avenged themselves on the oppressors. They seem to say, "You lord over us now; you are our masters and tyrants; but see you the Master and Tyrant in whose presence you will be as powerless as we are?" It is in the same spirit that the old French poet, Jacques Jacques of Ambrun, represents Death as proclaiming triumphantly the universality of his dominion:—

> "Egalement je vay regneant,
> Le counseiller et le sergeant,
> Le gentilhomme et le berger,
> Le bourgeois et le boulanger,
> Et la maistresse et la servante,
> Etla mère comme la tante;
> Monsieur l'abbé, monsieur son moine,
> Le petit clerc et le chanoine;
> Sans choix je mets dans mon butin
> Maistre Claude, maistre Martin,
> Dame Luce, dame Perrette," &c., &c.

The cloisters, in whose sacred shades Erasmus probably may have often walked and meditated, were erected in the fourteenth and fifteenth centuries (1332, 1400, and 1487). They extend to the brow of the hill overlooking the river, and to those who are fond of "meditations among the tombs" offer a very agreeable retreat. The monuments of three of the Reformers deserve a passing notice: Œcolampadius, who died in 1531, Mayer, and Grynaeus, who also died in 1531.

Behind the cathedral extends the terrace called the Pfalz. It is seventy feet above the river, and planted with chestnut trees, which in the May month hang the entire walk with blossom. The view which it opens up is very picturesque and extensive, including the broad sweep of the Rhine, the roofs and towers of the city, and the green slopes of the hills of the Black Forest.

From the remains of ancient walls and other ruins discovered in 1786 and 1836, it has been conjectured that the Minster stands within the area of the old Roman fortress of Robur or Basilia. Here, in an open space, is erected a monument to the reformer Œcolampadius. In one corner of the square stands a building called "Zur Mücke," of which nothing more need be said than that it was the meeting place of the conclave which, in 1436, converted Duke Amadeus into Pope Félix V.

Before proceeding further, we may as well glance at the other churches of Basel, none of which are characterized by any remarkable architectural beauty. In that of St. Martin, Œcolampadius preached the doctrines of the Reformation, addressing his hearers in their native German. In St. Peter's, restored in 1851, are the tombs of many of the Basel worthies, Zeillenden, Offenburg, Seevogel, Froben, and Bernoulli. St. Elizabeth's is a new and spacious edifice, erected within the last twenty years at the cost of an opulent citizen.

Passing into the streets, which are remarkable for their tall, narrow, and vari-coloured houses, we direct our steps towards the *Spahlen Thor* (unless, indeed, the spirit of iconoclasm abroad in Basel shall have accomplished its destruction), a narrow square tower, with two turrets and a pointed roof. The exterior of the gateway is adorned with a good statue of the Holy Virgin, to which the Catholic peasantry of the neighbourhood ascribe a peculiar sanctity, and certain traditional wonder-working powers. When the reformers attempted to destroy it, she struck her assailants dead with her sceptre of stone.

Under the scalloped cornice of the barbican, which covers the entrance to the town, a row of quaint little figures demands and deserves examination. "What a queer fancy must have been his who sculptured them! The Fischmarkt Brunnen, or "Fishmarket Fountain," which has been recently restored, is a graceful little structure, dating from the early part of the fifteenth century. We find a description of it done to our hand; it consists, says a recent writer, of a kind of telescopic prism-shaft, ornamented with fretted Gothic canopies for the statues which enrich its sides. The sculpture is excellent; the pinnacles canopying the figures are of the most delicate open tracery-work, and the little notched spire at the top of the column is crested with a miniature golden angel, so that the details are exquisitely varied, and the effect of the whole is as light and graceful as the lines formed by the glancing and shining water.

As we are not writing a guide-book, but simply endeavouring to seize the salient features of each place that interests us, we shall pass over unnoticed the new hospital, the new fountain, near the said hospital, the summer casino, customs-house and post-office, the missionary institute, and the botanical garden. With all these cannot the reader become acquainted in the pages of Baedeker, Murray, and Joanne?

But let us not be forgetful of the Spahlen Brunnen. Its sculptured figures are most felicitous. They were designed, it is said, by Albert Dürer, and represent the *Dudelsackpfeiffer*, or bagpiper, playing to a group of dancing peasants.

In the house "Zum Seidenhof" lodged strong-handed Rudolph of Hapsburg when he first visited Basel as emperor; his statue is shown there. That of "Zum Luft" was the dwelling-place of Erasmus, and the printing-office of Fröben; let every lover of letters reverently doff his cap as he passes by it. In the Burkhard'sche (formerly Ochsische), the treaty of peace was signed in 1795 between Prussia and France. And in the house This'sche, near St. John's Gate, the duchess of Angoulême was exchanged, in 1795, for certain members of the National Convention. The "Hôtel of the Three Kings" has been so called, it is said, since the year 1026, when the Emperor Conrad II., his son and chosen successor Henry III., and Rudolph of Burgundy, met under its ancient roof.

In the Arsenal is a small but not particularly valuable collection of arms and armour. The only thing of interest is the coat of mail worn by Charles the Bold at the battle of Burgundy.

We have dwelt at some length on the history and historical buildings of Basel, but we have yet to notice, before resuming our voyage, the New Museum, the Rathhaus, and the University.

The Museum, which contains all the art-treasures and science-treasures formerly scattered over various collections, is situated in the street of the Augustines. It contains at least seven different departments. As lovers of art we shall first visit the Museum, properly so called; that is, the Kunstammberg, which is under the direction of Herr Wackernagel.

The frescoes in the Entrance Hall are by Cornelius, designed for the church of St. Louis, at Merneil.

In the Vestibule are the paintings of Holbein, to which we have already alluded.

We next enter the Salle des Dessins, where, besides etchings and engravings by Brant and Jacques Callot, we may see some eighty-six pen and ink sketches by the immortal Holbein; the Death of the Virgin Mary, by Hans Grün, from sketches by Albert Dürer; and the Last Judgment, by Cornelius.

We count no fewer than thirty-six pictures in the Salle de Holbein, from the pencil of that indefatigable artist. Here are the Schoolmaster, portraits of Ammerbach and Erasmus, the Dead Christ (painted with ghastly fidelity), the Burgomaster Meyer, a Lais and a Venus, the printer Fröben, and the eight tableaux of our Lord's Passion, for which the Elector Maximilian had the magnificent good taste to offer 30,000 florins.

We have little admiration left for anything after dwelling so long on the masterpieces of a great and conscientious artist, but the Salle Allemande is not without attractions. The Eleven Thousand Virgins of Lucas Cranach exhibits a certain amount of rough but genuine power; and there is much to study in Albert Dürer's Adoration of the Magi. Observe, too, Peter Breughel's St. John preaching in the Wilderness (how gaunt and laidly frowns the great Precursor!), and the fragments of the Dance of the Dead, removed from the Dominican convent, and restored by Klander.

We pass quickly through the Salle Suisse and Salle Baloise. In the Quatrième Salle are two specimens of Jean de Mabuse; one of Teniers' cabaret-interiors, coarse but vigorous; a Quintan Matsys, and an Annibale Caracci.

In the Cinquième Salle the pictures best worth notice are Nicolas Poussin's Landscapes; a Birth of Christ, by Annibale Caracci; an Adoration of the Magi, by Jean de Mabuse, which may be profitably compared with Albert Dürer's presentation of the same subject in the Salle Allemande; a Landscape, by Ruysdael; a jovial group of Smokers, by David Teniers; and two landscapes, with figures, by E. van Heimskerk.

The library is under the superintendence of Professor Gerlach; it contains 80,000 volumes and 4000 MSS. Among the latter the enthusiast will know how to estimate an unique manuscript of Velleius Paterculus; the Acts of the Council of Basel in three great volumes, with chains attached to their covers, so as to secure them from felonious hands; the original Greek Testament of Erasmus; and a copy of his "Encomium Moriae," with marginal notes in his own writing, and charming pen and ink vignettes by Holbein.

To the attention of the archaeologist we may commend the collection of Roman antiquities discovered at Angst, and the collection, scarcely less interesting, of Mexican and Egyptian antiquities.

The Cabinet of Medals contains about 12,000. The Museum of Natural History is abundantly rich in minerals, fossils, and in birds from the Guinea coast. There are also a cabinet of Natural and Physical History, and a gallery of portraits of the most celebrated professors of the university.

The university was founded on the 4th of April, 1460, by a bull of Pope Pius II. (the ingenious and astute Æneas Sylvius, who as secretary to the great council had worked out his manoeuvres for his advancement with singular skill), and has always enjoyed a high and deserved reputation. It was re-organized in 1817, and again in 1835. Among its most eminent professors we may name Erasmus, Œcolampadius, Grynaeus, Ammerbach, Frobenius, Paracelsus, Plater, the two Bauhins, Daniel and John Bernoulli, and Euler.

The Rathhaus stands at the bottom of the Freie Strasse (the principal street), opposite the pinnacles of the Fischmarkt-brunnen. It was erected in 1508, and offers a pleasing example of the Burgundian or French Gothic. It was restored in 1825-27. The walls, of which the upper part is castellated, the lower part arched, are decorated with frescoes; and along the top runs a frieze, embellished with the arms of Basel, and of the cantons of Uri, Schwytz, and Unterwalden. The frescoes of the façade are descriptive of a hawking party, with groups of armed knights, and a characteristic figure of Justice carrying her sword. It is traditionally reported that they were designed by Holbein, and, at all events, their merit is such that their gradual decay cannot but be deplored. In the interior the artist cannot fail to admire some good old wood carvings, some painted glass, a picture of the Last Judgment, and a statue of Munatius Plancus, the traditional founder of Basel, and of the "colony" of Augusta Rauracorum.

The character of a city may be said to depend, in some measure, on the character of its immediate neighbourhood. For this reason we shall glance at some points in the environs of the towns we successively describe.

The village of St. Jacob by the Birs is situated about a quarter of a mile from Basel, on the Berne road. Here a Gothic column, thirty-six feet high, marks the last resting-place of the dead who fell in the great battle of St. Jacob, on the 26th of August, 1444, when a small Swiss force, not exceeding 1300 in number, heroically attacked the French army under the dauphin (afterwards Louis XL), though the latter were 20,000 strong.

Again and again, says Zschokke, the Swiss threw themselves upon the countless battalions of their enemies. Their little force was broken and divided, yet still they fought: 500 maintained the unequal struggle in the open field; the remainder behind the garden wall of the Siechenhaus at St. Jacob. Fierce as lions they fought in the meadow, until man after man fell dead on the heaps of slaughtered foemen. The dauphin won the victory by sheer preponderance of numbers, but it taught him a lesson. "I will provoke this obstinate people no further," said he, and full of admiration for such heroic courage, he met their representatives at Ensisheim, and concluded peace.

The young men enrolled in the various "Singing Unions" and "Federal Rifle Clubs" in this district, commemorate their Swiss Thermopylae yearly with vocal and rifle festivals. And the vineyard of Wahlstadt, not far from the battlefield, yields a red wine, which the people delight to call Schweizerblut, or "Swiss blood."

A marble tablet in the church of St. Jacob (a plain and unpretending edifice) bears an inscription to the following effect:—

     OUR SOULS TO GOD,
     OUR BODIES TO THE ENEMY.
     HERE DIED, UNCONQUERED,
     BUT EXHAUSTED WITH VICTORY,

THIRTFEN HUNDRED CONFEDERATES AND ALI IES,
IN CONFLICT WITH FRENCH AVD AUSTRIAN*,
26TH AUGUST, 1444.

We now take our leave of Basel. A few paces and we enter upon the French province of Alsace, which has figured so conspicuously in the present war, and which, at the time we write, seems fated to become a portion of the spoil of the conquerors.

Alsace, or Alsatia (in German, Ellsass), is supposed to derive its name from the *Ell* or *Ill* (Alsa), which waters two-thirds of the country, and constitutes its principal artery, and the German Sass, or "settlers." It formerly belonged to Germany, but by the treaty of Westphalia in 1648, and as a result of the victories of Turenne, was annexed to France, of which it forms the easternmost province. To the west lies Lorraine, separated from Alsace by the mountain-range of the Vosges, through whose defiles the Prussian Crown Prince so successfully carried his numerous battalions at the outset of the war of 1870. Its southern boundary, dividing it from Switzerland, is the chain of the Jura; to the south-west it borders on Upper Burgundy; to the east the Rhine separates it from Baden; and to the north the Lauter from Rhenish Bavaria.

Its surface being broken up by lofty mountains and deep valleys, and watered by numerous rivers, it is necessarily rich in bright and romantic landscapes. The slopes of the Vosges are covered with the ruined strongholds of the feudal barons; and an old saying is still popular, that in Alsace three castles are to be found on every mountain, three churches in every churchyard, and three towns in every valley.

The rivers of Alsace are many and charming, and the glens or hollows through which they trail their dark waters, present a succession of pictures bold in outline and rich in colour. The Ill is the largest and longest; it traverses a great part of the province, which is further intersected by the Monsieur or Napoleon Canal, connecting the Rhine with the Rhône, and, consequently, the North Sea with the Mediterranean. From the "bosom infinite" of the Vosges descends many a rippling river and tumbling torrent. In the department of the Upper Rhine, the Leber, which flows into the Ill near Schlettstadt; the Weiss, issuing from the Black and White Lake, and emptying its tribute into the Fecht; the Fecht, winding through the Münster valley, and after a course of thirty miles, falling into the Ill; the Thur, which brightens and enriches the vale of St. Amarin; the Doller, or Tolder, rising in a lake above the village of Dobern, and flowing into the Ill below Mühlhausen. In the department of the Lower Rhine, the Lauter, a Bavarian affluent, falls into the Rhine at Neuburg; the Moder, the Zorn, the Morsig, the Zunts, the Scher, the Andlau, the Ischer, and the Mayet are comparatively unimportant streams.

Alsace contains the important cities of Strasburg, Colmar, and Mühlhausen. In Caesar's time it was occupied by Celtic tribes; who, towards the decline of the Roman empire, were conquered by the Alemanni, and completely Germanized. For centuries it formed a part of the German empire. At the peace of Westphalia, some portions of it were ceded to Vienna, and the remainder was annexed by Louis XIV., whose seizure of Strasburg, in 1681, during a time of peace, was one of the most iniquitous acts of a reign in which the only recognized law was the law of might. By the peace of Ryswick in 1697, the cession of the whole to

France was unwisely confirmed, and Germany had the misfortune to see one of its finest provinces yielded to an aggressive and powerful neighbour, at a time when her arms were crowned with victory. At the downfall of the first Napoleonic empire, in 1815, an opportunity arose for the restoration of Alsace to Germany; but the Treaty of Vienna did nothing to redress an undoubted wrong in all its over-ingenious attempts to establish the European balance of power. Mr. Matthew Arnold has keenly remarked that the great object of the statesmen who concluded that famous treaty was to erect barriers against France. How did they proceed to carry out this object? "Instead of creating a strong Germany, they created the impotent German Confederation; placing on the frontiers of France the insignificant Duchy of Baden and an outlying province of Bavaria, and dividing the action of Germany so that her two chief powers, Prussia and Austria, must necessarily be inferior to France. They created the incoherent kingdom of Holland and the insufficient kingdom of Sardinia; they strengthened Austria against France, by adding to Austria provinces which have ever since been a source of weakness to her. They left to France Alsace and German Lorraine, which unity of race and language might with time have solidly re-attached to Germany. In compensation they took from France provinces which the same unity may one day enable her to re-absorb. The treaties of Vienna were eminently treaties of force, treaties which took no account of popular ideas; and they were unintelligent and capricious treaties of force."

Of late years, however, we have grown accustomed to see these treaties openly disregarded; and in spite of them Italy has become an united kingdom, and the isolated states of the Germanic Confederation have been welded "by blood and iron" into a compact and homogeneous empire. If at the close of the present war, victorious Germany puts forward a demand for the restoration of Alsace, it is difficult, say the pro-Prussian party, to see on what grounds the demand can be opposed by the neutral powers. Alsace, they tell us, is a German province, wrested from Germany by force and fraud; and the very principle of nationality to which so much prominence has been given since the war of 1856, would justify its annexation to the empire founded by Bismarck and Von Moltke. The German language is still spoken by many of its inhabitants, notwithstanding the efforts of the French to extirpate it, and in the smaller towns and villages German customs still prevail.

Alsace has given birth to some worthies who have attained an European reputation. Among these we may mention General Klèber, who distinguished himself in the French expedition to Egypt in 1798, and was left by Napoleon in command of the French army; Kellermann, and Rapp, two of Napoleon's favourite and most trusted lieutenants; Sebastian Brandt, of Strasburg, the author of the "Ship of Fools," well known in England through Barclay's vigorous but quaint translation of it; the poets Augustus and Adolphus Stöber, whose lyrics breathe a genuine German spirit; and the pious village pastor and enthusiastic philanthropist, Johannes Friedrich Oberlin (born at Strasburg in 1740, died in 1826). It is needless to say that in history it has played a conspicuous part, the thunder of battle having frequently resounded among its mountains, and the blood-red tide of war poured devastatingly over its fertile plains.

FROM BASEL TO STRASBURG.

On the Alsace bank of the Rhine.

A railway running parallel to the bank of the Rhine connects Basel with Strasburg. It was opened in 1841. The distance is 89 miles.

Soon after leaving Basel we perceive, on the right, the village of Grosse-Hüningen, so called to distinguish it from Klein-Hüningen, on the Baden bank of the river. In 1680, by command of Louis XIV., it was converted into a strong fortification by Vauban, the great military engineer; but the defences were razed in September, 1815, at the instance of the Swiss Confederation, and by the second treaty of Paris, France bound herself never to restore them.

We next arrive at the important and thriving town of Mühlhausen, situated on the Rhône and Rhine Canal, and famous for its extensive calico manufactories. The surrounding country is level but fertile, and its pastures are pleasantly refreshed by the windings of the Ill.

Mühlhausen, or, as the French call it, Mulhouse, owes its origin, as its name indicates, to a mill erected here on the bank of the Ill. We can easily imagine that in course of time other houses would spring up around the centre thus provided, until the hamlet grew into a village, and the village into a town. As early as the eighth century, this town was surrounded by walls. Having fallen into the hands of Rudolph of Hapsburg, it was elevated to the rank of an imperial free town in 1273. From succeeding emperors it received many privileges, and in 1293 Adolph of Nassau bestowed upon it a charter, in keeping, indeed, with the spirit of the times, though the superiority of its citizens over strangers or foreigners was pushed to the extent of waiving their responsibility for even the most criminal acts. Thus, no citizen could be summoned before a foreign magistrate. No citizen was required to defend himself against the accusation of an alien, nor was he allowed to render assistance to a foreigner against a fellow-citizen. All goods of which a citizen could prove that they had been in his possession for a year, were thenceforth to be regarded as his own property. If a citizen killed a foreigner, and it could be proved that provocation had been offered him, he was not condemned even to pay a fine. And lastly, no citizen, of whatever crime accused, could be arrested in his own house; a privilege surpassing the Englishman's proud boast, that his house is his castle; for the Englishman's house has always been open to the ministers of the law.

It cannot be said that the existence of such extraordinary immunities was altogether favourable to the prosperity of the town. They certainly attracted to it a numerous population; but what a population! Mühlhausen became the "Alsatia" of the surrounding country; the asylum of robbers and thieves, who were admitted to the rights of citizenship on taking an oath that they had not voluntarily committed a crime. As might be expected, its population was not deficient in energy, and it always evinced a marked hostility towards the nobles. In 1338 it joined the league of Alsace against them. In 1437, after gallantly repulsing an attack of the Armagnacs, it drove the *seigneurs* from its walls. Thenceforth it flourished as a democratic republic, and with undaunted intrepidity maintained its liberties, even venturing, in 1474, to resist Charles the Bold, who had threatened it with annihilation.

In its endless feuds with the nobles it had frequently demanded and received the support of the Swiss, with whom it was allied. In 1515 it renewed its treaty of perpetual union, and undertook, as a guarantee of its fidelity to the confederation, that it would enter upon no war, nor accept any foreign succour, without their consent. From these close relations sprung the natural result of the adoption of the Lutheran doctrines by the people of Mühlhausen, and this adoption, towards the end of the sixteenth century, leading to the interference of the house of Austria, a Swiss garrison was stationed in the town to protect it from attack.

In 1648 the treaty of Westphalia handed over to France the Austrian possessions on the Rhine, and the towns in the government of Haguenau. Mühlhausen was at the same time declared independent, like the Swiss cantons, and having no longer to arm against external power, was free to cultivate the arts of peace. A century elapsed, however, before it came to the front in the ranks of material progress. In 1746 the first manufactory of printed calicoes was established here by three worthies, whose names are still held in honour at Mühlhausen, Samuel Kcechlin, J. J. Schmaltzer, and Johannes Heinrich Dollfus. Twenty-five years later, and eleven new factories had been planted on the ruins of the palaces of the old nobility.

The busy city now throve amazingly. But its wealth attracted the greedy eyes of France, and though for some years it gallantly defended its freedom, in 1798 it was compelled to vote for its own extinction as an independent city. Under the influence of French bayonets, it gave 666 votes against fifteen, in favour of its annexation to France. Whether the whirligig of fortune will once more wrest it from France, and with the rest of Alsace, hand it over to victorious Germany, it is at present too early to conjecture.

Mühlhausen is distinguished by its great industrial resources; it is also distinguished by its noble benevolent institutions. It presents almost the only example in Europe of a Workman's City, of an independent community of operatives. Nowhere else has trade unionism been developed under such favourable auspices, and with such satisfactory results. Between Mühlhausen and Dornach, says Jules Simon, extends an ample plain traversed by the canal which winds round the city. Here, in a singularly healthy situation, and on both banks of the canal, the *Société des Cités Ouvriéres* has traced the plan of its new town. The ground is perfectly level; the streets, broad and spacious, are laid out at right angles. As each house stands in its own little garden-plot, the eye is everywhere greeted with trees and flowers, and the pure air circulates as freely as in the open country.

On the Place Napoleon, an open area in the very centre of this interesting town, and the point where the main thoroughfares terminate, are erected two houses of dimensions superior to the others; one of which is appropriated to the public baths and lavatory; the other to the restaurant, store-rooms, and library. On the opposite bank of the canal, in the square formed by the Rue Lavoisier and the Rue Napoleon, is located an asylum for the reception of 150 children; it is excellently managed, clean, and comfortable. There is no private school, because the managers have rightly judged that it could not surpass, or even equal, the communal school, which is one of the most admirable institutions in Mühlhausen.

At the restaurant and bakery every article is sold at wholesale prices. The restaurant is conducted on a most admirable plan. The charges are moderate, and differ greatly from those of the ordinary establishments. The dishes, too, are of a better quality, and sufficiently varied.

The conditions on which the houses become the property of the workmen are thus plainly stated by M. Simon.

The society, he remarks, makes no mystery about them. It says—"You see my houses are wide open; enter, and inspect them from the garret to the cellar. The ground cost me one franc twenty centimes per metre (about three yards three inches); including the architect's fees, purchase of materials, expense of erection, the houses cost 2400 to 3000 francs; I sell them to you at the same price. You are not in a position to pay me 3000 francs; but I, the society, can wait your convenience. You will deposit in my hands a sum of 300 or 400 francs to begin with; this will defray the legal and preliminary expenses. Afterwards, you will pay me eighteen francs (about 13$s.$ 10$d.$) per month, for a house worth 2400 francs; or twenty-three francs (about 18$s.$ 3$d.$) for a house worth 3000 francs. That is, you will pay about four or five francs more than you would for hired apartments. By continuing this payment for fourteen years you will have reimbursed the price of your house; it will be paid for, you will be its owner. Not only will you thenceforth live rent-free, but you will be able to leave it to your children or to sell it. By setting apart five francs monthly, which, if put in the savings bank, would not have realized 1400 francs, you will have acquired a house now worth 3000 francs, but which, in fourteen years, will probably be worth double that amount, and meanwhile, you will have been completely housed, without running any risk from a landlord's whims. You will have enjoyed the use of a garden, whose produce cannot be valued at less than thirty or forty francs per annum. We do not take into account the broad healthy streets, the tree-planted squares, the children's asylum—in a word, all the public and useful institutions which have been open to you, and which are not in anyway included in your rent."

It must be admitted that such terms as these present no ordinary attraction for the intelligent operative, and we are not astonished to find that out of the 560 houses belonging to the Société des Cités Ouvrières in 1860, 403 had been sold. Something of the same kind has been accomplished in London, and some of the larger towns of England and Scotland, but not, as it seems to us, on so liberal a scale or so enlightened a plan; and we commend the example of Mühlhausen to our British philanthropists in their efforts to promote the well-being and advance the interests of the working-classes. Fourierism and Owenism appear the empty theories of credulous philosophers when compared with the practical work so nobly conceived, and so admirably carried out, at Mühlhausen.

This enlightened town boasts also of a Société Industrielle, which carefully examines into the merits or demerits of every project brought forward for the amelioration of the condition of the working-classes. Then there are—a Société d'Encouragement à l'Epargne (for the encouragement of economy), a Société Alimentaire, a Société de Saint Vincent de Paul, a

Société des Amis des Pauvres, and a Société de Charité. In fact, Mühlhausen has become the arena where philanthropic designs are tested before the eyes of the public, and where those which possess intrinsic merit are immediately adopted, and energetically carried into execution.

Such a place will necessarily be provided with good schools. In addition to a college, a professional school, and an upper school, it possesses an admirable primary school, which the town supports by a yearly grant of 70,500 francs, and which has no equal in France, no superior on the Continent. The work of supervision and tuition is intrusted to a director, a sub-director, and forty-two masters, mistresses, and assistants, who take charge on an average of 3000 children of both sexes. The children of the operatives are admitted free. The educational course comprises French, German, English, Drawing, Geography, History, Arithmetic, and the Elements of Geometry.

France has a right to be proud of its radiant and intellectual Paris, of historic Tours, of regal Rheims, of sunny Bordeaux, and of many other towns and cities scattered over its fair and fertile land; but of none can it boast with greater justice than of industrious and philanthropic Mulhouse.

A few words will be sufficient to satisfy the reader's curiosity respecting its public edifices. Here, as in the preceding pages, we shall follow the guidance of Adolphe Joanne.

The new Catholic church, built in the ogival or pointed style of the thirteenth century, is a really graceful and yet majestic building, which we think would meet with the approval of the architectural purist, both in its general conception and principal details. It is above 270 feet in length by 110 in width at the transept, and seventy-five at the nave and aisles. Its height in the interior is seventy-five feet. The roof of the nave and transepts is of timber, and the general effect is very grand and impressive.

A new Protestant church, designed by the same architect, M. Schaere, has recently been erected. It measures 145 feet long, seventy-five feet wide, and sixty-five feet high.

M. Schaere is also the architect of the Jewish synagogue, which is built in the Oriental style, of red sandstone, and in the form of a parallelogram. The interior is divided into three aisles; in the central, which is of great width, sit the men; in the narrow lateral aisles, the women.

The town-hall is situated in the Place de la Reunion, in the oldest part of the town. It dates from 1551 to 1553. Its most original feature is its external double staircase. To the left of the entrance is a wall-painting, very striking and vigorous, of an old man in magisterial robes; on the right, a figure of a woman of the handsomest German type, crowned with roses, and bearing a crown of laurel in her hand. The great hall is adorned with three pictures representing the shields of the burgomasters or maires of Mulhouse. Above them is a row of the armorial bearings of the Swiss cantons. The glass windows are ancient and curious.

A lively and agreeable promenade is furnished by the long line of well-built quays which skirt the basin formed here by the Rhône and Rhine Canal. In most of the streets, however, the visitor will find much to amuse, and more to interest. The signs of rapid industrial progress are everywhere. To these, indeed, he may be accustomed in other towns; but in few towns will he find them accompanied by such abundant and satisfactory indications of moral advancement and artistic culture. Mühlhausen is French in aspect, German in character, English in spirit. In many respects it is a model of what a great manufacturing town ought to be.

The Industrial Museum is worth a visit. It is situated in the triangle of colonnaded mansions, which looks like a bit of Belgravia, erected in 1828.

Mühlhausen was entered by the Prussians in September, 1870.

The next station on our route is Dornach, a manufacturing town of about 4000 inhabitants. Here is the well-known establishment of Messrs. Dolfüs-Mieg and Company, whose printed calicoes are noted for their excellence.

At Dornach we cross the Ill, which formerly served as the boundary line between the Sundgau and Alsace, and the Rhône and Rhine Canal. At Lutterbach the railway strikes further inland, and opens up some striking views of the rugged peaks and deep ravines of the Vosges. A branch line diverges from this point to Thann (the ancient *Pinetum*), another manufacturing town, with a population of about 5000, partly Catholics and partly Protestants, as is the case in most of the towns of Alsace. Its situation is eminently picturesque, for it lies at the mouth of the St. Amarin Valley, while huge summits dominate over the foreground, and far away spreads a seemingly endless stretch of fair and fruitful country. Its special pride is its minster, dedicated to St. Theobald; a structure in the finest style of the German architecture of the fifteenth century, and not unworthy of the genius of Master Erwin of Strasburg, who is reported to have furnished the design. The spire, however, was erected by the architect Rumiel Vatel. The whole work, begun in 1430, was completed in 1516. An old tradition runs that the latter was an excellent year for the vintage, and that the beauty of the spire is owing to the circumstance that the mortar was mixed with wine.

The western gateway is magnificent. It is enriched with statues in decorated niches, and with a variety of ornamentation, which is not less graceful in design than conscientious in execution.

From Thann, following the course of the Thur, we return to Ensisheim, situated at the confluence of the Thur and the Ill. The latter river, it should be observed, from Mühlhausen to a point below Strasburg, incloses, in conjunction with the Rhine, a long and narrow peninsular strip of land, which is low, level, fertile, and well-cultivated.

Ensisheim is a town of about 3000 inhabitants. Jacob Balde, a Latin poet, whose odes have been translated by the German Herder, was born here in 1603. In its church is preserved a large aerolite, which fell in the neighbourhood on the 7th of November, 1492. It originally weighed 280 lbs., now only about 170 lbs.; portions having been gradually broken off by inquisitive curiosity-mongers.

Continuing our course at a distance of about ten miles from the Rhine, with the Vosges on our left hand, we reach, in succession, the town of Sultz, (3989), and Gebweiler (10,680), both inhabited by an industrial population. Near the latter, the Vosges culminate in the bold peak of the Belchen (4410 feet), or "balloon of Gebweiler."

We next arrive at Rouffach (the *Rubeacum* of the Romans), a busy and interesting town of a decidedly German aspect, with a population of 3917. Here was born Marshal Lefebvre, duke of Dantzig, one of Napoleon's safest and most skilful lieutenants, on the 25th of October, 1755. He was the son of a miller, who had formerly served in the army, and at the age of eighteen entered the Gardes Franchises, rising to the post of *premier sergent* in the year preceding the outbreak of the French revolution. In those stirring times every soldier carried a marshal's baton in his knapsack. His rise was rapid. In 1793 he was a general of brigade. For some years he served under Hoche, was appointed general of division, distinguished himself at Lamberg and Giesberg, and more especially at Stockach, March 25, 1799, where he kept at bay a greatly superior Austrian force. Afterwards he offered his services to Napoleon, and when the latter established the first empire, Lefebvre was made a marshal. At Jena, in 1806, he earned the imperial praise by his splendid valour, and in the following year was appointed to the command of the army besieging Dantzig. The city capitulated, and Lefebvre was created a duke. In 1808 he served in Spain, in 1809 in Austria and the Tyrol. In the disastrous invasion of Russia he commanded the imperial guard, and during the terrible retreat from Moscow his intrepidity and wonderful powers of endurance were strikingly displayed. He fought with equal courage and skill in the brilliant but unsuccessful campaign of 1814. It proved the close of his military career. After the restoration his services were not required, but he accepted the Bourbon rule with honourable loyalty, and was permitted to retain his hard-won honours. He died in 1820. A bust of the marshal, by David of Angers, is the principal ornament of the townhall of his native place.

Rouffach grew up round the old castle of Isenburg, one of the oldest in Alsace, where Dagobert II. frequently resided. At a later period it belonged to the bishops of Strasburg. It was seized by the Emperor Henry IV., whose men-at-arms, enjoying here an uncontrolled license, were guilty of the most abominable excesses. One day, the feast of the Passover, the governor of the castle carried off a young maiden of noble birth, while she was proceeding to church in her mother's company. The citizens heard with emotion the shrieks and exclamations of the distracted mother, but a craven dread of the imperial lances kept them silent. Their wives and daughters, however, more courageous, and more easily aroused to enthusiasm, hastened to the castle, broke through the gates, drove out the surprised garrison, and the emperor himself, who was at the time a resident within its walls. Terrified by the unexpected attack of the Alsatian heroines he fled, half-naked, to his harem at Colmar, leaving behind him his crown, his sceptre, and his imperial mantle, which his victorious assailants immediately offered up at the altar of the Virgin. In memory of this event, says Rouvrois, in his "Voyage Pittoresque en Alsace," the magistrates of the town conceded the right of precedence to the women in every public ceremony, and this proud prerogative they still enjoy.

Ashamed of his defeat, and furious at its disgrace, the emperor laid siege to the town with an army of 30,000 men, which he had collected for a campaign in Italy. It was now the turn of the men of Rouffach to come to the front, and they fought with so much resolution and intrepidity that the emperor was completely baffled. Unable to satisfy his vengeance by force, he had recourse to fraud. He demanded permission for his troops to pass through the town (1106), and when the citizens unsuspectingly opened their gates, he ordered it to be set on fire, and handed it over to the greed and lust of his mercenaries.

Towards the end of the thirteenth century, the men of Colmar seized upon Rouffach and plundered it. After this disaster, it was surrounded by strong walls, but the defence proved useless against the Armagnacs, who sacked it in 1444. Finally, in the seventeenth century, it was three times occupied by an enemy; on the first occasion by the Landgrave Otho; on the second by the Duc de Rohan; and on the third by Marshal Turenne, after his victory at Turckheim.

One cannot but pity the fate of these frontier towns, so frequently exposed to the ravages of war; nor can one help feeling some surprise at the vitality they have exhibited in surviving so many and such deplorable misfortunes.

In the thirteenth century Rouffach became unhappily distinguished by its cruel persecution of the Jews, many of whom were burned at the stake in a meadow still called *Judenfeld*. And, even at this day, not a single Jew inhabits Rouffach, or owns any property within it.

The church of Rouffach, dedicated to St. Arbogast, is an interesting monument of twelfth century date.

Its design and its decorative work refer it, according to M. de Rouvrois, to the second period of the Gothic style. The choir, with its remarkable boldness of construction, appears much more ancient than the remainder of the edifice. One of the baptismal fonts in a side-chapel on the right, arrests special attention as a masterpiece of subtle and delicate sculpture, in which every line seems informed with genius. Persons afflicted with epileptic fits are in the habit of resorting to the chapel of St. Valentine.

We must take the reader to Pfaffenheim (1700 inhabitants), situated at the very foot of the Vosges, in a sheltered and sunny land of vineyards, famous for the excellence of their vintage. The church is ancient, with a remarkable spire. Above the town rises the striking hill of the Schaumburg (1780 feet), from whose summit a view of the valley of the Ill may be obtained, which presents some striking features.

Gueberschwir (1500 inhabitants) was formerly a walled town, with a castle, the Mittelburg, of some celebrity. Its church, in the so-called Roman style, is an edifice of more than ordinary pretensions.

A line may be given to Huttstadt (1000 inhabitants) to refer the visitor to the romantic ruins of the old castle of Barbenstein.

Crossing the Lauch, a small swift stream, clear as a mountain torrent, and sparkling with an azure gleam in a dell of luxuriantly leafy character, we observe the stately castle of Hurlisheim (1100 inhabitants), erected in the last century on the site of an old robber fastness. Then we come to the interesting town of Eynisheim (1953 inhabitants), the birthplace, in 1049, of Pope Leo IX.

Of the castle in which, according to tradition, the pope was born, and which was built by the Count Eberhard, son of Duke Athic, the only remains are a grey hexagonal tower, gaunt and weatherworn, and some trace of the fosses which supplied the castle with water. To the west, on the cone-shaped mountain above the town, rise the three shattered towers of an ancient fortalice, called Drei-Exon. Each tower was severally named: thus, on the south stood the Wahlenburg; on the north, Dagsburg; in the middle, Weekmund. One of them is still some 125 feet in height; the others are in ruins.

This palace was erected by the first Count von Eynisheim, grandson to Duke Athic, and founder of several princely and royal dynasties, in whose successive generations our readers would take no interest. But, at least, it may be as well to note that among the number are included the princes of Teck, now, through the marriage of the Princess Mary of Cambridge, closely connected with our own royal house. Bruno of Eynisheim, son of Count Hugues IV., became bishop of Toul, and afterwards Pope Leo IX. His life has been written by his disciple and partisan, Archdeacon Wibert, with a credulity which leaves little to be desired. Whoever has a taste for the legendary and marvellous should turn to this narrative, as it appears in the valuable collection of Muratori. As a bishop, Bruno was notable for his fervent piety, his gentleness to those below him (he constantly washed the feet of the poor), his boundless charity, his eloquence as a preacher, and his knowledge of music. As pope, he showed a great talent for organization, an intense devotion, and an unwearied zeal for the interests of the church. Both as pope and bishop, however, he evinced a curious feature of character: he discovered reliques of saints wherever it was necessary to find them, he worked miracles, and he "saw visions." He died on the 13th of April, 1059, closing a saintly life with a sublime death. He ordered his coffin to be carried into St. Peter's; and laid himself down on a couch by its side. Then, having bestowed his last advice and admonitions on those around him, he received the last sacraments, and, rising with difficulty, looked stedfastly upon his future resting-place. "Behold," he said, "my brethren, the mutability of human things. The cell which I dwelt in as a monk expanded into yonder spacious palace; it shrinks again into this narrow coffin." The next morning he was dead.

Of his miracles we can but record a single example. A costly cup, presented to him by the archbishop of Köln, fell to the ground and was broken to pieces. At the bidding of Leo, these pieces came together, the cup was made whole, and the fracture was marked only by a thin thread (*capillo*). But the most wonderful thing was, that all the while not a drop of the wine which it contained was spilled!

The following account of the destruction of the pope's birthplace we borrow from the "Voyage Pittoresque en Alsace:"—

"It was in 1466. The year before, the nobles, whose oppressions the towns did not bear so patiently as in the preceding century, had been expelled from the senate of Mühlhausen. Enraged at this bold act of rebellion, they waited only for a pretext to re-assert their ancient domination, and avenge themselves on the presumptuous burghers. A miller's boy of Mühlhausen furnished them with the excuse they needed. Driven out by his master, and pretending that he was in great distress for a paltry sum of six oboli, which the latter refused to pay him, he carried his complaint before the nobles; and one of them, Peter of Eynisheim, purchased from him his debt.

"Strong in his legal title, and putting himself forward as a redresser of wrongs, he seized upon several citizens, and flung them into the lowest dungeon of his castle.

"Mühlhausen appealed to its allies, and a war, known as the Plappert-Krieg, or 'War of the Six Oboli,' broke out on this insignificant cause. The nobles, summoning to their aid all their friends and kinsmen, retired to the castle of Eynisheim, which they strongly fortified, and appointed Hermann Kliv, the miller, who had been the original cause of strife, to the chief command.

"The allied towns resolved to attack the castle, and under the leadership of a certain Stützel, they carried it by assault on the day of the Fete-Dieu (1466), and burned it to the ground. Then they crowned their victory by hanging up the miller and three of the most tyrannical nobles.

"It would seem to be tolerably certain that these three fortresses were never rebuilt, or inhabited after this event; for in 1568 a pretended sorceress, accused of having married her daughter to the devil, and celebrated the nuptial-feast among the ruins of Eynisheim, was brought to trial. The details of the evidence brought against this unfortunate victim of superstitious ignorance are very curious, very extravagant, and, as persons knowing anything of the history of witchcraft will readily believe, are frequently disgusting. We may mention, however, that it was stated as a fact, before a properly constituted court of judicature, that the wedding-feast had consisted of bats—cooked, we suppose, in a variety of ways—and that the concluding dance had been performed by imps and devils!

> "What thronging, dashing, raging, rustling!
> What whispering, babbling, hissing, bustling!
> What glimmering, spirting, stinking, burning,
> As heaven and earth were overturning!"

It is needless to add that the poor sorceress was put to death.

We resume our route. The Hoh-Landsberg, which rises above the chateau of Plixburg—the latter a thirteenth century building, with a cylindrical keep—was formerly, as its remains very plainly indicate, a fortress of great strength, and almost impregnable in the days before rifled cannon and mitrailleuses. In the history of Alsace it played an important part, as early as the thirteenth century. In 1281 it was captured by an imperial army, and thenceforth it remained a fief of the house of Austria. The Swedes took possession of it in 1638. It was dismantled by order of Louis XIV.

Logelbach, on the left, is famous for its large cotton mills, weaving, and calico-printing establishments. Wintzenheim, another manufacturing town, has a population of 4000.

Almost opposite the railway station of Colmar lies Turckheim (2946 inhabitants), where Marshal Turenne, on the 5th of January, 1675, gained a great victory over the imperialists.

Colmar is the principal town in the department of the Upper Rhine, and was the seat of the imperial court for the departments of the Upper and Lower Rhine.

This ancient and quaint old town is situated in the immediate shadow of the Vosges, on the small rivers Lauch and Fecht, and in a plain of great fertility, watered by innumerable rills which supply the motive power of many important mills and factories, and are carried through the busy streets of the town itself. In some they are reduced, however, to the modest dimensions of gutters. Its principal manufactures are cottons and printed goods.

Founded hi the sixth century, it was called Columbaria, or Colmaria, when the sons of Louis the Debonnair encountered in its vicinity their father, against whom they had rebelled, and forced him to surrender the crown he had received from Charlemagne (A.D. 833). The three brothers afterwards met in council at the royal vill of Colmar, and Lothair conveyed his father from thence to the monastery of Soissons, and treated him with the most shameful indignities. He was compelled to perform public penance in the church of St. Médard. There the father of three kings laid down upon the altar his armour and his imperial robes, and clothing himself in black, read the long and enforced confession of his crimes. Next, he laid the parchment on the altar, was stripped of his military belt, which was likewise placed there; and having put off his secular dress, and assumed the garb of a penitent, was thenceforth deemed incapacitated from all civil acts.

The field where the emperor had been deserted by his courtiers and army, was ever afterwards named Lügenfeld, *Campus Mentitus*, or "the field of falsehood."

In 1106 Colmar suffered severely from fire, but was soon rebuilt. In 1226 it was raised to the rank of a town by the Emperor Frederick II., and in 1282 declared an imperial town. In 1474 it was attacked by the French under Charles the Rash, but successfully repulsed its assailants. In 1552 it had grown so wealthy and prosperous, that it was thought advisable to fortify it with ramparts and towers. In 1632 it was taken by the Swedes; the majority of the citizens having embraced Lutheranism, compelled the imperialists to capitulate. Two years later it was annexed to France, and in 1673 Louis XIV. dismantled the fortifications, whose site is now occupied by pleasant boulevards, agreeably planted with trees, and surrounding the old, quaint, and obscure town with a belt of leanness.

Colmar has given birth to three eminent men, Pfeffel, Rewbell, and General Rapp.

Gottlieb Conrad Pfeffel was born in 1736. He became blind at the early age of twenty-one, while pursuing his studies in the university of Halle. By dint of unwearied perseverance he conquered the numerous obstacles which loss of sight throws in the way of the man of letters, and as a writer of fables attained a great and deserved distinction. He died in 1809, having for several years conducted with success a Protestant military academy.

Rewbell was one of the many whom the surging waves of the French Revolution carried into power. Having attained an influential position in the National Assembly, he had the courage to denounce the sanguinary excesses of the Jacobins, and was appointed one of the five directors to whom the government of France was intrusted by the constitution of 1795.

His character is concisely sketched by Alison:—An Alsatian by birth, and a lawyer by profession, he was destitute of either genius or eloquence; but he owed his elevation to his habits of business, his knowledge of forms, and the pertinacity with which he represented the feelings of the multitude, often in the close of revolutionary convulsions envious of distinguished ability.

For ourselves, we think that Alison does not do him justice. He was a man of principle, and advocated moderation at a time when to do so required considerable intrepidity. He was at all events a sincere republican, and had the sagacity to fathom the designs of

Napoleon, and the courage to oppose them as long as opposition was possible. In 1799 he retired from the Directory, and thenceforth made no sign.

Jean Rapp was born at Colmar on the 26th of April, 1772, of obscure parentage. He enlisted at the age of sixteen, served in the army of the Rhine, was four times wounded, promoted to the rank of lieutenant, and as aide-de-camp to Dessaix accompanied "General Bonaparte's" expedition to Egypt. Still following the fortunes of Dessaix, he stood by his side at the battle of Marengo, and supported him in his arms after he had received his mortal wound. It was probably his friendship with the one man whom Napoleon pre-eminently loved and trusted, that recommended him to the great conqueror's favour At the battle of Austerlitz he led one of the most dashing and successful cavalry charges ever made, and was rewarded with promotion to the rank of general of division. Henceforward he was admitted to Napoleon's special confidence, and was employed on several difficult and delicate missions. After serving throughout the disastrous Russian campaign, he was appointed military governor of Dantzig, and gained great distinction by his brilliant defence of that city in 1813; not surrendering until two-thirds of the garrison had perished. Being made a prisoner of war, he did not return to France until the restoration of Louis XVIII., to whom he offered his services. When Napoleon returned from Elba he could not refuse the claims of his old leader, and he took the command of the garrison at Strasburg, which city he held even after the crushing defeat of Waterloo. In spite of his tergiversation, he secured the forgiveness of the Bourbons, and was made a peer of France in 1818. He died in 1821, in his fiftieth year; leaving behind him the reputation of a gallant and trusty soldier, who was inferior to none in all the qualities which make an excellent lieutenant. He had no genius, but he had military talent; and he had a knack of doing whatever he had to do in a very sufficient and effective manner.

We can easily see all that is to be seen at Colmar in a few hours. A ramble along its streets will open up to us some quaint examples of domestic architecture; and if it be market day, we cannot but be amused by the no less quaint costumes of the peasants who stream into the town from the neighbouring villages.

The Minster, or St. Martin's church, is an admirable Gothic edifice, begun in 1265 and completed in 1360. Completed, that is, so far as the original design seems likely ever to be carried out; but of the two towers the southern one only has been commenced, and this rises but a little above the body of the building. A spire has been erected in the place of the ancient spire, destroyed by fire in 1572. The grotesque figures which decorate the portico and nave are worth examining; their carvers must have been men of a sly satiric humour! Not less notable is the altar-piece, by Martin Schön, or Schöngauer, a native of Colmar (died 1488), of the Virgin Mary with the Holy Child resting in a bower of roses, and attended by angels. The figures, larger than life, are set off by a background of gold.

Each window in the choir consists of three lancet lights with two mullions. They are filled with the remains of the superb painted glass which formerly adorned the ancient church of the Dominicans. It would be impossible to speak too highly of its depth and transparency of colouring.

The old Dominican convent (that of the Unterlinden) has undergone a deplorable transformation; the principal building being used as a corn-mart. The conventual church has been more fortunate; it contains the town museum and library, the latter numbering about 40,000 volumes. There are some interesting paintings in illustration of the life of Christ, by Martin Schöngauer; six subjects from the Passion, and an Annunciation and Adoration of the Magi, by the same artist; also various pictures attributed, with more or less foundation, to Albert Dürer and Grunewald. Here, too, are some fine specimens of medieaval carving, from the convent of Isenheim; the head of Peter of Hagenbach, embalmed, and preserved under glass; an aerolite which fell near Colmar in 1492; a Gallo-Roman mosaic from the choir of the minster; specimens of armour, and certain instruments of torture; besides many other things both rich and rare, and some which are neither rich nor rare.

The treasures of the library are, the first book printed in German, at Strasburg, by Eggenstein, in 1466; namely, a "Tractatus Rationiset Conscientiae," either printed by Guttenberg himself, or by his successor, Nicolas Becklermunze; and collections of medals (10,000 in number), ethnography, and natural history.

A bronze statue, by Bertholdi, to General Rapp, was erected on the Champ de Mars in 1855; and one in stone, by Friederich, to the fabulist Pfeffel, was placed beside the museum in 1859.

From Colmar a visit may be paid to Freiburg, in the Brisgau, and Neuf-Brisach (3456 inhabitants), on the banks of the Rhine. The latter is one of Vauban's fortified towns. In its vicinity is planted the Fort Mortier, a constant menace to Alt-Brisach, which suffered greatly, as well as the fort, in the Franco-Prussian War.

At four miles from Colmar we reach Bennwihr (1000 inhabitants), whence we proceed, by way of Ostheim, on the Fecht, to the Kaiserberg, and Rappoltsweiler (8000).

Kaiserberg is situated in a pleasant little valley at the foot of the ruined mountain fortress of the same name. Both fortress and town sprung into existence during the first quarter of the thirteenth century, under the Emperor Frederick II.

A short distance from the railway, and at the mouth of a vine-clad valley, lies Rappoltsweiler, better known by its French name of Ribeauvillé (population, 6081, of whom about one-seventh are Protestants). This town was the cradle of the once powerful family of Rappoltstein, who, after the annexation of Alsace to France, changed their name to Ribeaupierre. It was one of this family who, on the summit of the mountain above the town, erected the castle, now in utter ruin, of Hoh-Rappolstein, besieged in turn by Rudolph of Hapsburg and Adolph of Nassau. It is distinguished by its cylindrical tower. Lower down are the remains of two other castles, the Giersberg, and Niederberg, or St. Ulrich.

The parish church, dedicated to St. Germain, which contains the tombs of the lords of Ribeaupierre, and the town-hall, are the only two buildings of any particular interest or merit.

Along the crest of the foremost line of the Vosges runs the singular rampart, of unknown antiquity, called the Heidenmauer, or "Pagans' Wall." Its remains extend over an area of two leagues. It is composed of unhewn stones, uncemented, and about eight to ten feet high.

Philipp Jacob Spener, an eminent divine, who may justly be considered the founder of the Pietists, was born at Rappoltsweiler in 1635. He studied successively at Strasburg, Basel, and Geneva, imbibing the principles of the strictest Lutheranism, with, however, a strong attachment towards the Calvinistic ideal of church government and discipline. From 1666 to 1686 he laboured at Frankfort-on-the-Maine as senior pastor, with an enthusiasm and devotedness which revived in Germany the decaying spirit of evangelical piety. In 1675 he published his "Pia Desideria," which, according to Tholuck, is one of the most important productions in the whole theological literature of Germany. As a remedy for the religious lukewarmness then too prevalent, he urged that the laity should be taught to co-operate in the work of the Christian church, and that all the faithful, whether clerics or laics, should realize their spiritual priesthood by union in prayer, and by efforts for the well-being of their fellows. Hence arose the *collegia pietatis*, or private meetings for prayer and bible-reading, which originated the nickname of "pietists," bestowed on those who attended them.

From 1686 to 1691 Spener officiated as chaplain, or chief preacher, at the court of the Elector George III. of Saxony, but discharged his trust with a faithfulness which princely ears were unable to endure, and the connection was terminated abruptly, to the relief of both parties. Removing to Berlin, he filled the offices of provost of the church of St. Nicholas, and consistorial councillor, until his death in 1701. His influence extended over all Lutheran Germany, and he formed a school of zealous and able disciples, Breithaupt, Lange, Anton, Franck, and Freylinghausen, who took up and continued the movement which Spener had inaugurated, and infused a new life and inspiration into the German church.

According to Tholuck, and no man is better acquainted with the whole religious history of that age, Spener, of all who have attained to eminence in the Lutheran church, was the purest and most unblemished in personal character, and of all God's instruments in the seventeenth century the most signally blessed.

RAPPOLTSWEILER TO TUSENBACH.

A road lined with poplars conducts from Rappoltsweiler to a place of pilgrimage in much favour before the French Revolution, Tusenbach, so called from the noise (*tosen*) of a "brawling stream" which rushes past it. St. Mary of Tusenbach was the patroness of the musicians in all Alsace. These musicians formed a guild, which dated from the romantic era of the troubadours, when the singers and jongleurs wandered from castle to castle, and relieved the dull life of feudalism with flashes of poetry and song. The area over which the guild extended their operations lay between the Hauenstein and the Haguenau Forest, and from the extremity of the Wasgau to the Rhine. They placed themselves under the immediate protection of the lord of Rappoltstein, who assumed the title of King of the Jongleurs, constituting it a separate office, in subordination, at first to the Imperial, and afterwards to the French crown.

As late as the 10th of March, 1785, we find the royal council renewing the statutes which Eberhard von Rappoltstein had bestowed on his musical subjects in 1606.

Certain privileges, we had almost said prerogatives, belonged to the king of the jongleurs, and the jongleurs, in their turn, could claim certain rights. The former appointed a viceroy, or "piper king," who presided at the annual court. As the guild was very numerous, it was subdivided into three bodies, each of which had its separate rendezvous. Thus, the musicians from Hauenstein to Ottmensbühl assembled at Alt-Thann on the 8th of September; those from Ottmensbühl to Eppil came, with pipe and drum, to Rappoltsweiler on the same day; while those from Eppil to the Haguenau met at Bischweiler on the feast of Assumption.

On the 8th of September the musicians of the Rappoltsweiler district gathered together as early as nine in the morning, and set out from the Sun tavern, in a radiant procession, with music and banners, and the piper king at their head, and each man carrying a silver medal in his buttonhole, to hear mass at the parish church. Thence they marched to the castle, played a symphony in honour of their king, and drank his health in good red wine. Returning to the inn, a court of justice was held; complaints were heard, and in cases of the infraction of the brotherhood's statutes, suitable fines inflicted. The ceremonies of the day concluded with dances and songs.

TO HOH-KÖNIGSBURG.

After leaving Ribeauvillé, we pass Guémar (population, 1400) on the right, and Bergheim (population, 3100) on the left, and cross several streams, before arriving at St. Hippolyte (population, 2241), the point whence travellers frequently ascend the steep slopes of the Hoh-Königsburg.

On the summit are situated the extensive ruins of a castle of great antiquity. It was erected in 1469 by the Counts Oswald and Wilhelm von Thierstein. The view from the battlements is very fine. It is not often, even in the Rhine Valley, that so grand and striking a panorama, one so bold in its grand outlines and so rich in its details, is unfolded before the traveller.

At four miles from St. Hippolyte we reach Schlestadt; an important and prosperous town of 10,184 inhabitants.

Schlestadt was anciently a free town of the German empire, but did not receive its full civic privileges until the thirteenth century. The Frank kings, according to an old tradition, had a palace here, erected by Frederick II. In 775 Charlemagne spent his Christmas tide at Schlestadt. In the fourteenth century it was twice besieged by the warrior bishops of Strassburg. Alternately occupied by the Swedes and Imperialists during the Thirty Years' War, it fell, in 1634, into the hands of the French. At the peace of Westphalia it was again acknowledged as an imperial city; but in 1673 it was again captured by the French, and Louis XIV. ordered its walls to be razed, and new fortifications to be erected by Vauban. It is a place of considerable strength, and both in 1814 and 1815 successfully resisted the attacks of the allied armies. In the campaign of 1870 it was besieged and captured by a Prussian army.

Above the small town of Dambach rises, hoary and massive, the ruined castle of Bernstein, whose rapid decay Nature seeks to conceal with her freshest luxuriance. On the right is Ebersmünster, a village of 930 inhabitants, where Duke Athic founded, in 667, the *Apri Monasterium*, or Monastery of the Wild Boar, in place of a chapel built by King Dagobert.

And next, we arrive at Ebersheim (1900 inhabitants) the explanation of this Apri Monasterium.

Here, according to tradition, Sigebert, the son of Dagobert, was mortally wounded by a wild boar (eber); but through the potency of the prayers of St. Arbogast, then bishop of Strassburg, was restored to life. In grateful acknowledgment of the miracle, Dagobert erected in the vicinity the Chapel of the Boar, or Ebersmünster.

Benfeld is eleven miles from Schlestadt. It has a population of 2745 inhabitants, and is situated on the Ill. It appears to have risen on the ruins of the ancient Elcebus, the *Hellkebos* of the geographer Ptolemy, which the Goths destroyed in the fifth century. Here were interred the remains of St. Materne, the apostle and evangelizer of Alsace.

It was one of the most ancient demesnes of the bishops of Strassburg.

From Benfeld we proceed, by way of Matzenheim—leaving, on our right, the beautiful sixteenth century castle of Osthausen, belonging to the Zorn de Brulach family—to Erstein.

This quiet, old-world little town (population, 3705), pleasantly planted on the banks of the Ill, was anciently of some importance. The Frankish kings had a palace here, in which at a later date resided the two emperors, Otho I. and Otho II. It was at that time surrounded by walls, which, together with the castle, were destroyed by the stout citizens of Strassburg in 1333.

From Erstein the reader will permit us to diverge to Oberwin (population, 5150), an irregularly built but picturesque town, situated on the Ehn, with a fine background formed by the green acclivities of the Hohenburg. Formerly it was a royal demesne, belonging to the Merovingian kings; afterwards it became an imperial free town, of the sixth rank. It has four gates; but the only relics of its ancient importance are the remains of the strong towers that formerly flanked its walls. The town-hall, built in 1528, is rich in curious wood carving and ancient pictures.

From this point we proceed to ascend the Ottilienberg, or "Mountain of St. Odille;" the scene every year, on Pentecost Monday, of a pilgrimage famous throughout the length and breadth of Alsace. The Ottilienberg, apart from its associations, is worthy of a visit; its scenery is more than ordinarily picturesque and varied, and the prospect from its summit might fill the heart of a poet with gladness! To the left rise the ruins of the Rathsamhausen, which formerly belonged to a powerful Alsatian family, and the Lützelburg, which was built in the twelfth century, and whose two shattered towers are surrounded by a girdle of dark-green forest. To the south lies the Landsburg, which was occupied by a family of the same name down to the great Revolution of 1789. Its remains consist of two noble, cylindrical, five-storied towers, at the angles of the western enceinte; a mass of ruins on the eastern side; and, in the centre, the old, square, sandstone keep, with its grim eyeless walls, looking blankly out on a changed world.

From Erstein a journey of two miles brings us to Limersheim, a village with 500 inhabitants, and another two miles to Fegersheim, which, with a population of 1800, is situated at the confluence of the Little Andlau with the Ill. It is said to possess a spring whose waters are beneficial in ophthalmic diseases. Almost opposite it, above the old town of Rosheim (population, 3910), where there is a remarkable Byzantine church dating from the eleventh or twelfth century, rise the ruins of the stately pile of Guirbaden, the ancient castle of the Rohans, destroyed in the seventeenth century.

As we draw close to Strassburg we see on our right, between the railway and the Rhine, which here flows with a broad and noble current, the agricultural settlement of Ostwald, founded in 1839 by the city of Strassburg; and on the left the town of Entzheim (population, 1700), in whose vicinity, on the 4th of October, 1674, the Imperialists were defeated by the French under Turenne. The mountains of the Vosges, when seen from this point, assume a character of singular beauty, and the surrounding country is diversified by many rich and agreeable landscapes. In several villages the houses are decorated with double rows of tobacco-leaves drying in the sun; tobacco being cultivated here to a considerable extent.

THE BADEN BANK OF THE RHINE.

Basel to Kehl.

Having thus conducted the patient reader along the left bank of the Rhine, and the valley of the Ill, to the city of Strassburg, we now retrace our steps to Basel, cross the "exultant and abounding river," and proceed to carry him with us along its *right* or German bank, a route not inferior in interest or in beauty to the former.

The Rhine, in this part of its course, is frequently encroached upon by hills. It receives the Dreisam, the Elz, the Scbutter, and the Kinzig. Its surface is literally strewn with islands, more or less wooded, of various outline, and frequently very charming in aspect.

About a mile and a half from Basel, on the so-called Leopoldshöhe, or Leopold's Height, stands the Basel custom-house, to indicate that we have quitted the territories of republican Switzerland. Passing Hattingen and Efringen, through very bright and beautiful scenery, and crossing the small stream of the Kander, where we obtain a glorious view of the islanded river and the mountainous landscapes of Alsace, with the snow-peaks of the Jura rising beyond Basel, we penetrate the limestone cliff of the Isteiner Klotz in a succession of tunnels, and drawing near the river arrive at Schliengen.

Continuing our course along the vine-clad slopes of the Black Forest, we arrive at Mtihlheim (population, 3000), the seat of an "amstadt" or jurisdiction, and the nearest station for Badenweiler. Muhlheim is celebrated for the "Markgrafler "wine produced by the neighbouring vineyards. It is a town of great antiquity, the abbey of St. Gall having had possessions here as early as 758.

Badenweiler lies about three miles to the east. Its springs were known to the Romans, and the baths erected by them were discovered in 1748, in a state of excellent preservation. They consist of four large and eight smaller baths, including dressing and anointing rooms, a sudatorium, and other appurtenances. They are probably the most complete now in existence (out of Rome), and measure 324 feet in length by 100 feet in breadth. Badenweiler is now frequented by as many as 1500 visitors every season, and boasts of a handsome Cursaal. The water is impregnated to a large extent with common salt and gypsum, and reputed beneficial in cases of gout, consumption, rheumatism, hysteria, hypochondriasis, and intermittent fever. The temperature is 20° R.

About six miles from Badenweiler is the Belchen or Hochblewan peak, whose summit, 3597 feet above the sea, commands a fine view of the course of the Rhine as far as Strassburg, and of the country inclosed by the mountain chains of the Black Forest on the east, of the Vosges on the west, and the Jura on the south. Beyond the latter, on a clear day, may be seen the white crests of the Bernese Alps.

To the west of Mühlheim, at a distance of one mile and a half, and close to the rocky bank of the Rhine, lies Neuenberg, besieged by the chivalrous Duke Bernhard von Weimar, in 1633 to 1634.

Near Heitersheim, once the seat of the master of the Maltese Knights, are the ruins of Staufenburg castle, which can also be reached from Krotzingen. It was formerly the seat of a race of powerful nobles, whose line became extinct in 1602. From this point we may carry the reader, for a moment, to a town already mentioned—Alt-Brisach. Here the isolated volcanic mountain of the Kaisersstuhl throws out, as it were, a buttress of basalt, rising almost perpendicularly from the waters of the rolling river to a height of 758 feet. On the highest point of this singular eminence is planted the Gothic minster of St. Stephen, a notable example of thirteenth century architecture. The town of Alt-Brisach lies on the sides of the hill and in the valley beneath it. A flying bridge connects it with the opposite bank. Though now a quiet, lifeless place, with less than 4000 inhabitants, it was once a most important frontier fortress, and the key of Germany on the west.

As late as the tenth century, the Rhine is said to have flowed round the town, and isolated the rock on which it stands. From 1331 it belonged to Austria; but in 1638 was captured by Duke Bernhard of Saxe Weimar, after a blockade of twelve months, which inflicted the most dreadful sufferings on the garrison and citizens. After his death it was held by the French, to whom it was formally made over by the treaty of Westphalia in 1648. But it was impossible for Germany to rest contented with this important fortress in the hands of a hostile nation, and at the Peace of Ryswick, in 1700, it was recovered by the Austrians. In 1703 it was again taken by the French under Tallard and Vauban, nor was it restored until 1715. The Emperor Charles VI. greatly improved the defences, and erected a new fort. In 1743, when a new French invasion was apprehended, the Empress Maria Theresa ordered the Leopold and Charles forts to be destroyed, and the military stores removed to Freiburg. These steps were not taken too soon. In the following year the irrepressible banner of the fleur-de-lis once more crossed the Rhine, captured Alt-Brisach, and destroyed the remaining fortifications. Subsequently the bridge was removed. An Austrian garrison was not replaced in the town until 1768.

At the epoch of the French revolution the French once more attacked Brisach. On the bank of the river, opposite the unfortunate town, they had erected Fort Mortier, and from this position they bombarded the defenceless German town, on the 15th of September, 1793. A portion of the buildings having been restored, they again occupied it in 1796. In 1805 Napoleon resolved on converting it into a strong fortress, and the works were already in a forward condition when the treaty of Presburg gave Brisach to Baden.

About two leagues to the north of Brisach, on a spur of the Kaisersstuhl, which, projecting into the river, breaks up its regular flow into a swift and whirling current, are the ruins of Castle Sponeck. These owe more to their romantic position than to their extent or character, which is comparatively insignificant; but they command a fine view of the Rhine, the opposite bank, and the undulating sweep of the Vosges.

FREIBURG.

Freiburg, the ancient capital of the Breisgau, is situated about twelve miles from the Rhine, on the outskirts of the Black Forest, at the mouth of the romantic Höllenthal, or Valley of Hell, and upon the Dreisam, whose manifold ramifications extend into all the principal streets. It is elevated about 860 feet above the sea, so as to enjoy an unbounded view of the surrounding country, which is as bright, goodly, and diversified as eye can desire. The rich vale of the Dreisam, the boldly broken ground of the Black Forest, the fertile plain, which carries its stores of wealth and beauty up to the very foot of the vine-clad Kaisersstuhl, and the picturesque mountains, which raise their vapour-loaded crests against the horizon, form a picture of infinite light and loveliness.

Freiburg is the seat of a "jurisdiction" of the Imperial Court of the Upper Rhine Circle, of a university, and of the archbishop and chapter of the Upper Rhine ecclesiastical province. It has a population of 17,000, and is a busy and flourishing town; its prosperity being due in part to its position on the great German highways, and partly to its forming the centre to which the commercial and manufacturing industry of the Black Forest converges.

The history of Freiburg extends over about eight centuries. As late as 1008, and probably fifty years later, the area now covered by its well-thronged streets was a dense luxuriant forest. Gradually a clearing was made, and a few hunters and fishermen planted their huts on the bank of the Dreisam. The neighbouring hill was speedily seized upon as a suitable site for a castle, and the infant settlement began to extend under its protection. Then came an auspicious patron in the person of Duke Berthold III., of Zaringia, who, having visited Köln, and learned to admire its splendour, desired to establish a rival on the Upper Rhine. Accordingly, he raised the village to the rank of a town. From his brother and successor, Conrad, the new town received a charter of rights and privileges. It was under the rule of this energetic prince that the minster was commenced, and so diligently was it prosecuted that within its walls, in 1146, St. Bernard was able to deliver an eloquent harangue in favour of the Crusades.

In 1218 the male line of the dukes of Zaringia, who had done so much for the prosperity of Freiburg, became extinct. The town was then claimed as an imperial fief, but soon afterwards surrendered to Egon I., count of Hohenberg, who had wedded Agnes, the sister of Duke Berthold V., of Zaringia. His son, Egon II., called himself von Freiburg, and for the defence of the town erected the strong castle of Burghalden.

About the middle of the fourteenth century Freiburg became involved in a life and death struggle with Count Egon IV. She conquered, but the tax on her resources was so heavy, that to avoid any similar disaster she voluntarily parted with her independence, and surrendered her rights and liberties to the imperial house of Hapsburg. Some of her bravest sons afterwards followed the Austrian standard to the field of Sempach, and perished in that murderous battle. In 1457 the line of the counts of Freiburg ceased to exist.

In 1468 the Archduke Sigismund, whose extravagance had had its natural result, mortgaged all his possessions in Alsace, Sundgau, Breisgau, and the Black Forest, to Charles the Bold of Burgundy, for the sum of 80,000 florins. Freiburg then did homage at Ensisheim, and Peter von Hagenbach, a man of unbridled lust and cruelty, was appointed its governor. He was soon guilty of the most abominable excesses. In vain the towns complained to Charles; he listened to them with indifference. They then collected a sum sufficient to defray the mortgage, and encouraged Duke Sigismund to take up arms against the Burgundian tyrant. Hagenbach retired to Brisach with a considerable force; but continuing his exactions, the citizens rose against him, expelled his mercenaries, seized him, tried him according to the law of the empire, and beheaded him at night by torchlight. The towns then made common cause against their oppressor, who invaded Switzerland with a powerful army, but was defeated at Granson and Morat, and killed under the walls of Nancy, on the 5th of January, 1477.

During the famous Peasants' War, Freiburg was surrounded with twenty thousand insurgents, who were bribed to retire by a gift of 3000 florins and several pieces of artillery. In the Thirty Years' War, the Swedish army appeared before the gates of Freiburg on the 19th December, 1632. They were at first repulsed, but on the 26th of the same month their compact battalions once more gathered in front of the town, and Colonel Bernhard Schaffalitzki demanded its surrender in the name of Fieldmarshal Horn. In this extremity the citizens displayed no ordinary resolution. Supported by the students and country people, they manned the walls. For forty-eight hours the unfortunate town was bombarded with red hot balls, effecting so terrible a desolation that the Freiburgers found themselves compelled to surrender. On the 29th, Field-marshal Horn made his public entry, and immediately proceeded to levy a requisition of 30,000 florins.

After a brief interval of peace, Duke Bernard of Weimar appeared before the town (March 20, 1638). Under Escher von Bühningen it made a gallant defence; but on the 11th of April Freiburg surrendered. The Swedish colonel, Kanoffsky von Langendorff , was appointed governor. He treated its citizens with the utmost moderation; but in 1644, on the approach of the imperial army, ordered two of the suburbs to be razed. The Imperialists, 15,000 strong, under Field-marshal Mercy, invested the place, while Turenne, with 10,000 men, hastened to its relief. Mercy, however, delivered his attacks so incessantly and so furiously, that on the 28th of July the garrison was forced to yield. In recognition of its gallant defence, however, it was allowed to march out with all the honours of war, and retire to Brisach.

Turenne, reinforced by 10,000 men under the famous Condé, arrived on the scene soon after the capitulation had been concluded. On the 2nd of August he attacked the entrenchments which Mercy had raised along the neighbouring mountain, the Schinberg, but was repulsed with so severe a loss, that he retired upon Denzlingen during the night of the 5th of August. Mercy maintained himself in the town for several days, and then, leaving a strong garrison behind him, marched towards the Black Forest.

Freiburg now enjoyed a period of peace. By the treaty of Westphalia it was restored to Austria; but Louis XIV., in pursuance of his scheme of European supremacy, resolved to seize it. In the autumn of 1677, its garrison having been imprudently reduced, Marshal Crequi suddenly crossed the Rhine on the 10th, and made himself master of the place on the 16th, of November.

By the treaty of Nimeguen, in the following year, the city, so craftily won, was formally ceded to France. Louis XIV. proceeded to convert it into a fortress, after the plans of Vauban. In 1697 the treaty of Ryswick restored Freiburg to Austria; but in the condition of the town no improvement took place. On the 21st of September, 1713, Marshal Villars, with an army of 150,000 men, advanced against Freiburg, which was garrisoned by only 10,000 men under Fieldmarshal von Harsch. In little more than a week Von Harsch was forced to retire into the citadel, leaving the unfortunate inhabitants to take what steps they chose for their own protection. Villars had given orders to storm the town, but at the representations of the citizens he consented to accept terms of capitulation. An armistice was agreed upon until the garrison had communicated with Prince Eugene, and on the 17th of November the garrison marched out with all the honours of war, while the town paid a sum of 1,000,000 francs as an indemnity. Freiburg, however, quickly returned to its former allegiance, being restored to Austria by the treaty of Rastadt, in September, 1714. Harassed by these continual sieges, it declined more and more rapidly, until, with an expenditure exceeding its income by 5000 florins yearly, it owed a debt of 300,000 florins.

On the 17th of September, 1740, Marshal Coigny, with a French army of 56,000 men, crossed the Rhine, moved rapidly on Freiburg, and invested it. The town was at that time garrisoned by 8000 men under General von Damnitz, and its bombardment took place under the eye of Louis XV. The operations of the besiegers were pressed so vigorously, that on the 26th of October a breach had been effected, and on the 5th of November the garrison abandoned the town to the French, and withdrew into the castles. These, however, soon fell into the hands of the French, who captured 212 guns, besides eighty mortars and howitzers. They then razed the fortifications, and blew up the three castles.

The peace of Aix-la-Chapelle again restored Freiburg to Austria, when prosperity returned to the town, and it has since persevered annually in increasing its wealth and population. During the French Revolution it suffered comparatively little.

By the peace of Presburg, in 1801, Freiburg was annexed to the grand duchy of Baden, whose government used every exertion to promote its interests. In 1848 it was once more exposed to a partial bombardment. A body of revolutionists marched into the town during Passion week, proclaimed the republic, and barricaded the town gates. But on Easter Monday it was invested by the grand-ducal troops, by whom the insurgents were speedily put to flight.

Freiburg consists of the town, properly so called; of the Stephanie, formerly called the Schnecken (or Snail) suburb; and of a new district dating from 1826, which seems to be generally known as the Zaringian suburb. The cathedral, in boldness of design and perfectness of execution, in solemnity and grandeur of aspect, is inferior only to that of Strassburg. We are speaking, be it understood, of German cathedrals. Religious art has here produced a masterpiece, which seems to be informed, if we may venture on a somewhat fanciful expression, with the enthusiasm of a devout and lofty genius. It is surprising that an edifice, whose gradual erection spread over a couple of centuries, should everywhere exhibit so fine a harmony. It was begun between the years 1122 and 1152, in the reign of Conrad, duke of Zaringia. The nave, the west aisle, the tower, and the porch date from 1236-72. The new choir was begun in 1354, and not completed until 1513. In 1561 a portion of the spire was destroyed by lightning, but it was soon restored.

Built of red sandstone, which time and atmospheric influences have toned down sufficiently, the cathedral of Freiburg is, unquestionably, a structure of surpassing beauty. Its ground plan is cruciform, and it occupies the centre of an open area, in the direction of west to east. Its tower, crowned by a pyramidal spire, is 340 feet in height. The first stage forms a square; the second, above the gallery, a dodecagon, which quickly passes into an octagon, the whole ending in an "octagonal pyramid" of the most exquisite open work. The western entrance, at the base of the tower, which is of the same width as the nave, is enriched with eight and twenty columns, each adorned with a statue of admirable design and execution. The gateway is divided into two by a solid column, ornamented with a fine statue of the Virgin, and covered with remarkable sculpture. Finally, a bas-relief, inserted above the gate, represents, in four tableaux, some Biblical incidents and scenes from the life of our Saviour. The interior of the minster, from end to end, is 460 feet in length. The nave is divided from the aisles by six pillars (each about six and a half feet in diameter) on either side; and against these are erected, on pedestals, statues of the Twelve Apostles. Nave and aisles, taken together, measure ninety-five feet across. These dimensions alone will enable the reader to form some dim notion of the magnificence of the *coup d'oeil* which bursts upon the spectator as he passes through the entrance door; but to realize the scene he must fill the windows with richly painted glass, which sheds a "dim religious light" on pavement and statue and column, and embellishes each carved capital and the sculptured balustrade carried along the sidewalls, with the rarest dyes, "gules and emerald and amethyst."

The exterior of the cathedral, especially on the south, is not less impressive than the interior. Its flying buttresses, its balustrades, its statues, its niches and their Gothic dais, its curious and very various spouts, its side doors, its atriums, its interminable rows of windows, its Gothic *rosaces*, its carved pedestals, its abounding wealth of strange, quaint, monstrous, and beautiful sculpture, all so completely original, and, if we may use the expression, individual, would furnish the stranger with material for a whole day's investigation.

Worth visiting also, as Mr. Mayhew tells us, is the Munster Platz, or Cathedral Square, for the peculiarity of the costumes one sees congregated at the spot. This, continues our authority, is the principal market-place, and the head-dresses of the peasants here are of the most peculiar character. Most of the women wear two huge black ribbon bows perched right on the crown of the head, each bow being spread out fan-shape, and the two together seeming like the enormous wings of a gigantic black butterfly that has settled on the top of the skull. This is the time Margravia, or Breisgau fashion; the Catholics wearing the bows embroidered with gold at the back, and the Protestants preferring them plain. Other women, again, have straw hats of a most masculine shape, poised as it were on the head, and bright red handkerchiefs tied over their ears, while long Swiss tails hang down the back in double Chinese fashion, and are tied with ribbon that reaches literally down to the heels.

After the Cathedral, there are few buildings in Freiburg which the visitor cares to see. The Minster dwarfs as it were, and humiliates them. Still the Ludwigs (Protestant) Church, built in 1827-38, is worth a visit. It occupies the summit of a gentle elevation at the north end of the town, in the Zaringian suburb.

Then, among the sights of the town are, the archiepiscopal palace, east of the Kaufhaus; the fifteenth century fountain, in the Kaiser-strasse; the fountain in the Fish Market, built in 1807, and adorned with a statue of the founder of Freiburg, Berthold III.; the university, erected in 1454, and containing a valuable library of upwards of 120,000 volumes; the blind asylum; and the palace of the grand duke. The university has been rendered illustrious by the names of Capüton, Erasmus, and Philip von Engen; and in our own day by those of Hug the orientalist, Kotteck the historian, Welker the juriconsult, and Beck and Baumgarten the physicians. It has thirty-five professors, and 228 students.

By way of the Hollenthal the traveller may proceed from Freiburg to the Schauinsland or Erdkasten, whose summit, 4200 feet above the sea-level, commands the finest view in Baden; a view including not only the heights of the Black Forest, the Kandel, the Feldberg, and the Belchen, and the dim shadowy valleys which penetrate into their recesses, but the rich plain of the Rhine, fertile, sunny, and radiant, the Vosges, the mighty masses of the Jura and the Alps, from the Glcernisch and the Tcedi to the Dent-du-Midi and the "monarch of the mountains," Mont Blanc. The centre of this grand mountain chain is occupied by the white peaks of the Bernese Alps.

FREIBURG TO OFFENBURG.

We may now resume our journey along the Baden bank of the Rhine.

About three miles to the north lies the ruined castle of the dukes of Zaringia or Zähringen, the founders of the reigning family of Baden. It commands an attractive picture of the surrounding district of the Breisgau.

Passing Denzlingen, we soon come in sight of Emmendingen, a town of 2170 inhabitants. The only notable fact recorded in connection with it is that the astronomer Kepler, and the antiquary Schoepflin, were educated at its grammar-school.

From Emmendingen we make a detour to the Hochburg or Hochberg. The ruins are said to be the most extensive in Germany. The castle was founded by a family of the same name; sustained a siege during the Peasants' War; was occupied during the Thirty Years' War by the Margrave George Frederick, fortified after the peace of Westphalia by Frederick VI., and dismantled by order of the great French war-minister, Louvois, in 1689.

Continuing our route, we leave on the left the volcanic range of the Kaisersstuhl, and on the right the undulating ridges of the Black Forest, as we draw near to Riegel. From this station the Kaisersstuhl—so called because the Emperor Rudolph of Hapsburg, in his hunting expeditions, frequently rested on its summit—is usually visited. The highest point is indicated by nine lime trees (1950 feet). It lays bare to the eye the entire sweep of the Rhine, and of each side of its valley, from Basel to Strassburg.

Crossing the Elz, we reach Kurzingen (population, 2313), which formerly belonged to Austria; and crossing the Bleiche, we arrive at Herbolzheim (population, 2063). Leaving Ringsheim on the right, we come to Ettenheim (population, 2931), at the mouth of the valley of the Undiz; a place of interest as the scene of the forcible arrest of the young Duc d'Enghien, on the loth of March, 1804.

The summit of the steep conical Hohengerold is crowned by the ruins of a castle, destroyed in 1697 by the French under the Marshal de Créqui. The view from it is very beautiful, and the Rhine valley is seen inclosed between the Vosges on the west, and the Black Forest on the east, prior to its escape into the fertile plains of Baden, Hesse Darmstadt, and Rhenish Prussia.

Offenburg (with a population of 4408), is situated at the mouth of the valley of the Kinzig, about three miles above the junction of that river with the Rhine. It was formerly a free imperial town, but by the treaty of Presburg was ceded to Baden. At the end of the principal street the English visitor will be surprised to see a statue of the bold, bluff, sturdy Elizabethan sea-king, Sir Francis Drake, erected in 1583, apparently to commemorate his introduction of the potato into Europe.

At the Appenweiler station, a mile beyond Offenburg, a branch line strikes off on the left for Kehl and Strassburg (we adopt the German orthography), while the main line descends the bank of the Rhine to Carlsruhe, Mannheim, and Frankfort.

Kehl (population, 1903) attained a melancholy celebrity in the late war, having been laid in ruins by the batteries of Strassburg, during the siege of the latter by the German army under General Werder. It is situated at the confluence of the Kinzig and the Schutter with the Rhine, and was formerly an imperial fortress of some distinction.

The Rhine at this point is divided into two branches by an island, on which stood the French custom-house, and still stands the monument to General Desaix. The island is connected with the mainland on either side by a bridge of boats, blown up in 1870. The railway is, or was, carried across the river from Kehl to Strassburg by an iron lattice bridge on four piers, erected in 1861.

This connecting line between the French and German railways was opened on the 6th of April, 1861. It describes an immense curve around the city, for it first proceeds towards Paris for three-quarters of a mile, then connects itself with the Baden Railway by a branch of 800 yards in length, and follows up that of Basel for 2200 yards, as far as Koenigshofen. Beyond this village it assumes a "separate existence," crosses the Ill and the Rhône and Rhine Canal, and approaches the walls of Strassburg. Skirting the cemetery of St.

Urbain, and passing the south side of the citadel, it reaches the Porte d'Austerlitz station. On a light girder bridge it traverses the Little Rhine, opening up a view of the monument of General Desaix on the Ile des Epis.

CHAPTER III. THE CITY OF STRASSBURG, OR STRASBURG.

STRASSBURG, like most of the Rhenish cities, is of Roman origin; like Köln and Coblenz, Mainz, Bingen, and Speier. It was the old Romano-Celtic Argentoratum, and it is easy to understand that to the warriors of Rome its position would recommend itself as possessed of peculiar military advantages. It is situated at the confluence of the rivers Ill and Brieusch, about half a league from the Rhine; so as to hold the entrance to the valleys of both rivers. Hence, its possession has at all times been fiercely disputed by hostile armies endeavouring to obtain command of the Upper Rhine.

The strength of its fortifications, which were designed by Vauban, may readily be inferred from the resistance they offered, in 1870, to the Prussian arms. The siege was gallantly maintained; the defence was equally heroic; and the inhabitants suffered terribly before General Uhrich consented to relinquish the defence. The Prussian artillery had not only reduced the outworks to ruins, and effected a breach in the walls, but, at one time, had poured shot and shell into the doomed city, setting on fire the houses of inoffensive citizens, and slaying women and children, the old and young, the unarmed civilian as well as the soldier. For six weeks Strassburg held out bravely; but in the end, General Uhrich having done enough for his own fame, acted nobly in not prolonging a defence by which the unarmed and feeble must have been the principal sufferers. Happily, this terrible siege, in all its wide-spread devastation, has left comparatively uninjured the great pride, and boast, and ornament of Strassburg; its famous Minster has escaped the "storms of battle."

In outline as in details the cathedral of Strassburg deserves nearly all the praise that has been lavished upon it; and it is certain that no man of taste or fancy can look upon it without a very powerful emotion of reverent admiration. The spire rises 460 feet above the pavement; that is, one foot lower than the great Pyramid of Egypt, 104 feet higher than the cross of St. Paul's, 40 feet higher than the steeple of St. Etienne at Vienna, 28 feet higher than St. Peter's at Rome, and 258 feet higher than the monument of London. A doorway in the south side of the truncated tower leads to its summit. The next chief point of interest is the western façade, whose delicate and yet luxuriant beauty it would be difficult to overpraise; though we think it inferior to the corresponding parts of the cathedrals of York and Exeter. The effect has been compared to that of a netting of detached pillars and arches thrown—we had almost said spun—over the solid mass or body of the cathedral. And delicate as are the mouldings and sculptures, such is the hardness and excellent preservation of the stone, that they preserve all their original sharpness, and look "like a veil of the finest cast iron." The window is circular, and forty-eight feet in diameter.

After the spire and the west front, the principal object of interest to the traveller is the clock, whose origin dates as far back as 1352, in which year it was set up in its place in the south transept, under the auspices of Berthold de Buchek, then bishop of Strassburg. It was divided into three parts, of which the lowest exhibited a universal calendar. In the middle was an astrolabe, and in the upper section might be seen the figures of the Three Kings and the Virgin, carved in wood. When the hour struck the three kings bowed to the Virgin, while a carillon chimed a lively air, and a cock crowed and clapped his wings. In course of time, however, this ingenious mechanism got out of order, and in 1547 its repair was intrusted to Dr. Michael Herr, Chretei Herlin, and Nicholas Prugnor, three distinguished mathematicians. They died before the work was finished, but it was continued by Conrad Dasypodius, a pupil of Herlin, and completed in four years. Thenceforth the clock went merry as a marriage bell up to the year of the great French Revolution, when it struck for the last time, as if it felt it had been created in accordance with the "old order "of things, and was not in harmony with "the new."

Nearly fifty years passed away before any attempt was made to restore it to a working condition. During this time it fell into a state of pitiable dilapidation, and when the mechanicians came to examine it, they found that the works were eaten up with rust and verdigris, and that nothing could be done. At length, one Schwilgué, an artist and mathematician of Strassburg—who is still, or, at all events, was recently living—undertook to repair, modify, and reinstate the clock; which task, it is recorded, he commenced on June 24, 1836, and completed in 1840. The mechanism of the new clock was set up in the old framing, the number of the figures having been increased, and their appearance improved by jointed limbs. The quarter chimes are struck by figures representative of the Four Ages of Man, which move in a circle round the skeleton Time and his sweeping scythe. The hour bell is struck by a winged Genius, at the same moment that a figure of an angel turns an hour-glass, through whose narrow neck the sand continuously pours year after year. Daily, at noon, a procession of the Twelve Apostles wheels around a figure of the Saviour. Each one in passing bends towards him, and he, when the circuit is complete, extends his hands as if in the act of blessing. During the procession a cock claps his wings, opens his beak, and crows three times.

This singular and complex piece of mechanism exhibits the month and the day of the month, the sign of the zodiac, the Dominical letter, the sidereal time, the Copernican planetary system, and the precession of the Equinoxes; and the works are elaborated with so much ingenuity, that it also marks the 29th day of February in every leap year. Moreover, the various phases of the moon are shown, and the solar and lunar equations for the reduction of the mean movements of the sun and moon.

The façade of the cathedral is decorated by three porticoes. The central, ornamented with columns and with fourteen statues of the Hebrew prophets, is both the grandest and the most beautiful; though its gate of bronze, covered all over with the richest work, was melted down at the Revolution, converted into coin, and is now replaced by one of wood. The portico on the right hand is embellished with statues of the Ten Virgins, the Bridegroom, and Bride; that on the left, with figures of other virgins treading under their feet the capital sins. The tympana and pediments of all three portals are filled in with the most exquisite sculpture; and above, on the line where the second story commences, are set the spirited equestrian statues of Clovis, Dagobert, Rudolph of Hapsburg, and Louis XIV. The latter is of modern workmanship, and was not elevated to its present noble position until 1828. Also of modern workmanship and recent erection are the statues, on a somewhat higher level, of

Pepin the Short, Charlemagne, Otho the Great, and Henry the Fowler, each in his turn a ruler of the Holy Roman Empire.

Above the central gateway shines the glorious marigold window, which measures forty-three feet in diameter, and is filled with glass restored by Messieurs Ritter and Muller.

The north and south towers are each pierced with a noble window, enriched by numerous *rosaces*; and rosaces likewise embellish and beautify the pediments of the side doors. Statues of the apostles occupy a gallery raised above the great central rose. Higher still stands the majestic figure of our Lord, holding a cross and banner. On each side of this same stage may be seen a lofty ogival window behind a cluster of slender shapely pillars.

The third stage is occupied, between the two towers, by a massive belfry of late construction, inclosing four bells, of which the heaviest, cast in 1427, weighs 9000 kilogrammes. This portion of the façade was decorated in 1849 with a colossal sculpture, representing the Last Judgment. The entire story, except so far as the noble tower is concerned, is surmounted by a platform, where a small hut is erected for the keepers charged with ringing the bells, and raising an alarm in case of fire. From the north tower springs the münster, as it is called, or spire; this is supported by an octagonal tower; octagonal, yet, from a distance, apparently square, because four of the sides are concealed by winding staircases.

The spire is an eight-sided obelisk of the most exquisite open work, consisting of six tiers of small turrets, raised one above another in pyramid-fashion. A miracle of art, from its surpassing delicacy and admirable boldness! On the sixth tier or story rests the lantern, to which eight open winding staircases lead up; and thence, by steps constructed on the outside, the adventurous climber reaches the crown. Higher still, above another opening, poetically called "the rose," shoots the graceful spire in the form of a cross, five and a half feet high; finally, this cross terminates in a *bouton*, 460 millimètres in diameter, surmounted by a lightning-conductor.

The south doorway consists of two semicircular doors, and is ornamented with bas-reliefs and statues. Two of these were carved by the firm hand of Sabina von Steinbach, Erwin's daughter. On the parvise in front stands a statue of Erwin, executed a few years ago by M. Grass, the statuary of the cathedral. The old north doorway is masked by a façade, built in 1492 by Jacques de Landshut. The nave, covered with a copper roof, which suffered much during the great siege, is lighted by great pointed windows, ornamented with rosaces. Scarcely, indeed, is there a foot of stone which does not exhibit some more or less conspicuous effort of the carver's skill in statues, and gargoyles, and shapely pinnacles.

We now enter the interior; and the imagination recoils overpowered by the awful impression of that lofty aisle, whose vaulted roof soars heavenward with all the elasticity and strength of a forest arcade, and scarcely seems to lean on the double row of clustered columns which supports it. Rich glories dye the pavement; streaming in through many-coloured windows, which immortalize the names of John of Kirchheim, John Markgraf, Jacques Vischer, and the brothers Link. How soft and sweet the light which shimmers through each painted pane, and weaves a fine phantasmagoria of colour over wall and column! The pulpit is a masterpiece: it was carved in stone by John Hammern in 1406. The once-famous organ, built by Andrew Silbermann in 1714, was destroyed in the siege of 1870.

One of the columns supporting the roof of the choir is composed of a sheaf or group of pillars. It is known as the Angel's Column, and being of comparatively recent date is popularly attributed to Erwin of Steinbach. In the south transept, opposite a statue of Bishop Werner, stands the great clock which we have already described so fully.

The apse, intended to serve as a sanctuary, is, perhaps, too shallow. It is ascended from the choir by a flight of steps. The crypt, restored about eleven years since, contains a nave, a choir, and two apses. At the entrance we pause to contemplate a very ancient sculpture, representing our Saviour seized by the Roman soldiers on the Mount of Olives. The form of the pillars, the cubic capitals, the semicircular arches of the crypt, may be accepted as proofs that it was erected early in the eleventh century.

The chapel of St. Andrew, in the south aisle of the choir, contains the tombs of several bishops. Its columns and ornaments are very ancient.

In the chapel of St. John the Baptist, behind the north aisle, is the superb Gothic monument erected in honour of Bishop Conrad II., of Lichtenberg, who died in 1299. Near the entrance to this chapel our attention will be arrested by the baptistery, in stone, of Josse Dotzinger, of Worms: died 1449.

The chapel of St. Catherine, in the right wing, contains the tomb of a chevalier of Strassburg, remarkable for the number and excellence of the figures which decorate it, and for the singular manner in which they are grouped.

The cathedral contains several paintings by Strassburg artists; among others, the Adoration of the Shepherds, by Guerin; the Entombment of Christ, by Klein; and the Ascension, by Heim.

In a little court behind the chapel of St. John is the tomb of the sculptor Erwin, his wife, and son. In the north side of the cathedral, the St. Lawrence chapel is enriched with renovated sculptures, representing the martyrdom of the saints.

We now direct our steps to the Protestant church of St. Thomas, which occupies the site of a palace of the Frankish kings. After being twice burned, and twice reconstructed, it was completely rebuilt by Bishop Henry, in 1264. Externally, its characteristic features are its towers; the west is partly built in the Byzantine style; the east, in the Gothic. In the interior we shall find some admirable painted glass, and several curious monuments; among others, the celebrated monument of the Maréchal de Saxe, the masterpiece of the sculptor Pigalle, erected to the great soldier's memory by Louis XV., in 1777. A monument of very different character is the tomb of Bishop Adeloch, with its curious sculptures. It bears the date of DCCCXXX (830), but surely this is somewhat apocryphal.

The other churches are those of St. Peter the Elder (the most ancient in Strassburg, and easily distinguished by the graceful Gothic spire which crowns its dome); St. Peter the Younger (built in 1030, restored in 1290); St. William, so named in honour of William of Aquitaine, founder of the monastic order of the Guillelmites (here are the tombs of Counts Philip and Ulrich of Werden); the Madeleine (the choir is surpassingly beautiful); and St. Stephen, a Byzantine building of the eighth century, which in its time has played many parts, having been a church, a storehouse, a theatre, a tobacco manufactory, and again a church.

The Académie Royale was founded in 1538 as a Protestant school. In 1621 it was raised to the rank of a university, but it was suppressed at the Revolution. It was here that Goethe completed his studies, and took his doctor's degree in 1771. Indeed, the residence of the great German poet and philosopher at Strassburg is one of the most interesting associations of the place.

The offices of the Prefecture are worth a word of notice, on account of their own stately architecture, and because they occupy the site of the funeral pile on which ten thousand Jews were burned, in 1349, because they refused baptism. The founder of these buildings was François Joseph Klinglin, and the date of their erection, the early part of the eighteenth century.

Between the Ill and the south side of the cathedral stands the Château Imperial, formerly the episcopal palace, and one of the stateliest piles in Strassburg. In the same neighbourhood we find a rich and striking Renaissance mansion, the Frauenhaus, built in 1581. The chief object in its interior is a staircase of singularly light and elegant construction. Here are preserved the ancient plans, on parchment, of the cathedral: the works of the old astronomical clock; fragments of the cathedral, secured during its various alterations and repairs; and a collection of plaster casts of the most remarkable sculptures.

Strassburg has long and deservedly been quoted as a brilliant example of what may be done by a liberal city for the education of its children. Before the war it contained, besides its Academy, an Imperial Lyceum, a Protestant gymnasium, thirty-six primary schools, and twenty-four charities, supported by the town, and attended by 8000 pupils of both sexes; a normal primary school for schoolmasters; a normal primary school for Protestant mistresses; a municipal industrial school; a Jewish school; two institutions for the deaf and dumb; Catholic seminaries; a Protestant seminary; schools of design; a school of artillery; two schools to prepare young ladies for the work of tuition; four intermediate schools, into which, at a suitable time, the children passed from the charitable asylums; two evening schools for young artisans; a school of medicine; and a conservatory of music.

Our last journey conducts us to the Platz Kléber, where the convent of the Cordeliers, and a tower containing the archives and treasury of the city, gave way in 1767-68 to a vast public edifice of heavy design, formerly occupied by the governor's staff. In the centre of the open area, on a pedestal covered with inscriptions and vigorous bas-reliefs, stands a bronze statue of General Kléber, executed by Philippe Grass.

Besides Kléber, Strassburg gave Marshal Kellermann to the French army. François Christophe was born of an old and distinguished family, on the 30th of May, 1735. Entering the army in 1752, he served with good repute in the Seven Years' War, and in 1789, when the French revolution opened a career to men of talent, was a maréchal de camp. In 1790 he obtained the military command of the departments of the Haut and Bas Rhin, and early in 1792 attained the rank of lieutenant-general.

Dumouriez, at the head of the main body of the French army, was encamped at Grand Pré, in the forest of Argonne, and gravely threatened by the advancing Prussians. With a corps of twenty-two thousand men Kellermann hastened to his relief, and by a series of brilliant forced marches gained Valmy, a strong position on the right of Dumouriez. Here he was separated by a valley or ravine from the heights of La Lune, on which the Prussians were posted thrice as strong in numbers. About eleven o'clock on the 20th of September the latter assaulted in column, supported by artillery, Kellermann's position. A fierce struggle ensued, but the brilliant manoeuvres of the French general compelled the enemy to retire with considerable loss. It is noticeable that this victory was won on the day that monarchy was abolished in France. Its importance was immense. It saved the young republic from annihilation, and strengthened the heart of the people in their resolution to defy the coalition of Europe.

CHAPTER IV. STRASSBURG TO SPEIER.

LEFT BANK OF THE RHINE.

THERE are no steamers navigating this portion of the Rhine. The road from Strassburg is good, and very agreeable. The railway lies further inland, approaching very near the northern prolongation of the Vosges, and connecting Haguenau and Weissenburg, in France, with Landau, in Rhenish Prussia. From Strassburg to Weissenburg the distance is about forty-one miles.

At Vendenheim (population, 1362) we branch off from the Paris Railway—which proceeds by way of Nancy, Bar-le-Duc, and Châlons-sur-Marne, to the "capital of civilization"—and strike in a northerly direction; passing Haerdt (population, 1700), and Bischwiller (population, 8780), on the Moder. The latter is a busy and animated town, with those tall shafts rising above its roofs which invariably tell of commercial prosperity.

Traversing the "leafy shades" of the forest of Haguenau, we arrive at Walburg, a village of 600 inhabitants, on the Eberbach. Here the church is of great architectural interest. It belonged to an ancient abbey of Benedictine monks, founded, it is said, in the fifth century, and destroyed in 1525.

By way of Hoffen (population, 650) and Stundsbach (population, 750) we proceed to Wissembourg, or Weissenburg, a town of 5000 inhabitants, on the right bank of the Lauter, and at the base of the last buttresses or spurs of the prolonged chain of the Vosges. It was anciently one of the ten imperial free towns of Elsass. Captured by Louis XIV. in 1673, its possession was formally confirmed to France by the peace of Ryswick. Here, in 1870, the Prussians gained one of their earliest victories over the French.

Beyond Weissenburg the railway crosses the Lauter, an affluent of the Rhine, the "clear "river which marks the boundary of Alsace, and enters Germany in the territory of the Bavarian Palatinate.

Winden is the station for Bergzabern, a town of 3000 inhabitants, and the junction point of the branch-railway to Carlsruhe, which crosses the Rhine at Maxau.

Passing Rohrbach, we quickly arrive at Landau (population, 7500), on the Queich, a fortified town and depôt on the Germanic frontier. In the thirteenth century it was an insignificant village. In 1291 Rudolph of Hapsburg elevated it to the rank of a town, which was soon, much to its misfortune, surrounded by fortifications. Thereafter it became a military position of importance, and from the fifteenth century its history has been aptly described as a "succession of sieges, blockades, bombardments, captures, and surrenders." During the Thirty Years' War it was captured and pillaged eight times by the troops of Count Mansfeldt, the Spaniards, the Swedes, the Imperialists, and the French. By the treaty of Westphalia it was made over to France, who kept it for about three years. In 1678 it fell into the hands of the duke of Lorraine, but in the following year was recaptured by the French, to whom it was confirmed by the treaty of Ryswick. In the interval (1679-1691), its fortifications had been strengthened by the genius of Vauban, and the town nearly destroyed by fire (1689). During the profitless War of the Spanish Succession, its boasted impregnability was disproved, and it capitulated on four different occasions. In 1796 it was blockaded by the allies; but the victory of Weissenburg, won by Hoche and Pichegru, compelled them to raise the siege, and thence, until 1815, it remained in the hands of the French. By the treaties of Vienna it was given, first to Austria, and afterwards to Bavaria. Of late years its defences have been greatly neglected. The view from the church tower is extensive, and not deficient in the elements of the picturesque.

From Landau we proceed to Madenburg and Trifels, passing Arzheim, Ilbeseim, and Eschbach.

The Madenberg, or Madenburg, is the most perfect castle in the Rheinpfalz, and notwithstanding its ruined condition impresses the mind of the spectator by the singular dignity and magnificence of its aspect. The date of its foundation is unknown, and it first appears in history in the thirteenth century as the seat of the count of Leiningen. It was besieged, taken, and plundered by the Emperor Frederick the Victorious in 1470. In 1516 Ulrich, duke of Würtemburg, sold it to the archbishop of Spires (or Speier), but its ecclesiastical sanctity did not protect it from the insurgent peasants in 1525. Though almost razed to the ground, it sprang again into a splendid existence; again to be given up to the flames in 1552, by the margrave of Brandenburg, surnamed Alcibiades. Thrice, in less than a century, was the Madenburg ruined and rebuilt. Next came the horrors of the Thirty Years' War, and we read of it as alternately in the possession of the troops of Mansfeldt (1622), the French (1634), the Imperialists (1636), and the French again (1644). By the peace of Westphalia it was restored to the archbishops of Speier. It was once more restored, and on a very extensive scale; but in 1680 the French attacked, captured, and dismantled it. A stately ruin, it occupies the crest of a considerable and well-wooded ascent, and speaks with silent eloquence of the vicissitudes it has undergone in the stormy past. From its shattered battlements the traveller obtains one of those wide, bright, varied, and historic pictures which are met with nowhere else in such number and splendour as along the banks of the German river; a picture including the grim mountains of the Odenwald, the peaks of the Haardt, the irregular summits of the Vosges, with all their changing lights and shadows; the meanderings of the Rhine, the cathedral spire of Strassburg, and the old historic cities of Mannheim, Speier, and Worms.

An extension of our journey as far as Trifels will not fail to be of interest. The castle is now a complete ruin; it occupies, as its name implies, the summits of three conical heights, the Hauptberg (which is northernmost), the Anebos (to the south), and Trifels (in the centre). The chief remains now extant are those of a massive tower on the Hauptberg, in whose subterranean dungeon, according to tradition, Richard Coeur de Lion was imprisoned by Duke Leopold of Austria. In 1330 the castle of Trifels passed into the hands of the Princes Palatine. It is situated about 1422 feet above the sea-level. Even in its decay it is gravely imposing, and it commands a prospect of the richest and rarest character. On the adjoining hill of Scharfenberg rises a tower of 100 feet in height.

After leaving Landau, and passing the stations of Kerdningen and Edesheim, we arrive at Edenkoben, an industrial town of 4500 inhabitants. It is surrounded by extensive vineyards, but the wine is of inferior quality. On an adjacent hill, in the heart of vines and chestnut-trees, is situated the modern royal villa of Ludwigshöhe, and above it, on a higher eminence, bold and precipitous, moulder the ruins of the old castle of Rippburg, destroyed in the thirteenth century. To the north of the town wells a mineral spring, the Kurbrunnen.

From Edenkoben the traveller may repair to the Kropsburg, the Maxburg, and the Kalmit; or may ascend, through the western valley of the Modenbacher-thal, to the Steigerkoff, popularly designated the Schajnzel, whose summit, elevated some 2100 feet above the sea, commands what the guide-book calls a "magnificent panorama "of the valley-plain of the Rhine, and the heights which border on it.

The railway skirts the base of the Haardt Mountains, whose peaks and ravines offer many delightful vistas. On the opposite side, in clear and sunny weather, the long blue line of the summits of the Black Forest may be traced, like the undulating crest of a distant wave.

Maikammer is a town of 3000 inhabitants. On the right tower the massive and predominant bulks of the Maxburg, the Kalmit, and the Kropsburg. All the land seems burdened with their shadow, like a people lying under a great woe. But as their noble outlines rise more and more distinctly upon us, our heart seems to go forth towards the mountains, and we become sensible of their sublime associations of infinite silence and solitude, of purity, and majesty, and power.

From St. Martin, a village about two miles from Maikammer, the traveller most easily mounts to the Kropsburg, i.e., the "fine view," a castle of thirteenth century foundation, whose annals may be summed up in a few pithy phrases; it was frequently embellished and enlarged; it escaped the scourge of war; it did not escape the scourge of fashion, for some caprice induced its ancient lords to abandon and sell it, early in the present century. Thereafter it was partly demolished to furnish materials for the fortifications of Germersheim, and now it is occupied as a workhouse or benevolent asylum.

Above Maikammer, where, let us note, the church contains a good altar-piece by some German artist, rises the Kalmit (2300 feet), the culminating point of the mountains of the Palatinate, the Donnersberg alone excepted. An obelisk on the summit was erected by the people of Maikarnmer, in 1824, to King Maximilian Joseph.

The ascent of the wooded height of the Maxburg (1020 feet) may be made either from Oberhambach, from Mittelhambach, or by a path which skirts the southern acclivity.

The Maxburg, anciently known as the Hambacher Schloss, the Kaestelberg, and Kestenburg, is a stately, castellated pile, surmounted by a square turreted keep, which owes its present name to the circumstance that it was presented to King Maximilian by his subjects, on the occasion of his marriage to the Princess Mary of Prussia, October 12, 1842. It was then rebuilt on a magnificent scale by the architect Voit, of Munich, and a more splendid marriage-gift it would be difficult to imagine. It is not only a noble and majestic structure, with a richly-decorated interior, but it commands a wide and richly-coloured view of the mountains of the Haardt, and the beautiful valley-plain of the Rhine.

When the ancient castle of the Maxburg was founded, no German antiquary seems able to determine. From the Roman remains which have been discovered, it is allowable to suppose that the site was once occupied by a Roman camp. The castle afterwards erected on the same spot belonged, from the year 1100 down to the epoch of the French Revolution, to the cathedral-chapter of Speier; an instance of unbroken possession very unusual in Germany, whose castles generally changed hands once every half century. It was taken and plundered by the peasants in 1525; taken, plundered, and burned by the Margrave Albert of Brandenburg in 1552. The bishop of Speier showed no inclination to rebuild it, but in the great war of the Spanish Succession the French did what they could to complete its destruction. At the date of the French Revolution it became national property; and in 1823 was sold, on condition that the purchaser should not attempt to remove the ruins of the ancient pile. Here, on the 25th of May, 1832, was held the great popular demonstration of the Hambacher Fest, when the enthusiasm of a crowd of German students was fired by wild, vague ideas of consolidating German unity; a task only to be successfully accomplished, as we have seen, by "blood and iron."

Returning to Maikammer, we continue our railway route to Neustadt, sometimes called Neustadt an der Haardt, to distinguish it from other towns of the same name. It is a busy commercial and agricultural town, pleasantly situated at the foot of the well-wooded and vine-clad slopes of the Haardt mountains, and on the Rehbach, a small affluent of the Rhine. It forms the key of a valley which the conical bulk of the Königsberg apparently closes. On the height immediately above the town rise the ivy-shrouded ruins of the Castle Winzingen, or Haarsten Schloss, formerly the residence of the Electors Palatine, but reduced to decay in the Thirty Years' War and the War of Succession. The ruins are now attached to a handsome villa, and surrounded by blooming gardens, which command a view of the Rhine as far as Heidelberg.

The church of Neustadt is a stately Gothic structure, with massive towers, completed in the fourteenth century. It contains some interesting monuments of the Pfalzgraves, especially of Rudolph II. and Robert I., and some remains of ancient mural paintings in the fore-court, called the "Paradise."

In the neighbourhood of the town are the ruins of several castles, bearing mute and yet eloquent testimony to the desolation which a long series of wars effected in this fertile and beautiful region. The Wolfsburg was destroyed in the Peasants' War. Elmstein recalls the bitter memories of the Thirty Years' War. Some extensive quarries are here excavated in the Bunter sandstein and Muschelkalk; the latter, it is said, is rich in fossils.

LEFT BANK OF THE RHINE—LAUTERBURG TO SPEIER, BY RAIL.

The reader will remember that the route we have described in the preceding pages lies inland, at some miles from the Rhine, but forming the direct railway route from Strassburg to Neustadt. We now proceed to notice briefly a course that hugs more closely the bank of the great river.

From Strassburg the traveller makes his way to Lauterburg, by road, passing Germersheim, Fort Louis, Seltz, and Bernheim, and obtaining many glimpses of the broad and freely flowing Rhine, and of the picturesque wooded islands which occasionally diversify its channel. At Fort Louis, twenty-seven miles from Strassburg, a fine view of the celebrated spire of the cathedral may be obtained in clear weather. At a place called Knielingen, the railway to Carlsruhe is carried across the Rhine on a bridge of boats.

Below Lauterburg, a small fortified town of no great importance, and of less interest, the Lauter enters the Rhine.

A little lower down the river is crossed by another bridge of boats, and we arrive at Germersheim, a town of even less interest than Lauterburg, squalid, mean, and dirty, but surrounded by fortifications of great strength, which have been erected since 1834. This town was founded by the Emperor Rudolph of Hapsburg, who died here in 1291.

The country between Germersheim and Speier calls for no remark.

RIGHT BANK OF THE RHINE.—KEHL TO SPEIER.

From Kehl it will be convenient for the reader to return with us to Offenburg, and thence to descend the right bank of the Rhine by railway, visiting Rastadt (and Baden-Baden), Carlsruhe, and Philipsburg.

Passing the Appenweiler Junction, and the station at Renchen, we cross the Knisbis, and arrive at Achern, where there is a statue of Leopold, grand-duke of Baden, in the market-place.

At Sarsbach, two miles distant on the left, an obelisk of granite was erected by the French in 1829, to mark the spot where Marshal Turenne was killed by a cannon-ball, while reconnoitring the imperial army, July 27, 1675. Three previous monuments erected to his memory had been successively destroyed.

M. Charles Lallemand, in his elaborate work, "Les Paysans Badois," says, the vast plain which extends from the Rhine to the Black Forest, from Kehl to Appenweiler, has preserved its traditional costume and ancient manners. The Badish Hanau, he adds, is a kind of preface to the Black Forest. On quitting Kehl, and speeding along the branch line which, at Appenweiler, joins the great Baden railway, have you not a score of times admired those fertile levels, covered with crops, and meadows, and woods, which stretch afar on either hand, some with pretty villages where the peasant inhabitants move to and fro in a garb so picturesque and so elegant, that they seem the actors in an immense comic opera given by nature on this charming stage? And on Sunday especially, oh, then, nothing is wanting! neither idylls, nor merry ballads, nor harmonious choruses. So well defined, so distinct, and so individual is this picturesque country, in the heart of the uniformity which has crept over the surrounding plain, that the Badish people and writers preserve to it its ancient name of Hanauer-Lfendchen, though it has been formally incorporated into the Mittel-Rheinreis, or "Middle Rhine-circle." Hanauer-Laendchen (Laendchen being the diminutive of Land) signifies, the "little country of Hanau." The word seems to breathe an atmosphere of purity, freshness, and tenderness; it testifies to a love of country which is worth its weight in gold to artists, authors, and tourists.

We now come to Ottersweier, a town of nearly 2000 inhabitants, to the right of the railway, and close to the mouth of the Neusatzerthal, a pleasant and picturesque valley, watered by the Ambach. At about two miles from Ottersweier is the Hubbad, erected in 1811, after the plans of Weinbrenner. The thermal spring here is said to be efficacious in certain diseases of the stomach and bowels, in gout and rheumatic affections. In the neighbourhood lies the ruined castle of Windeck.

At Buhl, our next resting place, the most interesting object is the venerable church, the patriarch of the Badish churches in this part of the plain. The town has a population of 3000, and seems busy and prosperous; its fertile environs have been poetically but not untruly designated, *das goldene Land*. A stream called the Bühlotbach here flows down from the romantic valley of Buhl, which, by way of Herrenweise, communicates with the not less romantic valleys of Geroldsau and the Murz, and is famous for its vineyards and the "brave red wine "known as the Affenthaler.

Behind Steinbach, the hill of Yburg is crowned by the ruins of an old castle.

Leaving Sinzheim, a town of 2500 inhabitants, behind us, we cross the Oos rivulet, and speedily run into Oos junction, where we change carriages for one of the liveliest, gayest, and most beautiful of the German cities, the capital of the grand-duchy, Baden-Baden.

BADEN-BADEN.

The population of Baden-Baden is about 8000; that is, the permanent population; for the visitors in the season raise the total to 50,000.

Baden-Baden, the *Aurelia Aquensis* of the Romans, the queen of continental watering-places, is situated in a fair and well-wooded valley, watered by the Oos, at a distance of about six miles from the Rhine. It lies, in the form of an amphitheatre, on the slope of a mountain, whose summit is crowned by the old castle of Baden. It may not be, as some enthusiastic travellers assert, the most beautiful spot in Europe; but, as a French writer remarks, it offers the greatest number of pleasant walks,' especially for those who have eyes to see, and who love the bright long vista of fairy landscape and the deep shadows of wooded masses. If the forest were less luxuriant, and the waters more copious, the most enthusiastic of landscape amateurs would find nothing to displease them in this delectable region. And even as it is, there is such a freshness in the meadows, such a fulness and variety of vegetation, such a wealth of glowing colour in the picture, such a splendour and boldness of forms, that you can never weary of admiring them. Every day reveals to you a charm, a beauty previously unsuspected. In whatever direction you bend your steps, some secret surprise awaits and delights you.

And now for a glance at the history of Baden-Baden.

Note, as a preliminary, that the Oos or Oes (Oosbach), the comparatively insignificant stream which waters Baden, formerly separated the country of the Franks from that of the Allemanni. It still gives to this part of the grand-duchy—now a member of the North Germanic Confederation—the name of Oosgau or Usgau.

The origin of Baden, we are told by a learned authority, is referred to the most ancient times; and of all the towns on the right bank of the Rhine it has the oldest traditions, extending even as far back as the days of the Roman king, Tarquinius Priscus, when a Celtic colony is *said* to have settled here. At all events, it is certain that its sanative waters were soon discovered, and that they grew into repute among the Romans. According to an ancient monument which was discovered some years ago, its Latin designation was *Aurelia*

Aquensis; or, more correctly speaking, it would seem to have been called *Civitas Aquensis* by its founder, Augustus, and Aurelia by a later benefactor, Caracalla. It was also visited by Trajan (who greatly improved it), Hadrian, and Antoninus. It was connected by a military road with *Argentoratum* (Strassburg), *Salatio* (Selz), and Pforzheim; and was the headquarters, in succession, of the third, fifth, eighth, and fourteenth legions. Wine was first grown here in the reign of the Emperor Probus.

Having been destroyed by the Allemanni, Baden disappears from the page of history for some centuries. When we again hear of it, it is in the reign of Dagobert I., king of the Franks. From the Franks it passed to the monks of Weissenburg, the duchy of Suabia, the house of Zrehringen, Henry the Lion (by marriage), and Frederick Barbarossa (by exchange). The red-bearded emperor bestowed it as a fief on the Margrave Hermann III. His successor, Hermann IV., was the first who resided in the ancient castle. The town now rose from its ruins, became the capital of the margraviate, and in 1243 possessed, as we read, a church. It was also surrounded by fortifications, which proved of sufficient strength, in 1330, to repulse the troops of Berthold, bishop of Strassburg. In 1453 the church was converted into a "collegiate foundation." The Margrave Christopher forsook the residence of his ancestors, and in 1475 erected the new castle on the height immediately above the town. By this time the mineral waters had attained so great a renown, that as many as three thousand bathers yearly visited them. It is recorded that during the prevalence of the plague in 1551, the wafers were allowed to overflow and course through the streets; and owing, it was supposed, to the beneficial influence of their vapour, the pestilence never smote the town. It was less fortunate in its efforts to escape the plague of war. During the protracted struggle of the Thirty Years' War it suffered severely. In 1689 it was burned by the French under General Duras; its walls were dismantled, and the tombs of its margraves in the cloister church sacrilegiously broken open. After this event, the margraves retired to Rastadt, where they built a castle. In 1771 the branch of Baden-Baden became extinct in the person of the Margrave Augustus, and the line of Baden-Durlach inherited the ancestral territories.

The prosperity of Baden as a watering-place really dates from the epoch of the French Revolution, when numerous wealthy emigrés settled in its pleasant environs, and the fame of its baths spread among the higher classes of Europe. It was largely benefited by the Congress of Rastadt, for during the eighteen months its deliberations lasted, the different ambassadors gladly quitted the grim fortress to take up their abode in this attractive town. To meet the ever-increasing demand, new edifices sprung "like exhalations" from the ground; bath-houses, palaces, theatres, hotels. In 1822 was built the new "Conversation-house." At this date rouge-et-noir began to flourish, and Chabert paid 25,000 florins a year for the privilege of keeping a gaming-table. Purafit, who succeeded him in 1838, found it profitable to increase this abominable tribute to 45,000 florins.

For the idler and the adventurer Baden will lose its principal attraction when the public gaming tables are suppressed throughout the new German empire; but as it will still retain its delightful scenery and its baths, it is reasonable to expect that its prosperity will not be seriously affected.

The first visit of the "stranger in Baden" will be paid, we doubt not, to the Conversations-Haus and Trinkhalle. This splendid edifice is situated on the left bank of the Oosbach, at the foot of the Bentig, and the high hills of the Friesenberg, whose shady woods and verdant leas have been disposed in a kind of enchanted garden for the behoof of visitors. The building was erected in 1824 by Weinbrenner, but was considerably enlarged and embellished in 1854. It is now 350 feet in length, and has a portico of Corinthian columns. The interior is very richly, and yet elegantly, decorated. From the hall we pass into the assembly room, which is 150 feet long by 50 feet wide. Another magnificent chamber serves as the ball room (the "Salon des Fleurs"), and on either side are several smaller apartments, all decorated by Cielli and Sechan, and splendidly fitted up. The two wings are occupied as follows; on the right, by the Restaurant; on the left, by several new and partly private salons, namely, a ball and concert room, a "gallery of flowers," a "Louis Quatorze" salon, and a boudoir à la Loreis. ... At the end of the left wing are Marx's library and reading-rooms.

In front of the Conversations-Haus, beyond a wide and open area reserved for promenades, and furnished with seats, extends a beautiful verdurous lawn, on either side of which a "shady lane," bordered with noble trees, leads into the Lichtenthal road. The appearance of a fashionable bazaar, or fancy fair, is given to this agreeable promenade by the numerous shops, supplied with all kinds of *objets de luxe ou de nécessite*, which you encounter at every step. Of these *objets*, decidedly the most curious and the most artistic are the wood-carvings executed by the peasants of the Black Forest.

The Promenade, properly so called, stretches in front of the Conversations-Haus as far as the left bank of the Oosbach. At certain hours of the day all the fashionable world of Baden gathers at this rendezvous, where they can flirt and gossip to their hearts' content, while looking out upon one of the fairest prospects imaginable. The "season" begins on the 1st of May, and ends on the 31st of October, but even during the winter Baden is not wholly deserted.

North of the Conversations-Haus, and nearer the Oos, rises the new Trinkhalle or Pump-room, begun in 1839, from the plans of Hübsch, and completed in 1843, at a cost of 229,000 florins. It consists of a colonnade or portico, about 270 feet in length by 40 feet in width, and of a main building whose entrance is situated in the centre of the colonnade; this colonnade, we may add, being composed of sixteen Corinthian pillars of white sandstone. Fourteen commonplace frescoes, by Goetzenberger, the director of the Pinacotheca of Munich, form the principal decorations. They represent certain Black Forest legends, but are mean in conception and indifferent in execution. Over the main entrance is a good sculpture, by Reich of Hüfingen, representing the nymph of the spring surrounded by a crowd of eager worshippers. Above the north and south doors, inside, the designs are intended to illustrate the subjugation of Germania by the Romans, the Romans at Baden, and their expulsion from the city; the triumphal entrance into Rastadt of the Margrave Louis, the conqueror of the Turks; and the original sketch of Carlsruhe. The adjoining apartment is the Pump-room properly so called; the mineral water is brought here in pipes from the natural springs.

The temperature varies from 37° to 54° R. The springs, thirteen in number, emerge from rocks at the foot of the castle terrace, called *Schneckengarten*, behind the parish church; this part of the town is known by the name of "Hell," and in the coldest weather snow never rests upon the ground. A building in the form of a temple covers the principal spring ("Ursprung"), one of the hottest as well as most copious sources. The vault of masonry inclosing it is of Roman construction, and in the temple are preserved several relics of ancient sculpture, such as votive tablets and altars to Juno, Mercury, and Neptune (the patron-god of Baden). The Ursprung yields 7,345,440 cubic inches of water in twenty-four hours.

The other springs are:—The Hoellensprung, or Hell-spring, temperature, 52° R.; the Brühlquelle, or Scalding-spring, temperature, 50° 5′; the Jews' spring, temperature, 54°; the "Ungemach," temperature, 52° 3′; the Murrquelle, temperature, 50° 6′; the Fettq-uelle or "Fat Spring," temperature, 51°. There are also eight hot springs called the Butte; ten springs called the "cool fountain," 37° 5′ and 43° 7′ R.; and a chalybeate spring.

The Baden waters are recommended as beneficial in rheumatic and neuralgic affections, diseases of the skin and stomach, and sores and old wounds. They are both diaphoretic and diuretic, laxative and tonic; and are taken both externally and internally.

Of late years a new attraction has been added to the many attractions of this attractive watering-place; and Baden has its Races. It cannot be said that the course is very good, that the horses are of the best blood, that the stakes are hotly contested, or that, in a word, the glories of Ascot and Newmarket are reproduced in this little German town; but the scenes accompanying or originating in them—the outward procession and the homeward progress—are singularly characteristic and entertaining, and may be regarded as full-coloured pictures of "Life in Baden."

The Grand-duchess Stephanie—that is, in the Scottish peerage, the dowager duchess of Hamilton—has a superb palace near the Leopolds-platz; it was erected in 1809 from the designs of the architect Weinbrenner. In the Leopolds-platz was raised, in 1861, the bronze statue of the late Grand-duke Leopold, by Navier Reich; here commences a street called the Graben, ornamented with a central row of chestnut trees, and lined by splendid hotels and mansions. The Graben leads to what the French call *l'allee des Soupirs* (the *Seufzeraller*), and to the old Gernsbach road.

The parish church (*Pfarr-Kirche*, or Stifts-Kirche) was reconstructed in 1453, destroyed by the French in 1680, rebuilt in 1753, and restored in 1837 and 1861. Here are buried many of the margraves of Baden, and the choir contains their monuments; most of them in the rococo style, and covered with elaborate but unmeaning ornaments. They begin with Bernhard I., who died in 1631. To the left of the high altar are the tombs of Edward Fortunatus, died 1600; Bernhard III., died 1537: Friedrich, bishop of Utrecht, died 1515; Leopold William, died 1671, a great soldier in an age of great soldiers, and the comrade of Montecuculi and Stahremberg. Further off are those of Christopher I., died 1527, and his consort Ollibe; and of Jacob II., who died in 1511 as elector of Trèves, and whose corpse was removed hither from Coblenz in 1808. To the right of the altar stands the tomb of the Margrave Louis William, who died at Rastadt in 1707. He was a fellow-soldier of Prince

Eugene, Marlborough's companion-in-arms, and commanded in twenty-seven campaigns without sustaining a single defeat. The monument is by Pigalle, the sculptor who executed the monument of Marshal Saxe we have mentioned at Strassburg. As a whole, it is heavy and tasteless.

In the rear of the Trinkhalle stands a Russo-Greek chapel, built by Prince Michel Stourdza as a mausoleum for his son. The interior is lavishly enriched with paintings. The building is rather quaint than graceful.

Between the Conversations-Haus and the Lichtenthal road is situated the massive and richly decorated pile of the theatre, designed by Conteau, a French architect, and opened in 1862. Among the ornaments of the interior, the best are the busts of Auber and Rossini, by Dantan, and of Beethoven and Mozart, by Perrault. The theatre fills an important place in Badish sociology. The representations are well attended; the company is good, the music excellent, and the plays are well mounted.

We have now exhausted all the sights of the town but one: the *Neue Schloss*, or New Castle, the summer residence of the grand-duke of Baden; and called "new" for the same reason that America is called the New World, to distinguish it from the Old. The more ancient pile, which was inhabited down to 1471, is situated on the very summit of the hill; the new castle occupies a lower, but still commanding level. It was burnt and ruined by the French in 1689, and it is to be regretted that the grand-duke considered it necessary to rebuild so hideous a structure.

We do not visit it, however, from any architectural or artistic propensities, or with any intention of enjoying the prospect it commands, but simply on account of the very curious and remarkable dungeons beneath it. To these we slowly and painfully descend by a stair which winds under a tower on the right-hand corner of the inner court, through an ancient bath of Roman construction. This entrance has been broken through in modern times; originally, the dungeons were only accessible from above, by a perpendicular shaft running through the centre of the building, and still in existence. The visitor, in passing under it, can scarcely discern the daylight at the top. The old tradition asserts that prisoners, bound fast in a chair and blindfolded, were lowered by a windlass into these dim, chill, mysterious, and appalling vaults and corridors, which it is not improbable the Romans excavated out of the solid rock. Each cell closes with a massive slab of stone, nearly a foot thick, and twelve to twenty hundred pounds in weight, moving on a pivot, and ingeniously fitted.

In one chamber, loftier than the other, and called the Rack Chamber (*Fotter Kammer*), stood the dread instruments of torture; and a row of iron rings, still rusting in the wall, suggests most painful recollections of those dark and troublous times when the power of the oppressor was as yet unbroken. An adjoining passage contains the trap-door called the "Virgin's Kiss" (*baiser de la vierge*). The condemned was forced to kiss an image of the Virgin, when the trap-door giving way he fell headlong to a great depth below, on a machine armed with knives and spikes, which, slowly revolving, tore him to pieces. Not even the Oriental imagination, we think, could conceive of a punishment more diabolically cruel.

The last and largest of these vaults is the "Hall of Judgment," where, on stone benches, sat the members of the terrible *Vehmgericht*, or Secret Tribunal, and pronounced the terrible sentences from which there was no appeal. We have no space to dwell on the dark romantic story of this secret court; nor is it necessary, since the reader will find it dramatically related by Goethe in his "Goetz von Berlichingen," and Sir Walter Scott in his "Anne of Geierstein."

A road beginning behind the new castle winds up the richly wooded hill to the ruins of the more ancient pile (*das Alte Schloss*), the earliest residence of the margraves of Baden, where they sat secure, and looked down contemptuously on the toiling and moiling world below. It is a complete ruin, having been destroyed by the French during their ravages of the Palatinate. The view from the battlements of the square tower is simply a vista into fairy land: on one side rise the darkly wooded hills of the Black Forest, contrasting vividly with the bright fresh verdure of the valleys they inclose; while the foreground is filled up with innumerable villages, whitely-gleaming spires, convents, farms, and mills, clustering on the banks of winding streams; while, on the other side, the green declivities slope gently into the plain of the Rhine, and against the dark-blue sky breaks the sharp irregular outline of the Vosges.

Proceeding from the Alte Schloss, it is usual to visit the ruins of Ebersteinburg, near the village of the same name. These ruins are situated on a kind of rocky promontory, and seem to occupy the site of a Roman watch-tower, built, perhaps, in the third century. The masonry dates from the time of the Frankish emperors to the fourteenth century. From this castle a powerful family took their name, who afterwards, in the thirteenth century, removed to Neu Eberstein (or the "Boar Stone"). In a feud with Eberhard the Weeper, of Würtemburg, in 1337, the castle was burnt. Half a century later, the lands of the Ebersteins were sold to the margraves of Baden.

The castle was then rebuilt and enlarged, and for a century and upwards was the residence of one or other of the principal vassals of the margraves. But since 1573 it has been deserted, and nature has been left to embellish the ruined stronghold with her favourite growth of ivy and wild flowers.

The prospect from the ruins is bold, extensive, and animated; especially towards the rich and radiant valley of the lower Murz, and the pretty villages of Kuppenheim, Bischweier, Rothenfels, Gaggenau, and Ottenau.

To the east of Baden rise the Great and Little Staufenberg. The former, 2240 feet above the level of the sea, is also called the Mercury mountain; on its summit a Roman votive stone having been discovered, bearing a rude sculpture of Mercury with his caduceus and ram.

In 1837 a prospect tower, seventy-five feet high, was erected here by the Grand-duke Leopold.

From Baden some agreeable exclusions may be made in or about the Rhine valley, to which we shall briefly refer.

It is usual for the stranger at Baden to wander as far as Stephanienbad, where there are mineral waters and chalybeate waters, and to visit the monument to the poet Schiller, a mass of rock, surrounded by a pleasant shrubbery. He will find something to see at Lichtenthal. In the first place, its situation at the foot of the Klosterberg, and at the junction of the Oos with the Grobach, which comes sparkling and splashing down the pleasant vale of Geroldsau, is very pleasant. Next, there is an old convent, a very old convent, of Cistercian nuns, who renew their vows every three years. The vicissitudes which this convent has survived are remarkable. It was founded by Ermengarde, widow of Hermann V., in 1145; endowed by her sons and successors; and thus was raised into a position of repute and influence. In 1689 the French, under Duras, threatened to burn it, but it was saved at the intercession of one of the nuns. When the total suppression of monastic establishments took place, it lost all its fair estates; but a small annual pension was granted to its nuns, which is shared among about sixteen recipients.

There are two churches, and each has something to boast of: the larger, of the relics of the martyr-saints Pius and Benedict, with their skeletons attired in the most magnificent costume: the smaller (and more ancient), which was restored some fifteen years ago, and embellished with richly painted windows, of the tombs of several margraves of Baden-Durlach, and the quaint pictures of Hans Baldung Grün.

The Baden margraves descend to Rudolph VI., surnamed the Long, who lies on a stone bed of state, attired in full armour, in the middle of the chapel.

On the Rastadt road, about six miles from Baden, "in the green obscurity of a little park," is situated the grand-ducal summer palace, or lodge, called "the Favourite." Dr. Gaspey, in his volume on the "Upper Rhine," thus describes it:—It was built, he says, at a very considerable expense, in 1753, by the Margravine Sybilla Augusta, a princess of Lauenburg, and widow of Prince Ludwig, renowned for his successes against the Turks. In the evening of her days, when her eldest son had attained his majority, she withdrew from the pomp of a court life to this secluded residence. In the centre of the chateau a richly ornamented circular saloon, several stories high, is surrounded by a gallery, and receives its light from above; the design is not unlike that of the reading-room of the British Museum. The various apartments are cumbrously ornamented in the style of Louis Quatorze. In one of the side rooms the walls exhibit a crowd of the most curious fishes, flowers, and birds—you would suppose them to have sprung from the fancy of a Chinese artist!—and, in another, you may see the portraits of the margravine and her husband in seventy-two different dresses; while a third is more sensibly embellished with the miniatures of artists and men of letters of every country. A fourth apartment is wholly and truly in the Chinese style, with mimic pagodas and other incongruities; and a fifth bears witness, in its abundant embroideries, to the industry, if not the taste, of the margravine and her ladies. Most remarkable of all is the so-called "Show Kitchen," where a vast quantity of antiquated culinary apparatus, and a whole succession of dinner-services in Dutch porcelain, in the form of stags, birds, fishes, and garden fruits, never fail to interest the curious visitor.

Opposite the villa, in the densest shades of the park, stands a small quaint hermitage, and here, during Lent, the builder of the Favourite was wont to withdraw from her voluptuous life to undergo her self-imposed penances. She wore a horse-hair chemise and a prickly belt; and she slept on a straw-mat. The peasants, therefore, looked upon the margravine as a saint, though, in truth, she drank of the cup of pleasure to the dregs.

We shall now carry the reader to the south of Baden, and around the steep mountains of the Yburg (1767 feet), whose summit is crowned by the ruins of an old, old castle. Oh, what a glorious prospect do we enjoy from this lofty position! Yonder flows the noble river, winding through what is truly "enchanted ground"—through fields and groves, orchards, gardens, and vineyards, most pleasant to the eye, and dear to the memory from their legendary and historical associations. The ramparts of the castle overhang the very brink of the abrupt ascent; one of the towers, and a gateway, are also in excellent preservation. The story runs that the Margrave Edward Fortunatus coined bad money here, a most unprincely occupation; but, mayhap, the sole foundation for the story is the fact that his chemists, Pestalozzi and Muscaletta, had a laboratory in the castle, for the investigation, in all probability, of alchemical mysteries. Innumerable ghost stories, it is said, are connected with the ruins; originating, most likely, in the circumstance that all the storms coming from the direction of Strassburg pour their fury in the neighbourhood of the Yburg.

Yonder densely-wooded mountain, to the north of the Yburg, is known as the Fremersberg, and is only twelve feet lower than its castle-crowned rival. Some years ago its summit was occupied by a convent; on the site of the convent now stands, or did lately stand, a small inn.

Many other places and buildings of interest, many picturesque villages, and beautiful landscapes, are to be found in the neighbourhood of Baden; but as they mostly lie beyond the valley of the Rhine, we shall not introduce them into our present description.

RADSTADT.

We now proceed to Rastadt, one of the most celebrated fortresses on the German frontier. It is by no means a lively or picturesque town, and unless the traveller has military proclivities, he will find in it but few materials of interest. Its defensive works have been completed since 1840, under the direction of military engineers.

It is situated between Oos and Carlsruhe, at the confluence of the Oos and Murg, and on a kind of table-land which slopes gently towards the northeast. It is built with great regularity, most of its streets forming compact parallelograms, and has a population of about 7000 souls.

Rastadt was burned by the French in 1689, and rebuilt by Louis of Baden in 1701; it continued to be the residence of the margraves until the extinction of their line.

To the north of the town, and on a commanding height, rises the palace or castle founded in 1701 by the Margrave Louis William, the conqueror of the Turks, and the Margravine Sybilla Augusta, of whom we have already spoken. It was designed on the same plan as Versailles, but never completed; and a portion of it is now used as a barracks, while the park serves as a parade and exercise ground. It formerly contained a splendid collection of Turkish arms, housings, saddles, and standards, but this was pillaged and destroyed by insurgents in 1849. The apartments are decorated in the Louis Quatorze style. Above the main building rises a belvedere, or prospect tower, surmounted by a copper-gilt statue of Jupiter.

In this castle were held the two celebrated congresses of Rastadt; the first in 1713-14, and the second in 1797-99. The former brought to a close the great War of Succession, which had involved nearly all Europe in flames, and in which the military glory of England was raised to a prodigious height by the victories of Marlborough.

The second congress met in 1797, again with the view of negotiating peace between France and the imperial house. It began on the 9th of December, and the conference was protracted all through 1798, and into the spring of 1799; but with the lapse of time the French demands increased to such an extent that the emperor found himself unable to satisfy them. At length, indeed, the two contracting parties waxed less and less inclined to an agreement, and the congress finally declared itself dissolved. The departure of the diplomatic body was fixed for the 28th of April; but the commander of the Austrian garrison gave them orders to set out on the 10th, as the town on the following day was to be occupied by the imperial troops. An escort was demanded, but refused on the ground that it was unnecessary. Consequently, on the evening of the 10th, the French plenipotentiaries, Jean Debry, Ponnier, and Roberjot, set out for Strassburg; but scarcely had they passed out of the Rheinau gate when they were attacked by some drunken hussars, who seized them, dragged them from their carriages, murdered Ponnier and Roberjot, in spite of the frantic efforts of the wife of the latter to save her husband, and flung Jean Debry, severely wounded, into a ditch, where he escaped destruction only by promptly feigning to be dead. The assassins carried off all the papers of the legation, but committed no other robbery; and satisfied with the work they had accomplished, disappeared in the obscurity of the night: whereupon Jean Debry, though suffering severely from his wounds, contrived to crawl into Rastadt, and present himself, bleeding and exhausted, at the hotel of Herr Goertz, the Prussian ambassador.

In 1849 Rastadt was again the scene of a very sanguinary event. Here, on the 11th of May, began the Baden insurrection, and when, in July, the outbreak had been in a great measure suppressed, the rebels still held possession of the fortress, which was surrounded by the Prussians. The outrages which had disgraced the town in May and June were worthy of a signal punishment; and when the fortress surrendered on the 23rd of July, the Prussians shot the leaders Tiedermann and Micswoski, and a number of their principal followers.

Passing Muggensturm (population, 1770) and Malsch (population, 3261), we arrive at Ettlingen, a town of 5100 inhabitants, situated on the Alb, and famous for its paper manufacture. Near the bridge, in the wall of the town-hall, is inserted a Roman sculpture of Neptune, and other Roman remains have been discovered in the vicinity.

The railway here leaves the mountains, and approaches nearer to the Eider, which in this portion of its course is remarkable for its curves and angles, and is studded with numerous islands. We leave the little town of Ruppen on the right, and cross the Alb at Baluch, whose twin-towered church, built by Hübsch in 1S37, is adorned in the interior with well-designed and well-executed frescoes by Dietrich of Stuttgard. A journey of nine to ten miles from Ettlingen, and of eighteen miles from Rastadt, brings us to Karlsruhe (Carlsruhe, or "Charles' Rest ").

CARLSRUHE.

The population of Carlsruhe is about 28,000. The town itself is distant about five miles and a half from the bank of the Rhine, which is crossed by a branch line of rail, connecting the town with the railways to Paris, Strassburg, and the west of France.

There are few towns in South Germany, says Captain Spencer, which present a more cheerful appearance than Carlsruhe, the Liliputian capital of the grand-duchy of Baden. The streets are broad, airy, and cleanly-looking, and being here and there ornamented with public buildings of no slight architectural pretensions, it bears about it all the characteristics that usually distinguish a metropolis from a purely commercial town. It is the youngest capital in Germany, dating only from the beginning of the last century. In 1717 the site which it occupies was covered by the leafy masses of the Hartwald. In the depths of the woody solitude the Margrave William erected a hunting-lodge, or chateau, which he appropriately christened "Charles' Rest," or Karlsruhe. A town soon sprung up around it, and the forest annually dwindled in its proportions.

The present castle is a handsome pile of stone, raised by the Margrave Karl Friedrich in 1750. To this prince Carlsruhe owes its prosperity, if it owes its foundation to his grandfather. He encouraged by liberal concessions the erection of new houses; so that in 1793 his little capital numbered 630. In 1806 the margraviate became a grand-duchy, and received soon afterwards some accessions of territory, so that in 1814 it comprised a superficial area of 278 square miles, and a population of 1,000,000. Necessarily, its capital exhibited a corresponding increase in importance.

Carlsruhe is the very model of a quiet, sleepy, monotonous German capital. It is almost wholly dependent on the ducal court and its officials. Of late years it has essayed to become a manufacturing town, but with little success.

On arriving by the railway from Rastadt, we pass through the Ettlingen Gate, erected by Weinbrenner in 1S03. It is supported by twelve Doric columns, and ornamented with sculptures illustrative of the union of Baden and the Palatinate. Following up the Carl-Friedrichs Strasse, we come to an open square, the "Rondel," in whose centre stands an obelisk, raised to the memory of the Margrave William. To the right rises the stately palace of the margraves, built by Weinbrenner; it has a Corinthian portico of six pillars, and is two stories high.

Entering the market, which forms a kind of oblong, and may be considered "the handsomest part of Carlsruhe," we may glance at the monument of Duke Louis, who died in 1830; a statue in sandstone, by Raumer. Beneath a small pyramid rests the remains of the founder of the city, the Margrave Charles William. It bears the following inscription:— "Here, where formerly the Margrave Charles sought repose in the shades of the Hardt Forest, and built the town which perpetuates his name; here, on the spot where he found his last resting-place, this monument, inclosing his ashes, was erected in grateful remembrance by Ludwig William Augustus."

In front of the castle stands the statue of the Grand-duke Charles Friedrich, who died in 1811, after a reign of sixty-five years in duration. It was executed in bronze by Schwanthaler, and each angle of the pedestal is enriched by a female figure, representing one of the four circles of the grand-duchy; viz., the Lake circle, the Upper, Middle, and Lower Rhine circles.

The Schloss, or castle, was erected about 1750, in the "old Frankish" style, and, externally, is more remarkable for size than architectural splendour. It consists of a main building of three stories, with right and left wings of two, and is dominated over by the so-called "Lead Tower," which necessarily commands a broad and richly varied prospect. This tower, in the last century, was of scarcely less evil repute than the notorious Tour de Nesle of Paris in the fourteenth; being the seraglio of the Margrave Charles William. Internally, the Schloss is fitted up with a luxury and a richness not unworthy of the palace of a prince; but strangers wander "open-eyed," and with admiring looks, through a series of superb apartments. On these we shall refuse to dwell. There is matter more to our taste in the court library of 90,000 volumes, situated in the left wing; in the small but admirable cabinet of natural history; and in the theatre, in the right wing, erected by Hübsch in 1851-1853. The portico is embellished with well-executed busts of Mozart, Beethoven, and Gluck; of Goethe, Schiller, and Lessing; and an allegorical figure, the Genius of Dramatic Poetry.

Through an arcade in the right wing we pass into the gardens, where a graceful little monument commemorates the poet John Peter Hebel, born 1760, died 1826. He wrote some spirited and popular lyrics in the Allemannic dialect. The botanical garden is justly considered one of the most extensive in Germany; it owes its excellence to the unwearied care of the celebrated botanist, Charles Christian Gmelin.

Let us next conduct the reader to the Academy, or Kunsthalle, unquestionably the finest edifice in Carlsruhe. It is built of a cool gray sandstone, relieved by horizontal layers of red brick. The style is Byzantine, and the details have been well worked out by the architect Hübsch. The figures at the entrance, Painting and Sculpture, Raphael and Michael Angelo, Albeit Dürer, Holbein, and Vischer, are from the chisel of a native Badish artist, Navier Reich.

The apartments on the ground floor are crowded with statues and plaster casts, Etruscan vases, and Roman and German antiquities; among which the eye signals out, delightedly the exquisite Hebe of Canova, the very embodiment of grace, and mirth, and youth; a Nymph, by Sch wan thaler; and a Victory, by Rauch.

The grand staircase is ornamented by the boldly designed frescoes of Schwind, representing the Inauguration of Freiburg Cathedral, by Duke Conrad of Zaringia, and deriving a considerable interest from the number and fidelity of the portraits.

Of the Finance Office, erected by Hübsch in 1828, enough to say that it contains 110 rooms, and has 292 windows. The Polytechnic School, also built by Hübsch, is of very considerable extent; the façade extending 157 feet in length, and measuring 55 feet in height. Over the entrance are two statues in sandstone, Kepler, as the representative of science, and Erwin von Steinbach, as the representative of art. They were executed by Remfer.

The school, which contains about 500 pupils, was enlarged in 1863. It is very efficiently and yet economically managed.

The only place of importance between Carlsruhe and Philipsburg is Bruchsal, which has a population of 9500 souls. Philipsburg is a strong fortress on the bank of the Rhine, situated at an abrupt angle of the river, in a line almost due south of Speier.

The railway from Bruchsal strikes northward to Heidelberg, where it joins the Mannheim and Frankfort line. But we have now, in our descent of the river, arrived at a point nearly opposite Speier, and before we continue our journey that famous historic city claims the attention.

CHAPTER V. SPEIER AND HEIDELBERG.

SPEIER (the *Spire* of the French, and *Spires* of the English) is situated in a fertile plain, near the confluence of the Speierbach with the Rhine. "The tomb of the German Emperors," and formerly a free imperial city, it is one of the oldest, and, historically, one of the most remarkable towns on the great German river. True it is, that of its pristine magnificence few traces remain, but its associations are imperishable. It now contains a population of about 12,000, and it is still the capital of the Bavarian Palatinate, the seat of the provincial government, and of a cathedral chapter.

To the Romans it was known as *Spira*, and as *Augusta Nemetum* or *Noviomagus*. It remained under the sway of the Eagle until the breaking up of the Empire, when it was twice destroyed by the Northmen. The town soon sprung again into prosperity, and under the rule of the Franks abundantly flourished. At the partition of Verdun, in 843, it was awarded to Germany, "on account of the wine;" and passing under the supremacy of the Salic emperors, who resided at the castle of Limburg, within about eighteen miles of the city, it continued to was strong and wealthy.

The German princes seem to have affected it greatly; and it was so adorned and aggrandized by the Emperor Conrad II., that he obtained the surname of *der Speierer*, the Speier-man. One of his successors, Henry IV., bestowed on its bishop, not only the title of count of the Speiergau, but the rank and power of a secular prince. At a later date Henry V. placed the administration of the town in the hands of a municipal council, composed of twelve burghers. This step encouraged the growth of a spirit of independence among the citizens, and led to a series of struggles for supremacy between them and their bishops, terminating in the discomfiture of the latter in 1192. The bishops retired to Bruchsal, and Speier became a free imperial city.

From this epoch until the close of the seventeenth century its prosperity knew no check. Its population, like that of some of the old Flemish towns, was scarcely less versed in the arts of peace than of war, and though not exceeding 30,000 in number, were able to set on foot and maintain a well-equipped force of 6000 men. Placed at the head of the Confederation of Free Rhenish Cities which was formed in 1247, in opposition to the feudal nobility, it destroyed a considerable number of the strongholds and mountain-fastnesses, whence mediaeval knight and baron were accustomed to sally forth to pillage the defenceless merchant. So signal was its success, and so great its wealth, that its enmity was only less feared than its friendship was courted. The feudal princes, in 1315, in 1320, and again in 1422, armed against it, but their battalions were in each case repulsed with terrible slaughter. Protected by the martial spirit of its inhabitants, its commerce steadily increased; and of a rich, strong, and independent mediaeval city it would be difficult to find a more felicitous example than Speier. When the Diet of Worms abolished, in 1530, the atrocious right of private war, which had so long desolated the fair valley of the Rhine, the Imperial Chamber, or *Reichskammergericht*, instituted to watch over the full execution of this edict, was established at Speier, where it held its sittings for two centuries. In 1689 it was transferred to Wetzlar.

This astonishing course of prosperity was scarcely checked by the Thirty Years' War; for though Speier was alternately occupied by Swede and Imperialist, both parties seem to have agreed in treating it gently. But a very different fate befell it in the War of the Succession. It was then completely devastated by an army of Frenchmen, in the name of Louis XIV., and under the immediate order of his minister, Louvois. For two years Speier remained a heap of ruins; France would not suffer it to be rebuilt. At the peace of Ryswick, however, some of its former inhabitants returned, and rebuilt their shattered houses; but it never recovered its former splendour. It was doomed, moreover, to new misfortunes. In 1716, at the instigation of Bishop Hartand of Rollingen, it was plundered by a body of armed peasants. In 1734 it was stormed by a French army; and in 1794, another French army, commanded by the revolutionary general Custine, repeated the scenes of 1689. On this occasion the cathedral was again plundered, and the tombs of the Emperors Rudolph, Albert, and Adolph were desecrated.

By the peace of Lunéville Speier was annexed to France, and became a sub-prefecture in the department of Mont-Tonnerre. By the treaty of Paris it was restored to Germany.

The chief building, in truth the only building of interest in this ancient city, is the *Dom*, or cathedral, founded by the Emperor Conrad II. in 1030; continued by his son, Henry III.; and completed in 1061 by his grandson, Henry IV. It is a remarkable and magnificent example of the Byzantine style of the eleventh century, though it has suffered severely by successive fires, as in 1165, 1289, and 1450, and by the depredations of the French in 1689 and 1794. The principal entrance is through a porch called the *Kaisersaal*, or "Imperial Chamber," on account of the eight statues of the emperors which decorate it—the emperors buried under the roof of the ancient Dom. They are executed in white marble, of life size, and distinguished by an aspect of sovereign dignity. They represent Conrad II., Henry III., Henry IV., Henry V., Philip of Suabia, Adolph of Nassau, Albert of Austria, and Rudolph of Hapsburg.

The architecture of the interior is impressive, though somewhat overloaded with ornament. The broad and lofty nave is separated from the north and south aisles by twelve square pillars. Four stars of red marble, let into the pavement, indicate the place where St. Bernard preached a new crusade, in 1141, before the Emperor Conrad and his court.

At the entrance of the choir, to which we ascend by a flight of marble steps, two statues are kneeling on their tombs; Rudolph of Nassau and Rudolph of Hapsburg, sculptured in Carrara marble by Sch wan thaler. The imperial mausoleum, which has been carefully restored, forms an immense crypt. With torch in hand the visitor gropes his way into the dim, cool shades; a score of columns, rudely and roughly hewn, seem almost bent to the ground by the low and heavy roof. A long series of arches intersect each other in the obscurity. Lamps of baked clay, of ancient form, hang suspended from hooks of iron. Stone slabs, serving the purpose of altars, are planted on a couple of pillars, which are scarcely cut out of the stone. The mind involuntarily recalls those gloomy catacombs in which the Early Christians worshipped during the bitter days of persecution. Every year, on

Christmas night, the crypt grows alive; a hundred torches are kindled; and the bishop of Speier repairs hither with all his clergy to celebrate, according to the rites of the Romish Church, the Nativity of Christ.

Over the crypt is the Koenigchor, or "King's Choir;" and to the south of it, the Baptismal Chapel, containing the coloured sketches and drawings of Schrandolph for the frescoes with which he has decorated the cupola, the choir, and the aisles. They illustrate biblical personages and biblical scenes, and are very literal, cold, and inexpressive.

The Dom measures 480 feet in length, and 136 feet in width.

On passing from the Dom by the southern gate, we enter a leafy, shady garden, the ancient cemetery, where the only conspicuous object is a pile of stones, called the *Oelberg*, or "Mountain of Olives." It dates from the sixteenth century, is covered with figmes and sculptures, and owes its curious designation to the fact that it was formerly part of a chapel, whose interior represented the Garden of Gethsemane and the betrayal of our Saviour. It was partly destroyed by the French in 1689.

To the east of the cathedral rises the Heidenthürmchen, or "Pagans' Tower," which, with other Cyclopean ruins, tradition attributes to the Roman general, Drusus. It is most probable, however, that the tower was built by Bishop Rüdiger, about 1180, and was included in the fortifications of the city. It contains some antediluvian fossils, and various mediaeval relics. A staircase leads to its summit, from which a very bright and varied prospect may be obtained.

North of the cathedral stands the Hall of Antiquities, containing a valuable collection of Celtic, Roman, and Germanic antiquities, discovered in the Palatinate. It is divided into three sections, of which the central is the larger. An iron grating reveals a number of *milliaria*, statues, altars, and votive tablets. In the others, which are closed, vases, urns, amphorae, weapons, medals, and a legionary eagle, speak eloquently of the "brave old times" of Roman domination.

Opposite this treasure-house of curiosities is situated the chapel of St. Afra, the only one extant of the ten chapels which formerly surrounded the cathedral. It is connected with one of the most pathetic episodes in the history of Speier. The Emperor Henry IV. having died in profound distress, and under the ban of excommunication, his remains were deprived of the last solemn rites. Of all the priests who had flourished through his bounty, not one durst bury him. The men of Speier, more loyal and more grateful, collected his bones, deposited them in this chapel, and assiduously watched over them until the pope was induced to recall the terrible sentence, and the unfortunate emperor was permitted to sleep with his fathers in the imperial crypt.

The modern edifices of Speier are deficient in architectural beauty, and necessarily possess no historical interest. The reader will, therefore, be content with a simple enumeration—the Protestant church, the Episcopal palace, the government house, the town-hall, the lyceum, and the cavalry barrack.

From Speier we cross to the right bank of the Rhine, and by way of Schwetzingen proceed to romantic Heidelberg.

Schwetzingen is a comparatively insignificant town of about 3500 inhabitants, two-thirds of whom are Protestants. No one would spend an hour here but for the superb gardens, constructed at an amazing cost by the Elector Charles Theodore, and still maintained on a very sufficient and satisfactory scale. They are embellished with fountains and statues, Roman ruins, an orangery, a lake, temples to Mercury, Apollo, and Minerva; and a seventeenth century chateau contains some richly furnished apartments. A mosque, a theatre, and a restaurant are among the very varied and somewhat incongruous attractions offered to visitors.

The celebrated university town of Heidelberg is situated on the left bank of the Neckar, at the entrance of the fair Neckar valley, and at a short distance above the confluence of the Neckar with the Rhine. From its ruined castle a fine view is obtained of a position almost unequalled in picturesqueness of effect; while the prospect extends westward, across a plain so fertile and so fair that it has been called the "Garden of Germany," to the blue line of the Haardt Mountains in Rhenish Bavaria.

The town is about one mile and a half in length (population, 18,000), but exceedingly narrow in proportion. It lies between two wooded eminences, "higher than hills, and not so rugged as mountains." On a northern spur of one of these acclivities, the Koenigsstuhl, on the left bank, rise the grand but gloomy ruins of the old electoral castle. The Koenigsstuhl is 1893 feet above the sea-level, but the elevation of the castle does not exceed 313 feet. On the left bank soars conspicuous the vine-clad, "castled height" of the Saint's Mountain, or the Heiligenberg, whose summit has been crowned by the eagle of the Roman legionaries. Some authorities assert that the Romans fortified both the Heiligenberg and the Koenigstuhl. In the reign of Ludwig III. the Saint's Mountain was made over to the convent of Lorsch. Such Roman structures as were still extant were then destroyed, their materials being employed in the erection of religious edifices.

First, the chapel of St. Michael was built (about 863-870); and soon afterwards a Benedictine cloister was added to it. Next, a chapel dedicated to St. Stephen and St. Lawrence was built lower down the mountain. A second convent sprang up, whose rights and privileges were confirmed by Pope Alexander III. and by the Emperor Henry IV., in 1103. It was then the mountain acquired its present designation.

When the great irruption of the Germanic tribes swept away the Roman garrisons, their camp afforded an asylum and a stronghold to the barbarians. It is possible that some chieftain, weary of plunder and fighting, planted himself here with his followers, among whom he divided the surrounding lands. Then was heard the sound of the axe; the old patriarchal trees were felled, and golden harvests bloomed in the clearings effected by the industry of man. Want of water and of "free elbow-room" eventually brought them down to the banks of the Neckar, and Heidelberg was founded.

One day about the middle of the twelfth century (1155-1157), Conrad of Hohenstaufen, the count palatine, in the course of a journey through his dominions, arrived in this romantic neighbourhood, and resolved to build a castle here. Under his patronage the village of Heidelberg grew up into a town, which at the beginning of the thirteenth century had its guild of citizens, its magistrate, its governor, and its ramparts. Eventually it became the capital of the rich and beautiful Palatinate of the Rhine; and so continued until the last electors preferred to reside at Mannheim.

In the course of these five centuries, however, it passed through many vicissitudes. In 1248 it suffered from a dreadful famine: in 1278 it was devastated by an inundation of the Neckar, and so much as the gathering waters spared was soon afterwards swept away by a conflagration, until only one edifice remained extant, the church of the Blessed Virgin. In 1288, we are told, the town was visited by another conflagration; from which we must conclude that, in the ten years intervening between the two visitations, the town had been wholly or partially rebuilt. About the same date, the great Neckar bridge broke down while a procession was passing across it, and upwards of 300 persons were killed. About 1301, in the war with the Emperor Albert, and soon afterwards, in the war with the Emperor Ludwig, the country for many miles around was swept with fire and sword; and in 1313 or 1314 the unfortunate town was again blighted by plague and inundation.

It must have required all the tenacity and robustness of the German character to withstand such a series of misfortunes. Withstood they were; and in spite of all its sufferings, Heidelberg grew prosperous. In the fifteenth century, the Elector Robert III. commenced the erection of a feudal chateau on the very site of the ancient Roman walls, thus inaugurating that love of stately buildings which became a characteristic of the Palatinate family. It was the ambition of each elector to continue and surpass the work of his predecessor. Frederick the Victorious, Louis the Pacific, Otho, Henry, and Frederick V., were distinguished by their generosity and their love of dignified magnificence.

In 1414, on his way to the great Council of Constanz, the Emperor Sigismund was received at Heidelberg with a splendid welcome. In its castle the deposed pope, John XXIII., resided as a prisoner until 1418.

In 1461 the first mutterings were heard of the Palatine War. "Wicked Fritz," as his enemies called him, or Frederick the Victorious, as he was entitled by his partizans, when placed under the ban of the Empire, erected a stronghold on the height above the town, and boldly named it *Trutz-Kaiser*, or "Defiance to the Emperor." The surrounding country was ravaged by the troopers of Baden and Würtemburg. In preparation for the gathering storm the ramparts of Heidelberg were strengthened, and its garners filled; but the town was spared the horrors of a siege. Frederick met and completely defeated his enemies at Friedrichsfeld, between Seckenheim and Schwitzingen, on the 30th of June, 1462, making prisoners the Margrave Charles of Baden, Count Ulrich of Würtemburg, and Bishop George of Metz, whom he conveyed in triumph to the capital.

In 1613 the ill-fated marriage of the Elector Frederick V. (1610-1632), with Elizabeth, the daughter of James I. of England, the heroine of Wotton's beautiful lyric, and one of the most amiable and intellectual of the Stuart race, was celebrated with unusual magnificence. Nine years later the city was stormed by Tilly, whose fierce soldiers committed the most disgraceful excesses. For three days rapine was uncontrolled, while several of the public buildings and upwards of forty houses were sacked and burned. The university library was sent to Rome. In the following year victorious Bavaria attained the electorate, declared the Roman Catholic religion restored, and expelled the Lutherans from the country. Both town and castle remained in the hands of the Bavarian soldiers until 1633, when it was recaptured through an ably-conceived stratagem of the Swedish colonel, Abel Moda. Again the wheel of fortune revolved: in May, 1635, the Imperialists, under Count Clam Gallas, attacked and captured the town; and on the 27th of July the castle also surrendered, after an obstinate defence.

Few parts of Germany suffered more severely during the last five years of the Thirty Years' War than the Rhenish Palatinate, and on the conclusion of the peace of Westphalia the Elector Charles Ludwig (1632-1680) found his dominions in a condition the most deplorable; the towns half depopulated, the villages burned, the vineyards and corn-fields destroyed, commerce extinct, and industry almost at a standstill. The elector, however, was a man of more than ordinary capacity, and under his firm and enlightened rule the Palatinate was beginning to recover somewhat of its former prosperity, when it had to endure a heavier storm than ever, by Louis XIV. The French army was under the command of Melac, who excelled Tilly in cruelty, and whose name for years was so hated in the country he ruthlessly ravaged, that the peasants gave it to their dogs.

On the 26th of October Heidelberg was captured, and occupied until the spring of 1689 by a French army. The arms of France had been everywhere successful. They had overrun the entire Palatinate, and from Heidelberg spread even to the hanks of the Danube. But an event more disastrous to the French fortunes than any repulse in the open field, occurred at a critical moment. To the throne of England succeeded William of Holland, the resolute and mortal enemy of France; and his ability and steadfastness united all Europe in a formidable league against its common aggressor. France found itself called upon to combat, not only on the Rhine, but in Holland, in Savoy, in Spain, wherever the coalition formed at Augsburg could put an armed force in the field.

The French government, confronted by so powerful a league, conceived, as a French writer says, the most terrible resolution ever dictated by the genius of war: namely, to destroy every town they were compelled to evacuate, and to harry with fire and sword the territory they were forced to restore to the elector. This atrocious conception is generally attributed to the Marshal de Duras, but it was sanctioned, to his eternal infamy, by Louis XIV., and carried out with savage fury by the able and unscrupulous Louvois. The French generals, Mélac, Montclar, Tessé, Boufflers, and a score of others, were the executants, the hands; but Louvois was brain and soul. It is to the credit of the former that they occasionally experienced sentiments of remorse and pity; that they sometimes halted in their dreary course, and refused to proceed except under new and stringent orders. Duras openly cursed the fatal counsel which he had been evilly inspired to give, and implored the king, in "the name of his glory," to revoke the doom he had pronounced, and refrain from inspiring all Christendom with "a terrible aversion." But Louvois would not suffer him; not for one minute did this implacable statesman relent.

Heidelberg, says M. Durand, was the first to experience the consequences of the retreat of the French. In the month of March of this fatal year, Montclar received orders to burn the town, and expel its inhabitants. He selected for this mission the Count de Tesse", one of the heroes of the notorious Dragonnades. But neither the soldiers nor the generals were yet sufficiently hardened for the proper performance of their barbarous duties. The fire was not half kindled; and Tesse" hastened to quit the town before it was more than partially consumed. Its inhabitants immediately returned, extinguished the flames, and repaired their houses. They raised some palisades around the castle, which was spacious enough to accommodate 1000 imperial soldiers.

Four years later, and on the 22nd of May, Heidelberg, which had been hastily rebuilt and fortified, was stormed by the Marshal de Lorges, and this time it was utterly destroyed. The population were driven, foodless, without clothes, without shelter, to the other bank of the Neckar. The soldiery broke into the castle, plundered it of its treasures, desecrated the tombs of the electors, and scattered abroad their remains. Finally, several thousand pounds of gunpowder were deposited in the cellars, and all that remained of the magnificent work of four generations was blown to the winds of heaven.

Some years elapsed before any attempt was made to restore this unfortunate city. At the beginning of the eighteenth century, however, the ruined buildings were rebuilt, and many new ones erected. In 1712 the first stone was laid of the new University; soon afterwards St. Anne's Chapel and the Citizens' Hospital were commenced.

In 1735 Prince Eugene established his headquarters here; but the town and its neighbourhood escaped the usual ravages during the war of the Bavarian Succession, in consequence of the cautious neutrality observed by the Elector Palatine.

The Elector Charles Theodore (1742-1799), was desirous of returning to the seat of his ancestors. But an evil fortune pursued the chateau. On the 23rd of June, 1764, the walls being completed, and the following day fixed for the triumphant entrance of the prince, the tower was struck by lightning, and in a few hours three-fourths of the building were consumed. Thenceforth, the skill of man has turned aside from what seemed and seems to be "a house accurst;" and the ruined pile, standing erect on the desert slope of the mountain, reminds the traveller of those ancient imperial diadems which are preserved in our collections as the relics, not as the signs of royalty.

In the winter of 1784, that is, on the 18th of January, and again on the 26th and 27th of February, the town suffered greatly from an inundation: the bridge was carried away by the drifting ice; thirty-nine buildings were destroyed, and 290 greatly damaged.

During the long war of the French Revolution, this unfortunate city was frequently visited by hostile forces. The Austrian headquarters were established here, at frequent intervals, from 1794 to 1800. In September, 1799, it was occupied by the French, under Baraguay d'Hilliers, but they retired on the approach of the Imperialists. The French afterwards returned, under Nansouty and Sabbatier, and on the 16th October attempted to carry the bridge, but were beaten off, though the approach was commanded by only a single cannon.

In 1803 Heidelberg, with the Rhine Palatine, was annexed to Baden, and the grand-duke, Charles Frederick, immediately addressed himself to the task of resuscitating the university, which he endowed with new sources of revenue, and whose organization he remodelled in a liberal and enlightened spirit. Heidelberg is now one of the most prosperous, one of the brightest and most radiant, of the Badish towns; and to the cultivated mind its romantic beauty and historical associations will ever endow it with the gift of immortal youth.

Modern Heidelberg stretches along the left bank of the Neckar, and at the base of the final escarpments of the Koenigsstuhl, for a mile and a half, from W. to E., or from the Mannheim to the Karl gate. It consists in the main of two parallel streets, the Haupt Strasse, or principal street, and the Plock Strasse; behind which are found the Anlagen. On this promenade, which is agreeably planted, and lined with charming houses, stands a statue of bronze (by Brugger, in 1860) to the Bavarian Field-marshal Wrede, who earned considerable distinction in the Napoleonic wars. He was born at Heidelberg in 1767, and died at Ellingen in 1838. The railway terminus is situated near the Mannheim gate. The Haupt Strasse, the Plock Strasse, and the promenade, all lead to the castle, which is the great object of attraction to all visitors.

As the reader will suppose from our historical sketch, Heidelberg is a completely modern city. Of its ancient houses man and the elements seem to have spared but one, situated in the marketplace, opposite the church of the Holy Ghost. This was built by a Frenchman, Charles Belier, of Tournay, a Huguenot who had escaped from the massacre of St. Bartholomew's-day. It is now an inn, *Zum Hitter Sanct Georg.*

The church of the Holy Ghost, which we have spoken of as near this ancient mansion, is also of great antiquity. In truth, who built it, or when it was built, is not known; but it was certainly raised to the rank of a cathedral by Rupert III. in 1393, and completed under his son Ludwig early in the fifteenth century. Here were the tombs of numerous princes and electors palatine, unfortunately destroyed by the French in 1793. Divine service, after the Lutheran fashion, was first celebrated on the 3rd of January, 1546. Both Protestants and Catholics now worship under the same roof.

For nearly two centuries the university library was kept in the choir, and esteemed the finest in Germany. But when the town was captured by Tilly, Duke Maximilian of Bavaria despatched the books to Rome, where they were deposited in the Vatican. The Jesuits' Church was erected from 1712 to 1751. It is a spacious and imposing edifice.

The oldest church in the town is St. Peter's, also called the University Church. It suffered no great injury in the wars, but in 1737 its tower was greatly destroyed by lightning. Architecturally the interior is not remarkable, but it contains some interesting tombs; especially those of Marsilius von Inghen, the first rector of the university, and the noble and learned lady, Olympia Fulvia Morata, of Ferrara, who was appointed professor of the Greek language at the university in 1554 and died soon afterwards, in her twenty-ninth year.

The university, the celebrated *Ruperta Carolina*, owes its reputation chiefly to its faculties of medicine and jurisprudence. Not a few of its professors have acquired a European reputation. The number of students, prior to the war, varied from 500 to 600. It is one of the oldest universities in Germany, its foundation dating from 1386. Its buildings, however, are but of moderate extent, and of no special architectural merit. The handsomest edifice is the new anatomy school, in a street leading to the river. The laboratory is situated in the Academy Street; the botanical garden, outside the Mannheim Gate. Near the hospital, that is, to the east of the university, stands the library, a three-storied building, which now contains 150,000 volumes, 50,000 dissertations, and 1880 MSS. Some invaluable MSS., which from Rome had been carried to Paris, were likewise restored after the conclusion of peace. Among the bibliographical curiosities we may enumerate:—a Greek Anthology; a fine MS. of the eleventh century; MSS. of Thucydides and Plutarch, of the tenth and eleventh centuries; a translation of Isaiah, in the handwriting of Luther; his Exhortation against the Turks; an edition of the Catechism, annotated by the great Keformer; the Electress Elizabeth's Book of Prayers, ornamented with miniatures by Dentzel, of Ulm (1499).

Attached to the university is a mineralogical collection, containing more than 15,000 specimens.

We now proceed to the pride and glory of Heidelberg, its Castle, which from the distance appears a complete mosaic of ramparts and towers, and when seen more closely seems to deserve the title so frequently given to it, "the Alhambra of Germany." The story of its vicissitudes, reconstructions, and demolitions would fill a volume. We shall content ourselves with adding a description of the storm which destroyed the upper castle on the 25th of April, 1537. Its violence was so great that it tore up the trees in the neighbouring forests by the roots; and oaks which had braved the tempests of a hundred years, were dashed with surprising fury into the valley. The clouds from all points of the compass seemed whirling to a centre, with a wind which swept everything before it, and drew up the waters of the Neckar to such a height, that a fearful inundation was momentarily expected. Presently the most awful peals of thunder reverberated among the mountains, followed by heavy torrents of hail and rain, which completely deluged the earth. Suddenly, a vivid flash of lightning struck the tower of the castle, whose vaults were filled with many tons of gunpowder. Then it seemed as if the earth had been violently rent asunder, and the shock was like the simultaneous discharge of hundreds of cannons. The doors of the houses were lifted from their hinges; the windows dashed out into the streets; whilst the huge stones, the beams, and the entire roof of the venerable castle were precipitated into the town, destroying the houses, and crushing many of the wretched inhabitants. Even the valley was strewn with rubbish. The lower castle also was seriously damaged; and the Elector Louis V. narrowly escaped with his life. Of the venerable pile itself, only one or two insignificant walls were left standing.

We have already stated that the lower castle is first mentioned in the year 1329, in the treaty of Pavia. It was probably erected about the end of the thirteenth century, under the Palsgrave Ludwig the Severe, son-in-law of Rudolph of Hapsburg, who died in 1294. The palace was afterwards embellished and enlarged by successive electors, especially by the electors Otto Henry, Frederick IV., and Frederick V., the latter having erected the so-called "English Buildings," of which the remains are few. Then came the desolation of 1649, 1689, and 1692, and the splendour of Heidelberg vanished for ever. For ever, because when in 1764 the Elector Charles Theodore had resolved on restoring the ancient castle, it was struck by lightning, and the flames seized upon everything that would burn.

On entering through the principal gate—the Elizabeth Gate, built by the Elector Frederick V. in honour of his English bride—we pass into the Stückgarten, or Cannon-garden, so named because the Heidelberg artillerists were formerly drilled within its precincts. This, the westernmost part of the castle, commands an extensive and richly-coloured picture of the town, the Harst Mountains, and the valley of the Rhine. "Strictly speaking, it forms a large terrace, irregularly planted with tall lime trees."

Close adjoining the Cannon-garden is the so-called Theits Tower, of which only one-half is preserved. It was erected by the Elector Louis V., completed in 1533, and destroyed by General Melas in 1685, notwithstanding the thickness of its walls (twenty-two feet). In the ivy-shrouded niches may still be seen the remains of the stone statues of Frederick V. and his brother, Ludwig V.

In this vicinage stood the "English Buildings," erected in 1612 by Frederick V., in honour of his consort, Elizabeth of England. It was noble and majestic externally, and internally most sumptuous; but in 1689 it was set on fire by the French, and reduced to a heap of ruins.

On the east side of the castle court rise the two lofty triangular pediments of the sombre palace of Frederick IV., with its boldly-projecting entablatures, on which are erected, between four rows of windows, the beautifully executed statues of nine electors, two kings, and five emperors. To the right stands the exquisite Italian structure of Otto Henry, finished by that elector in 1566, ruined by the French in 1659, restored in 1718, and destroyed by fire in 1764. The plan is said to have been furnished by Michel Angelo.

Above the entrance, which is decorated with four statues, are the name, bust, and armorial bearings of the architect. The entire façade is adorned with niches, and these niches are filled with admirable statues. Thus, in the first stage we see Joshua, Sampson, Hercules, and David, a motley collection, with rhyming inscriptions; in the second, allegorical figures of Strength, Faith, Love, Hope, and Justice; and in the third, Saturn, Mars, Mercury, and Diana. The gable-ends are protected by Pluto and Jupiter, and near the pediments of the first tier of windows are the half-raised busts of Vitellius, Antoninus Pius, Tiberius, Nero, and four more Roman emperors.

The oldest part of the ruins is probably the Ruprechtsbau, or Rupert's Building, erected in the fifth century by the Palsgrave Rupert, restored by Ludwig V. in 1540, and embellished by Frederick II. Its hall contains a small collection of curiosities. In the rear rises a dilapidated structure, which is considered to be still older; and close beside it stands the Old Chapel, which Rupert I. erected in 1346, and amply endowed. Under Frederick I. it was restored; but the new castle chapel having been built by Frederick IV. in 1607, the former was converted into a throne room. More recently it has served as a cooper's shop.

Let us now proceed to the palace of Frederick IV., whose façade is overloaded with a profusion of heavy ornamental sculpture. It was commenced in 1603 by Frederick IV., and completed in 1607. On the inner façade, towards the court-yard, are sixteen statues, several of which bear the disfiguring traces of the Swedish bombardment in 1633.

On the ground-floor stands the new chapel, already referred to. The first-floor saloons are appropriated to the Graimberg Museum, containing, among other treasures, numerous specimens of the porcelain of the Palatinate; a picture, by Lucas Cranach; a manuscript diploma of Arnulph, grandson of Charlemagne, dated 896; a manuscript bull of Alexander IV., 1255; the plaster cast of the face of Kotzebue, taken immediately after he had fallen beneath the dagger of Sand; the portrait, and a lock of hair, of the murderer; portraits of Melanchthon, Luther, and Luther's wife; costly enamels; plans and drawings of the castle; a sword found in the Neckar paintings by Wohlgemuth and his school; coins seals, ornaments, arms, and household utensils There is also an elaborate model of the castle in cork

We now step into the broad balcony, raised by the same elector on the site of an old wall, and opening up a gorgeous view of the town of Heidelberg and the valley of the Neckar. A door in the west corner leads to the cellar containing the Great Tun, one of the most widely-celebrated of the curiosities of Heidelberg.

The first large tun seems to have been built about 1591. It contained 132 tuns, or nearly 133,000 quarts of wine, was an object of much popular wonder, and destroyed in the Thirty Years' War. In 1664 a new one was built, by order of Charles Ludwig, to hold 204 tuns, or upwards of 206,000 quarts.

In 1751 the present monster tun was constructed by the Elector Charles Theodore. It measures thirty feet five inches in length, and twenty-three feet in height, is kept together by eight massive iron and eighteen wooden hoops, and contains 236 tuns, or nearly 238,000 quarts. It was filled with wine on the 10th of November, 1752, which was subsequently repeated on three occasions, but since 1769 has remained empty. On either side a flight of steps leads up to it, while on the summit, and round the bung-hole, a flooring has been constructed, formerly reserved for the display of the light fantastic toe.

With a few brief words we must pass over the Octagonal or Bell Tower, completed in its present form by Frederick VI., about 1666; the Masted Tower, forming the Powder Magazine, erected by Frederick the Victorious about 1455, and blown up with gunpowder in 1689; and the four granite columns supporting a portico in the court-yard, which the pope gave to Charlemagne; which in the eighth century were removed from Ravenna to the banks of the Rhine, and in the fifteenth from the banks of the Rhine to those of the Neckar.

The castle gardens, at one time scarcely less famous for beauty than the castle itself for magnificence, were laid out in the formal French style by Solomon von Caux.

The finest views will be obtained from the Altau, or platform, constructed in 1346, beneath the chateau of Frederick IV.; from the Stückgarten; and from the great terrace in the gardens.

It is customary for every visitor to pass from the castle to the Wolfsbrünnen, passing on the right bank of the river the monastery of Newburg, and Zeigelhausen. In a little dell, under the shade of lofty trees, flows the Fountain of the Wolf: preserving the memory of a sorceress, named Jetta, who, it is said, was torn to pieces by a wolf while walking in this sequestered retreat.

CHAPTER VI. MANNHEIM TO MAINZ, VIA WORMS.

BETWEEN Heidelberg and Mannheim there is a railway, which strikes to the north-west, following at an irregular distance the left bank of the Neckar. On the right bank, nearly half-way, lies the small town of Ladenburg, in a plain of great fertility. It is conspicuous from its lofty church tower, the venerable church of St. Julius.

The Romans formed a settlement here under the name of *Lupodunum*. Next, the Franks got possession of it, and their kings built for themselves a palace. In 636 both town and palace were conferred by King Dagobert on St. Peter's Abbey of Worms, and in 1011 the bishops also obtained the jurisdiction. In the twelfth century the bishops made Ladenburg their place of residence.

In the Thirty Years' War it suffered severely: in 1621 it was occupied by Tilly; in 1622, by Mansfeldt; then came the Bavarians and Spaniards; and in 1631, Gustavus Adolphus. In 1641 it was seized by the French, who levied a heavy requisition; and in 1693 it was despoiled and devastated by Mélac. Towards the end of the seventeenth century the bishops of Worms quarrelled with the Elector Palatine about Ladenburg. Eventually the former gave way, and Ladenburg was awarded to the Palatinate, with which it afterwards fell to Baden.

The town has a population of 3000 souls, who are principally engaged in agricultural pursuits, and in the timber and tobacco trade. It boasts of a venerable Catholic church, which, in its turn, boasts of numerous sepulchral memorials of the barons of Sickingen and Metternich. A charity founded by the barons of Sickingen exists here. It is said that a young maiden of this family had, on one occasion, lost her way, and must have perished, but that, in her extremity, she was guided to the town by the welcome chime of a bell. The barons determined, therefore, that the bell should be rung every evening, and bread baked every week, so far as a bushel of corn would go, and distributed among the poor.

Mannheim, the largest town of the grand-duchy of Baden, has a population of nearly 30,000 inhabitants, and is situated on the right bank of the Rhine, opposite Ludwigshafen, at the point of junction between the stately Rhine and the rapid Neckar. It is situated in a flat, fertile, but uninteresting country. It has a circuit of about three miles, and three gates—the Neckar, the Heidelberg, and the Rhine gates. Like Washington, it is laid out in regular blocks or parallelograms, of which there are about 110.

Mannheim was founded in 1606 by the elector, Frederick IV. Unhappily for the town, he had scarcely begun to build it before he began to fortify it, and by so doing made it an object of attack in the various wars which have desolated Germany. Partly destroyed in the Thirty Years' War, it had risen from its ruins when the War of the Succession broke out. In 1688, when the French again invaded the Palatinate, it was under the command of Baron von Seligenkron, and the Lieutenant-colonels Strupp and Schenck. The works were put in good condition, and a force for their defence collected of 900 regulars, with cavalry and artillery, and 1050 militia.

On the 1st of November the enemy appeared before Mannheim. In less than a fortnight Seligenkron found himself compelled to surrender. The French immediately commenced the work of destruction. The houses were set on fire, the churches were blown up, and nothing was left of the town or fortress but blackened ruins. Mannheim seemed to have been swept from the face of the earth; and an old inhabitant, returning to its former site after the departure of the French, could with difficulty recognize the former position of the streets.

At the close of the war the Elector John William endeavoured to restore the town, and caused the plan of the new fortifications to be drawn up by the engineer Coehorn. In 1700 a council-house was built; in 1701 the Capuchin Church; about 1715 the Lutheran. To the Elector Charles Philip, however, Mannheim is principally indebted for its restoration. Had he not moved thither the court from Heidelberg in 1721, it would never have risen out of its insignificance.

Under Charles Theodore, on whose court enormous sums were lavished, Mannheim continued to improve in appearance. In 1746 the Kaufhaus, or Hall of Commerce, was completed; in 1754 the infantry barrack; in 1756 the Jesuits' Church; in 1772 the Citizens' Hospital and the Observatory; in 1777 the arsenal; in 1779 the theatre. Charles Theodore was no niggardly patron of the arts and sciences, but spent on their advancement not less than 35,000,000 florins. In 1754 was built the Anatomical Theatre; in 1756 a surgical hospital; in 1765 a maternity hospital. In the same year was commenced a cabinet of natural history, and in 1767 a botanical garden. In 1763 the Palatine Academy of Science had its beginnings; and in October, 1775, was founded the German Society for the Culture and Advancement of Literature, including among its members Lessing, Klopstock, Wieland, Schiller, Kästner. At this epoch, in truth, Mannheim was the Athens of Germany; it held among the German cities much the same position as Weimar afterwards held. It had its sculptor in Peter von Verschaffelt; its actors in Beck, Biel, and Iffland; its poet and dramatist in Schiller.

In 1777 Charles Theodore had succeeded to the throne of Bavaria, and his court and courtiers followed him to the Bavarian capital, Munich. The prosperity of the Badish city rapidly declined. In 1784 an inundation caused very considerable injury. Then, to complete its second overthrow, came the horrors of the French Revolutionary War. The Rhine entrenchments were captured by the French in December, 1794; and in September, 1795, a French army, under General Pichegru, appeared before the town. It was surrendered on the 20th, through the infamous treachery of the minister, Count Francis Albert von Oberndorf, and the governor, Baron von Belderbusch. A month later, and the Imperialists, under Clairfait, appeared before the city, after a series of successful actions along the Rhine, and in the vicinity of Coblenz and Mainz. Pichegru had left in Mannheim a garrison 10,000 strong, and taken up a position which enable him to communicate with the place by his right flank. So long as this communication was maintained, the Imperialists had little hope of reducing the city, and they resolved, therefore, to dislodge the French from their position. For this purpose Clairfait, having been reinforced with 12,000 men from the army of the Upper Rhine, attacked Pichegru's forces, and after a gallant action compelled them to retreat. He then proceeded to press the siege of Mannheim, covered by the main Austrian army under Wurmser. The French, under Jourdan, made an attempt to relieve it, but in vain, and the city capitulated on the 22nd of November.

By the peace of Lunéville, in 1803, it was given to the grand-duchy of Baden. Of late years it has grown into importance as a commercial town, and the Rhine harbour has assisted in developing its new-born energies.

The castle, or palace, formerly the largest in Germany, is more remarkable for its proportions than its architectural excellence. The façade was 1850 feet long, and the whole building contained 500 apartments, but the left or western wing was almost entirely destroyed during the bombardment of 1795. Strictly speaking, it consists of three courts or squares, of which the central and largest opens towards the town. The western portion was inhabited until her death by Napoleon's adopted daughter, the Dowager Grand-duchess Stephanie. The east wing is appropriated to the governor. Its picture gallery, since the removal of most of its treasures to Munich, does not present many valuable or interesting features.

The promenades of Mannheim are the terrace in the castle garden, which overlooks the excellent and abounding river; the Rhine jetty, or Rheindamm; the Neckarauer Wald; and the public garden of Muhlhausschlasschen, which forms a charming pleasure-resort on an island in the Rhine.

We cross the river at Mannheim to the small town of Ludwigshafen, whose advantageous position on the Rhine, and on the railways from Strassburg, Mainz, and Forbach, seems to insure it a prosperous future. Prior to the period of the French devolution, it was a fortress called Rheinschanze, the *tête-du-pont* of Mannheim. In 1794, 1795, and 1798 it was the object of desperate struggles, as it commands the passage of the Rhine at an important point. In 1798 it was razed to the ground, but the French reconstructed it in 1813, to abandon it, on the 1st of January, 1814, to the advanced guard of the Russian army. Until 1823 it held rank only as a fortress; but since that date commercial establishments have been founded here, new lines of streets erected, and many handsome houses built. Its rise has been carefully watched over by the Bavarian government, who made it a free port, and gave it the name of Ludwigshafen. Its fortifications have been demolished.

On the 15th of June, 1S47, and for several days, it was cannonaded by the Badish insurgents, after they had made themselves masters of Mannheim, and several houses were set on fire.

From Ludwigshafen, or Mannheim, there are two ways of reaching Mainz; by the Rhine, and by railway.

In descending the river, the following are the principal points of interest on either bank:— On the right, Sandhofen, which possesses two churches, neither of any peculiar architectural interest. But the situation of the village is charming. On the left, Frankenthal, a town of 5000 inhabitants, to which we shall duly refer. On the right, Lampertheim, in Hesse Darmstadt, a small sleepy town of 3500 inhabitants, with vineyards and orchards all about it; a town where any German Rip van Winkle, returning after an absence of fifty years, would find nothing changed. On the left, Roxheim, a town of 1000 inhabitants, situated on the old and original channel of the Rhine, which here, while winding and doubling like a snake in pursuit of its prey, preserves the broad calm aspect of a lake. On the left, the old historic city of Worms, respecting which we shall have much to record. On the same bank, Hernsheim, about two miles from the river; an old and lifeless town, encircled by ramparts. The castle belongs to the Duc de Dalberg. On the right, Gernsheim, a town of nearly 4000 inhabitants, famous as the birthplace of Peter Schoeffer, one of the first three printers. He was the son-in-law of Faust, and in 1454 invented metallic types. A statue, by Scholl, was erected to his memory in 1836.

Below Gernsheim a canal has been excavated, to avoid one of the longest *détours* made by the Rhine. Here, in the middle of the elbow formed by the river, on the right bank, near Erfelden, Gustavus Adolphus, the "Lion of the North," raised a monument to commemorate his successful passage of the Rhine on the 7th of December, 1631.

The Rhine approaches the railway very closely. We have on the left Oppenheim and Nierstein; then, on the right, Trebur or Tribur, where the Carlovingian kings had a palace, of which no remains are extant; and after having passed (left bank) Nakenheim, Bodenheim, Laubenheim, and Weissenau, and (on the right bank) Giersheim, near which point the Schwarz empties itself into the Rhine, we have on the right the embouchure of the Main, and beneath a railway bridge of very handsome erection sweep into Mainz.

We have now to speak of the railway route to Mainz. The first town we meet with is—

Oggersheim, with a population of 1500 souls, destroyed in the War of the Palatinate. Here, in the inn Zum Viehhofe, Schiller wrote his "Verschworung des Fiesco." At the time he was living in a condition of much distress, under the name of Schmidt; but soon afterwards he was invited to reside with the sons of Madame von Wollzogen, in her estate of Bauerbach, near Meinungen.

The chapel, or rather church of Loretto, at Oggersheim, is a centre of attraction to the surrounding country on Ascension Day. A convent of Minorites, endowed by the king of Bavaria, was founded here in 1845.

Our course now lies to the northward, across the Isenach, and brings us to Frankenthal (population, 4800), which is connected with the Rhine by a canal about three miles long. Both its origin and prosperity are due to sixty families of Flemish Protestants, who, expelled from the Low Countries by the tyranny of the Spaniards, established themselves here in 1562, in an Augustinian convent, founded in 1119.

When the Thirty Years' War broke out, the industrious little colony had increased to the number of 800 families, who introduced into this part of Germany industrial resources hitherto unknown, such as the manufacture of silk and cotton. It was then surrounded by walls, but its fortifications did not prevent it from being successively captured by the Spaniards, the Austrians, the Swedes, and the French. It was occupied for some months in 1622-23 by a small English force under Sir Horace Vere, despatched by James I. to sustain the failing cause of his son-in-law, the Elector Palatine. But the troops were too few in number, and their commander too deficient in military ability, to avail anything against the large Spanish army under Spinola, one of the first generals of his age, and accordingly they were compelled to surrender. When peace was re-established the electors rebuilt the town, which became in due time the great industrial depôt; but it has since fallen from its "pride of place."

On the site of the ancient convent, and after the model of the church at Karlsruhe, was built the Protestant church in 1820-23. The town, burned down in 1844, has since been reconstructed. The portico of the ancient conventual church is still extant.

Beyond Bobenheim we cross the Leininger; then we take leave of the Bavarian Palatinate, and enter into the grand-duchy of Hesse; cross the Alt and the Eis, and pass near the cemetery of "Worms, where we may distinguish the monument erected in 1848 to the memory of the old soldiers of the Grand Army of Napoleon.

WORMS.

The present population of Worms is about 11,000; it formerly numbered 40,000. The city is situated about a mile from the Rhine, which at one time washed its walls.

The one man with whom Worms is inseparably connected, and through whom it is something more than a decaying and dying city, is Martin Luther. The associations of Worms date from a venerable antiquity. A Roman fort was built here by Drusus. Here, too, in the Frankish era, were placed the scenes of the great German epic, the "Nibelungenlied." Christianity was introduced at a very early period, and Worms, in the fourth century, was a bishop's see. In the fifth century it was taken and plundered by Attila and his Huns; but it soon sprang erect from its ashes, and became a frequent residence of the Frankish kings. Dagobert I. built a palace, whose site is now occupied by the Trinity Church. Here Charlemagne declared war against the Saxons, and here, from 770 till 790, the famous May Assembly was held nearly every year. It was succeeded in due time by the Imperial Diet. At the Diet of Worms, in 1122, was concluded the treaty between the Emperor Henry V. and Pope Calixtus II., by which the bishops were thenceforth allowed to assume as episcopal insignia the sceptre, ring, and crozier. At the diet in 1495, under the Emperor Maximilian I., the right of private warfare was abolished, and public peace introduced into Germany. And it was the Diet of 1521 that summoned Martin Luther to answer the charges preferred against him by his opponents. The result of Luther's appearance before the Diet is too much a part of history to need description here.

FRANKFORT-ON-THE-MAINE.

In ancient German history there is no city, perhaps, which figures more conspicuously than Frankfort. It was an imperial city, a free city, and a city opulent and grave. Its gravity in those days became it, and was worthy of the sober burghers, its inhabitants, who played the game of life so decorously. And while it has lost its ancient renown, it still retains this dull and decorous air. At least so it seems to us, in spite of the newness which reigns about us; a newness due to its rich hotels, its broad bright boulevards, its open squares. But ancient Frankfort is no more; the narrow streets through which Charles V. and his cavaliers took their way, and the peaked gabled roofs, and the timber fronts of the houses, with all their quaint and curious carving, have vanished before that demon which reigns in every European town, and does its work not wisely, but too well—the demon of improvement. Whoever enters Frankfort, fresh from the pages of the old chroniclers, will be astonished how completely its past has disappeared; how little is left of the grand old mediaeval city.

Almost the only street which preserves what we may suppose to be its original characteristics is the Judengasse, or the Jews' Street. It has been well said that between it and its neighbours intervene 500 leagues and 500 years. The traveller, if he has wandered far, will be reminded of the muddy and miry Ghettos of Rome and Prague. It consists of two long rows of houses, black, gloomy, lofty, evil-looking, parallel, and almost alike. Between them runs a narrow, dim, and dirty causeway. On either side there is little to see but would-be doors, surmounted by an iron trellis-work fantastically wrought; and contiguous to these a grated *judas* partly opens on a gloomy alley. Wherever you turn you are greeted with dust, and ashes, and cobwebs, and worm-eaten crumbling timber, by a want and wretchedness more affected than real. But improvement has been in this street also—and, for once, let us own it was just necessary—and its ancient character will not be long in disappearing.

Here, on the right hand side, and in the house No. 118, was born the learned writer, Louis Boerne. Farther on, at No. 153, we come to the birthplace of the Rothschilds. As they grew wealthy they abandoned the old nest for more sumptuous residences; but their mother clung to it to the last, and died there in 1849.

The old synagogue of the Jews stands at the southern entrance of the street; at the northern extremity, in the Schützenstrasse, a new one has been erected in the Oriental style, and on a most superb scale. It was inaugurated in 1853.

From the Judengasse we turn to the quay of the Maine, and open up quite a different picture of the past. There still stand erect the ancient towers which strengthened the city walls, reminding us of the days when every man's hand was against his neighbour. The two banks of the river are connected by a narrow and high-pitched bridge. What tales its stones might tell if they could speak! for they are very ancient; we trace them back from generation to generation. The view from this bridge, and from the whole extent of the quay, is exceedingly picturesque and animated.

From the Main-Kai we turn up Neue Mainzer Strasse, and diverging on the right into Grosse Gallen Gasse, we soon find ourselves in the Rossmarkt, the largest open area in the town. Here is placed the Gutenburg *denkmal*, or memorial: a group of colossal statues representing the three first inventors of printing—Gutenburg, Fust, and Schoeffer; the medallions along the frieze reproduce the heads of the thirteen most celebrated German printers; and underneath the frieze are carved the armorial bearings of Mainz, Frankfort, Strassburg, and Verney, the four cities which most actively devoted themselves to the improvement and propagation of the new art; and, finally, the pedestal of the fountain is surrounded by allegorical figures of Theology, Science, Poetry, and Industry. The memorial was erected in 1845, and designed by Launitz.

In the Grosse Hirschgraben, close at hand, the house, No. 74, is for ever memorable as the house of Goethe, the greatest genius which Germany has yet produced. There he was born on the 28th of August, 1749, as the clock sounded the hour of noon.

Frankfort might well be content with the glory of having given birth to Goethe; but she has had other sons and daughters not unworthy of being remembered; as, for instance, Goethe's correspondent, Bettina von Arnim, the illustrious dramatist Oehlenschlager, Vogt, the great harmonist, Schlosser, Buttmann, and Feuerbach.

The handsomest, broadest, and liveliest street in Frankfort is the Zeil, where are situated the post-office, the residence of the grand-duke of Hesse, the house of De Rothschild, and at its lower end a foundry for bells and cannons. From hence we can take any one of the many streets leading into the other quarters of the town, and to the Rœmer (or town-hall), and the Dom (or cathedral).

The Roemer is an edifice of much interest, though it is difficult to say how much antiquity it retains, so frequently has it been repaired, restored, and reconstructed. It is said to have been originally used (and hence its name) as a kind of mart, or bazaar, where the Lombard merchants from Italy displayed their merchandise during the great Frankfort fairs. Others say it was erected on the site of one of Charlemagne's palaces. At all events, the city purchased it in 1403, and transformed it into a guildhall. Its façade is very curious. From a vast but low hall of the fifteenth century we ascend a broad staircase with a balustrade of iron, à la Louis XIII., and a lining of old tapestries, which are unworthy of attention, to the Kaisersaal, or imperial chamber. This is an irregular rhomboidal apartment, in which the emperors banqueted, with kings and princes acting as their attendants. The walls are covered with their portraits, fifty-two in number, and in chronological order, from Conrad I. to Francis II. These have been recently painted by Lessing, Burdeman, Rethel, and others, and are agreeable substitutes for the caricatures which formerly aroused the indignation of the visitor. Under nearly every one is the motto which the emperor adopted at his coronation. At the end of the hall is the Judgment of Solomon, by Steinde. In the Wahlzimmer, or election chamber, the senate of Frankfort, instead of the electors of the Holy Roman Empire, now hold their sittings. Here is preserved the famous Golden Bull, promulgated partly at Frankfort in the month of January, 1356, partly at Metz on Christmas day in the same year, by the august Emperor Charles IV., king of Bohemia, assisted by all the elector-princes of the Holy Empire, in presence of the reverend father in God, Theodore, bishop of Alba, cardinal of the Holy Roman Church, and of Charles, eldest son of the king of France, the illustrious duke of Normandy, and dauphin of the Viennois.

This document, whose appearance caused in its time a vast amount of excitement, is, after all, of little real importance; regulating, much less from a political than from a ceremonial point of view, the reciprocal relations of the electors and the head of the empire. In effect, it exalted the power of the seven electors, as they were called, at the cost of the imperial authority. It gave the king of Bohemia a place among the said seven; fixed Frankfort as the place of election; named the archbishop of Metz convener of the electoral college; gave to Bohemia the first, to the Count Palatine of the Rhine the second, place among the secular electors. In all cases a majority of votes was to be decisive.

"Peace and order," says Dr. Bryce, "appeared to be promoted by the institutions of Charles IV., which removed one fruitful cause of civil war. But these seven electoral princes acquired, with their new privileges, a marked and dangerous predominance in Germany.

They were to enjoy full regalian rights in their territories; causes were not to be evoked from their courts, save when justice should have been denied; their consent was necessary to all public acts of consequence. Their persons were held to be sacred, and the seven mystic luminaries of the Holy Empire, typified by the seven luminaries of the Apocalypse, soon gained much of the emperor's hold on popular reverence, as well as that actual power which he lacked. To Charles, who viewed the German empire much as Rudolph had viewed the Roman, this result came not unforeseen. He saw in his office a means of serving personal ends; and to them, while exalting by endless ceremonies its ideal dignity, deliberately sacrificed what real strength was left. The object which he sought steadily through life was the prosperity of the Bohemian kingdom and the advancement of his own house. In the Golden Bull, whose seal bears the legend—

'Roma caput mundi regit orbis frena rotundi,'

there is not a word of Rome or of Italy. To Germany he was indirectly a benefactor by the foundation of the University of Prague, the mother of all her schools; otherwise her bane. He legalized anarchy, and called it a constitution."

Since the days of Austerlitz Charlemagne's crown, until the present remarkable epoch, has rested on no imperial brow. Many of the losses which Austria had suffered at Napoleon's hands were repaired by the treaties of 1815; but the empire of Germany was not restored, and the Hapsburgs were forced to be content with the new imperial crown of Austria. In August, 1863, however, the present emperor made a bid, as it were, for the old leadership of Germany, which for some years had been divided between him and the king of Prussia; and in the ancient Germanic capital he convoked all the German kings and princes, to discuss with him the future interests of their fatherland, and the reforms required in her constitution. But the hostility of Prussia checked the move, and foiled the designs of the Austrian statesmen.

But at all events Frankfort could rejoice that for a moment the eyes of Europe were fixed upon her, as in the old historic days. And she had some reason to be proud with a civic pride when, before the princes assembled at the banquet, under the imperial roof of the Rcemer, the emperor of Austria pledged it in a cup of wine. The wealth of the old days once more poured into the treasuries of the Frankforters. Fifty thousand strangers were attracted from all parts of Europe by this gathering of kings, princes, grand-dukes, princelings, statesmen, soldiers, and courtiers. It was an imperial revival on a grand scale, but "for this occasion only." The emperor was lodged in the Roemer, as was the custom with his ancestors; but he was not to wield the sceptre of the Holy Roman Empire. It was a glorious dream, a dazzling mirage. As for practical result, it had none, unless we look for it on the field of Sadowa!

Amongst the ecclesiastical buildings of Frankfort, the first and foremost is necessarily the Dôm, or cathedral, also called the church of St. Barthelemy. This is a cruciform edifice, which has been erected at different epochs—the nave about 1238, the choir between 1315 and 1338, and the aisles somewhat later. The effect of the whole is certainly quaint and picturesque, but the details do not harmonize thoroughly. The Dom was restored in 1855. It measures about 310 feet in length, and 270 in width. On the right hand side of the principal entrance is conspicuous an enormous clock, with an astrolabe and a perpetual calendar, of the fifteenth century. The interior contains a number of objects more or less worthy of attention. The ancient tombs of the Holzhausen, with their remains of colouring, must not be overlooked. In the choir are some noteworthy frescoes of the sorrows of St. Bartholomew and the graces of St. Mary Magdalene, besides rude, bold wood-carving of fourteenth century date. In the chapel on the left, a fifteenth century sculpture, representing the Virgin on her death-bed, astonishes by its singularity of conception. The artist will find matter for criticism in a Christ on the Virgin's knees, attributed to Durer; an Assumption (over the high altar), by Veit, in the style of Rubens; and a Holy Family, after Rubens. For the simply curious spectator the objects of interest are many and varied; the ancient armour hanging from the walls; the painting, on leather, of the interior of St. Cecilia's tomb; some fine copper lamps; and, among other tombs, that of Gunther von Schwarzburg, elected emperor at Frankfort in 1349, and shortly afterwards poisoned. The monument was erected in 1352. It stands close beside the door leading to the old chamber of election. Observe, that in the centre of the Dom, and just at the entrance to the choir—that is, at the point where the nave intersects the transepts—the emperors have undergone the ceremony of coronation since the days of Maximilian II.

St. Leonhard's Church is memorable as occupying the site of the ancient palace of Charlemagne, who assembled, as the Chronicles tell us, the bishops and princes of the empire here at Frankensfurd, or the "Frank's ford." In the interior are some interesting objects. The altar-piece is by Stieler, a Bavarian artist.

The Sachsenhausen, founded by the Saxons about the epoch of Charlemagne, is chiefly inhabited by gardeners and vineyard-labourers. To the left, as we enter it, our eye rests on the Deutsche Haus, the residence of the knights of the old Teutonic order, but now degraded into a barrack.

The quay, which from the bridge runs along the right bank of the river, as far as the Obermainthor, is called the Schoene Aussicht, or "Beautiful Prospect." At its further end is placed the library, built in 1825. Among its bibliographical curiosities are a MS. Bible, purchased at Rome about 1350, and formerly in the possession of the Gutenberg family; the Mainz Bible of 1462, on parchment; and Gutenberg's Bible, the so-called Mazarin.

The Stadel Museum (of pictures) is situated in the Neue Mainzer Strasse, and named after its founder, a Frankfort burgher, who bequeathed all his paintings, drawings, and engravings to the city, besides a sum of £83,000 for the erection and maintenance of a public gallery. In the first room there is Moretto's admirable Virgin and Child, with the four Fathers of the Latin Church, purchased at an expense of 30,000 florins. In the second, the *chef d'oeuvre* is Lessing's Huss before the Council of Constanz. In the third, we remember an ancient and curious altar-piece, and a tasteless but cleverly composed Triumph of Christianity in the Arts, by Overbeck. In the sixth room, Schnorr, Schadow, and Steinle are represented.

The Fresco-Saal contains an allegorical fresco by Veit, representing Christendom introducing the Arts into Germany; and a terra-cotta composition by Andrioli (1561) of the Virgin and Saints.

Sinkenberg's Museum of Natural History is near the fine old Eschenheim Gate, and contains a tolerably well-selected, but not very large, cabinet of natural history specimens.

CHAPTER VII. FROM MAINZ TO COBLENZ.

MAINZ.

MAINZ (in French and English, Mayence), one of the principal towns of the German empire, is situated, at an elevation of ninety to ninety-five feet, on the right bank of the Rhine, almost opposite the mouth of the Main. Its population exceeds 40,000. With the left bank of the German river it is connected by a bridge of boats, and by a strong iron bridge at some slight distance from the city. This latter bridge was opened in December, 1862.

The circumference of Mainz, including its military outworks, may be computed at three leagues and a half. Three main gates, without including those of the quay, opening on the Rhine, provide a communication between the interior of the city and the country; namely, Neuthor, on the Oppenheim and Worms road; Gauthor, on the Paris road, *viâ* Algey and Kaiserslautern; and Münsterthor, on the road to Bingen, Coblenz, Trier, and Creuznach.

Now for a general description of the city.

A bird's eye view, could it be obtained—or an aerostatic voyage, which is equivalent to it—would show you Mainz in the form of a perfectly-defined arc of the circle, the chord being represented by the river, and the circle by the fortifications. These fortifications are founded on Vauban's system, but with many modifications, the fruit of modern engineering study. They are considered by the best judges to be of a very formidable character; and it will be observed that the river, on one side, acts as a deep, broad, and comparatively impassable fosse. In addition, a very powerful citadel, in front of the town, commands its passage, and threatens to overwhelm any assailant. Like a gigantic star, it projects in four angles, and its four bastions, bristling with artillery, bear these heroic or sinister names: Drusus, Germanicus, Tacitus, and Alarm. The latter, partly situated in the suburb of the city, is strengthened by a mine, and, from far or near, seems to say to the passer by, "Who goes there?"

Mainz is another example of the folly of converting populous cities into great military posts. It is literally choked within the strong grasp of its walls. Hence its streets are narrow and muddy, and its houses are carried to a great height to compensate for the want of superficial space. A busy and numerous population seem, in their marts and markets, to shoulder, to jostle one another.

The history of Mainz dates back to a period anterior to the Christian era. Whether the Germans had a settlement here, no antiquary seems able to determine; but thirty years before the birth of our Saviour, Martius Agrippa, one of the lieutenants of Augustus, constructed here an intrenched camp. This fortress, which was afterwards known as Moguntiacum, was rebuilt, twenty years later, by Agrippa's successor, Drusus Germanicus; who also raised, on the opposite bank of the river, a *castellum* (castle), and united the two by a massive stone bridge, some remains of which are visible to this day.

In A.D. 70 Moguntiacum was garrisoned by the twenty-second legion, which had conquered Judea and destroyed Jerusalem, under the orders of Titus. The ancient tradition affirms that St. Crescentius, who was one of the first to preach the religion of Christ on the banks of the Rhine, and who suffered martyrdom in 103, was a soldier in this legion before becoming a soldier of the church militant, and first bishop of Mainz.

In 235 Alexander Severus, while meditating a campaign against the Germans, was here waylaid by a small band of mutinous soldiery, incited, it is said, by his rival Maximinus, and murdered, along with his mother, in the thirtieth year of his age and the fourteenth of his reign.

After the crashing downfall of the Roman empire, Mainz successively fell into the hands of the Allemanns, the Vandals, and the Huns.

Destruction had swept over it, and it was but a heap of ruins when its bishop, Sidonius, with the help and patronage of Dagobert II., king of the Franks, began to rebuild it, but on a site nearer the river bank. It was surrounded with walls in 712 by Bishop Sigebert. Soon afterwards, by a vicissitude of fortune common enough in those days, it was seized by the Burgundians. These were driven out in 720 by the hammering blows of Charles Martel. Then it seems to have flourished apace; and in 745 the two kings, Carloman and Pepin, in agreement with Pope Zacarias, elevated its bishop to archiepiscopal rank, and made him the ecclesiastical metropolitan of all Germany. This new archbishop was no other than the sainted Wilfrid, better known under the name of St. Boniface. Born at Crediton, in Devonshire, of a wealthy and distinguished race, he became a monk in the Benedictine abbey of Nutsall, near Winchester, but speedily quitted it with eleven companions, to preach the gospel to the barbarous nations of Germany. His mission, interrupted by three voyages to Pome, lasted thirty years, and its influence extended from the Elbe to the Rhine, and from the Alps to the ocean. It is said to have accomplished, as its glorious result, the conversion of upwards of 100,000 pagans.

Glancing at the mediaeval history of Germany, we see two great facts standing out in conspicuous relief, both of importance, and one of them destined to exercise a social, moral, and intellectual influence over the whole civilized world. We refer, in the first place, to the League of the Rhine, founded by Arnold von Walboten in 1247, with the view of liberating commerce from the iron fetters imposed upon it by the tyranny of feudalism; the other, the invention of printing by Gutenburg in 1440. We know how the latter invention has affected every branch of our general life; how it has upset thrones and mitres and provoked revolutions, but, on the other hand, has encouraged reforms, and built up the fair structures of constitutional liberty and religious freedom.

We shall be right, perhaps, in considering that Mainz attained the climax of its prosperity in the fourteenth century. After the Reformation its history was one long course of vicissitude and disaster.

It was captured and set on fire in 1552 by Albert, margrave of Brandeburg. In 1631 the "Lion of the North," Gustavus Adolphus, appeared before it with that remarkable army of his, the prototype of Cromwell's "Ironsides." On the 13th of December, 1631, the king made his entry into the conquered town, and fixed his quarters in the elector's palace. In 1635 the Imperialists once more gained possession of the city, to give way to the French in 1644. When these had retired, it enjoyed some years of peace and prosperity; was rebuilt, embellished, and aggrandized by the Elector John Philip the Wise, who threw a bridge of boats across the Rhine. But in 1688 the French once more captured it, committing, according to French authority, "abominable excesses;" and in 1689, they being driven out, the Imperialists resumed possession. The Elector Lothair Francis, and his successors, resumed the work of John Philip, which had thus rudely been interrupted, and succeeded in effacing every sign of war and its ravages.

Then broke out the French revolution, and Mainz, as one of the great advanced posts of Germany, was compelled to endure a succession of calamitous sieges. It was taken by the French under Custine, in 1792; but in the following year they were forced to surrender by an Austro-Prussian army, more through the effect of famine than through the military skill of the commander of the allies. It was again besieged by the French in 1794, who were defeated under its walls. In 1795 they were also repulsed. In 1797, however, it was ceded to the French, and it remained a French fortress until 1814. Afterwards, and down to the present time, it belonged to the German confederation, and was garrisoned by an equal number of Austrians and Prussians. Now it is included within the boundaries of North Germany, and is solely occupied by Prussian troops. Its fortifications have been greatly strengthened and enlarged.

At Mainz begins the Lower Rhine.

We shall pay our first visit to the *Platz Gutenberg*, where, opposite the theatre, was erected in 1837 a bronze statue to Gutenberg, the first printer, executed by Thorwaldsen, at the cost of the citizens of Europe. Gutenberg was born at Mainz, about 1397, of a noble family, named Sulgeloch zum Gutenberg. The house where he was born stands at the corners of the streets Pfundhausgasse and Emmeransgasse. About 1424, having discovered the principles of the new art with which his name was to be associated, he betook himself to Strassburg, where he carried theory into practice, and made his first typographical attempts with movable types cut out of wood. He did not return to Mainz until 1443, when, being in want of funds, he associated with himself Fust, a wealthy goldsmith, and Schoeffer, a man of talent, and in the house *Hofzum Sungen*, which still exists, he printed his *Biblia Latina*.

The finest building in Mainz is its cathedral; a red sandstone pile of great extent, begun in the tenth, and completed in the eleventh century. It has gone through so many conflagrations, however, and suffered so much from the Prussian bombardment of 1793, and still more from having been used as a barrack and magazine by the French, that little is left of the ancient edifice except the eastern apse, which is flanked by two circular towers, one dating from 978, the other from 1137. The Pfarrthurm, at the east end, is an octagonal tower, surmounted by a cast-iron cupola, seventy feet high, designed by Moller. Like the cathedrals of Worms, Trier, and Speier, the church has a double choir, with high altars both at the east and west ends, and transepts.

The principal entrance is a low door in the side of the building. But the leaves of the door are eight centuries old, and on their bronze panels may still be read the characters of the charter granted to the city by Bishop Adalbert I., who ordered it to be here engraved.

Two domes, of different styles and proportions, crown the edifice. They might almost be called, in allusion to their form and ornaments, two papal tiaras. The older is the more severe and simple in construction, and the more imposing; the other, the more enriched, the more elaborate, and "perhaps" the more pleasing.

There are three naves in the interior, or rather a nave and side aisles, of which the central is remarkable for the boldness of its lofty arches. The great defect internally is the want of windows; they are few and narrow, and placed at too great an elevation. Hence the light is insufficient, and what there is falls in the wrong places, and injures the general effect. This has been not unjustly designated the capital vice of the Romanesque style. On the other hand, the Gothic architect delighted to open up windows wherever he could, and to flood his buildings with light, moderated and varied by the painted glass.

The cathedral was the place of sepulture of the electoral archbishops of Mainz, of the princes of the Holy Roman Empire, and of many other illustrious and distinguished personages. We cannot pretend to enumerate all these monuments. The most interesting are those which belong to the last years of the fifteenth and the earlier part of the sixteenth centuries. Among these we may point out Prince Albert of Saxony, 1484; the Canon Bernard of Brudenbach, 1497; Archbishop Berthold of Stenneberg, 1504; Archbishop Jacob of Liebenstein, 1508; and Albert of Brandeburg, 1545. In no case are the epitaphs more than pompous and verbose descriptions of the honours and dignities enjoyed by the deceased. A fragment of white marble, let into the wall, is all that remains of the tomb erected by Charlemagne to Fastrada, his third or fourth wife, who died in A.D. 794.

Another monument of historic interest is that of St. Boniface, raised to his memory in 1357. It consists of red sandstone, and is situated on the right side of the nave.

To the artist that of Frauenlob will also be attractive. Frauenlob (that is, "praise of women") was a canon of the cathedral, named Heinrich von Meissen, who lived towards the close of the thirteenth and in the early part of the fourteenth centuries. He was one of the first *Minnesingers*, or love-singers—the German troubadours; and he devoted his poetic genius to the laudation of women, and especially of the Virgin.

The church of Saint Stephen, in the Gauthor, is worth a visit. From the summit of its lofty tower, which is situated in the highest part of the city, the view is rich, extensive, diversified.

The old Electoral Palace, a stately red sandstone pile of the seventeenth century, was down to 1792 the residence of the electors. The throne room has been restored. Here are now collected, under a single roof, the library, the picture gallery, the museums of coins, antiquities, and natural history. The library possesses upwards of 100,000 volumes. Among these may be particularized, a bible, 1462; a catholicon, 1460; and a psalter, 1457. In the collection of antiquities, the most notable featured are the Roman altars, the votive stone, and the inscriptions discovered in the town and its environs. But the gallery of pictures contains things of beauty, which appeal to the heart and fancy of the largest number of visitors. Among about 270 works of ancient and modern artists, there are good specimens of Jordaens, Titian, Giordano, Albert Dürer, Tintoretto, Guido, Domenichino, Rubens, Murillo, Snyders, and others.

About a mile beyond the Gauthor are the remains of a Roman aqueduct, nearly 3000 feet long, which conveyed water to the Roman garrison from a spring five miles distant. Sixty-two piers, still extant, are admirable specimens of Roman masonry.

From Mainz to Coblenz extends what may aptly be called the "steamboat navigation of the Rhine," and this portion of the river is certainly best explored "by water." We enter now on the fertile country of the Rheingau, whose general aspect has been very faithfully described by a recent French writer. "The Rheingau," says Professor Durand, "is a region, half plain and half mountain, sheltered from the rough north and biting east by the thick masses of the Taunus and the Niederwald, while facing the south with its Rhine-washed hills. It is the vineyard of Germany. Places more poetical we *may* see; but none more prosperous or more flourishing. The intervals between the various villages are exceedingly short; and in their site, their structures, and the gleam of their lime-washed facades, there is an air of gaiety which greatly pleases the spectator. Most of them are planted at the very edge of the river, and are separated from it simply by a pathway. Thus, in winter, the inhabitants are driven from their homes by the floods. But as these floods are of periodical occurrence, no one seems to be disturbed by them. Everybody seems to have made up his mind to live on good terms with their regular visitor; and rather than depart from his paternal river, is willing to yield up to him once a year his room and bed. In the first sixty years of the present century, no fewer than thirty-three inundations have taken place, some of them of a terrible character. A church of greater or less antiquity, and generally of a pleasant architectural aspect, forms the central point of each village, and around it gathers a group of brick-built houses, adorned with vines."

The Rheingau's surest source of wealth is in the bounty of the vine, and, consequently, its cultivation has spread over every rood of ground. Rocky precipices, declivities, and precipices where it is a task to hold oneself erect, have been dug, and turned over, and fertilized. In default of vegetable soil, the cultivators have pulverized the friable rock. Far out of sight the vines extend their regular ranks, and all the outlines of the mountain bristle with them. Out of this flood or sheet of verdure rise at intervals large, gleaming Italian villas, with flat roofs and square walls, or Neo-Gothic castles, with crenelated turrets. These are the pleasant summer resorts of the opulent wine merchants of Mainz or Frankfort, erected in the midst of the vineyards to which their proprietors owe their wealth. Flags bearing the national colours float from every summit, and, as in a royal palace, indicate that the master is at home. But round these splendid edifices blooms scarcely any garden ground; the ground is too limited, the product too precious, for the agreeable to take the place of the useful. An oak, or a larch, gives only a little shade; but here, each foot of the vineyard is covered in autumn with pieces of gold. At the bottom of the terrace an elegantly decorated skiff balances on the waves. To have an estate in the Rheingau, and a boat on the Rhine, are the two extreme points of human happiness in this country.

Of all the vineyards in this part of the Rhine valley the most celebrated is the Johannisberg. After having belonged for some centuries to the abbey and convent of St. John, the original passed, early in the present century, into the hands of the prince of Orange; but the all-dividing Napoleon presented it as a gift to Marshal Kellermann. At the close of the first empire, it was given by the emperor of Austria to Prince Metternich to be held as an imperial fief. "The ground around is too precious as a vineyard to be laid out in gardens: no trees are allowed, as they would deprive the vines of the sun's rays; but on the north side of the houses there is a sort of vineyard planted with trees. The best wine grows close under the chateau, and indeed partly over the cellars. The species of wine cultivated is the Riesling. The management of it at all seasons requires the most careful attention. The grapes are allowed to remain on the vines as long as they can hold together, and the vintage usually begins a fortnight later than anywhere else. The vine-grower is not satisfied with ripeness; the grape must verge on rottenness before it suits his purpose; and although much is lost in quantity by this delay in gathering, it is considered that the wine gains thereby in strength and body. So precious are the grapes, that those which fall are picked off the ground with a kind of fork made for the purpose. The extent of the vineyard is about seventy acres, and it is divided into small compartments, the produce of each of which is put into separate casks: even in the best years there is considerable difference in the value of different casks. Its produce amounts in good years to about forty butts (called *stücks*), and of $7\frac{1}{2}$ ohms, and has been valued at 80,000 florins. The highest price ever paid was 18,000 florins for 1350 bottles, or upwards of thirteen florins a bottle."

THE RHEINGAU.

Generally speaking, the course of the Rhine, after leaving Mainz, is that of a river running in a deep mountain channel. On the right the Taunus, and on the left the Hundsrück, have neared each other as if they would absolutely arrest the progress of the waters. To the most superficial observer it is evident that, in ages long ago, the solid mountain mass must have been disrupted by some formidable convulsion; and in the chasm then created now flows the mighty stream—far mightier, it may be, in those days of earth's stir and turmoil. On either side it now washes a wall of rock, its narrow banks being covered with a scanty vegetation of firs and reeds, whose gloomy verdure communicates to the waters the colour of bronze. Here and there some persevering labourer has broken up the obdurate soil, and planted the fruitful vine. The live rock, wounded by the miner's pick, gnawed at by the waters, eaten by frost and rain, exhibits its marvellous strata of red and blue; and day and night, says a French writer, seem to encounter one another, without ever commingling, in the cavernous hollows of their declivities. At one point the eye is lost in a deep darkness; at another it rests on a surface flooded with light.

And mark how the river murmurs and plashes, as it eddies round a rock rising in the centre of its channel. Mark how it tumbles in a miniature cascade over the ledges which its waters have created. And now, behold, the mountains seem to hem it in, and the waters rest tranquilly in their sheltered basin, as in a far-off mountain tarn? We look in vain for its point of issue. When did it enter? whence will it escape? Is not this the termination of the Rhine? There is something attractive, and yet melancholy, in this deception. Were the heights loaded with snow, says Durand, you might think that the river had turned back towards its Swiss cradle, and had poured itself into one of the great lakes of the Alpine regions.

Thus, then, we have seen the Rhine in its wilder and gloomier beauty. There are no more villages after Bingen, few human habitations, scarcely any cultivation. An infinite grandeur is given to the picture by their silence and solitude; and as we gaze upon it our thoughts are raised to its own high standard. And the spectator, carrying his fancy back over the gulf of time, readily calls up the images of the primeval world, and traces through the ages the successive fortunes of the stream.

All Christian that it is, and though the spires and towers of a thousand churches are mirrored in its waves, the Rhine still gives birth to unnumbered pagan fables, unnumbered phantoms, of which it is both the cradle and the realm. Sylphs, and elves, and gnomes, loreleys, nixes, and ondines, spring into life along its banks, haunt its rocks, inhabit its crystal caverns, and contend with the priest for the empire of the river. The devil is on their side; the devil, who was ever-present to the mediaeval imagination, figures in at least onehalf of the legendary history of the Rhine. There is not a hermitage whose saint he has not tempted with his wiles; not a monastery to which he has not done some evil turn; not a cathedral but he has doomed it to remain unfinished for ever.

Simultaneously with the religious life, feudalism seized upon this fair countryside, to leave the indelible mark of its iron sway. The stir and conflict of the early centuries rendered necessary those innumerable burgs or fortresses which, from Bingen to Coblenz, form along the Rhine a belt of towers and battlements. Each summit, each rock, each mountain gorge, had its master. Entrenched behind walls six feet in thickness, separated from the commerce of men by draw-bridges, and bastions, and precipices, these warriors only quitted their falcons' nests to pounce upon a prey or to attack one another. It was an age of unrestrained violence. In no other country was mediaeval history characterized by so much blood, and rapine, and disorder; by so much turbulence on the part of the chief, by so much misery on the part of the peasant. And nowhere else has the image of those times been preserved with so much fidelity. Yon keeps, yon platform, yon shattered and crumbling walls, which, enthroned upon the rock, have so valiantly endured the weight of centuries—all these are the past, are feudalism, are history. It is as if an ancient theatre had remained erect, with the scenery almost uninjured of the drama formerly enacted within it. But where are the actors? where the movement, the sounds, the accents of human speech? Everything is alive in the past; everything is dead in the present.

FROM MAINZ TO COBLENZ BY THE EIGHT BANK OF THE RHINE.

Passing the long narrow islands of Petersau and Jugelheimerau, we arrive at Biberich, a small but pleasantly situated town of 5000 inhabitants, whose single attraction is the chateau of the duke of Nassau, a handsome structure of red sandstone, built towards the early part of the last century in the Renaissance style. Its richly decorated front faces the Rhine, and forms a conspicuous feature in the landscape. It consists of two main buildings, terminated by a couple of wings, and connected by a kind of circular projection or rotunda, ornamented with a group of statues. The interior is furnished with much taste and splendour, and the windows open up a number of beautiful views of the Rhine scenery.

Elfeld, or Eltville, bears the distinction of being the only town in the Rheingau. Its name is a corruption of Alta Villa, and indicates its conspicuous and elevated position. From afar it may be recognized by the lofty, four-turreted watchtower, which crowns the ridge of the acclivity, and is a part of the castle erected here in the fourteenth century by the archbishops of Mainz. These distinguished prelates were often glad of a safe refuge from their turbulent citizens. It was here that in 1349 Gunther of Schwarzburg, when beleaguered by his rival Charles IV., resigned his crown, and died, probably of poison. The castle was destroyed by the successive efforts of the Swedes and French. Of the town it may be noted that it possessed a printing press as early as 1465, and that its environs are unusually picturesque and attractive. There is a beautiful chapel of St. Michael in the Kedriel valley. It was built in 1440, and of the later Gothic is a valuable example.

The islands which here stud the expansive bosom of the river are named Rheinau, or Westphadau, Langwertherau, and Sandau. Charlemagne often resorted to them to fish, when he was residing at Jugelheim (of which hereafter). And upon one of them, probably Sandau, Louis the Debonnair, hunted to the death by his cruel sons, ended his wretched life in June, 840.

A little below Hattenheim the Rhine attains its maximum breadth, 2000 feet; and in the vicinity of this town, on the Strahlenberg, grows the celebrated Marcobrunnen wine, so named from the small fountain of Markbrunnen. Count Schönbom's château, Reichartshausen, is situated further down the river, in a pleasant but not very extensive park.

Through a country of vineyards, whose radiant smiling aspect it is impossible to describe, but of which one can never grow weary, we proceed to Geisenheim, distinguishable from a distance by the open Gothic towers recently added (1836) to its fifteenth-century church. Here lies the dust of John Philip, of Schoarbom, formerly elector of Mainz.

Of far greater interest than any of the vintage towns mentioned is Rüdesheim (sixteen and half miles by rail from Biberich), a place of great antiquity, of much importance, and picturesque situation. The neighbouring hills blush with the vines which produce the famous Rüdesheim liquor, the essence of the precious grape. Tradition ascribes the origin of these vineyards to Charlemagne, who, remarking from his palace at Jugelheim that the snow disappeared from the heights of Rüdesheim sooner than elsewhere, and detecting the advantageousness of the locality for vine-growing, ordered suitable plants to be conveyed thither from Burgundy and Orleans. And the grapes, we may add, are still called Orleans.

The great antiquity of Rüdesheim is the picturesque quadrangular keep, seated close to the bank of the Rhine, and known as the Brömserburg, which dates from 1100. It is also called the Neiderburg and the Oboeburg. It consists of three vaulted stories, and its walls are from eight to fourteen feet in thickness. It dates from the thirteenth century, and measures about 110 feet in length, ninety-five feet in width, and seventy-five feet in height—a formidable mass picturesquely adorned with ivy and shrubs. "What an admirable feudal castle!" cries Victor Hugo. "Romanesque caverns, Romanesque walls, a hall of knights illuminated by a lamp resembling that in Charlemagne's tent, Renaissance windows, iron lanterns of the thirteenth century suspended to the walls, narrow corkscrew staircases, frightfully gloomy cells or *oubliettes,* sepulchral urns ranged in a kind of ossuary—a complete accumulation of black and terrible things, at whose summit expands an enormous crest of verdure and flowers, whence we may contemplate the magnificence of the Rhine."

At first, the Brömserburg belonged to the archbishops of Mainz; next, to the nobles of Rüdesheim-Brömser (a family which died out in 1688); and afterwards it passed through the hands of various owners into those of Prince Metternich, who sold it to the Count von Jugelheim.

From Rüdesheim we always strike inland to the beautiful Niederwald, or Lower Forest. Here are Lagdschloss, a small hunting box; the Bezaubertu Haehle, or "Magic Grotto," affording three superb tableaux of the castle and church of Falkenburg, Rheinstein, and the Schweizerhaus. Thence we ascend to the artificial ruin of the Rossel, and "under the shade of melancholy boughs" to the Temple; which is situated on the very summit, 780 feet above the Rhine. Both from the Rossel and the Temple the views are grandly impressive; and though many others equal, few, if any, surpass them. They have a character of their own which prevents them from being forgotten, and once seen they are stamped upon the memory for ever.

Passing the confluence of the Nahe with the Rhine, we mark the old quartz rock which rises in the middle of the narrowing river, where the latter seeks to force a passage between the Taunus and the Hundsrück. The rock is crowned with the ruins of an old tower, the Maeusethurm, or Mouse Tower, or Bishop Hatto's Tower. Associated with it is a romantic legend, of which Southey has given a version. The tower was built in the thirteenth century, by Archbishop Siegfried, for the accommodation of the guards who levied the tolls inflicted on passing vessels. Hence it was called the Mauth or Maus, that is, the Toll tower. It was restored in 1856.

Continuing along the right bank, we come to Ehrenfels, the romantic ruins of a castle built in 1210, and frequently occupied by the archbishops of Mainz, when they and their treasures were in danger from their turbulent subjects. It was captured by the Swedes in 1635, and destroyed by the French in 1689. The most delightful and luxuriant vineyards embower these picturesque ruins.

Below Ehrenfels we cross the Bingerloch, an artificial canal excavated in a rocky dyke which, at that point, obstructs the bed of the Rhine. It was constructed by the Prussian government between 1830 and 1832.

We arrive at Lorch, the *Laureacum* of the Romans, situated at the confluence of the Wisper with the Rhine. In mediaeval times it was inhabited by numerous nobles, whose mansions are still extant. The church was founded in the twelfth century, but has undergone considerable reconstruction. It has a fine chime of bells, whose melody, gliding over the waters and echoing through the vineyard alleys, has a singularly impressive effect.

On the right bank of the Wisper rises, abrupt and precipitous, the terraced rock known as the Devil's Ladder—*Teufelsleiter*—crowned by the crumbling ruins of the castle of Nollicht or Nollingen. Even on this rude rock "the flower of a legend blows."

Below Lorch, a fair and well-cultivated little island breaks the waters of the Rhine. Below Bacharach, which will receive attention hereafter, the river plunges into a mass of rocks, with incessant clouds of spray and foam, and would be impassable for ships but for the canal excavated by the Prussian government in 1850. This *Wilde Gefoecht*, however, is one of the most picturesque points on the river.

At a bend of the stream, and on a rocky islet, stands the romantic castle of Pfalz or Pfalzgrabenstein, erected in the fourteenth century by the Emperor Louis the Bavarian. It completely commanded the passage of the Rhine, and levied a toll on all passing vessels. Here Louis le Debonnair died in 840, weary with the fatigues of empire, and longing only for a thatched lodge or leafy hut to shelter him in his last home. The "soothing music of the gurgling waters" lulled him to his rest. It was often used as a prison, and its dark and horrible dungeons lie below the level of the river. The castle is accessible by means of a ladder, and the solitary entrance is closed by a portcullis. The well which supplied its inmates with water is filled from a source far deeper than the bed of the Rhine. According to an old belief, the princesses Palatine always came here for their accouchements, and the mother and babe took their first airing in a boat on the surrounding waters.

Opposite Pfalz on the right bank of the Rhine, which, let us remind the reader, is the bank we have been descending, is Caub, with its important slate quarries. It was here, on the 1st of January, 1814, that the Prussian army, under Blucher, crossed the river, and commenced the invasion of France.

To the north of this little but remarkable town rises conspicuous the castle of Gutenfels. We hear of it as early as 1178, when the lords of Falkenstein sold it to the Palatinate, along with Caub, which, as was customary with the feudal towns, had grown up silently at its feet. It is said to owe its name—Guta's Rock—to the beautiful Beatrix Guta or Guda, the sister of Philip von Falkenstein, with whom our Richard of Cornwall, king of the Romans, became desperately enamoured, and whom he afterwards married. When the storm of the Thirty Years' War raged down the valley of the Rhine, Gustavus Adolphus attempted to dislodge a Spanish garrison which had previously been stationed in it; but the natural and artificial strength of the position foiled all his efforts.

As we descend the river grows narrower, and runs with pent-up waters in a rocky channel. A rock on the right bank, singularly shaped, arrests every eye. It looks as if giants had been constructing a staircase, and had failed in, or grown weary of, their task. The echo here is turned by the inhabitants to some account. It repeats every sound which strikes upon it seven times. As the steamboat passes, a man, standing on the left bank of the river, fires a few pistol shots, that the passengers may be amused with their repeated reverberations. It is a favourite jest with the German students to ask the hidden nymph, "Echo, what is the burgomaster of Oberwesel?" Echo answers, *Esel*, that is, "an ass."

Much of the poetry of the Rhine centres in this craggy rock. For *ley* means a rock, and *lore* is an old word for song, or music. Lurlei or Lorelei is, therefore, the "rock of song;" and the loreleys of the Rhine are singing maidens of great beauty, who, like the sirens of old, beguile the listener to his death. One legend relates that the boatmen sometimes descry on the summit of the rock a maiden of surpassing loveliness. She begins her enticing chant. In spite of themselves they are constrained to listen; and while they listen their boat dashes against the rocks, is shattered to pieces, and they are carried underneath the waves to the crystal halls of the Lurlei. A Count Palatine was desirous of seeing this siren, whose charms so far excelled all ordinary human beauty. He, too, fell a victim to her arts. His father immediately ordered his soldiers to bring the young magician to him, alive or dead.

But just as they thought themselves on the point of seizing her, she called upon the river to come to her rescue. Immediately it obeyed. From its foamy waves sprang two white horses, removed the stone on which she was seated, and dragged it down to the river-depth. On their return to the castle, they found that the siren had restored the young count to his home; Since this epoch, she has ceased to show herself; but her soft voice still awakens the murmurs of the evening breeze, and at times she will sport with the boatmen by mimicking their voices.

A small, and gradually decreasing fishery, is carried on in the neighbourhood of the Lurlei-bay.

We now pass by the fearful whirlpool of the Baik Bank, and the narrow and dangerous defile of the Gewirra—the Scylla and Charybdis of the Rhine. They prove no obstacle, however, to the progress of the Rhine steamers.

Our course now brings us to Sanct Goarshausen, opposite Sanct Goar. It is situated at the entrance of the beautiful and romantic Swiss valley, between the "Cat" and the "Mouse."

The "Cat" (die Katze) is an ancient castle, founded by the Counts von Katzenelnbogen ("cat's elbow") in 1392. It derived its name, perhaps, not from its lords, but because it watched the merchant vessels, in order to levy exactions upon them, as a cat watches a mouse. After this family died out, in 1470, it passed into the hands of various Hessian princes, until destroyed by the French in 1806. Its ruins command a view both rich and rare.

Opposite to it, but also in a ruined condition, stands the "Mouse" (die Maus), also called the Thurmberg or Kunoberg, built in 1363 by Kuno von Falkenstein, in order to keep the "Cat" under control. "Henceforth," said he, "I will be the mouse which frightens the cat!" And he was right, said Victor Hugo, for it is a formidable pile even to this day.

There is another of these eloquent memorials of feudalism far up the Swiss valley (which is by no means Swiss, though very picturesque in character). It is called the Reichenburg, and its history is easily summed up. As thus:—Built in 1280 by Count Wilhelm I. of Katzenelnbogen; destroyed in 1302; reconstructed by Baudoin of Trier in the Oriental style; destroyed by the ferocious Tilly in the Thirty Years' War; inhabited until 1806; sold, for purposes of demolition, in 1818; and now in possession of Herr Habel von Schierstein. Such are the phases through which a feudal castle seems generally to pass.

On the right bank we pass the little Gothic church of Wilmich, at the foot of the steep and broken rock crowned by the ruined fortalice of the Mouse. Lower down is Ehrenthal, with its silver, its copper, and its lead mines; and a short journey brings us to one of the "hallowed spots" of the Rhine—to the Castles of the Brothers, Liebenstein and Sternfels, whose story has been several times told by the poets.

"The mountains that inclose the river," says Mr. Mayhew, "are finely rugged, and ribbed with the schistose rocks that in some places protrude through the green hill-sides, and that in others apparently stream down from the top like a cascade of crags.

"Then there are the grand old ruins cresting the summits, and lending a hoary historic life to the neighbouring mountains—and the little bits of vineyards, crammed in among the stones whereon the sun can fall, and tinting the green-gray crags with many a golden streak—and the lovely repose of the valley openings, looking soft and cool in the rich 'clear-obscure' of the shade that hangs over them like a veil of dusky air, and with the steamy cloud of smoke that rises, as if it were so much morning mist, from the valley-hollows, telling of the peaceful homesteads that lie cradled within them; and the white frothy brooks streaming under the little archways beside the Rhine, and whispering of the many mills they give life and motion to as they come tumbling down the steep rocky dingles behind, and potiring over the walls of crag there in such a mass of foam that the very water seems no longer liquid, but to be a torrent of powdery particles, like snow, showered down from one ledge to another."

At Filzen the Rhine bends abruptly eastward, and washes the town of Ostersperg, resting in the cool green shadow of the Liebeneck. Then the Rhine resumes its northerly direction at Denkhers, famous for its mineral spring; and flows past Brauback and the grand castle of Marxburg.

Several hundred feet above the town of Braubach, on a rugged and rocky mountain height, stands its noble castle, which has been described as bearing some degree of likeness to that of Dover, but seems to us more closely to resemble the Scoto-Gothic castles of northern Britain. At all events, it is one of the most complete examples of a feudal castle along the whole course of the Rhine. Seen from the river, or from the village street, it possesses an indescribably grand effect, and one may be forgiven for fancying it the work of some ancient Titan, who, after piling rock upon rock, erected a stronghold for himself on the wind-swept summit.

THE MARXBURG.

Through long, narrow, and climbing alleys we reach the foot of the castled mountain, and then by a zig-zag path undertake the laborious ascent. It is right to add that the labour is much sweetened by the delightful glimpses you catch ever and anon of the flowing river and its wooded banks.

The first object to which your attention is directed after you enter the castle is the gloomy vault, the prison of the German Emperor Henry IV. The walls are bare and ochred, and there is only a "rude, little, conical chimney-place sunk in one corner of the apartment," while opposite a loophole, rather than a window, is inserted in a very small recess. On one side of this aperture a small stone slab, projecting from the massive wall, serves as a rude uncomfortable seat. Here Henry II. was imprisoned, after the rebellion of the German princes in favour of Rudolph, duke of Suabia.

From the prison-chamber you wind your way through dim, dark, and mysterious corridors, and across various apartments, and up steep and half-broken steps, to the gloomy dungeon called the Hundloch, or "dog-hole." After your eyes grow accustomed to its semi-darkness, you make out a beam slanted up on end, like a rude crane projecting from the ground, with a windlass attached to its base. This is the apparatus by which prisoners doomed to perpetual captivity, or, more truly speaking, to a lingering and terrible death, were lowered into the actual dog-hole, the pit below. The guide lifts up a trap in the floor, and standing on the edge and looking over, you see, by the glimmer of light let in through a chink or slit in the wall, that the pit resembles a well about thirty feet in depth. Into this most miserable of dungeons the poor wretch was lowered by the crane which we have spoken of; lowered, perhaps, with a crash which happily saved him from further suffering. Otherwise, provisions were let down in the same way, as long as the doomed man dragged on his wretched life.

From the dog-hole you ascend a narrow spiral staircase, hewn out of the massive masonry of the main tower, to the square platform which serves as roof; and from this elevated position you enjoy a picture of the Rhine, so bright, so beautiful, so rich in colour, that you forget at once the gloom of the scenes you have been looking upon. From this grand observatory we descend to the Fotterkammer, or Kack-chamber, another dark and dismal apartment, from which, however, the instrument of torture to which it owes its name has been removed. Thence we pass into the Speis-kammer, or Dinner-chamber; and the Ritter-saal, or the Knight's Hall, now used as a prison. Adjoining these another strong room is situated, whose white walls are covered with rude frescoes, drawn by the prisoners who, in the last century, were inmates of the place. Some of these consist of figures of warriors and princes, while others possess more of a grotesque than chivalrous character: such as wooden-legged fiddlers, peasants dancing, innkeepers carrying frothy cups of beer. In among these are scattered numerous inscriptions in prose and verse.

It is said that a secret passage descends through the live rock, connecting the Marxburg with a tower on the borders of the river. The castle is (or was until very lately) garrisoned by a corps of invalids.

Continuing our survey, we come to a little chapel, embosomed among trees, and nearly opposite the Königsstuhl (on the left bank), which calls for our special attention as the place where, in 1400, the four electors of the Rhine declared the deposition of the Emperor Wenceslaus, and elected in his stead the Count Palatine, Rupert III. This incident is a signal proof of the decay into which the Holy Roman Empire had by this time fallen, and of the virtual usurpation by the electors of the imperial power. The chapel, then, is literally one of the landmarks of the history of the Holy Roman Empire.

We next pause at Oberlahnstein (Upper Lahnstein), situated on a long bank of silted-up deposit facing the Rhine, its shore sanguine with heaps of red iron ore from the Nassau mines. 'Tis a picturesque old town, with stone rampart walls and old towers and turreted gates, and at the further end the palace of the electors of Mainz, rebuilt or enlarged. On the hill above moulder the ruins of the Lahneckburg, a castle of great antiquity, which figures in history as destroyed by the French in 1688, and in poetry as sung of by Goethe.

On the other side of the Lahn, which here comes down a romantic valley to join its waters with those of the Rhine, is Niederlahnstein (or Nether Lahnstein), and close by stands the structure of Johannis-kirche (St. John's church), with the tall lonely tower looking like the keep of some ancient stronghold, and reflecting its gray hoary walls in the silver mirror of the Lahn. It was destroyed by the Swedes, and after remaining for many years in a ruinous condition, was restored in 1857. Stolzenfels, rising so grandly on the opposite bank of the Rhine, will hereafter engage our attention.

On the right bank we pass Storchheim, the island of Oberwerth (or Upper Island, lying in a sheltered bay), and the village of Pfaffendorf. Opposite Coblenz rises Ehrenbreitstein, the "Gibraltar of the Rhine," the "Broad Stone of Honour." The best view of the steep mountainous rock, and the tremendous fortress which crowns it, is obtained from the opposite bank, just below the bridge that unites Coblenz with the Petersberg.

We now proceed to describe the left bank of the river from Mainz to Coblenz.

TO COBLENZ. BY THE LEFT BANK OF THE RHINE.

During the early portion of our course from Mainz to Coblenz, the railway closely hugs the romantic bank of the river, which is here studded with numerous islands. On the opposite shore all the beauties of Bieberich and the Rheingau are successively opened up to our gaze. Beyond the small village of Bredonheim, the iron road starts away from the river, and through a wood of murmurous pines reaches Heidesheim; of which I know nothing more than that all about it cluster prolific vineyards and not less prolific orchards.

The left bank is neither so romantic nor so interesting as the right until we reach Nieder Ingelheim, which lies about two miles inland from the river, on the Seltz, one of its minor affluents. It is a town to look at with curious interest, if it be true, as most historians assert, that Charlemagne, the most imperial of emperors, was born here. He seems to have regarded it with the affection one generally feels for one's native town; and he erected within its walls, between 768 and 774, a palace of more than usual splendour; a palace embellished, it is said, with one hundred columns of marble and porphyry which he had brought from Rome, and with the costliest mosaics, which Pope Hadrian had sent to him from Ravenna as a gift. Not a vestige of its ancient magnificence now remains.

It was here, on the 30th of December, 1105, occurred one of the most remarkable incidents in the history of the Holy Roman Empire. The bishops of Mainz, Köln, and Wurms pronounced the deposition of the Emperor Henry IV. Advancing towards him, they removed the "circle of sovereignty from his head," tore him from the throne on which he was seated, and stripped off his imperial robes.

To conclude our catalogue of the associations of this quiet little town, let us point to the small obelisk at its extremity, whereon two immortal names come into strange juxtaposition; both of them conquerors, and imperial founders, and great administrators, but how unlike in their fate, and in the fate of their work! This is the inscription on the obelisk:—

"Route de Charlemagne, termine'e en l'an ler du régne de Napoléon, empereur des Français." (The great road of Charlemagne, completed in the first year of the reign of Napoleon, emperor of the French.)

Through a beautiful country we make our way to Bingen, where the Nahe pours its waters into the Rhine. Confined on the left by the Nahe, on the right by the Rhine, it has developed itself in a triangular form around a Gothic church, set back to back against a Roman citadel. In the direction of Mainz sparkles the famous plain called Paradies, opening up the rich wine-garden of the Rheingau. On the side of Coblenz the sombre summits of Leyen rise against the horizon.

Bingen is the Roman *Bingium*, and its bridge across the Nahe is still called, as Tacitus called it, the "Bridge of Drusus." It was built by the Archbishop Wittigis in the eleventh century (1013), probably with the materials and on the site of the Roman bridge, which the Treviri had destroyed in A.D. 70. It was again rebuilt in the seventeenth century, and has been frequently repaired. The ruin called Klopp, on an eminence above the town, though of no greater antiquity than the days of feudalism, was probably raised on the site of one of the Roman forts built by Drusus. Bingen, commanding both the Nahe and the Rhine, was necessarily a military post of much importance before the invention of artillery. In the middle ages it belonged to the archbishops of Mainz and Trier. Its prosperity dates from its colonization by some Lombard merchants from Asti, in Piedmont—the Ottini, Pomario, Broglio, and others. In 1302 it was successfully defended against the Emperor Albert; but in the Thirty Years' War, and the War of the Succession, its position having ceased to prove formidable in defence, it passed from one of the belligerents to the other with admirable facility. It was included in the French territories from 1797 until 1813, and three years later was annexed to Hesse Darmstadt.

There is not much to be seen in Bingen, but around it the interesting features are very numerous. One of these is the Rochus Kapelle, or chapel of St. Roch, situated high up the hill—in truth, on its very crest, almost opposite Rüdesheim on the other bank. The ascent to it is neither very long nor very difficult; and were it both long and difficult, you would still be repaid for your labour by the magnificent prospect from the summit. The completeness of its beauty, its exquisite atmospheric radiance, its ever-changing effects of light and shade, its combinations or contrasts of colour, render the spectacle to the eye as if seen through a kaleidoscope. The Sunday following the 16th of August is St. Roch's day, when hundreds of pilgrims congregate from every quarter to pay their vows to the saint, who is famous as an averter of plague and pestilence.

There is a hill called the Scharlachkopf, which is easily accessible from Bingen or from St. Roch's chapel, and whose declivities are thickly planted with vines of good quality. From the terrace of this hill, too, the view is charming.

We resume our descent of the river, but do not halt again until we arrive at Bacharach, the mediaeval *Ara Bacchi*, long celebrated for the superior excellence of its wines. The true *Bacchi ara* is a rock in the bed of the river, adjoining the island a little below the town. Usually it is covered with water, but in very dry seasons its bare surface rises above the river-level, much to the gratification of the lord of the vineyard, who hails it as a sign of an auspicious vintage. It is said that Bacharach wine was of so delicious a flavour that Pope Pius II. imported a tun of it to Rome every year, and that the freedom of the city of

Nuremberg was purchased by the annual gift of a few casks of it to the Emperor Wenceslaus.

Victor Hugo's description of Bacharach is amusing. You would say, he remarks, that a giant, who dealt in *bric-à-brac*, wishing for a show-room on the Rhine, seized upon this mountain, cut it up into terraces, and piled upon these terraces, from top to bottom, and with all a giant's taste, a heap of enormous curiosities. In truth, he began under the very waters of the Rhine; for there, just beneath the surface, lies a volcanic rock, according to some authorities, a Celtic pulven, according to others, and a Roman altar, according to the few. There, on the bank of the river, moulder two or three old, worm-eaten hulls of ships, cut in two, and planted upright in the earth, so as to make decent cabins for fishermen. Next, behind these cabins, we come to a portion of the city wall, formerly crenellated, and supported by four square towers, the most ruinous and shot-battered that ever human eye beheld. After this, against the very *enceinte* itself, where the houses are all pierced with windows and galleries, and beyond, at the foot of the mountain, an indescribable pellmell of amusing edifices, fantastic turrets, preposterous facades, impossible *pignons*, whose double staircase carries a belfry pushed forward like a holy-water sprinkler on every stage, heavy timbers designing upon cottages most delicate arabesques, barns in volutes, balconies open to the day, chimneys fashioned like trains and crowns philosophically full of smoke, extravagant weather-cocks; but why need we continue the enumeration?

Amidst this most admired disorder there is an open area, a twisted space or place, made by blocks of mountains which have fallen from the sky haphazard, and which has more bays, islands, reefs, and promontories than a Norwegian gulf. On one side of this place stands a couple of polyhedrons, composed of Gothic constructions, overhanging, bent forward, grimacing, and impudently holding itself erect in defiance of all the laws of geometry and equilibrium. On "the other side, observe the beautiful Byzantine Church of St. Peter, with its handsome gateway and lofty belfry, and the host of tombs in the Renaissance style which crowd its interior. It was formerly a Templar church, and is interesting as an early example of mixed Round and Gothic.

Above this church, and on the road to the old castle of Stahleck, lie the ruins of St. Werner's church—windowless, roofless, doorless—yet a magnificent specimen of later Gothic, built of hard red sandstone in 1428. "It was demolished by the Swedes in the Thirty Years' War, but still shows in its east end a lantern, the highest and most elegant lancet style existing."

We come next to Schcenberg, the cradle of the family so named, whose most illustrious offshoot seems to have been the Marshal Schomberg who closed a long military career at the Battle of the Boyne, fighting for William III. Below Schcenberg is situated the picturesque town of Oberwesel, the *Vesalia* of the Romans, with its ivy-shaded, crenellated towers, its old, narrow, and quaint streets, and its two superb Gothic churches. The walls are in many places curiously romantic, and in the lower part of the town is the lofty round tower of the Ochsenthurm.

The church of Our Lady (Liebfrauenkirche), at the upper end of the town, is a simple but gracefully proportioned church, erected in 1331-38. Its roof is eighty feet in height, and rests upon plain square piers. Its porches are richly sculptured, and the vaulting of the cloisters is singular. In a side chapel are many monuments of the Schomberg family, bearing rudely carved effigies of knights in armour, ladies in ruffs and stomachers, and babies in swaddling clothes, like mummies or the larvae of insects.

The church of Saint Martin is still older, and its architectural details are full of interest. The altar-piece represents the Lowering of Our Saviour's Body from the Cross, by Diepenbeck, one of the pupils of Rubens.

Sanct Goar is opposite Sanct Goarshausen. The Hinter Rhein-strasse, which is the High Street of St. Goar, and the principal one of the two making up the long narrow town, has so few shops in it, that you would almost believe the simple villagers dealt with one another according to the primitive mode of barter. The church here is not a very interesting edifice, but the Protestant church is a well-looking structure near the centre of the town. It was built in 1468, contains some monuments of the Hessian princes, and stands over the crypt of the ancient church of St. Goar. It was restored in 1482. In this crypt Saint Goar was buried.

Above Sanct Goar towers the lofty castled crag of the Rheinfels, 368 feet high, the most extensive ruin on the banks of the Rhine. The earliest stronghold was founded by a Count Diesher of Katzenelnbogen, in 1245, for the purpose of a residence, and as a toll-tower, where he could levy toll on passing vessels. The appetite grew by what it fed on, and the bandit's exactions grew so colossal, that the citizens of the neighbouring towns plucked up spirit to rebel against him, and finally, to besiege the robber in his lair. The struggle was prolonged over fifteen months. Then was formed, on a broader base, the great Confederation of the Rhine, which destroyed so many of these robber-fastnesses, and set free the navigation of the river. Among the castles which the confederated burghers captured was the Rheinfels; it afterwards came into the possession of the Landgrave of Hesse, who converted it into a modern fortress of such strength that, in 1692, it successfully resisted a French army of 25,000 men, commanded by Marshal Tallard, though the latter had promised it as a New Year's gift to his sovereign. In 1794, however, it surrendered, before a shot was fired, to the French revolutionary army, who, about three years later, blew up its formidable defences.

Passing Salzig and its cherry orchards, we come to Boppard, the Roman *Baudobriga*, which in mediaeval times was an imperial free city. In 1312 the Emperor Henry VII. yielded it to his brother Baldwin, archbishop of Trier, who united it to the electorate. An attempt was made by some of its inhabitants to reconquer their liberties, but it failed. It now belongs to Prussia.

It is a pleasure to arrive at Rhense, for it is one of the most picturesque towns on the Rhine, and retains its mediaeval character with delightful freedom from modern improvements. Few of its houses, as the guide-book tells us, are newer than the sixteenth, while many are as old as the fourteenth century; a statement which, in itself, is sufficient to stir any true archaeologist's imagination. But Rhense has something more to boast of. Just outside of it is the Königsstuhl, or "King's Seat."

Here, says Victor Hugo, four men, coming from four different directions, assembled at intervals near a stone on the left bank of the Rhine, and at a tew paces from a grove of trees between Rhense and Kapellen. These four men took their seats upon the stone, and there they made, or unmade, the emperors of Germany. The place selected by them, Rhense, is nearly in the centre of the Rhine Valley, and belonged to the elector of Köln. In an hour, each elector could repair from Rhense to his own territories.

While Napoleon held the mastery of the Rhenish provinces the Königsstuhl fell into decay. In 1807 it was destroyed, and some of its materials used in the construction of a new road. But happily it was rebuilt in 1843 on exactly the same plan as the original, and to a great extent the original materials were employed.

Still pursuing the left bank of the river, we arrive at Kapellen, splendidly dominated over by the castle of the Stolzenfels, or the "Proud Rock," as it is appropriately named. The rocky promontory on which its walls and towers are planted rises about 330 feet above the Rhine. Destroyed by the French in 1688, the Stolzenfels remained in decay until 1823, when the city of Coblenz, which had become its owner, presented it to the present emperor of Germany, then crown prince of Prussia. From 1836 to 1845 the emperor expended upwards of £50,000 in restoring it, from the designs of Herr Schenkil. Looking southward from the Stolzenfels, at our feet we see the ruined Marxburg and the red roofs of Braubach; near Oberlahnstein, the white gleaming chapel of Wenceslaus; directly opposite, by the side of the picturesque town of Rhense, the Königsstuhl is barely visible through its screen of trees. Like the outstretched wings of a bird of prey, the shattered battlements of Lahneck still dominate over the ancient town of Oberlahnstein, where the palace of the elector of Mainz naturally attracts the eye. Farther away, in the remote and lonely valley of the Lahn, rises the Mountain of All Saints—the Allerheiligenberg—whose chapel is visited by numerous pilgrims. Before Niederlahnstein, and near the mouth of the Nahe, stands conspicuous the church of St. John. Northward, the woody isle of Oberwerth stretches itself at full length on the bosom of the Rhine. To the right, in the green cool shadow of verdurous mountains, rise the rocks of Ehrenbreitstein, or the "broad stone of honour," facing the formidable walls of Fort Alexander. Between the rocks and the fort a bridge of boats serves as a communication between Coblenz and Ehrenbreitstein. Finally, against the remote horizon are outlined the heights of Vallendar, the town and the church of the same name.

CHAPTER VIII. COBLENZ.

EHRENBREITSTEIN, a lofty rock, steep and abrupt on three sides, and on its fourth, or weakest, the north-western, protected by no less than three formidable lines of defence, is armed with upwards of 400 heavy guns. To the non-military observer it seems as if military science had here done its best and worst; and that no force could possibly advance in the face of the tremendous fire the garrison could pour upon them. The great platform on the summit of the rock is not only used as a parade ground, but artfully serves as a roof or cover for cisterns of immense capacity, which can hold a supply of water for three years, furnished by springs without the walls. Moreover, there is a well, sunk 400 feet deep in the rock, which communicates with the Rhine; but then, Rhine water is unwholesome, and would quickly lay low a garrison with disease.

We may conclude then, that Ehrenbreitstein could never be reduced by ordinary military operations, unless Coblenz was in the hands of an enemy; but that it might possibly surrender to a close and persistent blockade.

Ehrenbreitstein, the "broad stone of honour," seems to have been occupied for military purposes since a very remote period. In 1631 the Elector Philip Christopher, of Soetern, gave it up to the French, who retained possession of it for five years. In 1688 it was unsuccessfully besieged by Marshal Boufflers; in 1795 and 1796 by General Marceau; but in 1799 it surrendered to the French after a long and rigorous blockade. By the treaty of Luneville the French were compelled to restore it to Germany; but before abandoning it they blew it up, and converted it into the ruins so graphically commemorated by Byron.

Through the town of Thal-Ehrenbreitstein, and across the Rhine, we pass into Coblenz.

Coblenz owes its name to its position at the confluence of two great rivers—the Rhine and the Moselle. The Romans, who formed a camp here about 30 B.C., called it *Confluentia* , or *Confluentes*. Coblenz is situated on a triangular or wedge-shaped piece of land between the Moselle (north) and the Rhine (east). It may be divided into the Old Town and New Town. The former lies nearest to the Moselle; its streets are narrow and tortuous, and not unlike the wynds of Edinburgh. The New Town, or Clement's Town, lies behind the imperial chateau, built in 1778-86 by Clément Wenceslas, last bishop-elector of Trier; its streets are regularly laid out, its houses of good size and well built.

Here is a lively picture:—"The banks of the Moselle, opposite to Coblenz, are low, and a long plain stretches far away behind them towards Andernach, that has been, from Caesar's time, the scene of many a fierce battle; while close in front of them the river is floored with the rafts, which are here to be pieced together into one 'float 'before descending the broader part of the Rhine on their way to Holland: all along the shore, too, there are huge, square stacks of planks, and the air pants again, as it were, with the grating of the saws from the neighbouring timber yards.

"The Coblenz houses along the quay beside the Rhine are very different from those along the quay beside the Moselle; for the buildings facing the *Rhein-strom* are parts of the New Town, and consist chiefly of large white-fronted hotels, with their names painted all along them in gigantic letters; and the banks immediately under these are beset with many a landing-pier, beside which are grouped the steamers, with their piebald funnels; while beyond the dumpy round tower, with the Rhine crane, like a giant fishing-rod, projecting through its roof, and the square yellow-ochre turret of the Government House rising behind it, at the end of the quay, we can just catch sight of the tall red sandstone of the palace portico, as high as the building itself, and breaking, with a bold simplicity, the great length of the otherwise plain façade.

"The buildings, however, on the side of the city nest the Moselle, are all of an antiquated character, and there the gables of the narrow houses are huddled together, one above another, till the roofs look like so many black billows; and beyond these, the odd, old Exchange is seen, with its battlement-like turrets projecting from the upper corners of its walls; while farther on still, at the end of the quay next the bridge, the eye rests upon the ancient palace of the archbishop of Trier, with the lighthouse-like towers at either angle of its ochre-coloured front, and seeming more like the gate to some fortress than the residence of a Christian prelate.

"Then the Rhine-stream is crossed by a bridge of boats no higher than a floating pier, and whose platform stretches along the line of barges like an enormous lengthy plank, reaching from one side of the river to the other, and linking the valley village with the city. This is now all in pieces, for we can see large slabs of the floating roadway standing out in the river, far away from the bridge itself, and with two or three white-hooded peasant women upon them, as if they had been carried adrift in the hurry of crossing. Then, at either end of the gap in the "*Schiff-brücke*" we can distinguish the crowd of passengers dammed up, the brass-tipped helmets of the cluster of soldiers looking as if on fire in the sun, the market-women, with their baskets poised upon their heads, together with the white awning of the tilted carts, all brought together into one pretty group; while between the glittering opening in the platform we perceive in the distance some heavy, lazy-looking barge, with the yellow load of planks stacked high above its deck, and without a sail set, drifting down with the stream slowly towards the bridge."

In the Old Town, very close to the actual junction of the two rivers, is the church of Saint Castor. The church is associated with some memorable events. Beneath its roof the three sons of Louis le Debonnair—Lothaire and Louis of Germany and Charles the Bold—met to divide amongst them the grand heritage of Charlemagne's empire. And here, in the *platz* in front of the building, Edward III. of England, in 1338, had an interview with the Emperor Lewis of Bavaria, who installed him Vicar of the Empire, to enable him to secure the assistance of the imperial vassals on the left bank of the Rhine in his campaign against France. As a pledge of his honour, Edward deposited his crown in the church, where it was guarded night and day by an equal number (fifty) of Teutonic and English knights. To few Englishmen, we imagine, is this romantic incident known, which links English history with a quaint old church in a quaint old fortress-city on the bank of the Rhine!

In the New Town may be visited the Palace of the Government; the Hauptsteueramt (or tax offices), and the Royal Palace (Königliche Schloss), erected in 1778-1786 by the last elector of Trier, Clément Wenceslas. The Prussian government undertook its restoration some thirty years ago; and since 1845 it has frequently been inhabited by the present emperor of Germany and his wife. It commands a fine view of the Rhine, and the interior contains some really precious works of art. The service of the Church of England is performed here twice every Sunday, by permission of the emperor of Germany.

It has been well said by a recent French traveller, and must be apparent to every visitor, that Coblenz plays in the world a double part. Happily situated at the junction point of two rivers—the central ring of the vast chain of which the two extremities are formed in Köln and Mainz—it necessarily serves as the focus of all the commercial industry and agricultural wealth for thirty leagues around.

On the other hand, it is equally destined to the role of a military city. Its position is not less valuable to the defenders of Germany than formidable to its enemies; it commands the valley of the Moselle, it overawes the passage of the Rhine. It is one of the keys of Germany, and its conquest would be one of the first tasks imposed on an enemy invading the Prusso-Rhenish provinces. Hence it is doomed to see itself confined and imprisoned within a threefold line of forts and bastions.

There are many pleasant spots in its vicinity. The Petersberg contains within its wall a plain marble slab, with four corner stones, indicating the grave of the French revolutionary general, Hoche. Near at hand is the monument, a stone pyramid, erected to the memory of Marceau, another of the heroes of the Revolution. Translated into English, the inscription runs thus:—

"Here rests Marceau, born at Chartres, in the department of Eure-et-Loir, a soldier at sixteen and a general at twenty-two. He died [at Altenkirchen] fighting for his country, on the last day of the fourth year of the French Republic [September 21, 1796]. Whoever thou art, friend or foe of this young hero, respect his ashes."

THE RIGHT BANK OF THE RHINE TO BONN.

Along this bank extends a range of "smiling hills," never of any considerable elevation, but always of a very pleasant and picturesque aspect. Upon their slopes and at their feet are situated many little villages, which to the passer-by seem perfect Arcadias of peace, prosperity, and loveliness.

The first place, of any considerable importance in regard to population, at which we arrive, is Neuwied, a neat and cleanly town, with streets crossing each other at right angles; a town of 10,000 inhabitants, the capital of the principality of Wied, but now belonging to Prussia.

A writer speaks of it as "a pretty little town on the right bank of the Rhine, between Mainz and Bonn. The situation is agreeable, the air very healthy, and the country fertile. It lies in a plain of considerable dimensions, terminated by hills arranged in the fashion of an amphitheatre, and presenting to the eye a charming variety of fields, meadows, vineyards, and well-cultivated orchards." All the religions of Europe (Mohammedanism excepted) have found a meeting-place in this little town. In its factories, the Quaker and the Moravian work side by side, recognizable only by the different colour of their vestments.

The next place of interest is Andernach, the *Antenacum*—that is, the *statio ante Nacum*, or "advanced post of the Nette"—of the Romans. During the supremacy of Napoleon, Andernach was annexed to the French; it now belongs to Prussia. The neighbouring plain is one of the great historic battle-fields of Germany. Here Charles the Bold was defeated, in 876, by his nephew Louis the Younger. Here, after a bloody strife, the Franks prevailed over the Normans in 850. Here Otho the Great successfully withstood the freebooters of Duke Eberhard and Philip of Hohenstaufen. Here the Archbishop Frederick of Köln repulsed the soldiers of the Emperor Henry V. in 1114. And here, too, various battles were fought in the Thirty Years' War, the War of the Spanish Succession, and the French Revolutionary War. At present it is the scene, every three years, of the manoeuvres of a portion of the Prussian army.

The streets of Andernach are narrow and dirty, but these demerits are of little importance, as they are almost unfrequented. The great ornament of the town is its parish church, the Pfarr Kirche. The two tall towers, at the end of the nave, are pierced all the way up with light Romanesque arches, while in other parts the arches are Byzantine. There are in all four towers, with Byzantine belfries, which from a great distance serve as conspicuous landmarks. Beautiful sculpture enriches the south entrance to the transept. A bas-relief of curious design, but exquisite workmanship, represents the Adoration of the Lamb; another, the death of "some lady in a painted green dress, amid a crowd of priests and choristers, with archbishop-angels looking down upon her from the clouds above."

The shore of the Rhine, in the neighbourhood of the Crane Tower—which is lower down the river than the Watch Tower, and was built in 1554—abounds with dark-gray millstones, made of hard porous lava, and looking not unlike "so many cheeses" piled one against another. These are obtained from the curious basaltic lava quarries of Nieder Mendig; were well known to the Romans; and are now exported in considerable quantities to England, Russia, the East and West Indies, and all parts of the world. Andernach also produces a volcanic cement, or *trass*, from the quarries of Brohl and Krup; and a species of pumice, called oven-stone, from the Bell quarries, about five miles west.

Our course next brings us to Linz, a busy little town of 3500 inhabitants, surrounded by walls of basalt, and lying in a fruitful vineyard region. Charles the Rash captured it in 1475, the Swedes in 1632, the French in 1688. The tower near its Rhine-gate was erected in 1365 by the archbishop of Köln, for the exaction of a toll from boats ascending or descending the river; and also to defend the town against the burghers of Andernach, who cherished a bitter hatred against the Linzites. Linz lies opposite the mouth of the Ahr, and commands a charming view of the Ahr valley.

Below Linz we may visit the singular basaltic quarries of the Drattenberg, and the still more remarkable ones of the Minderberg, by way of the copper mine of the Sternhüter. In the latter, the columnar arrangement of the basalt is scarcely less beautiful than in Fingal's Cave or at the Giant's Causeway. The summit of the Minderberg is 1200 feet above the Rhine, and the prospect which it commands is magnificent and extensive. The castle of Ockenfels, on the river side, is now a picturesque ruin.

The basalt again appears on a grand scale in the precipices called Erpeler Lei, which rise to an elevation of 700 feet above the river. "The ingenuity of man has converted those barren rocks, which are almost inaccessible, into a productive vineyard. The vines are planted in baskets filled with mould, and inserted in crevices of the basalt. By this means alone can the earth be preserved from being washed away by every shower."

Carrying our gaze back to the bank of the Rhine which we are traversing, we find ample material for admiration and wonder. Here, at Königswinter, we obtain a fine view of the Drachenfels.

The Drachenfels (1056 feet) which, in conjunction with the island of Nonnenwerth and the Rolandseck, forms the most celebrated, and, perhaps the most perfectly beautiful of all the Rhine landscapes, is one of the volcanic group—remarkable not for height but for variety of outline—called the Siebengebirge, or Seven Mountains; the other six of which are, the Stromberg, 1053 feet; Niederstromberg, 1066 feet; Oelberg, 1453 feet; Wolkenberg, 1055 feet; Lowenberg, 1414 feet; and the Hemmerich, 1210 feet. There are several other, but less elevated and less conspicuous, summits. The general aspect of the whole group is singularly impressive; and seen from different points they break up into the wildest combinations, which fleeting lights and shadows invest with a mystical kind of air. Each peak is crowned with some old ruin, and commands a glorious prospect; but the view from the Drachenfels is considered the richest, as that of the Oelberg is the most extensive.

As you ascend the broken acclivities of the Drachenfels, your guide takes you aside to see, first, the quarry from which the blocks of trachyte were taken to build the cathedral of Köln, and hence called Dombruch; and, secondly, the "cave of the dragon" (whence the mountain is named), killed, according to the legend, by Siegfried, the hero of the national epic, the Niebelungen.

LEFT BANK OF THE RHINE. COBLENZ TO BONN.

After passing the "castled height" of Petersberg, and the pyramid marking the resting-place of Marceau, we traverse the plain of Andernach, and visit the chateau of Schönbomhist, which formerly belonged to the archbishop-elector of Trier. At the epoch of the great French Revolution it became the headquarters of the Bourbon princes and their partizans.

The village of Weissenthurm is so called from the square "white tower," erected by the archbishops of Trier to mark the boundary of their domains. Here the French forced the passage of the Rhine in 1797, in the face of an Austrian army. On an eminence behind it an obelisk has been raised to the memory of General Hoche, who accomplished the passage by throwing a bridge across to the island in the middle of the river.

The plain of Andernach is succeeded by a belt of undulating ground lying between the mountains and the river, which, from this point up to Bonn, forms a majestic lake, filling nearly the whole area of its valley.

Passing Oberbreisig and Niederbreisig we traverse the low, rich plain between the rail and the river, known as the "Golden Mile." We pause at Sinzig, an old walled town, about a mile and a quarter distant from the Rhine, in one direction, and the Ahr, in the other. It was the Roman *Sentiacum*, but Roman remains are scanty. Here, according to a more than doubtful tradition, Constantine the Great saw the luminous cross in the sky, and the legend, *In hoc signo vinces*, which indicated his coming victory over his rival Maxentius, and finally converted him to Christianity. A rough painting in the parish church, a curious semi-Byzantine, semi-Gothic building of the thirteenth century, commemorates the event.

Remagen is the *Regiomagum* of the Romans, and a valuable collection of Roman antiquities has been made here. The well-wooded hill which rises above this ancient Roman settlement is called the Apollinarisberg. Its summit is crowned with a modern church of very indifferent design, in which the head of the saint after whom the hill takes its name is duly preserved.

Below Remagen the Rhine makes a bold and abrupt curve. As we descend, and its course becomes less sinuous, we catch our first glimpse of the Rolandseck on the left, and the Drachenfels and its sister hills. On the right bank, Unkel forms the centre of a romantic landscape, which is matched on the left bank by the picturesque scenery of the Unkelstein, a mass of beautiful basaltic columns, which stretches far into the bed of the Rhine, and seriously obstructed its navigation, until a portion of the rock was blown up by the French. The current here flows with an almost dangerous rapidity.

Passing through Oberwinter, and by the sweet wooded island of Nonnenwerth, we arrive at another of the legend-haunted spots which have given so enduring a celebrity to the Rhine: the basaltic rock of Rolandseck, 340 feet high, with its feudal stronghold securely planted on its rugged summit. The Rolandseck is an everlasting monument to the memory of the famous nephew of Charlemagne—the Roland of song and story, the Roland of many a tradition and many a myth. In the old Frank ballads he is gay, brilliant, dashing, chivalrous; Germany has surrounded him with her own sentiment and mysticism.

In battle, on the banks of the Rhine, Roland fell grievously wounded, and the rumour of his death spread far and wide over many lands. Hildegund, his betrothed, took the veil in a monastery, feeling that she could never love again, and that the sole consolation in her overwhelming grief would be the strict performance of her religious duties. Meanwhile, the knight, being healed of his wound, hastened to obtain the reward of his valour from the sweet lips of his betrothed. He found her dedicated to heaven, and out of grief or emulation turned hermit. With a robe of sage about him, and his loins girt with a rope, he ascended the Rolandseck; not that he might be nearer, so to speak, to heaven, but that he might gaze from thence on the convent walls which imprisoned his Hildegund. And so his life flowed on in contemplation and earnest prayer. . . .

But one day the convent walls are covered with black; the knell resounds; on the brink of a new-made grave a company of veiled women deposit a coffin, wherein the dead is lying, with face uncovered, according to usage. Roland recognizes the death-calm features of his beloved. Falling on his knees, he follows with tearful eye every detail of the mournful ceremony; he sees the holy water sprinkled on the corpse; hears the ropes creak with the weight of the bier; as each spadeful of mould is thrown upon it a groan issues from hi3 bosom; and when the grave is finally filled, he himself falls prone upon the earth—dead!

Bonn is pleasantly situated on the side of a moderately steep hill, which slopes down to the very margin of the Rhine. Its houses are built in tiers, the lowest of which is washed by the waters, while the highest commands a magnificent perspective. The ascent from its base to the summit is, however, a difficult task for asthmatic visitors; and some of the streets are so steep that, if your foot slip, you must roll from top to bottom without hope of checking yourself in the *facilis descensus*. In this respect the town resembles Clovelly, in Devonshire, several times multiplied. Yet carriages ascend and descend, by some miracle of skill on the part of their Jehus. Bonn is a delightful place of residence. Not that this little city of 20,000 souls exhibits any extraordinary gaiety, or offers many objects of curiosity or interest. Its monuments scarcely rise above mediocrity. But its environs are "enchanting," and its walks are things of beauty. Life at Bonn is so smooth and easy; it glides along in such a transparent flowing stream. The good people of Bonn, moreover, are good-tempered and hospitable. Both mind and body are bewitched by an indefinable something in the air, the aspect, the habits of the country. Then, again, its university, the second in Germany in reputation, renders it a studious and "engaging "abode, from which you have no desire to tear yourself. We feel almost inclined to say, once at Bonn, always at Bonn.

One thing there is at Bonn which every Englishman will regard with pleasure; the care with which its inhabitants honour the memory of the celebrated men who have lived within its walls. In almost every street a marble tablet or an inscription calls upon us to do homage to the illustrious dead. Would so good an example were followed in London!

For example: in the Rheingasse, and close upon the quay, a tablet attached to the wall of an old house informs us that it was Beethoven's birthplace. Beethoven has sometimes been accused of having forgotten his country and his native city. It is true that three-fourths of his life were spent outside the walls of Bonn; but the following quotation will show that he was not wanting in patriotism:—"My country, my beautiful country, in which I first saw the light of day, is always present to my eyes, as full of life and beauty as when I quitted it. Happy will be the moment when I can see it again, and salute our father, the Rhine!" At all events, Bonn has not forgotten her wild, wayward, but Titanic genius. She has raised in his honour a statue of bronze.

We pass on to another house of interest to the English traveller, the house in which the late Prince Consort resided while a student at the university of Bonn.

It stands just within the university's gates, near one end of the Minster Kirche, and opposite a little grassy oval, called Martin's Platz. It is a homelylooking building, of a pale, green colour, set among tall fir-trees, and inclosed within a wall. The most noticeable thing about it is its steep slate roof.

You cannot help, says Mayhew, as you gaze at the humble dwelling, thinking of the wonderful change which occurred in the fortunes of the young student not long after he had drunk his "Bairioch Bier" (Bavarian beer) in the city of Bonn. Little, too, did he dream that a life of great usefulness to his adopted country, and a life of much domestic happiness, would be prematurely cut short at a moment when his queen-wife seemed most to need his counsel, and that the student of Bonn would die in the castle of our English kings.

Bonn is a clean and wholesome town. Its better streets and houses are all kept in excellent order. The present prosperity of Bonn is due to its healthiness, quietness, and agreeable situation, which draw thither a large number of English families, and, more particularly, to its university. The university buildings occupy an area of nearly a quarter of a mile in length. On the east they extend to the Coblenz-thor; on the south they occupy or include the palace of the electors of Köln, built in 1723 to 1761. They are situated at one end of a fine and well-wooded park, which originally belonged to the electoral palace, and where, according to tradition, Henry "the Fowler" was found bird-catching in the year 919, when the ambassadors arrived to announce his election to the imperial throne. The palace itself is now known as the University Museum of Natural History.

The various buildings comprise, according to the Guide-books:—A library of about 200,000 volumes, ornamented with a great number of busts; a Museum of Arts, or Plaster Casts, rich in about 500 copies of statues in plaster, bas reliefs, medals, and the like; a Gallery of Medals, remarkable for its fine Greek and Roman specimens; a grand Academical Hall, decorated with frescoes by Cornelius, and his pupils Harmann, Förster, and Götzenberger, which represent the four faculties—Philosophy, jurisprudence, Medicine, and Theology; Anatomical Theatre; and, finally a Museum of National Antiquities, discovered on the banks of the Rhine or in Westphalia, and comprising numerous memorials of the past.

At no great distance from the University Park blooms the magnificent chestnut avenue called the Poppelsdorfer Allée, leading to the old Electoral Palace, Lustschloss Klemensruhe, which King Frederick William III. presented to the university, and which now holds the University Museum of Natural History.

Hither it was, we are told, that the archbishop-elector of Köln, Engelbert von Falkenberg, removed his electoral court when the Köln burghers rebelled against his rule in 1268; and here it was, three centuries later, that a very different prelate, Count Gebhard von Truchsess-Waldburg, celebrated his marriage with the beautiful nun, Agnes, Countess von Mansfeldt, whom he had carried off from the noble convent of Gerresheim, near Dusseldorff.

Passing the village of Poppelsdorf, we proceed to ascend the Krenzberg, a finely wooded hill, 750 feet high, whose summit was formerly occupied by a convent of Servites, but is now surmounted by a church, erected in 1627 by the Elector Ferdinand. The pillared portico and commonplace façade are due, however, to the Elector Clément Augustus, who built it in 1725, as a screen or shelter for the *Scala Santa*, or Holy Steps, of Carrara marble, constructed about the same time. They were modelled after the *Scala Santa* at Rome—the sacred stairs (it is said) up which our Saviour was conducted into the presence of Pontius Pilate. Their ascent is permitted only on your knees.

Among the public edifices of Bonn, we do not feel called upon to direct the stranger's attention to any other than the Cathedral. Its foundation is attributed to the Empress Helena, mother of Constantine the Great; and it contains a bronze statue of the saint, characterized by no special beauty of workmanship. The present building was erected in 1270, and restored in 1845. The interior is very plain; but there are two bas-reliefs of more than ordinary merit; a Nativity and a Baptism of Christ by St John. Both are in white marble.

CHAPTER IX. COLOGNE.

FROM Bonn to Cologne, as the French, or Köln, as the Germans call it, the banks of the Rhine are low, flat, and devoid of the picturesque. The traveller becomes aware of the fact that he is drawing close to the frontiers of Holland; the Rhine has entered upon a plain extending to the sea, which grows duller and drearier the further you advance, and finally terminates in an immense morass. It has been well said, or it may be said, that the mode in which the traveller hurries over the latter portion of his Rhine-journey is a striking indication of his temperament and disposition. If he be restless and impatient, he escapes the infliction of a monotonous navigation by taking to the train. If he be an enthusiast, he continues his protracted voyage. Well: of whatever fatigue he may be sensible on the way, he feels himself amply repaid when he arrives in the magnificent port of Köln. The "city of the Eternal Cathedral," as a poet has called it, is accumulated, so to speak, on the river bank, and reflects itself in the broad mirror of the Rhine, which curves at its feet in a noble basin, incessantly furrowed with the tracks of busy keels.

The destiny of cities, says Durand, is singular. A colony of Ubians, situated on the right bank of the Rhine, being unable to oppose successfully the incursions of their predatory neighbours, sought the assistance of Rome—an assistance always readily given, but dearly purchased. Marcus Agrippa invited them to cross the river, and threw open to them the fortified asylum of the Roman camp. The change decided for awhile the course of history. The right bank fell into the occupation of barbarous peoples, and possessed neither towns, nor commerce, nor established societies: the left touched at every vantage point the Romanized Gaul, then in the full flush of civilization—a position admirably adapted to the necessities of commerce, and the interchange of so much as was then known of economical relations. Glance at the map, and you will see that nearly all the great cities of the Rhine are seated on its left bank.

A few years afterwards a daughter of Germanicus, the imperial and shameless Agrippina, who lived to become the mother and victim of Nero, was born within the walls of the Ubians. Their city then assumed, as a politic compliment, the name of the Roman commander's daughter; it called itself *Colonia Agrippina*, a name which is better preserved in the French Cologne than in the German Köln.

Köln preserved for several generations the traditions of its infancy; they were effaced neither by the fall of the empire, nor the great flood of barbarian invasion, nor the genial influences of Christianity, nor the complicated system of feudalism. For many centuries it called its nobles, patricians; its magistrates, senators; its burgomasters, consuls; its *huissiers*, lictors. It had even its capitol. Its inhabitants preserved the Roman costume as well as the Roman manners, and on its municipal banners were long inscribed, after the Roman usage, S.P.Q.C., *Senatus Populusque Coloniensis*.

Early in the fourth century Köln was captured and plundered by the Franks. Julian the Apostate (how history delights in nick-names!), recovered it, but they again made themselves its masters, and took care to keep it. Here the illustrious Clovis, the son and successor of Childeric, was crowned king. When at his death the empire he had laboriously built up was partitioned among his children, Köln remained one of the principal cities of Austrasia, a kingdom of which Metz was the capital. When, in their turn, the sons of Louis le Debonnaire divided the mighty realm of Charlemagne, it was comprised within Lotharingia, or the territory of Lothair, whence comes the well-known word Lorraine. Passing rapidly down the stream of Time, we find it ravaged by the Normans in 881 and 882. But escaping, without any serious injury, from all the turmoil of these early centuries, it was reannexed to the German Empire by Otho the Great, was endowed with extraordinary privileges, and placed under the special protection of his brother Bruno, duke of Lorraine, archbishop and elector of Köln.

Thenceforth it grew rapidly in importance, and increased wonderfully in population. Its safety became the peculiar object of the German emperors, and when it was threatened by Frederick Barbarossa, its ruler, the Archbishop Philip of Heimsberg, who had already enlarged it considerably by connecting it with its suburbs, surrounded it with solid walls, and with moats filled by the water of the Rhine. Its present fortifications are of a later date; belonging to the fourteenth, fifteenth, eighteenth, and even nineteenth centuries.

In 1212 Köln was declared a free imperial city. At this time it was one of the largest, most populous, and most opulent cities in Northern Europe and the Hanseatic League. She could put into the field, and maintain, an army of 30,000 soldiers.

In 1259 it obtained permission to levy a most extraordinary impost. Every ship entering its waters could only disembark its cargoes through the agency of boats or barges belonging to its merchants. These same crafty, wealth-amassing burghers enjoyed very great privileges in England. Its relations were scarcely less advantageous with France, Spain, Portugal, the North of Germany, and especially with Italy, which exported thither, not only its architecture and arts, but some of its characteristic customs, such as its wild gay Carnival, and its puppet theatres. Hence it acquired the distinctive name of the "Rome of the North" and "Holy Köln;" and hence it was induced to form in its own bosom a school of painting, the first with which Germany was enriched.

A traveller, whose Italian birth and culture were unlikely to dispose him to deal too favourably with the Germans, was astonished at the splendour of Köln, when he visited it in 1333. "I arrived there," he writes, "at sunset, on the eve of the Feast of St. John Baptist, and immediately betook myself, in obedience to the advice of my friends, to the bank of the Rhine, where a curious spectacle awaited me. A crowd of ladies had assembled; oh, such a gathering of beauties! How could one have avoided falling in love, if one's heart had not been already captured? I placed myself on an eminence to obtain a better view. Their heads were garlanded with fragrant branches; their sleeves were tied back to the elbow; in turn they dipped their white arms in the waters, uttering some words which had a singular charm. . I asked, as in Virgil:—

'Quid volt concursus ad amuem?

(What means this concourse on the bank of the stream!) I was told it was an old national custom; that the populace, and especially the women, were persuaded, that by washing themselves in the river on this particular day, they turned aside, they warded off, all the evils which threatened them, and secured a year of good fortune. The answer made me smile. 'Happy people of the Rhine! 'I cried, 'if the river carries away all your sorrows; oh, that the Tiber and the Po would do as much for us! '"

Köln had now attained the climax of her greatness, and thenceforth her wealth and power began to wane. The discovery of America opened up a new channel to the commerce of the East; but, perhaps, the chief cause of its decay was its incessant civil commotions. The Jews of Köln, who had done so much for its opulence, were cruelly massacred; the industrious and ingenious Protestants were banished; and a riot breaking out among the weavers, they were hung by the score, and 1700 looms were burned in the public place.

The survivors carried elsewhere, to more tolerant and equitable countries, the precious secrets of their industry; and so the harbour was no longer filled with ships, nor did the hammers ring in the deserted workshops. Workmen, without employment, wandered begging through the streets, and finding the trade of mendicancy productive, never again abandoned it. It became a scourge; one half the city lived on the alms of the other half, and thus they preyed upon the beautiful city which Petrarch had admired, until it became a wreck of what it was. And finally, to complete its ruin, the Dutch, in the sixteenth century, closed up the navigation of the Rhine, which was not again thrown open until 1837.

In 1794, when Köln was captured by the French, it still held the rank of a free imperial city, but its population did not exceed 40,000 souls. At that time a third of its population still lived by mendicancy. The French government, it must be owned, took prompt measures to repress this abuse; it secularized the convents, suppressed a great number of churches, and opened workshops and factories for the employment of the poor.

France held Köln until 1814. For twenty years it was the chief town of one of the arrondissements of the department of the Roer, of which Aix-la-Chapelle was the capital. The Russians occupied it militarily for a few months, after which the Treaty of Paris handed it over to Prussia. Let us admit that if the rule of Prussia be somewhat rigorous, it is also healthy and sagacious; and Köln, since 1815, has thriven greatly. The establishment of a steam-boat service on the Rhine, the reopening of the navigation of that river, and the construction of numerous important lines of railway which all find a terminus at Köln, have given a new impetus to its industry and commerce.

Köln is famous as the birthplace of Agrippina and St. Bruno.

The electorate of Köln, formerly one of the states of the German empire, and one of the three ecclesiastical electorates, was included in the circle of the Lower Rhine, and comprised numerous provinces and territories now belonging to Prussia. It was suppressed in 1794.

We shall borrow a general description of the city from the animated pages of M. Durand.

He will not allow that it is a beautiful city, at least in its present condition. It has all the inconveniences of the Middle Ages, but none of their picturesqueness. It is muddy, irregular, dull, badly laid out, and insufficiently paved. The best view of it is obtained from the river. There, indeed, its aspect is fair and pleasant; but both the fairness and pleasantness vanish when you plunge into its labyrinthine streets.

The truth is, everybody visits it for the sake of its cathedral, that immortal, that priceless, relic of the loftiest art.

The present edifice was preceded by two other cathedrals; one erected by St. Matema, the other founded in 784 by Hildebold, the first archbishop of the city, consecrated in 876, and set on fire in 1248. On the 14th of August in the latter year, Archbishop Conrad of Hochstetten laid the first stone of the present glorious building at a depth of 55 feet. Even before this event, the Archbishop Engelbert, count of Altona and of Berg, assassinated in 1225, had formed the idea of constructing a cathedral of unsurpassed grandeur. This idea was now realized, but strange to say, the name of the architect who designed the building and who laid down the plans which the labour of six centuries has failed to carry out, is wholly unknown.

This labour, however, was greatly impeded and delayed by the constant feuds in the thirteenth and fourteenth centuries between the city and its archbishops. A certain degree of progress was, nevertheless, accomplished, and on the 27th of September, 1322, the choir was consecrated by the Archbishop Henry II., count of Birnenburg. In 1437 the south tower had already been raised to the elevation which it now attains. But the work, so frequently impeded and interrupted for two centuries and a half, ceased completely in the year 1509.

Long forgotten and neglected, the cathedral of Köln was shamefully mutilated in the eighteenth century by the unintelligent and inartistic canons who then composed the chapter. For its beautiful altar a kind of Greek pavilion was substituted; its four bronze angels were transformed into rococo candelabra; heavy fauteuils replaced its beautiful stalls of sculptured stone; the stone chancel was demolished, that the choir might be surrounded with an iron railing; common glass was substituted for exquisite painted windows, which the canons pronounced too dark; and finally, the tabernacle, a masterpiece of sculpture, was destroyed and cast into the Rhine.

The French Revolution inflicted further injuries on this magnificent building. At last, the ravages of time which were added to those of man, not having been repaired for centuries, the general decay and dilapidation began to inspire serious fears for the solidity of the finished portions. The roof sunk in. A sum of 40,000 francs asked for the restoration of the edifice was refused by Napoleon. The French bishop of Aix-la-Chapelle, Berthollet, actually on one occasion congratulated the citizens that they possessed so fine a Gothic ruin, and advised them to plant it round with poplars to increase the effect. When, after the events of 1814, Köln was annexed to Prussia, a voice was raised on behalf of its cathedral in the *Mercure du Rhin;* no one listened to it. At last it happened that the old crane which from the summit of the incomplete tower had called fruitlessly on generation after generation to complete the work of their forefathers, fell to the ground through sheer decay. The incident awoke a tender interest in the heart of the citizens, who had not even been mindful of Berthollet's suggestion of a grove of poplar trees. They had been accustomed to see this crane every day; they could not dispense with it; and the municipal council, in 1819, voted the necessary funds for its re-establishment.

Meantime, the then Crown Prince of Prussia, afterwards Frederick William IV., visiting Köln, was powerfully impressed by the spectacle of the ruined cathedral. At his request the

Prussian monarch resolved to undertake the most urgent restorations, which between 1820 and 1840 absorbed no less a sum than 300,000 thalers. And after Frederick William IV. came to the throne, a society named the *Dombauverein* was formed under his royal patronage, not merely for the maintenance, but for the completion of the cathedral. Donations for an object so laudable flowed in from every quarter. The king promised an annual subscription of 50,000 thalers; and on the 4th of September, 1842, the second foundation of the cathedral was celebrated with the most imposing ceremonies. From that date to the present time, the works have been carried on under the direction of Herr Guirna and his successors, in strict harmony with the original plan, at an outlay already exceeding a million and a half of thalers. To sum up: the choir is completed; so are the transepts; the inner pillars of the nave, consecrated in 1648, have been raised to their full elevation; and strenuous exertions are being made to finish the vaulted roof and lofty towers, each of which will be about 500 feet from base to capital.

The cathedral is built on a cruciform plan, and rises about 60 feet above the Rhine, on an eminence, which, since the days of German supremacy, has formed the north-eastern angle of the fortifications. Its total length is 511 feet, its breadth at the entrance 231 feet; the former corresponding with the height of the tower when finished; the latter, with the height of the western gable.

The choir consists of five aisles, is 161 feet in height, and, internally, from its size, height, and disposition of pillars, arches, chapels, and beautifully coloured windows, resembles a poet's dream. Externally, its two-fold range of massive flying buttresses and intermediate piers, bristling with airy pinnacles, strikes the spectator with awe and astonishment. The windows are filled with fine old stained glass of the fourteenth century; the pictures on the walls are modern. Round the choir, against the columns, are planted fourteen colossal statues: namely, the Saviour, the Virgin, and the Apostles, coloured and gilt; they belong, like the richly carved stalls and seats, to the early part of the fourteenth century.

The fine painted windows in the south aisle of the nave were the gift of King Louis of Bavaria; those in the north aisle were executed in 1508. The reredos of the altar of St. Agilolphus, a quaint old combination of wooden carving and Flemish painting, is worth examination.

The apsidal east end is surrounded by some chapels. In the chapel immediately behind the high altar is placed the celebrated Shrine of the three kings of Cologne, or the Magi who were led by the star, loaded with Oriental gifts, to worship the infant Saviour. Their supposed bones were carried off from San Eustorjis, at Milan, by Frederick Barbarossa in 1162, and were presented by him to his companion and counsellor, Rainaldo, archbishop of Köln. We read in the invaluable Murray: "The case in which they are deposited is of plates of silver gilt, and curiously wrought, surrounded by small arcades, supported on pillars, inclosing figures of the Apostles and Prophets. The priceless treasures which once decorated it were much diminished at the time of the French Revolution, when the shrine and its contents were transported for safety by the chapter to Amsberg, in Westphalia. Many of the jewels were sold to maintain the persons who accompanied it, and have been replaced by paste or glass imitations; but the precious stones, the gems, cameos, and rich enamels which still remain, will give a fair notion of its riches and magnificence in its original state. The skulls of the three kings, inscribed with their names, Gaspar, Melchior, and Balthazar, written in rubies, are exhibited to view through an opening in the shrine, crowned with diadems (a ghastly contrast), which were of gold, and studded with real jewels, but are now only silver gilt. Among the antiques still remaining are two of Leda, and Cupid and Psyche, very beautiful."

Durand describes the choir as the consummate ideal of the Christian tabernacle. Columns slender as lances spring aloft to the very roof, where their capitals expand in flowers. All the rest is a splendid mass of glass-work (*verrière*), whose lancets are tinted over their whole surface with a rich colouring of azure, gold, and purple. The artist who constructed this magic wall must have remembered the words of the Psalmist, "My God, Thou art clothed with light," and has made for the Holy of Holies a dwelling-place not less resplendent than Himself.

There are numerous archiepiscopal tombs in the lateral naves. Like those of Mainz, they are overloaded with cumbrous epitaphs. The tomb of Conrad of Hochstetten, the founder of the cathedral, is regarded with special veneration.

"In the year of our Lord 1248, Bishop Conrad finding himself superabundantly rich in gold, in silver, and precious stones, and deeming his treasure inexhaustible, undertook the construction of the cathedral of this immense and costly edifice, on which we are labouring at the present moment." I take this extract from the "Chronicle of Cologne" for the year 1499.

Another bishop lies in a tomb fashioned like a fortalice, with a laurel at each angle. He reposes at their base in a semi-military, semi-ecclesiastic costume. Each archbishop of Köln kept his grave open throughout his archiepiscopate, to receive his dust, when needed. A fantastic custom, more honoured in the breach than the observance, demanded that every year of his rule should be marked by means of a small staff of white wood suspended to an iron hold-fast.

We follow M. Durand from the cathedral into the ancient Romanesque church of Saint-Martin; a church to be visited upon market-day, at the hour when the peasants of the neighbourhood abandon their fruits and vegetables to hear mass. In their temporary seclusion from worldly affairs, these rude and angular figures, with their fixed serious gaze, and solemn, stiff, and almost awkward air, seem to have stepped out of some old woodwork, or ancient German engraving, like those of Martin Schoen.

Verily, Köln, metropolis as it is of the banks of the Rhine, is still the city of the apostles and the princes of the Church, and even in these days of German Rationalism, the capital of Roman Catholic Germany.

What shall I say of its town-hall, which is situated between the Gürzenich (custom-houses) and the cathedral? I cannot do better than imitate my predecessors, and quote from Victor Hugo:—It is one of those enchanting harlequin-like edifices, he says, built up of portions belonging to all ages, and of fragments of all styles, which we meet with in the ancient communes, the said communes being themselves constructed, laws, manners, and customs, in the same manner. The mode of formation of these edifices and of their customs is curious to study. It is an agglomeration rather than a construction, a successive development, a fantastic aggrandizement, or encroachment upon things previously existing. Nothing has been laid out on a regular plan, or digested beforehand; the whole has been produced *au fur et à inesure*, according to the necessity of the times.

The general effect of this ancient structure is, however, very imposing. It was begun in 1250, and terminated in 1571, and is therefore a record of three centuries of architectural progress. Its portico is in the Renaissance style, and the second story is embellished with small triumphal arches made to serve as arcades, and dedicated by quaint inscriptions to Caesar, Augustus, Agrippa, Constantine, Justinian, and Maximilian. Among the sculptured bas-reliefs, you may remark a man worrying a lion. This man, named Gryn, was a mayor of Köln. The archbishop Engelbert III. had, to rid himself of a troublesome opponent, exposed him to combat with a lion. His courage brought him safely through the perilous experience. The inhabitants, rendered furious by his perfidy, avenged their mayor by hanging to a gate, which at this very day is called *Pfaffarthor*, or the Priest-gate, the first priest who fell into their hands.

The large and splendid hall in the interior, where the Hanseatic League formerly held its sittings, is adorned with nine large statues of knights.

Beside the town-hall stands the "Chapel of the Council," which formerly enshrined the Dombild, now preserved in the St. Agnes chapel of the cathedral. The Dombild, I may remark, represents, when thrown open, the adoration of the three kings, in the middle, and on the flaps (*volets*) St. Geryon with his companions, and St. Ursula with her virgins; when shut up, the Annunciation; it bears the date of 1410. The author of this remarkable picture is unknown; but it is generally attributed to Master Stephen Lotheren, of Köln, the pupil of Master William.

The "Chapel of the Council" contains a fine Roman mosaic, discovered when digging the foundation of the new hospital; and, also, a small collection of ancient pictures. In its fine tower, ornamented with many statues, and constructed in 1407, the municipal council was wont to assemble; at present it meets in the adjacent building, erected in 1850.

Near the Jesuits' church and not far from the quays of the Rhine, stands the church of Saint Cunibert, commenced, and consecrated in 1248, by the Archbishop Conrad. It stands on the site of an older church, built in 633 by the prelate whose name it bears. In its architectural character it is Romanesque; two portions only belong to the ogival style. Its small side-door presents a most remarkable combination of Oriental art and Gothic form. The front has been restored. The two Romanesque towers in the rear were formerly of a much greater height. The principal tower, having fallen into ruins, was rebuilt in 1850 in the ogival style; it has no other merit than that of magnitude. The most noticeable feature of the church is the thirteenth century stained glass in the apex; this is very rich and beautiful. There are also several small pictures on wood, by artists of the early German school.

Of course, no visitor to Köln fails to make a pilgrimage to that legendary edifice, the church of St. Ursula. From an artistic point of view it presents very little that is interesting or remarkable; except in the choir, the tomb of St. Ursula (dating from 1668), and her statue in alabaster on a pedestal of black marble, with a dove at her feet.

The legend runs that St. Ursula, daughter of a British king, set sail with a train of 11,000 virgins, to wed the warriors of an army which had migrated, under Maximus, to conquer Armorica from the Emperor Gratian. The ladies, however, losing their way, were captured at Köln by the barbarous Huns, who slew every one of them because they refused to break their vows of chastity.

This story is told in a series of most indifferent pictures, to the right of the visitor as he enters the church.

The reliques of the virgins cover the whole interior of the building; they are interred under the pavement, let into the walls, and displayed in glass cases about the choir.

As in St. Ursula's, so in St. Gereon's church, the principal ornaments are bones; its walls being lined with the remains of the 6000 martyrs of the Theban legion, who, with their leader Gereon, perished in the persecution under Diocletian, because they refused to renounce the Christian faith.

The church itself is one of the finest in Köln. The nave dates from 1262; the other portions, including the choir and crypt, are as early as 1066-69. Mr. Hope thus describes the decagonal nave:—"By a singular and theatrical arrangement, arising out of "these various increments, its body presents a vast decagonal shell and cupola, the pillars of whose internal angles are prolonged in ribs, which, centering in a summit, meet in one point, and lead by a high and wide flight of steps, rising opposite the entrance, to an altar and oblong choir behind it; whence other steps again ascend to the area between the two high square towers, and to the semi-circular east end, belted, as well as the cupola, by galleries with small arches and pillars, on a panelled balustrade. The entrance door, with square lintel, low pediment, and pointed arch, is elegant; and the crypts show some remains of handsome mosaics."

The baptistery, an elegant structure of the same date as the nave, contains a font of porphyry, said to be a gift of Charlemagne.

In the late Gothic choir of the semi-Romanesque church of St. Andrew are preserved the relics of the great chemist and necromancer, Albertus Magnus. The church of the Jesuits (1636) contains the crosier of St. Francis Navier, and the rosary of St. Ignatius Loyola.

Our space forbids us to dwell at any length on the numerous and interesting churches of this thrice-holy (and most odoriferous) city. But one of the most ancient—nay, I believe it wears the palm of unsurpassed old age—is that of Santa Maria di Capitolio. It is reputed to have been founded in 700, by Plectruda, wife of Pepin d'Heristal, and mother of Charles Martel, who erected a chanomy beside it. It is very clear that Plectruda's tomb belongs to an earlier date than the edifice which now enshrines it; and which, judging from its Romanesque style, was erected about the beginning of the eleventh century. It was restored in 1818 (the porch and choir in 1850), and enriched with stained glass windows. In addition to the curious tomb of its foundress, this church possesses an object of interest in an altar-piece attributed to Albert Durer. Painted in 1521, and placed in a side chapel, left of the choir, it represents in one compartment the Death of the Virgin, and, in the other, the

Dispersion of the Apostles. In the Hardenrath Chapel will be found some interesting mural paintings, portraits, and a Miracle of St. Martin, by Lebrun. The Schwarz Chapel contains the brass font (1594), surmounted by a figure of St. Martin on horseback.

The Church of St. Peter should be visited for the sake of the great picture of Rubens, forming its altar-piece, of the Crucifixion of the Apostle, with his head downwards. It was painted shortly before the master's death. Wilkie and Sir Joshua Reynolds both criticise it adversely; but the visitor who contemplates it, however, without any foregone conclusion, will be powerfully impressed by it, and will pronounce it, we think, not unworthy of Rubens.

The artist was baptized in this church, and the brazon font used on this occasion is still preserved.

Until he was ten years old (1587), he lived in the house, No. 10 Sternengasse where Maria de Medicis died in 1642.

The church of the Minorites, that of St. Mauritus, those of St. Pantaleon and St. Andrew, are well worth visiting. The same may be said—I wish that I had space to say more—of the double iron bridge (1352 feet long), across the Rhine; the noble quays; the house of the Templars, No. 8 Rheingasse; the new Rathhause, and the Wall-raff-Richartz Museum of pictures, founded and enriched by the two citizens whose name it bears.

So much for Köln. But stay, how can we leave the city without an allusion to its Eau de Cologne? To that celebrated perfume, which is nowhere more necessary than in Köln itself, though its evil odours are not quite so overpowering as they were in the days of Coleridge:—

> 'Ye nymphs, who reign o'er sewers and sinks,
> The river Rhine, it is well known,
> Doth wash your city of Cologne:
> But tell me, nymphs, what power divine
> Shall henceforth wash the river Rhine?"

"My eyes," says a traveller, "are still dazzled by the placards announcing in gigantic letters the sale of this precious perfume. Its distillation is the most important industry of the city. There are twenty-four manufacturers of it, and upwards of a hundred vendors. The annual production is estimated at from eight to nine million litres, worth about £6,000,000. But what a display of charlatanism for such a sum! The ancient Colonia Agrippina has no longer its consuls, its patricians, its princes, electors of the Holy Empire. It is swayed by the dynasty of the Jean Marie Farinas, an encroaching dynasty, swollen by usurpers and pretenders, who flood the streets with their products, their ensigns, their agents. Every wall is plastered over with provoking bills, which would be amusing enough if we were not weary with the 'posters 'of other cities. All the crossways are guarded by bill distributors and touters, who almost take you by the collar and force you to receive, at a moderate price, a flask coquettishly invested in an outer garb of white straw. There are upwards of thirty rivals, more or less legitimate heirs of the same name, sons and grandsons, nephews and great-nephews, disciples and successors of the illustrious Jean Marie Farina, inventor, in 1672, of *the* Eau de Cologne, sole possessors of his secret, sole manufacturers of the *true* 'water,' sole inheritors of his genius. Their lives are spent in decrying one another, *vivâ voce* or in writing. In fact, the question of *whose* or *which* is the genuine Eau de Cologne has quite a literature of its own, into which neither reader nor writer will be desirous of plunging."

We have now brought our readers to the point where the valley of the Rhine terminates, and the once grand and rolling river enters upon the low plains of Holland to creep sluggishly through winding channels, and finally mingle with the sea in two dreary estuaries. Soon after entering the Netherlands, the great river bifurcates into two arms—the left, called the Waal, and the right, the true Rhine. The Waal, near Fort Louvestein, is joined by the Maas, and forms the Merve or Mervede, which, below Dordrecht, takes the name of the Old Maas. The Rhine proper, a short distance above Arnheim, throws off the New Yssel, which was anciently a canal, cut by the Roman Drusus to connect the Rhine with the Old Yssel. At Wyk by Duerstede the Rhine again divides; one branch, the Lek, uniting with the New Maas near Ysselmonde; the other, the Kromme Rhine, separating at Leyden into the Vecht and the Old Rhine, the latter eventually reaching the North Sea to the north-west of Leyden. The delta of the Rhine is a low semi-inundated level, extending from lat. N. 51° 35' to 52° 20', and occupying nearly 50,000 square miles. It is protected from the ocean-floods by artfully disposed and solidly constructed dykes or embankments, varying from twenty to thirty feet above the river-level.

Here, then, as it is only with the German Rhine we had to deal—with that romantic and beautiful Rhine valley, which so abounds in old associations and chivalrous memories, and which has been so frequently the cause, the scene, and the prize of sanguinary wars—our task is done,

Made in the USA
Las Vegas, NV
30 June 2023

74076444R20430